9001

Short Story Criticism

Guide to Gale Literary Criticism Series

For criticism on	You need these Gale series
Authors now living or who died after December 31, 1959	*CONTEMPORARY LITERARY CRITICISM (CLC)*
Authors who died between 1900 and 1959	*TWENTIETH-CENTURY LITERARY CRITICISM (TCLC)*
Authors who died between 1800 and 1899	*NINETEENTH-CENTURY LITERATURE CRITICISM (NCLC)*
Authors who died between 1400 and 1799	*LITERATURE CRITICISM FROM 1400 TO 1800 (LC)* *SHAKESPEAREAN CRITICISM (SC)*
Authors who died before 1400	*CLASSICAL AND MEDIEVAL LITERATURE CRITICISM (CMLC)*
Authors of books for children and young adults	*CHILDREN'S LITERATURE REVIEW (CLR)*
Black writers of the past two hundred years	*BLACK LITERATURE CRITICISM (BLC)*
Short story writers	*SHORT STORY CRITICISM (SSC)*
Poets	*POETRY CRITICISM (PC)*
Dramatists	*DRAMA CRITICISM (DC)*
Major authors from the Renaissance to the present	*WORLD LITERATURE CRITICISM, 1500 TO THE PRESENT (WLC)*

For criticism on visual artists since 1850, see

MODERN ARTS CRITICISM (MAC)

ISSN 0895-9439

Volume 12

Short Story Criticism

Excerpts from Criticism of the Works of Short Fiction Writers

David Segal
Editor

Laurie DiMauro
Jennifer Gariepy
Drew Kalasky
Thomas Ligotti
Janet M. Witalec
Associate Editors

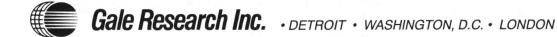

Gale Research Inc. · DETROIT · WASHINGTON, D.C. · LONDON

STAFF

David Segal, *Editor*

Laurie Di Mauro, Jennifer Gariepy, Drew Kalasky, Thomas Ligotti, Kyung-Sun Lim, Janet Witalec,
Associate Editors

John P. Daniels, Ian A. Goodhall, Margaret Haerens, Ted Mouw, Brigham Narins, Mali Purkayastha, Debra A. Wells,
Eric Williams, *Assistant Editors*

Jeanne A. Gough, *Permissions & Production Manager*
Linda M. Pugliese, *Production Supervisor*
Donna Craft, Paul Lewon, Maureen Puhl, Camille P. Robinson, Jennifer VanSickle, Sheila Walencewicz, *Editorial
Associates*

Sandra C. Davis, *Permissions Supervisor (Text)*
Maria L. Franklin, Josephine M. Keene, Michele Lonoconus, Shalice Shah, Denise Singleton, Kimberly F. Smilay,
Permissions Associates
Jennifer A. Arnold, Brandy C. Merritt, *Permissions Assistants*

Margaret A. Chamberlain, *Permissions Supervisor (Pictures)*
Pamela A. Hayes, Keith Reed, *Permissions Associates*
Arlene Johnson, Barbara Wallace, *Permissions Assistants*

Victoria B. Cariappa, *Research Manager*
Maureen Richards, *Research Supervisor*
Robert S. Lazich, Mary Beth McElmeel, Donna Melnychenko, Tamara C. Nott, *Editorial Associates*
Karen Farrelly, Kelly Hill, Julie Leonard, Stefanie Scarlett, *Editorial Assistants*

Mary Beth Trimper, *Production Manager*
Catherine Kemp, *Production Assistant*

Cynthia Baldwin, *Art Director*
C. J. Jonik, *Desktop Publisher/Typesetter*
Willie F. Mathis, *Camera Operator*

Library of Congress Catalog Card Number 88-641014
ISBN 0-8103-7955-4
ISSN 0895-9439

Printed in the United States of America
Published simultaneously in the United Kingdom
by Gale Research International Limited
(An affiliated company of Gale Research Inc.)
10 9 8 7 6 5 4 3 2 1

The trademark **ITP** is used under license.

Contents

Preface   vii

Acknowledgments   xi

Preface

A Comprehensive Information Source
on World Short Fiction

S hort Story Criticism (SSC) presents significant passages from criticism of the worlds's greatest short story writers and provides supplementary biographical and bibliographical materials to guide the interested reader to a greater understanding of the authors of short fiction. This series was developed in response to suggestions from librarians serving high school, college, and public library patrons, who had noted a considerable number of requests for critical material on short story writers. Although major short story writers are covered in such Gale series as *Contemporary Literary Criticism (CLC), Twentieth-Century Literary Criticism (TCLC), Nineteenth-Century Literature Criticism (NCLC),* and *Literature Criticism from 1400 to 1800 (LC),* librarians perceived the need for a series devoted solely to writers of the short story genre.

Coverage

SSC is designed to serve as an introduction to major short story writers of all eras and nationalities. Since these authors have inspired a great deal of relevant critical material, *SSC* is necessarily selective, and the editors have chosen the most important published criticism to aid readers and students in their research.

Approximately eight to ten authors are included in each volume, and each entry presents a historical survey of the critical response to that author's work. The length of an entry is intended to reflect the amount of critical attention the author has received from critics writing in English and from foreign critics in translation. Every attempt has been made to identify and include excerpts from the most significant essays on each author's work. In order to provide these important critical pieces, the editors will sometimes reprint essays that have appeared in previous volumes of Gale's Literary Criticism Series. Such duplication, however, never exceeds twenty percent of an *SSC* volume.

Organization

An *SSC* author entry consists of the following elements:

■ The **Author Heading** cites the name under which the author most commonly wrote, followed by birth and death dates. If the author wrote consistently under a pseudonym, the pseudonym will be listed in the author heading and the author's actual name given in parentheses on the first line of the biographical and critical introduction.

■ The **Biographical and Critical Introduction** contains background information designed to introduce a reader to the author and the critical debates surrounding his or her work. Parenthetical material following the introduction provides references to other biographical and critical series published by Gale, including *CLC, TCLC, NCLC, Contemporary Authors,* and *Dictionary of Literary Biography.*

■ A **Portrait of the Author** is included when available. Many entries also contain illustrations of materials pertinent to an author's career, including holographs of manuscript pages, title pages, dust jackets, letters, or representations of important people, places and events in the author's life.

- The list of **Principal Works** is chronological by date of first publication and lists the most important works by the author. The first section comprises short story collections, novellas, and novella collections. The second section gives information on other major works by the author. For foreign authors, the editors have provided original foreign-language publication information and have selected what are considered the best and most complete English-language editions of their works.

- **Criticism** is arranged chronologically in each author entry to provide a useful perspective on changes in critical evaluation over the years. All short story, novella, and collection titles by the author featured in the entry are printed in boldface type to enable a reader to ascertain without difficulty the works discussed. Also for purposes of easier identification, the critic's name and the publication date of the essay are given at the beginning of each piece of criticism. Unsigned criticism is preceded by the title of the journal in which it appeared.

- Critical essays are prefaced with **Explanatory Notes** as an additional aid to students and readers using *SSC*. The explanatory notes provide several types of useful information, including: the reputation of a critic, the importance of a work of criticism, and the specific type of criticism (biographical, psychoanalytic, structuralist, etc.).

- A complete **Bibliographical Citation,** designed to help the interested reader locate the original essay or book, follows each piece of criticism.

- The **Further Reading List** appearing at the end of each author entry suggests additional materials on the author. In some cases it includes essays for which the editors could not obtain reprint rights.

Beginning with volume six, *SSC* contains two additional features designed to enhance the reader's understanding of short fiction writers and their works:

- Each *SSC* entry now includes, when available, **Comments by the Author** that illuminate his or her own works of the short story genre in general. These statements are set within boxes or bold rules to distinguish them from the criticism.

- A **Select Bibliography of General Sources on Short Fiction** is included as an appendix. Updated and amended with each new *SSC* volume, this listing of materials for further research provides readers with a selection of the best available general studies of the short story genre.

Other Features

A **Cumulative Author Index** lists all the authors who have appeared in *SSC, CLC, TCLC, NCLC, LC,* and *Classical and Medieval Literature Criticism (CMLC),* as well as cross-references to other Gale series. Users will welcome this cumulated index as a useful tool for locating an author within the Literary Criticism Series.

A **Cumulative Nationality Index** lists all authors featured in *SSC* by nationality, followed by the number of the *SSC* volume in which their entry appears.

A **Cumulative Title Index** lists in alphabetical order all short story, novella, and collection titles contained in the *SSC* series. Titles of short collections, separately published novellas, and novella collections are printed in italics, while titles of individual short stories are printed in roman type with quotation marks. Each title is followed by the author's name and the corresponding volume and page numbers where commentary on the work may be located. English-language translations of original foreign-language titles are cross-referenced to the foreign titles so that all references to discussion of a work are combined in one listing.

Citing *Short Story Criticism*

When writing papers, students who quote directly from any volume in the Literary Criticism Series may use the following general forms to footnote reprinted criticism. The first example pertains to material drawn from periodicals, the second to material reprinted from books:

[1]Henry James, Jr., "Honoré de Balzac," *The Galaxy 20* (December 1875), 814-36; excerpted and reprinted in *Short Story Criticism,* Vol. 5, ed. Thomas Votteler (Detroit: Gale Research, 1990), pp. 8-11.

[2]F. R. Leavis, *D. H. Lawrence: Novelist* (Alfred A. Knopf, 1956); excerpted and reprinted in *Short Story Criticism,* Vol. 4, ed. Thomas Votteler (Detroit: Gale Research, 1990), pp. 202-06.

Comments

Readers who wish to suggest authors to appear in future volumes, or who have other suggestions, are invited to contact the editors by writing to Gale Research Inc., Literary Criticism Division, 835 Penobscot Building, Detroit, MI 48226-4094.

Acknowledgments

The editors wish to thank the copyright holders of the excerpted criticism included in this volume, the permissions managers of many book and magazine publishing companies for assisting us in securing reprint rights, and Anthony Bogucki for assistance with copyright research. We are also grateful to the staffs of the Detroit Public Library, the Library of Congress, the University of Detroit Library, Wayne State University Purdy/Kresge Library Complex, and the University of Michigan Libraries for making their resources available to us. Following is a list of the copyright holders who have granted us permission to reprint material in this volume of *SSC*. Every effort has been made to trace copyright, but if omissions have been made, please let us know.

COPYRIGHTED EXCERPTS IN *SSC*, VOLUME 12, WERE REPRINTED FROM THE FOLLOWING PERIODICALS:

The American-Scandinavian Review, v. LVII, September, 1969. Copyright 1969 by The American-Scandinavian Foundation. Reprinted by permission of the publisher.—*The Atlantic Monthly,* v. 166, July, 1940 for "Saki" by Elizabeth Drew. Copyright 1940 by The Atlantic Monthly Company, Boston, MA. Renewed 1968. Reprinted by permission of the author.—*Book World—The Washington Post,* November 21, 1971. © 1971 Postrib Corp. Reprinted by courtesy of the *Chicago Tribune* and *The Washington Post.*/ February 27, 1983. © 1983, *The Washington Post.* Reprinted with permission of the publisher.—*Boundary 2,* v. 10, Winter, 1982. Copyright © 1982 by Duke University Press, Durham, NC. Reprinted by permission of the publisher.—*Bulletin of Hispanic Studies,* v. LXIV, April, 1987. © copyright 1987 Liverpool University Press. Reprinted by permission of the publisher.—*Commentary,* v. 80, October, 1985 for "Reading Primo Levi" by Fernanda Eberstadt. Copyright © 1985 by the American Jewish Committee. All rights reserved. Reprinted by permission of the publisher and the author.—*Commonweal,* v. LXXXVIII, April 19, 1968. Copyright © 1968 Commonweal Publishing Co., Inc. Reprinted by permission of Commonweal Foundation.—*Contemporary Literature,* v. 16, Spring, 1975. © 1975 by the Board of Regents of the University of Wisconsin System. Reprinted by permission of The University of Wisconsin Press.—*Critique: Studies in Contemporary Fiction,* v. XXX, Fall, 1988. Copyright © 1988 Helen Dwight Reid Educational Foundation. Reprinted with permission of the Helen Dwight Reid Educational Foundation, published by Heldref Publications, 1319 18th Street, N.W., Washington, DC 20036-1802.—*Critique: Studies in Modern Fiction,* v. XIV, 1972; v. XVIII, Summer, 1976. Copyright © 1972, 1976 Helen Dwight Reid Educational Foundation. Both reprinted with permission of the Helen Dwight Reid Educational Foundation, published by Heldref Publications, 1319 18th Street, N.W., Washington, DC 20036-1802.—*Discourse: A Review of the Liberal Arts,* v. IX, Summer, 1966 for "Encounter with God in the Novella of Pär Lagerkvist" by Louis O. Kattsoff. © 1966 by the author. Reprinted by permission of the author.—*English Literature in Transition: 1880-1920,* v. 9, 1966; v. 21, 1978. Copyright © 1966, 1978 *English Literature in Transition: 1880-1920.* Both reprinted by permission of the publisher.—*English Studies,* Netherlands, v. XLVII, December, 1966. © 1966 by Swets & Zeitlinger B.V. Reprinted by permission of the publisher.—*Extrapolation,* v. 30, Spring, 1989. Copyright 1989 by The Kent State University Press. Reprinted by permission of the publisher.—*fiction international,* ns. 2-3, 1974. Copyright © 1974 by the Editors. Reprinted by permission of the publisher.—*French Forum,* v. 14, January, 1989. Copyright 1989 by French Forum, Inc. Reprinted by permission of the publisher.—*The French Review,* v. LVII, March, 1984; v. LVIII, October, 1984. Copyright 1984 by the American Association of Teachers of French. Both reprinted by permission of the publisher.—*French Studies,* v. XXVII, July, 1973. Reprinted by permission of the publisher.—*The Georgia Review,* v. XL, Summer, 1986. Copyright, 1986, by the University of Georgia. Reprinted by permission of the publisher.—*The Hudson Review,* v. XXXIX, Summer, 1986. Copyright © 1986 by The Hudson Review, Inc. Reprinted by permission of the publisher.—*Isis,* v. 77, June, 1986. Copyright © 1986 by the History of Science Society, Inc. Reprinted by permission of Chicago Press.—*The Journal of Narrative Technique,* v. 15, Winter, 1985. Copyright © 1985 by *The Journal of Narrative Technique.* Reprinted by permission of the publisher.—*London Review of Books,* v. 7, December 19, 1985 for "Aaron, Gabriel and Bonaparte" by Amanda Prantera. Appears here by permisson of the *London Review of Books* and the author.—*Los Angeles Times Book*

Miguel de Cervantes

1547-1616

(Full name Miguel de Cervantes Saavedra) Spanish novelist, short story writer, playwright, and poet.

INTRODUCTION

Best known for the novel *Don Quixote,* Cervantes is considered the first writer to compose what are now regarded as the modern novel and short story. Cervantes's collection of twelve stories, *Novelas ejemplares* (*Exemplary Novels*), is highly regarded for its portrayal of complex, realistic characters in conflict with society. Cervantes's use of dialogue to develop characters was considered revolutionary in his time, when authors of short fiction relied on stereotyped characterizations and narrative descriptions to present morals to the reader.

The son of an itinerant apothecary-surgeon, Cervantes began his career as a writer after heroic service in the Spanish Navy and a five-year period of captivity in North Africa at the hands of Algerian pirates. Upon his release and return to Spain, Cervantes fell into poverty, in which he would remain for the rest of his life despite his subsequent literary successes. While working for the Spanish royal government in various capacities, Cervantes produced a number of plays and *entremeses,* one-act comic interludes performed between the acts of longer plays. Though his plays were well-received, he was unable to compete successfully with the dramatic genius of his contemporary, the playwright Lope de Vega, who, unlike Cervantes, eschewed classical dramatic forms to produce scores of highly popular comedies. Cervantes instead turned to writing poetry and fiction. Eight years after completing *Don Quixote,* Cervantes published *Exemplary Novels* in 1613, claiming for them in his prologue the distinction of being the first original short stories written in the Spanish language. Critics continue to debate Cervantes's use of the apellation "exemplary" in the title of his short story collection. Because the short story was regarded in his time as a coarse form of entertainment fit only for the uneducated classes, some commentators have suggested that the title represents Cervantes's attempt to engage a wider audience by indicating that his stories were of higher quality than the usual tales. Others have maintained that the works are exemplary because they depict good triumphing over evil and thus provide moral examples for the reader. Such critics as Ruth S. El Saffar believe that Cervantes labeled his collection "exemplary" because he viewed the stories in *Exemplary Novels* as models of a new way of telling stories.

Commentators generally divide the stories in *Exemplary Novels* into two broad categories. The "idealistic" stories, including "El amante liberal" ("The Generous Lover"), "Las dos doncellas" ("The Two Damsels"), "La española

inglesa" ("The Spanish-English Lady"), "La fuerza de la sangre" ("The Force of Blood"), and "La señora Cornelia" ("The Lady Cornelia"), adhere more closely to the model of the traditional pastoral romance, presenting idealized heroes and heroines who triumph over adversity. The "realistic" stories—"El casamiento engañoso" ("The Deceitful Marriage"), "El celoso extremeño" ("The Jealous Husband"), "El coloquio de los perros" ("The Dialogue of the Dogs"), "El licenciado vidriera" ("The Glass Scholar"), and "Rinconete y Cortadillo"—draw characters, settings, and situations from Cervantes's observations of city life in Seville and Valladolid. Some of these works were considered shocking for their realistic portrayal of the poor and criminal classes and for their sharp satire of the Roman Catholic Church and other social institutions. The remaining two stories, "La ilustre fregona" ("The Illustrious Scullery Maid") and "La gitanilla" ("The Gypsy Maid"), are considered neither completely idealistic nor fully realistic. Like the idealistic tales, these stories end happily after a series of unlikely coincidences and reversals of fortune; however, their characters and settings are drawn not only from aristocratic circles but also from the world of peasants, gypsies, and criminals.

In many of his stories, particularly the realistic tales, Cervantes moved away from the traditional narrative technique of presenting stock characters from noble classes acting out idealized, conventional roles. Instead, he portrayed complex characters from different social classes. In such works as "Rinconete y Cortadillo," for example, Cervantes depicted characters who fall outside "respectable" circles yet have more integrity than the respectable people with whom they come in contact. The two main characters in this story are a pair of pickpockets who are driven from their hometowns for stealing and become involved with a group of organized criminals in Seville. Rincón and Cortado struggle against the rigid class definitions of their society, realizing that they belong with neither the peasants whom they cheat, the criminals with whom they associate, nor the wealthier, more educated people whom they victimize. In this and other tales, Cervantes allowed the thoughts and conversations of characters to move the story and convey his thematic concerns. His characters display a profound sense of isolation and a critical outlook on their culture. Such portrayals of individuals in conflict with society and with themselves have become central to the modern conception of the short story, as have Cervantes's techniques of conveying themes through character development.

PRINCIPAL WORKS

SHORT FICTION

Novelas ejemplares   1613
  [*Exemplarie Novells,* 1640; also published as *Exemplary Novels* in *The Complete Works of Miguel de Cervantes Saavedra,* vols. VII and VIII, 1902]

OTHER MAJOR WORKS

"Yo que siempre trabajo y me desuelo" (poetry) 1569; published in *Historia y relación verdadera de la enfermedad, felicísimo tránsito, y suntuosas exequias fúnebres de la serenísima Reina de España Doña Isabel de Valois, nuestra señora, con los sermones, letras, y epitafios á su túmolo*
La Galatea (romance) 1585
  [*Galatea: A Pastoral Romance,* 1791]
*El ingenioso hidalgo Don Quixote de la Mancha (novel) 1605
  [*The History of the Valorous and Wittie Knight-Errant, Don Quixote of the Mancha,* 1612]
Viage del Parnaso [adaptor; from the poem "Viaggio in Parnasso" by Cesare Caporali di Perugia] (poetry) 1614
  [*Voyage to Parnassus* published in *Voyage to Parnassus, Numancia, and The Commerce of Algiers,* 1870; also published as *Journey to Parnassus,* 1883]
Ocho comedias y ocho entremeses (drama) 1615
  [*Pedro, the Artful Dodger* (partial translation) published in *Eight Plays of the Golden Age,* 1964]
*Segunda parte del ingenioso cavallero Don Quixote (novel) 1615

[*The Second Part of the History of the Valorous and Witty Knight-Errant, Don Quixote of the Mancha,* 1620]
Los trabaios de Persiles y Sigismunda (romance) 1617
  [*The Travels of Persiles and Sigismunda. A Northern History. Wherein, amongst the Variable Fortunes of the Prince of Thule, and this Princesse of Frisland, are interlaced many Witty Discourses, Morall, Politicall, and Delightfull,* 1619]
†*El cerco de Numancia* (drama) 1784
  [*Numancia,* 1870; also published as *The Siege of Numantia* in *The Classic Theatre,* 1961]
‡*El trato de Argel* (drama) 1784
  [*The Commerce of Algiers* published in *Voyage to Parnassus, Numancia, and The Commerce of Algiers,* 1883]
Obras completas de Cervantes. 12 vols.   (novels, short stories, romances, dramas, and poetry) 1863-64
Interludes (dramas) 1964

---

*Since first publication and translation, these works have appeared as the single work *Don Quixote.*

†This work was written ca. 1585.

‡This work was performed sometime after 1580.

CRITICISM

William J. Entwistle   (essay date 1941)

[*In the following essay, Entwistle maintains that Cervantes's long novels may be divided into separate short stories, many of which closely resemble* Exemplary Novels *in style and intent.*]

To understand the place of the exemplary novel in Cervantes' life we must remember that few were written so late as the date of publication, and many are not contained in the ***Novelas ejemplares.*** The date 1613 is significant for Cervantes' readers and imitators, but not for himself. It will appear prominently when we think of Spanish literature as a series of historical achievements, but will be effaced as we proceed to causes. Not in 1612 or 1613 only, but during thirty years of an active literary life, Cervantes was fashioning his new literary technique. During most of the same time he was writing plays, some of which have intimate relations with his novels. For the drama he lacked flair, and he worked under conventions already established to his hurt. His plays, therefore, stand to his novels as a false dawn to a true dawn. In the one set of works he misconstrued his genius, in the other he grew to gigantic stature. It is in the *Galatea* that we encounter the first of the exemplary novels, and their style and technique is then scarcely to be distinguished from the pastoral. The first part of *Don Quixote* is a combination of what might have been two exemplary novels of the second epoch, into which are avowedly inserted certain others. The urge for unity is felt strongly in the second part, and the plot is closely knit; yet it includes narratives which are separable, if not separate as in the first part. For certain reasons the attempt to fashion a prose epos in the *Persiles* failed. The main plot cannot hold our attention, which therefore shifts towards the score of separate stories—mostly exemplary—which the main plot embraces. In short, all Cervantes' exercises in the grand style of novel writing are reducible to units of the same nature as his exemplary novels.

In view of the stress laid in the published collection on the historicity of these narratives, we may well exclude from the list of exemplary novels all pieces, long or short, in the pastoral manner. The essence of the pastoral, as Cervantes admitted in the preface to the *Galatea,* is disguise. These shepherds are not real shepherds, nor are their adventures real adventures. At most they are allusive to reality. But the *Novelas ejemplares* are certified true by the sons or grandsons of their *dramatis personæ;* and in one case so high an authority as that of an archbishop is daringly alleged. Mere shortness, therefore, should not entitle the *Historia de Grisóstomo y Marcela* or the *Bodas de Camacho* to be included in our list of exemplary novels. Yet these pieces and other exercises in the pastoral vein are not distantly related to this genre. The whole *Galatea* purports to relate how the respectable poet-shepherd Elicio contested Galatea's affection against a richer claimant. That is also the history of Lauso in *La casa de los celos* and of Basilio in the *Bodas de Camacho.* The theme is virtuous poverty versus the undue influence of wealth—a theme congenial to him who, at the height of his fame and at the age of 68, was "viejo, soldado, hidalgo y pobre." Similarly, the story of Grisóstomo treats of disdain and despair. Such topics afford examples of conduct, conducive to social doctrine. They are acted by characters of specific moral values. There is the 'desamado Lenio,' the 'rústico Erastro,' the 'lastimado Silerio,' not to mention the 'gallardo y enamorado Elicio.' Cervantes imports even into the pastoral style his strong ethical urge.

The exemplary novels have to do with moral doctrine. The author's words are too strong to be discounted as hypocritical or ironical; 'el manco de Lepanto' would not lightly hazard his right hand. But there are many modern readers who say, with M. Hazard, "A vrai dire, ces exemples ne seraient pas toujours bons à suivre." Such criticism, however, is too restricted. The Venerable Bede held that history offers examples of virtues to copy and vices to shun. With Cervantes there is the same dualism, and it has even, by and large, a certain chronological value. His first novels are examples of commendable virtues, but those of his second (Sevillan) period analyse vice, morbidity or mental infirmity. They speak of things to be avoided, whether they be larceny or jealousy or a judgment perturbed by fiction. Their author does not suppose they are 'bons à suivre,' though he has a large-hearted sympathy with all God's children. If he engages for them and their doings our sympathy—well, we, his readers, are supposed to be able to distinguish between good and evil! But there is also a third interpretation of the word 'exemplary' which applies (again by and large) to his novels of the third era. They are morally profitable—not merely tolerable—because they provide honest recreation. Recreation

is re-creation; it is, as it were, doing again in our own persons the work of God. For this reason entertainments and entertainers are necessary in any well-ordered republic; and if we cannot see in **"La Gitanilla,"** for instance, any specific virtue to be imitated or vice to be avoided, the contemplation of so honest a maid is recreative, and she is not slow to pronounce highly moral discourses.

The author does not pretend that the episode of Timbrio and Silerio, which forms the subplot of *La Galatea,* is an affair of shepherds and shepherdesses. He announces an exemplary subject in his first words:

> Basta saber que, no sé si por la mucha bondad suya, o por la fuerza de las estrellas que a ello me inclinaban, yo procuré por todas las vías que pude serle particular amigo, y fuéme en esto el cielo tan favorable, que casi olvidándose a los que nos conocían el nombre de Timbrio y el de Silerio, que es el mío, solamente *los dos amigos* nos llamaban, haciendo nosotros con nuestra continua conversación y amigables obras que tal opinión no fuese vana.

Cervantes offers us a title: *Los dos amigos.* Let us take it, for his theme is the Renaissance virtue of friendship, so much superior to love. Silerio sacrifices love for the friendship of Timbrio; Timbrio requites this friendship by bringing love to Silerio. It is a history of virtue in excess, as **"El amante liberal"** is of excessive magnanimity in a lover. Virtues to be copied. The two novels have internal dates: 1576 for the first, 1574 for the second. *Los dos amigos* was completed with the rest of *La Galatea* in 1583, though published in 1585. **"El amante liberal"** belongs to the interval between *El trato de Argel* (certainly written in Madrid) and *Los baños de Argel* (probably written early during the Sevillan period). There is a common plot running through these three pieces, and a fourth of the series is the *Historia del capitán cautivo* inserted in *Don Quixote* (I), completed by 1604. **"La fuerza de la sangre"** seems to me to exemplify, if anything, discretion, and *El gallardo español,* though a play, defines and illustrates military honour.

We may characterize this first style as follows: the intention is to commend virtue; the characters are typical of certain virtues, and hardly more complex than the labelled abstractions of the pastoral novel; the plot is contrived to convey a moral, at whatever cost to the likelihood of the incidents; the style is altisonant, as in *La Galatea;* there are monologues, but no true dialogues; the guarantee of historicity comes from the use of minor episodes drawn from Cervantes' experience as a marine and captive.

For the novels of the second period we have two important points of reference. **"El curioso impertinente"** is included in *Don Quixote* (I), and **"Rinconete"** is named. **"Rinconete"** was submitted to the archbishop of Seville in 1606 by Porras together with **"El celoso extremeño"** and *La tía fingida.* **"La española inglesa"** seems to have been prepared by its author for submission to the same prelate, but it may be counted an example of overlapping styles. It is authenticated in the first manner, by means of a Cervantine sea-fight; and it is romantic, in what I believe to be the third manner. The duration of this second style was probably from about 1589, when Juan Sarmiento de Valladares was Asistente in Seville, or 1597-9 when the Conde de Puñonrostro suppressed the gangsters, to 1609 ("Coloquio de los perros") or 1610 ("Licenciado Vidriera"). It is an extremely important period, since it covers the elaboration of the first part of *Don Quixote,* and the planning of the second. An unwritten unit of this group would be that *Vida de Ginés de Pasamonte* of which Cervantes speaks in his great novel; and in dramatic form we have the first act of *El rufián dichoso* and such an *entremés* as "El viejo celoso" or *El rufián viudo.*

This second period has many sides, since it is that of the plenitude of Cervantes' power. The general characteristics are these: vices to be avoided; characters studied from life and themselves the causes of their histories; authentication of the plot itself as true to life, particularly that of Seville; diminution of verse and monologue, and development of dialogue; language powerfully reinforced from colloquial and even base usage. The author's interest has shifted slightly from the moral problem to the pathological. "Rinconete and the "Coloquio" do reveal the misgovernment of Seville and the harm done to the young by evil communications, but they are primarily analyses of ruffianly life in Andalucía. So is the picaresque part of "La ilustre fregona"—a novel in two styles—and, of course, the first act of *El rufián dichoso.* These are studies in the pathology of society; but others deal with the individual. The *entremés* of "El viejo celoso" treats amorally the same theme as "El celoso extremeño." Jealousy causes the unfaithfulness it fears. In the *entremés* Cervantes accepts the fact and embodies it; in the novel he penetrates into the jealous man's mind, shows how his conduct leads to Loaisa's assault, and concludes by pointing a moral. It is true that the moral is somewhat obscure. The novel exists in two forms: in one the author seeks, but against his better judgment, to excuse the lady's conduct; in the other he merely warns his readers against intriguing duennas! Similarly, prurient curiosity leads to grief ("El curioso impertinente"). The evil arts of the procuress are studied in *La tía fingida* and her punishment is consummated. Esperanza, more sinned against than sinning, escapes the usual consequence of her life through the effect of 'beauty and discretion' (the latter a Cervantine virtue of very vague contours), but light maidens are warned that such escapes are rare.

The main body of "El licenciado Vidriera" consists of a collection of social jests, forming a more conventional and bookish criticism of society than we find in the "Coloquio de los perros." The same line is followed in parts of the play *Pedro de Urdemalas.* But the more interesting opening chapters are pathological. They resemble the madness of Don Quixote. The scrutiny of Don Quixote's library shows that he cultivated to excess not merely the literature of chivalry, but also pastoral novels and epic poems. He had given his mind over to fiction so unrestrainedly that he could no longer recognize reality face to face. His sane counterpart, Don Diego de Miranda, had a library of books of devotion and history in Spanish and Latin, but not a work of fiction among them. There is a definite moral warning to be drawn from the case of Don Quixote, but there is also an intensely interesting study of morbid pa-

thology. The datum is far richer than that used for the "Vidriera," and the novel swelled. Cervantes had imagined continuations for "Rinconete" and the "Coloquio." In *Don Quixote* he set out to write an exemplary novel of the pathological sort, but was swept into a long novel by the richness of the inspiration. Its fullness at first escaped his embrace, and he had recourse to his characteristic device of inserting a second plot. The history of Cardenio is also pathological. His misfortunes are severally and collectively the consequences of his timidity. Timidity Cervantes studied again in his comedy *La Entretenida,* with a change of plot, but with another Cardenio and another Dorotea.

The second part of *Don Quixote* contains the exemplary *Historia del moro Ricote,* not to mention the sanguinary episode of Clara Eugenia, and the separable adventures of Sancho Panza in his government of Barataria. The chapters devoted to Roque Guinart distantly resemble the novel of "Las dos doncellas," and it is possible that we should reckon also "La señora Cornelia" among late novels. But for the typical work of the third style we should select "La Gitanilla" (1611). Its plot had been announced first in the "Coloquio de los perros," and worked out in an ungracious form in *Pedro de Urdemalas.* The characteristics of "La Gitanilla" are these: a novel of honest recreation with only incidental doctrine; realism and idealism commingled; romantic optimism, ready to overleap the probabilities to round off the story with a happy ending; diminution of dialogue and restoration of poetry and altisonance, though with more grace than in the first period. These characteristics are to be noted in *La historia del moro Ricote,* in "La española inglesa" and "La ilustre fregona" (though not in the picaresque parts). The third manner thus overlaps the second for several years, but it is quite distinct. It shows that the author had wearied of observation and longed to liberate his creative fancy, even at the cost of reality. He wished to shape plots and evolve characters at will. His ageing mind was more tolerant, and more ready to promote peace and felicity. The last works have not the strength of "Rinconete" or the better parts of *Don Quixote,* and many a critic has registered his protest. But are the critics right? Would they not do better to give thanks that the author of the "Coloquio de los perros" had genius enough to create, in quite a different style, "La Gitanilla"?

There were enough plots in Cervantes' imagination to have furnished *Las semanas del jardín,* despite the prodigal effusion in *Persiles y Sigismunda.* This book contains a score of exemplary novels. It was devised, as the author tells us, on the model of Heliodorus, and with the earnest hope of producing an epic in prose. It begins *in medias res* and has the prescribed beginning, episodes, middle and end. Persiles and Sigismunda are exemplars of princely virtue, as the epic theory demanded—and therein lay the author's fallacy. For the spectacle of immaculate virtue is, to us sinful men, not edifying but boring. We know our brothers by their infirmities. We know Don Quixote, and laugh and revere him; but we cannot know Persiles or feel the slightest interest in his courtship of the equally nebulous Sigismunda. The epic intention fails because of what one might call the exemplary fallacy in heroic poetry; and because of the failure of the whole, we are the more free to rummage among the parts. The parts include embodied vices (*lujuria*-Rosamunda, *maledicencia*-Clodio), anecdotes like that of the *Cautivos fingidos* (III), and exemplary novels of varying types and lengths. Some of them may be early. That of *Antonio el bárbaro* (I and III) is dated internally by a reference to the wars of Charles V against the German Protestants. It exemplifies a point of honour, namely, the use and abuse of the pronoun *vos;* and this may be a reminiscence of a Cervantine experience in 1568 or 1569. Similarly the story of *Renato y Eusebia* is dated by a reference to Charles V's retirement to Yuste, and deals with a point of honour. A lady's virtue is falsely impugned, and she is put to trial by combat. It is the history of Elsa of Brabant or Sevilla Empress of Germany or the Gunhild of our *Aldingar* ballads. In *El laberinto de amor* (which is assuredly the same as *La Confusa* of 1585) Cervantes applied his ingenuity to this plot by inventing a new datum. The accuser is the true lover, anxious (with her consent) to keep the lady for himself. Renato is not an accuser of Eusebia, but a defender like Lohengrin or Mimecan; but Cervantine ingenuity asks what happens to a chivalrous hero if, as may readily happen in real life, he is overthrown. The affiliations of this plot seem to be with an early part of Cervantes' activity.

There are novels for which it would be imprudent to suggest a date: *Rutilio el bailarín italiano, El enamorado protugués D. Manuel de Sousa Coutiño, Transila* or *jus primœ noctis*, etc. But one cannot fail to see in the histories of *Isabel Castrucho* and *La liviana talaverana* (III, IV) typical novels of observation. The adventure of *Ortel Banedre y Doña Guiomar* (III) exemplifies the virtue of magnanimity, and in the tales of *Feliciana de la Voz* and *Ruperta la escocesa* (both in III) we notice the tendency to accept too optimistically a conventional happy ending. The skill with which these manifold stories in many styles are woven together shows that Cervantes' hand had not lost its cunning, even if his eye had dimmed. The novel flows smoothly from chapter to chapter. It is only that the main conception is too thin to sustain our interest. With the *Persiles*, however, we see that the exemplary technique, which had given not only the *Novelas ejemplares* but also *Don Quixote*, outlived its creator, leaving a surplus that was never exploited. Cervantes died with his music still in him. (pp. 103-09)

William J. Entwistle, "Cervantes, the Exemplary Novelist," in Hispanic Review, *Vol. IX, No. 1, January, 1941, pp. 103-09.*

Frank Pierce (essay date 1953)

[*In the following excerpt, Pierce observes that although Cervantes breaks with certain conventions of the Italian courtly* novelle, *his* Exemplary Novels *affirms traditional standards of conduct.*]

The **Exemplary Novels** have not proved an easy subject of criticism because of their obviously disparate form, and recent attempts to explain their "intention" have tended to emphasize this fact. Professor Casalduero has much of value to say, as when he rejects any attempt to fit the Cer-

vantine tale within the narrow confines of nineteenth-century realism, or when he insists upon the need to keep in mind the beliefs and the way of life of the seventeenth century if we wish to examine the characters and plots of these stories in any depth. When, however, he proceeds to analyze their structure, his imagination tends to run away with him into a private world of geometric patterns, personifications and semi-allegorical meanings. One puts his monograph down in puzzlement and the precise nature of Cervantes' realism—that is, his verisimilitude—remains undefined [*Sentido y forma de las "Novelas ejemplares,"* 1943]. Professor Atkinson has also tackled the problem of the significance of the **Exemplary Novels** in an interesting study ["Cervantes, El Pinciano and the *Novelas ejemplares,"* Hispanic Review XVI, 1948]. This critic puts aside five of the stories (**"El Amante liberal," "La Española inglesa," "La Fuerza de la sangre," "Las dos Doncellas," "La Señora Cornelia"**) as having "no bearing on the business of life", nor any "claim to be either new or exemplary". Thus, only certain of the **Novels** would merit serious consideration today. It is true that a recognition of experiment and of development of the area of imaginative reality within the whole collection is a prerequisite to any understanding of the total achievement. At the same time, it is doubtful if the progress is from pure romance unrelated to "the business of life" towards a fictional realism that bespeaks "experience", that is, a new and close approximation of Cervantes' imaginative vision to his remembered extra-literary life.

There can be no doubt that the twelve tales do divide into unequal halves of five and seven, but there are strong reasons against making this division into a boundary between two distinct conceptions of the genre. Professor Casalduero appears to strike the truer note when he holds that the matter of the **Exemplary Novels** deals largely with the relations between the sexes. That is, as the present writer sees it, they are predominantly social in their relevance. In this matter the Spanish critic proceeds in the same illuminating direction as that recently taken by students of the *comedia* and the picaresque novel. Golden Age literature is now rightly seen as reflecting the intimate doctrinal and moral preoccupations of a society and an age unusually theological, and philosophical, in its conscious statements. This is a view that tends to conflict with those first set out by Professor Américo Castro in his *Pensamiento de Cervantes* (and followed by Professor Atkinson), although, ironically, it might be argued that the earlier critical opinion has prepared the way for the more recent. As for Cervantes' short stories, the present writer sees therein much more evidence of the author's orthodoxy than of his liberal philosophy. Thus, the entire collection may be viewed as presenting problems and situations of choice and conflict, whether in the fantastic adventures of the hero and heroine of **"La Española inglesa"** or in the disreputable carryings-on of Rinconete and Cortadillo.

It is suggested, then, that Cervantes' progression from a traditional and overworked novel form to a freer and richer medium of fictional reality is not accompanied by a corresponding change in his perception or judgment of human conduct. Whatever the development of form and plot, the inner content remains the same, since the same set of beliefs would seem to inform each of the tales in turn. [The critic adds in a footnote: "One should not forget that Américo Castro, in his famous monograph on Cervantes, drew attention to the consistency of the writer's ideas and beliefs throughout all his works, although Castro's precise formulation of Cervantes' 'philosophy' would not now meet with the unanimous agreement of a younger generation of Hispanists."] This appears to be substantiated by the publication of all the stories together as one work, by their common title of "exemplary", and, some would have it, by the order in which they are set out.

It is here proposed to attempt to illustrate some of the above points with reference to **"La Gitanilla," "La ilustre Fregona"** and **"Rinconete y Cortadillo."**

If it be admitted that man in his social setting is the characteristic subject of the ***Exemplary Novels,*** what, then, is Cervantes' view of society in these three stories, which can conveniently be studied together? It is a frankly aristocratic one, which stands in marked contrast to the detached position taken up in *Don Quixote* in which the reader is allowed to witness the juxtaposition and the fusion of several social types. The tolerance and naturalness of human intercourse are best typified in *Don Quixote* by the elevation of Sancho to a place of near-parity with his master. Whereas this mellow atmosphere has endeared Cervantes to generations of readers and helped to win wide affection for his long novel in a world of increasingly egalitarian tendencies, the flavour of the shorter tales is, it must be conceded, traditionalist and their emphasis that of a conservative believer in social values. This difference of tone may help to explain why the first generations of readers, belonging to an aristocratic dispensation, regarded *Don Quixote* as a farce, even a satire. For these same readers the ***Exemplary Novels*** would present an undisturbed picture of society even if the latter might be submitted to exceptional strains and adventures.

In **"La Gitanilla"** there are two planes of conduct, that of the high-born in Madrid and, later, Murcia, to which D. Juan (Andrés) belongs, and that of the gipsies in which Preciosa is brought up. On the former we meet the guardians of Christian morality, on the latter the free life, albeit with its own sanctions, of the nomads. The contrast is stated unequivocally, and with a bias far removed from any romanticizing of this picturesque community, at the outset:

> Parece que los gitanos y gitanas solamente nacieron en el mundo para ser ladrones: nacen de padres ladrones, críanse con ladrones, estudian para ladrones, y finalmente salen con ser ladrones corrientes y molientes a todo ruedo; y la gana de hurtar y el hurtar son en ellos como accidentes inseparables, que no se quitan sino con la muerte.

"La ilustre Fregona" divides similarly between the world of the young noblemen Carriazo and Avendaño and that of the inn and the alleys and dens of Toledo. In **"Rinconete and Cortadillo"** the "heroes" early draw their moral self-portrait in a dialogue of light-hearted cynicism and preserve throughout a precarious middle position, typifying the deep irony of the whole tale, between the life of the

noblemen they briefly serve and the outrageous parody of society in Monipodio's fraternity which they enter but never fully join.

An initial dissection of the three stories also reveals the nature of Cervantes' experiment in terms of novelistic genres. The remains of the courtly *novella* are easily identified, while the use of the pastoral technique in the introduction and wooing of Preciosa and Constanza, and the controlled development of such picaresque elements as "autobiographical" material and the farcical distortion of naturalistic detail, betray the conscious blending of established novelistic conventions.

How are the two planes kept together within each story? In **"La Gitanilla"** and **"La ilustre Fregona"** the heroes seek adventure among the lower social order, D. Juan for the worthy motive of his love for the peerless Preciosa, Avendaño and Carriazo for less commendable and more frivolous reasons (although Avendaño's passion for the unapproachable Costanza soon gives his and his companion's rather aimless exploits the very acceptable purpose of all true love literature). These young bloods transform themselves for their escapades by means of various disguises: D. Juan turns gipsy, Avendaño and Carriazo elude their families and their tutor in turn, then travel south to Toledo and assume the humble callings of inn-servant and water-carrier. The young aristocratic *picaros* remain relatively untouched by their adopted surroundings. D. Juan avoids complete "gipsification" by declining to thieve and by generously making up for his honesty (or adherence to a superior code) and the deprivation it causes his fellow-gipsies by gifts from his personal fortune. Carriazo is introduced to the reader as one who has already enjoyed his adventures in Madrid and southern Spain but has yet kept himself essentially uncontaminated:

> . . . pero con serle anejo a este género de vida la miseria y estrecheza, mostraba Carriazo ser un príncipe en sus obras: a tiro de escopeta en mil señales descubría ser bien nacido; porque era generoso y bien partido con sus camaradas; visitaba pocas veces las ermitas de Baco, y aunque bebía vino, era tan poco, que nunca pudo entrar en el número de los que llaman desgraciados, que con alguna cosa que beban demasiada, luego se les pone el rostro como si se le hubiesen jalbegado con bermellón y almagre. En fin, en Carriazo vió el mundo un pícaro virtuoso, limpio, bien criado, y más que medianamente discreto . . .

Here Cervantes indulges in the fantasy of a Prodigal Son who visits the far country but keeps himself from sinning. Later, when Carriazo is joined by Avendaño, the same self-control is evident in their rejection of the advances made by the Galician wenches. Indeed, they indulge in their own humorous self-criticism:

> "¿Bien cuadra un don Tomás de Avendaño, hijo de don Juan de Avendaño, caballero lo que es bueno, rico lo que basta, mozo lo que alegra, discreto lo que admira, con enamorado y perdido por una fregona que sirve en el mesón del Sevillano?" "Lo mismo me parece a mí que es," respondió Avendaño, "considerar un don Diego de Carriazo, hijo también de caballero, del Hábi-

to de Alcántara el padre, y el hijo a pique de
heredarle con su mayorazgo, no menos gentil en
el cuerpo que en el ánimo, y con todos estos
generosos atributos, verle enamorado ¿de quién,
si pensáis? ¿de la reina Ginebra? no por cierto,
sino de la almadraba de Zahara, que es más fea,
a lo que creo, que un miedo de santo Antón."

Thus, the reader is conducted on an exciting tour of dangerous places by his equals, who carefully avoid outraging the former's feelings by making it clear that no real harm is intended. Both sets of adventures are also kept unmistakably within the bounds of propriety and good breeding by the creation of the quite unnaturalistic heroines, who may be taken to symbolize very clearly the ideal of feminine beauty and virtue to which a young man of gentle upbringing would aspire. The visit to the lower world is carried out strictly from the point of view of those coming into it, with adequate safeguards and with neither desire nor intention to write a piece of *costumbrismo*. Further, the portrayal of the two heroines, who come to dominate the action each in her own way (the positive, involved Preciosa, the passive, aloof Costanza), lends itself to a semi-allegorical interpretation, as is the case with any love story deriving ultimately from the mediaeval tradition of erotic literature. Both girls are preserved from the evils of their surroundings by the jealous and zealous care of their foster-mothers, and Cervantes allows himself the luxury of a romantic *dénouement* (with parallels in the *comedia*) according to which the poor but very beautiful girls are shown to be of noble origin after all. Thus alone can the kind of adventure in question be acceptably terminated. Neither **"La Gitanilla"** nor **"La ilustre Fregona"** can be regarded as an example of naturalism; in fact, the success of these experiments with the *novella* required a flight of fancy which would bridge a social chasm that was unbridgeable in the real world of the reader's experience.

The **"Rinconete"** belongs to the same kind of experiment, if by implication or at one remove. Rinconete and Cortadillo are *pícaros* not yet beyond redemption since they remember their fall, even if they only joke about it. Their link with the reader consists in their joining only temporarily a community so sunk in sin that it is no longer conscious of its guilt. For the moment, however, Rinconete and Cortadillo must adopt their disguises. They change their names to the diminutive (does this symbolize their conditional absorption into Monipodio's world?), on signing their names they omit those of their parents, and they endeavour to learn the new language of *germanía*. Rinconete's superiority to his new master is seen when he is called upon to read for the illiterate Monipodio, while his final judgment on the *cofradía*, half of scorn and half of moral censure, puts a legitimate limit to the author's fancy and satisfies the conscience of the scrupulous reader:

. . . especialmente le cayó en gracia cuando dijo
[Monipodio] que el trabajo que había pasado en
ganar los veinte y cuatro reales lo recibiese el
cielo en descuento de sus pecados; y sobre todo
le admiraba la seguridad que tenían y la confianza de irse al cielo con no faltar a sus devociones, estando tan llenos de hurtos y de homicidios y ofensas de Dios. . . . No menos le suspendía la obediencia y respeto que todos tenían a Monipo-

dio, siendo un hombre bárbaro, rústico y desalmado. Consideraba lo que había leído en su libro de memoria, y los ejercicios en que todos se ocupaban: finalmente exageraba cuán descuidada justicia había en aquella tan famosa ciudad de Sevilla, pues casi al descubierto vivía en ella gente tan perniciosa y tan contraria a la misma naturaleza; y propuso en sí de aconsejar a su compañero no durasen mucho en aquella vida tan perdida y tan mala . . .

The fact that his lack of experience leads him to return to Monipodio for a further period does not affect the author's view of the "infame academia" nor minimize the importance he gives in the closing words of the story to the lesson to be learned from it.

There is yet another way of looking at the structure of these three tales of social adventure. This is by an examination of what might be referred to as Cervantes' moral geography. It will have been noted how the one-class society of the *Novels* of a clear Italianate type gives way here to a wider view and an unusual bringing together of social extremes. Conversely, the far-flung area of action traversed in, for example, **"El Amante liberal"** or **"La Española inglesa"** is replaced by a closer and more familiar scene in the three under study. The journey, which Professor Atkinson sees rightly as a significant element in most Cervantine fiction, is from north to south of the Peninsula (in **"La Gitanilla"** from Madrid to Murcia, in **"La ilustre Fregona"** from Burgos to Toledo, in **"Rinconete y Cortadillo"** from villages near Segovia and Salamanca to Seville), as if the southern half of the country were the natural refuge of adventurers and the abode of evil-doers. The departure from home is a descent which for D. Juan, Carriazo and Avendaño ends in return and reintegration and for Rinconete and Cortadillo is left in doubtful suspension. This peripatetic quality yet again invites an allegorical interpretation; such a significance would link Cervantes with his predecessors in the novel of the fifteenth and sixteenth centuries and would herald tendencies of later seventeenth-century fiction. These short tales do, in fact, pose problems or present situations which in most cases are solved by the triumph of virtue and the righting of wrongs.

It would appear, then, that for Cervantes the Spain of Old Castile, Leon and New Castile as far south as Madrid, the new capital, was the home of the time-honoured social and personal virtues. And, in fact, the historical reality of his day would not seem to belie this attitude. The centre and, in particular, the south had been the scene of mixed life for a very long time; certain parts of southern Spain, notably the great port of Seville and the poverty-stricken land of Estremadura, were in the author's time the places of origin of many adventurers, conquistadors of all kinds, who emigrated to the New World. Andalusia was still a land of social fluidity and dubious ways of life and was becoming a common scene of picaresque fiction; the Moriscos of the Alpujarras had risen in Cervantes' own youth. The fact that Cervantes spent in the south some of his most distressing, if imaginatively fruitful, years after his return from North Africa emphasizes the meaning to be attached to its rôle in the *Exemplary Novels*: Seville again stands for a city of evil ways in **"El Coloquio"** and in **"El celoso Extremeño."**

This use of the social and geographical reality of his own and his readers' country in the three tales examined here undoubtedly increases their verisimilitude and their interest. Cyprus, North Africa, England or Italy, with their altogether hazier associations for the average Spaniard of the age, served as suitable backgrounds for the more remote and more "literary" adventures of **"La Señora Cornelia," "El Amante liberal"** and **"La Española inglesa."** The fictionally more unusual yet more credible adventures of **"La Gitanilla," "La ilustre Fregona"** and **"Rinconete y Cortadillo"** took place in more immediate settings. Cervantes appears to have moved nearer home the more he explored the possibilities of the *novella* and the more he departed from this form as he found it. One can trace this ever greater emergence of a new novelistic reality from **"La Gitanilla"** through **"La ilustre Fregona"** to the **"Rinconete."** The passage, that is to say, from the upper to the lower social world is more emphatic in the second than in the first of these stories, while in the last-named an almost complete absorption into the society of outcasts takes place. Cervantes' ground-plan for each of the three would appear to be the same, and one is tempted to regard them as a real trilogy that marks a special stage in his writing at a time when he was fascinated by a particular aspect of the social and the literary situation as he saw it. Could it be held of Cervantes as of Dickens that he tended to portray the humbler social order with more intensity and truth than he did the upper? If this is so, and it is arguable, it should not be taken to mean that even the **"Riconete"** is a naturalistic transcript of society, any more than is either of the others, or for that matter the **"Coloquio de los perros."** The fantastic quality of our three tales is a necessary part of their success, since without the idealistic Preciosa and Costanza the two to which, significantly, they give the titles would be as formless as the **"Licenciado Vidriera,"** and without the ironic comment of the author and the awareness of the chief character the **"Rinconete"** would be a pointless piece of realism.

The exemplarity of the three stories we have analyzed would appear to take the form of a social lesson. The highborn—in this the forerunners of the bourgeoisie of the novel of a later epoch—are the natural guardians of virtue and righteous living and it is their duty and their privilege to live up to their birth-right: the confession of his sin by D. Diego de Carriazo the elder and his magnanimous recognition of Costanza as his natural daughter thus add emphasis to the exemplarity of **"La ilustre Fregona"** while supplying a sentimental intrigue with which to enrich the ending of the tale. Exposure to the ways of the poor and the vicious ought to refresh belief in one's own professed standards of conduct and to allow of comparison favourable only to the aristocratic way of life. This is a hierarchical concept of society which finds its earlier literary expression in such works as the *Celestina* and which, in any case, was current in Europe for several centuries. There is in Cervantes' **Novels** no middle class between the lower orders and the nobility, and, whatever the facts of the gradual emergence of a bourgeoisie, this view of life must be taken as substantially true of Golden Age Spain. The

"Rinconete," coming at the end of the experiment, if its connexion with **"La Gitanilla"** and **"La ilustre Fregona"** be admitted, might seem to elude such a reading of these two and of almost all the other *Exemplary Novels.* It should be remembered, however, that in **"Rinconete and Cortadillo"** Cervantes never gives us the unsmiling and generally one-dimensional picture of society to be met with in several of the other tales of the collection; rather do we encounter at every step an ironical patina which produces not an unblinking realism but a gay, amused vision, as if Cervantes the writer of aristocratic views were deriving huge fun from his experiment and meant us to do the same. The lesson of the **"Rinconete"** is even more explicit than that of the other two stories and it is, in the present writer's opinion, of exactly the same kind.

Finally, it may be pointed out that Cervantes' imaginative growth and increasing emancipation from his own surroundings of class can be measured by the fact that he so transcended the reality of the *Exemplary Novels* as to create Sancho Panza in his fulness. (pp. 134-42)

> *Frank Pierce, "Reality and Realism in the 'Exemplary Novels'," in* Bulletin of Hispanic Studies, *Vol. 30, No. 119, July-September, 1953, pp. 134-42.*

Karl-Ludwig Selig on Cervantes and the Boccaccian novella:

In his *Novelas exemplares,* Cervantes/author/creator explores various and variegated possibilities of the novella form: each text is a different artistic and formal exploration of the form and a different articulation and experimentation of and with the form and tradition. While there might be a total unity and design to all the *Novelas exemplares,* that is, to the entire and total opus as one textual unit, in dealing with these texts, one obviously has to take into account the single unity and organicity of each novela, being conscious at the same time, that there is a web, a nexus, and an inter-relationship, that some novelas may inter-relate and reach out to other texts and that referentials and referential affinities may exist and/or may be established. In this respect, the following parallel may be useful and valid: keeping in mind the rather enigmatic phrase "yo soy el primero que he novelado en lengua castellana," just as the *Decameron* can be considered an artistic and intellectual exploration of the variegated possibilities of the form and a codification of the form and the tradition, a similar matter occurs in the *Novelas exemplares;* in a way these texts present a challenge to the Boccaccio tradition, and furthermore this quest and exploration of the form can also be considered an important aspect of their exemplariness.

> *Karl-Ludwig Selig, in his "Some Observations on Cervantes' 'El amante liberal'," Revista Hispanica Moderna, 1978-79.*

Bruce W. Wardropper   (essay date 1957)

[*Wardropper is a Scottish-born American educator and critic specializing in Spanish literature. In the following essay, he asserts the relevance of the short story "The Impertinent Curiosity" to the novel* Don Quixote.]

Cervantine criticism is divided on the question whether **"El curioso impertinente"** is relevant to the total context of *Don Quixote*. Américo Castro, writing in 1925, compiled a list—which he declared to be "not exhaustive"—of six critics who were opposed to the interpolation of the short story, and five who welcomed its inclusion. He himself created a tie by accepting **"El curioso impertinente"** as a further exemplification of the theme of error and its consequences; the tale, that is, was seen to reinforce the thematic structure of *Don Quixote* as Castro then interpreted it [*El pensamiento de Cervantes*, 1925]. Since the making of this classic summary of opinion a stalemate has reigned; no significant contribution to our understanding of the problem has been made. Some random examples from later commentators will establish this point.

G. Boussagol, in 1926, held that **"El curioso impertinente"** was a *novela ejemplar* which Cervantes published as a part of his great novel because he had it on his hands, and because literary tradition authorized the inclusion of extraneous episodes in works "de longue haleine" ["Quelques mots sur la genèse de *El curioso impertinente*," *Revue de l'Enseignement des Langues Vivantes*, XLIII (1926)]. J. D. M. Ford, in 1928, adopted substantially the same view as Boussagol, adding hesitantly in a note that "though the **'Curioso'** is outside the movement of the main plot of the *Don Quixote*, it has none the less an appropriateness of its own in that it provides another illustration of monomania" ["Plot, Tale and Episode in *Don Quixote*," *Melanges Jeanroy* (Paris, 1928)]. Twenty years later Robert L. Pendley wrote that the intercalated *novelas* portray the same "unconventional behavior" as the main plot ["Unconventional Behavior in the *Novelas intercaladas* in *Don Quijote*," *Library Chron. Univ. Texas* III (1948)]. Joaquín Casalduero (1949), insisting more strongly than any previous critic on the thematic pattern of *Don Quixote*, regarded the short story as an integral part of the *Quijote de 1605*, though his account of the relation of part to whole is hardly convincing [*Sentido y forma del Quijote*, 1949].

This controversy presents the student of Cervantes with two alternative opinions: (1) the writer inserted a short story into his novel for no good aesthetic reason; or (2) he used it to give another—an extra, gratuitous—illustration of a point he was laboring. The first choice is inadmissible a priori: in judging a work of art the critic must assume first the relevance of every detail. Moreover, it is scarcely flattering to the world's idea of a masterpiece or of the genius who wrote it to suppose that he threw it together like a bad cook making a cake. The weakness of the second argument is that no agreement seems possible on the theme that Cervantes was supposedly hammering home with an additional gratuitous illustration. The critical confusion about **"El curioso impertinente"** merely underscores the fact that there is still a general disagreement about the nature of *Don Quixote* itself.

The more one reads *Don Quixote* the more one is driven to the conclusion that this mystification is of Cervantes' own making. The author seems—for motives best not speculated about here—to delight in pulling the wool over his readers' eyes. He disparages, for example, the "rastrillado, torcido y aspado hilo" of his plot—a kind of modesty topos that has fooled many Cervantine scholars. And when he alludes in Part II to critical objections to Part I—really made? invented by the author?—he is meek and submissive, conceding points and promising to do better in the future.

One of the charges that Cervantes does not seek to answer effectively is that the first part sinned with its episodes and interpolated stories. **"El curioso impertinente"** bears the brunt of this type of criticism. Why? Obviously because, as Cervantes admits, it is attached to the plot somewhat more loosely than the other tales. But is it not singled out for blame also because the title suggests that it is an irrelevance? While it is logically the inquisitive man who is described as "impertinent," a secondary meaning—that the tale of this **"Curioso"** is "irrelevant"—echoes from the words. I suspect that this ambiguity is deliberate, a part of the process of confusing the reader.

The *bachiller,* an unimaginative literalist for all his play-acting, introduces this criticism: "Una de las tachas que ponen a la tal historia . . . es que su autor puso en ella vna nouela intitulada: **"El Curioso Impertinente,"** no por mala ni por mal razonada, sino por no ser de aquel lugar, ni tiene que ver con la historia de su merced del señor don Quixote." Don Quixote then launches into an attack on the ignorance of the author of his *historia*. "La historia es como cosa sagrada, porque ha de ser verdadera," he observes. Since this is so, he does not know what "le mouio al autor a valerse de nouelas y cuentos agenos, auiendo tanto que escriuir en los mios." But it is a monomaniac who is speaking. From Don Quixote's egocentric point of view **"El curioso impertinente"** is an irrelevance, but is it necessarily so when seen from the point of view of Cervantes and his readers?

The problem is focused somewhat differently by Cide Hamete Benengeli. He is reported, in Chapter xliv of Part II, to have lamented the dullness of his task. The history he is writing is dry and limited because he must always write about Don Quixote and Sancho "sin osar estenderse a otras digresiones y episodios mas graues y mas entretenidos." In an attempt to give variety to his theme "auia vsado en la primera parte del artificio de algunas nouelas, como fueron la del **"Curioso Impertinente,"** y la del *Capilan cautiuo,* que estan *como* separadas de la historia, puesto que las demas que alli se cuentan son casos sucedidos al mismo don Quixote, que no podian dexar de escriuirse." A key word in this quotation is the italicized *como.* The fictitious Arabic historian does not admit that these tales are divorced from the main plot; they are only separated *as it were.* Another key word is "artificio," which corresponds to a fundamental concept in Renaissance and baroque aesthetics. Cide Hamete returns to this idea in his next sentence. It has occurred to him that many readers, engrossed in the adventures of Don Quixote, might skip over the *novelas* "sin aduertir la gala y artificio que en si contienen, el qual se mostrara bien al descubierto, quando por si solas, sin arrimarse a las locuras de don Quixote, ni a las sandezes de Sancho, salieran a luz." He resolves therefore to remain within "los estrechos limites de la narracion"—the *historia*—in Part II, resisting the temptation of *el artificio*. The sacrifice of art to history is a hard one to make, and Cide Hamete begs the reader's applause "no por lo que escriue, sino por lo que ha dexado de escriuir."

From these two passages it is clear that the interpolated tales produce a different reaction in the writer (Cide Hamete) and the protagonist (Don Quixote). It is implied that the reader who sees only Don Quixote and Sancho in the work has failed to respond as the writer intended. In the aesthetic terminology of the time the history must not detract attention from the art.

Is it not legitimate to deduce from this argument that Cervantes considered *Don Quixote* to be a combination—not necessarily a blend—of history and art? The reader fails to understand the whole if he neglects the artifice—a category which must surely include the Marcela-Grisóstomo episode and the pairs of lovers in the Sierra Morena as well as the specifically mentioned tales. The author, in Part I, has used two styles to project two different types of illumination on his subject. If he relinquishes this plan in Part II it is because he has failed, as we say today, to "communicate," because the pressure of an ignorant public—verbalized or imagined—has forced him to do so.

This interpretation of Cervantes' words justifies those who have maintained a unity of theme in tale and novel: monomania, unconventional behavior, and other related characteristics. But merely to see a single theme linking story and history is too unsubtle an interpretation of Cervantes' expressed intention. The fact that **"El curioso impertinente"** is based on a theme found in the *torcido hilo* of the main plot is subordinate to the fact of the differentiated treatments: the artistic and the natural. The very realization of this dichotomy helps to reveal what the identical theme is.

The comments cited so far were made *post hoc* by the author. But, Cervantes, being a self-conscious writer, referred to the problem in Part I, before smarting under the acrimony of criticism—if indeed the objections reached his ears. There, in Chapter xxviii, he held that "our age needed merry entertainments," among which he singled out "la dulçura de su verdadera historia" and "los cuentos y episodios della, que, en parte, no son menos agradables y artificiosos y verdaderos que la misma historia." This is a difficult passage: it concedes that there is *artificio* and *verdad* in both the *historia* and the *cuentos*, that the two styles are never absolutely segregated. The *historia* and the *cuentos* complement one another, but at the same time they overlap, encroach on each other's territory. The statement comprises a subtle truth, but it forms too a part of the mystification process.

The repeated affirmation that *Don Quixote* is a *verdadera historia* raises the question as to what kind of truth is to be found in it. Dramatists at that time, of course, used the phrase lightly, attaching no more importance to it than they did to the cliché *verdadera comedia*. But Cervantes is not content with a casual introduction of the formula: he insists on it, repeats it *ad nauseam*. It must have had some significance for him. Partly, like Lucian in his fantastic *Vera Historia*, he may have been amused at the irony

of it: he was proclaiming the historical accuracy of what every intelligent reader must know was a fiction; and he was doing this in a context that was describing the mad world that results from just such a confusion of life and letters. Not only his hero but the inn-keeper and several other characters in the novel believe in the historical truth of the stories they read. History and story are one for these characters, just as they are for the Romance tongues in which they are written. But Cervantes must have been impressed by more than just the irony of it all, for this was indeed a serious problem. In Cervantes' time there was Lope de Vega and his "Literarisierung des Lebens" [The reference is to Leo Spitzer, *Die Literarisierung des Lebens in Lopes Dorotea,* 1932]. Later Cadalso would find his life and writing inextricably mingled [José F. Montesinos, "Cadalso o la noche cerrada," *Cruz y Raya,* 1931]. And these are merely the more spectacular and best known cases. Students of Cervantine criticism will recall the more obscure case of the student who slashed the wine skins; others will bring to mind the young Teresa de Cepeda y Ahumada planning a chivalric expedition against the Moors. Cervantes aggravates for his readers this natural tendency to confuse fiction and reality by his ever more convincing repetition of the idea that Don Quixote really lived and really did have the adventures attributed to him in his *verdadera historia*.

But aside from this confusionism, complicated by aspersions cast on the veracity of the Moorish chronicler, the term *verdadera historia* is to some extent justified. In Renaissance nature-aesthetics a true history is one which is written without art, which is allowed to follow its meandering course, which is not forced into a preconceived mold: something akin to Unamuno's conception of a viviparous story; a prose cousin of the *romance*.

In contrast to the *verdadera historia* we have the *novelas* or *cuentos*, an art form. These, we are told, are as true as the main story, but this truth, I suggest, is of a different order. *Don Quixote* treats of natural truth, which includes verisimilitude and psychological observation, the truth of Cervantes' world of *experiencia;* **"El curioso impertinente"** treats of artistic or artificial truth, truth in the abstract, the truth of the philosopher rather than the truth of the proverb.

The short stories, then, are artificial compositions in contrast to the natural main plot. They serve, I believe, to present similar themes to those of the *historia* under a different guise. The short story is set in a metaphysical framework; the history is made out of experience, out of the obsessive verbal expressions "ver con los ojos," "tocar con la mano," "tomar el pulso."

The debate between the proponents of natural and artistic writing was the burning question in the aesthetic thought of the first quarter of the seventeenth century. One might favor one side of the issue, or one might progress from nature to art, as Lope de Vega did [R. Menéndez Pidal, "Lope de Vega: El Arte Nuevo y la nueva biografía," *RFE* XXII (1935)]. Cervantes, however, adopts in all controversies a position of quasi-neutrality that has become his trademark. He "sees both sides of a question." This is not to say that he makes ineffectual compromises. He seldom fails to make clear his own views, but he scrupulously gives a hearing to the other side. He is anything but dogmatic. He says, as it were: "I personally incline to this opinion, but I recognize that there is a lot to be said for the other side." The intellectual texture of his writing is founded on opinions, rather than on beliefs. His characters move in a world of moderate skepticism. Thus, in the debate between arms and letters, Cervantes weights the scales slightly in favor of the military life, but he does not fail to do justice to the intellectuals. So, too, in the debate between art and nature—less explicitly argued in *Don Quixote* except in the rather enigmatic discussion between the canon and the priest—Cervantes leaves one with the impression that, while he rather prefers the viviparous style of his major novel, he sees also the potentialities of the artistic prose forms. For this reason he has recourse to both modes, much as in his life he switched from the career of arms to that of letters. Cervantes' debates are conducted with utmost fairness: he himself argues for and against each motion, and the result is always a near-tie. The debate between art and nature embraces, of course, a number of other clashes of opinion: literacy versus illiteracy, proverb versus adage, and the like. It is an essential part of the stuff of his novel. In Part I he cannot refrain from inserting contrasting artificial episodes; neither can he in Part II, however much he may pretend to be writing solely from nature. Let us see, then, the effect of reducing to artistic order some of the themes that are conveyed naturally in the "true history."

Among the major themes explored in *Don Quixote* are: (1) the consequences of accepting as a rule of life, not "unconventional," but upturned values, values unacceptable to society because experience or common sense has shown that they are *wrong;* (2) the debate between the fictional reality of books and the physical reality of life, between the imaginative world of the reader of books (Don Quixote) and the everyday world of the illiterate (Sancho); (3) more generally, the debate between truth and falsehood, and the various methods of perceiving them, such as experience, reading, or hearsay. In a sense the third great theme subsumes the first two.

The word *debate,* used in this statement of themes, is not quite accurate in its application to the *historia* of *Don Quixote* because it suggests a polarization. Cervantes, in the natural *historia,* does not present a series of *cruces y rayas,* but rather many gradations between the possible extremes. It is in this capacity for nuance that nature excels art. The art story must be constructed around an artificial polarization.

But if nature is superior to art in its capacity for nuance, it is also more baffling. The issues discussed may be so complex that they are submerged in the plot—barely perceptible, in need of underlining. That this is so is demonstrated by the inability of readers, since Cervantes' day, to agree on a "meaning" for *Don Quixote.* The art story, too, often skipped, provides the clue to the thematic structure of the *historia,* by simplifying it and reducing it to an orderly pattern. There need be no doubt about the "meaning" of **"El curioso impertinente,"** in the sense that the themes are easily apparent, as is the pattern into which

they fall. The short story is a pointer, a clear indication of at least some of the things that *Don Quixote* is about.

Let us illustrate the two modes of writing by examining the way in which the theme of upturned values is treated "naturally" and "artistically."

Don Quixote presents a world in which normal values—the interpretation of physical reality, accepted ethical standards, and so on—are turned inside out as a result of the confusion of life and letters. Don Quixote is a kind of Alice in Wonderland. His affirmations of belief, his professions of faith, are grounded in nonsense. When in the Sierra Morena Sancho doubts the "truth" of the life he and his master have been living Don Quixote replies: "¿Que es possible que en quanto ha que andas conmigo no has echado de ver que todas las cosas de los caualleros andantes parecen quimeras, necedades y desatinos, y que son todas hechas al reues?" This apparently inside-out world of nonsense—this Wonderland—is accounted for, falsely, by "vna caterua de encantadores." But, illusory or not, the Wonderland has to be lived in; and since Don Quixote and Sancho are not innocent little girls like Alice, living in Wonderland poses problems: that of adjustment to the nonsense, that of revising normal ethical standards. Alice was able to adapt herself to her fantastic environment by being cross and feeling superior; Don Quixote's fantasy world, however, includes normal human beings who must either partly yield to his world (by play-acting, like Sansón Carrasco, the Priest, the Duques) or clash violently with his world (the merchants of Toledo, the Santa Hermandad).

But sometimes Quixotic nonsense infects the human being whom the Knight encounters; wrong values breed other wrong values, nonsense breeds nonsense. As an example of this contamination one might cite the shepherd boy Andrés, as he reviews the rough treatment meted out to him by his master as a result of Don Quixote's intervention. It was natural enough, says Andrés, for his master not to obey Don Quixote's instructions once he had departed, "mas como vuestra merced le deshonró tan sin proposito y le dixo tantas villanias, encendiosele la colera, y como no la pudo vengar en vuestra merced, quando se vio solo descargó sobre mi el nublado, de modo, que me parece que no sere mas hombre en toda mi vida." Does this passage "make sense"? "Vuestra merced" [a knight, a man of honor] "le deshonró" [dishonored him, a *villano,* a man without honor]. This same *villano* is outraged by the *villanias* of the Knight. The sympathy for the victim of the master's rage was misplaced ("tan sin proposito"), *therefore*—in this Wonderland logic—this misplaced interference must be followed by a misplaced act of revenge ("como no la pudo vengar en vuestra merced . . . descargó sobre mi el nublado"). This boy, not yet a man, then says: "no sere mas hombre en toda mi vida." From this piece of nonsense Don Quixote draws a flawless conclusion: he had erred by treating a *villano* as though he had been a man of honor, thereby contravening the teaching of "luengas experiencias."

These few illustrations reveal the complexity of the "natural" nonsense in *Don Quixote.* The "artistic" nonsense in **"El curioso impertinente"** will be seen to be sharper in outline, because the physical world is stable in the eyes of all the characters, leaving only the moral values upturned. Moreover, the normal moral values, those of Lotario at the beginning of the tale, are explicitly stated; they stand in clear contrast to the upturned values of Anselmo. For example, Lotario establishes a threefold analysis of the possible ends of life: those who strive in the world aim at the acquisition of *bienes de fortuna;* those who strive in the religious life aim at saintliness; those who strive in the military life share the two former aims. At least, in discussions of this sort one knows where one stands. Terra firma has replaced the quicksands of the main plot. The arms-and-letters debate has been clarified in Lotario's statement, even though it is left somewhat falsified by oversimplification. Lotario also gives a precise definition of divine friendship and honor as limits to the extent to which human friendship may be tested. Anselmo will be in error to the degree that he departs from these clear norms; he has had his warning. His conduct will be measured against Lotario's assertions of normalcy.

Anselmo's moral values are warped from the moment he disregards Lotario's warning that friendship may not be tested in matters of honor. He continues, like Andrés in the *historia* (but more obviously), from one *non sequitur* to another. In a conversation with his friend he learns that Lotario has failed to deceive him, as instructed, by making love to his wife: "¿para qué me engañas?" he asks. Logically this question should have been phrased in the negative. Anselmo does not understand that a single rent in the moral fabric weakens the whole. He angrily sees a deceit within the deceit; he does not realize that his rejection of traditional values requires their rejection by the friend who is committed to uphold them. This is an abstract Wonderland, a proving ground for nonsense. It inevitably involves even Lotario in its madness, for he is eventually described as "casi como tomando por punto de honra el auer sido hallado en mentira."

From this point on Anselmo cannot think straight. When a letter from Camila assures him that Lotario is at last attempting to seduce her he is "alegre sobremanera de tales nueuas." And so he forges the chain of false reasoning that leads to his dishonor and death: "yua añadiendo eslauon a eslauon a la cadena con que se enlazaua y trauaua su deshonra, pues quando mas Lotario le deshonraua, entonces le dezia que estaua mas honrado." Honor here is not very important in itself; it is merely the exemplar of the process of Quixotic unreasoning, the point of departure for an incursion into upturned values. It is the device that converts the confusing and complicated Wonderland of Don Quixote into Anselmo's Wonderland with its ideal simplicity and artistic clarity.

The words *verdad* and *mentira* appear insistently in every chapter of *Don Quixote*. Cervantes is fascinated by the idea that certain events, doctrines, or statements are true and others false; and by the idea, too, that some of these events, doctrines, and statements appear to be true though they are not, and vice versa. This preoccupation obliges him continually to speculate on the means of differentiating between the true and the false, on the means of metaphysical cognition. In this concern he differs from most of

his contemporaries. It is a fact that the *verdad-mentira* oscillation is a typical theme of baroque literature: Góngora's *letrilla* using these words as an alternating refrain is a classic example. But Góngora, Quevedo, and other poets of the time are content to rely on their intelligence and on authority for the discernment of truth; they are dogmatists, however far-fetched their paradoxes may at times seem to be. They know all the answers. Cervantes does not pretend to know the answers. The recognition of truth and falsehood is for him a problem defying a simple solution. His refusal to be doctrinaire is at the bottom of his fairness in debate, and of his respect for opinion as such.

The metaphysical problem is given literary form in *Don Quixote,* and it acquires thereby an aesthetic relevance. Cervantes identifies literary creation with lie: characters in *Don Quixote* repeatedly assert that books of fiction—chivalric or pastoral novels—are lies, *mentiras.* The shepherds of the pastoral convention "mas son encarecimientos de poetas que verdades." The equation—fiction equals lie—is restated in **"El curioso impertinente."** Camila asks:

> "Luego ¿todo aquello que los poetas enamorados dizen, es verdad?"
>
> "En quanto poetas, no la dizen," respondio Lotario; "mas en quanto enamorados, siempre quedan tan cortos como verdaderos."

This firmly maintained position implies that life is true and art is false—a view consonant with Cervantes' views on arms and letters.

It is reasonable to suppose, then, that the "toying with truth" in *Don Quixote* covers an earnest attempt to introduce this undefined truth into literature, to do what is by definition impossible. Is this the meaning of the phrase *verdadera historia?* I suspect that something of the kind stands behind the phrase and the author's attitude, for there is undoubtedly seriousness concealed by the playfulness.

Serious or not, the game of mixing up truth and falsehood confuses the reader. This confusion into which he is plunged may be salutary, but it would be irresponsible of Cervantes as a writer not to point toward the exit from the maze. A direction is given, among other places, in **"El curioso impertinente."** The point is that the *verdadera historia* is a plasma, potentially true, and about potentially real people, though it contains lies; the tale is actually a lie, and founded on an actual lie worked out with puppets who are fully under the author's control. The first action might have happened to the reader; the second is a performance in which he could never participate.

The initial truth from which the lie emerges in this spectacle is that Lotario is a good friend of Anselmo—"mi amigo verdadero" and that Camila is as good and faithful a wife as Anselmo thinks she is. Unnecessarily he submits these two truths—matters of honor, and therefore of life and death—to a test, not realizing that certain truths, if tested, cease to be truths. This is the point at which belief enters the scale of assent. Both Anselmo and Lotario believe in Camila's virtue, and affirm it to be "la mesma verdad." "¿Para qué quieres poner esta verdad en duda?"

asks Lotario. He realized that if truth is converted into doubt it is no longer truth. The result is foreseeable: Lotario and Camila really fall in love, really deceive Anselmo, and cause his experiment to miscarry. They reach such a degree of intensity in their clandestine affair "que hizieran los dos passar aquella mentira por mas que cierta verdad." In Lotario's analogy, the gem believed to be a diamond does not increase in value if it withstands the blows of a hammer. If on the other hand it breaks, the "known truth" is destroyed with the stone. It is as though Cervantes maintains that even in the physical world of precious stones the genuine article may be changed to paste by reason of the very fact that it is subjected to experiment. In matters of life and death belief is shown to be superior to experience as a means of cognition, despite the obvious merits of experience in everyday existence.

This account of the problem of truth and falsehood may not find many supporters, but it is a clear, reasonable one which may serve to explain why the masquerading of Dorotea, the Priest, and Sansón Carrasco is futile in dissuading Don Quixote from his adventurous life: lies breed lies. Without the oversimplification of this theme in **"El curioso impertinente"** the constant appeal to it in the history of Don Quixote and Sancho passes almost unnoticed, dissolved in a current of amusing adventures.

The short stories can produce their effect of clarifying the issues of the main plot only if the reader attaches at least the same importance to the *artificio* as he does to the *verdadera historia*. Cervantes' disappointment on suspecting that his readers were failing to read as he had intended is expressly stated in Part II. Much as we sympathize today with Cervantes' endeavor we still cut his text in our abridged editions and in our reading habits. If we continue to mutilate in this way we deny ourselves the possibility of fully understanding and fully enjoying—*Don Quixote*. (pp. 587-600)

> Bruce W. Wardropper, "The Pertinence of 'El Curioso Impertinente'," in PMLA, *Vol. LXXII, No. 4, September, 1957, pp. 587-600.*

Ruth S. El Saffar (essay date 1974)

[*El Saffar is an American educator and critic who has written several books on* Exemplary Novels. *In the following excerpt, she contrasts Cervantes's early and late fictional works.*]

A basic thread that runs through all of Cervantes's fiction from *Don Quixote* Part I to the *Persiles* is the notion that the world is bigger than any single view of it by a protagonist in his works. The difference between the early and the late works in their treatment of this common theme is that in the late works the central protagonists are exemplary in their acceptance of their given role in life and in their devotion to a transcendent reality. [The critic adds in a footnote: "Although it remains to be conclusively proved, I will be using in subsequent discussions the terms "early" to refer to the works whose elements reflect *Don Quixote* Part I and "late" to refer to the works more similar in style and content to *Don Quixote* Part II and the *Persiles*."] In the early works, on the other hand, the main characters

try to remake their lives. They reject the circumstances into which they have been born and show no faith in any reality beyond the one they perceive. From this single difference, a number of corollary distinctions between early and late works can be derived. The main characters' faith, in the late works, allows them to persevere through great hardship and suffering without yielding to the many pressures and temptations to which they are exposed. Since the character, in his exemplarity, remains unchanged, his development and his perceptions are no longer the central focus of the story. The scenes in the later works are richly described by a narrator who appears to be most preoccupied with the tasteful arrangement of incidents and an author who sees all earthly events as abstract representations of a reality which stands in changeless, timeless perfection against the chaos of existence in time. Opposing the serenity of the transcendent reality toward which the later characters aspire is the agitation and confusion they are forced to suffer. The later stories are filled with high adventure. The dizzying movement and action portrayed devalues the importance of the lived moment by the sheer quantity of its representation.

The fixation on a transcendent reality also affects the structure of the story. Rather than allowing the reader to move with the character, sharing his uncertainties, toward an undefined end, the characters' submission to a higher reality causes the reader's attention to focus, in the later stories, on the plot construction itself. We are asked to admire the author's skill in inventing new and different twists and surprises; to watch him begin the story in the middle and then work back toward the beginning before finally bringing the threads of the plot into perfect resolution. Since the characters' reactions are predictable, it is now the author's skill that must draw our attention.

Emphasis on the plot and the way in which it is developed also supposes that the story will have an ending. Since the main characters are exemplary, the ending will be happy. In all of the late stories the main characters are moved out of their normal circumstances, placed in situations in which their lives and honor are threatened, and then returned, through recognition and peripety, to a settled state within society in reward for their faith and dedication.

The early stories appear to have a much less planned development. The characters, while also living their lives in fiction outside the bounds of society, do so not because they are forced but because they choose to escape what they feel to be society's oppressive nature. In their escape they are constrained to start, in fiction, out of nothing: to recreate themselves and the society they are rejecting. Because the story builds from an initial choice by a character to recreate himself, it appears to have only the design developed by the character himself. In the early stories the narrator's role is severely restricted. He introduces the main protagonist with a brief statement of his prehistory, often omitting even the most rudimentary information concerning his character. The character then seizes upon some plan of his own devising and proceeds to impose that plan on himself and the others in the story. The early characters convert themselves, within a few paragraphs, from characters in someone else's story to authors of their own stories. Since the stories which they create are, from their point of view, unique and unrelated to their pasts, the ending to the early stories remains uncertain.

The prehistory outlined by the narrator at the beginning of the early stories reveals in every case a character whose escape into self-creation is instigated by a sense of alienation and lack of fulfillment in the normal context of his life. His invention must be unique because it must offer him a new route, an escape from everyday life. And because his existence depends upon it, he will seek to perpetuate the fiction into which he has cast himself.

The later characters, on the other hand, endure their fictional state. They neither choose it nor invent it. Though a flaw in their own personalities, or a mistaken choice, may have participated in causing their subsequent alienation, their prehistory is desirable and peaceful, and the later characters do not consciously seek escape from it. They work for and wait for the end of their trials. They seek a way out of fiction. The story leads the character through a maze of circumstances which interrupt the fulfillment of his wishes for peace and marriage and return to society.

Of the early stories, all end either with the destruction of the central character or with no conclusion at all. Anselmo, in the **"Curioso impertinente,"** Carrizales, in **"El celoso extremeño,"** and the Licenciate, in **"El licenciado Vidriera,"** all die after having seen their dreams shattered. All, having planned to create their futures by the force of their ingenuity, must face the absolute disintegration of their plans, recognize their folly in having tried to control reality, and die. In **"Rinconete y Cortadillo," "El coloquio de los perros,"** and *Don Quixote* I, the ending is suspended. By the end of **"Rinconete y Cortadillo"** the two young protagonists have achieved a certain distance on the thieves' life they have chosen, but, we are told at the end, they remain in Monipodio's confraternity for several months beyond the end of the story. The promised continuation will deal, according to the narrator, with Rinconete and Cortadillo's subsequent adventures with Monipodio's gang, not with their life beyond Monipodio's world. The ending, therefore, is no ending. The story simply dissolves into the continuing reality beyond its fiction. **"Rinconete y Cortadillo"** is nearly static, a copy of a moment of reality which, because the copy must reflect the reality exactly, has no right even to impose the arbitrary limitations of beginnings and ends. For such limitations belong to the imagination of the writer and not to the reality which he is reproducing. The absence of ending in *Don Quixote* I is identical to that in **"Rinconete."** In both cases the narrator anticipates a final end: Rinconete and Cortadillo will eventually leave Monipodio; Don Quixote will eventually die. But in both cases the narrator emphasizes that the second part will deal not with that ultimate end, but rather with the continued adventures that connect the present moment with the end. In other words, the continuation promised in each case would be a repetition in structure of the present story, not a conclusion. The **"Coloquio de los perros"** also ends in the middle, the two talking dogs anticipating another night in which they will be able to enjoy conversing with one another.

A picture begins to emerge regarding all the characters who appear in Cervantes's pre-1606 fiction. All are in flight from a reality with which they cannot successfully deal. All are cerebral in that they rely on their intelligence, ingenuity, or understanding to fill up the emptiness of their lives; all fail in fact to understand their past or to control their future; and all find that the present state of suspension in which they have willfully sustained themselves is an illusion from which all—some happily and some tragically—must fall before their story ends.

The irony in the early characters' apparent autonomy and voluntarism is that their reliance on their mental constructs—their faith in their own understanding—actually immobilizes them. Monipodio's world threatens to absorb Rinconete and Cortadillo entirely. The Licenciate's wisdom is swallowed up in his madness; and Don Quixote's reforming zeal is rendered useless by those who, having been rejected by Don Quixote, reject him in return. Cardenio and Dorotea (*Don Quixote* I), each wrongly convinced that their love and honor have been permanently destroyed, decide to give up even trying and are found, semi-wild, living alone in the mountains. Anselmo (**"El curioso impertinente"**) and Carrizales (**"El celoso extremeño"**), having established the outlines of their stories, drop out of the picture, only to be overwhelmed by real forces which are in fact beyond their grasp.

The later characters, in contrast, are far more successful in their life projects, despite their apparent passivity. Though many major characters in the later stories (i.e., Leocadia [**"La fuerza de la sangre"**], Teodosia [**"Las dos doncellas"**], Recaredo [**"La española inglesa"**]) face seemingly impossible situations, they do not base their actions upon any intellectual assessment of their chances to extricate themselves successfully from their problems. Because they do not conceptualize or invent for themselves a future in which present despair is justified, they maintain hope and act in every way to free themselves from their suffering and alienation. As a result, many of the later characters are highly active. Recaredo and Ricardo (**"El amante liberal"**) exert their energies strenuously, despite repeated failures and disappointments. They are shown engaged in a constant struggle against an unacceptable present circumstance, but never worried about understanding or reinterpreting the past or predicting the future.

The series of distinctions between early and late stories began with a comparison of the characters who appear in each type of story. Whereas the characters in the early stories were captured in fiction because of their flight from reality and were unsuccessful in recreating themselves because of their insistence on self-reliance and their belief in their own apprehensions regarding their past, present, and future, the characters in the late stories were shown to be in fiction not out of choice but because of circumstances beyond their control. Rather than running from society, they are shown constantly seeking release from their alienation from it, constantly striving to reintegrate themselves with society. The attitude of the early characters results in stories which appear autonomous, moving forward toward an undefined goal by the actions and reactions of the characters. In the later stories, the controlling hand of the author is so evident that the characters appear almost as puppets, victims rather than creators of the plot that complicates their lives.

Any change involves all the basic elements of the story. The differences in character attitude cannot truly be separated from the way the plot develops, the way the narrator presents himself with respect to his characters, or the way the major characters are related to the minor characters. Even such questions as the organization of the events narrated and the setting of the stories cannot be divorced from the other elements. It is surely no accident that historical detail is much more evident in the early than in the later stories. It is significant that the story's development in the early works follows a more or less chronological pattern, with the narrator rarely anticipating the story's outcome or rearranging the events in his presentation, while in the later works the chronology is destroyed by the controlling organization of the narrator. To determine, among the intertwining elements of fiction, which one caused the others to change would be a hopeless task. The story is an organic unit. The conventions of criticism which separate it into plot, characterizations, setting, diction, etc. are useful for discussing the way the story is designed, but they do not suggest a causal relationship between them. For causes we must look behind the changes.

In the later works, as they have been described here, Cervantes appears to have adopted a view of society greatly at variance with the one reflected in such works as **"El licenciado Vidriera"** and **"El coloquio de los perros."** The problem that must be resolved, if we are to avoid the conclusion that the idealistic tales represent Cervantes's capitulation to the dominant forces of society, is why marriage, nobility, and happy endings become persistent elements in Cervantes's post-1606 novelas, while the early works tend to champion rebellious heroes whose exertions lead only to failure. The change that mutes social criticism and exalts social conformity cannot be explained by Cervantes's personal recovery from ill-fortune after 1606. From the prologue to *Don Quixote* II, as well as from the *Viaje del parnaso,* we know that Cervantes still suffered from attacks on his character, poverty, and personal troubles at the end of his life. What appears to have changed, as a result of the fame and literary recognition he finally achieved after 1606, is his own perspective on his personal fortunes.

It is well known that *Don Quixote* I poses questions concerning the nature of reality and the relation of reality to fiction. From the way authors become readers and readers become authors and characters become alternately authors and readers; from the way basins become helmets and nags become steeds, it is likely that not only Don Quixote, but Cervantes, is challenging the commonly accepted meanings of words and suggesting that words are actually independent of the things they represent. Don Quixote's devotion to words and his blind faith in their truth; the attention he gives, as author of his life as knight-errant, to naming; his love for poetry; and his concern that Sancho and the others whom he meets speak properly, is only humorous because the words and names he believes in so fully are not in accord with those commonly accepted by

everyone else he meets in the novel. The more verbally careless and illiterate Sancho and the more skeptical Barber, Curate, and Canon appear closer to an understanding of truth than Don Quixote. Lotario, in **"El curioso impertinente,"** speaks out most eloquently against empiricism as a source of knowledge, and Anselmo's total delusion after Camila's pretended statement of her fidelity reveals the fallacy of reliance on sense impressions for true information. In *Don Quixote* I no one, including the original narrator, the "second author," Cide Hamete, Don Quixote, Sancho, the Curate, or the Canon, has a privileged position of greater knowledge within the novel. All are shown as limited and struggling, through language and their own understandings of each other, to maintain their autonomy and independence. Cervantes does not choose between them because he includes himself within their confusions, being as uncertain as they about reality and truth.

At the base of that confusion lies a nihilism and an individualism which threaten to destroy art and communication. The only way out of chaos and uncertainty is the affirmation of a truth that transcends language, society, everyday experience, social customs, and sense impressions. Human hardships lose their intensity when viewed as temporary, as unreal in comparison with a reality of greater meaning beyond life. Cervantes appears, for reasons on which we can only speculate, to have achieved such a faith sometime after 1606.

The novelistic expression of this position in Cervantes's works appears as an abrupt break from the earlier individualism and character autonomy. The early works represent an intense exploration of the consequences of individualism. Cervantes's alienated and cerebral characters, no matter how sympathetic the author may be with them, fail in their projects, doing damage to themselves and to those around them. The later works, starting with **"La ilustre fregona"** and **"La gitanilla,"** and continuing through **"El amante liberal," "La fuerza de la sangre," "La española inglesa,"** *Don Quixote* II, and the *Persiles* show a detachment from everyday reality and an increasing effort by the narrator to distance himself from the characters. Reality in Part II of *Don Quixote* becomes elusive rather than vindictive, as it had proved to be against *Don Quixote* in Part I. The minor characters in the *Persiles* who allow themselves to be beguiled by the world of reason or of sense perception are clearly presented as negative examples to be compared with Persiles and Sigismunda's chastity and single-minded devotion to their goal of reaching Rome in fulfillment of their pledge. The seven years Leocadia (**"La fuerza de la sangre"**) spends in pretense after her rape and the birth of her illegitimate child pass as nothing in the story which is devoted not to her suffering but to the nearly miraculous salvation of her honor. The evil characters in whose charge Ricardo and Leonisa find themselves in **"El amante liberal"** are, like the minor characters in the *Persiles,* to be regarded as symbolic of the evil passions which control men and women divested of a sense of transcendent truth. Recaredo, in **"La española inglesa,"** proves the emptiness of sense impressions in his pledge of love to Isabela when her face has lost all of its beauty after her poisoning by the jealous Arnesto's mother. As in **"La**

fuerza de la sangre" and **"El amante liberal,"** years pass before the characters' desires are fulfilled in **"La española inglesa."** Adventures become more variegated and fantastic, and the spatial and temporal distances covered by the characters are larger because the entire experience that makes up the work is understood by both the author and the major characters to be fiction. The vain search for truth in this life—the search that marked the project of characters and narrators alike in the early stories—gives way in the later stories to a conviction that life itself is inimical to truth—that all reality within the reach of human reason and human senses is, by virtue of that reason and sense perception, false. Life itself becomes a fiction. Cervantes's literary fiction then becomes a meta-fiction—a fiction whose truth resides in its exposure of both itself and the reality it is supposed to reflect as fiction.

Ironically, it is the stories which emerge out of this view of life's unreality and of man's inability to perceive it which appear to be structured most carefully and in a most ordered way. The narrator's voice is much more assured and authoritative in the later stories. In a reversal of the early relationship between narrator and character, the central characters in the later stories are made to rely on the narrator to unravel their entangled lives. In the early stories the narrator appeared to rely on the character to develop his own life and initiate his own adventures. The new relationship between narrator and character, however, accurately reflects Cervantes's changed metaphysical position. The later stories are teleological, presenting a fiction and an existence justified by its ending. The later stories enclose longer stretches of time and space and present disoriented characters because they reflect life viewed as a totality, as struggle and confusion relieved only by the faith that the struggle has a transcendent significance not apparent in time. In the later stories the narrator is sure of himself and of his craft because he reflects the author's view that God is also a reliable narrator weaving a fiction of infinite complexity in which the characters will be saved if only they trust in His mercy and act in accordance with their faith.

In the later works social criticism is not absent, but simply relegated to a position of lesser importance. When Cervantes reworked **"El celoso extremeño"** for publication in the *Novelas ejemplares,* he omitted a long and bitter section criticizing the young rakes of Seville. The same type of character appears in **"La fuerza de la sangre"** in the figure of Rodolfo, Leocadia's abductor. However, in the later version of the **"El celoso extremeño,"** as in **"La fuerza de la sangre,"** the wrongs of these characters are individualized, not attributed to only one class or type of person. In **"La fuerza de la sangre,"** Leocadia's father does not notify the authorities about his daughter's rape because he does not trust their dedication to the cause of a poorer man against the very wealthy. Preciosa, in **"La gitanilla,"** sings and dances for a group of noble men and women who are too penurious to pay her anything. They are shown to be vain, selfish, and exploitive of Preciosa's talents.

The lessened importance of social criticism in the later stories should not be regarded as acceptance of social corruption or blindness to it. It is rather indicative of a change of perspective. From reform of society, from the hope of rediscovering truth in literature, Cervantes has moved in the later fiction toward a concern for personal salvation through faith in a truth not understandable in human life. All of life comes to be viewed as a fictional journey through which one must pass on his way to salvation. Social corruption is only one manifestation of life's delusive nature and deserves no special attention. Not only is the bailiff who colludes with the underworld in **"El coloquio de los perros"** corrupt because of the distance he establishes between appearance and reality, but all things that man sees and touches and experiences are corrupt. For appearance is antithetical to reality, and understanding is antithetical to truth. The particular examples of fraud and deception in social life have been generalized in Cervantes's later work. Social corruption is only the most obvious symbol of the unbridgeable separation in life between individual perspective and truth. By making this a universal condition, Cervantes undercuts his earlier suspicion of a particular group who specialize in deceiving others and his resentment of the wealth and prestige of some of his rivals.

The liberation this new perspective on human life offers does not, however, catapult Cervantes into the next world or make him privy to the truths he intuits as existing beyond life. If the nature of living and writing is to be caught up in a journey through life whose appearances are all snares and delusions for the unsuspecting, then Cervantes must still undergo those hazards. As a writer he must try to capture transcendent reality through symbols. Nobility and marriage become the social and literary correlatives of the elect of God who achieve union with Him after death. Marriage is represented as salvation and is achieved in the later works not automatically or easily, but only after long struggle and peregrination. Later characters—both male and female—face temptations and obstacles which they reject and overcome without losing faith in the achievability of their ultimate goal. All the later stories, as the specific analyses in subsequent chapters will show, force the major characters to break down their sense of uniqueness and individuality and to accept the other—the loved one—as independent of himself, as having a meaning and a reality that transcends and enriches his own. This process is most clearly evident in **"El amante liberal,"** but is essential to all the stories of love and marriage. This sense of the other's reality, this breaking out of selfishness and isolation as a precondition of marriage, is symbolic of the type of conversion necessary for faith and true belief in God.

In all the late stories, the chaos and uncertainty in which the characters live end at the point when marriage is achieved and the main characters return to stability within the social order. This again is a symbolic, necessarily earth-bound representation of the chaos and uncertainty which is life's fiction and the ending in death and salvation which marks the return to reality.

A story without an end is inconceivable in the later works. Both early and late works express a relationship between fiction and reality. The open-endedness of many of the early works—of **"Rinconete y Cortadillo,"** *Don Quixote* I, and **"El coloquio de los perros"**—suggests that only the particular point of view of each individual can determine whether an event is true or only imagined. Fiction flows into reality and reality flows into fiction, but there is no truly distanced vantage point from which an absolute determination can be made. Just as Cide Hamete is, for Don Quixote, the "real" author—the scribe and enchanter who alternately records Don Quixote's deeds and befuddles his intentions—he is, for the reader, fictitious. The books which for the Canon are fictitious are real for Don Quixote. Don Quixote slashes the wine skin which he says is the head of the giant whom Dorotea had commissioned him to kill in order to free her for marriage. The others wink (or, in the case of the owner of the wine skin, get angry), yet the reader has another laugh when he sees that it is precisely after Don Quixote has slain the imaginary giant that the real Dorotea is released from her predicament and the way is in fact opened for her marriage. At the end of Part I, Don Quixote remains essentially unchanged. In the struggle for self-assertion that marks all of the interrelationships of Part I, Don Quixote neither wins nor loses. He is returned home in a cage, but still refuses to give in to Alonso Quijano and prosaic, everyday reality. The world view that produced *Don Quixote* I could not resolve the struggle. For the author is no more an authority than anyone else. Each character is equally right. Don Quixote is not juxtaposed against his essence in Part I, but against a society which, like him, is a mixture of pretense and reality. It is only when Cervantes conceives of his characters' struggles as oriented toward the problems of salvation and transcendent truth rather than toward society that resolution becomes possible. In Part II, Don Quixote comes to see all of reality as appearance and finally recognizes that he himself is another appearance—a mask that must be shed before reality can be glimpsed. His return to Alonso Quijano, like the characters' return to society, in the idealistic stories, is not capitulation. It is, rather, symbolic of a rejection of pretense and self-invention, a return to origin which within life means society and one's given name and circumstances, but in religious terms means eternity and God's will. In the later stories the characters end where they began. Only for the span of the story—which symbolizes the span of their lives—are they alienated from their origins. The main characters are pilgrims of life whose story ends when their goal of salvation is achieved.

Not only the characters and milieu, but the disposition of the story elements undergoes change in the later works. In the early works the stories develop chronologically. Because time is seen as endless movement along a continuum which has neither a beginning nor an end, the narrator does not anticipate the fate of the characters. It is this time orientation that permits many of the works to remain without an ending. For endings, like beginnings, are arbitrary in a world seen as continual flux. The conventions of beginning and ending are just as false as the conventions of author, reader, and character, or of naming, or of any of the processes by which man breaks up, for his own convenience, a continuum that permits any subdivision, but substantiates none of them. In the **"Coloquio de los perros"** Cervantes chooses arbitrarily the duration of a single night to limit Berganza's discourse, though presumably Berganza could continue to speak indefinitely if such an

external limit were not imposed on him. Don Quixote's defeats in Part I become part of the stimulus for his next effort, tracing a pattern of alternations: of defeat and victory, of rest and struggle, of discourse and action, leading nowhere. There is no indication at the end of Part I that a development has taken place.

In the late works, the narrator, clearly separated from the characters, does not present the story of their lives in the order in which they experience it. The *in medias res* beginning, characteristic of the Greek novel and present in the *Persiles,* is more than just a literary convention. It is part of the new metaphysical orientation reflected in the later works. By beginning in the middle of the story and working simultaneously toward the beginning and the end, the narrator further distinguishes himself from the character about whom he is writing. For the character, as a creature in fiction, like man in life, must experience events through time, chronologically. But the narrator is free, since he already knows the character's history as well as his destiny, to present the story to the readers in any way he chooses. This disjunction between the character's time and the time of the work further emphasizes the character's fiction, and the arbitrariness of the events which affect him. Finally, the story's organization suggests the eternity beyond human time and offers a perspective on chronology that reveals its ultimate unimportance. The character must save himself by his ability to intuit a pattern beyond the one apparent to him in his experience. He must be able to detect an essentiality in the present that undermines his sense of sequence and determinism. Adherence to this unseen essence will save him from both corruption and despair.

Another indication of the changelessness that the later works seek to express within change is the pattern of naming characters. All Cervantes's major characters in early and late works appear in fiction in disguise. Alonso Quijano truly enters fiction when he recreates himself as Don Quixote. Tomás Rodaja at the beginning of **"El licenciado Vidriera"** marks his progress through life by a constant change of names: from Tomás Rodaja to the Licenciado Vidriera to Tomás Rueda. Rincón and Cortado become Rinconete and Cortadillo according to Monipodio's wishes, and the once libertine Carrizales becomes "the jealous" upon entering the fictional world of **"El celoso extremeño."** In all early stories, the main protagonists continue within their fictional roles until the end. Anselmo and Carrizales repent of their folly, but die without returning to their prefictional state. Tomás Rueda dies in a new role, his original one long since forgotten, and Don Quixote's and Rinconete and Cortadillo's stories end with them still suspended within their fictional roles and names.

In the later works the characters also live out their lives in disguise. Preciosa turns out to be Doña Constanza de Meneses at the end of **"La gitanilla,"** and Costanza, in **"La ilustre fregona,"** discovers herself to be the daughter of Don Diego de Carriazo. Tomás de Avendaño and Diego de Carriazo, in the same work, become Tomás Pedro and Lope Asturiano during the course of their adventures, only to return to their original names at the end. Teodosia and Leocadia adopt men's names in **"Las dos** doncellas" during their struggles and return to their correct names when they have succeeded in their efforts. In **"La fuerza de la sangre,"** Leocadia must pretend to be Luisico's cousin until the moment when she finally marries Rodolfo. Sometimes, as in **"La fuerza de la sangre"** and **"Las dos doncellas,"** the disguise is conscious, while other times, as in **"La gitanilla"** and **"La ilustre fregona,"** it is unconscious. But in all cases the main protagonists feel a disparity between the roles they are playing and their essential selves. While Preciosa and Costanza do not know they are of noble birth, they do know that they do not belong fully to the situation in which they find themselves. The disparity between the existential situation of the main characters in the late works and their true being constitutes the tension which marks their lives. Their struggles are in all cases directed toward relieving this tension not by yielding to the existential situation, which is always known to be false, but by striving to bring that situation into harmony with their true selves. Therefore, since the major characters are exemplary, when their stories end they find themselves rejoined to their original selves. "Teodoro" becomes Teodosia again; Costanza and Preciosa find their true parents. The late stories end when the protagonists are free to cast off their disguises and return to the destiny promised by their birth.

The circular pattern of the late stories, the search for and achievement of return, does not suggest changelessness, however. The infant Constanza de Meneses, whom the gypsies robbed, was born only potentially noble. Her noble birth was no guarantee of her nobility of character. When, at the end of the novel, she returns to adopt her original name, it is with a sense of fulfilled promise. The Constanza at the end is truly noble, for her actions during the period of her disguise brought her external faith into accord with her internal worth. That nobility is not a condition of blood, as many have wrongly interpreted **"La gitanilla"** as saying, can be seen in the vapidity of the noblemen for whom Preciosa performs at the beginning of the story. Nobility is the label Cervantes applies to a condition achieved only *a posteriori* through, and as a result of, struggle. This is true for all of the characters in the later works. Marriage, after the trials of Isabela and Recaredo in **"La española inglesa,"** is not the same as their marriage would have been prior to the struggles. This point is important because it reveals the role of existence within essence. It is through time, through living and struggle, that the essence is both proved and made possible. Though time and human life may be fiction when viewed from the standpoint of eternity, just as the character's chronology is meaningless when viewed from the point of view of the novelist, or the character's name is false from the point of view of the reader and often of the character himself, chronology and deception are absolutely essential to the character's salvation. The character must take seriously his deception. Leocadia must hide from others the fact she is Luisico's mother or lose all chance actually to regain her proper status; Recaredo must hide his Catholicism from the Queen of England in order to be given the opportunity later to express it fully; Mahmut, in **"El amante liberal,"** must pretend loyalty to Alí Baja in order to survive to return to Christianity and to save Ricardo and Leonisa. The late characters engage in a dialectic of a most delicate nature. From the perspective of existence, the dialectic is established between a pretense that keeps a character within the appearances demanded by society and the truth which, because it is apparently impossible to find, may be abandoned or forgotten. Too much giving in to either the pretense or to the absolute truth would destroy the ultimate goal of uniting the two publicly. In the context of Cervantes's fiction the dialectic is established between the character in chronological time and the author outside it. The character must act according to the immediate demands of his situation and at the same time believe, often against appearances, that the immediate situation belongs to a larger plan that will ultimately lead to his salvation. Recaredo's release of the captured Spanish sailor in **"La española inglesa"** is a most dramatic example of the delicacy of the characters' position. Despite the urging of his men that he kill the Spanish captives so that they would not be able to alert the Armada and pursue them, Recaredo lets the captives go, because as a Catholic he could not kill other Catholics. His action threatens to reveal that he is a covert Catholic and exposes the entire ship to attack by the Spanish navy. His courageous taking of the right choice, however, was rewarded by the author's plan for his success.

All life, in the later works, is seen as fiction. Perceived reality, when measured against transcendent reality, is as a fiction. The fiction, however, is not devoid of meaning, for it is part of a dialectical process through which transcendent reality is finally achieved. The return to origins, the circular pattern suggested by the joining of ending to beginning, is not antithetical to growth and progress through time. For only through time can the end be rejoined to the beginning. The ending is at the same time a transcendence of time and a fulfillment of the beginning. The circle is an earth-bound representation of eternity. But since eternity is beyond human grasp, existing on a higher plane than temporality, the circularity suggested involves a vertical component. The movement through time produces a vertical trajectory which is expressed novelistically by completion. Time conceived of horizontally, as the early stories showed, has no beginning or end. When, in a story, beginning and end meet beyond fiction, time can be viewed as having both horizontal and vertical components: horizontal within the space of fiction and vertical in the ultimate ceding of fiction to a reality beyond it. The difficulty is in seeing that, rather than being isolated and disjoined, the horizontal and vertical components are interconnected. The origin provides for the possibility of chronological time. Proper understanding of chronological time in turn provides for the possibility of an ending which fulfills the promise of the origin by transcending chronology.

Just as he does in the early works, in the later works Cervantes builds an implied interchange between character and narrator, between truth and fiction. The difference is that in the later works the character and narrator exist on two clearly distinguished planes. The narrator no longer confuses himself with his characters and no longer pretends to be victim of the same uncertainties as they. This distance, clearly defined, between narrator and character does not, however, obviate their interaction. The characters appear to be on trial in the later works, yet free to choose their actions. Each proper choice by a character appears to be rewarded by the narrator by the presentation of a new circumstance which will make his ultimate goal more possible. Works like the *Persiles* are filled with minor characters who, having made the wrong choices, are left unfulfilled. The plot, then, is not so much an abstract pattern as a collaborative effort of an autonomous character oriented toward salvation and a benevolent narrator who both tests and rewards the character at each juncture. . . .

Fiction has a role in the later works. The role is to define the province of illusion and to reveal the dual nature of reality and time. Truth, salvation, and peace are not the province of fiction. But they are the realities toward which fiction can point and which the chaos of fiction can create as desirable. The wild adventures, the shipwrecks, the pilgrimages, the peripeties and changes of fortune, the recognition scenes, the presentation of an elaborately deceptive reality, and the creation of rhetorical pirouettes become the hallmark of Cervantes's later fiction because he no longer believes in words or temporal reality as truth. The exaggerated invention of the later stories emphasizes his lack of concern with everyday reality and reveals his vision of all of life as chaotic deception. But this highly imaginative literature can be exemplary because it represents not the author's madness . . . but the essential confusion and diversity, the empty plentitude of human existence. The calm which surrounds the late stories, the social order serenely confident of itself, suggests that beyond fiction, beyond alienation, struggle, and disappointment, is order, an order which fiction cannot, by its very nature, depict. In the same way, we are led to see by analogy that beyond the chaos and struggle there is peace. The struggle is meaningful only because it makes one desire an end, and the end is possible only because an intuition of it in the struggle keeps life and fiction going.

Time enters into a dialectic with eternity, and fiction enters into a dialectic with life. In the resultant totality life is identified with fiction. Neither, in itself, is true, and both, being limited by time and individual perspective, are equally imaginary. A study of the liberation of the imagination in Cervantes's late fiction cannot be divorced from its metaphysical implications. For that liberation does not suggest divorce from life, but rather a new way of relating to it. Cervantes's late work reflects both his sense of the chaotic multiplicity on the surface of life and the promise of its invisible underlying and overriding truth. (pp. 13-29)

> *Ruth S. El Saffar, in her* Novel to Romance:
> A Study of Cervantes's "Novelas ejemplares,"
> *Johns Hopkins University Press, 1974, 189 p.*

David M. Gitlitz (essay date 1981)

[*In the following essay, Gitlitz discusses the strict structural symmetry and the characterization of Rodolfo in Cervantes's "The Force of Blood."*]

Two aspects of Cervantes' **"La fuerza de la sangre"** interest me here: the details of and reasons for the novel's extraordinary symmetry, and the reason why in spite of the novel's apparently happy ending, we are left with the im-

> I am the first to essay novels in the Castilian tongue, for the many which go about in print in Spanish are all translated from foreign languages, while these are my own, neither imitated nor stolen. My genius begat them, and my pen gave them birth.
>
> —*Miguel de Cervantes in the preface to his* Six Exemplary Novels, *1613.*

pression that Rodolfo is a libidinous S.O.B. This statement, which seems a wild anachronism along the lines of those which are analysed by Anthony Close in his book about the legacy of romantic attitudes on Cervantes criticism of the last century [*The Romantic Approach to 'Don Quijote',* 1977], really is not anachronistic, for it is rooted in textual evidence and in principles of construction common in the seventeenth century.

Although many critics have dealt with this novel's symmetry, no one speaks of its highly paradoxical resolution, in which the rhetorical tone of felicity and harmony contrasts sharply with identification of Rodolfo as a man piloted by undisguised and uncontrolled sexuality. We will see how this interpretation of Rodolfo, and of the novel's significance, is derived from the symmetry of the work. My interpretation builds on the investigations of three critics who in recent years have contributed greatly to our understanding of this novel: Joaquín Casalduero [*Sentido y forma de las Novelas ejemplares,* 1962], Robert Piluso [" 'La fuerza de la sangre': un análisis estrutural," *Hispania* 47 (1964)], and Ruth el Saffar [*Novel to Romance,* 1974].

Typical of Golden Age art is its predilection for symmetry derived from Aristotelian principles of composition. Golden Age painters, architects, musicians and poets conceived of each work of art as a closed, balanced, harmonious system whose geometry was carefully sketched long before pen touched paper or brush dipped into paint. A good example would be the rigorous symmetry of motifs in Salicio's and Nemoroso's songs in Garcilaso's "First Eclogue"; or the meticulous geometry of the Escorial; or the logical development of any of Diego Ortiz's compositions for the *vihuela;* or the intersecting triangles of Velasquez's "Coronation of the Virgin," or the receding planes of his "Spinners." What all these examples, chosen over a span of about 150 years, have in common are the notions that (1) beauty is an intellectual and thus to some extent abstractable quality, and that (2) artistic unity of the whole is a function of the proportioned symmetric distribution of the parts. These are some of the Aristotelian precepts which infuse Cervantes' work, and which he occasionally alludes to directly, such as when he says in the *Galatea:* "Corporeal beauty . . . occurs when all parts of the body are by themselves beautiful, and when all of them together make a perfect wholeness, and form a well proportioned harmony of members."

"La fuerza de la sangre," at first glance one of the simplest *Exemplary Novels,* typifies the Golden Age preoccupation with geometry and with artfully decorated architectural forms. Its plot relates two events accompanied by emotional crises—a rape and a reconciliation—separated by a hiatus of seven years in which Luisico, who is engendered as a result of the rape, grows up. It is remarkable how regularly Cervantes distributes the stuff of his novel—anecdotes, characters, descriptions, themes, and symbols—with almost perfect symmetry. For example, each of the three sections of the novel is divided into three scenes, and those of the first and third sections are related in both setting and plot:

Part one narrates the rape and Leocadia's subsequent dishonor.

Part three narrates the reconciliation of Leocadia and Rodolfo with the restoration of her honor.

The first scene of each part occurs in the street: in the first Leocadia is violently kidnapped, in the second Luisico is injured by a runaway horse.

The second scene of each part occurs in Rodolfo's room: in the first Leocadia is raped by an unknown assailant, and then she carefully registers the contents of the room; in the third she once again inventories the room, recognizes it, discloses the rape and identifies the rapist.

Each third scene occurs at home, in the presence of family: in the first part Leocadia confesses to her family what has happened, and is warmly reconciled with them. In the third part Leocadia joins Rodolfo in his home, where they are both subsequently united with their families.

Although in **"La fuerza de la sangre,"** as in most of Cervantes' so-called "idealistic novels" there is little conversation, here the climactic moments are marked by speeches: twice in the second scene of each part, and once in the third scene of each part. The themes of these speeches,—honor, death, and justice—are repeated in the two parts.

Towards the end of **"La fuerza de la sangre,"** Cervantes gives us an explicit clue for interpreting its structure. Leocadia, awaking in Rodolfo's arms from the last of her faints, says:

> When I woke up and came to myself after that other faint, I found myself, sir, in your arms without honor; but I consider it well occasioned, since when I awoke from my most recent faint, I found myself in those selfsame arms, but with honor.

This passage indicates how Cervantes has structured his novel around a series of repeated events (like the fainting spells), which sometimes have opposite interpretations (honor/dishonor). In the first of the fainting scenes, for example, we see that Leocadia fights to escape Rodolfo's attempt to repeat the rape; then later on, when Rodolfo's intentions are matrimonial, Leocadia says that she "would like with honest strength to untie herself from Rodolfo's arms," but that it is no longer necessary.

This play of dualities, sometimes in parallel and sometimes in opposition, dominates the novel's structure to an astounding extent. Ruth el Saffar, in her analysis of just the first paragraph of the novel, has clarified the binary opposition of the two groups, each composed of five people, who meet that night in Toledo: the sheep and the wolves; the old men and the young; family and the loose company of youth; intentions well inclined and twisted; those who descend on horseback and those who climb the hill on foot, the immediacy of rape and the projection of dishonor many years into the future.

In the field of anecdote it is easy to find similar pairs of events. In the first part of the novel Leocadia carefully registers Rodolfo's house, noting the bed, the hangings, the desk, and a window with a grate which opens onto a garden, all details which she recounts again when she returns to the house in the third part. In the first part the wild companions of Rodolfo disguise themselves, and Rodolfo binds Leocadia's eyes so that she will not recognize him; in the third part it is Rodolfo who is ignorant of the true identity of his future wife when he is deceived first with the portrait and then when no one will tell him who the beautiful woman at the banquet really is. Early on Rodolfo's companions aid in the kidnapping; later they aid in the reconciliation. On the thematic plane, as Robert Piluso notes, "the physical kidnapping of Leocadia by Rodolfo . . . is avenged with the spiritual kidnapping of Rodolfo by Leocadia." In the first part Leocadia steals a crucifix; she prays to it and finds that her prayers are answered in the third part when she uses the crucifix to prove her story.

There are also numerous examples of symmetry through antithesis, such as the series of disharmonies in the first part which are harmoniously resolved in the third. The squadron of insolent wolves which steal Leocadia from the sheep gives way to a family scene where, with Biblical and Virgilian echoes, those who were sheep dine in peace with the former wolves. In a similar fashion, the scene of the kidnapping ends with the dichotomous separation of the two groups, one happy and the other sad, into their respective houses. The novel ends with the joyous reunion of all in the house of Rodolfo. The terrible night of the rape becomes the happy wedding night. And so forth.

Cervantes deploys the images associated with the main moments of his novel in a symmetrical fashion. By conceiving of violence and sin in terms of disharmony and darkness, and by identifying the harmonious resolution of the plot with images of radiant light, Cervantes follows a solid Renaissance tradition. The rape occurs at night when it is impossible to see clearly. Leocadia awakes surrounded by shadowy darkness. She says that she prefers that the darkness should last forever, that her eyes might never again see the light of the world, that her dishonor might be perpetually hidden in shadow. Rodolfo binds her eyes once again and sets her in the street before the first light of dawn. This literal darkness in the first part of the novel has a figurative counterpart: Leocadia faints, losing the light of her eyes. Her parents are rendered blind by the tragedy, "without their daughter's eyes, which were the light of their own." Rodolfo, at the instant of committing the rape, was "blind to the light of understanding." In the last part of the novel all this darkness and blindness becomes light. Leocadia counts the steps in Rodolfo's house and brings all her suspicions to light. When Luisico recovers, he restores to his grandparents the light of their eyes. At the banquet Leocadia appears with her hair decked with diamonds which "clouded the light of the eyes of those who gazed upon them." Over dinner the two young people flash radiant glances at each other.

The rigorous symmetry of this novel impels us to take into account the relationship between two elements which at first seem dissimilar, if it were not for the fact that because of their arrangement within the scheme of the novel they must be considered related. I am referring to the horse which runs down Luisico in the street, shedding his blood, and to Rodolfo, who kidnaps Leocadia in the street in order to rape her, shedding her virginal blood. It is well known how Golden Age writers used the horse to indicate sensual passion out of the control of reason. The most famous example is the "hipogrifo violento," the violent hypogryph which opens *Life is a dream* where, to quote Valbuena Briones, the horse represents "passionate instinct . . . , primordially carnal appetite and pride" ["La Caida del caballo," in his *Perspectiva crítica de los dramas de Calderón,* 1965]. The extraordinary parallelism of **"La fuerza de la sangre"** indicates that here the horse should be interpreted the same way. This horse, whose rider, Cervantes says, "was unable to hold in check the fury of his running," represents the unbridled passion of Rodolfo, whom Cervantes also describes as having "twisted inclinations," "too much freedom," and of being moved by the "unchaste impetus of youth." At the beginning of the novel Rodolfo and his band are horsemen, while Leocadia climbs the hill on foot. Rodolfo is continually characterized by his taste for sensuality, while Leocadia, on the other hand, seems to be the personification of chaste discretion, of the domination of intellect and restraint over carnal appetites.

Is it legitimate to associate the horse symbol with Rodolfo? In spite of Anthony Close, who casts doubt on the validity of any allegorical or symbolic interpretation of Cervantes' prose (especially *Don Quijote*), I would say that it is legitimate for three reasons.

First, Golden Age art, from the *autos* of Calderón to Valázquez's paintings to emblem books to much of Cervantes' other work, attests to the popularity of symbolic interpretation. We remember the allegorical carriages of the Countess Trifaldi, the literary battles of the *Viaje al Parnaso,* or the allegorical characters who figure in many of Cervantes' plays. Second, the finely elaborated symmetric structure of this novel allows us to suppose that Cervantes took such care in physically joining diverse elements in the story so as to link them thematically as well. Third, of the twelve *Exemplary novels,* this is the only one whose title does not directly name the protagonist (**"Las dos doncellas," "El celoso extremeño," "La gitanilla"**) or refer to a key event (**"El casamiento engañoso"** and **"El coloquio de los perros"**). The title of this novel not only lends itself to symbolic interpretation, it invites it.

But to what force is it referring? And to what blood? It seems to me that these questions may have at least five plausible answers: (1) The blood can be that of Christ, evoked in this novel by the stolen crucifix to which Leocadia entrusts herself, and its force, its strength, is to lead the protagonists to a happy resolution and even to absolve Rodolfo of his sin, although this is not stated explicitly. (2) Or the blood can be that of lineage, the mixture of bloodlines which produce Luisico, and its strength is such that Luisico's grandparents recognize him as their own. (3) The blood can refer to the nobility of the two protagonists, whose strength makes Leocadia behave the way she does and leads Rodolfo to correct his error by marrying her. (4) Or the blood may be that which Leocadia sheds when she is raped and that Luisico sheds when he is run down in the street by the horse, the two moments in the novel when strength and violence win out. (5) Or the blood can refer to the hot sexual instincts of Rodolfo, which force him to make use of force to achieve his ends. It seems clear that all these interpretations of the novel's title are justified, and to some extent all are operative simultaneously, which helps to explain the thematic richness of the novel. Particularly these last two interpretations, which link Leocadia's blood with Luisico's, and associate Rodolfo with the horse, suggest that we take another look at the ending of the novel and at Rodolfo's role.

To the three critics that I referred to at the beginning of this talk, **"La fuerza de la sangre"** has a happy ending. Casalduero, in his exegesis of the novel, advances a religious allegorical interpretation: the rape scene itself (original sin) contains the germ of the sinner's redemption (symbolized by the crucifix), and after a period of expiation (the seven years) the sin is "purified and redeemed by the sacrament of marriage." Robert Piluso reaffirms this interpretation when he notes that **"La fuerza de la sangre"** presents sacramental marriage as a reward following a period of trial [*Amor, matrimonio y honra en Cervantes,* 1967]. And Ruth el Saffar, whose interpretation is far from Casalduero's Catholic allegory, considers that this marriage, which is the end result of a chain of natural and divine causes, mitigates our possible condemnation of Rodolfo. "For this reason," she writes, "Rodolfo's acceptance of Leocadia as his wife is viewed with benevolence and is taken as sacramental, despite the fact that it was motivated by desires originating out of his lust and love for beauty."

But as I have said, I think that the evidence presented in this novel argues for an essentially negative interpretation of Rodolfo's character, and thus for an ending which is more ambiguous than happy. Piluso, referring to the beginning of the novel only, calls Rodolfo an egotist, a "slave to his sexual appetite," and I think this harsh judgment should be extended to the end of the novel as well, for lust continues to be Rodolfo's dominant characteristic. When his mother indicates that his intended bride is beautiful, Rodolfo hurries home from Italy, motivated by the "sweet delight of enjoying such a beautiful woman" ("la golosina de gozar tan hermosa mujer"). When he sees the portrait of the ugly woman, he confesses to his mother that his only interest in marriage is the conjugal bed, "el justo y debido deleite que los casados gozan," and that among all the possible graces that a woman might have—nobility, wealth, and discretion—he only cares for physical beauty. At the wedding banquet, when Leocadia faints for the third time, Rodolfo rushes to take her in his arms in order to rest his face on her breast. When he learns that Leocadia is his real bride to be, Rodolfo is inflamed by desire, and abandoning all pretense of modesty, he kisses her passionately ("llevado de su amoroso y encendido deseo, y quitándole el nombre de esposo todos los estorbos que la honestidad y decencia del lugar le podían poner, se abalanzó al rostro de Leocadia, juntando su boca con la de ella") and even after they are married, Rodolfo protests that night comes limping on crutches, so eager is he to take his new wife to bed. It is clear that marriage has not bridled the horse of Rodolfo's lust.

We have here another case of Cervantean moral ambiguity of the kind that abound in his works. We know, for example, that Roque Guinart is a thief, an outlaw and a murderer, but we also see him perform as an able administrator and effective knight errant who aids Claudia Jerónima. Although Maritornes is a whore, and thus a kind of anti-María, when she buys wine for Sancho Panza after his blanketing she is the only true Christian at the inn. Ricote the *morisco* is an enemy of the state, but at the same time he feels a profound love for Spain, to which he has returned in search of his lost daughter. Are these characters good? Bad? Normally Cervantes does not resolve this ambiguity, neither in the events nor in the rhetorical trappings that clothe them, but merely poses the moral issue and lets each reader decide for himself.

Much nearer Rodolfo's case is Fernando's in the first part of *Don Quijote*. Although Fernando does not rape Dorotea, he does seduce her, and later abandons her as well. Dorotea is just as intelligent, *discreta*, as Leocadia, and like her, with the help of her friends she confronts the wrongdoer and forces him to marry her. In *Don Quijote*, as Américo Castro has shown, all evidence indicates that Fernando is not really repentant, that he still desires Luscinda and not Dorotea, and that he consents to marry Dorotea only because he would publically lose his honor as a gentleman and Christian if he did not [*De la edad conflictiva,* 1972]. The Fernando episode leaves a bitter aftertaste, because although we realize that Dorotea will at last have her husband, this husband will be Fernando. Dorotea has done the best she could. For her, given Fernando's character, the solution is optimistic, and at the same time very human, which is to say flawed, and not unambiguously satisfactory.

The same thing happens in **"La fuerza de la sangre."** Leocadia's honor is restored by her marriage to Rodolfo, and in addition she is genuinely attracted to him. From the beginning of the banquet scene, rhetorical cues and the tone of the novel suggest that its ending is to be interpreted as happy. But it must also be noted that Cervantes does not adopt either of the two strategies that would resolve the ambiguity: he neither condemns nor absolves Rodolfo, either of which would have been easy to achieve. He might, for example, have inserted a reference to a contemporary law that orders that rapists, even if they later should marry their victims, none the less will be "excommunicated, and perpetually infamous and ineligible for any dignity: not only the rapist himself but all those who aided or abetted him" [López de Ayala, "El Concilio de Trento,"

cited by Agustín G. De Amezúa y Mayo in his *Cervantes: Creador de la novela corta española,* 1958]. Or, on the other hand, Cervantes might have had Rodolfo repent. But Rodolfo never does, not even in the scene where he frankly confesses to his mother his innermost thoughts about love and marriage.

The rigorous symmetry of the story emphasises how nearly every other element in the novel changes, but that Rodolfo does not. The dark night of the rape, when all is shrouded in gloom, becomes the gleaming nuptial feast. The desperate shouts and laments turn to joyous congratulations. The families are finally united. Leocadia's shame and dishonor are abrogated by her marriage. At the end of the novel the wolf and the sheep lie down together.

But, of course, the wolf is still a wolf. Nor does anything dissolve the association of Rodolfo with the horse, an equation suggested by the artful symmetry of the rape and the violence done to Luisico by the runaway horse. Rodolfo is always what Calderón would call an *hipogrifo violento,* and we would call a libidinous S.O.B., which is the same thing three centuries later.

Leocadia has done the best she could: this ending, like that of the Fernando and Dorotea episode, is essentially human, which is to say imperfect, for there is no indication that Rodolfo has changed, or will change, his nature. (pp. 113-21)

> *David M. Gitlitz, "Symmetry and Lust in Cervantes' 'La fuerza de la sangre,'" in* Studies in Honor of Everett W. Hesse, *edited by William C. McCrary and Jose A. Madrigal, Society of Spanish and Spanish-American Studies, 1981, pp. 113-22.*

Ruth S. El Saffar on the interrelatedness of the stories in *Exemplary Novels:*

The *Novelas ejemplares* capture, in a way similar to the two parts of *Don Quixote*, the trajectory of Cervantes's development as a man and as an artist. The strong differences that separate the stories into groups represent not authorial schizophrenia or senility or hypocrisy or a response to monetary pressure, but, through their intermixture in the collection, an organic whole built up through struggle and confusion toward release in a full acceptance of transcendent truths. The stories are not opposites, as their very different styles would suggest, but complementary parts of a totality perceived by Cervantes when, near the end of his life, he gathered them together in one "exemplary" collection, the value of which was to be derived "from each one in itself and from all together."

Ruth S. El Saffar, in her Novel to Romance: A Study of Cervantes's Novelas ejemplares, *1974.*

Juan Bautista Avalle-Arce   (essay date 1981)

[*An Argentine-born poet and scholar of Spanish literature, Avalle-Arce has especially distinguished himself as editor of the works of Lope de Vega and Cervantes. In the following essay, originally delivered as part of the Dartmouth Study Group in Medieval and Early Romance Literatures in 1981, he studies Cervantes's experiments with literary conventions in* Exemplary Novels.]

In the year 1613 Miguel de Cervantes Saavedra brought out in Madrid a collection of twelve short stories, which he entitled collectively *Exemplary Novels.* After a slow and dubious start in the literary world, Cervantes was then at the height of his fame. His years in the Spanish army were far behind him in time, and so were his years of captivity in Algiers. His first published novel had come out more than a quarter of a century earlier. That book, *Galatea,* a highly experimental pastoral novel, had met with an all too modest success, although Cervantes clung to the pastoral theme to his, literally, dying days. He had written an unspecified number of plays, which he chose not to publish until a few years after the *Exemplary Novels.* But the competition with Lope de Vega, the Monster of Nature, had proved too strenuous, and Cervantes had given up writing for the theater. In 1605 he had published the most successful novel in literary history: the first part of *Don Quixote.* Its success had been immediate and immense, and Cervantes had left the reading public dangling with the written promise of a second part, whose very sketchy outline appeared at the end of *Don Quixote* of 1605.

It is interesting to reconsider the fact that Cervantes deliberately chose not to follow up the success of *Don Quixote.* He decided not to publish the promised continuation, to postpone it, and this decision had the gravest consequences. The continuation was destined to come out all right—not written by Cervantes but by an imitator who called himself Alonso Fernández de Avellaneda, whose real identity will remain unknown forever, short of a literary miracle. But Avellaneda's continuation would not appear until the year after the publication of the *Exemplary Novels.* It was a strange and fateful decision for Cervantes to postpone the obvious and imminent success of the second part of *Don Quixote* in favor of publishing these short stories. His decision underscores the special place that the *Exemplary Novels* had in the literary estimation of their author.

He had been at work on them since before the publication of *Don Quixote* in 1605. We know this because **"Rinconete y Cortadillo,"** the third of the *Exemplary Novels,* is mentioned in chapter 47 of the *Don Quixote* of 1605. Furthermore, we have a different manuscript version of **"Rinconete y Cortadillo"** from the one Cervantes chose to publish in 1613. And we have a very different version of **"El celoso extremeño"** as well, thanks to the literary curiosity of a priest from Sevilla named Francisco Porras de la Cámara, who, no later than 1605, collected in a manuscript the two above-mentioned short stories. I cite some of these facts to bring into perspective the artful and deliberate care with which Cervantes treated his collection of short stories. He was at work on two of them before 1605, and when he published these same two stories in 1613 the revisions were more than considerable.

In the preface to the *Exemplary Novels* Cervantes goes out of his way to call the reader's attention to the literary revolution he is about to start. As he writes in the preface (I should point out that I use throughout this paper Harriet de Onís's translation): "I am the first to essay novels in the Castilian tongue, for the many which go about in print in Spanish are all translated from foreign languages, while these are my own, neither imitated nor stolen. My genius begat them, and my pen gave them birth." This, far from being a show of literary arrogance, is nothing but the naked truth, as the slightest consideration of the Italianate short stories of Juan de Timoneda (d. 1583) makes very evident. I mention Timoneda's name because he was the most successful of Cervantes's predecessors in this genre. In other words, Cervantes set out in the *Exemplary Novels* to invent a new literary genre in Spanish. He was fully aware of the novelty of the experiment, and he wanted his reader to be equally aware.

Let me briefly consider the first and the last of the *Exemplary Novels* to emphasize my point. The first one is **"La gitanilla" ("The Gypsy Maid")**, and it should be obvious that Cervantes set a very special store by it, since he chose to give it the place of honor in the collection. Why? It should be clear that the first story in a collection must successfully ensnare the reader and not let him wander. Which qualities contributed to making **"La gitanilla"** a successful reader-trap? I think that the most successful single quality is the literary typology contained in that short story. Gypsies had arrived in Spain by the early fifteenth century, and they had been officially outlawed by the state as early as the reign of the Catholic kings. Officially condemned as vagrant and thieves, gypsies had no room in literary history, save for a few bit parts in the earliest Spanish theater. Cervantes broke with this literary condemnation, bringing gypsies into full focus in the first of his *Exemplary Novels.* The success of this experiment would be attested to by Victor Hugo in *Notre Dame de Paris,* whose female protagonist is the gypsy girl Esmeralda, and in our century by Federico García Lorca in his *Primer romancero gitano,* where the second *romance* is precisely called "Preciosa y el aire," Preciosa being the name of Cervantes's protagonist in **"La gitanilla."** To this day the gypsy remains a social outcast, but he has been saved from literary oblivion by the magic art of Cervantes.

But there is more to it than that. **"The Gypsy Maid"** begins with these words: "It would seem that gypsies, men and women alike, came into the world for the sole purpose of thieving." By 1613, the date of publication of the *Exemplary Novels,* Spanish literary history knew a canonical literary form dedicated to thieves and thieving—the *novela picaresca,* the romance of roguery, adumbrated by *Lazarillo de Tormes,* that anonymous novel published in 1554, and brought to full fruition by Mateo Alemán in his two-part *Guzmán de Alfarache* of 1599 and 1604. So **"The Gypsy Maid"** begins with the clear insinuation that the reader is about to enter a picaresque world sui generis. But the world we enter is one of romantic love and travel. If we look at Spanish literary history again, we will see that the literary genre dedicated to narrating travels and studying romantic love was the Byzantine novel, which I prefer to call the novel of adventures, which would constitute, precisely, the subject of the posthumous novel of Cervantes, his *Persiles y Sigismunda.* So **"The Gypsy Maid"** offers the reader kaleidoscopic literary possibilities, incarnated in a group of social pariahs, redeemed by love. I think that Cervantes was quite right in thinking that **"The Gypsy Maid"** would be the successful snare to keep the reader glued to the pages of the *Exemplary Novels.*

Now let us turn to the last piece in the collection, **"El coloquio de los perros" ("The Dialogue of the Dogs").** This "novel" has two immediate and distinctly unique qualities, which I want to emphasize now, although I will return later to the narrative as a whole. First, let us consider that this text is exactly what its title implies: the dialogue between two dogs, Cipión and Berganza, outside the hospital in Valladolid. The subject of their dialogue is, mainly, the autobiographical reminiscences of Berganza, interspersed with philosophical comments by Cipión. Talking animals, of course, will take us to the opposite extreme of literary realism and, for that matter, completely outside the realm of reality. We are in a world of fantasy and satire that had been previously explored, many centuries earlier, by the Greek satirist Lucian. But it is highly unlikely that Cervantes could have known Lucian, because the very few works of Lucian that circulated in Spanish had been printed outside Spain, in Lyon and in Strasburg. Cervantes could have known, however, *The Golden Ass* of Apuleius, translated into Spanish by Diego López de Cortegana in 1513, with various reprintings. The golden ass, however, is a former human being now devoid of the faculty of speech, and he does not come into contact with any other animal of similar characteristics. The possible model for talking animals in the medieval, Aesopic fables was too elementary in its conception and functions to be of effective use to the Cervantine imagination. In other words, when reading **"The Dialogue of the Dogs"** we are confronted with the imagination of its author completely untrammeled and in absolute freedom, abandoning the norms of realism and from the outlines of reality. These have been the boundaries of the other eleven *Exemplary Novels,* but upon reaching the last one, the one that will act as a golden brooch to close the collection so auspiciously opened by **"The Gypsy Maid,"** Cervantes will abandon reality as a literary nourishment, and with the most graceful of intellectual pirouettes will openly embrace fantasy. Plato never dreamed of putting one of his philosophic dialogues to the use that this one is being put to by these two Cynic philosophers, and when I say Cynic I am referring to all possible meanings of the word.

The second unique characteristic of *The Dialogue of the Dogs* is that it literally has no beginning, an extraordinary occurrence in the annals of literary history. The way that Cervantes has manipulated things for this remarkable occurrence to take place has to do with the characteristics and plot of the eleventh of the *Exemplary Novels:* **"El casamiento engañoso" ("The Deceitful Marriage").** The protagonist of this novel is a soldier, Alférez Campuzano, who illustrates in his life and artistic development the folkloric tale of the deceiver deceived. On the streets of Valladolid, Campuzano meets an old friend of his, Licenciado Peralta, who asks him about his dejected and sickly appearance. The gist of the story told by Campuzano concerns his plan to deceive a woman, who in turn tricks and

dupes him, leaving him with a most embarrassing social disease. To cure himself of this, Campuzano repairs to the local hospital. The treatment he undergoes there puts him in a feverish state, and in the ensuing delirium he thinks or imagines that he hears two guard dogs, under his window, exchanging in human voices their life stories. When he comes out of his delirium Campuzano jots down the conversation he thinks he has heard, and at the moment of the narrative he brings forth his jottings and places them in front of his friend, Licenciado Peralta. Peralta sits down comfortably, takes the sheaf of papers, and tells his friend that he will read the notes, out of curiosity if for no other reason. And he begins his reading. So, *sensu stricto,* **"The Dialogue of the Dogs"** is nothing but the act of reading on the part of the Licenciado Peralta. This process of reading has already begun in **"The Deceitful Marriage,"** which ends with the following words: "The Alférez leaned back, the Licenciado opened the notebook, and at the very top he read the following title." Thus **"The Dialogue of the Dogs"** begins with no formal beginning.

But this is not the only structural innovation that Cervantes makes in **"The Dialogue of the Dogs."** He engages in structural telescoping carried to dizzying extremes. Let me try to explain myself. As I said before, the subject matter of the dialogue is mainly the autobiographical reminiscences of Berganza. At one point in his narrative Berganza recalls how he got to the Andalusian village of Montilla, famous at that time for its witches. There he ran into a witch named Cañizares, who recognizes him, in his canine form, as the long-lost son of another witch named La Montiela. At this point we are told that Berganza's real name is Montiel, and we get an outline of the life of La Montiela. Now the story of La Montiela is a function of the story being told of his life by Berganza, which functions as only part of **"The Dialogue of the Dogs,"** which, as we have seen, is the product of the reading of Licenciado Peralta, a secondary character in **"The Deceitful Marriage,"** which is in turn the product of the retelling of his own recent past by Alférez Campuzano to Licenciado Peralta. So we have this dizzying structural telescoping: a story (that of La Montiela) within a story (that of Cañizares) within a story (the life of Berganza) within a story (the dialogue of the dogs) within a story (the reading of Licenciado Peralta) within a story (the artful deceit played on the sickly Alférez Campuzano). At this point we can say that we are light-years away from the elementary structure of the folk motif of the deceiver deceived, or of the Aesopic fable, which is where it all began.

Now I wish to turn to some of the other uses to which Cervantes put literary tradition in his *Exemplary Novels.* I will try to be very specific, and to that end I will concern myself with only one literary tradition and the imaginative uses Cervantes made of it. The literary tradition I have in mind is that of *la novela picaresca,* the rogue's story, which I have mentioned earlier. As I said before, this tradition was set into motion in the Spanish peninsula by the anonymous author of *Lazarillo de Tormes* in the year 1554. Three editions came out in that year, in Alcalá, Burgos, and Antwerp. This little masterpiece was immediately continued by various authors, but in the climate of new moral and religious strictures during the reign of Philip II

(1556-98), it lost its popularity, was thoroughly censured and refurbished, and reappeared as *El Lazarillo castigado* ("Lazarillo Punished"), attributed to the pen of the royal officer Juan López de Velasco. Nowadays there is a raging polemic as to whether *Lazarillo* is a picaresque novel or not. I will not take sides, at least not here. I will only point out that Cervantes recognized it as such (more about this later), which allows me to consider it as such for my purposes. Whatever its dominant genre, *Lazarillo* effectively outlined the standard form of the picaresque novel, which was brought to its perfection in the *Guzmán de Alfarache* of Mateo Alemán.

The narrative form of the picaresque novel became conventionalized and canonized in a hieratic form from the first moment. Its subject matter was intended to seem autobiographical. The picaro, the rogue, told his life from birth to a time that usually did not coincide with the actual moment of writing. For example, *Lazarillo* ends at a time considerably prior to the time of writing. As Lázaro is made to say: "At that time I was at the height of my good fortune"; these are the last words of his autobiography. *Guzmán de Alfarache,* with its illusion of autobiography, ends with the repentance of the picaro, that is to say, his metaphorical death; the repentant Guzmán will write his life to set an example for others.

In dealing with his first moments in life the picaro dwells especially on his ancestry. Lázaro tells us that his father was a thieving miller, captured, tried, condemned, and sentenced, while his mother quickly became the concubine of a Negro slave. It is at this point that Lázaro sets out into the world. Guzmán de Alfarache, for his part, was the son of a Jewish, Genoese merchant, with the very serious consequences that such a background had in Golden Age Spain, given the national, suicidal obsession with *limpieza de sangre,* blood purity. As if these factors were not sufficiently alienating, the Genoese, Jewish merchant becomes a convert to Islam, marries a rich Moorish woman, steals all her money, escapes to Spain, and reconverts to Christianity. At this point he meets the woman who is to become Guzmán's mother. She is the concubine of a very rich and very old nobleman. Although her ancestry, as far as it can be traced, consists of whores, she deceives her old paramour with Guzmán's father, and Guzmán is, naturally, born out of wedlock.

The elements that the picaro wants to stress about his ancestry are those that will accentuate the sense of infamy *a nativitate.* But, as can also be seen, the infamy of Lázaro is only social, whereas the infamy of Guzmán is social, racial, and religious. This gradual stress on the all-pervading infamy of the protagonist will become a characteristic of the genre as it unfolds in time, as has been richly demonstrated by the fine study of the late Marcel Bataillon.

The autobiography of someone who is an infamous scoundrel from birth cannot but have a very jaundiced outlook on society. The point of view of the picaro, as Francisco Rico has suggested, is exclusive and completely negative. This is of paramount importance to the texture of the picaresque novel as a genre, for the point of view of the picaro is the only functional one in his autobiography. This last characteristic is, of course, proper to all autobiographies

as a literary genre. Furthermore, the autobiography of the picaro will be highly selective, another characteristic of the genre. In the case of Lázaro, for example, the speaker selects from his life only those elements that in his own opinion, will serve to explain his success in life. For Lázaro success in life consists of the fact that he no longer has to work for a living, because his wife is the concubine of a priest from Toledo.

That Cervantes knew well the models of the picaresque genre is a foregone conclusion. Although he paid no compliments to Mateo Alemán and his *Guzmán de Alfarache* (not even in his all-embracing literary catalogue of Spanish men of letters, which he entitled *Viaje del Parnaso*), this was due to the fact that *Guzmán* had preceded his *Don Quixote* and was its main competitor in the novelistic field. But Cervantes did mention and praise *Lazarillo de Tormes,* in a passage to which I shall return.

In the works of Cervantes we can collect a rich gallery of roguish types. Leaving aside the ***Exemplary Novels,*** two of his literary characters are very particular prototypes of the picaro as interpreted by his creative mind. The first one is Pedro de Urdemalas, the protagonist of a play of the same title, who winds up his life of roguish antics as the head of a tribe of gypsies, which should draw our minds subtly back to **"La gitanilla"** (**"The Gypsy Maid"**). The other wonderful picaro created by Cervantes is Ginés de Pasamonte, a character in both parts of *Don Quixote,* a special and distinguishing characteristic since he is one of the very few characters, other than the two protagonists, to appear in both parts. In *Don Quixote* of 1605 Ginés de Pasamonte is a galley-slave, and his antics in that part will lead to a tremendous textual confusion that should not concern us today. Because of his many crimes Ginés has been sentenced to the galleys, but while in jail he has been writing his autobiography, which, as he says, will enter into direct competition with *Lazarillo de Tormes.* He is then asked if his autobiography is finished. He laughs this off, asking how he could have finished it when he is still alive.

This last observation is worth considering from a few different viewpoints. In the first place, Ginés alludes to his autobiography, but we never see it, it is unfinished. In point of fact, Cervantes never wrote any kind of autobiography, fictional or nonfictional, a point I will have to return to later on. In the second place, Ginés appears in the novel in midlife, as a full-fledged picaro, a tried and sentenced criminal; we do not follow his education in crime but rather see its consequences. And in the last place, the novel focuses on Ginés de Pasamonte at a time in his life when he is totally unrepentant—he is almost proud of being a galley slave—a fact which places him at the opposite extreme from Guzmán de Alfarache, who had by then become the picaro par excellence. In the second part of *Don Quixote* Ginés de Pasamonte continues to be completely unrepentant. In 1615 Ginés makes his reappearance as Maese Pedro *el titerero,* Master Peter the Puppeteer, and in this guise he hoodwinks his audience, most particularly Don Quixote and Sancho Panza, his main victims in the first part.

I said that Cervantes had an obvious dislike for autobiography as a literary genre, since he never wrote one. The closest he came was in the first part of *Don Quixote,* in the story of the captive captain, and even then his story, told in the first person by the captain himself, centers on the episode of his captivity in Algiers and his escape. Before passing on to the analysis of the picaros in the *Exemplary Novels,* I want to approach briefly this Cervantine dislike for autobiography. As I said before, and this is by way of insisting on a basic truth, autobiography presents us with but one viewpoint, that of the author of the autobiography. In the course of the narrative other viewpoints might be presented, but they are always subordinated to the teller's point of view, because of narrative exigencies if for no other reasons. That is to say, autobiography constitutes an extreme form of literary dogmatism, because it presents one point of view to the exclusion of all others.

José Ortega y Gasset, the famous twentieth-century Spanish philosopher, once said that truth is but a point of view. And if that point of view remains motionless, truth will inevitably be distorted, with parts of it out of focus; it will suffer. A conjunction of points of view, on the other hand, will enhance truth, will help to clear up its outline. In an intuitive and artistic way Cervantes knew this long before Ortega y Gasset; multiple points of view constitute the fundamental tenet of his narrative art. This is why he spurned autobiography, which is the presentation of truth and reality from a single point of view, without the possibility of a challenge. On the contrary, he favored dialogue, explicit or implicit dialogue, because dialogue, as Plato had so admirably demonstrated, is the presentation of two or more different points of view. If Cervantes had but known it, he would have enthusiastically subscribed to Plato's statement in the *Republic:* "Dialogue is the coping stone of the sciences."

This is why *Don Quixote* as a novel really gets under way only after the creation of Sancho Panza, who becomes immediately a verbal sparring partner for his master. From now on, nature, reality, and truth will be seen from at least two different points of view. This, of course, is enhanced by the hallucinatory nature of Don Quixote's mind, which distorts reality while in the process of apprehending it, whereas Sancho's prosaic nature refuses any distortion whatsoever. This is why *Don Quixote* has become the greatest novel-dialogue ever written. The novel is conceived and executed as an exchange of viewpoints, as an immense dialogue, which can take place even at a great distance, as when Sancho, in the second part, goes to govern the famous island of Barataria. While discharging this illustrious duty Sancho is aided and abetted by the ever-present advice and letters of his master, which is a way of maintaining alive an implicit dialogue. There is no point in illustrating the almost eternal, explicit dialogue that occurs between master and servant at other points in the book, so full of merry verbal pranks and most serious intellectual queries.

This is another way of saying that Cervantes's mind had an intellectual thirst for dualities, dualities at minimum, because he considered the presentation of a single viewpoint a pauperization of reality. This was the great discovery of *Don Quixote,* and Cervantes would remain faithful to it throughout his creative career. This is why he could never bring himself to write a picaresque novel, which in its autobiographic, canonical form represented precisely that pauperization of reality that inhibited his creative imagination. The intellectual necessity for multiple viewpoints very likely explains Cervantes's love for the theater, an early love that he still avowed very late in life, when he published a selection of plays in 1615, the year before he died. In the prologue he wrote for this selection, *Ocho comedias y ocho entremeses nuncal representados,* he confirms much of what has just been said.

There is no point in going any further into Cervantes's dual intellectual necessities or his demand for multiple viewpoints. It can be seen even in the titles of so many of his texts. I will choose but a few, taken exclusively from his *Exemplary Novels*—**"The Two Damsels,"** for instance, or **"Rinconete y Cortadillo,"** or **"The Dialogue of the Dogs."** The last one, to be sure, appears in explicit dialogue form. All this should explain why Cervantes had an actual abhorrence to writing a truly picaresque novel.

This is not to say that Cervantes restrained himself from experimenting with the picaresque genre. I have already mentioned some of the wonderful picaresque types he created. The creation of these types was bound to lead him to experiment with the genre, to see if it could yield the possibility of multiple viewpoints. One thing to remember, at this juncture, is the fact that from the start of his literary career Cervantes demonstrated a wonderfully fertile, experimental turn of mind. One must only look back to *Galatea,* his first published novel, a pastoral, which at the opening of its idyllic, bucolic world presents a brutal murder of one shepherd by another shepherd.

The frustrated autobiography of Ginés de Pasamonte could be considered one such experiment with the picaresque genre. But in the *Exemplary Novels* we have two such full-scale experiments, which it is time to consider. I am referring to **"Rinconete y Cortadillo"** and to **"The Dialogue of the Dogs."** I have mentioned the fact that **"Rinconete y Cortadillo"** is known to us in two different versions, one printed in 1613 and one before 1605, both contained in the manuscript of Francisco Porras de la Cámara. I repeat this because it demonstrates the early intellectual need that Cervantes felt to experiment with the picaresque genre. And also because it demonstrates the artful care that Cervantes took with his literary experiments.

"Rinconete y Cortadillo" tells the story of two teenagers who meet by happenstance at an inn in La Mancha and decide to make their way together to Sevilla. There they perform some minor thefts in San Salvador Square. But they are detected by Ganchuelo, a member of the fraternity of thieves and criminals presided over by Monipodio; Ganchuelo decides to take them to the house of Monipodio to be examined, pay their dues, and join the fraternity. This is precisely what happens. The last two-thirds of the novel are dedicated to the description of the kind of human beings who attend a soirée in the patio of Monipodio's house. That is to say, we are dragged into the heart of the criminal life of Sevilla, which is an extension of the kind of life into which Guzmán de Alfarache was born. But the presentation of this world could not be more diametrically opposed to the technique adopted by Mateo Alemán. The consideration of these differences will serve to emphasize the dimensions and scope of Cervantes's experiment with the picaresque genre.

From the very first words of Cervantes's tale we can detect a veritable gulf between his concept of the picaresque and that of his predecessors: "One of these hot days of summer two lads chanced to find themselves in the Molinillo Inn." This is to say, the fate of these two boys is going to be molded by chance ("acaso," in the original). But the action, the intervention, of chance, fortune, or whatever you want to call it is unthinkable in the picaresque genre. The life of the picaro is governed exclusively by predetermination, indeed by predestination, as is made only too clear by the morose care with which the speaker describes his criminal ancestry. The picaro is a criminal because he cannot be any other way; he faces a destiny of crime because he was predestined to it by his ancestry. To a certain extent this literary predestination can be seen as a result of the original conception of the picaresque novel as an antichivalric novel. Amadís de Gaula, the greatest chivalric hero produced in Spain, was predestined to be such, for he was the son of the heroic king Perión de Gaula and of the most beautiful princess Elisena. Similarly, Lazarillo de Tormes was predestined to be a petty criminal, because his father was a thieving miller and his mother something just this side of being a prostitute. Chance cannot play any part whatsoever in any picaresque novel; if it did, then by chance the picaro might turn out to be good—in other words, he might cease to be a picaro. Hence the novel would lose its raison d'être. The conversion of the picaro, Guzmán, for example, has nothing to do with chance; it is, instead, allied with the contemporary theological polemic *de auxiliis*. But from its first line **"Rinconete y Cortadillo"** opens its doors widely to the action of chance, because Cervantes, as I have demonstrated repeatedly, had an almost religious respect for human free will in its literary representation. The life of Don Quixote richly demonstrates this: on account of physiological reasons he becomes mad, and after he is mad he chooses to call himself Don Quixote—but much later, on his deathbed, he chooses freely to abdicate, to give up, his freely chosen identity of Don Quixote.

The role of chance in the first line of **"Rinconete y Cortadillo"** serves a purpose analogous to free will in the world of Don Quixote. But it also serves its own very definite and subtle literary purpose. At the end of the novel Rinconete "made up his mind to advise his comrade that they should not linger in that vicious and evil life." In other words, Cervantes's picaros are free to abandon their evil way of life at any time they feel like it; the entrance into, and the exit from, the picaresque life of Sevilla is an exercise of the will for Rinconete and Cortadillo. Neither Lázaro nor Guzmán were given, or could have been given, that option, for the reasons already mentioned.

The criminal life into which Lázaro and Guzmán were born is described only from their viewpoint, since each is writing his own autobiography, as is the case in the canonical picaresque novel. But, obviously, such is not the case with **"Rinconete y Cortadillo,"** which spurns the simplis-

tic approach to literary reality by having a double protagonist and, consequently, a double perspective on literary reality. For example, upon their entrance into Sevilla each youth enters the life of crime in his separate way, and the narrative thread will at first follow one and then the other. During the long episode on the patio of Monipodio's house, the literary viewpoint will alternate between youthful protagonists. And at the end of the novel the literary point of view will rest squarely with Rinconete. The last paragraph begins: "Although nothing but a boy, Rinconete had a good head on his shoulders, and was decent by nature." Toward the end of the same paragraph the author intervenes to tell us that "we must leave for some other occasion the account of his life and adventures," with the implied promise of a future unicity of literary viewpoint. Let us note in passing that this personal intervention of the author in the novel, this sort of narrative distance and control, is impossible by definition in the picaresque novel, where the distance is permanently fixed by the autobiographer's point of view.

Another significant divergence from the canonical picaresque lies in the fact that the *novela picaresca* is eminently an urban novel, because to practice his tricks the picaro needs the city mobs. By contrast, **"Rinconete y Cortadillo"** begins with a completely rural setting: "One of those hot days of summer two lads chanced to find themselves in the Molinillo Inn, which stands on the outskirts of the famed plains of Alcudia on the way from Castiel to Andalusia." Only after this significant start does the novel move leisurely to its urban setting of Sevilla.

For the sake of brevity I will point out one last divergence, this time between Cervantes's tale and *Guzmán de Alfarache*. Upon leaving his house, Guzmán's first adventure is his encounter with a mule driver who victimizes him and steals from him. Guzmán asks for the help of justice, but gets no redress, which demonstrates his complete impotence before the world. He has to learn and practise deceit in order to defend himself in the world. The first adventure of Cervantes's youthful protagonists also involves a mule driver at the Molinillo Inn, but here it is the boys who trick the mule driver, steal his money, and when attacked by the mule driver defend themselves successfully against him. The importance of the different dénouement to identical adventures is considerable. The young boys do not need to learn deceit in order to defend themselves successfully against the world; they fall back upon their combined strength and succeed; they are self-sufficient. At the bottom of this significant difference lies the fact that on account of Guzmán's early impotence and defeat, the tone of his tale is pessimistic, melancholy, and bleak. But the early show of self-sufficiency and victory makes the tone of the lives of Cervantes's characters happy, gay, graceful.

Now to **"The Dialogue of the Dogs,"** which I consider to be Cervantes's other experiment with the form of the canonical picaresque tale in the *Exemplary Novels*—and by far the most ingenious and artful. The audacity of this experiment is extraordinary. To point out just some of the most obvious differences with the canonical picaresque, one need only recall that the protagonists are not human beings but rather two dogs, a most original and unique development of an Aesopic fable. The lonely protagonist of the *novela picaresca* is replaced by two, and its autobiographical form by a dialogue, with its consequent alternation of viewpoints.

But Cervantes has left enough characteristics of the picaresque genre in **"The Dialogue of the Dogs"** to make it easily identifiable as his most audacious and daring experiment with that genre. I will go one step farther and state that **"The Dialogue of the Dogs"** is Cervantes's travesty, ironization, and reworking of Mateo Alemán's *Guzmán de Alfarache*. Some other points of comparison will emerge later, but for the moment I want to stress only one. A major criticism addressed to the *Guzmán de Alfarache* is that each adventure is followed by lengthy passages of moralizing and philosophizing, passages invariably longer than the adventure itself. To be sure, this characteristic makes the reading of *Guzmán de Alfarache* quite an arduous experience. Of course, adventure and moral are all related from the same first-person viewpoint, with its categorical denial of any possible variation in the narrative tone. But in **"The Dialogue of the Dogs"** Berganza tells his own life from the moment of birth, with a passing reference to his ancestry ("this would lead me to believe . . . that my parents must have been mastiffs"), but his main role is to attend to the narrative of his life. He does not usually stop to philosophize or moralize about himself or his adventures. Such philosophical commentaries are usually supplied by Cipión. Such alternating viewpoints and functions give variety and spice to the sum total of the narrative, solving in the most dexterous and innovative way the enormous artistic problem that Alemán had created for himself in adopting the single point of view of an autobiographer's narrative.

As I have just mentioned, as in any picaresque novel Berganza begins the story of his life with a reference to his ancestry. He tells us, also, that he was born in Sevilla, like Guzmán; like Guzmán he was born into a life of crime. Berganza was born in the slaughterhouse of Sevilla, which he describes in the following terms: "All who work there, from the lowest to the highest, are persons of elastic conscience, cruel, fearing neither man nor devil; most of them are married without benefit of the clergy; they are birds of prey, and they and their doxies live on what they steal."

In a way analogous to Guzmán de Alfarache, the first adventure of Berganza consists of being tricked and duped, not by a muledriver, but by a beautiful girl, in a way somewhat reminiscent of *La Celestina*. The deceit into which he has fallen brings about the wrath of his first master, and gets him into deep trouble with the master, a butcher from Sevilla. Berganza runs away to save his skin and goes into the service of some shepherds, safely removed from the city. This suggests two characteristics of **"The Dialogue of the Dogs,"** each worthy of comment. First, with each new master he serves, Berganza changes his name. At various times he is known as Gavilán, Barcino, Montiel, or Berganza, the name under which he is known in Valladolid. I have discussed at length this characteristic in relation to *Don Quixote,* and my conclusions will remain the same. Cervantes gives his protagonist various names, or, better still, the protagonist gives himself various names, to

identify some deep-set, vital change. From the semi-anonymity of the beginning (what was his real name after all? Quijada? Quesada? Quejana?), the protagonist proceeds to call himself Don Quijote de la Mancha, and at various times in his life he will be known as The Knight of the Sad Countenance, The Knight of the Lions, Shepherd Quijotiz, and finally, on his deathbed, he will identify himself forever as Alonso Quijano the Good. This *polionomasia,* this changing of personal names, has its roots in the Judaeo-Christian tradition, and we know that Israel is the name given in the Old Testament to Jacob after he wrestled the angel of the Lord. In the New Testament, Saul of Tarsus was a bitter Christian-hater, but after the vision on the road to Damascus and his conversion, he came to call himself Paul. The use to which Cervantes puts this form of *polionomasia* is analogous, in the sense that the change of personal name differentiates the various stages of a man's life, or of a dog's life, for that matter. This, of course, goes against the grain of the picaresque, because the life of the picaro is one continuous reality, that of the life of crime.

The second characteristic that I want to point out is that in telling his autobiography we see Berganza serving various masters. Beside the two already mentioned, Berganza serves, to mention just a few, a rich merchant in Sevilla, a constable, a soldier, and a dramatist. This characteristic of the picaro serving a chain of masters became canonical in the picaresque genre as early as *Lazarillo de Tormes,* where we see the protagonist first serving a blind beggar, then the stingy priest of Maqueda, then the hungry and miserable nobleman of Toledo, then a friar of dubious reputation. In fact, each of the seven chapters of *Lazarillo de Tormes* presents the protagonist serving a different master. This characteristic became so ingrained in the picaresque genre that it was to serve as the title of a late Spanish picaresque novel: *Alonso, mozo de muchos amos* ("Alonso, servant of many masters"), by Jerónimo de Alcalá, who published the first part in 1626 with such great success that he quickly had to publish a second one later the same year. To this extent, Cervantes is quite willing to go along with classical features of the canonical picaresque. This one feature he found most useful to air his views on literature, narrative technique, contemporary society, and even the burning issue of the day, the expulsion of converted Moors, which was going on at the very time of the publication of the *Exemplary Novels.*

There is no question, having read **"The Dialogue of the Dogs"** with the picaresque structure in mind, that Cervantes utilizes the *novela picaresca* with the same overwhelming irony as he utilizes in *Don Quixote* the romances of chivalry. There were standard situations and human types in both genres that he could use, imitate, parody, ironize. He did all of these things to the canonical picaresque in his minor masterpiece of **"The Dialogue of the Dogs."** Maybe the most valuable lesson that this tale can present to us lies in the demonstration that Cervantes could put to some remarkable uses the autobiographical form of the picaresque. The truth of the matter is that in **"The Dialogue of the Dogs"** he invented a new literary genre of such extraordinary novelty that it has had no followers: the autobiography in dialogue form. (pp. 197-214)

Juan Bautista Avalle-Arce, " 'Novelas ejemplares': Reality, Realism, Literary Tradition," in Mimesis: From Mirror to Method, Augustine to Descartes. *Edited by John D. Lyons and Stephen G. Nichols, Jr., University Press of New England, 1982, pp. 197-214.*

George Ticknor on *Exemplary Novels*:

All of these stories are, as [Cervantes] intimates in their Preface, original, and most of them have the air of being drawn from his personal experience and observation.

Their value is different, for they are written with different views, and in a variety of style and manner greater than he has elsewhere shown; but most of them contain touches of what is peculiar in his talent, and are full of that rich eloquence, and of those pleasing descriptions of natural scenery, which always flow so easily from his pen. They have little in common with the graceful story-telling spirit of Boccaccio and his followers, and still less with the strictly practical tone of Don Juan Manuel's tales; nor, on the other hand, do they approach, except in the case of the "Impertinent Curiosity," the class of short novels which have been frequent in other countries within the last century. The more, therefore, we examine them, the more we shall find that they are original in their composition and general tone, and that they are strongly marked with the individual genius of their author, as well as with the more peculiar traits of the national character,—the ground, no doubt, on which they have always been favorites at home, and less valued than they deserve to be abroad. As works of invention they rank, among their author's productions, next after *Don Quixote;* in correctness and grace of style, they stand before it.

George Ticknor, in his History of Spanish Literature, *Vol. 2, 1891.*

Alban K. Forcione   (essay date 1982)

[*Forcione is an American educator and critic who has written several book-length studies of Cervantes's works. In the following excerpt, he contrasts* Exemplary Novels *with the* novelle *of Cervantes's time.*]

In his literary testament, the mock-epic *Viage del Parnaso,* Cervantes describes his frustration when, on entering Apollo's dazzling garden, he finds himself excluded from the ceremonial gathering of the great poets beneath the laurels of Parnassus. Likening the indignity to the mistreatment of Ovid in his exile, he allows his "Juvenalian anger" to vent itself in the composition of some autobiographical verses. Addressing his complaint to the god of poetry, he reminds him of the authenticity of his vocation and proceeds to pass review of his considerable achievements as a writer. Cervantes prefaces his surrender to anger with an acknowledgment that the literary products of the indignation of fools are generally full of perversity. But a more interesting note of self-deprecation sounds in the middle of his list of accomplishments, in the qualification attached to his defense of his collection of short stories, *Las novelas ejemplares:*

Yo he abierto en mis Nouelas vn camino,
por do la lengua castellana puede
mostrar con propriedad vn desatino.

(In my novels I have opened a way,
Whereby the Castilian tongue can display
An absurdity with propriety.)

In its reference to the "desatino con propriedad," the tercet presents the exemplarity of the tales in an odd perspective, a perspective that is all the more striking when one considers it beside the emphatically doctrinaire pronouncements of Cervantes's prologue to the tales: "I have given them the name of *Exemplary,* and if you look at it well, there is not one of them from which a profitable example could not be extracted . . . perhaps I would show you the savory and honest fruit which could be derived from them. . . . If in any way it comes to pass that the reading of these novels could tempt one who should peruse them to any evil desire or thought, rather should I cut off the hand with which I wrote them than bring them out in public." The paradoxical understatement of the *Viage* is much more elusive than the closed, conventional discourse of the prologue, but its ambiguities might, in fact, tempt us to suspect disingenuousness in the latter and to read both as implying Cervantes's awareness that the exemplarity of his tales is not to be sought where expected.

If we look at the testimony of one of Cervantes's most illustrious contemporary readers, we discover a striking failure to find any notable exemplary content in the tales. Introducing his own collection of novellas, *Novelas a Marcia Leonarda,* Lope de Vega praises the formal excellence of Cervantes's tales, but adds: "I confess that they are books of great entertainment and that they could be exemplary, like some of the *Tragic Histories* of Bandello, but they should be written by men of learning or at least by great courtiers, men who are able to discover in a 'disillusionment' (*desengaño*) remarkable *sententiae* and aphorisms." Apart from what it reveals about Lope's ambivalent personal feelings toward the literary successes of his great rival, the commentary is most interesting in its insistence that the excellences of Cervantes's short stories are to be found exclusively in their pleasant fictions. Quite explicitly, Lope refuses to acknowledge that the *Exemplary Novels* offer any edifying doctrine commensurate with their entertaining effects, and in making his judgment, he invokes a narrow and well-defined conception of exemplarity in short fiction. His emphasis on erudition, wit, courtly philosophy, and a type of discourse in which univocal doctrinal content can be clearly isolated and indeed even dissociated from its fictionalization through reductive *discursus,* aphorism, and *sententia* recalls methods of novella writing which had developed in courtly circles of Italy in the sixteenth century and were to flourish in the academic novellas of seventeenth-century Spain. As Walter Pabst has demonstrated in his comprehensive account of the historical development of the early European novella, the sixteenth century witnessed a striking transformation of the genre in its form, its social function, and its reception by its readers. The change paralleled an increasing interest throughout Europe in the vulgar tongues as the proper instrument of self-expression and communication for the new culture of court and city, and it was undoubt-

edly a response to the ascendance of the courtly society
with its widely orchestrated ideal concerning the individual
al as a socially perfectible being. Castiglione himself gave
the genre a type of canonization which was to be frequently
ly repeated and which we find echoed in Lope de Vega's
observations on Cervantes. If the courtier is indeed to
achieve the polish required to distinguish himself within
his society, he must master the arts of good speech ("bel
parlare") and the strategies of competitive conversation.
The proper models for wit, verbal resourcefulness, propriety,
ety, and grace in the use of Italian lie in the tales of Boccaccio, and the successful courtier would do well to study
them in order to cultivate the arts of extemporaneous
composition [*Novellentheorie und Novellendichtung: Zur
Geschichte ihrer Antinomie in den romanischen Litera-
turen,* 1967]. While such a conception of the art of the
short story brought with it the elevation of a genre which
had been traditionally consigned to the marginal and even
subliterary spheres of man's reading experience, it undoubtedly blinded its adherents to the numerous possibilities which the form had cultivated in its historical development and excluded from serious consideration all narrative procedures and even types of tales that failed to focus
on the social graces and urbane wisdom of "courtly philosophy." It is surely such a blindness which Lope, the most
worldly of Spain's great writers, reveals in his failure to
find any exemplarity worthy of comment in Cervantes's
tales. It is even possible that Cervantes's refusal to employ
the traditional frame—a courtly society of teller and recipient—with its conveniences for both reader and author as
a closed, determining structure which reduces the contained fictions to a univocal exemplarity and thereby fixes
the reader's response to them, was for Lope a sign that the
Novelas ejemplares belonged to a conventional type of
writing aiming at the modest goal of entertaining its audience.

If Lope and, presumably, numerous readers who shared
his expectations concerning the form and proper subject
matter of the novella were inclined to discount the exemplarity of Cervantes's tales, we must consider the possibility that Cervantes's allusion to the "proper *desatinos*" of
his fiction was in fact an admission of their modest intention of supplying permissible entertainment for a public
which did not always welcome the edifying assaults on its
sensibilities of traditional devotional readings or of the
more austere genres of "honest entertainment." Apart
from the salaciousness of some of the tales in the collection, Cervantes's willingness to use the designation "*desatino*" may be his way of acknowledging and dealing with
the disdain which the short story had suffered in official
circles from its very beginnings and which persisted
through the sixteenth century despite the peculiar sanction it received in the courtly society of Italy. The authors
of early novella collections frequently had to recognize the
embattled status of their fiction, its disruptive subject matter, its potential for debasing its readers, and the contempt
that it excited in orthodox quarters. The excesses of their
justifications can, in fact, be read as testimony to the validity of their opponents' claims. If the genre was generally
looked upon as a vulgar form of entertainment, the designation *novella* and its cognates were themselves occasionally invoked as terms of derogation. For example, Chré-

tien de Troyes, Ramón Lull, and Juan Manuel suggested
that one of the worst insults a knight could endure was to
be regarded as a *novelero,* a teller of novellas. One of Cervantes's predecessors in Spain, Juan de Timoneda, intitled
his volume of tales and anecdotes "the collection of lies"—
El patrañuelo—, suggested to his reader that his creations
should be taken purely for "pasatiempo y recreo humano," and added: "my native Valencian tongue intitles
such confusing imbroglios (*marañas*) *Rondalles,* and the
Tuscan calls them *Novelas.*" And it is possible that Lope's
introduction to his collection of novellas, which attributed
their composition to the persuasiveness of a "woman reader," his beloved Marta de Nevares, remarking: "I never
thought that it would occur to me to write novellas," is
to some extent motivated by the traditional scorn with
which the genre was treated in academic circles.

At the same time, in referring to his absurdities as *proper,*
Cervantes may well have been adopting a defensive posture, ironically acknowledging the traditional disrespect
for short fiction and carefully reminding his audience that
his own tales should not be judged according to conventional prejudices. His words may in fact be simply a translation into a more severe paradox of a contradiction latent
in the phrase *"novela ejemplar"* and as such a characteristically indirect way of pointing simultaneously to the literarily revolutionary and the morally legitimate character
of his literary undertaking. The same intention could well
have motivated the exaggerations and reiterations concerning their exemplarity in the prologue. Cervantes, as
we have noted, is prepared to cut off his hand before allowing it to write a word that might provoke an evil thought
in his reader. E. C. Riley is certainly right in suggesting
that "the excessive insistence of Cervantes undoubtedly
reflects anxiety," and that he may have been eager to dissociate himself from the notoriety enjoyed by the classical
Italian *novellieri,* whose names, well known in Spain, had
become "bywords for salaciousness" [*Cervantes's Theory
of the Novel*]. However, there is something yet more revealing in the paradox which he voices while complaining
of his mistreatment in the garden of Parnassus, and it explains in part why for Lope de Vega the true exemplarity
of the tales may have passed unnoticed. It is perhaps well
to recall Cervantes's self-deprecatory discussion of the literary merits of *Don Quixote* I on the eve of Don Quixote's
third sally. In the midst of the various denunciations of the
work—the improvisational monstrosity resembling Orba-
neja's formless paintings, the masterpiece for an audience
composed of the "stultorum infinitus numerus," the
hodgepodge of "baskets and cabbages"—Don Quixote
notes that "to say amusing things and to write humorously
is the gift of great geniuses" because "the cleverest character in comedy is the clown, for he who would make people
take him for a fool, must not be one." In its association
of the "discreet madman" and the *Quixote,* the phrase
casts a revealing light on the "proper absurdities" which
Cervantes offers as the designation of his tales, and in both
cases the paradoxes look back to the fundamental paradox
animating the thought and writings of the Erasmian reformers, men inspired by their profound sense that ultimate truth lies beyond the canonized forms of culture—
the deadening letter—and that it can be reached only if
one transcends the logic of the letter. As Erasmus asked

repeatedly, was not the most sublime source of truth veiled in the humble form of a carpenter's son in Nazareth? And did not the wisest of the ancient sages pronounce his universal truths from an oafish face and a slovenly figure laughable to all who gazed upon it until they beheld the wonders of the spirit concealed within?

Cervantes's description of his tales as *"desatinos"* is, then, neither the defensive invocation of a *topos* of novella composition nor an admission that his tales are primarily aimed at furnishing pleasing entertainment. In the tradition of Erasmus's meditation on the *Sileni Alcibiadis,* it is rather an invitation to look for the truth beneath the surface, in the remote or concealed areas where Lope de Vega, a man of radically different disposition and a man whose spiritual formation was the product of very different historical circumstances, was temperamentally unprepared to look. As Cervantes insinuates in his prologue, "lofty mysteries" lie concealed within his trifles: "they hold hidden some mystery which elevates them" ("algún misterio tienen escondido que las levanta"). "He who says 'mystery' says 'pregnancy' (*preñez*), an impending truth which is hidden and recondite, and any truth which exacts a price in its communication is more highly esteemed and more pleasureable," Gracián was to say in his poetics of wit [*Agudeza y arte de ingenio*] a few years later. For the critic, a reader whose business it is to transcend, insofar as it is possible to do so, the historical rootedness that inevitably mediates and conditions our/perception of the past, Cervantes's words offer not only an invitation to look within, but a challenge to look backward in history as well, to the humanist writings of nearly one hundred years earlier, the writings of Cervantes's spiritual fathers, men who understood that the loftiest teachings concerning man's religious, ethical, political, social, and domestic life could be conveyed perhaps most effectively in the disjointed discourse of a fool. (pp. 3-10)

The European novella came into existence in Boccaccio's *Decameron* as one of the most flexible and multifarious of literary forms, assimilating a variety of traditional narrative structures and techniques, incorporating a considerable range of aesthetic effects, and, as it was widely regarded as an undignified conveyer of amusement, gossip, and novelties, escaping the confining concepts of decorum and the limitations on compositional procedures which canonization in the official poetics of the period would no doubt have brought to it. If such variety had always been a characteristic of the early novella collections, there was, nevertheless, a uniformity visible in the general tendency of the individual tales toward brevity, swiftly paced movement to a climactic point, and spareness in the use of any detail—whether descriptive, rhetorical, psychological, or thematic—that might delay the reader in his movement toward the point. Based on one of the most primitive elements in man's literary experience, the stability of the genre was to a certain extent dependent on severe limitation, and it proved increasingly precarious as writers of the sixteenth century attempted to exploit the fictional resources of the form for radically new purposes and effects. While courtly circles continued to find its traditional qualities well-suited to their cultivation of wit and conversational charm, such writers as Marguerite de Navarre and

the French adaptors of Bandello's sensational tales, Belleforest and Boaistuau, were expanding its narrow confines by introducing elements that were ultimately incompatible with its traditional constitutive features: the consideration of philosophical and social problems, the cultivation of sentiment, the exploration of complex psychological motivation, an increased attention to description, and the elaboration of striking narrative units—e.g., the scene of pathos, the rhetorically striking declamation, the generalizing excursus by character or narrator—as independent and hence discontinuous elements within the traditional tightly ordered design. In short, the form, which had always been open in its assimilation of different socioeconomic milieus, different types of character, and different tones, settings, and historical periods, now opened up in a way which was much more radical and which threatened its foundations and hence its very existence. The century preceding Cervantes's decision to *novelar* for the first time in Castilian would appear to be a period of crisis in the historical evolution of the genre, a period of breakdown and redirection in its response to new expressive needs, themselves the result of the complex historical pressures of this age of transition in European history. More than any other collection of short stories of the period, Cervantes's **Novelas ejemplares** would attest to the profundity of the alteration which the genre experienced in this period. On the one hand, they represent the full realization of the effort, initiated sporadically in Marguerite de Navarre's *Heptaméron,* to turn the novella into a vehicle capable of engaging with the most urgent ideological and social preoccupations of the moment. As a novelistic monument to the humanist vision, analogous perhaps in its "belatedness" within its spiritual tradition to Milton's *Paradise Lost* in Renaissance epic literature, Cervantes's collection of tales is a true descendent of the *Heptaméron,* and one can not begin to account for the evolution in narrative fiction represented by both collections without giving some attention to the possible impact on the novella of the most highly influential fictionalizations of profound ideas in Europe of the sixteenth century—the *Colloquies* of Erasmus. On the other hand, Cervantes's tales represent the culmination in the quest for new forms that marked the experimentalism occasionally visible in sixteenth-century short fiction as it turned from the brief, pointed forms that had been dominant during the first centuries of the genre's historical life. Viewed within the tradition of the early European novella, Cervantes's collection is remarkable not only for the length of the individual tales included, but also for the variety of their forms and the generic models to which they point.

While Cervantes's aspirations to be the first to *novelar* in Spanish were high, his imagination was obviously not inhibited in the slightest by an awareness of a particular model to be imitated or a set of codified rules of composition to be followed. His admirers immediately hailed his collection of novellas for its variety:

> aqueste florido abril,
> cuya variedad admira
> la fama veloz, que mira
> en él variedades mil.

This flowery April,

Whose variety is admired by
Flying fame, who looks upon
A thousand varieties in him
[prefatory poem by Fernando Bermúdez Carbajal].

At the same time there are indications that his contemporary audience was somewhat bewildered by his claims to offer a collection of novellas. As we have seen, Lope, who in his willingness to consider *Amadís de Gaula* and *Orlando furioso* as distinguished examples of the genre seems not to have had a very precise awareness of what a novella was, nevertheless drew attention to the deviations in Cervantes's tales from a type of story which was familiar to him and could be invoked as representing the norms of the genre, Bandello's *Tragic Histories.* The observations of the conservative Avellaneda similarly indicate the disorienting effect which Cervantes's designation of such narratives may have had on his contemporary readers. The works are not only improperly called exemplary, since they are "más satíricas que exemplares," but they are also inaccurately described as novellas since nearly all of them are in reality "comedias en prosa." At the same time, in the enthusiastic reception which greeted Cervantes's tales in France, there are clear indications that their failure to match readers' expectations based on established conventions of the short story was so thorough that they were viewed as representing an entirely reconstituted novella, or, in fact, a new literary form. Le sieur d'Audiguier introduced his French translation of the tales as offering his public a completely new type of fiction, and Tallemant des Réaux expressed the view that the Cervantine novella must be considered as a literary form sui generis.

Modern readers and literary historians have found the variety of Cervantes's tales no less challenging than his contemporary readers, but their attempts to render it intelligible in terms of familiar generic categories have been only slightly more helpful than those of his seventeenth-century readers. If one considers the various attempts at systematic classification of the *Novelas ejemplares,* one quickly discovers that critics and literary historians have been content to account for the differences in the tales by invoking some rather vaguely formulated dualistic typology—such as romantic and realistic, fantastic and *costumbrista,* idealistic and skeptical, Italianate and Spanish, imitative and original, literary and representational, normative and vitalistic, early and late, and so on—a duality that in fact turns out to be a translation into the terms of literary genre of the more basic biographical dichotomy that Cervantists continue to cling to—the "two Cervanteses." On scrutinizing it closely, one then discovers that this dichotomy, as well as the various others which it underlies, is in reality the expression of literary preferences of the modern reader, and that it carries with it a strong value judgment. There is, on the one hand, the authentic, "original," and genuinely creative Cervantes, writing the literature that significantly altered the history of prose fiction and man's literary experience, creating, through the ironic engagement with nearly all traditional forms of fiction, the great representational genre of the modern novel. On the other hand, there is a conservative, conformist, and imitative Cervantes, the man of letters who bowed to the conventional literary tastes and values of his society and its repressive institutions, such as the Inquisition, and wrote such perishable imitations of its escapist, naively idealizing forms as *La Galatea, El Persiles,* and the so-called Italianate novellas. (pp. 21-6)

The fact is that Cervantes, one of the great experimenters in the history of fiction, was receptive to a wide variety of literary forms. There was nothing exclusivistic about his reading preferences; as he himself put it, he was a man who could not resist picking up, reading, and rescuing from oblivion, as it were, the scraps of paper he found in the streets, and one need only look at the immense variety of forms and styles which he incorporates into the *Quixote* to get some idea of the catholicity of his literary tastes. Neither the single generic designation *novella,* which Cervantes himself offers us, nor the various dualities which literary historians have thus far invoked can account for the variety of the tales or, for that matter, for the form, structure, and effects of a single one. Indeed, in the failure of such attempts at classification Walter Pabst has found confirmation of his thesis concerning the nonexistence of a "classical" European novella and his general view that little is to be gained in literary study by the invocation of such insubstantial entities as types and genres. On examining the tales, Pabst goes on to remark that perhaps the most apt designation for Cervantes's collection of short fiction would be a "labyrinth" (an *Irrgarten*), a metaphor which resurrects the very *topos* by which authors and commentators, from the *Decameron* to the ***Novelas ejemplares,*** declared the freedom of the form in its unbounded variety. Certainly one must agree with Pabst that a healthy critical nominalism which leaves the eyes open to the integrity of the individual object of study is far preferable to the facile typologies which mediate the object through a screen of modern prejudices concerning literary value. Fortunately, however, one does not have to resign oneself at this point to the choice of these two counterproductive positions. Over the past thirty years our insight into the generic possibilities of prose fiction has increased enormously, and numerous valuable studies of neglected genres, ranging from the simple minor literary forms of folktale, parable, fable, and aphorism to such inexhaustibly rich creations of man's literary imagination as romance and satire and their various subspecies—for example, chivalric, Byzantine, and hagiographic; Menippean, Lucianesque, and picaresque—have rewarded us with an increasingly sophisticated and precise knowledge of the specific forms that make up that gigantic area of non-novelistic narrative fiction, forms which can be viewed both as stable, definable literary systems and as objects with particular historical existences, involving origination, evolution, transformation, and, in some cases, death and oblivion. Anybody who reads *Don Quixote* quickly recognizes that Cervantes's consciousness of the literary conventions of traditional literary genres is highly developed, so developed in fact, that the novel itself, and particularly Part I, draws its imaginative vitality from the reiterated process of disclosing the artificiality of literary convention in its opposition to reality. The ***Novelas ejemplares,*** of course, assume a much less subversive attitude toward traditional generic systems, but they are no less wide-ranging in their incorporation of available forms, and they are just as subtle and, in a different way, just as original in their engagement with generic codes as is the great novel. . . . Far from being inhibited by the pressures of his culture and captive to its most reactionary literary preferences, Cervantes, in his aspiration to be the first to *novelar* in Spanish, proceeds with absolute freedom and sovereign control of his medium. His engagement with all available literary resources is that of a writer who understands thoroughly their potentialities and exploits them independently for his own particular needs. His methods of adaptation are always original, and they range from unprecedented hybridization, in the combination of traditional forms of disorder in **"El casamiento engañoso y el coloquio de los perros,"** and skillful accommodation, in **"La Gitanilla"** 's complex fusion of ideas and romance conventions, to unraveling and reconstitution, in the critical engagement with a prestigious hagiographic form in **"La fuerza de la sangre,"** and violent deconstruction, in the unexpected formal disarticulation of **"El celoso extremeño."** As the latter case would indicate, Cervantes's tales can become structurally most intricate and elusive precisely when they appear to be most doctrinaire and conventional. Indeed there is hardly a tale that fails to deviate in some radical way from the expectations that its traditional ingredients would arouse in its audience. The disorienting *desatinos*—the "swerves from the destined mark"—are clearly intended. Cervantes, whose stories so frequently strike one as childlike in their simplicity, is at once the most indulgent and the most exacting of authors, and the numerous efforts, from Avellaneda to Unamuno, to rewrite his fiction so as to eliminate "superfluous" or "absurd" elements, while commemorating certain readers' failures to respond fully to the challenge in its refusal to close in the readily intelligible way according to an insinuated "destination," are, nonetheless, continuing testimony of its power to activate its reader and enlist his energies in its own creation. In the sense that the irregularities of Cervantes's "Sileni" refuse to allow their reader the comforts of a stock response and instead burden him with the obligation to cope with unsettling violations of his vocabulary of genre, the *Novelas ejemplares* stand as one of the fullest literary realizations of the characteristic nonlinear discourse of the great humanist writers of the sixteenth century, who turned to dialectical, ironic, and paradoxical modes of exposition in their efforts to explore the complexities of truth, to provoke their readers' collaboration in that exploration, and to revitalize perceptions blunted by the tyranny of familiarity and appearance. The man who thoroughly understands the "familiar" beliefs which he adopts and on which he acts is in a very fundamental way a truly liberated man. To the extent that the *Novelas ejemplares* are composed in this deceptive, demanding discourse, their ultimate message may well lie in the freedom with which they dignify their reader and in the example of the creative use of freedom set by their author. In this sense they are no less progressive in the history of literature than the much more overtly revolutionary *Don Quixote,* for, while the language of its phrasing is frequently quite remote and calls for translation and mediation by the literary historian, the ultimate message to be recovered is no less valid in 1980 than it was in 1613. (pp. 26-30)

Alban K. Forcione, in his Cervantes and the Humanist Vision: A Study of Four Exemplary Novels, *Princeton University Press, 1982, 410 p.*

Harriet de Onís on *Exemplary Novels:*

In the prologue to the *Exemplary Novels* Cervantes assures the reader that of the twelve tales there is not one "from which thou couldst not derive a profitable example." In this there is perhaps a touch of the dissimulation typical of the period, when it was important to render virtue at least lipservice. Cervantes was too great an artist to have edification as his main objective. What he was depicting was human nature, the infinite workings of the human heart, which may often be less than exemplary but always interesting. With his glorious humor he laughed humanity's foibles, weaknesses, even vices, not to scorn but to love. The judgment the great critic Samuel Taylor Coleridge passed on *Don Quixote* applies equally to the *Exemplary Novels:* " . . . he blends with the terseness of Swift an exquisite flow and music of style, and, above all, contrasts with the latter by the sweet temper of a superior mind, which saw the follies of mankind, and was even at the moment suffering severely under hard mistreatment, and yet seems everywhere to have but one thought as the undersong—'Brethren! With all your faults I love you still!' "

Harriet de Onís in her introduction to Six Exemplary Novels *by Miguel de Cervantes, Barron's Educational Series, Inc., 1961.*

Albert A. Sicroff   (essay date 1984)

[*In the following essay, originally delivered at the Fordham Cervantes Lecture in 1984, Sicroff questions the "exemplary" behavior portrayed in Cervantes's short stories.*]

Students of Spanish literature may have been impressed at one time or another by the fact that so many of its universally recognized masterpieces are not accepted as such for universally recognized reasons. Scholars who have given special attention to *El libro de buen amor, La Celestina, Lazarillo de Tormes, Guzmán de Alfarache* and *Don Quijote* still argue about the fundamental thrust of any one of them. Cervantes' *Novelas ejemplares*—although not ranked among the aforementioned masterpieces, perhaps unjustly so—stands on no more firm critical ground than they do. Here, a principal obstacle to understanding them derives from the very title with which their author sent them out into the reading world. If they are supposed to be exemplary in a moral sense—as is suggested, although not perfectly clearly stated, in the Prologue—not all of the *novelas* bear that out. Some are, at best, ambiguously exemplary and others appear to contradict the very notion of exemplarity.

Fully aware that distinguished hispanists who have attempted to deal with the problem of the exemplarity of the *Novelas ejemplares* have generally been met with about as much criticism as acceptance of their explanations, let me muster all the courage I can to suggest an approach to the question that, as far as I know, has not yet been essayed. I would propose investigating what happens to the idea of exemplarity in the *novelas* when read seriatim, in the order that Cervantes had them published, which we know does not correspond to the chronology of their composition. Such a reading immediately makes us recognize that the first story, **"La gitanilla,"** certainly is a *novela ejemplar*—most completely so, as I shall attempt to establish. The last one—actually the last pair of stories, **"El casamiento engañoso"** which leads into **"El coloquio de los perros"**—are the radical misfits of the collection, to the point of actually being "anti-exemplary." The question then arises whether Cervantes capriciously included them under his "novelas ejemplares" rubric. One critic—Agustín G. de Amezúa y Mayo—long ago proposed something to that effect with regard to **"Las dos doncellas"** and **"La señora Cornelia"** which, according to him, were included simply to add bulk to Cervantes' publication. Another possibility, which has not been considered, is that the order in which he published the *Novelas ejemplares* traces a line of development that takes us from the summit of the exemplary gypsy story to the annihilation of exemplarity in the final pair of *novelas* dealing with the treacheries of a deceitful marriage and an account of a dog's life.

We may find some justification in seriously considering the latter possibility in Cervantes' declaration in the Prologue that there is something to be gained from each story individually and all of them taken together, all of which he could explain but will not for the sake of brevity. Of course, we cannot know exactly what Cervantes had in mind or why his explanation would have been so long. Nevertheless, when we do take the time to do what Cervantes did not do for us—examine each story individually and consider the impression with which they leave us in their totality—perhaps we can make some contribution to the understanding of exemplarity in the *Novelas ejemplares.*

I have already suggested that **"La gitanilla"** is the most exemplary of the *novelas* gathered under that rubric. It is that, I think, because it takes place in a well-ordered world in which virtuous characters can function and ultimately be rewarded for their exemplary behavior. Paradoxically, Cervantes unfolds this exemplary story in the gypsy world—a world of outcasts against whom severe penalties were constantly being legislated. Cervantes makes no more of the disrepute of the gypsies than to mention that they are all considered thieves and somehow mitigate their thievery by treating it (no doubt with a smile of insinuation) as an occupation that in no way affects the exemplary community in which they live. Their life, as described by the old gypsy when he is initiating Juan de Cárcamo who is joining them in order to win the hand of Preciosa, is one of rigorous order sustained by justice, honesty and sincere friendship among them. There are even echoes of Don Quijote's discourse on the Golden Age as the gypsy tells Cárcamo (soon to take the name of Andrés Caballero) that there is no want among them since they all live from nature's abundance. Nor is there "mine" and "thine," for everything is owned communally without jealousy, desire for honor or the ambition to increase it. Only one's conjugal partner is exclusively one's own and

that relationship is entered into by mutual agreement of both partners, to judge by the conditions Preciosa imposes on Cárcamo before she will marry him. In this idealized community, vicious behavior may occur, but it is dealt with swiftly by the gypsies themselves, without appeal to the courts, which the reader knows did not enjoy the best reputation for effective justice and honesty.

From this almost idyllic community emerges the figure of Preciosa, who, if she does indeed turn out not to be a gypsy by birth, certainly has not suffered in her upbringing among gypsies. Approximately one third of the *novela* is taken up with a portrait of her many virtues and admirable characteristics—discretion, wit, intelligence and above all her sense of herself as a free and independent being. Indeed the problem that furnishes the narrative thread of the story derives from her very virtue rather than from some evil deed that must be overcome, as happens in the later stories. Preciosa that she is, she will be won by Juan de Cárcamo only after he has served a novitiate as a gypsy to prove that his is a true love and not mere passion.

As the gypsy Andrés Caballero, Cárcamo not only meets the demands Preciosa has imposed upon him but also acts as the honorable *caballero* he is by birth. Thus, if he must play the gypsy in order to win Preciosa, he cannot bring himself to engage in stealing, their normal occupation. Instead, he buys what he must claim to have stolen as his contribution to the communal holdings of the gypsies. In the end, evil does enter into the story—be it noted, from outside the gypsy community—in the persons of Juana Carducha, who tries to ensnare Cárcamo, and the Alcalde and his nephew. But it only serves to bring the story to a crisis whose resolution leads to the exemplary *dénouement.* All ends well. Cárcamo's noble identity is reestablished and Preciosa turns out to be his equal in lineage so that they can marry and live happily ever after. Virtue, love, and justice have been fully served in this exemplary novel that ends without a single note that would threaten its pure harmony.

"El amante liberal" takes us into a much more turbulent world, fraught with perils that were entirely absent in the previous *novela*. Ricardo will have to overcome difficulties and dangers that Cárcamo never knew, in order to win Leonisa. She has none of the qualities of Preciosa; rather, as her name indicates and Ricardo says, she is a lioness for him, rejecting him for the foppish Cornelio of the soft hands who lacks the courage to defend her when she is carried off by the Turks. To rescue her, Ricardo must go forth into a world that bears no resemblance to the benign, orderly one Cárcamo knew among the gypsies. He will have to survive tempests at sea and their counterparts on land in the confounding treacheries he encounters among the Turks who hold Leonisa captive. At one point, she aptly describes the labyrinth in which misfortune has caught them without hope of escape unless they resort to lies and deceptions, even though such behavior is unbecoming to them. To free Leonisa, Ricardo will indeed stoop to tricks that were never forced on Cárcamo: remember that, as a gypsy, he would feign rather than actually steal. Nevertheless, having survived all sorts of disasters, Ricardo returns in triumph to Sicily with Leonisa whom he will win for himself with a final grand gesture as an "amante liberal." He restores her to Cornelio and also offers to contribute to their happiness his share of the booty—more than 30,000 escudos—with which they have returned. But on second thought comes realization that he can hardly be liberal with that which is not his. It is not for him to hand Leonisa over to Cornelio: he can only restore her to freedom—which she promptly exercises to choose him in marriage. Thus, she says, she will show that not all women are "ingrates." The reader has once more been left with an edifying tale, this time of an exemplary "amante liberal" who has been rewarded by a grateful woman, whose rare example of discretion, honesty, composure and beauty continues, according to the narrator, to resound beyond the confines of Sicily. But it has all occurred in a world beset with turmoil and disorder, and only through the intervention of sheer good luck, or a compassionate heaven.

After the tempestuous story of Ricardo and Leonisa, Cervantes leads us from the "mundanal ruido" to Monipodio's patio where exemplarity will be problematized in another way. In the company of Rinconete and Cortadillo, we are spectators to the goings on in the underworld. Surprisingly, we are once more in an orderly community held together by friendship, love, religious devotion and quickly dispatched justice. But this time, in contrast to the way he treated the gypsies, Cervantes does not spare the opportunity to make fun of these evil-doers ("maleantes") who are thieves, as one of them says, "to serve God and good people" ("para servir a Dios y a las buenas gentes"). The author also raises the question of the worth of good deeds by those who, as Rinconete observes at the end, are confident they will get to heaven as long as they do not fail in their religious devotion, even though they fill their lives with robberies, homicides and other offenses against God. Nevertheless, the reader may be left rather perplexed when Rinconete ends by condemning the neglectfulness of such a famous city as Seville for permitting the almost open existence of such pernicious people so contrary to Nature itself ("gente tan perniciosa y tan contraria a la misma naturaleza"). For we have seen the exemplary behavior that is the rule among that pernicious gang and we have also learned that one of their principal occupations is doing the dirty work they are commissioned to perform for the respectable citizens of the city.

In **"La española inglesa,"** the fourth and last of the *novelas* that may still be considered exemplary, Cervantes returns to the world of intrigue and treachery which he conjugates with the lesson of uncertainty we learned in **"Rinconete y Cortadillo"** about from whom we may expect exemplary behavior and those who may be the agents of evil. This time Cervantes does not include an observer like Rinconete who will point out the confusion he sees. Thus there is no one to call our attention to the "primordial sin" from which the story originates: the kidnapping of a seven year old Spanish girl by Clotaldo, an English Catholic, during the raid on Cádiz, in flagrant disobedience to the orders of the English Protestant, Count Leste, who has led the expedition. Nor do we find anyone to comment on the absurdity of the Catholic Englishman's triumphant return to his country with the Spanish child hidden in the hold of

the ship, a child he intends to present to his wife as a most precious prize ("un riquísimo despojo") of the raid on Cádiz. In passing, Cervantes has touched on what must have been a poignant note for some Spaniards: the Spanish child has had the good fortune to fall into the hands of clandestine Catholics who outwardly appear to follow the opinion of the queen, as Cervantes puts it ("seguir la opinión de su reina"). Such perseverance of clandestine Catholics in an officially Protestant kingdom had to remind the Spanish reader of his country's own two-century old preoccupation with *conversos* suspected of clandestine judaizing.

From such uncertain beginnings, it soon becomes evident that Cervantes does not intend to focus on the English Catholics as the exemplary figures of the story. Instead he pursues a line of development that will once more make the point that virtue and exemplary behavior may be found where least expected—in this respect, the Protestant Queen Elizabeth joins the gypsies and thieves of previous stories. Moreover, he now suggests defiantly that the Catholic may be a less admirable figure than the Protestant. Queen Elizabeth—the one whom Lope de Vega, that vox-populi of the theater, called a "Gorgon Medusa"—is, in this sense, the morally most attractive figure in the *novela*. Thus, when she orders the Spanish girl, now grown up as a beautiful woman, to appear at court, Clotaldo and his wife are trembling because they are certain of the Queen's ire when she learns that Isabela has been brought up as a Catholic. The Queen does remonstrate gently with the Catholic couple for having kept such a treasure of beauty and graceful comportment hidden from her. Most surprising is her reaction upon discovering that Isabela was brought up secretly as a Catholic for, in spite of the opinion the Catholic Spanish reader may have had of her, Queen Elizabeth declares that she esteems the young woman all the more for having remained faithful to the religion her parents taught her ("la estimaba en más, pues tan bien sabía guardar la ley que sus padres le habían enseñado").

Later on, when the forces of evil have been unleashed by the Queen's lady-in-waiting in revenge for seeing her son, Arnesto, being denied Isabela's hand in marriage (Clotaldo's son Ricaredo is to marry the Spanish girl), the Protestant queen's superiority, in wisdom and virtue, is again demonstrated. Elizabeth's "camarera" has poisoned Isabela, leaving her monstrously ugly. Clotaldo and his wife, rather than see their son married to such a hideous creature, renew negotiations they once had undertaken to marry Ricaredo to a Catholic Scotswoman. Only Queen Elizabeth is sympathetic to Ricaredo's continued love for Isabela and encourages him in his determination to marry her. She agrees with Ricaredo that "if Isabela lost her beauty, she could not have lost her infinite virtues" and gives him permission to carry off one who, in the Queen's words, is "a most precious jewel enclosed in a rough-hewn wooden box."

Without entering into further details, suffice it to observe that once more virtue will triumph, although in the face of apparently overwhelming obstacles: Ricaredo's parents' insistence that he forget Isabela and marry the Scottish

Clisterna; the adventures he must undertake at sea to show he is worthy of Isabela; his pilgrimage to Rome in order to assure his conscience for having broken the commitment to marry Clisterna, from which he returns to Seville to reclaim Isabela at the very moment she is entering a convent and would thus be lost to him forever.

The *novela* of **"El licenciado vidriera"** now appears at a point where we have seen virtue prevail in four stories—exemplary in this sense—but not without an ever-increasing gathering of the dark clouds of human perversity that threatens but never quite manages to eclipse exemplarity. It is the Licenciado—suddenly fallen into a peculiar "vitreous madness"—for whom the unexemplary nature of those he encounters becomes all too apparent. Giving voice to all the ills that are transparent to him, he is at the same time a quixotic figure of madness who amuses others with his fearful awareness of his own fragility. No one must touch this man of glass lest he be shattered. He begs those who would ask questions of him to do so at a distance. And to his fragile clairvoyance no rosy hues filter through from life about him. On his long unclean laundry list of life, no aspect of existence seems to be missing: mischievous boys in the street, the *converso,* the house of prostitution, poets, painters, booksellers, muleteers, pharmacists, doctors, judges, tailors, shoemakers, pastry-makers, puppeteers, actors, "dueñas," notaries, sheriffs are but a sample of those denounced for their less than exemplary contributions to life. The last ones to appear on the list—gossipers ("murmuradores")—may be the most significant ones taken to task, as I shall soon attempt to show.

In general, the Licenciado's gloomy views will continue to make themselves felt in the stories that follow. Cervantes will still present them as ***Novelas ejemplares*** which *appear* to leave the reader with an edifying example of his literary characters' behavior. But closer examination will always reveal—as we shall soon see—a disconcerting flaw that mars what appears to be an exemplary resolution of the story.

Before taking up this point in some detail, we should observe that the most crucial moments of the action of all of the post-**"Licenciado"** stories—**"La fuerza de la sangre," "El celoso extremeño," "La ilustre fregona," "Las dos doncellas"** and **"La señora Cornelia"**—take place for the most part in the darkness of the night. Even more significant is the fact that all of these *novelas* have embedded in them the problem of honor. From our point of view this is important for two principal reasons. First, it links them to one of the last problems we heard the Licenciado Vidriera denouncing in the previous story: that of the "murmuradores," gossipers. For honor, especially as played in the theater where it was a primary problem, always depended on the opinion one enjoyed among others which in turn was always endangered by wagging tongues. Perhaps of even greater importance, was the fact that honor problems never did achieve a fully cathartic solution, regardless of the efforts that might be made to give the impression that all had turned out right. The irreparable harm suffered by honor once lost—or even when only apparently placed in jeopardy—was expressed in numerous ways in the *comedia,* perhaps the best known was by way

of the idea that honor was like a fragile glass that once broken could not be repaired without showing the seams of the break. The post-**"Licenciado"** stories I have mentioned are all left with such a mark, sometimes apparently ignored by the author of the *novelas* that would be *ejemplares* and sometimes with a trace of mocking humor that gives us to understand that the author is in effect saying to his reader "al buen entendedor, pocas palabras," i.e. few words are needed for the one who catches on easily to what goes on.

In **"La fuerza de la sangre,"** the first of the more troublesome stories that follows that of the **"Licenciado,"** Cervantes evidently did so good a job in giving it the appearance of an exemplary story that a modern critic declares it to be "Cervantes' most extreme affirmation of faith in the harmony which beauty and virtue can produce" (Ruth El Saffar). I must confess I find no such affirmation in this *novela* whose very beginning would render anything resembling such optimism unlikely if not impossible. No pre-**"Licenciado"** story has begun with the violence we now find. Rodolfo rapes Leocadia, not even feigning a promise of marriage to gain his end, one summer night when she is returning from an outing with her family by the banks of the river in Toledo. Despoiling Leocadia of her "most precious jewel" and leaving the family dishonored, he flees—ultimately to Italy. Leocadia does manage to take away from the chamber where the assault took place a small silver crucifix. Are we to see this as an indication that Cervantes has in mind an exemplary ending in which, perhaps, Rodolfo will return, repent for his crime and sin, marry Leocadia and claim as his own the son she has borne in his absence? At best that will be the apparent *dénouement,* but not what really happens.

Rodolfo will return to Toledo in response to a letter from his father who informs him that he has arranged for him a marriage with a lady of extraordinary beauty. The one intended for him is none other than Leocadia. The father, don Luis, accidentally discovered the misdeed of his son, is sheltering Leocadia and her son and hopes to right the wrong through marriage. Rodolfo departs for home, hardly a candidate for redemption. He can hardly wait to partake of the tasty dish his father has described to him ("con la golosina de gozar tan hermosa mujer como su padre le significaba"). Upon his return to Toledo he is shown a less than attractive portrait of the one who *supposedly* has been chosen to be his future spouse. He is quite disconcerted, for knowing that the portrait painters usually enhance their subject's beauty, the lady he sees portrayed must be ugliness incarnate! Rodolfo pleads with his parents to remember that he is a young man who craves beauty above all other qualities—i.e. nobility, discretion and wealth—usually sought in a marital partner. The sacrament of matrimony, he contends, does not forbid pleasure in marriage. And how can there be pleasure when one is constantly faced with ugliness—in the living room, at the dining table and in bed?

Leocadia enters the room and is indeed a "human angel." Rodolfo, still unaware that she is the one he had raped, can hardly contain himself. The word "esposa" removes all inhibitions, and he hurls herself on Leocadia with a soulful kiss. Finally, Leocadia does produce the silver crucifix in order to establish that she was actually Rodolfo's victim in that dark room. The story then ends with jubilation at the marriage—rather grotesque, considering the circumstances, particularly that of Rodolfo's continued libidinous condition with nary a thought for repentance for the wrong he committed. If there is any doubt about his condition, one has but to recall how he chafes during the banquet because, although the evening's hours were flying by, says the narrator, for Rodolfo they were moving on crutches. This, because he cannot wait to get Leocadia into bed again, where they evidently were to spend a good and pleasureful share of their married life, to judge by the many children they had and the illustrious line of descendants they bequeathed to Toledo.

The **"Fuerza de la sangre"** story has set the course that will be followed in the following four *novelas* which, in turn, will lead to those of **"El casamiento engañoso"** and **"El coloquio de los perros."** In those intervening stories, the honor problem is present in one way or another. And with its presence—as we have noted, fragile and irretrievable once lost—Cervantes seems to have given up on the possibility of constructing a convincingly exemplary tale. At best, he can lead us to the disastrous lesson to be learned from the mad obsession of the **"Celoso extremeño"** to safeguard his honor. Comic notes—which become more blatant in subsequent stories—creep in as we read of Felipo de Carrizales' cloistering of his wife in an isolated house, with windows that look out only on the sky and from which all trace of masculinity has been banished; only females serve his wife, cats and dogs are female and the tapestries and paintings portray women, flowers and woodland scenes—but no males. Carrizales himself spent sleepless nights making the rounds, guarding his wife with the hundred eyes of an Argus. And for all his zeal, the *extremeño* only succeeded in attracting those who would despoil him of what he was guarding so closely. Loaysa is overcome by curiosity and in turn overcomes all of Carrizales' precautions—to end up in bed with Leonora. The narrator underscores the futility of it all: while Carrizales slept and Loaysa and Leonora struggled in bed—for she did try to resist him—the point is made of the uselessness of all of Carrizales' extraordinary measures when there are enemies against whom neither precaution nor the sword can prevail.

When the story has been brought to a close with Carrizales recognizing that he brought his disaster on himself, with Leonora again cloistered—this time in a convent—and Loaysa gone off to the New World, the narrator tells us how anxious he was to get to the end of the tale which was an example of how little faith may be placed in keys and high walls when the will remains free. In an "exemplary" sense it really is an "anti-example example," one about which nothing can be done. Regarding the question of honor—that lifeblood of Cervantes' society—the reader has been left with little edification: honor is at risk if unguarded and no less so when zealously protected. No wonder that the narrator was so desirous of getting to the end of a story that bore such a disturbing message.

One of the most curious of all the *Novelas ejemplares* is

"La ilustre fregona." It begins as if it were going to narrate the picaresque adventures of Diego de Carriazo and then, when accompanied by his friend Tomás de Avendaño, takes up the story of their stay in Toledo at the "posada del Sevillano." Avendaño's courtship of Costanza, the *ilustre fregona,* seems to be the central thread of the story, although she is such an unsociable, nay-saying, harsh character that there does not seem to be much that her wooer can do to win her. The reader's attention has to be directed to the shenanigans of Carriazo in Toledo while waiting for the outcome of Avendaño's interest in Costanza. We have no time to go into too many details of what happens. Suffice it to note the bizarre ending, which is being passed off in a would-be exemplary tale. The pretender to the hand of Costanza is getting nowhere and yet everything will suddenly be resolved happily when his father and Carriazo suddenly show up at the inn. The latter is seeking to verify whether Costanza is his daughter, born of his brutal rape of a lady of very high estate he had encountered quite by accident. Carriazo, the elder, confesses he had his way with her against her will and by sheer force. Since she never spoke a word to him he did not learn who she was at the time and only recently—twenty days ago—learned that the daughter of his violence was probably the *ilustre fregona* of the *posada del Sevillano.*

The facts are soon established. Costanza is his daughter. The elder Avendaño learns that his son is at the inn courting her. We are now about to witness a multiple happy ending, three marriages which in different ways make a mockery of the way honor plays frequently ended. In a not very convincing scene, Costanza is betrothed by her father to Tomás de Avendaño and she accepts with tears of joy at having been found by her father. The Corregidor's son who also sought to marry the *fregona* will content himself with marriage to a daughter of Juan de Avendaño and, to leave no loose ends, the younger Carriazo will marry the daughter of the Corregidor. All of this neat tieing up of couples has been made possible by the "exemplary" reclaiming by the elder Carriazo of a daughter born of a woman he raped.

Hardly more edifying are the remaining two pre-"Casamiento engañoso" stories. In **"Las dos doncellas"** both ladies were deceived by the same man, Teodosia to the point of sexual surrender to Marco Antonio and Leocadia only as one to whom he had not fulfilled his written promise of marriage. Again the reader is left to "celebrate" disconcerting endings. The aggrieved *doncellas* catch up with Marco Antonio, Teodosia accompanied by her brother Rafael who is committed to help her avenge the harm she suffered. Marco acknowledges the wrong he has done both women and agrees to marry Leocadia since, with her, promises had been consummated in deeds. Teodosia comes away not entirely empty-handed; she will marry Rafael—for whatever sense that makes, and as the story ends we are told that "poets of that time found occasion to employ their pens exaggerating the beauty and the happenings to that pair of damsels, as bold as they were *honestas* (sic!), which is the principal subject of this strange occurrence."

Finally, Cornelia became **"La señora Cornelia"** when, despite the vigilance of her brother, she bore a child to the Duke of Ferrera. The narration begins as two Spanish noblemen, Don Antonio de Isunza and Don Juan de Gamboa in Bologna as students, become involved in the matter in mysterious nocturnal goings-on too complex and too long to describe. Cornelia appeals to Don Antonio to help her because of the courteous behavior that characterizes those of his nation. (She evidently has not read the preceding three *Novelas ejemplares*!) Antonio agrees to shelter her in his house while helping her to work out her problem. It is that, having borne the Duke's child out of wedlock, his promise to marry her cannot be carried out while Cornelia's brother is out to kill him in revenge and the Duke's mother is opposed to the marriage and he must wait for her to pass away before he is free to act.

As the story moves toward its resolution, Cervantes seems to find more than one occasion to expose the absurdity of the honor intrigue as well as the exemplary reputation the two Spaniards enjoy. Antonio travels to Ferrara to try to convince the Duke to do the honorable thing by Cornelia only to find he already has every intention to do so. He is only waiting for his mother, now near death, to pass on to a better life so that he can carry out his intention. But, although so close to solution, Cervantes still has a few tricks with which to amuse us.

Throughout the story there has been constant re-iteration of those Spanish virtues: their courtesy, their trustworthiness, their valor (to have a Spaniard at one's side is like having the armies of Xerxes as allies), their generous heart is only motivated by honor, etc. But as the *novela* is reaching its resolution, Cervantes, always irrepressible, cannot resist placing all that fine reputation in, at least, momentary jeopardy. Thus when they bring the Duke to the house where they left Cornelia and the child, they are gone. The housekeeper has convinced her she is not safe there and has carried her off for safer-keeping to the house of a priest in a nearby village. When the Duke arrives not only is Cornelia gone, but the pages, who do not know she had been smuggled into the house, deny she was ever there. With which the "generous," "virtuous," "valiant" Spaniards see themselves in danger of being reduced to liars and impostors, if not worse, in the eyes of the Duke. To make matters worse, the latter is informed that Cornelia is in the house, in an upstairs room with one of the pages. That bit of embarrassment is cleared up when it is discovered that the one with the page is another Cornelia. But there is more. The Duke accidentally comes upon his Cornelia in the house of the priest, who is an old friend of his. A joyful reunion takes place but when Lorenzo, his new brother-in-law who is out for revenge, shows up, the Duke decides not to let on that he has found his wife. He claims that not having been able to locate her, he cannot give Lorenzo satisfaction to restore the latter's honor. For how can he marry one whom he cannot find. Instead, he announces he will now make good his promise to marry a certain peasant girl he knew before he met Cornelia. While the Duke leaves the room to fetch his *labradora* so that Lorenzo and the Spaniards who have joined him may see for themselves the sacrifice he had made in turning from the peasant girl out of love for Cornelia, the brother and his Spanish cohorts plot revenge. The Duke simply

cannot be permitted to abandon his search for her so lightly. True Spaniard that he is, Don Juan de Gamboa swears "By Santiago of Galicia . . . and by his faith as a Christian *caballero* he will as soon let the Duke carry out his intention as turn Moorish." In short, if the Duke does not fulfill his promise to Cornelia he will leave his life in Don Juan's hands here and now.

After all that bragadoccio, the Duke returns, not with a peasant woman but with Cornelia and their child. Threats are dispersed, joy returns and the Spaniards confess that the Duke has played a most clever and delectable trick on them. One more bit of a Cervantine wrinkle before it all ends. In gratitude, the Duke offers his Spanish friends two cousins of his in marriage. But they cannot accept because they are Basques whose custom it is to marry among themselves. Cervantes thus concludes his story touching on a sensitive point no contemporary reader could possibly have missed: Basque pride in considering themselves the most noble and pure Old Christians—without "taint" of Jewish or Moorish ancestry—in all of the Iberian peninsula. It is precisely this point that has been shown by modern students of the period to be the original source of Spain's excessive preoccupation with honor—in life as well as literature.

As we turn to the final stories, we may reflect on what has happened to exemplarity in the post-**"Licenciado"** *Novelas ejemplares.* It certainly does not function the way it did in **"La gitanilla"** and its more immediate successors, overcoming obstacles of varying difficulty so that the exemplary figure could carry the day without a shadow of a suggestion that all had not turned out well. Now we no longer find figures of the purity of a Preciosa, a Juan de Cárcamo, a Ricaredo (the *amante liberal*) or even of a Queen Elizabeth of England or a Monipodio who made their contributions to the maintenance of an orderly world. After the Licenciado Vidriera's outburst against what is wrong in the world, the subsequent stories appear to be marked with a sort of "original sin" without possibility of a redemption that is more than illusory. For the creation of literature to reflect such a notion, the honor theme has served Cervantes well, albeit not without a touch of humor typical of him, as I have attempted to indicate.

Now, with **"El casamiento engañoso"** we enter a world which is a jungle of human existence with no room for that which would even appear to be exemplary. The **"Casamiento"** and the **"Coloquio"** to which it is linked can only offer an unmitigated and unrelieved gloomy view of life. In the first of this pair of *novelas,* treacherous deception is all-pervasive so that the agent becomes the victim who in turn becomes the agent of betrayal which promises to continue even beyond the confines of the story. As Campuzano confesses to Peralta, he entered into a relationship with Doña Estefanía "with such a twisted and treacherous intention" that he would prefer to be silent about it. But it so happens that Estefanía's thoughts were no less maliciously self-serving than his. Skipping the details of their mutual deception, suffice it to recall that she carries off all of Campuzano's possessions—as he intended to do with hers. In the end it is difficult to measure who, if anyone, gained or lost more from the *casamiento engañoso.* If she has stripped the old soldier of all he owns, she has yet to discover that the valuables he flashed before her were all glitter and no gold. Should she attempt to sell them she will find they will bring no more than ten or twelve *escudos.* Campuzano, on the other hand, having lost everything, nevertheless was left with a "gift" from Estefanía, a disease that has stripped him of his hair. Peralta has run into him as he emerged from a cure in the hospital, hardly recognizable without hair, without eyebrows or eyelashes, beardless and bald. It was while in the hospital that he overheard the conversation that will constitute the last of the *Novelas ejemplares.* This close narrative linking of the stories will have its counterpart in the linking of their content. Campuzano has narrated a single case of evil that in the **"Coloquio"** proliferates into a whole world of evils.

From the outset it is evident that Berganza, the dog who will be telling the story of his life, has nothing good to say about what he knows about human existence. For, ever since he was old enough to gnaw a bone, he has been accumulating things he would have wanted to say and now that he has suddenly gotten the gift of speech he will get it all off his chest. Despite Cipión's repeated admonitions that he refrain from backbiting, life as he has known it allows him to do little else. The only good word he has is for the Jesuit school in Seville where the Jesuit teachers dedicate themselves with care and skill to set young people on the path of virtue. He also speaks well of the Sevillian merchants who send their children to the school, thus seeking to display their wealth and authority in the education of their children rather than on their own person; a most generous ambition, says Berganza, which is indulged in without bringing harm to third parties. (CURIOUS NOTE: On Sept. 1, 1572, Francisco de Borja, General of the Society of Jesus, was informed that the Jesuit *colegio* at Córdoba was in disrepute because so many of its students were of Jewish origin, a stain we know was considered indelible in Cervantes' time. Was the author then taking a roundabout swing at the Spanish obsession with "Jewish blood" and the negative opinion the Jesuits suffered because they were not squeamish about ex-Jews in their midst? The fact that he has Berganza praise the *merchant* class for sending its children to be educated by the Jesuits would suggest that the thrust is at Spain's anti-Judeo-Christian stance.)

As for everyone and everything else: the denunciation is total and devastating. Some things about which the Licenciado made negative comments with epigrammatic lightness, Berganza now deals with in somber detail. All value seems to have disappeared as even those dealt with glowingly in the pre-**"Licenciado"** stories are now treated harshly. The gypsy world of **"La gitanilla"** now gives way to gypsies who are totally malicious; the house of Monipodio reappears but now it is filled with ruffians, thieves, tricksters who are at each other constantly. Even the pastoral world comes in for its share of "de-exemplarification." It bears no resemblance to the descriptions of it in pastoral novels. Real live shepherds are not named Elicio, Fílida, Sireno, etc. but rather Antón, Domingo, Pablo or Llorente. The latter make harsh sounds on crude instruments rather than the beautiful harmonies one reads about in books about shepherds. Furthermore,

those who really live the pastoral life spend most of their day repairing their sandals or delousing themselves rather than in the pleasant diversions described in fanciful pastoral novels.

We need not retrace all the negative portrayals—of poets, mathematicians, witches, alchemists, *moriscos,* actors and others—in order to make the point that in this last *novela* Cervantes has eliminated exemplarity as definitively as he terminated the chivalresque career of Don Quijote at the end of Part II of his novel. Indeed, we could, if we wanted to end with a risky conjecture, suggest that the *Novelas ejemplares* might have served Cervantes as a rehearsal exercise for composing the Second Part of his *Quijote* as a sequence of events that would problematize radically his protagonist's role until he finally abandoned his belief in chivalry and knight errantry. Was not an analogous development worked out with regard to exemplarity as a protagonist that starts out brilliantly and slowly is in effect being entombed until done away with completely in the last of the *Novelas ejemplares* where it now lies stretched out full length (as was Don Quijote in the end) so that no one can resurrect it? (pp. 345-60)

> *Albert A. Sicroff, "The Demise of Exemplarity in the 'Novelas ejempares'," in* Hispanic Studies in Honor of Joseph H. Silverman, *edited by Joseph V. Ricapito, Juan de la Cuesta, 1988, pp. 345-60.*

William C. Atkinson on the content and purpose of Cervantes's fiction:

[Cervantes] has no interest in dogmatic truth, but only in stimulating the reader to a concern for truth, in making him reflect on the nature of life and of man. For himself he believes in an inner harmony, of the individual within himself, and in a larger harmony, of men with one another and with Nature, and this is often, but not invariably, his theme. Before that ultimate goal can be reached mankind must realise what are the barriers that separate us from it: the beginning of knowledge is self-knowledge. Herein lies the exemplariness of the *Novelas ejemplares.*

William C. Atkinson, in his "Cervantes, El Pinciano, and the Novelas ejemplares," *Hispanic Review, 1948.*

Adriana Slaniceanu   (essay date 1987)

[*In the following essay, Slaniceanu probes the "calculating woman" motif in* Exemplary Novels, *focusing on the character Leocadia in "The Force of Blood."*]

The choice of the term 'calculating' to describe the protagonist of **'La fuerza de la sangre'** may seem hazardous, even capricious, given this novel's reputation as a repository of idealistic statements concerning virtue, honour and marriage. It is easier, to be sure, to point to more overt examples of calculating women who attempt to manipulate men and place them in a compromising position. La Carducha of **'La gitanilla,'** the *dueña* Marialonso of **'El celoso extre-**

meño,' and the two *mozas de mesón* of **'La ilustre fregona'** readily come to mind. Doña Estefania, the protagonist of **'El casamiento engañoso,'** is an excellent example of the scheming woman who weaves an intricate web of deceits in order to marry the ensign Campuzano. Certainly, the shadowy figure, the 'dama de todo rumbo y manejo' of **'El licenciado Vidriera,'** who tries to drive Tomás Rodaja mad with desire by giving him a poisoned quince, qualifies as a manipulative woman.

The fact that the results are disastrous for all of them has generally prompted critics to regard the ineffectual use of deceit as a source of humour, whereby the unsuccessful schemers serve as a foil to morally superior male and female protagonists. Often the characters' motivation for aggressive and deceitful behaviour can easily be attributed to normal incitements, such as the desire for amorous dalliance and the sting of jealousy; in this respect, the commonplace about Cervantes' natural antipathy to lascivious women offers a simple explanation for their well-deserved failure.

On the other hand, we cannot view the role of certain conniving women exclusively within the confines of the episode in which they appear. Carducha's function in **'La gitanilla,'** for example, goes beyond that of the scorned woman venting her fury on the indifferent man: her false denunciation of Andrés amplifies the motifs of lying and stealing, which are central to the novel's ethical and artistic intention. In **'El licenciado'** and **'El casamiento,'** even though the woman's role may appear to be minor, particularly in the first story, it is the catalyst of the entire novelistic action. In both instances, the lady who causes Vidriera's madness and doña Estefanía, who brings her husband perilously close to death by infecting him with syphilis, seem to have designs which extend beyond the ephemeral pleasure of an hour's love-making. The narrator strongly implies their desire to marry at all costs: in an almost simplistic form of transaction, they offer their worldly goods, real or counterfeit, in return for the social status with which the scholar and the soldier can endow them. Since the man's position itself is tenuous and ambiguous, it cannot offer an anchor against constantly-changing circumstances. Their failure is tragic, for their commitment is as complete as it is illusory. Both men and women learn the bitter lesson that society will resist any attempt to change it forcibly, and will relegate any would-be intruder or reformer to the oblivion of the social outcast.

In the seven *novelas* which end in marriage, Cervantes' treatment of the female protagonist differs considerably, in keeping with the narrative genre. In the romance, the woman is always successful in her enterprise to gain the commitment of the man, and she achieves her goal in a manner which is palatable to the reader's sense of propriety, and acceptable to him under the conditions of this genre's structural conventions.

My choice of **'La fuerza de la sangre'** in order to analyse the nature of the calculating woman is prompted by its obvious romance features: the woman's dominant role in the action, the blood-will-tell motif, the opposition of violence and fraud, exemplified by the act of rape, and its vindication by the heroine's enormous resourcefulness. Another aspect of primary interest is the specific setting in the city of Toledo, which permits strong overtones of social criticism to intermingle with the protagonist's peripeties. By underlining the standard episodic fare of the romance genre, I hope to show that Cervantes' intention was to match a pre-existent literary form in an ironic manner, as he did so admirably in the *Quijote.* In the *Novelas* this pitting of one literary form against another has been neglected, except by those who have looked beyond the commonplace in the boast of originality in the *Prologue* [Bruce W. Wardropper, "La eutrapelia en las *Novelas ejemplares* de Cervantes," *Actas del Séptimo Congreso de la Asociación Internacional de Hispanistas,* 1982].

My premiss is that the purposive mystification about the protagonist's origins—so evident in the Alonso Quijano-Don Quijote transference—is, to a greater or lesser extent, exploited in all the *Novelas.* Preciosa is neither gypsy nor noblewoman, Costanza is neither noblewoman nor scullery maid. The women who disguise themselves as men to search for their seducers are perceived, at least temporarily, as neither male nor female. The studied indifference regarding the woman's prehistory is a means of denying her a specific identity, of making her a marginal being who exists at the pre-ethical level, free of any ties of responsibility. Her need to forge an identity, her desire to occupy a place in society with security, demands the adoption of a role which she will create according to circumstances.

In **'La fuerza'** Leocadia is introduced as a generic sixteen-year-old, whose beautiful face has a shattering impact on Rodolfo: 'La mucha hermosura del rostro . . . comenzó de tal manera a imprimírsele en la memoria, que le llevó tras sí la voluntad y despertó en él un deseo de gozarla, a pesar de todos los inconvenientes que sucederle pudiesen'. Man's organic impulse to enjoy beauty, in its innumerable literary treatments, has generally been shielded from total exposure by the cloak of literary convention. The ironic subterfuge behind the use of idealized love terminology was very much in evidence in Cervantes' novelistic progenitor, *La Celestina.* It is understandable that this author of counter-reformation Spain might chide his predecessor for not sufficiently disguising the all-too-human traits of his characters, but it is undeniable that he realized the possibilities which the use of irony offered for the purpose of unmasking human motivations.

Rodolfo's immediate determination to commit violence against the unknown girl produces a double shock in the reader: the first is emotional, the immediate effect of the inherent immorality of the act; the second is mental, and threatens to invalidate the metaphor of beauty as spiritual inspiration. In spite of the reader's acceptance of the neo-Platonic commonplace as a necessary safeguard for the verisimilitude of the final reconciliation between Rodolfo and Leocadia, many persist in finding the end emotionally repugnant, for their tendency is to overlook Cervantes' more than occasional use of irony in the romance.

The opposition between the young man and woman is established with great rhetorical economy. To Leocadia's family, belonging to the 'bien inclinada gente', Rodolfo is juxtaposed as a 'caballero a quien la riqueza, la sangre ilustre, la inclinación torcida, la libertad demasiada y las compañías libres le hacían hacer cosas y tener atrevimientos que desdecían de su calidad y le daban renombre de atrevido'. The antithesis is intensified by a symbolic encounter between 'los dos escuadrones, el de las ovejas con el de los lobos'. The inference which seems to be demanded of the reader is that the behaviour of each group will follow the instincts with which nature has endowed them: one tends towards a peaceful existence, the other to prey upon others. The argument that Rodolfo's will to victimize Leocadia must inevitably be realized seems irrefutable.

Yet the 'sheep and wolves' antithesis should be analysed in its multiple ironic facets. The narrative action confirms, to be sure, the simile about the two natural arch-enemies. Critically, however, the author provides us with certain tools to 'exonerate' overt behaviour: Rodolfo is the product of a 'twisted' inclination, aided and abetted by the excessive freedom that wealth and social status afford him. They are 'making' him behave outrageously, and his actions 'belie' his quality. There is little, then, that is 'natural' about Rodolfo's evil. From this perspective, the rape is symbolic of impotence, for Rodolfo is unable to perceive the human and ethical quality of love: socially, he is an unproductive individual, who mistakes property and the security of status for power. He is a wolf among men externally, while internally he is a sheep. As such, he has succumbed to the stimulus of the girl's beauty without understanding its true potential.

The family's reaction to Leocadia's abduction is equally important in reinforcing the antinomy between force and submission. The narrator states that the father's anguish at the loss of his daughter is aggravated by the realization that one social group can overcome another with impunity. He seeks no aid from the forces of law and order, for *hidalgos pobres* have no recourse to official justice. This tacit acceptance may represent the understanding of the power which property exerts over all sectors of society. On the other hand, it may signal a much deeper perception that the *hidalguía,* that most nebulous of social classes, is devoid of any specific identity by which the demand for human rights is possible. By not seeking police protection, the father is showing less abnegation than the narrator would have us believe; his family's security depends on not exposing itself, on maintaining a silence which may be broken only in appropriate circumstances. This discretion is the principle which the father will instil in his daughter, and which will inform all her actions subsequent to the rape.

In the contrasting characterization of the two groups the reader can glimpse the disjunction between the real and the ideal world. Both Leocadia and Rodolfo, for different reasons, lack a personal identity: her innocence is amorphous, and needs to be reduced to a specific mould in order to become real; his lawlessness is devoid of intentionality. Their confrontation establishes the necessity for building social identities and practising public virtues; it will shape Leocadia's character and alter Rodolfo's sufficiently to allow it to become a fully-fledged personality.

Leocadia's awakening after the rape, her act of 'volver en sí', represents the birth of her ethical identity, the beginning of the process of defining who she is. As a newborn,

she begins to perceive reality through the senses, most specifically that of touch, since, in the darkened room, she obviously cannot see. The narrator exploits the play on light and shadow in order to emphasize the girl's greater sensitivity to a spiritual crisis: '¿Estoy en el limbo de mi inocencia o en el infierno de mis culpas?' When Rodolfo touches her, she has her answer, and 'sees' herself in a dramatic light, as if she were in a state of dishonour: 'Ya me imagino y veo que no es bien que me vean las gentes'. Leocadia's instantaneous evaluation is unrealistic if measured by any standard other than that of fiction's convention, whereby ideas are presented with greater clarity, simplicity, and unity than are observable in experience. As a literary construct, the girl's lightning-quick deliberation is entirely verisimilar. She distinguishes between the reality of innocence and the appearance of guilt, fully perceiving the disparity between an existential situation not of her choosing and her own self. Her objective is to make an expedient adjustment to the role imposed upon her.

The choice to play a role, to calculate all its phases scrupulously, is crucial to the possibility of transcending it. Leocadia's first step is to attempt to communicate to her victimizer the enormity of his abuse. Killing her would be a compassionate act, in comparison with the cruelty of having deprived her of her honour: 'en un mismo punto, vendrías a ser cruel y piadoso'. The concept of the reconciliation of opposites, which adumbrates the dénouement, is beyond Rodolfo's understanding; Leocadia's words leave him confused and speechless. The narrator attributes this confusion to his nature as 'mozo poco experimentado', and the girl forgives him because his youth has made him behave irresponsibly. But, in fact, Rodolfo's inexperience has little to do with his age, nor, we surmise, with his lack of expertise with women. If seduction and violence are habitual inclinations, sanctioned by his peers, why should Rodolfo hastily retreat to seek his friends' advice?

The man's lack of understanding harks back to his total adherence to a spiritual model which has been deformed by social custom. His Platonic apprehension of the girl's beauty incites his will to follow the image of beauty, but he confuses adoration with possession, and allows carnal desire to take over. Rodolfo automatically equates image with object: he is a foolish believer, whose devotion to beauty represents the slavish acceptance of a principle which has been emptied of its symbolic substance.

The final segment of Leocadia's monologue outlines how she intends to cope with dishonour. Since by his silence and inertia Rodolfo has denied her the option to die, she must continue to live according to the terms she has imposed upon herself: to isolate herself from society, not to publicize her shame, provided that he promise not to follow her home, nor inquire about her family's name. Her declaration that 'yo haré que no nací en el mundo' sums up the nature of her surrogate existence: it is that of a social outcast.

Rodolfo reacts to her words in a manner which shows his inability to perceive her critical detachment. She can make a value-judgement on the offence, and dispassionately overcome grief; he, unaware of Leocadia's second dimension as spectator now to her own tragedy, continues to see her as a beautiful woman, and tries to embrace her. Her rhetorical mastery, as well as her physical attack on him, are concerned with denying her moral involvement, should a second rape take place. Her ability to forgive him is contingent on his willingness to strike a bargain with her: silence for silence. She will acquiesce in his deceitful existence born of ignorance, if he will grant her a deceitful existence born of need.

Rodolfo apparently desists from the second attack because her valiant defence weakens his strength and makes his sexual ardour wane. In a moralizing interjection, the narrator notes that impulses born of lasciviousness, not love, are quickly diffused, leaving only a 'tibia voluntad'. This lukewarm, mechanical application of the will explains the 'inclinación torcida' which led the seducer to his first aberration. His wish to possess is not generated by hope, and it lacks a goal; it exists in an isolated moment of pleasure, which is quickly destroyed. The only way in which the violent act can be 'redeemed' is through his understanding that free will is bound by intentionality.

Leocadia's deceitful existence begins when Rodolfo leaves her in the bedroom to seek out his friends. The narrator's reprise about the girl's desire to die is perfunctory: she opens the window, the moonlight illuminates the room, and her attention is quickly diverted. She gathers all the material evidence about its owner: the rich adornments, the golden bed with opulent covers which 'befit a prince'. She counts chairs and tables, studies the floor plan, the position of the locked door in relation to the window, which, providentially, turns out to be guarded by bars. The garden itself is enclosed by a high fence. Clearly neither death nor escape is possible.

Leocadia exhibits none of the despair that a normal young woman would feel under the circumstances. Her reaction is much too sanguine, for she resembles a thorough investigator at the scene of a crime. Her behaviour would strike a comic note, except that her purpose is carried out in deadly earnest. She has in fact plundered the room, in order to gather all the necessary evidence to fashion her revenge. The last, and most useful find, a small silver crucifix, is quickly hidden in her sleeve, 'no por devoción ni por hurto, sino llevada de un discreto designio suyo'. Her careful scrutiny accomplished, she carefully locks the window, returns to the bed, and awaits the 'end of the unfortunate beginning of the event'. On his return, Rodolfo will believe that she has done absolutely nothing during his absence; instead, in the half-hour lapse, she has made maximum use of time.

The attempt to redeem her honour naturally fits into the role she is to play in society, and is confirmed by her suggestion that the cross be shown in churches, in the hope that the owner will claim it. Leocadia's father rejects the idea as impractical: first of all, it might fall into the wrong hands, making identification impossible; besides, the crucifix, as the only witness to her shame, will eventually produce a judge to render justice. The crucifix has been associated with a proverb, 'A buen juez, mejor testigo', in Zorrilla's *Leyenda de Toledo* [John J. Allen, 'El Cristo de la Vega y *La fuerza de la sangre*,' *MLN,* 1973]. The legend, of medieval origin, deals with the divine retribution meted

out to a recalcitrant seducer, guilty of breach of promise. The crucifix detaches itself from the cathedral altar and falls on the sinner's head, in answer to the dishonoured girl's prayers.

From the beginning, Leocadia has claimed that she will express her grief only in private discourse with God; her father amplifies the premiss by spurring her to show a true devotion to the cross: within Providential design there always exists the possibility of salvation. In the here-and-now fashioning of Leocadia's life, that possibility is realized, paradoxically, by the testimony of silence. The girl's performance is sanctioned by the father's observations on the nature of honour:

> Advierte, hija, que más lastima una onza de deshonra pública que una arroba de infamia secreta. Y pues puedes vivir honrada con Dios en público, no te pene de estar deshonrada contigo en secreto: la verdadera deshonra está en el pecado y la verdadera honra en la virtud.

Their conspiracy of silence does not stem from a banal preoccupation with the *qué dirán,* but from a profound understanding of their society's false conception of honour. Honour's natural and essential affinity to personal rectitude is corrupted by placing it in an unnatural context, in the marketplace of public opinion. If society will be satisfied by fakery, then silence is the only appropriate response to the absurdity and hollowness of its principles.

The trust both father and daughter place in the cross does not exclude the role of God as the ultimate judge. There is, however, a strong suggestion of distrust about the place where it might normally be shown—the church. The narration of their conversation takes up an inordinately long space within the scope of a short novel. The elder *hidalgo* states his misgivings about the possible loss of the cross, and ignores totally the role that religious authorities might have in its restitution. In the exchange between father and daughter the cross is reified, deprived of its symbolic value, and the mysterious workings of Providence are equally divested of their mystical power. Leocadia will use the cross simply as a recognition tool, by which she proves to be a most self-possessed witness to her tragedy.

The irony of Leocadia's life in isolation affirms her excellence and creativity. She models her existence upon the fiction of respectability, and the fact that it is a surrogate makes it powerfully subversive: it carries weight because, as a fiction, Leocadia can control it as an author controls his creation. The parodic analogue is based on an artificially created disharmony, in that the family's social integration exists solely by deceit. The revolutionary aspect of it is that the deceit is directed by the will of the participants, in feigned acquiescence in social conventions, but totally directed by the laws of expediency. The manipulation would be tantamount to anarchy, were it generalized to an entire society: it would sap the security felt by those who accept social custom as a necessary defence against individual rivalries.

The preservation of silence becomes a *tour de force;* all social contact is avoided before, and during the girl's pregnancy. The safeguards are carried to extremes, for Leocadia's mother herself acts as midwife, and the child is immediately dispatched to a village where he is brought up by relatives until the age of four. When he returns, it is under the guise of cousin. Caution has the purpose of creating the respectability which will be the child's only worldly patrimony.

The illusion is highly successful. Luisito's gentle appearance and disposition, as well as his cleverness, earn him copious blessings from all observers. Society showers applause on a model child who is, in reality, a bastard. The noble traits which Luis is said to have inherited from an illustrious father are ascribed to nobility of blood, whose transcendental value, however, is diminished by the real blood shed by the child, as he is almost killed by his paternal grandfather's horse. With the accident true nobility comes to the fore: as the rider looks into the face of the wounded child, he is reminded of his son. Moved by compassion, he brings Luis into his house, thus initiating the process which will enable Luis to claim his birthright.

When Leocadia is fetched to care for the child, she immediately recognizes the house and the bedroom where he was conceived. It seems that she is not so distraught as not to be able to count again the number of steps which lead to the entrance, as she had when Rodolfo hastily brought her out. Only now does the narrator disclose this detail, and applauds her 'advertencia discreta' of seven years before. The ludic undertone which runs through the recounting of Leocadia's plight clearly indicates Cervantes' highly original application of the concept of verisimilitude. The 'weakness' of romance is its reliance on the inverisimilar occurrence, and Cervantes exploits this very weakness to create subtle interplay between the unlikely event and the critical check of self-parody.

Leocadia's entrance into the aristocratic household brings to an end the necessity for the silence she has sustained for seven years. The suspicions harboured by Rodolfo's parents, which have now progressed beyond intuition, are confirmed by the testimony of the silver cross. In Leocadia's words, the design of divine justice has brought her to this house 'para que . . . hallase yo en ella, como espero que he de hallar, si no el remedio que mejor convenga (y cuando no), con mi desventura, a lo menos medio con que pueda sobrellevalla'. The girl's 'hope' for the restoration of her honour is more than a vague wish: her appeal for a 'remedy' or a 'means' is a plea for a response by the seducer's family. She has played her role well in establishing an honourable existence for herself and her son; now, the family should take equitable action.

The second fainting spell, a timely reaction to grief, fear, and helplessness, represents Leocadia's genuine state of submissiveness, as it had at the time of her violation. In this instance, it is an overt, if unconscious, statement about the type of power she still lacks in order to complete her self-creation. She possesses all the prerequisites for an individual existence couched in ethical values, but it cannot blossom fully in isolation.

The rebel who alienates himself from the traditional establishment might well be the harbinger of a heresy, but the revolutionary rejects solipsism, since it lacks the force to project the potential for change beyond the individual. Sensorially, doña Estefanía responds to the girl's need for solidarity: 'Como mujer y noble, en quien la compasión y misericordia suele ser tan natural como la crueldad en el hombre . . . juntó su rostro con el suyo, derramando sobre él tantas lágrimas, que no fue menester esparcirle otra agua encima para que Leocadia en sí volviese'. The two women are surprised in this posture by the husband and grandson, who join them in grieving. Thus begins the active integration of the outsider into the family nucleus, a union which can only become complete with the presence of Leocadia's rightful husband.

Rodolfo's return from Italy is effected by his parents' offer of a beautiful bride. As they correctly surmised, 'la golosina de gozar tan hermosa mujer' brings rapid results. In fact, the alacrity with which their son answers the call makes them fear that his travels abroad have not changed his worldly nature. Since truth must be ascertained gradually, doña Estefanía decelerates his son's actions by staging a complication. While Leocadia and the child are hiding, Rodolfo is shown the portrait of an ugly woman, and told that what she lacks in physical beauty she more than makes up in virtue. It is a harsh test for virtue indeed! But it appears that Rodolfo has gained a good measure of discretion, and the calculated risk of 'disenchanting' the bride pays off. Rodolfo perceives the disharmony in the unfair exchange of ugliness of virtue, and eloquently rejects it: since the sacrament of marriage is an indissoluble tie which cannot be undone except by death, its bonds must be of the same fabric. Virtue, nobility, discretion, and riches in a woman may well please the eyes of the mind, but ugliness cannot comfort the human eye, and hinders man from enjoying the benefits of marriage, which, besides the responsibility of procreation, promises a lifetime of pleasure. Without 'el justo y debido deleite que los casados gozan . . . cojea el matrimonio y desdice de su segunda intención'. He seeks the only thing he still lacks: 'La hermosura busco, la belleza quiero, no con otra dote que con la de la honestidad y buenas costumbres que si esto me trae mi esposa, yo serviré a Dios con gusto, y daré buena vejez a mis padres'.

Because Rodolfo has been placed in a precarious position, he has reacted by making the necessary connection between ideal love, by nature atemporal, and temporally conditioned marital love. If the latter is not to be destroyed by time's progress, it must include the characteristic vitality of sensual pleasure, subsumed to the control of the spirit. As a sacrament, marriage has no transcendental value, unless accompanied by human faith. Rodolfo has successfully added the dimension of intentionality to his desire for pleasure by the exercise of free will.

Man's perception of the true nature and application of free will signals an imminent behavioural change. With the union with his beloved begins a process of mutual transformation by means of a barter system: one concept of personal identity is exchanged for another. Woman has already forged her identity by recognizing the double fiction which dominates the social condition; the first is the fiction enshrined in social, literary and spiritual tradition, the second is the fiction by which we lead our daily lives.

The judicious practice of the second type, more 'real' because of our familiarity with it, can lead us to achieve a just perspective on the values of the first. By dint of this particular superiority, woman offers man a model to follow. In accepting the model, man places himself under the obligation not to follow it slavishly, but to begin, by imitation, to learn that there exists no schematic method which makes all things simple.

Cervantes' use of the mother figure in 'La fuerza' is a unique case in the *Novelas ejemplares;* usually, in the stories involving honour restoration, the woman's defender is a brother, as in 'Las dos doncellas' and 'La señora Cornelia.' Even if we consider two surrogate mother characters, Preciosa's putative grandmother in 'La gitanilla,' and Queen Elizabeth in 'La española inglesa,' we must conclude that both male and female defenders of the heroine's virtue merely share the role of mediators. In this *novela,* dona Estefanía's well-delineated character can be attributed in part to the story's very specific surroundings. While the peripeties of other stories hurl the protagonists into the amorphous social spaces of foreign countries or the neutral ground of inns and strangers' homes, 'La fuerza' 's action takes place entirely in Toledo.

Doña Estefanía bears the characteristics of a 'real' mother, perturbed by the actions of a young son, cognizant of the family's and society's realities. She is no less painstaking than Leocadia in gathering material evidence to ascertain the truth about Rodolfo. Soon after his arrival, she questions the two friends who accompanied him to Italy, and receives the needed confirmation. Should we infer that, even after deciding to make Rodolfo face up to his iniquities, the mother still regards Leocadia as an intruder who can destroy their social position? The care with which Leocadia determined her seducer's social status confirms her awareness that he might provide her with vindication as no member of any other social group could. Doña Estefanía's careful scrutiny parallels Leocadia's, and shows her insight into the subversive power generated by the girl's existential mode.

The novelist has done nothing to underplay the material nature of both women's calculatedness. On the contrary, the emphasis on trivial details, such as examining room decorations and counting steps, on the one hand, and questioning witnesses, on the other, reinforces it. Doña Estefanía becomes the judge whom Leocadia and her family had so earnestly hoped to find; she deems the girl's exemplary existence worthy of imitation, follows through in creating her own deceit, and thus initiates the lovers' rightful union. In order to fulfil her promise to Rodolfo that he will be married according to his wishes, he must first be able to see in the same person the object of his desire and his intended bride. The synthesis of the ideal and the real is achieved by a subtle transformation of nature. Doña Estefanía belatedly remembers her secret guest, and calls for servants to usher her in; Leocadia herself had anxiously awaited her dramatic entrance: 'Poco tardó en salir Leocadia y dar de sí la improvisa y más hermosa muestra que pudo dar jamás compuesta y natural hermosura'. Here beauty, as well as the woman, are submitted to a critical evaluation. A winter dress of black velvet provides the best background for gold and pearl buttons, a diamond necklace and belt. To rival their brilliance, long, 'not too blond' hair, with its ingenious arrangement of ties, curls and diamonds, offers the perfect frame for the face. The overall effect of brilliant light is heightened by the candles held by two servants showing Leocadia the way.

By this excellent example of literary portraiture the narrator accounts for the bystanders' extreme reaction; they perceive an image of beauty which is, somehow, beyond the pale of humanity: 'Levantáronse todos a hacerle reverencia, como si fuera alguna cosa del cielo que allí milagrosamente se había aparecido . . . Rodolfo, que desde más cerca miraba la incomparable belleza de Leocadia, decía entre sí: "Si la mitad de esta hermosura tuviera la que mi madre me tiene escogida por esposa, tuviérame yo por el más dichoso hombre del mundo. ¡Válame Dios! ¡Qué es esto que veo! ¿Es por ventura algún ángel humano el que estoy mirando?" ' In negating the commonplace that beauty needs no adornment, the narrator points to the necessity of 'playing up' natural characteristics so that these may have a permanent impact.

The dénouement exhibits a typical acceleration of action, with rapid untying of the threads of complication. Leocadia, in an intense speculation about how close she may be to either happiness or despair, faints in doña Estefanía's arms; Rodolfo, in his haste to assist her, trips and falls twice. Since no effort to revive her succeeds, everyone concludes that she is dead. The news spreads through the household, and brings out of hiding three guests, Leocadia's parents and a priest. It is the latter, concerned with the girl's state, for the sake of her soul's salvation, who discovers that Rodolfo has also fainted.

Leocadia's third fainting spell, with its abdication of the senses, is symbolic of yet another change of identity. She has been transformed twice: once into a being of exemplary virtue, the second time into a woman of exemplary beauty. After her experience of near-death, she emerges as a real woman, in whom exemplary and concrete qualities are perfectly integrated. Rodolfo's requirement that a woman's virtue coexist with physical beauty has been fulfilled.

Rodolfo's own loss of consciousness signals the bringing together of 'lo justo', the happy conformity with his parents' wishes, and 'el gusto', the free and willing acceptance of his bride. The priest hastens to consecrate the union by the couple's simple statement of intention, for, as the narrator explains, 'sin las diligencias y prevenciones juntas y santas que ahora se usan, quedaba hecho el matrimonio'.

With his brief gloss on marriage customs in pre-Tridentine Spain, the narrator strengthens the reader's awareness that the story has reached a sensible ending. Yet, this thrifty conclusion to the sustained and calculated pursuit of marriage cheats the reader of the pleasure of witnessing its celebration. In the *Novelas* which end in marriage, the narrator generally limits his reporting to the statement that the happy pair 'got married'. 'La gitanilla' and 'El amante liberal' respectively introduce a bishop, and a 'bishop or archbishop' to waive the legality of the waiting period after the publication of the banns. In 'La española 'inglesa' the dénouement gives a slightly different twist to the final reunion. Recaredo finds his intended bride Isabela in a monastery: in the presence of a 'suffragan bishop' and the monastic order, the last complication is cleared up, to the delight of the former, who embraces the couple and her parents, and two of the ecclesiastics, who request that the girl put her story in writing for the archbishop. The couple ask the assistant bishop to honour their wedding: 'Holgó de hacerlo así el asistente, y de allí a ocho días, acompañado de los más principales de la ciudad, se halló en [las bodas]'.

Is the mystification about the ecclesiastics' titles and their pseudo-official rites casting a playful shadow on the celebration of 'Christian marriage' [Marcel Bataillon, 'Cervantes y el "matrimonio cristiano",' *Varia lección de clásicos españoles,* 1964]? There can be little doubt that Cervantes scrupulously chose this coda to his compositions ending in marriage for the purpose of undermining the authority of those figures normally associated with its formalities. The only authority with any validity is that of the lovers, since they are the sole agents of their union. Through it, they have acquired the most valuable property of self-hood, even though they have reached the point of disillusionment regarding its true nature. They know that individual creation is an illusion which alternately meshes with and grates against collective fictions.

The only thing that Cervantine characters can learn from their experiences is the consciousness that their only power is the potential for change. They are destined to remain in a peculiar state of faith, whose ardent expression is the only possible reply to those who believe too innocently in the human capacity for goodness. The author leaves it up to the reader to derive his own benefit from their example, provided he interprets the signs correctly: truth is deliberately revealed in a most undignified manner, by gesturing and posturing, to make the point that man is at his most authentic when he welcomes the doubt about who he is with a smile. (pp. 101-09)

> *Adriana Slaniceanu, "The Calculating Woman in Cervantes' 'La fuerza de la sangre',"* in Bulletin of Hispanic Studies, *Vol. LXIV, No. 2, April, 1987, pp. 101-10.*

FURTHER READING

Bibliography

Drake, Dana B. *Cervantes' Novelas Ejemplares: A Selective, Annotated Bibliography,* 2nd. ed. New York: Garland, 1981.
    Lists selected criticism from the seventeenth century to the present day.

Biography

Entwistle, William J. *Cervantes.* 1940. Reprint. Oxford: Clarendon Press, 1965, 192 p.
    Literary biography of Cervantes.

Fitzmaurice-Kelly, James. *The Life of Miguel de Cervantes Saavedra.* London: Chapman and Hall, 1892, 396 p.
    Important nineteenth-century biographical and critical study. This work contains an authoritative, chronological bibliography of Cervantes' works in Spanish and in translation, from original appearance through late nineteenth-century editions.

Watts, Henry Edward. *Life of Miguel de Cervantes.* Ann Arbor, Mich.: Plutarch Press, 1971, 185 p.
    Major nineteenth-century biography that contains balanced criticism of Cervantes's works.

Criticism

Donato, Clorinda. "Leonora and Camila: Female Characterization and Narrative Formula in the Cervantine Novela." *Mester* XV, No. 2 (Fall 1986): 13-24.
    Contrasts the female protagonists in Cervantes's "The Jealous Husband" and "The Impertinent Curiosity."

Fox, Dian. "The Critical Attitude in 'Rinconete y Cortadillo'." *Cervantes* 3, No. 2 (Fall 1983): 135-47.
    Maintains that point of view in "Rinconete y Cortadillo" is used both to create sympathy for the two young thieves and to criticize their criminal acts.

Hart, Thomas R. "Versions of Pastoral in Three *Novelas ejemplares.*" *Bulletin of Hispanic Studies* LVIII, No. 4 (October 1981): 283-91.
    Analyzes "The Gypsy Maid," "The Illustrious Scullery Maid," and "Rinconete y Cortadillo" as stories adhering to a traditional pastoral scheme of exile, rejuvenation, and return.

Herrero, Javier. "Emerging Realism: Love and Cash in 'La Ilustre Fregona'." In *From Dante to García Márquez,* edited by Gene H. Bell-Villada, Antonio Giminez, and George Pistorius, pp. 47-59. Williamstown, Mass.: Williams College, 1987.
    Argues that "The Illustrious Scullery Maid" parodies the conventions of classical comedy and romance.

Keightley, Ronald G. "The Narrative Structure of 'Rinconete y Cortadillo'." In *Essays on Narrative Fiction in the Iberian Peninsula in Honour of Frank Pierce,* edited by R. B. Tate, pp. 39-54. n.p.: Dolphin Book Co., 1982.
    Examines the narrative structure of "Rinconete y Cortadillo."

Martinez-Bonati, Felix. "Forms of Mimesis and Ideological Rhetoric in Cervantes's 'La gitanilla'." In *Textual Analysis: Some Readers Reading,* edited by Mary Ann Caws, pp. 64-73. New York: Modern Language Association, 1986.
    Applies the methods of phenomenology to analyze the rhetorical devices and ideologies apparent in "The Gypsy Maid."

Murillo, L. A. "Narrative Structures in the *Novelas Ejemplares:* An Outline." *Cervantes* VIII, No. 2 (Fall 1988): 231-50.
    Examines the narrative structures in *Exemplary Novels.*

Pabon, Thomas A. "Courtship and Marriage in 'El amante liberal': The Symbolic Quest." *Hispanófila* 26, No. 76 (September 1982): 47-52.
    Views Leonisa and Ricardo's courtship in "The Generous Lover" as a process of trial and purification leading toward their "spiritual triumph in marriage."

Riley, E. C. "Cervantes, Freud, and Psychoanalytic Narrative Theory." *The Modern Language Review* 88, No. 1 (January 1993): 1-14.

> Studies the similarities between Freud's psychoanalytic theory and Cervantes's "Dialogue of the Dogs." Riley argues that Freud's reading of the short story may have influenced his thinking when he later formulated his theories about psychoanalytic principles.

Soons, Alan. "Three *Novelas ejemplares* of Cervantes: Diptych Pattern and Spiritual Intention." *Orbis Litterarum* XXVI, No. 2 (1971): 87-93.

> Finds similarities in structure between certain classical and medieval spiritual works and Cervantes's "The Spanish-English Lady," "The Force of Blood," and "The Illustrious Scullery Maid."

Weber, Alison. "Tragic Reparation in Cervantes's 'El celoso extremeño'." *Cervantes* 4, No. 1 (Spring 1984): 35-51.

> Psychoanalytic study of Cervantes's portrayal of guilt and atonement in "The Jealous Husband."

Willtrout, Ann E. "Role Playing and Rites of Passage: 'La ilustre fregona' and 'La gitanilla'." *Hispania* 64, No. 3 (September 1981): 388-99.

> Examines the function of social status and role playing in two of Cervantes's short stories.

Additional coverage of Cervantes's life and career is contained in the following sources published by Gale Research: *Literature Criticism from 1400 to 1800,* Vol. 6; and *World Literature Criticism.*

Arthur Conan Doyle

1859-1930

English short story writer, novelist, essayist, historian, and poet.

INTRODUCTION

Doyle is best known for his collections of stories featuring Sherlock Holmes. Detailing the exploits of the world's first consulting detective and his friend Dr. Watson, these works are among the most popular in literature. During his multifaceted career, Doyle also wrote a variety of other long and short fiction works, including adventure and science fiction stories, supernatural tales, and historical romances.

Doyle was born in Edinburgh and educated in Jesuit schools. He took his medical degree in 1881 and eventually established a struggling practice as an ophthalmologist, a profession he abandoned to pursue a literary career. His early medical experiences were the basis for *Round the Red Lamp,* a collection of short stories published in 1894. His first work featuring Sherlock Holmes was the novel *A Study in Scarlet,* which did not garner immediate attention; however, the short stories relating the exploits of the famous detective captured the reading public's interest in 1891 when they first appeared in the newly founded *Strand* magazine. These early stories were collected in *The Adventures of Sherlock Holmes* and *The Memoirs of Sherlock Holmes.*

Modeled on Edgar Allan Poe's detective Auguste Dupin and Emile Gaboriau's Inspector Lecoq, Holmes is described as "cold, precise, but admirably balanced" and his milieu is a stylized version of late Victorian London which abounds with gas lamps and thick fog. The early stories deal primarily with crimes that are the result of greed and threats to the social order. For example, in "The Speckled Band," Dr. Grimesby Roylott covets his stepdaughter's property. "A Scandal in Bohemia" examines the arrogance and hypocrisy of a king who believes he is the victim of a blackmail scheme. While the Holmes adventures were very popular with British and American readers, Doyle grew bored with his creation and weary of the contrived plots of detective stories. He also wanted to devote more time to what he considered his important work, the writing of historical fiction. In "The Final Problem" Holmes is killed during a struggle with the villainous Dr. Moriarty. However, public outcry and repeated requests from his publisher led to Holmes's resuscitation ten years later in *The Return of Sherlock Holmes.* The exploits of Holmes and Watson continued in *His Last Bow* and *The Case-Book of Sherlock Holmes,* collections noted for their unusual violence and grotesque characters. The plot of "The Cardboard Box" revolves around a package containing two human ears, one male and one female. The protago-

nist of "The Creeping Man" attempts to regain his youth through injections of a serum that turns him into a creature described as half-man, half-monkey.

During the decade-long hiatus between *The Memoirs of Sherlock Holmes* and *The Return of Sherlock Holmes,* Doyle produced historical fiction, war histories, and adventure novels. He had some success with *The Exploits of Brigadier Gerard* and *The Adventures of Gerard,* two volumes of short stories about a gallant soldier of the Napoleonic period. A sports story, "The Croxley Master," reflects Doyle's sense of decency and fair play, traits that critics see reflected in all of his work. His science fiction stories, particularly "When the World Screamed" and "The Disintegration Machine," emphasize adventure rather than scientific veracity.

Critics observe that Doyle's portrayal of Holmes and Watson was influential in the development of the detective story. The brilliant but cold detective and his affable colleague became a stock pairing in the detective genre and remain among the most recognizable figures in Western culture, much like Don Quixote and Hamlet. As Don Richard Cox has asserted, Holmes "brings with him his lantern of rational thought and repeatedly flashes it into the dark corners of human existence, showing us that the shadows lurking there are not to be feared."

PRINCIPAL WORKS

SHORT FICTION

Mysteries and Adventures 1889; also published as *The Gully of Bluemansdyke, and Other Stories,* 1893
The Captain of the "Pole-Star," and Other Tales 1890
The Adventures of Sherlock Holmes 1892
The Memoirs of Sherlock Holmes 1894
Round the Red Lamp: Being Facts and Fancies of Medical Life 1894
The Exploits of Brigadier Gerard 1896
The Green Flag, and Other Stories of War and Sport 1900
The Adventures of Gerard 1903
The Return of Sherlock Holmes 1905
His Last Bow: Some Reminiscences of Sherlock Holmes 1917
Tales of Ring and Camp 1922; also published as *The Croxley Master, and Other Tales of Ring and Camp,* 1925
Tales of Terror and Mystery 1922
Tales of Twilight and the Unseen 1922
The Case-Book of Sherlock Holmes 1927

OTHER MAJOR WORKS

A Study in Scarlet (novel) 1888
Micah Clark (novel) 1889
The Sign of Four (novel) 1890
The White Company (novel) 1891
The Refugees (novel) 1893
The Stark Munro Letters (novel) 1895
Rodney Stone (novel) 1896
Songs of Action (poetry) 1898
The Tragedy of the Korosko (novel) 1898; also published as *The Desert Drama,* 1898
The Great Boer War (nonfiction) 1900
The Hound of the Baskervilles (novel) 1902
The War in South Africa: Its Cause and Conduct (history) 1902
Sir Nigel (novel) 1906
Songs of the Road (poetry) 1911
The Lost World (novel) 1912
The Poison Belt (novel) 1913
The Valley of Fear (novel) 1916
The British Campaign in France and Flanders. 6 vols. (history) 1916-20
The New Revelation; or, What Is Spiritualism? (essays) 1918
The Wanderings of a Spiritualist (essays) 1921
Memories and Adventures (autobiography) 1924
The History of Spiritualism. 2 vols. (nonfiction) 1926
The Maracot Deep (novel) 1929

CRITICISM

Pierre Nordon   (essay date 1964)

[*In the following excerpt, originally published in French in 1964, Nordon examines the origins, structure, and social background of the Sherlock Holmes stories.*]

Sherlock Holmes's appearance in *The Strand Magazine* was the actual starting-point of the cycle, or at least of the phase leading to its success. . . . George Newnes, who had handed over the editorship of *The Review of Reviews* to William Stead, decided that his new monthly magazine must have an illustration on every page, thus firmly staking all on a formula which was to have an incalculable effect on literature, directly or indirectly. *The Strand Magazine* was an immediate success. It is difficult today to separate the triumph scored by Holmes from the popularity of the magazine itself, and of the image created by Sidney Paget's illustrations. We should not conclude from this that *The Strand Magazine* contributed to any great extent to Conan Doyle's success. It was Conan Doyle who made the fortune of *The Strand Magazine.* We know that the editors offered him large, afterwards fabulous sums of money. Less concrete perhaps, but just as eloquent, is the evidence of Basil Hastings, the editor-in-chief:

> Alone of all the great and popular authors in that astonishing flowering of letters which marked the beginning of this century, and the beginning of the popular illustrated magazine, Conan Doyle writing Sherlock Holmes, was the only one—Kipling and Wells *not* excepted—whose name on the cover as a contributor was sufficient to justify the publisher in increasing by many thousands the print run for that particular issue. I can think of only one contributor who, if we had the paper, and the author were willing, could put thousands on the sales of any one issue of a magazine to-day. And that is Winston Churchill.

Of course it is more difficult to analyse the multiple factors contributing to an artistic success than to treat the artist like a tradesman in terms of supply and demand. 'He was greatly admired by the intelligentsia,' wrote Somerset Maugham of Conan Doyle, 'they couldn't help enjoying his stories, but felt that it was hardly literature,' Conan Doyle was to some extent the victim of the prejudice against detective fiction, a prejudice he shared himself; and he maintained a somewhat ambiguous modesty about this part of his work. Perhaps he did his reputation a disservice by attracting our attention to the formula he believed he had invented:

> It had struck me that a single character running through the series, if it only engaged the attention of the reader, would bind that reader to that particular magazine. On the other hand, it had long seemed to me that the ordinary serial might be an impediment rather than a help to a magazine, since, sooner or later, one missed one number and afterwards it had lost all interest. Clearly the ideal compromise was a character which carried through, and yet instalments which were each complete in themselves, so that the pur-

chaser was always sure that he could relish the whole contents of the magazine. I believe that I was the first to realize this and the Strand Magazine the first to put it into practice.

Conan Doyle was unaware that this last statement was not exactly true, and that others before him, Dickens in particular, had thought of a similar formula.

Nor do his reflections really explain why Sherlock Holmes continued to flourish in the pages of *The Strand Magazine* until as late as 1927, nor why in two cases, *The Hound of the Baskervilles* and *The Valley of Fear,* published respectively in 1901 and 1914, the formula was abandoned without the slightest ill effect. It had already been exploited before the founding of *The Strand Magazine* in *The Sign of Four,* a story about the same characters who had appeared in *A Study in Scarlet.* The only appreciable result of transferring the Sherlock Holmes stories to the restricted area of a monthly magazine was to reduce them in scale. In its turn, this necessary reduction simplified the plots and directed Conan Doyle's mind towards less impersonal subjects than those of the two previous stories.

It is difficult to analyse the sources of a writer who is both very imaginative and a great reader. The simplest plot lends itself to innumerable comparisons. For instance that of **'The New Catacomb,'** published in 1898, could be traced to the influence of three separate authors, as well as to a theme already treated by Conan Doyle and an incident from his own life.

From 1891 on, however, literary reminders are very few; the similarities that can be traced between Conan Doyle and Poe in **'The Musgrave Ritual'** or **'The Dancing Men'** are inherent in the cipher theme as Conan Doyle himself pointed out.

> Not only is Poe the originator of the detective story; all treasure-hunting, cryptogram-solving yarns trace back to his 'Goldbug,' just as all pseudo-scientific Verne-and-Wells stories have their prototypes in the 'Voyage to the Moon,' and the 'Case of Monsieur Valdemar.' If every man who receives a cheque for a story which owed its springs to Poe were to pay a tithe to a monument for the master, he would have a pyramid as big as that of Cheops.

We can therefore definitely say that many more of the plots came from life than from books, and the origin of a story will often be found in some incident experienced or observed by the author, some echo of a suggestion or memory of a conversation.

Can the first of the Sherlock Holmes Adventures to appear in *The Strand Magazine* be said to have a plot at all? The beautiful adventuress Irene Adler has in her possession compromising letters from the King of Bohemia (as imaginary a figure as Shakespeare's dukes), who is afraid that the scandal created by their publication will prevent his proposed marriage to a 'Scandinavian' princess. He begs Sherlock Holmes to help him get back the letters, which Irene Adler refuses to return. It is a situation slightly reminiscent of 'The Purloined Letter,' but Conan Doyle projects a very different light on it. Not only do the incidents have no relation to those in Poe's story, but the reader's interest is gripped by Irene Adler's character and Sherlock Holmes's deductions: 'To Sherlock Holmes she is always *the* woman. I have seldom heard him mention her under any other name. In his eyes she eclipses and predominates the whole of her sex.'

Conan Doyle has not made her a commonplace adventuress, influenced by sordid motives. She in fact refuses to sell the letters, and once she realises that her feelings for the King have changed she is ready to give up any attempt to interfere with his marriage plans. Although at the mercy of her own impulsive but generous nature, she never becomes unreasonable; and she shows Sherlock Holmes that she is an adversary worthy of his steel. She succeeds in frustrating his plans—no mean success. In a word she is as nearly as possible the detective's feminine counterpart, as he freely admits. The concise irony of his comment on the subject escapes his clumsy and obtuse client: ' "From what I have seen of the lady, she seems, indeed, to be on a very different level to Your Majesty," said Holmes, coldly.'

Irene Adler's personality is the pivot of the story, and it is unnecessary to look far for the model Conan Doyle took her from. She was Lola Montès. Born in 1818, this adventuress had appeared on the London stage before she became the mistress of Louis of Bavaria. Her political influence alarmed the Jesuit party, and the King was forced to part from her. For the purposes of his story Conan Doyle shifted the events to a time forty years later, but the similarity between Irene Adler and his model remains. Both are English by birth and connected with the theatre. Like Lola Montès, Irene Adler is the mistress of a central European sovereign, whose heart has to submit to considerations of State. Both become exiles. Why should the romantic legend of Lola Montès have induced Conan Doyle to make Irene Adler the incarnation of the eternal feminine in Sherlock Holmes's eyes? Of course the story of Lola Montès would have made an impression on him as an adolescent, and it will be remembered that at seventeen he was in Austria in the Jesuit school at Feldkirch. It is permissible to suppose that in this small world and in this small town the amazing story of Lola Montès could still be the subject of conversation in 1876, particularly among school-boys: and in 1891 Conan Doyle and his wife spent the winter in Vienna. This new taste of Austrian life may well have revived his adolescent memories, and **'Scandal in Bohemia'** was probably written in Vienna. In any case the story was published a few weeks after his return.

The next Adventure introduces a new dramatic element—mystification. In **'A Case of Identity'** the detective finally discovers that the man he is looking for, who is supposed to have disappeared, never in fact existed at all. Instead of the incidents being scattered through the story, the surprise is reserved entirely for the conclusion; and in order to make it as sensational as possible Conan Doyle makes the enquiry begin in the most colourless and ordinary way. The plots of the stories were gaining in simplicity and consequently in aesthetic perfection. This led to their being based on current events, and we already notice a prosaic quality in **'A Case of Identity,'** both in the characters and the problems they set Sherlock Holmes. We find the inspiration for many of the stories in the newspapers for the year 1890. It has been shown for instance that the young Earl of Arundel and Surrey, who had been forced by illness to live in isolation at Norbury not far from South Norwood where Conan Doyle was living at the time, may well have given him the idea for 'The Yellow Face.'

In 'The Stockbroker's Clerk' Conan Doyle seems to have been thinking of the case of a swindler called Isidor Gilka in November 1888; and in 'The Naval Treaty' of Charles Marvin, a Foreign Office official who sold the text of a secret treaty between England and Russia to *The Globe.* Among other references to current events, one should include a photograph of a false horse-shoe in *The Strand Magazine,* or a figure seen more than once in the City, or a house whose situation made it of interest to bank robbers in 'The Red-Headed League.' Real-life memories also throw light on some of the plots: the harpooners in 'Black Peter' are the men Conan Doyle lived with on board the *Hope.* In the same way the village of Birlstone and its manor-house described in such detail in *The Valley of Fear* are the village and manor-house of Groombridge, seven miles from Crowborough, where Conan Doyle had several times stayed. Other stories were inspired by conversations or correspondence with friends. In 1903 Sir Arthur accepted a device suggested by Jean Leckie to account for Holmes's return after his long absence and apparent disappearance in the falls of Reichenbach. *The Hound of the Baskervilles* arose from a conversation followed by a visit to Dartmoor. Fletcher Robinson, a friend he had made in South Africa, was intrigued by a legend about a phantom dog told him by Max Pemberton; he passed it on to Conan Doyle, who dedicated the book to him. There was some question of a collaboration, but Robinson backed out, though Conan Doyle took him with him for long days on the moors. Hearing that an escaped Dartmoor convict was hiding in this remote region, he organised his different impressions and observations round an old local legend about a certain Richard Cabell.

Any anecdote, however unexpected and comical, could be the germ of one of Sherlock Holmes's Adventures. Soon after the famous occasion when General Humbert asked if Sherlock Holmes was a private in the British Army, Conan Doyle replied by writing the story which brought his hero's career to an end. This was 'His Last Bow,' first published in *The Strand Magazine* with the sub-title 'The War Service of Sherlock Holmes.'

How can one sum up the sources of the Sherlock Holmes Adventures? The formula he used to make them suitable for a magazine resulted in a success he had never dreamed of, nor even perhaps desired. As the cycle grew he came under more and more pressure from his own creation, and for a great many years the thread on which his days were strung was tightened by the fact that his imagination was caught in a trap. The intimacy this wove between the author and this series of stories during nearly forty years, gave them very visible organic unity. Technically speaking, the need for the plots to be as short and lucid as possible helped to build up the character of Holmes—the central point where all the threads met. But we must now go on to study the background, which will raise the question of the nature of detective fiction in general.

Every novel in which police and detectives play an important part is not necessarily a detective-story. One might mention works as different from each other as *Moll Flanders, Les Misérables, Crime and Punishment, Le Procès, Sanctuary* and a great many more. What is it about the Sherlock Holmes stories that makes them so typical of detective fiction? Firstly, it would seem, that everything to do with the investigation is given primary importance, to the detriment of the rest of the action and descriptions of persons and places. Also that in the detective story in general, and the Sherlock Holmes cycle in particular, time factors, characters and plot are controlled by aesthetic considerations belonging more to the domain of the theatre than the novel. We have to do with several hundred characters, almost all of whom appear in only one of the stories. What they are and what they do only interests us in so far as it concerns the hero. Later on we will describe Conan Doyle's treatment of his characters; for the moment we will confine ourselves to making clear that whatever their status in the action, whether the plot requires them to be princes or pariahs, they are technically speaking mere satellites. They fall into two groups or camps, according as to whether the hero is on their side or against them—a dualism that inevitably results in an almost Manichaean simplification of their psychological make-up. To know all is to forgive all: but criminals cannot be allowed to justify their crimes, the plot requires them to remain as they are. All that is necessary is to attribute their actions to one of the two motive forces to which all behaviour can be reduced—love or gain.

Let us consider the whole cycle of fifty-six short and four long stories, disregarding the distinction between innocent and guilty. In twenty of them either the central or subsidiary action depends on a love affair. Among eight murders motivated by jealousy, the rival is the victim in six and the unfaithful spouse in two. In these two last, one of the murderers is the husband ('The Retired Colourman') and one the jilted fiancée ('The Musgrave Ritual'); but the crime of passion plays only a secondary part in the plots. In only one story, 'The Abbey Grange,' do we find a drama of jealousy of the traditional type, and the victim is presented in such an unfavourable light that Sherlock Holmes allows the criminal to escape from justice.

If we examine these twenty plots we find that it is generally the victims who are involved in love affairs, whereas the criminals are invariably inspired by more sordid motives. We see from this that love is treated extremely unrealistically, never losing its pure and even sacred character, and in one case it is allowed to triumph over the law of the land. It must not therefore dominate the action. More often than not, whenever the plot seems to hinge upon a love affair, the final explanation brings more sordid motives to light. However there is one story, 'The Missing Three-Quarter', in which exactly the opposite happens, and any reader familiar with the previous stories is as much surprised as the author evidently intended him to be.

The great majority of Holmes's adversaries are in complete control of their emotions, perfectly aware of what they are doing and therefore responsible; at least this is so in all the stories written before 1910. They represent the most formidable threat to the safe and well-organised class who profited from the established order in Great Britain before the First World War—the threat to property. Sometimes they are ordinary burglars, counterfeiters, or treasure-seekers; sometimes blackmailers, hired thieves or swindlers. It is not surprising that such characters as these should often have scores to settle among themselves, nor that three of the novels and nineteen of the Adventures should centre round the essentially dramatic theme of revenge.

The cycle is concerned with crimes of blood, but we never have to face unbearable scenes of slaughter, nor do we come across those 'chain' murders so commonly found in detective-stories written after 1930. Some of the stories even make do without a corpse. Among the twelve stories of the first series of Adventures, nine contain no blood-thirsty crime at all. It is true that they become more common in the later stories, figuring in nine out of eleven stories in the *Memoirs* and ten out of thirteen in the *Return.* But the murders are used to give accent, or are too episodic in character to create a macabre atmosphere. It is rare to find Holmes's investigations beginning with a bloody crime. Only seven stories start with a murder; the story called 'Thor Bridge' seems to be an eighth but in reality is not.

Holmes's task is not therefore always to unmask or arrest a murderer. Very often the problems he is given to solve are nearer comedy than tragedy. Perhaps this is why Sherlock Holmes is so ready to describe them as 'grotesque'— by which he means tragicomic. For instance the criminal may use a deliberate confusion of identity to achieve his ends: someone is forced to play the part of victim ('The Copper Beeches,' 'Shoscombe Old Place'), or else the criminal passes himself off as the victim ('A Case of Identity,' 'The Man with the Twisted Lip,' 'The Stockbroker's Clerk,' 'The Norwood Builder') and deceives the reader, as well as Holmes and Watson. Or the detective may be asked to find a valuable piece of jewelry or a stolen document. But whether it is a question of finding insufficiently well guarded State secrets ('The Naval Treaty,' 'The Second Stain,' 'The Bruce-Partington Plans') or of acting for private individuals, we find ourselves accompanying Holmes on a treasure-hunt that is exciting rather than really dangerous.

The unexpected appearance of someone after a long absence in a remote country is a specifically theatrical device, and Shakespeare, Molière, Racine and Beaumarchais among others have accustomed us to it. Whether he is the criminal, an inconvenient witness, or a redresser of wrongs, this individual is always a 'skeleton in the cupboard' for the other characters, and the *deus ex machina* of the story. It will be noticed how frequently this theme occurs in the stories published between 1900 and 1910, when the author was having to make an effort to renew the series, and most of all in the *Return* stories, the first of which brings the detective once more on the scene. Perhaps it is too convenient a contrivance to satisfy aesthetic

principles, but it at least allows Conan Doyle to conjure up an exotic and romantic background and give the Holmes cycle its epic quality.

The mysterious confines of the criminal world sometimes contain secret societies, whose activities do not escape Sherlock Holmes's vigilance, and introduce a disturbing note, as also do the cases of kidnapping he exposes in the course of his investigations. The criminal may perhaps want to get by force the services of someone with a particular skill ('The Engineer's Thumb,' 'The Greek Interpreter'), or conceal the victim of some infirmity from inquisitive eyes ('The Yellow Face,' 'The Blanched Soldier'). And there are five stories in which a guilty or innocent person tries to remain hidden or else pass for dead. Critics have amused themselves by pointing out the classical treatment of plots and situations; with this we find an atmosphere belonging more to the theatre than to the novel. It is hardly surprising that within the very narrow scope of these plots, Conan Doyle has only rarely introduced a sub-plot; but with the exception of 'The Musgrave Ritual' (perhaps the most successful and characteristic of all the stories) when he does so this second plot spoils the balance. He nearly always preserves the unity of action, and this does not interfere with the intricacies of the plot, but facilitates them. Since these involve Holmes's adversaries as well as himself, an apparent equilibrium is maintained between the different forces in play. To destroy this equilibrium long before the *dénouement* would be to deprive it of all tension and therefore of interest.

The simplest stratagem used by Holmes is disguise. Dr. Watson, who is taken in every time, insists that his friend is a gifted actor with a talent for changing his walk or tone of voice. Holmes's love of disguise and stage-production even leads him to use a wax image of himself as a bait. But other characters in the stories share his taste for disguise. Some of his enemies use camouflage of a different sort, for instance in 'Silver Blaze.' Hiding-places also play an important part in their plans, and so sometimes do houses that have been faked, rather like boxes with double bottoms. Holmes never hesitates to fight his adversaries with their own weapons, force his way into a private house in disguise, or arrange a false alarm with or without the help of the official police ('Scandal in Bohemia,' 'The Norwood Builder'). If the criminals set a trap to get him out of the way, Holmes and his devoted friend Watson divert their suspicions by pretending to follow the false trail. His sense of artistic perfection makes him aim at ingenious or spectacular *dénouements* ('The Dancing Men'), or indulge in the innocent pleasure of mystifying his own clients. The *dénouements* are particularly dramatic, and all with two exceptions ('The Yellow Face' and 'The Missing Three-Quarter') turn out favourably for Holmes.

The aesthetics of the Holmesian cycle have the same advantages and disadvantages as those of the theatre. The psychological field is strictly limited, but situations and incidents can be exploited by good organisation and balance. A writer like Chesterton may have greater aesthetic subtlety, but whatever the merits of his detective-stories they have not the formal perfection we find in Conan Doyle. The danger of the theatrical treatment is that it may end in melodrama or *grand guignol.* It must be admitted that some of his *dénouements* are not free from melodrama—those of **'The Yellow Face'** or **'The Beryl Coronet'** for instance—but this is exceptional. As for *grand guignol,* it is hardly apparent in the stories written before 1910, which contain few scenes of horror, and those strictly subordinated to the needs of the action. However, after 1910 this element becomes much more common; the last fifteen stories are different from the rest both in their atmosphere and the part Sherlock Holmes plays in them.

In contrast to the problems in the earlier stories, we now find some actually morbid ingredient in the plots: for instance, a disease having all the appearance of leprosy (**'The Blanched Soldier'**), a case of mental abnormality in a child (**'The Sussex Vampire'**), a fantastic physical mutation of a Jekyll and Hyde description (**'The Creeping Man'**), a horrible mutilation (**'The Veiled Lodger'**). Some of the other Adventures are burdened with scenes of violence quite disconnected with the action. More or less imaginary poisons are used in some of the murder stories, and there are scenes involving gruesome discoveries. Conan Doyle only returns to his normal manner in the novel *The Valley of Fear* and the story of **'Thor Bridge'**; the investigation develops in a similar way in both of these, and ends with the discovery of important evidence in a moat and a lake. Except for these two, the detection has lost some of its dramatic tension, the incidents are shorter and less numerous. The analysis is generally longer however, and in four of the stories Dr. Watson is no longer the narrator. We leave the glare of the footlights and move into a region of disturbing semi-obscurity, with something of the atmosphere of modern science-fiction about it. Holmes's personality suffers from these developments. He now gives us the impression of being a passive witness of events, rather than dominating and directing them. Henceforth we do not feel sure of his omnipotence. Of course he has sometimes been outwitted before (**'Scandal in Bohemia,' 'The Missing Three-Quarter'**), but at least he did not then give the impression of having lost the initiative.

The plots of some of the final stories of the cycle are so paradoxical that he is obliged to be relatively inactive. In **'Shoscombe Old Place'** and **'Thor Bridge,'** for instance, though there are apparently two murders to be solved, they in fact turn out to be natural death and suicide. The situation in **'The Three Gables'** corresponds with that of the first story of all, **'Scandal in Bohemia,'** but Sherlock Holmes's role is reversed. Instead of being commissioned to find papers which would compromise his client, he is asked to forestall a burglary organised by an adventuress, far less attractive and alive than Irene Adler, in search of a document incriminating her. Moreover the story is bathed in an extremely changeable atmosphere, at times almost scabrous, at others frankly improbable. It is as if Sherlock Holmes's dwindling stature had thrown the story out of balance, with the result that these last stories do not have the eminently reassuring quality his resplendent presence conferred on the Adventures of the great period. (pp. 232-42)

If it is true, as the experts in Holmesian studies maintain, that Sherlock Holmes was born in 1854, he must have been the contemporary within two years of the greatest chemist of his day, Sir William Ramsay; and judging by F. G. Donnan's article on Ramsay in the *Dictionary of National Biography,* the two men had various points in common: 'He was gifted with rare scientific insight and imagination, and was the possessor of a most wonderful skill and dexterity in the devising, constructing and use of apparatus . . . A man of sanguine and courageous temperament, of tireless energy, and power of instant action, he fearlessly attacked problems the experimental difficulties of which could have dismayed and deterred most men.'

On more than one occasion, Holmes describes a method of reasoning founded on a rationalistic conception of the universe. In spite of his pretended ignorance of astronomy, he talks like a follower of Le Verrier, the mathematician who put astronomers on the track of the planet Neptune: 'From a drop of water . . . a logician could infer the possibility of an Atlantic or a Niagara without having seen or heard of one or the other. So all life is a great chain, the nature of which is known whenever we are shown a single link of it.' Or again: 'As Cuvier could correctly describe a whole animal by the contemplation of a single bone, so the observer who has thoroughly understood one link in a series of incidents, should be able accurately to state all the other ones, both before and after.'

We also find him stressing the importance of mathematics and the authority of Euclid. He feels an inventor's pride in his 'methods' ('You know my methods, Watson' is one of the leitmotivs of the Adventures), and insists on the importance of observing details: 'Never trust to general impressions, my boy, but concentrate yourself upon details. My first glance is always at a woman's sleeve, in a man it is perhaps better first to take the knee of the trouser.'

His skill in reading objects, character and thoughts, confirms the excellence of this rule, and it must be said that in practice he gets much more conclusive results from observation than from logical processes. Perhaps a problem such as that of **'The Beryl Coronet'** offers somewhat unsystematic proof of the value of the study of foot-prints; nor does it justify the distinction Holmes tries to make between his own methods and those of his predecessors. He shows his superiority over the Scotland Yard detectives less by the originality of his methods than by his greater skill in analysing the clues. Thus for example, in **'The Norwood Builder,'** a thumb-print leads him to make an exactly opposite deduction to Inspector Lestrade's: ' "The thumb-mark, Lestrade. You said it was final; and so it was, in a very different sense. I knew it had not been there the day before. I pay a good deal of attention to matters of detail, as you may have observed, and I had examined the hall, and was sure that the wall was clear. Therefore, it had been put on during the night." '

As though the events of the plot were not enough to show the importance of apparently insignificant details, a certain number of allusions to imaginary cases are used to show off the acuteness of Holmes's powers of observation. For instance: You will remember, Watson, how the dreadful business of the Abernetty family was first brought to my notice by the depth which the parsley had sunk into the butter upon a hot day.' Humorous though these often are, they still serve to stress the subtlety of the famous 'methods.' And it is almost always under a veil of humour that Conan Doyle describes Holmes lecturing his listeners on objectivity. In 'The Noble Bachelor' a message scribbled on the back of a hotel bill puzzles the detectives. Holmes puts them on the right track by showing them that the bill itself contains much more useful evidence.

We have already remarked on the restraint and lack of bloodshed in the plots. Sherlock Holmes is not interested in notorious crimes alone; he also sets himself to end scandals and solve problems, whether criminal or no. He admits to a special taste for unimportant cases, when he can indulge his curiosity without anxiety. In his search for clues and documents, his efforts to extract evidence from them and reconstruct the situation objectively, he shows the attitude of an archaeologist or historian. But where the archaeologist makes old records or inscriptions speak', Sherlock Holmes asks questions of objects that appeal to the popular imagination, like the stone used by the criminal as a weapon, or the disguised handwriting on an envelope. From the point of view of the mental processes brought into play by both author and reader, the Sherlock Holmes stories have something in common with Conan Doyle's historical novels and also with the movement to popularise science which was already beginning to appear in the last years of the nineteenth century, as only one of the forms taken by the general spread of education and culture, notably in the illustrated magazines, with *The Strand Magazine* well to the fore.

On the pretext that Sherlock Holmes's 'deductions' are really 'inductions,' that chance is too often on his side and that his hypotheses are not always flawless, there have been attempts to minimise the influence of science on the Holmes stories. They may not have much to do with the actual content of scientific thought, but that does not prevent their showing a debt to the preoccupations of the period. The fictitious world, to which Sherlock Holmes belonged, expected of him what the real world of the day expected of its scientists: more light and more justice. As the creation of a doctor who had been soaked in the rationalist thought of the period, the Holmesian cycle offers us for the first time the spectacle of a hero triumphing again and again by means of logic and scientific method. And the hero's prowess is as marvellous as the power of science, which many people hoped would lead to a material and spiritual improvement of the human condition, and Conan Doyle first among them.

As with every other heroic figure, the reader is tempted to identify himself with Sherlock Holmes, as the incarnation of the spirit of his age. The setting and the details of the stories also facilitate identification. The public, particularly the London public, could live through Sherlock Holmes's Adventures in imagination, without making any great change in their normal way of life. The cycle may be said to be an epic of everyday events. The reader can put himself in the hero's place without much difficulty, and be actor and spectator at the same time in an adventure that he knows will turn out well. (pp. 244-47)

It is clear that all the inhabitants of [the world of the Sherlock Holmes cycle] are keenly aware of where they belong—are 'class-conscious' in fact. It is rare for this to be explicitly remarked on—it would be out of keeping with Watson's style; but it is implicit in the way the characters reveal themselves in the dialogue, or by the choice of their surnames. The aristocracy are represented by Holdhursts, St. Simons, Holdernesses, Musgraves, Mount-Jameses, Baskervilles, Brackenstalls or Prendergasts. Such resounding names are not allowed to the lower orders, among whom we find housekeepers called Porter or Warren (who must not be confused with Bernard Shaw's heroine); a grocer named Francis Prosper; Mrs Oakshott, a poultry-seller; Morton, an electrician; and Pycroft, a young bank clerk:

> The man whom I found myself facing was a well-built, fresh-complexioned young fellow with a frank, honest face and a slight, crisp, yellow moustache. He wore a very shiny top-hat and a neat suit of sober black, *which made him look what he was*—a smart young City man, *of the class who have been labelled Cockneys, but* who give us our crack Volunteer regiments, and who turn out more fine athletes and sportsmen than any body of men in these islands [italics added].

Watson's 'but' is admirable, and this portrait reveals from what a distance the members of his world observed the rest. The narrator practically tells us what rank young Pycroft may hope to reach—but not to pass—as a volunteer.

Between the aristocrats by birth and the almost anonymous but numerous group of 'little men,' we find the true middle-class as represented by Dr. Watson—and they are the majority. Holmes stands for the landed gentry. From the point of view of their criminal guilt the different worlds are treated with complete impartiality. Each has its honest and dishonest members. It is not surprising that there are fewer dishonest men among the aristocracy, nor is it grounds for charging the Adventures with being perversely 'bourgeois.' Quite the reverse, for it is the representatives of the aristocracy in the stories who are judged most severely. But by the end of the last century they had lost the aura of absolute respect which surrounded them forty or fifty years earlier.

The historian G. M. Young writes that in 1890: 'It would have been hard to find even a Conservative who felt for a rich man, or a titled man, as such, the respect which Early Victorians had, not wrongly, paid to the founders of great industries or the heads of historic houses, on whose capacity they depended for good government and progress.'

Except for an extremely discreet allusion to Queen Victoria at the end of 'The Bruce-Partington Plans,' royalty is only represented by the King of Bohemia in 'A Scandal in Bohemia.' He gets somewhat rough treatment, but he is after all only a foreign sovereign. Baron Gruner and Count Sylvius are the only representatives of the foreign nobility, and Watson's portraits of them lack indulgence to say the least of it. The aristocrats we are asked to judge severely are never those with political power. The Prime Minister and Secretary of State in 'The Second Stain' (their names are Lord Bellinger and the Right Honourable Trelawney Hope) are both likeable and in the highest degree honourable men. But whenever the taboo on affairs of State is removed, the Adventures show great freedom of judgement, and describe, as G. M. Young puts it: 'The supersession of the aristocracy by the plutocracy, a process masked by the severe and homely court of Victoria, but growing precipitate, after the agricultural depression, with the influx of South African money and American brides.'

As well as the tyrannical and degenerate Lord Brackenstall, John Clay, the black sheep grandson of a royal prince, and the Duke of Holdernesse (who is involved in kidnapping his own son), we have the vulgar Lord St. Simon, younger son of the Duke of Balmoral, announcing his marriage to Miss Hetty Doran, 'the fascinating daughter of a Californian millionaire.' Holmes reads *The Morning Post*'s significant comment aloud to Watson: 'There will soon be a call for protection in the marriage market, for the present free-trade principle appears to tell heavily against our home product. One by one the management of the noble houses of Great Britain is passing into the hands of our fair cousins from across the Atlantic.'

All the fore-mentioned characters in their different ways exemplify the only reproach levelled at the aristocracy by their admirers the middle-classes: they sometimes fail to set a good example.

The Holmesian cycle pays much less attention to the social behaviour of the lower orders. Watson lets them voice their feelings and ideas themselves, and they do so in a very characteristic manner, but also so prosaically and with such vapidity, that we begin to wonder whether the Southsea doctor is having his revenge, at Holmes's expense, for the interminable and confused confidences he may have had to put up with from some of his patients. Watson hits the nail on the head when he says: 'I had expected to see Sherlock Holmes impatient under the rambling and inconsequential narrative.' In Holmes's world, as in our own, the surest sign of social stability is the rarity or complete absence of people who have changed class—either upwards, by becoming *nouveaux riches,* or downwards, by becoming new poor. The aristocratic young criminal in **'The Red-Headed League'** belongs rather to the type of 'gentleman cracksman' whose exploits were described by Conan Doyle's brother-in-law, William Hornung. Jonathan Small in *The Sign of Four* is a much more interesting character. It will be remembered that he is the villain of the story and that Holmes eventually arrests him after an exciting chase on the river Thames. In the last chapter Small tells us his own life story. He was guilty of taking advantage of the general confusion during the Indian Mutiny to become involved in the murder of a rich merchant whom it was his duty to protect. He describes his long years of suffering in a convict settlement to Holmes and Watson: 'Twenty long years in that fever-ridden swamp, all day at work under the mangrove-tree, all night chained up in the filthy convict-huts, bitten by mosquitoes, racked with ague, bullied by every cursed black-faced policeman who loved to take it out of a white man.'

Small deserved to be sent to this hell upon earth, not only because of the blackness of his crime, but also because, by agreeing to be an accomplice in a native plot, he had debased his status as a 'sahib.' However his downfall has not entirely obliterated his sense of honour: it was his loyalty to his companions in crime that destroyed him and also explains the significance of 'The Sign of Four' of the book's title. He is a figure reminiscent of Conrad—the exception that confirms the rule of solidarity with class and way of life.

Censoriousness about morals was another characteristic of the Victorian mentality. In Conan Doyle's works it is an expression of his own personal chastity. The shattering entry of the deplorable prostitute in **'The Illustrious Client'** must be attributed to Conan Doyle's efforts to start a new series of Adventures. The story was written in 1925 and shows what vain attempts he made to distort his own fastidiousness. In a page of literary criticism, Conan Doyle tells us what a fascination the female characters in Richardson's and Fielding's novels had for him. Can all eighteenth-century women have had the piquant charm of Pamela, Harriet Byron, Clarissa, Amelia and Sophia Western? he asks. He sets against their attractions the 'negative charm' of that innocent and insipid creature, the amiable doll of the nineteenth century. We can be more objective than Conan Doyle here, and ask whether the difference does not come from the eye of the beholder rather than the subject seen. Except for Lady Hilda Trelawny Hope, quivering with a sense of her own aristocratic grandeur, most of the women in Holmes's world are in fact very insipid and incredibly innocent. The author does not seem to want to interest us in them. They merely perform the dramatic function of being 'young girls in danger,' and Conan Doyle shows his casualness about differentiating them even in the choice of their Christian names: Violet Smith, Violet Westbury, Violet de Merville, Violet Hunter. This name is as common in the stories as dukes in Shakespeare's comedies.

Perhaps the fact that these young women seem almost disembodied conduces to their intuitive awareness of their fate. Holmes remarks on the spirituality of Violet Smith's features. Helen Stoner foretells her twin sister's tragic fate: 'A vague feeling of impending misfortune impressed me. My sister and I, you will recollect, were twins, and you know how subtle are the links which bind two souls which are so closely allied'; while Mrs. St. Clair is sure that her husband is alive, despite all appearances to the contrary: 'There is so keen a sympathy that I should know if evil came upon him.'

Just as the Holmes cycle depends on a Victorian view of the social order, it appeals also to a corresponding moral code. The Holmesian ethics are revealed in the judgements the reader is invited to make, and also in Holmes's character considered as a model of conduct. (pp. 254-57)

On a slightly lower level, and in a minor key, we find what might be called 'The Watson chronicle,' in contrast to 'the Holmes saga.' Here science and heroism have been exchanged for facts and domesticity. Instead of a wide but impersonal vision of city life, we have the picturesque aspect of London and Baker Street which appealed to Dr.

Watson. The Adventures of Holmes and Watson sometimes take them out of London for a longish period, as in *The Hound of the Baskervilles;* occasionally it is only for a few hours, as when they visit Birmingham in **'The Stockbroker's Clerk'** But in more than half the stories the whole investigation takes place in London. London is never forgotten; every enquiry begins in the Baker Street flat, and we are brought back to Baker Street at its conclusion. Holmes and Watson are such complete Londoners that we even share their sense of exile during their trips to the country. Let us listen to the reflections the sight of the countryside inspires in Holmes in **'The Copper Beeches'**:

> 'Good heavens!' I cried. 'Who would associate crime with these dear old homesteads?'
>
> 'They always fill me with a certain horror. It is my belief, Watson, founded upon my experience, that the lowest and vilest alleys in London do not present a more dreadful record of sin than does the smiling and beautiful countryside.'
>
> 'You horrify me!'
>
> 'But the reason is very obvious. The pressure of public opinion can do in the town what the law cannot accomplish. There is no lane so vile that the scream of a tortured child, or the thud of a drunkard's blow, does not beget sympathy and indignation among the neighbours, and then the whole machinery of justice is ever so close that a word of complaint can set it going, and there is but a step between the crime and the dock. But look at these lonely houses, each in its own fields, filled for the most part with poor ignorant folk who know little of the law. Think of the deeds of hellish cruelty, the hidden wickedness which may go on, year in, year out, in such places, and none the wiser. Had this lady who appeals to us for help gone to live in Winchester, I should never have had a fear for her. It is the five miles of country which makes the danger. Still, it is clear that she is not personally threatened.'

London is the focus of the Adventures, but it also reassures the town-dwelling reader about the moral context of his society. It is impossible not to remember the very different charges James Joyce levels against town life in *Dubliners*!

In the purely London stories, the topography is usually so precisely indicated that certain passages will give anyone who knows the city well the pleasure of re-discovery. With Watson as guide we visit in turn fashionable London, the London of hotels and theatres, literary London, business London and finally London the sea-port. Stories like *The Sign of Four,* **'The Red-Headed League,'** **'The Blue Carbuncle,'** **'The Greek Interpreter,'** *The Hound of the Baskervilles,* **'The Six Napoleons'** and **'The Bruce-Partington Plans'** bring out these different aspects of London in a panorama as kaleidoscopic as Watson's view of Londoners themselves. Long descriptions are unnecessary: a few impressionistic notes are quite enough to revive the very endearing and individual personality of the vast city: 'At half-past five a cab deposited us outside 104 Berkeley Square, where the old soldier resides—one of those awful

grey London castles which would make a church seem frivolous.'

One of Holmes's most picturesque 'readings' of objects takes place in a cab carrying our two friends to an unknown destination:

> Sherlock Holmes was never at fault, and he muttered the names as the cab rattled through squares and in and out by tortuous by-streets.
>
> 'Rochester Row,' said he. 'Now Vincent Square. Now we come out on the Vauxhall Bridge Road. We are making for the Surrey side, apparently. Yes, I thought so. Now we are on the bridge. You can catch glimpses of the river.'
>
> We did indeed get a fleeting view of a stretch of the Thames, with the lamps shining upon the broad, silent water; but our cab dashed on, and was soon involved in a labyrinth of streets upon the other side.
>
> 'Wandsworth Road,' said my companion. 'Priory Road. Larkhall Lane. Stockwell Place. Robert Street. Coldharbour Lane. Our quest does not appear to take us to very fashionable regions.'
>
> We had indeed reached a questionable and forbidding neighbourhood. Long lines of dull brick houses were only relieved by the coarse glare and tawdry brilliancy of public-houses at the corners. Then came rows of two-storied villas, each with a fronting of miniature garden, and then again interminable lines of new, staring brick buildings—the monster tentacles which the giant city was throwing out into the country.

Here we have that effect of speed so reminiscent of the cinema; it is produced by the rapid succession of Holmes's remarks punctuated by the staccato rhythm of the style. Watson's eyes move more slowly and are more attentive to detail; he analyses what he sees and conveys an eminently pictorial and personal impression to our imaginations.

The people of London are just as briefly, precisely and vividly described. Their habits, the places they frequent, their clothes, never go unobserved. Here is Miss Mary Sutherland in her boa, her straw hat, worn like the Duchess of Devonshire's, her simple plum-coloured dress with collar and cuffs of purple velvet; here is her pseudo-fiancé in black frock-coat, grey Harris tweed trousers, brown gaiters and elastic-sided boots. Here again is that aristocratic bachelor, Lord St. Simon: 'His dress was careful to the verge of foppishness, with high collar, black frock-coat, white waistcoat, yellow gloves, patent-leather shoes, and light-coloured gaiters. He advanced slowly into the room, turning his head from left to right, and swinging in his right hand the cord which held his golden eye-glasses.'

In the heart of the city, and (like Watson) 'the only fixed point in the centre of an ever-changing universe,' are the Baker Street rooms which the chronicle has made so familiar. Baker Street is the permanent stage-set in which Watson has granted us the privilege of living in intimacy with his illustrious friend; it is the mute witness of conversations or long silences between the two. Everything in it speaks of Holmes to our imagination: 'There were the chemical corner and the acid-stained deal-topped table. There upon a shelf was the row of formidable scrap-books and books of reference which many of our fellow-citizens would have been so glad to burn. The diagrams, the violin-case, and the pipe-rack—even the Persian slipper which contained the tobacco—all met my eyes as I glanced round.'

Chemist, archivist, artist, dilettante and bohemian—Holmes is all of these; we can use his 'methods' to translate this description at sight, so clearly is his personality given off by it. But these rooms are also an observation-post. Let us follow Watson to the window and watch the London scene beside him:

> It was a bright, crisp February morning, and the snow of the day before still lay deep upon the ground, shimmering brightly in the wintry sun. Down the centre of Baker Street it had been ploughed into a brown crumbly band by the traffic, but at either side and on the heaped-up edges of the footpaths it still lay as white as when it fell. The grey pavement had been cleaned and scraped, but was still dangerously slippery, so that there were fewer passengers than usual. Indeed, from the direction of the Metropolitan station no one was coming save the single gentleman whose eccentric conduct had drawn my attention.

In spite of the variable weather, Conan Doyle likes best

Sherlock Holmes receives Miss Mary Sutherland in "A Case of Identity." Illustrated by Sidney Paget.

to show us Baker Street in the morning dimness of all-pervading, mysterious fog:

> It was a cold morning of the early spring, and we sat after breakfast on either side of a cheery fire in the old room in Baker Street. A thick fog rolled down between the lines of dun-coloured houses, and the opposing windows loomed like dark, shapeless blurs, through the heavy yellow wreaths. Our gas was lit, and shone on the white cloth, and glimmer of china and metal, for the table had not been cleared yet.

Among all the kinds of weather that Conan Doyle excels in describing with an ever-alert, exact and restrained pen, the London fog has double significance. Why should the reader so often associate Baker Street with the fog, described even more insistently in **'The Bruce-Partington Plans'**? asks Gavin Brend [in his *My Dear Holmes*]. Because it is a feature of the London weather, of course; but also because it belongs to a literary tradition of which the reading public is more or less consciously aware. Ever since the rediscovery of Shakespeare during the romantic period, we have known what a dramatic and moral function fog can assume. It is not necessary to have read *Macbeth* to associate the word 'fog,' like the word 'shadows,' with the idea of crime, and so with the notion of a blurred, confused and disordered perception of moral values. The idea of fog is inextricably involved with a very rich and complex cultural experience. And the London fog in particular, its aspect and its evocative power, have been enlarged upon by Dickens to such an extent that it has become permanently linked with his novels. So that it is not surprising that Conan Doyle's descriptions of it raise echoes of special significance in every English reader's mind.

A chronicle of London, the chronicle of an epoch, and also of course an impressionistic chronicle. Because he wanted to keep Watson's chronicle distinct from those of the historians, the chronicles of political and current events, Conan Doyle was careful, as we have seen, not to mix reality too exactly and too brutally with fiction. How then did he succeed in making the stories give such a vivid sense of the period? Simple repetition and frequent allusions to the manner and spirit of the age certainly illuminate the whole Holmesian cycle; but are they enough to create such a definite impression? It is difficult to be sure, and we must therefore consider the stories from a purely temporal point of view.

We know that they were published between 1887 and 1927, but that this is not the period covered by the Adventures themselves. We also know that their internal chronology does not correspond to the order in which they were published. It is this internal and fictitious chronology that H. B. Bell amused himself by establishing from direct or implied evidence in the text [in his *Sherlock Holmes and Doctor Watson: The Chronology of their Adventures*].

I do not propose to discuss his methods nor the exactness of his conclusions in detail. With certain reserves, due to the extremely fantastic nature of some of his conjectures and the uncompromising precision with which he presses his points, his conclusions are acceptable, and lead to a certain number of assumptions of which he was apparently unaware himself. The story of Sherlock Holmes's first campaign, which Bell places in 1875, is to be found in **'The 'Gloria Scott.'** The detective's career ends in 1914 during the first days of the war. But if one amuses oneself by drawing up a diagram of his activities, it soon becomes clear that its intensity varied greatly, and two main phases can be distinguished—one lasting six years, the other nine, the interval between them explained by Holmes's reserve after his duel with Professor Moriarty.

NUMBER OF SHERLOCK HOLMES'S INVESTIGATIONS

1875-9	2	1895-7	14
1880-5	6	1898-1904	11
1886-91	23	1905-14	2
1892-4	2 (*Disappearance of Holmes*)		

This table shows clearly enough the relation between Sherlock Holmes and several generations of his public—those who reached the reading age between 1886 and 1904. These dates indicate the limits of the social reverberations of the Holmes stories more accurately than do the dates of publication. But if we accept Bell's theories as to the time-lag between the fictitious date and the date of publication, we can construct a very illuminating diagram, showing the mutual fidelity between Sherlock Holmes and his public. In fact we may say that as the dates of publication advanced in time, the interval between them and the fictitious dates steadily increased.

Series	Number of stories	Minimum interval	Maximum interval	Average
Adventures (1892)	12	1 year	10 years	3 years 11 months
Memoirs (1894)	11	2 years	18 years	7 years 8 months
Case-Book (1927)	12	18 years	31 years	24 years

The whole Holmesian cycle is thus concentrated in time in a way that gives readers the illusion of being Sherlock Holmes's contemporaries, and of taking part in the Adventures. The stories have the further attraction of touching their imaginations by appealing to their personal memories. This simple conclusion helps us understand the nostalgia that so many readers of 'Sherlock Holmes's generation' feel for the earlier stories, and the fact of their finding them preferable to those published later. We believe this to be something subjective, and in which aesthetic judgements only play a secondary part. It does not matter if a story published in 1922 is technically better than another published thirty years earlier, if what we feel today is the echo of yesterday's youthful response. For the benefit of his chosen public, Watson's chronicle occasionally refers to some recent event or contains a topical pastiche, to create atmosphere and appeal to all the resources of 'magazine aesthetics.' Holmes and Watson are not the only characters who reappear in the stories. Other old acquaintances turn up at less regular intervals: Moriarty, Mycroft Holmes, Mrs. Hudson, the 'Baker Street Irregulars' and a few more. The stories contain frequent references to one another, sometimes explicitly, sometimes by inference. For example in **'The Empty House,'** the brief reference to an air-gun reminds one of **'The Final Problem.'** In this way the Holmes cycle develops that piquant sense of initiation, that enjoyable esoterism which is one of the chief attractions of the 'Holmes Clubs.' Sometimes the stories even presuppose the reader's fidelity or com-

plicity. Some of the dramatic effects are based on this. Our surprise at the *dénouement* of **'The Missing Three-Quarter,'** for example, largely depends on our having grown accustomed to a very different sort of conclusion. We have seen that a great many different aesthetic elements combine on the epic canvas of the Holmes saga. Whether through the London background or the atmosphere of some of the stories, the Sherlock Holmes cycle draws upon a collective literary inheritance and a sediment of popular ideology without its readers knowing it. (pp. 261-67)

Pierre Nordon, in his Conan Doyle, *translated by Frances Partridge, John Murray, 1966, 370 p.*

Doyle on the Sherlock Holmes stories:

People have often asked me whether I knew the end of a Holmes story before I started it. Of course I do. One could not possibly steer a course if one did not know one's destination. The first thing is to get your idea. Having got that key idea one's next task is to conceal it and lay emphasis on everything which can make for a different explanation. Holmes, however, can see all the fallacies of the alternatives, and arrives more or less dramatically at the true solution by steps which he can describe and justify. He shows his powers by what the South Americans now call "Sherlockholmitos," which means clever little deductions, which often have nothing to do with the matter at hand, but impress the reader with a general sense of power. The same effect is gained by his offhand allusion to other cases. Heaven knows how many titles I have thrown about in a casual way, and how many readers have begged me to satisfy their curiosity as to "Rigoletto and his abominable wife," "The Adventure of the Tired Captain," or "The Curious Experience of the Patterson Family in the Island of Uffa." Once or twice, as in **"The Adventure of the Second Stain,"** which in my judgment is one of the neatest of the stories, I did actually use the title years before I wrote a story to correspond.

Arthur Conan Doyle, in his Memories and Adventures, *1924.*

Gavin Lambert   (essay date 1975)

[*Lambert is an English critic. In the following excerpt, originally published in Great Britain in 1975, he discusses themes, plots, and characters in the Sherlock Holmes stories and in Doyle's supernatural tales.*]

When Conan Doyle finally decided to abandon his medical career and concentrate on writing, his wife had just given birth to a daughter. **'A Scandal in Bohemia'**, the first Holmes short story, was born of financial need. Written a year after *The Sign of Four* appeared, it was conceived as one of a set of six for *The Strand* magazine.

At the same time an imaginative stimulus arrived from a writer nine years older than Conan Doyle, but in many ways younger. Many of Stevenson's stories were first published in the magazines. In open revolt against wordiness and slack, they offered the alternative of verbal marksmanship and the quick direct hit at the small centre. Although fascinated by the detective as a phenomenon of the times, a man who 'from one trifling circumstance divines a world', Stevenson deplored the long and laboured mechanics of the popular detective novel. He felt the pull of melodrama but liked it glamorous or unearthly, under the spell of buried treasure or the supernatural. *Dr Jekyll and Mr Hyde* was both instant folklore and seductive evidence of the short story's power of compression. It had the allure of a legend or fairytale, larger than life though small in scale. **'The Suicide Club'**, one of Conan Doyle's favourites at this time, revived the spirit of *The Thousand and One Nights*. The tales of Scheherazade were preoccupied with escape and pursuit (not surprisingly, since she invented them to distract her husband from murdering her), and they exist on the borderline of magic and reality. The stories of Prince Florizel, a young visitor to London who disguises himself in search of adventure, reproduce their pace and twists of plot, their last-minute rescues from the trap about to close. In the first short story that begins the Holmes cycle their imprint is clear.

King Wilhelm of **'A Scandal in Bohemia'** comes from the same country as Prince Florizel. On a winter's night his carriage stops in front of 221B Baker Street and he steps out wearing a long cloak, fur-trimmed boots and a black mask over his eyes. We are at once in a different world from the novellas. The surface is more fantastic, with a fairytale aura—but the power of reason will ferret out a logic and an actuality behind the most extraordinary events. The black magic of the old fairytale becomes an ingeniously planned crime, conquered by a greater marvel, the scientific spirit. Behind the mental curtain where he first thought of Holmes, the young Conan Doyle sifted through different layers of experience—inherited beliefs and acquired doubts, wide reading of books and of life, pressures, memories, fears. They connect in a final superimposition of form that allows the cycle to develop like a miniature epic, reaching from the personal to the collective unconscious. 'These are much deeper waters', as Holmes likes to remark, 'than I had thought'.

Like the King of Bohemia subsequent visitors turn up at Holmes's apartment at all hours of the day and night, blown in by the wind, tramping through snow, umbrella'd against the rain. Veiled, breathless, cagey, indignant, all are in some kind of danger, threatened by murder or blackmail or involved in unnerving events they don't understand.

> 'Ha! I am glad to see that Mrs Hudson has had the good sense to light the fire. Pray draw up to it, and I shall order you a cup of hot coffee, for I observe that you are shivering'.
>
> 'It is not cold which makes me shiver', said the woman in a low voice, changing her seat as requested.
>
> 'What, then'?
>
> 'It is fear, Mr Holmes. It is terror'.

As well as cross-examination of his story the client must expect intense personal scrunity:

> 'Beyond the obvious facts that he has at some time done manual labour, that he takes snuff, that he is a Freemason, that he has been in China, and that he has done a considerable amount of writing lately, I can deduce nothing else'.

The enormous success of the first stories led to another six and then another complete set of twelve for *The Strand* magazine. Collected as **The Adventures** (1892) and **The Memoirs** (1894), this first part of the cycle ends with Holmes's apparent death at the hands of his arch-enemy Moriarty.

In **'A Scandal in Bohemia'** the opening suggestion of masquerade develops as Holmes disguises himself as a groom and a clergyman, while his opponent, the brilliant adventuress Irene Adler, disguises herself as a man. At the end she rather surprisingly outwits him, and Holmes asks for her photograph as a memento of the experience. Watson comments that she remains '*the* woman' for his friend, but Holmes's admiration seems more intellectual than romantic. It has no real bearing on his celibacy, which always remained a matter of principle. 'As a lover he would have placed himself in a false position'. Holmes cut himself off from sexual feeling to protect his reputation for objectivity.

The idea of a king being blackmailed by his former mistress, whom he met when she was an opera singer, was suggested by the affair between the dancer Lola Montez and King Louis of Bavaria. Many of the stories that follow are derived from newspaper items, gossip, fragments of anecdote, and a few impose an original twist on a situation from Collins or Poe. **'The Naval Treaty'**, one of the most ingenious puzzles, comes from an actual case of a Foreign Office employee turned spy. The theft of **'The Beryl Coronet'** carries vibrations from *The Moonstone*. The crime is not always murder and in a few cases not even technically criminal—like the woman in **'The Yellow Face'** whose first husband was a negro and who keeps their child hidden in a cottage bedroom and a strange white mask. Settings divide evenly between London and the country. Disguises and impersonations recur. Some stories (like **'A Scandal in Bohemia'**) are more adventure than puzzle, and in others the basic mystery is human behaviour. The most powerful reiterated motive is greed. Desire for money and land provokes four memorable accounts of murder and cruelty. **'The Reigate Puzzle'** involves two country squires in a death feud over property rights. Girls with inheritances find themselves in particular danger. In **'The Speckled Band'** a stepfather contrives a diabolical murder with the aid of a trained snake. **'In The Copper Beeches'** a governess forced to cut her hair and wear a blue dress discovers that she's been hired to impersonate her employers' daughter, locked away in a barricaded wing of the house. In **'The Engineer's Thumb'** a group of counterfeiters traps the mechanic who threatens to reveal their secret in a nightmare dungeon reminiscent of *The Pit and the Pendulum*. Notably inspired by the challenge of **'The Speckled Band'** and **'The Reigate Puzzle'**, Holmes admits a preference for the bizarre. Its force will grow stronger and darker in the great stories of the later cycle.

Another recurring theme is of people living under false names to escape a criminal past. It leads to murders of revenge, of which **'The Resident Patient'** is a savage example, echoing the horror of *A Study in Scarlet:*

> I have spoken of the impression of flabbiness which this man Blessington conveyed. As he dangled from the hook it was exaggerated and intensified until he was scarce human in his appearance. The neck was drawn out like a plucked chicken's, making the rest of him seem the more obese and unnatural by the contrast. He was clad only in his long night-dress, and his swollen ankles and ungainly feet protruded starkly from beneath it.

In this story Holmes is again at his most inventive. From a few insignificant details—cigar butts, a screwdriver, the angle of a footprint, a piece of rope—he reconstructs a murder made to look like a suicide, deduces the number of people involved, how they entered the house and in what order they went upstairs, even their movements in the room before Blessington was killed.

These tales dominate *The Adventures* and *The Memoirs* even though the lighter and non-violent ones in fact outnumber them. But the bizarre note and the profit motive persist in the absence of physical violence or punishable crime. In **'The Man with the Twisted Lip'** and **'A Case of Identity'**, a single clue—a missing coat and a typewritten letter—enables Holmes to expose outrageous dramas of disguise. An ex-actor pretends to be a businessman but really makes his money posing as a hideous and pitiable beggar every day in the London streets. To keep control of his stepdaughter's legacy and deter her from marriage, a wine salesman impersonates a gas fitter with tinted glasses, side-whiskers and moustache. He meets the lonely short-sighted girl at night, makes cautious love to her, then 'disappears' and breaks her heart. A precise sense of place and social background reinforces these fantastic situations, and pivotal touches make the central characters oddly plausible. Cosmetic scars stripped away, the beggar reverts to a sad young man with an apologetic and bewildered air. The suburban girl's myopic good-natured face, her clumsy and timid movements, mark her out as one of life's victims. Ironic examples of Holmes's belief that life is infinitely stranger 'than anything which the mind of man could invent', these two stories also expound his basic theory of detection. When the impossible has been eliminated, he explains to Watson, 'then whatever remains, however improbable, must be the truth'.

In the professional melting pot of pawnbroker and racehorse trainer, engineer and wine salesman, doctor and plumber, army officer and servant, governess and politician, only the derelict and the unemployed are absent. Halfway through the century Disraeli had called the rich and the poor 'the two nations', Conan Doyle reflected the nation he knew and a state of affairs that had hardly changed by the 1890s. The upper classes still formed the garrison of power and the Labour Party had not yet been created. The 'great conservative politician' of **'The Naval Treaty'** represented an overwhelming type. Because Conan Doyle's imagination and experience stopped somewhere short of the poverty line, and he never suggested

hunger or desperate need as a criminal motive, he has been criticized for giving a falsely secure impression of the period. But he was aiming at a different kind of impression. Watson sums it up when he remarks that Holmes's cases offer 'a perfect quarry for the student not only of crime but of the social and unofficial scandals of the late Victorian era'. Holmes takes the political system for granted because he operates in the world as he finds it. His attitude to crime is not exactly reassuring, but in the light of subsequent ideas and events it seems at times prophetic.

The two nations have now become two worlds, yet there is less crime in Morocco than in California. Economic motives defer to psychic problems, genes and hidden instinctual drives. **'The Copper Beeches'** and **'The Reigate Puzzle'** describe the greed of affluent people, and today their impulses would be classified as aggression by Konrad Lorenz, and as the territorial imperative by Robert Ardrey. In one of his rare general statements, Holmes refers to tensions created by 'the artificial state of society' and to the influence of heredity, under which 'the person becomes, as it were, the epitome of the history of his own family'. He sees the criminal as a symbol of psychic unrest and biological destiny at work in the tightly structured Victorian world. He leaves us to see a connection between the obsessive use of disguise and the houses with locked and guilty rooms.

The masked child, the imprisoned daughter, the false beggar and lover, the assumed names, the wigs and cosmetics are all cover-ups, literal and figurative. They point to the buried lives and secrets that haunted Wilkie Collins. The stepfather in **'The Speckled Band'** guards his house with a baboon and a cheetah, and the couple in **'The Copper Beeches'** train a huge dog to fly at enemy throats. In **'The Reigate Puzzle'** the land-hungry father and son react to the threat of exposure by violently attacking Holmes, one trying to break his arm and the other to strangle him. Extreme security measures do not suggest a secure period.

Watson's normality provides the reassuring note. One of Conan Doyle's most subtle effects is to make Holmes's biographer a man about whom the detective complains that he lacks imagination. The ideal solid citizen, Watson's virtues are common sense, dependability, and a cautious but open mind. Resisting the unpredictable only to face the shock of proof, he connects the man in the street with the deadly snake gliding through the ventilator. **'The Musgrave Ritual'** shows how much is lost when Holmes himself narrates a story. Without Watson's honest and sometimes dazed mental filter, only a technician solving a puzzle remains. Watson not only animates the character, he breathes his own fear and anxiety into the situation, then offers a touch of comfort. After the bloated corpse hanging from the ceiling, the Baker Street sanctuary with its brightly lit windows at night and the great man's thoughtful silhouette glimpsed behind the drawn blind.

While the 'quiet thinker and logician' becomes almost unrecognizable in action, examining footprints and sniffing clues with 'a purely animal lust for the chase'. Watson always returns to the detective as artist and the eye as antenna of the mind. 'You see, but you do not observe', Holmes tells him. 'That is the difference'. And again, when Watson says, 'You see everything', he is briskly corrected: 'I see no more than you, but I have trained myself to notice what I see'. The trained eye leads first to a particular deduction—that a man takes snuff and has been to China—and then to a commentary on life. Since the improbable and the true are so often the same, the eye warns Holmes not to look for revelation in the commonplace but in the dangerous and unexpected and bizarre. Watson learns to apply this method when he examines Holmes's personal habits. The detective's untidiness—unanswered letters and residues of chemical experiments everywhere—reflects not a vague but a fantastically disciplined person. Working at constant high pressure, his brain has no time for middle-class proprieties and is completely indifferent to the cigar in the coal scuttle or the criminal relic that turns up in the butter dish.

Watson instinctively avoids treading on private ground. After the discussion about cocaine in *The Sign of Four* he drops the subject for many years. He records without protest the celibacy, the rejection of social life, the moodiness and driven quality that leads Holmes to the edge of breakdown. He's not even surprised that Holmes has no other friends besides himself, and accepts the fact that for the detective their friendship is simply another habit. He admits his own slowness but sees that it excites Holmes's 'flame-like intuitions' to burn even more fiercely. Most important of all, his devoted and admiring records will make Holmes into a legend, and the detective knows it. Although he disclaims interest in money and fame, Holmes agrees with Watson's view of himself as an artist and hopes for the approval of a trained eye beyond his own, for the nod of posterity.

Until the last but one story of *The Memoirs,* Watson describes a man who reasons strictly from cause to effect, discounts the supernatural and remains indifferent to the idea of God. In **'The Naval Treaty'** a moment occurs that seems all the more significant because it has no bearing on the plot. The detective takes a rest from trying to unravel an espionage case and picks up a rose:

> 'There is nothing in which deduction is so necessary as in religion', said he, leaning with his back against the shutters. 'It can be built up as an exact science by the reasoner. Our highest assurance of the goodness of Providence seems to me to rest in the flowers. All other things, our powers, our desires, our food, are all really necessary for our existence in the first instance. But this rose is an extra . . . It is only goodness which gives extras, and so I say again that we have much to hope from the flowers'.

Logically this is below the master's standard and sounds out of character. A mosquito, after all, is an 'extra', but it points to divine malice rather than goodwill. The idea comes from Conan Doyle himself, not Holmes, and provides the first sign of the author at odds with his protagonist. Conan Doyle's notebooks show that by the time he came to write **'The Naval Treaty'** his trained eye had begun to look beyond the visible. The struggling young doctor had attended a few spiritualist meetings. He came away mildly sceptical, but they sparked a fascination. By the mid-1880s he was reading Swedenborg and corre-

sponding with Frederic Myers, the founder of the Society for Psychical Research. Approaching the occult like his detective, he set off on a long search for conclusive evidence. He wrote to Myers for advice on how to distinguish the genuine table rap from the accidental creak, and noted that if the truth of spiritualism could be proved it might 'break down the barrier of death'. The creator of the supreme rationalist was also privately investigating all aspects of the paranormal, mediums, clairvoyance, animal magnetism, extra-sensory perception. Although identified with an apostle of logic, he was slowly edging towards the unknown 'extra' missing from his life since he rejected the Christian church.

The situation has a touch of *Frankenstein,* and so has the way out that Conan Doyle chose. Naturally the Ma'am was the first to be told. 'I am in the middle of the last Holmes story, after which the gentleman vanishes, never to return'! He had already complained that Holmes interfered with his more important work as a historical novelist, but this in itself hardly justifies attempted murder. The hasty concoction of **'The Final Problem'** suggests a desire to be free at all costs from a character whose basic point of view is now in conflict with his own. A new and fanatic enemy of Holmes appears on the scene. Moriarty, the head of a secret murder network, pursues Holmes and Watson to Switzerland. The great criminal and the great detective are left alone at the Reichenbach falls. After both of them disappear, the police conclude that they toppled into the cataract together during a struggle. But there are no bodies. Holmes is only declared missing and presumed dead. In a farewell letter discovered by Watson on a rock, he confesses that his career has run its course and he finds the prospect of death perfectly acceptable. None of this works. The episode is clumsily contrived and the transformation of Holmes into a fatalist sounds unconvincing. All that survives is the image of a confrontation on the edge, the two antagonists above a black chasm and a torrent of melting snow. A touch of guilt is suggested in the way Conan Doyle left the country for a vacation before **'The Final Problem'** appeared in *The Strand.* He avoided some extraordinary public scenes, hundreds of outraged letters and black armbands worn in the street. (pp. 40-9)

The Hound of the Baskervilles (1902) appears as a Holmes novella set in the pre-Moriarty years, and the actual **Return of Sherlock Holmes** (1905) naturally causes a sensation, though as a whole it's the least satisfactory collection in the series. But some of Conan Doyle's most personal and surprising work is contained in a few short stories mostly written around the turn of the century, all dealing in some way with the fantastic and the supernatural. (They were eventually collected as **Tales of Terror** and **Tales of Twilight and the Unseen.**) Their emphasis is on violence and the grotesque, those increasingly powerful hallmarks of the later years. **'Playing with Fire'** describes a spiritualist séance in which the writer makes his first imaginative statement on the possibility of two worlds existing at the same time, and on people moving like amphibians between them. The medium breathes and hisses, a strange luminous vapour hovers around the table in the ordinary surburban room, while cabs pass in the street outside, voices are heard in a sidewalk argument and dogs bark in the distance. A hideous monster is unaccountably conjured up, a huge black unicorn-like thing that stamps and snorts and rushes 'with horrible energy from one corner of the room to another'. In **'The Terror of Blue John Gap'** the monster is real, and much larger. A survivor from prehistoric times, it lives in a subterranean lake reached by a cave opening out of the peaceful countryside. Even more loathsome than the apparition of **'Playing with Fire'** or the Baskerville hound painted with phosphorus, it is ten times the size of a bear, has immense fangs and claws and pale malignant eyes like light bulbs. Local farmers finally block up the entrance to the cave, burying the creature in its own dark.

The prevalence of monsters is the most striking feature of these years. Glaring, snarling, smoking, they erupt with the force of unconscious images. When Conan Doyle describes the labour involved in sealing up the Blue Gap monster—dozens of people rolling boulders into the cave—the metaphor is unmistakable. It is also misleading, for the monsters have not been buried and in fact will never go away. They develop on a vicious human level in the later Holmes stories, and the theme of dark surviving prehistoric agencies will be explored in the science-fiction masterpiece, *The Lost World.* Meanwhile the public figure keeps up its impassive appearance. In a painting done as the century ends he sits very upright in a dark leather chair, pencil in hand, notepad on knee, a correct monument of the age: rich moustache with long waxed ends and a silver chain looped across his vest. You look at the stiff yet genial face and wonder how much he knows. Part of the fascination is that he will never tell. Occasionally he throws out a remark that may or may not be a hint. 'The best literature', he tells his audience at a lecture, 'is always the unconscious literature. . .'

Was Conan Doyle unconsciously motivated when he killed off Holmes and failed to produce a body? In any case it eased the technical problem of a return to life, and the moment itself was clearly signalled in advance. While the detective remains missing and presumed dead, his creator is still haunted by the subject of crime. In 1901 he publishes a series of articles in *The Strand* that discuss some recent murder cases. *The Hound of the Baskervilles* appears a year later and proves that Holmes is still alive in the writer's mind. Although set in the past, this story naturally excites demands for Conan Doyle to reconsider the future. Big offers from America and British magazines for the return of Holmes are certainly an inducement. But they are not conclusive, for he will continue the cycle when he no longer needs the money. The strongest clue to a change of heart lies in the work itself.

Watson opens **'The Empty House'**, the story in which Holmes reappears, with a confession that seems to echo Conan Doyle's own situation: 'It can be imagined that my close intimacy with Sherlock Holmes had interested me deeply in crime, and that after his disappearance I never failed to read with care the various problems which came before the public. . .' The best tales in the new collection show a darkening view of the criminal world. The imagery becomes fiercer. London is compared to a jungle in which monsters have to be tracked down like wild beasts. Unlike

the shadowy Moriarty, the master-criminal Moran and the blackmailer Milverton emerge as antagonists with an appetite for evil far beyond any characters in the earlier part of the cycle. Holmes gives signs of a deep pessimism about human nature. In the context of the darkening view, Conan Doyle tries to close the religious gap between himself and his creation by making Holmes a kind of lay brother, using the detective to ventilate his belief that a special dominating force is now necessary to oppose the criminal. And since the British have always enjoyed staking the amateur against the professional, Holmes's status gives him a unique and rather mysterious position. His superior talent recognized by Scotland Yard and the government, both of whom frequently seek his help, he becomes like an elected mediator between authority and crime. On the side of the law, he is still powerful enough to break or ignore it when he feels inclined. For Wilkie Collins the main objective was never the solution but the experience of the mystery. Conan Doyle believes in the solution at all costs. A practical and symbolic act, it preludes the removal of an infection in the system.

The detective returns appropriately in disguise, and when the hunchbacked book-collector reveals his identity Watson faints for the first and last time in his life. Only Moriarty died in the struggle at the falls, but to avoid the professor's associates Holmes has been obliged to live in hiding. Now only one of the murder gang survives, Moran of the scarred face, iron nerve and cruel eyes. Speculating on how a man who was once an 'honourable soldier' could become a paid assassin, Holmes suggests that a secret deforming process may be at work in nature. 'There are some trees, Watson, which grow to a certain height and then suddenly develop some unsightly eccentricity. You will see it often in humans. . .'. With Watson's help the enemy is cornered and Holmes takes up his profession again.

Several unusually tame case-histories follow, then halfway through the collection gathers force. The plump and dandyish blackmailer in **'Charles Augustus Milverton'** has touches of Fosco [the villain in the Wilkie Collins story 'The Woman in White'] in his frozen smile, glittering eyes and smooth conceit. To convey his peculiar repulsion, Holmes evokes memories this time of venomous serpents at the London zoo. In a surprisingly ruthless climax, Holmes and Watson witness the blackmailer's murder, hidden behind a curtain while an elegant and aristocratic lady empties her revolver into his shirt-front:

> He shrank away, and then fell forward upon the table, coughing furiously and clawing among the papers. Then he staggered to his feet, received another shot, and rolled upon the floor. 'You've done me', he cried, and lay still. The woman looked at him intently and ground her heel into his upturned face.

A draft of night air blows into the room and the beautiful avenger slips away with a rustle of skirts. Holmes makes no effort to detain her. When the police later ask his help in solving the case, he refuses. Milverton had ruined the woman's life—when she couldn't meet his price he sent some 'compromising' letters to her husband—and the detective feels that such a case reverses the usual identities of criminal and victim.

He feels it again in **'The Abbey Grange'**. A drunken aristocrat brutalizes his wife, even setting fire to her dog. Then someone murders him. Holmes discovers that Lady Brackenstall has a lover. He learns that Captain Croker kissed nothing more than the ground on which his lady trod, but killed Brackenstall after seeing him beat his wife across the face with a stick. As judge and jury Holmes and Watson pronounce pardon, and allow the young sailor to flee the country. Two cunning puzzle stories that show Holmes at his most alert also incline to the same view of criminal and victim. In **'The Second Stain'** a foreign agent blackmails a politician's wife on account of an indiscreet but 'innocent' event in her past. He forces her to help him steal a state document, but Holmes recovers it and again sets up his own court of justice. Respecting the lady's secret, he refuses to incriminate her. In **'The Golden Pince-Nez'** he is even prepared to be sympathetic to a murderous lady nihilist from Russia whose husband betrayed her to the police, but she resolves his dilemma by killing herself.

Condoning acts of private revenge, Conan Doyle begins to accept the inevitability of violence in the world around him. Defending 'pure' passion, he refers to the situation with Jean Leckie and perhaps even confesses his own fear of blackmail. In Milverton and Brackenstall he discovers a form of life low enough to justify the private executioner. But the really new element in these criminal fables is their underground of suffering. When he shows people trapped in situations from which the only way out is through violence or betrayal, he moves to the edge of a bitter territory that Simenon will later explore. More personally involved than before with the predicaments of clients and criminals, Holmes is often pictured by Watson as stern, haggard, preoccupied. His friends make the same point about Conan Doyle at this time. Resurrected and forgiven, the imaginary character seems closer than ever to the real one. Holmes in **'The Second Stain'** is deeply concerned when the prime minister describes Europe as an armed camp and admits his fears of a major war. Conan Doyle's private life apart, his interest in military tactics and propaganda on behalf of British rearmament betrays a quickening anxiety for a world he feels to be threatened. Soon after *The Return* is published, the author even turns detective himself. The case of a near-sighted and rather dim young Indian convicted of mutilating cattle suddenly arouses doubts in his mind. He conducts his own investigation, sifting through clues of weapons and bloodstains, brilliantly demolishes the police evidence, exposes the real criminal and frees an innocent man. Later he will rescue a gambler and pimp accused of murdering a rich old lady, will solve a jewellery theft and the mystery of a man who vanished apparently without trace from a London hotel. United by their drive to forage for truth and correct injustice, Conan Doyle and Sherlock Holmes are now moving together to confront some final experiences on what the detective calls a great and sombre stage.

> 'What is the meaning of it, Watson'? said Holmes, solemnly, as he laid down the paper. 'What object is served by this circle of misery and violence and fear? It must tend to some end,

or else our universe is ruled by chance, which is unthinkable. But what end? There is the great standing perennial problem to which human reason is as far from an answer as ever'.

This epilogue to **'The Cardboard Box'**, one of Conan Doyle's most disturbing inventions, sums up the mood of the great final tales in *His Last Bow* (1917) and *The Case-Book of Sherlock Holmes* (1927). The story that opens this last part of the cycle, **'Wisteria Lodge'**, finds Holmes discussing with Watson the associations of the word 'grotesque'. He detects in it some 'underlying suggestion of the tragic and the terrible', and remarks how often the grotesque deepens into the criminal. The cycle has already been laced with witty references to some bizarre cases that Watson feels for various reasons cannot be made public. Sealed away for ever is the journalist staring in terminal insanity at a matchbox that contains a new species of worm, the banker sucked to death by a red leech, the affair of the giant rat of Sumatra and of the aluminum crutch. But now Watson releases a few other hauntingly strange episodes from the archives, and at moments they almost crack the composure of Holmes himself.

The last stories were written between 1912 and 1925, but with two exceptions the period is still late Victorian and early Edwardian England. Not only time and distance affect the view. Since *The Return* appeared, Conan Doyle's world has passed from the threshold to the centre of shock. Now he reexamines an earlier age in the light of the First World War and the 'feverish' twenties. The final part of the cycle also coincides with the years of his finest imaginative writing, the Professor Challenger series beginning with *The Lost World* (1912), a classic ghost story called **'The Brown Hand'**, and the extraordinary **'Horror of the Heights'** in *Tales of Terror*. During these years he also exhausts his long investigation of spiritualism and becomes a convert, certain that he's found the secret to 'the bridge of death, the assured continued journey in the world beyond'. Meanwhile the colours of the actual world grow darker and the atmosphere of violence and danger surrounding Holmes turns as thick as the fumes from his chemical experiments.

Mutilations and psychoses are uncovered in the old country houses and suburban villas. Many characters exist on the edge of deformity: a dwarflike creature with a bulbous head, a man with a curved back and convulsively twitching hands, a woman like a huge clumsy chicken. Holmes has developed a particularly sharp response to physical oddity. When Watson embarks on a rather imprecise visual catalogue of a murder suspect, he interrupts—

> 'Left shoe wrinkled, right one smooth'.
>
> 'I did not observe that'.
>
> 'No, you wouldn't. I spotted his artificial limb. But proceed'.

Holmes seems almost manic-depressive now. He slumps into near-despair: 'We reach. We grasp. And what is left in our hands at the end? A shadow . . . '. Then he rouses himself to feverish activity, reaching the climax of a case after an attack on his life, pale as a ghost with a bandage around his head. One year finds him so exhausted that his doctor orders complete rest. During another case he feels so energized and relaxed that he can write a monograph on the medieval composer Lassus in the intervals of stalking prey. He watches Watson drowsing in an armchair, and from the expressions that cross his friend's face can deduce what he's been thinking about (getting a picture framed, and then the American Civil War). The portrait of the artist suggests a presence that broods over everything, on or off stage.

At the same time we seem to penetrate beyond the stare of the author's poker face, the patriot, the sportsman, the justice-collector, the family man, that composite 'normal' image purveyed by so many biographers and cultists. On the other side is a human being of extraordinary gifts, admired and successful, happy in his personal relationships, with a great capacity for pleasure, and yet in a deep sense alienated. No one who spends years searching for proof of a future life, then advertising his discovery of it, can be at ease with his present one. Even at his most secure Conan Doyle finds the ground giving way beneath his feet. He is haunted by that 'underlying suggestion of the tragic and the terrible'. In his newly discovered relation to the universe he looks across the bridge of death to a state of eternal progression, a movement farther and farther away from all human dangers and terrors, from the existence that Holmes now calls 'the schoolroom of Sorrow'.

Here are some events occurring in the schoolroom. In **'The Cardboard Box'.** Holmes solves a murder of jealousy which begins with a suburban spinster receiving through the mails a package that contains two human ears, one male and one female, freshly severed and packed in salt. In **'Wisteria Lodge'** he confronts a ferocious political vendetta involving the former dictator of a South American republic. Before the final assassination there is one barbaric murder and an attempt at another by a mulatto who practises voodoo in his kitchen, where Holmes discovers a pail of blood, a mutilated rooster and a disgusting fetish that suggests a 'mummified negro baby'. In **'The Devil's Foot',** a sister and two brothers are found sitting around a table in a farmhouse, their faces convulsed with horror. The sister is dead and the brothers have been driven out of their minds. Chanting idiotically, they are removed to the nearest asylum. There will be yet another victim before Holmes exposes a drama of revenge in which the criminal uses a poison derived from the root of an African plant. Thrown on the fire, its powder induces hallucinations that result in either madness or death. Jealousy with a circus background is the secret behind **'The Veiled Lodger'**, a woman who hides herself in a suburban apartment and always wears a thick veil to conceal the ruin of her mutilated face.

The cycle also describes some parallel acts of inner violence. In **'The Creeping Man'** a distinguished middle-aged professor falls in love with a young girl and goes to Europe to try a rejuvenation drug. Injections of monkey serum turn him into a kind of missing link, clambering up the walls of his house, attacked by his dog, flying into chattering rages. 'When one tries to rise above Nature', Holmes drily remarks, 'one is liable to fall below it'. In **'The Sussex Vampire'** a man sees his wife attack her stepson, then suck blood from the neck of their own baby. When Holmes solves the mystery, appearances are almost magically reversed. 'Did it not occur to you', he asks the husband, 'that a bleeding wound may be sucked for some other purpose than to draw the blood from it'? The young stepson, adoring his father and jealous of the new wife, has tried to kill their baby with an arrow dipped in poison. In **'Thor Bridge'** a woman commits suicide but makes it look as if she's been murdered by a girl with whom her husband is in love. Although there has been no affair, only a close friendship, the wife suffered from a 'soul-jealousy' as passionate as any 'body-jealousy' Holmes remarks that he's never come across 'a stranger example of what perverted love can bring about'. Even the idea of a mental rival drove the wife to revenge and suicide.

Just below the level of these tales are two others in which the vicious and the grotesque make an equal impact. **'The Illustrious Client'** provides Holmes with another superantagonist, the murderer and sexual adventurer known as Baron Gruner. This sinister creature, with languorous eyes and waxed tips of hair under the nose that suggest an insect's antennae, exploits a rich young girl who finds him attractive. The beauty and the beast situation is resolved when a prostitute throws vitriol in Gruner's face, and it turns into something blurred and inhuman, like a painting 'over which the artist has passed a wet and foul sponge'. In **'Shoscombe Old Place'** a country squire has reasons for concealing the death of his wealthy invalid sister. He burns her body and hides it in the family crypt, then hires a manservant to impersonate her. Holmes becomes suspicious when he learns that the squire has given away his sister's dog. He retrieves the animal and sets it on the impersonator as 'she' appears on one of her rare outings, riding in a carriage:

> With a joyous cry it dashed forward to the carriage and sprang upon the step. Then in a moment its eager greeting changed to furious rage, and it snapped at the black skirt above it.

> 'Drive on! Drive on'! shrieked a harsh voice.

Even disguise has become macabre. Physical horrors in these stories are tersely but unsparingly described. They seem to spring from that awareness of spreading violence first noted in *The Return,* but are heightened by the new element of psychosis. **'The Sussex Vampire'** contains an unforgettable image of the father fondling his baby while Holmes glimpses the young stepson's face, maniacal with jealousy, reflected in a window that looks out on a peaceful garden. An even more chilling moment ends **'The Veiled Lodger'** The woman has confessed how she and the circus strong man planned to kill her husband. The plan failed on account of her lover's cowardice, and she was left alone to be attacked by a lion. Angered by the memory of the strong man's weakness but still in love with him, the passionate relic compares herself to a wounded animal crawling into its hole to die. Moved to a rare and rather awkward display of sympathy, Holmes pats her hand and murmurs something about patient suffering:

> The woman's answer was a terrible one. She raised her veil and stepped forward into the light.

'I wonder if you would bear it', she said.

The curious link between sexual desire and physical disfigurement is echoed by Gruner's fate in **'The Illustrious Client'** and by the lovers' in **'The Cardboard Box'**, of heads battered to a pulp and ears cut off. (It recurs even more brutally in **'The Case of Lady Sannox'**, from the *Tales of Terror,* with a surgeon tricked into mutilating his mistress.) Lust also motivates the apelike regression of **'The Creeping Man'**. The final revelation is often of a submerged but violent sexual guilt, just as the 'soul-jealousy' in **'Thor Bridge'** alludes to Conan Doyle's fear, after his first wife died, that she might have suspected his love for Jean Leckie. Severed ears, squashed heads, dissolved and ruined faces, the academic capering wildly from branch to branch of a moonlit tree—the cycle closes with some terrible and grotesque symbols that ironically recall their author's remark about unconscious literature.

The same externalized fears continue in the final stories: violence, corruption, war. In **'The Three Gables'** Conan Doyle moves valiantly beyond his range to a sleazy underworld of prize fighters and gun molls. His subject is the rise of organized crime in London. But the portrait of the American millionaire in **'Thor Bridge'** is blunt and sardonic. The Gold King stands on the vanishing frontier between big business and gangsterdom and imposes like a prefiguration of one of Marlowe's rich ambiguous clients. Like many English writers, Conan Doyle has problems with American dialogue, but he brings off his effects all the same. Looking like a villainous Abe Lincoln, the millionaire talks about his interests—'they are large, Mr Holmes, large beyond the belief of an ordinary man'—and warns of his power to influence not only individuals but 'communities, cities, even nations'. He tries to bribe Holmes and is deeply shocked to find one individual exempt from his influence.

The title story of *His Last Bow* is an inferior work, but ends with a strange elegiac scene on the eve of the First World War. Holmes has been called out of retirement to unmask a German espionage network. Mission accomplished, he stands with Watson on the terrace of a country house and gazes out at the moonlit sea:

> 'There's an east wind coming, Watson'.
>
> 'I think not, Holmes. It is very warm'.
>
> 'Good old Watson! You are the one fixed point in a changing age. There's an east wind coming all the same, such a wind as never blew on England yet. It will be cold and bitter, Watson, and a good many of us may wither before its blast . . .'.

From this bleak future with its suggestion of 'God's curse' hanging over the world, Holmes has already decided to retire. He returns to his farm and absorbs himself again in philosophy and bee-culture, studying the insects' 'little working gangs as once I watched the criminal world of London'. (pp. 51-61)

> *Gavin Lambert, "Final Problems," in his* The Dangerous Edge, *Grossman Publishers, 1976, pp. 31-78.*

Charles Higham   (essay date 1976)

[*Higham is an English poet, critic, and nonfiction writer best known for his controversial books on Hollywood celebrities. In the following excerpt from his* The Adventures of Conan Doyle, *he discusses the sexual and spiritual themes of Doyle's supernatural stories.*]

[The turn of the century] was a rich period for the tale of terror, with some of the finest work of H. G. Wells and M. P. Shiel being published, and Conan Doyle created quite a stir with his contributions to the genre. In **"The Story of the Brazilian Cat"** (1898), the heir to a fortune is trapped by his sinister cousin in a cage in a sober country home; the other occupant of the cage is an alarming jungle feline with phosphorescent eyes, which toys with its victim before attempting to tear him to pieces. A touch of the perverse makes the story work: despite himself the prisoner is drawn to the animal, finding its supple, muscular figure painfully alluring. It is clear that the cat is an unconscious symbol of sexuality, at once menacing and attractive, primitive and releasing.

In **"The King of the Foxes,"** revised in 1903 from a draft written in 1888, . . . fox hunting is given a bizarre literary treatment. At the end of an exciting chase, the "fox" jumps out at the hounds; it is actually a Siberian wolf, a creature the size of a donkey, with a huge gray head, dripping fangs, and tapering jaws, which savages the hounds and sends them squealing for cover. Both these creatures, monsters stalking through a dignified English country scene, were to be echoed in the even more horrendous form of the Hound of the Baskervilles.

Some stories written in this period suggest more extreme and rarefied terrors. In **"The Story of the Beetle Hunter"** (1898), the entomologist Lord Linchmere and his demented brother-in-law Sir Thomas Rossiter live in a country house crammed with countless specimens of dead beetles, in display cases, which they have brought back from the jungles. The insects suggest a primeval horror which these aristocrats cannot escape. Indeed, Rossiter, obeying some atavistic instinct, prowls through the beetle-filled rooms at night and attempts to smash his relative's head with a hammer. In **"The Story of the Japanned Box"** (1899), a crazed knight, bereaved by the death of his wife, keeps her dying words on a tin record in a small black portable phonograph, relaying her voice deafeningly through his house at night.

The supernatural is dealt with more alarmingly in the story **"Playing with Fire"** (1900). In this extraordinary work, the author suggests that beasts, like humans, may survive the grave. At a straightforward séance in London, with little more expected than conventional table raps and flying tambourines, the sitters are dismayed when a vibrating luminous fog swirls through the room and a mysterious form materializes through the mist:

> Some huge thing hurtled against us in the darkness, rearing, stamping, smashing, springing, snorting. The table was splintered. We were scattered in every direction. It clattered and scrambled among us, rushing with horrible energy from one corner of the room to the other.

This monstrous unicorn seems to come from the same stable as the great horses of the Apocalypse. And indeed the horsemen were riding when Conan Doyle wrote the story in the autumn of 1899. War was breaking out in South Africa, as the British Empire was challenged by its most vigorous adversary since Sher Ali, of the Second Afghan War. (pp. 155-57)

Despite travel, service in the war, and the experience of public acclaim, Conan Doyle never stopped writing for a day. And he did not neglect the horror story in those years at the turn of the century. In his study at Undershaw, as he gazed out across the rolling Nutcombe Valley, strange visions swirled in his brain. Just before 1900, he had written one of his most extraordinary tales of terror, **"The Brown Hand,"** which resembles some of Kipling's ghost stories. The narrator this time is a member of the Society for Psychical Research, reminiscent of Podmore, with a wide experience of haunted houses. He is called in to investigate a ghost pursuing Sir Dominick Holden, a distinguished surgeon . . . who has just been in service in India. Sir Dominick's house, Rodenhurst, in Wiltshire, oddly anticipates Conan Doyle's later home, Windlesham, in Sussex. Surrounded by prehistoric fossils, the house itself is by contrast a microcosm of contemporary science. (p. 176)

Conan Doyle builds the atmosphere marvelously, describing the stench of methylated spirits floating through the rooms, glass cases filled with relics of disease and suffering, and along the shelves at night a spectral Indian gliding with a dangling arm that ends in a useless knotted stump. The dead Indian obsessively returns again and again, looking for his hand, which was amputated by Holden. But the hand has long since been destroyed. The narrator travels to London to obtain a substitute hand. He secures it at a hospital, and places it in a glass container. Conan Doyle now shows a characteristic touch of macabre humor. The Indian appears, examines the hand, and with a cry of disappointment returns it to its place; it does not correctly match the mutilated arm—it is a *left* hand. Not until the correct member is supplied can the ghost find final satisfaction.

A most significant passage illustrates Conan Doyle's feelings at the time about departed spirits. He tells us that they "are the amphibia of this life and the next, capable of passing from one to the other as a turtle passes from land to water." This curious concept suggests that the dead are condemned to an existence both bloodless and sexless, adrift in a mindless vacuum, impelled only by some overwhelming need.

A bizarre story, **"The Sealed Room,"** shows a person obtaining a kind of life after death by entirely material means. A young man contacts the narrator in a desperate attempt to locate his father, who has disappeared to Europe, sending letters periodically. At the end of the story, the narrator and his friend burst into a secret room, where they find a ghastly presence. It is the corpse of the father, covered with a layer of dust that has built up over years. Overwhelmed by debts, the father long ago committed suicide, first contriving to give his son the illusion of his continual existence by writing numerous letters which he has arranged to have mailed at regular intervals from the continent.

In **"The Great Brown-Pericord Motor,"** a story on a somewhat higher level, the terror springs from the transformation into an engine of death of a new invention—the flying machine. The story appeared in *The Pictorial Magazine* in January, 1904, only three weeks after Orville and Wilbur Wright had made the first flight in a heavier-than-air machine on December 17, 1903, at Kitty Hawk, North Carolina. Francis Pericord, a great inventor, has created a weird device with flapping yellow metal wings, which buzzes about with alarming intensity. The implication is that Pericord has violated the code of life by creating a grotesque facsimile of a bird, which can only bring misery to the world. Pericord's reason is affected when his chief mechanic steals his designs. As an act of poetic justice, and at the risk of his own device, he murders the thief, attaches him to the infernal miniplane, and sends him on a last journey:

> For a minute or two, the huge yellow fans flapped and flickered. Then the body began to move in little jumps down the side of the hillock, gathering a gradual momentum, until at last it heaved up into the air, and sailed off into the moonlight.

Months later, Pericord is found to be insane, and is confined to a New York asylum, where he constructs new-fangled flying machines in his rare moments of lucidity.

The resemblance to H. G. Wells is obvious, but there is a difference. Though Wells does not ignore the possible menace presented by the new age of science, he at heart welcomes science. In many ways, he becomes its spokesman and apostle. By contrast, Conan Doyle has a more ambiguous attitude. He is fascinated by science, but frightened by it. The Brown-Pericord Motor, a sinister giant metal moth, is seen chiefly as an engine of death; its only act of transportation is to convey a corpse to its last resting place in a moonlit ocean.

In one story a belief that obsessions can drive individuals back from the grave; in another, that the only immortality is achieved through post-dated letters; in a third, that the dead are carried not by angel's wings but by the infernal wings of an airplane: these stories reflect Conan Doyle's constantly changing attitudes toward the survival after death of the human spirit.

His interest in the occult is again reflected in his finest story of the period. **"The Leather Funnel"** (1900). This tale shows the author's concern with psychometry, a power whereby, supposedly, gifted individuals are enabled to perceive the history of objects when they are close to them. William Denton, Professor of Geology at Boston University in the 1840's, had reported seeing astonishing images of ancient Hawaii after examining a fragment of lava at Kilauea. His wife had examined a mastodon tooth, and in a dream seemed to become the creature itself. Denton's account of his experience must have provided much of the inspiration for Conan Doyle's later novel *The Lost World.* Subsequent examples of psychometry were frequent. Toward the end of his life Conan Doyle compared psychometric impressions to shadows on a screen. He believed that the screen was the ether, "The whole material universe being embedded in and interpenetrated by this subtle material which would not necessarily change its position since it is too fine for wind or any coarser material to influence it."

In **"The Leather Funnel,"** the occultist Lionel Dacre presents the funnel to a guest for a psychometric experiment. His guest sleeps next to it and experiences a horrifying nightmare, described with all of Conan Doyle's mastery of atmosphere and suspense. He sees a woman, brooded over by black-clad inquisitorial figures, presented with the leather object; it is about to be thrust into her when the dreamer wakens. He has recalled the torture of the infamous Marquise de Brinvilliers, a mass murderess of the period of Louis XIV. Historically, the torture known as the "Question" involved forcing quantities of water by funnel into the mouth and the stomach only. But the author gives this story a typically perverse twist. By not specifying the orifice into which the funnel is pushed, he supplies an unexpected note of sexual terror. The result here is, not for the first time, a hint of Conan Doyle's equation of sexuality and death. (pp. 176-79)

> *Charles Higham, in his* The Adventures of Conan Doyle: The Life of the Creator of Sherlock Holmes, *W. W. Norton & Company, Inc., 1976, 368 p.*

Stephen Knight   (essay date 1980)

[In the following excerpt, Knight discusses the Sherlock Holmes stories in the context of late Victorian society.]

The contents of early copies [of *The Strand*] define the magazine's ideology: prominent are the biographies of successful men, stories about courage and adventure, features about new machines. But there are also stories that realise bourgeois sentimental morality, and sections for housewives and children regularly occur. The magazine was to be read and taken home by the white-collar man who worked in London. It was a central piece of middle-class ideological literature, oriented towards the family and respectable success in life. The cover of the magazine brought form and content into a masterly union: an etching from a photograph of The Strand itself, taken just where the head office was located. The busy and then fashionable street had rich symbolic meaning: it stretched from the city where the purchasers mostly worked to the West End where they might one day aspire to live. The anxious, alienated, upwards-looking white-collar workers of the capital were caricatured in the Grossmiths' tellingly titled *The Diary of a Nobody;* in *The Strand Magazine* they could find a validation of their morality and a prospect of all they could look forward to, in dreams at least.

There are many relations between the meaning of the Holmes stories and the world-view of *The Strand* and its purchasers. It is best to assess first how the form of the stories worked, how Doyle affectively created patterns that supported, even developed, the attitudes of his audience. With these formations in view, it will be easy to understand how the nature of the plot and detail shapes a prob-

lematic responding to the concerns of the audience and resolvable in comforting terms.

The titles of the short stories have the crisp materialism, the briskly objective, unemotive quality that Doyle first encapsulated in the title of *The Sign of Four.* This final version was itself just a little firmer and more mysterious than 'The Sign of the Four,' the title of the original American publication, commissioned by *Lippincott's Magazine.* Most of the short story titles are briskly specified: **'The Beryl Coronet'**, **'The Noble Bachelor'**, **'The Blue Carbuncle'**. Some titles use a material but unexpected qualifier to create an enigma: **'The Engineer's Thumb'**, **'The Five Orange Pips'**, **'The Speckled Band'**. The early titles **'A Scandal in Bohemia'**, **'A Case of Identity'** and **'The Boscombe Valley Mystery'** include a less material term that suggests the genre of the stories. But they too have an objective aura, clearly abandoning the manipulative rhetoric Doyle sought in his first title *A Study in Scarlet.* That was originally 'A Tangled Skein', a weakly emotive title, and the final choice is reminiscent of Gaboriau's melodramas, especially *L'Affaire Lerouge* (although Lerouge is the murdered woman's surname). The rejection of this emotive element is quite conscious: in *The Sign of Four* Watson refers to the 'somewhat fantastic title' of the previous adventure.

The early stories show a brisk attack from the beginning. Like *The Sign of Four* the first three adventures all use Sherlock Holmes's name in the opening sentence. The initial paragraphs are increasingly crisp and briefly suggestive. One of the motives is Doyle's conscious production of a series, encouraging regular purchase of the magazine; he assumed that readers of the later stories would know the established patterns and characters. But at the same time he wanted to grip the audience, plunge them into the matter with less of the narrator's comment than opens **'A Scandal in Bohemia'**. The direct openings bring the hero into active involvement with problems, reducing his earlier aloof distance from the reader and his world. This effect is also created by the greater simplicity of the endings. In the two novellas and in **'The Red-Headed League'** Doyle continues Poe's pattern, giving his detective a final comment, separated from the action both by its lofty, judging tone and its foreign language. In **'A Case of Identity'** the comment is translated, and from then on they disappear; the final disengaging remarks, when they occur, are English and moralistic, not isolated pieces of intellectualism.

These features all tend to involve the hero in action, not isolate him in cerebration like Dupin. This model responds to the worldview of a basically uncerebral audience, and it is most fully created by the varied and dramatic action. The pace accelerates as Holmes comes to grips with his problem: the paragraph where he studies the King of Bohemia's notepaper is a fine example of a vigorous and object-dominated presentation which enacts the worldly involvement of the hero. Watson examines the paper and sees some letters in its watermark:

> 'What do you make of that'? asked Holmes.

> 'The name of the maker, no doubt; or his monogram, rather'.

'Not at all. The *G* with the small *t* stands for 'Gesellschaft', which is the German for 'Company'.
It is a customary contraction like our 'Co.'. *P,*
of course, stands for 'Papier'. Now for the *Eg.*
Let us glance at our Continental Gazeteer'.

He took down a heavy brown volume from his
shelves.

'Eglow, Eglonitz—here we are, Egria. It is in a
German-speaking country—in Bohemia, not far
from Carlsbad. "Remarkable as being the scene
of the death of Wallenstein, and for its numerous
glass factories and paper mills". Ha, ha, my boy,
what do you make of that'? His eyes sparkled,
and he sent up a great blue triumphant cloud
from his cigarette.

Details flow out, under the control of Holmes's supreme
knowledge—did he know all the time, and just gave Watson a lesson in method? Or was he really looking something up? The passage does not make it clear: the method
is a little clouded in mystery. Built into the passage are
Holmes's special and amazing powers, and also information perfectly comprehensible to anyone with common
sense. But the vitality of the passage, the expressive dynamism of the created personality, make us believe he has
brought off a triumph. Where Poe expressed an almost
prophetic mystery in the smoke that wreathed Dupin,
Holmes's signal is of victory over a material enigma—and
one located in notepaper, an object straight from the everyday experience of the white-collar worker.

The speed of the stories derives not only from a vigorous
style. The fast-moving and interlocked plot has its own
meanings. First, since nothing is accidental, and cause and
effect control the relationship of events, the incidents converge with rapidity and increasing sureness on the climax
of the story. This convergence brings all the satisfaction
of organic unity, and true to the attitudes that lie behind
the development of that structural pattern, . . . the convergence is only made possible by the power of a single intelligence. The hero—and behind him the author—is the
individual understanding and resolving contemporary
problems, so realising in shapely and persuasive fictions
the motives that led Doyle to deplore Gaboriau.

Doyle's plots are not only organic and rapid; they also
present many puzzling incidents in a short space for hero
and form to resolve. They are dense enough to seem valid
representations of the packed experience of everyday life.
Doyle knew well that a full and tightly connected plot was
essential to his success, saying accurately: 'every story
really needed as clear-cut and original a plot as a longish
book would do'. Many later crime novels use less actual
puzzle-plotting than Doyle puts into six or seven thousand
words. His action and dialogue are rarely extraneous to
the mystery; the long sequences of description, comedy or
emotion that fill out a novel by, for example, Dorothy Sayers are absent here. The brief sequences of characterisation
or setting operate in close connection to the central mystery and this strict sense of relevance etches deeply the effect of the stories. Doyle recognised the importance of a
tight, stylised manner when he wrote of 'the compact handling of the plots' and said that Holmes's character 'admits of no light or shade'.

An early portrait of Sherlock Holmes by Sidney Paget.

With a vigorous material style and a compressed, rapidly
linked structure, the emphasis of the presentation falls all
the more sharply on events and objects. These tend to be
less exotic and essentially melodramatic than the phenomena of the novellas; even the royal romance of the first
story centres on nothing more recherché than a cabinet
photograph, and the objects used for deduction—a watch,
a typist's sleeve, a letter—make the superior powers of the
detective operate in a very familiar and real world. It is not
only the evidence of the detail itself that establishes this;
Doyle presses the point through Holmes himself. 'It has
long been an axiom of mine that the little things are infinitely the most important' he tells Watson when discussing nothing further from the ordinary business world than
a typewriter, in **'A Case of Identity'**. The set of the stories
towards enigmas of the ordinary world, materially presented, is given specific and authoritative expression by
Holmes in the opening of the same story:

We would not dare to conceive the things which
are really mere commonplaces of existence. If we
could fly out of that window hand in hand, hover
over this great city, gently remove the roofs, and
peep in at the queer things which are going on,
the strange coincidences, the plannings, the
cross purposes, the wonderful chains of events,
working through generations, and leading to the
most *outré* results, it would make all fiction with
its conventionalities and foreseen conclusions
most stale and unprofitable.

The passage is fascinatingly double in its tone. The image
of flying and the notion of peering into other people's lives
reveals an alienated intelligence dramatising its own isolated power; the romantic artistic consciousness is created,
and ratifies itself not only in the image but also in the final
reference to Shakespeare—and that to Hamlet himself,
prince of alienated intelligence. Yet the interest is real, and
the subtle mind elevates the everyday. The power of
Holmes is not only to resolve the problems of ordinary life,
but to make that life seem rich in itself, and therefore emotionally fulfilling.

A world is created where people enmeshed and to some extent daunted by the puzzling and the mundane nature of their experience can find comfort both in the Holmesian resolutions and in the aura of grandeur, the sheer heroism and enrichment he brings with him. In terms of epistemology we have a materialistic model, which can read off from physical data what has happened and what will happen. The succession of incidents in explained and necessary relationship to each other expresses the ideas of material causation and linear history so important to the Victorian world-view. The perception of these patterns by the heroic individual manages to balance those essentially deterministic attitudes with the basically contradictory idea of the individual as noble and free, untrammelled by the laws of material causation. A deeply satisfying and heavily ideological view of the world is made in the stories by concealing the fissure between heroism and materialism; this illusory resolution will be discussed further in terms of content but it is brought to life in the crisp and compressed creation of those two forces by Doyle's mastery of lively and suggestive writing.

The structuring of the narrative units within an organic, convergent model is in some ways simple, in others quite complex; here too the effect is dual. At its barest, analysis of the Holmes story would have three parts: relation, investigation and resolution of mysterious events. This reveals an unchanging basic structure, but, like a lot of structural analysis, tells us little about what the stories mean as they are communicated. In the early Holmes stories there is surprising flexibility in presenting relation, investigation and resolution. Not until later stories does a fixed pattern emerge, the structural system so well remembered. In that formula, the story opens with Holmes and Watson at Baker Street; a client arrives; Holmes deduces from the client's appearance; the problem is outlined; Holmes discusses the case with Watson after the client leaves; investigation follows—usually some is conducted by Holmes alone, but most occurs at the scene of the crime with Watson and the police looking on; Holmes identifies what has happened, normally in action of some kind; Holmes explains all to Watson, back at Baker Street. This formula is used in the skilful pastiches by Adrian Conan Doyle and John Dickson Carr, but it is by no means a constant pattern in *The Adventures,* nor even in the second book of stories, *The Memoirs of Sherlock Holmes.*

As you read through *The Adventures,* the elements often seem familiar but there is no sense of formulaic repetition; each story has something different in its structure or in the context of some of the structural units. The effect is much more lively, varied and interesting than the usual remembered model which is established in the later collections. Two of *The Adventures* never go to Baker Street at all—'The Boscombe Valley Mystery' and 'The Man with the Twisted Lip'. These variations are outside the basic pattern of relation, investigation, resolution and include them, but within those bare categories there is also much variety.

The dominant pattern in relation is for the client to explain what has happened, but in three cases Holmes himself outlines the problem—'The Boscombe Valley Mys-

tery', 'The Blue Carbuncle' and 'The Man with the Twisted Lip'. Investigation has a whole set of variable features. It can be very sketchy, when Holmes thinks about events taking their own course, as in 'The Five Orange Pips', 'The Man with the Twisted Lip' and 'The Copper Beeches'. Or he may just put himself in the right place to find the answer, as in 'A Scandal in Bohemia' and 'The Blue Carbuncle'. Other stories present detailed investigation and so approach the later 'clue-puzzle' where a great amount of detected data is put before us, but only the detective can see the pattern that gives the answer—'The Red-Headed League', 'The Boscombe Valley Mystery' and 'The Speckled Band' are of this sort, and 'A Case of Identity' as well, though in it most of the data comes out of the relation.

If the intensity of investigation varies, its methods also have considerable flexibility. There are three types: armchair analysis at Baker Street, often with the use of reference books; Holmes goes alone to make inquiries, sometimes in disguise; Holmes and Watson go together to the scene of the crime. No story in *The Adventures* has all three of these methods; most have two, a few rely entirely on a joint field investigation. You gain a sense of a common pool of methods, of familiar patterns being re-enacted, but the reader of *The Strand* would not have found this month's story quite like the previous one. This commercial skill has wider meaning. Holmes's abilities are flexible enough to make him a convincing respondent to the variety and difficulty of the problems he tackles; the varying form creates an aura of spontaneity, of resourceful vigour that strengthens the hero's authority.

The resolutions of the stories are formally more similar than the investigations, but two differences can be seen, one of context, one of content. As to the first, five of the stories are resolved at Baker Street and the dénouement of the others occurs in the field. This is merely a non-significant varying of pattern, but the second, contentual variation has considerable impact on meaning. In some stories Holmes is not fully triumphant: he understands the crime but has not brought the criminal to justice. At the end of 'The Five Orange Pips' comes a report that the ship carrying the criminals has sunk; justice has been done, but not through Holmes's hands, and the story also shows his failure when John Openshaw is murdered after consulting him. This reduced control by the hero appears in 'A Scandal in Bohemia' and 'The Engineer's Thumb' where the perpetrators escape. This does not necessarily weaken the hero's authority: an analysis of the content-meaning of these endings will be offered later, but here it should be noted that Holmes's relative uncertainty can itself be an element of variety in the narrative.

The overall structural pattern is one of fairly intense variation within an unchanging order; in no story do the three basic units, relation, investigation and resolution, change position. Even in 'The Man with the Twisted Lip', where Holmes has worked on the case off-stage for days before explaining the problem to Watson, his successful investigation occurs in the story, as he sits up all night and smokes his way to the resolution. Overriding order and intrinsic variation are common enough features of popular story, of course. V. I. Propp has shown in his well-known analysis of Russian folk tales that "functions" (the controlling actions) come in the same order, and while some may be omitted, the normal series will continue in order from where the story picks it up. In this way Holmes's solitary investigation, if it occurs, will come before the climactic field investigation with Watson. The compulsive order causes some slightly odd plotting in **'The Boscombe Valley Mystery'**, where Holmes has to visit a prison at night because fieldwork is scheduled for the next morning. This order creates the ideologically important meaning of a hero whose individual, isolated action in response to problems is always a means towards a social end; his lonely researches must be realised in the setting of a public inquiry, shared with Watson who represents the public, and with the ineffectual police authorities looking on. This rigid order emphasises the active movement of the story and hero from knowledge of a problem towards its resolution. A dynamic model of applied intelligence is created in the structure, quite different in its vigorous, engaged effect from the retrospective explanatory structures that Poe and Freeman (especially in his 'reverse' stories) were led to create by their valuing of the quite isolated intelligence.

And if the permanence of structural order is meaningful, so is the consistent absence of a feature ever-present in fairy tale. . . . [Most of the stories] that have come down to us from the past have an essential 'Provider' function. That is, as the hero is about to undertake his quest or has just started on it, a 'Provider' gives him a magical object which will help him in a crisis. This is obviously present in the James Bond stories where the armourer gives the hero items of technological magic to rescue him from danger. The 'Provider' helps heroes who need supernatural aid to bring order to a troubled world. But Holmes is his own provider: self-help, that great Victorian virtue, is embodied in his power to succeed with no more than his own abilities.

Skilful variation within the structural order itself emphasises that resourceful independent power. The emphasis may arise affectively, as from changes of location and from the variety in presenting the relation and the resolution; or it may be directly created by the varied ways of investigating. In both cases the strength and ideological force of the figure come together with the inventive variety to please the audience.

A modern audience's pleasure in innovation is not a free-floating phenomenon. The idea that originality in art is a virtue is itself modern, rising from the concept that the individual artist communicates something of a special, private and inventive nature. It also relates to the marketplace situation of the artist, needing to distinguish one product from another to sell his wares for cash. The copyright act which recognised originality in law was passed to cover the situation of emerging market-artists like Hogarth: uniqueness was not sought or even much approved in earlier work, just as the idea that a human individual could triumph alone was not then entertained. Repetition formulae and supernatural assistance together are actively pursued and applauded in art outside the consciousness of

bourgeois individualism, like the stories of Gaelic shanachies or the narratives of medieval chroniclers.

In its varied, original-seeming construction, in its materialist presentation and in its stylistic vitality Doyle's art found formal patterns that were valid fables about a problem-solving hero who works in a recognisable world with essentially graspable and credible rational methods. The linked plotting, the driving pace and the dominance of the hero over the action (patterns which were fully developed in *The Sign of Four*) have been compressed in a short story form to combine richness with speed into a mixture both ideologically satisfying and easily readable for people who bought *The Strand* and who subscribed to the values the stories ultimately dramatise and support. These values are specifically realised, the formal energies are channelled, by the selection and the details of content, and it is now appropriate to examine this process, starting with the characterisation of the hero himself.

The notes Doyle first jotted down about his detective establish some crucial features. Holmes has a private income of £400 a year—a decent, but not enormous sum, enabling him to live in reasonable comfort without relying on his chosen profession for support. He is in, but not enclosed by, the world of bourgeois professionalism. The notes also imply Holmes's arrogance and commanding nature; a brief piece of dialogue is given: ' "What rot is this," I cried—throwing the volume petulantly aside . . . ' This forceful, quasi-professional hero is qualified for success by his mastery of science. The opening pages of *A Study in Scarlet* made the point at length, but in the first short story Doyle works more subtly, realising these qualities in images rather than action. Watson describes Holmes as 'the most perfect reasoning and observing machine that the world has seen'. This power involves a certain distance from human normality; in particular, feeling would damage the scientific force: 'Grit in a sensitive instrument, or a crack in one of his own high-power lenses, would not be more disturbing than a strong emotion in a nature such as his'.

The importance of science—more exactly, of the aura of science—in Holmes's methods is well-known; it mobilises for the audience's fictional protection the contemporary idea that dispassionate science was steadily comprehending and so controlling the world. But Holmes's power does not only reside in his well-known romantic scientific insights. The steady collection and analysis of data was in itself the basis of nineteenth-century science and a strong feature of other areas of thought—such as Doyle's own beloved history. And Holmes, it is less well-known, is also a master of the data of his subject. He has collected thousands of cases, can remember them and see the patterns of similarity in new problems: this power is in itself part of the Victorian romance of knowledge. Holmes does not 'deduce' in a vacuum; he understands through his materialist, association-based science the probable meanings of physical data and through the patterns of criminal action. This latter part of his armoury is, like his science, expressed in detail in *A Study in Scarlet* and touched on more lightly, but insistently, in the short stories.

The dispassionate isolation arising from Holmes's scientific powers meshes with his aloof, sometimes arrogant personal qualities. His drug-taking was, at that time, seen as an excitingly dangerous means of elevating and isolating the consciousness, closely bound up with the romantic artistic persona. His moody reveries, strangely atonal violin-playing, arrogant, dismissive tone to Watson are all other parts of the model of a superior being, a superman whose world differs from that of limited and often baffled people like Watson. The trenchant style Doyle gives to Holmes realises this aspect of his personality well, as does his occasional sarcasm, threatening Watson, and the audience, that he might cut himself adrift from their mundane realm. But he does not; Holmes is never the self-indulgent dandy American and French presentations of his figure have made of him, he is that familiar figure in English fable, the stern, distant yet ultimately helpful patronising hero.

The importance of this figure in nineteenth-century culture has been documented in W. E. Houghton's chapter on 'Hero Worship' in *The Victorian Frame of Mind*. Great emotional value was found in an individual who seemed to stand against the growing collective forces of mass politics, social determinism and scientific, super-individual explanation of the world, all of which appeared as mechanistic threats to the free individual. A figure like Holmes, who treated all problems individualistically and who founded his power on the very rational systems which had inhumane implications was a particularly welcome reversal of disturbing currents. Aloofness, self-assertion, irritation with everyday mediocrity were not merely forgivable—they were necessary parts of a credible comforting hero.

The crucial device by which Doyle makes this figure so effective is the limit he sets to Holmes's distance. The passage quoted above, where Watson tells how this machine-like scientist avoids emotion, ends by almost reconciling him with ordinary human feeling: 'And yet there was but one woman to him'. The story tells how Irene Adler can not only match his skill, but inspire something suspiciously like affectionate admiration in the hero. The whole characterisation of Holmes contains many dualities of this sort, that assert both his isolation and his contact with normality. He chooses to be a lone agent, but he takes cases, neither a mundane policeman nor a self-gratifying amateur. He is a self-confessed Bohemian, yet he lives in busy professional London, not in a Dupin-like romantic hermitage. He shares his lodgings with Watson, being neither a solitary nor matched by a partner. For all their eccentricity his rooms are cosy, filled with masculine gadgets for comfort. He will not eat when the hunt is up, but good meals are available, with a decent English housekeeper to provide them. He travels in normal conveyances, not some special heroic vehicle, yet his movements are sudden and dramatic. His atonal violin playing can give way to amusing Watson with favourite sentimental pieces, and he is a keen concert-goer—for him music is both private incommunicable reverie and social activity. His chemistry is smelly and dangerous, but can be practical and applied. His explanatory language, for all its learned aura, remains materialist, never withdrawing into the idealist intellectualism of Dupin. He works alone, often in disguise, but will

use agents and the street arabs of the Baker Street Irregulars, so revealing his demotic touch. His world is modern, real London, not some imagined or mistily foreign city.

These details make the critical link across the fissure between the special hero and the 'dull routine of existence' that at his most isolative he claims to abhor. The action of the stories sets this dualism in motion. In 'A Scandal in Bohemia'—Holmes's reasoning is interwoven with active investigation, disguise, play-acting and the dramatic activity of smoke bombs and mock blood. The thoroughness with which Doyle makes Holmes a dual figure is clear when he examines his client in 'A Case of Identity'. 'he looked her over in the minute and yet abstracted fashion which was peculiar to him'. It is his special power to embrace both detail and analysis. The mixture of modes is constant and intimate: Doyle's hero is never bogged in mundanity or lost in etherealness. Doyle never lets the audience forget either aspect of the hero.

The special, distant features of Holmes's personality are threaded through the stories. He has a copy of Petrarch on the train in 'The Boscombe Valley Mystery', he quotes Cuvier in 'The Five Orange Pips'. Yet neither writer is so abstruse to be unknown to the average reading man; the spread of science and the medieval tendency of much Victorian art made both figures known generally as the sort of thing knowledgeable people comprehended. The physical aloofness that authorises Holmes's greatest efforts is also touched on. He does not eat all day in 'The Five Orange Pips', he thinks with his eyes firmly closed in 'The Red-Headed League', he smokes all night in 'The Man with the Twisted Lip'.

Holmes's heroic quality is exerted in a professional direction. He accepts fees for his work, though only unusual rewards tend to be mentioned. But this mystification of his income does not mean he will not work for the public. Where Dupin's heroic action made him strangely, passively transformed, Holmes is enlivened when he engages with human problems. His eyes glitter on the chase in 'The Boscombe Valley Mystery' they sparkle through the smoke when he cracks the enigma of the notepaper in 'A Scandal in Bohemia'. Activity is often quite hectic, even when he is following, rather than elucidating events. Withdrawal is the state in which he activates his special resources of knowledge and insight, but these episodes are only the inspiration and impetus for busy, involved implementation of that almost oracular knowledge.

Apart from Holmes's involvement in ordinary life there are many occasions when he openly shares the values of his clients. To the lady typist in 'A Case of Identity' he shows 'the easy courtesy for which he was remarkable'. He often belittles his own ability with a proper English modesty and feels the threat of failure in a very native way. In 'The Man with the Twisted Lip' he says 'I think, Watson, that you are now standing in the presence of one of the most absolute fools in Europe. I deserve to be kicked from here to Charing Cross.' It is a demotic, physical, London-based self-deprecation. Holmes can feel restrained chagrin at a degree of failure; in 'The Five Orange Pips' when he hears of John Openshaw's death ' "That hurts my pride,

Watson," he said at last. "It is a petty feeling, no doubt, but it hurts my pride." '

This human side of Holmes is shown in his deference to Irene Adler, and he often has attitudes like a normal man about London. As the King of Bohemia arrives at Baker Street, he says 'A nice little brougham and a pair of beauties. A hundred and fifty guineas apiece. There's money in this case, Watson, if nothing else.' And as he reads the biography of Irene Adler from his files he deduces her status as a retired mistress with a slightly prurient amusement: ' "Contralto hum. La Scala, hum. Prima Donna Imperial Opera of Warsaw, yes. Retires from operatic stage—ha. Living in London—quite so." ' We find in Holmes many signs of the 'knowledge of the world' that he praises at the end of **'A Case of Identity',** and we also find disenchantment with aristocrats—a feature shared by many middle-class people, who felt both attraction and jealousy towards those of the undeniably upper-class. He is drily sharp to Lord St Simon in **'The Noble Bachelor'**.

> 'I understand you have already managed several delicate cases of this sort, sir, though I presume that they were hardly from the same class of society'.
>
> 'No, I am descending'.
>
> 'I beg pardon'?
>
> 'My last client of the sort was a king'.

But as the story develops we find this is not just an instinctive dislike of a lord; St Simon has dismissed a mistress with the inhumanity of the King of Bohemia. Holmes's rudeness turns out to be a moral evaluation, just as his ironic shaft at the King of Bohemia has a critical basis. The king asks of Irene Adler ' "Would she not have made an admirable queen? Is it not a pity she was not on my level?" ' Holmes's reply has fine irony: ' "From what I have seen of the lady, she seems, indeed, to be on a very different level to your Majesty," said Holmes coldly'. It is highly likely that this royal figure, like that in **'The Beryl Coronet'** is a transparent disguise for the Prince of Wales. Holmes is the agent of middle-class feeling against the manipulative, immoral hedonism of aristocrats. Sir George Burnwell in **'The Beryl Coronet'** is another; he leads both son and daughter astray and, according to his suggestive name, is headed for the everlasting bonfire.

Holmes's power to evaluate is ratified by his wide experience as well as his personal authority. He is in touch with all levels of society. In **'The Noble Bachelor'** a letter from St Simon, the son of a duke, reminds Watson that the morning's letters came from a fishmonger and a tide-waiter, that is a beachcomber in the tidal mud of the Thames. The extraordinary breadth of his experience, the story suggests, is one of the sources for Holmes's insight, just as he can turn street urchins into an effective force of detectives.

This contact with the lower reaches of London life is really a rhetorical flourish on Doyle's part, not crucial to the plotting; it is an extension of the complex by which Holmes is partly an ordinary man, partly a very superior figure. A similar piece of rhetoric, taken effectively from

Poe, is the simple-subtle paradox, as when Holmes speaks of 'those simple cases which are so extremely difficult'. These are finishing touches to the solidly created dual figure, aloof and yet available, who is constantly recreated and was clearly in Doyle's mind from the opening of the first story. The situation is put lucidly in **'The Red-Headed League'**, when Holmes says ' "My life is spent in one long effort to escape the commonplaces of existence" ' but he is reassured by Watson, high priest of the commonplace, ' "And you are a benefactor of the race." ' Doyle himself has sent up a cloud of triumphant characterisation, a smoky illusion concealing the real nature of detecting crime and the difficulty of controlling contemporary threats to order. To read further into the appropriateness of Doyle's image of Holmes, his cigarette smoke was blue, and the whole creation fulfils the implications of that colour in the period. The aura of chivalry, of patronising autocracy and essential conservatism is a pervasive feature of the heroic personality and its function.

The effect is not only Doyle's work. Sidney Paget's dramatic illustrations of the hero did much to create the incisive and consoling image. He provided the legendary deer-stalker hat that naturalised Holmes's hunter-protector element, and by the time of **'The Boscombe Valley Mystery'** Doyle had altered his earlier description of Holmes's features to fit Paget's authoritative version. Paget's flair linked Doyle's imaginative creation to the exciting new force of the illustrated medium, and he caught exactly the aloof nobility and material bourgeois setting so important to the duality that is central to the power of Holmes as a figure. Paget used as his model his elder brother, in itself a relevant image of authoritative familial guidance. His brother was the man [George Newnes, founder of *The Strand*] had meant to commission for the illustrations, but by a most irrational error the job went to Sidney instead. It is a fine revealing irony; inside the all explaining image are fragments of human chaos: beneath the production of the text lie the strains the text is dedicated to resolving.

The creation of Watson does not have the weight that the more overt feeling and greater length of the story gave him in *The Sign of Four*. In the early stories Watson is married, but by various plot devices is with Holmes through most of the action. From **'The Speckled Band'** on Doyle goes back in time before Watson's wedding. This does not diminish him as the representative of family solidity and bourgeois morality: Doyle has settled down for a long series of stories and presumably did not want to explain each time how Holmes and his narrator came together.

Watson personifies the virtues of middle-class manhood: loyal, honest and brave—these features come out especially in **'The Red-Headed League', 'The Speckled Band'** and **'The Copper Beeches.'** Holmes explains all to him, and so to the audience, but Doyle avoids letting Watson stand as the presence of the audience in the story. His characterisation enables the reader to see him as a little foolish, and so to by-pass him and construct the one-to-one relation with Holmes that the underlying individualist epistemology requires. Doyle achieves this delicate and important effect largely through a careful modelling of Watson's voice. At times it is a hopeful imitation of Holmes's decisiveness, a deferential recognition of his mastery; but he can also be sharp enough to remind Holmes of the values of common humanity. But between these two tones that indicate the limits of Holmes's dual personality lies the tone that is Doyle's triumph, the one that Watson adopts to comment at a story's beginning. It is the voice of a mildly self-satisfied bourgeois who feels he has a mastery of things: a slightly wordy style, a little too much insertion of the first person pronoun and his own self-conscious opinions, along with a delicately banal rhythm. The opening of **'The Beryl Coronet'** is a good example: " 'Holmes," said I, as I stood one morning in our bow-window looking down the street, "here is a madman coming along. It seems rather sad that his relatives should allow him out alone." ' The fussy inversion of said I', the flat prepositional phrases that follow, the carefully limited 'rather sad' all sketch the figure with almost subliminal effect. The reader can like him, admire his virtues, but also can suspect the situation is more complex and threatening than Watson can really handle. The hero's greater incisiveness is needed to control anxieties. The closeness Watson has to Holmes links the detective firmly to the actual bourgeois world; the crucial difference between them, the definite diminishing of Watson through his own mouth are the features which make the hero distant from and also immediately, personally accessible to an anxious, individualist bourgeois audience.

The major effect of Doyle's characterisation is a duality of the familiar and the exotic: this exists between Watson and Holmes and within Holmes himself, as has just been demonstrated. It is no surprise, then, to see that the methods by which Holmes solves problems are themselves dual in effect, a set of fairly simple procedures within an aura of elaboration. In the novellas Doyle carefully described 'The Science of Deduction'—a chapter heading in each book—and established Holmes's credibility as a master of scientific and criminological knowledge. Then he went on to show him making fairly straightforward, commonsense deductions. In the short stories a similar illusion is at work, but the higher qualifications are not clearly realised. There are general statements like 'He was still, as ever, deeply attracted by the study of crime, and occupied his immense faculties and extraordinary powers of observation in following out those clues, and clearing up those mysteries, which had been abandoned as hopeless by the official police.' This appears in the opening of **'A Scandal in Bohemia'** and sets the tone for the series in *The Strand.* Later on, in **'The Five Orange Pips'** Watson mentions 'those peculiar qualities which my friend possessed in so high a degree' Less stress is laid on science and information, more on 'those deductive methods of reasoning by which he achieved such remarkable results' (in **'The Engineer's Thumb'** or 'severe reasoning from cause to effect' (in **'The Copper Beeches'**). (pp. 70-86)

Pierre Nordon is one of the few critics to have discussed Doyle's work along socio-cultural lines; he has pointed out the special selection of the crimes involved, but his analysis of the situation seems over-simple. He suggests a line is drawn between the rich and the poor, and that villains in the stories before 1910 tend to be 'the calculating enemies of order'. There are figures who emerge in the second collection of stories who fit such a description, notably Charles Augustus Milverton and Professor Moriarty himself. But these ogres simplify Doyle's meaning by naturalising evil, giving it an incorrigible presence in dedicated villains, and in the opening volume of stories that first gripped the reading world things are not so simplistic. The evil that arises from selfishness in *The Adventures* is often expressed in calculating terms and does usually seek money; it is also certainly a threat to order as well as property. But Nordon's summary wrongly identifies an embattled class seeing and facing enemies outside itself. Doyle is more self-conscious, more attuned to middle-class worries about the ability to protect and reproduce itself. His stories do not present the foreign, loathsome enemies encountered by Sexton Blake, Bulldog Drummond or, in the modern period, by James Bond. Doyle offers fables in which the class whose language, epistemology and values are enacted can examine the dangers that arise if its members are untrue to its codes.

It is important to recognise that doubt and fear are firmly directed at other members of the class, their potential failure to remain faithful to the shared morality. Yet none of the stories imply a sense that the individual might himself fail to maintain these standards; this is achieved through the absolute trustworthiness of Watson and the clients who bring the problems to Holmes. Watson never fails in morality, however inadequate his intellect might be. Through him the stories express self-confidence in bourgeois ethics and by recognising his limitations they clarify the need to know more, to improve the educational skills of the audience to defend their personal moral fortresses. The clients who invoke Holmes's special intellectual force are always puzzled, but never dishonest or immoral. Agatha Christie will develop a sense of disquiet about the self by using unreliable or criminal narrators, and Raymond Chandler will isolate the hero by making his clients untrustworthy. But here a series of respectable people experience disorder, and an unfailingly honest narrator and a comforting reliable hero close ranks with them. At the same time, the stories never invoke intelligence in the clients, never suggest the reader can match the hero's intellectual power: he is accessible, but not imitatable. Later writers allow the reader to doubt the existence of a shared and automatically restorative morality and also suggest the reader can match the intellectual skill of the hero; the next chapter will discuss this pattern.

The only enemy clearly identified outside the class is the aristocrat who does not subscribe to middle-class values—an interesting corroboration of the fact that through the nineteenth century the upper-class had steadily become more bourgeois in outlook. Here too Doyle could sense and realise the forces of his period. This fear of a distinct aristocratic class and its different values is a part of the uncertainty that arose from the middle-class awareness that it had 'made itself', and that its successful position depended on vigilance, on a sustained defence and propagation of the virtues that seemed central to its continued security. The fact that they 'seemed' central is important. Doyle's stories are concerned with property and money, but they do not show acquisitiveness and protection of money as virtues in themselves. Money and property are considered the natural result of correct ethics, and failure in morality causes the attack on property and even on life. Dr Roylott, the memorable villain of **'The Speckled Band'** is an eccentric irascible man as well as greedy for his step-daughters' property; John Clay is a renegade gentleman and a thief; James Ryder is weak and so tempted by the great carbuncle; Sir George Burnwell is a profligate first and a thief second—and the nobleman who puts the beryl coronet in pawn and triggers the whole crime has himself acted badly to come to this state.

Weber argued that protestant ethics were a substantive cause of bourgeois financial success; others have agreed with Marx that the pervasive bourgeois morality was an ideological screen for the acquisitive and self-defensive instincts of a newly self-conscious class. Whatever the truth of the dispute, Doyle's stories dramatise the dialectic effect of that morality: it both justifies the possession of property and is shown protecting the possessors in their comfort.

The nature of the resolutions themselves is an important part of the ideology of the stories. Only rarely does the legal system operate at the end of a case. An arrest is made in **'The Red-Headed League'** but we hear no more of the criminals; they are out of sight and out of interest. Comprehension of their attempt has been enough to dissolve their threat. In **'The Blue Carbuncle'** and **'The Boscombe Valley Mystery'** for Holmes to know all is for him to pardon: one criminal dies naturally, the other is set on what we are asked to believe will be a life of reform. In several stories punishment is autonomous, rising from the machinations of the criminal. The grisly fates of Dr Roylott and Jephro Rucastle, attacked by their own savage animals, are satisfying self-created judgements, and in **'The Five Orange Pips'** the stormy weather that broods over the whole story is the indiscriminate agent of fate, sinking the ship *Lone Star*—apparently with all hands, innocent as well as guilty. In **'A Scandal in Bohemia'** and **'The Noble Bachelor'** no actual penalty falls on those who have directly caused the disorder; Holmes's scorn punishes the aristocrats judged to have been most at fault—and this kind of resolution operates in **'The Beryl Coronet'** as Sir George Burnwell gets away with a mere £600 for his boldly immoral crime and feels Holmes's contempt. Doyle, like many middle-class people, cherished ideas of his family's past grandeur—his mother was obsessed with heraldry, especially that of her family. His scorn for aristocrats who failed in their moral duty was strong and expresses both the middle-class dislike of and impotence towards the classes they admired and sought to join. Such class values cause Holmes's contempt for James Windibank in **'A Case of Identity'**. He has shown improper greed and broken familial ties; the threatened beating is the traditional punishment for a man who betrays a woman. The only criminals who escape unscathed are the coiners of **'The Engineer's Thumb'**; the destruction of their press is certainly a handicap to them, and it may be the real purpose of the story, as will be discussed below. (pp. 91-4)

The emphasis here has been to establish the social meaning of the patterns of form and content in Doyle's stories.

This crucial aspect has been too little observed. But as with Poe's stories, the ideology, however much a shared one, is essentially that of personal achievement and personal morality threatened in a subjectively perceived way—and ultimately defended by an individualistic hero to whom the audience relates on a one-to-one basis. It would be surprising, then, if there were not some resonances in the stories of Doyle's own anxieties. One obvious channel for these, so clearly present in Poe, lies in the hints that respond to Freudian analysis. Neither the space nor the expertise is available here to identify these features in any satisfactorily full way, but two aspects of male anxiety seem to thread their way through the stories.

Loss of masculinity is the fear behind some details. For all his vigour the King of Bohemia is crucially weakened because Irene Adler (her name in his own language means that rapacious bird, the eagle) has locked away a power totem in her most secret compartment. Jabez Wilson, whose head is aflame with virility, is suborned in his own house, and his betrayers penetrate the bank, that fastness of security, by a suggestive back passage. The vigorous, phallic-necked animal that would make James Ryder as powerful as his surname implies, is found to be empty of its stone. Victor Hatherley loses his thumb, a prime phallic symbol; Neville St Clair becomes hideous and deformed in the quest for money; Lord St Simon finds his wife has disappeared and belonged all the time to someone else.

This last case perhaps moves away from sheer loss of masculinity to the other main anxiety, the fear of supplanting that is most firmly felt by the father for the daughter; several stories act out this family drama. James Windibank not only desires his stepdaughter to stay at home and allow him to control her person and property, he actually provides a suitably weak-voiced and unthreatening rival to himself. Dr Roylott goes so far as to attack his stepdaughter with a snake, forced through a hole he has pierced in her wall. Alexander Holder (a tenacious man?) finds his daughter's virtue is stolen along with the jewelled coronet that symbolises it as well as wealth and honour; the tug of war between the supplanter and the son who, though suspected by the father is still his own image, shatters the perfect circle. **'The Copper Beeches'** also presents a possessive father whose neck, well-known phallic object, is savaged by the beast kept in his own home as his daughter is finally lost. There may well be many more such details, and a close analysis would chart the meaning more fully. But the presence of such material can hardly be denied; here too Doyle has the power to realise the fears and urges that seethed in the respectable personality and that needed to be contained by normative influences like the unperturbable yet comprehending hero Sherlock Holmes. If there were any doubt of Doyle's artistic sense of these topics, they would be dispelled by a glance at his novella *The Parasite*. Written in 1894, this vivid case study of a man possessed by the id only achieves the triumph of the superego by the foreclosing coincidental incursion of Victorian moralism. The vicar arrives just before the hero is about to destroy his proper, respectable lady friend for the sake of the ugly but powerful and sensual woman who has possessed him. (pp. 95-6)

When *The Adventures* had been running for only six months Doyle wrote in his diary 'Holmes keeps my mind from better things'. But even before this his interest in Holmes was limited. After completing **'The Boscombe Valley Mystery'** Doyle had a bad attack of influenza, and on recovering decided to be a full-time writer. It was not the Holmes stories he saw as his métier—his mind was on another historical novel, to be *The Refugees*. But he did complete the promised half-dozen Holmes stories. The next was **'The Five Orange Pips'** where the strong resonance of the past-crime plot of the novellas suggests the barrel is being audibly scraped and where Holmes comes close to failure. The sixth story was **'The Man with the Twisted Lip'**. In this and **'The Engineer's Thumb'** Doyle appears to be dramatising his dislike of the Holmes phenomenon, his sense that it weighs him down and interferes with his real work and his self-respect.

The two stories are linked by unusual structural features—which first drew my attention to them as a pair. In both stories Watson controls the opening action, pushing Holmes into the background in a surprising way and when he appears his powers are considerably reduced, as they were in the preceding adventure. He is mistaken for most of **'The Man with the Twisted Lip'**, saving himself by a quite unexplained piece of overnight deduction, and in **'The Engineer's Thumb'** he makes only one simple piece of analysis (that the villains drove round in a circle). Holmes's limitations and Watson's added weight suggest a doubt in Doyle's mind about the validity of the hero. The symbolic meaning of the stories' content makes it clear that this arises from Doyle's unusual element of self-expression.

'The Man with the Twisted Lip' tells the story of a respectable reporter who, in the course of a special commission, finds he can earn more disguised as a deformed, sharp-tongued beggar in the city than in his real employment. When he is short of money he takes up the role again and begging becomes his livelihood. Ultimately his wife sees him in circumstances that will reveal his shameful state. He is unable to reappear as himself, and so is accused of his own murder.

The parallels with what Doyle felt he was doing are obvious. A respectable writer, for the sake of gaining large sums of money in a way he has accidentally discovered, degrades himself and takes profits made in the street from City workers. Doyle, *The Strand* and the Holmes phenomenon are effectively symbolised. The beggar reveals Doyle's projected fear. A handsome body is distorted and a mouth that should produce decent speech is twisted into a sneer to bring in more cash; this shameful practice amounts to a murder of the real self, a betrayal of the family. 'It was a long fight between my pride and my money, but the dollars won at last' says the disgraced man. When Holmes finally sifts the matter he wipes clean the soiled face, restoring honour and clean upright life to the money-dazzled reporter.

It is a fascinating allegory, revealing Doyle's growing dislike of what he saw as vulgar potboilers which kept him from the scholarly and overtly moralising work of his historical novels. Watson's introduction itself offers an even

more alarming model, a respectable well-connected man who, becoming a drug-addict was 'an object of mingled horror and pity to his friends' and was no more than 'the wreck and ruin of a noble man'.

Apart from these patent traces of meaning and the reduced power of Holmes himself, there is a quite unusual intensity of feeling in the writing. Doyle rarely works with imagery, but this story is rich with motifs of light and dark more intense even than those of *The Sign of Four*. Holmes and Watson drive through 'sombre and deserted streets' across 'the murky river' through 'a wilderness of bricks and mortar' and the reporter's wife stands 'with her figure outlined against the flood of light' from her warm respectable house. When he begins to grasp the case Holmes says 'the clouds lighten' and when he has cracked the problem he and Watson go out into 'the bright morning sunshine'. This sort of emotional landscape has been used generally in the novellas, but here it is locked into the meaning of the man defined by his own situation, by his own filth that is washed away and, above all, by being called Neville St Clair. The aristocratic Christian name and the holy light of the surname have been besmirched in shameful money-grubbing—the fact that it came as a sudden, unexpected and eventually troubling gift may well be subconsciously expressed in his beggar's name, Hugh Boon.

The problem is still resolved by Holmes, limited though his powers might be. This clarifies Doyle's ambiguous relationship with his hero. Though he is still writing stories he dislikes, he actually uses the distasteful hero to resolve the problem that, symbolically at least, has been set by that figure. In his own anxiety Doyle employs the absolving force of the hero who combines isolated intellectualism and social service: in the story Holmes does for Doyle just what he did for Doyle's kin among his audience.

Having worked out his feelings in this manner Doyle refused to provide more stories. But as the public and Newnes clamoured for more he weakened, demanding £50 a story in the hope of a refusal. Newnes agreed gladly and Doyle had to set to work again. His professionalism and the relief found in the previous story set the next two, **'The Blue Carbuncle'** and **'The Speckled Band'**, among his most brilliant efforts, vigorously written and inventively plotted. Yet the shadow of Holmes was not so easily dispersed, as the later events reveal, and as is plain in **'The Engineer's Thumb'**, a more deeply troubled story than **'The Man with the Twisted Lip'**.

Here Holmes is distanced further from events at the start of the story, as Watson actually brings the case to him. Watson is himself consulted and acts with Holmesian decisiveness. This reduction of Holmes's force in the action leaves an emotive gap filled by Doyle himself: the figure of Victor Hatherley, the client, is very much like the author. Hatherley is a consulting scientific specialist with few clients, seduced by a lucrative offer that turns out to be disabling. The Doyle who has just decided to give up his specialist's role for writing, but who has Newnes's money to weigh him down is clearly enough presented. More sharply still Hatherley has shown the link between his own engineering knowledge and medicine in his ability to treat his wound; his 'suit of heather tweed with a soft cloth cap' and 'strong masculine face' could come straight from a surviving photograph of the young Doyle. The client's disturbing involvement is not, as was Neville St Clair's, a matter of impersonation and losing self-respect. The threat is deeper and more damaging; Hatherley has been seduced into dealing with people who, for all their vigour and apparent respectability, are criminals, and their crime is literally to make money with a press—of all things. (pp. 97-100)

The plot tells how the press closes in on the young idealist just as he discovers the false villainy of the whole operation. The light he has, literally, brought in burns down the press but though he escapes with his life he leaves behind his thumb—a clear sign that he has lost his masculinity in the process. The story has the wish-fulfilling power to illuminate and destroy the whole of Newnes's establishment, but the villains themselves are untouched. They do vanish: they are exorcised from consciousness at least, but not destroyed. True to the legends of Victorian manhood, a good woman has saved the hero; but the crippling wound remains. Holmes has watched all this happening without any real act of analysis, but the authority of his final words gives comfort to the client as if he really were an author: 'you have only to put it into words to gain the reputation of being excellent company for the remainder of your existence'.

This final comment shows Doyle's anxiety to avoid being the shameful outcast pictured twice in the earlier story, and his desire to gain and hold respect through his chosen profession of author. The greater disturbance of this story, compared with **'The Man with the Twisted Lip'**. is shown by the increased obscurity and distancing of the symbolism, by the client's career being that of the Doyle who was not a writer, and in the failure of Holmes or any other agency to find the villains. There is no renewal here, just a wished for destruction of the press, and a remaining sense of emasculation. The debilitation that gave rise to the story seems to have lasted; the next, **'The Noble Bachelor'**, continues the theme of impotence though it is distanced further from Doyle because the client is a feeble aristocrat. In spite of this partial recovery, the story shows how Doyle was exhausted by his exegesis of anxiety: it is one of the weakest of all the Holmes stories, as Doyle later admitted.

The pattern covertly present in these two stories is fascinating. Firmly in the grip of contemporary moralistic ideas about what was good art, Doyle could not see the ideological function for a particular audience (including himself) of his work. Critics can be as blind as authors; Charles Higham, in his recent book *The Adventures of Conan Doyle,* can do no more than trace these two stories to fairly similar events in contemporary news reports. This approach, itself reifying and fragmenting the force of fiction, belittles both the imaginative power Doyle possessed and the neurotically urgent pressure of the stories. (pp. 100-01)

The Holmes stories, especially in the period when Doyle's success and Holmes's nature were formed, are a contemporary analogue to a series of folk-tales, or a set of epic lays in which a figure fitted to be a culture-hero of his peri-od was presented in a medium and form technologically and epistemologically valid for a contemporary class. The function of epic and folk-tale has been well described by anthropologists and folklorists; a most succinct account of their social meaning, along with other human behaviour, has been given by Clifford Geertz (who describes himself as an anthropologist of culture). Man, he says, is an un-completed animal who completes himself through culture. Through his habits, rituals and fictions he explains the world to himself and justifies his place and his actions in that world. Month by month in *The Strand Magazine* readers could see, through the plots, the crimes and the criminals of the Holmes stories, an account of what they felt might go wrong in a world that was recognisably theirs and which was, through the force of omissions and the formation of its problematic, one where their own sets of values would work. The consolations were great, and the wit and verve of Doyle's writing give those comforts the illusory vitality of a living system. The essential functions of folk-tale are to explain the world, to protect the folk against psychic and physical threats, to offer escapist entertainment and to be socially normative—to urge that these values will keep society on an even keel, resist dis-commoding change. All of these functions are manifest in the Holmes stories: we find scientistic and rational explanation of a materially known world; the psychic protection of a powerful hero and the exclusion of real physical threats from the plots; lively dialogue, wry jokes and sensually sharp presentation of admired objects and valued feelings; and above all central bourgeois values which operate through Holmes as the tools of maintaining order,

---

Doyle's interest in science fiction:

There seemed to be no special reason why Doyle should have returned to the serious writing of science fiction, as he did in 1912. If it had happened in 1909 it might have been attributed to his presiding at the centenary dinner at the Metropole of the birth of Edgar Allan Poe, in which he paid homage to the memory of a man whose inspiration had profoundly influenced every aspect of his early work. Perhaps it was the example of H. G. Wells, a friend and correspondent, who had established his reputation in the world of the scientific romance. Whatever the reason, he wrote to Greenhough Smith, editor of *The Strand,* regarding *The Lost World:*

> I think it will make the very best serial (bar special S. Holmes values) that I have ever done, especially when it has its trimming of faked photos, maps, and plans. *My ambition is to do for the boys' book what Sherlock Holmes did for the detective tale. I don't suppose I could bring off two such coups. And yet I hope it may.*

A goal had been set. A. Conan Doyle was determined to build for himself a reputation in science fiction as great as the one that caused him to be canonized by detective story lovers.

Sam Moskowitz, in his Explorers of the Infinite: Shapers of Science Fiction, *1963.*

and through the victims as the qualities that earn Holmes's care and deserve the correction of disorder about them. (p. 103)

> Stephen Knight, " '. . . A Great Blue Triumphant Cloud'—'The Adventures of Sherlock Holmes'," in his Form and Ideology in Crime Fiction, *Indiana University Press, 1980, pp. 67-106.*

George E. Slusser   (essay date 1981)

[*Slusser is an American educator and critic with a special interest in science fiction and fantasy literature. In the following essay, he examines Doyle's science fiction stories.*]

At first glance Conan Doyle's tales might seem to have little to do with science fiction. Indeed, in those stories that deal with the otherworldly, the author appears more interested in occult phenomena than in scientific occurrence, turned more toward the prehistoric past than the future, toward lost worlds rather than new ones. And yet, despite surface appearances, these stories clearly address what many theorists still consider the central problem of the genre: what Isaac Asimov calls "the impact of scientific advance upon human beings." What is ultimately important is to determine the manner in which his works address this problem and to define the thematic and formal configurations that result. The tales in question span, essentially, a period from the *fin de siecle* to the 1920s, a historical moment dominated by World War I and marked by the final extension and beginning dissolution of empire. In them, science is not considered as an epistemological problem so much as an agent of change and movement, as technology. And if then this science, in turn, has become a menace, it is again not to man's perceptual or conceptual security but to his physical existence itself. During this period changing and increasingly violent social and cultural conditions not only give new urgency to the theory of evolution, but in doing so seem to bring about a greatly altered relationship between positivistic science and a natural world suddenly become more than simply recalcitrant, but now terrifyingly atavistic, cataclysmic even. Throughout more than four decades of work in diverse story forms—many like the "lost-race" and "future-war" narrative and the tale of occult "science" considered forerunners of the genre or tangential to it—Conan Doyle develops consistent strategies to deal with the contradictory impact of contemporary science, with simultaneous belief in technological progress and fear of evolutionary regression. This preoccupation places Doyle firmly in the British tradition of science fiction that reaches from Wells to recent writers like Aldiss and Clarke.

Less a purist than Asimov, Kingsley Amis sees as the fundamental condition for the creation of science fictional situations "some innovation in science or technology, or pseudoscience and pseudotechnology." And to be sure, in the tales considered here, pseudoscience always seeks to cover the supernatural, and instead of mediums and seances we have "psychometry." The technological innovations they describe, on the other hand, are very real: new motors, dynamos, airplanes, submarines. Be it pseudoscience or real technology, however, practical concerns invariably take precedence over speculative or purely theoretical ones. The reason for this is that both science and technology seem to have, for Doyle, the same function: to uncover and ultimately harness the primal powers of nature. To this end, both provide means of actual physical exploration. Psychometry, for instance, posits that spirit inheres in objects in such a way that they may act as vehicles to carry one elsewhere, or even back in time, to the place where they were first charged with the emotional energy they convey. Yet this search to control primal forces can and does lead to an unleashing of the uncontrollable, the pursuit of innovation paradoxically to resurgence of some horrible primitive past. Thus in **"The Leather Funnel,"** a story bearing many similarities with the ones in this Collection, the psychometric exercise summons nameless terrors that cause the experimenter to retreat to his well-ordered present: "I writhed, I struggled, I broke through the bonds of sleep, and I burst with a shriek into my own life. . . . Oh, what a blessed relief to feel that I was back in the nineteenth century—back out of that medieval vault into a world where men had human hearts within their bosoms." Emblematic perhaps of the paradox of scientific "research" in Conan Doyle is the climactic scene of the novel *The Lost World,* too long to be included here, although the collection contains two stories featuring its protagonist. Here Professor Challenger, the archetypal scientist whose very name is innovation, comes to unleash—in the guise of scientific demonstration, as "proof " of the existence of the world he has discovered—a hideous pterodactyl in the midst of the assembled Zoological Society.

The obverse of science then seems to be horror. And again and again in Conan Doyle we see the importance of horror to a genre which Darko Suvin, in a recent definition, claims has always been dominated by a rationalist vision. "Estrangement" in science fiction, for Suvin, exists to serve cognition. As a formal device it is used to generate a fictional *novum,* a new world which must be validated by cognitive means, for only cognition can guarantee such concepts as purposive change, progress, futurity. Conan Doyle's tales turn these terms around. Cognition quite literally serves estrangement, for to pursue rational inquiry or orderly advance, such as the aviator rising step by calculated step in **"The Horror of the Heights,"** invariably leads to an encounter with regressive, atavistic forces that shatter all pretense at cognitive advance. Suvin may be wrong then to place his generic boundary at a point separating science fiction and horror as cognitive and anticognitive modes. What we seem to have, rather, are elements in the same generic system. The presence of the anticognitive need not signal a qualitative shift from the empirical to the supernatural realm, but rather a reversal occurring entirely within natural space, the assertion of an irrational and monstrous "nightside" to the idea of scientific progress. In fact, this dayside and nightside is portrayed with such acuity in Conan Doyle's fiction that it forms, as a set of contrasting images, its distinctive organizing polarity. Loving and detailed descriptions of man-made objects, such as the Paul Veroner monoplane in **"The Horror of the Heights"** with its "ten cylinder rotary Robur engine" and "all the modern improvements—

enclosed fusilage, high-curved landing skids . . . gyro-scopic steadiers, and three speeds, worked by an alteration of the angle of the planes upon the Venetian blind princi-ple," constantly call forth nightmare images from the bio-logical realm. The "horror" encountered in the upper air is both "loathsome" and predatory: "The vague, goggling eyes which were turned always upon me were cold and merciless in their viscid hatred." Likewise, the creature Professor Challenger retrieves and unleashes on civiliza-tion in *The Lost World* summons from the narrator a se-ries of atavistic images. It has a face "like the wildest gar-goyle," a savage mouth full of a "double row of shark-like teeth"; it is "the devil of our childhood," emitting a "pu-trid and insidious odor" as it soars from the room. In a sense, this monstrous reversion of airplane to flying mon-ster symbolizes what is, generally in Conan Doyle, retreat from the future to the past, from science to myth. What is more, the cause of such reversals appears to be cognition itself, the process of knowing or seeking to know. With the rigor of an equation, the aviator's obsessive search for knowledge through his machine in **"The Horror of the Heights"** releases the implacable hate of the airborne monster that displaces him. In like manner, Challenger's rational demonstration culminates by invoking the ulti-mate irrationality, a devil in flesh and blood.

At work here then is a particular compensating dynam-ic—where technology, mind-imposed order, calls forth or-ganic monstrosity, mind-shattering chaos—probably born in the renaissance of conflict between an emerging modern science and a resisting medieval world order, and repre-senting a psychic need on the part of man to maintain him-self, as creature formed of mind and body, at the norma-tive center of a natural world now conceived in terms of process and change. Indeed, a system of compensation is already fully at work in Swift's *Gulliver's Travels,* where the projective schemes of science invariably lead to those monstrous physical regressions symbolized by the endless-ly decaying *struldburgs*. This dynamic was given greater amplitude, however, by the accelerated rhythm of scientif-ic speculation in the 19th century, especially by the hopes and fears raised with evolutionary theory, where all excite-ment at man's intellectual domination of nature is perpet-ually dampened by vistas of purposeless, monstrous forces called forth by this bold theorizing itself. In this context Conan Doyle's tales, which as "popular" works seem so open to the collective fears and aspirations of this scientific century, force comparison with the narrative mode most probably their true successor—the science fiction film. Not only are both dominated by the same system of im-ages—and Doyle's stories are eminently "filmic" in their structure, based on sharp visualized contrasts—but they are essentially cathartic in nature, affecting reader and viewer alike as rites of humbling which paradoxically do not displace man from the center so much as reinstate him (if in diminished form) in that position. Both modes then are, in essence, antievolutionary in nature, governed not by a complex rhythm of struggle and change so much as by a simpler binary logic reminiscent of the Pascalian "contrariety"—as man rises he is lowered, as man falls he is raised up.

In a sense, the dynamic of the science fiction film could serve as gloss for Conan Doyle's tales. It centers on the constant relationship of man to machine and organism, to his extensions and his origins, to the future he would build in hopes of escaping his biological destiny by using and perhaps ultimately becoming a machine, and the past he would renounce only to have it recur in the most primitive forms to remind him of his median position between these two impulses. Increasingly, from the 19th century on, organic process has been seen in an evolutionary light as random tooth-and-claw violence in need of control through technology, the construction of a mechanized landscape to replace the natural one. To do so, however, is to invite resurgence of this repressed organic force—in forms all the more monstrous for their repression—through some unexpected or forgotten chink in the mech-anistic structure. In the film, in fact, we learn that the most frequent channel of reentry is "dehumanized" man him-self, to whom the organic recurs as "thing" from his cul-tural, racial, or biological past. Thus, within the ordered world of *Metropolis,* the mechanized future city with its upper and lower layers, emerges a parallel structure from the dark Gothic past, also with its upper and lower areas, Rotwang's primeval hut and Maria's catacombs, an in-verted funnel through which black magic invades white, then explodes as destructive, organic chaos into the city itself. A recent film like *Alien* places this dynamic on a basic morphological level, where expulsion of the organic becomes the direct cause of its monstrous resurgence. Into the overly mechanized world of their spaceship—a metal womb and tomb presided over by a travesty of the procre-ative forces, a family unit where "father" is the Company, "mother" the central computer that does its bidding, their offspring the robot science officer Ash—the crew in pur-suit of its mission reintroduces a primal organic form whose subsequent (and destructive) evolutionary course literally transforms machine landscapes into writhing liv-ing shapes, turns cords and cables into intestines, digestive rather than thinking entities.

If anything, Conan Doyle's science fictional vision is even more restrictive in its depiction of the dilemma of modern technological man. As vision, it not only radically quali-fies the turn-of-the-century myth of empire built on tech-nological mastery of the natural environment, on the tam-ing of elemental and racial savagery into institutionalized civility, but also contradicts the world view that sustains Doyle's own creation, Sherlock Holmes, the age's most popular incarnation of rationalistic positivism. Instead we have man cleaving in almost agoraphobic fashion to the streamlined shells he has constructed—the well-ordered world of social conveniences and railroad schedules—in terror of primal forces lurking beyond. Yet in his isolation he must be reminded that he too—both in his body and in the very energy that drives him to achieve "progress"— not only partakes of these forces but even provides, in the act of moving to exclude them, a conduit for their violent reentry into the closed spaces his technology has built. With Doyle then we have, more than simply a dionysian "underside," a total encirclement of fragile human order akin to the landscape of *Beowulf,* where man's efforts are a feeble point of light surrounded on all sides by Grendel's darkness. In most of Conan Doyle's science fiction tales, technology has provided merely the thinnest film of order, a delicately suspended *status quo*. From this plane the least foray into surrounding spaces, each act of scientific curiosity or exploration, leads to the monsters Doyle sees lurking everywhere—in the earth or in the air, in the past and in the future. Only this flattest of presents is safe ground. And it is safe, apparently, only because it is continually reaffirmed by these incursions into monstrous space, through almost ritualistic encounters with chaos that lead to those miraculous reprieves epitomized by the last line of **"The Lift"**: "By Jove, that was a close call!"

And yet, however restrictive the landscape of Doyle's tales may seem, the pattern that emerges from this interplay of basic images—man, machine and monster—is ultimately both complex and suggestive. This interplay suggests first of all, on its simplest level, the ambiguity of technology as a mode of action. For the force that constructs present order by banishing the chaotically organic into the past or the future at the same time provides both the lure and the means of adventuring out of that present to lands that time forgot or, through controlled transmission of spirit, toward worlds to come. The machine then that would expel monsters actually begets them, in both directions indiscriminately, and in spatial and temporal realms alike. In this sense, then, Doyle provides a link between Wells's entropic future in *The Time Machine* and a work like Brian

Sherlock Holmes and Professor Moriarty struggle in "The Final Problem." Portrait by Sidney Paget.

Aldiss's *Cryptozoic!*, which posits absolute reversibility of future and past and offers the possibility that our evolutionary end is actually one with our beginning in primal chaos. It is, in fact, just such a possibility that raises for Doyle a second, deeper question. For technology here appears in danger of becoming a self-regulating process, an automatic exchange on the machine-monster axis from which man, at the point where he ceases to use machines and begins to be used by them, vanishes altogether as active term, becomes at best a passive onlooker or victim. In his insistence, however, on locating man in this otherwise binary landscape as a third connecting term, Doyle not only asserts man's involvement in the process of making machines but raises the question of human responsibility as well. Paradoxically, many so-called parables of technology actually seek to efface the question of technology—the relation of man to machine—by excluding man from the equation through this very act of revealing the machine itself to be the monster. The pivot here is often a concept like "sentience," which delineates the moment when, magically, the machine is given independent will and turns to dominate its maker. We see this sudden, unmediated conflation of poles in a tale like Harlan Ellison's "I Have No Mouth and I Must Scream," where a giant computer "born" of man's hate finally effaces man altogether by making him a monstrous blob of flesh, and thus suspending the struggles of technological man in a juxtaposition of machine and monster as mirror doubles. The same fusion constantly operates in the imagistic configurations of films: Rotwang's robot is instantly transmuted into the monstrous "false" Maria; the Frankenstein monster, spawned of the apparatus in the film's famous laboratory, emerges an amalgam, with plugs on its head and creaking gait, of the organic and the mechanical; finally the gradual animation of the machine landscape in *Alien* reduces man to the role of horrified spectator, unable to reflect that he, initially, built the machine that begat the monster. With Doyle, however, a different pattern of imagery occurs. Here the process of conflation turns upon the inclusion of man rather than his exclusion, and the result is a series of hybrid forms whose position is determined by this common term, a system of shifts built on such couplings as beast-man and man-machine, and distributed along an axis that remains centered in man. Literally, visually, in Doyle man cannot make a machine and loose it on the world without remaining part of it himself, thus through this hybridization marking it as an extension of his will rather than a separate entity. The difference here is subtle but crucial, for man in making his machine does not simply make a monster so much as he, in the process of creating it, becomes a monster himself. Monstrosity here then is ultimately of a very different form, one which visually, in these hybrids, both subsumes and mirrors man's moral responsibility by grotesquely distorting it, by insistently linking the sought-for extremes of machine and primal organism to a perniciously abiding human center. In a sense then this rhythm, at the price of restoring homocentricity, delineates these extremes, and by doing so resists the dehumanization of technology that increasingly marks later science fiction.

This particular mode of resistence is not unique to Conan Doyle, however, but rather places him solidly in a tradition of British science fiction that runs from Wells to Clarke. Let us work backwards from a striking, and very Doyle-like example in Clarke, "A Meeting with Medusa." At the core of this story's action we have the clear formation, become now almost a formulaic exercise, of a balancing set of hybrid forms. The prophesy of a machine future ("Someday the real masters of space would be machines, not men.") instead leads cyborg Howard Falcon to encounter his biological past on Jupiter in the monstrous form of the great floating "Medusa," an alien that ironically resembles this most primitive of earth creatures. What is more, his atavistic terror and fall in the face of this "Medusa"—a literal reversion to the beast-man—renders all the more grotesque his subsequent assertion of mechanically aided superbeing, rising "on his hydraulics to his full seven feet of height." The pattern that emerges is neither regressive nor progressive, for Falcon is as unable to abandon the machine as he is to become one. In fact, beneath a pretense of evolutionary drama, Clarke's shifts in perspective actually reinstate a static view of man as unchanging norm. In its vertical rhythm of rising and falling forms, Clarke's tale reminds us of Doyle's **"The Horror of the Heights."** Here an aviator exceeds what he sees as the limits set by the "Creator," and reaches the "jungles" of the upper air only to be hurled back to earth by the very real monsters that exist there. Once again, however, the outer rhythm contains an inner one, where the accent has shifted from man meeting monster to man actually becoming one, both in his technological ascension and in his subsequent atavistic fall. The aviators in this story in fact, in their obvious physical love of their airplanes, literally meld with them as if they were mechanical extensions of their inquiring spirit. But as these explorers are hurled back to earth, the body of one, Lt. Myrtle, is found missing its head. In a very real sense then, the being who through mind would become a machine has instead become a monster without a mind at all. Another Doyle story of flight, **"The Great Brown-Pericord Motor,"** transposes this same dynamic onto the horizontal plane. Published a month after the Wright brothers' success at Kittyhawk, this story tells how the ethereal genius Pericord conceives his great flying motor only to be forced, in order to build it, to associate with the crude and brutish engineer Brown. This titular association, on one hand, proves a most unstable hybrid, for Brown's attempt to steal the patent unleashes in Pericord a repressed animal violence that finally destroys him. On the other hand, however, and in contrary fashion, this title suggests that a union of body and spirit may be the proper fabric of human endeavor after all. Indeed, as each of these terms claims absolute status in the story, this union reasserts itself in the most grotesque manner. For just as Pericord's dream of disembodied machine flight is forced to bear, on its first and only voyage, the organic charge of Brown's dead body, so the inventor himself, as one who would sacrifice flesh to machine, discovers in turn that even mechanisms are not immune from organic inbalance, in this case his own ensuing madness: "It is the most delicate machine which is most readily put out of gear." The "flying machine" becomes, as its name suggests, a literal hybrid of organic and mechanical elements, and the final image of a "black bird with golden wings" heading out to sea simply points to the

Byzantean nature of the construct, a machine that claims monstrous existence, a travesty of life.

At the heart of this dynamic of cancellation lies a paradoxical view of the machine itself, seen simultaneously as a progressive and a static entity. This paradox is immediately visible in a work like Clarke's *2001: A Space Odyssey,* where the machine not only leads man forward and backward at the same time—the use of tools is also the cultivation of destructive violence—but also becomes, through the ever-present slabs, man's total environment, the envelope that encompasses and ultimately preserves him. Much the same pattern dominates Conan Doyle's narratives: the machine is constantly a force that moves only to assert itself as a fixed point, the dislocating menace that becomes at the same time man's huddling place, his sanctuary. In almost ritualistic fashion in these stories, machine becomes monster and monster machine, future summons past and pure mind organic chaos only so that these cancelling forces may drive man back to the center, reaffirm that comfortable present which technology has achieved yet fears forsaking to adventure in either direction. In **"The Great Brown-Pericord Motor"** it is precisely because of these counterthrusts of organism and mechanism, of mind and body, that ultimately nothing moves, that the progress of Kittyhawk is suspended and the world spared the effects of manned flight and potential destruction from the air. And in a much later tale, **"The Disintegration Machine,"** we find the same paradox: fascination with the possibility of change through technology, here raised to cataclysmic power, countered by the desire to reverse directions entirely, to affirm a present unchanging in its power to balance and cancel opposing forces. As a figure, the inventor in this story combines the extremes of Brown and Pericord in one form: below the eyebrows he is pimply, slobbering, hunchbacked, above he displays a "splendid cranial arch." Morally, he is a hybrid of great "philosopher" and "vile crawling conspirator." His search to "disintegrate"—on the high level to reduce solid bodies to pure essence, on the low to destroy London and a political enemy—leads him to encounter the solid figure of Professor Challenger, who functions here less as Europe's leading scientific speculator or as incarnation of man's instinctual past, than as their stable union, the guardian of the status quo. Significantly, he does not disintegrate the would-be disintegrator so much as execute him by tricking him into his machine, which in the act comes to resemble one of those electric chairs that so fascinated Conan Doyle as terrible instruments of social order.

The result is a fictional dynamic that celebrates stasis. Indeed, behind the paradoxical destinies of these technological explorers—be they aviators or inventors—lies a precise literary model, one often invoked in the context of modern science from Tennyson to Clarke, Ulysses, the hero whose fabulous voyage is simultaneously a homecoming, whose travels join the poles we ultimately encounter in Conan Doyle—the alien and the mundane. Interestingly, however, the archetypal incarnation of this Odyssean rhythm in British science fiction is not a man but a machine: Wells's time machine chair. Here the mechanical vehicle, conspicuously opposed to the monstrous shapes it encounters, remains all the while an obvious extension of the contemporary Englishman's domestic immobility, a seat onto which the traveller can "clamber" in safety. In Wells's novel, it is this time machine then which resumes all opposite impulsions, taking man to meet the monsters of the future and in the same movement thrusting him back, a disshevelled monster himself, into the polite dinner-table world from which he started. In its very form the time machine equates the going out with the coming home, and frames the fabulous sweep of technology and man's fears of terrible encounters in time in a thoroughly domestic space. This time-space nexus is defined, emblematically, as the returning traveller recrosses the path of his forward-moving housekeeper Mrs. Watchett and reverses it: "I think I have told you that when I set out . . . Mrs. Watchett had walked across the room, travelling . . . like a rocket. As I returned, I passed again across that minute when she traversed the laboratory. But now her every motion appeared to be the exact inversion of her previous ones. The door at the lower end opened, and she glided quietly up the laboratory, back foremost, and disappeared behind the door by which she had previously entered." It is not, then, that we have never moved, or that our movement through technology is a dream. Rather technological man, in works from Wells through Doyle to Clarke, seems to move only to bestow on his own present a sacred, almost numinous quality: Mrs. Watchett's banal trajectory transfigured by its marvelous acceleration and reversal.

The world of Doyle's tales may itself then seem a self-regulating machine, a structure resumable in the very objects, the motors and lifts, that mark their titles and excluding man altogether as purposive agent. Ultimately, however, Doyle does grapple with the possibility at least of some Odyssean being, unifying the contrary impulsions of past and future, technology and organic vigor, emerging at the focal point of this triple rhythm of man, machine and monster. Even so, most of his stories focus on the negative aspect of this problem, on that tenacious split between body and mind faced by modern man, that extension of the primal fall of man caused by the scientific enterprise itself. This is an abiding preoccupation that ties together the most diverse categories of tales in Conan Doyle. The problem of the separation of mind and body is perhaps most apparent in his pseudoscientific tales of spiritual transmigration. Interestingly, these function in quite the opposite manner from stories in the occult tradition of Hoffmann. For where the latter present (and applaud) the constant attempts of spirit to throw off its material trammels, Doyle's celebrate instead the process whereby the wandering spirit is inexorably drawn back to the precise material object that gave rise to it originally. Some of Doyle's tales are cautionary in this respect, and would show us this: if the spirit in its scientific investigations would wander away from its proper place, it will discover that some other, more horrible, force may occupy that place instead. In the farcical German student story, **"The Great Keinplatz Experiment,"** that place is literally shown to be here or no place. The experiment that would prove the spirit can exist apart from its body results only in a grotesque transposition of minds, which leads in turn to a slapstick of drunken brawls and pratfalls. The implications of a tale like **"Through the Veil,"** however, are much more ominous, for it is suggested here that the or-

dered surface of contemporary society itself holds only by suspending some deeper relation between spirit and body, in this case between modern man and his racial memory rooted in the native soil. Again it is science—here the archeological excavation of an old Roman ruin in Scotland—that leads to the protagonist's terrible dream and the realization that her present marriage may conceal the barbarous murder of her former self's Roman lover by the past incarnation of her present husband. The savage, twisted violence of these beginnings has not resolved itself in time, but on the contrary remains incarnate in the marked racial opposition of husband and wife, ever ready to erupt into the seemingly placid present. We find similar warnings in Doyle's "future war" tales. In **"Danger!,"** written eighteen months before the outbreak of World War I, technology in the form of the submarine raises dark subterranean forces—a reversion from the chivalric codes of warfare to a Darwinian struggle for survival—to attack an empire built on overextension, the dissipation of spirit, through conquest and economic exploitation, away from its proper roots in the soil of the homeland, now neglected and unable to sustain its own. **"The Last Galley,"** a future war tale in reverse, again places the prophesied decline of the British empire in a general context of the necessary split between the quest to conquer and the pull of the native soil. The lesson here is less the fall of Carthage that the spectacle of the "lean, fierce galleys" of the Roman conquerer, himself now forced to roam far from home, pulled down by the dying gesture of the dark rover captain in sight of Carthage. Here again the bright future is engulfed in the dark vortex that opens at the feet of those who would turn their back on the past.

Doyle's "lost world" tales are similarly cautionary. The difference, however, is that they locate this relation of mind to body in time rather than in space. If in **"The Horror of the Heights"** man pursues his space flight future only to be hurled back to earth, in **"The Terror of Blue John Gap"** he seeks his prehistoric past in this dark subterranean realm beneath the old Roman mine. But in his utter revulsion at the incomprehensible, shapeless form he encounters, the modern explorer remains irrevocably cut off from a being less his evolutionary ancestor than his exact opposite, an absolute, detached physical force, the sightless dweller in dark regions the sighted can never penetrate. The story **"The Lift"** is even more interesting, for it sets this same divergence of mind and body, of dark and light impulsions, squarely within the temporal frame of the present. Here, in a post-war world returned to blue-sky happiness, on an observation tower in a mechanized pleasure garden which actualizes the desire of modern man to elevate himself above the primal soil, Commander Stangate's dark premonitions announce the eruption of organic chaos into this well-ordered world. In the figure of Jim Barnes, the mechanic who would hurl this holiday crowd to their deaths, we see an atavistic physique—great straggling limbs, a hooked nose and flowing beard—twisted into madness. Ironically, it is the new perspective afforded by modern technology that reawakens irreconcilable, primitive visions in the heart of "peaceful England." Original sin reenters the garden of technology as Jim looks down at the crowd from the girders and sees "the wicked dotting the streets" beneath him.

These are all tales of separation. But are there any, finally, that explore the possibility of union between mind and body, between man's past and his future? Where such union is hinted at, it occurs invariably in an individual rather than a social context. **"The American's Tale"** is an interesting case in point. We find more here than just another lost world in the strange "Arizona" covered with "orchidlike umbrellas" and man-eating flytraps. We have instead an odd interpenetration of forces: the uneducated American enters the world of polite London scientific societies to tell of the quiet Englishman Tom Scott, who on the American frontier seems able to mingle civilized codes of honor with an uncanny affinity for monstrous flytraps. Though this story ends with a plea to unite the American eagle and the British lion, this hybrid merely covers the fact that any true fusion here takes place on the level of the lone figure of Scott, who seems to have harnessed organic monstrosity in the service of human order. In another American tale, **"The Los Amigos Fiasco,"** organized technology's attempt to eradicate dark chaos is opposed by the figure of the amateur scientist Peter Stulpnagel, who alone sees that larger and larger doses of electricity will not kill criminal Duncan Warner, but on the contrary fortify and rejuvenate him. And yet this triumph merely serves to transpose the initial rift onto another level. For though he can proclaim that "electricity is life," Stulpnagel remains a harmless, foolish figure isolated from this force incarnated by Warner with his tangled locks and black flowing beard. The one figure in Doyle who unites, at least iconically, these two extremes is Challenger himself, the figure who remains not only his ultimate science fictional character but his ultimate character in every sense. Challenger is "a primitive cave man in a lounge suit"; he is "the greatest brain in Europe, with a driving force behind it that can turn all his dreams into facts." The unity of body and mind found in Challenger, however, is in many ways more bravado than conviction. For his absolute experiment, and culminating act of union, remains, in the story **"When the World Screamed,"** little more than a rape. In thrusting the dart of technology into what he has discovered to be the living epiderm of our Earth, this physical center of Doyle's fictional universe reveals himself to be an emotional child: "I propose to let the earth know that there is at least one person . . . who calls for attention." (pp. vii-xix)

> *George E. Slusser, in an introduction to* The Best Science Fiction of Arthur Conan Doyle, *edited by Charles G. Waugh and Martin H. Greenberg, Southern Illinois University Press, 1981, pp. vii-xix.*

Don Richard Cox   (essay date 1985)

[*In the following excerpt, Cox discusses the plots and themes of the Brigadier Gerard tales.*]

After Holmes and Professor Challenger, Doyle's next most popular fictional creation was [a French cavalryman, Brigadier] Gerard. Doyle wrote a total of sixteen stories about this gallant soldier of Napoleon. The first eight were published in *The Strand* in 1894-95 and collected as *The Exploits of Brigadier Gerard* (1896); the second eight stories were published in *The Strand* in 1900-03 and collected as *Adventures of Gerard* (1903). During most of this time, it should be noted, Sherlock Holmes was "dead" and not a character Doyle was planning to resurrect.

Although at first Gerard seems to resemble no other major character in Doyle, if one looks closely one can see resemblances to an assortment of military figures sprinkled throughout his historical fiction. Gerard is a braggart who is never more happy than when singing his own praises. He is also an excellent swordsman, the best rider in Napoleon's entire army, and a lover who bewitches (and is in turn bewitched by) every attractive woman he meets. Although Gerard's bravado might put off readers at times, this flaw in his character is more than offset by his overwhelming sense of loyalty to his emperor Napoleon, and his intense belief in honor and chivalry.

It is somewhat ironic that Doyle the patriot chose as a hero a French soldier, particularly a soldier who fought directly against the British in one of their most bitter struggles. Yet it is perhaps because the French cause was defeated by the British that it seemed more romantic to him. Gerard represents an attitude about war that Conan Doyle always found glamorous, and whether the French soldiers were in fact more dashing, more reckless, and more devoted to achieving glory for its own sake than were the more pedestrian and businesslike British soldiers (whom Gerard regularly refers to as "English beef"), Doyle seems to have believed that they were and thus was able to incorporate Arthurian ideals into a work of fairly recent history. The British, after all, were led into battle by a bureaucracy of generals; the French were led by a single man, an emperor who, like Caesar or Alexander or Arthur, could be found on the battlefield as well as in court; it was the scope and daring of Napoleon's struggle against most of Europe that caught Doyle's imagination. Gerard, by frequently being a special envoi for the emperor, is freed from the mundane necessity of being tied to a specific unit or military action. He is free to wander through most of Europe (and his exploits take him everywhere—Russia, Italy, England, Germany, Spain, Poland) in a series of swashbuckling episodes, accompanied only by one of his fast and faithful horses.

The stories are told in the first person by an elderly Etienne Gerard, whom we usually find sitting in a café drinking wine and reminiscing over his past. The stories he tells span the period from 1807 to 1815, taking him from the rank of lieutenant to colonel. The first story in the series, **"How the Brigadier Came to the Castle of Gloom,"** establishes that he is both a fearless fighter (he has recently dueled with six fencing masters) and a reckless soul when the safety of a woman is involved. Gerard, imprisoned in a cheese cellar, sets off an explosive charge to blast his way free, even though a nearby powder magazine might also explode and bring the whole castle down. When the fire does spread to the magazine Gerard is outside, but the ensuing blast renders him unconscious for weeks. Such a mishap is a fairly minor occurrence for Gerard, however, whose life is threatened regularly in the rather bloody series.

In **"How the Brigadier Slew the Brothers of Ajaccio,"** for example, Gerard is asked by Napoleon to serve as the emperor's bodyguard on a secret mission. Gerard is not alert enough, however, to prevent an assassin from sinking a dagger to the hilt in the emperor's chest. A furious and humiliated Gerard kills the assassin and his companion, then learns that the murdered man was not Napoleon but a servant Napoleon had asked to masquerade as himself. The assassination attempt, like other nonfactual elements of the series, was "kept secret" by Napoleon and Gerard during Napoleon's lifetime, and can only be told now that many years have passed.

In the next story in the series, **"How the Brigadier Held the King,"** Gerard is taken prisoner. He then plays cards and wins his freedom, but meets Wellington who refuses to honor the arrangement and grant that freedom. "See, my lord," cries Gerard, "I played for my freedom and I won, for as you perceive, I hold the king." To this plea Wellington only responds, "On the contrary. . . . It is I who won, for, as you perceive, my King holds you." Thrown into Dartmoor prison in **"How the King Held the Brigadier,"** Gerard languishes only briefly, then effects a breathtaking escape (involving both an attractive lady and an English prizefighter), is recaptured, and finally exchanged for an English colonel and returned to France where he can begin his adventures anew.

In **"How the Brigadier Played for a Kingdom,"** we find Gerard betrayed by a German princess and nearly hanged while trying to deliver a message for Napoleon. In **"How the Brigadier Won His Medal"** he resolutely and against all odds delivers what turns out to be a false message that Napoleon assumed would be intercepted and would deceive the enemy. Gerard, in tears, tells Bonaparte, "Had I known that you wished the despatch to fall into the hands of the enemy, I would have seen that it came there. As I believed that I was to guard it, I was prepared to sacrifice my life for it. I do not believe, sire, that any man in the world ever met with more toils and perils than I have done in trying to carry out what I thought was your will." Napoleon's response to this is to give Gerard a special medal of honor, because, in Napoleon's words, "if he had the thickest head he has also the stoutest heart in my army."

Such a stout heart is remembered by Bonaparte in **"How the Brigadier was Tempted by the Devil,"** the last story in *The Exploits.* In it Gerard is summoned and asked to join in a coup against Napoleon because the fight looks lost. Gerard refuses, absolutely indignant, and it is this loyalty to his emperor that causes him to be sent on yet another secret mission (involving yet another beautiful countess) to retrieve important papers. After a perilous adventure Napoleon and Gerard bury the papers in a secret hiding place and Gerard explains that he understands Napoleon thrice attempted to write Gerard from St. Helena about them. Because these letters were intercepted, Napoleon's secret documents remain buried, their exact location known only to Etienne Gerard who has remained loyal to his leader and silent about their whereabouts. Gerard promises to tell how he dug these papers up in a later story (in fact, Doyle never relates that episode), and the first series of adventures ends.

In the second volume, *Adventures of Gerard* (1903), Doyle quickly reestablishes the gallant nature of his hero in **"How the Brigadier Lost His Ear"** by having Gerard, who is imprisoned by Venetian terrorists, exchange cells with a young female prisoner, who is to be punished for fraternizing with him by having her ear cut off. The ear is removed in the dark (inexplicably), so no one notices that Gerard is in her place until too late. French soldiers arrive to release him and the young woman retires to a convent. "Youth is past and passion is gone," the elderly Gerard muses at the tale's conclusion, "but the soul of the gentleman can never change, and still Etienne Gerard would bow his grey head before her and would very gladly lose this other ear if he might do her a service."

In two stories in this volume Gerard experiences the British sensibility firsthand. In **"How the Brigadier Slew the Fox,"** Gerard, while in Spain, infiltrates an English fox hunt and finds himself both emotionally and physically caught up in the pursuit. As the best horseman in Napoleon's army, Gerard is able to outdistance the British riders and kills the quarry before breaking off from the hunt and rejoining his companions. Tongue in cheek, Doyle creates his conversion of Gerard to a "British sportsman" in a high-spirited fashion. "Then it was that the strangest thing of all happened," proclaims Gerard. "I, too, went mad—I, Etienne Gerard! In a moment it came upon me, this spirit of sport, this desire to excel, this hatred of the fox. Accursed animal, should he defy us?" Gerard, not as familiar with the details of the hunt as he might be, uses his saber to cut the "accursed animal" in two; in the next story he receives the dismembered fox as a present from the English along with a note urging him to eat it now that he has slaughtered it.

In **"How the Brigadier Triumphed in England,"** Gerard returns to the sojourn he spent in England as a prisoner, an adventure described in *The Exploits.* While waiting to be exchanged for an English colonel he becomes embroiled in a duel fought over a beautiful woman. When the woman intervenes before the duel is completed, Gerard attempts to show off by discharging his pistol in a playful fashion and nearly kills a bystander. His gracious and charming apology gets him out of this scrape and wins him the praise of his rival, Lord Dacre, who says "I never thought to feel towards a Frenchman as I do to you. You're a man and a gentleman, and I can't say more."

"How the Brigadier Bore Himself at Waterloo" is a two-part story that covers Gerard's heroic action in Napoleon's last battle. In the first part, Gerard infiltrates enemy lines where among the soldiers he meets he encounters an English officer who remembers him from the fox hunt. Surrounded by the enemy on all sides, Gerard takes refuge in the loft of an inn and is able to escape when the wife of the innkeeper creates a diversion. In the second part of the story he passes back through the Prussian army to the front by posing as a Prussian messenger carrying a special dispatch. Reaching the front lines, he discards his Prussian disguise and crosses to the French side to rejoin Napoleon, who first disbelieves, then grudgingly accepts, the bad news Gerard brings. While on the other side Gerard has learned that a select crew of nine horsemen has been picked from the Prussian army and assigned to capture Bonaparte. Seeing this team approaching, Gerard suddenly shoves Napoleon into his carriage, takes Bonaparte's overcoat and white horse, and rides off hoping to decoy the raiders away from their true quarry. The trick works and in a hair-raising chase Gerard systematically eliminates and eludes eight of the nine horsemen while Bonaparte effects his escape. Finally having Napoleon's horse shot from beneath him, Gerard arrives safely in a French encampment just as the last pursuer closes in. The action, of course, only temporarily staves off the inevitable, for Napoleon surrenders a few weeks later. "Had others been as loyal as I," Gerard remarks, "the history of the world might have been changed."

Although Gerard called his Waterloo ride his "last and most famous exploit," his adventures, like those of Watson and Holmes, were hard to conclude. In **"The Last Adventure of the Brigadier"** Conan Doyle brought him back for an attempt to rescue Napoleon from St. Helena. Put ashore with the assignment of escorting Napoleon back to the rescue ship, Gerard discovers that the attempt is ill-fated. He arrives to find his emperor has just died. Sadly, Gerard views Napoleon lying on his bier surrounded by rows of burning candles. Gerard pulls himself to attention, gives his fallen leader a final salute, and solemnly takes his leave.

"You have seen through my dim eyes something of the sparkle and splendour of those great days" Gerard says in his closing remarks, "and I have brought back to you some shadow of those men whose tread shook the earth." In this series of stories Doyle creates some of his best historical fiction, perhaps proving once and for all that he was far better at writing short stories than writing novels. There is an excitement and dash to these adventures that appears only episodically in the longer fiction, largely because Doyle keeps the plot uppermost and does not bury himself under a mass of historical description, detailing the technicalities of chamfrons, arbalests, or greaves.

Instead he is left to sketch the portrait of a man who is the abstraction of an age, or at least an age as Doyle idealized it. "Long after Etienne Gerard is forgotten," the old soldier muses, "a heart may be warmed or a spirit braced by some faint echo of the words that he has spoken." This is essentially how Conan Doyle viewed the tales, as moral and psychological props to brace the spirit of an age that seemed to be in need of heroes. The aftermath of the Boer War brought a good deal of criticism to the British military, an organization that Doyle knew from his firsthand experience had performed heroically on the battlefield. Histories, such as Doyle's own books on the Boer War and World War I, could record the factual data, but in fiction Doyle could record the emotional truths of heroism, the "sparkle and splendour" of great days and actions where gallantry was recognized no matter what uniform it was wearing.

Gerard is not so much a French soldier as he is an ideal soldier, devoted to principles he will never abandon. It is because Gerard represents these ideal truths that Doyle chose to make him French—the enemy in the eyes of most of Doyle's countrymen. Making him British could have

turned the series into another nationalistic gesture on Doyle's part, and perhaps have tempted him to repeat the patriotic stereotypes one might expect in such fiction. In these stories Doyle is trying to do something much larger than reinforce the average Englishman's stereotyped responses to queen, flag, and country. In Gerard he creates a figure—not completely noble and perhaps therefore more believable—who represents the true embodiment of a chivalric code. To what end? "As the tree is nurtured by its own cast leaves," notes Gerard, "so it is these dead men and vanished days which may bring out another blossoming of heroes, of rulers, and of sages." By Gerard's example, . . . Doyle hopes to invoke such an age. (pp. 26-33)

Don Richard Cox, in his Arthur Conan Doyle, *Frederick Ungar Publishing Co., 1985, 251 p.*

The popularity of the Sherlock Holmes stories:

[It] is not what Holmes and Watson actually do that accounts for their enduring popularity. There are other factors inducing addicts of these characters in particular and detective fiction in general to return compulsively for more. Adults know that they cannot tear those who offend them limb from limb. Hostile wishes pervade everyday life, but they must routinely be consigned to the level of fantasy. Residual rage and feelings of helplessness are sublimated through art. Detectives in fiction act as intermediaries between what society dictates and what the individual really desires. They move freely between upper and underworlds, often having closer ties to the lower echelons than they do to the forces of law and order.

Then, as now, contrary to the adage, crime pays very well, and the public knows it. The detective acts in fantasy as the reader's surrogate; the aberrations of his personality and the mythic charisma that surround him encourage the reader's identification. But the detective is also accepted because he differs from the reader. If he were too similar, it might be necessary to reject him as threatening. After all, if the reader were forced into a direct confrontation with his own wishes for vengeance, perhaps mixed with sadistic overtones, without considerable personal insight, the suddenly acquired self-awareness might lead to consumer rejection—a kind of modern "kill the messenger" reaction. Surely, with Holmes and Watson such an eventuality is unthinkable.

Mary Wertheim in Columbia Library Columns, *1986.*

Jacqueline A. Jaffe   (essay date 1987)

[*In the following excerpt, Jaffe analyzes the form and content of Doyle's early adventure and supernatural stories.*]

Doyle's early experience as a fashioner of magazine stories was instrumental in the final shaping of him as a writer. He learned much about the art of writing and his talent continued to develop as he continued to practice his craft. These early stories are not all good, although some are very entertaining indeed. Their interest to the contemporary reader lies in the emergence of what were to be characteristic themes in Doyle's work: the heroic code of behavior with its attendant costs and benefits, a love of physical action, an emphasis on male camaraderie and friendship, and a delight in adventure and excitement.

Doyle's writing is also an attempt to invent or impose coherence within the boundaries of the finite entity that is narrative. His portrayal of the heroic code and his archetypal protagonists who subscribe to or violate that code are all attempts to give meaning to the chaos that he believed lay just beneath the surface of existence. As Northrop Frye [in his Anatomy of Criticism] has pointed out, the romance is "the champion of the ideal," a form which imposes this order. Doyle was drawn to stories of adventure and romance because he wanted a fictional world more hopeful, more heroic, and more moral than the real world and because he was attracted by a fictional form whose structure gave coherence.

"The Mystery of the Sasassa Valley," "The American's Tale," and **"The Gully of Bluemansdyke"** (published in 1879, 1880, and 1881 respectively) were all inspired by and modeled on popular Bret Harte stories. Doyle calls them "feeble echoes of Bret Harte," but they are better than that. **"The Mystery of the Sasassa Valley, a South African Story,"** is presented by a first-person narrator as a true account of his adventure. The storyteller, Jack Davis, is one of two young men who have left England to search for fame and fortune in South Africa. Initially the two school friends, one English, one Irish, have no success, but just as they are about to return to England, they are told a story by a traveler who has seen a one-eyed ghost in a valley that, according to native superstition, is haunted. The Irishman, Tom Donahue, deduces that the one eye must be a diamond that glows in a strange, lifelike way when it is struck by moonlight. After convincing Jack that they should search for it, Jack and Tom start out and, one false trip and a series of adventures later, find the diamond and ensure their prosperity.

"The American's Tale" is also presented as a true story by someone who witnessed the events. Set in the American West, the story concerns a giant man-eating plant, like an enormous Venus's-flytrap, which, fortunately, snaps up the villain just as he is about to bushwack the young English protagonist. The notion of a large plant that could devour a man was a familiar one to the Victorian reader, for it appeared over and over again in a variety of popular articles that dealt with the wonders and sensations of nature. Doyle's version of the machinelike plant is an especially terrifying one, however, as he has his victims impaled on long spikes hidden inside the leaves before their flesh is devoured.

The third story, **"The Gully of Bluemansdyke,"** set in the Australian outback, deals with a young man's coming of age while riding with a posse that is tracking down a band of vicious murderers. The trooper, Jack Braxton, has already proved himself to be a courageous and skillful tracker, but in this story, he has to learn to accept the help of an older and more experienced woodsman before they can capture the entire gang.

Central to Doyle's first stories is the notion of a strong male friendship that operates as part of a heroic code of behavior. This is less evident in **"The American's Tale"** where the friendship between the protagonist and narrator is only part of a general background of male friendship and fighting against which the horror of the man-eating plant can be more clearly detailed. Indeed, the clanlike aspect of the men in the American West seems totally insignificant in light of the decisive action that nature takes. But in the other two stories male camaraderie is more explicitly detailed. The protagonists are connected by such a strong bond of sympathy that their relationship goes beyond the normal bonds of friendship; they are blood brothers. Even the generational competition that exists between the brash young Braxton and the older, more experienced woodsman in **"The Gully of Bluemandsdyke"** is not sufficient to change the nature of the bond that links them.

The friends in **"The Mystery of the Sasassa Valley"** are also strongly linked in spite of various differences, the most obvious being that Tom Donahue is Irish and Jack Davis is English. In this story the cultural differences of English and Irish are translated into a distinction that was to become familiar to the Victorian reader in the relationship between Mr. Holmes and Dr. Watson—the distinction between an ordinary person, the narrator, and his extraordinary friend, the hero. Jack, who tells the story, is a loyal, kind man of average intelligence. His friend Tom is a man of visionary intelligence, mercurial, decisive, and active. Like Dr. Watson, Jack is fully sensible of his friend's talents. When Tom embarks on what appears to be an incomprehensible course of action, Jack comments: "I had, however, seen so many proofs of my friend's good sense and quickness of apprehension that I thought it quite possible that Wharton's story had a meaning in his eyes which I was too obtuse to take in."

Like Holmes, once Tom had perceived the truth, he will not stop until the mystery is solved. When their first effort to find the diamond fails, the uncertain and fearful Jack wants to give up: " 'There is no diamond here,' I said, 'Let's return and get a nights sleep.' " But the impassioned Tom will not let them rest, " 'Let's have one more try,' he said, 'I believe I've solved the mystery.' " In ways like these, the two friends, who foreshadow the partnership of Holmes and Watson, illustrate the special closeness of male camaraderie.

That this masculine bonding takes place best in faraway places, free from the restraints of social conventions, is no surprise. For Doyle, as for most adventure-story writers, the charm of exotic lands lies in their freedom from the demands of a known place in the present time. Society's constraints, in particular the demands of domesticity, have to be removed so that the emphasis can fall, where it rightly belongs, on individual male action and adventure. Doyle's stories are thus set in unknown places or in places that are intentionally geographically vague, like the American West.

Having chosen the adventurous place, Doyle does not have his hero go alone into that timeless country. He puts men together (either as a pair, or as members of a small group) as comrades and blood brothers to illustrate best how the heroic code works. Doyle uses the adventure convention of out of time, out of place to emphasize the permanent nature of male comradeship, and to show how it develops and sustains the participants under every kind of condition. The emphasis is still on individual action, but in Doyle's case the action directly benefits the male familial group, not the male alone, as well as presumably indirectly benefiting the larger society left behind.

Doyle achieved his first critical success in July 1883, when *Cornhill* magazine bought his story **"Habakuk Jephson's Statement."** Doyle wanted the accolade of being accepted by James Payn, the demanding editor of that prestigious magazine. He also desperately wanted to be in the company of other writers that he admired, and the *Cornhill,* formerly edited by Thackeray, and the publication that had printed Edgar Allan Poe's stories and, more recently, the works of Robert Louis Stevenson, provided access to this inner sanctum of literary excellence. James Payn, "the warden," as Doyle described him, "of the sacred gate," was to be a mentor whose influence was to be felt in all Doyle's work for most of his life. As an early indication of Payn's standing with Doyle, he tells us that "[what] for the first time made me realize that I was ceasing to be a hack writer and was getting into good company was when James Payn accepted my short story."

Although **"Habakuk Jephson's Statement"** was published anonymously, some of the reviews suggested that Stevenson had written it, a suggestion which was to Doyle, "great praise" indeed. There was another kind of notoriety that developed around **"Habakuk Jephson's Statement,"** however, the kind more readily associated with an Edgar Allan Poe story. **"Habakuk Jephson's Statement"** is a tale that purports to explain the real-life mystery of the abandoned ship, the *Mary Celeste.* Unfortunately, or fortunately as it turned out, a Mr. Flood, Her Majesty's Advocate-General at Gibraltar, read the story and mistook fiction for fact. He first sent off a telegram to the newspapers calling the story "a fabrication," and followed this up with a written report to the government which was also circulated to the newspapers. (pp. 18-22)

Although Doyle continued to write adventure stories, the fervor of his new burst of writing led him to explore a genre that he enjoyed as much if not more: the supernatural tale of terror. Some of his earlier works like **"The American's Tale"** and **"The Gully of Bluemansdyke"** play with the possibility of a supernatural explanation for the mysterious happenings, but this suggestion is part of the foil against which the superior human intelligence of the adventurers can come into play; in fact, the existence of devils is disproved in these adventure stories. In his horror stories the situation is reversed. Doyle treats the supernatural seriously. His tales of terror are not, as Charles Higham points out [in his *The Adventures of Conan Doyle: The Life of the Creator of Sherlock Holmes*] "what one would expect from the pen of a young, uncomplicated extrovert," but they show an important side of Doyle's character. The heroic and optimistic world of adventure in which a mystery is used only to "intensify and complicate a story of triumph over obstacles" is replaced, in the tale

of terror, by a mystery so powerful and terrifying that Doyle confronts not only the limitations of heroic action but "the limitations of mortality" [John Cawelti, *Adventure, Mystery, and Romance*]. Furthermore, his Gothic tales of mystery and terror, often ending in madness or death, express the darker side of the writer's vision and suggest depths to his character that are not quite evident in his seemingly open and frank memoirs.

It appears as if once having espoused the value of action, and the clarity of the sequential form of the adventure story, Doyle could then freely explore the power of the psyche by allowing it to range freely, unfettered by any code of heroic idealism or social behavior. The need for action and the clarity that action brings are set aside in these mystery stories for the clarity that is achieved only when feelings dominate the intellect, when the single-mindedness of the emotionally obsessed determines all behavior. The protagonists of Doyle's tales of terror all demonstrate this steadfast purpose. Nicholas Craigie in **"The Captain of the 'Pole-Star,'"** Sosra, in **"The Ring of Thoth,"** Cowles in **"John Barrington Cowles,"** and Ourganeff in **"The Man from Archangel"** are all strange, solitary men dominated to the point of insanity by a singular fixation—their love for a dead woman. And like the earlier Gothic protagonists that these characters so clearly resemble, they fail in their various attempts to overturn the natural order because they are finally consumed by their obsession.

"The Captain of the 'Pole-Star'" (published in *Temple Bar* magazine, 1883) is the first of these tales that Charles Higham explains, "reach beyond the boundaries of normal experience into a no man's land between life and death." Set on a whaling ship bound on a hazardous journey into the frozen Arctic, this story, which begins in a manner strongly reminiscent of Mary Shelley's *Frankenstein,* uses material that Doyle collected in a diary while he was on a similar voyage. However, Doyle embellishes his experience by portraying the captain of the *Pole-Star,* Nicholas Craigie, as a man haunted by the spectre of the dead woman he used to love. She is a sirenlike figure, who calls to him and beckons him and the ship further and further into the middle of the treacherous ice floes. Several members of the crew hear the ghost crying, but she is visible to no one except the captain. This vision separates the captain from the society of the men with whom he travels, producing moments of desperate isolation. " 'Look!' he gasped, 'There, man, there! Between the hummocks! Now coming out from behind the far one! You see her—you *must* see her!' " Finally, the captain keeps his tryst with his lover: " 'Coming, lass, coming,' cried the skipper in a voice of unfathomable tenderness and compassion,' " while he runs "with prodigious speed" across the ice and into her arms. The captain's passion for his long-lost love transcends the natural boundary between life and death, for when the crew members find the captain's frozen body, they see the shape of a woman, fashioned out of "little crystals of ice and feathers of snow" bending over the corpse to kiss it. As the crew reports, this reunion has made Craigie happy, even in death; "Sure it was that Captain Nicholas Craigie has met with no painful end, for there was a bright smile upon his blue, pinched features and his hands were still outstretched as though grasping at the strange visitor which had summoned him away into the dim world that lies beyond the grave."

A refusal like Craigie's to accept the fact of physical death also characterizes the Egyptian, Sosra, in **"The Ring of Thoth"** (published in the *Cornhill* in 1890). In this tale, a student of Egyptology, John Vansittart Smith, is mistakenly locked in the Louvre at night when he falls asleep while studying the mummies. He is awakened by an approaching light from a lantern, carried by an attendant who Smith has noticed earlier because he bears a marked physical resemblance to the ancient Egyptians. "It was indeed the very face with which his studies had made him familiar. The regular, statuesque features, broad brow, well-rounded chin, and dusky complexion were the exact counterpart of the innumerable statues, mummy cases and pictures which adorned the walls of the apartment. The thing was beyond all coincidence." While Smith watches, the attendant unwraps one of the mummies and embraces what appears to be the perfectly preserved body of a beautiful young woman.

In the confrontation that follows the Egyptian's discovery of Smith, Smith learns that the attendant, Sosra, was a priest of Thuthmosis, who lived sixteen hundred years before the birth of Christ. During his priestly studies Sosra had discovered a wonderful potion that gave eternal life. After Sosra had swallowed this potion, he met and fell in love with a beautiful woman, Atma, and she returned his love. But before he could convince Atma to take the mixture and join him in life eternal, she fell ill and died. Since her death, Sosra has been searching for the ingredients for another potion that would counteract the first and enable him to "shake off that accursed health which has been worse to me than the foulest disease."

Sosra finally finds the potion that he has so long sought in a ring—the ring of Thoth—which was hidden in Atma's burial garments. Vansittart leaves and Sosra drinks the liquid while clasping the unwrapped Atma in his arms. As in **"The Captain of the 'Pole-Star,'"** when the lovers are found in the morning, Smith reports that "so close was his embrace that it was only with the utmost difficulty that they were separated."

Published in 1886, **"John Barrington Cowles"** is a story of a man who, like Sosra and Craigie, dies for love; however, in this case, the love is misplaced. A handsome and sensitive young man, John Cowles suddenly falls in love with a beautiful but mysterious woman, Kate Northcott. No one seems to know who she is, where she comes from, or what her past contains. The narrator, a medical student and close friend of Cowles's, tries to find out about the woman, but he is only able to uncover some unsavory rumors about her former lovers. The narrator does, however, know that Kate is a strong-willed and determined young woman, for he sees her one day cruelly punishing her little dog "with a heavy dog whip," the dog "shining piteously" was "evidently completely cowed."

Although the narrator tells John to give Kate up, the obsessed Cowles proceeds with his plans for an early marriage only to discover on his wedding eve that his bride-to-be is a creature so terrible (some form of vampire is hinted at) that her true nature cannot be revealed. Indeed, the knowledge alone is so terrible that it is enough to drive Cowles to the edge of madness. In a vain attempt to recover his sanity and to escape from Kate's influence, Cowles and his friend travel to Scotland. But the spectre of Kate Northcott haunts Cowles wherever he goes, calling to him and allowing him no sleep, until one moonlit night, unable to bear his obsession any longer, he breaks free from the restraining arm of his friend, runs to embrace Kate's beckoning figure, and plunges over a cliff to his death.

This story is the first one in which Doyle shows the obsessional object to be evil. In **"John Barrington Cowles,"** Doyle explores, as Charles Higham explains, "The Gothic writer's feelings of terror about women, who are often portrayed as vampires, luring men to doom," in a way that reverses the pattern of Doyle's other tales of terror. Craigie, Sosra, and Ourganeff, the protagonist of **"The Man from Archangel,"** all actively seek death because it will reunite them with the women they love, and—happily—break the power that their obsession holds over them. These characters are only waiting for the right signal from beyond the grave so that they can go to the death that they welcome. By contrast, John Cowles tries to escape from Kate and to break free from her relentless embrace. But he is unable to do so, perhaps because this obsession is imposed from outside and thus involves forces beyond the power of his own will. Kate is too strong, too determined to have her own way, and too imbued by supernatural powers to be challenged; the sensitive Cowles is broken by that combination.

"John Barrington Cowles" demonstrates the voluptuous nature of the loss of control. There is a sensuous quality in Cowles's inability to act that implies that, at least in this story, Doyle finds total passivity attractive. Cowles is, interestingly, the most effeminate of these possessed men, the one who bears the least resemblance to what Kiely calls that "darkly masculine race of nineteenth-century demon-heroes: Manfred, Melmoth, Rochester . . . Heathcliff," who are his literary predecessors. Cowles, who is slight and fair, handsome but frail, is in contrast to the strong, passionate Craigie and Sosra.

A more important distinction between the two kinds of obsessional stories lies in the fact that Cowles is innocent. He is the passive victim of evil, whose innocence is shown to be dangerous, for it renders him powerless. The attraction of passivity is here linked to a warning about the naiveté that leads to such a surrender. Unlike Craigie, Sosra, and Ourganeff, who maintained the ability to act throughout the story, Cowles is never heroic. He is always the victim, never an instigator. The sexual element in Cowles's surrender to Kate should not obscure the warning implicit in the story: naiveté and innocence are not admirable qualities, for they lead to passivity, powerlessness, and death.

In another and more interesting fictional experiment, **"The Man from Archangel"** (1885), Doyle tried to find a way in which he could portray a protagonist ruled by passion in a story that would question his obsession. **"The Man from Archangel"** was one of Doyle's own favorite stories, for it was, he said, "perhaps as good honest work as I have ever done." It is also especially interesting, in the light of the other stories, for the way it questions the grand gesture of surrendering one's life to a fixed desire. Doyle achieves this double purpose of exploring the nature of an obsession and suggesting an alternative to it by dividing his Gothic hero into two, the doomed lover, Ourganeff, and the narrator, M'Vittie.

M'Vittie is a misanthrope who removes himself from society by going to live in a small cottage on a bleak tract of land next to the sea in the Scottish Highlands. M'Vittie is a scientist who has committed his life to a search for the answers to certain scientific questions. He is also a romantic in the tradition of Manfred, Heathcliff, and Ballantrae, all of whom were embittered by the puny nature of modern man, and were portrayed, as Robert Kiely points out, as part of the "myth of a lost giant in an uncongenial world." M'Vittie is such a character, except that he is not contemptuously taking the world on: he is contemptuously leaving it to its own mediocrity.

M'Vittie establishes his life in such a way that he can continue his experiments while seeing no one and speaking to no one. This continues until one day, during a violent storm, a ship is wrecked at sea and a beautiful Russian girl, Sophie, is washed upon the beach next to his cottage. M'Vittie reluctantly gives her food and shelter and learns that she has been abducted from her wedding to a "soft-skinned boy" by Ourganeff, the captain of the doomed ship, a man who had been Sophie's intended husband until he was presumed lost at sea. The captain is obsessed by Sophie and has vowed not to live without her. M'Vittie, the obsessed scientist, insists that such a passion for another human being is incomprehensible to him.

Apart from their choice of obsessional objects, though, the two men are remarkably similar. They are physically alike—tall, dark, and very strong—and also alike in their personalities—determined, active, and inordinately proud men with violent tempers. Sophie's obsessed lover, Ourganeff, has forcefully abducted Sophie from her wedding, and M'Vittie has fled to the Highlands because: "I had nearly slain a man in a quarrel, for my temper was fiery and I was apt to forget my own strength when enraged." Their duality is actually established at their first sight of each other. M'Vittie sees the ship go down and catches a glimpse of a man who is behaving differently from the other sailors: "He was a tall man who stood apart from the others, balancing himself upon the swaying wreck as though he disdained to cling to rope or bulwark . . . He stood dark, silent and inscrutible looking down on the black sea and waiting for whatever fortune Fate might send him."

When they meet face to face, they find that they are physically similar: "I suddenly became aware of a shadow which interspersed itself between the sun and myself. Looking around, I saw to my great surprise a very tall powerful man who was standing a few yards off." Except for the fact that they are obsessed by different passions, M'Vittie by his experiments and Ourganeff by Sophie, the two men are mirror images of each other. At the end of the story Ourganeff once again abducts Sophie and drags her from her rescuer to a death that only the lovers can share. In the aftermath of another violent storm, M'Vittie finds their bodies: "It was only when I turned him over that I discovered that she was beneath him, his dead arm circling her, his mangled body still intervening between her and the fury of the storm."

The ending to the story of Ourganeff and Sophie is the traditional romantic one of love conquering death: "I fancy that death had been brighter to him than life had ever been." But **"The Man from Archangel"** is interesting not for the expected death of the lovers but for the life of M'Vittie. In this story Doyle has divided his obsessed protagonist into two, one dominated by his love for a woman and one dominated by his love for science, so one manifestation of the usually doomed Gothic hero is left alive. M'Vittie's love for science and for rational explanations to mysteries is clearly the safer, more productive passion.

Yet his encounter with Ourganeff has taught him something about human nature, so that after the death of the lovers, his misanthropy is abated. In a gesture that emphasizes his change of heart, he allows wild flowers to be put on the graves of the lovers. "No cross or symbol marks their resting place, but Old Madge puts wild flowers upon it at times and when I pass on my daily walk and see the fresh blossoms scattered over the sand, I think of the strange couple who came from afar and broke for a little space the dull tenor of my sombre life."

Although M'Vittie's experience with the passion that one human being can feel for another alters him and makes him more sympathetic to the human plight, his passion for scientific experimentation is unabated. In this sense, his story runs counter to those of Dr. Frankenstein and Dr. Jekyll, those other nineteenth-century men of intellect whose pursuit of knowledge eventually ruins them. Unlike the heroes of Mary Shelley and Robert Louis Stevenson, however, the passion for knowledge evidenced by Doyle's hero does not lead to his death. M'Vittie becomes a better scientist because he now appreciates the strength of human attachment and understands science's obligation to serve human needs. In fact, it is love that saves M'Vittie. The lonely researcher's loathing for his fellow creatures, another kind of passion which might have destroyed him, has been mitigated by his experience of the love of Ourganeff and Sophie. "I sometimes have thought that their spirits, flit like shadowy sea birds, move over the wild waters of the bay."

In this way **"The Man from Archangel"** represents something of a turning point in Doyle's career. Out of his stories about passion has evolved M'Vittie, a man whose passion is yoked to the service of science. When **"The Man from Archangel"** resolves itself in a kind of qualified approval of the life lived in the impassioned service of the intellect, it points the way to Doyle's most famous exemplar of that life, the master detective Sherlock Holmes.

Doyle's tales of terror show that there are things that cannot be known, or can only be half-known, and that these secrets are dangerous to us. In their qualified resolutions, these tales seem to suggest the need for another form, one in which these uncertainties can be faced squarely and in which mysteries are solvable and secrets understood.

Doyle found this form in the detective story and in the invention of a character, the detective, who would make a practical and social application of the knowledge that the scientist pursued in lonely experimentation. Through a combination of induction and deduction, the scientist and the detective solve the mysteries with which they are faced. But while the scientist, alone in his remote laboratory, runs the risk of wasting his life in pursuit of sterile knowledge, the detective brings that knowledge into the realm of the social. In so doing he is charged with protecting the truth and undertakes, as the editors of a recent collection of essays on detective fiction point out, "the full facing of criminality, even horror, and all its implications."

In turning M'Vittie back from the pursuit of sterile knowledge by humanizing his research, Doyle marked the beginning of his turn toward a character whose scientific pursuits would have social application. In 1886, the year after the publication of **"The Man from Archangel,"** he took the next step toward alleviating the Gothic pattern of failure and death into which his characters had been locked. He decided to write a story using a scientist in a structure that assumes that the solution to mysteries can be found. The horror story which, as Dorothy Sayers says, "must always leave us guessing" was to be replaced by the detective story which "seeks to leave nothing unexplained." The ambiguous M'Vittie was to be overshadowed by the heroic Holmes. (pp. 22-30)

Jacqueline A. Jaffe, in her Arthur Conan Doyle, *Twayne Publishers, 1987, 148 p.*

Ely M. Liebow   (essay date 1987)

[*In the following excerpt, Liebow traces the autobiographical elements in* Round the Red Lamp.]

In 1894 Conan Doyle published a volume of stories dealing with medical life, **Round the Red Lamp** (the visible symbol of a doctor's residence in Victorian England). The stories nearly all deal with Conan Doyle's medical school days or early practitioner's life, and there are many traces of Edinburgh. The one based most obviously on his medical education there is **"His First Operation,"** wherein a third-year man brings a squeamish first-year student to witness an operation for the first time. On the way to the clinic, the older student greets a fellow outpatient clerk:

> "Anything good?"
>
> "You should have been here yesterday. We had a regular field day. A popliteal aneurism, a Colles' fracture, a spina bifida, a tropical abcess, and an elephantiasis. How's that for a single haul?"
>
> . . . The tiers of horseshoe benches rising from the floor to the ceiling were already packed, and the novice as he entered saw vague curving lines of faces in front of him. . . .
>
> "This is grand," the senior man whispered; "you'll have a rare view of it all."

When the neophyte asks about two men at the operating table, he is told:

> "One has charge of the instruments and the other of the puffing Billy. It's Lister's antiseptic spray, you know, and Archer [a surgeon] is one of the carbolic acid men. Hayes [another surgeon] is the leader of the cleanliness-and-cold-water school, and they all hate each other like poison."

What the neophyte—read Conan Doyle—was learning is that not all the doctors at the famed medical school accepted the great Lister's antiseptic technique. Conan Doyle's mentor Joe Bell believed in Lister's theory, but Conan Doyle also knew that the celebrated Dr. James ("Dismal Jeemy") Spence led the opposition to the germ theory of Lister, Pasteur, etc.—even eminent scientific men may refuse to believe in a thing if they cannot see it, a lesson Conan Doyle no doubt remembered years later when debating other scientific men about the validity of Spiritualism.

(While Conan Doyle acknowledged Sherlock Holmes' debt to Joe Bell's analytical and diagnostic method, he said relatively little about Bell outside his autobiography and a couple of magazine articles. But in **"The Recollections of Captain Wilkie,"** Conan Doyle did allude to his keen, grey-eyed professor with the sharp aquiline profile. "I used rather to pride myself on being able to spot a man's trade or profession by a good look at his exterior," says the story's Holmes-like protagonist: "I had the advantage of studying under a Professor at Edinburgh who was a master of the art, and used to electrify both his patients and his clinical classes by long shots . . . and never very far from the mark.")

One autobiographically interesting story—because of what it says about Conan Doyle's attitude toward women—seems on the surface not autobiographical at all. Conan Doyle was opposed to the suffrage movement. None of his medical classmates had been women. But in 1894 he published **"The Doctors of Hoyland."** Dr. James Ripley practices in a small town. Because of his modern methods and scientific spirit, he easily vanquishes his few rivals. For some years he reigns unchallenged, but then he learns of a Dr. Verrinder Smith newly arrived in town—educated with distinction at Edinburgh, Paris, Berlin, and Vienna, culminating in the coveted Lee Hopkins scholarship.

Anticipating a kindred mind and welcome company, Ripley calls on the newcomer and meets "a little woman, whose plain, palish face was remarkable only for a pair of shrewd, humourous eyes." He is shocked to learn that *she* is Dr. Smith. "He had never seen a woman doctor before, and his whole conservative soul rose up in revolt at the idea. He could not recall any biblical injunction that man should remain ever the doctor and the woman the nurse, and yet he felt as if a blasphemy had been committed." What makes it worse is that her scientific knowledge is obviously more up to date than his. In a fairly adroit manner, Conan Doyle has the young lady save Dr. Ripley's leg after an accident on the road; we see him not only change his mind about her but even prefer her ministrations to those of his brother, a London surgeon. Finally he proposes to her, whom he had thought of as "an unsexed woman." "What, and unite the practices?" she asks. She finally tells him she intends to take a position in Paris. And so once again there is only one doctor in Hoyland—a wiser but lonelier one.

Undoubtedly Conan Doyle had in mind Sophia Jex-Blake and the turmoil in Edinburgh over her medical ambitions. After failing to gain admission to Harvard Medical School in 1865, Jex-Blake had been allowed to enroll at Edinburgh but had to take classes alone. Told that such an arrangement was prohibitively expensive for the school, she returned with six other qualified young ladies, all of whom were reluctantly admitted. They were reviled, humiliated, spat upon, and sued. Sophia Jex-Blake took Edinburgh University on in the courts for five years, leaving bloody-but-unbowed for Paris and Bern and returning a few years later as a doctor to establish a women's hospital in Edinburgh. Conan Doyle came along at the tag end of the litigation. Women doctors were on everyone's minds. He was well aware of the role played by the young women's great champion, Joe Bell's mentor and probably Edinburgh's greatest surgeon—Dr. Patrick Heron Watson.

The final **Red Lamp** story we will take time to consider, **"Behind the Times,"** is about a figure depicted by Conan Doyle in many of his novels and stories: the old and out-of-date, but strangely able, family doctor. In Conan Doyle's own life it was Dr. Reginald Ratcliffe Hoare, of Birmingham, with whom he did several stints of assistantship as a student. In a few stories Conan Doyle calls him "Dr. Horton," but here he is Dr. Winter. The narrator is a clever, competent new doctor, who was brought into the world by Dr. Winter. No one knows the old man's age. He is opposed to the use of chloroform, just as many of the "lightning-fast" school of surgeons of that day were leery of the stuff. Dr. Winter refers to the stethoscope as "a new-fangled French toy" and "the germ theory of disease set him chuckling for a long time, and his favourite joke in the sickroom was to say, 'Shut the door, or the germs will be getting in.' " Joe Bell tells us that Dismal Jeemy Spence used to holler (always in Baron Lister's presence) "Shut the door; ye'll let the germs oot!"

If there is anything in the idea that Arthur Conan Doyle projected himself into many of his literary creations, not much effort was required when he wrote **"The Croxley Master"** in 1899. A medical student, strapped for funds because of a fouled-up bursary (scholarship), takes a job with an established practitioner in Sheffield. Conan Doyle suffered the same financial problem as a student, and his first assistantship was with a Dr. Richardson in Sheffield. Like Conan Doyle, the student is trying to cram five years' work into four, and is overworked by his mentor. To make ends meet, the husky young fellow agrees to box a local dreadnought, the Croxley master. Conan Doyle did not earn his tuition with his fists, but as a student sailing as ship's surgeon on the Greenland whaler *Hope* he put on the gloves more than once, and his fists won him many admirers. Conan Doyle's account of the young student's relationship with the parched Dr. Oldacre matches his own unillustrious three-month stint with Dr. Richardson in Sheffield. Both young men found little time for themselves; rolled countless pills; lived on skimpy diets; prided themselves on their cricket game; and removed themselves

from the unpleasant situation as soon as possible. (pp. 27-30)

Scholars have made use of autobiographical content in Conan Doyle's fiction—but incompletely, sometimes uncritically, and too often without enough knowledge of Conan Doyle's life to obtain full benefit from the clues he scattered throughout his literary output. The latter is indispensable, for without the navigational assistance afforded by a sound working knowledge of Conan Doyle's life, uninformed biographical mariners can all too easily sail past items of interest in his fiction or run aground on the reefs of his undeniably fertile sense of creativity. (p. 37)

> *Ely M. Liebow, "Experience Veiled in Pseudonyms," in* The Quest for Sir Arthur Conan Doyle: Thirteen Biographers in Search of a Life, *edited by Jon L. Lellenberg, Southern Illinois University Press, 1987, pp. 25-37.*

FURTHER READING

Bibliography

De Waal, Ronald Burt. *The World Bibliography of Sherlock Holmes and Dr. Watson: A Classified and Annotated List of Materials Relating to Their Adventures.* Boston: New York Graphic Society, 1974, 526 p.
>Inclusive bibliography of books and essays on Holmes and Watson.

Green, Richard Lancelyn, and Gibson, John Michael. *A Bibliography of A. Conan Doyle.* Oxford: Clarendon Press, 1983, 712 p.
>Bibliography of books and essays on the works of Doyle.

Biography

Carr, John Dickson. *The Life of Sir Arthur Conan Doyle.* New York: Harper & Brothers, 1949, 304 p.
>Anecdotal biography of Doyle.

Nordon, Pierre. *Conan Doyle.* Translated by Frances Partridge. New York: Holt, Rinehart & Winston, 1966, 370 p.
>Considered the best biographical and critical study of Doyle.

Pearson, Hesketh. *Conan Doyle.* London: Methuen & Co., 1943, 193 p.
>Critical biography.

Criticism

Batory, Dana Martin. "The Rime of the 'Polestar'." *Riverside Quarterly* 7, No. 4 (December 1985): 222-27.
>Compares Doyle's "The Captain of the 'Polestar' " to Mary Shelley's *Frankenstein* and Samuel Coleridge's "The Rime of the Ancient Mariner."

———. "The Climax of 'When the World Screamed'." *Riverside Quarterly* 8, No. 2 (March 1988): 124-28.
>Calls Doyle's story "a lascivious account of one man's search for the ultimate in copulation."

Berger, Arthur Asa. "Sherlock Holmes: Master Semiotician/Semiologist." In his *Signs in Contemporary Culture: An Introduction to Semiotics,* pp. 9-19. New York: Longman, 1984.

Applies the principles of semiotics to the Sherlock Holmes story "The Blue Carbuncle."

Bleiler, E. F. "Arthur Conan Doyle and His Supernatural Fiction." In an introduction to *The Best Supernatural Tales of Arthur Conan Doyle,* by Arthur Conan Doyle, pp. v-xiv. New York: Dover Publishers, 1979.

Provides bibliographical and biographical background relevant to Doyle's supernatural stories. Bleiler concludes that Doyle "was not the towering figure in supernatural fiction that he was in the detective story or the historical novel."

Green, Roger Lancelyn. "Adventures in the Past." In his *Tellers of Tales: British Authors of Children's Books from 1800 to 1964,* pp. 168-81. New York: Franklin Watts, 1946.

Discussion of the Brigadier Gerard stories, asserting that "for sheer excitement and suspense some of Etienne Gerard's escapes rival anything that [Doyle] wrote."

Hennessy, Rosemary, and Mohan, Rajeswari. "The Construction of the Woman in Three Popular Texts of Empire: Towards a Critique of Materialist Feminism." *Textual Practice* 3, No. 3, (Winter 1989): 323-59.

Analyzes "The Speckled Band" from a feminist perspective.

Jann, Rosemary. "Sherlock Holmes Codes the Social Body." *English Literary History* 57, No. 3 (Fall 1990): 685-708.

Investigates Sherlock Holmes's methodology, maintaining Doyle's logic is a "positivistic triumph."

Maurice, Arthur Bartlett. "The Romance of the Ring." *The Bookman* XI (May 1900): 223-25.

Review of *Green Flag, and Other Stories,* concluding that Doyle "is absolutely unrivalled as a chronicler of the romance of the [boxing] ring."

Moskowitz, Samuel. "Arthur Conan Doyle: A Study in Science Fiction." In his *Explorers of the Infinite: Shapers of Science Fiction,* pp. 157-71. Cleveland: The World Publishing Co., 1963.

Offers biographical information and a survey of Doyle's science fiction.

Rosenberg, Samuel. *Naked Is the Best Disguise: The Death & Resurrection of Sherlock Holmes.* Indianapolis: Bobbs-Merrill, 1974, 202 p.

Argues for previously unconsidered influences on the Sherlock Holmes stories, especially that of Friedrich Nietzsche as the model for Professor Moriarty.

Truzzi, Marcello. "Sherlock Holmes: Applied Social Psychologist." In *The Sign of Three: Dupin, Holmes, Peirce,* edited by Umberto Eco and Thomas A. Seboek, pp. 55-80. Bloomington: Indiana University Press, 1983.

Asserts that Holmes's "application of rationality and scientific method to human behavior is certainly a factor in the detective's ability to capture the world's imagination."

Stanley Elkin

1930-

(Full name Stanley Lawrence Elkin) American novelist, short story writer, essayist, and scriptwriter.

INTRODUCTION

Considered one of the most entertaining stylists in contemporary American literature, Elkin is known for such frequently anthologized stories as "I Look Out for Ed Wolfe" and "Criers and Kibitzers, Kibitzers and Criers." Like his novels, Elkin's short fiction depicts protagonists whose obsessive personalities are expressed through intense, humorous, and often eloquent rhetoric that commonly derives from their chosen vocations. Although usually isolated from the social mainstream, these characters are viewed by critics as representatives of American society, presenting the ways in which individuals interact—commercially, emotionally, and psychologically—with popular culture.

Elkin was born in New York City and grew up in Chicago. After serving in the United States Army from 1955 until 1957, he studied at the University of Illinois and completed his doctorate in 1961 with a dissertation on William Faulkner. Elkin describes his father, a traveling salesman with a gift for storytelling, as an important factor in his decision to pursue a literary career and as an influence on his writing style, which often possesses the manic rhythm of pitchmen and stand-up comedians. Elkin's first collection of short fiction, *Criers and Kibitzers, Kibitzers and Criers,* was published in 1966. He completed two novels—*A Bad Man* in 1967 and *The Dick Gibson Show* in 1971—before his second collection, *Searches and Seizures,* was published in 1973. After several highly respected novels, including *The Franchiser, The Living End,* and *George Mills,* Elkin's third collection of short fiction, *Van Gogh's Room at Arles,* appeared in 1993.

In *Criers and Kibitzers, Kibitzers and Criers,* the protagonists are isolated individuals obsessed with affirming themselves, committing, as a result, extreme actions with irreversible consequences. In some of the stories, the theme of self-definition acquires the aspect of heroism, anticipating Elkin's later works, especially his novels, in their allegorical treatment of the problems individuals experience in confronting their mortality and alienation.

Many critics consider *Searches and Seizures,* a group of three novellas, to represent Elkin's best short fiction. The protagonists of these narratives are maladjusted bachelors, a common character type in Elkin's writing. In "The Condominium," Preminger, a failed lecturer and perpetual graduate student, goes to Chicago to tend to his father's funeral, but stays on at his father's place in the hope of changing his life. Preminger discovers, however, that the

condominium complex, in its exclusive isolation, seems more suitable as a place to die, and he suffers a nervous breakdown that leads to his suicide. The second novella, "The Making of Ashenden," begins as a parody of a cross-cultural romance, which critics observe recalls the work of Henry James and Noël Coward in its subject and style. The novella's hero, Ashenden, civilized to an extreme, is told by his fiancée to "purify" himself by renouncing his sexual history. Having brought himself to the point of self-loathing through introspection, he goes for a walk through the grounds of his friend's estate, where he has a sexual encounter with a she-bear that results in his plan to reject all connections with civilization. In "The Bailbondsman," Alexander Main's fascination with crime as a mystery and his hunger for strange, obscure forms of knowledge have led him into his role as a professional bailbondsman. When he finds his business declining, however, he becomes obsessed with his power to dictate the freedom of others, and finally shoots his assistant, who is a fugitive and the only person over whom Main has any real control. Commentators also have noted the inherent tension of the novellas that results from the vigorous rhetoric of Elkin's characters and their sensitivity to style and language in the face of their acute awareness of death. Thomas LeClair has commented: "[Because the obsessions of Elkin's heroes] arise from areas of mass fascination and because they expend their energies within recognizable—if sometimes dislocated—systems of value, their private thoughts and public careers reveal truths particularly relevant and available to the American present. Theirs is the singleness that illuminates multiplicity, the focus that creates perspective, and Elkin uses them to examine both the normalities and aberrancies of our time."

PRINCIPAL WORKS

SHORT FICTION

Criers and Kibitzers, Kibitzers and Criers 1966
Searches and Seizures 1973; also published as *Eligible Men,* 1974
Early Elkin 1986
Van Gogh's Room at Arles 1993

OTHER MAJOR WORKS

Boswell (novel) 1964
A Bad Man (novel) 1967
The Dick Gibson Show (novel) 1971
The Living End (novel) 1979
The Franchiser (novel) 1976
George Mills (novel) 1982
Stanley Elkin's The Magic Kingdom (novel) 1985
The Rabbi of Lud (novel) 1987
The MacGuffin (novel) 1991
Pieces of Soap (essays) 1992

CRITICISM

Raymond M. Olderman (essay date 1974)

[*Olderman is an American critic and educator. In the following review of* Searches and Seizures, *he praises Elkin for his vitality in portraying contemporary life.*]

I don't know if *Searches and Seizures* is Stanley Elkin's best book, but I'll tell you one thing—it's terrific. I feel as if I should write this in capital letters. No. Not capitals, headlines, maybe: READ ALL BOOKS WRITTEN BY STANLEY ELKIN. That's a little pushy; but if you want to learn to embrace multitudes, or construct catalogues of the crazy, lists of the looney, read Elkin. You'll learn to see pimples on the earlobes of the enormous, and to occasionally try and write bad imitations of Elkin just to touch the totem of his vitality. Elkin's works are profound and filled with stuff and ideas and visions and all the stimulations that make a critic want to examine him in depth, but above all he is a first-rate writer, a man of deep, almost Shakespearean compassion for the life of the individual no

matter who he/she is, and he has one of the best eyes for detail of anyone writing now. Like Alexander Main, The Bailbondsman, the moving mover of the first novella in *Searches and Seizures,* Elkin seems to say:

> I know everybody I have had dealings with, their names and faces, their heights and weights, each identifying characteristic, every wart and all pimples, perfect pitch for human shape and their voices in my head like catchy tunes. What a witness I would make, a police artist's dream with my eye for detail, the crease of their gloves and the shine on their shoes like so many square inches of masterpiece in an art historian's noggin. Not "male Caucasian, mid-twenties, sandy hair and slightly built, five foot ten inches and between 130 and 135 pounds." That's given, that's understood; I do that like the guess-your-age-and-weight man at the fair. But the weave of his trousers and the pinch of his hat, which hole he buckles his belt and the wave in his hair like the force number on the Beaufort scale. A marksman's eye for his pupils and its length to a fraction of the cuff rolled back on his sweater. I have by heart the wrinkles on his trousers and know the condition of his heels like a butcher his fillets. Everything. The roller coaster of his flies when he sits, where his hands get dirty, which teeth need attention, the sunsets on his fingernails. Everything.

But Elkin sees even more than Alexander Main. His books are filled with sustained comic and serious metaphysical flights of rhetorical salesmanship on people, on crayons, on consumer products, on the look of a hairdo, on one man's range of moving experiences, on hard luck, on low places and dirty deals, on high places and "plenty of plentitude." And the extent of his observations is matched by the genuine vigor of his descriptions. His work is filled with lust, with hunger, with hot juices burning his brain to know more, to see more, to live. Can you imagine Walt Whitman, Henry James, William Faulkner, Charles Dickens, and Woody Allen all pitching in?—Elkin is something like that.

Even when he contends with death, when he speculates on the future, when he examines the fuel that drives him, he doesn't think in terms of grand schemes and galactic dreams. He worries about all the details he hasn't seen. "But what hurts," Alexander Main tells us,

> I mean what really *hurts*, is that if I had a brain as big as the Ritz I still wouldn't know anything. We die dropouts. All of us. Disadvantaged and underachievers. I have questions. I'm up to *here* with questions. I never needed to be happy; I only needed to know. Simple stuff. A dopey kid of the next century could tell me. If I could only live long enough I would sit at his feet as if he was Socrates and he'd tell me . . . What? Whether Dubuque ever made it into the majors. If there's crab grass on distant planets. Who won the war and what they were supposed to be fighting for and old Uncle Tom Cobbly and all. He'd rattle off the damn fool slogans of his time and I'd take them in like the Ten Commandments. What do I do with my wonder, I wonder?

Because Elkin's books have grown progressively more involved with wonder and mystery, they have continued, each in different ways, to grapple with death.

What is more important, for now, is to recognize that Elkin's love affair with life—in his novels—does not come out of political naiveté or faddish affirmation. It is wrung from a deep knowledge of human suffering given only to those who see in such detail that they are tortured into frantic searches and seizures. "Listen, disdain's easy, a mug's game, but look close at anything and you'll break your heart." It is hard to embrace a torturous world. Few authors can look so closely at the texture of America and come away moved but still hungry for more. It is Elkin's great talent that when he sees plastic-motel America—consumer garbage, and piles of plenty, neon lips advertising the look of love, and all the detritus that most of us see and are repelled by—he also sees the human imagination, the human victims, the humans themselves standing somewhere behind the mess we all make. It can break your heart. But Elkin makes us embrace it all. Despite myself, I am forced to rise above my political acrimony—of which I have an unhealthy supply. I am forced to remember that love of life and morality are not the same thing. He imposes on his readers the necessity of the imaginative leap. Feldman, in *A Bad Man,* tells us that "The paper ribbon in deference to my ass across the toilet seat breaks my heart." Why? I ask. The answer is surely a history of human folly, ugliness, exploitation, and playfulness. But still, I think about the person who first thought of the paper ribbon, of the maid or steward that replaces it there after each ass has left. I remember a man I saw on television—a thirty second live spot in between reels of the late show—he was selling pots, something like nineteen pots for $12.95; he talked fast trying to convince me that the pots were perfect, indestructible, but he had to go so fast that he burst into inspiration and started pounding his pots together to prove their durability. The thirty seconds ended with a final shot of his puckered face and a battered pot in each of his hands. I think of him often. What happened afterwards, backstage? I worry about him. Elkin makes me do it.

The balance necessary for so close a look at contemporary life comes, in Elkin's books, from variations on his concept of style. On one level I mean that the energy of his rhetoric is not just manic; it is infectious. But discussions of style on that level are of interest, I believe, only to students of technique and structure and rhetoric—to writers and some critics. For many readers the question is really: how does style help gain balance in a plastic world? In this sense, style has something to do with behavior. Everybody in Elkin's world seems to have some movie role in mind, but Elkin reveals these roles to us as a technique actor would reveal them—from accumulated outside detail that finally reaches inside. His best characters are not method actors—they are Olivier not Brando. But, the large supporting casts in his novels are often mediocre actors—types. We are given the set they work on, the costumes, the gestures, the clichés, grimaces, all the accumulated externals that shallow people mistake for inner personality or soul. Then we see them clearly: a mafia man who says softly, "it's Command Performanceville." We know how

he looks, the gun under his camel coat, a businessman's look with only the minimum of lip movement. We have him. We've seen him in the movies, on TV—*Mission Impossible,* The Watergate Hearings, maybe. We really do see Elkin's characters everywhere, minor players, mostly letting their roles be thrust on them, never getting beyond the externals they imitate. They are Marcuse's one-dimensional humans, but to Elkin they are playing it the best they can.

On the other hand, Lawrence Olivier can play all the roles, and that is the secret of most of Elkin's manic heroes. They bear down on life by knowing all the roles, from outside in, from jargon to the edge of a breaking heart. Their energy comes from their drive to know all the movies, to shift roles as quickly as possible. They are acquainted with flux—who knows who'll come on stage next?—and they hunger for the challenge, for the knowledge. This perception of human experience usually depresses us. Don DeLillo in his third novel *Great Jones Street* has a rock star who discovers that to cope with plastic America, he must reduce, diminish—if you live in shit, learn to love it till your taste is made of toilet paper. But this is disdain, and it is, as we have been told, easy to disdain. Elkin's manic stars do, however, need strength. (pp. 140-42)

[*Searches and Seizures*] is a collection of three very fine novellas, and it presents some new explorations for Elkin. I believe he is examining the former givens of style itself. How is it connected to taste, to behavior, to attitude, and to action? The first story picks up the manic hero once again, **The Bailbondsman,** hungrier than ever for the gusto of knowledge, but tiring. Better than Gibson [in *The Dick Gibson Show*], but ready to admit, "I'm called on to make colorful conversation in my trade. Don't think I enjoy it. I'm a serious man; such patter is distasteful to me." But he does it well and although tired, he carries on to the end, both touched and touching, keeping the movie in motion. In the second story, Elkin departs somewhat, playing a little Henry James with **The Making of Ashenden.** Here, the hero is a man of exquisite taste on every level. Neither the most ardent leftist could fault his activism, nor could the moneyed-set fault his manners. He has style as balanced as the best of James' beautiful people. But when he meets the woman who is his match, he needs to purify himself of his discreet but nonetheless unvirginic past. So, of course, he goes into a wilderness that turns out to be like a series of art works—as in *The Ambassadors* or in *Madame de Mauves*—and there in a setting he believes to be Edward Hicks' *The Peaceable Kingdom,* he lies down with a bear. Well, the rest is pure Elkin with a different style and the same wonderful embrace of life. Brewster Ashenden is purified, but while Faulkner might have loved the encounter, this is one he could never have written.

In the last novella, **The Condominium,** Elkin gives us another departure, a little bit of a Bellow-type character. I mean there is a little of that angst, a little of that lost diamond, scuffed by a bad old world. Here, style, place, and placidity are examined. But the whole book deserves study. . . . Let me leave it by saying, I believe Elkin is undergoing some change, and **Searches and Seizures** provides a great deal of provocation to understand his direction in depth. Read Elkin, please; he may come near breaking your heart, but you'll skip around too, right there in your office, on your rug—swinging and swaying right there as if you had hold of Melville's Catskill eagle, who "can alike dive down into the blackest gorges, and soar out of them again." Because, even if you don't soar, you can certainly laugh. And you can wait till later to worry—like the hero of *The Condominium,* flying from the fifteenth floor—about "the hole I'm going to make when I hit that ground!" (pp. 143-44)

> Raymond M. Olderman, "The Politics of Vitality," in fiction international, *Nos. 2-3, Spring-Fall, 1974, pp. 140-44.*

Thomas LeClair   (essay date 1975)

[*In the following excerpt, LeClair discusses the prominence of "obsessional heroes" in Elkin's fiction.*]

"There are only two kinds of intelligences, the obsessive and the perspectual," says James Boswell, hero of Stanley Elkin's first novel, *Boswell.* In statement and act Boswell affirms the obsessive and thereby points to what I believe is the single most important theme—and description of technique—in Elkin's work. In Elkin's fictional world, the perspectual intelligence—rational, balanced, Apollonian—gives way to the obsessive imagination, the willful, kinetic force that destroys accepted perspective with its compulsively straight and irrationally jagged lines. For Elkin, perspective means objectivity, ordinariness, and compromise. Obsession is subjective, strange, and extreme; it is characterized by a narrow focus on fixed ends, by intense desire and extravagant means, and by the lack of relations and options. Elkin does create perspectives on his characters' actions through comedy and invites the reader to analyze the nature and effects of obsession. But within the work itself, "Drive drives the world," obsession dominates. It rules character, dictates structure, and permeates the voices Elkin loves to throw.

Elkin's protagonists are ordinary men with extraordinary purposes and singular dreams, men who become obsessed with the improbable possibilities of the self's expansion. Isolated by their obsessions, these manic heroes mount single-minded assaults upon the world and force themselves toward ultimate fulfillments. Although development is their end, plot becomes the compulsive repetition of action and complex situation is reduced to simplicity by their obsessions. Even setting is defined by the radical subjectivity of the obsessive inhabiting it. Sellers of singleness, pitchmen of transcendence, Elkin's narrators and heroes have a high-energy, repetitive rhetoric, an exclamatory prose that intensifies the ordinary, presses the impossible, and registers the urgency of their fixations. The result is a unity of effect, a Siamese connection of substance and style.

It is probably a truism that characters in contemporary American fiction are obsessional, but Elkin's heroes, unlike those, say, of Mailer, Hawkes, or O'Connor, develop their obsessions from natural authorities, common needs, or the promises of a popular culture rather than from some social, psychological, or religious ideology. Elkin's

are not the exotic products of a subculture nor the constructs of an experimental theory but the distortions of the American almost-ordinary. Because their obsessions arise from areas of mass fascination and because they expend their energies within recognizable—if sometimes dislocated—systems of value, their private thoughts and public careers reveal truths particularly relevant and available to the American present. Theirs is the singleness that illuminates multiplicity, the focus that creates perspective, and Elkin uses them to examine both the normalities and aberrancies of our time. (pp. 146-47)

Much of Elkin's short fiction . . . deals with the obsessional character. . . . [Many] of the protagonists in *Criers and Kibitzers, Kibitzers and Criers* (1966) are passionate loners with obsessional projects of extraordinary selfhood. Driven by inescapable needs, they use extravagant means to rise above their contemporaries. In **"I Look Out for Ed Wolfe,"** the title character divests himself of goods and relations in a desperate search for "the gleaming self beneath." In **"The Guest,"** a young misfit named Bertie cultivates an unremitting hipsterism and takes credit for the destruction of his friends' apartment to prove his self-importance and special difference from the herd. Four of the stories in this collection go beyond this theme of self-definition through simplification to heroism as an explicit subject. **"In the Alley"** presents a man named Feldman who, dying of cancer, decides "he must (it reduced to this) become a hero." **"On a Field, Rampant"** has a protagonist who believes he is the "World's Last Pretender" to a throne, any throne. Obsessed with the "restoration of the hero," he searches the globe for the place he thinks he has lost. A more banal kind of hero, but one equally affixed to transcending the mass and personifying authority, is Push the bully in **"A Poetics for Bullies."** "God of the Neighborhood," Push is an irreconcilable youth who cannot be moved to compromise his adopted role. The last story, **"Perlmutter at the East Pole,"** features Morty Perlmutter, the anthropologist in *Boswell.* Having seen the rest of the world, Perlmutter comes to New York City to "synthesize the universe." He finds in Union Square a group of professional obsessives, all believing they have the single answer to the world. At the end of the story, Perlmutter takes his place among them and prepares to give *his* encompassing statement, which will be the definition of his heroism. (pp. 158-59)

[These] characters push themselves toward the ultimate gesture or irreversible act of selfhood, only to fail or to be left in uncertainty. In their obsession to achieve the impossible, they deprive themselves of friendships and relationships; they have only their knowledge of an attempt that should not have been made. The sources and effects of their obsessions are not always clear, for Elkin presents them at a crisis point and often leaves an open ending. This focus on the crisis of obsession gives the stories dramatic intensity but also tends to make the characters into passionate curiosities. In [his] novels, Elkin's techniques of repetition and comprehensive development defined the nature of the obsession and established sympathies for the hero. The length of the novel allowed for subtle rhetorical variations—shifts from comedy to seriousness and back again—that gave the reader perspective on the characters.

In the short stories, the characters more often seem simply pathetic or comic because the causes and development of their obsessions are necessarily excluded. Several of these stories (**"I Look Out for Ed Wolfe"** and **"On a Field, Rampant"**) are excellent fables of fixation and several (**"A Poetics for Bullies"** and **"Perlmutter at the East Pole"**) have the excitement of Elkin's distinctive rhetoric, but I think the short story form works against the theme of obsession, which, by its very nature, is large, repetitive, and extravagant. Elkin is an adder and multiplier, not a subtracter or divider; the expansive characters he creates and the verbal performances that are his strength need the length and openness of the novel.

The novella form Elkin uses in *Searches and Seizures* (1973) gives him a compromise: the crisis excitement of the short story and some of the possibilities for development of the novel. As do several of the stories in *Criers and Kibitzers,* one of the three novellas in *Searches and Seizures—The Condominium*—presents the obverse of Elkin's obsessed hero: the man who surrenders to circumstances. Marshall Preminger comes to Chicago to his father's funeral, stays to live in his condominium, has a nervous breakdown, and finally commits suicide. Preminger has some of the markings of an Elkin obsessive—he is childish, self-conscious, proud, and covetous—but he lacks the energy and the imagination to live anything but a qualified life. Instead of willing a "gleaming self " or insisting upon some exceptional end, Preminger contemplates the environment that enfolds him. As he falls to his death, he recites synonyms for necessity rather than Elkin's more characteristic series of possibilities: " 'Cage,' he shouted. 'Net,' he screamed. 'Pit, sheath, vesicle, trap,' he roared above gravity. 'Cell, cubicle, crib and creel.' " In his weakness and lassitude, Preminger represents other Elkin characters—Boswell's uncle and son, Feldman's wife and friend Dedman, Richard Preminger in *Criers and Kibitzers,* people who have capitulated to the ordinary. Elkin's obsessed men are also frustrated or defeated, but, unlike these victims, their lives are exceptional.

If Preminger is obsession's obverse, *The Making of Ashenden* is heroism's parody. Elkin satirized Greatness in *Boswell,* made some fun of American Hero Dick Gibson, and parodied the questing hero in **"On a Field, Rampant,"** but *The Making of Ashenden* submits all three varieties of heroism to ludicrous parody. Brewster Ashenden has a redwood genealogy, wealth, and public recognition; he is an honorable gentleman and "glad to be a heroic man." When his parents die, he searches for and finally finds the perfect mate, one Jane Löes Lipton. Unfortunately, she insists he become pure (he is honorable but "experienced") before she will have him. Ashenden's test comes when a bear in rut captures him and insists he mate her. Although he is trying "to undo defilement," Ashenden mates the bear and fails the test of purity as no other hero, Lancelot included, ever has. But the title *The Making of Ashenden* alludes to more than the bear's successful wooing. Ashenden's vow to go "someplace wild, further and wilder than he had ever been" signals a change from his life of accepted adventure and conventional courtship; the real "making of Ashenden" is his freedom. The Jamesian pattern of events, the formalized language of gentility, and the pallid notion of heroism all contribute to the parody, but it is the bear's extravagant demands that make Ashenden's obsession ludicrous and the story a successful tour de force.

The Bailbondsman is a day in the life of a classic Elkin obsessive, Alexander Main, a Cincinnati bailbondsman. Main is the Elkin omnivorous man: "I have no taste, only hunger." Student of the past and imaginer of the future, close watcher of the present, Main is a man to whom the world is an affront because he and it are separate. He is also a professional rhetorician, a persuader of prostitutes and lawyers, a mix-master of diction. Main has become a bailbondsman because of his curiosity about the mysteriousness of crime and his desire "to doodle people's destiny . . . to loose the terrible, to grant freedom where he felt it was due, more magisterial than a king, controlling the sluices and locks of ordinary life. . . ." Now in his mid-fifties, Main faces declining business and powers, but finds his curiosity and desire mockingly strong: "Where are my muscles, my smooth skin? Why doesn't desire die? . . . Why do I have this curiosity like a game leg? How can I cross-examine the universe when it jumps my bond?" In his decline, Main becomes obsessed with his power over freedom. He dreams of Oyp and Glyp, the only men who ever got away from him; he volunteers, in his dream, to go a twenty billion dollar bail for tomb robbing to regain control of them. Finally admitting that Oyp and Glyp are beyond his reach, Main goes to his assistant's hotel room to talk. Main realizes that Crainpool, whom he has harbored from prosecution, is "the only man in the world [he is] allowed to kill." The story ends with Main shooting Crainpool in the hand and chasing him into the Cincinnati night. Dictating or destroying another's freedom, Main demonstrates his own, and satisfies his obsessive need to control life from the oasis of self.

The Bailbondsman does not have the philosophical and cultural significance of Elkin's three novels—none of his stories has—but it shares with the novels qualities that make Elkin's fiction important, qualities I want to summarize here: an imaginative inclusiveness of vision, a hero whose obsessional angle of perception reveals "the range of the strange" in American life, a psychology that registers dynamic multiplicity and contradiction, an understanding of the way ideas get translated into gestures and actions, a voice to express primal discontents without jargon, a careful attention to the transactions of an individual and the popular culture, a perspective-giving verbal and

---

Elkin on character in the short story and the novel:

The short story is about *acute* character, and a novel is about *chronic* character. A short story is like a myocardial infarction: you live or you die. A novel, on the other hand, you live, or you live and you live, or you die and die. The character's always the same, the situations change. Most good novels don't depend upon a crisis situation, whereas the short story is *about* a crisis.

Stanley Elkin, in "A Conversation with Stanley Elkin and William H. Gass," The Iowa Review, 1976.

situational comedy, and an extended rhetorical intensity to express the fullness of his world. Like the anthropologists in his fiction, Elkin combines significant general ideas with a marvelous knowledge of specific fact and creates perspective on both with characters whose obsessions test ideas and confront the necessity of fact. (pp. 159-62)

Thomas LeClair, "The Obsessional Fiction of Stanley Elkin," in Contemporary Literature, *Vol. 16, No. 2, Spring, 1975, pp. 146-62.*

Doris G. Bargen   (essay date 1980)

[*In the following excerpt, Bargen examines the themes that dominate Elkin's short fiction.*]

While Stanley Elkin's involvement with Metafiction has hitherto gone unnoticed, his relationship with Black Humor has been noticed but misunderstood. Critics have in fact confused his distanced Metafictional approach to Black Humor with an active commitment to the movement. And this despite his repeated statements, in interviews, that he is no Black Humorist. His theory of fiction resembles most closely that of William H. Gass in that the hero's perceptiveness manifests itself in his immersion in the gratifications of language. Gass [in his *Fiction and the Figures of Life*] contends that plot should be abandoned in favor of the writer's *complete* devotion to language: "by means of metaphor, the artist is able to organize whole areas of human thought and feeling, and to organize them concretely, giving to his model the quality of sensuous display." Gass even goes so far as to divest the customary notion of character from its associations of personality: "anything, indeed, which serves as a fixed point, like a stone in a stream or that soap in Bloom's pocket, functions as a character." Although Elkin shares Gass's high evaluation of metaphor, although he likes to think of himself as a stylist, he differs fundamentally from Gass on precisely this question of character. Gass seeks to make fiction an independent form made up of sentences and paragraphs rather than of plot and character, but Elkin returns again and again to "the hard edge of personality." On another occasion, he refers to his characters' centrality and says, "At the core of the fictive sensibility is character and style, but character is really what it's all about."

In his insistence on character, Elkin parts company with most of the Black Humorists, whose response to what they see as an absurd reality is best dramatized through caricatures. But Elkin goes further. The Elkin hero must possess a faculty for moral conflict. Elkin's emphasis on style rarely functions as an end in itself but rather as a means of exploring the characters' moral qualities. This generalization can be best exemplified by **"A Poetics for Bullies"** (1965), a story which seems to combine both Metafictional and Black Humorist elements, which actually demonstrates Elkin's interest in the first category and his distance from the second. The author has confirmed the strategic importance of the story for his work:

> anybody who wants to understand my works would have to understand **"A Poetics for Bullies"** first [. . .]. I wouldn't recommend it as the best thing I've written, but I'd recommend

it as the central thing. Push in that story undergoes, willfully, all the stratagems of most of my protagonists.

In this story, Elkin's theory of fiction and his position vis-à-vis Black Humor are demonstrated rather than stated. Although the title is overtly Metafictional, the concern for literature as literature is secondary. Although the story may seem at first to contain Black Humor, the moral thrust is opposite to that of [Kurt] Vonnegut and [Bruce Jay] Friedman.

Push, the protagonist of the story, is the archetypical kibitzer whose faith is built on "Sleight-of-mouth, the bully's poetics." His bullying and poetic teasing actually *benefit* his victims by bringing them to self-knowledge. Indeed, Push's motives are vindicated, curiously enough, by the cooperative behavior of his victims. Their relationship is based on mutual need. For all the "torment" that is bestowed upon the children with defects, "*especially* cripples," Push's attention to their troubles resembles the attention the psychiatrist shows for his patients. Push's tactics lie somewhere between the psychiatrist's tactful secretiveness and the conventional bully's physical violence: "(I'm a pusher, no hitter, no belter; an aggressor of marginal violence, I hate *real* force)."

The morality of this hero is determined neither by society's ethical codes nor by religious credos. Push has consciously made a choice as to "what his life must be." It is only when he encounters John Williams, a neighborhood rival with conventionally "good" morals, that his own motives are sharply defined.

John Williams sets himself up as an idol, a "*prince*," whose coat-of-arms casts a temporary spell even over Push. The status emblem resembles the medal the anonymous hero of **"On a Field, Rampant"** (1963) wears over his heart. Although the same type of pretentious character is described in both stories, the eventual dethronement of John Williams is less tragic than that of Khardov's son in the earlier story. The latter deserves more sympathy because the instigator of his foolish quest for a non-existent kingdom is his own father. John Williams, on the other hand, has only himself to blame for his pretentiousness.

In **"A Poetics for Bullies,"** Push gradually exposes the arrogance of his rival. Push cannot tolerate anybody who deems himself superior to others. Therefore, he is neither sentimental nor cynical when he puts himself on the same level as his victims, as a matter of principle, even before the arrival of John Williams: "(Do you know what makes me cry? The Declaration of Independence. 'All men are created equal.' That's beautiful)."

Unlike the model boy, Push takes the criers for what they are, neither embellishing nor covering up their defects. In his painful way, he demonstrates that he is not indifferent to their problems:

> I held them to the mark. Who else cared about the fatties, about the dummies and slobs and clowns, about the gimps and squares and oafs and fools, the kids with a mouthful of mush, all those shut-ins of the mind and heart, all those losers?

He does not spare them the reality of their situations whereas John Williams nourishes their illusions by teaching them alternative skills:

> I see him with Slud the cripple. They go to the gym. I watch from the balcony. "Let's develop those arms, my friend." They work out with weights. Slud's muscles grow, they bloom from his bones.
>
> I lean over the rail. I shout down, "He can bend iron bars. Can he peddle a bike? Can he walk on rough ground? Can he climb up a hill? Can he wait on a line? Can he dance with a girl? Can he go up a ladder or jump from a chair?"

Weightlifting does not solve Slud's problems. Push cannot, either, but at least he does not ignore them. When he first begins to lose his criers to the "prince" with the ordinary name who captures their attention with exotic tales, he must admit his own vulnerability:

> I have lived my life in pursuit of the vulnerable: Push the chink seeker, wheeler dealer in the flawed cement of the personality, a collapse maker. But what isn't vulnerable, *who* isn't? There is that which is unspeakable, so I speak it, that which is unthinkable, which I think. Me and the devil, we do God's dirty work, after all.

After many embarrassing failures in his effort to defeat the "paragon," Push finally succeeds in provoking him to an act of violence. Although Push's former victims still stand by John Williams, Push's personality has left its mark on the intruder who until then had had the "perfect" manners of a Sid Sawyer but also the talent of a Tom Sawyer to excite the imagination of a crowd. Towards the end of the story, the hero's moral stance becomes more powerful than ever—his character evokes the "real magic at last":

> John Williams mourns for me. He grieves his gamy grief. No one has everything—not even John Williams. He doesn't have *me*. He'll never have me, I think. If my life were only to deny him that, it would almost be enough. I could do his voice now if I wanted. [A sign of Push's new power.] His corruption began when he lost me.

Like many other Elkin protagonists, Push's initial attraction to and skepticism of magic had referred to charlatanry. Yet even then he had suspected that "the bully's poetics" were a gift of his character rather than magic itself which, after all, is "only casuistical trick." The "real magic" he takes pride in at the height of his power is therefore not simply a trick but the essence of his being: "the genuine thing: the cabala of my hate, of my irreconcilableness." In the end, the hero appears more confident about controlling John Williams and about recapturing the loyalty of the criers who

> moan. They are terrified, but they move up to see. We are thrown together. Slud, Frank, Clob, Mimmer, the others, John Williams, myself. I will not be reconciled, or have my hate. *It's* what I have, all I can keep. My bully's sour solace. It's enough, I'll make do.
>
> I can't stand them near me. I move against them.

> I shove them away. I force them off. I press them, thrust them aside. *I push through.*

Through his **"Poetics for Bullies,"** Push—in the fashion of a Metafictionist—has demystified "white magic" and shown it to be a hoax. Hard truths are morally better than easy illusions.

This type of aggressive—and vulnerable—hero appears in much of Elkin's fiction. Unfortunately, the actions of Push and his literary kinsmen have been denounced as inhuman in numerous reviews. As a result, many critics have been led to believe that Elkin is a Black Humorist, while others have been more cautious in using the term. Although many vignettes from any work by Elkin could be cited as examples of Black Humor, the context in which they appear and the attitude of the protagonists towards American cultural values refute such an affiliation. Most importantly, the Elkin hero neither displays an "emotional coolness" nor "a seeming indifference to the remediable ills of mankind" most commonly associated with Black Humor.

In **"A Poetics for Bullies,"** Push often strikes terror in the hearts of his victims, but not in order to hurt them. On the contrary, he invests his energy in reviving their damaged self-respect: "I love nobody loved." In other words, in a world that ignores people's physical and mental problems in order to peddle the soft soap of a John Williams, Push's rough counteraction may actually be a valuable instruction in the nature of reality. One episode from the story illustrates Push's effect of touching the most vital nerve of the criers, of mobilizing their dulled senses:

> "Push is the God of the Neighborhood." [Push says.]
>
> "Go way, Push," the kid says, uncertain.
>
> "Right," Push says, himself again. "Right. I'll disappear. First the fingers." My fingers ball to fists. "My forearms next." They jackknife into my upper arms. "The arms." Quick as bird-blink they snap behind my back, fit between the shoulder blades like a small knapsack. (I am double-jointed, protean.) "My head," I say.
>
> "No, Push," the kid says, terrified. I shudder and everything comes back, falls into place from the stem of self like a shaken puppet.

This may seem like Black Humor's enjoyment of the grotesque, but it is not. Elkin's remarks on the suffering of Faulkner's characters also apply to his own, to both criers and kibitzers:

> They seek suffering because it fixes identity. I bleed; therefore I am. [. . .] Since *it is pain which assures Faulkner's characters that they are alive at all,* the awareness of life, purchased as it is by the awareness of pain, becomes an expensive but absolutely necessary object.

Because Push inflicts pain, there can be no doubt that he is not morally indifferent but rather that he moves in controversial moral territory for the definite purpose of showing people their limits, or better, of pushing them to reaching their limits. In defending his heroes and Push in particular against charges of cruel behavior, Elkin has once again credited his Muse with rhetoric, the primary source of energy, while refusing to reduce his protagonists' moral position simply to one of either good or evil:

> Energy is what counts. It is what is on the good side of the ledger for Feldman [in *A Bad Man*] and for Push. Whoever has the better rhetoric is the better man, and since Feldman by and large tends to have the better rhetoric, he is as far as I'm concerned the more sympathetic character. And to the extent that Push has better rhetoric than John Williams, he is the more sympathetic character. But in moral terms I don't care whether these people are good or bad. What draws me is rhetoric, and the need for resistance, and of course the ability to do that.

Another story that might be mistaken for Black Humor is **"In the Alley"** (1959). The hero, another member of the Feldman "family," feels threatened by the standard elements of Black Humor—sickness, sexuality, and death. Moreover, Mr. Feldman's Jewish origins indicate an affinity between Black Humor and American-Jewish fiction. The two literary movements are supposedly linked through the concept of suffering and laughter. The hero's suffering, however, is not restricted to the suffering of a particular ethnic group, nor is laughter likely to be the reader's response to the story.

Mr. Feldman is deathly ill. Understandably, he takes his fate seriously. Death is a grave matter. He intends to carry the burden of his death alone rather than tell anybody. Mr. Feldman will be "a hero." After his brave decision, however, the tense situation takes unexpected, comic turns that are mostly out of Feldman's control. Instead of Feldman's mocking his impending death, as a Vonnegut character might, it is he himself who is mocked for doing just the opposite—for taking his death seriously, too seriously. Not only had the doctor erred in his prognosis of only one more year to live but a note of hubris had also been revealed in the hero's secret attempt to cope with death all by himself. Yet the opportunity for grandeur that Death respresents for Feldman, the chance for expanding the self one more time, cannot be fulfilled. In the end, Death inevitably reduces Feldman to his human stature. The typical Black Humor protagonist would never experience the tragic, pitifully human showdown Feldman does when he dies in a filthy alley with a note on his jacket, "STAY AWAY FROM WHITE WOMEN." Panicky about his prolonged struggle with death, Feldman had ventured into a strange neighborhood where he had been beaten for confessing his approaching death to a local woman in a lower-class bar and, more importantly, for proposing intimacies to her. The Black Humorist's laughter concerning death is cynical:

> death becomes a crime, an unforgivable denial of the American myths of potency and expansiveness. [. . .] Black Humor is a simultaneous advance upon and retreat from death; it both endangers and protects its readers' consciousness in its fusion of death and comedy.

By the end of the story, the comedy of the hero's initial egocentricity has turned into a sad irony rather than an occasion for more malicious, sadistic laughter. The object

is not to detach the reader from the hero's fate, as in Black Humor, but to develop the reader's empathy even for a goal as foolish and presumptuous as Feldman's.

Shortly before he dies amidst the alley's garbage, he realizes that neither the heroic pose in front of his relatives nor his humble confession to the woman in the bar had been the decent thing to do. Neither by hiding nor by proclaiming his prospective death has he been able to avert people's disrespect. Although Feldman finally dies absurdly in a place that is unflatteringly symbolic of the end of all things, he is the greatest opponent of the specific attitude towards death commonly associated with Black Humor: "The threat to the body is part of the omnipresent threat of death in grotesque black humor. Death dominates, but it occurs in a ridiculous manner and is never dignified." Quite contrary to this concept of Black Humor, Feldman stands (and falls) with Ben Flesh (in *The Franchiser*), another major Elkin hero who must cope with the approach of death: "There are no ludicrous ways to die. There are no ludicrous deaths."

Once Feldman has overcome a momentary feeling in the bar that "dying was essentially ludicrous," he can finally come to terms with his mortality and the true nature of his heroism: "nothing came gracefully—not to heroes." What hurts him most is mockery. Having been in agreement with Ben Flesh's view all along, except for his moment of doubt, Feldman cannot endure the disgrace he had been trying to avoid so hard:

> The men from the factories lifted him from the floor where he lay and carried him into the street. It was dark now. Under the lamplight they marched with him. Children ran behind and chanted strange songs. He heard the voices even in his sleep, and dreamed that he was an Egyptian king awaking in the underworld. About him were the treasures, the artifacts with which his people mocked his death. He was betrayed, forsaken. He screamed he was not dead and for answer heard their laughter as they retreated through the dark passage.

Even in this dark story, then, Elkin picks up Black Humor themes, like sickness, sexuality, and death, only to refute the Black Humorists' assumption that these are matters which our society permits us to ridicule. Not even in his almost bashful attempt to attract the attention of the woman in the bar does Feldman stoop to the sexual abuse, or violence, often found in the Black Humor protagonist. On the contrary, it is he who is made to suffer under the woman's black humor:

> "I'm dying," he said again. "I don't know what to do." He could no longer hear himself speaking. The words tumbled out of his mouth in an impotent rage. He wondered absently if he was crying. "The doctor told me I'm supposed to die, only I don't do it, do you see?"
>
> "Go to a different doctor," the girl said.
>
> She joked with him. It was impossible that she didn't understand. He held the worm in his jaws. It was in his stomach, in the hollows of his arm-

pits. Pieces of it stoppered his ears. "No, no. I'm really dying. There have been tests. Everything."

In this early story as well as in his story, **"The Conventional Wisdom,"** the author aims at a critical literary evaluation of a literary movement rather than a promotion of it. In both stories the heroes come into contact with a world that is ruled by Black Humor, are victimized by it but never convert to it.

"The Conventional Wisdom" features a continually robbed liquor-store owner who refuses to succumb to the temptation of a Black Humorist point of view as a way out of his misery. Black Humor is prevalent all around him. He hears it from his profit-oriented wife, from the greedy wives of his former clerks (who are either killed or badly beaten in the stick-ups), and from the robbers who victimize him. Everybody seems to tell Ellerbee that it does not pay to be the good guy.

When the story takes a surrealistic turn after Ellerbee's death in still another hold-up, the ultimate test of his conventional wisdom presents itself first in Heaven and then in Hell. There the hero discovers that the conventional wisdom, that is, the fantasy of Heaven and Hell, is all true, despite the clichés. Although Ellerbee bitterly accuses God of a petty Catch-22 manner and of not rewarding him for his good will, he never regrets having lived the life of cliché, of having distinguished between the good and the bad. The grotesque clash between Ellerbee's adamant defense of his good will and the cynical world surrounding him makes this story one of the harshest condemnations of the philosophy of Black Humor.

Indeed, Stanley Elkin agrees in theory with those critics who disapprove of the goals of Black Humor—violence, blasphemy, pornography, the debasement of human dignity for satirical purposes, or merely for the sake of poking fun at people's weaknesses, the repetitiveness of their motifs, all most obtrusively and obnoxiously combined in Joseph Heller's *Catch-22* (1961). Elkin remains, even in 1977, enough of a Metafictionist to turn *his* protest against Black Humor into a story vindicating literature as a moral act. (pp. 46-53)

. . . . .

In American-Jewish fiction, the rhetorical mode often appeared in the form of salesmanship. Stanley Elkin has worked within and enriched this tradition, not only in his Jewish or half-Jewish protagonists, but, more remarkably, also in his non-Jewish ones. **"I Look Out for Ed Wolfe"** dramatizes the rhetoric in the figure of Ed Wolfe whose ethnic identity is cast in doubt. Just as Faulkner's Joe Christmas is permanently uncertain about his race, Ed Wolfe must forever remain uncertain about the Jewishness ascribed to him during his stay in a Jewish orphanage. While the salesman theme is traditional in Jewish fiction, the episodic structure the author chooses for this story links the hero to another literary tradition, that of the picaresque.

The major critical complaint against Stanley Elkin has been that his fiction has, at best, an episodic structure. For these critics, a series of episodes must be a failure of plot in any piece of fiction except the picaresque novel, but there is no literary law requiring all treatments of the orphan theme to take the form of the picaresque novel. In fact, most of Elkin's characters fit Robert Alter's conception of the modern picaroon:

> It is only because of his imagination [i.e., the picaroon's and the artist's imagination] that he can get along so well in what is, after all, a precariously marginal existence. It is his imagination that enables him to be a nimble deceiver, a protean role-player and master of disguise [. . .]

Protean and diverse as the modern picaro may be in his appearance, attitudes, motivations, problems and aspirations, compared to his traditionally restricted ancestor, Elkin's heroes have rarely been classified as belonging to this contemporary version of the picaresque. May it suffice here to speculate in moderation: it does not seem inconceivable that Elkin's novels, with the exception of *A Bad Man* (1967), should bear more or less pertinent traces of the picaresque in so far as their protagonists, like Bellow's Augie March, are roguish orphans on the road, obsessed with some not completely understood spiritual quest.

While Stanley Elkin considers **"A Poetics for Bullies"** to be his most programmatic piece of fiction, with **"On a Field, Rampant"** as its "companion" story, **"I Look Out for Ed Wolfe"** distinguishes itself by revealing the prototype for his orphan characters. In his early recognition of "Stanley Elkin's Orphans," Allen Guttmann suggests that many of Elkin's characters are defined, either literally or metaphorically, by their orphanhood. So important is this concept to the story, and to Elkin's work in general, that failure to understand it has led many critics to confused dissatisfaction.

Central to **"I Look Out for Ed Wolfe"** is the ramification of orphanhood. The crisis which sets the picaresque story in motion does not warrant a novelistic exploitation of the theme but presses the hero for a short-term solution of his suddenly unhinged, dangling existence. Neither from a Thoreauvian impulse "to live deliberately and Spartanlike" nor from a parody thereof, not even from the traditional picaro's mockery of "the mysterious birth of the traditional hero," does Ed Wolfe divest himself of all his possessions but from a desperate search for the limits of his orphan's lack of social ties and obligations.

The episodic structure of **"I Look Out for Ed Wolfe"** holds together as a complicated argument does, with every point made as a logical step toward its inevitable conclusion. As a matter of fact, the story's tense, critical atmosphere is enhanced by a flavor of determinism. It is emphasized by the hero's fixed outsider position and by the Quixotic principles that Ed Wolfe tries to follow, sometimes sheepishly, sometimes doggedly. If Ed Wolfe's behavior appears to be rather fickle from episode to episode, it is because he needs to approach his monomaniac goal from every possible angle. The extraordinary, existential premise of the orphan hero and the matching episodic structure of an obsessive quest are the bases for Stanley Elkin's expansive inventiveness. It is unfortunate that the reviewers of Elkin's work have been unable to attribute any meaningful function to such powerful imagination as it explores the ramifications of identity.

Ed Wolfe's orphanhood is indeed the one steady, undisputable factor in his life: "He was an orphan, and, to himself, he seemed like one, looked like one." As this first sentence of the story indicates, Ed Wolfe is self-conscious about his orphan identity. By virtue of his orphanhood, he is bothered by an uncertainty of status to which he, at age twenty-seven, has managed more or less to adapt. He survived sixteen meagre years spent in an orphanage, where he was given his name and his marginal Jewishness. He has put up with an unpleasant job at Cornucopia Finance Corporation, a job which he alone, with his background, knew how to appreciate. Who is better suited for a loan company than an orphan with a borrowed identity? Critics who condemn his harsh technique of admonishing delinquent debtors to cope with Cornucopia overlook the origins of his righteous indignation about deadbeat behavior. Ironically, it is Ed Wolfe's professional efficiency that leads his admiring boss to fire him: "Your technique's terrific," [says Mr. La Meck.] "With you around we could have laid off the lawyers. But Ed, you're a gangster. A gangster."

Once fired from his job with the loan company, he recovers quickly, as if he had never expected to be kept long in the first place:

> La Meck gave him a check and Ed Wolfe got up. Already it was as though he had never worked there. When La Meck handed him the check he almost couldn't think what it was for. There should have been a photographer there to record the ceremony: ORPHAN AWARDED CHECK BY BUSINESSMAN.

It is only La Meck's mean reference to his orphanhood that arouses vengeful thoughts in Ed Wolfe. La Meck puts forth his views more brutally than any remark Ed Wolfe ever made to his clients, who truly deserved a harsh word for reckless spending and borrowing. La Meck bleats: "You're not supposed to be happy. It isn't in the cards for you. You're a fall-guy type."

Jobless, he sets out into the world as "Ed Wolfe, the Flying Dutchman, the Wandering Jew, the Off and Running Orphan," with nothing but his severance pay and La Meck's advice: "You've got to watch it. Don't love. Don't hate. That's the secret. Detachment and caution. Look out for Ed Wolfe." La Meck's motto is echoed throughout the story, evoking a variety of responses in the hero. It is a sad, perhaps even traumatic moment when he is first seen at the complete mercy of the motto:

> in a moment he was out of La Meck's office, and the main office, and the elevator, and the building itself, loose in the world, as cautious and as detached as La Meck could want him.

Detachment, however, requires a cynicism that Ed Wolfe, despite his harsh evaluation of people, cannot sustain.

Once let loose, the protagonist launches upon a seemingly contradictory series of immense and bold enterprises. Each one he takes up with great passion, as he had previously been obsessed with his job. First he envisions a life of infinite luxury and "obedience," but such a life is not for him. Unlike La Meck, he needs a passion to thrive on. What strikes his fancy, almost like a revelation, is a simple advertisement by a used car dealer. He realizes—like many of Elkin's heroes—that there is magic in merchandise and in buying and selling, a drama he too can play a part in. In a haggling scene with "an automobile *buyer*," he does in fact get the upper hand.

In the next phase of his quickly shifting, hectic pursuits, he decides to sell out, to divest himself of his possessions. He will live on the "orphan's nutritional margin." Like the typical Elkin hero, he acts out his obsessions to the extreme. Determined to perfect his orphan identity and embody La Meck's doctrine of "detachment and caution," he sells his possessions as if they were parts of his own body and mind and future. The sell-out foreshadows the even greater sacrilege at the end of the story—his symbolical death. Leo Feldman in *A Bad Man* learns from his supersalesman father Isidore that one can only sell a dead body and that "the unsalable thing" is the living human being. Consequently, the son takes his father up on the lesson he taught him by selling his father's dead body. Ed Wolfe's logic works in similar ways. Blindly following La Meck he shrouds himself in delusion:

> It was a time of ruthless parting from his things, but there was no bitterness in it. He was a born salesman, he told himself. A disposer, a natural dumper. He administered severance. As detached as a funeral director, what he had learned was to say good-by. It was a talent of a sort. And he had never felt quite so interested. He supposed he was doing what he had been meant for—what, perhaps, everyone was meant for. He sold and he sold, each day spinning off little pieces of himself, like controlled explosions of the sun. Now his life was a series of speeches, of nearly earnest pitches. What he remembered of the day was what he had said. What others said to him, or even whether they spoke at all, he was unsure of.

When he has sold everything and thus learned the exact "going rate for orphans in a wicked world," he cannot stop. There is now money to dispose of. Ed Wolfe moves forward with fateful determinism. At this point in the inevitable course of events he can already sense what is in store for him. It is as if only some "special grief" could redeem him from his isolation and indifference:

> He longed for a special grief, to be touched by anguish or terror, but when he saw the others in the street, in the cafeteria, in the theater, in the hallway, on the stairs, at the newsstand, in the basement rushing their fouled linen from basket to machine, he stood, as indifferent to their errand, their appetite, their joy, their greeting, their effort, their curiosity, their grime, as he was to his own. No envy wrenched him, no despair unhoped him, but, gradually, he became restless.

Consequently, he now enters a spending phase which is nothing but another desperate attempt to rid himself of Self, for "He had come to think of his money as his life." When he finally and dangerously approaches the limits of his marginal existence, he once more shrinks back, only to try another angle of his self-destructive path, repressing any emotion and denying himself the most minimal convenience:

> In the darkness he walked through a thawing, melting world. There was something on the edge of the air, the warm, moist odor of the change of the season. He was touched despite himself. "I'll take a bus," he threatened. "I'll take a bus and close the windows and ride over the wheel."

However, the ascetic pose is of no avail. He has been fooled by La Meck's Cassandra prophecy of the "fall-guy" fate. More importantly, he, like Khardov's son in **"On a Field, Rampant,"** believes in his specialness to the point where he himself becomes incredulous:

> there was a suggestion [. . .] that his impregnability was a myth [. . .] He strove against himself, a supererogatory enemy, and sought by a kind of helpless abrasion, as one rubs wood, the gleaming self beneath. An orphan's thinness, he thought, was no accident.

At the slightest encouragement from a figure of authority, however, he is reaffirmed in his belief. Just as Khardov inspires the illusions of his princely son in **"On a Field, Rampant,"** La Meck saddles Ed Wolfe with a false consciousness. Despite the diametrically opposed directions the protagonists take on their quests—one approaching the limits of his orphan existence and the other aspiring to the crown—they both end up in utter defeat and disillusionment.

Ed Wolfe's last adventure—the boldest of them all—is initiated by his adoption of the professional role that seems to come most easily—and passionately—to him. Pompously, he walks into a hotel lobby and introduces himself: " 'Nice town you got here,' he said expansively. 'I'm a salesman, you understand, and this is new territory for me.' " His ebullient mood is immediately shattered by his encounter with a Negro sitting in the hotel lobby and reading *The Wall Street Journal*. The black man, by doing what "looks good for the race," mirrors Ed Wolfe's own pretentious effort to become what he is not; the black draws attention to his race just as Ed Wolfe makes a point of his orphanhood. In his defensiveness and embarrassment, Ed Wolfe blunders comically:

> In the lobby a man sat in a deep chair, *The Wall Street Journal* opened wide across his face. "Where's the action?" Ed Wolfe said, peering over the top of the paper into the crown of the man's hat.
>
> "What's that?" the man asked.
>
> Ed Wolfe, surprised, saw that the man was a Negro.
>
> "What's that?" the man repeated, vaguely nervous. Embarrassed, Ed Wolfe watched him guiltily, as though he had been caught in an act of bigotry.
>
> "I thought you were someone else," he said lamely. The man smiled and lifted the paper to his face. Ed Wolfe stood before the opened paper, conscious of mildly teetering. He felt

lousy, awkward, complicatedly irritated and ashamed, the mere act of hurting someone's feelings suddenly the most that could be held against him. It came to him how completely he had failed to make himself felt. "Look out for Ed Wolfe, indeed," he said aloud. The man lowered his paper. "Some of my best friends are Comanches," Ed Wolfe said. "Can I buy you a drink?"

Kurt Dittmar considers the remark about the Comanches tasteless and irrelevant; he sympathizes with the black's good-natured but deceitful intentions and ignores Ed Wolfe's guilty confusion. Yet, nothing could describe Ed Wolfe's state of incompatible emotions—of arrogance and embarrassment—more perfectly than this clumsy cartoon phrase. He tries to be friendly and appears pushy. Finally, he literally forces himself on the man, thereby making the first—and unusually gentle—physical contact since he shook hands with the despicable La Meck. He is moved by the whole scene, proving that he is not the inhuman creature critics have made him out to be.

While the moment of kinship with the Negro lasts, the protagonist is uniquely involved and no longer an "indifferent" incorporation of the La Meck doctrine. They go off to a party as pals. Half-drunk, Ed Wolfe is awed by the Negro's helpfulness: He lets the Negro guide and entertain him. Soon, however, he becomes afraid of this untrue-to-an-orphan dependency and begins to develop hostile thoughts, prompted by fear: "Fake. Fake, Ed Wolfe thought. Murderer. Nigger. Razor man." This hostility makes him feel "gently detached" again. The world of the Negro and his friends is meant to be a replica of the white *goyim* world that he hates. Because the replica is a poor and pathetic one, it enrages and saddens him even more.

He asks Mary Roberta, a black girl, for a dance and is shocked by her vitality: "Sick, he remembered a jumping bean he had held once in his palm, awed and frightened by the invisible life, jerking and hysterical, inside the stony shell." Simultaneously attracted and frightened by her protected, unattainable life, he is irritated by her questions concerning his own life. He immediately falls back into his tough-orphan role.

> "I'm a pusher," he said, suddenly angry. She looked frightened. "But I'm not hooked myself. It's a weakness in my character. I can't get hooked. Ach, what would you *goyim* know about it?"

To his own fearful astonishment he excites the crowd with his loud confessional outcries against his lonely existence. He feels threatened by people's curiosity and seeks refuge in the "La Meck Plan." Holding on to Mary Roberta as a kind of hostage, he addresses the crowd from the bandstand in a wild speech about his salesman-pusher commitment and mentality. In his explication of his orphan identity, he clings to his basic human value: his salesmanship.

> "Brothers and sisters," he shouted, "and as an only child bachelor orphan I use the term playfully, you understand. Brothers and sisters, I tell you what I'm *not* going to do. I'm no consumer. Nobody's death can make me that. I won't consume. I mean, it's a question of identity, right?

Closer, come up closer, buddies. You don't want to miss any of this."

In order to prove his point, he tries to auction off the black girl to the Negro audience. The offensive scene is, of course, a macabre, contemporary reenactment of slave auctions. It can only be understood, as the despairing protagonist himself points out, by his orphan privilege to be "Rough!", the social assignment to do the dirty jobs:

> "Look," he said patiently, "the management has asked me to remind you that this is a living human being. This is the real thing, the genuine article, the goods. Oh, I told them I wasn't the right man for this job. As an orphan I have no conviction about the product. Now, you should have seen me in my old job. I could be rough. *Rough!* I hurt people. Can you imagine? I actually caused them pain. I mean, what the hell, I was an orphan. I *could* hurt people. An orphan doesn't have to bother with love. An orphan's like a nigger in that respect. Emancipated. But you people are another problem entirely."

Indeed, he has been outraged, almost feels betrayed, by their inauthentic behavior, starting with the black man reading *The Wall Street Journal,* by their emulation of white *goyim.*

When they crowd in upon him in indignation, he panics and tries absurdly to distract them by pretending to be brother, father, and son to some imaginary person. This scheme, of course, holds them off only momentarily. When they then demand the black girl back, he decides to sell himself—Elkin's unpardonable sin—rather than release her into their custody. Although he was initially ready to turn her over to them, the "parents"—despite his feeling of kinship for her and his awe at her vulnerability "inside the stony shell"—he acted in self-defense. At their threat to take her away from him, he changes his whole strategy. He symbolically sells himself into adoption (or slavery, as the dramatic setting also suggests). The act of shifting loyalty from himself to her involves, in his estimation, a noble sacrifice.

Ed Wolfe has come to believe in the symbolic equation of money and self. Therefore, by parting with his money—which has come to stand for all he is "worth"—he experiences a spiritual death. Moreover, instead of selling himself, he practically has to give himself away, because the crowd does not even bother to take an active part in Ed Wolfe's faked bidding. In his theater, the protagonist goes through the most humiliating of all his sell-outs. **"I Look Out for Ed Wolfe"** is a one-man-show and the hero gets what he, at heart, really wants. At last, he gives himself the final blow by parting from the girl, from life itself:

> He faced the girl. "Good-by," he said.
>
> She reached forward, taking his hand.
>
> "Good-by," he said again, "I'm leaving."
>
> She held his hand, squeezing it. He looked down at the luxuriant brown hand, seeing beneath it the fine articulation of bones, the rich sudden rush of muscle. Inside her own he saw, indiffer-

ently, his own pale hand, lifeless and serene, still and infinitely free.

The deepest significance of this enigmatic story lies in the conjunction of the basic Elkinesque themes of orphanhood and salesmanship. The link between these two concepts is found in a third concept—that of the self. In a common American phrase, people are urged to "sell themselves," as if the self were some commodity to be wholesaled or retailed to the public. Of Ed Wolfe, Elkin writes, "He sold and he sold, each day spinning off little pieces of himself." Thus Ed Wolfe's orphanhood and his salesmanship are intricately related. His salesman's passion makes him, in a sense, an orphan to the second power. The orphan, by definition, lacks the identity and sense of self which derive from having a family; the salesman divests himself of self. In Ed Wolfe's case, the apparent contradiction between the orphan's traditional search for a more powerful sense of self and the salesman's divestiture of self is tragically cancelled. The hero is torn by the socially ascribed identity of orphanhood and his dream identity of the outgoing, independent salesman personality type. His choice of salesmanship as a vehicle for making social contact—with the customers—apparently defies the orphan's deterministic fate of loneliness and dependence. However, he discovers that the two roles of orphan and salesman put him in a vicious circle. While his *self-image* as a salesman had given him the illusion of an inflated, strong ego, *being* a salesman had confronted him with the requirement of selling himself, of deflating the ego again. When Ed Wolfe, in the climactic auction scene, tries to sell someone else, the black girl, and meets the crowd's resistance, he despairingly commits a kind of salesman's version of suicide—he gives himself away. He fails to strengthen his orphan position by abandoning himself in his salesman passion. His orphanhood cannot be escaped or endured through a salesman's prostitution of the self. In his eagerness to overcome the orphan's loneliness, he gives away what little self an Elkin's orphan has to start with. It has been too difficult, after all, to look out for Ed Wolfe. (pp. 83-91)

. . . . .

Alexander Main, bailbondsman, is another of Elkin's obsessed professionals. Like Leo Feldman and Ben Flesh, he is—at least metaphorically—a salesman. He thinks of his business transactions as acts of salesmanship: "I have the route salesman's heart." Unlike Feldman and Flesh, however, he sells no "product." What he "sells" to the indicted and imprisoned is their freedom, their temporary release from the law's captivity. But the freedom is also a bondage to him. And, to make the paradoxical situation even more complicated, he places himself in bondage too. If *they* abscond, *he* loses. Since Main is a typically Elkinesque protagonist, the loss is more a matter of professional pride than it is of cold cash. Main is totally absorbed in his difficult profession. He sacrifices his private life to his role as bailbondsman. In fact, he lives by his collection of business calendars, whose official red-letter days he ignores on behalf of his clients' unofficial ones, i.e., their appointment in court. His profession furnishes him not only with the means for personal aggrandizement but also with an aura of myth:

I love a contract like the devil, admire the tall paper and the small print [. . .] I beat no one with loophole. Everything spelled out, all clear, aboveboard as chessmen: truth in advertising and a language even the dishonest understand. No, I'm talking the *look* of the instrument, texture, watermark, the silk flourish of the bright ribbon, the legend perfected centuries [. . .], the beautiful formulas simple as pie, old-fashioned quid pro quo like a recipe in the family generations. My conditions classic and my terms terminal.

A bailbondsman's success requires an abundance of criminal suspects and Main is determined to be successful:

Stuff the jails I say, crowd them. Shove in the innocent with the guilty. I don't want to see educational programs in the pens, I don't want to know from rehabilitation. That shit knocks down recidivism. Shorter sentences, that's something else, a different story entirely. Shorter sentences are *good* for business. That gets 'em back on the streets again, the villains and stickup guys. That's what we call turnover, and I'm all for it.

Nothing seems sacred to the bailbondsman. Emma Lazarus' poem on the Statue of Liberty he perverts to his use: "So give [me] your murderer, your rapist, your petty thief yearning to breathe free." His bailbondsman's toast is "To hard times and our golden age of blood!" For psychological survival, a modicum of detachment is necessary, even for the obsessed professional:

But I forget. When it's finished I forget, chuck it in the mind's wastebasket as you'd throw away a phone number in your wallet when it no longer has meaning. Well, what am I? The rogues' gallery? A computer bank? Must I walk around with sin like a stuffed nose? Of course I forget.

Detachment is achieved through rhetoric. Slogans are adapted to Main's purposes; lingos change with changing clients. No matter what the situation, Main responds with a spectacularly varied and forceful flow of language. Even his momentary expressions of ambivalence sparkle with rhetorical energy:

"We would rather be a banker in a fine suit. We would rather conduct discreet business over drinks at the club. Heart to heart, man to man, gentlemen's agreements and a handshake between friends. We would prefer silver at our temples and a portrait in oils in the marble lobby. *But . . .* "

It is doubtful that Alexander Main would actually prefer to be "a banker in a fine suit," but the suggestions of the slightly old-fashioned are not accidental. Although Main is immersed in the frantic hurly-burly of contemporary life, several aspects of the novella link him to the recent, the distant, and even to the prehistoric past. That Main is a part of the present needs little comment. He rattles off the slang and jargon of his profession, he is "in the know" vis-à-vis the law, and he is cognizant of modern criminal practice. Fully integrated into the modern *Gesellschaft*, he is professionally enthusiastic.

Or so it seems. Upon closer scrutiny, we discover an interesting, almost anachronistic pattern. Like the heroine of **"Fifty Dollars,"** Main resists the trend to huge, impersonal, strictly functional commercial office centers. He refers to his office as the "shop" and has made it look slightly decadent. He attaches great importance to the shop's little bell, as in "a bakery or an old candy store." Mr. Crainpool, Main's secretary, is compelled to wear clothes that are suggestive of the homely dignity of the shop: "It gives him the look of a clerk in Dickens and lends tone to the place." Crainpool is forced to sit at a nineteenth-century desk, to wear a green eyeshade, and to write with a quill pen. Main's fondness for the Victorian appears along with his conception of himself as a Phoenician. To this ancient people he attributes the very idea of bailbond and of the bailbondsman. Main relishes the nickname given to him by his colleagues, "The Phoenician." Antiquity appears also in a crucial dream (discussed below), in which the bail-jumpers Oyp and Glyp burglarize a Pharaonic tomb.

A fascination with the prehistoric past appears in a mysterious visit to the Museum of Natural Sciences. There, the bailbondsman studies—teeth. Main's comical obsession with teeth is full of original and apparently irrelevant insights. The scientific information he gathers from cards is immediately translated into some strikingly appropriate and often funny comparison taken from a more familiar frame of reference: "A root thicker than the wire in a coat hanger rises a full inch above the awful terraces of decay which surround it." To him, the various teeth symbolize "the distillate of the animal's soul, the cutting, biting edge of its passion and life." The visit to the museum is an overwhelming experience. "He is weeping." The entire episode suggests a primitive substratum beneath the modern *Gesellschaft*. Psychically, we are all survivors, still linked by our unconscious to "nature red in tooth and claw." No wonder that Main's study of the prehistoric teeth releases an inspired flow of rhetoric. At the mere sight of the teeth he becomes inventive and poetic in his choice of similes, always a sign, in Elkin's work, of emotional involvement. The museum teeth, in their powerfulness and present "terrible disrepair," bring Main to meditation on the ultimate:

God sees through my bright caps, knows what's beneath them, sees right down to the gums, the pink base of my being, the cloudy tracings in which the teeth stand parallel as staves. And under the gums the cementum-sheathed roots hooking bone, seeking wild handhold and purchase like some apraxic mountaineer. God knows my jaws.

Unconsciously, perhaps, he is moved so much because the museum experience mirrors his unforgotten passion for pursuing Oyp and Glyp (whose names resemble those of the cavemen in popular literature). That they have successfully absconded, that they continue to elude him, that they have ruined his otherwise perfect record—these facts are extremely important and Main's reaction to them forms the central action of the novella. The two fugitives seem to have invaded the bailbondsman's peace of mind: "Oyp and Glyp. They're alive. Alive and loose and flouting my extraditionary will."

The dream of Oyp and Glyp requires close analysis.

Main's subconscious shows their significance to be of truly unreasonable dimensions. By means of an associative dream logic events and impressions are linked together and magnified by the subconsious. A logical sequence of events is kept within the framework of the major action. The tomb robbery is followed by an arrest, the denial of bail and the release of Oyp and Glyp. Throughout the dream, the baffled bailbondsman plays an unsuccessful and helpless role, quite uncharacteristic of the self-assured image he projects in his everyday business deals.

Through the dream he hopes to regain control of the two fugitives who were only car thieves in real life but are now promoted to tomb robbers. They are after gold, which exercises a strong power on him as well. Yet the usual connotations of gold are absent. The image is rather of "golden blight" and "ruinous disease," as if the tomb violators' false values were a warning to Main about his own. Main takes the warning to heart. What frightens him in the world of reality is reflected in his dream, and vice versa, for such dreams have occurred to him before:

> He sees their light before he sees them, refracted, rolling off the walls like a sand dune, breaking like a wave, caught, confirming as it comes the gold surfaces he had smelled, felt, tasted and heard before he had seen.

Anachronisms, however, tend to burlesque what might otherwise terrify and to provide the comedy of the three-part dream, especially in the crime section. Past and present are curiously mixed. The ancient site of the Pharoah's tomb is invaded by contemporary tourists who are content with staring at the props, the hollowness of the "golden blight":

> the now empty storerooms and holy chambers and chapels where the Pharaoh's painted double stood in mimic life in the picture-book rooms viewing his faded family album, fooled into feasting on images of food, hunting cartoon deer and fishing cartoon fish from cartoon rivers, copulating with cartoons and waiting for the dead man's soul to invade the ka's body like a virus.

Only Oyp and Glyp defect from the group for the real gold in the still undiscovered tomb. They speak a modern gangster lingo and are equipped with their car mechanics' tools for breaking the car-like sarcophagus. After all, they are only car thieves. As a preliminary to the major crime, Oyp and Glyp break the amphoras for the "Pharaoh's unguents and liquors." Main's excitement at this point results in "a wet dream," as he realizes when he wakes up. The robbers become rapists in a quasi-defloration scene of the amphora which, ironically, contains the Pharaoh's "ejaculatory final ethers." In a state of intoxication, the team moves on to the breaking of the sarcophagus. The more experienced and ruthless of the two finally gets down to the solid gold layer of the chinese box arrangement of coffins: "He is exactly like the attendant in a filling station whose fingers seek a clasp which will raise the hood of your car."

Reminiscent of the Easter decorations in the streets of Cincinnati is the "shell of the dead king" which, despite its splendor as the "priceless golden Easter egg of a Pha-

raoh," is not declared the thieves' booty. Unlike Main, they seem to have learned how to deal with phenomena of the "golden blight." As a consequence, the king's "shell" becomes at most the subject to their detailed study and their awe. However, the unscrupulous leader— against the protest of the younger thief—wants to escape with no more and no less than the "Pharaoh's natron-dried, embalmed heart." They penetrate and abandon all the gold for the symbolical essence of the deity. The bailbondsman witnesses the crime with wonder. He is continually puzzled by hieroglyphs he cannot decipher. This inability definitely adds to the immensity of the mysterious crime.

Oyp and Glyp are caught and tried for their crime. In the trial scene, the bailbondsman refers to their inadequate equipment in order to play down their crime. Main makes light of their trespass, but the judge refuses bail, for the crime of Oyp and Glyp is truly so immense as to be "unthinkable." Paradoxically, the judge decides on aquittal because no punishment is commensurate with the crime. Main is not permitted to exercise his professional power. Therefore, his "fugitives from fugitiveness itself" still remain a challenge to him. By the end of his dream, he must realize that "there were limits to his power and his own precious freedom." Main must acknowledge that Oyp and Glyp are and will always be ahead of him just as he prides himself of being ahead of his fellow bailbondsmen: "the tomb robbers always got there first, breaking the chain of expectation, spoiling eternity with the fierce needs of the present."

Oyp and Glyp escape. They are not the only ones. The novella ends with the escape of Crainpool, whose mysterious subservience to Main is finally explained. Indeed, the riddle of the Dickensian clerk is revealed in its full impact only at the very end of the novella. Technically, the shift from the mystery of Oyp and Glyp to that of Crainpool manifests itself in a shift of narrative technique. Those sections dealing with Main's business and his secretary are controlled by the narrative "I" of the hero himself, whereas the supernatural and the nightmare are marked by the third-person narration of the authorial voice. The reader is therefore cautioned to distinguish between the clues he receives from the two modes of narration. It is significant, however, that Main does not, contrary to what one might expect, regain possession of the narrative after his nightmare. The loss of voice means—and this is underlined by Main's treatment of his secretary—that Main is indeed a changed man.

He goes from the nameless hotel in which he dreamed of Oyp and Glyp to the Vernon Manor Hotel, which has the appearances of a relic of the past. It is as old-fashioned as Main's shop, and its residents are old, which, of course, is why Main ordered his secretary to live there. Main is counteracting modern taste, tying Crainpool to a symbolical past.

The puzzled secretary hopes that his employer's visit be just another joke, but a single allusion to Oyp and Glyp suffices, with a side reference to himself, to alarm him. He is shocked by Main's motives for the visit: " 'To what do I owe this honor?' [Crainpool] says at last. 'To bad dreams. To my poor scores in hard subjects. To your vulnerable history.' " Crainpool had once before been terrified of the bailbondsman, whose victimizing had become "routinized" over the years. Now, Main once again strikes to the bottom of Crainpool's fear. It is only at this juncture that Elkin reveals the origins of Crainpool's servitude. Crainpool too had jumped bail. Caught by Main, who has the legal right to shoot him, Crainpool serves his time as clerk rather than go to prison. Now, threatened by Main's allusions, Crainpool is relieved to hear of the "bailbondsman's statute of limitations." His relief is premature.

Main announces that he is going to shoot Crainpool, possibly in lieu of Oyp and Glyp, who seem to have escaped him forever. The helpless "stunt man" now falls back in despair upon their old comedy routine. An unconvincing actor under such pressure, Crainpool does not succeed in making Main's threat of murder as exciting and theatrical as the bailbondsman desires. For one thing, he does not have his master's relentless, torturous imagination. Accordingly, Main is as disappointed in his potential victim as Feldman is in Dedman, despite his own, proudly announced cowardice. There is, of course, comedy in the incongruity between Main's demand for theatrical performance and Crainpool's bottomless fear. Main explains:

> "[. . .] I'd want scenario, demand explanation like a last cigarette, civilized denouement like a detective's professional courtesy in the drawing room and even the murderer's glass filled. Do you feel any of that?"

> "I do. Yes. A little. I do."

> Main looks at Crainpool suspiciously. "I hope you do. There are conventions, ceremonies. The mechanics are explained but never the mysteries. Foh. Look at me. I'm a parade. At bottom I've a flatfoot's heart [. . .]"

As is frequently the case in Elkin's work, victimizer and victim express their need for each other. Main needs to provoke Crainpool, whom he looks down upon as "a disciple to his own destroyer." On the other hand, Main now resents the fact that Crainpool has used him as a substitute for a term in prison: "I am his life's work, the Phoenician thinks. I have rehabilitated him. He has gone straight man."

Feeling Crainpool morally free from his influence and accepting the fact that Oyp and Glyp are no longer within his reach, Main is resolved to bring matters to a head. He will become a hunter, like the prehistoric beasts whose teeth so impressed him. Crainpool will be his game. To give the hunt greater significance, he pauses for the sake of overwhelming Crainpool with metaphysical questions that the poor secretary is unable to answer. It is theater of the absurd, with Main moved by Crainpool's fears, with Crainpool alternately egging him on and angrily challenging him.

The bailbondsman admits his own sense of inferiority and terror of the unknown and the future: "What do I do with my wonder, I wonder?" Intentionally missing a deadly shot, he orders the still incredulous Crainpool to flee: " 'Run,' the Phoenician commands, hisses. 'Run, you bas-

tard.' " Only then can Main go searching for the fugitive, the one thing that he can be sure of, among the falseness of "the golden blight" and "the golden bedsprings in the Cincinnati trees." It is doubtful, however, that Crainpool will provide a hunt as exciting as that for Oyp and Glyp. The bailbondsman's fervor is that of an old man:

> "OYP," he shouts, "AND GLYP," he shouts, "ARE DEAD," he shouts. He starts after the clerk in his old man's gravid trot. "LONG," he roars, "LIVE CRAINPOOL!"

In a world where no better bonds exist to create a human family, Main will cling to his professional substitute. (pp. 169-76)

> *Doris G. Bargen, in her* The Fiction of Stanley Elkin, *Peter D. Lang, 1980, 338 p.*

Elkin on language in fiction:

Okay. Yes. Certainly. Right. Let men make good sentences. Let them learn to spell the sound of the waterfall and the noise of the bathwater. Let us get down the colors of the baseball gloves—the difference in shade between the center-fielder's deep pocket and the discreet indentation of the catcher's mitt. And let us refine tense so that men may set their watches by it. Let fiction be where the language is. Let it *be* a language, as French is, or Bantu. And let it be understood that when we talk about fiction we are finally talking about the people who write it, about all those special talkers in tongues like Shakespeare or Faulkner or Melville or Gass. Let us enlist in Vocabulary, Syntax, the high grammar of the mysterious world.

Stanley Elkin, in "A Conversation with Stanley Elkin and William H. Gass," The Iowa Review, 1976.

Peter J. Bailey   (essay date 1985)

[*In the following excerpt, Bailey argues that the preoccupation with both language and mortality found in* Searches and Seizures *determines certain aspects of Elkin's style.*]

Elkin's style is nothing if not elaborately and self-consciously poetic in its concern with the sound of the English language and in its dedication to vitality and evocativeness; it is tirelessly committed to visualization and novelty, precise and all-but-exhaustive descriptions of objects tumbling breathlessly upon outbursts of puns, neologisms, comic solecisms and barbarisms, apostrophes and similar rhetorical pyrotechnics. John Gardner's description of "Elkin at his best," though itself somewhat overwrought, accurately gauges this aspect of Elkin's characteristic conjunction of form and content: "It's raw energy that Elkin loves—in prose and in characters. He's Ahab smashing through the mask with jokes, an eternal child whose answer to oppressive reason is to outperform it, to outshout it." Elkin has himself made similar comments about the centrality of energy—often rhetorical energy—as a value in his work, and it is not difficult to connect this aspect of the prose with the thematic strain in his fiction that counters its leveling, normalizing tendencies—the affirmation of the isolate individual or, as Elkin summarized the theme in an interview, the notion that "The SELF takes precedence." It is not surprising to discover that the primary conflict . . . in Elkin's fiction (which might be variously described as a confrontation between uniformity and individualism, communality and self, the ordinary and the particular or the personal) reduplicates itself in antinomies discernible on the formal level, but it is a point worth examining because of its special importance in the novellas of *Searches & Seizures,* works that dramatize the tension between these contraries in remarkably explicit terms.

The protagonists of **"The Bailbondsman," "The Making of Ashenden,"** and **"The Condominium"** have two important characteristics in common. They are all (as Elkin's prefatory note points out) men extraordinarily aware of their own mortality, men whose actions arise in large part out of that very recognition; but they are also extremely sensitive to the language through which they present themselves to the world, constantly considering how the language works, what it means, and what it commits them to. These three novellas, then, represent three different versions of the confrontation between the contraries that underlie Elkin's style, that constitute its paradox and give it its sense of tension—the antitheses of the awareness of death and the ability of language to hold death off, to pit form, structure and meaning against their ultimate dissolution. Or, to put the opposition in different terms, these novellas dramatize the self's confrontation with the fact of its own extinction, and its attempt to at once deny and reconcile itself to this fate through the self-assertions of language. This basic antithesis is not expressed in such Manichean terms in the novellas, of course: the language can be put to the service of death, of dissolution and the extinction of the self, and the assertion of self can, conversely, leave the self-asserter with no choice but self-destruction. The basic antinomy, manipulated or qualified as it might be, remains crucial to the understanding of these novellas, however, as language offers the only medium through which the self can be reconciled (and then only tentatively, temporarily) to the imminence of its own extinction. The paradox of and tension in Elkin's prose is attributable to its denial of distinction and difference on the one hand, and its simultaneous claims to distinctiveness on its own terms on the other. The style becomes an argument against death and the dissolution of structures and forms, even as it demonstrates that everything succumbs to, is leveled and rendered uniform by, these forces in the end.

Of the three protagonists in *Searches & Seizures,* the one least concerned with death and least consistently self-conscious about his use of language is Brewster Ashenden, the central character of the collection's second work, **"The Making of Ashenden."** The relative unimportance of these themes, compared to their centrality in the other two works, is perhaps attributable to the fact that only after he finished **"The Making of Ashenden"** did the idea of a sequence of novellas occur to Elkin. The simplicity and directness with which these themes are addressed in this no-

vella tends to make them more distinct and immediately graspable than in the other two works, where they are more firmly embedded in metaphors and analogies.

Brewster Ashenden doesn't initially think very much about death, but he knows very well what language is and what it is for. Language for him is simply an index of one's social standing and a barometer of one's taste. Ashenden's social standing is very high and his taste refined to an extreme, for he is the scion of a wealthy family, a well-educated and highly civilized young man who is welcome in the most exclusive jet-set homes on all continents. His breeding and good taste are, of course, reflected in his language, which permits nary a "damn," "hell," or "pain-in-the-ass" (his prissy hedge is "pain in the you-know-what") to intrude, and which insists upon the euphemization and sublimation of any term or subject that might be judged unpleasant, physical, or crude. He teasingly tells his dying mother, for instance, that she is a "naughty slugabed" for failing to leave her deathbed and join him in a round of golf, his only explanation for such deliberate fatuousness being that "a code is a code."

It takes very few pages of Ashenden's hyperbolically civilized patter to convince the reader that he is no mere adherent of a code but an utterly encoded being, one for whom taste is a fit substitute for experience and whose every action, verbal and otherwise, is mediated by the best guides to etiquette and social deportment. Having no need to earn a living, Ashenden dedicates his days to the obligatory aristocratic ritual of self-seeking, ultimately finding himself in the person of Jane Loes Lipton, a wealthy socialite so perfectly suited to him that each can anticipate precisely what the other is going to say before he or she says it. She is the "perfection" that has eluded him in his lifelong journey from one estate to another, the embodiment of the "magnetic, Platonic pole, idealism and Beauty's true North" for which he has searched. Her only drawback (which is, within the aristocratic romance tradition in which Ashenden and the story are operating, a definite advantage and seductive virtue) consists in the fact that she is dying, a case of *lupus erythematosus* causing her body to produce antibodies against itself, making her progressively allergic to her own chemistry. To marry her would be to inflict himself with the same necessarily fatal illness. Inspired by the poetry of this romantic doom, Ashenden presses his suit, only to be rejected as unworthy of her hand because he is not a virgin, while she is. She sets him a task: to purify himself or lose her forever, her challenge uniting her with all the fairytale princesses who demand similar (if less earthy) tests of their suitors' ardor and fidelity. Ashenden resorts to mere rhetorical trickery to uncorrupt himself, deciding that he has attained to a "self-loathing" so extreme that "it *is* purity." Too excited to sleep away the hours before he can bestow his newly chastened self upon Jane, he wanders out into the game preserve that surrounds the estate where he and she are staying to pass the time until dawn.

He is not, as it turns out, fated to escape with a simple self-confrontation, the mere joining of self with its feminine mirror image. Instead, his initiation suddenly becomes a much more menacing confrontation of self and other, the other being, in this instance, a bear in heat. Nor is this a task that he can finesse with language, as he had the initial one, for the bear has a language of its own:

> Again it made its strange movement, and this time barked its moan, a command, a grammar of high complication, of difficult irregular case and gender and tense, a classic aberrant syntax. Which was exactly as Ashenden took it, like a student of language who for the first time finds himself hearing in real and ordinary life a unique textbook usage. God, he thought, I understand bear!

Whereas Jane has demanded that he uncorrupt himself if he wants to become one with her in death, the bear is telling him that he must sully himself in sexual contact with her if he hopes to live. Even Ashenden's attempts to reduce the situation to allegory and thus dismiss it ("What this means, he thought, is that my life has been too crammed with civilization. . . . I have been too proud of my humanism, perhaps, and all along not paid enough attention to the base") cannot save him from the necessity of satisfying the beast. He subsequently discovers that he desires the bear, but by this point his ardor has cooled and he has to whip himself back up by regaling her with conventional endearments, offering seductive smalltalk and predictable verbal inducements (" 'I love you. I don't think I can live without you. I want you to marry me' "), exciting himself into tumescence with the cheap sentiments of ordinary courtship.

His experience with the bear changes not only his language—" 'We are all sodomites,' " he tells himself in midcoitus, " 'all pederasts, all dikes and queens and mother fuckers' "—but also alters his plans, convincing him to renounce the aristocratically romantic death he had resolved to share with Jane in favor of travel to places "further and wilder than he had ever been." What he is repudiating here is not merely death but a solipsistic kind of self-extinction, a death engendered by the self's mating with its mirror image and one characterized, appropriately enough, by a chemical pathology in which the victim's system poisons itself. His coital adventure with the bear has also accomplished the very purpose Jane set him in his task—it has revirginized him through a purification by soiling. He is pure not in the sense that she demanded, of course, but pure in the sense that his sodomy has redeemed him from a life thoroughly insulated by formalities and dictated by codes. In choosing the language of sensuality and anti-social impulse over the lure of romantic self-annihilation, Ashenden frees himself into possibility, tempering his taste with the awareness of the bestial in himself and expanding his notions of heritage to include among the air, earth, water, and fire one additional element—honey.

If it is through activating the language of bear within himself that Ashenden manages to escape the prison of forms and formalities in which he has lived, it is though a similar process that Elkin's language leads his reader in the novella. The excessively refined, fastidious prose with which Ashenden narrates the first two-thirds of the novella gives way to a third-person narrative in the bear fuck scene, where Ashenden's particularity is replaced by evocative

precision, his delicacy abandoned in favor of the immediacy of dramatization. The scene is one of the most ambitious, exuberant, and (as numerous reviewers were quick to point out) moving moments in Elkin's fiction, a triumph of language so striking that it fairly overwhelms the protagonist whose experience it describes. The novella not only depicts the situation of one whose expanding lexicon emancipates him from a sterile life, then—it also dramatizes this process by giving the reader a word experience as extreme, as affecting, and as imaginatively liberating as the one that is, in both senses of the phrase, the **"Making of Ashenden."**

The most lighthearted of the *Searches & Seizures* novellas, **"The Making of Ashenden"** is also the one most consistently and comically permeated by the mediating presence of other voices, other books—fairytales and Henry James novels conspicuous among them. **"The Condominium,"** which follows it, is the darkest of the three, largely because it permits, neither the reconciliatory movements nor the peripeteia that allow **"The Bailbondsman"** and **"The Making of Ashenden"** to conclude in redemption and the rediscovery of possibility, however qualified. It is also, consistently enough, the novella in which language is revealed to have no redemptive value, no power to pit against the inevitability of death. Language, instead, comes to play a contributing role in the protagonist's suicide. **"The Condominium"** makes no more final statement than the other novellas, of course, and if its placement at the volume's end gives it a kind of emphasis, its real authority is grounded less in its location than in the unremitting bleakness of its depiction of human existence.

Whereas both **"The Bailbondsman"** and—in a different sense—**"The Making of Ashenden"** close upon paroxysms of language that free their protagonists into possibility once again, **"The Condominium"** opens with a lengthy passage neither capable of redeeming nor reflective of redemption for its writer. The narrative suggests more than anything else the psychological and emotional problems facing Marshall Preminger, a professional lecturer inspired to discourse upon the human instinct toward homebuilding, toward the ownership of shelter, on the occasion of his inheritance of his father's Chicago condominium. " 'A place to live, to be' " is his theme, his lecture's central question being " 'Out of what frightful trauma of exclusion arose this need, what base expulsion from what cave during which incredible spell of rotten weather?' " He never completely answers this question—or, to put it more precisely, he never becomes conscious that he is answering it—because he doesn't complete the lecture, putting it aside when responsibilities attached to his new property demand his time. What the fragment of the lecture does address itself to is the evolution of a New Jersey summer resort at which his parents had once rented, then owned, a bungalow when he was a boy. In his account he traces the decreasing importance of the open air in the lives of those who inhabit the resort every summer; the canoes, tennis courts, and baseball diamond fall into disrepair through lack of use, as if the residents " 'had no interest in the out-of-doors at all, had repudiated it, as if life were meant to be lived inside and the games they once played as bachelor boys and bachelor girls—"The Good Sports,"

"The Merry Maidens"—were over, literally, the scores frozen, more final than Olympic records.' " What Preminger is unintentionally prefiguring here is his own fate as a thirty-seven-year-old virgin who has never played the games that "bachelor boys and bachelor girls" play, and who will be driven more and more emphatically inside—not only inside the condominium that he has involuntarily inherited, but further inside still, into the absolute solitude of the lonely, irreducible self. His suicide, then, becomes a partial answer to the question, " 'Out of what frightful trauma of exclusion arose this need, what base expulsion from what cave during what incredible spell of rotten weather?' " But that answer is necessarily a limited and partial one, and the actual source of the specific trauma remains to be revealed.

Preminger's lecture not only addresses itself to the problem that will prove fatally insoluble for him, it also dramatizes it. As he traces the year-by-year growth of the resort and its bungalows, he becomes less capable of cleaving to those issues that make his oration interesting to others, "solipsism" (as Dick Gibson would put it) "drowning out inquiry" over the course of his remarks. At various points in writing the lecture he wanders off into nostalgic reminiscence of his own childhood, becomes so excited about the accuracy of his insights that he must stop and cool down for a day or two before continuing, and generally proves that ordered discourse, the subjugation of self to subject, is no longer within his power. But he begins work on this lecture well after his father dies and he takes possession of the condominium, and only after we understand what his father's death means to him can we begin to see what the apartment and all that comes with it will come to signify.

Preminger is summoned to Chicago by an acquaintance of his father's, and he arrives for the funeral only to suffer two immediate surprises. First, he sees that his coffined father has grown long hair, sideburns, and a mustache since Preminger had last seen him; second, he learns that the estate he had anticipated consists of the condominium and a backlog of unpaid maintenance assessments. The financial disposition of the unit is such that Preminger cannot sell it without forfeiting a third of his father's investment, and thus he resolves to move into the condominium, having his belongings forwarded from Missoula, Montana, because, as he admits to himself, "a life like his could be lived in Montana or Chicago. It made no difference." In an important sense Preminger is not so much transferring his life as exchanging it for another's: "He was in his father's skin now," we are told, "plunging into Pop's deepest furniture, but all along the attraction had been that it was someone else's, that he'd been granted the dearest opportunity of his life—to quit it, a suicide who lived to tell the tale. (But to whom?) Wrapping himself in another's life as a child rolls himself in blankets or crawls beneath beds to alter geography."

The urge of the son to escape his own life and symbolically or literally enter the life of the father is a familiar one, and we are not surprised to find distinct allusions to the archetypal version of this situation appearing shortly following this passage. A neighbor named Evelyn Riker comes to

Preminger's door, asking to be let in so that she might explain her relationship with his father, and Preminger is immediately reminded of the women who began coming to his parents' home after the rise of his father's fortunes, women whose appearance he "associated with the TV, and the new gadgets and the other merchandise. Perhaps his own low-level sexuality had to do with his being broke, the hard-on [which he experiences when Mrs. Riker embraces him in grief] . . . with his being in his father's house again. Which made him an Oedipus of the domestic for whom jealous of his father's place meant just that: *place*." This tacit disclaimer notwithstanding, the two senses of place (as home and as sexual access to the wife/mother figure) prove difficult for Preminger to differentiate; his search for the man whose life he is taking over culminates in the discovery of tawdry details of that man's sexual life. That sexual life is then revealed to have its roots in the upward mobility and achievement of financial security with which Preminger earlier associated it.

Mrs. Riker divulges, in her explanation, that she and the elder Preminger were only friends, residents of the same building who would occasionally talk together at the pool. As they became better acquainted, she would write him letters articulating her views on literature and politics, agreeing in return to keep a key to his condominium so that he might fantasize about her using it one evening. The two responded to each other, she insists, purely as "outlets," their relationship never exceeding the limits of pen pal from one side and object of fantasy from the other. He approves her version of their relationship, surrenders her letters that his father had saved, and accepts her promise that she will return his key as soon as she locates it. Satisfied with this exchange, Preminger rededicates himself to the new life he has moved into, convinced that he can finally elude the "tourist condition" of his old life and rid himself of the "unsavory quality of displaced person" that he has up to now given off.

All that initially prevents him from fitting in with the "ordinary life, H.O. scale" of the condominium is his temper, his tendency to lash out against regulations. He admonishes himself, "If I don't stop violating the dress codes I'm a dead man. Where do I get my fury? he wondered. What nutty notions of my character have come on me? What is it with me? What do I think I am—where three roads meet?" This second allusion to the Oedipus story pushes the reference's significance beyond the previously established analogue and aligns the father (the victim of the son's rage at the spot where the three roads meet) with the condominium whose regulations Preminger lashes out against. The aptness of this parallel becomes increasingly clear as it becomes more obvious to Preminger how thoroughly his father had internalized the condominium's ethic and become indistinguishable from the world that it implies.

Preminger proves as capable of turning his anger in upon himself as he is of projecting it outward upon the world, and this trait more than any other dooms his efforts to live a normal life among normal people in the condominium. When a group of chairmen of the complex's association committees visits Preminger to acquaint him with their functions and activities, he is deeply moved. He is impressed, too, by their united front, their reasonable speeches, their "low-court style like foreign language converted in dreams." They express the hope that he will become active in committee work, and he seizes the occasion to answer (" 'I think I can give you assurances now,' " he grandly begins) in the identical civic tone. But only a sentence or two into his remarks his gratitude for their concern quickly shades into self-deprecation, and before long he is discomfiting them all by explaining his lamentable circumstances and bemoaning his fate, much as he does in the autobiographical intrusions in his lecture: " 'My life is a little like being in a foreign country,' " he tells them. " 'There's a displaced person in me. I feel—listen—I feel . . . *Jewish.* I mean even here, among Jews, where everybody's Jewish. I feel Jewish.' " (The association's spokesman responds to Preminger's confession by pointedly citing a few of the association's regulations, emphasizing particularly that its members must approve all new residents: " '. . . no chinks, no PR's, no spades,' " he insists, as if he has just found one of these living on the premises in disguise.) To be the one alienated man in a community of the supposedly alienated is Preminger's fate. His loneliness and concomitant certainty that that loneliness is his just desert convince him that his fellow residents must "have his number"—one.

His isolation is temporarily interrupted by his appointment as lifeguard at the condominium swimming pool when a fall hot spell necessitates its being kept open past Labor Day. The role gives him the comforts of a prescribed code of behavior and involvement with those who use the pool. He is encouraged, too, by a letter from Mrs. Riker in which she discusses aspects of "our permissive society," a Philip Roth novel, Mike Nichols's films, and the heat wave, concluding with a postscript noting that she has not yet located his key, but that she will return it to him as soon as she can "lay her hands on it," which she anticipates will be soon. He responds enthusiastically, convinced that she is cryptically promising him that she will soon use the key, sending her a lengthy telegram inviting her to bring the key whenever she finds it. Gradually the hopes he had placed in his pool duties and in Mrs. Riker prove groundless, and he is forced back into himself, bearing a devastating knowledge as the only result of his foray into the world of others.

The pool proves a disappointment because his role allows him only peripheral involvement in the community that gathers there. The bathers and sunners are content to have him listen in on their conversations dealing with the buying of their condos, the gas mileage of their automobiles, their cleaning women, and other concerns of the settled in and secure, those whose apartments give them a platform from which to speak contentedly of life's trivia. Preminger, of course, has achieved no such foothold, his ownership of a condominium notwithstanding. When he is directly addressed by any of the poolside kibitzers, it is usually as a representative of the younger generation whose values aren't their own and whose sympathies they find abhorrent. Normally defensive about the position in which they have placed him, Preminger finally embraces it while attacking those who have imposed it on him. On

the pool's closing day he criticizes them for voting Sunday rules into effect for weekdays, thus denying use of the facilities to sons, daughters, and grandchildren, and for never discussing or exchanging pictures of those whom their Sunday rules have excluded. His own father, he angrily insists, could not have lived this condominium life with its implicit denial that the residents had ever had families; he must have proudly displayed pictures of Marshall around this very swimming pool, Preminger is certain, and surely he talked avidly of his son's success on the lecture circuit. But Preminger suddenly recognizes that his father would have concurred in the rules change and talked little of his son, so thoroughly had he bought into the condominium ethos. " 'Shit,' " he complains through his revelation, " 'He never said a word. Like the rest of you. You should see the place. A swinger. He had hair like a pop star.' "

Underlying Preminger's petulant outburst is his conviction that the bonds of posterity have been utterly eliminated in the condominium, that the elderly have abandoned completely their parental and grandparental concerns, seeking instead only the gratification of their own private needs and desires. This sour insight into the significance of his father's Danish modern furniture and altered styles of dress and hair is the first of two revelations so devastating to Preminger's sense of the fitness of things that, if they don't actually unhinge his mind (he tells the poolside contingent that he is experiencing a nervous breakdown), they do deprive him of any reason to go on living.

The final revelation takes the form of a second letter from Mrs. Riker. He finds it under his door upon returning from his emotional outburst at the pool. This letter is not unlike its predecessor in its discursiveness, disingenuous humility, and banal cordiality; her narration of a trivial argument she once had with her former husband is presented in the same stiffly informal, platitude-ridden prose in which she had commented on the work of Roth and Nichols. Nor is that style altered significantly when she shifts from this anecdote to the discussion of the circumstances of Preminger's father's death, a death she not only witnessed but actually caused.

She had decided to return the key, she explains in the letter, and she used it to let herself in when no one answered her knock. She found the senior Preminger, dressed only in briefs, lying on his bed looking seriously ill, and she decided to stay with him despite her awareness that he had misinterpreted the impulse behind her visit. She called a doctor and agreed to lie in bed with the sick man until he arrived, believing that this would calm him. Fearing that the erection resulting from his seizure was exacerbating his discomfort, she "reluctantly" submitted to his entreaties, undressed, and copulated with him. The exertion of coitus killed him. She cleaned away all traces of their intercourse and departed, leaving the dead man to be found by the doctor she had summoned. Her explanation complete, she asks Preminger not to answer her letter, and she promises in a postscript to get his key back to him.

Nervous breakdown notwithstanding, Preminger understands this letter quite fully; he realizes completely, too, with a rising sense of horror, the conflicting impulses of attraction and repulsion that her narrative has inspired in him. What he comprehends only intuitively is the fathomless banality of the document he has just read, its outrageously unintentional dramatization of the extent to which its writer has rationalized into ordinariness her unquestionable complicity in his father's death. Her bland recounting of the event reflects absolutely no hint of awareness of what impact such revelations would have on the victim's son. That her letter is an exercise in unimaginable self-delusion is established by her continued reluctance to surrender the key, with its implicit unwillingness to abandon the hope that the game she played with the father can also be (and is being) carried on with his son. Preminger, however, is concerned with the letter less as a revelation of the bland vileness of Mrs. Riker than as a vehicle of self-confrontation, his reaction to its contents—his hope that the accomplice in his father's death will use the key now, his awareness that this hope reduces him to the same desperate circumstance in which his stricken, tumescent father hopelessly and terribly waited out his final minutes listening for the sound of the key in the lock—manifesting the abject helplessness of his own situation. Her second letter, then, closes off a series of revelations that began with his surprise at his father's modish wardrobe, hairstyle, and apartment, that continue in his realization that the man was not the familiar dad whose life revolved around his pride in his son but a late-middle-aged bachelor desperate to get laid, and that culminate in the disclosure that his reckless and frantic priapism, in concert with a self-deluded, obliging neighbor, resulted in his death.

Preminger also understands the relationship between his father and his father's final home, seeing that the condominium in which they have consecutively lived represents a retreat into private worlds of fantasy and self-gratification. With this recognition comes the related revelation that the condominium can never be a foundation upon which to build the ordinary life to which Preminger has aspired, for, despite the complex's surface communality, its poolside neighborliness and appearance of social interaction, it is ultimately a place of withdrawal into the self, a place that allows its residents to turn away from the concerns of the world and to trivialize themselves so thoroughly that they will no longer be obliged to notice their lives slipping away. Less clearly connected in Preminger's mind is his sense that sexuality is somehow related to financial success, to the rise of one's economic fortunes, with his father's death in the home that signifies the achievement of retirement security; involved here, too, of course, is the fact that his father died in the arms of a woman whom Preminger had associated with those women who appeared at the Premingers' home during his father's working life. It is safe to say that he intuits these connections, however, and understands through them that he must push beyond his father's retreat into a condominium death by withdrawing so thoroughly from the world that he himself becomes his home. He eliminates all purchase in space by leaping from his apartment's twelfth-floor balcony, intent upon destroying the self's last refuge—the body. As he falls, he tries to deliver his habitation speech, but the wind stops the words on his lips. His one final go at articulating the world into some kind of co-herence is jammed back down his throat, the lecture halted by his ultimate commitment to silence and death. His suicide, clearly enough, represents a kind of response to his lecture's crucial question, then, but the only trauma it points to is his own, the only "spell of rotten weather" the one that led him toward the discovery of his own hopelessness. For Preminger, anthropological questions—all questions—must become autobiographical, and it is against this final turning inward, or in complicity with it, that he hurls himself to his death.

In **"The Condominium"** the language that prevails is Mrs. Riker's epistolary prose, a prose blithely unconscious of and indifferent to its own effects, a prose chatty yet artificial and consummately bland, a deadly language that destroys extremity by trivializing it. Hers is, without question, the banally seductive siren song of the condominium, and Preminger must succumb to it because his own sense of self is too crippled to counter that voice's tendencies toward trivialization and sameness with its own force of articulation, differentiation, and self-expression. Of the three protagonists of *Searches & Seizures,* then, Preminger the lecturer strikes the poorest bargain between style and substance, proves least able to reconcile the inevitable human conflict between self and other, word and world. Alexander Main, a man of primitive impulses, learns the necessity and value of sublimating that impulsiveness into a style, of formalizing it into a constructive verbal means of bearing down on the world, it having become clear to him that such compromises with the world's terms are unavoidable if that world is to be counted upon to restore his "sense of his possibilities." Brewster Ashenden, by self-proclamation "one of the three or four dozen truly civilized men in the world," learns to mediate the emptiness of style-for-its-own-sake with a bit of carnality and impulse, the bear having awakened in him the awareness of his forgotten grammar of animality. Only Preminger fails to reconcile the opposing strains, retreating further into the self as the world rejects him and the sibyl of the condo seduces him, perhaps unknowingly, toward the same annihilation of self into which her sour, banal epistolary song had ultimately led his father.

The bleakness of this conclusion to *Searches & Seizures* is balanced by the qualified affirmation of the opening novella, and the two are mediated by the manic energy of the tour de force resolution of **"The Making of Ashenden,"** itself a dramatization of language's ability to overcome the gravitational forces of formlessness and dissolution. None of the three is intended to represent an absolute statement or concluding vision, yet it is difficult not to find Main's reconciliation of the tension between self-expression and dissolution, between style and nothingness, the most convincing and resonant, perhaps because it most closely approximates Elkin's own response to these antinomies.

Main—**"The Bailbondsman"**—has a very clear notion of what the language his profession imposes upon him is and how he feels about it. "I'm called upon to make colorful conversation in my trade," he explains early in the novella. "Don't think I enjoy it. I'm a serious man; such patter is distasteful to me. When day is done I like nothing better than to ask my neighbor how he's feeling, to hear he's well and to tell him same here, to trade what we know about the weather, to be agreeable, aloof and dull. Leave poetry to the poets, style to the window trimmers. I'm old." What makes his occupation repugnant to him is not the high-handedness connected with his role as determiner of what felons will be set free, liberated back into their criminality, nor is it the strongarming he must occasionally resort to with fugitives who have jumped his bond; these are his exuberant means of "controlling the sluices and locks of ordinary life," his chosen way (to use a favorite term of Leo Feldman's) of "bearing down on the world." It is the rhetoric the job demands that he finds hateful, the obligatory use of "colorful rhythms" and "salty talk" a burden that nothing else in the trade can make up for, "not the viciousness or the seamy excitements or my collective, licey knowledge of the world." In the course of the novella Main's attitude toward his shoptalk, this "flashy grammar of body contact," changes considerably, language ultimately becoming the only medium of redemption he can know.

Main requires redemption for a number of reasons. First, his hard-edged, unforgiving bad man's perspective on the world has entered into a losing competition with an emergent cultural perspective characterized by humanitarianism, charity, and compassion; his own cherished ideals of impulse and revenge have been largely subordinated to the values of rehabilitation, sublimation, and order. This cultural shift manifests itself primarily in the fact that business is bad. The Federal Bail Reform Act of 1964 (which empowered federal courts to act as their own bondsmen, thus eliminating airplane hijackers, interstate kidnappers, and other federal criminals from the independent bondsman's rolls), the compassion-inspired legislation introduced by coalitions of social scientists, civil libertarians, and a left-leaning Supreme Court, and the increasing politicization of crime have all combined to reduce drastically both the number of felons available for bonding and the profit margin involved in bonding them. Main's Cincinnati colleagues discuss this situation at their weekly luncheon in Covington, Kentucky, agreeing that henceforth they will work in concert rather than in competition, facing adversity with a united front. In addition, they resolve to soften their hard-guy image by changing tactics: they will agree on a lottery system to determine which bondsman will get which prisoner, and they will talk any bail jumpers (upon whom they are empowered by law to use force) back to prison, rather than using violence. While they are formulating their democratically established concessions to the fact that "heart is winning the battle of history," Main is off in a Cincinnati museum, skipping the lunch so that he can study the teeth of extinct animals. He periodically visits this exhibit of the jaws of long-dead beasts, gaining inspiration and sustenance from the display of an untempered ferocity that he feels has fled the world. He examines the skull of a young jaguar, noticing that "skin still adheres to the palate, the concentric tracery as distinct and fine as what he touches with his tongue at the roof of his own mouth. It is teeth he comes back again and again to see, as if these were the distillate of the animal's soul, the cutting, biting edge of its passion and life." While his colleagues are fraternally agreeing upon policies of capitulation, then, Main is being nourished by an oppo-

site vision, his sense of his isolate's integrity reinforced by the realization that the jaguar's palate is as singular in its detail as his own, "the cutting, biting edge" of his own "passion and life" confirmed as well by his recognition of its reflection in the jaguar skull's menacingly sharp teeth. It is from a world too sold on sublimation and too suspicious of impulse that Main wants most to be redeemed, his own drive for life finding no fulfillment in a culture gone slack with convenience, communality, and an incapacitating relativism.

The earlier Elkin protagonist whom Main most conspicuously recalls is Leo Feldman [in *A Bad Man*], partly because their irascible, uncompromising natures are similar, and also because they both assume positions mediating between law and lawlessness, Feldman supplying contraband goods and services through his department store basement, Main monitoring the passage of criminals off and back into the city streets. Both are also explicitly associated with older, more primitive worlds and civilizations: Feldman is linked with the severity of the medieval world, with "a distant, Praetorianed land, unamiable and harsh," while Main proudly and repeatedly invokes the memory of his Phoenician ancestors, a desert people whom he credits not only with the development of the bailbond but also with the invention of the oasis, innovations that, from one point of view, could be said to be one and the same. Their "horned, spiky skin," Main explains, "took the sunburn and converted it into energy," energy that they put to the services of resourcefulness, becoming "sand and water alchemists," "conservationists of the bleak," undauntable creators in the desert's arid wastes, "growing a world." The etymological relationship that links Phoenician to phoenix is, quite clearly, what Elkin has in mind in this description of the creation of oases from the desert's barrenness; it lies, too, behind his decision to give Main the nickname "The Phoenician," in anticipation of the character's ultimate rebirth from a condition of failed possibilities.

That condition is brought about in part by Main's displeasure with the law's increasing laxity toward criminals, but it has more to do with his overall disillusionment with crime itself. He offers a parable of that disillusionment ("My thoughts explode in words," he muses) to Crainpool, his secretary, appraising him of "the progress of a liver fluke through a cow's intestine to a human being." His account races the trematode's journey from cowflop to the blade of grass in which it waits, "a befouled phoenix," for the appearance of the sheep whose liver it will attack and sicken, the sheep's poisoned excrement giving it still another bourn in which to await the arrival of the barefoot human offering his unprotected soles to its capacities for corkscrew penetration and spiral intrusion. The point of this delineation of " 'Nature's nasty marathon, its stations of the cross and inside job' " is that " 'What the liver fluke can do man can do. The fix is in, it takes two to tango, all crime's a cooperation. This I wanted to see. I've seen it, show me something else. Phooey. A Phoenician's phooey on it all.' " What disappoints Main, obviously, is the recognition that crime is communal, that even the liver fluke needs assistance in undertaking its nasty, instinctual break and entry; neither desire nor impulse is sufficient to liberate it from its dependence upon other living things.

Not until the late pages of the novella, however, is Main's comment (" 'This I wanted to see' ") clarified and the extent and meaning of his disillusionment with crime fully explained. He became a bailbondsman, we learn there, when he decided that "Crime was the single mystery he could get close to"—when it occurred to him that mastering the disciplines that address the most profound questions of the universe and of man was beyond his abilities, and that he must settle for a field in which the mysteries ("Who done it? What's the motive?") are more manageable but no less obscure. His chosen field ends up disappointing him, leaves him bitterly asking his secretary, who has himself been a lawbreaker and jumper of Main's bond, " 'What does crime come to at last? Nothing. Crummy hornbook, lousy primer. Slim volume, Crainpool, pot fucking boiler, publisher's remainder. You taught me nothing, mister. And where did I get the idea that by getting next to aberration I could. . . . ' " Main's ellipsis might be completed with "make more sense of the world, understand the normal and the social by becoming expert in deviations from them." He had hoped, in other words, to find criminals as representative of primal, irrational human urges as he has found prehistoric animals' teeth reflective of the primitive impulses of those beasts, and he had convinced himself that the study of both could only reinforce his own raw hunger for life and help him to discover what that life is. He has, in the intervening years, read all the words in crime's "slim volume," however, and he has had to recognize that crime is merely ordinary, that it reflects no "cutting, biting edge" of outlaw "passion and life" but represents only a dull, laughably circumscribable form of mystery that sheds practically no light on the larger mystery, the "Mystery that kept him going."

Although his experiences in the actual world have been supplying him with compelling evidence of crime's ordinariness, it takes a dream representation of this fact to convince Main (who had earlier dismissed dreams as containing "trivial enigma[s] we forget on rising") of its indisputable truth. In his dream he witnesses the violation, robbery, and desecration of the tomb of a pharoah by two men whom he subsequently recognizes to be Oyp and Glyp, the only two criminals ever to have jumped his bail and to have eluded his attempts to recapture them. Outdoing the robbery of Tutankhamen's tomb (upon whose crime Elkin has modeled theirs), Oyp and Glyp not only destroy priceless artifacts in the chamber, spill the pharoah's invaluable unguents on the floor, and collect all that is portable; they actually exhume the pharoah himself, breaking through his sarcophagus, splitting his outer and inner coffins, penetrating his golden shell, and finally unwrapping his mummy so as to get at the riches it contains, pocketing not only rings and jewels but the pharoah's bandage-swathed heart as well. The two are immediately apprehended by local authorities, and Main, who has witnessed the entire crime, follows them to court. Once they have been arraigned, Main feels obligated to try to win them their freedom once again, and he appears before the presiding magistrate to make his case. This effort compels him to argue what he has known professionally but has never before

acted upon: the notion that even the most heinous crime is only ordinary, that even the violation of God's burial ground and the desecration of his corpse are merely mundane sorts of transgressions committed by common, banal men in—as Main puns—"under their heads." His argument fails to persuade the judge, but it does convince the dreaming Main completely. What Oyp and Glyp had come to represent to the waking Main was a romantic sense of crime as that which exists beyond the boundaries of civilized life, and of criminals as those who feed upon the experience of extremity, those who press human limits to the edge and are exalted by their daring defiance. His dream allows him to eloquently and persuasively talk himself out of this misconception. In the dream, the judge lets Oyp and Glyp go free; in waking from it, Main understands that in fact, or perhaps only to him, Oyp and Glyp are dead. The progression, as he sees it in the dream's end, goes like this: they were "fugitives once from his scrutiny and control, then from his intercession, and now from the earth itself. Fugitives from the bullying freedom he needed to give them who till now could stand between the law and its violators, having that power vouch-safed to him, the power to middlemen, to doodle people's destiny." His dream oration leaves him bereft of the one remaining absorbing passion of his life—the belief that the whereabouts of Oyp and Glyp continues to be one of life's soluble mysteries, that they are still out there, a two-ply exception to and repudiation of the ordinary. The dream forces him to recognize that they have disappeared without a trace into the ordinary, that the ordinary has claimed another source of his interest, his life, his passion. From this worst of all losses he must be redeemed at the novella's close.

The ordinary and the exceptional are not the only contraries that **"The Bailbondsman"** (and for that matter, the bailbondsman) must reconcile if Main is to achieve his promised redemption. His preferences in animals as well as his pride in his ancestors reflect his attachment to the past, a partiality suggested, too, by his insistence that his secretary act and dress like Bob Cratchit and that his own office duplicate exactly the look of a bailbondsman's office in film noir. He objects to the present because it is only the present, the omnipresence of taste, style, and fashion attesting to its temporal one-dimensionality, to its willing capitulation to the fact that now is only and immutably now. Main is offended by contemporaneity as he is by crimes generated by the law's permissiveness, explicitly linking the two as he walks through Cincinnati's downtown shopping district: "They spoke of the breakdown of law and order," he muses, "but what a discipline was in these streets, what a knuckling under and catering to the times." The shops "burst with an egoism of the present tense," the city is "pickled in taste," but Main has "no taste, only hunger. I have never been fashionable, and it's astonishing to me that so much has happened in the world. The changes I perceive leave me breathless." The rapidity of change has led him to conclude, "It's as if he lives trapped in the neck of an hour-glass. Style, he thinks. As a young man he wanted it, hoped that when he awakened it would be there like French in his mouth. Now he sees it as a symptom of a ruinous disease." And so he walks the city streets, noticing the Easter decorations being hung in the trees ("long strips of gold foil in light rigid frames, exactly the size and appearance of bedsprings . . . inching their way the long length of the avenue like a golden blight"), morosely deciding, "It's too much for me—spring, style, the future."

His argument with the future is that he can't know it—it eludes him as Oyp and Glyp once eluded him, evades his "scrutiny and control" and thus "limits his power and his precious freedom." What he would know are those simple things that "a dopey kid of the next century could tell him," basic facts concerning the alignment of the major leagues, what songs become hits, who would be assassinated, what the new political slogans would be. " 'Everything I don't know and never will know leans on me like a mountain range,' " he tells his secretary, " 'It creams me, Crainpool. It potches my brain and rattles my teeth.' " It threatens, that is, the symbolic locus of his "passion and life."

When he tries to foresee the future he is foiled by the unavoidability of contemporary analogues as well as the time-boundness of words, and he consequently becomes "depressed by language, the finite slang of his century. . . . He needed new endings, new punctuation, a different grammar." He gets no new language, of course, but by the end his attitude toward the language he does have has changed considerably. The difference between his earlier feelings toward his rhetoric (his idea that "it was only a foreign language he had learned to speak, the flashy grammar of body contact, a shoptalk of which he is weary because no one has yet bested him at it") and his subsequent, altered view is that he comes increasingly to mean what he says and to feel what he means. His addresses to Miss Krementz, a client, and Crainpool progressively reflect his willingness to use his "foreign language" as a medium through which to present his deeply felt concerns and fears. Neither of these speeches is marked by an ingenuous simplicity, of course; both of them treat a variety of subjects, express a number of contradictory moods, and rely heavily upon rhetorical maneuver, their combined effect being to dramatize what Main is feeling more than to directly express it. For Miss Krementz he delivers an account of his life that is intended as an explanation of why he is refusing to post bail for her boyfriend. For Crainpool he expounds upon his frustration at not being able to know the future as a kind of prefatory explanation of his imminent banishment of his secretary back into fugitive status. Both monologues mix autobiography with business, as the habitual, indifferent shoptalk is gradually compelled to accommodate itself to more personal rhythms and more visceral concerns. This shift reflects Main's tacit awareness that language is the only means through which he can possibly resolve the primary tension underlying his personality—" 'who wired this tension in me between ego and detachment?' " he asks Crainpool—and the only agent capable of mediating between the other contraries that plague his life. Language, he comes to understand, is his only tool for mediating between himself and the world in the same way that he has placed himself "between the law and its violators." He recognizes, too, how crucial language is in resolving necessary conflicts between self and role.

This insight into the power of language is reinforced by Main's subsequent realization of the significance that language—what he calls his rhetoric—has had for him throughout his life. The two occasions upon which he mourns the success of Oyp and Glyp in evading his apprehension are both characterized by his image of the pair hiding in places so remote and forbidding "that the inhabitants have no language," or in exotic locales where they go undetected and undisturbed because "they don't speak the lingo." To escape him, Main's fantasies seem to suggest, the fugitives must escape the sphere of his language, perhaps even lose language as a social tool altogether, and leave behind the civilized world that empowers him to undertake his bailbondsman's role. Completely consistent with this sense of language's circumscribing powers is Main's realization that what has immobilized his other bailjumper, Crainpool, has been his rhetoric, the "foreign language he has learned to speak" having "held [Crainpool] all these years, kept him in town while the Phoenician was out rounding up jumpers." The secretary has ultimately become a "connoisseur of the Phoenician's abuse." Main has used language, then, to give others freedom by arguing for and winning them the right to be bailed out, and he has used it to keep Crainpool and other clients where he wants them. Now he must use it to free himself from the pall that has descended upon his life, the feeling that "I could only recover with drugs the sense of my possibilities."

He achieves his redemption through the monologue he delivers for Crainpool's benefit, a monologue that has as its primary object the discovery of a means by which he can "recover the sense of his possibilities," but that turns out to have been the very means for which he was searching. Main wakes Crainpool in the middle of the night to tell him that Oyp and Glyp are dead; then he pulls a gun, threatening to kill him because he jumped Main's bail years before. (When Crainpool objects that his eleven years of devoted service to Main has been restitution enough, Main responds that he is going to shoot him anyway because, as the law defines the relationship between bailed fugitive and bailbondsman, " 'You're the only man in the world I'm allowed to kill.' ") Main's ensuing monologue careens from the description of his sense of life's loveliness to accounts of the latest scientific theories of " 'the universes . . . leaking into each other . . . this transfusion of law in the sky' " to his despair over the mundane facts of a future he can never know and the facts of a present he will never know, his ecstatic narrative culminating in the admission that, until now, " 'There was always someone to hunt. . . . A mystery I was good at. My line of country. But if Oyp and Glyp are dead . . .' " (He shoots at his secretary's hand, grazing him, and threatens to shoot again, sending the man into wild flight.) " 'LONG LIVE CRAINPOOL!' "

Main's secretary is being catapulted out into the world as a replacement for the now extinct Oyp and Glyp. His whereabouts will become the manageable mystery that Main may never be able to solve, but he will have the consolation of knowing it is soluble. Crainpool will provide Main with future opportunities for search, with reasons to remain interested in a world that is closing down all around him. Propelling Crainpool back into the world is only the offshoot, the consequence, of a more significant movement Main undertakes (or, to use the collection's title, seizure he experiences). His monologue is based on the tacit assumption that the universe, for all its mysteriousness and inaccessibility to the human mind, must nonetheless be perpetually confronted, must be attacked again and again with our only weapon capable of piercing its imperturbability and silence—words. In his peroration on new scientific discoveries about man and the universe, Main refers to the theory that " 'all life is merely four simple compounds arranged on a spiral spring of sugars and phosphates,' " his description recalling, and tacitly likening human beings to, the liver fluke, whose spiraling, foul progress toward his goal he so patiently depicts in his parable of the communality of crime. The analogy's unavoidable implications are comically vulgar: if one must live in excrement in order to progress toward the ideal state of being, then one must indeed live in excrement, be it that which provides a temporary home for a liver fluke or that which is produced by a hyperarticulate bailbondsman. Or, to put the idea less scatologically, all of life strives toward some form of completion, some achievement of an ultimate which must be gained through the only means that the organism has at its command, be it the capacity for spiral locomotion or the ability to best everyone else with one's use of language.

The liver fluke is recalled here, of course, because of its explicit association with the Phoenix and with the novella's whole notion of rejuvenation. Its recovery from a state of torpor and paralysis prior to the sheep's arrival parallels Main's similar ascent from the despair of a world without possibility. The association of Main and the liver fluke with the Phoenix and the idea of rejuvenation is given reinforcement in the novella's final image, which also reflects a resolution of a number of the contraries that have undergirded Main's personality and have become central thematic antinomies. As he exits the hotel from which he has rejected Crainpool, Main looks around, lazily wondering where his new quarry might have fled: "East towards the railroad tracks? Or did he double back? To the street where he himself had walked that afternoon? Where the people were more like film stars than the film stars were, as everybody was these days, handsomeness creeping up the avenues of the world like the golden bedsprings in the Cincinnati trees?"

The "befouled Phoenix" of a liver fluke, the "spiral springs of sugars and phosphates" that are all life, "the golden bedsprings in the Cincinnati trees"—all these are symbols of hope, possibility, life. The novella's final image adds the last requisite notion to the symbolic complex: the bedsprings are Easter decorations, suggestive of rebirth and redemption in the world. These "golden bedsprings" and the handsomeness with which they are associated recall the modernity that Main rejected earlier but embraces here, his restoration of possibility having reconciled him to the less subtle, more communal form that possibility can take for others—contemporaneity, fashion, the new and the now. By the end, then, he has come to accept (tentatively, at least) two of the three things he had earlier described as being "too much for him." Spring now has a personal, immediate meaning and no longer represents

merely an inducement to mediations upon how little in his life is susceptible to regeneration. Style no longer seems "a ruinous disease" but has saved and restored him, his paroxysm of language having dramatized the realities of his situation and having led him to recognize that through the idiosyncratic, highly imaginative manipulation of language he can (for himself, at any rate) keep possibility alive in the world. (Crainpool, in fact, very nearly understands the point of Main's monologue, even if he does misanticipate its culmination. " 'You always have to have the last word,' " he complains, interrupting Main's speech. " 'You always have to do things big, don't you? Big shot. You'd kill me for nothing, for the sake of your style.' ") The future has not been brought under Main's control, of course, but he has gained a small victory over it by exchanging a distant future in which incalculable and unimaginable things happen for a more immediate, more manageable future, one whose primary (and possible) object is the recapturing of a fugitive he has himself released.

On a number of levels, then, **"The Bailbondsman"** suggests that language allows us a few tentative victories over our circumstances, allows us to reconcile personal conflicts like those of ego and detachment, self and role, being and style, and even occasionally permits us to articulate ideas and images that will be, perhaps only symbolically, perhaps only temporarily, redemptive. This is the argument of the most effective and impressive of the three *Searches & Seizures* novellas, and it is not in any way surprising that Elkin has admitted, "I, myself, am closer to Main than any other character [in my work]." The upbeat conclusion of Main's narrative is not final in terms of its relation to *Searches & Seizures* as a whole, but it could be said to represent most accurately the deal Elkin has struck with language. Like Main, he has resolved to use language as his way of bearing down on the world, not because language will alter the future, but because it can occasionally be made to effect a seizure of the present. That the process is no less circular than that of seeking a fugitive whom the seeker has set free is a contradiction that Elkin, like his protagonist, has learned to live with. It is, after all, a gesture, and gestures are crucial. Dick Gibson could very well be describing Main's action of sending Crainpool out into the world to embody possibility when he presents this apostrophe: "Gestures, gestures, saving gestures, life-giving and meaningless and sweet as appetite, delivered by gestures and redeemed by symbols, by necessities of your own making and a destiny dreamed in a dream." (pp. 139-64)

Peter J. Bailey, in his Reading Stanley Elkin, *University of Illinois Press, 1985, 220 p.*

Alan Wilde   (essay date 1987)

[*In the following excerpt, Wilde examines "The Making of Ashenden."*]

The elusive but inescapable presence of the world, or its meaning, is . . . the subject of Stanley Elkin's **"The Making of Ashenden,"** which . . . engages in a send-up of its central character. Surely one of the most outrageous figures in contemporary literature, Brewster Ashenden acts out the fall from innocence that is the novella's most obvious if, finally, only its enabling theme. But the innocence is at the same time (for the two are by no means incompatible) a matter of extravagant pride and self-deception; and no sooner do we hear Ashenden begin to speak than we anticipate not only the inevitability but the precipitousness of his descent. "One of the blessed of the earth," as he describes himself, one among its *only three or four dozen truly civilized men,*" he is, by his own estimate, the cynosure of the universe: "I come of good stock—" he says, referring to the source of his ancestors' considerable fortunes, "real estate, mineral water, oxygen, matchbooks: earth, water, air and fire, the old elementals of the material universe, a belly-button economics, a linchpin one."

It is clear already that Ashenden sees himself mythically and his world aesthetically. "A heroic man," he becomes a character in his own elaborate romance. But if, as he puts it, he is "classical, drawn by perfection as to some magnetic, Platonic pole, idealism and beauty's true North," he is still more emphatically a romantic, his potentially glacial assurance neatly compromised by what is, given his age, a somewhat incongruous search for identity. For Ashenden is, and is meant to be, considerably less tragic than comic in his fall; and his need to know, indeed his assertion that he "know[s] *everything,*" is in reality hostage to a more urgent need for stability and order, which betrays itself in the hilarious credo that is his final comment on the world's balky diversity: "You can learn almost all there is *to* learn," he tells a friend, "if you leave out the mystery and the ambiguity. If you omit the riddles and finesse the existential."

Whether or not it was so intended, Elkin's novella provides . . . a virtual compendium of modernist themes. And when it introduces Jane Löes Lipton, its second major character, it engages what is perhaps the most suggestive of them: the projection of the ego into its double. As the object of Ashenden's quest for perfection and as his mirror, Jane is our major clue to him and to the underside of that vaunted civilization to which both pay tribute. The fact that the two come together for the first time at an estate whose park is an enormous private zoo and whose owner inclines to see his friends in terms of his beasts ("A man concerned with animals must always be conscious of who goes into the cage with whom," he says, worrying about the meeting of his guests) gives us our first hint of what has so far been hidden. The revelation that Jane suffers from *lupus erythematosus*—"The intelligent, wolfish mask across her beautiful face"—is the next. And the last, which proceeds from Jane's refusal of Brewster's proposal (because he has been impure) and which sets him off "to undo defilement and regain innocence, to take an historical corruption and will it annulled, whisking it out of time as if it were a damaged egg going by on a conveyor belt," this final one lets us know for certain that we are in the presence of Romanticism's and modernism's pervasive primitivist dream. For Jane's rejection bespeaks a claim to innocence even greater than her lover's and, since they are doubles, indicates the unwillingness of both to accept the conditions of the fallen world, the imperfections of life in time. Typically, since he is adept at self-justification, Ashenden achieves the impossible (it is the farcical climax of

the novella's first part), "the self-loathing that *is* purity" and that, in restoring him to innocence (as he sees it), makes him worthy of Jane: "See, morality's easy, clear, what's the mystery?" But Jane, that flawed emblem of completeness, disappears now, too static to interest us for long, leaving behind unsettling whiffs and intimations of an otherness that will in time overtake and overmaster Ashenden himself. In other words, whereas Jane embodies the state of unreal perfection, Ashenden figures its pursuit: the quest that reveals him, over and again, as a prig of the extraordinary and the victim of his own heroic myth.

"Ashenden"'s swerve, its *écart,* is effected by a switch in point of view, as we move, suddenly and unexpectedly, from first to third person about two-thirds of the way through the work. But though we now see Brewster from the outside, the world remains what it has always been, *his* mirror: "a crèche of the elements," an image of "paradise," a landscape that charms him by its resemblance (here at least he is right) to the works of painters. "I am in art, he thought, and thus in nature too," he adds with a Popean delight in order. The eruption at this point of a ruttish bear into the frame that methodizes nature as Ashenden's myth aestheticizes his life promises a challenge different from any he has heretofore known and, it is to be imagined, one that will lay waste his awesome self-satisfaction. So it does up to a point, urging him into emotions he has not known till now. But habits of mind die hard; and though he is hardly in a position to deny the fact of the bear, the interpretation of the encounter, Elkin indicates, remains very much his: "The confrontation was noble, a challenge (there's going to be a hell of a contest, he thought), a coming to grips of disparate principles. . . . He believed not that the bear was emblematic, or even that he was, but that the two of them there in the clearing . . . somehow made for symbolism, or at least for meaning."

Not surprisingly, since nothing for Ashenden can be simply itself, the presence of the bear repeatedly translates itself (an affectionately parodic allusion to Faulkner here?) into a test: "Oh Jesus, he thought, is this how I'm to be purified? Is *this* the test? Oh, Lord, first I was in art and now I am in allegory." And if in what follows—his unavoidable lovemaking with the bear, the description of which is one of Elkin's most prodigious tours de force—he is at last forced out of his complacence, it is only superficially so. Even while stretching to encompass a new content—"But then I am a beast too, he thought. . . . What this means . . . is that my life has been too crammed with civilization"—his mind retains its fundamental structures of thought and perception. Fatuous to the end, he manages at once to glimpse the truth about himself ("I have the tourist's imagination, the day-tripper's vision") and to transform it into a matter for self-congratulation: "God, how I honor a difference and crave the unusual."

Brewster's post-coital resolution (Jane is now not only out of sight but out of mind) to "book passage to someplace far, someplace wild, further and wilder than he had ever been" testifies both to his inexhaustible capacity for fantasy (still finessing the existential, "fleeing the ordinary," he will, we recognize, always be en route and possibly *en rut*) and to the wonderful plasticity of his innocence. Reconstituted in the aftermath of Jane's rejection ("So innocence is knowledge, not its lack"), it undergoes a more bizarre and paradoxical recovery during his "ecstatic, transcendent" union with the bear, for, as he thinks later: "Maybe *I* was the virgin. Maybe *I* was. It was good news." Good news indeed: a gospel of infinite possibility, renewal, and redemption. But Elkin's final comment ("He started back through art to the house") ensures that we will not miss the irony—not only that Ashenden is off on the track of still wilder myths; or that like Dick Gibson's, in another of Elkin's novels, Ashenden's is an apprenticeship that will never end; and not only that his taste for the extraordinary is undiminished; but that (it is Elkin's most illuminating insight into modernism's thematic ideals and resolutions) the aesthetic and the primitivist are two sides of a single coin: the one, *pace* Forster, Lawrence, Woolf, and Joyce, the echo rather than the antithesis of the other.

At this point, with Ashenden dispatched and unchanged, everything seems to have fallen into place. But has it? Does this reading account for all of the work's complexity and does it account for my use of it as an example of midfiction? In the light of Elkin's other works, even of some elements of "Ashenden," and especially of remarks made by him in various interviews, some doubts begin to obtrude. "All characters," he says in one of these interviews, "all protagonists, are ultimately sympathetic," and in another: "Energy is what counts. . . . Whoever has the better rhetoric is the better man. . . . He is as far as I'm concerned the more sympathetic character." Ashenden? Sympathetic? Is that what these comments imply? At stake is Elkin's well-known fascination with obsession, a subject to which he returns repeatedly: "I'm attracted to the extreme. . . . I'm attracted to extremes of personality too. . . . I stand in awe of the *outré*. Those characters who are exaggerated seem, to me at least, more vital than the ordinary character, certainly more energetic. It's this energy which engines my work." And again, speaking once more of his characters: "I don't regard them as losers. The fact that they may be unhappy doesn't mean that they're losers. The fact that they may be outrageous or immoral doesn't mean that they're losers. The fact that they're obsessed, that they have obsessions which would get real people arrested, doesn't mean that they're losers. It means that they are simply demonstrating the kind of extravagance—the kind of *heroic* extravagance, if you will—that makes them, in my view, winners—winners, inasmuch as they impress me."

Brewster Ashenden clearly belongs in the well-stocked gallery of Elkin's obsessive characters. And though he is less intense than, say, Alexander Main in "The Bailbondsman" or *The Franchiser*'s Ben Flesh (largely because the treatment of him is so frequently broad-stroked and farcical), still he does have an incontrovertible vitality, which derives from the fact that Elkin endows him—successfully, if in defiance of even the most minimal verisimilitude—with his own energetic, vivid, and disruptive language. . . . [If Elkin] reacts ambivalently to his protagonist, and if, as he does, he clearly revels in the bizarre and improbable not only for their ironic potential but for their own sake, how are we to gauge the novella's attitude

toward the central question it poses about the ordinary and the extraordinary? The answer is anything but obvious, since "The Making of Ashenden" does not itself tell us unambiguously what—if it were not contravened by Brewster's aesthetic and primitivist impulses—the ordinary might be. Nor, until recently and especially in *The Living End*, does any of Elkin's fiction. His works are—and the image doesn't seem excessive—a battleground in which the lure of the extraordinary, made attractive by an obsessive concern with death, time, and the unknown, is only gradually and never completely countered by a celebration, still wild and fantastic, of what Larry McCaffery [in his "Stanley Elkin's Recovery of the Ordinary," *Critique: Studies in Modern Fiction* (1979)], refers to as "the beauty and wonder that is normally locked within the vulgar and ordinary."

Perhaps the most one can say is that the good life according to Elkin steers a difficult course between a desired intensification and a possible distortion of the ordinary and that his fiction demonstrates a willingness to risk failure rather than remain passive in the face of life's ineluctable mysteries. . . . Elkin seeks at most—since "there is no conventional wisdom . . . [since] truth comes in fifty-seven day-glo flavors"—a mitigation of inherent contradictions, a way, finally, of coping, which leaves the world in its essence unchanged and us, in part at least, with the job of making sense of it. (pp. 30-4)

> *Alan Wilde, "The Midfictional World: Elkin, Apple, and Barthelme," in his* Middle Grounds: Studies in Contemporary American Fiction, *University of Pennsylvania Press, 1987, pp. 24-40.*

Elkin on the genesis of "I Look Out for Ed Wolfe":

[One] day, apropos of absolutely nothing at all, I found myself wondering what would happen if a person, not unlike myself, decided to see exactly what he was worth and undertook to convert everything he owned back into cash. His clothes, his appliances, his geegaws and coat hangers, back into cash. He surrenders his phone and gets back the twenty-five-dollar deposit; he sells his furniture, his sheets, and his pillowcases. He converts his policies. He dumps his car, pulls his savings out of the bank, and sells his postage stamps back to the post office, everything must go. I called the story **"I Look Out for Ed Wolfe. . . ."**

Stanley Elkin, in his Preface to Stories from the Sixties, *1971.*

Stanley Elkin   (essay date 1990)

[In the following essay, originally published as the foreword to Criers and Kibitzers, Kibitzers and Criers, *Elkin comments on his use of realism in the collection of short stories.]*

For reasons not in the least clear to me, ***Criers and Kibitzers, Kibitzers and Criers*** has turned out to be my most enduring work, if, by "enduring," one refers not to a time scheme encompassing geological epochs or, for that matter, scarcely even calendrical ones, but to those few scant handfuls—twenty-four since it was first published by Random House in hardback in 1966—of years barely wide enough to gap a generation. Not counting downtime, when it was out-of-print, or the peculiar half-life when it was in that curious publisher's limbo known (but never entirely understood, at least by this foreworder) to the trade as "out-of-stock," it has been in print under sundry imprimaturs (Berkley Medallion, Plume, Warner Books, and, until I actually looked it up in *Books in Print* where I couldn't find it, I had thought Dutton's Obelisk editions, and, now, Thunder's Mouth Press), oh, say, eighteen or nineteen years. Set against the great timeliness of history this ain't, of course, much, not in the same league with astronomy's skippy-stony'd light-years certainly, or even, for that matter, the same ball park as the solar system, but we're talking very fragile book years, mind, which are to life span approximately what dog years are to the birthdays of humans. At a ratio of seven-to-one (seven doggie years equaling forty-nine bookie years), that would make my criers and kibitzers, depending on how the actuaries count that half-life, either eight hundred eighty-two or nine hundred and eleven years old. A classic, antique as Methuselah—the test, as the saying goes, of time.

In addition—more new math—two of these stories, **"Criers and Kibitzers, Kibitzers and Criers"** and **"The Guest,"** were adapted for and produced on the stage. **"Criers"** has been a radio play on the Canadian Broadcasting System—and one, **"I Look Out for Ed Wolfe,"** was bought for the movies, though it never made the cut. (**"Ed Wolfe,"** published in *Esquire* in 1962, was my first mass-market sale and put me, quite literally, on the map. Well, at least *Esquire*'s rigged 1963 chart about America's "Literary Establishment," where I found myself in shameless scarlet, short-listed among a small, arbitrary bundle of real writers—realer, in any event, than me—in what that magazine deemed to be "The Red Hot Center." [Just Rust Hills and Bob Brown kidding around.] It thrilled me then, it embarrasses me now. Had I had more sense it would have embarrassed me then, too. God knows it angered a lot of important critics who wrote letters to the editor, columns, even essays about it, a short-lived tempest in a tea bag not unlike the one old John Gardner provoked when he made his pronouncements about moral fiction. Not art for art's sake but hype for hype's. Like the PENs and Pulitzers, NBAs and National Book Critics Circle Awards, and all those other Masterpieces of the Minute that might not last the night.) **"A Poetics for Bullies"** was recorded on an LP by Jackson Beck, the radio actor and famous voice of Bluto in the Popeye cartoons, and somewhere loose in the world is a cassette tape of **"The Guest"** that I recorded for an outfit called The Printed Word. Oh, and eight of the nine stories in *C & K*—**"Cousin Poor Lesley and the Lousy People"** is the exception—have been anthologized, a few of them—the criers, guest, Ed Wolfe, and bully stories—several times—almost often. **"Criers"** and **"Ed Wolfe"** were in *The Best American Short Story* annuals back in the days when Martha Foley was Martha Foley. Indeed, for many years during the late sixties, the decade of the seventies, and into the eighties (it's starting to fall off), the stories have provided me and my family with a

kind of widow's mite, a small annuity—"sky money," I like to call it. I regard myself as a serious writer, even a professional one, but deep in my heart I think of most of the money I receive from my writing as essentially unearned. This isn't, as you may suppose, a poetic wimp factor kicking in—I'm no art jerk—so much as the heart's quid pro quo, all ego's driving power trip, the rush, that is, many writers get out of their almost sybaritic wallow in the unfettered luxury of their indulged imaginations. (What, they'll pay for this? I may be a badass, but I'm an honorable badass.) Anyway, it, the money on the stories, all sources, never amounted to *that* much. I come cheap, after all. Maybe, top-of-the-head, all-told, thirty or thirty-five thousand dollars since 1966, my going rate for having passed the test of time. Nothing solid as a fortune, I admit, but tighter than loose change, something like the cumulative yield on a small CD, say.

What isn't clear to me, though, is why. Why this book, why these stories? Surely I've written better books. Surely I'm a better writer now than I was when I wrote these stories. (Five of them, including the title story, one of my favorites, were written when I was still back in graduate school, for Christ's sake, and only three, **"The Guest,"** **"A Poetics for Bullies,"** and **"Perlmutter at the East Pole,"** were published after I'd published my first novel and before I'd written a second one.) So why? Why, really? I'd like to know.

One thing, certainly, is the accessibility of their style and (not behind that—indeed, quite the opposite—in absolute hand/glove relationship to the relative simplicity of the style) plain speaking's package deal with realism, time's honored literary arrangement between ease and verisimilitude. Here, for example, is Feldman, the butcher, returning to his store after a quick trip to the bank for change for his cash drawer. (In the story, had I been a better stylist in the realistic tradition, I would have used the word *silver*.)

> The street was quiet. It looks like a Sunday, he thought. There would be no one in the store. He saw his reflection in a window he passed and realized he had forgotten to take his apron off. It occurred to him that the apron somehow gave him the appearance of being very busy. An apron did that, he thought. Not a business suit so much. Unless there was a briefcase. A briefcase and an apron, they made you look busy. A uniform wouldn't. Soldiers didn't look busy, policemen didn't. A fireman did, but he had to have that big hat on. Schmo, a man your age walking in the street in an apron. He wondered if the vice-presidents at the bank had noticed his apron. He felt the heaviness again.

There's something comforting, almost soothing, about realism, and it's nothing to do with shocks of recognition—well it wouldn't do, would it, since shocks never console—or even with the familiarity that breeds content, so much as that the realistic world, in literature, at least, is one that, from a certain perspective, always makes sense, even its bum deals and tragedies, inasmuch as it plays—even showboats and grandstands—to our passion for reason. The realistic tradition presumes to deal, I mean, with cause and effect, with some deep need in readers—in all of us—for justice, the demand for the explicable reap/sow benefits (or punishments), the law of just desserts—all God's and Nature's organic bookkeeping. And, since form fits and follows function, style is instructed not to make waves but merely to tag along, easy as pie, taking in everything that can be seen along the way but not much more and nothing at all of what isn't immediately available to the naked eye.

My point, then, is that the stories in *Criers and Kibitzers, Kibitzers and Criers* are right-bang smack-dab in the middle of realism. I may get things wrong or even silly—as I do in the improbable scene in **"In the Alley"** when my protagonist, top-heavy with incurable cancer, checks himself out of the hospital to wander the city and goes into a bar to die in an unfamiliar neighborhood, or, in red-hot-centered **"I Look Out for Ed Wolfe"** where, ending the story, as stories never should end, with a gesture, I have Ed throw his money away—but most of the stories have conventional, realistic sources. Only **"On a Field, Rampant"** and **"A Poetics for Bullies"** owe less to the syllogistic, rational world—though they're not experimental, none of my writing is; I don't care for experimental writing and, in my case at least, experimental writing would be if I did it in German or French—than they do to some conjured, imaginary one and, sure enough, only in those stories am I more preoccupied with language than I am with realism's calmer tropes. I offer the battle of the headlines from **"On a Field, Rampant"**:

> " 'DOCKER WOULD BE KING,' " a man said, reading an imaginary headline. "IMMIGRANT CARGO HANDLER SAYS HE'S RIGHTFUL MAJESTY!' "

> " 'PRETENDER HAS MEDALLION WHICH TRACES LINEAGE TO ANCIENT DAYS OF KINGDOM.' "

> " ' "AMAZING RESEMBLANCE TO DUKE" SAYS DUKE'S OWN GATEMAN.' "

> " 'DOCKMAN DEFIES DUKE, DARES DUKE TO DUEL!' "

> " 'MAKE-BELIEVE MONARCH.' "

> " 'CARGO CON MAN CLAIMS KINGDOM!' "

> " 'KHARDOV CREATES KINGDOM FOR CARGO KING.' "

> " 'WHO IS KHARDOV?' "

And the abrasive, brassy up-frontness of the opening paragraph in **"A Poetics for Bullies"**:

> I'm Push the bully, and what I hate are new kids and sissies, dumb kids and smart, rich kids, poor kids, kids who wear glasses, talk funny, show off, patrol boys and wise guys and kids who pass pencils and water the plants—and cripples, *especially* cripples. I love nobody loved.

The point here is that a "higher" or more conscious—if not conscientious—style is not only less realistic than the sedate and almost passive linears of the butcher's quiet street but much more aggressive and confrontational. (Only consider the two operative words in the titles of those two stories—*rampant,* with all its up-in-your-face forepawardlies and dug-in hind-leggedness, and *bullies*—and you'll take my meaning.) In fiction and style not formed by the shared communal linkages between an author and the compacts, struck bargains, and done deals of a reasonable, recognizable morality—my law of just desserts—it's always the writer's service. Whatever spin, whatever "English" he puts on the ball is his. It's his call. He leads, you follow. He leads, you play catch-up. (It's that wallow in the ego again, self 's flashy mud wrassle.) Obviously this makes for difficulties with which most readers—don't kid yourself, me too—don't much care to spend the time of day, let alone hang out with long enough to pass any tests of time.

Who's afraid of the big bad wolf?

Damn near everyone.

Now I don't know how true this next part is, but a little true, I should think. I'm trying to tell what turned me. Well, delight in language as language certainly. (I'd swear to that part.) But something less delightful, too. It was that nothing very bad had happened to me yet. (I was a graduate student, protected, up to my ass in the ivy.) My daddy's rich and my ma is good lookin'. Then my father died in 1958 and my mother couldn't take three steps without pain. Then a heart attack I could call my own when I was thirty-seven years old. Then this, then that. Most of it uncomfortable, all of it boring. I couldn't run, I couldn't jump. Because, as the old saying *should* go, as long as you've got your health you've got your naïveté. I lost the one, I lost the other, and maybe that's what led me toward revenge—a writer's revenge, anyway; the revenge, I mean, of style.

One final word about the stories in this collection and I'm done. I'm particularly fond of at least four of them, **"Perlmutter at the East Pole"** for its main character and the curses he invents, **"The Guest"** for its situation and humor, **"Criers and Kibitzers, Kibitzers and Criers"** for its situation and humor, and the truth, I think, of its perceptions and characters, and **"A Poetics for Bullies,"** for its humor and energy and style. I like the **"Ed Wolfe"** story a bit less but I like it—for the imagery in the opening paragraph, for a lot of its dialogue, and for a reason no one could guess. Remember Polish jokes? I could be absolutely wrong about this, but I think I may have invented them in this story. It was published in the September 1962 issue of *Esquire*. In August of that year I went off to Europe to write my first novel. Up to that time I'd never heard a Polish joke, but when I returned to America in June 1963, they were all the rage. Everyone was telling them. A serendipity, of course, like penicillin or certain kinds of clear plastic, but *my* serendipity. What a claim to fame—to have invented the Polish joke. But it proves my point, I think, the one about the distance to which a writer's ego will stoop to have, whatever the cost, to him, or to others, its own way. (pp. 240-45)

Stanley Elkin, "Foreword to 'Criers and Ki-

bitzers, Kibitzers and Criers'," in his Pieces of
Soap: Essays, *Simon & Schuster, 1992, pp.
240-45.*

Meg Wolitzer   (essay date 1993)

[*In the following excerpt, Wolitzer reviews* Van Gogh's
Room at Arles.]

The cover of Stanley Elkin's 1985 novel read *Stanley
Elkin's The Magic Kingdom,* which brings to mind titles
like *Stephen King's "It"* and *Jacqueline Susann's Once Is
Not Enough.*

Now, eight years later, Mr. Elkin has written ***Van Gogh's
Room at Arles,*** a subtle, complicated, often astonishing
collection of three novellas. This time around, it almost
makes sense to think of the book as "Stanley Elkin's Van
Gogh's Room at Arles," not because it feels showy and
sensational, but simply because the collection is so singular to its author, and the room in its title seems to belong
as much to Stanley Elkin as to Vincent van Gogh.

The first novella, an exercise in helplessness and rage
called **"Her Sense of Timing,"** takes place far from Arles.
Jack Schiff, a professor of political geography at a university in St. Louis, is a victim of a debilitating disease that
has left him a virtual invalid, largely dependent on the care
of Claire, his wife of 36 years: "Even in restaurants Claire
paid the check, figured the tip, signed the credit-card slip.
His disease turned him into some sort of helpless, old-
timey widow, some nice, pre-lib, immigrant lady."

At the beginning of the novella, Claire has just announced
that she's leaving Jack, and she proceeds to pack her suit-
cases and scram. What follows is a maddening and riotous
account of Schiff's struggle to reconcile himself to being
on his own for the first time in years. Not only has Claire
left him in the lurch, but, even more horrible, she's departed on the eve of Schiff's annual party for his graduate students: a big, messy affair that Claire has always overseen.
What will he do? How will he cope?

Schiff (and, cleverly, Mr. Elkin) turns to one of those companies that install emergency aid devices in the homes of
the elderly or disabled. The S.O.S. Corporation swiftly dis-
patches a team to Schiff's house, and his relationship with
its members, Bill and Jenny, becomes the source of much
broad, dark humor. He's forced to rely on them for every
little thing, and when it's time for him to pay for their services, he enlists them to go rummaging around the house
for his checkbook:

> "I think it may be in one of the drawers in the
> tchtchk."
>
> "Say what?"
>
> "The cabinet in the hall. We call it the tchtchk."
>
> "That's a new one on me. You ever hear that,
> Jen? The choo-choo? Heck, I can't even pro-
> nounce it. How do you say that again?"
>
> "Tchtchk. It doesn't mean anything."
>
> "Just a pet name, eh? From your salad

> days. . . . It's just something you ought to bear
> in mind. . . . Well, that you *had* salad
> days. . . . That's why the good Lord usually
> lets us hold on to our memories. . . . So we can
> remember the times before our wives had to
> carry us around piggyback."

The word "tchtchk" summons up the private shorthand
used by longtime couples, the secret language of marriage
that usually can't be shared with anyone else, or even fully
translated. Later in the novella, when Jenny casually refers to the "tchtchk" as though it were a common word,
the moment is surprisingly affecting. Schiff starts to grow
attracted to her, to come alive for the first time in years.
Although he's in a wheelchair, in a position of potentially
humiliating vulnerability, this "pre-lib, immigrant lady"
slowly gains back a good measure of his American male-
ness and bravado.

That night at the graduate students' bash, which takes
place despite his protests, Schiff finds himself attracted
once again, this time to a student named Molly Kohm:
"He was gathering courage, putting together a sort of
schoolkid's nerve he hadn't used in years. . . . Yes, Schiff
thought, I'm going to touch her. I'm going to reach over
and hold her."

Mr. Elkin, who teaches at Washington University in St.
Louis and who has written eloquently elsewhere about his
own multiple sclerosis, here explores the ramifications of
degenerative illness, from the purely physical difficulties
of the smallest everyday actions to the roaring anger and
frustration of not being in charge. The novella gamely confronts weakness and strength, and ends with—no surprise—a really good punch line.

Mr. Elkin's second novella, **"Town Crier Exclusive, Confessions of a Princess Manqué: 'How Royals Found Me
"Unsuitable" to Marry Their Larry,'"** brings us a bit
closer to France, at least in terms of geography. This is a
tour de force about a woman who falls in love with Lawrence, Crown Patriciate of England. Coming as it does on
the heels of a major British monarchy shakedown, the novella is timely and funny, although inhabiting the mind of
Louise, the commoner who briefly nabs Prince Larry, is
at least as arduous as occupying the body of Prof. Jack
Schiff. Louise rambles on, relating choice tidbits to a su-
permarket tabloid, Town Crier, that has bought the rights
to her story. As Mr. Elkin portrays her, Louise is a kind
of breezy, souped-up Fergie-Diana hybrid, an ordinary
woman plucked from the normal world and brought into
the palace nuthouse. **"Town Crier Exclusive"** is a witty
piece of work, studded with bits that lampoon the royal
family. Some are based on actual events, such as a reference to an intruder sneaking into the Queen's bedroom to
watch her sleep, while others are pure Elkin, as in a scene
in which the Prince's relatives discuss the upcoming wedding with the prospective bride and groom:

> "Would it be all right, do you think, if we wore,
> well, jeans, to the wedding?"
>
> "Jeans? To a Royal Wedding? In Westminster
> Abbey?"
>
> "I told you he wouldn't go for it."

"Well, not jeans, or not jeans exactly. Regular morning coats and top hats for the boys, actually."

"And gorgeous gowns for the ladies. With these ravishing big hats and really swell veils."

"Just *cut* like jeans."

"From stone-washed denim."

"Oh, it would be such fun! The Sloane Rangers would just die!"

"Town Crier Exclusive" is often truly funny, but at times it's a little too thickly packed with ludicrous humor and circumlocutious side trips, and it does go on somewhat longer than it should. After a while, the clutter of Mr. Elkin's version of royal life becomes a little too much to take and, like Fergie and Diana bolting the palace gates for good, the reader finally wants out.

Mr. Elkin's strongest stuff is saved for last. The title novella concerns a professor named Miller who's won a foundation grant and been sent to an academic retreat in Arles, where, by a stroke of luck, he's assigned to van Gogh's bedroom. All the accouterments of the great man, depicted in his famous painting of the room—the basin, the pitcher, the bed—have been left for the less-than-great man to use. Miller is out of his element in every way; the retreat in Arles is a think-tank hideaway for intellectuals from all the great institutions: Harvard, Yale, Princeton, Booth Tarkington Community College. *Booth Tarkington Community College?* That's where Mr. Elkin's protagonist teaches.

All around him, other institute fellows proudly describe their work: "Myra Gynt, a composer from the University of Michigan, explained how it was her intention to set the lyrics of various Broadway showstoppers to the more formal music of the 12-tone scale." "Farrell Jones held forth regarding his conclusions about the parallels between the mood swings of manic-depressives and babies." A man in a wheelchair is in Arles to research a project on his theory that "world-class cities were almost never found on mountaintops." (Although he's not named, we can guess that he is meant to be Jack Schiff of **"Her Sense of Timing,"** whose reappearance is a self-referential wink to the reader.)

Finally, when it's Miller's turn in this game of rarefied show and tell, he fails miserably. He's been invited by the foundation to work on a study of the image of the community college among academics from prestigious universities, and at the end of his description of this vague, bogus-sounding project, Miller faints dead away.

A doctor is summoned who turns out to be Félix Rey, the great-great-grandson of van Gogh's own doctor, Félix Rey. The young Rey is the spitting image of his ancestor, right down to the tips of his reddened ears. Over the course of Miller's stay in Arles, he becomes aware of other members of the Club of the Portraits of Descendants of People Painted by Vincent van Gogh. These characters haunt the edges of the novella like apparitions, creating an atmosphere reminiscent of parts of Joyce's story "The Dead," invoking the greatness of what's past and the mundane but moving humanness of what's still living.

In this novella, Mr. Elkin muscularly demonstrates his talents through his easy transitions from shtick to art and back again. He has great fun listing the catalogue of intellectuals, getting their names just right: "Samuels Kleist, a vernacular architect in his late 60's, Yalom and Inga Basset, pop psychiatrists. . . . Jesus Hans, statistics adviser to the third world." Mr. Elkin can also be highly poetic, a kind of borscht belt visionary who reaches for a real epiphany near the close of the novella: "Miller decided to turn off the light. Low as the light had been, his eyes still had to adjust to this new black dark. What he saw now, the almost colorless configuration of shapes and masses, made a different and still stranger picture and, as dawn came and the light turned milky, and then, as the sun rose higher and the room experienced its gradual yellowing, it seemed almost to go through a process of queer simultaneity, of aging and renewal at once." This time, Mr. Elkin doesn't go out with a punch line, but the humor lingers even as the novella closes with a long passage of charged and beautiful writing.

The three novellas in **Van Gogh's Room at Arles** are linked through shared themes and obsessions, with Mr. Elkin the ironic geographer lurking in a corner, overseeing the landscapes of his characters' lives. Mostly, though, the novellas are connected by Stanley Elkin's distinctive and unflagging voice. In his new book, that voice is big enough to fill the whole room. (pp. 3, 19)

> *Meg Wolitzer, "The Roaring Anger of Not Being in Charge," in* The New York Times Book Review, *March 21, 1993, pp. 3, 19.*

FURTHER READING

Bibliography

Robbins, William M. "A Bibliography of Stanley Elkin." *Critique* 26, No. 4 (Summer 1985): 169-84.
    Bibliography of primary works, including Elkin's reviews, introductions, and prefaces, and of the criticism of his works.

Criticism

Bargen, Doris G. "Modern Man in Consumer Culture—Elkin's Orphans, Salesmen, and Consumers." In her *The Fiction of Stanley Elkin,* pp. 81-98. Bern and Frankfurt, Germany: Lang, 1980.
    Examines the problem of survival in a modern consumer culture in three of Elkin's short stories—"I Look out for Ed Wolfe," "Fifty Dollars," and "A Sound of Distant Thunder."

———. "An Interview with Stanley Elkin." In her *The Fiction of Stanley Elkin,* pp. 220-304. Bern and Frankfurt, Germany: Lang, 1980.
    Conversation with Stanley Elkin regarding his novels

and short fiction, the significance of their characters and themes, and the ways in which he has developed as a writer.

Brickner, Richard P. "Born Losers." *The New York Times Book Review* (23 January 1966): 40-1.

Review of *Criers and Kibitzers, Kibitzers and Criers,* criticizing the stories in the collection for their preoccupation with failure and futility.

Clapp, Susannah. Review of *Eligible Men,* by Stanley Elkin. *The Times Literary Supplement* (13 December 1974): 1405.

Reads the three novellas in *Eligible Man (Searches and Seizures)* as taking place in a "more or less prosperous American Eden," where the male protagonists of each narrative seem interchangeable.

Cohen, Robert. Review of *Early Elkin,* by Stanley Elkin. *The New York Times Book Review* (18 May 1986): 24.

Praises the short stories in *Early Elkin* for the ways in which they anticipate characters and themes in Elkin's later fiction.

Ditsky, John. "Stanley Elkin." *The Hollins Critic* 19, No. 3 (June 1982): 7-11.

Considers the novellas in *Searches and Seizures* to present "specialized modes of existence" that determine the ways in which characters respond to their situation.

Dougherty, David C. "A Conversation with Stanley Elkin." *The Literary Review* 34, No. 2 (Winter 1991): 175-95.

Examines Elkin's views of his fiction and where they differ from critics' conception of his writing.

Duncan, Jeffrey L. "A Conversation with Stanley Elkin and William H. Gass." *The Iowa Review* 7, No. 1 (Winter 1976): 48-77.

Elkin and Gass informally discuss their interests and aims in writing fiction, with Duncan moderating.

Edwards, Thomas R. Review of *Searches and Seizures,* by Stanley Elkin. *The New York Times Book Review* (21 October 1973): 3.

Praises Elkin for the aggressive nature of his writing and his depiction of the ways in which the fate of individuals is determined by "the general fate of humankind" in *Searches and Seizures.*

Koenig, Rhoda. Review of *Van Gogh's Room at Arles,* by Stanley Elkin. *New York* 26, No. 10 (8 March 1993): 84.

Asserts that the stories in *Van Gogh's Room at Arles,* while sometimes brilliant in their treatment of the theme of cultural crossover and exchange, "somehow add up to less than the sum of their parts."

Thompson, John. "From Out of Nowhere." *The New York Review of Books,* no. 6 (3 February 1966): 12-13.

Review of *Criers and Kibitzers, Kibitzers and Criers* that finds fault with Elkin's portrayal of characters who experience unrelieved suffering.

Additional coverage of Elkin's life and career is contained in the following sources published by Gale Research: *Contemporary Authors,* **Vols. 9-12, rev. ed.;** *Contemporary Authors New Revision Series,* **Vol. 8;** *Contemporary Literary Criticism,* **Vols. 4, 6, 9, 14, 27, 51;** *Dictionary of Literary Biography,* **Vols. 2, 28;** *Dictionary of Literary Biography Yearbook: 1980;* **and** *Major 20th-Century Writers.*

William H. Gass

1924-

(Full name William Howard Gass) American novelist, short story writer, and essayist.

INTRODUCTION

Gass is included among a prominent group of American writers whose work is often described as "metafiction." In contrast to realistic fiction, which employs narrative devices in order to present an accurate rendering of individuals and events, metafiction plays with the conventions of style and narrative to draw attention to the process of reading and to focus on language as an end in itself rather than as a means for conveying subject matter. Gass's fiction is particularly noted for its use of rhyme, alliteration, cadence, and elaborately developed metaphors, qualities which are more commonly associated with poetry than with fiction.

Gass was born in Fargo, North Dakota, and raised in Warren, Ohio. While this Midwest background is reflected in the characters and locales of his fiction, Gass has asserted that "though people try to label me as a local midwestern writer . . . I never had roots; all my sources are chosen." By the age of eight, Gass has remarked, he was determined to become a writer. He attended Kenyon College and later Cornell University, where he received a doctorate in philosophy in 1954. Subsequently Gass has taught philosophy at Purdue University and Washington (Mo.) University. Regarding the relationship between his studies in philosophy and his fiction, Gass has stated: "It is not surprising, I suppose, that philosophical ideas, used as a painter might use pigment, have always colored, if not clouded, my work." This influence, critics note, is especially evident in Gass's emphasis in his fiction on the way language reflects his characters' perception of the world.

In his critical essays Gass illuminates his principles as a writer through his view of the distinction between fiction and nonfiction. He argues that while nonfiction works such as biographies and histories consist of representations of people, objects, and events in the actual world, works of fiction are composed solely of literary elements and are significant for their artistic form rather than for their correspondence to anything in real life. Although both nonfiction and fiction employ the same materials, Gass contends that the purpose of fiction is to structure those materials in an artistic manner using metaphors, symbols, and other literary devices. As Gass has explained: "I am principally interested in the problems of style. . . . I try to make things out of words the way a sculptor might make a statue out of stone." The result of this approach, critics observe, is a body of fiction in which the act of writing itself forms the dominant subject matter.

This concern for artistic form is evident in Gass's short fiction. For instance, in "The Pedersen Kid" the content of the story becomes less important than the poetic language Gass uses to construct it. Bruce Bassoff has commented that in this story, "the metaphor, the anapestic rhythm, and the alliteration . . . call our attention away from what is said to the saying itself." A further example is the title story of *In the Heart of the Heart of the Country*. Critics have demonstrated how this story's poetic language and formal configuration—the narrative is fragmented into several individually titled sections—takes precedence over its subject of life in a small town in Indiana. Gass's emphasis on form is perhaps most evident in the novella *Willie Masters' Lonesome Wife*, which employs various type faces, photographs, and unconventional layout to make the reader particularly aware of both its structure and its attempt to render consciousness in print. In *Willie Masters' Lonesome Wife* the emphasis on literary devices and formal structure is developed to the point that this work cannot be adequately described without reference to these properties.

Gass's contribution to the "metafiction" school resides in his ability to incorporate ideas from his aesthetic philosophy into his fictional work. In the words of Larry McCaffery: "Certainly no other writer in America has been able to combine his critical intelligence with a background as a student of both the literary and philosophical aspects of language and to make this synthesis vital."

PRINCIPAL WORKS

SHORT FICTION

In the Heart of the Heart of the Country, and Other Stories 1968
*Willie Masters' Lonesome Wife 1971

OTHER MAJOR WORKS

Omensetter's Luck (novel) 1966
Fiction and the Figures of Life (essays) 1971
On Being Blue: A Philosophical Inquiry (essay) 1976
The World within the Word (essays) 1978
Habitations of the Word (essays) 1985
A Temple of Texts: Fifty Literary Pillars (nonfiction) 1991

* Originally published in *TriQuarterly Supplement* 2, 1968.

CRITICISM

George P. Elliot (essay date 1968)

[*In the following excerpt from a review of* In the Heart of the Heart of the Country, and Other Stories, *Elliot observes that the stories in the collection take the reader inside an abnormal mind in a tenuous relationship with reality.*]

Gass's fiction may be phenomenological as all get out, and if phenomenology is what you want, more power to you. Myself, I like his stories because they are interesting as narrative and verbal constructs and because at their best they say something strange and worth listening to about the world.

In all five of [the stories in *In the Heart of the Heart of the Country, and Other Stories*], Gass has modified Robbe-Grillet's technique for representing the contents and motions of a highly abnormal mind; but then Gass has put this technical facility to the service of what seems to me a worthy fictional end—not "new" but not old exactly either and certainly not old-fashioned: just literary, human. The essence of this technique is fictionally to present everything as it impinges on the quite abnormal mind of a person who is in a peculiar, unstable relationship with the other persons in his world, with social institutions, even with beasts and inanimate objects. The least impressive of these five stories, **"Icicles,"** is in the third person;

the other four, all in the first person singular, take you much further into the consciousness of the central character, the aim of all Gass's fiction.

Now there is, I believe, a natural reluctance in many or most readers against coming very close to or going very far into the mind of another when that mind is as peculiar as all five of these are, and a considerable part of the job of a writer of such fiction is to overcome this reluctance. In the two middling stories in this book, **"Mrs. Mean"** and **"In the Heart of the Heart of the Country,"** Gass accomplishes this by the rather easy strategy of presenting a character of much sensitivity and intelligence being stretched on the rack of Midwest smalltown neighbors and customs. The title story, in fact, reads rather like the ruminations of one of the more bilious contributors to the *New York Review of Books* if he had been condemned for a long stretch in such a town, well past his breaking point. It is not that in actuality such towns are not living graveyards—I came from one and they are. It is just that they have been literarily stereotyped almost beyond the possibility of serious use—as, at the other end of the scale, Paris has been used too often as the city to which the sensitive young intellectual from the killing provinces flees for his life.

"The Pederson Kid" is a good notch above these two (please understand that it is a high standard by which I am judging these stories, the highest). In this long story, long enough to be labeled a novella, that nonform, Gass takes you into the consciousness of a normal-seeming boy, but then subjects him to such extreme experiences, emotional, moral, physical, that you have little difficulty believing in his disappearance into a deranged state of mind, and are willing to sympathize with him as he goes off into it. My only reservation about the story is that Gass makes it impossible for you to know exactly what happens at the end. To me as reader, it matters whether the boy actually kills the others or only thinks they have been killed by somebody (he is not clear by whom), and I resent the author's obscuring this knowledge from me. If he wanted me to feel a literary confusion equivalent to the boy's confusion about what was what, he succeeded. But instead of deepening my empathy with the character (or teaching me some sort of phenomenological lesson?), it turned me against the author for trickery.

Identity is the issue common to all these stories, and Gass's investigation of the minds of people who are uncertain or confused about their identities is powerfully carried out; this is especially successful in **"The Pederson Kid."** My only serious complaint is that Gass seems, a little, to be trying to call my identity into question too, and this I consider an illegitimate literary endeavor; in my own person, I resist it.

The masterpiece of these stories, in my opinion, is the shortest, **"Order of Insects."** It consists of a housewife's strange reflections on the insect bodies that keep appearing in the house that she and her family are renting, her relation to them, to all *those others,* to her role in the world. The tone is lyrical; the story is a dramatic monologue, and the effect is poetic. It is one of the best stories I have ever read, as well as one of the oddest.

For in it, as not always in the others, the language is wholly successful. **"The Pederson Kid"** is the most narrative of the five, and in it the language is plainest, up to the point where the narrator alters into madness. The title story is hardly narrative at all, and its language is highly stylized. Gass turns out, in all his fiction, splendid sentences by the dozen; but rather too often, as in the title story, he falls into an obtrusively iambic rhythm which leads to a plodding life of its own, neither taking the reader into the character's mind particularly nor taking him anywhere else either. But in **"Order of Insects"** everything comes together magically, and the reader rides the poetic prose with the character to a region where he has never been before and wants to go again—I've read the story three times already and look forward to reading it many more. (pp. 573-74)

> *George P. Elliott, "Stretched on the Rack of the Midwest," in* The Nation, *New York, Vol. 206, No. 18, April 29, 1968, pp. 573-74.*

Irving Malin   (essay date 1968)

[*In the following review, Malin focuses on the relationship between consciousness and reality that he considers the basis for the stories in* In the Heart of the Heart of the Country, and Other Stories.]

William H. Gass is interested in the "texture" of consciousness. He believes that plot is less important than insightful flashes because it is "well ordered" and artificial—it is divorced from the way we actually experience "the heart of the country." Thus he writes stories which have no fixed point of reference (except the narrator's consciousness). These stories are, in effect, *imagistic essays on the mind* and when they work, they disturb our conventional responses to life and literature.

It can be argued that **"The Pedersen Kid"**—one of the five stories in [*In the Heart of the Heart of the Country*]—does have a plot. But the various physical actions—the journey in the blizzard; the search for the intruder; the entry into the house—are significant only as they impinge upon the "center of consciousness." It is the boy's mind at work which patterns (and is patterned by) the outside world. When he describes the snow-scene, he interprets it; and because he is disturbed by real and imaginary fears, he is a difficult, elusive being—he cannot be categorized; he responds in quirky ways. It is fitting that he "slips" out of himself—all of Mr. Gass' narrators distort reality—because this transformation of personality is, perhaps, the only stable "fact" in the universe.

Mr. Gass uses the blizzard as the symbol of violent consciousness. Objects and motives are dim; boundaries are violated. The entire situation becomes dreamlike and hallucinatory, especially when the mysterious appearance (of the Pedersen kid) and disappearance (of the intruder) reinforce ambiguities. I think that the narrator is a bit too pleased about finding himself—"I had been the brave one and now I was free"—but even here Mr. Gass may suggest that he cannot rest at home—he will be caught in the snow again.

In **"Order of Insects"** we meet a wife (as narrator) who does not undergo the brutal journey of the boy. She stays at home; she stablizes the family order. But she also begins to recognize another world—not of snow, but of insects—and as she broods about this new "order," she "slips" out. She spends unnecessary time examining the beauties of insect-structure—"I no longer own my own imagination"—and when we last see her, we realize that she can never be as "tidy and punctual" as before. She is "suspended"—like a spider?—and she must not tell her family (or herself) the underlying causes. In less than ten pages Mr. Gass captures her fascination with insects and her surrender to them.

Perhaps the most unorthodox story in the collection is **"In the Heart of the Heart of the Country."** It is, superficially, a series of vignettes about life in one Mid-Western town. It offers glimpses of "People," "Businesses," and "Politics"—a comforting, almost-cliché newsreel. But we realize that a "mad" or "unhappy" narrator is describing the scene. The vignettes emphasize distortion, dislocation, and inversion; business, people, and politics suddenly become different. Not only does the narrator compel us to question the picturepostcard reality we have always accepted—he makes us unsure of his reliability (and personality). Does he view things bleakly because of an unhappy love affair? Or can he "strike through the mask"—to use Melville's phrase—because of his now-heightened perception? Both "the heart of the country" and the heart of the narrator remain wonderfully obscure: "There's no one to hear the music but myself, and though I'm listening, I'm no longer certain. Perhaps the record's playing something else."

The publisher gives us a blurb by John Hollander which implies that this treatment of the "relation between self and things is unique in American writing." This statement is easy—the important American novelists from Poe to Flannery O'Connor have dealt with obsessive designs which distort reality—but I think that at his best, Mr. Gass makes us remember these writers. His stories question the relation between consciousness and reality, and they make us wonder about our tense situation in an alien (?) world. They stun us. (pp. 154-56)

> *Irving Malin, in a review of "In the Heart of the Heart of the Country," in* Commonweal, *Vol. LXXXVIII, No. 5, April 19, 1968, pp. 154-56.*

Paul West   (essay date 1971)

[*In the following review, West praises Gass's experimental narrative technique in* Willie Masters' Lonesome Wife *for its rendering of consciousness in print.*]

A lot of what is visually verbal in our society isn't paginal at all, but bombards the eye in various ways through neon or through posters, labels, buttons, postmark legends, and so on. The eye wearies, but it nonetheless absorbs information from what might be thought of as being beyond the traditional visual field, the page (or the TV screen). In other words, our reading habits in the largest sense are more elastic, more three-dimensional, than they used to be, so it's inevitable that we should approach the format of the printed page with an acute sense of its limitations—of its top-to-bottomness, its left-to-rightness, its essentially chronological mode. We miss, perhaps, the random grouping of the non-paginal, and what it has in common with the randomness of what is non-verbal.

Not surprisingly, writers have acknowledged these changes in our ways of looking at print. Stultifying to read in bulk, concrete poetry nonetheless delivers and emphasizes something morphological in individual letters, and a goodly number of novelists have resorted to visual devices that recall [Laurence] Sterne and Lewis Carroll, not so much supplanting word with icon as augmenting the one with the other. No doubt of it, the writer in the third third of this century is in the interesting position of, as a communicator, having at his disposal not only all the orthodox deployments of typography but also what, by now, are the orthodoxies of advertising (giant lettering and lettering in color; fast-registering logos and subliminal residues), not to mention those of the comic strip (words in balloons) and the movie (the subdivided screen). It's only reasonable that the writer should add to his arsenal in this way, winning for himself some of the still-surviving visual impact there is in Japanese or Chinese, and fortifying his semeiology with something graphic or even sculptural.

All very well, many readers and some writers might say, but visual gimmicks are a feeble supplement to printed texts and run contrary to the principle of reading, which is to chart your way painstakingly from line to line, registering the connected argument as you go, all startling effects having to be made in the same material and not imported from an alien medium. Well, I for one don't buy that: There are no rules about mixing media, not even about which mixtures work and which don't. And here comes William Gass, an established and respected novelist, with a performative text that's something between collage and recitative, a text that regales the eye with combinations of italics and bold face, footnotes and headnotes, asterisks and treble clefs, placards that tend to dominate the page and parabolical tails of words that go wagging off it, lines that curve up and down as if seen through a distorting lens or arrange themselves into the shape of a Christmas tree, a page faced by its mirror-image, pages ringed brown-maroon by coffee cups, and interleaved shots of nudes that sometimes have the text itself elbowed into a corner as if in parody of Life's ousting Art. All in all, it's a defiant, ingeniously staged typographical concerto for eye and berserk compositor, in the course of which Gass keeps the mind at full stretch as he feeds it information from all quarters of the page and sustains as many as three parallel streams of narrative all competing for simultaneous attention.

Ostensibly this is a lament uttered by Babs Masters on the occasion of her recognizing what the onset of aging can do to any woman, and a lonely one in particular. Ranging as far and wide as she mentally can, she plucks the joys and monotonies of her life together into an erotic, uncouth, and sleazy synopsis which is as centrifugal as the typography. On one hand, this is a case history volunteered by the case herself; on the other, it's an essay on the mind-body inexus. You would expect the first from the au-

thor of *Omensetter's Luck*, in which Gass's reverence for unmetropolitan eccentricity develops into an eloquent general summation, and you would expect the second from the professional philosopher which Gass happens to be. What's new, at least from him, is the liberties taken for the sake of making a prose monologue seem, on the page, less rehearsed, less glib, and less groomed than usual. Let's face it: The lonely Mrs. Masters has an untidy head whose quality could not, I think, have been gotten convincingly across in conventional prose conventionally set out. It's no accident that the sixty-odd pages are unnumbered and that all but the last eight (which are glossy white and where Gass more or less speaks in his own person) are a matte gray; the telling is as much tactile as verbal, and as much visual as it is either.

I mentioned Gass's beginning to speak in his own person, and he makes it clear that Mrs. Masters, once again (but this time verbally rather than sexually), is being used: "I," she is made to say towards the end, "am that lady language chose to make her playhouse of." And what we have, after finishing the book, is a retrospective sense of having witnessed—assisted at—a ventriloquial showpiece of literary style in which Gass, by juxtaposing the humdrum with the histrionic, has worked compassion into a just rhetoric that runs the gamut of human commotion from spit to spirit. Mrs. Masters tells you to

> expectorate into a glass . . . Drink . . . Analyze
> your reluctance. And wonder why they call sali-
> va the sweet wine of love,

a bit of perception from which, although in a footnote, we soar into an anthem on the notion of whiteness:

> marbles, japonicas, and pearls, as in a joyful day,
> the innocence of brides, benignity of age, superi-
> ority of race, the robes of the redeemed, the bear
> of the poles, albino seas, their sharks and squalls,
> their whales; and thus universals . . .

Predictably, the peroration to all this is earthy and urbane:

> It's not the languid pissing prose we've got, we
> need; but poetry, the human muse, full up, erect
> and on the charge, impetuous and hot and loud
> and wild like Messalina going to the stews, or
> those damn rockets streaming headstrong into
> stars.

To my mind, Gass here proves that straight, rectilinear prose is no longer sufficient for the writer who wants to discuss the spirit of the age with the people most aware of it. How right and fitting it is that one of the evoked ghosts in **Willie Masters' Lonesome Wife** is "Sam" (not Johnson or Beckett, but Samuel Taylor Coleridge, high priest of imagination, the "esemplastic" or unifying power). For here raises that power to its highest and, in so doing, sets an alternative standard for American narrative prose. It's no longer useful to try to imagine imagination in the act of imagining, for this is just what Gass makes happen here, low-level through the sluttish Babs, high-level when she tries to think—like a performing flea in Emma Bovary's navel—what it might be like to have a high-caliber litr'y gent talking on your behalf while feeling you up. The book's unity transcends its hectic gesturing, and the subtlety of Gass's mind the real dog he's saddled himself with on this creative occasion. (pp. 12, 14)

Paul West, "From Spit to Spirit," in Book World—The Washington Post, *November 21, 1971, pp. 12, 14.*

Patricia Kane   (essay date 1972)

[*In the following essay, Kane offers an analysis of "The Pedersen Kid."*]

Tales of boys' coming to manhood or an awareness of evil so abound in American literature that to write such a story without its being commonplace and repetitious requires skill of the sort William Gass demonstrates in **"The Pedersen Kid."** The story, narrated by an adolescent boy named Jorge, tells of a journey through a Plains' blizzard that ends in death and madness. Jorge does not discover evil; he has always lived in a brutalizing environment. His life suggests what Huck Finn's might have been if Pap and his mother had settled on a Dakota farm. Here Jorge meets no gentle teacher, but only a hired man as cruel and corrupt as his father. Neither offers refuge from the hostile natural environment.

The story begins with Hans, the hired man, putting the nearly-frozen body of the Pedersen kid, a neighbor's child, on the kitchen table and asking Jorge to wake his drunken father. Jorge, jealous of the attention the kid gets and resentful of the admiration accorded for his feat of coming through the snow, resentfully helps. Throughout the opening section of the story, Jorge recalls and experiences typical episodes of his own brutal, ugly life with his drunken Pa, a mother who has retreated into mindless domesticity (more interested, Jorge believes, in the cleanliness of her kitchen than in her son), and the cruel, teasing Hans. During a brief moment of consciousness the kid tells Hans of a killer in yellow gloves. Pa, Hans, and Jorge set out for the Pedersens, not out of any concern for them, but to punish each other over a bottle of Pa's liquor Hans used to try to revive the kid. In the second part of the story they endure a terrible journey through the snow. Jorge begins the trip feeling like a knight "setting out to do something special and big," but soon is overcome by the cold, and his warm feeling changes to a burning hate. In the final section, at the Pedersens, Pa is shot, Hans disappears, and Jorge remains alone feeling with a mad joy that he has been brave and deserves the warm feeling of "burning up, inside and out, with joy."

Because Jorge ends in madness, several matters remain uncertain at the conclusion of the story. Perhaps, as he says, a killer with yellow gloves came to the Pedersens, killed them, returned after his horse died in the storm, killed Pa but let Jorge live, and finally simply left. But there is no sign of the Pedersens' bodies, the killer has built no fire in their house despite the freezing weather, he mysteriously spares Jorge, and Hans simply disappears. We see Pa being shot, but it could be Jorge who shoots him.

One can locate several points in the story at which Jorge may have hallucinated the rest. Such alternatives provide semi-rational explanations, but the story remains enigmat-ic and fails to lend itself to neat exegesis. One's first response, to credit Jorge's narration, with the restriction only of obvious mixing of memory and desire, provides a reading terrible enough in its implications. Locating the moment that Jorge's tenuous hold on reality slips remains as inexact as the moment itself. Several times the characters speak of the madness produced by the snow. During the journey Jorge has pointed his gun at Hans and imagined he had shot Hans and his parents earlier; when he is alone at the Pedersens' he feels haunted by the reproaches of his dead father. Most simply, and probably most accurately, the killer does for Jorge what he wishes done, and his final exuberance is that of freezing to death. Gass has said that in dealing with naturally strong situations, such as violence, one must "disarm them." The blurring of fact and wish may represent such disarming.

Gass on his motivation for writing:

If someone asks me, "Why do you write?" I can reply by pointing out that it is a very dumb question. Nevertheless there is an answer. I write because I hate. A lot. Hard. And if someone asks me the inevitable next dumb question, "Why do you write the way you do?" I must answer that I wish to make my hatred acceptable because my hatred is much of me, if not the best part. Writing is a way of making the writer acceptable to the world—every cheap dumb nasty thought, every despicable desire, every noble sentiment, every expensive taste. There isn't very much satisfaction in getting the world to accept and praise you for things that the world is prepared to praise. The world is prepared to praise only shit. One wants to make sure that the complete self, with all its qualities, is not just accepted but approved . . . not just approved—whooped.

William Gass, in an interview with Thomas Le-Clair in The Paris Review, *1977.*

Jorge imaginatively identifies himself with the kid. If he were in the kid's supposed situation of coming into the house and finding a killer pointing a gun at his parents, forcing them into a freezing cellar, he asserts to his mother that he would not have run. As he journeys to the Pedersens, during his exalted sense of being worth remembering, like a knight, he sees himself taking on the killer in his own kitchen. At the end of the story, when he thinks he has to bury everyone, including his mother, his dream of heroism may explain his certainty that he and the kid alone survive. A further explanation of his belief that all are dead except the kid and himself lies in his conviction that the killer honors them for having done great things, that is, journeyed through the snow. Jorge imagines the killer arriving at his house, seeing Hans, his mother, and the kid on the table. The killer makes them disappear like the Pedersens, "but he'd leave the kid, for we'd been exchanged, and we were both in our own new lands." At the end Jorge says he need not grieve because he has been brave and now is free. He and the kid have done brave things.

Jorge sometimes identifies himself with the killer. At the

end of the story he plans to "bury pa and the Pedersens and Hans and even ma if I wanted to bother." No previous indication has been made, except in his fantasy, that Hans and ma die. Jorge may confuse them with the Pedersens, whose deaths are only surmised. Earlier, at the time Jorge waits in the Pedersens' basement expecting the killer to find him, just after he discovers the Pedersens are not there, he thinks, "the kid for killing his family must freeze." The killer carries out for him, and by extension for the kid, the wish to be free of parents and the restrictions they represent. If Jorge shoots his father (he has a gun and orders him to die between the first and second shots), he projects any guilt to the killer. More probably, Jorge only wishes all their deaths to complete his sense of freedom.

Jorge as narrator expresses himself in a simple language, filled with unpleasant, although almost never violent, images. They grow from his experience and center around his life on the farm—the household, nature, animals, and farming. In the first and third sections, when he is at his house and at the Pedersens, he uses fewer household similes than he does during the second or journey sequence. In all the sections, however, the images fall almost evenly into domestic, including food, images and those of nature, farming, and animals. Two sets of images recur: variations on the kid as food (because he was placed on the table) appear throughout, although they cluster in the first section, and images of burning, especially the sun burning the snow, begin on the first page, occur throughout, and conclude the story. These burning images come to be associated with snow and the killer, assuming a disproportionate significance.

Although Jorge's images rarely express violence, they reveal the harshness of his experience. Unpleasant images occur throughout the story more than twice as frequently as the few neutral images, such as ma scaring Jorge by moving "like a combine through the fields," and the even fewer pleasant images. Even the occasional pleasant images often contain negative references. For example, the exalted sense of high adventure produces a feeling "warm as new bath water and just as hard to hold." A pleasant image functions occasionally as contrast: "It wasn't like a sleigh ride on an early winter evening when the air is still, the earth warm, and the stars are flakes being born that will not fall."

Pleasant or neutral images are buried among such descriptions as Pa asleep looking like "dung covered with snow," the kid looking "like a sick shoat," Ma lifting the kid's clothes "like you would the flat, burned, crooked leg of a frog dead summer." Pa has a head "fuzzed like a dandelion gone to seed," a nose that looks white "like a part of him had died long ago," sometimes smiles "like he's thought of something dirty." Hans holds a liquor bottle "like a snake," has a red face "swollen like the skin around a splinter," and expresses meanness that is like "a blister on my heel, another discomfort, a cold bed."

A specifically violent image occurs, interestingly, in the only completely pleasant episode, Jorge's memory of summertime and companionship with his father. He recalls it after coming from the Pedersens' basement to the kitchen

and seeing a figure he believes to be the killer depart. Once, he remembers, he "went in the meadow with an old broom like a gun . . . [and] flushed grasshoppers from the goldenrod in whirring clouds like quail and shot them down." He rode the broom and "with a fist like pistol butt and trigger" shot an imaginary Indian. He watched his father on the tractor, then "with a fist like a pistol butt and trigger, going fast, . . . shot him down." Jorge's memory of childhood play continues with a description of his father's sharing water with him, talking with him, expressing concern. The violent images of broom and fist like a gun in this context seem innocent, but Jorge has witnessed and wished for his father's death before he recalls the episode and has recalled numerous harsh and violent events involving his father. The impact thus seems less nostalgic than part of the ugly pattern of his life.

Shortly after his pleasant memory of his father and after dreaming that the killer made his mother and Hans disappear, Jorge imagines his father reproaches him over his death. It begins with a conversation about the habits of horses and how Pa doesn't know anything because he's always drinking. Pa reminds Jorge that he never drank except in the winter. Jorge replies, "It's winter now and you're in bed where you belong." Pa notes that the bottle made it spring for him, "just like that fellow's made it warm for you." After this explicit connection of the killer's acts and Jorge's pleasure, Jorge decides he will not give grieve because Pa is "no man now" with his bottle broken in the snow. He accuses Pa of being "always after killing" him, and complains that he was cold in Pa's house. Pa replies, "Jorge—so was I." Jorge denies this common bond, insisting he was the one "wrapped in snow," who even in summer would sometimes shiver. He concludes by telling Pa he shouldn't be haunting him because he did not touch him; "*He* did." After thus dismissing his father, Jorge imagines the return of the killer.

Jorge next grabs his gun and crouches behind a chair, feeling "alone with all that could happen," knowing he is "all muddled up and scared and crazy." He soon builds a fire, concluding that the killer was not meant to harm him and has left. He looks out, sees the sun flash from the barrel of Pa's gun, decides again he need not grieve, and feels warm. He has clearly lost his hold on reality, creating his own sanctuary where he feels heroic and free.

Jorge's movement from harsh reality to what he calls his own country is laced with images of burning and the association of the killer and snow. On the first page of the story, Jorge notes that the sun burns the snow; he repeats this observation directly three other times, often refers to it indirectly, and uses it as an image. Thus from the beginning he connects burning and snow. A violent association comes early when Jorge, sent by Hans to wake his father and ask where he has hidden his whiskey, hates Hans because "I was thinking how Pa's eyes would blink at me—as if I were the sun on the snow and burning to blind him." Burning sometimes has pleasant connotations, as when he thinks of a stove or when he burns with joy at the end, but Jorge links burning usually with cold, speaking, for example, of how his ears burn from the snow. As they approach the Pedersens' and see no smoke from their chimney, Jorge experiences the snow shifting strangely in his eyes, feels "alone, frightened by the space that was bowling up" inside him, a space he describes as "a white blank glittering waste like the waste outside, coldly burning." The cold burning sense transfers to his father; Jorge says he hates him "no more like a father," but "like the burning space".

Snow, usually associated with the killer and the cruel cold, sometimes suggests refuge to Jorge. He imagines the snow slipped over the kid "like a sheet," and once thinks of the snow as like a cave. During the journey he feels the pull of giving in to the snow: "I wanted to sit down. Here was the sofa, here the bed—mine—white and billowy. . . . I had the cold storm in my belly, and my pinched eyes. There was the print of the kid's rear in the dough. I wanted to sit down." In this comment Jorge links his wish for escape to snow, snow to cold, cold to his hate, snow to the dough the kid lay in. Thus snow, burning (hate), the kid, the killer, his fate all join in a confused unity.

The killer has explicit connections with the snow. He comes during the storm, stays at the Pedersens' because the storm kills his horse, departs without trace because the snow covers all. Jorge calls him a snowman at the time Pa is shot. He muses that the killer might "live in snow like a fish in water." The snow and the killer provide Jorge the sanctuary of his own country, free of his parents and Hans, where he can burn with joy. The killer has made it warm for him.

Jorge's journey into manhood leaves him feeling he has a new identity and has been given a country, "a new blank land." He notes that as they traveled, "I'd been slipping out of myself, pushed out by the cold, maybe." He feels that if they had turned back during the trip, he would have come to himself again at home, warm by the stove; but as he reflects, it no longer appeals: "I didn't want to come to myself that way again." As the story ends, he enjoys his new self in his new land, feeling brave and free with the snow to keep him. The killer has done him and the kid "a glorious turn," making him "think how I was told to feel in church." He believes the winter finally "got them all." The winter and the killer have fused for Jorge, destroying his enemies, creating a kinship with the kid, protecting him, leaving him "burning up, inside and out, with joy."

Jorge lives close to nature, observes it carefully, and responds to its power. His central image of the sun burning the snow develops from an ordinary fact of his experience. His journey, so different from Huck Finn's river voyage or Ike McCaslin's yearly sojourn in the big woods, has its share of remarks on landscape and animals. Snow looks "stiff and hard as cement" as well as "blue as the sky." He observes the "sick drawn look of a winter dawn," the sun throws down "slots of orange like a snow fence had fallen down." But the landscape he recalls most vividly exists on a calender picture of an idyllic January scene of skating and sliding. He express fondness for the family's horse, but recalls most acutely the animals in a picture book that Pa destroyed. Jorge's language, like his experience of family and nature, is harsh, often violent, cruel. With no river, territory, or woods for refuge, he creates his own country where he burns with joy, alone in a snowstorm. (pp. 89-96)

Patricia Kane, "The Sun Burned on the Snow: Gass's 'The Pedersen Kid'," in Critique: Studies in Modern Fiction, Vol. XIV, No. 2, 1972, pp. 89-96.

Michael Wood   (essay date 1972)

[*In the following excerpt, Wood regards the experimental typography of* Willie Masters' Lonesome Wife *as only partially successful in conveying the work's theme of loneliness.*]

The Midwest . . . in William H. Gass's story **"In the Heart of the Heart of the Country"** . . . becomes a metaphor for loneliness, for a sense of the self as stranded in a symbolic geography, almost before the writer has done anything to make this happen. Lives are "vacant and barren and loveless," Gass writes, "here in the heart of the country." "Who cares," he asks later, "to live in any season but his own?"

I suspect that it is because this last question is so central in American writing, and so perfectly rhetorical, not expecting an answer, that the Midwest, with its physical spread and relative emptiness, slips so easily into allegory, has a hard time sustaining itself as a real place in fiction. There is no mention of the Midwest in Gass's *Willie Masters' Lonesome Wife,* but the location is recognizably that of Gass's earlier story: the heart of the heart of the country, the lonely heart of a person looking for love, a lonely mind reaching out for us, then shrinking back, complaining of its isolation even as it wriggles further into the solipsism.

Willie Masters's wife, a former burlesque actress and stripper, is in bed, it seems, with a man named Phil, and broods over the business in a monologue. "I can't complain," she reminds herself. "You're supposed to be lonely getting fucked." She goes over her past life, worries about the inadequacies of language, quotes Dryden, enjoys the word *catafalque,* pastes pages from old novels, some great and some not so great, into her memories. "Well, Prince," we read without warning, "Genoa and Lucca are now no more than private estates of the Bonaparte family." She reveals herself as a front for the writer himself, who has had his printer reproduce in the text the muddy ring his coffee cup left on the manuscript: a mocking image of the writer's dream of contact, since such simulations of intimacy can only emphasize distance. We know the dark, circular stain only *looks* like the mark of a coffee cup—but then a book only *looks* like a piece of writing personally addressed to us.

Gass is asking us to consider, though, the desperation such tricks bespeak, and behind the fussiness of much of the book there is a real urgency, a powerful vision of the loneliness inherent in writing (you write because you can't speak, for whatever reason) and of writing as a useful and articulate image for loneliness of other kinds.

> These words are all I am. Believe me. Pity me.
> Not even the Dane is any more than that. Oh,
> I'm the girl upon this couch, all right, you
> needn't fear; the one who's waltzed you through
> these pages, clothed and bare, who's hated you

for her humiliations, sought your love, just as the striptease dancer does, soliciting male eyes for cash and feeling the light against her like a swelling organ. Could you love me? Love me then. . . . My dears, my dears . . . how I would brood upon you: you, the world; and I, the language.

The typography of the book is a kind of light-show in black and white, what Kenneth Koch describes in another context as a field day for the technician, and is only partly worth the printer's, or our, trouble, I think. There are pictures, tilted typefaces, pages of asterisks, letters simulating a convex surface, letters growing larger or smaller as they proceed up or down the page, even a change of color in the pages themselves. The pictures, which portray, presumably, the lonesome wife in a range of provoking postures, make effective punctuation of the text: harsh assertions of the reality of flesh amid the safe abstraction of print—or at least of the relative reality of photographs.

There is a splendid moment when the book's footnotes (the narrator is offering us the script of a burlesque act about a man who finds a limp, unowned penis in his breakfast bun) almost crowd the text off the page, force the frightened words, cramped and bent, to find a precarious refuge in a top corner; and another when a series of footnotes to footnotes traps us at the bottom of the page and the narrator crows over our poor chance of ever getting out again, back into the text: "Now that I've got you alone down here, you bastard, don't think I'm letting you get away easily, no sir, not you brother. . . ."

For the rest of the time the switching styles of print tend to advertise far too clearly that a shift of mood or voice is taking place—either the text on its own makes such shifts work or it doesn't, it seems to me. The text has to be trusted with its meanings. Occasionally the purpose of the swinging typography seem merely decorative: arbitrary exercises in layout. Still, there are verbal equivalences for that in Gass's prose, frequent touches of the clogged, the baroque, or the grandiose, not quite managed by the irony and intelligence which is usually in control, so the physical book doesn't seem to let him down in any serious way.

> *Michael Wood, "Great American Fragments,"* in The New York Review of Books, *Vol. XIX, No. 10, December 14, 1972, p. 12.*

Bruce Bassoff   (essay date 1976)

[*In the following essay, Bassoff offers a close reading of the short stories from* In the Heart of the Heart of the Country, and Other Stories.]

William Gass's **"The Pedersen Kid,"** the first story in *In the Heart of the Heart of the Country,* reads at times like a story by Hemingway. After a snow storm, the handy man of the Segren household discovers the body of a neighbor's son in the barn, brings him inside, and revives him with rubbing and whisky. Upon regaining consciousness, the young man tells Hans, the handy man, a terrible story of a stranger dressed in black cap, green mackinaw, and yellow gloves who has murdered the young man's

family. Hans, Jorge (the young narrator), and Jorge's alcoholic father start out for the Pedersen place, where Jorge's father is shot; Hans runs away, and Jorge survives to contemplate his independence. The dialogue is most often terse and realistic although the narrator's speech sometime assumes the hardboiled lyricism of Raymond Chandler: "He was as good as dead. I held him and I felt him. Maybe in your way he was alive, but it was a way that don't count." The narration is also figural in a way uncharacteristic of Hemingway: "I was thinking how Pa's eyes would blink at me—as if I were the sun off the snow and burning to blind him." The metaphor, the anapestic rhythm, and the alliteration of *s's* and *b's* call our attention away from what is said to the saying itself, away from the narration of the adventure to the adventure of the narration. One consistent theme in Gass's criticism is that fiction is not mimetic but configural; if true of supposedly "realistic" fiction, it is patently true of fiction in which substance is clearly an illusion of imaginative reticulation. Since Gass wants to end fiction's dependence on the form of history, his desubstantiation of character reveals the text under the patina:

> Anything . . . which serves as a fixed point, like a stone in a stream or that soap in Bloom's pocket, functions as a character. Character, in this sense, is a matter of degree, for the language of the novel may loop back seldom, often, or incessantly. But the idea that characters are like primary substances has to be taken in a double way, because if any thing becomes a character simply to the degree the words of the novel qualify it, it also loses some of its substance, some of its primacy, to the extent that it, in turn, qualifies something else.

On the symbolic level—where semantic traits float freely in a world of fluid identifications—Gass's stories work most powerfully. **"The Pedersen Kid"** is a good beginning for such consideration.

As one node of the fiction, Big Hans and the Pedersen kid are associated with Christ. Hans' last name, "Esyborn," is a vaudevillian version of "He's born," and "Big Hands" sounds like a good epithet for God: "The bottle and the glass were posts around which Big Hans had his hands." The narrator, moreover, accuses Hans of feeling "like a savior." The disguised "Peter" in **"Pedersen"** is elicited by Hans' characterization of the boy's father as "Holy Pete" and by the imagery of stones that qualifies both him and others. The narrator imagines the kid being uncovered in spring "like a black stone," and while the horse that the family takes to the Pedersen house is called Simon, a horse's head is described as being "uncovered like a rock." After the Pedersen kid is found in a crib, his resurrection is described in terms that evoke communion: the kitchen table on which he is revived is covered with dough, "pasty with whisky and water, like spring had come all at once to our kitchen." Earlier the narrator thinks, "We were getting him ready to bake."

The narrator's father also becomes part of the complex: he "looks like a judge," which suggests the Old Testament ruler; his name is "Magnus," and "Mag" (used once in the story) suggests the Magi. At one point the narrator says,

"I hated him. Jesus, how I did. But no more like a father. Like the burning space." The father, in turn, accuses Pedersen of having brought on one of the Biblical plagues: "Pedersen *asked* for hoppers. He *begged* for hoppers." Finally, the father seems like a seasonal god at times: his hair is "fuzzed, like a dandelion gone to seed," and he is later "another snowman" who will melt. The killer is also associated with Biblical imagery. The narrator imagines him falling when the horse runs into a barberry, rearing "as the barbs go in." He is later identified with both the narrator and the horse: "He was in the wind now and in the cold now and sleepy now like me. His head was bent down low like the horse's head must be." He is also "worn like a stone in the stream."

The story is full of fluid identifications and double exposures. In the Pedersen household the counterpart of Big Hans is Little Hans, who is "no fool" according to Big Hans but is "no kin" to Big Hans according to Jorge's father. Jorge is identified with Big Hans not only on an anecdotal level (through his former hero-worshipping) but on the figural level: Jorge's father instructs him, "Hey, get your hands in it, *your hands.*" Jorge is identified with the Pedersen kid even as he rejects him—having considered him dead. He and the Pedersen kid are part of the same circuit of exchange: "The Pedersen kid—maybe he'd been a message of some sort. No, I like better the idea that we'd been prisoners exchanged. I was back in my own country. No, it was more like I'd been given a country." Unlike his father, however, Jorge is "no judge" although he is familiar with "the spirits": "The spirits, the spirits, Jorge Segren . . . ha. He's had a few he says. He's had a few." Both Jorge and the Pedersen kid, indistinguishable from each other, are identified with the killer: "They were all drowned in the snow, weren't they? The kid for killing his family. But what about me? Must freeze." Through the squinting use of "his," Hans is identified with the horse: "Later in the winter maybe somebody would stumble on his shoes sticking out of the snow. Shooting Hans seemed like something I'd done already"—"his" referring anaphorically to horse and cataphorically to Hans.

The killer, as a composite of all these characters, is himself transparent: "Then why did he stand there so pale I could see through?", having no more substance than the hieroglyphs of dreams analyzed into language. His most salient aspect is the colors in which he is figured: "Green, black, yellow: you don't make up them colors neither," Hans remarks. These colors take on a particular significance when Jorge sets out "like a knight" for the Pedersens, having experienced the initial excitement of the quest as a feeling "warm as new bath water." Bloodied from sacrifice, the questing knight achieves the gold of glorification, the yellow of which appears in an ironically debased mode when the "sour yellow sick insides" of Jorge's father are described and when Jorge accuses both Hans and his father of being "yellow." But the gold is present in the "golden tail" of Jorge's fantasized horse; in his memories of summer and childhood; in the sun, a dominant motif of the story; and in the yellow gloves Hans seems to create by rubbing—like Aladdin's lamp. As the action begins, the colors on the towels used to warm up the Pedersen kid begin to run, anticipating the thawing of spring that would

have revealed the Pedersen kid's body. Just before the men decide to go to the Pedersen house, the mother is described as "moving like a combine between rows" as the frost melts. If the colors run, Jorge wants to convince everyone that he (whose name Segren—sea green) would not have run. Later, having called Jorge a little "smart-talking snot," Jorge's father "wisely" says, "Cold makes the snot run"; omnipresent, vacant, and cold is the heavenly color of blue: "Sometimes the snow seemed as blue as the sky. I don't know which seemed colder."

These colors, associated with the various aspects of the knight's quest, associated also with the changing seasons (and with the lives and deaths of the gods) are generated by the sun. With the sun withdrawn the world is "black and white and everything the same," the killer's horse circling aimlessly in the snow. The conflict between Jorge and his father is conveyed as follows: "You were always after killing me, yourself, pa, oh yes you were. I was cold in your house always, pa. Jorge—so was I. No. I was. I was the one wrapped in the snow. Even in the summer I'd shiver sometimes in the shade of a tree." If, as Freud claimed, the rite of communion is both an expiation of the son's crime against the father and a replacement of the father by the son, Jorge's unexpiated guilt haunts him in the specter of the killer: "And pa—I didn't touch you, remember—there's no point in haunting me. *He* did. He's even come round maybe."

At the beginning of the story, these conflicts are suggested by the configuration of sun, darkness, and snow: "The barn was dark, but the sun burned on the snow. Hans was carrying something from the crib." The frozen birth in the dark of the barn is also a death—Jorge and the Pedersen kid being exchanged for each other, and Jorge being given a "new blank land." While the killer is described as a "bump of black," the black stove is a source of heat: "black . . . god . . . black . . . lovely sooty black . . . and glow[ing] rich as cherry through its holes." While the Pedersen kid has been resurrected from the depths of the world—whether from under ground or from the sky, the energy from the sun thaws the body. The sun's burning, however, does not always seem benevolent. Early in the story Jorge anticipates the way his father's eyes will blink at him, "as if I were the sun off the snow and burning to blind him." If we hear "sun" also as "son," the threat of blinding is later reversed. After telling himself not to look at the dead body of his father, he experiences the "painful" glare closing "the slit in [his] eyes"—also the "crack" in his father's face. The father in his archetypal dimensions ("no more like a father") is "like the burning space." Remembering the importance Freud placed on mourning in the formation of the ego, we can understand the following passage:

> I stood as still as I could in the tubes of my clothes, the snow shifting strangely in my eyes, alone, frightened by the space that was bowling up inside me, a white blank glittering waste like the waste outside, coldly burning, roughed with waves, and I wanted to curl up, face to my thighs, but I knew my tears would freeze my lashes together. My stomach began to growl.

"Rough with waves" is one translation of "Segren," now

both his own and his father's "glittering waste" as he approaches the moment of rebirth—in a fetal position, his clothes "tubes" from which he will emerge. Just at the moment when "the snow" becomes "my snow," when death becomes *Jorge's* death, the killer is seen leaving.

The sun, as well as the sacrifices in the story, can be seen in a still more general context: "The way that fellow had come so mysteriously through the snow and done us such a glorious turn—well it made me think how I was told to feel in church. The winter time had finally got them all, and I really did hope that the kid was as warm as I was now, warm inside and out, burning up, inside and out, with joy." Like the "tiger, tiger burning bright," Jorge is a point of extreme incandescence, and in the general economy of life his incandescence has been ignited in the depths of the sky, in the consumption of the sun. If man through his work founded the world of *things* and became himself one of the things of that world, through his strange myths and cruel rites he is in search of a lost intimacy. Only in consumption—in a kind of expense which provides no compensatory return or profit, as in the *potlatch* or in human sacrifice—can man reveal to his fellows what he is *intimately*. If malediction removes the victim from the order of things (since his sacrifice is pure expense), and if his figure then radiates intimacy, agony, and profundity to those who partake of his sacrifice, the consciousness of the moment is the beginning of self-consciousness—a consciousness which no longer has anything for object. The ending of **"The Pedersen Kid"** conveys such a moment of joy and lucidity.

If the story is recursive in the looping of language, it is also recursive in its use of embedded story or image. In ironic contrast with the cruel expense of sacrifice are the seasonal calendars and the storybook picture Jorge describes. Arresting the menace of the moment in which the "reality" of the killer is being affirmed is Jorge's vision of January's picture: three men in the snow, a red scarf and some mittens, some ice and coal, and Jorge, smiling, learning to skate. Later, having expressed the need for expiation in the alliterative "the kid for killing his family must freeze" (where "killing" and "kid" seem to exchange semantic properties, as do "family" and "freeze"), Jorge envisions himself sleighing off the roof and floating "around a dark star" rather than skating. His vision of death is not, he says, the calendar for March. Beside the reassuring banality of the seasonal calendar is the storybook picture of a line of sheep down a long green hill, which contains no people. The lamb of innocence is torn and deposited in the privy, however, by Jorge's malevolent father.

The most interesting embedded story, however, is Jorge's memory of childhood and summer. During the winter Jorge's father burns "inside himself" and drinks whisky to make it summer for him, while during the summer he does not burn inside and drinks water with Jorge. During the winter the dandelions are used to qualify the frizzled head of Jorge's father, while in the summer those that have begun to seed seem primary—as if the "cracked" face of the father in winter has become the "cracked" low ground of summer. Early in the story Jorge says to Hans, "Something besides the kid came through the storm"; he

then notes, "Something, it looked like whisky, dripped slowly to the floor and with the water trickled to the puddle by the pile of clothes." Later, as Jorge follows his memory of summer with the memory of spring, he says, "I'd a habit, when I was twelve, of looking down. Something sparkled on the water." Although earlier looking up and down was associated with the Pedersen kid, the rubbing of whose body generated the yellow gloves, the "something" here is the father's whisky bottle, which transforms winter into summer. That "something" is itself later transformed into "nothing" and "nowhere": "Nowhere Pedersen's fences had kept bare he might be lying huddled with the horse on its haunches by him; nothing even in the shadow shrinking while I watched to take for something hard and not of snow and once alive." Gass's "nowhere" is the place of fiction—a utopia, a possible world. Even as the killer's continued existence is denied, the description of this "nowhere" and "nothing"— cemented by alliteration—gives reality to the fiction. The consumption of fiction is also, after all, an expense— useless and gratuitous.

While **"The Pedersen Kid"** enacts a sacrifice, an expense that solarizes the world and restores our sense of intimacy, **"Icicles"** enacts the contrary process of reification, in which the boundaries between men and things break down. Charlie Fender is a real-estate salesman who begins to take his boss's valorization of "real" estate so seriously that it becomes all reality. Properties are like people, we are told—Mr. Pearson can "pass judgment" on a street and read its future. The names "Fender" and "Pearson" are revealing: Fender ends up by withdrawing from the world, "fending" the world off in the "persons" of mailman and newspaper boy who threaten his icicles; "Pearson," combining "peer" and "person," suggests the omniscience and *im*personality of a god. Fender, although oppressed by him, feels anxious when Pearson is not watching him. Pearson says of property: "This is your person, Fender . . . the body of your beloved." Since everything is property, "living in harmony with nature" becomes living in harmony with the fluctuations of the real-estate market. Such absolute reification results in a kind of sympathetic magic: when Glick, Fender's colleague and double, divides a piece of paper on which he has computed the salient aspects of some piece of property, "The land [represented] parts cleanly." The division, in turn, is duplicated by Fender's cut finger, whose stinging gives him pleasure as a kind of temporary reprieve from total anesthesia.

The pervasiveness of the reification can be seen in Gass's use of alliteration, where "Prop-purr-tee" generates passages of p's and b's (part of the same phonetic family); and the name of Fender, who is himself becoming property, generates *f*'s: "Buy at the bottom. Fill your freezer. Fortunate . . . to take advantage of the time. . . . People pass on. In the midst of life, you know, Fender . . . well . . . but property, property endures." Alliterations proliferate like the icicles in the story, which "multiply like weeds." The foci of these icicles are the "points" on which "drops of water were wavering"—the alliterating w's being generated by the winter to which Fender is assimilated: "Fender was weary—weary of winter" (the repeated rhythmic configurations also underline the assimilation). Pearson advises Fender to keep everything "at the tip—the tip"; Pearson himself is imagined dying "on the impertinent pick of an icicle"; facts are as "sharp as needles," "a golden row of pencils [come] to points," and Fender's life disappears "like a stick on a river." The phallic aspect of these images is seen in the fear with which Fender regards the icicles: "What would people think if they saw him . . . anyone passing . . . Pearson conceivably? He wished his icicles were growing on the other side—within—where he might measure them in private, examine them in any way he liked. But if one broke off. . . . The thought was dismaying." His narcissistic fear is reinforced later when he wishes that he could grow the icicles "inside himself," icicles the beauty of which is "a sign of the beauty of their possessor."

In this parable of reification, people become things. Fender's customer, who is muffled up in fur that seems to have been stained mahogany, is referred to as "the muff." Glick, who is a pickle, is also a "click"—the focusing of Fender's attention that objects bring about; and he is also *monstrosum* like his dried flowers, "cut when young, bound in loose bunches, hung upside down, cold dry place, where a breeze would be helpful"—flowers that also resemble icicles. Although Fender protests that he is "not green" like Glick, not "countably discrete" like the peas in his pot pie, he is obsessed with counting the peas and pieces of beef in the pie as a way of getting at its "quality." He also wallows imaginatively and homeopathically in the pie when he can no longer stand Glick's insane inventory of properties.

Other aspects of that "false consciousness" associated with reification are a loss of temporality and a paranoid concern with being seen by the Other. Fender says to himself, "There's no one to help you, Fender, you have no history, remember? Log in the stream." Time as productive of values does not seem to exist for him, living under the eye of Pearson, whose belief in property is "better, absolutely," is a "beautiful belief." In addition, contemplating the purity of the icicles, which have a "hard dry gleam," he feels as conspicuous as a "fish in a bowl" and draws the curtains of his living room: "better to live like a mole out of eyeshot." Later, Glick, a kind of parodic double of Fender, surfaces his "troubled, obsequious face like a fish" to receive Pearson's joke and then submerges himself again. If Fender becomes a house at the end, he also becomes one of his own organs—as if he is the pie and the peas in the pie at the same time: "Was he an organ looking out" from his place of refuge?

If the icicles are property, if they are connected somehow to Fender's list of tasks and to his narcissistic fears, if the strings of icicles are also the "wires" of clients' worries, if they appear like "elbows" and "arms," they are also associated with "laws that build beauty out of change." "Perishing," Fender says, is the word for icicles. When the day clears and the "dazzling" sun begins to melt things, icicles form—first thick and opaque, then glittering brilliantly. All four elements eventually become involved in these transformations: when snowlight makes Fender's eyes burn, "moisture" appears in their corners; when the icicles "blaze," the "breath goes out of him"; when lights

"pierce the pie," the gravy oozes and bubbles. As Fender contemplates throwing a fit in order to interrupt Glick's parody of real-estate listings, he thinks, "What was epilepsy . . . but a struggle with the powers of the air." Light on the snow resembles urine although it *seems* diaphanous rather than corrosive—light for Gass often has a corrosive, transforming quality. Light, moreover, is transformed as it goes from within to without and from without to within. Glick, contemplating the wounding of Pearson by an icicle, says, "Everyone will wonder, when it's melted from the puncture, as much at how he let the air out of his life as they ever had before at how he's pumped it in her." The sense of Heraclitean flux and conflict disturbs the reified surface of the story—the effect that "dwarf[s] the causes" of Pearson's social activity—just as the blinding light of the snowfields and the stinging of his cut are pleasant experiences for Fender, who demurs occasionally against his anesthesia. The clarity of those snowfields is contrasted with the "cave" of Ringley (the house Fender shows), in which Fender imagines worms, spiders, and bats; and the earth and water of the cave are contrasted with the fire of the mountain and the "glittering air"—air and fire being the active elements, earth and water the passive ones. The conflict is conveyed by the word "prospects" (potential buyers), which refers to "gold" and "clean air" but also to "dirt" and "deceiving air." If false consciousness involves a violation of certain boundaries. Fender contrasts the mess in his drawer (or psyche) with a "radiant order, each thing bespeaking its place through its nature." The suggestion of sublimation in the contrast between cave and mountain is amplified in the story **"Mrs. Mean,"** as is the erotic function of the four elements. Here Fender thinks, "Even now you're melting down. True—but those icicles gather the snow as it softens, oppose their coldness to the sun, and turn their very going into . . . Isabelles"; the longing for Isabelle (another colleague in the office), like the crystallization of the icicles, is opposed to the immediately ensuing description of Fender's reification: "Look, Fender: feet flat on the floor. Keep. Them. There. Arms in the arms of the chair. Armchair."

Pearson, like Big Hans in **"The Pedersen Kid,"** is a magician. He "twist[s] the ring" and by "the power of imagination" turns everything into a commodity—while Hans had revived a thing into a living person. Fender, like the narrator of **"The Pedersen Kid,"** refuses such wizardry for himself, but just as Jorge participates in the sacrifice that anticipates the thawing of a frozen world, Fender sees the icicles "firing up, holding the sun like a maiden in her sleep or a princess in her tower—so real, so false, so magical. It was his own invention, that image, and he was proud of it." While Pearson's imagination is really Hobbes' "decayed sense," Fender's is that of an artist. Like Jorge who envisions himself sleighing off the roof, Pearson, Glick speculates, may have "swooned clean away like the slope on a steeple." The disappearance (and sacrifice) of Pearson, however, results only partially in the combustive glow of **"The Pedersen Kid"** since Fender's anxiety and withdrawal counteract his ebullience before the icicles: "Yes, he thought, I do not even occupy myself."

"Order of Insects," since its structure is almost a reduced version of **"Icicles,"** will not be considered here at length. It concerns a kind of (possibly recurring) psychic breakdown in which a housewife can "no longer own [her] own imagination." The separation of one's imagination from what one "owns" is the "point of view of a god," a "temptation" of which the housewife feels she is not "worthy" as the "wife of the house." Since Gass's stories seem to enact the dialectical reversals of identification and dissociation, a kind of pilgrim's progress (or treadmill) through the "dark soul of the world" itself, we can discover the kinds of reversals taking place in this story. The housewife says, "Well I always see what I fear," which reverses her earlier assertion that she fears what she sees. In the earlier passage the disquieting bodies of insects are transformed into "rolls of dark wool or pieces of mud from children's shoes," into ink stains or deep burns that terrify her. In the later passage mud, stains, burns, and broken toys (a variation of "children's shoes") are ordinary objects transformed into "threatening" ones. The threatening aspect is normal, "the ordinary fears of daily life," the narrator tells us, and the bug that "frightens housewives" is the fear with which the housewife identifies so thoroughly she cannot "study" it: "It's no study for a woman . . . bugs." The process of identification and dissociation works again in the final two stories of the volume.

The title story, **"In the Heart of the Heart of the Country,"** is composed of reflections of a poet-teacher on his situation in Middle America and on his failed love affair. It is also a fiction about the relation between poetry and false consciousness. The protagonist of **"Icicles"** was a type in whom poetry and false consciousness met; while Fender seemed to accept Pearson's view that everything is property, which was "the power of [Pearson's] imagination," his own invention created "a princess in her tower" out of the icicles—a kind of objective correlative for his feeling of entrapment. The narrator of **"In the Heart of the Heart of the Country,"** explicitly a poet, suffers from the same kind of narcissistic withdrawal: on the one hand he says, "I would rather it were the weather that was to blame for what I am and what my friends and neighbors are—we who live here in the heart of the country"; on the other he says, "Who cares to live in any season but his own?"—the climate being an objective correlative for his inner state. If lovers, poets, and madmen are, in fact, near allied, we can see that Fender is more the madman, the narrator here more the poet—and both are frustrated lovers.

The story opens with an echo from "Sailing to Byzantium": "So I have sailed the seas and come . . . to B. . . ." Yeats' assertion that "Once out of Nature I shall never take / My bodily form from any natural thing" is echoed ironically in Gass's observation: "Tell me: do they live in harmony with the alternating seasons? It's a lie of old poetry. The modern husbandman uses chemicals from cylinders and sacks, spike-ball-and-claw machines, metal sheds, and cost accounting. Nature in the old sense does not matter. It does not exist." Here again poetry and false consciousness are near allied—the artifice of Yeats' Byzantium echoed by the antinature of Gass's technology. The narrator of Gass's story calls into question poetry's "lies" (or fictions), among which are man's harmony with

nature and the whole and immediate experience of childhood. Other echoes of Yeats' poem are the "old men" whose "consciousness has gone" and who provide the vehicle for the following figure: "Our eyes have been driven in like the eyes of old men. And there's no one to have mercy on us." One character, Billy Holsclaw, resembles Yeats' "paltry thing, / A tattered coat upon a stick": "He wobbles out in the wind when I leave him, a paper sack mashed in the fold of his arm"—the metaphor of Yeats' poem becoming the metonymy of Gass's passage. Billy Holsclaw, like one of Yeats' beggarmen, is described as violent in his "eagerness for speech."

Like the withdrawn Fender of **"Icicles,"** the narrator is living "in." With the house a metaphor for the body, "living in" is presented as a kind of Orphic fall; it is also a form of mourning: "My house, this place and body, I've come in mourning to be born in." The narrator says, "I am in retirement from love" (173), which translates, "I have retired my love." As he contemplates one of his many projections, the lonely and shabby Billy Holsclaw, he notes that poetry is "no answer"—either in a dialogue or as a solution to the lovelessness he evokes in "the heart of the country" and in the heart of that heart: himself. The "claw" in "Holsclaw" is taken up later when the narrator sinks his "claws" into the cat's fur, and when the cat in turn becomes a figure of poetry: "Mr. Tick, though, has a tail he can twitch, he need not fly his Fancy Claws, not metrical schema, poetry his paws"—those claws suggesting poetry's desire for *ad*herence to reality, just as the alliteration embodies poetry's *co*herence. Another passage reveals both of these dimensions: "He steps away slowly, his long tail rhyming with his paws. How beautifully he moves, I think; how beautifully, like you, he commands his loving, how beautifully he accepts." The narcissism of the poet calls into question poetry's adherence: "How well this house receives its loving too"; it becomes more explicit as the story goes on and the narrator notes, "We meet on this window, the world and I, inelegantly, swimmers of the glass; and swung wrong way round to one another, the world seems in." The glass suggests a barrier between self and world, which is compensated for by imaginary gratification: "All poets have their inside lovers. Wee penis does not belong to me, or any of this foggery. It is *his* property which he's thrust through what's womanly of me to set down this." The "foggery" refers us to another version of the poet as mourner, Mrs. Desmond, whose "thin white mist of hair, fine and tangled, manifests the climate of her mind." Like the poet, "It is herself she hears," and her "talk's a fence" as she mourns those she has lost.

The relationship between sex and writing is elaborated at length in the story. Fender's narcissistic fear of castration in **"Icicles"** is a fear everywhere diffused in **"In the Heart of the Heart of the Country."** Behind the narrator's house is a row of "headless maples" which have been cut to "free the passage of electric wires," later described as "words wound in cables. Bars of connection." The past participle "wound" (implying the communication of poetry) is later punned on with the noun "wound": perhaps Billy Holsclaw is "a surgeon cleansing a wound or an ardent and tactile lover," and "my window is a grave, and all that lies within it's dead. . . . Downwound, the whore at wagtag clicks and clacks"—the poet having become a surgeon for his own wound, and the whore "downwound" suggesting the nature of the wound. In addition to the "headless maples," a single tree—a "larch" stands in the middle of the field. The narrator knows "moments—foolish moments, ecstasy on a tree stump—when [he's] all but gone, scattered . . . like seed." Later, the poet's ambivalent attitude toward his paradoxical fecundity is expressed as follows: "A cold fall rain is blackening the trees or the air is like lilac and full of parachuting seeds. Who cares to live in any season but his own?" After the potency of such fall-out is questioned, "The flakes as they come, alive and burning, we cannot retain, for if our temperatures fall, they rise promptly again, just as, in the summer, they bob about in the same feckless way," the ensuing fantasies of exploding trees and scorching temperatures renew the desire for potency, just as "keeping warm" is Billy Holsclaw's "one work." Although the wires are "bars of connection," they serve to "fasten" the narrator, whose "platform" is on his "stump," from which his chanting keeps out the world, "enclosing the crows with the clouds." The obstacle has numerous variations in Gass's work, the fence and the window being the most salient.

Returning to the sexual aspect of the poet's "living in," the narrator notes, "I think I shall hat my head with a steeple; turn church; devour people." Earlier, the church in "B" has been described as having "a steeple like the hat of a witch, and five birds, all doves, perch in its gutters." If the witch and the narrator's ogre-like orality suggest the darker aspects of the poet's love, the church and the birds suggest its sublimation. The five birds undergo variations in the story: five gas stations also, in their way, suggest flight since they go in a line through town; the vertical variation is the ferris wheel, which climbs "dizzly into the sky" but which is also threatened by children: "The irritated operators measure the height and weight of every child with sour eyes to see if they are safe for the machines." In the Midwest, anyway, "the sky in the winter is heavy and close," and the gray haze of summer reminds us of Mrs. Desmond's "mist of hair"—the figures in the story being overdetermined as in dreams. The poet's assertion about hatting his head is followed by his address to the cat: "O Mr. Tick, I know you; you are an electrical penis," whose potency is distasteful to Mrs. Desmond, representing the more otiose aspects of the poet. That penis is later transformed into the worm which has "swallowed down" the poet's parts and "still throbs and glows like a crystal palace"—a transformation of the narrator's house and a symbol of the work of art.

The narrator's assertion that "poetry, like love, is—in and out—a physical caress" is perhaps the central statement of the story. The groping of Billy Holsclaw, who is compared both to a surgeon and to an "ardent and tactile lover," is juxtaposed to the erotic memories of the narrator: "He [Billy] bends the down on your arms like a breeze"—like the earlier "winds" of the narrator's grandfather, thinking of which the narrator becomes "all [his] ages." If the beloved is the ground on which Billy gropes, she is also the page on which the poet writes: "A bush in the excitement of its roses could not have bloomed so

beautifully as you did then. It was a look I'd like to give this page," as if poetry could have such presentness. The narcissism of the poet's love is emphasized by the following sequence of statements: "The country became my childhood"; the narrator knows the small Dakota town of his childhood, he says, "as I dreamed I'd know your body"; and "childhood is a lie of poetry." Poetry is mourning; it is nostalgia for a sense of presence and oneness that is itself a "lie of poetry." The story thus generates a contrast between "politics" and "love": "For all those not in love there's law: to rule . . . to regulate . . . to rectify. I cannot write the poetry of such proposals." If politics is an anal phenomenon (like the Miss "Jakes," the town teacher) and love (or poetry) genital, both are also oral phenomena: like the politician, the narrator says, "I chant, I beg, I orate, I command, I sing." The poet, after all, is "in retirement from love," which may not be recollected in tranquility but is recollected. The beloved is "bread in [his] mouth" when he works on his poetry; when he does not, he is "out of bread and out of body," Like the Midwest, which is "a dissonance of parts and people" and "a consonance of Towns," the poet is a consonance, an alliteration of those things he has died to: "I think when I loved you I fell to my death"; "my window is a grave, and all that lies within it's dead." The real caress in **"In the Heart of the Heart of the Country"** is "fearful," the caress of flies: "No caress could have been more indifferently complete. . . . They would explosively rise, like monads for a moment, windowless, certainly, with respect to one another, sugar their harmony." The story ends with a similar vision of *agape* in a church during a high school football game.

Seemingly opposed to the regulations of politics is the "diffuse" consciousness and will associated with the oneiric aspects of poetry. The cat is "all ooze," "spilled" by the narrator. One of the names the narrator gives to his friends is "Fitchew," a European polecat with animal sperm in its etymology, and the narrator also feels "spilled, bewildered, quite mislaid." When he describes one of the figures of *mnemosyne* in the story, Uncle Halley (who is also a liar), he notes of the latter's memorabilia: "They flowed like jewels from his palms"—an image of blood and stigmata, of cruci-fiction. Politics and poetry come together in these wounds.

The theme of *eros* and *poiesis* is continued in the final story, **"Mrs. Mean,"** begun with an act of naming: "I call her Mrs. Mean," an act also associated with the verbs "see," "surmise," and "wonder"—verbs that delimit a kind of primal scene as the story goes on. The artist's Pegasus is associated with children's toys: "I remember with fondness my own tricycle, capable of tremendous speed or so it seemed then, and because it was not fangled up by paid imaginations, it could be Pegasus, if I liked, and it was." Then immediately the Means' house is evoked as a cave in which the father floats "white as animals long in caves, quiet as a weed," and later the narrator in front of the Means' garage is like a child "frightened by the cold air that drifts from a cave to damp the excitement of its discovery." The sense of fear and repression is conveyed by similar sensations derived from a childhood memory. Having noted again the coolness and dampness of the

THE EYE
BY WHICH I
SEE GOD IS THE
SAME AS THE EYE B
Y WHICH GOD SEES ME.
MY EYE AND GOD'S EYE A
RE ONE AND THE SAME
—ONE IN SEEING,
ONE IN KNOWING
AND ONE IN
LOVING.

I believe I was discussing why they call saliva the sweet wine of love, though I can't imagine who "they" are. Would you call saliva the sweet wine of love? Nor should I. Nor should I call it nectar or mead, denominate it cider. It goes back to birds, vomiting in their babies. Perhaps it consists in the ritualization of attack—these bared teeth neutralized. But nothing I say will prevent it, no description mar the quality or lessen the force of its attraction. No one can imagine—simply—merely; one must imagine within words or paint or metal, communicating genes or multiplying numbers. Imagination is its medium realized. You are your body—you do not choose the feet you walk in—and the poet is his language. He sees his world, and words form in his eyes just like the streams and trees there. He feels everything verbally. Objects, passions, actions— I myself believe that the true kiss comprises a secret exchange of words, for the mouth was made by God to give form and sound to syllables; permit us to make, as our souls move, the magical music of names; for to say Cecilia, even in secret, is to make love. How

Page from Willie Masters' Lonesome Wife.

Means' house (his common-sensical wife says that the house is "cool and dry and airy"), the narrator remembers when he was playing around the family porch: "I accidentally placed my hand upon a cold wet pipe which rose out of the ground there and saw near the end of my nose, moist on the ridge of the post, four fat white slugs. I think of that when I think of the Means' house and of pale fat Mr. Mean, and the urge to scream as I did then rises strongly in me." Out of such repressed eroticism come the kind of condensations and displacements characteristic of dreams: Mr. Mean is a father floating in the cave, but his damp pallor associates him also with those "four fat white slugs" that suggest drops of semen. The Means also have four children whose dispersion is contrasted with the concentrated essence of Mrs. Mean—another hieroglyph of erotic repression and expression. A similar hieroglyph (whose concentration is suggested by the name of the motherly figure, Mrs. "Cramm") occurs in the final sequence of the story, where the narrator begins his walk "through the alleys by the backsides of the houses," where "trash spills over the cinders and oil flavors the earth." Earlier, after Mrs. Mean has denied the narrator's "preternatural power" as an idol and the narrator feels that he does not exist, Mrs. Mean "burns and burns before me.

She revolves her backside carefully against a tree"—as if she were both Apollo and Daphne or the relation between them. The aggression and exclusion suggested by Mrs. Mean's denial are characteristic of the "mirror stage" of our development, where we achieve a coherent image of ourselves—particularly of the topology of our body— through imaginary identification with another: the "oil" of the final sequence and the "tree" of the Daphne sequence (combined in the "oiled ash" found in the garage) are the keys in this instance.

The Oedipal suggestions of "oiled ash" are conveyed by the composite figure of Mrs. Mean and Mr. Wallace. On two occasions Mrs. Mean is described as "hobbling," and at one point "her arm points accusingly at [her son's] eyeless back. She curses him." Mr. Wallace, an old man totally involved in the weather and in his inner climate of pain, uses a cane, which gives the narrator occasion to say, "The cane came out of his belly" and "the cane rises with difficulty." When Mr. Wallace "hurls the cane like a spear," and when he tells his wife that he "tried to kill a squirrel," one is reminded of Laius and Oedipus at the crossroads. A similar figure of aggression appears in **"In the Heart of the Heart of the Country"**—Aunt Pet, who has broken the back of a dog with her stick and who recalls the incident by raising "the knob of her stick to the level of your eyes." That the narrator identifies with Mr. Wallace is shown by the images of their bellies: "But Mr. Wallace has a strong belly. It is taut and smooth and round, like a baby's, and anything that Mr. Wallace chooses to put into it mashes up speedily," and "Mrs. Mean wanted my attention. She passed across my vision, brilliant with energy, like the glow of a beacon. Each time my stomach churned." The narrator, alternating between dreading Mr. Wallace and claiming that Mr. Wallace dreads him, notes finally, as he does with Mrs. Mean, "There was, in him, no respect for my mysteries." If the narrator is a spider ready to "mend or suck dry intruders," Mr. Wallace, a whale to the narrator's Jonah, is associated with the "smell of oil and the sound of water," which function almost like a symptom formation—the oil occurring again in the final sequence in which the narrator notes, "I tell myself I have fallen into the circle of my own spell." If Mr. Wallace is a "burnt blind Polyphemus," emerging from the cave evoked continually in the story, the narrator says of himself, "Singleness of sight has always been my special genius"—as well as his special blindness.

That the mirror stage of imaginative identification is involved here is revealed by the massive patterns of identification and mutual aggression. Consider the theme of swallowing: the narrator as a spider swallows others, Mr. Wallace as a whale swallows the narrator, and Mrs. Mean's "beak" of a hand swallows the bolls of dandelions—also identified with her children. As a god, the narrator can observe without being observed; he can objectify the others and play with their possibilities; as an idol, however, whose eyes are treated like "marbles" by them, he seems desirous of impressing his objective being in the wax of their subjectivity. Such intersubjective process is revealed also in the narrator's observation: "Mrs. Mean is worse for witnesses. She grows particular"—more and more the essence of meanness to be penetrated. That the narrator is trapped in his mirror image is revealed by his having withdrawn from purposeful activity, measuring time by playing Achilles to the Other's tortoise. Mrs. Mean's "reality" is not only mechanical; it is geological: "Following her gyrations in the grass . . . I forgot her geological depth, the vein of meanness deep within her earth." Meanness has density, although the paradoxical density of an abstraction. Its increasing density corresponds to the narrator's increasing compulsion to penetrate it, a compulsion that he calls "prophecy" since his future is the distance he can create in order to cross it, the shadow he can cast in order to enter it.

As we have noted, the cold wet pipe is an important part of a scene of repressed eroticism. Among many other references to the elements, we are told that "hurts are all fires. Keep you warm" and that "freezing's quiet . . . it's warm." When the narrator fantasizes a cramp for Mrs. Mean, the day is both warm and humid, and she, feeling a dryness and a "blaze," goes toward the house for a glass of water. When the narrator, having imagined Mrs. Mean's son as David to Mr. Wallace's Goliath, now imagines himself in that role, he senses "the wet and dry together." Among the four elements everything that happens is either union or disunion, love or destruction. War is really only another form of love—the love of similars—while cosmic harmony results from the love of opposites. From a cosmic point of view, both creation and destruction are equally necessary; from a human point of view, an orderly love—particularly between men and the gods—must be fostered. Through sacrifices one can appease the gods and even improve them. In **"Mrs. Mean"** the narrator creates beings of gigantic proportions: the Goliath, the Polyphemus, the whale of Mr. Wallace, and the Mrs. Mean whose "anger is too great to stand obedience"—embodied by the narrator in a malevolence that gives her density, an inside to penetrate. Since he uses divination in order to penetrate and torment them, all he discovers (like the reversal of fisherman and fish in the Puritan poem he remembers) is his own otiose tyranny: "There was a time when my hand, too, held heat and when its touch left a burn beneath the skin and I sought beauty like the bee his queen; but it was a high flight for an old tyrant, and not worth wings." The narrator's discovery of his same in the other—his trap in an imaginative identification—inevitably leads to paranoid aggression since he is not the other that he is. The poet is again in this story a surgeon for his own wounds: "I . . . cut surgically by all outward growths, all manifestations, merely, of disease and reach the ill within."

The fictive self of imaginative identification dissolves into fog and mist. Identifying imaginatively with Mr. Wallace, whose account of the weather during the night is taken over by the narrator under the sign of Gemini, the narrator reports: "And the dawn was gray as soapy water. Fog lay between garages." In the final sequence, the narrator passes a "house of love," sees the letters of a Puritan slogan "swallow at the light," feels the fear of a child before a damp cave, sees the "oiled ash" become "splintered wood," and discovers that he has "fallen into the circle of [his] own spell"; he breaches the Means' "fortress" and then sees the maternal figure of Mrs. Cramm as a "thin gray mist" before she engages in surreptitious colloquy

with Mrs. Mean's son. As he contemplates the colloquy—the "vague, tantalizing murmurs"—Mrs. Cramm also becomes as "gray and grotesque as primitive stone," the stone David uses to attack the giant since the narrator then wonders, "Have I gone down before the giant? Mrs. Cramm is suddenly gone and I slink home." The narrator then becomes the "fog between the garages," his self spilled out, his only hope for recuperation being "to see, feel, to know, and to possess." The redbud tree by which he stands recalls the "bud in the blood of her back, in the bend of her legs" when the narrator insinuates himself into Mrs. Mean as a kind of cramp.

The dynamics of Gass's narrative are revealed by the narrator's view of the Means' Calvinism: "Their meanness must proceed from that great sense of guilt which so readily becomes a sense for the sin of others and poisons everything." That the narrative is a projection of the narrator's guilt and fear of castration is clear: "There is no pleasure. There is only the biological propriety of the penis"—the *p* words are further transformed into the "Slovenly Peter" of the cautionary tale and into the "promise" of a "painful" disease tailored by "Providence" and revealed in a "poem of our Puritan ancestors." A fisherman is himself fished in the poem, just as the narrator is caught in his imaginative projections. Although he disclaims the creations he has driven together, he is reassuring himself when he says, "Mr. Wallace has displayed a certain strength. I had thought him shorn but he has joined the Means." The narrator says further of the "toad," "warts," "blemishes," and "stars" about which he is divining truths: "Stigmata. The world of air is like the skin and sings without are only symbols of the world within." When Mrs. Mean holds up her "soiled hands"—a gesture associated with the rampant sexuality of the dandelions—we translate that gesture into the narrator's wish to "disclaim our dirt."

While the theme of Calvinism suggests the way in which the poet's *pathos* is translated into *poiesis,* the story's Orphic theme takes us back to the force of instinct. The poet's Pegasus is the most sublimated example of the force—but toads, bears, cats, insects, and bleached animals inhabit the interior of the Means' world, as does the following mythical creature: "his cow-chested, horsenecked, sow-faced mother." The narrator says of his relation to this world: "Our surprise is symbolic. It is a gesture of speech. . . . I am, in these remote engagements, as fearsome, as bold and blustering as a shy and timorous man can be." He does not want his wife to "strike up friendships" so as to "find out" about this world: "That must be blocked," the narrator says, "It would destroy my transcendence." Despite his ambition for transcendence, he also has the desire to be engulfed by the Other: "To be properly swallowed, then, was the secret; to cause, in going down, the oils to flow that would convulse the membranes of the stomach." The narrator, having sacrificed his concrete freedom, wants to recover a sense of existence by being the responses he stimulates in the Other, whose gigantism makes the secret meaningful. Being swallowed, however, is a return to primal unity, and being swallowed by one's own creation is the narcissistic gratification of art. (pp. 36-57)

Bruce Bassoff, "The Sacrificial World of William Gass: 'In the Heart of the Heart of the Country'," in Critique: Studies in Modern Fiction, *Vol. XVIII, No. 1, Summer, 1976, pp. 36-58.*

William H. Gass   (essay date 1976)

[*In the following excerpt taken from Gass's preface to* In the Heart of the Heart of the Country, and Other Stories, *he describes the origin of the stories in this collection while giving insights into his creative process and relationship to the reader.*]

Franz Kafka and Lewis Carroll, Lawrence Sterne and Tobias Smollett, James Joyce and Marcel Proust, Thomas Mann and William Faulkner, André Gide and Joseph Conrad: what could a poor beginner do?

Begin. And I began by telling a story to entertain a toothache. To entertain a toothache there has to be lots of incident, some excitement, much menace. When I decided to write the story down, I called it "And Slowly Comes the Spring," because that fragmentary phrase seemed somehow appropriate and poetic (it wasn't); but it was some weeks before I began to erase the plot to make a fiction of it, since one can't count on the ear of an everlasting toothache. I titled it, then, **"The Pedersen Kid,"** and because I believed it was good for me (it was), I tried to formulate a set of requirements for the story as clear and rigorous as those of the sonnet. From the outset, however, I was far too concerned with theme. I hadn't discovered yet what I would later find was an iron law of composition for me: the exasperatingly slow search among the words I had already written for the words which were to come, and the necessity for continuous revision, so that each work would seem simply the first paragraph rewritten, swollen with sometimes years of scrutiny around that initial verbal wound, one of the sort you hope, as Francois Mauriac has so beautifully written, "the members of a particular race of mortals can never cease to bleed."

But what do beginners know? Too much. It is what they think they know that makes them beginners. Anyway, here are some of the instructions I drew up (or laid down) for myself during that January of its commencement nearly twenty-five years ago.

> The problem is to present evil as a visitation— sudden, mysterious, violent, inexplicable. All should be subordinated to that end. The physical representation must be spare and staccato; the mental representation must be flowing and a bit repetitious; the dialogue realistic but musical. A ritual effect is needed. It falls, I think, into three parts, each part dividing itself into three. The first part is composed of the discovery of the boy, the discovery of what the boy has seen, the discovery (worst of all) that they will have to do something. The second part is composed of efforts—the effort made to reach the farm; the effort needed to build a tunnel; the effort made to gain the house from the barn. The point here is that the trio, who have come this far only through the social pressure of each other, and in shaky bravado, must go on, knowing that they

are ignorant of causes—of the force itself—("He ain't there"). But the shooting leaves Jorge alone in the house. The pressure which had moved him this far is removed, and the pressure of fear—the threat of death—substituted. The third part contains Jorge's attempt to escape and his unwilling stalk through the house, his wait through the blizzard and the night, and his rescue in the morning. The force has gone as it came. The Pedersens are missing and the great moral effort of the Jorgensens, compelled at every step as it was, is wasted and for nothing.

Though I dropped the rescue, I did not so much depart from this conception as complicate it, covering the moral layer with a frost of epistemological doubt. In any case, during the actual writing, the management of monosyllables, the alternation of short and long sentences, the emotional integrity of the paragraph, the elevation of the most ordinary diction into some semblance of poetry, became my fanatical concern.

Working through the summer, I finished the story in September, and it was seven or eight years after that—and you can imagine how many refusals (it seemed like thousands), and how many broken chairs and bitter bottles and household quarrels, black thoughts and stubborn resolutions, intervened—before John Gardiner generously published it in his magazine, *MSS.*

Writing and reading, like male and female, pain and pleasure, are close but divergent. Although writing itself may be a partial substitute for sexual expression, during adolescence, at any rate, sexual curiosity propelled my reading like a rocket. Over how many dry pages did I pass in search of water? Beyond the next paragraph, around the turn of the page, an oasis of sensuality would materialize, fuzzy in the desert light at first, but then clear, precise, and detailed as a dirty drawing. My sexual puzzles would undo like bras, mysteries would fall away like underpants passing the knees. Alas! such a hot breath blew upon the page that every oasis withered. What did I learn from Pierre Louÿs? Balzac? Jules Romain? . . . *their* puzzles and *their* mysteries, *their* confusions and *their* lives. I didn't understand. I didn't realize. I wanted dirt or purity, innocence or cynicism, never the muddy mix, the flat balance, the even tones of truth. I carried a critic with me everywhere who rose to applaud the passionate passages with a shameless lack of discrimination, and during that throbbing din I couldn't honestly feel or sharply sense or clearly think. Of course, sexual curiosity remains the third lure of reading, yet what an enormous amount of the body's beautiful blushing is wasted on the silliest puerilities when writers write for the reasons reader's read.

> He wondered how her breasts were really formed. Guess, she said. Did the nipple rise like a rainspot on a pond, and were the hollows of her thighs like cups which would contain his kisses? Imagine what will pleasure you, she said. Her clothing always fought him off. His fingers could not construct the rest of what they touched, even when one, slipping beneath the boundary of her underwear, traversed a sacred edge. She would permit him every liberty so long as cloth was wrapped like a bandage between

them, but his hands or his lips or his eyes on anything but customary flesh caused her to stiffen, sucking at her breath until it drew like a bubbly straw. He realized he was as much ice water as a wound. One day, indeed, she had taken all her upper garments off but a soft thin blouse of greenish Celanese, and through its yielding threads he had compressed her. His protests were useless. Guess, she always said. And finally when he had with sufficient and extraordinary bitterness complained how hard her teasing was on him, she'd firmly ordered his phallus from its trousers as you might order a dog from a tree. Dear thing, she said; I'll free you of me. Ultimately, this became their love, like shaking hands, and he had eventually accepted the procedure because, as he explained, it was so like the world. She smiled at this and slowly shook her head: you still have your dream, she said, and I have my surprise.

In a sense, **"Mrs. Mean"** is a story of sexual curiosity translated, again, into the epistemological, although it had its beginning in an observation I never used.

> 3 August '54. The following tableau at the house of Many Children: father is going to work and is standing by the car talking with his wife. He is tall, thin, dark, heavily bearded so that, though he shaves, he always has a heavy shadow, almost blue, across the sides of his face and chin. She is large, great breasted, fat, pig-eyed, fair. The children annoy father who yells at them in a deep carrying voice, cuffs one hard and shoos the rest away with a vigorous outward motion of his arms (like chickens). The children flee, crying and screaming and carrying on. Then father departs. Mama waves and when he's gunned the car furiously away (it stalls twice), she turns to the house; the children's heads pop into place. She makes her voice deep and gruff like his and shouts at them. She swings at one or two (missing widely), and makes his shooing motion with her arms. The children roar delightedly. She goes in and they all troop gaily behind her.

I was to observe this scene, played with only slight variations, many times, and what interested me about it, finally, was the triangle formed by mother, children, and private public-me; but I didn't begin to invent a narrative Eye, my journal tells me, until July 12, 1955, when the first words of the story appear in an unwhelped form. Empty of any persuasive detail, the focus wrong, order inept, rhythms lame, these initial early sentences are aimless, toneless, figureless, thin.

> We call her Mrs. Mean, my wife and I. Our view of her, as our view of her husband and each of all her children, is a porch view. We can only surmise what her life is like inside her little house, but on warm, close Sunday afternoons, while we try the porch to stay cool and watch her hobbling in the hot sun, stick in hand to beat her children, we think a lot about it.

I notice that by November I have begun writing little encouraging notes to myself: buck up, old boy, and so on. It has become a drab affair, like the writing of all my fic-

tions. Imagine an adultery as full of false starts, procrastination, indecision, poor excuses, impotence, and, above all, *plans*.

> The idea I must keep in mind is how I can (a) tell the story of the public Mr. & Mrs. Mean, as seen by the "I" of the story, (b) make "I" more than a pronoun—rather a pronounced personality, (c) slowly, imperceptibly shift from the factual reporting of it to the imaginative projections of "I." The problem is as knotty as PK, and as nice. The ending will be, of course, unsatisfactory, as it will end in the imagination, not in the fact, as if the imagination had filled in the gaps between facts with more *facts,* whereas only fancies are there. All stories ought to end unsatisfactorily.

A month later I had a page, and I completed the piece at some unspecified time in 1957.

I write down these dates, now, and gaze across these temporal gaps with a kind of dumb wonder, because I am compelled to acknowledge the absurd manner in which my stories have been shovelled together: hodge against podge, like those cathedrals which have Baroque porches, Gothic naves, and Romanesque crypts; since the work on them always went slowly; time passed, then passed again, bishops and princes lost interest; funds ran out; men died; shells shattered their radiant windows; they became victims of theft, fire, priests, architects, wind; and because they were put in service while they were still being built, the pavement was gone, the pillars in a state of lurch, by the time the dome was ready for it, gilt or the tower for its tolling bell; so the difficulty for me was plain enough: as an author I naturally desired to change, develop, grow, while each story in its turn wanted the writer who'd begun it to stick around like a faithful father to the end. This dilemma, like drink, nearly destroyed the work of Malcolm Lowry. The absurdity enlarges like the nose of a clown, too, when one realizes that the structure which eventually gets mortared and plastered and hammered together more nearly resembles some *maison de convenience* than even the most modest church. Still, needs are served as much by the humble and ridiculous as by the lordly and sublime.

In any event, it became necessary (it is always necessary) to rewrite earlier sections of whatever I found myself finally trapped in, according to the standards and style of the part presently underway; because, though time may appear to pass within a story, the story itself must seem to have leaked from a single shake of the pen like a blot.

There is much fright. One tries to stick one's words together well, but perhaps, as I write this, the sentences these sentences are supposed to front are melting like icicles, and pointedly passing away; so that, reader, when you turn the final page of this preface, you will be confronted with a pale, pretentious blank; and if that happens, I know which of us will be the greater fool, for your few cents spent on this book are a small mistake; think of me and smile: I spent a life.

My journal begins to sputter—goes out. No more little plans, no more recorded glooms or glorious exhortations, and no more practice paragraphs either, like scales run over in the street. For several years before I began **"The Pedersen Kid,"** I had practiced them (and single sentences, too, and imaginary words, and sounds I hoped had fallen out of Alice); three of which I have put in this preface like odd bits of fruit in a pudding—just a change of texture and a little action for the teeth—and these exercises were another idiocy, because I knew that words were communities made by the repeated crossing of contexts the way tracks formed towns, and that sentences did not swim indifferently through others like schools of fish of another species, but were like lengths of web within a web, despite one's sense of the stitch and knot of design inside them.

Once more right about art and wrong about the world, the Idealist philosophers had argued the same way; but was a sentence like that flower in its crannied wall, and could one see inside its syntactically small self the shape of a busy populace? I guess I hoped so.

Hours of insanity and escape . . . hours inventing expressions like "kiss my teeth" and then wondering what they meant . . . hours of insanity and escape . . . hours spent looking at objects as if they were women, sketching ashtrays, for instance, and noting of a crystal one

> . . . the eyes, the lines of light, the living luster of the glass—the patterns, the ebb and flow—shadows, streaks—the flowing like water in the quiet streams with the sun on it—the foam and bubble of the glass . . .

and concluding the study grandly (Who was I pretending to be? Maupassant tutored by Flaubert?) with this command:

> Never mention an ashtray unless you can swiftly make it the only one of its kind in the world.

A rule I obeyed by never mentioning an ashtray.

Obscurely and fortuitously, chance brought these stories forth from nowhere. Icicles once dripped solidly from my eaves, for instance. I thought them remarkable because they seemed to grow as a consequence of their own grief, and I wondered whether my feelings would freeze to me by the time they had traveled my length, and whether each of us wasn't just the size of our consciousness solidified; but these fancies scarcely crept into the story which, like **"Order of Insects,"** and everything I've written since, is an exploration of an image. I was impressed not only by their cold, perishable beauty, but by the feeling I had that they were *mine,* and that, though accident had fixed them to my gutters the way it had hung them everywhere, no one had a right to cause their premature destruction. Yet where may the eye fall now its sight is not bruised by vandals? No matter. The story merely began from this thought, it did not create itself entirely as an icicle should, so that passions warmed elsewhere would cool as they passed along the text until, at the sharp tip, they became themselves text. That would have been ideal.

Hours of insanity and escape . . . collecting names in the hope they'd prove jackpotty, and stories would suddenly shower out like dimes . . .

> Horace Bardwell, Ada Hunt Chase, Mary Persis

Crofts, Kelsey Flowers, Annie Stilphen, Edna Hoxie, Asher Applegate, Amos Bodge, Enoch Boyce, Jeremiah Bresnan, James G. Burpee, Curtis Chamlet, Decius W. Clark, Revellard Dutcher, Jedediah Felton, Jethro Furber, Pelatiah Hall, George Hatstat, Quartus Graves, Loammi Kendall, Truxton Orcutt, Plaisted Williams, Francis Plympton, Azariah Shove, Peter Twiss; and in addition the members of the cooking club of Mt. Gilead, Ohio, 1899: Dean Booher, Floy Buxton, Nellie Goorley, Ira Irwin, Bessie Johnson, Clara Kelly, Sadie McCracken, Clara Mozier, Josie Plumb, Sarah Swingle, Maude Smith, Anna, Belle, Deane and Ivan Talmage, Roberta Wheeler.

Round, ripe, seedful names such as these are seldom found and cannot be invented, though they might be more sweetly arranged. I could not have shaken them from any local tree because I have no locality. I am not a man from Warren. What is it to be from Warren? or weakly half-Protestant, half-Catholic? nondescript in white? of German and Scandinavian blood so pale even pure Aryans are disgusted? and with a name made for amusement, and one which, even in German, means "alley." I am no one's son, or father, it appears. Not Northern, not American, not a theosophist, not a scholar, not Prufrock, not the Dane. Yet I gathered these names all the same. From a book . . . the pages that are my streets.

Nature rarely loops. Nature repeats. This spring is not a former spring rethought, but merely another one, somewhat the same, somewhat not. However, in a fiction, ideas, perceptions, feelings, return like reconsiderations, and the more one sees a piece of imaginative prose as an adventure of the mind, the more the linearities of life will be bent and interrupted. Just as revision itself is made of meditative returns, so the reappearance of any theme constitutes the re-seeing of that theme by itself. Otherwise there is no advance. There is stagnation. The quiet spiral of the shell, a gyre, even a whirlwind, a tunnel towering in the air: these are the appropriate forms, the rightful shapes; yet the reader must not succumb to the temptations of simple location, but experience in the rising, turning line the wider view, like a sailplane circling through a thermal, and sense at the same time a corkscrewing descent into the subject, a progressive deepening around the reading eye, a penetration of the particular which is the partial theme of **"Mrs. Mean"**—at once escape and entry, an inside pulled out and an outside pressed in, as also is the case with **"Order of Insects."**

Hours of insanity and escape . . . in which I write inadequate verse, read, rage . . . record anecdotes which fade into the page like stains . . . beat time with my pencil's business end . . . cast schemes and tropes like horoscopes . . . practice catachresis as though it were croquet . . . grrrowl . . . realize that when I picture my methods of construction all the images are architectural, but when I dream of the ultimate fiction—that animal entity, the made-up syllabic self—I am trying to energize old, used-up, stolen organs like Dr. Frankenstein . . . grrrind . . . Ohio: I hear howling from both Os . . . play ring agroan the rosie . . . rhyme . . .

Thus the idea of an audience returns like an itch between the toes, because now we have words watching words—not surprising—what should Berkeley's trees do, hidden in their forest, if they learned, if they believed, if they knew that unnoticed they were likely to be nothing? encourage birds? grow eyes and ears and rub remaining leaves like foreign money?

When Henry James, bruised by his failure in the theatre, returned to the novel with *The Awkward Age,* he wrote in the scenery himself; he created his actors and gave them their speeches and gestures. More than that, he filled the spaces around them with sensibility—other observations—the perfect vessel of appreciation—himself, or rather, his roundabout writing. His method has become a model. Now, on the page, though the stage is full, the theatre is dark and empty. Red bulbs burn above the exits. And when the theatre is empty, and the actors continue to speak into the wings and walk from cupboard to sofa as if in the midst of emotion, to whom are they speaking but to themselves? Suddenly the action is all there is; the made-up words are real; the actors are the parts they play; questions are no longer cues; replies are real replies; there's no more drama; the conditions of rehearsal have become the conditions of reality, and the light which streams like colored paper from the spots is all there'll ever be of day.

1. Continue work . . .
2. Study the masters . . .
3. Do deliberate exercises . . .
4. Regularly enter notes . . . sharpen that peculiar and forgetful eye . . .
5. Take to sketching . . . details . . . exactitude . . .
6. Be steeped in history . . .
7. . . . the better word . . . the better word . . . the better word . . .
8. Figure it will be five years before any . . .
9. Wait . . .

A former student, who had reached the lower slopes of a national magazine, charitably wrote to ask if I would do a piece on what it was like to live in the Midwest. Without quite knowing whether my answer would be yes or no, I nevertheless began to gather data on that subject, although it became plain soon enough that the magazine was not interested in the logarithmical disorders of my lyricisms. I had always avoided the autobiographical in my work, reasoning that it was one beginner's trap I'd not fall into (more witless wisdom), and by now I had become suspicious of my own detachment. Could I write close to myself, or would the letter B, which my narrator said he'd sailed to, stand for bathos?

I was living in Brookston, Indiana, then, but I called it B because that's how it was often done in the old days. Turgenev's characters sometimes wait on some small porch fastened like a belt around an inn which rises as a low bump on the road to S, though nothing is yet in sight when we encounter them. Like the reader, they are waiting for the book to begin. (On the other hand, Beckett's roads are letterless, and his figures are waiting for the text to terminate.) I also wanted, quite ironically, to invoke the golden boughs of Yeats' Byzantium. The subjects are slyly the same. Furthermore, I knew that when I'd finished, it wouldn't be Brookston, Indiana, anymore, but a place as full of dream and fabrication as that fabled city itself. Inside my cautious sentences, as against Yeats' monumental poetry, it would become an inverted heaven for man's imagination.

I certainly didn't resort to the letter out of shyness or some belated sense of discretion; but as I got my "facts" straight (clubs, crops, products, prospects, townshape, bar and barnsize), I remembered how eagerly I'd come to the community, how much I'd needed to feel my mind—just once—run free and openly in peace, in wholesome and unworried amplitude, the way my legs before in Larimore, N. D., had carried me through streets scaled perfectly for childhood; and I slowly realized, while I drew my lists (jobs, shops, climate), marking social strata like a kid counts layers in a cake, that I was taking down the town in notes so far from sounding anything significant that they would not even let me find a cow; yet I figured my estimates anyway (population changes, transportation, education, housing, love), and I took my polls (of churches and their clientele, of diets and diseases); I made my guesses (fun, games, finance—pitch or catch, cadge, swap or auction), just as any geographer would, impressed by the seriousness of habit, too, of simple talk or an idle spit or prolonged squat; and as I started to distribute my data gingerly across my manuscript, a steady dissolution of the real began, because the more precisely one walks down a verbal street, the more precisely trash and shadow, weed and feel and walkcrack are rendered; when all that can conceivably enter consciousness, snowflash and harness, tin taste and grain spill and oil odor, hedge and grass growth, enters like a member of an orchestra, armed with an instrument, bee hum and fly death—the more completely, in short, we observe rather than merely note, contemplate rather than perceive, imagine rather than simply ponder—then the more fully, too, must the reader and writer realize, as their sentences foot the page, that they are now in the graciously menacing company of the Angel of Inwardness, that radiant guardian of Ideas of whom Plato and Rilke spoke so ardently, and Mallarmé and Valéry invoked; since a sense of resonant universality arises in literature whenever some mute and otherwise trivial particularity is experienced with an intensely passionate particularity—through a ring of likeness which defines for each object its land of unlikeness, too . . . though who says so, aside from Schopenhauer, who was also wrong about the world? . . . and consequently the heart of the country became the heart of the heart with a suddenness which left me uncomforted, in B and not Byzantium, not Brookston, far from the self I thought I might expose, nowhere near a childhood, and with thoughts I kept in paragraphs like small animals caged.

Hours of insanity and escape . . . tear paper into thread-thin strips—not easy . . . then to slide lines of words from one side of a page to another, vainly hoping the difference will be agreeable . . . instead of a passionate particularity, to try for a ringing singularity . . . cancel, scratch, xxxxx . . . stop.

So I am still the obscure man who wrote these words, and

if someone were to ask me once again of the circumstances of my birth, I think I should answer finally that I was born somewhere in the middle of my first book; that life, so far, has not been extensive; that my native state is Anger, a place nowhere on the continent but rather somewhere at the bottom of my belly; that I presently dwell in the Sicily of the soul, the Mexico of the mind, the tower at Duino, the garden house in Rye; and that I shall be happy to rent, sell, or give away these stories, which I would have furnished far more richly if I could have borne the cost, to anyone who might want to visit them, or—hallelujah—reside. In lieu of that unlikelihood, however, I am fashioning a reader for these fictions . . . of what kind? well, skilled and generous with attention, for one thing, patient with *longeurs,* forgiving of every error and indulgence, avid for details . . . ah, and a lover of lists, a twiddler of lines. Shall this reader be given occasionally to mouthing a word aloud or wanting to read to a companion in a piercing library whisper? yes; and shall this reader be one whose breathing changes with the tenses of the verbs? yes; and shall every allusion be caught like a cold? no, eaten like a fish, yes; and shall there by eyes and eyebrows raised at rhymes? and the thoughts found profound and the sentiments felt to be of the best kind? yes, and the patterns applauded . . . but we won't need hair or nose or any other opening or lure . . . not a muscle need be imagined . . . a body indifferent to time, to diet . . . what? oh, a sort of slowpoke singer, finger tracer, then, mover of lips. . . . And shall this reader, as you open the book, shadow the page like a palm? perhaps (mind the strain on the eyes); and sink into the paper? become the print? and blossom on the other side with pleasure and sensation . . . from the touch of the mind and the love that lasts in language? yes. Let's imagine such a being. And begin. Begin. (pp. 17-31)

> *William H. Gass, in a preface to his* In the Heart of the Heart of the Country and Other Stories, *Pocket Books, 1977, pp. 9-31.*

Charles Caramello   (essay date 1980)

[*In the following essay, Caramello examines* Willie Masters' Lonesome Wife *in terms of the aesthetic principles outlined in Gass's critical writings.*]

William H. Gass calls a brief encounter with Wittgenstein "the most important intellectual experience of my life"; he is vitriolic on the topic of Sartrean *engagement* in literature; he describes himself as "very much a Valérian", and he consistently argues that art "teaches nothing. It simply shows what beauty, perfection, sensuality, and meaning are. . . ." The title of his collection of stories, *In the Heart of the Heart of the Country,* implies a position: there is neither heart nor Conradian void at the center of fiction; the final reduction is to language—to the phrase, "the heart." The title of his recent collection of essays, *The World Within the Word,* neatly encoding both an aesthetics and a metaphysics, appears to express that position.

The epistemic shift that Derrida associates with "the end of the book and the beginning of writing" and that Roland Barthes designates as that "from work to text" has considerable relevance to the issues raised by Gass' fiction. Derrida speaks of the cultural categories of "a good and a bad writing: the good and natural is the divine inscription in the heart and the soul; the perverse and artful is technique, exiled in the exteriority of the body." Predicated on a metaphysics of presence and Authority—on an idea of the Book—the dichotomy collapses once one acknowledges the decentered play of Writing. William Gass would seem to have done so. But if we can consider Barthes' "work" and "text" as *analogous* to Derrida's "book" and "writing"—keeping in mind his use of "work" to refer to the concept of literature as that which is produced by a discrete authorial presence and "text" to refer to the concept of literature as that which is produced largely in its reception, that which is cut loose in the intertext, that which participates in the phenomenon that he describes as "the death of the author," that in which there is "no other origin than language itself, language which ceaselessly calls into question all origins"—then we might have to place Gass on the side of book, work, and authority.

Indeed, Gass' work reveals an ambivalence on this matter of textuality and authority—an ambivalence that obtains in much of postmodern American fiction. His brief novella, ***Willie Masters' Lonesome Wife,*** published over a decade ago, both treats and exemplifies this ambivalence.

It is appropriate that the first line of the Preface to Gass' first collection of essays, *Fiction and the Figures of Life,* refers to Valéry, for Gass presents himself as among the most formalistic of contemporary American writers. We recall that for Valéry poetry is to prose as dancing is to walking; that poetry "stimulates us to reconstruct it identically"; that a poem should reveal "an intimate union between the word and the mind"; that "a poem is really a kind of machine for producing the poetic state of mind by means of words." While ordinary spoken language is transparent and autodestructive—"*Its task is fulfilled when each sentence has been completely abolished, annulled, and replaced by the meaning*"—"poetic language must preserve itself, through itself, and remain the same, *not to be altered by the act of intelligence that finds or gives it a meaning.*" The poet himself "is no longer the disheveled madman," but "a cool scientist, almost an algebraist, in the service of a subtle dreamer." He must dream, that is, but he must also transform this dream into "an artificial and ideal order by means of a material of vulgar origin": common language. He must, moreover, be as precise as possible, for the inherent multivalence of poetic language predisposes it to violation—allows the reader to "corrupt" or "disfigure" its meaning. The extreme of interpretation—the reduction of a poem to its prose statement—"*to make of a poem a matter for instruction or examinations*"—is "no slight matter of heresy," but "a real perversion."

Now, Gass is a consistent defender of poetry as a special discourse: he argues that words undergo "ontological transformations" when shifted from common language to contextualized poetic forms. He feels likewise about prose literature: that "there are no descriptions in fiction, there are only constructions"; that "the lines of the novelist . . . are not likely interpretations of anything, but are the thing itself"; that "there are no events but words in fiction." He argues that "the novelist, if he is any good, will keep us kindly imprisoned in his language," and that the reader should "feel the way he feels when he listens to music—when he listens properly, that is." Although Gass wants the reader's "effort of understanding a work," he does not want his or her "creative co-operation." "Anything that the reader is creatively going to be asked to put in," he says, "I'll put in. I don't want him meddling around with my stuff." He opposes "pretensous claims for literature as a source of knowledge," and believes, generally, that the work is a closed spatial construction with, at best, an indirect relationship to the world. One of Gass' preferred metaphors for fiction is sculpture. Fiction, he writes, is like a statue pointing with "outstretched arm and finger": "Though pointing, the finger bids us stay instead, and we journey slowly back along the tension of the arm. In our hearts we know what actually surrounds the statue. The same surrounds every other work of art: empty space and silence."

Although the metaphor of sculpture literally describes Gass' *Willie Masters' Lonesome Wife*—a book that presents itself as the body of a woman—metaphors of performance may be, finally, more appropriate. *Willie Masters'* is crucial to the question of the book in postmodernism for two reasons. First, Gass has exploited the physics of the book to flesh out fiction—to make the book a body, to render concrete his aesthetics of an opaque, palpable language. Second, his metaphysics of the Book reveals an ambivalence—concentrated in this virtuoso performance—with respect to the positions of author and reader in relation to the literary text. Gass, that is, makes the book perform in the play of textuality, but he remains authoritarian about the status of the performing selves associated with it.

The interior monologue of a woman named Babs, the narrative of *Willie Masters' Lonesome Wife,* is printed with varied typographies on pages of varied colors and textures—pages enclosed within front and back cover photographs of a nude female torso. The book becomes the sculptured body of a woman, self-contained and self-generated. At the same time, however, this book as woman is obsessed with sexual penetration and claims to want to remain open to it. On the one hand, we have Gass, coupling with his own imagination, creating an interior monologue seamless with its physical vehicle—a perfect union, it would seem, of mind and word, of intelligence and body. From this perspective, Gass remains in control—orchestrating language and graphics—of a purely formalistic fiction. On the other hand, we have the reader faced with a highly discontinuous text, a fiction he or she cannot fulfill, a fiction whose varied designs, colors and textures, whose metaphoric flights and narrative dislocations, whose elaborate fabric of reference (in just sixty pages: Homer, Dante, Shakespeare, Dryden, Goethe, Tolstoy, Gogol, Lawrence, Hardy, James, Flaubert, Baudelaire, Apollinaire, Stein, Joyce, Beckett, and others), all resist reading as anything less than writing. From this perspective, author relinquishes his control to the fortuities of the intertext. On the one hand, we have a voyeur's art; on the other hand, we have an appeal for book and reader

to come together. And between clashing conceptions of the writer as master and the reader as lover stands the ambiguous literary text itself: a book as woman that seems to dissociate itself from both Molly Bloom and Anna Livia Plurabelle while clearly dependent on their priority; an erotic text that oscillates between, in Roland Barthes' terms, *plaisir* and *jouissance.* If we consider the problematics of writer, reader and book separately, we will see how ambivalent Gass' postion is.

The novelist, Gass has written, wants language to be "an utterly receptive woman"; his business is not "to render the world," but "to *make* one, and to make one from the only medium of which he is a master—language." In *Willie Masters'* itself we read that the penis is "the very instrument and emblem of the imagination," and someone in this theater of voices adds: "Yet I have put my hand upon this body, here, as no man ever has, and I have even felt my pencil stir, grow great with blood. But never has it swollen with love. It moves in anger, always, against its paper." We also read that the "man of imagination"

> experiences his speech as he does himself when he's most fit, when he is *One*—and moving smoothly as a stream. Imagination is, as Sam said, the unifying power, and the acts of the imagination are our most free and natural; they represent us at our best.

The elements of this vision reach an apotheosis in the work's final lines:

> It's not the languid pissing prose we've got, we need; but poetry, the human muse, full up, erect and on the charge, impetuous and hot and loud and wild like Messalina going to the stews, or those damn rockets streaming headstrong into stars.

In sum, we find an attitude that Charles Rosen has characterized well with reference, appropriately, to Liszt's fantasy on themes from Mozart's *Don Giovanni:* "the virtuosity of Liszt's fantasy," Rosen notes, "acts as a symbol of virility and dominance, a displacement of erotic mastery." Gass points to this displacement himself in his titular wordplay: Will he master his lonesome wife?

The title, however, alludes not only to the romantic impulse (Goethe's *Wilhelm Meister*) and, perhaps, to the idea of the pure poem (Mallarmé as *le Maître*), but, more importantly, to Shakespeare. With reference to the Sonnets, Northrop Frye has articulated a crucial element of sexual/textual mastery:

> The true father or shaping spirit of the poem is the form of the poem itself, and this form is a manifestation of the universal spirit of poetry, the "onlie begetter" of Shakespeare's sonnets who was not Shakespeare himself, much less that depressing ghost Mr. W. H., but Shakespeare's subject, the master-mistress of his passion. When a poet speaks of the *internal* spirit which shapes the poem, he is apt to drop the traditional appeal to female Muses and think of himself as in a feminine, or at least receptive, relation to some god or lord, whether Apollo, Dionysus, Eros, Christ, or (as in Milton) the Holy Spirit.

The poet, that is, can invert his masculine posture and claim to be receptive to all of poetry as a context and to the things of the world. Gass refers to such an inversion when he writes of D. H. Lawrence: "Yet when Lawrence felt he *could* go unprotected, when he allowed things, landscapes, people, to enter *him* . . . then there was no greater sensualist, no more vital, free, and complete a man, no more loyal and tender a lover." He also practices it in *Willie Masters' Lonesome Wife.* We recall that a central theme of the book is that the wife's lovers "protect" themselves with condoms; that as she strives for "completion," she complains of her having to "complete" her lovers ("I dream like Madame Bovary. Only I don't die during endings. I never die. They fall asleep on me and shrivel up. I write the *finis* for them, close the covers, shelf the book"); that her principal objection is that her lovers lack "tenderness." The ambiguity with regard to the question of mastery as it pertains to the master-writer, then, also informs the question of completion as it pertains to the lover-reader. As complement to the wordplay on the husband's name (Will he master his lonesome wife?), Gass has another wordplay based on the principal lover's name, Phil Gelvin: Will Phil fulfill her by filling her with Phil?

When Larry McCaffery—in a fine essay called "The Art of Metafiction: William Gass's *Willie Masters' Lonesome Wife*"—identifies "the central metaphor of the whole work: that a parallel exists—or should exist—between a woman and her lover, between the work of art and the artist, between a book and its reader," he identifies the problem correctly. But in his determination to interpret this work as a "remarkably pure" metafiction, McCaffery effects a reduction of its ambiguity that, in my opinion, causes him to misformulate important implications of this metaphor.

I do not believe that *Willie Masters'* finally coincides with McCaffery's reading of it:

> Gass, thus, invites one to enter his work of art—a woman made of words and paper—with the same sort of excitement, participation, and creative energy as one would enter a woman's body in sexual intercourse. . . . Unfortunately, as we discover with Babs, all too frequently those who enter her do so without enthusiasm, often seemingly unaware that she is there at all.

It does not because there is a fundamental ambiguity in this work *as a book:* it is *here,* as a physical object, but, as Gass has elsewhere argued, a book is also *not here:* it is a platonic idea, separate from its physical manifestation and from its reader who, when similarly abstracted, "is just as far away and metaphysical as the book."

The identity of the wife / book, then, is also ambiguated internally, not only because she / it is "created" by an author and a reader whose statuses are ambiguous, but because her / its status as self-creator is ambiguous. The wife / book appears to be autotelic:

> Departure is my name. I travel, dream. I feel sometimes as if I *were* imagination (that spider goddess and thread-spinning muse)—imagination imagining itself imagine. Then I *am* as it *is,* reflecting on my own revolving, as

though a record might take down its turning and in that self-responsive way comprise a song which sings its singing back upon its notes as purely as a mirror, and like a mirror endlessly unimages itself, yet is none the less an image (just as much a woman, gauzy muse and hot-pants goddess quite the same), for all that generosity—for all that giving of itself and flowing constantly away.

(The passage, printed on a page whose opposite mirrors it, is rife with images of reflexivity, mirroring, and turning.) Rendering visually Gass' fiction-as-sculpture metaphor, a photograph of a woman's arm emerges from the binding on the first page after the cover and points to the title *Willie Masters' Lonesome Wife.* This is not Michelangelo's finger of God instilling vitality in Adam—which it echoes and which would be consistent with the idea of the author as Master—but the finger of the wife creating herself as a self-inspired Eve. She is imagination imagining herself imagine in a masturbatory play that, as she says, does not require cheap and mimetic pornography or fetish objects to produce pleasure:

> . . . when I am masturbating I—by Christ—call, witch up, conjure images and pictures, visions, fancies, wishes . . . wishes! They're obedient to no one. I have faeries straddle me, and angels, demons, stallions, dogs, as well as women. I will translate, just as Bottom was, my poor homeless lonely finger into anything.

As desiring machine, the wife is actually less desirous of her reader—despite her protests—than she is of herself.

And who is this wife—this imagination imagining itself imagine—if not the book as textual performance? McCaffery goes wrong, I believe, when he identifies her only as "lady language." That identification results from a misreading of this important sentence: "I am that lady language chose to make her playhouse of. . . ." The "lady" is not "language"; "language" is also feminine ("her"), but it is not the predicate noun of the "I" of the sentence. "I" and "lady" refer to something *of which* language makes a playhouse: that something appears to be imagination performing itself in a book *as* text. The book is the playhouse of imagination in both senses of the word "playhouse." It is a place for games: a place where the play of language plays (with) itself; and it is a theater: a performance space for the *presumably* interacting performances of writer, book, and reader.

We recall that Babs, the wife, is not only a "whore," but that she was a stripper. She also says, however: "Until my flesh began to lose its grip, I danced in the blue light with the best, and then I married Willie so I could dance the same dance still, the dance I'm dancing now, and not feel lonely. . . ." She *remains* a performer, performing the stripper's dance in language, the dance of the tease, which she also performs as a sexual performance that defers orgasm. It is not the case, unfortunately, that "in performance, all difficulties disappear." If I can do so with good humor, I would say that McCaffery—as the book reminds its reader—has "BEEN HAD . . . FROM START TO FINISH." As Willie (the whore) Master, Gass no more invites the reader to enter his woman than she herself extends such an invitation. To her, the reader is a "sad sour stew-faced sonofabitch" whom she holds in considerable contempt. ***Willie Masters'*** is a stripper's art, but what disturbs is not simply its deferral of orgasm: it is that the deferral—the dance—also seems to lack an affirmative joy.

In *The Pleasure of the Text,* Roland Barthes writes:

> The pleasure of the text is not the pleasure of the corporeal striptease or of narrative's suspense. In these cases [texts of pleasure], there is no tear, no edges: a gradual unveiling: the entire excitation takes refuge in the *hope* of seeing the sexual organ (schoolboy's dream) or in knowing the end of the story (novelistic satisfaction). Paradoxically (since it is mass-consumed), this is a far more intellectual pleasure than the other: [it is] an Oedipal pleasure (to denude, to know, to learn the origin and the end), if it is true that every narrative (every unveiling of the truth) is a staging of the (absent, hidden, or hypostatized) father—which would explain the solidarity of narrative forms, of family structures, and of prohibitions of nudity, all collected in our culture in the myth of Noah's sons covering his nakedness.

Perhaps what disturbs about ***Willie Masters'*** is that it appears to be a striptease within a striptease, revealing the apparatus of revealing—"the staging of an appearance-as-disappearance"—but that it does not, finally, effect this apparent unmaking. For crucial to Barthes' idea of the text as tissue is that it does not veil a truth; it is, rather, a "perpetual interweaving; lost in this tissue—this texture—the subject unmakes himself, like a spider dissolving in the constructive secretions of its web."

Now, the wife as subject certainly unmakes herself ("a mirror endlessly unimag[ing] itself ") in this fashion, as, more importantly, ***Willie Masters' Lonesome Wife*** appears to unmake the reader as subject in terms that Barthes uses to describe the *plaisir / jouissance* overlap:

> Text of pleasure: the text that contents, fills, grants euphoria; the text that comes from culture and does not break with it, is linked to a *comfortable* practice of reading. Text of bliss: the text that imposes a state of loss, the text that discomforts . . ., unsettles the reader's historical, cultural, psychological assumptions, the consistency of his tastes, values, memories, brings to a crisis his relation with language.

Gass' book guarantees such a loss for the reader, who must chase asterisked footnotes several pages ahead of the text's body, who must balance multiple narrations on the same page, who is accused of being a footfetishist for reading the footnotes, and who is told in one particularly nasty note that he (the implied reader of this work is clearly male: a Baudelairean double: "dear brother, lover, fellow reader") is a "bastard" hated with "a niggerish hate," an "ass-plugger" trapped "deep inside me like they say in the songs, fast as a ship in antarctic ice." "Even the reader who *has* played the game, who has *not* been a literalist at loving," is told "YOU'VE BEEN HAD . . . FROM START TO FINISH." ***Willie Masters',*** moreover, *sounds* like the "writing aloud" (*l'écriture à haute voix*) that

Barthes identifies with textual *jouissance:* "we can hear the grain of the throat, the patina of consonants, the voluptuousness of vowels, a whole carnal stereophony: the articulation of the body, of the tongue, not that of meaning, of language."

What disturbs, I think, is that Gass does not unmake himself as master, does not subvert his own authority (although he does render it highly ambiguous), does not disrupt our cultural or sexual assumptions. Gass, that is, exposes the nudity of the wife (on the cover) without shame, but he forces her to strip *beyond* her legitimate attack on the male reader to this sentiment: "But let's not quarrel. Though you'll [Phil Gelvin] not be back, your brother will. Tell him he is responsible for me, and that I give as good as I receive. If he will be attentive, thoughtful, warm and kind, I shall be passionate and beautiful." Gass, in short, must force her to capitulate to the male reader's fantasy because that reader, Gass knows from Baudelaire, is *his,* the writer's, double. Even more, Gass forces her to mouth the phallic plea for metaphor at the book's end. Gass does not stage his unveiling as a master, or father, in the text, nor (his formalism) through the text. He does not reveal Noah's nakedness, allowing the reader the traumatic but gratifying glimpses that Joyce does in the closure / disclosure apparatus in *Finnegans Wake.* But neither does he quite stage an appearance-as-disappearance. He displaces erotic mastery as virtuosity; he makes the woman speak his voice, the voice of the male: what disturbs in this book is its sexual encroachment, its hegemony of the female voice. Chronologically posterior to *Ulysses* and the *Wake,* it may be ideologically anterior to them.

What Gass does not unmake is himself as Master: as Author. Important to Barthes' theory of textual / sexual play is his perception of the text as a dismembered body: "the text itself, a diagrammatic and not an imitative structure, can reveal itself in the form of a body, split into fetish objects, into erotic sites." Gass dismembers the wife in this way, but a writer who says in an interview, "Whenever I find myself working at white heat, I stop until I cool off. I write very slowly, laboriously, without exhilaration, without pleasure, though with a great deal of tension and exasperation," and who adds:

> I am . . . a Protestant, wholly inner-directed, and concerned only too exclusively with *my* salvation, *my* relation to the beautiful, *my* state of mind, body, soul. . . . The interactions which interest me tend to be interactions between parts of my own being.

(pp. 56-63)

This would be consistent with Gass' aesthetics: that "where language is used as an art it is no longer used merely to communicate. It demands to be treated as a thing, inert and voiceless"; that the writer is the "maker" of a totally self-contained verbal world beyond which "there is literally nothing"; that language is "opaque"; that theories "which think of fiction as a mirror or a window onto life" are "absurd"; that "Relevance is meaningless to [art]. A work of art is made to last as a valuable being in the world. As such it may develop, over time, useful relations to the world; but just as human beings ultimately must find their value in themselves, so works of art must *be relevant by being*"; that, finally, "books are more real than the world, that they're more high-powered ontologically." Gass essentially divorces from history both the production of the text and its reception. Although Barthes, for example, explores the disruption of narrative structure and of the physical book in personal and erotic terms, he has also seen this disruption as politically significant. In an early essay, "Literature and Discontinuity," he writes (with reference to Michel Butor) that *"the Book-as-Object is materially identified with the Book-as-Idea,* the technique of printing with the literary institution, so that to attack the material regularity of the work is to attack the very idea of literature." It is to reject the metaphysics of the Book and its sacred / sacrosanct Author, and it is to subvert—at least indirectly—the social institutions that depend upon that metaphysics for their legitimacy. Although Gass clearly practices such disruption, he seems not to obviate but to continue to mystify Authority.

The mystification is linked, in Gass as in Barthes, to an erotics of literature. Gass writes, for example:

> The purpose of a literary work is the capture of consciousness, and the consequent creation, in you, of an imagined sensibility, so that while you read you are that patient pool or cataract of concepts which the author has constructed; and though at first it might seem as if the richness of life had been replaced by something less so— senseless noises, abstract meanings, mere shadows of worldly employment—yet the new self with which fine fiction and good poetry should provide you is as wide as the mind is, and musicked deep with feeling. . . . Because a consciousness electrified by beauty—is that not the aim and emblem and the ending of all finely made love?
>
> Are you afraid?

Consciousness as the end of love: we read in **Willie Masters'** that "there's no woman who's not, deep inside her, theoretical"; and later: "how close, in the end, is a cunt to a concept—we enter both with joy." The most curious ambiguity of **Willie Masters'** is that it embodies woman as book only to then disembody both as pure consciousness. This is the consciousness of Willie Master(bator): ceaseless reverberations between Narcissus and Echo. We can begin to see why Gass also warns of mistaking the word for flesh, of living in fiction "when on our own we scarcely breathe"; why he criticizes Gertrude Stein's work as revealing a "desire to gain by artifice a safety from the world—to find a way of thinking without the risks of feeling"; why he "see[s] no reason to regard literature as a superior source of truth, or even as a reliable source of truth at all"; and why the final injunction of **Willie Masters'** is: "YOU HAVE FALLEN INTO ART—RETURN TO LIFE."

Freed from the tics of his nervous prose and the archness of his critical pre / proscriptions—concentrated in **Willie Masters' Lonesome Wife**—Gass' ambivalence is compelling. He seems reluctant, finally, to accept a metonymical textual play of language that fragments the body into erotic sites as he is to accept a metaphorical presence of language that, as in Norman O. Brown, unifies the mind and body as a sensual whole: "Everything is only metaphor; there is only poetry." For Gass, the bottom line remains *separation:* fiction as the vehicle of a metaphor whose subject is the world of the reader. The imagining that is the wife seems to be, as McCaffery suggests, *here,* in the language and in the book:

> No one can imagine—simply—merely; one must imagine within words or paint or metal, communicating genes or multiplying numbers. Imagination is its medium realized. You are your body . . . and the poet is his language;
>
> I'm only a string of noises, after all—nothing more really—an arrangement, a column of air moving up and down . . . ;
>
> The usual view is that you see through me, through what I am really—significant sound;
>
> This moon, then, is something like me. For one thing, I'm an image.

This wife, in Gass' Langerian view, is "significant form," a complete image in herself, and separate from the world: the split between "you, the world; and I, the language," continues to gape. "I can't complain," she says. "You're supposed to be lonely—getting fucked."

But complain of separation she constantly does: her lover "even carried his sperm away in a little rubber sack"; "he puts his penis in a plastic bag"; "Thus we never touched, nor would have, though he feared me greatly, when we fucked. Afterward, he carried his seed off safely in a sack." Separation is absolute between writer and reader:

> The muddy circle you see just before you and below you represents the ring left on a leaf of the manuscript by my coffee cup. Represents, I say, because, as you must surely realize, this book is many removes from anything I've set pen, hand, or cup to. . . . All contact—merest contact— any contact—is impossible, logically impossible (there's not even a crack between us) . . . ;

between reader and book:

> As you see, its center's empty [the same circular stain, now inscribed "This is the moon of daylight"], no glow there. And I am lonely. This stupid creature who just now has left me . . . did not, in his address, at any time, construct me. He made nothing, I swear—nothing. Empty I began, and empty I remained;

between writer and book:

> When a letter comes, if you will follow me, there is no author fastened to it like the stamp; the words which speak, they are the body of the speaker. It's just the same with me. These words are all I am. Believe me. Pity me. Not even the Dane is any more than that.

When this letter—this woman as letter, as "I"—comes, she comes alone. The four sections of the book may represent stages of sexual excitation, as McCaffery suggests, but these are not stages of intercourse. This is soft-core porn. Unfulfilled by Phil, from whom she is eternally separated,

Babs is left with her own finger—the finger of the statue, of the masturbator—a finger that has been *allowed* her: "But can you imagine any woman thinking: I've Phyllis folded up my in-between? It's not such a bad idea, though."

Melville's "dead letters," separated from origin and end, would seem to have reappeared in American fiction, this time as "French letters," for the brown circular stains in *Willie Masters'* are also condom stains. The final one encircles the navel of the (photograph of the) woman's body—a woman who is neither, finally, the navel-less Eve associated with Molly Bloom, nor the omphalos of Anna Livia Plurabelle: a phallic OM as the originary Word made feminine. But neither is she their joyful decentering. She is the book that we can open but cannot penetrate (the navel as false vagina): the physical book as the metaphysical Book that we, in fact, cannot enter with joy.

The Gass of whom I have been speaking is, of course, more a persona than a person, more a construction of quotations than a living writer. And the position of even this Gass is difficult to state with certainty, for the disposition of voices in *Willie Masters'* is complex. Gass speaks as Babs, as Willie's wife, "in a feminine, or at least receptive, relation to some god or lord." But he also speaks "silently"—in the composition itself—as Willie. Willie is his double, just as Phil Gelvin is Willie's double, just as the reader is Phil Gelvin's double. "Responsible" for the wife's existence, Gass implies through this chain of substitutions that he is also as "responsible" for her loneliness as the reader is.

Gass has criticized Nabokov's novels as being attacks upon their readers, though not like . . . Baudelaire's, who called his *lecteur* a hypocrite, because he also called him his double, his *frère*. He has also written that these "novels are frequently formless, or when form presides it's mechanical, lacking instinct, desire, feeling, life (nostalgia is the honest bloodstream of his books, their skin his witty and wonderful eye). . . ." What Gass seems not to admire in Nabokov is the gamesmanship, especially when it is pedantic and when it does not sever itself from a conception of author as Master so much as refract this mastery in elaborate mirrorings. "Even a sentence which fails the demands of the body," Gass writes,

> which calls upon only the deductive faculty, which does not fuse the total self in a single act of sense and thought and feeling, is artisitically incomplete, for when the great dancer leaps, he leaves nothing of himself behind, he leaps *with,* and *into,* all he is, and never merely climbs the air with his feet. Nabokov's novels often . . . seem like those Renaissance designs of flying machines—dreams enclosed in finely drawn lines—which are intended to intrigue, to dazzle, but not to fly.

> Form makes a body of a book, puts all its parts in a system of internal relationships so severe, uncompromising, and complete that changes in them anywhere alter everything; it also unties the work from its author and the world, establishing, with them, only external relations, and never borrowing its being from things outside it-

self. A still umbilicaled book is no more formed than a fetus.

In his quest for "significant form"—for a self-contained book / body—for an *un*-umbilicaled "wife"—Gass creates a work that is intended to intrigue, to dazzle, *perhaps* to come with its reader, but *not* to conceive a perpetually open textuality. We might wish to say of Gass what one character in John Rechy's *City of Night* says of another: "And where his heart should be, there is a novel." Nostalgia, however, is also the honest bloodstream of Gass' book.

Gass' ironic comments on what Derrida might term the cultural rejection of writing as primary often take a curious expression:

> That novels should be made of words, and merely words, is shocking, really. It's as though you had discovered that your wife were made of rubber: the bliss of all those years, the fears . . . from sponge. . . . For the novelist to be at all, in any way, like a mathematician is shocking. It's worse than discovering your privates are plastic.

We may recall how often penises and breasts appear as balloons in *Willie Masters',* how pivotal the image of the "plastic sack" is, and how Babs positions herself as imagination imagining itself imagine against men who no longer can imagine without outside stimuli: "and so they need some flesh-like copy, some sexy pix and rubber lover, a substitute in plasti-goop or blanket-cloth to keep them safe, to keep them clean of fact and fancy." It is impossible to tell, finally, whether Gass champions textuality as sexuality or whether he seeks the metaphoric speech of love's body: an honest nostalgia.

It is also possible, however, that this dichotomy does not apply: that this nostalgia is the sentimental underbelly of a brilliant but brittle aesthetic surface: that Gass sustains a Modernist dream of form, a dream that his ambivalence operates within, disrupts, and finally begins to subvert. Gass wants to leap, unified, into the dance of art, "leaving nothing of himself behind"; but he also wants to stage himself as a Master—as a performing self—in a stripper's dance. The two desires may be incompatible. Gass—as he says of Nabokov—does not so much disappear as withdraw behind his multiple refractions. In this, he may participate in what Herbert Blau views, negatively, as a Postmodern solipsism:

> The solipsistic self is a tautology—all assertions curving back upon themselves in a kind of metaphysical redundancy. If the self is neither body nor soul but only self, not anything else in the world, it is only a metaphysical subject—it vanishes behind the mirror of thought. . . . It would seem as if in this mirror there is only one future, and that is the future of an illusion.

I would say that in *Willie Masters' Lonesome Wife,* Gass is at the extreme verge of Modernist authority as it withdraws into a Postmodern funhouse of mirrors—a funhouse from which it may emerge in yet another transformation. (pp. 63-7)

Charles Caramello, "Fleshing Out 'Willie Masters' Lonesome Wife'," in Sub-Stance, *Vol. IX, No. 2, 1980, pp. 56-69.*

Eusebio L. Rodrigues (essay date 1980)

[*In the following essay, Rodrigues examines Gass's "Order of Insects."*]

William Gass's **"Order of Insects"** is a translation into fiction of Plato's observation that perception is a form of pain. A Kafkalike piece, it focuses on a moment of vision that breaks up a whole way of existence. A woman tells of this breakup, which she cannot explain.

Gass compels the reader into his fictive world by using intense focusing. The woman has no face, no name, no real past. Not a character, she is a state of consciousness, deeply shocked by the mysterious nightly appearance of large dead roaches on the carpet of a house the family recently moved into. Gass endows her with a voice and a language that convey the vibrations of this shock. The voice is at first calm and neutral, clearly striving to maintain a difficult equilibrium. Gradually the listener becomes aware of its subtle rhythms, its hidden intensities, its sudden ebbs and flows. The language of this voice, like the identity of its speaker, has been stripped clean of local and national accents. It uses unusual nouns like "startle" and "caesar" (with a small c), turns "museum" into a verb, borrows Shakespeare's use of the verb "beggar," and employs a startling turn of phrase as in "the skull-shaped skull" or "a stream of pins." It is a language put together by Gass to project the woman's trembling sensibility and the strange logic of her intuitions.

The woman speaks to herself trying to understand what has happened to her. Gass avoids monotony by charging the soliloquy with tensions, deliberately unresolved. There is the woman that was and the woman that is. Her impulse to change battles against her impulse to resist change. Gass makes the reader aware of these conflicts by seesawing the past and the present tenses, and by the adverbial time-signals, "at first" opposed to "now." "Order of Insects" enacts the complex tangled process (which the reader has to linearize) by which the woman strives painfully towards an understanding of the "recent alteration" in her life.

At first she had shuddered when she saw those "fierce, ugly, armored things." She relives the first moment of shock: it was the middle of the night; she had shouted at the children warning them that the bugs were "infectious and their own disease"; with a handkerchief to her face she had glanced at them with horror and repulsion. The next day, haunted by guilt and angry with herself, she "screws" her eyes onto the bugs. Gass's metaphor dramatizes the immense effort involved.

Her eyes cone down to see not bugs but embodiments of "gracious order, wholeness, and divinity." The nymphs (a technical term for insects in a stage of transition) are golden in color; the adults have wingsheaths with a dark shine. Their legs look like the canes of a rose. She notes the intricate gauzelike meshwork on their wings, the geo-metrical precision of their button-like compound eyes. Wonderstruck, she can touch them and collects their marvelously preserved shapes.

She now has a totally different perspective on the world. Her former world had been one of suburban routine with its usual jingle of worries: "Is the burner on under the beans? the washing machine's obscure disease may reoccur, it rumbles on rinse and rattles on wash; my god it's already eleven o'clock; which one of you has lost a galosh?" Her life, measured by her daily chores, had been patterned and meticulous. This order, she now realizes, is false, man-imposed, an act of reduction: "What do we live with that's alive we haven't tamed—people like me?—even our houseplants breathe by our permission." Technology has compelled man into an existence symbolized by the identical blocks he lives in; it has created an order she is now horrified of: "It is the sewing machine that has the fearful claw."

The reader has to hold in suspension the woman's implied feelings about her own and human existence, for the story is not about the order of insects but about human disorder. "Corruption, in these bugs, is splendid," the woman states. The implication is that the corruption of the human body after death and burial is ugly and shocking. The difference in the supporting structures of man and insect is significant: while man's skeleton is internal, an insect wears its skeleton on the outside of its body. The internal flesh of an insect decays after death, but its tubular structure *lives*. Man's outer features, which he so loves, perish and his skeleton, his permanent and beautiful part, is cast into the oblivion of the grave. A curious logic, this. But behind the logic can be heard a lament on human mortality and impermanence.

In contrast the bugs are mysterious and immortal. So taken is she with the marvel of their being that she is a woman possessed. Her dreams are so intense that her waking life seems a mere dream. She imagines the roaches summoned into existence out of nowhere, dead as soon as materialized, translated into immortality by her household cat. But death does not spell decay, for they remain intense and "immortally arranged." The experience is beautiful, profound and terrible.

It is beautiful because insects are living works of art (as all textbooks of entomology proclaim). Their glistening shells are like the gaze of Gauguin's natives' eyes. The profundity of the experience is indicated by a phrase the woman uses for the true soul of a roach—"the dark soul of the world." The phrase (which leaps catlike into her consciousness) suggests the vibrant oneness which the earth shares with the roach, the "darkly invisible" cat, and the woman. The roach is the most primitive of insects, having crawled out originally from the womb of the earth. A cat is a mystical manifestation of the pure animal spirit. The woman feels instinctively drawn to these two creatures, as she did to Gauguin's natives, because they appeal to the most primitive and natural level of her being. The manmade world of technology has polluted this being but not rooted it out. That is why the thick rug makes her wish her bare feet would swallow her shoes. When her husband vacuums the red ants in her kitchen (she could never kill any insect), she has a nightmare about being one of them trapped in the suction tube.

The experience of beauty and of natural order leads, strangely, to a pure terror. The woman has always lived in a state of fear. Convinced that life is one of turmoil and confusion and that it has to be endured, she had spun around herself a cocoon of deadening routine. Now she can perceive a superior order and permanence she never knew existed: "But this bug that I hold in my hand and know to be dead is beautiful, and there is a fierce joy in its composition that beggars every other, for its joy is the joy of stone, and it lives in its tomb like a lion." It is this perception that causes the keen pain, for accompanying it is the realization that she (and all human beings) can never achieve such supreme order. Only briefly does she experience this order when her mind stops functioning at night and when she lies, shell-like, turned inside out like an insect.

"Order of Insects" presents an oblique, bitter view of the human condition. Human life is seen as a disease (the word recurs throughout the story). Human order is unnatural and sterile. A human being, subject to decay, can never experience peace because of the split between his body, which belongs to the natural world, and his soul (mind, consciousness) which gives him "the point of view of a god." The roach does not suffer from such a division, its body and soul are one, its joy is the joy of stone. The woman is aware of the painful conflicts within her being: "Nonetheless my body resists such knowledge. It wearies of its edge." Torn between the two orders, this "nymph" is in torment. "O my husband, they are a terrible disease," she shouts silently, using the same word she had flung at her children. The word now indicates that the bugs have invaded her being and have infected her own life.

For now she collects insects and loves them. She watches the perfect rounds squeezed from the rectal ends of caterpillars and notes the graceful curves they make when they crawl. At times she studies the roaches with a "manly passion" like an entomologist, but this kind of knowledge does not satisfy her. At other times she tries to reassure herself that what she has seen is merely "a squat black cockroach after all, such a bug as frightens housewives." But she knows that she has undergone a metamorphosis and developed "a pair of dreadful eyes." Eyes like Galileo's, who watched the swinging lamp in the Pisa cathedral and discovered the wonderful laws of mathematical physics. Eyes like Gauguin's, who created the beautiful order that art imposes on existence.

Such a mode of vision makes the woman feel that she has been "entrusted with a kind of eastern mystery, sacred to a dreadful god." "I am not worthy," she says, the Biblical phrase implying that such divine knowledge should not have entered under her womanly roof. For her state now is one of endless anguish. The story is a woman's prayer for deliverance and for peace, a cry of pain that erupts from one who knows the bleak truth about man's fate and the human condition. Gass leaves the woman poised on the edge of temptation: she tilts dangerously towards a nonhuman world of peace, order and beauty, but is pulled back by the order she still inhabits as a wife of the house

(not of a man), "concerned for the rug, tidy and punctual, surrounded by blocks." (pp. 348-51)

Eusebio L. Rodrigues, "A Nymph at Her Orisons: An Analysis of William Gass's 'Order of Insects'," in Studies in Short Fiction, *Vol. 17, No. 3, Summer, 1980, pp. 348-51.*

Larry McCaffery   (essay date 1982)

[*In the following excerpt, McCaffery discusses the ways in which Gass makes the reader aware of the physicality of the printed word in* Willie Masters' Lonesome Wife.]

Shattering conventional expectations about how we read or how a work of fiction should be organized, *Willie Masters* is an especially clear and ambitious representation of a metafictional work—and a virtual casebook of literary experimentalism as well.

Interestingly enough, *Willie Masters* is actually only one section of a much longer work which Gass began in the early 1960s. Before he abandoned the project as being impractical—it was originally to have dealt metafictionally with almost every narrative mode known to Western literature—two other short excerpts appeared: **"The Sugar Crock"** and **"The Clairvoyant."** Like *Willie Masters,* these pieces are metafictional reflections on the nature of fiction making with self-conscious narrators pondering their relationship to their creations. Although they do not provide much background for *Willie Masters,* they do introduce a few of the people who appear in the later work. Ella Bend, mentioned in passing in *Willie Masters,* is the central character in both stories; we also meet Phil Gelvin, the unresponsive lover in *Willie Masters,* as a rakish shoe salesman and "Baby Babs" Masters herself, mentioned only in an unflattering comparison with another character ("fat in the belly like a sow, thick through his thighs like Willie Masters' Lonesome Wife").

Gass's basic intention in *Willie Masters* is to build a work which will literally embody the idea with which he opens his essay, "The Medium of Fiction":

> It seems a country-headed thing to say: that literature is language, that stories and the places and the people in them are merely made of words as chairs are made of smoothed sticks and sometimes of cloth or metal tubes. . . . That novels should be made of words, and merely words, is shocking really. It's as though you had discovered that your wife were made of rubber: the bliss of all those years, the fears . . . from sponge.

Just as he does in his essays, in *Willie Masters* Gass reminds us that literature is made of words and nothing else. Here the words themselves are constantly called to our attention, and their sensuous qualities are emphasized in nearly every imaginable fashion. Indeed, the narrator of the work—the "Lonesome Wife" of the title—is lady language herself. Although the narrative has no real plot or even any fully developed characters, the book's "events" occur while Babs makes love to a particularly unresponsive lover named Gelvin; this introduces the central metaphor of the whole work: that parallels exist—or should exist—between a woman and her lover, between the work of art and the artist, between a book and its reader. The unifying metaphor is evident even before we open the book: on the front cover is a frontal photograph of a naked woman; on the back cover is a corresponding photograph of the backside of the same woman. Thus Gass invites his readers to enter this work of art—a woman made of words and paper—with the same sort of excitement, participation, and creative energy that a man would ideally have in entering a woman's body in sexual intercourse. The poetnarrator in Gass's "In the Heart of the Heart of the Country" explains why this metaphor is so appropriate when he says that "poetry, like love, is—in and out—a physical caress." Babs puts it more bluntly: "How close in the end is a cunt to a concept; we enter both with joy" (white section). As we discover from Babs, all too frequently those who enter her do so without enthusiasm, often seemingly unaware that she is there at all. Indeed, like all of Gass's major characters, Babs is an isolated, lonely individual who longs to make contact with the outside world but is unable to do so. Thus, as Tony Tanner suggests, Gass's title introduces a paradoxical notion into the work:

> We may note immediately that a lonesome wife is already a potential paradox suggesting both solitude and connection, a lapsed contract, a failed union, and the text concerns itself with those things which both join and separate us—lips, sexual organs, dances, words. There is a hovering parallel between semen given and taken away (in a contraceptive) and semantics, meanings which we own and lose.

As an appropriate extension of the metaphor, the central orderings of the book are loosely based on the stages of sexual intercourse. In order to embody these parallels more closely, Gass uses the color and texture of the page rather than relying on traditional chapter divisions and pagination to indicate subtle alterations in Babs's mind. Even the page itself is not ordered in the usual linear fashion; instead, typographical variations establish a different visual order for each individual page. The first eight pages are printed on blue, thin paper with very little texture; these pages suggest the rather slow beginnings of intercourse and Babs's playful, low-intensity thoughts and remembrances. The next twelve pages are thicker, more fully textured, and olive in color; this section, which is also the most varied in typography and graphics, corresponds to the rising stages of Babs's sexual excitement and her wildly divergent thoughts. Next follow eight red pages, with paper of the same texture as the first section, suggesting the climax of intercourse and the direct, intensely intellectual climax of Babs's thoughts about language. Finally, the fourth section uses a thick, high-gloss white paper like that of expensive magazines; these pages parallel Babs's empty, lonely feelings after intercourse when she realizes how inadequate the experience has been. Reinforcing the feelings produced by color and texture are the photographs of Babs's nude body interspersed throughout the book. The first section opens with a picture of her upper torso and face, with her mouth eagerly awaiting the printer's phallic S-block (not coincidentally, a similar S-block opens Joyce's *Ulysses*). As the book continues, her face becomes less prominent and her body itself is emphasized. The photo at the beginning of the white section shows Babs curled up in a fetal position, her head resting upon her knees in a position indicating her sad, lonely feelings of resignation and rejection.

But by far the most intricately developed method used by Babs to call attention to her slighted charms is the wide variety of type styles with which she constructs herself. One of the functions of these typographic changes—at least in the blue and red sections—is to indicate different levels of Babs's consciousness. The opening blue section, for instance, is divided into three monologues printed mainly in three separate, standard typefaces: roman, italic, and boldface. With these typographic aids, we can separate the strands of Babs's thoughts roughly as follows: the roman sections deal with her memories about the past and her concern with words; the italic sections indicate her memories of her first sexual encounter; and the boldface sections present her views about the nature of bodily processes (another obsession of many of Gass's characters) and their relation to her aspirations for "saintly love." The blue section can be read largely as an ordinary narrative, from top to bottom, left to right; the different typefaces, however, enable us to read each of Bab's thoughts *as a whole* (by reading all the italics as a unit, then reading the boldface sections, etc.). In the olive and red sections, however, the graphics and typography destroy any linear response by the reader.

Gass's aim in using such techniques is to achieve, like Joyce in *Ulysses,* a freedom from many of our language's traditionally imposed rules of syntax, diction, and punctuation. To help emphasize the incredible versatility of human consciousness, Joyce relied on a wide range of linguistic parodies of earlier literary styles (most notably in the "Cyclops" and the "Oxen of the Sun" episodes). Like his fellow Irishman, Laurence Sterne, Joyce was also quite willing to use unusual typographical devices to help present his parodies. Such devices—Sterne's blank and marbled pages, Joyce's headlines, question-and-answer format, the typographic formality of the "Circe" episode—are foreign to the "pure" storyteller but are available to modern writers by the nature of books and print alone. Hugh Kenner persuasively argues that Joyce hoped to liberate the narration of *Ulysses* from the typographical conventions of ordinary narratives and notes that the linear, one-dimensional method of presenting most books simply could not do justice to Joyce's expansive view of language: "There is something mechanical, Joyce never lets us forget, about all reductions of speech to arrangements of twenty-six letters. We see him playing in every possible way with the spatial organization of printed marks." Kenner's remarks are perceptive, although he overstates his case when he says that Joyce experimented with printed marks "in every possible way." Gass's more directly metafictional work, written fifty years later in the age of McLuhan (himself a Joyce scholar), carries the methods of typographical freedom to a much fuller development.

Gass's intentions in ***Willie Masters*** can be compared to Joyce's in other ways. Like Joyce's presentation of a parodic history of English styles in the "Oxen of the Sun" section, Gass's work is practically a history of typography. One of Gass's original intentions for *Willie Masters* was to reproduce the first-edition typefaces of any lines taken from other works, something which would have visually emphasized the highly diverse natures of those voices who have "used Babs" in the past. This intention proved to be impractical, but type styles can be found here from nearly every period since Gutenberg, ranging from pre-printing press calligraphy to old German gothic, Victorian typefaces, and modern advertising boldface.

In addition to mimicking typefaces, Gass presents many other typographic conventions, often with parodic intent. One amusing example is found in the olive section in which a one-act play is presented with all the rigid typographical formality usually found in a written transcription of a play. Babs provides asterisked comments and explanations about stage directions, costumes, and props. These remarks begin in a very small type, but as the play progresses the typeface becomes larger and bolder. Gradually the number of asterisks before each aside becomes impossible to keep up with, and the comments themselves become so large that the text of the play is crowded off the page—to make room for a page containing only large, star-shaped asterisks. Gass thus pokes fun at typographic conventions much as John Barth does with his manipulation of quotation marks in "The Menelaid." Gass also uses the asterisks for reasons we do not usually consider with a work of fiction: for their *visual* appeal. As Babs notes, "These asterisks are the prettiest things in print" (olive section). Throughout the olive and red sections there are many other examples of typographic variations: concrete poems, quoted dialogue inscribed in comic-book "balloons," pages which resemble eye-charts, a Burroughs-like newspaper "cut-up," and even the representation of coffee stains.

In addition to drawing attention to the visual qualities of words, Gass also forces us to reexamine the whole process of how we read words. In particular, Gass reminds us that the Western conventions of reading—left to right, top to bottom, from first page to last—are all merely conventions that can be altered. Indeed, as Michel Butor has pointed out, even in Western cultures we are probably much more familiar than we probably realize with books which do not rely on linear development (books like dictionaries, manuals, telephone directories, and encyclopedias): "It is a misconception for us to think that the only kinds of books are those which transcribe a discourse running from start to finish, a narrative or essay, in which it is natural to read by starting on the first page in order to finish on the last." In *Willie Masters,* especially in the olive and red sections, Gass typographically makes ordinary reading procedures impossible. In the red section, for example, Babs begins four or five narratives on a single page. In order to follow these largely unrelated narratives, each presented in a different typeface, we cannot begin at the top of the page and read down; instead, we are forced to follow one narrative from page to page and then return to the beginning of the section for the second narrative. Like Joyce, who requires us to move backward and forward to check and cross-check references, Gass takes advantage of what Kenner terms "the book as book." This disjointedness is an advan-

tage; the use of asterisks and marginal glosses indicates Gass's willingness to take advantage of the expressive possibilities of literature's form as words on the printed page. Kenner has pointed out the effect of using such typographical methods to deflect the eye from its usual horizontal / vertical network in a discussion of the use of footnotes:

> The man who composes a footnote, and sends it to the printer along with his text, has discovered among the devices of printed language something analogous to counterpoint: a way of speaking in two voices at once, or of ballasting or modifying or even bombarding with exceptions his own discourse without interrupting it. It is a step in the direction of discontinuity: of organizing blocks of discourse simultaneously in space rather than consecutively in time.

Throughout *Willie Masters* Gass never allows our eyes to move easily along the page from left to right and top to bottom; instead, we turn from page to page, moving backward and forward, moving our eyes up and down in response to asterisks or footnotes, from left to right to check marginal glosses, and occasionally standing back to observe the organization of the page as a whole (as when we note that one page is shaped like a Christmas tree, another like an eye chart). The effect is remarkably close to Kenner's description of "blocks of discourse" organized "simultaneously in space rather than consecutively in time."

The last and most significant method used by Babs to call attention to herself is also probably the least radical of her strategies. It involves the sensuous, highly poetic quality of the language which she uses to create herself. Of course, a fundamental aspect of most poetry is a focus on words, but in ordinary discourse and in the language of literary realism, the "utility function" of words is usually primarily emphasized. As Babs explains, "The usual view is that you see through me, through what I am really—significant sound" (red section). Babs, however, is extremely vain about her physical qualities and resentful when she is used but is not noticed. In suggesting that when words are placed into an aesthetic context their utility is sacrificed in favor of a unity of sound and sense, Babs is also paraphrasing one of the key features of Gass's own aesthetic stance:

> Again there is in every act of imagination a disdain of utility, and a glorious, free show of human strength; for the man of imagination dares to make things for no better reason than they please him—because he *lives*. And everywhere, again, he seeks out unity: in the word he unifies both sound and sense; . . . between words and things he further makes a bond so that symbols seem to contain their objects.
>
>   (Red section)

A bit earlier in the same section, Babs even goes so far as to suggest that of all the methods of discourse available to man, only her language—"the language of imagination"—allows man to fully express his human qualities:

> Well then: there's the speech of science and good sense—daily greetings, reminiscences and news, and all those kind directions how-to; there's the speech of the ultimate mind, abstract, soldierly,

efficient, and precise; and then there's mine, for when you use me, when you speak in my tongue—the language of imagination—you speak of fact and feeling, order and spontaneity, suddenness and long decision, desire and reservation—all at once. It is the only speech which fills the balloon of the whole man, which proceeds not from this part or from that, in answer to this isolated issue or that well and widely advertised necessity, because, although it may have a focus . . . nevertheless, it is always—when right, when best, when most beautiful—an expression of a unity, and ideal and even terrible completeness—everywhere rich and deep and full—and therefore—let me warn you, let me insist—can only come from one who is, at least while speaking in that poet's habit, what we— what each of us—should somehow be: a complete particular man. That's why imaginative language can not be duplicated; why it is both a consequence of enormous skill, of endless art, but also a sign in the speaker of his awesome humanity.

(Red section)

But like Barthelme's Snow White, who says, "Oh I wish there were some words in the world that were not the words I always hear!" Babs is bored with her own existence. "Why aren't there any decent words?" she exclaims in the blue section; and in a footnote to the play in the olive section, she compares the "dreary words" of ordinary prose to ordinary action in the theater which often loses all subtlety and beauty as it strains to make itself understood to an audience "all of whom are in the second balcony." Babs shares with Gass the opinion that both readers and writers are too often unresponsive to the body of literature—a body made of language. At one point she comments on the writer's necessity to accept the medium in which he works. The passage is typical of the lyrically expressive, highly poetic language favored by Babs throughout her monologue:

> You are your body—you do not choose the feet you walk in—and the poet is his language. He sees the world, and words form in his eyes just like the streams and trees there. He feels everything verbally. Objects, passions, actions—I myself believe that the true kiss comprises a secret exchange of words, for the mouth was made by God to give form and sound to syllables; permit us to make, as our souls move, the magic music of names, for to say Cecilia, even in secret, is to make love.
>
> (Olive section)

These remarks not only emphasize the purely verbal nature of the poet's enterprise, they also reinforce the sexual parallels between writing and lovemaking. Even as we read these words, we have "in secret" been making love to Babs—and one hopes our response has been better than Gelvin's.

If poetry is the language in which Babs tries to realize herself, she admits that she rarely finds lovers appreciative enough to create her properly. Apparently her encounter with Gelvin is a typically unsatisfactory one, for when he leaves, Babs says, "He did not, in his address, at any time,

construct me. He made nothing, I swear. Empty I began, and empty I remained" (white section). Indeed, she even anticipates various inadequacies on our own part, as when she asks us, "Is that any way to make love to a lady, a lonely one at that, used formerly to having put the choicest portions of her privates flowered out in pots and vases?" (red section). The main problem, as Babs observes, is simply that we have forgotten how to make love appreciatively: "You can't make love like that anymore—make love or manuscript. Yet I have put my hand upon this body, here as no man ever has, and I have even felt my pencil stir, grow great with blood. But never has it swollen up in love. It moves in anger, always, against its paper" (red section). Today readers and writers alike approach lady language in the wrong spirit, looking for the wrong sorts of things. And the pencil—the writer's phallic instrument of creation—grows great nowadays only with blood or anger, never with love. After intercourse, Babs is left alone to contemplate the sterile whiteness of the last section; here she sits and ponders her fate: "They've done, the holy office over, and they turn their back on me, I'm what they left, their turds in the toilet. Anyway, I musn't wonder why they don't return. Maybe I should put a turnstile in" (red section).

Lonely, misunderstood, and often ignored, Babs spends a good deal of her time considering her own nature and the relationship between words and the world. In the olive section, for instance, she half-quotes John Locke's discussion of the way in which language develops from sense to impression to perception to concept. Locke shows how our understanding sorts out our perceptions; he concludes that we give proper names to things "such as men have an occasion to mark particularly." Babs has taken Locke's view to heart, for she constantly muses over the appropriateness of names in just this fashion. She wonders, for instance, why men do not assign proper names to various parts of their anatomy:

> They ought to name their noses like they named their pricks. Why not their ears too?—they frequently stick out. This is my morose Slave nose, Czar Nicholas. And these twins in my mirror, Reuben and Antony, they have large soft lobes. . . . If you had nice pleasant names for yourself all over, you might feel more at home, more among friends.
>
> (Blue section)

As this passage indicates, Babs confers upon language the same magical potency which Stephen Dedalus gave it in *A Portrait of the Artist as a Young Man:* she exalts the habit of verbal association into a principle for the arrangement of experience. And, of course, she is right—words do help us arrange and particularize our experience. In this sense words are connectors, for if we have a means of touching and naming something, then we are given a sort of power over it; we become master of a situation, in part, by simply being able to put it into words. Babs is also proud of the fact that although men die (both literally and sexually), language does not. "I dream like Madame Bovary," Babs says in the blue section. "Only I don't die, during endings. I never die." In the olive section she compares her own ethereal existence ("I'm only a string of noises, after all—nothing more really—an arrangement of air moving up and down") with the unfortunate, mortal condition of man: "You see? a man, a mere man, mortal, his death in his pocket like a letter he's forgotten, could not be that, could not be beautiful. . . . Oh you unfortunate animals—made so differently, so disastrously—dying." If it is immortality we seek, she tells us, we can find it only in the community of concepts: "Only here in the sweet country of the word are rivers, streams, woods, gardens, houses, mountains, waterfalls and the crowding fountains of the trees eternal as it's right they should be."

On the other hand, Babs is also haunted by what she terms "the terror of terminology" (blue section), that is, the failure of language to adequately express or suggest what it is supposed to. As noted earlier, words are one means of "touching" reality, embracing it, and just as Babs is made lonely by the failure of her lovers to embrace her ardently, so too is she continually depressed by the failures of language adequately to embrace reality. Tony Tanner summarizes the implications of this idea in *Willie Masters:*

> We are creatures of ever-attempting, ever-failing modes of attachment. We try to adhere ourselves to other bodies through embraces and holdings and adhere to the world through words and concepts. Yet the text constantly touches on the dread involved in the sense of failure of all our adhesions and adherences.

As might be expected, when Babs offers some examples of the way in which words fail us, they are typically drawn from sexual contexts: "Screw—they say *screw*—what an ideal! did any of them ever? It's the lady who wooves and woogles. Nail—bang—sure—*nail* is nearer theirs" (blue section).

Because of her envy of poetic language, Babs is especially interested in circumstances—as with the language of any great poet such as Shakespeare—where the words become something more than simply Lockean devices for calling to mind concepts. Babs's concept of the poetic ideal coincides almost exactly with Gass's own view of the ideal language in literature: words in literature lie midway between the "words of nature" (which constitute reality) and the words of ordinary language (which are nothing in themselves but arbitrary symbols directing our minds elsewhere). In the olive section Babs explains her view of the qualities of ordinary words:

> What's in a name but letters, eh? and everyone owns *them.* . . . The sound SUN or the figures S, U, N, are purely arbitrary modes of recalling their objects, and they have the further advantage of being nothing *per se,* for while the sun, itself, is large and orange and boiling, the sight and the sound, SUN, is but a hiss drawn up through the nose.

At times Babs exploits the sound of words at the expense of their sense (or referential quality) in a way which may remind us of Poe's poetry or that of the French Symbolists. For instance, she takes one of her favorite words—*catafalque*—and repeats it for several lines just because she likes the way it sounds. She then creates a lovely-sounding but totally nonsensical poem: "catafalque cata-

falque neighborly mew / Ozenfant Valéry leonine nu" (olive section). What Babs really seems to be searching for, at least in her own creation, is the kind of fusion of sound and sense that can be found in the best poetry. As she says admiringly of Shakespeare, "Now the language of Shakespeare . . . not merely recalls the cold notion of the thing, it expresses and becomes a part of its reality, so that the sight and sound, SUN, in Shakespeare is warm and orange and greater than the page it lies on" (olive section). It is precisely this sort of fusion, of course, that Gass is searching for in his own writing.

Willie Masters, then, is one of the purest and most complexly developed metafictions to yet appear. If Babs (Gass) has succeeded, our attention has been focused on the act of reading words in ways we have never before experienced. As Tony Tanner puts it, "Gass's text takes us into the heart of the heart of the desolations of our corporeal existence, but it also takes us into 'the sweet country of the word'—writer and reader talking and dying alike, the lonesome self losing and recreating itself in language, the prisonhouse turning itself into the playhouse before our very eyes." At the end of the book, we encounter a reminder from Gass stamped onto the page: "YOU HAVE FALLEN INTO ART—RETURN TO LIFE." When we do return to life, we have, hopefully, a new appreciation of—and perhaps even love for—that lonesome lady in Gass's title. (pp. 171-83)

> *Larry McCaffery, "William H. Gass: The World Within the Word," in his* The Metafictional Muse: The Works of Robert Coover, Donald Barthelme, and William H. Gass, *University of Pittsburgh Press, 1982, pp. 151-250.*

Arthur M. Saltzman (essay date 1986)

[*In the following excerpt from his study* The Fiction of William Gass: The Consolation of Language, *Saltzman discusses the "Pedersen Kid," "Order of Insects," and "In the Heart of the Heart of the Country."*]

Despite the ambition and complexity of *Omensetter's Luck,* William Gass's notoriety as a writer of fiction is typically attributed to his collection of short stories, *In the Heart of the Heart of the Country.* These stories appeared in 1968, two years after the publication of his novel. By Gass's own estimation, *In the Heart* contains much of his most successful writing to date; in addition, several of the stories—namely, the title piece, **"The Pedersen Kid,"** and **"The Order of Insects"**—are among the most consistently anthologized works of recent "experimental" fiction, ranking Gass alongside John Barth, Donald Barthelme, and Robert Coover in terms of visibility on college syllabi. (p. 57)

Jethro Furber, the dominant consciousness of *Omensetter's Luck,* can be seen as a precursor of the narrators presented in [Gass's] stories. Each narrator is a mind in retreat, or, as the unnamed storyteller in the concluding story refers to himself, an eye driven inward; each hopes to secure a reliable refuge (resembling Furber's verbal architecture) that serves as an alternative to a world characterized as violent, tedious, loveless, or downright inscrutable.

Surely the environmental circumstances surrounding **"The Pedersen Kid"** seem to vindicate the flight of the narrator, young Jorge Segren, into the interior life. In contrast to Furber's thickly-worded garden, however, the words here barely emerge intact. Language is spare and brittle. Articulation, the definitive achievement of the fictional artist, withers against the frozen backdrop, where a ponderous silence rules.

> Big Hans yelled, so I came out. The barn was dark, but the sun burned on the snow. Hans was carrying something from the crib. I yelled, but Big Hans didn't hear. He was in the house with what he had before I reached the steps.
>
> It was the Pedersen Kid. Hans had put the kid on the kitchen table like you would a ham and started the kettle. He wasn't saying anything. I guess he figured one yell from the crib was enough noise. Ma was fumbling with the kid's clothes which were stiff with ice. She made a sound like whew from every breath. The kettle filled and Hans said,
>
> Get some snow and call your pa.
> Why?
>
> Get some snow.

The bleak landscape exerts a petrifying influence on the language generated there, and we might infer a metaphorical connection between the slow, ritualistic revival of the Pedersen Kid after his rescue from the snowstorm and Jorge's private establishment of consciousness and free will, which is described throughout the story in terms of a growing warmth inside him. As if to demonstrate Jorge's need to define himself apart from his environment, Gass reserves the lyrical passages of **"The Pedersen Kid"** for interior monologue—the sole context where beauty can develop uncontaminated.

Of the five stories in the collection, the first is the one most ostensibly indebted to the realistic tradition: conventions such as a powerfully realized setting, discreet characterization, and the familiar plot structure of a journey leading to some pivotal revelation are prominent components of **"The Pedersen Kid."** Relentlessly convoluted in design, as though the all-encompassing blizzard in the story were rendering all perception hesitant and indistinct, **"The Pedersen Kid"** is replete with allegorical options for the discerning reader and is equally accommodating to Freudian, Christian, and heraldic archetypes. Nevertheless, these designs are merely scaffolds for the language they occasion. Despite Gass's surface adherence to the tenets of literary realism, according to which the tale takes priority over the technique, the shaping of a narrative detachment ultimately precedes the particulars of whatever "actually happened."

As he did in *Omensetter's Luck,* Gass delves into a well-worn motif—a rite of initiation—to focus his symbolic analysis of the awakening of artistic temperament as exhibited by the unfolding of language. One dismal morning in North Dakota, Big Hans discovers the half-dead body

of the Pedersen kid, a boy from a nearby farm, lying in the snow outside the Segren place. Once inside, Hans and Jorge return the frozen boy to consciousness with the aid of massage and Pa Segren's precious whiskey. The kid struggles to tell them that a stranger broke into his house and was holding his parents captive in the fruit cellar; the boy had managed to escape into the blizzard, but he feared that the menacing stranger had murdered his parents. After an argument with Jorge's brutish, alcoholic father, the three of them—Jorge, Pa, and Big Hans—grudgingly board their wagon and head for the Pedersen place. Finding the stranger's frozen horse, Hans and Pa, whose mutual antagonism is apparent throughout the story, become temporary allies in the dubious project of tunneling through the snowdrift on the far side of the house as a surprise tactic. That effort proving useless, they advance to the barn, but they are reluctant to risk crossing the open space and entering the house. Jorge finally does so, but when his father follows, a gunshot drops him. The boy breaks through a basement window and huddles in anxious expectation of a confrontation with death. Curiously, the stranger never appears, and Jorge is left to contemplate his isolation, the presumed deaths of all the adults at the hands of the killer, and the sudden wellspring of joy he feels burning within him.

So goes the plot. But to be seduced by the naturalistic skin of the story into trying to burrow past the dense language in order to uncover the message buried beneath it is to discard the story's greater import, which has to do with the accumulation and patterning of the words themselves. Clearing away language so as to better view plot is self-defeating. Indeed, instead of illuminating the symbolic structure of the plot as the story progresses—a common aim of realistic fiction, in which perseverance is rewarded with the reliable dismantling of mystery—Gass steers us into cul-de-sacs, lets loose ends dangle, and plunges without warning into subjective distortions. Given his theoretical position that the verbal configuration itself (the pointing statue, rather than where it points) is the justification for fiction, we may well be to blame for our own misguided frustration. The identity of the yellow-gloved killer and the fates of the rest of the characters, both discoveries toward which the story seems to be directed, are not resolved; suspense is not relieved, as though the story purges itself of external distractions as it moves forward and refines out everything but the narrator's churning consciousness. Mental activity ultimately takes priority over the amenities of plot, and the central theme becomes the attempt to deliver oneself, if only psychologically, from the rigors of daily existence.

The dominant metaphors of heat and cold give continual evidence of this desire. Every character yearns to somehow create "spring inside": Big Hans secludes himself with his pictures of naked women; Pa fondles his whiskey bottle; his wife finds her solace in the maintenance of the household routine and in organizing her meager kitchen; and Jorge consoles himself with intricate dreams of prowess and liberation. Furthermore, these secret comforts provide the main source of self-worth for these characters. At times, for example, Pa displays a physical affection for his bottles—surely no person elicits such devoted feelings from him; paranoid about pilferage, he hides them about his property. "He took pride in his hiding," thinks Jorge, fearing his father's reaction to the fact that his mother had quickly rooted out a bottle for the failing Pedersen kid. "It was all the pride he had." Pride in hiding applies equally well to Jorge, who must always be alert to the incursions of hatred from his elders. He still recalls with pain and furor Pa's mutilation of his story book; it is a response very much in keeping with that of his father to the discovery of his own most precious possession. "I was cold in your house always, pa," the boy silently accuses, for the lack of intimacy and compassion there makes it little better than the wintry landscape outside.

No wonder that Jorge's immediate reaction to the arrival of the helpless Pedersen kid is one of resentment, for the frozen child commands center stage in a way Jorge, who regularly dodges physical abuse, never has. Jorge takes some satisfaction in having a larger penis than the competition, and he extends his hatred for Big Hans and Pa to young Pedersen; whose dying supplants his own status in the Segren household: "I decided I hated the Pedersen kid too, dying in our kitchen while I was away where I couldn't watch, dying just to pleasure Hans and making me go up snapping steps and down a drafty hall." Pa smacks his son for waking him, and Jorge blames the Pedersen kid for that as well. In short, the appearance of the Pedersen kid emphasizes for Jorge his peripheral position. He has always been invisible because the adults around him are either incapable of or unwilling to see him; he predicts how his sodden father will blink at him "as if I were the sun off the snow and burning to blind him." Jorge targets his peer for scorn, boasting to himself that *he* would not have run if an intruder threatened his family, although in a house where he does not count, neither love nor duty seem appropriate motives for heroic sacrifice. Convinced that Pedersen's stupidity is the original cause of the kid's drinking his whiskey, Pa spews curses at him, and Jorge, in a rare display of solidarity, echoes his father's condemnations.

The decision to accept the Pedersen kid's tale results from complex and thoroughly self-centered impulses on the part of the "avengers." The fact that the warming operation performed by Big Hans is described in terms of kneading dough—the boy is resuscitated on the bread table, where he acquires a second skin of flour—is significant in the sense that the kid, as well as the plot he introduces, is being prepared for digestion. For what does **"The Pedersen Kid"**—the story and the human presence in the Segren kitchen—mean? Gass's characters are essentially faced with a malleable text, and they all take advantage of their opportunities to exercise subjective interests so as to develop a private understanding. Big Hans, Pa, and Jorge may be viewed at this point as fiction-makers, not just as an audience for the Pedersen kid. Bringing the boy to consciousness is, in addition to an act of restoration, an act of creation; it imitates Gass's construction of the text and our efforts to recapitulate and evaluate the ambiguous material before us.

Therefore, the identity of the yellow-gloved intruder, initially obscured by the Pedersen kid's fear, is buried deeper and deeper by the various prejudices of his potential benefactors. Such is Gass's layering technique: "The problem is to present evil as a visitation—sudden, mysterious, violent, inexplicable. All should be subordinated to that end. The physical representation must be spare and staccato; the mental representation must be flowing and a bit repetitious; the dialogue realistic but musical. A ritual effect is needed." Accordingly, the preternatural incarnation and menacing silence of the killer steep him in a mist of unreality; he is the abominable snowman, winter's harshness in human form.

Hans is alone in accepting the kid's story without qualification, perhaps because, having been the instrument of his salvation, Hans is compelled to unite his version of reality with the one proposed by the kid. Jorge recognizes Hans's perturbation when Pa insists that the kid was simply making the whole thing up to excuse his "fool stunt" of running off into a snowstorm: "Hans didn't like that. He didn't want to believe the kid any more than I did, but if he didn't then the kid had fooled him sure. He didn't want to believe that either." To his chagrin, Hans realizes that the truth he advocates requires him to follow through, to go to the Pedersen house and face the danger waiting there—a terrifying consequence with which Jorge delights in plaguing Hans. The kid lives for Hans and because of Hans's attention, which thereby requires him to acknowledge the killer's reality as well: "Rubbing. You didn't know what you were bringing to, did you? Something besides the kid came through the storm, Hans." So Hans grimly takes on the challenge to his pride. As for Pa, his motive for joining the expedition is to release his wrath (his own pride having been damaged by the discovery of his hidden whiskey) in the form of leering disdain for Hans.

Jorge has no personal stake in this plan at first. His Pedersen kid is dead, so the story the kid gives is negligible. Instead, Jorge is bullied into the plot by the men. (Free will must be supported by physical might in order to be respected by men like Pa and Hans.) But almost imperceptibly, Jorge's attitude toward the Pedersen kid changes as the plot unfolds. Competition slowly turns to emulation. Jorge imagines that the crawling coldness he feels in the snow matches the sensation that must have crept over the Pedersen kid earlier. Furthermore, in reversing the kid's journey, Jorge figures to reverse his fortune; he welcomes the chance to prove himself better than the kid in a crisis:

> It was like I was setting out to do something special and big—like a knight setting out—worth remembering. I dreamed coming from the barn and finding his back to me in the kitchen and wrestling with him and pulling him down and beating the stocking cap off his head with the barrel of the gun. I dreamed coming in from the barn still blinking with the light and seeing him there and picking the shovel up and taking him on. That had been then, when I was warm, when I was doing something big, heroic even, and well worth remembering. I couldn't put the feeling down in Pedersen's back yard or Pedersen's porch or barn. I couldn't see myself, or going slowly up and down in ma's face and ma shooing

it away and at the same time trying not to move
an inch for getting shot.

Beyond Jorge's wish to save his family, of course, is the
desire to endanger them in the first place. Ultimately,
Jorge embraces the shadowy killer who shoots his father
as an embodiment of vengeance for years of mistreatment;
he is the instrument by which Jorge seizes the role of protagonist in his own life. In the end, warming in the Pedersen basement, he muses about the possibility that Hans
and Ma are also dead now, which would grant him by default the prominence he seeks.

There is, of course, the reality beyond artistic manipulation to be considered: the hard journey through the snow,
the dead horse in the snowdrift, and finally, the unavoidable presence of the killer himself. All of these details are
incontrovertible; their weirdness or unpleasantness resists
redefinition. They all require that the kid's story be credited. The tiny peculiarity of the killer's yellow gloves is
enough to initiate a feeling of being caught up in a reality
that overmatches the fictionalizing impulse: "It's like
something you see once and it hits you so hard you never
forget it even if you want to; lies, dreams, pass—this *has*
you; it's like something that sticks to you like burrs, burrs
you try to brush off while you're doing something else, but
they never brush off, they just roll a little, and the first
thing you know you ain't doing what you set out to, you're
just trying to get them burrs off." Inexplicably, but beyond
doubt, there is the killer, and asking how or why he'd
come through the blizzard to assault the Pedersens cannot
remove that "burr": "He was in it now and he could go
on and he could come through it because he had before.
Maybe he belonged in the snow. Maybe he lived there, like
a fish does in a lake. Spring didn't have anything like
him." There is no mistaking the admiration which overshadows Jorge's fear at this moment. Later, from the confines of the Pedersen cellar, Jorge will be able to fashion
a truce with the cold, his life-long symbolic adversary, because it has struck Pa and Big Hans down.

Jorge's inner warmth—the physical manifestation of an
energized consciousness—develops only after the trial by
winter. Pitted against the cold are a series of images of
wombs, tunnels, and shelters which serve as psychological
attempts to marshal his waning resources. Unfortunately,
memories of warmth are evanescent: "I tried to hold the
feeling but it was warm as new bath water and just as hard
to hold." The cold, however, is always present, and its
main effect on Jorge is to paralyze his imagination, to confront him with his enslavement to insensitive men, and
thus, to stir him to helpless rage. Forced out of the wagon
to stab about in the snow for the bottle his father dropped,
Jorge consoles and fortifies himself with dreams of vengeance: "It was frightening—the endless white space. I'd
have to keep my head down. Winded slopes and rises all
around me. I'd never wanted to go to Pedersen's. That was
Hans's fight, and Pa's. I was just cold . . . cold . . . and
scared and sick of snow. That's what I'd do if I found it—
kick it under a drift." His hatred intensifies, pervading the
scene like the weather. Treated as an appendage in the employ of adults who show greater affection for horses and
inanimate possessions than they do for Jorge, he suspects
the cold of having conspired with his enemies, since it

seems as if the cold, like Pa's wrath and Hans's sullenness,
is directed against him personally. In spite of concentrating on an image of a kettle steaming on the stove, Jorge
cannot neglect for long the sense of his "breath coming
slow and cloudy and hanging heavy and dead in the still
air."

To counter his environmental and human oppressors,
Jorge envisions the pleasures of sanctuary, which his alter
ego, the Pedersen kid, has already attained by having
made his way through the snow. Ironically, the snow itself
tantalizes him with this very promise. The makeshift tunnel, which turns out to be useless as a means of approaching the Pedersen house, does have the psychological appeal of being a barrier against the elements: "It would
have been wonderful to burrow down, disappear under the
snow, sleep out of the wind in soft sheets, safe." In fact,
throughout the story, the snow's opposing connotations
wage war in Jorge's mind: it is both hazard and refuge; its
coldness burns.

This paradoxical linkage particularly asserts itself after
Jorge, partly to show his bravery and partly to escape the
domination of the men, challenges the vast open space and
makes it into the cellar. The symbolic circuit between the
Pedersen kid and Jorge Segren, who has retraced and mirrored the kid's adventure, is complete, and the narrator,
along with his imaginative sensibilities, begins to thaw out.
From his fetal position in a dark, moldy corner, fantasies
are released from deep freeze: "But I stayed where I was,
so cold I seemed apart from myself, and wondered if everything had been working to get me in this cellar as a
trade for the kid he'd missed. Well, he was sudden. The
Pedersen kid—maybe he'd been a message of some sort.
No, I liked better the idea that we'd been prisoners exchanged. I was back in my own country. A new blank
land. More and more, while we'd been coming, I'd been
slipping out of myself, pushed out by the cold maybe. . . .
Suppose the snow was a hundred feet deep. Down and
down. A blue-white cave, the blue darkening. Then tunnels off of it like the branches of trees. And fine rooms.
Was it February by now?" Note the concept of "a new
blank land," a profound contrast to the sensation of fear
that Jorge felt outside from "the space that was bowling
up inside me, a white blank glittering waste like the waste
outside, coldly burning." What had earlier been the white
of bleakness and despair is transformed into the white of
unbridled possibility—the artist's open canvas awaiting
his unique imprint.

Despite the looming danger of an unseen killer—and were
the dead bodies of the Pedersens behind the next door?—
Jorge settles into the rare ease of nostalgia. He recalls an
idyllic summer when he roamed carefree over the plain,
pretending to shoot any unwitting passerby with a
broomstick. He was enjoying the game of ascendancy over
his father (one of the "shooting" victims), the liberty it afforded, and the sensual pleasures of a warm, bright day;
it would be "a special shame" to forego this satisfaction
"on the edge of something wonderful" to return to the
snow and his father's snarling commands. That peaceful
summer, he realizes, was the last time he felt so free, until
now; when the summer ended, winter and the mutual an-

tagonism of Pa and Hans set in. Jorge also remembers Pa's desecration of a favorite picture book, whose pieces the vicious man scattered in the privy; having once emptied the contents of his chamberpot on Hans, Pa is regularly associated with excrement in Jorge's mind, and he is initially described while he is sleeping as "dung covered with snow." Why go back to that, now that his own body seems a new, intriguing territory to be explored? How can Jorge surrender his refuge, now that the cellar air is suddenly sweet?

How hospitable of the killer to free him from that responsibility! Jorge's "proposal" that the killer visit the Segren house—ostensibly to provide a test of Jorge's mettle, but also to relieve him of the stifling authority of adults, as the killer had already done for the Pedersen kid—comes true in his mind after the actual shooting of Pa. However, as the storyline frays into uncertainty, the circumstances of Pa's death cloud over: perhaps it is Jorge himself who shoots his father, fulfilling the wish he had intimated in his summer reverie, while the yellow-gloved man stands as a needed screen to protect him from the awful guilt. "The kid for killing his family must freeze" is one uninvited thought that darkens Jorge's celebration of awakening selfhood. Indeed, Jorge may be freezing to death, and doubt thereby veils the entire closing section of his narrative. It remains questionable whether the "melting away" of the threats that surround him in this strange seclusion is a delusion; what is most definite about the final paragraph of **"The Pedersen Kid,"** of course, is Jorge's alliance with the "heroic" stranger: "I had been the brave one and now I was free. The snow would keep me. I would bury pa and the Pedersens and Hans and even ma if I wanted to bother. I hadn't wanted to come but now I didn't mind. The kid and me, we'd done brave things well worth remembering. The way that fellow had come so mysteriously through the snow and done us such a glorious turn—well it made me think how I was told to feel in church. The winter time had finally got them all, and I really did hope that the kid was as warm as I was now, warm inside and out, with joy."

Jorge manages to create and interpret the plot that contains him; that is the nature of his heroism. He seizes destiny imaginatively, and that is the wellspring of power. (He can even choose which of the other characters he'll bury!) Speaking of the fiction of Borges, Gass declares, "Any metaphor which is taken with literal seriousness requires us to imagine a world in which in can be true; it contains or suggests a metaphorical principle that in turn gives form to a fable." Although he has Borges' fictions in mind, the procedure Gass outlines applies to Jorge Segren's method as well. By preferring the realm of metaphor over physical environment, Jorge creates a surrogate world, in which his own aspirations can be attained and are the dominant, actual ones. (pp. 57-70)

"The Order of Insects" is the shortest work in *In the Heart,* and it dramatizes in miniature the critical instant when consciousness is first arrested by structure. In fact, the drawbacks of artifice which compromise its attractiveness in Gass's other works are not so apparent in this story; whereas the various refuges inhabited by

Furber . . . and the others are often seen as reductive, stifling, or unwholesome, the order which beckons the unnamed female narrator of **"The Order of Insects"** is beautiful, even majestic, despite its being manifested as carcasses of bugs.

José Ortega y Gasset, a prominent touchstone in Gass's criticism, provides the term "infrarealism" to define fiction that focuses on what usually escapes notice. In this story, a woman is confronted with the ineluctable "thereness" of highly organized microstructures that seem to signify the natural existence of the coherence which Gass's artists try to produce synthetically.

The choice of a woman protagonist for the story is particularly important. The drabness of life, a decisive impetus for several characters of artistic temperament who opt for imaginative alternatives that promise to be more conducive to their sensibilities, is in her case intensified by having been programmed into the confining stereotype of the housewife. Not only her daily activities, but also her emotional and intellectual responses to her environment are so routine that she is incapable at the beginning of the story of acknowledging profounder experiences than those traditionally associated with her limited role. Clearly, she has learned to evade potential disturbances by retreating into a tightly circumscribed self-concept: she prides herself on the fastidious way she goes about her housework, carefully sealing out the dirt and organizing the cupboards. As a woman, she is privileged, or forced, to edit out intrigue. Time and again her incipient fascination with the insects is hampered by the suspicion that the subject is too indelicate for the weaker sex: "It's no study for a woman . . . bugs," she reasons, and she later worries that the growing revelation she allows herself is something no woman is worthy of.

Appreciating the order of insects, then, requires a broadening of the self—a significant change from the contractions of self which so frequently prove to be the price of withdrawal in Gass's fictions. The woman is actually thrust into a limbo between the mundane, "appropriate" affairs and the superior order of "the dark soul of the world itself."

That her earlier order was just a kind of incarceration is evidenced by the superficiality of the artistry it enables her to practice and by the automatic way she recoils from strange encounters. She is, quite literally, wife of the house, relegated to pettiness. Even her fears are ordinary: "Womanly, wifely, motherly ones: the children may point at the wretch with the hunch and speak in a voice he will hear; the cat has fleas again, they will get in the sofa; one's face looks smeared, it's because of the heat; is the burner under the beans? The washing machine's obscure disease may reoccur, it rumbles on rinse and rattles on wash; my god it's already eleven o'clock; which one of you has lost a galosh?" Mired in this relentlessly unpoetic state of mind, she has only revulsion for the tiny corpses which have infiltrated her home, as mysteriously and inexorably as they will soon invade her consciousness. (For had not a similar episode of pestilence driven her family to move out of one house—"after all we had been through in the other place," she ruefully recalls—into this one?) She shudders before the "fierce, ugly, armored things," looking away as the vacuum cleaner sucks them up: "I remember the sudden thrill of horror I had hearing one rattle up the wand. I was relieved that they were dead, of course, for I could never have killed one, and if they had been popped, alive, into the dust bag of the cleaner, I believe I would have had nightmares again as I did the time my husband fought the red ants in our kitchen." Final escape from the infestation of her mind is impossible; in her dreams, she joins the bugs "in the dreadful elastic tunnel of the suction tube" which her husband wields, confirming her psychological correspondence with the suppressed, not with the suppressor.

Her struggle against the insects is short-lived and unavailing because her buried self is not in it. Though she defends herself against infection with a handkerchief in front of her mouth, there is no denying them access: "At first I had to screw my eyes down, and as I consider it now, the whole change, the recent alteration in my life, was the consequence of finally coming near to something." She determines that the ugliness she had shunned had been an optical illusion caused by the distance she had maintained from the insects. Now, they merit glorification. Not even death robs them of their essential grace. Our narrator praises the durability of order that inheres in their exoskeletons (while our bones are worn secretly within, their structure surfacing only in the grave where the poor flesh anonymously decays). It is, quite simply, a glimpse of divinity that renders her own life small: "But this bug that I hold in my hand and know to be dead is beautiful, and there is a fierce joy in its composition that beggars every other, for its joy is the joy of stone, and it lives in its tomb like a lion."

Suddenly, inevitably, previous satisfactions are exposed as shallow. Like Henry Pimber in *Omensetter's Luck,* the woman falls under the spell of marvelous self-possession and quiet coherence; like Brackett Omensetter, the insects exhibit the joy of stone. Just as Omensetter conferred magical weightlessness upon the stones he skipped across the water's surface, the insects themselves seem astonishingly light now that the burden of life has been lifted from them; stony, too, is their immortal arrangement, especially when contrasted with human perishability.

In the tradition set by her predecessors in Gass's fiction, the narrator tries to digest this stunning, new reality in the form of language. She encloses the insects in a series of admiring adjectives, and she reinforces her conception of them with elegant foreign phraseology describing their body parts and functions. She borrows the enchanting structural rigor of the natural sciences, then strives to improve upon it, reformulating it into an intensely personal artistic order; the advantage of the latter is what Gass terms "freedom from the *esthetically* senseless." Thus occupied, she translates purely descriptive activity into creative activity.

The narrator begins to drift out of the normal circumstances of her daily life. Lying "shell-like in our bed, turned inside out, driving my mind away," she most closely approaches the ironically superior insect status; the insects "played caesar to my dreams." By no means has her

husband ever possessed her so fully. Under his jurisdiction of the old, discredited order, everything was tamed, deemed disgusting, or just neglected. Innocence itself was a work of art under perpetual construction. Thanks to her metamorphosis, however, whereas she once had to force herself to look at the insects, she now has "a pair of dreadful eyes, and sometimes I fancy they start from my head." How can her family continue to recognize her, much less claim her? And how can such eyes ever again view their habitual setting with the old complacency?

Still, as suggested earlier, **"The Order of Insects"** does not conclude the exchange of one equilibrium, which is presided over by the husband, for another which is comparatively rewarding and privately administered. Instead, the story concludes with the woman caught between, uncertain yet yearning. The splintered reality of home and family continues to exert its influence strongly enough to make her doubt her revelation: "It is a squat black cockroach after all, such a bug as frightens housewives, and it's only come to chew on rented wool and find its death absurdly in the teeth of the renter's cat." Conventional duties and role restrictions reassert themselves: a woman does not have the right to indulge in these frivolities; her husband, certainly, would deem them nonsense. "How can I think of such ludicrous things—beauty and peace, the dark soul of the world—for I am the wife of the house, concerned for the rug, tidy and punctual, surrounded by blocks." Children and toys are formidable barriers that verify the woman's interior position. "Tidy and punctual" describes a brand of order which is in no way as remarkable or impressive as the order of insects, but at least for now, it remains intact. So our narrator has not resolved her situation in the telling. Increased perception does not guarantee increased potential, and we cannot predict with confidence whether or not she will be able to enter the provocative, "extra-suburban" realm completely, nor how that reconstituted self would appear. The very existence of her narrative does suggest, whatever her fate, that, that the temptations of the dark soul of the world have not been erased by logic, habit, or shame.

The title story of Gass's collection is recognized as one of the hallmarks of recent American fiction and has earned a deceptive reputation as a clinically precise depiction of Middle America. In the stark surface of the piece, which emphasizes the bleakness of the landscape and the paltriness of its pleasures, many readers have found a singular example of literary documentary which would appear to betray the author's debt to the literary realist program.

In fact, Gass is quick to complain of the regular misreading of his best-known work. To assume that **"In the Heart of the Heart of the Country"** copies a geographical location cheats the work out of its reality *in words*. It falsifies both plan and product:

> The first thing I had to do was to get rid of any intention to be truthful about the place. That would have been exceedingly difficult and would have required all kinds of other operations. What you could say is, yes, something like certain of these things happened in a town like this but that was only part of what happened, not the whole thing, and I frequently get letters which

say, 'You really captured how it was to live in this small town in Utah, in Indiana.' That just means they weren't seeing their town fully enough because it isn't the way it was. Again, they are doing something people frequently do, taking the complexities of experienced reality and bringing them down *not* to the complexities of the language which is, I hope, a rival, but to the complexities of something they then lift out of that language, simplify and then suppose that they have got a picture of their world. I find that dismaying.

Regarding **"In the Heart of the Heart of the Country"** from the perspective we have employed toward his other fictions, according to which the dynamics of the lexical system rather than verisimilitude take precedence, we can recognize how representative of Gass's writing this story actually is. If the heart of the country is that familiar setting of the small midwestern town—the place, plot, characters, and style so often visited by the realists—the "heart of the heart" is an essence of consciousness, an inscape instead of a landscape, which derives from that setting and which is realized as the province of language.

The unnamed narrator of the story, a poet "in retirement from love," pits his language against the vast vacancy that surrounds and frustrates its generation. He justifies his insularity as staving off contamination by the desolation that his neighbors, who are uniformly decrepit, seem to have inherited from the town. "And I live *in*" he proclaims. He lurks inside his house in the same manner as the narrator of "Mrs. Mean"; also, he is ducking inside his own body, a self in hiding from self-awareness (while his cat brims to its skin with natural, uninhibited vitality and ease); and finally, to complete this nest of boxes, he skulks within the words themselves, atrophying like sperm in a jar in "my spew, the endless worm of words I've written, a hundred million emissions or more" until, like one of Beckett's spectral wretches, "there is nothing left of me but mouth."

In addition to defeat in love, a world of dim vistas also causes his retreat. Of course, we have seen that world elsewhere in Gass's writing. The Gilean of *Omensetter's Luck* is just as uninspiring, as are the photographs which trace a "Wisconsin Death Trip": "The loneliness trapped in these figures is overwhelming, and one thinks of the country, and how in the country, space counts for something, and how the individual is thrown upon his own resources, how he consequently comes to sense his essential self; and then you notice with a guilty twinge three generations posed in front of a small unpainted shack, and you realize that these families are as closely thrown together as potatoes in a sack; that, like men on a raft, space is what confines them; and that the tyranny of the group can here be claustrophobic crushing, total."

So the poet shrinks into artifice to confirm his detachment from a world which is barren of love, energy, and potential. **"In the Heart"** opens by invoking Yeats's Byzantium, that poet's own dignified alternative to deterioration. But while the paradise Yeats contrives is a place of hammered gold, Gass's narrator has "sailed the seas and come . . . to B . . . a small town fastened to a field in Indiana." "B" is the diminished, unregenerate version of Byzantium, the

eternal city of art. Furthermore, the poet's creation has come to embody the poet himself—an artistic project made spiritual project, in the sense of being the supreme projection of the artist's personality. As Frederick Busch explains, the poet is the town's spiritual complement; B is as inalienably fastened to his being as it is to the barren field, or as Yeats's famous heart is "fastened to a dying animal." Busch asks us to be guided by the pun on "to be" in the story's opening line, according to which the poet takes on the features of the world to which he has been exposed: "So I have sailed the seas and come to be a small town fastened to a field in Indiana."

So our narrator has fallen headlong into his art and thereby succumbed to a terrible irony: the distance he has hoped to effect through narrative activity has not saved him from identification with his surroundings. Love's absence has hollowed out his handiwork, trapping him in the same fate that the other residents of the story—all of them relics, all wasting away—suffer daily. He interprets one of the inarticulate citizens as saying "that there were many wretched love-ill fools like me lying alongside the last bone of their former selves, as full of spirit and speech, nonetheless, as Mrs. Desmond, Uncle Halley and the Ferris wheel, Aunt Pet, Miss Jakes, Ramona or the megaphone; yet I reverse him finally, Billy, on no evidence but Braggadocio, and I declare that though my inner organs were devoured long ago, the worm which swallowed down my parts still throbs and glows like a crystal palace." Because he must, the narrator convinces himself that his potency survives the contagion of decrepitude; nevertheless, the steady accumulation of data spooks him. What difference is there between his own airless, obsessive existence and Uncle Halley's junk collection? And Billy Holsclaw, who wobbles in aimless distraction through the town's debris, is consistently recognized as the poet's exposed self. Trying to treat him as an object of contemplation, the poet discovers that Billy resists the advances of poetry. He is unbeautifiable. All the poet can muster under the sway of this Muse is a litany of grays: "For we're always out of luck here. That's just how it is—for instance in the winter. The sides of the buildings, the roofs, the limbs of the trees are gray. Streets, sidewalks, faces, feelings—they are gray. Speech is gray, and the grass where it shows. Every flank and front, each top is gray. Everything is gray: hair, eyes, window glass, the hawkers' bills and touters' posters, lips, teeth, poles and metal signs—they're gray, quite gray. Cars are gray. Boots, shoes, suits, hats, gloves are gray. Horses, sheep and cows, cats killed in the road, squirrels in the same way, sparrows, doves, and pigeons, all are gray, everything is gray, and everyone is out of luck who lives here."

Once again, however, we are counseled by the narrator not to mistake the Indiana that his predilections distort for the so-called "real world." He creates whatever suits his gray mood—"I must stop making up things. I must give myself to life," he resolves, feebly—and *that* Indiana is damnable, worse than any Gopher Prairie. To commit himself freely to life would be to capitulate to the town's poverty. Stripped of his lover's inspiring attentions—"Yet I was not a state with you, nor were we both together any Indiana," he broods—he cannot work on poetry, and he turns venomous. If the town seems hardly conducive to artistic enterprise, it can also be argued that, at least in part, it catches its disease from him: "Of course there is enough to stir our wonder anywhere; there's enough to love, anywhere, if one is strong enough, if one is diligent enough, if one is perceptive, patient, kind enough—whatever it takes; and surely it's better to live in the country, to live on a prairie by a drawing of rivers, in Iowa or Illinois or Indiana, say, than in any city, in any stinking fog of human beings, in any blooming orchard of machines. It ought to be." Perhaps it ought to be easier to live apart from the swollen crowds of people, but the theory does not avail him. For one thing, "It's impossible to rhyme in this dust." Whereas the bucolic life and pastoral sweetness are debunked as "a lie of old poetry," so, too, is the romantic theme of a sensitive man keeping his chalice aloft among the philistines. Thus, the sterile poet condemns a world he cannot redeem; lyricism brought low, the poet trades the dream of Keats's "viewless wings of Poesy" for the desire "to rise so high . . . that when I shit I won't miss anybody." Impotently raging, he imagines the trees exploding, shaking off the joyless dust; the snow is like mass depression, "a pale gray pudding thinly spread on stiff toast, and if that seems a strange description, it's accurate all the same."

This is the hardest irony to bear: having retired to revitalize his waning powers of imagination, the poet is further stifled by retirement itself. With his beloved, so his nostalgic remembrances run, his words were buoyed by every caress; he could depend upon escaping along the slope of her body like a skiff on a river, and every interlude renewed his perceptivity: "You were so utterly provisional, subject to my change. I could inflate your bosom with a kiss, disperse your skin with gentleness, enter your vagina from within, and make my love emerge like a fresh sex." Now there is nothing to uplift him to where the sky only rarely "allows the heart up." He confronts a cold windowpane: devoid of interest, vision stunted. "We meet on this window, the world and I, inelegantly, swimmers of the glass." Poetry initiates no change because the poet's words barely consult the world; stuck in the window, they seem to turn in upon their fog-bound creator.

In the section entitled "Politics," our narrator notes the narrow-mindedness and short-sightedness of "the badly educated, who squander their passions on trivial matters, then senses that he has formed a treaty of sorts with them by hemming himself into his own idiosyncracies. Nostalgic longing is just as limiting, just as fanatical, a pastime similar to gabbing about the local sports scores. If the anonymous "they" are held back by mindless pursuits, the poet's eyes are "driven in" by a hypersensitive self-consciousness. His inventory of the aged contains no one whose deafness and implacability is any more intense than his own. (What a contradiction of the title "Vital Data" is the desolation of hope that succeeds it!) In short, he has come to be defined by the closed space he occupies. He is as static and opaque as the house he occupies. It is not surprising that he thinks of transforming himself into a church, for that act would verify his psychological situation and would validate his vigorous self-worship, as his ego dominates the vicinity.

How far he has drifted . . . from natural ease. . . . [While his cat] benefits from unselfconscious ease. The cat shames its owner, who cannot seem to copy its lesson of how to live: "Mr. Tick, you do me honor. You not only lie in my lap, but you remain alive there, coiled like a fetus. Through your deep nap, I feel you hum. You are, and are not, a machine. You are alive, alive exactly, and it means nothing to you—much to me. You are a cat—you cannot understand—you are a cat so easily. Your nature is not something you must rise to." Calling his cat Mr. Tick is yet another of the poet's sophistries, for it remakes the animal into a clock; if its "electrical penis" is a rebuke against the ascetic poet, its rhythmically twitching tail is a metronome that reminds him that he is dying daily into greater identification with a dying community. "I am learning to restore myself, my house, my body, by paying court to gardens, cats, and running water, and with neighbors keeping company," he rationalizes; but gardens mock his emptiness, cats his incessant ramblings about the past, and running water his inertia.

As for neighbors, they are withered premonitions of his own demise. He blasts them for embodying the anxieties and failures that brought him into their company:

> For I am now in B, in Indiana: out of job and out of patience, out of love and time and money, out of bread and out of body, in a temper, Mrs. Desmond, out of tea. So shut your fist up, bitch, you bag of death; go bang another door; go die, my dearie. Die, life-deaf old lady. Spill your breath. Fall over like a frozen board. Gray hair grows from the nose of your mind. You are a skull already—*memento mori*—the foreskin retracts from your teeth. Will your plastic gums last longer than your bones, and color their grinning? And is your twot still hazel-hairy, or are you bald as a ditch? . . . bitch. . . . . . bitch. . . . . bitch. I wanted to be famous, but you bring me age—my emptiness. Was it *that* which I thought would balloon me above the rest?

Despair determines his interests as well as his prejudices. He cannot empathize with anyone but the old and lonely; youth, once celebrated in his love affair, is currently represented by the town's ugly scheming children.

Gass seems to be saying that one option for any artist is to foster his sense of importance by sneering at mass access and mass engagement, thereby reassuring himself that his gestures are reserved for the aesthetically-initiated elite. The extreme version of this logic takes the shape of an exclusively narcissistic art, composed in shadows and tucked away in drawers. (The strictest elitism is solitude). As it happens, the rest of B accepts and reflects self-obsession. For example, there is the ancient Mrs. Desmond, who, although she is frightened by the scrape of flies against the screens and by the sound of "her own flesh failing," is hardly aware of the poet's presence: "Her talk's a fence—a shade drawn, a window fastened, door that's locked."

The structure of **"In the Heart"** imitates the fortress the poet has tried to erect for himself: a stylistic blockhouse. (Consolidating one's world so efficiently at least allows for *organized* solipsism.) Ronald Sukenick argues that the as-

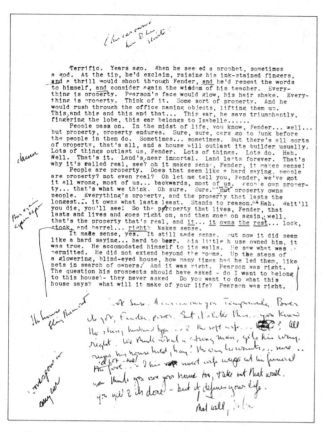

Manuscript page from In the Heart of the Heart of the Country.

cendancy of spatial over temporal reality on the page changes the fate of description in contemporary fiction and neatly applies to our narrator's method of "composing" himself in prose: "Since it is no longer the novelist's business to 'make us see' as it was in terms of imitation theories, description in fiction would seem to be pointless, but this is not the case. Description is too deeply embedded in the tradition of the novel ever to be lost, but its present significance is ironically antithetical to its former one. The contemporary novelist describes things with whose appearance we are already perfectly familiar (through photography, film, travel, or simply the modern quotidian) not to make us see those things but to test the language against them, to keep it alive to visual experience. The pleasure of description is the pleasure of a linguistic skill, not that of a genre painting." The rigid appearances of these notecards is also consistent with Gass's analysis of a quality of human nature which the artist simply exteriorizes: "We are inveterate model makers, imposing on the pure data of sense a rigorously abstract system. The novelist makes a system for us too, although his is composed of a host of particulars, arranged to comply with esthetic conditions, and it both flatters and dismays us when we look at our own life through it because our life appears holy and beautiful always, even when tragic and ruthlessly fated." Metaphor confers relevance upon all the strange particulars by coaxing them into familiar files. No matter how peculiar the river, to borrow Gass's image, man gropes for trouts, even if he has to recontrive them to fit

his nets: "He arranges everything he hears, feels, sees, in decorous ranks like pallbearers beside him, and says he's 'informing' his visual field. He lives a lot like a pin in a map—he calls it 'growing up'—and there he indicates the drains. No, he does not copulate, he counts; he does not simply laugh or sneer or shout, he patiently explains. Regardless of the man or woman he mounts, throughout his wildest daydreams and even in the most persistent myths of his pornography, he will imagine in amounts." For want of a woman, the poet takes pencil and paper to bed. By abstracting the world into catalogues, it is replaced with a language that treats everything and everybody like literary fodder; secured in the heart's heart of words, the poet indulges his "desire to gain by artifice a safety from the world—to find a way of thinking without the risks of feeling."

To some extent, he achieves that privilege. When, at the end of the story, reality is epitomized by the metallic strains of "Joy to the World" emanating from a worn-out phonograph record, we do tend to prefer the triumph of withdrawal from reality; nevertheless, if the poet's convalescence is made possible within the house of language, it may also be unhealthily prolonged confinement, and any affirmation of the world, even one tempered by skepticism, might ultimately serve him better than do loneliness and inertia. Poetry loses its redemptive powers in direct ratio to its removal from community. The drowsy rhythms of the sentences that constitute the narrative "islands" concretely display the inability to resolve to move. As Tony Tanner points out, "The great empty space which surrounds the town is visible in the blank lacunae between the narrator's several entries."

"In the Heart" explores a mental realm where content is never expendable; because the mind's life is the only source of energy detectable here, every detail is precious fuel. Gass assesses the value of fictions whose catch-all style—he calls it a "redounding of reference"—is the last-ditch effort of the artist to join into some sort of contract with the world at large: "Let nothing be lost. Waste not even waste. Thus collage is the blessed method: never cut where you can paste. No question it works. It works wonders, because in collage logical levels rise and fall like waves." Parodically updating Henry James's advice to aspiring writers, which stemmed from confidence in the abundance that was available, our narrator hopes to draw meaning out of a blasted environment by personalizing it. He purges its foreignness to a degree by subordinating its inherent reality to the reality of his own devastated condition. Again, Ronald Sukenick supplies a useful corollary to the creative strategies of this narrator in his analysis of Wallace Stevens, in which he suggests how the sensitive personality can bear the rigors of contemporary American life: "When, through the imagination, the ego manages to reconcile reality with its own needs, the formerly inspired landscape is infused with the ego's emotion, and reality, since it now seems intensely relevant to the ego, suddenly seems more real." Relevance to the self defines reality; the world is asked to make the principal accommodations. Clearly, the sections of **"In the Heart"** entitled "Business," "Politics," or some other public generality contain selective, personal impressions of details, rather than objective factsheets (although the accounting-ledger technique of presenting information tends to obscure subjective interference). Under one "Business" section, a tawdry carnival is described as a dinky, noisy waste; "Weather" compels a catalogue of lucklessness; "Politics" includes declarations of outrage at the Russians for having shut up a dog in a satellite; "Education" digresses into an excoriation of the hapless Mrs. Desmond; "A Person" inevitably traces the perorations of Billy Holsclaw, the poet's second self cast adrift outside his house.

Billy's looming presence is especially provocative. Cast as "The First Person," and so, by extension, as the stand-in for the narrator's "I," Billy also represents the whole collection of "love-ill fools like me lying alongside the last home of their former selves"—he bears the standard of their desolation. That the poet is implicated by association is an awful thought to confront, so he reverses it into a more palatable one, conjuring up the image quoted earlier which speaks of the continuing vitality of his "glowing" inner organs inside the worm that swallowed them down. Reclamation projects in the heart of the heart of the country concentrate on the internalized Indiana, but the charms of a vigorous worm are limited, no matter how fertile it may make the self it burrows through for the production of memories. As the poet himself admits, "When I've wormed through a fence to reach a meadow, do I ever feel the same about the field?" Means contaminate ends; the exasperating rules of refuge daily detract from the achievement of refuge.

Gass on the relationship between life and fiction:

I feel it *is* a moral obligation not to write about people in such a way that they would ever recognize themselves, not to use your art and your relationship to people in that sense. Now there are two sides to this question. A lot of people have read ["In the Heart of the Heart of the Country"] and have said to me, "gee, I come from so-and-so Texas or such-and-such Oklahoma or such-and-such Missouri, and you describe small town life exactly the way it is." They saw the life; they lived there; and they approved of this—as opposed to people, say, seeing and either hating it or disavowing it or whatever. But these people who approve of what I've done in this way are making the same mistake, I would say, as somebody who looked at the story and said, "oh, he's slandering me or libeling me," because they're not there. What I find when people say "you caught the life of a small town" is that they didn't see any more of that small town than my narrator does: my narrator has a narrow point of view; he's a driven-in person, and I hope *I* saw more life in small towns than he does.

William Gass, in an interview in Modern Fiction Studies, *1983.*

And so, the poet clings unsteadily to his presumed vantage point like a vulture brooding over the dying, nourished by a dead love; meanwhile, "sparrows sit like fists" on the ubiquitous telephone wires which, though they may be "bars of connection" for others, fasten him to the spot. (His intercourse, communicative and sexual, is solely "by

eye.") The childhood adventure of "Household Apples" lends evidence to the argument that life can flourish in the midst of decay, but it shows just as plainly that even flies "are so persistently alive," as is Mr. Tick, that the poet's existence pales in comparison. While the poet lives like an outlaw in the recesses of his house and body, and like Israbestis Tott in his wall, insects consume the sweet fruit. He confesses that his arms "had never been more alive" than when flies clustered about it like a humming sleeve as he picked the apples; however, he cannot finally afford the epiphany which tells him that his current aesthetic stronghold does not compare. "What have I missed?" he wonders, but only for a second before deeming those sensations false. Instead, he seals up his fiction: "Childhood is a lie of poetry."

In this way, **"In the Heart of the Heart of the Country"** completes Gass's volume by making unanimous the presentation of the artistic consolation as a double-edged alternative. Yes, art has the ability to rescue beauty and coherence from a world which will not sustain them, but rescue is expensive: immediacy and the intensity of direct experience are lost in the bargain. Only a soberly practical perspective keeps sanctuary from seeming like a prison, or transcendence from withering into trite unpoetic loneliness. There is always the danger that one's artwork may start to stink of artificiality, as do the "wood or plastic iron deer" that the narrator of **"In the Heart"** detests for their betrayal of nature. A closed cathedral, an endlessly repeating phonograph record that no one else hears, much less cares to hear—these images cast doubt upon the solipsistic creations which get trapped in the glass or on the mirrored page, until "all that lies within it's dead." The artist lies and suffers the consequences of counterfeit experience: life, which is tantalizing and dreadful, courses just beyond him, though it may as well be miles. And the pane's kiss is cold. (pp. 84-101)

Arthur M. Saltzman, in his The Fiction of William Gass: The Consolation of Language, *Southern Illinois University Press, 1986, 194 p.*

Charlotte Byrd Hadella   (essay date 1988)

[*In the following excerpt, Hadella analyzes the narrator of "In the Heart of the Heart of the Country" as someone trapped within a solipsistic "wasteland" of art.*]

"Models interfere with the imagination," William Gass insists in response to a question about how or where he gets the material for his fiction. In this same interview, however, Gass confesses: "The only time I ever used a 'model' in writing was when, as a formal device, and to amuse myself, I chose to get the facts about 'B' in **'In the Heart of the Heart of the Country'** exactly right." An important connection exists, I believe, between Gass's theory about the stifling effect of models on the imagination and the fact that he uses a model to create "B" in **"In the Heart of the Heart of the Country."** The narrator in that story, a "teacher, poet, folded lover," constantly seeks models for his work and his life, and these models certainly interfere with his imagination. He shuns human connections and seeks literary ones; he hides behind an image of himself that he has fabricated from literary models: he is W. B. Yeats's aging artist and the etherized patient from T. S. Eliot's "Prufrock"; at various times throughout the narrative, he is Whitman's oratorical singer or Rilke's "poet of the spiritual." Yet this narrator/poet is miserable, lonely, and lost in a fragmented world, much like the world of Eliot's *The Waste Land,* because he fails to participate fully in either art or life.

The reference to Yeats's Byzantium in the opening lines of the story signals that the narrator has left one world and entered another—the world of his own imagination. This first segment of **"In the Heart"** is titled "A Place," and it characterizes the world of the story, "B," as a place that is stagnant and decaying behind a veneer of progress and pleasantness. "B" is "fastened to a field in Indiana," and it "always puts its best side to the highway"; for instance, on one lawn stands a "wood or plastic iron deer," a mock representative of the artifice of Yeats's Byzantium—a substitute for the natural, sensual world that is subject to decay. Also in "B," according to the narrator, the lawns are green in spring; but a careful reader will realize that spring never arrives in the story. As Gass leads us into his story, we move away from the best side of town and into an unmistakable wasteland where "gravel dust rises like breath behind the wagons." "A Place" concludes with the narrator's announcement that he is "in retirement from love," an indication that we are, indeed, in an emotional wasteland **"In the Heart of the Heart of the Country."**

With the fragmented structure of his story, Gass conveys a subliminal message of the isolation, loneliness, and departmentalized perception of his narrator. The thirty-six segments offer descriptions of, and/or observations about such varied topics as weather, church, politics, education, business, people, and wires, indicating that the narrator is somehow trying to "measure the whole." [In] his book of critical essays, *The World Within the Word,* after defining words as "deposits of meaning made almost glacially over ages . . . names for thoughts and things acts and other energies which only passion has command of," Gass refers to T. S. Eliot's coffee spoon metaphor in "The Love Song of J. Alfred Prufrock" to illustrate his definition:

> Prufrock did not measure out his life One/Two, One/Two, but carefully, in coffee spoons, from which the sugar slid, no doubt, like snow, and the beverage circled to their stir as soundlessly as a rolled eye. Morning, noon, evenings, afternoons. There was the polite chink as they came to rest in the saucers—chink chink chink . . . a complete world unfolds from the phrase like an auto map reveals its roads. In metaphor, meanings model one another, wear their clothes. What the poet tries to measure is the whole.

However, Gass's narrator, more like Prufrock the character than Eliot the poet, slips into pools of words that drown his "measurements" in solipsistic emotional paralysis. Because Gass's poet has retired from love, he lacks the passion to command language and his stifling self-consciousness renders him unable to maintain a metaphorical vision.

In the first "Weather" section, Gass introduces the infor-

mation that the narrator is a writer and that he blames the weather for his mood. Thus, the narrator reports that "it is a rare day, a day to remark on, when the sky lifts and allows the heart up. I am keeping count, and as I write this page, it is eleven days since I have seen the sun." Bruce Bassoff aptly observes in "The Sacrificial World of William Gass," that the climate of **"In the Heart"** is an objective correlative for the inner state of the narrator." That this inner state is winter, the season of stasis, of withdrawal from life, is in keeping with the wasteland imagery that opens the story of a place whose inhabitants are "lonely and empty" and "barren and loveless." The next "Weather" section (segment 15) emphasizes the ubiquitous grayness of winter—even "speech is gray." This segment also includes a hellish description of summer:

> The heat is pure distraction. Steeped in our fluids, miserable in the folds of our bodies, we can scarcely think of anything but our sticky parts. Hot cyclonic winds and storms of dust criscross the country. . . .

Through the narrator's obsessive attention to weather, Gass emphasizes a controlling irony in the story: though the narrator complains about the weather, he is the one who is responsible for the world in which he lives. His complaints suggest that he does not accept this responsibility.

Frederick Busch argues that in **"In the Heart of the Heart of the Country,"** the narrator's world is "the refuge or prison he creates for himself. So we have a man who has fled the world of nature, who has somehow fallen, and who is now trapped (or hiding, or both) in his imagination. This little story is a saga of the mind." Therefore, the present-tense season for "B" is always winter because the narrator's mood is a perpetual winter. The poet/narrator avoids thinking of spring as the season of rebirth and renewal. Thus, even when he does mention spring rain, the rain mentioned is only a memory, and it is not associated with desire or awakening to life; instead, he insists that "in the spring it rains as well, and trees fill with ice."

By the time he narrates the final "Weather" section of the story, Gass's poet has begun to realize the fallacy of blaming the weather for his barren, loveless predicament. He claims: "I would rather it were the weather that was to blame for what I am and what my friends and neighbors are—we who live here in the heart of the country"; but he equivocates in the next sentence with "better the weather, the wind, the pale dying snow . . . the snow—why not the snow?" In the following paragraph, however, the poet again attempts to accept responsibility for his world by stating, "a cold fall rain is blackening the trees or the air is like lilac and full of parachuting seeds. Who cares to live in any season but his own?" But he backs away immediately from the frightful prospect that he has created his own sickness and answers himself: "Still I suspect the secret's in this snow, the secret of our sickness, if we could only diagnose it, for we are all dying like the elms in Urbana." Thus, we are back to winter again in the heart of the country of this story.

Gass's poet, finding himself in a dormant winter state, attempts to gain a new perspective in the section titled "My

House" (segment 3) by climbing the high stumps of the headless maple trees behind his house "like a boy to watch the country sail away. . . ." Here he has the revelation that "I think then I know why I've come here: to see, and so to go out against new things." But his resolution lasts only as long as he is perched upon his tree stump. By the next "house" section (segment 7), the poet has retreated from his perch; he has moved inside where he faces his inability to create; he seems to have abandoned his resolution to "go out against new things." Here we find that "leaves move in the windows," and the narrator cannot tell us "how beautiful it is, what it means." The next "house" section, "My House, This Place and Body" (segment 13), illustrates the narrator's final retreat from his previous resolution. Here, he explains: "I've fallen as fast as the poet, to the sixth sort of body, this house in B, in Indiana, with its blue gray bewitching windows, holy magical insides. Great thick evergreens protect its entry. And I live *in*." Following this announcement of total withdrawal, Gass reasserts his narrator's connection to the land with "this country takes me over in the way I occupy myself when I am well." But the poet is not well; he has not been able to re-create the "ecstasy on a tree stump," which originally inspired him to "go out against new things."

In fact, he has achieved the reverse of meaningful interaction with humanity or movement toward new knowledge: he now "lives in" and his thoughts are dominated by his past, and particularly his failed love affair. But in spite of his self pity and narrow perception, the poet continues to make metaphors. He calls his love a fiction, "a figure out of Twain"; and later, as Busch notes, "the beloved is on a raft with the poet and is simultaneously the river on which they drift. She becomes a metaphor for the Finn-like journey from the real and noxious world." Gass's achievement in this metaphor is twofold: he demonstrates that his narrator still has creative powers, the recuperative powers necessary to deliver himself from his living hell; however, the narrator's creative production is clearly limited by his solipsism, and thus incapable of becoming something new, something separate from its maker: a work of art.

The section that follows "My House, This Place and Body" consists of one paragraph titled "The Same Person" (segment 14) that intensifies the theme that the narrator's ability to make metaphors cannot save him as long as he lacks love and flees from commitment to his community. In this passage, the narrator encounters Billy Holsclaw at the post office. The details of the segment contribute to Gass's portrait of his narrator as a person who deliberately cuts himself off from humanity. The setting is ironic since the post office itself represents connections with the world outside of the character's immediate sphere—communications, messages sent forth, messages received. And here Billy Holsclaw talks "greedily" to his neighbor "about the weather." The narrator observes: "His [Billy's] head bobs on a wild flood of words, and I take the violence to be a measure of his eagerness for speech." But instead of responding to Billy's need for fellowship, the narrator retreats: "I leave him . . . and our encounter drives me sadly home to poetry—where there's no answer."

The two remaining sections that deal specifically with Billy, "That Same Person" (segment 23) and "The First Person" (segment 33) support the interpretation that Gass employs "fluid identifications" for his narrator, and that Billy is one of these identifications. The narrator, therefore, expresses his own desire for stasis when he says about Billy, "Quite selfishly I want him to remain the way he is—counting his sticks and logs, sitting on his sill in the soft early sun—though I'm not sure what his presence means to me . . . or to anyone." Immediately following this passage, the poet reasserts that "Byzantium" desire to become a work of art and thus remove himself from the world of senses and decay. He speculates, "whether, given time, I might someday find a figure in our language which would serve him [Billy] faithfully, and furnish his poverty and loneliness richly out." Here he projects onto Billy that which he desires for himself—immortality through art.

That Gass's narrator shuns Billy because he shuns the natural forces of life is expressed most clearly in "The First Person." The poet confesses that by severing himself from humanity, "I did not restore my house to its youth, but to its age." Though Billy is old, tattered, and almost blind, the narrator says, "I'm inclined to say you [Billy] aren't half the cripple I am, for there is nothing left of me but mouth." But he retracts this metaphor as just "another lie of poetry" before finally declaring: "My organs are all there, though it's there where I fail—at the roots of my experience." Here the poet recognizes that he has the equipment to be human (bodily organs), but that he has cut himself off from the community of human experience, the roots of humanity. Thus Gass articulates in **"In the Heart"** perhaps the most important theme from Eliot, the central question in *The Waste Land:* "What are the roots that clutch?" Eliot suggests that the roots, which keep modern man alive, are the roots of myth, of death, and of rebirth. Christ's sacrifice is part of this continuum, and Christ's message merges in *The Waste Land* with the Vedic order: "Give. Sympathize. Control." When Gass's narrator says that he has failed at the roots of his experience, he is recognizing that his experience has not been human: his love has been a fiction, his childhood a lie of poetry, and his present existence is a retirement from love.

Admittedly unsuccessful at both art and life, the poet/narrator of **"In the Heart"** cannot see that his failure results from his unwillingness to give to either of these processes the central ingredient of both—love. He tries, instead, to substitute order. Beginning the first of three "Politics" sections (segment 8) with the half sentence "for all those not in love," the poet signals that he is actually addressing himself. He proceeds, then, with a brief paragraph about two political figures, Batista and Castro, who have been engaged in a power struggle for control of Cuba. Perhaps because he identifies with Batista, a man who has lost his power, the poet's commentary in "Politics" degenerates into egocentric metaphor with "A squad of Pershing Rifles at the moment, I make myself Right Face: Legislation packs the screw of my intestines. Well, king of the classroom's king of the hill. You used to waddle when you walked because my sperm between your legs was draining to a towel."

Finally, this section turns into a Whitman parody with "I chant, I beg, I command, I sing—." Alluding to the conclusions of the first and second sections of *The Waste Land,* Gass's poet sings:

> Good-bye. . .Good-bye. . .Oh, I shall always
>   wait
>   You, Larry, traveler—
>   stranger,
>   son,
>   —my friend—
> my little girl, my poem, my heart, my self, my
>   childhood.

This conflation of the conclusions to "The Burial of the Dead" and "A Game of Chess" suggests that the poet of **"In the Heart"** is trying desperately to unify his own experiences through another writer's consciousness.

But none of his literary models can contain the material that Gass's narrator would like to pour into them, and the attempt at narrative control in "Politics" fails by breaking into a lamentation of personal bewilderment and ineffectiveness. Interrupting the political discussion, and introducing the Whitman parody and the Eliot allusion, the poet whimpers: "I cannot write the poetry of such proposals, the poetry of politics, though sometimes—often—always now—I am in an uneasy place of equal powers which makes a state." The "uneasy place" for the narrator is a zone of his own invention. Caught between the equal powers of life and death, he finds himself in a state of living death. Escape requires change, and change is what this character fears the most. Therefore, instead of venturing forth into the unknown, making new relationships, Gass's narrator tries to enter the world of literature and thus escapes death.

In "Politics" and similar sections containing spliced allusions and frustrated rantings, Gass demonstrates the futility of his character's attempt to find a formula for his feelings or a system of values through literature. As Charles Newman explains Gass's theory of fiction, "it [fiction] is a process of signification which does not unify experiences but is its own experience." According to Gass, truths exist within the world of a piece of fiction that apply to that fiction. When we sever these truths from their fictional universe, we inevitably distort what we have extracted by trying to fit that fragment of fiction into our lives in any meaningful way. The work itself is truth, complete and whole, and the process of reading it is the process of discovering the world of truths within the words. Gass will allow that good works of literature deal with ambiguities that "can be made into an orderly revelation of meaning"; but readers are to measure their lives against that meaning, not extract that meaning to live by. Thus, the poet/narrator of "In the Heart of the Heart of the Country" fails to find meaning in his life because he refuses to participate in the process of living.

At times, however, the poet of this story appears to be committed to his quest for physical, spiritual, and emotional restoration. In the fourth "house" section, "My House, My Cat, My Company" (segment 18), he declares resolutely, "I must organize myself," which reveals that he is attempting to exert some kind of control over his life.

This control is manifest through language as the poet divides his existence into titled sections that vary in content, structure, and point of view. But his search is characterized generally by directionless commentary that invariably slips away from objective observations or rational discourse into narcissistic whining. As he casts about for topics of discussion, the "folded lover" admits his lack of control:

> My will is like the rosy dustlike light in this room: soft, diffuse, and generally comforting. It lets me do . . . anything . . . nothing. My ears hear what they happen to; I eat what's put before me, my eyes see what blunders into them; my thoughts are not thoughts, they are dreams. I'm empty or I'm full . . . depending; and I cannot choose.

Here, the narrative voice of control discloses itself as a mere pose, the echo of modern consciousness.

When Gass's narrator announces in "My House, My Cat, My Company" (segment 18) that "I am learning to restore myself, my house, my body, by paying court to gardens, cats and running water, and with neighbors keeping company," he seems to have reached beyond himself to make a meaningful human connection. He refers to his eighty-five year old neighbor, Mrs. Desmond, as his "right-hand friend" and describes her obsession with loss and death. In the next paragraph of this segment, however, the poet reveals that he and Mrs. Desmond do not really communicate, that there is no real relationship between them: "We do not converse. She visits me to talk. My task to murmur. . . . Her talk's a fence—a shade drawn, window fastened, door that's locked. . . ." Thus, in his "listening posture," the narrator retreats to his past, remembers listening to his grandfather talk, compares himself to "badly stacked cards," and recalls his lost love affair in terms of a card game. This scene underscores the fact that the only character with whom the narrator even pretends to keep company is a character who, like himself, uses language as a protective fence to bar any real contact with others.

Gass describes his poet as "one person who's having a lot of problems looking at certain things in the town in a certain way"; he adds that his poet, in fact, "is suffering from a lack of perception of the world." Everywhere the narrator looks in "B," he sees himself, his own inadequacies, metaphors for blindness and failure. One of three "Business" sections (segment 22), for instance, focuses on failed enterprises. A particularly vivid image in the section is a torn campaign poster that blocks the windows of a watch repair shop and urges viewers "to vote for half an orange beblazoned man who as a whole one failed two years ago to win at his election." Significantly, this poster blocks the narrator's view of a watch repair shop, a place where broken timing mechanisms can be restored. This image draws attention to the fact that the poet is stuck in time, suffering from a perpetual winter, fearing both life and death.

The very next passage articulates explicitly the narrator's fear of the unknown:

> What do the sightless windows see, I wonder, when the sun throws a passerby against them? Here a stair unfolds toward the street—dark,

rickety, and treacherous—and I always feel, as I pass it, that if I just went carefully up and turned the corner at the landing, I would find myself out of the world. But I've never had the courage.

The poet himself is the half man on the poster who "failed two years ago to win at his election." Instead of going on with his life, "going out against new things," he clings to his past failures and shuns pathways that lead to unknown experience. In this passage, Gass's poet echoes Prufrock's question: "Do I dare/Disturb the universe?"

By beginning the story with words lifted from Yeats, then relying upon images, patterns, and themes from Eliot, Rilke, Whitman, and others, Gass underlines an important impulse of his narrator's character: he approaches art, as well as life, selfishly, with a limited consciousness that attempts to appropriate words, experiences, and emotions from other sources because his own creative and procreative faculties are paralyzed. In *The World Within the Word,* Gass exhorts readers to "watch out for images which are merely telephonic sums, for explanations which aren't really meant but are, like plastic bosoms and paste gems, only designed to dazzle. We confine ourselves to too few models, and sometimes live in them as if they were, themselves, the world." In the narrator of **"In the Heart,"** Gass creates a character who dramatically cripples himself with explanations only designed to dazzle, a character who confines himself to too few models and lives in those models as if they were the world. His attempt to find his own poetic voice is obstructed by the clutter of poetic images, phrases, and postures that he borrows from the world of literature and tries to piece together to make his own statement.

That the narrator's own words out of which he models his wasteland world are barriers to his renewal is most evident in the final "house" section, "House, My Breath and Window" (segment 28). In this segment, consisting of one long single paragraph, the narrator explains that his window "is a grave, and all that lies within it's dead." What lies within this death frame is not only the view of the world outside, but also the narrator's reflection that merges with the outside setting by the end of the paragraph. The poet's breath becomes visible on the glass, he says, to "befog its country and bespill myself." In this scene, Gass dramatizes how his narrator's words blur the outside world and drive him in upon himself. The poet speaks to his own reflection here; he becomes his own audience: "Ah, my friend, your face is pale, the weather cloudy: a street has been felled through your chin, bare trees do nothing, houses take root in their rectangles, a steeple stands up in your head. You speak of loving; then give me a kiss. The pane is cold."

The narrator's narcissistic gesture epitomizes the personal limitations that trap him in his cold, static world. The poet cannot find his way out of this wasteland because his vision encompasses only himself. He grasps only a fragment of Eliot's climactic message at the end of *The Waste Land.* He gives to no one; he sympathizes only with himself; and his attempt to control his world through language fails because he lacks love, the vital ingredient needed to trans-form language into art. At the end of the story, Gass's poet/narrator remains, still, in the wasteland winter of his own imagination. (pp. 49-57)

> *Charlotte Byrd Hadella, "The Winter Waste-land of William Gass's 'In the Heart of the Heart of the Country',"* in Critique: Studies in Contemporary Fiction, *Vol. XXX, No. 1, Fall, 1988, pp. 49-58.*

Reginald Dyck   (essay date 1991)

[*In the following essay, Dyck analyzes Gass's short fiction in relation to the literary schools of Modernism and Postmodernism.*]

> I don't regard myself as a postmodernist. . . . I prefer to think of myself as a purified modernist. In architecture that would mean modernism without social content: Corbusier not building for society.
>
> —William Gass

When William Gass claims, "I think that literature is not a form of communication," he seems to preclude a social interpretation of his work. "Serious writing must nowadays be written for the sake of the art," he asserts. Baudelaire made this claim in the context of his resistance to the commodification of art; Gass in his formalist rhetoric is resisting the traditional ways of reading fostered by the fiction of realism. Yet while his critical writing works to convince his readers to resist the old ways, it also acknowledges that his fiction has a significant relationship to the social world.

Most people, Gass states, read fiction as history without graphs or dates, an approach that falsifies by creating expectations fiction does not intend to fulfill. "I object to so-called extraliterary qualities because they get confused with the merit of the book." The word *because* is important; Gass's point is not that extraliterary qualities do not exist, but that they are too easily misread. The danger is that literature "provides a sense of verification (a feeling) without the fact of verification (the validating process)." For example, although Gass did careful research for **"In the Heart of the Heart of the Country,"** the story should not be read simply as an exposé of rural Midwestern towns or American society as a whole. Gass explains that "the story is not an accurate picture: it's an accurate construction. Not even 'accurate': just a construction of one person's way of looking at things." Rather than an objective report, the story presents the consciousness of a particular type of character in a particular type of place.

Another way that readers misread is by emphasizing plot as the central quality of fiction. The well-constructed plot as a moral equation has been for novelists a way of making sense of the chaos of life, and readers have accepted that construction as the import of the novel. Consequently, the novelist as artist is slighted in favor of the novelist as philosopher or sociologist. Gass has been challenged most vigorously by John Gardner, who argues for the inescapably moral nature of literature: "In literature, structure is the evolving sequence of dramatized events tending toward understanding and assertion; that is, toward some meticulously qualified belief." It is not that Gass is un-aware of the moral views fiction presents, but that his interest is in the dramatic tensions those views create rather than their correctness. Nabokov's *Lolita* is to be read in this way as well. Both authors want readers to look at their fiction as objects of art, not as moral treatises.

Therefore Gass calls himself a "purified modernist." In an essay subtitled "Demystifying the Ideology of Modernism," Fredric Jameson asks "what kind of society it can be in which works of art have become autonomous to this degree, in which the older social and cultic functions of literature have become so unfamiliar as to have made us forgetful . . . of the power and influence which a socially living art can exercise?" Sociologist Todd Gitlin, in describing the helplessness reflected in post-1960s culture, provides an answer: "Self-regarding irony and blankness are a way of staving off anxieties, rages, terrors and hungers that have been kicked up but cannot find resolution." When Gass began to publish his short stories in the midfifties, the modernist belief in the autonomous power of imagination, part of the Romantic view of the artist, had turned to doubt. Yet even if the imagination is understood as inevitably shaped by its social milieu, how can an artist fulfill the traditional bardic function of making sense of the world in a seemingly meaningless, mass society that does not take artists seriously?

Postmodern art has responded to this loss of meaning in two ways: with a sense of liberation or with a sense of isolation and betrayal. Although Gass's criticism celebrates the first, his fictional characters experience the second. The celebration stems from his claim to have separated beauty from truth, or fiction from society. However, Gass's escape into the artistry of language is not complete, nor does he intend it to be.

Gass on metaphor:

My complaint about Barth, Borges, and Beckett is simply that occasionally their fictions, conceived as establishing a metaphorical relationship between the reader and the world they are creating, leave the reader too passive. But such words are misleading. I have little patience with the "creative reader."

I mean this: some metaphors work in one direction—the predicate upon the subject. When I say that her skin was like silk, I am using the concept silk to interpenetrate and organize the idea of skin. Some metaphors, however, interact—both terms are resonant. If Hardy writes, "She tamed the wildest flowers," then not only has "she" become an animal trainer, the flowers have become animals. Nor has "taming" been left untouched, for such taming is now seen in terms of gardening. Now if fictions are metaphors or models, then perhaps they should occasionally "fictionalize" the reader.

William Gass, in an interview with Carole McCauley in The New Fiction: Interviews with Innovative American Writers.

To the extent that novels are forms of communication, Gass explains, they work not as direct descriptions but as constructed metaphors for our world. Metaphors are models of reality that posit conceptual connections among data. As much as novelists might strive for concreteness, they can only use words, which can never directly describe but must interpret. Thus, "The purpose of a literary work is the capture of consciousness, and the consequent creation, in you, of an imagined sensibility, so that while you read you are that patient pool or cataract of concepts which the author has constructed."

The opening of **"In the Heart of the Heart of the Country"** emphasizes the idea of the story as a model of consciousness. Echoing Yeats's "Sailing to Byzantium," the poet/narrator states, "So I have sailed the seas and come . . . to B. . . ." Gass plays on "to B" not only as an ironic reference to Yeats's Byzantium as an "artifice of reality," but also as a verb of being which alerts the reader that what follows is not literal description of a particular rural town but the creation of a fictional character's consciousness. The reader is presented with a model of what it would be like to be a poet "in retirement from love" and living in "a small town fastened to a field in Indiana." However, this does not preclude a social reading of the story; B is in the state of Indiana, and we do recognize the poet as our contemporary. The models Gass creates are as embedded in culture as their creator's imagination inevitably is.

Metafiction, such as Gass writes, openly exposes itself as a constructed model by showing us characters in the process of creating "a system of meaning which will help to supply their lives with hope, order, possibly even some measure of beauty." These metafictional models-within-models offer more than just aesthetic pleasures to the characters that create them. For example, at the end of **"The Pedersen Kid,"** we see Jorge creating a world of the imagination as an alternative to the mean, narrow one in which he lives with his parents and the hired man. In reading we are moved not only by Gass's display of craftsmanship but also by his presentation of the pain that drives his young character into this imaginary world. Through the story, we also understand something about the motivations and methods for the model-building process. In a sense Jorge confirms Gitlin's analysis of postmodern culture. Jorge's helplessness as a young boy in a violent, uncaring world motivates him to imagine a world of snow, the Pedersen kid, himself, and no adults. Patricia Waugh gives this explanation of metafictional model-building:

> Metafiction, then, does not abandon "the real world" for the narcissistic pleasures of the imagination. What it does is to re-examine the conventions of realism in order to discover—through its own self-reflection—a fictional form that is culturally relevant and comprehensible to contemporary readers. In showing us how literary fiction creates its imaginary worlds, metafiction helps us to understand how the reality we live day by day is similarly constructed, similarly "written."

Gass explains that the point for the reader is not to assess the accuracy of the model that either a character or the story as a whole creates. "I think of the text you are read-ing as the metaphorical model that reassesses yours, rath-er than the other way around." In claiming this privileged position for art, Gass shows his modernist affinities. He also guardedly claims fiction as an agent for change. The novel both displays and argues, and thus challenges our own conceptions of the world. But Gass gives a continual warning, "Still for us it is only 'as if '." The novel remains a world of words.

Although modernist in its formalist aesthetic, Gass's world of words reflects a postmodern perspective on con-temporary culture. A comparison of Wright Morris's *Cer-emony in Lone Tree,* a late-modern novel, with Gass's story **"Icicles"** makes this clear. Both writers wrote these works at about the same time, experimented with nontra-ditional forms and understand fiction as a model of con-sciousness. Yet the model Morris creates in *Ceremony,* published in 1960, and Gass's in **"Icicles,"** which first ap-peared in 1963, suggest significantly different worlds. The central characters, Boyd in *Ceremony* and Fender in **"Ici-cles,"** best exemplify this difference.

The modernist revolt against tradition deeply marks Boyd's outrageous actions; he wants to shock others out of the "hereditary sleeping sickness" of their middle-class lives. If the modernist faith in the artist's ability to change society has been depleted—Boyd's self-exile in Mexico suggests this—his return to Nebraska indicates his contin-uing stake in it. His bringing along a young friend whom he calls Daughter, a gesture he seems to have borrowed from *Lolita,* is one attempt to shock his friends' sense of propriety, and thus awaken them to the emptiness of their unreflected lives.

In "The Culture of Modernism," Irving Howe describes modernist writers as "an avant-garde marked by aggres-sive defensiveness, extreme self-consciousness, prophetic inclination, and the stigmata of alienation." Although true of Boyd, none of this characterizes Gass's Fender. Because he cannot believe that his actions matter, he is not one of those who "chose and oppose." Instead, he is a "confused self," "a diffuse, unfocused protean self which cannot de-fine issues in any determinate way." As a postmodern character, Fender is not oppressed by tradition as Boyd is, but by the "meaninglessness and triviality of freedom itself, which is unable to locate any bearings amid the in-coherent and apparently aimless massiveness of society."

Because Fender's world seems to have experienced the ef-fects of cultural entropy longer than Boyd's, Fender no longer has the energy for rebellious, audacious acts. Even if Boyd's idealism is largely exhausted, his rebellion keeps him in a dynamic relationship with society. Whereas Boyd brazenly attempts to walk on water and then creates a public account of his failure, Fender counts the contents of his pot pie but only thinks about writing a letter of com-plaint. Boyd has the energy of restlessness; Fender has the lethargy of listlessness.

Because Boyd's energy pushes him outward and Fender's lethargy focuses inward, they turn to aesthetics with dif-ferent intentions. Boyd transforms his water-walking fail-ure into a play and a novel; his inner struggle directs him

toward an audience. Fender develops a private aesthetic of icicles which estranges him from others because it al-lows him to escape from the public world. Coming home from a humiliating real-estate job, Fender becomes fasci-nated by the icicles that block part of his picture window. At first he reacts professionally, considering them a nui-sance and a sales problem. Then he creates images out of them: parsnips, the insides of caves, sets of teeth. Al-though he is surprised and embarrassed at his new inter-est, he soon becomes protective of it. Finally he does not care that his appreciation is not socially acceptable: "Only the icicles mattered." He wants to bring their beauty in-side himself. The icicles stand in opposition to the social world where, because "Everything is property," Fender comes to see himself as a decrepit piece of real estate. Al-though the outside world still threatens to intrude, he re-treats as much as he can into a private, aesthetic world of icicles. As he does, a sense of comfort displaces his listless-ness.

This retreat is made easier by Fender's lack of personal history. He jokes at a party, truthfully he realizes after-ward, that "he couldn't tell the story of his life because he couldn't in the least remember it." Although this frees him from Boyd's struggle to extricate himself from the re-straints of his past, Fender also lacks history's consola-tions. The present must carry the whole weight of his exis-tence, and when it fails to support him, Fender can only escape into a world of imagination: "There's no one to help you, Fender, you have no history, remember?"

Analogously, Fender is more disconnected from society than Boyd in spite of leading a more conventional life. Boyd may drop out of society, but his need to shock his childhood friends reveals his contradictory desire to be-long while asserting his difference from their deadening middle-class lives. Fender has the trappings of that mid-dle-class world, a job and a house, but neither provides him with social relationships. His dinner, here an ironic symbol of disconnectedness, illustrates his passive isola-tion. Rather than enjoying conversation and friendship, he eats in silence without even a television to bring in the out-side world. The pot pie establishes only a pathetic com-mercial connection.

Because of his helplessness, Fender finally stops struggling with society, leaves his job, and retreats into a self-contained world of icicles and language. Boyd also retreats into language, but he uses it as a defensive weapon, not as a blanket in which to hide himself as Fender does. In not taking an antagonistic stance against society, Fender moves beyond alienation. Instead of the heroic alienation and anxiety of modernism, he lives with the fragmentation and decentering of postmodernism. Thus he goes gently into that good night of death-in-language while Boyd rages against the dying of the light by setting off fireworks with his wit in order to expose his society's emptiness.

Boyd chooses to stand outside of society; Fender finds himself invisible within it. The census did not miss Fender because he refused to be counted: he was bitter that he had to call attention to his own existence. His escape into imagination is by default and provides him little comfort because the social world continues to impinge. The values of real estate insinuate themselves so that he comes to think, "I do not even occupy myself." Rather than having escaped, he discovers that "his inner exclamations were like advertising signs." Therefore he wants to "drive himself into wordlessness."

As a result, Fender, like Jacob Horner in Barth's *End of the Road,* becomes paralyzed. At the end of the story he protects himself by turning the children playing outside into a field of colors, yet his world of icicles is still vulnerable to their attack as "they [come] down the hill like a snowfall of rocks." **"Icicles"** ends with Fender's aesthetic world threatened by the world that surrounds him. Caught between these worlds, Fender can do nothing to save himself. This conclusion contrasts with the ending of *Ceremony:* rather than paralysis there is a sudden awakening as Boyd's audacity has its effect. Following his example of doing "something crazy" as "the only way to leave an impression," Lois shoots a pistol—symbol of violence and sexuality—and startles the others out of their habitual responses. Even if Morris does not imply that the changes are permanent, he does suggest that the paralysis of his characters' cliché-filled lives is not inevitable. A sense of powerlessness and inevitability does mark **"Icicles,"** thus placing it beyond the modernist energy of resistance.

Like his characters, Gass also stands between two worlds. While working within the modern aesthetic of a unique and personal style, his fiction engages a world that offers little opportunity for individualism. The "bourgeois ego," if liberated from the anxiety that drives Boyd to audacity, is also "liberated from every other kind of feeling as well, since there is no longer a self present to do the feeling" but instead only " 'intensities' . . . free-floating and impersonal." That is Fender's dilemma.

Rather than as a purified modernist, "Corbusier not building for society," Gass can better be understood as a modernist engaging a postmodern, mass society that does little to encourage artists, or any individuals, to think that they can affect their world. His fiction does celebrate the artistic possibilities of language, but just as Yeats's poet sails for Byzantium as a paltry old man who can no longer find a place in his native country, Gass's characters—Fender, Jorge, the poet in B, Rev. Furber—escape into an imaginary world as a retirement from love and a retreat from a world that is too much mere real estate.

Denis Donoghue claims that in Gass's fiction "the sentences make an arbitrary festival, a circus of pleasures, satisfactions corresponding to the smile with which desperate remedies, duly considered, are set aside." I read that smile as a wince and find the festival less arbitrary, the pleasures more troubling, and the desperate remedies still being desperately held to. (pp. 124-29)

> Reginald Dyck, "William Gass: A 'Purified Modernist' in a Postmodern World," in The Review of Contemporary Fiction, *Vol. 11, No. 3, Fall, 1991, pp. 124-30.*

Melanie Eckford-Prossor   (essay date 1991)

[*In the following essay, Eckford-Prossor comments on the construction of multiple "realities" in the narrative of "The Pedersen Kid."*]

Jorge and Hans have a problem: the Pedersen Kid, lying half frozen on the kitchen table, has told them of a killer who placed his family in the root cellar. Before they decide to act on the Kid's story, though—and possibly confront the killer—they must decide if what the Kid says is true. They must confront the apparent reality of language. Hans begins his rhetoric:

> Is it something you make up? Is it something you come to—raving with frostbite and fever and not knowing who's there or where you are or anything—and make up?

> —Yeah.

> No it ain't. Green, black, yellow: you don't make up them colors neither. You don't make up putting your folks down cellar where they'll freeze. You don't make up his not saying anything the whole time or only seeing his back or exactly what he was wearing. It's more than a make-up; it's more than a dream. It's like something you see once and it hits you so hard you never forget it even if you want to; lies, dreams, pass—this has you.

Jorge considers this:

> What Hans said sounded right. It sounded right but it couldn't be right. It just couldn't be . . . . Whatever was right, the Pedersen kid had run off from his pa's place. . . . I knew he was here. I knew that much. I'd held him. I'd felt him dead in my hands, only I guess he wasn't dead now.

In this rather abased version of a Platonic dialogue, Jorge raises the fundamental question of epistemology, but instead of the convenient epistemological distinction between *res cogitae* and *res extansae,* thinking substance versus physical substance, Jorge finds himself unable to distinguish between such basic physical facts as whether or not the kid is dead or alive. He tries to reason through this problem by expressing known "facts" in clear language. But as we see above, it doesn't work. In this way Gass simultaneously exploits and undercuts the predisposition of both readers and characters to believe that we "see" things clearly when they're clearly expressed. Gass capitalizes on this predisposition by layering his text with surfaces that may seem "real" and clear, but which are not to be trusted. To do so, and to consequently believe that one has somehow reached the meaning of the story, would be to agree that at root **"The Pedersen Kid"** is a story about creation and psychology. But the gaps in the surface of the text—gaps in logic and language—demand to be read more closely. By inspecting four crucial breaks in narrative logic, we see that in **"The Pedersen Kid"** Gass experiments with epistemology, certainty, and phenomenology. Thus, because the narrative, and the very language it's carried out in, mediates among these levels of philosophical experimentation, the entire story can be seen as a philosophical exercise in layered appearances and the ridiculing of both the characters' and the readers' desire to locate *a* truth and *an* explanation. Rather, what we should see is the contingency of a fictional world upon certain philosophical groundings.

Strangely enough, even though **"The Pedersen Kid"** is one of Gass's earliest stories and therefore probably most influenced by his Ph.D. work, few critics have taken account of Gass's philosophical influences. Instead they have examined his language from an aesthetic point of view or probed the story for psychological themes. Such approaches deny the complexity and many-layered depth of the story. This is especially true of psychological readings, which may provide another dimension or layer to the text, but which do so by unlocking the story using a rather simple key. The best of such articles is Bruce Bassoff's "The Sacrificial World of William Gass"; here Bassoff explains that the "story is full of fluid identifications and double exposures." Those which Bassoff wishes to reveal to us show the symbolic and psychological side of the story. Thus Bassoff explains that "as one node of the fiction, Big Hans and the Pedersen kid are associated with Christ." Later he argues that Jorge fulfills his own version of the "knight's quest." These two points, however, are subsumed by Bassoff's argument that "if, as Freud claimed, the rite of communion is both an expiation of the son's crime against the father and a replacement of the father by the son, Jorge's unexpiated guilt haunts him in the specter of the killer." Such a psychological injunction, however, poses a problem because it violates one of Gass's most ardently held beliefs. In "In Terms of the Toenail: Fiction and the Figures of Life" he tells us that any fictional world is only "a metaphorical model of our own." To forge a correspondence between a fictional world—which is a "metaphorical model" of a world—and our world, is to make a great blunder as the reader. To apply Freudian psychology, itself influenced by the study of literature but then assimilated into our culture as a way of coping with "real" problems, then, violates precisely this idea that a fictional world is a metaphorical model.

A strong alternative to the thematic psychological approach is a focus on Gass's language; when done well such an approach begins to give a sense of the amount of different interpretive levels of the story. One of the best of these is written by Arthur Saltzman, who argues that we should see Jorge as a figure of the author who, once driven into himself by the snow, authors his own world, one in which language becomes for Jorge a consolation for the physical brutality he has suffered. Saltzman founds his argument on the caution that we are not "to be seduced by the naturalistic skin of the story into trying to burrow past the dense language in order to uncover the message buried beneath it." If we do this we have discarded "the story's greater import, which has to do with the accumulation and patterning of the words themselves. Clearing away language so as to better view plot is self-defeating. Indeed, instead of illuminating the symbolic structure of the plot as the story progresses—a common aim of realistic fiction, in which perseverance is rewarded with the reliable dismantling of mystery—Gass steers us into cul-de-sacs, lets loose ends dangle, and plunges without warning into subjective distortions." Here Saltzman writes about **"The Pedersen Kid"** from the outermost layer: he sees it as a whole, a story written by William Gass. Later, he switches

levels and moves inwards, looking instead at Jorge as a figure of the author. There Saltzman explains that those "cul-de-sacs" and "loose ends" demonstrate "the reality beyond artistic manipulation . . . the hard journey through the snow, the dead horse in the snowdrift, and finally, the unavoidable presence of the killer himself. All of these details are incontrovertible; their weirdness or unpleasantness resists redefinition. They all require that the kid's story be credited."

The question that arises is should we be using different standards for different levels of the text? On the one hand Saltzman cautions us not to look beyond language, yet on the other, he accepts crucial problems in the plot, which we see precisely because of detail, as demonstrating "a reality beyond artistic manipulation." On this level, whether we look past the language to the plot or whether we look at the "reality beyond artistic manipulation," we still find ourselves determining a meaning from the text based on precisely the details that set the realist trap he cautions us to avoid. But there is an alternative. I suggest that the surface of the text and the plot are not seamless—Jorge may try to author the text, but he leaves gaps: we should recognize all the layers of the narrative not as incontrovertible, nor as demonstrating a reality beyond Jorge's artistic manipulation, but as made by Jorge. If we refuse to see the story as made and refuse to acknowledge the gaps in logic as failures of artistic manipulation, then we have implicitly assented to viewing the language as dense though ultimately transparent and representational.

To look "through" language toward some object or "reality" recalls Saltzman's warning not to read the "skin" of the story as real: both approaches depend upon our notions of language and how they, in turn, persuade us to believe, paradoxically, in a fictional reality. In our postromantic universe, the challenge presented to both the reader and the characters consists not in attaining the "willing suspension of disbelief," but in attaining precisely the opposite: the willing suspension of belief. It is just this difficulty that Gass exploits here by structuring Jorge's narrative—at least early on—in such simple sentences. Samuel Weber in his translator's note to Adorno's *Prisms* addresses this point when he writes of the difficulty of expressing German dialectics in English. Weber argues that English exemplifies a strong literary tradition that asserts a "criterion of clarity [that] is rigidly enforced by a grammar which taboos long sentences as clumsy and whose ideal remains brevity and simplicity at all costs." If we take Weber's point a step further we can see that, rightly or wrongly, clarity and brevity at the level of syntax are not only esteemed in English, they are connected with accurate judgment and honesty. From the story's opening, once Jorge suffers his confusion about the Kid's status, Gass probes the implications of this predisposition to see truth in clear syntax. Because both the majority of the readers and all of the characters are uninitiated into the philosophy of language, both groups tend to trust briefer and more direct language. This language game widens to the more general issue of language's ability to lend structure to our perceptions and to aid discovery of knowledge.

To the extent that Jorge grapples with expression and

order in language, he works through certain philosophical problems that Wittgenstein, prompted by Moore's "defence of common sense," probed in *On Certainty*. There Wittgenstein constructs a comment similar to Weber's insights into English. He cautions us to "remember that one is sometimes convinced of the *correctness* of a view by its *simplicity* or *symmetry*, i.e., these are what induce one to go over to this point of view." Jorge feels disquietude about Hans's propositions because they do seem too clear and too simple, but when he tries to puzzle out the Kid's physical state he is pretty much trapped by his own use of language. And he further complicates things when he keeps insisting on what he knows. This use of "I knew" recalls Wittgenstein's point that

> 'I know' has a primitive meaning similar to and related to 'I see' ('wissen', 'videre'). And 'I knew he was in the room, but he wasn't in the room' is like 'I saw him in the room, but he wasn't there.' 'I know' is supposed to express a relation, not between me and the sense of a proposition (like 'I believe') but between me and a fact. So that the *fact* is taken into my consciousness. (Here is the reason why one wants to say that nothing that goes on in the outer world is really known, but only what happens in the domain of what are called sense-data.) This would give us a picture of knowing as the perception of an outer event through visual rays which project it as it is into the eye and the consciousness. Only then the question at once arises whether one can be *certain* of this projection. And this picture does indeed show how our *imagination* presents knowledge, but not what lies at the bottom of this presentation.

Thus, to read the story from a psychological point of view, or from a perspective that positions Jorge as the figure of the author does not go far enough. Insofar as the issues of fundamental importance to the story are knowledge and its connection to fact, belief and imagination, the story enters into the realm of phenomenology, itself a movement poised between Husserl and Moore. According to A. J. Ayer, Husserl's "language was strange, but the intuition of essences need not have amounted to anything very different from Moore's analysis of concepts. It all depended on the details of the performance and the assumptions that went with it. What separated Husserl from Moore was the belief which grew on Husserl after the publication of his *Logical Investigations* that entities of every sort are not only hospitable to consciousness but constituted by it." Thus, conversations that pepper the opening pages, conversations about the Kid's physical status, force the reader to question the basis of the knowledge about "facts" that are stated in clear and simple language. Divided into three parts, and explored on at least three levels of the text (philosophy, narration, and interpretation), the story is actually an investigation of three realms of "knowledge": fact (whatever that may be—perhaps the "fact" of the kid's death—and the story shows us precisely the way empirical "fact" may be denied and how subject it is to interpretation), belief (in the face of fact and in the rightness of one's actions), and imagination (as a way of providing alternatives to "facts"—Jorge's skating "in" to his imagination). When it comes to answering the three

main questions posed by the text—Who shot Pa? What happened to the Pedersen family? and Is there really a Yellow Hands?—we see Jorge testing each of these approaches to knowledge and certainty. What must be stressed is that he tests these approaches by constructing a world that justifies the action his narrative actually disguises.

For readers, this means that Gass's doubts about the sophistication of his readers becomes, in **"The Pedersen Kid,"** an elaborate plot to separate able readers from those who so believe in brevity and clarity—both of language and the metaphorical "clarity" of supposedly "realistic" fiction—that, ironically enough, they become blind to the biases of their language. For the characters, their language games hold the same threat of blindness: they make the same mistake as the unwary reader when it comes to establishing truth. From the opening of the story both readers and characters confuse philosophical categories—logic and ordinary language—because they believe that clear thinking and simple syntax can reveal truth. Hans and Jorge think that if they can make their language clear and brief—if they can impose order on the Kid's ramblings—things will make sense; similarly, some readers believe that with the right key they can gain the secret of the text. To this extent they yearn for exactly what Weber decries about the "tendency of English syntax to break thought down into its smallest, self-contained, monadic parts . . . this has helped the English-speaking world to keep its feet on the ground." It is exactly this hope—and this preference for small, self-contained parts—that Jorge enacts when in the quotation above he tries to get a handle on what exactly it is that he does know: "I knew he was here. I knew that much. I'd held him." As this short string of sentences progresses, it gets simpler and simpler as Jorge struggles for a base of empirical knowledge. To use Wittgenstein's terms, Jorge is struggling to be "*certain* of this projection"—this "fact" that the Kid is dead. If the Kid were dead then Jorge's perception of it would be a "perception of an outer event." The problem is that he can't be certain. So unfortunately once he reaches the point of holding the kid in his narration he has reminded himself of his complex epistemological problem. From this point, then, the syntax of the sentences becomes more complex as he strives for an answer to his epistemological dilemma: "I'd felt him dead in my hands, only I guess he wasn't dead now." Confusion abounds.

In the above instance, Jorge imposes language to yield order and clarify perception from fact, but there's another capability of language: characters can use it to create, thus further confusing and therefore foregrounding issues of perception and "reality." In the second section of part 1 Jorge overhears Big Hans talking to himself:

> Just his back. The green mackinaw. The black stocking cap. The yellow gloves. The gun.

> Big Hans kept repeating it. He was letting the meaning have a chance to change. He'd look at me and shake his head and say it over.

> "He put them down the cellar so I ran."

Hans filled the tumbler. It was spotted with whiskey and flecks of flour.

"He didn't say nothing the whole time."

In Big Hans's invocation we hear and see the power of language to build a "fact." The facelessness of Yellow Hands, his silence and the bizarre colors he wears remove him from the human and into the realm of evil, which, Gass says in the "Revised and Expanded Preface" to *In the Heart of the Heart of the Country,* was precisely his object: "the problem is to present evil as a visitation—sudden, mysterious, violent, inexplicable." Yet though these details and Gass's stated goal seem to indicate that Yellow Hands is a mirage, we must see that by chanting the phrases Hans gives Yellow Hands such a strong verbal presence that for Hans he coalesces into a fact. Though Jorge explains Hans's repetition of the description as a way of "letting the meaning change," it in fact rigidifies the meaning. So rather more than letting "the meaning have a chance to change" is at stake here: if such a person exists, and through his invocation Hans makes him exist, Hans, Pa, and Jorge must do something about him. The moral code of their society demands that one always be right and that one never be a coward. When Jorge explains that Hans "didn't want to believe the kid any more than I did, but if he didn't then the kid had fooled him sure. He didn't want to believe that either" we see just the influence of strong verbal creations.

On the level of the story, the characters and the readers must determine what's real; on the level of the story's philosophy, comments made by Weber and Wittgenstein, as well as the idea of phenomenology itself, force us to question realism—an ambiguous and deceptive term itself—and the problematic issue that must be confronted when trying to determine various states of being, the existence of characters or the plausibility of explanations and ravings. What Gass counts on is what Linda Nochlin summarizes as the general belief that "Realists were doing no more than mirroring everyday reality." In **"The Pedersen Kid"** we have an extreme event, but with ordinary people in a remote and ordinary place, and at least in the opening, an event expressed in "clear" everyday language. Or that's what Gass counts on us thinking, at least initially. What it seems to me he's really getting at is the distinction between realism and reality, and our desire to confuse the two—to believe that "what you see is what you get" can be transposed into fiction's "what you hear/read is what you get." Hans hears the Pedersen Kid's description of Yellow Hands and he chants it into actuality. But instead of accepting this platitude we should try to see the other, rather Platonic side of realism that does not trust perception. How do we know what we see? How do we know the object we think we see is the object we want? And so on. Even within the fiction of **"The Pedersen Kid"** fiction and reality are problematic and *dangerous* issues.

The depth of these layers of "reality" is particularly clear in part 2 when Hans, Pa, and Jorge move from the warmth of the house into the snow. After a battle of wills among the three, Jorge finally stumbles upon a horse's hoof and starts a fight about whose horse this is. Jorge forces Hans and Pa to say whose horse they believe it to be—then tests the story by comparing the hooves they remember with the one they found. Despite the facts of the hoof—its color and size and so on—the characters entrench themselves in their belief that the hoof is something other than what Jorge maintains it to be . . . the hoof of Yellow Hands's horse. The incident is one of Saltzman's "cul-de-sacs," but to try to determine the source of the hoof or the owner of the horse is to force the story into coherency, even though Gass himself says that the evil in the story is "inexplicable." This desire for explanation doesn't work, even for Jorge who tries to achieve maximum distance from the consequences of the hoof by seeing the three characters as a winter scene from a calendar:

> Hans and Pa were silent. I looked up at them, far away. Nothing now. Three men in the snow. A red scarf and some mittens . . . somebody's ice and coal . . . the picture for January. But behind them on the blank hills? Then it rushed over me and I thought: this is as far as he rid him. I looked at the hoof and the shoe which didn't belong in the picture. No dead horses for January. And on the snowhills there would be wild sled tracks and green trees and falling toboggans. . . . Hans and Pa were waiting behind me in their wool hats and pounding mittens . . . like a picture for January. Smiling. I was learning to skate.

A product of the imagination imagines himself as a component of a winter calendar scene, which itself evokes a rather Breughelesque scene and therefore adds yet another layer to the imaginative production within the story. Interestingly, when Jorge imagines this world, he for once rejects language as the prime component of that world, and instead tries to enter a mute world of images. Although he may not be able to sustain the calendar image for long, he manages to change and revise it. He elaborates. As Saltzman points out, he's author of this imagined world, though he knows that he must make some decision about his action in "this" world. What he finds is that he is able to shift back and forth between worlds: he is "learning to skate." Jorge skates deep into this other world when he imagines himself killing his family. Listening to Pa and Hans argue about the horse's hoof he discovers, Jorge burns with hatred and violence. He skates into an unreal world where he tells us "Of course I shot them all—Pa in his bed, ma in her kitchen, Hans when he came in from his rounds. They wouldn't look much different dead than alive only they wouldn't be so loud." He skates further into the world—imagining standing alone in every room—imagining looking at Hans's magazines—imagining standing warm by the stove. But though his mind is in this other world, his body is in this one and Hans and Pa both back away from Jorge as he points his gun at them. By exposing his unpredictability Jorge guarantees that neither Pa nor Hans will heed his wishes. And it is at this point that the reader again is forced to question the layers of appearance and their suggestion of certainty. The idea of shooting his family, of playing the role of Yellow Hands himself, appears to be a direct result of the cold and the extreme circumstances of the story, yet by the end of the story we find Jorge alone in the Pedersens' house narrating the "facts" of the story.

To the degree that he centers his narrative on such questions of reliability and a determinate reality, Gass seems to be using **"The Pedersen Kid"** to test Hegel's point that "True reality lies beyond immediate sensation and the objects we see every day" and that "Only what exists in itself is real." Jorge's problem, of course, is that he does not want to admit, though he recognizes reluctantly, that "true reality" lies beyond *res extensae.* And throughout the course of the story he has the increasing problem of holding on to his sanity. In these terms, then, the plot of the story traces Jorge's coming to terms with Hegel's proposition by using Wittgenstein's aphorisms. After all, once he can no longer distinguish what's alive from what's dead, what's said to be here from what is here, what he knows from what he sees, he then searches for something "beyond immediate sensation" to ground him. He has moved from empiricism to concepts. To use the phenomenological term, he is consumed with bracketing.

Nevertheless, there is another layer to the story, one that Saltzman begins to get at with the idea that Jorge authors his own reality: as Hegel puts it, "Art digs an abyss between the appearance and illusion of this bad and perishable world, on the one hand, and the true content of events on the other, to reclothe these events and phenomena with a higher reality, born of the mind. . . . Far from being simple appearances and illustrations of ordinary reality, the manifestations of art possess a higher reality and a truer existence." Within the framework of fiction, Gass shows us Jorge authoring not only himself, as Saltzman maintains, but, more ambitiously, this other world, this "higher reality and a truer existence." Yet he does not do it flawlessly. Indeed he leaves his mark upon the made fiction. The cul-de-sacs that Saltzman notes are not the proof of a reality beyond artistic manipulation but the stigmata of the manipulation and creation itself—of the patching together of "reality." That reality, however, is what Bachelard calls "a phenomenology of the imagination. By this should be understood a study of the phenomenon of the poetic image when it emerges into the consciousness as a direct product of the heart, soul and being of man, apprehended in his actuality." Gass places this concept of the phenomenology of the imagination in the mind of an imaginary character who realizes he is imagining, but who finally realizes this and is able to narrate what appears to be a coherent set of events. The levels of layering here mimic the layering of Jorge, the imaginary character, imagining himself moving into a calendar—a created image—which itself evokes a Breughel—a "real" product of an imagination. Because the entire narrative exploits the reader's ability to believe in fiction, it almost parodies Bachelard's idea that the poetic image is "a direct product of the heart, soul and being of man, apprehended in his actuality." And yet the narration is Jorge's "direct product of the heart, soul and being" of a fictional character who very much wants to author a "real" unproblematic self, but who fails to do so.

While the first part of the story sets up the explanations and reasons for action, and the second part uncovers the hoof and shows how the dynamics of the trio force them into staying at the Pedersen farm, the third part opens with the shooting of Pa—either by Yellow Hands or by Jorge. If the reader has, like the characters, accepted the existence of Yellow Hands, then he is the person who killed Pa. Yet Jorge, now in possession of his gun, could also have done it. Standing with his back to the house, Jorge gives the all clear to Pa and Hans. "Pa came carefully from the barn with his arms around his gun. He walked slow to be brave but I was standing in the open and I smiled." Until the last clause of the second sentence, Jorge's narration in this short passage seems clear and unequivocal—as honest and as true as the simple syntax: it seems that Pa tries to demonstrate his bravery by walking slowly. In the final clause of the second sentence, though, "but" immediately follows "brave," therefore questioning Pa's bravery. If Jorge's standing in the open was meant to encourage Pa there would be no need for the "but." Instead there is an opposition between Pa and Jorge who stand at either end of the snow bank, either end of the sentence. Jorge implies that he was the braver because he stands in the open. Jorge's first smile of the story intensified the sense of ominous rivalry. Jorge continues his narration of Pa's shooting: "Pa sat hugging his knees as I heard the gun, and Hans screamed. Pa's gun stood up. I backed against the house. My god, I thought, he's real." Something has happened between the sentences to make Pa hug his knees before he was shot, but the only thing that has transpired is Jorge's smile. Pa "sat" as Jorge "heard" the gun. Why does Pa sit before Jorge hears the shot, unless it is because Jorge himself pulls the trigger? Jorge finishes the description of his father's death by describing how "Pa bumped as I heard the gun again. He seemed to point his hand at me." Does Pa point at Jorge to indicate his guilt or to ask for a drink? Gass deliberately chooses not to solve the puzzle, leaving it instead up to the reader, who must work his or her way through Jorge's narration. To determine the reality of Yellow Hands we have to rely on Jorge, who hears the shot and *thinks* "My god, I thought, he's real." But is he really?

Once inside the house, Jorge searches the fruit cellar for the Pedersen family, and consequently for proof of Yellow Hands. He finds neither. This encourages the supposition that Yellow Hands was made up, as does Jorge's later discovery that the Pedersens are nowhere to be found in the house. Indeed, Jorge himself begins to encourage the idea that both he and the Kid are forms of Yellow Hands when he comments "the kid for killing his family must freeze." Soon after this, however, Jorge narrates seeing footprints in the snow on the porch, a point he mentions only once before he retreats into his imagination. The only other "real" sighting of Yellow Hands occurs when Jorge peeps from a crack in a door and from there looks through a window. Though Jorge interprets what he sees as Yellow Hands's black stocking cap, he adds to his observation the phrase "I thought." He runs to the window to confirm the sighting. Like the kid, he sees not a face but "his back upon a horse. I saw the tail flick. And the snow came back. . . . He was gone." How much can we trust Jorge? He admits to fleeing inside so as to avoid the reality of possibly freezing to death. But nearly freezing to death, how clear is he on the distinction between imagination and reality? "The snow came back," but is this the exterior snow or the interior snow that allows him to skate? It is when Jorge fantasizes seeing Yellow Hands shooting his family we understand the workings of his imagination: "why did he stand there so pale I could see through?." He stands there pale and ghostly because he is not real—he has no substance apart from the imagination. Jorge himself adequately assessed the reality of Yellow Hands back in part 1: "something besides the kid came through the storm . . . I ain't saying yellow gloves did neither. He didn't. He couldn't." He couldn't because he is not real. He is an apparition—a representation of mindless evil—the mindless evil within each of the characters that Gass says in his preface was the goal of writing the story.

Abused by his family, alienated from them, Jorge finally achieves the ultimate alienation: alienation from himself. His perceptions—of which he is now completely sure—force the reader to question his sanity and the basis of his epistemology. The reader is subject to Jorge who suggests possible turns and explanations for what happened—justifications for his primal actions. To this extent we see the influence of Poe and Faulkner: we watch a mind crumble without acknowledging its own destruction. Indeed, one of the interesting points about the story is that as readers we experience Jorge's disintegration for the first time, but as narrator Jorge had experienced it first, and has created an apparently coherent narrative that disguises his illness and his crimes.

This sophisticated, intricate, layered narrative may not appear as metafictional as Gass's *Willie Masters' Lonesome Wife* or even **"In the Heart of the Heart of the Country."** But if we define metafiction as fiction about writing fiction, what **"The Pedersen Kid"** presents is a fictional character who creates events and explanations about the way in which he authors not only himself but his fictional world in a way that deliberately fools us into "believing" it's "real." To this extent not only is **"The Pedersen Kid"** a more subtle—but more daring—experiment in layered narration than Gass's more physically dazzling works of metafiction, its concern with epistemology, certainty, and phenomenology prefigure his interest in ontology. And if we consider the sections of *The Tunnel* that have been published, it's an experiment to which Gass has returned. (pp. 102-12)

Melanie Eckford-Prossor, "Layered Apparitions: Philosophy and 'The Pedersen Kid'," in The Review of Contemporary Fiction, *Vol. XI, No. 3, Fall, 1991, pp. 102-14.*

FURTHER READING

Bassoff, Bruce. "Getting Even, With William Gass." In his *The Secret Sharers,* pp. 99-122. New York: AMS Press, 1983.
    Discussion of Gass's work that focuses on his short fiction.

———. "The Sacrificial World of William Gass: *In the Heart of the Heart of the Country.*" *Critique* XVIII, No. 1 (Summer 1976): 36-58.

    Detailed analysis of Gass's short story collection.

Blake, Nancy. " 'Out of Time, Out of Body': An Erotic Map of the 'Heart of the Heart of the Country'." *Revue française d'études américaines,* No. 20 (May 1984): 265-74.
    Explores Gass's representation of time and space through the language and structure of "In the Heart of the Heart of the Country."

Bruss, Elizabeth W. "William H. Gass." In her *Beautiful Theories: The Spectacle of Discourse in Contemporary Criticism,* pp. 139-202. Baltimore, Md.: Johns Hopkins University Press, 1982.
    Analyzes the relationship between Gass's literary theories and his fiction with particular emphasis on the difference between literature and historiography.

Busch, Frederick. "But This Is What It Is to Live in Hell: William Gass's 'In the Heart of the Heart of the Country'." *Modern Fiction Studies* 19, No. 1 (Spring 1973): 97-108.
    Argues that "In the Heart of the Heart of the Country" resembles Malcolm Lowry's *Under the Volcano* in that both are works of profound innovation that strive to affirm the finality of death while simultaneously transcending it through art.

Dettmar, Kevin J. H. " 'yung and easily freudened' ": William Gass's 'The Pedersen Kid.'" *The Review of Contemporary Fiction* XI, No. 3 (Fall 1991): 88-101.
    Claims that Gass has anticipated certain positions of Freudian criticism of "The Pedersen Kid" by incorporating them within the story itself.

French, Ned. "Against the Grain: Theory and Practice in the Work of William H. Gass." *The Iowa Review* 7, No. 1 (Winter 1976): 96-107.
    Claims that the central tension in Gass's fiction is the desire to escape the capitalistic mass-production of art while also avoiding the solipsism of art that exists only for its own sake without reference to reality.

Hicks, Granville. "Fragments of Life." *The Saturday Review* 51, No. 38 (21 September 1968): 29-30.
    Reviews *Willie Masters' Lonesome Wife.*

Merrill, Reed B. "The Grotesque as Structure: *Willie Masters' Lonesome Wife.*" *Criticism* XVIII, No. 4 (Fall 1976): 305-16.
    Examines Gass's fiction in light of theories defining the grotesque as an aesthetic style.

Morton, Frederic. "Inside Trivia, Armageddon Simmers." *The New York Times Book Review* (21 April 1968): 4-5, 59.
    Discusses *In the Heart of the Heart of the Country, and Other Stories* with respect to the pessimism of contemporary literature.

Scholes, Robert. "The Range of Metafiction: Barth, Barthelme, Coover, Gass." In his *Fabulation and Metafiction,* pp. 114-23. Urbana: University of Illinois Press, 1979.
    Compares Gass's short fiction to that of Donald Barthelme.

Tanner, Tony. "On Reading 'Sunday Drive.'" In *Facing Texts: Encounters between Contemporary Writers and Critics,* edited by Heide Ziegler, pp. 205-14. Durham, N. C.: Duke University Press, 1988.
    Analyzes Gass's attention to language in the short story "The Sunday Drive."

Wilson, Lucy. "Alternatives to Transcendence in William Gass's Short Fiction." *The Review of Contemporary Fiction* XI, No. 3 (Fall 1991): 78-87.

Describes the tension in Gass's short stories between the "tendency of his language to slip the bonds of reference and signification in an orgy of self-reflexive wordplay, and the less powerful but still discernible effort to penetrate 'the particular'."

Wolfshohl, Clarence. " 'The Text is Oozing Out': William H. Gass and Transliteracy." *Studies in Short Fiction* 26, No. 4 (Fall 1989): 497-503.

Describes the design of *Willie Masters' Lonesome Wife* as an interaction between the physical and literary aspects of the book.

Additional coverage of Gass's life and career is contained in the following sources published by Gale Research: *Contemporary Authors New Revision Series,* **Vol. 30;** *Contemporary Authors,* **Vols. 17-20, rev. ed.;** *Contemporary Literary Criticism,* **Vols. 1, 2, 8, 11, 15, 39;** *Dictionary of Literary Biography,* **Vol. 2; and** *Major 20th-Century Writers.*

Pär Lagerkvist

1891-1974

(Full name Pär Fabian Lagerkvist) Swedish short story writer, playwright, novelist, and poet.

INTRODUCTION

Recipient of the 1951 Nobel Prize in literature, Lagerkvist is one of the foremost Swedish literary figures of the twentieth century. Throughout his career he displayed a concern with conflict between good and evil, faith and nihilism, and the mundane and the spiritual. Proficient in many genres, Lagerkvist garnered an international appeal based largely on his short stories and allegorical novellas, which often incorporate elements of folklore and mythology. Winston Weathers has noted: "Lagerkvist, perhaps more than any other twentieth-century author, has dealt consistently and artistically with the truly eternal questions: What is the meaning of life? Is there a God? What is death? What is the rationale of existence?"

Lagerkvist was born and raised in the city of Växjo in a religiously conservative household where such customs as daily readings from the Old Testament were strictly observed. Following a year of study at the University of Uppsala, he traveled to Paris in 1913. There he became acquainted with the Fauvist, Cubist, and "naivist" movements in the visual arts. Impressed with both the intellectual discipline and aesthetic innovations of these groups, Lagerkvist issued the pamphlet *Ordkonst och bildkonst,* in which he contrasted what he considered the "decadence" of modern fiction with the "vitality" of modern art. Calling for a renunciation of the documentary methods of nineteenth-century Naturalism, Lagerkvist endorsed an approach that employed the epic style and symbolic narratives of classic Greek tragedy, Icelandic sagas, and the Bible. Lagerkvist first incorporated these principles in his novella *Människor,* his collection of short stories *Järn och människor,* and *Ångest,* a volume of poetry often considered the first expressionist work in Swedish literature.

Lagerkvist lived in Denmark during most of World War I and spent much of the 1920s in France and Italy writing plays and poetry. In 1930 he settled with his family in Lidingö, an island community near Stockholm. Lagerkvist continued to write, and he steadily rose to prominence in the Swedish literary world: in 1940 he was elected to the Swedish Academy (the body which awards the Nobel Prizes) and in 1941 received an honorary doctorate from the University of Göteburg. However, Lagerkvist remained virtually unknown outside of Sweden until he was awarded the Nobel Prize. He wrote his most famous works, a cycle of six novellas, in the 1950s and 1960s. Lagerkvist died in 1974.

Lagerkvist's literary output during and immediately after

World War I has been characterized by Holger Ahlenius as "one single cry of despair over the bestiality of man." From the 1920s onward, Lagerkvist's works consistently exhibit his preoccupation with spiritual questions. In the novella *Det eviga leendet* (*The Eternal Smile*), souls of the deceased ponder the mystery of existence and undertake a journey to confront God. In the autobiographical novella *Gäst hos verkligheten* (*Guest of Reality*), Lagerkvist chronicled a child's growing awareness of his own mortality. The allegorical novella *Bödeln,* which may be translated both as "The Hangman" and "The Executioner," was inspired by the political upheaval that swept Europe during the 1930s. Set in Nazi Germany, this work uses the social and political climate of the time as a springboard for observations on the nature of society and the role of evil in its development.

In his series of six loosely related novellas with biblical themes, Lagerkvist addressed many religious and existential issues. *Barabbas* recounts the spiritual tribulations of a condemned thief in whose place Jesus of Nazareth is crucified. The title character remains a restless and loveless man despite his reprieve, although he dies possibly having found the spiritual truth and peace he sought. *Sibyllan*

(*The Sibyl*) focuses on the apocryphal character Aha-suerus, the Wandering Jew, who is condemned to roam the earth forever as punishment for his refusal to allow Jesus to rest beside his house on the road to Calvary. Aha-suerus discusses his fate with a disgraced priestess of the Delphic oracle, and their conversation explores the multi-faceted nature of gods and the relationship of gods to hu-manity. *Ahasverus död* (*The Death of Ahasuerus*), *Pilgrim på havet* (*Pilgrim at Sea*), and *Det heliga landet* (*The Holy Land*), often called the "Tobias Trilogy" after the com-mon protagonist, chronicle quests for redemption in which the goal is the quest itself. *Mariamne* (*Herod and Mariamne*) declares the necessity of both virtue and wick-edness in human experience. Lagerkvist's novellas, as well as his short stories, persistently relate the search for the meaning of existence, leading Gunnel Malmström to com-ment: "The sense of alienation from existence is a major theme in twentieth-century literature, and as one of its in-terpreters Lagerkvist is akin to writers like Kafka and Camus. He belongs among those whose struggle against the dehumanization of mankind has led them to seek for *the hidden God,* a solution to the metaphysical riddles of life."

PRINCIPAL WORKS

SHORT FICTION

Människor   1912
Järn och människor   1915
Kaos   (short stories, poetry, and drama)   1919
Det eviga leendet   1920
    [*The Eternal Smile,* 1934; also published in the collec-
        tion *The Eternal Smile and Other Stories,* 1954]
Onda sagor   1924
Gäst hos verkligheten   1925
    [*Guest of Reality,* 1933]
Bödeln   1933
Barabbas   1950
    [*Barabbas,* 1951]
The Eternal Smile and Other Stories   1954
The Marriage Feast and Other Stories   1955
Sibyllan   1956
    [*The Sibyl,* 1958]
Ahasverus död   1960
    [*The Death of Ahasuerus,* 1962]
Pilgrim på havet   1962
    [*Pilgrim at Sea,* 1964]
Det heliga landet   1964
    [*The Holy Land,* 1966]
Mariamne   1967
    [*Herod and Mariamne,* 1968]

OTHER MAJOR WORKS

Ordkonst och bildkonst   (criticism)   1913
Motiv   (poetry)   1914
Ångest   (poetry)   1916
Sista människan   (drama)   1917
Teater: Den svåra stunden   (drama and essay)   1918

    [*Modern Theatre: Seven Plays and an Essay,* 1966]
Hjärtats sånger   (poetry)   1926
Han som fick leva om sitt liv   (drama)   1928
Konungen   (drama)   1932
Vid lägereld   (poetry)   1932
Mannen utan själ   (drama)   1936
Genius   (poetry)   1937
Låt människan leva   (poetry)   1939
Seger i mörker   (drama)   1939
Midsommardröm i fattighuset   (drama)   1941
    [*Midsummer Dream in the Workhouse,* 1953]
Dvärgen   (novel)   1944
    [*The Dwarf,* 1945]
Aftonland   (poetry)   1953
    [*Eveningland,* 1975]
Antecknat: Ur efterlämnede dagböcker och anteckningar
    (notes and journals)   1977

CRITICISM

Lucien Maury   (essay date 1951)

[*In the following preface to the 1951 English translation of the novella* Barabbas, *Maury praises the work as the culmination of Lagerkvist's artistic and intellectual de-velopment.*]

In a body of literature which has been for the most part preoccupied with national background, with painting the manners of Stockholm and of the Swedish countryside, and—apart from its exploitation of a rich lyric strain— with folklore and epic fantasy, Pär Lagerkvist, since his early "Expressionist" days, has stood as representative of an intellectualism which, like himself, has remained some-what remote and dignified, somewhat unresponsive to the noisy methods of modern publicity.

In the world of Swedish and Scandinavian letters, Lager-kvist occupies, as poet and thinker, a position of eminence which has long been recognized by his compatriots and by the educated public in the countries which adjoin his own. To paint the portrait of this remarkable man, whose work takes rank with the most significant productions of con-temporary Scandinavia, is as tempting as it would be diffi-cult.

Except for a few short stories, and one piece of dramatic narrative, *The Dwarf,* which was highly praised by our lit-erary critics, the French public knows next to nothing of his writings.

Before saying anything else, it is well to draw attention to characteristics which are pre-eminent in the whole body of his work—to a nobility of tone and of style, to an un-questioning devotion to independence of mind, to an un-equivocal sense of vocation which, for half a century, has assured for him a deserved reputation as one of the "ad-vance guard."

There is scarcely a single æsthetic problem in the realm of literature which Lagerkvist has not striven to define and resolve—not only theoretically, but in the practice of his art—whether in the theatre, the short story, or works of meditation, and verse. He has passed through many stages, from his early concern with the art of the theatre at a time when Copeau and Gordon Craig were making their first experiments, a concern which led to conclusions as daring and as relevant now as they ever were, to those hybrid productions, sometimes published simultaneously in the form of narratives or plays—*The Man Who Lived Again; The Dwarf; The Man Without a Soul;* **The Hangman**; *Victory in Darkness; The Philosopher's Stone.* He has travelled far from the *Tales of Cruelty*—which have only a title in common with the stories of Villiers de l'Isle-Adam—or the deeply moving short pieces marked by an eloquent simplicity which the French writer Louis Philippe would not have disowned; from those chapters of autobiography which reveal a meditative childhood already haunted by strange presentiments, and a curious hankering after death, to those essays and poems marked by a thrilling tenseness of unease, and filled with metaphysical ardour. It has been a far cry with him from anguish to serenity, to that interior joy which triumphs over all despair; from early revolt to an acceptance which has never been mere resignation, though often it is not far removed from a mood of burning adoration, from a religious sense at one with reason, from faith in the existence of a principle to be found at the source of all our human destiny. Many phases mark his pilgrimage, and the victories he has won are numerous in battles joined on the fields of ethics and æsthetics, in the perpetual struggle to attain to those realms of thought where the spirit can find its ultimate well-being.

Had Pär Lagerkvist written in a language more easily accessible to Western readers, he would undoubtedly have been acclaimed as one of the leaders of our time, as one of those few, those necessary, men who can hold aloft a light to guide our footsteps through the obsessive darkness of our world. (pp. v-viii)

[*Barabbas*] proves abundantly that he has never lost touch with the tragedy of the contemporary mind, that, in spite of his philosophy, he is familiar with the devastating terrors of our problems, and has been brought face to face with the insoluble problem of Man's predicament, with the horror of that blindness in which we are compelled to face the problem of the universe and of ourselves.

In this enigmatic and unforgettable *Barabbas,* with its sense of spiritual torment, its deep stirrings of faith, its sure response to the movements of the human mind, is expressed the riddle of Man and his destiny, the contrasted aspects of his fundamental drama, and the cry of humanity in its death throes, bequeathing its spirit to the night.

In this, his latest work, we see the final development of an art which has reached the limits of elliptic suggestion, of austerity, and of a form that has been pared down to essentials.

Barabbas is the last phase in a process of thought which has moved beyond mere literature, of an art which, with

its admirable sobriety, embodies the emotional climate of our times. (pp. viii-ix)

Lucien Maury, in a preface to Barabbas *by Pär Lagerkvist, translated by Alan Blair, Random House, 1951, pp. v-ix.*

André Gide   (letter dated 1951)

[*Many critics regard Gide as among France's most influential thinkers and writers of the twentieth century. In his fiction, as well as his criticism, he stressed autobiographical honesty, unity of subject and style, modern experimental techniques, and sincere confrontation of moral issues. In the following letter, Gide praises the novella* Barabbas, *particularly complimenting Lagerkvist's description of Barabbas's spiritual crisis.*]

My Dear Lucien Maury:

Pär Lagerkvist's **Barabbas** is, beyond all possibility of doubt, a remarkable book. I am deeply grateful to you for giving me an early opportunity to read it, as you did in the case of the same author's *The Dwarf* which received, last year, so enthusiastic a welcome from critics and public alike.

When you brought me the translation of **Barabbas,** you spoke of it in such a way as to make me feel the liveliest desire to read it. But I had no idea then how deeply it would interest me. I was, as it so happened, marvellously (I dare not say, providentially) prepared for the experience of its perusal owing to the fact that I had been buried, for the past month, in a study of *l'Histoire des Origines du Christianisme*. Renan had, in masterly fashion, made it possible for me to realize with what intelligent precision Pär Lagerkvist has shown the mysterious springs of an emerging conscience secretly tormented by the problem of Christ at a time when the Christian doctrine was still in the process of formation, when the dogma of the Resurrection still depended on the uncertain evidence of a few credulous witnesses who had not yet bridged the gap between superstition and faith.

From what you told me then, my dear Maury, I derived a very imperfect idea of the extent to which the adventure of Barabbas was involved in the story of Our Lord's crucifixion, of the degree to which the troubled movements of the robber's mind were bound up with what he had seen, or thought he had seen, at Golgotha, and with the various rumours which followed hard upon the Divine Tragedy—an event upon which the destiny of well-nigh the whole of humanity was, eventually, to hang.

It is the measure of Lagerkvist's success that he has managed so admirably to maintain his balance on a tightrope which stretches across the dark abyss that lies between the world of reality and the world of faith. The closing sentence of the book remains (no doubt deliberately) ambiguous: "When he felt death approaching, that which he had always been so afraid of, he said out into the darkness, as though he were speaking to it:—To thee I deliver up my soul." That "as though" leaves me wondering whether, without realizing it, he was, in fact, addressing Christ, whether the Galilean did not "get him" at the end. Vicisti Galileus, as Julian the Apostate said.

I have your word for it, dear Maury, that this ambiguity exists also in the original text. The Swedish language has given us, and is still giving, works of such outstanding value, that knowledge of it will soon form part of the equipment of any man calling himself well-educated. We need to be in the position to appreciate the important part likely to be played by Sweden in the Concert of Europe. (pp. x-xii)

> *André Gide, in a letter to Lucien Maury in 1951, in* Barabbas *by Pär Lagerkvist, translated by Alan Blair, Random House, 1951, pp. x-xii.*

Richard B. Vowles   (essay date 1954)

[*Vowles is an American educator and critic who has edited works by Lagerkvist and other Scandinavian authors, including August Strindberg and Peder Sjogren. In the following essay, which is a version of the introduction to the 1954 English edition of* The Eternal Smile and Other Stories, *Vowles divides Lagerkvist's short fiction into two types: moral tales and "choral fiction"—defined by Vowles as rhythmic and patterned stories that have humanity as their subject.*]

It is a habit of critics and historians to deplore the passing of the tragic spirit, that sharp sensitivity to the violence and the transient beauty of life. But the tragic spirit persists in some men, among them in the brooding, isolated personality of Pär Lagerkvist. In awarding him the Nobel Prize, the Swedish Academy might have erred in honoring a man whose conceptions were too privately Swedish for world-wide recognition and enjoyment; they did not. However close his affinity to the sweet smelling woods and myth-rich earth of Småland, Lagerkvist is a universal spirit. The complaint has even been voiced that Lagerkvist belongs to no common Swedish heritage. That is, perhaps, our gain, for without sacrificing the validity of his soil and people, he has projected his thought into a fabulous world of human inquiry, now grim and twisted, now tender and idyllic. Deep religious searcher that he is, his writing life has been one long attempt to cut his way through anguished reality to a new belief. "It is the measure of Lagerkvist's success," observed the late André Gide, "that he has managed so admirably to maintain his balance on a tightrope which stretches between the world of reality and the world of faith."

Lagerkvist is a very dwelling place of dualisms, of contending opposites: darkness and light, good and evil, the cosmic and the familiar, life and death, comfort and despair. While many of these contrasts, impossible of resolution, enrich the *chiaroscuro* of his art, one has worked itself out in the evolution of his style. When Lagerkvist began to write, early in the decade of the first world war, the note of torment, of hectic anxiety, was dominant:

> Anguish, anguish is my heritage,
> wound in my throat,
> my heart's shriek in the world.
> Lather of sky now stiffens

> in night's gross hand,
> and now the woods
> and hardened heights
> rise barrenly toward heaven's
> stunted arch.
> How hard is all
> how steely, black, and still.

Happily, the fever of this harsh Wertherism was curbed by a growing sense of form which Lagerkvist learned in large part from the French cubist painters and began to apply to his literary art. The result is a style compounded of emotional drive and taut, architectonic control, expressionistic in that realism is translated into a rhythm of bold, often theatrical, symbols. Thus Lagerkvist arrived at artistic maturity as early as 1920.

Lagerkvist is chiefly known in England and America as a writer of fiction, and this is perhaps as it should be. The vigor of his poetry is more rhythmic than metaphoric and thereby loses much in translation. His drama—and he has written some twelve plays since *The Last Man* in 1917—is, I suspect, too austere and abstract for a realistic theatre. It is rather lean fare compared to the warped opulence of the later Strindberg, to whom Lagerkvist is, however, manifestly indebted. American readers know Lagerkvist best as the author of those two finely artisaned novels, *The Dwarf* and *Barabbas.* The sinuous malignancy of the dwarf's monologue, recording as it does the day-to-day activity of a Renaissance household somewhat like that of the early Medici, is impressive as a portrait of evil. *Barabbas* admirably examines the crucifixion of Christ through the eyes of a deeply involved bystander (as we are all involved), who moves through a series of episodes resembling the stations of a medieval morality play.

> [Lagerkvist's literary style is] compounded of emotional drive and taut, architectonic control, expressionistic in that realism is translated into a rhythm of bold, often theatrical, symbols.
>
> **—Richard B. Vowles**

But these two novels, told as they are in rather traditional narrative, give only partial indication of the depth and breadth of Lagerkvist's prose. The remaining prose is largely of two types: *moral tale* and what might be called *choral fiction.* The first is a hard-bitten perpetuation of the pithy moral account in a world which gives little encouragement to it. The second is rhythmic and architectonic. Accomplished by a fusion of expressionism and cubistic form, it is Lagerkvist's chief claim to fictive originality. Both types are worth examination, particularly as Lagerkvist almost from day to day acquires a more international audience.

The high moral content of Lagerkvist's shorter prose is compacted in a mold of half parable, half fable. It by and large lacks the moral tag of the one and the utter brevity of the other. Frequently it is a myth turned inside out, as in **"Paradise,"** which appeared in 1935 in a volume entitled *In That Time.* Retelling the Biblical account of Eden, Lagerkvist rejects the divine prohibition placed on the tree of knowledge, one suspects because it appears to him an arbitrary act, deliberately designed to keep a people in ignorance. Lagerkvist may be permitted scholarly as well as fictive license in such treatment of a perplexing Biblical crux. At any rate, for Lagerkvist mankind's sin becomes the misuse of knowledge.

"The Children's Campaign," from the same volume, presents a detailed account of warfare as conducted by an army of tender six-year-olds. It is Lagerkvist's best exercise in the manner of measured Swiftian fury; though, conditioned as we now have been by the sight of fascist youth troops, the brutality and bloodshed of these "little men" may seem almost civilized. But there is no mistaking the vigor of satiric thrust in such incidents as the spanking administered one small lieutenant by an angry washerwoman and the execution of another soldier for his unmanly behavior at the sight of a Christmas tree. Unfortunately, they have not been conditioned, like Aldous Huxley's delta babies, into a properly compliant citizenry.

Lagerkvist has never made any bones about his preference for fantasy. It is significant that in their short prose both Lagerkvist and E. M. Forster have persisted with fantasy, in spite of a world more interested in its own realistic contours. "Fantasy now tends to retreat, or to dig herself in, or to become apocalyptic out of deference to the atom," Forster has recently observed. Lagerkvist's fantasy, however, is timeless. While Forster's is whimsical and elfish, Lagerkvist's is seriously, solemnly moral, tending to perpetuate itself in parable upon parable. But its method is various, as may be best seen in the *Evil Tales* (1924).

The opening sketch, **"Father and I,"** is a revelation of the unknown. The country idyll of childhood is punctuated by a frenzied, unscheduled locomotive in the night, reminiscent of the headless horsemen and pale riders of the past, which to the youth of the story is the anguish ahead, the hurtling unknown. In **"Saviour John"** Lagerkvist uses the sustained soliloquy very beautifully to explore a case of messiah madness. Tenderly done, without insistent reference to the Christ myth, it manages to contain more narrative than one would expect within its brief scope. The pathetically weak-minded John, who wears the picture of a woman on the lid of a cigar box tied around his neck ("I can't remember now what it means") and a tin star on his forehead, addresses the crowd in the market place.

> They listened attentively; I think they were comforted by my words. I don't understand why they laugh. I myself never laugh. For me everything is serious. . . . Oh, it was glorious to stand like that and feel them gathered around me. . . . I think that I was filled with the spirit today and that they understood me.

So "Saviour John" works for the redemption of humanity even to his own end when he dies attempting to rescue his workhouse companions from a frenzy of flame.

Lagerkvist's concern with the dwarfed, the truncated, and the misshapen asserts itself repeatedly. While, more often than not, such figures are human grotesques, as in the mad cycloramic play *Heaven's Secret,* or personifications of evil, as in *The Dwarf,* the portrait of Lindgren, the man with the withered legs in **"The Basement,"** is a study in harmony and adjustment. The speaker of the story visits him in his flat below street level, where everything is curiously foreshortened and compressed in proportion to the dwarf's size, and there learns a lesson about the fulness of life. On leaving he remarks, "The old man's lamp was the only one burning; it lighted me nearly all the way home." While the method is quite explicitly allegorical, the realistic context is not abandoned. Though God is represented by the vague person of "the landlord," this tale is in every other respect an affectionate, near-Christian myth. **"The Evil Angel"** is equally optimistic, in its portrayal of superstition "in blood-red mantle," scratching crosses on door, the while shouting "You shall die. You shall die." One may have some confidence in humanity. For the people knew quite well they were going to die, they said. "There was so much else of greater importance of which to remind them." In this fashion, many of the *Evil Tales* are sculptured enigmas, concretions of myth, milestones along Lagerkvist's path through a dark moral universe.

In *Struggling Spirit* (1930), a collection of four long stories, one finds Lagerkvist circling realism with no great affection for it. **"The Marriage Feast"** makes of the love of Frida Johansson, haberdasher, with her false teeth and sunken cheeks, and Jonas, village ne'er-do-well, "a heavenly song of praise, a hosanna of light." So Lagerkvist glorifies two simple souls. Much the longest of these tales is **"The Masquerade of Souls,"** a love idyll which presents the intense affinity that a sensitive lame girl and a slightly feverish young man have for each other. Love evolves through its passionate physical condition, unrealized in children, to a spiritual state in which both deny the reality of the world. Lagerkvist seems to consider the sublimation desirable, since "one's whole existence [is] filled with a thousand small things, chopped up into seconds, tiny-tiny, into innumerable small *nows.*" Such is the fragmentary nature of reality. When, in the end, the young man takes his life on a park bench, the commentary of the real world is provided by the passing dog who noses his sock and urinates on him. Unfortunately, with all its charm, essential purity, and immateriality, the love affair does not, I think, leave quite the impression that Lagerkvist intended. Rather than sublimation we seem to have a love that consumes itself in inanition and allows self-pity to render it unfit for this or any other world. The paradox is further heightened by the setting of a partially realistic story in the souls' land where everything is beautiful and sublime, "where there is always masquerade." It is not quite clear what Lagerkvist is masquerading other than his intent. But the undeniable effect is much like that described by Yeats in *The Tragic Theatre:*

> If the real world is not altogether rejected, it is but touched here and there, and into the places we have left empty we summon rhythm, balance, pattern, images that remind us of vast pas-

sions, the vagueness of past times, all the chimeras that haunt the edge of trance. . . .

And trance best describes the mood of this story.

Perhaps the condition of trance may best be seen in its germinative phase in *Guest of Reality* (1925), thinly veiled autobiography, which represents an indeterminate stage between the moral tale and what I choose to call choral fiction. Depicting as it does the youth of Anders in an apartment over a rural railway station where his father is station-master, it is not only quite charming as reminiscence but significant as a repository of those luminous images of childhood that become the symbols of later vision. The book may be regarded as a fair portrayal of Lagerkvist's pietistic upbringing and of Swedish provincial life, though it is much more. The very title asserts the theme of transiency recurrent in Lagerkvist. (I remember another, rather bizarre, tale in which man, the traveler, finds himself in a Kafkan dream hotel where everything is in a state of mad renovation.) In *Guest of Reality* Lagerkvist rejects family reality, the warm corners of childhood, as an elaborate deceit. A nearly pathological awareness of death in the young Anders stretches nostalgia into a taut membrane. Details take on unexpected meaning: The empty bandstand with its music rests heaped like skeletons in the corner, the dark womb of the ice house, the marsh landscape, the revival service. It is a world that one experiences rather than sees with any visual particularity, even in this most realistic of Lagerkvist's fiction. One revealing vignette is a portrait in miniature of the mature writer. Anders is

> sitting hunched up on the ledge, making drawings in the soot on the window-sills. When he'd finished with one he'd move over to the next; there was one to each little window and the fine soot lay thinly everywhere. He didn't seem to see the trains that came in at the platform. But he felt them, gliding and gliding, changing and changing without break. He didn't need to see.

He did not need to see. Nor does Lagerkvist need to see, for he has the moral sentience which surpasses sight.

Lagerkvist's greatest originality lies in what I prefer to call "choral fiction." The earliest effort in this medium is *The Eternal Smile* (1920), Lagerkvist's *divina commedia* to the extent that the title is even a gently ironic paraphrase. Through a collection of loosely joined baroque tales, fabliaux, testimonials, confessions, and case histories—many of folk origin—Lagerkvist creates a representative humanity. Then, the assorted principals of his stories, after the rhythmic crescendo of their various accounts, join like so many striking workers, in a march of protest against the divine mystery. If it is the progress of humanity toward God, it is also the progress of the poet's soul. Geographically indeterminate, quite without dimension, Lagerkvist's limbo reflects a modern world which possesses no such neat gradation of sin as Dante's meticulous hierarchy. Finally, the anger of the multitude is somehow assuaged by the discovery of God in the person of a little old man sawing wood, whose only answer to the chorus of shouts and queries is "I have done the best I could." This presiding, almost obsessive, symbol springs from Lager-

kvist's childhood, from the figure of old Jonsson in *Guest of Reality,* who saws the family wood and observes "It's bitterly cold in this world if you haven't got fires, I can tell you that." It is characteristic of Lagerkvist to discover faith in humble mankind at work.

The Eternal Smile has depth and space, but it is by the dictates of its subject somewhat amorphous. This is by no means true of Lagerkvist's other distinguished piece of choral fiction. *The Hangman* (1933) has the power and impact of the central figure around which all action is grouped, the monolithic presence of the hangman. The image of the hangman was quite possibly suggested by Strindberg's play *The Bridal Crown;* the folk materials were derived from a Danish cultural study, Hugo Matthiessen's *Hangman and Gallows Bird* (1910). But the conception is entirely Lagerkvist's. The hangman becomes a complex symbol of guilt and violence in the first, or medieval, section of the story; and of ritual hysteria in the second, or modern, section of the story. Hence violence is portrayed as man's eternal heritage. While medieval man resorted to and remained in awe of it, modern man is capable of worshipping it with *heils* and genuflections, making of it a very saviour. Figures come and go, now whispering their curiosity, now stopping to pay their respects. A well-fed dowager remarks on the way to the lady's room (the milieu shifts from medieval tavern to modern nightclub): "Well you don't say! It's the hangman! Wait till I tell Herbert about this! My son is simply mad to meet you. Dear child, he loves bloodshed so!"

Strangely enough, the hangman is to some degree a sympathetic character. How is this compatible with the dominant symbolic meaning? It may be said that he plays the role of social scapegoat. Man mistakenly seeks salvation through violence; hence he sees violence as beneficent when it is not. However ambiguous the social statement may be, Lagerkvist builds up his fictive structure with great skill. Simple story merges into dialogue, dialogue gives way to ensemble movement, and movement to dynamic soliloquy—that of the protagonist:

> Again you call me, and I come. I survey the land—a land lying feverish and hot—and in the air I hear the screams of sick birds. It is the rutting hour of evil. It is the hangman's hour.

Thus the fiction progresses through a phantasmagoria of light and brutal color, theatrical to a high degree. It is not surprising that the dramatized version of *The Hangman* was a high moment of Scandinavian theatre in the mid-thirties. It was not merely a profound study of the nature of evil, but one of the first attacks on European totalitarianism.

I have heard it said that the Swedes are only mediocre artists in two dimensions, but that in three they excel. This, like most generalizations, is as arresting as it is glib; for Swedish glass, architecture, faïence, and the sculpture of Carl Milles are powerful arguments. Lagerkvist's literary art is, in the last analysis, three dimensional. He seizes upon the elemental, the typical, and the organic. His short tales have the purity of concretions, his longer ones the mass of sculptured groups and monoliths. They compose a classical landscape, a moral landscape, somehow reassuring in our time.

Such reassurance is perhaps unexpected in the pervading climate of despair. What, among many paradoxes, does Lagerkvist finally believe in? Eternity, for one thing; however dark and bottomless it may be. An imminent presence, for another; though it be man's own creation. And man himself; for Lagerkvist sees in man infinite possibility. Finally, the good, "a quiet, everyday radiance in life that mankind always has difficulty noticing and setting a value on. The evil is so conspicuous and seems to have more reality." The problem is that most of us live in the limbo between good and evil. Ours is the torpid soul of Barabbas dully examining the mystery of life. Dark symbols have obsessed Lagerkvist, it is true; but a recent poem of his suggests the explanation. Reality is pictured as a stagnant water, yielding no relief to the parched soul. Yet in its surface is visible the naked infinitude of stars. Here lies the depth and dark serenity of Lagerkvist's vision. (pp. 111-17)

> *Richard B. Vowles, "The Fiction of Pär Lagerkvist," in* Western Humanities Review, *Vol. 8, No. 2, Spring, 1954, pp. 111-17.*

Mark Schorer   (essay date 1954)

[*Schorer was an American critic and biographer who wrote the definitive life of Sinclair Lewis. In his often anthologized essay "Technique as Discovery" (1948), Schorer put forth the argument that fiction deserves the same close attention to diction and metaphor that the New Critics had been lavishing on poetry. In the following review of* The Eternal Smile and Other Stories, *he points out what he considers the characteristic theme of the collection.*]

Pär Lagerkvist who won the Nobel Prize in 1951 and is highly esteemed in Sweden as the author of over thirty-five books in nearly all the literary forms, is little known in this country, his work in translation until now having been limited to two short novels, *The Dwarf* (1945) and *Barrabas* (1951). [*The Eternal Smile and Other Stories*] should do much to familiarize us with Lagerkvist's quality and, more important, his range, for the collection contains stories written not only over quite a long period of time (from 1920 to the mid-thirties) but also in a variety of forms and moods—from a one page fable like **"The Adventure"** to the moderately realistic novelette of well over a hundred pages called *Guest of Reality.* Between these extremes in length and kind, Lagerkvist presents himself in many moods and modes: solemn and whimsical, idyllic and satirical, questioning, outraged, resigned.

In spite of the variety of which Lagerkvist is capable, one can pin down a central man, a single imagination, even a characteristic form. Lagerkvist is a man who never asks less than an ultimate question. His prose (perhaps the translated prose) makes us feel that in his questions, life and reality are words that always present themselves to him in the upper-case. "What does life mean?" every story by anybody probably asks, however indirectly, but Lagerkvist's stories ask, "What does LIFE *mean?*"

His emphasis is relentless, and on the evidence of this great sheaf of stories, one's impression is that his examination of the ordinary in daily life has not been close enough to permit of the perpetual solemnity with which the very tone of his voice passes judgment upon it. All this is simply to say that in this translation, at least, the rhetoric overshadows the intensity of perception. Or one may wish to say instead, with Richard B. Vowles, who has written an extended introduction to this collection, that Lagerkvist is "a mystic and a seer, rather than a writer of fiction." I think that we would be saying the same thing.

What *does* life mean? The great virtue of Lagerkvist's stories is that he opens fiction up in such a way that he challenges us again to ask ourselves this question directly. His answers are not obscure. It means, first of all, something more than mere endurance if it holds love—love between man and woman. The last story in the collection, another brief fable, this one called **"The Wave of Osiris,"** pictures a great Egyptian king waking from death to present himself to Osiris, and finding that all the accoutrements of his daily life that had been placed in his tomb are unrecognizable objects to him, but that the golden statue of a woman sends through him again a pulsation of life.

A very long story—a novel, in fact—that appears not much before this last one, a work called *The Masquerade of Souls,* deals with a man and woman who enjoy a perfect love, but when one of them dies, there is nothing for the other to do but die too for without love, life is unendurable. This love, lived in "the land where the souls are," where "it is not like here," is necessarily without relation to any of the accoutrements of daily life: when love goes, there is nothing else, for love itself has been rooted only in another soul. This dilemma would seem not only to make of *The Masquerade of Souls* a work of philosophical irony, but also to point to Lagerkvist's necessary second value, his second answer to the question that all his fiction insists upon.

This answer is simply that reality is the humblest detail of actuality. In the opening story of the book, *The Eternal Smile,* which Mr. Vowles calls "Lagerkvist's *divina commedia . . .* the progress of humanity toward God *. . .* also the progress of the poet's soul," God himself appears at the end of the journey as "a little old man sawing wood, whose only answer to a chorus of shouts and queries is 'I have done the best I could.'" A piece not made public until the Nobel Prize banquet in 1951, called **"The Myth of Mankind,"** asserts that "human happiness . . . began when man took possession of the world as it is. The earth is man's home; human happiness lies in the acceptance of this world and our life in it."

When Lagerkvist described himself as "a religious atheist," he probably meant that he apprehended transcendental values but had no dogma within which to locate them. He may even have meant something like this: the idea that the nobility of man's humblest activity, of work, is endless, extending even as far as "God," and that "God" works in man through love alone. Man works up to "God," "God" works down to Man: the point at which they meet marks Man's fullest realization of his life in the world. Love gives work meaning, but work gives Love a world.

This is an abstract notion that Lagerkvist prefers to handle in abstract forms, forms that often carry the tone of the folk-tale, which provides many of his narrative sources, but forms also that have the structure of the parable, which gives them the portentous overtones of philosophy. If his faith lies in the familiar realities, the reality of his fiction lies in his faith. (pp. 4-5, 18)

Mark Schorer, "Many Moods and Modes," in The New York Times Book Review, *June 13, 1954, pp. 4-5, 18.*

Robert Donald Spector   (essay date 1961)

[*Spector is an American critic, poet, editor, and the author of a study on Lagerkvist's life and work. In the following excerpt, he analyzes Lagerkvist's symbolic use of physical deformity in his short fiction.*]

An English editor, aroused by Lagerkvist's use of deformity in *The Dwarf,* grimly remarked that he had no intention of introducing his readers to anything so horrible as this disgusting author. Admittedly, Lagerkvist, like Swift, sometimes employs such symbolism for the shock value that is necessary to the moralist's purpose, but generally his object is never so simple, and certainly his intention is hardly sensationalistic. The "concern with the dwarfed, the truncated, and the misshapen," which, as Richard Vowles has pointed out [in his introduction to *The Eternal Smile and Other Stories*], "asserts itself repeatedly" in Lagerkvist's work, serves a multiplicity of purposes, ranging from the allegorical, symbolic, and philosophic to the structural. For Lagerkvist, it is not only the perfect metaphor for what Walter Gustafson has called his tales of "suffering souls, persons who might be called men of anxiety" ["*Sibyllan* and the Patterns of Lagerkvist's Works," *Scandinavian Studies* XXX (August 1958)], but it has implications that are metaphysical and ethical as well as aesthetic.

Some of this range presents itself in the fiction gathered in *The Eternal Smile.* To be sure, there is the moralist's technique that attaches evaluative significance to the shocking image of the betrayed husband with the bullet wound displayed in his temple in **"The Lift that Went Down into Hell,"** just as there is in the ironic contrast between the physical healthiness and the social corruption in **"A Hero's Death."** Indeed, Lagerkvist often uses this contrast between bodily fitness and spiritual decadence to achieve his irony. In **"The Children's Campaign,"** it is a soul-less society that emphasizes physical soundness for its destructive purpose. Lagerkvist conveys his scorn through his matter-of-fact style and his understatement in describing the victory celebration for the child warriors and the spectators' inability to distinguish between artificial and normal limbs:

> Some of the loudest cheering was for the small invalids at the rear of the procession, blind and with limbs amputated, who had sacrificed themselves for their country. Many of them had already got small artificial arms and legs so that they looked just the same as before. The victory

salute thundered, bayonets flashed in the sun. It was an unforgettable spectacle.

But more significant is Lagerkvist's use of deformity in the title story. Here the marred figures are intended to suggest the lack of communication of human beings, absorbed in themselves, lost in their own problems, unaware of the defects in others, and therefore isolated by their lack of sympathy. The more trivial the deformity, the more absurd their behavior. A man born without a thumb permits it to become a barrier between himself and his neighbors. One with a black spot on his nail, unnoticed by anyone else, allows it to become a burden. The very fact that these deformities carry beyond life and are deep in their souls indicates the degree of their self-absorption, and, indeed, they cannot even communicate with each other. Yet salvation for both can come only through their merging in a common cause, a common understanding. For, as another character remarks, "It is a fact that a hunchback is born into the world every minute. It seems, therefore, that there exists in the race a definite need to be in part hunchbacked." That is as much as to say, as the dwarf does in Lagerkvist's novel, there is none of us without some kind of deformity.

Perhaps because of its symbolic significance, Lagerkvist's use of the misshapen is never sentimental. He accepts it as a natural part of the human condition. Lindgren, the man with the withered legs in **"The Basement,"** a story that Vowles has characterized as "a study in harmony and adjustment," is no more unnatural than the man who is outwardly seemingly erect and healthy and says, "We don't take much notice of him . . . it is as though he should be here, as though he belonged to our world . . . as though he were a part of ourselves." In the same way, Jonas in *The Guest of Reality* has a strength of soul that is more important than his amputated arm. The generosity of his nature and his self-reliance have made normal his relationships with others, despite his need to greet them with only his left hand.

The only time that Lagerkvist permits physical deformity or abnormality to appear a handicap is when it manifests spiritual decadence. Throughout the early part of **"The Masquerade of Souls,"** Arna's lameness is at most a reminder of reality amid the idyllic atmosphere of the narrative, perhaps a foreshadowing of her failure in childbirth, but it is no deterrent to the love affair, and indeed permits a greater emphasis on the kinship of the lovers' souls. Only with the suggestion of some spiritual disturbance does the bodily imperfection manifest itself in the story. Her limp increases with the untidiness of her soul, and with the disintegration of her spiritual strength, she becomes "more of a woman who was lame."

While these examples of Lagerkvist's treatment of the subject illustrate the importance it plays in what might be called his philosophy, another story in *The Eternal Smile* demonstrates as well its structural function in Lagerkvist's work. In both the narrative and dramatic versions of *The Hangman,* examples of physical deformity abound. That Lagerkvist here relates them to moral defects is apparent. He connects the dirty pock-marks with the evil smile of the hangman's child, and he joins the father's great scars with his brutal and savage look. But in the transference of the hangman's brand on his sinful wife to the birthmark on her child, Lagerkvist extends the meaning of the moral symbol so that it becomes a commentary on social injustice, just as the mutilated figure of Gallows Lasse depicts the extent of man's inhumanity to man.

Yet these are only the surface function of Lagerkvist's symbols. They serve as well to unify the structure of both the play and story through an ironic point of view that is accomplished without the author's direct intervention. To be sure, Vowles is accurate when he describes the hangman himself as "a complex symbol of violence, the center of superstition in the first section of the story, and of ritual hysteria in the last." Nevertheless, the ironic contrast between these unhealthy symbols in the superstitious world of the first part and the emphasis upon physical soundness in the Hitlerian doctrine of the second part not only unifies the work but underscores the depth of the sickness of the Nazi mind in the modern world.

How much more revolting is the spiritual mark described in the Nazi's comment that "war stamps the sign of nobility on a man's forehead" than the hangman's brand which Vowles says denotes him as a "necessary social functionary" and thus makes him "in Lagerkvist's conception, a sympathetic figure"! Can all the shocking details of physical disfigurement match the comment of the "healthy" assassin who looks upon his victim and says, ". . . but you could see clearly enough from his body that he wasn't one of us"! That Lagerkvist is making moral judgment on the greater criminality of the totalitarian mind than anything that has gone before is clear in the Nazi assertion that "Violence is the highest expression not only of the physical but even of the spiritual forces of mankind!" As the one afflicted character in this second part indicates by his revelling in war, his blindness of soul is more serious than his lack of sight.

But even more than these stories, Lagerkvist's novels display the same varied and extensive use of deformity. To support the sibyl's assertion that her lover had been an ordinary mortal, his amputated arm imposes limitations on his ability to possess her fully. The contrast between his imperfection and the beautiful formation of her son's hands and feet is crucial to the boy's identification with the sibyl's god so that there shall be no mistaking the child's divine origins.

Divinity is involved as well in the meaning of Lagerkvist's symbols in *Barabbas.* Perhaps it is dangerous, as critics have pointed out, to emphasize the philosophic message of his work, but it is equally undesirable to treat it as an aesthetic vacuum, and *Barabbas* is a good example of the relationship of Lagerkvist's artistic methods to his fundamental beliefs. Using deformity primarily for an exposition of theme, he contrasts both Christ's attitude toward the unselfishness of the hare-lipped girl and her conduct with the unchristian behavior of supposedly Christian disciples, sound and unsound. There are the blind man's lack of sympathy for the lepers, his uncharitable opposition to their cure, and his fear for his own safety. There is the uneasiness of Christ's followers who find in her testimony for Christ only a mockery of their Lord. For them, Lagerkvist

says, "it was as if she had ridiculed what they were about. And perhaps she had. Perhaps they were quite right. Their only thought after this seemed to be to put an end to their meeting as soon as possible."

She had indeed ridiculed their belief by unwittingly exposing their hypocrisy. They are out of all charity with her, ashamed of and embarrassed by a being whose own conduct was as selfless as Christ's own martyrdom. Instead of asking Jesus to perform a miracle for her, she would not trouble Him with anything so trivial. There were others, she felt, "who really needed help; his were the very great deeds." And what had been Christ's response? He had asked her to bear witness for Him. It is a measure of the difference between the Christian ideals and those who profess to practice them that Christ had had no difficulty in understanding her, but her words of testimony for Him fall like a jumble on their Christian ears. What is so important in the mean view of men is of no consequence in the sight of the God they worship. As Lagerkvist describes her after she has been stoned to death, the "scar in the upper lip had become so small, as though it didn't in the least matter. And it didn't either, not now."

> Perhaps it is dangerous, as critics have pointed out, to emphasize the philosophic message of [Lagerkvist's] work, but it is equally undesirable to treat it as an aesthetic vacuum. . . .
>
> —*Robert Donald Spector*

Significantly, Barabbas himself is never closer to Christianity than when he is in her presence. She acts as a lure, and it is apparent that he, the outsider, wants to believe. Yet how can he believe in the efficacy of Christian doctrine when he has witnessed Christian behavior? After her testimony has been rejected and scorned by the Christians, after their platitudes about faith, Barabbas turns away, and he is "glad to be well away from it all. The mere thought of it made him feel sick."

For the outsider theme itself, Lagerkvist also uses deformity as a symbol. The scar, flaming red, marks his apartness. The boldness and daring that have come to him only after this disfigurement are related to his break from his father. If it is a sign of his maturity in an active life, however, it is also a measure of the variations in his faith. When Barabbas is closest to yielding to Christianity, the scar pales and becomes unnoticeable, a symbol of his turning from the ways of men, deep in blood, to the ways of Christ. But with the negation of his belief in Jesus, the scar on Barabbas's face grows burning red and signifies once more his individuality. It is an indication of Barabbas's inability to accept Christ that the final mention of the scar, after his imprisonment, marks him as a man apart. (pp. 209-14)

Lagerkvist's use of deformity . . . is no more revolting or disgusting than the values upon which it is a moral comment. If it is shocking, it is only because the truths that it unmasks are difficult to look upon with equanimity. For Lagerkvist, it represents a fundamental technique to express his philosophy, one dedicated to a search for truth which cannot be dissuaded by the harshness of reality. (p. 217)

Robert Donald Spector, "Lagerkvist's Uses of Deformity," in Scandinavian Studies, *Vol. 33, No. 4, November, 1961, pp. 209-17.*

Richard M. Ohmann (essay date 1962)

[*Ohmann is an American educator and critic, as well as the author of a work on the theory of literary language. In the following excerpt, he contends that Lagerkvist's best short fiction denies the possibility of spiritual resolution.*]

It is over forty years now since the appearance of Pär Lagerkvist's first piece of extended fiction, **The Eternal Smile.** In that tale the dead sit talking desultorily of their lives and their sufferings, until, stirred by one of their number to hatred of "life's insult to man," they decide to seek out God, to "call him to account for everything." After wandering for thousands of years through desolation and darkness, they come on God, a tired old man sawing wood, who answers their outraged "Why?" by quietly repeating "I have done the best I could."

Their anguish erupts: "But what did you mean by it all then? You must have meant something. What did you intend by this that you set going, by all this unimaginable life? We must demand a complete understanding of everything, and also the confusion which is in everything . . . We must demand coherence in everything, peace for our thought, for our tormented struggling heart, and also we must demand that there shall be no coherence, no rest, no peace. We must demand everything."

In humility, God replies, "I am a simple man. I have worked untiringly. I have stood by my work day after day for as long as I know. I have demanded nothing. Neither joy nor sorrow, neither faith nor doubt, nothing. I only intended that you need never be content with nothing." Somehow this dark riddle soothes the millions; they trek back to where they came from, content with a quotidian "life" which is "the one thing conceivable among all that is inconceivable."

If a writer *begins* with the stark metaphysical encounter with God and nothingness, where does he end after forty years and eight novellas (his plays and verse are not my concern here)? Lagerkvist's new book, **The Death of Ahasuerus** published in Sweden in 1960, leaves us in pretty much the same place, or rather the same no place. God's name is spelled with a small letter now, and he never appears in person; he dropped from sight after **The Eternal Smile**, as Lagerkvist moved still farther away from religious certainty. But the central pattern is still the same: an endless quest for meaning, represented by a physical journey; confrontation with suffering; a defiant approach to God; a paradoxical revelation of God's finiteness; and

a final reconciliation to death, which is at the same time a reconciliation to life.

Ahasuerus, the Wandering Jew, is of course the archetypal wayfarer, and as such, a natural symbol for Lagerkvist, who used him before in **The Sibyl.** Now we meet him near the end of life, with centuries of drifting behind him, at an inn for pilgrims to the Holy Land. His eyes are desolate; he stares into darkness. For all his experience he has learned nothing, except that he is incomprehensibly and endlessly persecuted by God. He falls in with one of the pilgrims, a hardened ex-soldier named Tobias, who never kneels, except once, involuntarily, in the presence of a dead woman who bears the stigmata. Under the strange compulsion of this vision Tobias is making a pilgrimage he does not understand; he too, as Ahasuerus would have it, is *chosen* by God: in God's power. With him is a woman, once a virgin huntress, whom he raped and turned into a harlot.

This nondescript party of outcasts lags behind the rest of the pilgrims and is further delayed by a mountain snowstorm. A mysterious arrow, apparently aimed at Tobias, is intercepted by the woman, and she dies. The two men reach the port of embarkation just after the pilgrims have sailed. Tobias, wild with disappointment, gives all his money to three scoundrelly-looking men who claim they are sailing for the Holy Land in their battered yawl. He embarks on his dubious voyage, perhaps to be destroyed in a tempest, perhaps to be killed by the sailors, perhaps to arrive at his goal; we do not know which. Ahasuerus languishes and dies in a monastery at the port.

That's all that happens. As often in Lagerkvist's fiction, the burden rests not on narrative, but on spare, iconographic scenes (the shriveled woman with the stigmata, the arrow in the mountain pass), on the emotions of the characters and, preeminently, on metaphysical speculation. For Lagerkvist is a relentlessly philosophical writer, and his theme is always the same: man's suffering and its relation to a greater power than himself. The entire story of this book seems merely a scaffolding erected to hold the deathbed of Ahasuerus, and his final thrust at understanding. To what insight is he raised? That all mankind, not Christ alone, is crucified: "I understand this; I discovered it at last: man lies forsaken on his bed of torment in a desolate world, sacrificed and forsaken, stretched out upon a little straw, marked by the same wounds as yourself . . . though only you are called the Crucified."

Christ, who cursed the Wandering Jew, was actually his brother in pain. A crucifixion requires a crucifier, and that role Ahasuerus assigns to God: "He sacrifices men! He demands continual sacrifice—human sacrifice, crucifixions!" The hateful revelation is, paradoxically, a release for Ahasuerus, a release from the power of God. By his own strength he has "vanquished god"; the discovery of divine wickedness lifts the centuries-old curse of ignorance, solves the onerous riddle, and writes a coda to the endless wanderings. At last Ahasuerus can die.

But there is a final twist to the argument. Though the pilgrim's quest is futile, his intuition must be valid. "Beyond the gods, beyond all that falsifies and coarsens the world

Lagerkvist is a relentlessly philosophical writer, and his theme is always the same: man's suffering and its relation to a greater power than himself.

—*Richard M. Ohmann*

of holiness . . . there must be something stupendous which is inaccessible to us." It is that holy thing, hidden from men by God, which Ahasuerus embraces in dying, in passing into mystery. He dies happily in a miraculous burst of light, which he values no less for the knowledge that it is simple diurnal sunlight.

An imprecation that is a triumph and an affirmation, an understanding that is no understanding, a commonplace miracle: the paradoxes suit Lagerkvist's agnostic temperament, and they are strongly felt. But the reader may wonder if the strange affirmation which ends this book is adequately contained by the main action, whether the metaphysical position has in the story itself what T. S. Eliot calls an "objective correlative," a hard-won concreteness that stands for and evokes the abstract feeling or thought. And he may wonder, too, whether cosmic affirmation, even of this ambiguous cast, is a possible consequence of Lagerkvist's tormented search.

The two points are related. All his fiction is freighted with philosophy, but in the best of it narrative structure and scene finely support the burden. And in the best of his fiction that burden is overwhelmingly one of doubt and brooding evil, not of reassurance. Uncertainty and suffering are woven into the very fabric of experience as Lagerkvist most powerfully feels it; affirmation in his world is like a candle in the outer darkness.

In the autobiographical *Guest of Reality* (1925) the boy Anders is besieged by reminders of death. His family lives above a railway station restaurant, where the casual guests and the passing trains speak of transiency and impermanence. The beer garden, festive at night, is desolate and frightening during the day.

At play, Anders digs a hole in the sand, and a well-intentioned man tells him that when children dig holes someone in the house is going to die. The boy has a nightmare of the living and the dead, all in one huge grave, with a mighty but incomprehensible voice speaking overhead. In the yard is an ice house, cold and windowless, which terrifies Anders, but curiously attracts him too. He goes in, and stands shivering but immobilized by fear of death. A dismal old woodcutter, a thunderstorm, his grandfather's wrinkles, these too threaten the perilous security of family and home.

Yet around the humble labor of the father, the graceful domesticity of mother and sister, there is an aura of almost unbearable beauty (like that in *Our Town,* or Agee's *A Death in the Family*)—unbearable because so fragile. Anders prays in the woods: "let none of them die, for certain,

not one. Let Father live, let Mother, let his brothers and sisters . . . Let not one possibly die. Let everything be as it was. Let nothing be changed!" But the equilibrium *is* shattered; his grandmother does die, and even before, while she wastes away, Anders thinks of her as dead. To live is to be dying; to be dying is to be dead; this is the one certainty.

After this tale Lagerkvist never again dwells so forcefully on the poignance of ordinary existence, but the certainty of death is with him for good—and the uncertainty of nearly everything else. For above all, Lagerkvist is the apostle of uncertainty and ignorance. A "religious atheist," he has called himself: one who is temperamentally religious, but who finds nothing to pin his faith on. That man should yearn for comprehension, yet be sunk in a world of suffering which is incomprehensible: that condition rankles as an outrage in the hearts of Pär Lagerkvist's compelling anti-heroes. (pp. 170-71)

[The universe is incomprehensible to the heroes of Lagerkvist's best fiction, including] *The Hangman* (1933), *Barabbas* (1950), and *The Sibyl* (1956). The hangman confronts God with an indictment and a question, but for an answer there is only God's stony gaze and "the icy wind of eternity. . . . There was nothing to be done. No one to speak to. Nothing." Barabbas asks himself, at last, if there has been any meaning in his life, and can find none: "But this was something he knew nothing about." And the Sibyl, though she has been possessed a hundred times by the divine spirit, can only say "I know nothing."

In the chaos of life, God should be a pole of certainty, of order; thus the dead who seek God in *The Eternal Smile* are seeking "what is always true." But they find only the enigmatic old wood-cutter. Similar figures are the silent, stone-faced God whose stare mocks the hangman's query, and the silent, smiling, idiotic son whom the Sibyl has borne to God. . . . Behind God's inscrutability is his multiformity, the very reverse of system and order. For the Sibyl, her god is "both evil and good, both light and darkness, both meaningless and full of a meaning which we can never perceive, yet never cease to puzzle over." This jumble of opposites she can neither hate nor love.

Others in Lagerkvist's books, however, are not content with a riddle, particularly one that implicates human beings in senseless pain. Hence Ahasuerus' conviction (in *The Sibyl*) that God is evil, heartless, malignant, and his final defiance of God in the new book. Hence the dwarf's nausea at talk of divine harmony. And hence Barabbas' hate for Christ, the sacrificer of men.

These figures, along with the hangman, radiate an extraordinary malignance. They hate man, too, for his cruelty, for his arrogance, or for his ignorance. The Christian message, "love one another," falls with extreme oddity on their ears. Who can understand such words, within the human landscape of these books—the torture, thievery, rape, battle, and slavery that fill Lagerkvist's pages? And his heroes, through whose eyes and whose words we see the world (since Lagerkvist rarely intrudes an authorial point of view), have been especially ill-treated by it. . . .

[The] hangman, with his blood-red clothes and his symbolic responsibility for human cruelty; Barabbas, whose mother hated him at his birth, and who must move through incredible scenes of Roman inhumanity toward his eventual crucifixion, strangely drawn to those very Christians who most despise him; the Sibyl, wrenched from a simple life to be the uncomprehending mouthpiece of the god, who jealously kills her lover and impregnates her with an idiot son; Ahasuerus, alone denied the blessing of death, because of what seems to him a random and trivial act: all are outcasts, set off from other men, hated by them, persecuted by God, and deprived even of knowledge. Their lives are moved by forces they do not understand, or, worse, by no force at all, by chance (Barabbas lives, Christ dies: "it just turned out that way"; Barabbas' crucifixion, too, "just turned out like that"). Isolation and hate are the air they breathe.

In these, the strongest of Lagerkvist's tales, there are to be sure some traces of beauty, but a beauty that reaches us gravely qualified by the rancor or skepticism through which it sifts. There is the Sibyl's passionate love idyll—but we hear it from the lips of a ruined old woman who knows what a jealous god can do. There is the simple nobility of the early Christians—clouded over by the blank skepticism of Barabbas. . . . The only nobility that survives, finally, is that of the tormented heroes themselves. It issues in uncertainty and rebellion, at best.

But uncertainty and rebellion are not dishonorable conditions. In any case, the world as Lagerkvist sees it offers no other terms: take it or leave it, take it or die. In his best work—and it ranks with the best in contemporary Europe—there is no compromise with them. Reassurance and peace, as in *The Death of Ahasuerus,* are not materials he is at home with. (p. 172)

> *Richard M. Ohmann, "Apostle of Uncertainty," in* The Commonweal, *Vol. LXXVI, No. 7, May 11, 1962, pp. 170-72.*

Sven Linnér   (essay date 1965)

[*In the following excerpt, Linnér compares Lagerkvist's novellas* The Eternal Smile *and* The Sibyl *to examine the philosophic development evident in his writings.*]

When *The Sibyl* (*Sibyllan*) was first published in 1956, several Swedish critics pointed out its close relation to Lagerkvist's earlier book, *The Eternal Smile* (*Det eviga leendet*) of 1920. One passage in *The Sibyl* particularly brought that title to mind. Ahasuerus thinks of the sibyl's demented son who has disappeared so mysteriously:

> [Suddenly he knew of what that perpetual smile reminded him. It was the image of a god which he had seen yesterday, down in the temple at Delphi: an ancient image standing somewhat apart as if to make room for newer, finer images. It had the same smile, enigmatic and remote, at once meaningless and inscrutable. A smile neither good nor evil, yet for that very reason frightening. It represented the same god as did the other images, no doubt—her god and the temple's—but it was evidently very old, and so was the riddle of its stone smile.

> Yes, god was incomprehensible, cruel and frightening. (translated by Naomi Walford)]

In *The Eternal Smile* the symbolism of the title can hardly be related to any particular phrase or scene, but its meaning seems fairly clear: it stands for reconciliation, peace, and acceptance of life. We cannot help wondering whether Lagerkvist had this in mind when he wrote the lines about the smiling stone god in the temple at Delphi. But we don't know. The writer himself *may* never have reflected upon the parallel. But it is there before us, nevertheless, and we have the right to ask ourselves—if not the writer—whether *The Sibyl* should be read as an ironic refutation of the young author's all too easy acceptance of life, his "belief in life" or his *livstro.*

There are still more reasons to compare the two books, separated by half a lifetime. Thus, the character of the sibyl is anticipated in *The Eternal Smile.* In the Giuditta-episode, one of the most beautiful parts of this remarkable book, we are told about the meeting between the young lovers and an old woman who lives high up on the mountain:

> [. . . an ancient creature, a hunched woman, sooty and lean. She sat poking the fire; she was one-eyed. We have lost our way, we said. Yes, she replied, as if she knew it. I could see that she was not one of our people. It was oppressive and strange. I wanted to get away from it, down to the valley again, to sun and trees, to houses and people. I knew I could get there alone once it was light again. But Giuditta sat down and stared like the old woman into the fire. She asked her who she was. The old woman said she was no one. Then you are not human? No, said the old woman, I keep watch over human beings. (*The Eternal Smile and Other Stories,* 1954, translated by E. Mesterton and D. W. Harding) [Giuditta said, but you have only one eye? "Yes," replied the old woman, "I have but one, I can only see that which is true, of the rest I know nothing." "Isn't it enough to know that which is true," asked Guiditta. "Here on earth it is enough," said the old woman.] (The lines within brackets have been omitted in later versions of *The Eternal Smile.*)]

Like the sibyl, this old woman lives above the existence of ordinary people, not only physically but also symbolically, keeping watch over them, and she looks, as does the sibyl in the final scene of that novel, out over the valley where they experience their joys and sorrows. One detail in the description is particularly fascinating, her one-eyedness. It is tempting to speculate upon the meaning of this within the frame offered by the book itself. The fact that the old woman sees only what is true and knows nothing of the rest, may not only mean that she is free from illusions and daydreaming, but also that there *is* "a rest" to be known, real although not "true" in her sense of the word. Such a reading is supported by phrases from the last pages of the book like the following:

[Perhaps there is something other than us; perhaps there is something other than living. But of that I know nothing. It is not me. We sense everything but we exist in what is ourselves.

. . . . .

The wealth of life is boundless. The wealth of life is as great as we can grasp. Can we ask for more? When nevertheless we do ask for more, then all the incomprehensible exists as well, all that we cannot grasp. As soon as we are able to reach out our hands for something, as soon as we get the feeling that something is, immediately it is. Can we ask for more? (translated by Mesterton-Harding)]

Thus, it seems, that the old woman in *The Eternal Smile* does not, in spite of her power of divination, stand for such a total vision of life as does the sibyl.

An important field of study opens up here: the tracing of Lagerkvist's knowledge of folklore and religious history. In spite of some valuable contributions, little has been done so far. An investigation would not only shed light on Lagerkvist's technique in using external material for his own artistic purpose, but also locate his position in a European tradition, where writers—often the most sophisticated ones, like Thomas Mann—turn to myth and the imaginings of the primitive mind.

I am not sure, however, that such a study would help us substantially in understanding the relation between the two stories under discussion. Our main source remains the texts themselves. It is obvious that they have much more in common than is indicated by particular phrases and figures such as the ones mentioned, namely, a fundamental outlook on life which can most easily be—if not caught—at least circumscribed in abstract terms. Some of these abstract ideas are advanced by Lagerkvist himself in the concluding pages of *The Eternal Smile,* and represent an answer to what might be called Ivan Karamazov's question: how are we to accept God's creation knowing the evil it contains? Above all, the following statement:

[I allow that life can be good and evil; I thank it for everything. I thank it for darkness and light, for doubt and belief, for evening and morning. In me it is the one; in my brothers everything else. (translated by Mesterton-Harding)]

A similar thought, albeit on a more bitter note, is expressed by the sibyl:

[My life is what I have lived in you [i.e., God]. The cruel, bitter, rich life you have given me. May you be cursed and blessed! (translated by Naomi Walford)]

Propositions like these may be studied and compared, and still others, which are implied rather than explicitly stated, may be extracted from the text. Thus, we can in each book discern a philosophy of life—that is, if the term philosophy is taken in its most untechnical sense. Still, what the writer presents to us is not just a "philosophy"; it is also an attitude toward life; and his words contain more than an intellectual opinion; they are the summing up of an experience. These two things, the opinion and the experi-

ence, may certainly be regarded as two aspects of the same totality, but they are still not identical. Thus, the first approach may lead us to a discussion of the development of Lagerkvist's religious thought, especially in its relation to the Christian faith. Such a study, if strictly limited to the intellectual content and stripped—as far as it could be done—of all emotions and concrete elements, would certainly be rewarding, but not fully so. The skeleton is much less interesting than the whole man, and we get to know a writer only when we turn our attention to that unity where intellectual ideas are blended with attitudes, reminiscences, and fragments of concrete experience.

That is why I hesitate to talk about the writer's religious thought, and prefer to talk about his religious attitude or belief. A comparison between the belief (in this broader sense) of *The Eternal Smile* and that of *The Sibyl* is obviously of the greatest interest. I wish here only to summarize my opinion on the earlier book by saying that neither a Christian nor a non-Christian reading can easily be refuted. The religious meaning of this legend is "open." The same can be said of *Barabbas* and the collection of poems, which follows, *Evening Land (Aftonland)*; otherwise André Gide would not have issued his famous dictum about Barabbas that perhaps the Galilean "got him" in the end. (See Chap. 7 in my *Pär Lagerkvists livstro,* 1961.)

It seems that Lagerkvist, toward the end of his life, has begun a revision of his religious positions, and *Barabbas* and *Evening Land* may be taken as indicating a return to—or at least a movement toward—the faith of his childhood. *The Sibyl,* however, again points away from that faith. In my opinion a "Christian" reading of the book is possible only if the religious terms are so extenuated as to be misleading. This seems still more clear in the light of Lagerkvist's two latest books, following upon *The Sibyl.* Thus, in *Ahasuerus' Death (Ahasverus död,* 1960) the dying man in his last words talks of "the divine" itself, which must exist beyond all holy rubbish of religions and superstitions: ["Yes, God is that which separates us from the divine."] Lagerkvist here takes up the theme which he so eloquently expressed in his profession of a (non-Christian) faith, in *Life Vanquished (Det besegrade livet,* 1927).

But this leads me away from my main concern. The point where a difference between *The Eternal Smile* and *The Sibyl*—and thus a development in the writer—can be seen most clearly, has not yet been mentioned. In *The Eternal Smile* the accusations against God, which remind us of Ahasuerus' lamentations in *The Sibyl,* and the acceptance of life, which anticipates the sibyl's final words, are pronounced by characters who are almost anonymous. We hear voices but we do not see their owners, as we see Ahasuerus and the sibyl. Still, *who* says something is often as important as what is said; the same belief professed by an old man and by a young person is really not the same. In the first, and larger, part of *The Eternal Smile* we get to know several characters, among them Giuditta and her lover who visit the old woman on the mountain slope. But it would be almost meaningless to ask what the meeting with God means to them, or whether the old woman now sees with both eyes also the things which are not "true."

The representatives of mankind who stand before the woodsawing god, are invisible, having no bodies, no pasts. This is not to deny that the concluding pages of *The Eternal Smile* are magnificent as poetry and vision: I think they are. I wish only to point out that Lagerkvist, who is so much of a realist in the larger part of the story, changes style and genre in the end, as radically as does Dante when he moves from the *Inferno* to the *Paradiso*. There is no such shift within *The Sibyl:* the woman who has seen and suffered all is also the one who accepts all, and, if she influences Ahasuerus, it is not through the logic of her argument, but by virtue of her experience.

It may thus be said that the sibyl has reached the quality we usually call maturity. I mean by that a working out, instead of an escaping or suppressing, of our experiences and an integration of them in our minds. Of course, we may regret the bitterness in the sibyl's final comment: ["May you be cursed and blessed!"] and assert that this is not yet wisdom. The fundamentally happy acceptance of life in *The Eternal Smile* may seem to us a better alternative. Still, the fact remains that this acceptance is not represented as being borne out of experience; in this sense the earlier book is not a work of maturity.

Lagerkvist was, of course, a young man when he wrote it, but an aging man in his sixties when he conceived *The Sibyl.* It is tempting to identify him with the main characters in the latter novel. One detail may serve as an illustration here. In *Evening Land* the poet talks about himself as having "old eyes": ["With old eyes I look back," "My hand covering my old eyes, once those of a child."] The phrase returns in Ahasuerus' words about himself, that it has been his lot [" . . . to look about me day after day, year after year, for centuries and tens of centuries, with these old eyes that see through everything and perceive the vanity of all things."] A few pages later Ahasuerus looks at the Sibyl's face: ["He looked at her in silence; at her dark face, which seemed ravaged by fire, and at her inscrutable old eyes which had seen god" (translated by N. Walford).] It seems natural to say that Ahasuerus in his accusations against God and, more apparently still, the sibyl in her resignation represent the writer himself.

> [The] same themes and symbols recur all through Lagerkvist's work with rare consistency, but they are connected with characters and situations of such great variety that it is hard to point at any one of these characters as representing "the writer himself" or as "coming out of his own heart."
>
> —*Sven Linnér*

But what do we mean by that? We should not be surprised to find that in *The Dwarf* (*Dvärgen*, 1944), Lagerkvist's novel from the second world war, not only Maestro Ber-

nardo, the genius and artist, has those old eyes which have seen everything [(" . . . the strange weariness in his aged eyes" (translated by Alexander Dick)], but also the dwarf himself. This is how he looks at Boccarossa, the condottiere: ["As though bewitched, I stood and scrutinized him with that ancient gaze of mine which already witnessed everything, with my dwarf's eyes in which all the centuries dwell" (translated by Alexander Dick).] For anyone who is well read in Lagerkvist, it seems clear that all these characters who have "perceived everything" have something fundamental in common with their creator, but in no case is there simple identification and direct projection of self. It is true that the same themes and symbols recur all through Lagerkvist's work with rare consistency, but they are connected with characters and situations of such great variety that it is hard to point at any one of these characters as representing "the writer himself" or as "coming out of his own heart." Really, terms like these are not much more than metaphors or semantic shortcuts standing for, and often confusing, a relation of utmost ambiguity. If we wish to speak with greater precision about *The Sibyl,* we may say that here Lagerkvist has given us a "personal expression"—thus indicating a quality in the text, rather than a biographical fact—of an attitude toward life more mature than the one represented in the great legend of his youth. (pp. 160-67)

Sven Linnér, "Pär Lagerkvist's 'The Eternal Smile' and 'The Sibyl'," in Scandinavian Studies, *Vol. 37, No. 2, May, 1965, pp. 160-67.*

Louis O. Kattsoff   (essay date 1966)

[*Kattsoff is the author of such works as* The Design of Human Behavior *(1953),* Logic and the Nature of Reality *(1956), and* Physical Science and Physical Reality *(1957). In the following excerpt, he studies humanity's relationship to God as presented in four of Lagerkvist's novellas:* Barabbas, The Sibyl, The Death of Ahasuerus *and* Pilgrim at Sea.]

Like Sartre, Camus, Kierkegaard, and the Existentialists in general, Lagerkvist is concerned to depict the agony of man in his existence. The existential situation demonstrates clearly that freedom and self-assertion are fundamental traits of mankind, but above all man is immersed in an agony of bewilderment in the face of his apparent destiny, Death, which is nothing. The spiritual climate of human living, today, is as confused and chaotic as the physical climate is hopeful and orderly. When the steady, intoxicating, advance of the physical sciences is contrasted with the rapid and stupefying decline of the religious domain of existence, the explanation for human despair and agony is obvious. Man is less and less certain of his future destiny. Nothing makes sense from a human point of view. Man is not merely all too human, he is all too insignificant—except for his freedom and he is no longer sure what that means. Indeed, modern Existentialism regards freedom and its risks, as well as the threats to that freedom as perhaps the most significant concept in any theory of the nature of man. Lagerkvist's purpose in [*Barabbas, The Sybil, The Death of Ahasuerus,* and *Pilgrim at Sea*] is basically to support Sartre's and Camus' thesis that the greatest threat to freedom is God. To support this Lagerkvist depicts the encounter with God of Lazarus, Barabbas, Ahasuerus, the Sibyl, a sailor Giovanni, and a pilgrim.

Except for the Sibyl, the god encountered is the god who desired to be crucified. The reference is manifestly to Jesus, but in none of the books is Jesus' name ever given. He is always referred to as "the crucified one," or "the son of God," or "the god who wanted to be crucified." And, always, the word 'god' is spelled with a small letter 'g.' The impression is left that neither Jesus nor the "god at Delphi," are much different. In both cases, they are gods and not God.

Lazarus is mentioned only in the first book, **Barabbas.** His encounter with god was a "long-distance" one, for he was resurrected to bear witness to "the crucified one," and this not because he had asked for resurrection, but because, apparently, the crucified one desired someone to testify for him. But the outcome of this resurrection, for Lazarus, is hardly one of joy. His existence is a shadow of death. He lives as though he were still dead; alienated from all that he was and all that he loved. The "crucified one" had not really resurrected Lazarus—he had merely brought him back to the realm of the living, and left him there. "Barabbas had never thought a face could look like that and he had never seen anything so desolate. It was like a desert." Lazarus' eyes expressed nothing at all. Raised from the dead, Lazarus continues in a living death. True, he says he thanks this "son of god" for having raised him from the dead. But death, says Lazarus, is nothing. "I have merely been dead. And death is nothing . . . The realm of the dead isn't anything. It exists, but it isn't anything." And then he adds the strange remark "But to those who have been there, nothing else is anything either." Lazarus' encounter with god is not a joyous one. It is a tragedy! If a musical accompaniment were provided to this picture of Lazarus, it would be rather a funeral dirge than the song of angels rejoicing. Somehow in his encounter with god, Lazarus ends up less a man, less a human, and not more.

Barabbas' encounter with god was, in its way, also a defeat. His existence after the encounter is radically undermined and transformed into a kind of living death. Like Lazarus, Barabbas' encounter was not of his own willing. He was saved from the cross, and in his stead "the crucified one" died. Barabbas did see this man who was called the "son of god." Indeed, he never could forget the crucified one after that. It was strange and beyond comprehension to Barabbas, that the son of god could be crucified in his stead, if he was the son of god. For Barabbas this enigma is never answered. But, like Lazarus, Barabbas' salvation from death is not anything over which to rejoice. He too is now isolated from all he did and all he was. Barabbas was not only saved from death, he was transformed. He was no longer Barabbas as before. He was a stranger to his associates and to himself. He wanders about alienated, bewildered, at times in despair; no longer the free, strong man; strongly drawn to those who worshiped "the crucified one," and apparently enslaved by him. Barabbas' very thoughts cannot leave the memory of "the crucified one." Barabbas' existence is such that one of his friends

is led to say, "if a man is sentenced to death, then he's dead, and if he's let out and reprieved he's still dead, because that's what he has been and he's only risen again from the dead, and that's not the same as living and being like the rest of us." So, Barabbas is dead, while alive! Barabbas' alienation is complete. Even the Christians will have nothing to do with him when they discover he was released instead of the Master—even though it was not Barabbas' fault at all that this thing had happened to him. As a final sign of his alienation, Barabbas, when brought before the Roman who is seeking to find out if he is a Christian, says, "I have no god"; whereupon the Roman scratches the name of "Christus Jesus" from the slave's disk Barabbas was wearing. This is, in fact, symbolic. The slave disc indicates to whom the wearer belongs. And on one side of Barabbas' disk was the insignia of Rome, on the other that of Jesus. Scratching out the name of Jesus was a sign of his diremption from god. At this instant, Barabbas' eyes take on an expression of hatred. It is as if Barabbas' act of final renunciation released him to himself. Where before his eyes, like those of Lazarus, were dead and staring, they now awoke to human emotion. But only for that moment. Barabbas could not really free himself from god. As if to underline this terrible fact that an encounter with god results in slavery and leaves everything transformed, Barabbas is finally crucified along with, but not among, the Christians because he wishes to do the god's word and destroy the Romans! In a burst of frenzy he seeks to set fire to the homes of the Romans, as the Romans set a trap for the Christians. Barabbas is caught with a fire-brand; and Barabbas' presence among the Christians serves to condemn all to the cross.

So, Barabbas dies on the cross next to the Christians, but not of them; as if to demonstrate his alienation once again. At the crucifixion, " . . . it was a long time before it was all over. But the crucified spoke consolingly and hopefully to each other the whole time. To Barabbas, nobody spoke." "And Barabbas was left hanging there alone . . . "

In a definite sense, Barabbas is typical of modern man. He wants desperately to believe, but cannot. He tries to see what the girl with the hare-lip sees, but does not. Even though he waits outside the cave where "the crucified one" lies, and which later is empty, he sees nothing except the empty cave. At the crucifixion, he sees the darkness; but there was no darkness elsewhere, so he attributes it to a trick of his eyes. He cannot understand Christian belief, nor the Christians themselves. Hasak, the slave, who dies willingly rather than deny god, is utterly incomprehensible to him. And Barabbas dies alienated, entering the realm of death which Lazarus, who did believe, said was nothing—nothing at all.

The story of Ahasuerus, which begins in **The Sibyl** and ends in **The Death of Ahasuerus,** is another dramatic picture of the disastrous effects of an encounter with god. Unlike Lazarus and Barabbas, however, Ahasuerus' encounter and its results, although also in a sense accidental, are partially his own fault. But, and this is important in understanding Lagerkvist, the terrible punishment inflicted upon Ahasuerus is the fulfillment of the curse pronounced

Pär Lagerkvist.

by "the crucified one," the "son of god," who preaches love and forgiveness, and who died on the cross for the salvation of all sinners. Ahasuerus lived on the street along which men condemned to crucifixion dragged their crosses on the way to Golgotha. How was he to know that the unhappy man who stopped to lean against his house was "the son of god?" Ahasuerus, fearing the Romans as well as the Jews, had brusquely ordered this unhappy man to move on lest he bring ill fortune to his house. The son of god, thereupon, looked at Ahasuerus and uttered the terrible curse, "Because I may not lean my head against your house your soul shall be unblessed forever . . . you shall never die. You shall wander through this world to all eternity, and find no rest." In a sense, this was a strange curse since it gave Ahasuerus something people ordinarily desire—immortality. But immortality is not in itself a blessing. From then on Ahasuerus was no longer a free man. Neither his paths nor his thoughts were his own. And he was not even free to die, as any mortal is. Ahasuerus heard the rumor that this had been "god's son" later on. He tried not to believe this; for, if the "crucified one" were the son of god, why were they who really believed in him in hiding. For Ahasuerus the world takes on an air of "ashen gray" desolation, as his wanderings begin and he seeks to find his destiny. He was doomed to wander for all eternity, "and eternity was something limitless, endless, a realm of death which the living must look into with horror." Ahasuerus himself viewed his immortality as a form of death,

for he says, "That was my death sentence: the most cruel that could be devised." He was powerless to prevent, or do anything to offset, this curse. Even his attempt to rebel, to refuse to accept this destiny invoked by the son of god, failed. From that point on, his unhappiness increases as he realizes all that is meant when even the love of his wife is taken from him. "This is the result of an encounter with god! god? To me," says Ahasuerus,

> he was no god, but just a criminal . . . Compassion? Love of mankind? Maybe. But I'm not a loving man, and have never pretended to be. . . . Of his doctrine of love I know little—only enough to be sure that it's not for me. And besides, is he himself really so loving? To those who love him he gives peace, they say, and he takes them up with him into his heaven; but they say, too, that he hurls those who don't believe in him into hell. If this is true, then he seems to be exactly like ourselves, just as good and just as bad."

So, Ahasuerus wanders through the centuries. Bound to god, he is not free. He is immortal now, as god is; but, is not free. His fate, the Sibyl points out, is forever bound with god.

Significant too, in this respect, is the death of Ahasuerus which is described near the end of *The Sibyl.* Ahasuerus, like Orestes in *The Flies* is able to re-assert himself—to defy god, with the words, "I care for no one but myself, as god cares for no one but himself. If he has cursed me, then I curse him, too. I will not bow . . . And my hatred [for god] is as immortal as his." It is this assertion of himself through his defiance of god, that brings Ahasuerus to realize (in *The Death of Ahasuerus*) that god and man are not too unlike, if that is what god is like. Ahasuerus challenges a god who so incongruously demands the sort of things god does. He then realizes that the son of god is not the only one to suffer. The crucified one is not the only one to have been crucified. Many others have ascended the cross, and endured the anguish of crucifixion. These thoughts lead Ahasuerus to reject the crucified one as the son of god. His rebellion is now victorious, as Ahasuerus cries out. "Now I have torn down the veil of the holy of holies and seen who he is. Now at last he has lost his power over me. At last I have overcome him—at last I have vanquished god. I have lifted the curse from my own shoulders. I have delivered myself from my destiny and mastered it. Not with your help or anyone else's but my own strength . . . I have conquered god."

These words are important. They constitute the heart of Lagerkvist's argument. Ahasuerus is able to assert himself only in so far as he rejects god. He becomes aware of the fact that he who claims to be god, is like himself. Nothing but a brother in disguise, so to speak. This puts Ahasuerus on the same footing as the son of god. He too, therefore, is a son of god. As such, Ahasuerus is free, he is the master of his own destiny. Only by conquering god, i.e., rejecting him, can Ahasuerus stand up as a free man. And, if he can be free by conquering god, then surely god is no god, but only an imposter obstructing man's view of the divine. For, continues Ahasuerus,

Beyond the gods, beyond all that falsifies and coarsens the world of holiness, beyond all lies and distortions, all twisted divinities and all the abortions of human imagination, there must be something tremendous which is inaccessible to us. . . . Beyond all the sacred clutter the holy thing itself must exist. . . . god is nothing to me. Indeed, he is hateful to me, because he deceives me about this very thing, and hides it from me. . . . Yes, god is what divides us from the divine. . . . To god I do not kneel—no, and I never will. But I would gladly lie down at the spring to drink from it. . . .

As if to underline and accentuate the basic argument he is proposing, Lagerkvist offers two additional bits of evidence, the life of the Sibyl (in *The Sibyl*) and the life of Giovanni (*Pilgrim at Sea.*) The reasons for both of these stories are clear. The Sibyl is the prophetess of a pagan god—the god at Delphi. Giovanni was the servant of the Christian god—a defrocked priest. Yet, there are common elements in both of their lives, chief among which is the disastrous consequence of the encounter with god, and the cruelty and ingratitude of their gods. In the case of the Sibyl, moreover, there are astounding and shocking parallels to the story of Jesus, even to the ascending into heaven of the son of god born of a mortal woman. The Sibyl from early childhood is dedicated to the service of god. But her child is born of a rape in the cave of the god while the Sibyl is prophesying. Presumably the goat-god who inhabits the cave had committed this act against her. The child is, however, witless, and sits in the sibyl's miserable house in the mountain grinning—until he ascends to heaven. This is the Sibyl's reward for her service to god!

Giovanni, too, had dedicated his life to the service of god from early youth. But he finds the love of a woman too strong for his vows. As a result, he, too, is outcast, defrocked, and forced to leave his home. The service of god does not allow for the human experience of love, just as the Sibyl discovered when she gave her love to the stranger in the woods. But the Sibyl remains tied to god, while Giovanni on the ship has discovered that the sea serves as the paradigm of freedom. At the beginning of the Sibyl's story, she remarks "There is no joy in serving god,' but at the conclusion she shows her strong attachment in the following words,

What would my life have been without him? If I had never been filled with him, with his spirit? If I had never felt the bliss that poured from him, the anguish and pain that is his also, and the wonder of being annihilated in his blazing arms, of being altogether his? Of feeling his rapture, his boundless bliss, and sharing god's infinite happiness in being alive?

. . . . .

Yet I cannot forget all the evil he has done me, and the horror. How he took possession of my whole life and took from me almost every earthly joy. How he opened his abysses to me, his evil depths. I don't forget that, and I don't forgive!

While Giovanni says to the pilgrim:

Can one grab anything of life . . . until one has

learnt from the sea? . . . Until one has learned to be carried along by the sea, to surrender to it utterly, and cease fretting about right and wrong, sin and guilt, truth and falsehood, good and evil—about salvation and grace and eternal damnation—about evil and god and their stupified disputes. Until one has become as indifferent and free as the sea and will let oneself be carried, aimless, out into the unknown—surrender utterly to the unknown—to uncertainty as the only certainty, the only really dependable thing when all's said and done.

Here is the crux of the matter. To be free! And to be free means to reject goals, purposes, objects; only to find peace—the peace of the sea. Giovanni, being unfrocked, has regained his freedom—for he is now a godless man. There is a sharp contrast between the character of Barabbas and the Sibyl and that of Giovanni and Tobias the Pilgrim. Barabbas breaks away from god by recognizing the divine—and dies—but now he is free. The Sibyl never breaks away from god. Indeed, her recognition that she has given birth to god's son only seems to tie her closer to her god, for, finally, she remains seated at the door to her abode watching the temple below as a new priestess enters it. Giovanni, on the other hand, does break away and becomes free, while Tobias, the Pilgrim, apparently remains with the ship—a free man—and surrenders his pilgrimage. It is remarkable, however, how closely this freedom so vividly described by Giovanni resembles death.

And this is also the striking fact about so many existentialists' interpretation of freedom. Man makes his own fate! Yes, but in order to do this, he must be completely free. And complete freedom involves a rejection of all responsibility, all morality, all subjection to any law except those one chooses from one's own inner freedom. Such a condition of absolute lack of compulsion can only be achieved in a state of complete isolation. This makes of *human* existence a transitory moment that appears and vanishes like a comet bursting through the skies.

Lagerkvist's argument can be phrased as follows. If god exists, and is as the Christian says he is, then an encounter with god should be not only meaningful but rich and full of joy. But an encounter with god results in mystification, enslavement, tragedy, and sorrow. It follows, therefore that either god does not exist, or he is not as the Christians describe him. The evidence for the second premise is in the lives of those who have encountered god (or say they have) in an intimate fashion. Here are no logical or metaphysical arguments for or against the existence of god. These Lagerkvist presumably leaves to the philosophers and theologians. Here is an argument stated in terms of human existence and its problems—of man's quest for himself. As such, it attempts to meet the problem at a vital point. God's existence must have widespread impact on human living. If god is only a transcendent and transcendental observer with no influence on human affairs, then he is irrelevant and man can in no way be subject to him. But, if, as the Christian believes, god does interfere in human affairs; if Christ was the saviour; if salvation is a fact; then the conflict between human freedom and god's power is not only real but urgent. In other words, Lagerkvist's argument against the existence of god is existential and concrete.

There is, however, a real weakness in such an argument. Even if we suppose that most encounters with god are disastrous and end in slavery and a denial of freedom, this would demonstrate not that god does not exist, but only either that god must be rejected and defied, or that such are the consequences of an encounter with god. If god is rejected, not merely denied as existing, then this would mean that man is stupid. For is it not stupidity to deny the facts? Is it being truly free, to act as if something which is, is not? To defy god, is, perhaps, to assert one's freedom; but this is only an illusory freedom. It amounts to saying, "I am free" when the fact of the matter is that I am not. These are not merely conceptualized rebuttals of Lagerkvist's thesis; they are thoroughly grounded in existence. For, if god exists, and does touch human lives, then the very human situation itself is incomprehensible if it fails to take these things into account. (pp. 380-88)

> *Louis O. Kattsoff, "Encounter with God in the Novella of Pär Lagerkvist," in* Discourse: A Review of the Liberal Arts, *Vol. IX, No. 3, Summer, 1966, pp. 378-88.*

Winston Weathers   (essay date 1968)

[*Weathers is an American critic, educator, and author whose works include* Pär Lagerkvist *(1968),* The Archetype and the Psyche: Essays in World Literature *(1968), and* William Blake's "Tyger": A Casebook, *(1969). In the following excerpt from the first-named work, he discusses Lagerkvist's rejection of conventional religion in his novellas and short stories.*]

Against the dark background of human nature and universal mystery, Lagerkvist discusses the fundamental issues of God, Christ, and the church. Lagerkvist is primarily a religious writer after all, and though he finally rejects man's conventional concepts of God and Christ and rejects the validity of the Christian church, Lagerkvist himself never becomes the secular philosopher who would reject the realities of human experience upon which conventional theology and religion are based.

Lagerkvist's theology begins with a distinction between divinity and god—divinity, a real and experienceable force in the universe, and god, a horrifying projection of man's own secular nature. Lagerkvist distinguishes, as it were, between a True God and a False God; and it is the False God that he rejects in his own form of contemporary atheism—a religious atheism that does not deny a transcendent reality and divinity but denies a limited and artificial godhead.

Two major works in which Lagerkvist discusses the diverse natures of god and the divine are *The Sibyl* and *The Death of Ahasuerus,* two of the novels in his great postwar pentalogy. In these novels, Ahasuerus and the Sibyl enter into theological conversation, Ahasuerus in particular articulating a great deal of Lagerkvist's theological thought.

Ahasuerus, the wandering Jew burdened with eternal life, expresses the distinction between god and the divine when

he says, "Beyond the gods, beyond all that falsifies and coarsens the world of holiness, beyond all lies and distortion, all twisted divinities and all the abortions of the human imagination, there must be something stupendous which is inaccessible to us." The "something stupendous" is the True God and the "twisted divinities" are the False God. And it is the false and twisted that Ahasuerus refers to when he makes the key theological observation in all of Lagerkvist: "Yes, god is what divides us from the divine."

Lagerkvist believes that man is separated from the True God by a False God of man's own invention. Man, truncated and dwarfed, cannot see and cannot reach the True God; like the Dwarf, he cannot see the stars in the sky; and out of his own secular limitation and short reach, man has of necessity created a god of his own that he *can* lay hands and mind and eyes upon in order to make sense out of the enigmatic universe.

Secular man finds the True God inaccessible, disinterested, ambiguous, and a constant mystery. From man's perspective it is as though True God was absolutely impersonal, a distant light filtering into our world only by accident. And Lagerkvist has tried in various ways to describe this indescribable divinity. In the play *Let Man Live* (1950), Jesus talks of the divinity in this way:

> He is, in one way, a stranger in His own life, in the life He has created. And you are right in saying that He is very remote. He is far, far away. He lives in an entirely different world, you might say in an altogether different universe from the one you call yours.

Frequently, Lagerkvist presents his divinity as a lonely old man—sawing wood by lantern light in **The Eternal Smile;** sawing wood, oblivious to the action around him, in *The Secret of Heaven;* called a "very lonely man. And He is an old man, too," in *Let Man Live.*

Perhaps one of the most dramatic of Lagerkvist's depictions of the indescribable divinity is given in one of his very fine short stories, **"Father and I,"** in which a father takes his son for a walk along the railroad tracks, a walk that lasts late into evening. On the way home the boy grows frightened of the darkness, but his father explains we need not fear the darkness since we know that god is present; this observation is, however, unsatisfactory to the boy; it actually frightens him even more: "It was horrible that he was everywhere here in the darkness, down under the trees, in the telegraph poles which rumbled—that must be he—everywhere. And yet you could never see him." Then suddenly, the father and son hear the mighty roar of an unscheduled train behind them; they jump off the tracks just in time; and they see blaze past them a darkened train, with only the fire in the engine glowing upon the engineer, who stands "there in the light of the fire, pale, motionless, his features as though turned to stone." We are surrounded by a frightening mystery, by the ever present yet inexplicable force of the divine, and from our narrow perspective, from our "childhood," we see the inexplicable as frightening and horrifying.

Indeed, the True God in Lagerkvist is always distant, difficult to discern and understand, pictured often as a statue with an "eternal smile," both gentle and mocking, both kind and cruel, beyond our comprehension. We do not understand God's purposes, if there are purposes at all; and our own crooked lives . . . complicate our human reception of the straight light that may be shining out from the divine. Peering out at the distant divine, we, in our secular blindness, see something split, divided, and paradoxical. We see a god terrible and wonderful at once, and we decide, as the Sibyl does, that God "is the most inhuman thing there is. He is wild and incalculable as lightning. . . . With him anything may happen. . . . The divine is not human. . . . " Unable to see the True God, we finally begin to describe him as the Sibyl does: "And so far as I comprehend it he is both evil and good, both light and darkness, both meaningless and full of a meaning which we can never perceive. . . . A riddle which is intended not to be solved but to exist."

Secular man does not like riddles, of course. He is committed to reason, order, and solutions. He insists upon a universe of definable and describable phenomena. And by means of definitions and descriptions he reduces the inaccessible divine into accessible god. In *The Hangman* secular man explains that "it's absolutely essential for us to get a god for ourselves," a god fitting our specifications. Barabbas (in the novel *Barabbas*), one of the great representatives of secular man in Lagerkvist, is completely baffled by the idea of Christ and the Messiah, simply because of the matter of definition: "How can they talk like that! . . . The son of God! The son of God crucified! Don't you see that's impossible!" Christ cannot be Messiah: "Didn't she know what a Messiah was? . . . he would have come down from the cross and slain the lot of them." Barabbas, one of the least educated and least capable of men in Lagerkvist's myth, is nevertheless certain that he knows what god is and should be.

It is this very delimiting activity on the part of man that finally produces the False God, made in the image of man. And obviously, a god in the image of man is of man's nature. Ahasuerus says:

> To those who love him he gives peace, they say, and he takes them up with him into his heaven; but they say, too, that he hurls those who don't believe in him into hell. If this is true, then he seems to be exactly like ourselves, just as good and just as bad. Those we love we too treat well, and we wish the rest all the evil there is.

Not only is he "like ourselves," but he is—like us—more easily evil than good. Ahasuerus says, "For he is a malignant power which never releases me from his talons, and gives me no peace." The Sibyl says, "He was unrest, conflict, and uncertainty. Those things were god." . . . We conceive god in our own dimension; and since we are become dwarfs, we see him as the dwarfish murderer of the universe, the god who "let you hang there when you cried out to him in your deepest despair," and whom "there is no joy in seeing."

The divine, in secular hands, becomes False God, then Cruel God, and finally, of course, Dead God. Long before Hamilton and Altizer, Lagerkvist was putting such words into the mouth of the Hangman as these: "You have turned your God to stone. He's long been dead now. . . . Now he is crumbling on his throne like a leper and his dust is spread over the waste of heaven by the desolate wind of eternity." The divine is not dead, but our vision of the divine is dead, and the secular god whom we erected is a stone-dead god without any significance whatsoever in our secular wasteland. This secular god is simply a Thing, an idol. (pp. 19-23)

In a universe in which a divine reality is obscured by the presence of man-made god, what is the status of Christ? In many ways, Lagerkvist provides an ambiguous answer, as though he himself were not sure what the role of Christ might finally be in the spiritual drama of mankind. Yet Lagerkvist does feel something about the man from Nazareth: Christ is much in Lagerkvist's writing—especially his late novels—and is not a despised creature.

Christ, as he appears in *Barabbas,* is a lean and spindly man, the queer, weak man, sparse of beard, with hairless chest, the unlikely god. But does Lagerkvist even suggest that Christ is God? The Christians in Lagerkvist's novels do acknowledge Christ as the "Son of God"—but Lagerkvist himself would seem to suggest a Christ, not the "Son of God," but the son of the divine, a distinction of major importance.

Is not Christ simply that part of our humanity that can make contact with the Divine Reality? Is not Christ, rather than the incarnation of God, the achiever of divinity? Certainly Lagerkvist sees Christ as the great representative of all men: "All mankind is crucified," Ahasuerus says, "like you; man himself is crucified; you're just the one they look up to when they think of their fate and their suffering." And as our representative sufferer, Christ is our brother. "Now I understand: you were my brother. He who pronounced the curse on me was my own brother, himself an unhappy, accursed man."

Yet Christ may be more than simply a *representative* figure. Is he not the special man who has managed to break from the secular prison and partake of the divine, so that his death—more than all other deaths in the world—is significant? Jesus himself says, in *Let Man Live,* "The meaning of my death is that it should serve a greater purpose than the others." Christ is the human being who has made contact with or been receptive to real divinity and who, even though destroyed by the secular world, has had that ultimate spiritual vision and illumination that become a gospel for the world, a gospel of a freedom that can truly transform and elevate the lives of those who accept it. Indeed, in Lagerkvist, Christ is man at his most significant moment. Christ is man, in the process of becoming divine, achieving transcendence out of his carnate adventure rather than succumbing to the secular darkness. And again perhaps Lagerkvist anticipates the radical Christians of our day by envisioning a human Christ.

The tragedy of Christ is, of course, that he is the victim of a secular world. He is hailed by some as the "Son of God," but always that god is the False God—and who has really recognized Christ as the son of the divine? Christ is not only sacrificed by a secular world; even worse, he is misunderstood and exploited by the secular world.

And thus Lagerkvist moves on to his great attack upon institutionalized, secularized religion. . . . Always man takes the divine and limits it to a secular god and to a secular behavior whereby "once again the old altar was soiled with blood." Lagerkvist's attack is upon all religiosity—pagan, Jewish, Christian—for he sees all organized religion simply as the evil angel saw mankind: "This craven mob, stinking of faith in a pack of lies." (pp. 23-4)

The image of superficial religiosity is graphically presented in *The Sibyl* in terms of the temple of Apollo at Delphi; a shining, beautiful temple on the mountainside hides a dark, stinking cave beneath; the gilded temple above is for public use and worship; the dark, sacrificial hole is where the reality of the Apollonian religion takes place. Shining surface; dark undertruth.

Even more terrible than religious superficiality, however, is the secular tendency to contain spiritual experience within structure—within community, organization, and institution. When Barabbas encounters St. Peter in Jerusalem, after the crucifixion of Christ, he hears St. Peter say that "he didn't trust these people here in Jerusalem, not an inch, he made no bones about it; he was sure most of them were downright robbers and scoundrels." And when St. Peter finds that he has been talking not to a simple stranger but to the criminal Barabbas, he "released Barabbas's hand and looked from one to another, unable to conceal his dismay. The newcomers showed their feelings even more plainly, breathing violently in agitation." As Barabbas leaves, the early Christians cry out at him fiercely, "Get thee hence, thou reprobate." Already the Christian community has been established: it distinguishes between insiders and outsiders. Lagerkvist, in *Barabbas,* makes this indictment:

> They for their part kept together in every way through their common faith, and were very careful not to let anyone in who did not belong. They had their brotherhood and their love feasts. . . . But whether they loved anyone else who was not one of themselves was hard to say.

Lagerkvist gives us a picture of a Christian community, encircling and containing the divine revelation, narrowing its effectiveness and its meaning into a social structure. Even later, in Rome, when the Christians are crucified, they spoke "consolingly and hopefully to each other," but they will not speak to Barabbas, their companion in death.

The religious community is absolutely secular. It is exclusive. And it is social in the worst sense. When Barabbas sneaks into one of the Christian meetings in Jerusalem to listen to their witnessing, he observes the pathetic harelip girl, among the lowest of the low, attempting to give her testimony for Christ. Not really one of the Christian community, she snuffles out her faith, speaking in ignorance. And her fellow Christians "showed clearly that they were ill at ease, that they thought it was embarrassing; some turned away in shame." Already the Christian community has a sense of good taste and propriety; the Christian community is embarrassable.

Lagerkvist implies that, out of religious organization, with its social structure, comes the privileged class of the priesthood. . . . [In] *The Holy Land* we see in the primitive, primordial world of man's development the bald man reading the entrails of a bird in the first gestures of sacerdotal mystery, initiating the whole idea of blood and sacrifice, beginning the drama of secular religion. And the Sibyl learns, once she is privy to the inner workings of the Apollonian religion at Delphi, that the priests "lived not for god but for his temple—that it was the temple they loved and not him—and for its prestige and renown in the world." She becomes aware of the corruption surrounding the religion, a corruption tolerated and encouraged because of its economic contribution to the religious order in which "everyone in it lived on god."

Lagerkvist questions, obviously, the sincerity and purpose of the official churchman (as T. S. Eliot does of the True Church in his poem, "The Hippopotamus"); and at one point, in *Pilgrim at Sea,* we hear the fierce denunciation of such churchmen, a group of official pilgrims on board their pilgrim ship, on their way to the holy land:

> What are you doing here? Scared to put to sea because it's blowing a bit? You weaklings—you cringing curs! Running for port just because there's a little sea on—and in that great ship of yours! . . . Weren't you supposed to be going to the Holy Land? . . . To his tomb—to the place where he was tortured and where he died? . . . You miserable bastards, seeking shelter on your way to Golgotha! Did *he* do that—did they let him?

Lagerkvist indeed deplores the vice of community and society, those great secular concepts that pervert the vision of the divine into a closed circle of top dogs and plaster saints who darken whatever divine illumination may be seeping into the human condition.

Lagerkvist comes to the only possible conclusion: that religious experience, if it is genuine, can never be achieved through organization. All spiritual events are finally private and individual. The official god, the official misunderstanding of Christ, and the official organization of the church are always corruptingly secular. One must follow a private road, an uncharted way. The mystery of the divine cannot be structured and mapped out for us. God, Christ, and the church—in their conventional forms—play no significant or meaningful part in our spiritual quests. (pp. 25-7)

> *Winston Weathers, in his* Pär Lagerkvist: A Critical Essay, *William B. Eerdmans, 1968, 47 p.*

Robert Donald Spector (essay date 1969)

[*In the following essay, Spector analyzes literary techniques employed by Lagerkvist in his short fiction.*]

Like the large body of his poetry, drama, and novels, Pär Lagerkvist's short fiction presents an odd combination of limited range in subject matter or areas of interest and a remarkable variety of literary techniques even within a particular form. To be sure, over the years, Lagerkvist's short fiction, like his work in the other genres, has shifted its emphasis and adjusted its moods according to changing conditions in the world and in his personal life, and there has been a deepening philosophical understanding as he has matured as a writer; but the focus has remained essentially unchanged: a concern for the mysteries of existence; an investigation of the dualities of life; and a constant probing into the nature of good and evil.

It is a narrow range, but the varied literary treatment—although Lagerkvist maintains a fundamentally fabulist role throughout—has made its fictional possibilities appear unlimited. That literary treatment has kept critics searching for an appropriate nomenclature to describe some of its forms. [In his introduction to *The Eternal Smile and Other Stories*] Richard Vowles, who has difficulty even in labeling Lagerkvist as "a writer of fiction," describes his work as "the creations of a mystic and a seer." He hesitates in naming what he calls Lagerkvist's "most common prose vehicle" as either "parable [or] fable, for it lacks the moral tag of the one and the utter brevity of the other." Individual short works by Lagerkvist have been called "choral fiction," "antiphonal poems," and "cosmic fantasy"—names that suggest the impossibility of ordinary classification. Writing [in *A History of Swedish Literature,* 1961] about the last three collections of Lagerkvist's short fiction, Alrik Gustafson emphasizes their great diversity in forms and types, "symbolical episode and the fable, . . . moralizing fairy tales and grimly satiric sketches, . . . realistic tales and lurid episodic sequences. . . . "

Here, to make the subject simple enough for discussion of Lagerkvist's techniques, I shall group my examples into three categories: the fable, the short story, and the novella, although the last does not truly concern us in this [essay]. The first stresses a particular moral point; the second, a sudden insight or a character assessment; the third devotes itself to an explication of a way of life, a philosophical or social problem, or a question about the relationship of illusion and reality. Within these groupings, Lagerkvist's infinite variety of treatment is striking.

Even in the fable, where it would seem that the fictional possibilities are most limited, Lagerkvist proves inventive. **"Paradise,"** a brief narrative, does have the pronounced qualities of a parable, concluding with man's exile from Eden and God's luxuriating beneath his best-loved tree of knowledge after man's ouster. Yet the form itself combines parable and parody, in some ways foreshadowing Lagerkvist's technique in his later biblical-historical novels: appearing to retell a biblical or historical episode while altering its meaning as well as its details. Lagerkvist's God does not prohibit man from eating the fruit of the tree; indeed, He urges it as the means for man's becoming sensible, and what enrages Him is man's inability to use his knowledge constructively. The message is hardly derived from the Bible, but instead is consistent with Lagerkvist's own philosophy that fixes upon man the responsibility for the way he lives his life.

Parables like **"The Adventure"** and **"The Experimental World"** do not have a moral tag, but briefly outline Lagerkvist's vision of man's failures as being no more than attempts at finding the right way to exist, holding out the prospect of further opportunities despite the errors. These are not developed narratives, but rather abstract comments or aphorisms on the nature of mankind. Their tone is straightforward, but the details are vague, their characters abstractions, maintaining the qualities necessary for the effect of a vision.

But Lagerkvist's little fables are also capable of richly ironic tone. In **"Love and Death,"** a single paragraph, Lagerkvist introduces a Cupid who is "a large man, heavy and muscular, with hair all over his body," and the arrow that strikes the lover does not unite him with his sweetheart, but leaves him lying pathetically behind her, his life's blood oozing, as she walks on. In the same way, in **"The Evil Angel,"** an angel, fettered for centuries in a village church, escapes and warns the town's inhabitants that they are to die, but the warning is to no avail, no more than an anti-climax, since it is something they have always known.

Only in **"The Princess and All the Kingdom"** does Lagerkvist pursue the traditional form of the fable, using the formulaic "Once upon a time" and pointing his moral that power demands the assumption of responsibilities not bargained for in the quest to achieve it.

Yet Lagerkvist also writes fables that have nothing to do with this vague fairy-tale world about men in some bizarre locale or princes and princesses or biblical settings. These are tales firmly rooted in contemporary events, concerned with modern materialistic greed, ludicrous patriotism, and inane warfare.

If **"A Hero's Death"** does have some of the vagueness in its detail, such as the failure to name the place or the hero who has been hired to dive to his death as a public entertainment, it is grounded in the values of the real world. Lagerkvist maintains the simple expression characteristic of the fable, but plays it off against the harsh reality of a public that assents to the spectacle until it has ended and then the question of responsibility for the hero's death arises. Moreover, the fundamental motivation for the willing suicide is offered in the commonest cliché of modern society. Asked by sensation-seeking journalists why he is willing to perform his act, the hero replies, "But one does anything for money," an incisive comment on modern values.

In **"The Venerated Bones,"** too, Lagerkvist maintains the fabulist's technique of generalizing his material by refusing to specify places or persons. Yet once again he grounds his fantasy in the reality of the modern world. Here the groundwork is the senseless emotionalism of a patriotism disturbed by rumors of fraternizing among the dead of the two nations. Even Lagerkvist's concluding irony—the satisfied relief when the living learn that all that has been going on is the exchange of bones between the two sides—depends for its effect on the actual stupidity that characterizes chauvinism.

"The Children's Campaign" is Lagerkvist's most sustained use of the fable. His Swiftian irony about a children's army that gains national prominence as it successfully wages the country's war requires no moral tag. Instead, Lagerkvist achieves his moral through the device of irony and through the rhythmic repetition of phrases. Scaling down the sizes and ages of his warriors, Lagerkvist has no need to make a direct statement about their symbolic representation of real soldiers involved in real warfare. When he remarks on how children are naturally suited to the pursuit of war, it becomes a comment on the nature of war. His report on the battle casualties on both sides, setting the figure precisely at 12,924 for each, ridicules the statistical game that converts human lives into abstract figures. Lagerkvist derides the rhetoric of war by calling his infants "men" and turning the cliché "armed to the teeth" into "armed to the very milk teeth." Beyond the fantasy of Lagerkvist's story stands the actuality of the youth movements in Mussolini's Italy and Hitler's Germany. The allusion itself acts as a moral comment. The love of spectacle in the parades of those totalitarian nations becomes the object of ridicule in Lagerkvist's repeated phrase, an "unforgettable spectacle," to describe the horrifying sight of the mutilated children returning to march before an enthusiastically applauding nation.

Lagerkvist's fables are clearly the work of a moralist, whether they are cast in the forms of visions, parodies, or satires, but just as his moral code is no mere repetition of orthodoxy, neither is his literary technique bound to the conventional. What is true of the fables is equally true of his short stories, which retain his fabulist's mannerisms, eschewing modern naturalism and psychologizing, while refusing to fall into traditional patterns. What, for example, is an appropriate label for **"Saviour John,"** a kind of dramatic monologue or a soliloquy dealing with the Messianic impulses that end in a sort of crucifixion or self-immolation? Ordinarily such material would be used for a psychological probing of the character, but Lagerkvist, who does show the vacillation between faith and despair in this modern Christ, concerns himself less with the character than with the confusion in modern religious and social attitudes.

In **"The Lift that Went down into Hell,"** Lagerkvist again displays the complexity of his technique. The story combines harsh reality with fantasy in sending adulterous lovers down into Hell, confronting them in their sordid surroundings with the bizarre figure of the woman's husband, who has just committed suicide. Another modern writer would have concluded his narrative at that point, depending on the epiphany for his shocking effect. Lagerkvist, however, proceeds to a deliberate anticlimax, allowing the illicit lovers to return to their customary behavior as they ascend to their own world. It is the fabulist's rather than the short-story writer's technique, but again Lagerkvist creates his own form, for, instead of adding the moral tag himself, he allows the action to become the comment on their conduct. Indeed, throughout the work, he has combined the simple narrative development of the fable with a subtle set of ironic contrasts in detail and a continual word play on their visit to Hell, both devices natural to the short-story form.

This odd combination of the realistic short story and the illusion of fable characterizes two more ambitious works by Lagerkvist—**"The Marriage Feast"** and **"God's Little Traveling Salesman."** Both are well-developed, full-length

stories, allowing for considerably more detail than a fable offers. In **"The Marriage Feast,"** Lagerkvist uses this detail to achieve verisimilitude in a story about two unlikely lovers, two outsiders for whom marriage seemed the remotest possibility. Their oddity sets them off from the others, makes their romance a movingly pathetic experience. Inherent in their tale, however, is an emotionalism dangerously open to sentimentality. By surrounding them with townspeople crudely realistic and by relying on wit and irony in his narrative, Lagerkvist manages to maintain the balance. The realism belongs to the realm of the short story, but Lagerkvist manages to point his fable element toward an unforced conclusion, the very language of which combines the disparate qualities of his story:

> They lay there together in the darkness, near each other, with burning cheeks and their mouths half open for a kiss. And like a heavenly song of praise, like a hosanna of light around the only living thing, the stars rose around their bed in mighty hosts, their numbers increasing with the darkness.

"God's Little Traveling Salesman," too, contains many elements of the fable in its study of religious faith in our times. Despite the particularities of his circumstances, the salesman of religious tracts serves as a kind of modern Everyman as he wavers between devotion and doubt. His position at the end of the story, as he returns to his religious beliefs a more honest man, though no saint, represents Lagerkvist's attitude toward man's possibilities. In a kind of moral tag, Lagerkvist concludes: "With him, as with so many others, it was just that he had a slovenly soul." Even the manner of statement, while having an appropriateness to the fable, suggests Lagerkvist's ability to combine two forms—the sense of an epiphany, the ironic tone (which characterizes, as well, the manner throughout a story heavy with criticism of social and religious hypocrisy), these belong less to the fable than to the technique of the modern short story.

With both **"Father and I"** and **"The Basement,"** Lagerkvist demonstrates his ability to write effectively what we regard as the modern short story. At the same time, in both works he concerns himself with material that is familiar throughout his writing: the mystery of existence, the dualities of life, and the nature of good and evil. Both employ balances and contrasts which are his technical devices in all his fiction, and the sense of moral commitment in the two stories is the persistent tone throughout his created fictional world.

"Father and I" belongs to a genre of revelation that includes James Joyce's stories about a child's maturation in *Dubliners.* Like Joyce's famous story "Araby," **"Father and I"** uses a narrator who tries to capture the experience of youth although maintaining the point of view of an adult. Lagerkvist's narrative line is thin, no more than a young boy out for a walk with his father and suddenly confronted by the terror of night. Narrowly escaping from the tracks as an unscheduled train hurtles by, the boy identifies the experience as a foreshadowing of life, a portent of "anguish to come, the unknown, all that Father knew nothing about, that he wouldn't be able to protect me against."

But the richness of Lagerkvist's story does not come from the epiphany. The revelation is meaningful because it emerges from the contrasts that Lagerkvist has previously developed: a contrast between the warm, live world of day and the dreadful fear of dark and abyss in the night; a contrast between generations, the father's confidence and security in God and the boy's skepticism and insecurity in his rejection of his ancestors' faith.

"The Basement," too, depends for its effect on the contrasts that provide the structure of the story. While the narrator appears to be recounting the story of Lindgren, a beggar with withered legs, whom he accompanies home, the major concern is with the character of the narrator himself. The deformed beggar has adjusted to life; the seemingly healthy narrator suffers from spiritual malaise. Walking behind Lindgren, the narrator mentally notes his movements, and while apparently praising the cripple uses language that patronizes and makes metaphorical comparisons in animal imagery. And yet, Lindgren is more a man than the narrator.

Lagerkvist employs an epiphany to drive home the point of his story. Leaving Lindgren's apartment, the narrator notes that only the cripple's light burns, and rather despairingly he remarks, "it lighted me nearly all the way home," indicating still the despair within himself. The epiphany here, as in **"Father and I,"** serves instead of a moral tag, but Lagerkvist remains the fabulist even though the form masks the character of his preaching.

Add to these varied stories the complexity of Lagerkvist's forms in the novella, which are equally the work of a fabulist and moralist, and the wonderful variety that he achieves in treating similar materials is astounding. In *The Eternal Smile,* where Lagerkvist uses the quest itself to provide unity in his narrative about a group of souls seeking God, the method, as I have described [in "The Structure and Meaning of 'The Eternal Smile,'" *MLM* (March 1956)], is akin to Hebrew antiphonal poetry, in which the individual voices come together as though in single argument. The structure of *The Hangman,* Lagerkvist's study of evil, is a dramatic confrontation between the Middle Ages and the modern period. Indeed, its dramatic qualities were sufficient to allow Lagerkvist to convert his narrative into a successful play. By contrast *The Guest of Reality,* his autobiographical novella, consists of a series of episodes each in itself not unlike **"Father and I,"** but achieving in its totality an impact drawn from the rhythmical repetition and expansion of its theme. So unlike the structure of *The Hangman* is that of *The Guest of Reality,* that when it was adapted as a drama on Swedish television, it required the constant intrusive presence of a narrator. Finally, in **"The Masquerade of Souls"** Lagerkvist uses a fabulist's prologue and epilogue to frame his idyllic tale about two lovers who come together through the kinship of their souls and seek to remain aloof from the world's realities. Throughout his novella, Lagerkvist allows hints of the real world to interrupt their bliss, and then, in his final comment, denudes the masquerade of all its pretenses.

In these novellas, as in his fables and short stories, Lagerkvist maintains many of the devices of the fabulist to en-

force his moral concerns. And yet, it is the mark of his craftsmanship that the form never permits the similarity of content and intention to pall through familiarity, but rather each new work seems fresh and distinct from others even within the same genre. (pp. 260-65)

> *Robert Donald Spector, "Lagerkvist's Short Fiction," in* The American-Scandinavian Review, *Vol. LVII, No. 3, September, 1969, pp. 260-65.*

Ray Lewis White   (essay date 1979)

[*In the following excerpt, White summarizes the critical reception of Lagerkvist's short fiction in America.*]

For three hundred years Americans had made best-selling books of biblical legends retold (typically, *Life of Christ, The Story of the Bible, The Day of Doom, The Life of Our Lord*) and fiction extrapolated from biblical stories, such as *Quo Vadis?* by Henryk Sienkiewicz, *Ben-Hur* by Lew Wallace, *The Nazarene* and *The Apostle* by Sholem Asch, and *The Robe* by Lloyd C. Douglas. Invariably minatory in message and minimal in literary finesse, these devotional works quite successfully fed the spiritually easily satisfied; and when the prestigious company Random House published Lagerkvist's *Barabbas* in English in 1951 (one year after publication in Sweden) many reviewers found the work quite recommendable as another devotional tract to comfort the converted and convert the discomfited. Hence *Barabbas* was called awe-inspiring, mystical, thoughtful, philosophical, and doctrinally sound on the problem of reason-faith, good-evil, guilt-sacrifice, and anomie-community. But wiser reviewers defined *Barabbas* by describing it as unlike both the typical popular biblical story and the epical historical romance; *Barabbas* resembled instead the artfully simple dramas of Strindberg or the classical tragedies of the Greeks, particularly because Lagerkvist's novel was ironic, unsentimental, questioning, dignified, and seemingly of bleakly ambiguous dénouement. Again—almost universally—Lagerkvist's modernistic but uncomplicated prose drew great acclaim; and Americans liked to know that this Swedish author had been "second to William Faulkner" for the 1950 Nobel Prize for Literature. Chosen for subscription sales by both the Book-of-the-Month Club and the Religious Book Club, *Barabbas* was already moderately successful when reviewers learned, in November of 1951, that Lagerkvist was himself now a Nobel Laureate—and *Barabbas* received a renewed wave of publicity. For good or bad results, after 1951 Pär Lagerkvist's publications would be advertised as the works of a Nobel Prize winner: future books would surely be admired and praised, but they would seldom be judged on simple merit instead of on the author's Nobel fame.

Proud of Lagerkvist's world fame and of the critical reception of *Barabbas,* the Random House company naturally wanted to publish this author's future works; but until Lagerkvist wrote further novels to be translated into English, the publisher had to find another way to establish a more solid foundation in readers' memories than *The Dwarf* and *Barabbas* had built. Fortunately, Lagerkvist had in his

early career written a large number of short stories and novellas; and the rapid working of four translators produced
enough material for publication in 1954 of almost four
hundred pages of Lagerkvist's prose from 1920 through
1935. Probably because of the generous variety of works
now available and surely because in these older works Lagerkvist was less susceptible to appropriation by religious
true-believers, American reviewers of 1954 dared to write
many negative judgments of the Swedish author. He might
indeed own a Nobel Prize, but his fiction was obscurantist,
too heavily ironic and mystically confused, élitist in symbolism, macabre and humorless in plot, and pretentious
and sententious in rhetoric. For comparison—usually to
the disfavor of Lagerkvist—reviewers brought up the satires of Jonathan Swift, George Orwell, and Aldous Huxley; the macabre tales of Ambrose Bierce, Edgar Allan
Poe, Hans Christian Andersen, and Sherwood Anderson;
the gloomily portentous works of such Russians as Anton
Chekhov; and the well-developed characters of Stendhal
and James Joyce. To Lagerkvist's credit, there were comparisons by reviewers to fiction by Ernest Hemingway,
Katharine Mansfield, and Franz Kafka and notice of
"Scandinavian" qualities in Lagerkvist like those in
Strindberg, Lagerlöf, Undset, Grieg, and Sibelius. The
wise critic of 1954 appreciated in *The Eternal Smile and
Other Stories* Lagerkvist's universal fables, his modernistic bitterness, his cosmic mysticism, and his complex fictional speculations on life's dualisms, insolubilities, and
paradoxes. This large anthology gave Americans the opportunity to know Pär Lagerkvist as more than the "religious" novelist of *Barabbas;* and yet almost no reviewer
was ever to describe Lagerkvist's later novels as obvious
developments and continuations of style and theme inherent in his fiction since 1920. What the public expected was
apparently more books like *Barabbas.*

What the American public got next from Pär Lagerkvist
was indeed a "religious" novel but not just a sequel to *Barabbas. The Sibyl* (1956), published in 1958, attracted far
less attention than had the earlier novel. Reviewers could
think of few works by other authors comparable to *The
Sibyl;* perhaps Lagerkvist's purpose was like John Milton's in *Paradise Lost* ("to justify the ways of God to
man") or perhaps his subject of godly possession resembled that of C. S. Lewis in *Till We Have Faces.* The nature
of Pär Lagerkvist's prose, which in *Barabbas* had seemed
merely an extrapolation of the Bible, here seemed too abstract, too artificial, too unpeopled for the popular American taste. The new-world dislike of pessimism, "Scandinavian" gloom, and unresolved paradox found full expression against *The Sibyl;* and a truly negative reviewer declared *The Sibyl* no better than the traditional historical
novels *Ben-Hur, Quo Vadis?,* and Edward Bulwer-
Lytton's *The Last Days of Pompeii.* Reviewers who liked
The Sibyl praised its lyrical sublimity; its inspired simplicity; its cold, brilliant grandeur; its cosmically mythic philosophy. The apparent themes were identified as Lagerkvist's usual studies of dualities: divine-human, thought-
ful-unthinking, living-existing, and Christian-pagan.
Wary of being unjust or unkind to a Nobel Prize winner
or too opinionated about unusually intellectual fiction,
American reviewers received *The Sibyl* with a general po-

liteness, surely hoping that future Lagerkvist novels would
be more accessible to interpretation and enjoyment.

Such an understandable hope was not to be fulfilled, for
if Americans felt vaguely cheated of plot and characters
and clarity in *The Sibyl,* Lagerkvist's next three novels—
the "Tobias" trilogy *The Death of Ahasuerus* (1960), *Pilgrim at Sea* (1962), and *The Holy Land* (1964)—
published in America in 1962, 1964, and 1966 respectively—invited readers into an even more unrealistic and uni-
versalized fictional world of seemingly total abstraction.
Lagerkvist was still publicized as the Swedish Nobel Prize
winner, author of the well-remembered *Barabbas,* self-
styled "religious atheist," and creator of deceptively simple fiction. So often were the volumes in the Tobias trilogy
called "deceptively simple" that the phrase became an irritating stock-epithet for all of Pär Lagerkvist's fiction. Reviewers of the three parables about Tobias' quest found a
few different writers to whom Lagerkvist could be compared: favorably to John Bunyan, Francis Thompson,
Nikos Kazantzakis, and Isak Dinesen; unfavorably to the
American authors of violent fiction Mickey Spillane and
Robert Ruark, and of sentimental good-evil drama Arthur
Miller and Paddy Chayevsky. A few reviewers found artistic comparisons to be made to Giotto and Edvard Munch;
but—finally, and surprisingly late in Lagerkvist's career—
comparisons were made to the film techniques of Ingmar
Bergman and to the "deceptively simple" designs of modern Scandinavian furniture and modern architecture. As
for the intrinsic merit of *The Death of Ahasuerus, Pilgrim
at Sea,* and *The Holy Land,* American reviewers were disappointed anew over Lagerkvist's opaque philosophizing,
lack of realism, needless perplexity, foggy metaphysics,
murky symbolism, and overwhelming (now "Arctic")
gloom. The three novels received increasingly negative
criticism as they appeared in the 1960's; defenders of Lagerkvist's work increasingly cited his great humanitarianism, his brilliant prose, and his hauntingly memorable
plots. They easily identified the author's continuing theme
of the soul's search for meaning/God, but few were unrelieved when Random House advertised *The Holy Land* as
the last of the Tobias novels. And perhaps Random House
was tired of carrying Pär Lagerkvist as one of its many distinguished authors, for, after publishing *The Holy Land*
in 1966, Random House relinquished any future books by
Lagerkvist to Alfred A. Knopf, an equally prestigious
American publisher.

Only one additional Lagerkvist novel received commercial
publication in America, *Herod and Mariamne* (1967),
which Knopf published in 1968. This translation of
Mariamne received scant critical attention, least comment
of any of the Lagerkvist books published in America. The
national taste for religious subjects had diminished, seemingly along with the politeness to be accorded Nobel Prize
winners, even when their fiction was uncomfortably obscure and gloomy. Historically aware reviewers chided
Lagerkvist for misrepresenting the real Herod and
Mariamne, and ordinary reviewers called on the Swedish
author for more realistic detail and more rounded characters. Admirers of *Herod and Mariamne* found nothing
new to say about Lagerkvist's simple prose, with its clarity, brevity, and originality; and they found only one new

specific comparison to make: to the "less is more" architectural dictum of Ludwig Mies van der Rohe! Had reviewers of *Herod and Mariamne* in 1968 known that there would be no more Lagerkvist books for commercial publication in America, they would not particularly have been sorry. Thereafter, the eight Lagerkvist books that appeared in America from 1945 through 1968 would become—like the author's poetry and drama—subject to scholarly study but not popular attention. (pp. 5-11)

Ray Lewis White, in his Pär Lagerkvist in America, *Humanities Press, 1979, 149 p.*

Gweneth B. Schwab   (essay date 1981)

[*In the following essay, Schwab compares Lagerkvist's novellas* Herod and Mariamne *and* Barabbas, *finding that both works convey the complexity, ambiguity, and difficulty of life while presenting different perpectives on the significance of Christianity.*]

The world recoiled from World War I only to instigate the forces which would produce World War II. The pattern of crisis of the twentieth century is well known: the crisis of faith in God, of faith in science, of faith in history, and of faith even that man can learn from or correct his own errors. The holocaust soiled the century with a horror nearly indescribable. The crisis of the century repeated itself over and over in the crises of individual consciences. Yet, out of these ashes of faith emerged a kind of beauty as men continued to live and artists continued to create. Pär Lagerkvist is one of the many who created in spite of and inspired by the crisis of his world and of his personal world view. Using the two thousand year only division of history as a touchstone, Lagerkvist explores the reality of the human condition in many of his novels. Two such novels, *Barabbas* (1951), and *Herod and Mariamne* (1967), portray humanity against the backdrop of Christ's incarnation. The first begins at the crucifixion; the second ends with the nativity. In the novels, Lagerkvist depicts mankind with reference to one of the most significant events in religious history and reveals the same turmoil, confusion, and incompleteness that has always defined man. He dramatizes that God is not a significant variable in the human equation.

Barabbas depicts the convict who was acquitted when Christ was crucified. Barabbas is forever scarred by his view of Calvary: the man dying, the women watching, and the darkness descending. He stays in Jerusalem for a while, living distantly from others as he probes the mystery of this event. He speaks with some of the disciples of Christ, including Peter, but is excluded from their circles when word spreads of his identity. He never regains his former life, and his bandit cohorts and his mistress think it is because of his prison experience. Barabbas wonders himself if the darkness he had witnessed was not perhaps merely a result of slow recovery of his eyes from the prison gloom. After spending a brief ineffectual time with the robber band, he is no longer heard of until he becomes a slave in copper mines, chained to another slave who is a believer in the crucified one. When Barabbas eventually confides to him that he had seen Jesus die, the old slave

draws him into an alliance of belief. Yet, Barabbas backs away from his profession of belief, and later, after being released to lighter duty on the governor's estate, is *not* crucified with the slave when the owner discovers the slave's Christianity. One night, after the household has moved to Rome, Barabbas, while looking for a Christian meeting in the catacombs, gets lost and becomes terrified until he is finally able to make his way out. In that mood, he comes across a home burning and a hired mob accusing the Christians. In a final violent effort to join them, he torches several homes thinking that the world was to be burned and that their Savior had come. Later, in prison, he again meets Peter, a fellow prisoner, who tells him that he was only helping the worldly god, Caesar, and that the Christians' 'Lord is love'. In a poignant final scene, Barabbas, odd man out, trails the chained pairs of Christians out to be crucified. His cross hangs farthest out in the rows of crosses, and no one speaks to him. When he dies, as he lived, it is as if to the darkness that he delivers up his soul.

Herod, the principal character in *Herod and Mariamne,* is also affiliated with Christ through death. It is this Herod who, when three men following a star come to the temple to seek a newborn king, decrees that all the infants be slaughtered. Soon after, he dies. The story can be outlined even more simply than *Barabbas.* The King, Herod, builds and beautifies the Jewish temple, and yet is hated by the people. The cruel and violent Herod sees the elegant, gracious Mariamne and is stunned by her beauty. He finally meets her when she petitions him to release a young kinsman, a twelve year old Maccabean boy who had tried to stab a cruel soldier. He agrees to release him, and Mariamne continues in the following months to ask for the release of several others whom people implore her to help. Eventually, Herod proposes marriage, and she accepts out of a desire to help others through her softening effect upon him. The effect lasts for a while, but Herod cannot learn to love and Mariamne cannot love without a sense of duty to him and to the others. His passion eventually cools and he fills the palace with women again. Unfettered from his wonder of her, his suspicion of what is different from himself and of what he cannot control by force causes him to hire someone to murder her. His cruelty and power increase until his death, yet Mariamne continues to perplex him also. He dies 'stretching out his arms into the darkness' crying 'Mariamne! Mariamne!'

Most liberties which Lagerkvist takes with the histories of Herod and Barabbas are of addition rather than alteration. Most sources agree that, as the Oxford scholar, Alfred Edersheim, states, 'Bar-Abbas belonged to that class, not uncommon at the time, which, under the colourable pretence of political aspirations, committed robbery and other crimes'. Nothing is known of his subsequent history. However, Herod's history is more interesting. History claims him to be every bit as cruel as the portrait in the novel. He did, apparently, love Mariamne, a Maccabean princess, 'in his own mad way'. It was through a complex intrigue of jealousies and the fear that Mariamne might become someone else's wife that Herod was finally brought to the point of killing her. History reports that she received a mock trial before her execution, rather than being killed by a hired assassin as Lagerkvist describes.

According to *The Interpreter's Dictionary of the Bible,* 'Herod was never able to accept sanely the reality that Mariamne was dead'. History also affirms Herod's contribution to the construction of the temple. Herod embellished the temple as no other had done. According to Jewish tradition, 'He that has not seen the Temple of Herod, has never known what beauty is'. Edersheim explains the many ways that the reign of the Jewish King Herod paralleled the reign of the earlier King Solomon. In a comparison relevant to this study, he declares, 'Herod was not the antitype, he was the Barabbas, of David's Royal Son'.

The many close similarities between the two novels are worth noting specifically. The two characters, Barabbas and Herod, parallel each other in more than a relationship to Jesus. They are similar men in temperament. Herod is described in the novel 'as the cruellest, most ungodly man who ever lived—as the scum of the human race', 'a monster in human form'. Even his joy in life is described as wild, as 'joy in violence, blood, and battle; joy in rampant horses trampling bleeding enemies underfoot; joy in killing . . . in the capture and rape of women . . . in success, gold, power—in a word, joy in life entire'. Usually Herod led his army not only by command but by fighting at the front as well: 'If anyone delighted in battle it was he . . . and . . . fury . . . usually distinguished him'. If not king, Herod could have easily led a band of robbers such as the one Barabbas led. Such a life was to Herod 'the life of his forebears, such as they had led in their desert realms to the south, with raids into Judea and attacks on the caravans bound thither. It was a hard, cruel life, and . . . the life that had given him his soul'.

Barabbas, although not known particularly for his cruelty and not possessing a royal sceptre, was a rough and amoral bandit:

> He it was who used to plan most of their ventures and be the first to carry them out. Nothing seemed impossible for him, and he used to pull it off too . . . and they had grown used to relying on everything turning out well. He became a kind of leader . . .

During one raid on a wagon of tithes he 'cut down' two of the temple guards and 'afterwards he even outraged their bodies, behaving so incredibly that the others thought it was going too far and turned away'. He had already used the help and inexperienced emotions of a girl with a hare-lip, had impregnated her, and subsequently deserted her.

Herod is constantly described as a 'desert' man. He takes solitary nocturnal walks in the temple he is renovating. In fact, he is 'easily bored and repelled by the people he gathered around him'. Consequently, he dies in 'utter solitude'. The desert and the darkness are repeated throughout the novel to enforce Herod's solitude. Barabbas, too, is an outsider and man of the desert, often referred to as a stranger. He is never more than a sexual partner to his mistress in Jerusalem. He had always been distant from the other bandits, but becomes even more inexplicably strange to them after the Jerusalem acquittal: 'He was just like a stranger to them and he too must have thought they were strangers . . . '. He is characterized by his perpetual si-

lence and his eyes which are so sunk into his head as to be hardly seen. The closest Barabbas comes to anyone is to the Christian slave, Sahuk, with whom he is so long chained. In his old age he dreams of Sahuk and wakes with tears in his eyes to find no one sleeping bound next to him: 'He was not bound together with anyone. Not with anyone at all in the whole world'. At his crucifixion, he is 'out' from the others in every way possible, and it is significantly as though to darkness that he gives up his soul. Herod and Barabbas share the solitude of the desert and the dark.

Although Lagerkvist, in ***Barabbas,*** says that the appearance of a man is of little consequence, the similarity even in the appearance of Herod and Barabbas is significant. Both are large, powerfully built men. Barabbas' complexion is sallow, while Herod's is described as yellow. Herod's hair is blackish-red; Barabbas' hair is black, but his beard is red. Their eyes give no relief or consolation to anyone. Barabbas' eyes are so deep-set, 'hidden away', that they reflect nothing. Herod's brown eyes with lighter flecks make men uncomfortable and are not soon forgotten; his gaze is 'dangerously observant'. There is also about the appearance of each something menacing. In the case of Barabbas it is the famous mark of a Hollywood 'bad guy', a deep scar which disappears into his beard. In Herod's case it is a heavier tread with his right foot than with his left. It is described as giving 'more force and somehow more menace to his figure . . . '.

Herod and Barabbas, although both outsiders, differ significantly as to what each desires. Barabbas is outside belief. He tries to believe, to convince himself of the facts in which others believe. Too much uncertainty and lack of proof prevents him. He later attempts to join the slave, Sahuk, in his belief. It is almost as if he wants the reverence of Sahuk, to draw him, too, into the circle of slaves to Jesus. But this does not occur. Finally, his confusion in the catacombs and perhaps his desperation cause him to join enthusiastically in the burning. Barabbas gropes for belief throughout the novel, aptly illustrating Irene Scobbie's comment [in 'The Significance of Lagerkvist's *Dwarf*', *Scandinavica* (1971)]: 'One can dismiss religion, but not man's need for it'. The closer Barabbas gets to the inside of a group that believes, such as the imprisoned and crucified Christians at the end, the farther out he remains.

Herod, however, is outside of love. He is described as loving no one, and as being loved by no one. He is so far outside of love that it suffers a transformation to something else when it contacts him. Several times the narrator clarifies that for Herod love itself is evil. His difficulty is clearly explained:

> He had never experienced love before, and knew nothing about it. It was foreign to his nature. He knew that he loved her, but did not know what this should imply. And love wrought no change in him.

The novel explains that Herod's desire for her is what he believes to be love, since it is not the same lust as he feels for whores, nor is she like any other woman, but is 'new to him, and his very opposite'. Although outside of love, he comes close to love, and when retreating from a sexual relationship with Mariamne, ironically reveals a degree of real care for her.

The gap between Herod and love is analogous to the gap between Barabbas and belief. The close parallel is revealed through many incidents of the plots. The closer both come to the ends they seek, the less personal power each has. When Barabbas admits Sahuk, his fellow slave, into some of his own privacy, when he allows the name of Christ to be scratched on the back of his slave medallion, he is in the worst possible bondage—'the most ghastly punishment imaginable' of the Cyprian copper mines. When he thinks that the Christians are burning the world and he runs to join the burning, he only ends in prison. When Herod is first entranced with Marimane and during the beginning of their marriage, before the truth of her mere fondness for him dawns on him, his usual cruel inclinations are tempered by the mercy he extends at her request. He admits his reasons to her and acknowledges, 'I ought not to do it—I know that very well'.

Even while personal power is lost, a degree of catharsis occurs concurrently. Mariamne wonders about Herod's continual softening and thinks of him as a captive in his own fortress. After meeting Mariamne, Herod clears the whores from his palace in language reminiscent of scripture: 'He had cleansed his whole house'. There were many signs of change. Mariamne eventually 'induced him to be gentler and more considerate with her' in sexual relations. The palace begins to look more like a home; 'she dispelled its desolation'. At one climactic point in their marriage, after he had spitefully killed her young Maccabean relative, he reached his most vulnerable point:

> When Herod beheld her and perceived what he had done to her—perceived how much she had borne on his account—he fell down at her feet with a groan, and the sweat of anguish broke out upon his forehead. He held up his arms, but without touching her, and looked at her imploringly with bloodshot eyes. Wordlessly he begged forgiveness for his wickedness, for being what he was.

She eventually strokes his head until 'he seemed to find a kind of peace'. But within a page Lagerkvist implies the end of this release into peace: 'For a while Herod was calmer'. As Roy Swanson expressed so well [in 'Lagerkvist's *Dwarf* and the Redemption of Evil', *Discourse* (1970)], 'His love proves to be an inescapable love of self and his elevation is seen to be merely apparent and abruptly transitory.'

Barabbas also experiences partial release from bondage concurrent with his lack of personal power. After temporary acceptance of the Christian bond with the slave to whom he is chained in the copper mine, he is also released above ground to lighter slave labour. That he had escaped an earthly hell on the strength of the word of another is clear. Another liberation, less positive certainly, occurs at the end of the novel, when, after a last misguided attempt to join the believers, he is freed from the burden of his quest by death. When Barabbas attempts belief, he is thwarted, and fails to believe. When Herod attempts to love, he, too, fails to achieve much more than self-serving

lust and distant melancholy. Even though he uses the language of Christianity, Barabbas gives his soul up as though to darkness, and Herod's despair is impenetrable even to the desire for love.

Finally, Barabbas and Herod are both intimately involved in others' deaths. In **Herod and Mariamne,** the old serving woman from Mariamne's former home and the young kinsman rebel are killed either directly by Herod or on his orders. The deaths in Barabbas are not *caused* by him, yet, because the girl with the hare-lip and the slave both die for the belief that he cannot accept, he is intimately involved as he watches both die. The one whom they die for is Jesus. Yet Barabbas seems uncertain about Jesus even up to his own death despite the momentous truth that Jesus had literally died for him. Mariamne, too, dies instead of Herod—or so he thinks. Freed from his fascination for her by his realization of her lack of love, his suspicious nature causes him to doubt her. His doubt becomes an obsession, until he thinks 'the unthinkable', that Mariamne wanted his life. Although he rides back to Jerusalem in a mounting fury which can remind one of Barabbas' fury to burn Rome, he can only watch her die and repeat over and over, 'Beloved'.

Several of the symbols of both **Barabbas** and **Herod and Mariamne** work in similar ways to reinforce the novels' meanings. Similar to the circuitous dark catacombs in which Barabbas loses his way are the palace and temple of Herod. The palace is essentially empty, except for whores and officials, and is only temporarily made liveable by Mariamne. The temple more nearly parallels the catacombs, for, as Herod habitually walks there at night, he is always in darkness, and always alone:

> Why did he do it? He himself could not have said: There was no object in it. And yet he went there, and walked for a long time in the darkness. Then he would stand outside for a while, looking up at the fiery night sky.

> He had no link with the divine. Inwardly he was a wilderness, and the stars drove their cold spears into his soul.

The cold spears communicate nothing more to him in his wanderings, than the gleams of light Barabbas sees, follows, and loses in the catacombs. These lights do not lead to the Christians' meeting that he looks for, nor do they lead him to the earth above. If anything they only confuse him, making him more desperate to escape, which he finally does on his own. And who would be surprised that Herod, who only experiences stars as cold spears, should react to a larger star leading to some new born king as a challenge to be opposed? Even the cool silvery qualities of Mariamne remind Herod of the cold silvery starlight realm that he walks under so often. She, too, is essentially unattainable to him.

The night and darkness of both novels work in the same way, and the desert home and habits of both male protagonists identify a metaphorical wasteland. But the temple that Herod builds, greater and more beautiful than Solomon's, to a God he barely gives even lip service to, should remind the reader of Barabbas' medallion. Barabbas, too, in his more limited way, controls an outward sign, a physical entity reflecting a relationship with the divine. For Barabbas, too, it is emptied of any security. He wears a name crossed out, and Herod wanders in an unfinished house of God, staring at soul-piercing stars.

Herod and Barabbas remain outsiders until their deaths: one through lack of love, the other through lack of belief. Love links the death of Jesus, who, Peter tells Barabbas, is the Lord of love, to the death of Mariamne, whom Herod finally addresses as beloved after her death. But one must be careful of oversimplistic statements. Lagerkvist's fiction, for all its parallels, presents an ambiguous world both AD and BC. The novel, *Barabbas,* never decides the 'Lordship' of the Jesus who dies for Barabbas. And Herod's Mariamne represents the possibility of love, but is not representative of love itself. She is, rather, throughout the novel, representative of sacrifice and goodness, for she knows from the beginning that 'she could never love him; but she could feel pity. And in feeling this she felt also the need to sacrifice herself. . . . Of love she knew nothing; she believed only that she would sacrifice herself'.

Mariamne is more nearly a representative of goodness than of love. Her goodness is dramatized by her inability to live in a palace with the dungeon of condemned men beneath her and by the reaction of the Jerusalem people to her even after they realize that she no longer has influence over Herod: '. . . they smiled at her whenever they saw and recognised her, and many continued to kneel and kiss the hem of her mantle'. It is also dramatized by her inability to have believed, even if told, that her kinsfolk hated her for her marriage to Herod. Much of the attraction of Herod towards Mariamne is the rare quality of her goodness, a complete lack of guile, so different from himself and anyone he had ever encountered. The novel describes her as simply but regally dressed with garments edged in silver, with silver thread, sash, and sandal straps. The people call her 'Mariamne the silver-clad'. She seems to care little for the temple Herod builds, and remains as a temple unto herself. The novel also compares her to a tree 'which has no consciousness of itself, and is a secret'. Truly she is selfless and good.

Just as Mariamne does not represent pure love, neither is Mariamne's goodness or sacrifice the pure antithesis of Herod's evil. Viewing the two as direct opposites will cause one to miss the irony. Mariamne is sometimes sexually aroused by Herod, and even, despite his violence with her, sometimes fulfilled. And just as Herod, when realizing that her feeling for him was not like his own, proudly forces himself to no longer approach her (only in fact to reveal his love for her in so doing), so, too, does Mariamne in trying to please him, try even harder to pretend a need for him, only to further convince him that she feels little. In trying not to show love, Herod reveals a degree of love. In trying to show love, Mariamne reveals the lack of it. They share the same, sometimes frustrating, humanity.

The characters who people *Barabbas* are more clearly a blend of good and evil than are either Herod or Mariamne. Barabbas murders a fellow bandit but carries the hare-lipped girl's body to an appropriate grave. He burns a Roman neighbourhood but dreams nostalgically of a for-

mer friend. Herod's evil is nearly total. His accidentally revealed 'lustlove' and accompanying mercy are momentary. And Mariamne's goodness seems nearly pure, only slightly marred by the pretense of real love. The 'chiaroscuro' world of fiction, the light-dark dualism described by D. G. Kehl [in 'The Chiaroscuro World of Pär Lagerkvist', *Modern Fiction Studies* (1959)], is *within* Barabbas and *between* the characters, Herod and Mariamne.

To discuss Lagerkvist in terms of his ambiguity is no new idea, yet it is a constant reminder that even though individual characters are less complex in the later work, no easy conclusions are possible. Adolph Benson's statement [in 'Pär Lagerkvist: Nobel Laureate', *College English* (1952)] that Pär Lagerkvist reveals 'a firm belief that good will conquer evil' is indefensible. [In his *Pär Lagerkvist,* 1973] Robert Spector describes the novelist's 'deliberate ambiguity': 'For Lagerkvist, Christians do not exist without doubt; doubt cannot have meaning without faith. Death and life, love and hate, fidelity and betrayal—these exist simultaneously for mankind'. Fifteen years between *Barabbas* and *Herod and Mariamne* did not wash this quality from Lagerkvist's fiction. He is reported to have said at one point, 'I constantly conduct a dialogue with myself; one book answers the other' [quoted by Gunnel Malmström in 'The Hidden God', *Scandinavica* (1971)].

The style of both novels reflects the theme of ambiguity. The ambiguous language of *Barabbas* has been noted by many and commented upon fully. It can be represented by the phrase 'as though', used to describe Barabbas at Sahuk's crucifixion and at his own ' . . . he gave a gasp and sank down on his knees as though in prayer', and ' . . . he said out into the darkness, as though he were speaking to it: 'To thee I deliver up my soul'. Such tentative language is also characteristic of Herod and Mariamne. The narrative continually repeats words such as 'yet', 'perhaps', 'surely' and 'probably'. It continually uses the verbal structure which includes the probable 'may': 'he may have been right', 'so far as may be conjectured', 'this may have been'. The passive voice sometimes increases the possibility of doubt: 'It was believed by all who watched the temple rise—and is believed to this day'. Other phrases reflecting uncertainty recur such as 'One could not be sure. One could never be quite sure'. Even words of certainty are ironically used with uncertain factors: '*Certainly* it *promised* to be a fair, rich temple' (emphasis added). One sentence describing Herod's life illustrates well the continual layering of ambiguous language: 'A vicious life, no doubt; yet perhaps not exactly for the reasons given by the people'.

One of the features of Barabbas which prevents the scepticism from controlling the novel, other than the attraction of belief, is the possibility of resurrection. The bleakness of *Herod and Mariamne* is also countered by more than its attraction of love. There are nearly as many deaths in *Herod and Mariamne* as in *Barabbas;* in fact, the darkness, the sense of death as pure extinction, is strong. However, even though no one is resurrected, someone is, at the end, born. And not just anyone, but Jesus, already escaping death at the powerful hand of Herod, the cause of all the other deaths in the novel. Perhaps some would view this as a possibility of 'saving grace'. Victory over death some may see represented in the scene of the threesome foiling the great Herod by a trip to Egypt. However, the novel lends no support to this causality.

If Lagerkvist's work indeed answers itself, and if, in the case of Herod and Mariamne, the characters are fewer and less complex while continuing Lagerkvistian ambiguity, how does the novel with a pre-incarnation setting fit into the total fiction? It has been termed an 'independent epilogue', 'a variation of the major themes' [Malmström] of Lagerkvist's work and 'an underscoring of the theme of the separation of man from God' [Spector]. The first novel after the crucifixion pentology (as the five preceding novels beginning with **Barabbas** have been labelled) portrays the same difficulties, searches, painful perplexities, and, ambiguities of the human condition that are portrayed in the earlier fiction.

By moving the characters from AD to BC, however, Lagerkvist has accomplished much more. D. G. Kehl's incorrect statement should alert the reader to the problem. He claims that 'the controlling obsessive symbol of the crucifixion appears in some form in all Lagerkvist's novels'. But it does not. That is the point. By placing the novel in an era before Christ, Lagerkvist has removed Christ from inside the circle of man's quest to somewhere outside this circle. For Barabbas, Jesus was the problem which nagged him until his own death. Herod's dealings with the star followers, however, are subordinate to his central concern for his own death and his memories of Mariamne. The novel subordinates the birth to Herod's death. Christ may be one aspect of the total picture, but he is not a significant variable in the human equation.

In addition, the unique contribution of Herod and Mariamne to the whole of Lagerkvist's fiction suggests itself by the more extreme and less complex characterizations of the two characters. One might wonder if the quest for meaning and happiness in Lagerkvist's fictional world was complicated even further by the arrival of Christianity. Did life become more ambiguous and even less certain as divine characteristics, before reserved for consideration in temples and dogmas, became mixed with human characteristics in a man claiming to be God? Is it easier and more clear when love can be aspired for from humans and when worship and obedience can be given to God in temples? Does the incarnation muddy waters already tumultuous with human dilemmas? Mankind is a mixture of good and evil. Herod and Mariamne may coalesce more of one quality within themselves than another, but it is love they are immediately concerned with, not the concept of love resulting from belief about someone who died, who might have risen, and who might have been God. In the world before Christ in Lagerkvist's fiction, the human dilemma is seen more clearly. As a self-confessed 'religious atheist', Lagerkvist does not leave God out of the picture. Herod, after all, builds a temple, and tries to kill a baby familiar to the readers as 'Immanual' (God with us). Yet, Lagerkvist in **Herod and Mariamne** relegates Jesus to a less significant role in the story, and may, therefore, be making a statement about the elements which contribute to man's confusion in an age of crisis.

The human equation is no simple formula, and Lagerkvist knows it. He implies in all his fiction that it may require a 'higher calculus' than mankind knows in order to solve it satisfactorily. He may be suggesting with his last novel that Jesus is perhaps a variable in the equation rather than a constant, and not a significant one at that. In a century born in crisis and reared in conflict, the word crisis doesn't cause the sharp pain it once did. But like a bad tooth, the ache is still there. Lagerkvist prods his readers and probes the ache of the human dilemma, sometimes roughly, sometimes gently, reminding them always that suffering, struggling, and searching is the triple heritage of Christianity and crisis. (pp. 75-83)

> *Gweneth B. Schwab, "Herod and Barabbas: Lagerkvist and the Long Search," in* Scandinavica, *Vol. 20, No. 1, May, 1981, pp. 75-85.*

FURTHER READING

Bibliography

White, Ray. *Pär Lagerkvist in America.* Atlantic Highlands, N.J.: Humanities Press, 1979, 149 p.
    Indexes reviews of Lagerkvist's works published in the United States, including the novellas *Barabbas, The Sibyl, The Death of Ahasuerus, Pilgrim at Sea, The Holy Land,* and *Herod and Mariamne,* and the short story collection *The Eternal Smile and Other Stories.* Brief excerpts accompany each citation.

Biography

Sjoberg, Leif. *Pär Lagerkvist.* New York: Columbia University Press, 1976, 52 p.
    Summary of Lagerkvist's life and early works.

Criticism

Ahnebrink, Lars. "Pär Lagerkvist: A Seeker and a Humanist." *The Pacific Spectator* VI, No. 4 (Autumn 1952): 400-12.
    Traces Lagerkvist's development as a writer.

Benson, Adolph B. "Pär Lagerkvist: Nobel Laureate." *College English* 13, No. 8 (May 1952): 417-24.
    Discusses Lagerkvist's short fiction within the framework of an introduction to his works and philosophy.

Bloch, Adèle. "The Mythical Female in the Fictional Works of Pär Lagerkvist." *The International Fiction Review* 1, No. 1 (January 1974): 48-53.
    Analyzes Lagerkvist's use of the mythical mother figure in his short fiction.

Ellestad, Everett M. "Lagerkvist and Cubism." *Scandinavian Studies* 45, No. 1 (Winter 1973): 38-53.
    Studies Lagerkvist's "development of literary cubism from theory to practice," concentrating on the style and technique of his fiction.

Fuller, John. "Apings." *New Statesman: The Week-End Review* LXVII, No. 1,717 (7 February 1964): 219-20.

Unfavorable review of the "absurdly overplayed" and "comically portentous" novella *Pilgrim at Sea.*

Gustafson, Alrik. "Pär Lagerkvist and Barabbas." *The American Swedish Monthly* 45, No. 11 (November 1951): 11, 23, 25.

Highly favorable review of the novella *Barabbas* introduced by a brief overview of Lagerkvist's career.

———. "Realism Renewed and Challenged." In his *A History of Swedish Literature,* pp. 345-473. Minneapolis: University of Minnesota Press, 1961.

Presents Lagerkvist's short fiction within the context of his entire career.

Gustafson, Walter. "Pär Lagerkvist and His Symbols." *Books Abroad: An International Literary Quarterly* 26 (Winter 1952): 20-3.

Examines recurring motifs in Lagerkvist's works, including the novellas *Barabbas, The Eternal Smile,* and *The Executioner.*

Hicks, Granville. "Pär Lagerkvist's *The Sibyl:* A Novel with Many and Profound Meanings." *The New Leader* XLI, No. 2 (13 January 1958): 16.

Primarily plot synopsis. Hicks praises *The Sibyl* as "a work of manifold meanings and unmistakable profundity."

Kehl, D. G. "The Chiaroscuro World of Pär Lagerkvist." *Modern Fiction Studies* XV, No. 2 (Summer 1969): 241-50.

Argues that Lagerkvist's recurring themes and techniques create "a world of dualisms, of contending opposites, of darkness and light, . . . evil and good, death and life."

Lowry, Robert. "A Timeless Parable." *The New York Times Book Review* (7 October 1951): 4.

Favorable review of the novella *Barabbas.* Lowry notes Lagerkvist's "dry-point style" and his depiction of Barabbas as a "skeptical Everyman."

Malmström, Gunnel. "The Hidden God." *Scandinavica* supplement (1971): 57-67.

Studies Lagerkvist's novella cycle and his poetry collection *Aftonland* in order to determine his perception of humankind in relationship to God. Quotes from Lagerkvist's work are in Swedish.

Scobbie, Irene. "An Interpretation of Lagerkvist's *Mariamne.*" *Scandinavian Studies* 45, No. 2 (Spring 1973): 128-34.

Focuses on the relationship between Mariamne and Herod in the novella *Herod and Mariamne,* observing that "through the purity and the suffering of Mariamne it has been possible for Christ . . . to be born into Herod's wastelands." Quotes from the text are in Swedish.

———. "The Origins and Development of Lagerkvist's *Barabbas.*" *Scandinavian Studies* 55, No. 1 (Winter 1983): 55-66.

Reconstructs—using diaries, drafts, and letters—the creative process which resulted in the novella *Barabbas.*

Spector, Robert. "The Structure and Meaning of 'The Eternal Smile'." *Modern Language Notes* LXXI, No. 3 (March 1956): 206-07.

Comments on the harmony of structure and theme in *The Eternal Smile.*

———. "Lagerkvist and Existentialism." *Scandinavian Studies* 32, No. 4 (November 1960): 203-11.

Uses the short fiction, poetry, and drama of Lagerkvist to demonstrate that his writings display existential qualities.

———. *Pär Lagerkvist.* Twayne, 1973, 196 p.

Biographical and critical study of Lagerkvist and his work, including his short fiction.

Sundén, Hjalmar. "Tobias's Pilgrimage." *Scandinavica* supplement (1971): 69-80.

An analysis of Lagerkvist's pilgrimage novellas—*The Sibyl, The Death of Ahasuerus,* and *Pilgrim at Sea*—focusing on the function and psychology of the spiritual pilgrimage. Quotations from texts are in Swedish.

Swanson, Roy. "Evil and Love in Lagerkvist's Crucifixion Cycle." *Scandinavian Studies* 28, No. 4 (November 1966): 302-17.

Discusses the themes which run through Lagerkvist's novella cycle and the search for the Kingdom of Heaven by its major characters: Barabbas, Ahasuerus, Giovanni, and Tobias.

"Whither, O Splendid Ship?" *The Times Literary Supplement,* No. 3,232 (6 February 1964): 101.

Argues that *Pilgrim at Sea* has a vague mystical emphasis that denies the novella relevance to the "predicament of twentieth-century readers."

Trotter, Stewart. "Morality, Monsieur." *The Listener* 85, No. 2,189 (11 March 1971): 312.

Criticizes Lagerkvist's "unassertive" point of view and "tiresome" use of anecdotes in *The Eternal Smile and Other Stories.*

Weathers, Winston. "Herod and Mariamne." *Commonweal* LXXXIX, No. 14 (10 January 1969): 478-79.

Examines human qualities represented by the title characters in the novella *Herod and Mariamne* and the philosophical implications of their relationship.

Additional coverage of Lagerkvist's life and career is contained in the following sources published by Gale Research: *Contemporary Authors,* Vols. 49-52, 85-88; *Contemporary Literary Criticism,* Vols. 7, 10, 13, 54; and *Major 20th-Century Writers.*

Ursula K. Le Guin

1929-

(Full name Ursula Kroeber Le Guin) American short story writer, novelist, poet, author of children's books, editor, and scriptwriter.

INTRODUCTION

A highly respected award-winning author of fantasy and science fiction, Le Guin is best known for her stories in which alternative societies serve as the backdrop for discussion about philosophic and social issues such as morality, individual identity, political ideology, and racial interaction. Perhaps unexpectedly, Le Guin's works seem to be shaped more by the social sciences than the physical sciences, as evidenced in her writing by the prominent inclusion of historical context, varied political and economic systems, diverse cultures, and psychological characterizations.

Le Guin wrote short stories during her youth and had unsuccessfully submitted both science fiction and fantasy tales for publication by the age of twelve. While studying French and Italian Renaissance literatures in 1951 in the graduate program at Columbia University, Massachusetts, she began composing some of the stories that were later gathered in 1976 as *Orsinian Tales.* Le Guin married in 1953 and abandoned her academic career to concentrate on writing. "An die Musik," one of the pieces included in *Orsinian Tales,* is her first published short fiction, originally appearing in the journal *Western Humanities Review* in 1961. The "The Dowry of Angyar," included in a 1964 issue of *Amazing* magazine, provided the seed for Le Guin's first novel, *Rocannon's World,* in which the story was altered and incorporated as the chapter "Prologue: The Necklace"; this revised version was also published in the 1975 collection *The Wind's Twelve Quarters* as "Semley's Necklace." "The Winter's King," included in *The Wind's Twelve Quarters,* established the milieu for her first major critical success, the 1969 novel *The Left Hand of Darkness.* Le Guin's literary reputation originated with her novels of the late 1960s, but she has received considerable attention for her short fiction of the mid-1970s, most notably the 1973 Hugo Award novella *The Word for World Is Forest* and the short stories "The Ones Who Walk away from Omelas" and "The Day before the Revolution," which won the 1974 Hugo Award and the 1974 Nebula and Jupiter Awards, respectively. Of her more recent works, the 1982 collection *The Compass Rose* contains stories that previously had been published independently and, similarly, *Buffalo Gals and Other Animal Presences* reprints some earlier works, but also comprises new stories, as well as poems; *A Ride on the Red Mare's Back* is a 1992 novella for young adults.

Le Guin's writing saliently features political concerns. For

example, *The Word for World Is Forest* is by Le Guin's own admission an analogy for American military involvement in Vietnam; the novella depicts a heavily forested environment and the subjugation of native people by means of force. "The Diary of the Rose," the 1976 Jupiter Award story in *The Compass Rose,* involves a politically liberal individual who is alienated by a repressive society. The novella *The New Atlantis* also describes a government that tyrannizes those who do not assimilate; in addition, the state prohibits marriage and treats fidelity with suspicion. Some commentators have criticized Le Guin's work as overtly polemical, a charge commonly leveled at the novella *The Eye of the Heron,* which details the response of pacifists to the threat posed by a violent group with whom they share their space colony. However, works such as *Orsinian Tales,* which comprises stories set from 1150 through 1965 in an imagined Central European country, are judged subtle renderings of political climate: in a description of the efforts of one person to assist people past the border patrol, "A Week in the Country" intimates the slightly dystopian temper of the government.

Le Guin frequently gives a psychological emphasis to her work. "The Good Trip," from *The Wind's Twelve Quar-*

ters, is about a man whose wife suffers from insanity. He hallucinates a meaningful conversation with his wife and, after initially ascribing the visionary encounter to the effects of LSD, recognizes the experience as the result of his fervent, unwavering love for his wife. From the same collection, "The Day before the Revolution" provides a character portrait of an aging woman on the last day of her life. "The First Report of the Shipwrecked Foreigner to the Kadanh of Derb," included in *The Compass Rose,* is an intensely personal evocation of Venice that seems dreamlike. The stories in *Orsinian Tales* have been widely praised for their depiction of individuals growing from youth to maturity, searching for physical and spiritual freedom, and—most fundamentally—enduring; generally acknowledged as a focal tale of the collection, "Imaginary Countries" chronicles a composer's examination of the duty of an artist. Le Guin's stories sometimes present general philosophical observations. She has suggested that "The Masters" and "The Stars Below," both from *The Wind's Twelve Quarters,* can be interpreted as allegories in which the suppression of science represents the rejection of art and creativity. Compiled in the same collection, "Schrödinger's Cat" emphasizes the uncertainty inherent in life and dismisses the belief that science can be an alternative to or substitute for spiritual hope. "The Ones Who Walk away from Omelas," from *The Compass Rose,* uphold moral responsibility, condemning happiness that depends on the suffering of even one person.

Le Guin's fiction commonly presents encounters with the unfamiliar, a theme that critics assert is greatly molded by the anthropological work of her parents, who published several works about North American Indians and introduced their daughter to the culture and history of those people. The *Compass Rose* story "Mazes" depicts a scientist who attempts to test the intelligence of an alien yet comprehends neither the alien's behavior nor dietary needs, a misunderstanding that leads to starvation of the creature. From the same collection, "The Pathways of Desire" describes an expedition to observe the culture of a seemingly primitive alien race on an idyllic planet. Similarly, "Vaster Than Empires and More Slow," which appears in both *The Wind's Twelve Quarters* and *Buffalo Gals and Other Animal Presences,* relates the mutual unease of an exploration team and the vast sentient vegetable organism inhabiting the planet that they are scouting; one explorer, however, comes to understand and appreciate the creature. By contrast, *The Word for World Is Forest* provides no optimistic resolution of confrontation between colonialists and the forest people whose planet they have commandeered. "Nine Lives," in *The Wind's Twelve Quarters,* describes the unlikely friendship that develops between a genetically engineered, constitutionally superior clone and a feeble human. Le Guin places great value on diversity and bonds that transcend differences; yet Theodore Sturgeon, when inquiring whether a single common denominator can be identified in the work and thought of Le Guin, asserted: "Probably not; but there are some notes in her orchestrations that come out repeatedly and with power. A cautionary fear of the development of democracy into dictatorship. Celebrations of courage, endurance, risk. Language, not only loved and shaped, but investigated in all its aspects; call that, perhaps, communication.

But above all, in almost un-earthly terms Ursula Le Guin examines, attacks, unbuttons, takes down and exposes our notions of reality."

PRINCIPAL WORKS

SHORT FICTION

The Word for World Is Forest   1972; published in *Again, Dangerous Visions,* ed. Harlan Ellison
The New Atlantis   1975; published in the anthology *The New Atlantis,* ed. Robert Silverberg
The Wind's Twelve Quarters   1975
Orsinian Tales   1976
Very Far away from Anywhere Else   1976; also published as *A Very Long Way from Anywhere Else,*   1978
The Eye of the Heron   1978; published in *Millennial Women,* ed. Virginia Kidd
The Compass Rose   1982
Buffalo Gals and Other Animal Presences   1987
A Ride on the Red Mare's Back   1992

OTHER MAJOR WORKS

Planet of Exiles   (novel)   1966
Rocannon's World   (novel)   1966
City of Illusions   (novel)   1967
The Wizard of Earthsea   (novel)   1967
The Left Hand of Darkness   (novel)   1969
The Lathe of Heaven   (novel)   1971
The Tombs of Atuan   (novel)   1971
The Farthest Shore   (novel)   1972
The Dispossessed: An Ambiguous Utopia   (novel)   1974
Wild Angels   (poems)   1975
"No Use to Talk to Me"   (drama)   1976; in *The Altered I: An Encounter with Science Fiction by Ursula K. Le Guin and Others*
The Language of the Night: Essays on Fantasy and Science Fiction   (essays)   1979
Leese Webster   (novel)   1979
Malafrena   (novel)   1979
The Beginning Place   (novel)   1980
Always Coming Home   (novel)   1985
King Dog   (drama)   1985
Dancing at the Edge of the World   (criticism)   1989
Tehanu: The Last Book of Earthsea   (novel)   1990

CRITICISM

Ian Watson   (essay date 1975)

[*An award-winning English author of science fiction, Watson has written such works as* The Jonah Kit *(1975),* The Gardens of Delight *(1980), and numerous noted short stories. In the following excerpt, he compares*

Le Guin's novella The Word for World Is Forest *and short story* "Vaster Than Empires and More Slow," *observing that the works present a metaphor for varying stages of a burgeoning transcendental consciousness.*]

In the Afterword to **The Word for World Is Forest** (**WWF**) Le Guin remarks that writing this story was "like taking dictation from a boss with ulcers. What I wanted to write about was the forest and the dream; that is, I wanted to describe a certain ecology from within, and to play with some of Hadfield's and Dement's ideas about the function of dreaming-sleep and the uses of dream. But the boss wanted to talk about the destruction of ecological balance and the rejection of emotional balance." The story accordingly describes the conflict between the forest-dwelling natives of the planet Athshe—who possess a sane and balanced, if (to a prejudiced eye) "primitive," social order—and the Terran colonists who exploit and brutalize them and their world.

The Terrans, having already reduced Earth to a poisoned wasteland, regard the forests of Athshe purely as a source of lumber, and the native Athsheans as a pool of slave labour. The Bureau of Colonial Administration on Earth may issue benevolent guidelines, and a hilfer (high intelligence life form specialist) such as Raj Lyubov may be genuinely concerned with native welfare, woodlands and wildlife; but, till the coming of the ansible instantaneous transmitter, there is no means of investigating complaints or introducing reforms within less than half a century. Thus the tone is set by the Terran military on Athshe, represented at its most paranoid and oppressive by Colonel Davidson. "They bring defoliation and they call it peace," to amend Tacitus.

The analogy between Terran conduct on Athshe and the American intervention in Vietnam is explicit, ironically underlined by the provenance of Earth's Colonel Dongh—and a considerable relief from other reflections of America's war experiences in SF, which, albeit the moral is one of futility and savagery, nevertheless frequently intoxicate the reader with the gungho mood of combat and the lavishly presented technology *per se* (as in Joe Haldeman's widely admired set of stories, collected as *The Forever War*). At the same time, the obvious Vietnam analogy should not blind one to other relevant contemporary analogies—the genocide of the Guyaki Indians of Paraguay, or the genocide and deforestation along the Trans-Amazon Highway in Brazil, or even the general destruction of rain-forest habitats from Indonesia to Costa Rica. Le Guin's story is multi-applicable—and multi-faceted.

The political facet aside, **WWF** is a vivid presentation of the dynamics of a sane society which lives in harmony with its natural environment because its members are themselves in psychological equilibrium. The Athsheans practice conscious dream control, and having thereby free access to their own subconscious processes, do not suffer from the divorce that Terrans exemplify between subconscious urges and conscious rationalizations. To the Athsheans, the Terrans—deprived of this dream knowledge—seem to be an insane people, their closest approach to self-knowledge being the undisciplined confusion brought on

by the hallucinogens they entertain themselves with obsessively (the "drug problem" faced by American forces in Vietnam is here savagely presented as the military norm).

The Athsheans' proficiency in the dream life is directly imaged by their physical residence in the dark tangled forests of the planet: these latter function metaphorically as a kind of external collective unconscious. The Terrans, whose unconscious is an impenetrable jungle in which they are far from being at home, react to the Athshean forest with confusion, fear and dislike. Deforestation is their technological response to the mysteries of the wood. Indeed, one might fairly argue that the metaphorical significance of the Terran deforestation is primary and the economic or factual significance quite secondary:

> men were here now to end the darkness, and turn the tree-jumble into clean sawn planks, more prized on Earth than gold. Literally, because gold could be got from seawater and from under the Antarctic ice, but wood could not; wood came only from trees. And it was a really necessary luxury on Earth.

The paradox of "necessary luxury" neatly capsulates the confused thinking of the Terrans, and goes some way towards explaining the essential implausibility of hauling loads of wood over a distance of 27 light years; but on balance, just as the metaphorical sense precedes the economic in this passage, so it does in the story as a whole, intensely verisimilar though the story is in presentation.

The metaphorical structure operates on a primary opposition of light and darkness: the arid light outside the forests, where the aggressive and exploitative Terrans feel falsely safe, and the shiftingly many-coloured darkness within, where the integral Athsheans wake and dream. The forest paths are "devious as nerves"—a neural simile which supports the impression that the forest itself is conscious; that it represents the subconscious mind, the dark side of awareness. Being tangled and dark, no superficial reconnaissance of it is possible—no fast overflight surveys beloved of Herman Kahn's "flying think tanks" (Kahn's thermonuclear catechism is rehearsed by the rabid Colonel Davidson, reflecting "by God sometimes you have to be able to think about the unthinkable." "Nothing was pure, dry, arid, plain. Revelation was lacking. There was no seeing everything at once, no certainty." Lyubov, initially oppressed by the world-forest with its impenetrability and "total vegetable indifference to the presence of mind," eventually comes to terms with the forest (and its implications), and reflects that, whereas the name "terra" designates the soil of his own world, "to the Athsheans soil, ground, earth was not that to which the dead return and by which the living live: the substance of their world was not earth, but forest. Terran man was clay, red dust. Athshean man was branch and root." The Athshean word for "dream," indeed, is the same as the word for "root."

Out of the original impetus to write about forest and dream, then, has come a world-forest that—while nonsentient itself—nevertheless functions metaphorically as mind: as the collective unconscious mind of the Athsheans. However, the story (at "the boss's" behests) is oriented politically and ecologically; hence it must be primarily verisimilar rather than metaphorical. Consequently there is a surplus of energy and idea, attached to the central image of a forest consciousness, which cannot find a full outlet here. At the same time, *WWF* is exploring an alternative state of consciousness, in the conscious dream; yet this is not a paranormal state of mind—something which Le Guin has treated extensively in her previous Hainish-cycle works. The "Forest mind" theme, controlled and tempered to politics and ecology in *WWF,* finds its independent outlet only within a *paranormal* context, in another long story of this period, **"Vaster than Empires and More Slow"** (VTE). The two stories are closely linked thematically—the latter involving a general inversion of the situation of the former. If . . . Le Guin's 1971 novel *The Lathe of Heaven* represents a discharge of paranormal elements built into the framework of the Hainish cycle, then, outside of that cycle, **VTE** represents a parallel working-out of a conflict between verisimilitude and metaphor in **WWF.** VTE uses the paranormal element from the Hainish cycle as a way of validating a forest-mind which is a verisimilar actuality rather than a metaphor.

Whilst Earthmen in general are regarded as insane by the Athsheans, the Extreme Survey team of the second story are of unsound mind by the standards of Earth—and Hain, and any other world. Only people who are radically alienated from society would volunteer for a trip lasting five hundred years, objective time. The most alienated of them, Osden, is paradoxically an empath. He possesses the paranormal skill "to pick up emotion or sentience from anything that felt." Unfortunately, the feelings of his fellows only serve to disgust him. Le Guin adds that properly speaking this faculty could be categorised as a "wide-range bioempathic receptivity"—which seems to be a way of suggesting that this is not in fact a paranormal skill, comparable to telepathy, since all human beings possess a certain degree of what can only be termed, "bioempathic receptivity" in relation to kinesic body-signals and phero-mone scent-signals (even though most of the time they are unaware of this consciously). However, the fact that a teachable technique for telepathy exists (on Rocannon's World, otherwise Fomalhaut II—locale of Le Guin's first Hainish novel) is deliberately introduced into the story at this point, to rout the skeptic voice that would separate empathy off from telepathy. As the events of the novel *Rocannon's World* are supposed to take place some 300 years after the events of this story, the paranormal comparison is conceivably more important than strict adherence to chronology. But in any case, sharing "lust with a white rat, pain with a squashed cockroach and phototropy with a moth" is hardly classifiable as a natural talent. Clearly this represents a qualitative leap into the beyond of the paranormal—a movement away from a mere extension of everyday (if rarely noted) experience, to a radically different level of perception.

The psychological disconnectedness of the **VTE** survey team contrasts sharply with the total connectedness of the vegetation on World 4470. There is nothing but vegetation on this world—tree, creeper, grass; but no bird or beast, nothing that moves. The interconnected roots amid creepers function as slow neural pathways binding the whole complex of forest and prairie into a slow vegetable consciousness, whose awareness is a function of this connectedness.

It is aware; yet not intelligent. Slowly realizing the presence of rootless, mobile intruders in its midst, the vegetable mind reacts with an anxiety that grows to terror in the minds of the survey team as they sense it, and which is only absorbed and transcended by the empath Osden. His only psychological defence against the flood of feelings from others, that threaten to swamp his own personality, is to reject these others, and then masochistically thrive on his own rejection by others which this provokes. Thus rejection becomes his salvation.

One might clearly relate Le Guin's use of the forest as metaphor for a mental state to Henry James' use of a similar image in his story "The Beast in the Jungle." Not only does a lurking "psychic beast" lie in wait for James' protagonist John Marcher, to be sensed also by Le Guin's Porlock as "something moving with purpose, trying to attack him from behind." Not only does John Marcher's response, of hurling himself violently facedown in his hallucination, as though he has been physically leap upon, pre-echo what happens to Le Guin's Osden. But even the very nature of Marcher's beast—which represents a lifelong atrophy of affect, of emotional cathexis with other people and the outside world—parallels Osden's autism.

At the same time, one can find in previous SF several "forest-minds" and vegetable intelligences. Perhaps the most lucid and insightful are Olaf Stapledon's Plant Men in *Star Maker* (1937). Stapledon's "vegetable humanities" are specifically associated with the mystical, and even the redemptory. ("Till sunset he slept, not in a dreamless sleep, but in a sort of trance, the meditative and mystical quality of which was to prove in future ages a well of peace for many worlds.") Stapledon is here closest to Le Guin in mood of the various arboriculturists of SF—and it is Stapledon, that mystical atheist, who remains the writer best able to articulate the sense of cosmic mystery as well as to indicate the nature of possible higher-order intelligences, or superminds, without falling into either naive bravura, or will to power. Van Vogt, who, with his assorted slans, silkies, nexialists, etc. can be relied on for an operatic, mystificatory demonstration of the will to power, has described in his short story "Process" a forest-mind that is slow-thinking, yet fast-growing, a ravening leviathan of hostility, yet slothful and stupid, a forest replete with contradictions which visiting spacemen (who remain invisible) insert their impervious ship into, from time immemorial, to steal some riches (in the form of uranium) and fly away. This story, by contrast with Le Guin, is *unconscious* metaphor. The tangled, fearsome, stupid forest "reads" quite blatantly as the hidden, unconscious area of the mind, into which the masterful creative consciousness plunges—well-armoured—to extract necessary wealth; and the story remains an absorbing one, for all its contradictions, precisely because it is about the process of creation, and at the same time about Van Vogt's own willful refusal to be analytically aware of this. The story is about the betrayal of full consciousness.

Van Vogt's short story "The Harmonizer" describes a supertree which angrily manufactures a stupefying perfume whenever its "sensitive colloids" catch "the blasts of palpable lust" radiated by any killer—whether carnivorous animal, or hate-drunk soldier. Such trees, deposited on Earth by a space-wreck, are responsible for the disappearance of the dinosaurs. Latterly, their one survivor, re-emerging after 80 million years, halts World War III, introducing a malign, brainwashing pseudo-pacificism. This time, the tree is overtly associated with the militant spread of a form of consciousness. A similar manipulatory—though paranormal—situation occurs in Kris Neville's short story "The Forest of Zil," where a world-forest responds to Terran intrusion by retrospectively cancelling the time-line of Homo Sapiens, sending a creeping ontological amnesia back along the time axis. Manipulatory, too, is the symbiotic diamond wood forest in James H. Schmitz's short story "Balanced Ecology." It too encapsulates both violence and somnolence—twin associations which link these four stories, suggesting that the subconscious, the time of sleep, is indeed underlying these various tree-minds in one form or another, and that the time of sleep, furthermore—when dreams take place—is feared as a time of ignorance and violence. This can certainly not be said of Stapledon's treatment of the theme—nor of Le Guin's.

Theme and image, event and illusion, bind Le Guin's two forest-mind stories together. The title of **"Vaster than Empires and More Slow"** is but one of a series of references to the work of Andrew Marvell, especially his poem "To His Coy Mistress": "My vegetable love should grow / Vaster than empires, and more slow." Another allusion to this same poem occurs at the end of the story ("Had we but world enough and time . . .") while another familiar line from the poem presides over Lyubov's headache in *WWF*: ". . .ow, ow, ow, above the right ear I always hear Time's winged chariot hurrying near, for the Athsheans had burned Smith Camp . . . ." Again, in **VTE,** Osen's reflecting that the vegetation of World 4470 is "one big green thought" echoes the famous "a green thought in a green shade" from Marvell's poem "The Garden."

The second story also picks up the military argot of *WWF* where Colonel Davidson is obsessed with the idea of people going "spla"—crazy. Osden uses the word more than once of the effect the forest is producing; while the comment that "the chitinous rigidity of military discipline was quite inapplicable to these teams of Mad Scientists" recalls the behaviour of the Terran military on Athshe, at the same time as it turns it upside-down.

The hallucinatory quality of Athshe—a world "that made you day-dream"—recurs in the "Hypnotic quality" of the woods of **VTE** World 4470, where imagery binding root and dream is reinforced. The woods are dark, connected; nightmare passes through the roots as the visitors are sensed; the visitors themselves relapse increasingly into sleep, to dream dreams that are "pathless" and "dark-branching." When awake, the visitors are still scared "blind." The path leading Osden to his self-sacrifice commences with a fall in the forest that injures his face, and lets his blood mingle with the root-nerves. Thereafter his countenance is "flayed" by scars that parallel the injured

face of Selver the Athshean, beaten up by Colonel Davidson. But Selver, the flayed one, becomes thereby a "God" in Athshean terms—dreamer of a powerful new collective dream. Osden, too, through psychic identification with the "immortal mindless" forest—an idiot God absorbed in its own Nirvana beyond Maya, the changes of the world—transcends the human level, and at the same time becomes a "colonist" of World 4470. This word, the very last of the story, would seem an odd choice indeed for Osden's fate as castaway did it not reflect back to the Terran ambition to colonize Athshe—which the Terrans signally fail to achieve, precisely because of their disconnectedness. Osden succeeds where they failed; but only in a mystic apotheosis achieved by a paranormal "wild talent"—a fictive dimension ruled out of court by the politically conscious, this-worldly "boss" of *WWF,* and henceforth to be purged from the Hainish universe of Le Guin.

However, it is apparent from this story that there is an authentic "mystical" strain in Le Guin—an authentic strain, as opposed to the various gimmick-ridden mystifications that frequently pass for mysticism in our times, from the conjuring tricks of Uri Geller or the "grokking" of Charles Manson, via the musico-hagiology of the pop Orient, to the opening of the third eye of confused Western disciples by cult gurus. Whether this authentic mystical strain is necessarily radically at odds with the socio-political strain, as metaphor may be at odds with verisimilitude, is another matter. It might be truer to say that this mystic element has hitherto been falsely expressed through the traditional paranormal gimmickry of SF and that it is here in the process of breaking free (though it is not yet free). Just as *The Lathe of Heaven* is discharging the tension generated by use of the paranormal in the Hainish cycle, so **VTE,** structurally attached as it is to the politically "correct" partner story presided over by the "boss," may be seen now as an attempt to discover a permissible locale for the mystical—stripped, as it were, of a phoney mysticism of supermen and superminds. Hence the caginess as to whether Osden's empathy is paranormal or not; hence the need to remark on this and draw the problem to our attention.

The story opens (in the original version at least [—the version in *The Wind's Twelve Quarters* omits the first four paragraphs]) with a meditation on the nature of eternity as experienced during NAFAL time-distortion starflight, which is directly compared to the time, outside time, of dreams: "The mystic is a rare bird, and the nearest most people get to God in paradoxical time is . . . prayer for release," comments Le Guin, coining a phrase clearly suggested by the "paradoxical sleep" of the dream researchers. The story ends with a return to this same keynote mood. Osden is absorbed into the eternity, the no-time sought by those rare birds, the mystics:

> He had taken the fear into himself, and accepting had transcended it. He had given up his self to the alien, an unreserved surrender, that left no place for evil. He had learned the love of the Other, and thereby had been given his whole self. But this is not the vocabulary of reason.

The final sentence is revealing. Le Guin has inverted the

main values of **WWF** to give suppressed material a veri-similar outlet. She has swung as far away as possible from the military domain into the realm of the "speshes" (specialists). Dream has become nightmare, and sleep a form of catatonic withdrawal from reality. She has made her visitors to the stars overtly mad. She has created an alien life-form—as opposed to the various humanoids of Hainish descent, that have been her theme hitherto. She has pushed beyond the limits of Hainish expansion to describe a world that has nothing to do with Hain. Forest as metaphor of mind has here been translated into narrative reality. The grudging military surrender of the Terrans on Athshe has become the "unreserved" spiritual surrender of Osden, who thus becomes the only true colonist: not so much of World 4470—for how can one man colonize a world?—as of the Beyond, of the dream time (*pace* Raj Lyubov's shade stalking Selver's dreams). Yet, in the end, this transcendent territory is unchartable by rational discourse. Stripped to the bare minimum of the paranormal trappings that do duty for it elsewhere (however successfully—one thinks of Genly Ai's encounter with Foretelling in *The Left Hand of Darkness*), it is inarticulable. Or rather, to draw a distinction that Wittgenstein draws, it may be shown forth, but not stated. The ending of **VTE** recalls the terminal aphorism of the *Tractatus*: "What we cannot speak about we must pass over in silence" [Ludwig Wittgenstein, *Tractatus Logico-Philosophicus*]. The essentially silent world-forest of **VTE** shows forth, yet cannot state, the para-rational elements implied by **WWF** though sternly suppressed in that story.

It might seem, then, that whilst the mystic area of experience may be an authentic area, there is nothing profound one can say about it. Least of all should one attempt to do so by invoking the paraphernalia of the paranormal from the lumber-room of SF, for this only alienates one from the physical—and from the social—universe. Yet the sense of insight into the infinite is not thereby necessarily lost. It returns, in *The Dispossessed,* with Shevek's creation of a General Theory of Time—within a context of positive social, political and emotional practice. It returns, having been chastened by the "boss" of **WWF,** and then by contrast—in the partner story **VTE**—allowed free rein to test out the mystic Pascalian silences where the vocabulary of reason becomes void. To the world-forests of these two stories, both metaphors for mind—one overt, one covert—corresponds Shevek's Theory: which is, within the verisimilar setting of the book, also *metaphorical* to a large extent. Yet, whereas the forest-mind is presented as something concrete that lies in wait out there for us, Shevek's Theory arises only out of the complex dialectic of his own life as scientist and utopian. As he discovers his own unity, so his theory becomes possible; and only so. This is the vocabulary of reason—which turns out to have far greater scope and depth than that other vocabulary, of unreason, or parareason. But it is a vocabulary of a *subversive* reason, which has therefore had first to pass through the false, non-reasonable and by themselves non-cognitive expressions of parareason. The two forest minds of **WWF** and **VTE** are—beyond their intrinsic interest as bases for two shrewd and powerful stories—necessary stages in a development from ur-SF to the mystico-political theory of time and society in *The Dispossessed.* (pp. 231-36)

Ian Watson, "The Forest as Metaphor for Mind: 'The Word for World Is Forest' and 'Vaster Than Empires and More Slow'," in Science-Fiction Studies, *Vol. 2, No. 3, November, 1975, pp. 231-37.*

Paula Deitz (essay date 1977)

[*In the following essay, Deitz discusses the theme of "borders and boundaries of the land and of the mind" in the stories of Le Guin's* Orsinian Tales.]

There comes a time in reading *Middlemarch* when you finally grasp the geography of it—names and positions of towns, villages, estates and parishes as well as the connecting roads and lanes. An actual map is visualized that stays with you until you complete the novel, and for a long time thereafter. The same is true for Ursula K. Le Guin's *Orsinian Tales,* a finely crafted collection of eleven stories which are joined in part by their sense of a locale. Krasnoy is the capitol city of her region, which has smaller towns with names like Foranoy, Rákava, Aisnar, Sfaroy Kampe, and villages, Sorg, Kolle Verre, Vermare, on the border, and Prevne, beyond the border. The country may be Hungary, or not, Le Guin does not say, but it is certainly Middle European. (And here I will note that, perhaps to produce the effect of a foreign idiom, her language is stilted, like that of a translation, which sometimes helps and sometimes does not.)

There is a difference, however. Although we are always (with the exception of one story set in Paris) in the same region, we are never there at the same time. We pass back and forth through time, mostly in the twentieth century but once in 1150 and once in 1640, walking the same streets on golden autumn afternoons or early spring evenings but with different people in different situations. Each story gives you a new memory of a time and a person to carry with you to the next one. **"A Week in the Country"** is about a grandson of the man in **"Brothers and Sisters."** Also in the story **"A Week in the Country,"** we hear a scream coming from an upper floor and are reminded of a similar scream that echoed eight centuries before in the same town in **"The Barrow."** What a strange and beautiful experience it is in 1939 to cross the bridge at night in the city of Foranoy with a composer and see through stone arches the river dividing the city. And then to compare that experience with that of crossing, with a revolutionary-to-be, the bridge in Krasnoy that divided the city in the '56 revolution. The effect is cumulative as we move backward and forward in time.

Architecture is central to the atmosphere of these stories, as are Le Guin's minute descriptions of seasonal weather and changing times of day. Nothing is permanent. Her towns are always in stages of decay. Buildings where important events take place in one story appear as ruins in another. The freedom of summer houses, farms and villages is contrasted everywhere with the cramped quarters and lack of privacy of urban dwellings and crowded courtyards, though in turn the anonymity provided by these latter, particularly in the city of Krasnoy, may give one of her people an only chance at survival. And this brings us to her major theme, the meaning of the circumscription of space, both outer and inner, or, in other words, the borders and boundaries of the land and of the mind.

Le Guin delineates man's preoccupation with territorial borders and the boundaries of rigid social and political systems, relying here on our preconceived notions about the Eastern European region she has chosen as her stage. For the castle walls, protected border crossings and bridges dividing cities are all symbolic of the deeper psychological borders within ourselves. The stunning climax of each story is the pivotal moment at which the persons cross over to a new level of awareness, a kind of freedom, leaving behind the constriction of their previous state. For the young people, about whom she writes so well, this is the moment which marks their maturity. So subtle is the imaginary line crossed that we as readers sometimes see it first and watch with absorbing interest the dawn of realization. Throughout there are such phrases as: " . . . it was at this moment, though he was unaware of it, that he defected" (**"The Fountains"**); "She knew . . . her will . . . set him free; . . . she must go with him into freedom, and it was a place she had never been before" (**"Conversations at Night"**); " . . . as if at each step she crossed, unwillingly, a threshold" (**"Brothers and Sisters"**) or " . . . in this one recognition by one man, he was strong and he was free" (**"An die Musik"**).

These transitions sometimes come about spontaneously and sometimes as a reaction to other people, as when a whole border patrol in **"A Week in the Country"** attempts and fails to stop one man from helping people escape across the border. People pass from one state into another just as paganism passes into Christianity (in **"The Barrow"** and **"Ile Forest"**); as the world is revealed to the blind (**"Conversations at Night"**); as night becomes day (in one of the best passages from the same story):

> Outside the dreams, outside the walls, the city Rákava stood still in daybreak. The streets, the old wall with its high gates and towers, the factories that bulked outside the wall, the gardens at the high south edge of town, the whole of the long, tilted plain on which the city was built, lay pale, drained, unmoving. A few fountains clattered in deserted squares. The west was still cold where the great plain sloped off into the dark. A long cloud slowly dissolved into a pinkish mist in the eastern sky, and then the sun's rim, like the lip of a cauldron of liquid steel, tipped over the edge of the world, pouring out daylight. The sky turned blue, the air was streaked with the shadows of towers. Women began to gather at the fountains. The streets darkened with people going to work; and then the rising and falling howl of the siren at the Ferman cloth-factory went over the city, drowning out the slow striking of the cathedral bell.

—or as, at the end of a story about a carefree summer, the awareness of winter sets in:

> He saw, at the end of the smoke and the shining tracks, the light of candles in a high dark dining-room, the stare of a rockinghorse in an attic corner, leaves wet with rain overhead on the way to school, and a grey street shortened by a cold,

foggy dusk through which shone, remote and festive, the first streetlight of December.
> ("Imaginary Countries")

In only one story, **"The Lady of Moge,"** does the heroine reach her greatest moment of self-awareness while still confined within walls. Because her departure from her castle was not on her own terms, her imprisonment begins only upon her arrival in the outside world. But in the rest, particularly those about the emergence of youth, about which Le Guin is so knowing and tender, the new awareness is only the beginning of lives in which people really connect, fall in love and make decisions. In brief, they know what action is even against great odds, and at the risk of sounding fashionable, I must say for the most part it is the women, brave and determined, who know what to do.

Le Guin's book is not about happiness, though there are brief happy moments in it. But here is a writer who can reveal her knowledge of the inner joy of maturity and the subsequent release into full awareness. She portrays better than most, too, the sharp sense of perception we all possess when we are alone, and she knows how it really feels to be alone, particularly when we are walking along a city street at nightfall. (pp. 106-08)

> *Paula Deitz, "Outside the Dreams, Outside the Walls," in* The Ontario Review, *No. 6, Spring-Summer, 1977, pp. 106-08.*

James W. Bittner   (essay date 1978)

[*Bittner is an American educator and the author of* Approaches to the Fiction of Ursula K. Le Guin *(1979). In the following essay, Bittner provides an overview of* Orsinian Tales *and examines two stories collected therein, "Imaginary Countries" and "An die Musik," as works that provide special insight into Le Guin's fiction as a whole.*]

In 1951, the year Ursula Kroeber entered Columbia to begin graduate work in French and Italian Renaissance literature, she invented an imaginary Central European country and wrote her first Orsinian tale. The country's name—Orsinia, or the Ten Provinces—and its creator's name have the same root; *orsino,* Italian for "bearish," and *Ursula* came from the Latin *ursa.* Le Guin explains rather dryly that "it's my country so it bears my name."

After marrying Charles Le Guin in 1953, she abandoned her academic career to concentrate on writing. By 1961, she says in an autobiographical essay, she had completed five novels, four of them set in Orsinia, "as were the best short stories I had done." When these novels and stories, classifiable as neither fantasy nor realism, were submitted to publishers like Knopf or Viking, or to magazines like *Harper's, Cosmopolitan,* or *Redbook,* they came back with the remark "this material seems remote." It *was* remote, says Le Guin:

> Searching for a technique of distancing, I had come upon this one. Unfortunately it was not a technique used by anybody at the moment, it was not fashionable, it did not fit any of the categories. You must either fit a category, or 'have

a name,' to publish a book in America. As the only way I was ever going to achieve Namehood was *by* writing, I was reduced to fitting a category. Therefore my first efforts to write science fiction were motivated by a pretty distinct wish to get published.

Orsinia did not go entirely unnoticed. [The poem "Folksong from Montayna Province" and the story **"An die Musik"**] were published in little magazines in 1959 and 1961. But just as a couple of Le Guin's minor Orsinian pieces were appearing in print, she discovered Cordwainer Smith, rediscovered science fiction, which she had read as an adolescent, and, intent on getting published, started writing fantasy and science fiction for *Fantastic* and *Amazing.* By 1963 she had begun her explorations of Earthsea and the Hainish worlds, and was on her way to Namehood. Now, of course, with numerous awards from both inside and outside science fiction, she has achieved it; twenty-five years after her Orsinian tales started collecting rejection slips, her **Orsinian Tales** received a nomination for the National Book Award for fiction.

I go into all this—the date of the earliest Orsinian tales, and their place vis a vis categories like "realism," "fantasy," and "science fiction"—to dispel the notion that **Orsinian Tales** is Le Guin's attempt to extend the range of her talents beyond the boundaries of fantasy and science fiction. If anything, the opposite is the case. **Orsinian Tales** includes chunks of the bedrock that lies beneath Le Guin's other imaginary countries and worlds. Or, using another metaphor, I would suggest that a trip through Orsinia may lead us to those underground streams that nourish the imagination that created the Earthsea trilogy, *The Left Hand of Darkness,* and *The Dispossessed.*

Relationships between **Orsinian Tales** and the rest of Le Guin's fiction will be one of my concerns here. Some of these tales were written before Le Guin discovered-invented Earthsea and the Hainish worlds, some were written at the same time she was writing fantasy and science fiction, and they were all collected, arranged, and published after she had written the works that brought her Namehood. We cannot, therefore, try to understand **Orsinian Tales** as a discrete stage or step in Le Guin's development, for the parts and the whole were composed at different times. Accordingly, my approach will be eclectic. In the first section below, I will treat the book as a whole, discussing Le Guin's synthesis of aesthetic and historical perspectives, and arguing that Le Guin's historical understanding is mediated by the literary form that structures most of her fiction, the circular journey or romance quest. Then, I will look at the country Orsinia as an imaginary construct whose fluid boundaries enclose enclose both fantasy and realism, and also as a *paysage moralisé* which manifests the same qualities we find in Le Guin's other imaginary landscapes. In the final two sections, I will concentrate on **"Imaginary Countries"** and **"An die Musik,"** two tales Le Guin wrote in 1960, before she turned to fantasy and science fiction, reading the first as the central tale in the collection, and the second as an early formulation of a problem that continues to be prominent throughout Le Guin's career, the conflict between her deep devotion to art and her strong commitment to ethical principles.

1. **Orsinian Tales,** Le Guin's second collection of short fiction, is radically different from her first. In her "Foreword" to **The Wind's Twelve Quarters,** Le Guin explains that it is "what painters call a retrospective": the stories are assembled in the order they were written to give us an overview of her artistic development. The tales in **Orsinian Tales,** however, are *not* arranged in order of their composition, so this is not another Le Guin retrospective. But if "retrospective" does not describe the collection, then another word from painting, "perspective," may indicate something about the nature of the tales and may help to reveal the ordering principles embedded in their arrangement.

After we finish reading any story, we step back from it as though we were stepping back from a painting, adjusting our vision to get an impression of its total design and meaning. This is aesthetic perspective, the desired effect of any technique of distancing. The distancing technique Le Guin uses in **Orsinian Tales,** the technique she developed in the fifties before she began writing for *Amazing* and *Fantastic,* is derived from Isak Dinesen's tales and from Austin Tappan Wright's *Islandia.* This technique does something more than create an aesthetic perspective; it creates a twofold perspective—aesthetic and historical.

Le Guin achieves aesthetic distance from her materials by writing *tales,* not stories (notwithstanding the publisher's dust jacket subtitle "A Collection of Stories"). **Orsinian Tales** does not belong in a class with Joyce's *Dubliners* and Anderson's *Winesburg, Ohio;* rather, its title recalls the tradition that includes Scott's *Tales of My Landlord,* Hearn's *Tales Out of the East,* Dunsany's *A Dreamer's Tales,* and Dinesen's *Seven Gothic Tales* and *Winter's Tales.* Le Guin's title is a clear echo of Dunsany's and Dinesen's titles. A tale does not pretend to represent everyday reality as faithfully as a story does; more than a story, a tale calls attention to itself as a work of art, closed off from the world, and in its tendency to state a moral more overtly than a story usually does, it has affinities with fables, parables, and legends. A tale offers a clearer understanding of the shape and action of the moral order we dimly perceive in our sometimes disordered daily experience, and it does this because it detaches itself from the contingencies of a particular time and place. The discovery and delineation of moral laws, in fact, may be the most important goal of the teller of tales, and the pattern of those moral laws cannot be separated from the aesthetic forms which enable the artist to discover them and communicate them to others. As ethical choices in our everyday lives are not free from history, those in a tale are bound by aesthetic forms. A tale offers a perspective that combines aesthetics and ethics in a single vision.

Yet at the same time that Le Guin creates this aesthetic perspective, she negates it by regrounding her tales in history, seemingly contradicting, yet really complementing the ahistorical qualities of the tale with precise historical connections. Le Guin sets her tales in an imaginary country, to be sure, but that country is in *Mitteleuropa,* not *Faerie:* Orsinia is in the "sick heart" of modern Europe and knows at first hand what Mircea Eliade, a native of Romania, calls [in her *Myth of the Eternal Return*] the "terror of history." Le Guin therefore evokes as the larger setting of her tales some of the darkest, most chaotic, and most violent history available. Like Hardy's Wessex, Faulkner's Yoknapatawpha County, and Wright's Islandia, Le Guin's Orsinia may be imaginary, but it is profoundly affected by real historical forces.

At the end of each tale we discover a date; these dates, ranging from the early Middle Ages (1150) to the recent past (1965), locate each tale at a precise moment in Orsinia's (and Central Europe's) history, and invite us to step back from our involvement with a character's experiences, to insert those experiences in a definite historical context, and to understand them in a historical perspective. It is significant that the the dates are at the *end* of each tale; they appear *at the very moment* we are stepping back from the tale to see aesthetically. At that moment, history and aesthetics, two modes of seeing and knowing, become one.

The process of reading the eleven pieces in *Orsinian Tales,* then, is the process of forming and re-forming this two-fold aesthetic and historical perspective, progressively enlarging our understanding of the relationships among individual tales and deepening our understanding of the relationships between any one moment in the lives of individual Orsinians and the whole web of Orsinian history. As we finish the collection, we realize that the two perspectives are not contradictory, but complementary; the one being the dialectical negation of the other, art and history combine to create a single vision. "Heroes do not make history," says the narrator of **"The Lady of Moge"**—"that is the historians' job." *Orsinian Tales,* however, offers abundant evidence that the job is not the sole responsibility of historians: it is shared by artists. Le Guin's tales are as historical as Scott's Waverly novels are, and her history is as much an aesthetic invention as are Dinesen's finely crafted tales. As Le Guin's art in *Orsinian Tales* redeems her history from meaningless contingency and hopeless determinism, her history redeems her art from amoral escapism.

Le Guin's arrangement of the tales embodies a complex organic vision of history. If they are not arranged as they were written, neither are they arranged as history courses are, to give the impression that chronology and historical causality are somehow synonymous. Nor are they randomly mixed up just to give us the exercise of reconstituting Orsinia's history. Le Guin's ordering of the tales guides us through the history of Orsinia so that we move forward *only* by circling back to the past; we understand any present moment only as we understand it to be an organic part of its past and future. After beginning in 1960 (**"The Fountains"**), we return to 1150 (**"The Barrow"**), move forward to 1920 (**"Ile Forest"** and **"Conversations at Night"**), then on to 1956 (**"The Road East"**), back to 1910 (**"Brothers and Sisters"**), forward beyond 1956 to 1962 (**"A Week in the Country"**), back to 1938 (**"An die Musik"**), forward beyond 1962 to 1965 (**"The House"**), back to 1640 (**"The Lady of Moge"**), and finally forward to 1935 (**"Imaginary Countries"**), coming to rest, at the end of the collection, at the chronological *center* of these eleven tales: five are set before 1935, and five after 1935. As I will show later, this is not the only way in which

"Imaginary Countries" is the central tale in *Orsinian Tales.*

The pattern of this movement through these tales that *are* Orsinia's history—a synthesis of circularity and linearity, a series of returns which are also advances—is not only the configuration of Le Guin's sense of history; it is also the aesthetic structure that informs most of her fiction. The romance quest which is at once a return to roots and an advance is Ged's path (way, Tao) in Earthsea; it is the route taken by Genly Ai and Estraven from Karhide over the Gobrin Ice to "The Place Inside the Blizzard" and back to Karhide; and it is the form of Shevek's journey from Anarres to Urras and back home again. In *Orsinian Tales,* this pattern is present not only in the shape of the whole collection; it is present also in individual tales: Freyga, Count of Montayana, returns to pagan sacrifice then advances the cause of Benedictine monks; Adam Kereth returns to Orsinia after "defecting" at Versailles; and Mariya returns to her husband Pier Korre in Aisnar after searching for independence and freedom from marriage in Krasnoy.

These circular journeys are in one way or another versions of the Romantic quest for home, freedom, and wholeness. What Le Guin's characters learn on their quests is that freedom and wholeness are not to be found in individualism, but in partnership, and further, that freedom from historical necessity comes not from escaping history, but from returning to roots. This is the moral message that takes shape when we see Le Guin's fiction from the perspective created by her distancing techniques. It is the ethical principle discovered by Sanzo Chekey and Alitsia Benat, by Stefan Fabbre and Bruna Augeskar, and by Mariya and Pier Lorre. In Le Guin's fantasy and science fiction it is discovered by Ged and Vetch, Tenar and Ged, Arren and Ged, Genly Ai and Estraven, George Orr and Heather Lelache, Shevek and Takver. In *The Dispossessed,* we find Le Guin's most concise statement of the principle, chiseled into Odo's tombstone: "to be whole is to be part: / true voyage is return." It is the ethical foundation of Le Guin's fiction, even as it is aesthetic form and historical consciousness.

> **What Le Guin's characters learn on their quests [in *Orsinian Tales*] is that freedom and wholeness are not to be found in individualism, but in partnership, and further, that freedom from historical necessity comes not from escaping history, but from returning to roots.**
>
> **—James W. Bittner**

Ethics, art, and history, along with religion, philosophy, politics, and science, are what Joseph Needham [in *Moulds of Understanding: A Pattern of Natural Philosophy,* edited by Gary Werskey] calls "moulds of understanding." Each one, taken by itself, offers a limited and limiting mode of comprehending and experiencing the world. *Orsinian Tales* is one of Le Guin's attempts to formulate a unified mould of understanding that integrates artistic, ethical, and historical modes. Convinced that the worlds we experience, from subatomic to cosmic levels, whether material or imaginative, are all integrated parts of an ordered whole, a continuous process, Le Guin has from the beginning of her career tried to fashion fictional techniques to comprehend that order. The hybrid of realism and fantasy in *Orsinian Tales,* the fantasy of the Earthsea trilogy, and the science fiction of the Hainish novels are all different means to the same end: a realization of the unity of the world we live in. The end, unity, and the formal means, a circular journey, are cognate. In one sense, Le Guin uses different genres; but in another sense, those genres are merely distinct, though not radically different, constellations of moulds of understanding. Just as the artist and historian in Le Guin collaborate in *Orsinian Tales,* artist and scientist work together in her science fiction. Genly Ai opens his report from Gethen with these remarks:

> I'll make my report as if I told a story, for I was taught as a child on my homeworld that Truth is a matter of the imagination. The soundest fact may fail or prevail in the style of the telling: like that singular organic jewel of our sea, which grows brighter as one woman wears it and, worn by another, dulls and goes to dust. Facts are no more solid, coherent, round, and real than pearls are. But both are sensitive. [*The Left Hand of Darkness*]

Ai then proceeds to weave together his own story; extracts from Estraven's journal; an anthropological report; and Gethenian legends, folktales, and myth. Each presents only a partial view of the truth; together they come closer to Truth. For Le Guin, the real and the fantastic, fact and value, art and history, myth and science are neither separate nor even separable realms and modes of discovery; they are complementary and internally related parts of the same realm. "How can you tell the legend from the fact?" asks the narrator of *Rocannon's World.* The answer, of course, is "you can't." Another answer, an ethical one, is "you shouldn't." Le Guin's fiction denies the walls we build with different moulds of understanding; it denies the reification and dehumanization that a fragmented and compartmentalized way of life produces. Like the music Ladislas Gaye hears at the end of **"An die Musik,"** "it denies and breaks down all the shelters, the houses men build for themselves, that they may see the sky."

2. The Italian sociologist and economist Vilfredo Pareto was disturbed by the shifting and sometimes contradictory meanings of Marx's words and concepts:

> If you raise some objections against a passage in *Capital,* a passage whose meaning seems to you incontestable, someone can quote another, whose meaning is entirely different. It is the fable of the bat all over again. If you embrace one meaning, someone tells you
>
> I am a bird; see my wings;
> Long live the flying things!

And if you adopt the other, someone tells you

> I am a mouse; long live the rats;
> Jupiter confound the cats!

Much the same can be said—indeed has been said, though in a positive rather than in a negative sense—about the ideas and concepts in Le Guin's fiction. In his essay on the Earthsea trilogy ["The Magic of Art and the Evolution of Words: Ursula Le Guin's Earthsea Trilogy," *Mosaic* 10 (Winter 1977)], T. A. Shippey may not argue that Le Guin's words are, like bats, both birds and mice, but he does note that Le Guin's story embodies an "argument" against "conceptual barriers" that result from "the very sharpness and hardness of modern concepts." Not only does Le Guin make "covert comparisons between 'fantastic' and 'familiar,' " says Shippey, she also shifts the meanings of familiar concepts: at times magic in Earthsea seems to be a science, at other times an art, and at still other times, it is ethics. The "oscillation between concepts" that Shippey sees in the Earthsea trilogy is not peculiar to Le Guin's juvenile fantasy; it permeates nearly everything she has written, from her individual sentences to her major themes, images, and even characters. Were Pareto alive, he might consider Le Guin's Gethenians just as bat-like as Marx's concepts: if he tried to see them as men, they would become women, and if he tried to see them as women, they would become men. Le Guin wants to teach readers like Pareto (and characters like Genly Ai) to think both-and (or even, perhaps, neither-nor) rather than either-or. She started doing just that in the fifties and sixties when she was writing her Orsinian tales.

Long before Le Guin wrote a sentence like "The king was pregnant" [*Left Hand of Darkness*], she was writing sentences like this one in *Orsinian Tales*: "On a sunny morning in Cleveland, Ohio, it was raining in Krasnoy and the streets between grey walls were full of men." This sentence first situates us in a familiar time and place, then erases the distinctions we make between a real country like the USA and an imaginary country like Orsinia. Cleveland and Krasnoy do not exist in the same world. Or do they? Le Guin's sentence creates a new world, neither our familiar one, nor an entirely fantastic one, but a world which is both realistic and fantastic. The point of this sentence is not that one thing is real and the other is imaginary; the point is that they are both in the same sentence. The world of Le Guin's fiction is not a realm of well-defined, discrete things and places and times and ideas; rather, it is a realm where categories and perspectives are fluid, a world which is ordered process in which nothing, except change itself, can be taken for granted as certain. Orsinia's location, its political history, even its geology, are all in flux.

Orsinia can be placed on two different maps. Darrell Schweitzer says [in "The Vivisector," *Science Fiction Review,* No. 20 (1977)], that "in *Orsinian Tales* Le Guin seems to be trying to do a *Dubliners* set in an unnamed central European country (clearly Hungary, complete with a revolution against foreign conquerors in 1956)." Le Guin's brother Karl Kroeber, on the other hand, tells us [in "Sisters and Science Fiction," *The Little Magazine* 10 (Spring/Summer 1976)] "not to seek in Bulgaria for the setting of **'Brothers and Sisters.'** The curious growthless plain of limestone quarries is not East of the Sun and West of the Moon, just a little south of Zembla and north of Graustark." Though Kroeber is mostly right in placing Orsinia on the same map with Nabokov's distant northern kingdom in *Pale Fire* and McCutcheon's Balkan kingdom, rather than in a totally fantastic realm ("East of the Sun and West of the Moon"), and though Schweitzer is mostly wrong in identifying Orsinia with Hungary, neither of these two mappers takes full account of Le Guin's "oscillation," as Shippey might call it, between Joycean naturalism and the escapism of McCutcheon's *Graustark* or Hope's *The Prisoner of Zenda*. Literary naturalism and Ruritanian romances were contemporary phenomena at the turn of the century when many writers and readers were making clear distinctions between realism and romance. Le Guin's fictional techniques dissolve those distinctions; the boundaries between the real and the fantastic disappear when we understand them to be complementary and internally related parts of the imaginary.

Le Guin herself says that Orsinia is an "invented though non-fantastic Central European country." Le Guin's invented worlds, whether set in Europe or in the Hainish universe, still contain accurate and naturalistic facts, history in the first instance, science in the second. To make the transition from writing Orsinian tales to writing science fiction was no major step for Le Guin; all she had to do was replace one social science (history) with another (anthropology), and integrate some elements from the hard sciences. In fact, some of the Orsinian tales were written at the same time she was writing the Hainish novels.

There are, certainly, ample naturalistic facts in *Orsinian Tales* to justify looking for Orsinia on a map of Europe. We visit Versailles, hear of Croatian microbiologists, get a glimpse of the conflict between Teutonic paganism and Christianity in the early Middle Ages; we see the social and economic dislocation caused by late nineteenth-century industrialization, watch the suffering of a World War I veteran, and hear about an insurrection in Budapest in October, 1956. But just when we become secure with our identifications between the fictive and the real, the things we see change (like Pareto's bat), and we're in places that appear on no map of Europe. Conversely, when we suspend disbelief and get comfortable in Krasnoy or Sfaroy Kampe or Aisnar, we learn, with a clerk-composer in Foranoy (who has a sister in Prague), that Hitler is meeting Chamberlain in Munich in September, 1938. One city in Orsinia seems to have a foot in both worlds: Brailava could be as real as Bratislava, Czechoslovakia, or it could be as imaginary as Sfaroy Kampe. The point, however, is this: we must not read *Orsinian Tales* the way blind men read an elephant. To avoid seeing either a tree trunk or a wall or a rope, we must see the whole, be sensitive to the *relationships* among parts that characterize an organic whole. Relationships, not discrete things, are the subject of all of Le Guin's fiction. In **"A Week in the Country,"** Stefan Fabbre recalls the story of a Hungarian nobleman. The wars between the Ottoman Empire and Hungary were real; the story is a legend; and Stefan Fabbre is a product of Le Guin's imagination. They are all re-

lated. "How can you tell the legend from the fact?" "Truth is a matter of the imagination."

The political entities in Central Europe, like the boundaries between the familiar and the fantastic, have been fluid, and this is probably one reason that Le Guin chose Central Europe as the location of Orsinia. Orsinia's name does more than play on it's creator's name; it echoes names like Bohemia, Silesia, Moravia, Galicia, and Croatia. The singular fact of political experience for these people is that while they have tenaciously preserved their nationality, they have never had lasting political independence. Orsinia shares with these countries a position on the battlegrounds of European and Asian imperialism, from Attila to the present. Orsinia may have come under Hapsburg domination in the sixteenth century (Isabella, "the Lady of Moge," has a Spanish-sounding name) and was probably threatened by the Ottoman Empire in the sixteenth and seventeenth centuries. In the eighteenth century Austria and Prussia could have fought a war in Orsinia; in the nineteenth century, Napoleon probably crossed Orsinian soil; and up to World War I, Orsinia was probably part of the Austro-Hungarian Empire. Then in the twentieth century, after a short-lived political independence, Orsinia was probably overwhelmed from the west by Hitler, and then a few years later, from the east by Stalin. This long historical nightmare of violent political change and oppression by authoritarian states only brings into sharper relief one of the major themes, if not *the* major theme, of these tales: the struggle of the individual to win a sense of freedom and wholeness in a prison-like society, and his heroic (the word is not too strong) efforts to maintain a sense of identity and self-respect. It is but a short step from this to the thematic center of *The Dispossessed*.

Le Guin's imaginary countries are not finished creations in which the landscape, geological or moral, is set for all time. The glaciers and volcanoes on Gethen, the earthquakes on Anarres, as well as Orsinia's limestone bedrock, are notable examples of geological flux. As Genly Ai and Estraven are ascending a glacier (a fluid solid) past the active volcanoes Drumner and Dremegole to reach the Gobrin Ice, Estraven records in his journal,

> We creep infinitesimally northward through the dirty chaos of a world in the process of making itself.

> Praise then Creation unfinished.

Orsinia's topography may not change as dramatically as Gethen's, but it is nevertheless also in flux; it too is "in the process of making itself." One of the striking features of the Orsinian landscape is the Karst, the setting of **"Brothers and Sisters."** Karst topography is characterized by rocky barren ground, caves, sinkholes, underground rivers, and the absence of surface streams and lakes, resulting from the work of underground water on massive soluble limestones. Originally the term "karst" was applied to the Kras, a limestone area along the Adriatic coast of Yugoslavia. (The principal city of Orsinia, Krasnoy, may take its name from the Kras, and the name of Foranoy may be related to foraminiferan tests, the raw material from which limestone is formed.) There are no hymns like "Rock of Ages" in Orsinia. The rocks dissolve in water.

Like all of Le Guin's imaginary countries, Orsinia is a *paysage moralisé.* The moral and psychological resonance of the settings and landscapes in Le Guin's science fiction has already been recognized. What she does in the Hainish worlds and in Earthsea is anticipated in **Orsinian Tales.** Like the chasm beneath the Shing city in *City of Illusions,* like the forests in **"Vaster than Empires and More Slow"** and *The Word for World Is Forest,* like the islands and seas of Earthsea (another solid-liquid combination), the Karst in **"Brothers and Sisters,"** the forest in **"Ile Forest,"** and the mountains in **"The Barrow,"** as well as the decaying house and garden on the Hill in Rákava in **"Conversations at Night,"** are both images and symbols: they are at once themselves even as they refer beyond themselves to moral and psychological values and meanings. If Orsinia's bedrock can be dissolved and reconstituted, so can moral values. Dr. Adam Kereth steals freedom and is then drawn back to Orsinia by mere fidelity; Count Freyga sacrifices a Christian priest then aids Christian monks; and Dr. Galven Ileskar, who believes that murder ought to be an unpardonable crime, loves a murderer who turns out to be his brother-in-law, and brother, too.

The thematic significance of the fluidity of Le Guin's political, topographical, psychological, and moral landscapes is this: her human actors are free to choose and to be personally responsible for their choices. No less than the rocks in her landscapes, Le Guin's characters are "in the process of making themselves." Neither reality nor ethics is handed to them on adamantine tablets (though some of them may think they are); whole cultures as well as individuals dissolve and reconstitute themselves as they change and grow. This happens repeatedly in her science fiction: Terrans and Tevarans cease to exist as independent cultures in *Planet of Exile,* Gethenian cultures are on the brink of a major change in *The Left Hand of Darkness,* and reality itself is repeatedly reconstituted by George Orr's effective dreams in *The Lathe of Heaven.* It goes without saying, of course, that the society on Anarres is a society in the process of making itself which offers the individual the most freedom to make himself (thereby re-making the society), as long as it does not petrify. Faxe the Weaver speaks for Le Guin when she-he says "the only thing that makes life possible is permanent, intolerable uncertainty: not knowing what comes next" [*The Left Hand of Darkness*]. Life is making choices; if we knew what comes next, we could not choose.

But what certainties can Le Guin offer in the midst of all this flux? Human relations: fidelity, constancy, and love. In **"A Week in the Country,"** Stefan Fabbre and Kasimir Augeskar, on their way to visit the Augeskars' summer home, exchange these words in a train compartment:

> "So here we are on a train to Aisnar," Kasimir said, "but we don't know that it's going to Aisnar. It might go to Peking."

> "It might derail and we'll be killed. And if we do come to Aisnar? What's Aisnar? Mere hearsay."—"That's morbid," Kasimir said . . . —"No, exhilarating," his friend answered. "Takes a lot of work to hold the world together, when you look at it that way. But it's worth-

while. Building up cities, holding roofs up by an act of fidelity. Not faith. Fidelity."

What at first appears to be merely an academic discussion by two students to pass the time takes on new meanings by the end of the tale. After Stefan falls in love with Bruna Augeskar, after he hears Joachim Bret sing an English lute song,

> You be just and constant still, Love may beget a wonder,
> Not unlike a summer's frost or winter's fatal thunder:
> He that holds his sweetheart dear until his day of dying
> Lives of all that ever lived most worthy the envying,

after he sees Kasimir killed by the secret police, and after he is tortured himself—after all that, when Bruna comes for him, he knows that there is "No good letting go, is there. . . . No good at all." Fidelity—being just and constant still—and love hold the world together in ways Stefan had not imagined. And the more precarious existence becomes, the more necessary fidelity becomes. In **"Conversations at Night,"** Sanzo Chekey and Alitsia Benat are little more than beggars, and their hope, like Stefan's and Bruna's, lies in the personal fidelity that holds their world together:

> "Lisha," he [Sanzo] said, "oh, God, I want to hold on . . . Only it's a very long chance, Lisha."

> "We'll never get a chance that isn't long."

> "You would."

> "You are my long chance," she said, with a kind of bitterness, and a *profound certainty.* . . .

> "Well, hang on," he said. . . . "If you hang on, I will." [my emphasis]

"Betrayal and fidelity were immediate to them," Le Guin says of the Augeskar family in **"A Week in the Country."** Like many Le Guin characters, the Augeskars live out on the edge; they live near the Iron Curtain, in a political climate that makes their existence as perilous as the Gethenians' is in their barely habitable natural climate. It is worth remembering that Le Guin says that *The Left Hand of Darkness* is "a book about betrayal and fidelity." Betrayal and fidelity are as immediate to Ai and Estraven when they trek across the Ice and when they seek aid from Thessicher, as they are to the Augeskars in Orsinia. And finally, the best example in Le Guin's fiction of personal fidelity against a background of flux and uncertainty comes in *The Dispossessed.* Just as Shevek is coming into Chakar to rejoin Takver and Sadik after a four-year separation, an earthquake hits the region. He finds Takver's domicile, and knocks. She answers the door:

> She stood facing him. She reached out, as if to push him away or to take hold of him, an uncertain, unfinished gesture. He took her hand, and then they held each other, they came together and stood holding each other on the unreliable earth.

Just a moment before, Shevek had thought that "the earth itself was uncertain, unreliable. The enduring, the reliable, is a promise made by the human mind." Human relations are no different on Orsinian soil.

A good analogue, perhaps a source, for Le Guin's use of landscape in **Orsinian Tales** is another *paysage moralisé,* Auden's "In Praise of Limestone":

> It is form the landscape that we, the inconstant ones,
>   Are consistently homesick for, this is chiefly
> Because it dissolves in water. . . .
>
> It has a worldly duty which in spite of itself
>   It does not neglect, but calls into question
> All the Great Powers assume; it disturbs our rights. . . .
>
>   when I try to imagine a faultless love
>   Or the life to come, what I hear is the murmur
> Of underground streams, what I see is a limestone landscape.

Le Guin knows Auden's work, and may have read "In Praise of Limestone," which appeared about the time she was inventing Orsinia. Even if Le Guin was not directly influenced by Auden, there are unmistakable elective affinities here, and these might be explained by the fact that both Auden and Le Guin have been influenced by Rilke. Like Rilke, both Auden and Le Guin rely on concrete settings and naturalistic landscape detail to express moral values and emotions. When Dr. Kereth returns to his hotel in Paris after having "stolen" freedom at Versailles, "kingly he strode past the secret-police agent in the lobby, hiding under his coat the stolen, inexhaustible fountains."

In a review of Rilke's *Duino Elegies,* Auden wrote that Rilke is

> almost the first poet since the seventeenth century to find a fresh solution [to the poet's problem of] how to express abstract ideas in concrete terms. . . . He thinks in physical rather than intellectual symbols. . . . Rilke thinks of the human in terms of the non-human, of what he calls Things (*Dinge*), a way of thought which, as he himself pointed out, is more characteristic of the child than of the adult.

What Auden says of Rilke applies to Le Guin, and may help to account for the artistic superiority of the Earthsea trilogy over the science fiction. Science fiction, as many have pointed out, is a literature of ideas. Le Guin succeeds as well as anyone in finding concrete images for the abstract ideas of modern science, but this success falls short of what she accomplishes in her juvenile fantasy, and in many of the pieces in **Orsinian Tales.** In her "Response" to the Le Guin issue of [*Science-Fiction Studies*] Le Guin says that she

> can't even think one stupid platitude without dragging in a mess of images and metaphors, domes, stones, rubble [Rilkean *Dinge*?]. . . . This lamentable concreteness of the mental processes is supposed, by some, to be a feminine trait. If so, all artists are women. And/or vice versa.

Or children. Whenever Le Guin succeeds in expressing human values and abstract ideas in vividly sketched landscapes, or with a "mess of images and symbols," she creates superior art.

Le Guin succeeds as well as anyone in finding concrete images for the abstract ideas of modern science, but [in her novels] this success falls short of what she accomplishes in her juvenile fantasy, and in many of the pieces in *Orsinian Tales.*

—James W. Bittner

In his discussion of Auden's moral landscapes and "psychic geography," Monroe K. Spears notes that "for Auden, as for Rilke, the distinction between inner and outer worlds is tenuous and interpenetration is constant." He could say the same of Le Guin, for the Earthsea trilogy is as much about Le Guin's own inner world as an artist as it is about Ged. Le Guin herself says as much in "Dreams Must Explain Themselves," her essay recounting the genesis and growth of the Earthsea trilogy:

> Wizardry is artistry. The trilogy is then, in this sense, about art, the creative experience, the creative process. There is always this circularity in fantasy. The snake devours its tail. Dreams must explain themselves.

In the same sense that Ged *is* Le Guin, Orsinia *is* Ursula; the "true name" of her country, a pun on her own name, is one more instance of this "circularity in fantasy." And that circularity can be seen clearly in the last and central tale in **Orsinian Tales,** "Imaginary Countries."

3. "Imaginary Countries" is a family portrait. Baron Severin Egideskar, his wife, and their three children Stanislas (fourteen), Paul (seven), and Zida (six) are in the last few days of their annual stay at "Asgard," their summer home in the country. The baron will return to his chair as Follen Professor of Medieval Studies at the University of Krasnoy. Josef Brone, his research assistant, has been with them throughout the summer, helping the professor with the documentation for his history of the Ten Provinces (Orsinia) in the Early Middle Ages. Rosa, the maid, and Tomas, the caretaker, complete the group. The family that sat for this portrait is the A. L. Kroeber family, who used to spend summers at "Kishamish" in the Napa Valley, 60 miles north of Berkeley, where Kroeber was Professor of Anthropology at the University of California. Like Kroeber, who spent his summers in the thirties working on a huge study in comparative cultural anthropology (*Configurations of Culture Growth*), Egideskar is at work on a "history [that] was years from completion." And like Ursula Kroeber, born in 1929, Zida Egideskar is six years old in 1935; so **"Imaginary Countries"** is, among other things, a portrait of the artist as a young girl.

Le Guin has written a tale about the family of a professor

who is writing a history of Orsinia, a country she invented; the professor has a daughter who is a portrait of the girl who grew up to invent an imaginary country where, in 1935, a professor is writing a history . . . and so on. The snake devours its tail. In addition to recognizing the uroboros, though, we might also see Chinese boxes: Le Guin includes in a collection of tales set in an imaginary country a tale entitled **"Imaginary Countries,"** which includes characters who live from time to time in imaginary countries. . . . **"Imaginary Countries"** is the central tale in the collection in the same sense that the point at which the snake's tail disappears into its mouth is central; or, it is central in the way that the intersection of two mirrors that produce an infinitely regressing image is central.

So **"Imaginary Countries"** is central in *Orsinian Tales* in more ways than just being the middle tale chronologically. If we read Le Guin's Orsinian tales as Ursuline tales, then our reading of them becomes at once a journey into Orsinia's history and a journey into the history of Le Guin's invention of Orsinia's history. The work created and the creative work become one. Just as Le Guin's arrangement of the tales directs us back into Orsinia's past even as we move forward into the collection, **"Imaginary Countries"** returns us to the roots of the imagination that created the book we have just finished reading: the last tale concludes the collection at the same time it looks toward the creation of the collection by showing us a portrait of the artist as a young girl. When Le Guin placed **"Imaginary Countries"** at the end of *Orsinian Tales,* she was saying, in effect, "In my beginning is my end" and "In my end is my beginning" (the first and last lines of T. S. Eliot's "East Coker"). *Orsinian Tales,* then, has the same organic structure that *The Dispossessed* has. The alternating chapters on Anarres and Urras are put together so that when we come to the end of Shevek's story on Anarres, he is ready to begin the trip to Urras that opens the novel; and when we come to the end of Shevek's story on Urras and his return to Anarres, we see him ready to leave Anarres. Le Guin would probably accept what another Romantic, Coleridge, says [in a letter to Joseph Cottle, March 7, 1815] about the function of poetry:

> The common end of all *narrative,* nay of *all,* Poems is to convert a *series* into a Whole; to make those events, which in real or imagined History move on in a *strait* Line, assume to our Understandings a *circular* motion—the snake with it's Tail in it's Mouth.

Orsinian Tales does this for the imaginary history of Orsinia at the same time it does it for the real history that is Le Guin's career as a writer.

It could be that Professor Egideskar, who writes narratives of "real" history, as well as his creator, who writes narratives of imagined history, would agree with Coleridge. An observer of history as sensitive as the baron would have seen that the idea of Progress, the ever-ascending "strait Line" of history that was born in the Enlightenment, was not working in the ethics and politics of the twentieth century; by studying early medieval times, he may be trying to understand history not in strictly linear terms (chronology and causality), but in circular terms

as well (returns and rebirths). The baron could not be unaware of the goings on to the west of Orsinia in the thirties. Nazi barbarism, in fact, may be the silent subject of his history of Orsinia in the Early Middle Ages. Among the events he is studying and interpreting would be incidents like the one Le Guin describes in **"The Barrow,"** set in 1150. His assistant Josef Brone reads from "the Latin chronicle of a battle lost nine hundred years ago"; one of the incunabula Josef and the baron pack in a trunk probably contains the "bad Latin of [the Benedictine] chronicles of Count Freyga and his son," mentioned at the end of **"The Barrow."** Count Freyga lived at the time when pagan ethics and Christian ethics clashed; although he is nominally a Christian, he reverts to sacrificing a priest to "Odne the Silent" to relieve his terrifying anxiety about his wife and unborn child. The baron lives at a time when a nominally civilized culture is reverting to barbarism. Understanding medieval Orsinia, going to historical roots, may help Egideskar understand twentieth-century Europe.

Some readers may think that the baron, who calls his wife Freya and his summer home Asgard, is implicated in the revival of Norse myth used by the Nazis to legitimate their ideologies. That would be doing the baron a disservice, for he does know the difference between a unicorn's hoofprint and a pig's, and there is as much difference between a true myth and a false myth as there is between a unicorn and a pig. The baron faces the problem that any serious student of history and culture sooner or later faces: he is part of what he is trying to understand. He needs a technique of distancing. He can get it by spending his summers away from Krasnoy, by participating in his family's imaginary countries, and by studying the history of Orsinia in the Early Middle Ages. In order to get free of the distorting fog of subjectivity and ideology, he needs an Archimedes point from which he can get "a view in"; he needs to see from a place "a very long way from anywhere else" [The quoted phrases are borrowed from the titles of an essay and novella, respectively, by Le Guin]. The baron, that is to say, encounters the same problems as a historian that Le Guin faces as a writer, and this is yet another way in which **"Imaginary Countries"** is the central tale in *Orsinian Tales.* In a book that is in many ways about history, we have a portrait of a historian: still another instance of the circularity of fantasy.

But **"Imaginary Countries"** is more than the central tale in the collection. Earlier I said that a trip through Orsinia may take us to the underground streams that nourish the roots of the imagination that created Earthsea and the Hainish worlds. Coming at the end of the trip, **"Imaginary Countries"** brings us as close as we are likely to come to those streams, Le Guin's childhood experience of Norse myth and folklore.

Written in 1960, after Le Guin had been exploring Orsinia in novels and tales for a decade, and before she turned to stories that fit publishers' categories, **"Imaginary Countries"** is a tale in which Le Guin returned to the myths that informed her childhood play and nourished her imagination. Like "the Oak" in Stanislas' "kingdom of the trees," the whole body of Le Guin's fiction can be seen as

Yggdrasil, the Norse world-tree, with its roots in Orsinia and its branches and leaves in the far-away galaxies of the Hainish universe. When Josef follows Stanislas into "the Great Woods," Stanislas guides him to "the Oak":

> It was the biggest tree [Josef] had ever seen; he had not seen very many. "I suppose it's very old," he said; looking up puzzled at the reach of branches, galaxy after galaxy of green leaves without end.

In this story, which precedes by three years Le Guin's invention-discovery of the Hainish universe, she was already using the language of science fiction with Norse myth. That is exactly how she created the Hainish worlds: in **"The Dowry of Angyar"** ("Semley's Necklace" in *The Wind's Twelve Quarters*), she wove together the Einsteinian notion of time-dilation with the Norse myth of Freya and the Brisingamen Necklace. That story became the germ of *Rocannon's World,* her first novel, and from that the rest of the Hainish novels followed. The Earthsea trilogy evolved in much the same way.

After Le Guin started writing science fiction, she returned to Yggdrasil again and again. In *Planet of Exile,* Rolery gazes at a mural representing Terra and "the other worlds":

> The strangest thing in all the strangeness of this house was the painting on the wall of the big room downstairs. When Agat had gone and the rooms were deathly still she stood gazing at this picture till it became the world and she the wall. And the picture was a network: a deep network, like the interlacing branches in the woods, like interrunning currents in water, silver, gray, black, shot through with green and rose and a yellow like the sun. As one watched their deep network, one saw in it, among it, woven into it and weaving it, little and great patterns and figures, beasts, trees, grasses, men and women and other creatures, some like farborns and some not; and strange shapes, boxes set on round legs, birds, axes, silver spears with wings and *a tree whose leaves were stars.*

Here is an actual landscape (spacescape?) painting (which, incidentally, describes Le Guin's fiction as well as any critical article has), a *paysage moralisé,* representing an imaginary landscape, the Hainish worlds, seen through the eyes of a native of Gamma Draconis III, a person whose ways of seeing have been shaped by the landscape of her native world, itself another of Le Guin's *paysages moralisés.* The tree in this painting, "the Oak" in **"Imaginary Countries,"** and all the other trees in Le Guin's fiction, from the rowan tree in *The Farthest Shore* in Le Guin's "Inner Lands" to the forests on Athshe in *The Word for World Is Forest* in her "Outer Space"—they all have the same roots.

Like the painting we see through Rolery's eyes, Le Guin's prose landscapes are full of *things.* Could it be that her artistry in representing abstract concepts derives from her childhood moulds of understanding, moulds like those of Zida Egideskar, who builds a unicorn trap from "an eggcrate decorated with many little bits of figured cloth and colored paper . . . a wooden coat hanger . . . an eggshell painted gold . . . a bit of quartz . . . a breadcrust"? Rilke,

who believed that thinking of the human in terms of *Dinge* is characteristic of the child, would answer yes. Like Zida's unicorn trap, Le Guin's fiction is built by an artisan from a "mess of images and metaphors, domes, stones, rubble" to catch imaginary beasts, imaginary people, imaginary countries, androgynes, mythic archetypes, truth. Zida Egideskar is indeed a portrait of the artist as a young girl.

When Josef Brone asks Stanislas what he does in "the Great Woods," Stanislas answers, " 'Oh, I map trails.' " That answer is profoundly meaningful, for it describes what Le Guin herself does in her fiction. Her discovery-invention and mapping of imaginary countries has been her artistic solution to the epistemological problem that confronts everyone in the human sciences: like anthropologists, historians, psychologists, sociologists, and students of art, Le Guin is part of the social and cultural and historical situation she wants to write about. In this position, objectivity and truth seem impossible ideals, especially when the culture debases language and fictional forms, the writer's only tools for discovering truth. Because Le Guin is an artist, this philosophical/ideological/political problem presents itself to her as an artistic problem requiring an artistic solution. And because artists are supposed to tell the truth, it is an ethical problem. Inventing imaginary countries and mapping them has been Le Guin's solution to her artistic/ethical problem. Lies are the way to truth. The real subject of Le Guin's fiction is not life in any of her imaginary countries, in Orsinia or on Gethen or Anarres or Gont or Havnor; these are metaphors, landscapes, *Dinge,* thought experiments, what Kafka (in a letter to Max Brod) calls "strategic considerations":

> It sometimes seems to me that the nature of art in general, the existence of art, is explicable solely in terms of such 'strategic considerations,' of making possible the exchange of truthful words from person to person.

Seen in this light, **"Imaginary Countries"** is not only the central tale in ***Orsinian Tales***; it is also central to the whole body of Le Guin's writing, and more than that, to the act of writing itself.

4. Even if Le Guin's strategic considerations do make possible the exchange of truthful words, what if no one wants to publish them? What good are truthful words if they are not exchanged? What's the use of writing? What's the use of art? Questions like these may have been in Le Guin's mind around 1960 when she wrote **"An die Musik."** Like Ursula Le Guin herself, who had been writing Orsinian novels and tales for ten years without seeing them in print, Ladislas Gaye (whose name faintly echoes his creator's) has been writing songs and a Mass for ten years and has very little hope of ever hearing them performed. If **"Imaginary Countries"** includes a portrait of the artist as a young girl, **"An die Musik,"** written at the same time, includes an oblique portrait of the artist as a grown woman. Like the Earthsea trilogy, it is "about art, the creative experience, the creative process." **"An die Musik,"** however, is much more than self-portraiture, for it raises questions about the relationship between art and politics—questions fundamental not only to any serious discussion of Le

Guin's later works, but fundamental also to any serious discussion of the social role of art in the twentieth century.

The tension between [what John Huntington calls in his "Public and Private Imperatives in Le Guin's Fiction," *Science-Fiction Studies* 2 (1975)] "public and private imperatives" in Earthsea and the Hainish worlds is a reflection or a projection of an ethical conflict in Le Guin herself, and that conflict—between her duty as an artist to serve her art and her commitment to a social ideal—is at the center of **"An die Musik,"** and continues to be prominent in her later fiction, even when an artist is not the central character. A theoretical physicist like Shevek or a mathematician like Simon in **"The New Atlantis"** is as much an artist as are the musicians that appear throughout Le Guin's fiction. Le Guin does, of course, define the problem in radically different ways in **"An die Musik"** and in *The Dispossessed* or **"The New Atlantis."** But even if her formulations of the artist's problem have changed, her conception of the purpose of art has remained constant and steady. With Auden, she believes that the end of art, its final cause, its *raison d'être,* is to persuade us to rejoice and to teach us how to praise. Answering Tolstoy's question "What is Art?" Le Guin defines the job of art with one word: "celebration."

If Le Guin's trilogy of imaginary countries—Orsinia, Earthsea, and the Hainish universe—manifests the same circularity that her fantasy trilogy does (and I think it does), then we can apply her injunction "dreams must explain themselves" to the whole body of her fiction. In order to begin an exploration of the problematic relationships in her later fiction between creativity and politics, between the demands of the imagination and the demands of everyday life, or, more broadly, between the individual and society, we can do no better than return to **"An die Musik,"** her first published story. It is the first of many works in which Le Guin dramatizes the problems she herself faces whenever she sits down to write. This is not the place to make a comprehensive survey of the ways Le Guin has handled these issues in all of her fiction; all I will do here is look carefully at one of her earliest formulations.

As she would do in *The Left Hand of Darkness* when she constructed a thought experiment to explore sexuality, in **"An die Musik"** Le Guin creates a character—a composer with an "absolutely first rate" talent—and places him in a setting—Foranoy, Orsinia, in 1938, a "dead town for music . . . not a good world for music, either"—in order to ask three related questions: (1) should an artist, as a private individual, ignore the demands of his family to meet the demands of his art, (2) should an artist use his public voice to serve art or a political idea, and (3) what is the function of art.

When Le Guin puts Gaye in a cramped three-room flat and gives him a bedridden mother, an ailing wife, and three children to support on his wages as a clerk in a steel ballbearing factory, and when she makes him a talented composer with a compulsion to rival Berlioz and Mahler by writing a grandiose Mass for "women's chorus, double men's chorus, full orchestra, brass choir, and an organ," she formulates the question in such stark either-or terms

that Gaye's conflicting ethical duties are simply irreconcilable. At the same time, she dramatizes each of these claims on Gaye so skillfully that neither can be denied: Gaye cannot abandon his Mass because, as he tells Otto Egorin, "I've learned how to do what I must do, you see, I've begun it, I have to finish it," and he cannot abandon his family because he is "not made so." If neither obligation can be denied and if their conflicting claims are so polarized that they cannot be reconciled, then Gaye's moral dilemma cannot be resolved; it can only be transcended, and then only for a moment. Moreover, by setting the tale in 1938, Le Guin polarizes the artist's public duties as severely as she polarizes his private ones. His only choices are to write apolitical music (*Lieder* or a Mass) or socialist realism (a symphony "to glorify the latest boiler-factory in the Urals").

Le Guin's formulation of Gaye's moral/aesthetic dilemma is thoroughly dualistic: it rests on the belief that a devotion to art, like the devotion to a religious creed, is absolutely incompatible with everyday life. In **"An die Musik"** art is religion; if it traffics in social issues, it debases itself. Just as Jesus Christ called on his disciples to abandon all family ties if they wanted to follow Him (Matt. 10:34-39; Mark 3:31-35; Luke 14:25-26), Egorin, who believes that "if you live for music you live for music," suggests to Gaye that he "throw over . . . [his] sick mother and sick wife and three brats" if he wants to write his Mass and hear it performed. And then quoting Christ directly, he tells Gaye:

> You have great talent, Gaye, you have great courage, but you're too gentle, you must not try to write a big work like this Mass. You can't serve two masters [Matt. 6:24; Luke 16:13]. Write songs, short pieces, something you can think of while you work at this Godforsaken steel plant and write down at night when the rest of the family's out of the way for five minutes. . . . Write little songs, not impossible Masses.

But Gaye, like Kasimir Agueskar, another Orsinian musician, is an "enemy of the feasible." He must write the Mass. He will continue to serve art and his family, Godly art and a Godforsaken steel plant, even if the tension tears him in two. All he wants from Egorin is the recognition of his identity as a musician; that gives him the strength and freedom he needs to endure the conflict he can neither escape nor resolve.

Finally exasperated by "the arrogance, the unreasonableness . . . the stupidity, the absolute stupidity" of artists, yet recognizing Gaye's talent and wanting to encourage him and to produce some of his work, Egorin gives Gaye a volume of Eichendorff's poetry. " 'Set me some of these,' " he tells Gaye, " 'here, look, this one, 'Es wandelt, was sir schauen,' you see—that should suit you.' " It is one of Eichendorff's religious lyrics:

> Es wandelt, was wir schauen,
> Tag sinkt ins Abendrot,
> Die Lust hat eignes Grauen,
> Und alles hat den Tod.
>
> Ins Leben schleicht das Leiden
> Sich heimlich wie ein Dieb,

Wir alle mussen scheiden
Vor allem, was uns lieb.

Was gäb' es doch auf Erden,
Wer hielt' den Jammer aus
Wer möcht' geboren werden,
Hielt'st du nicht droben haus!

Du bist's, der, was wir bauen,
Mild über uns zerbricht,
Dass wir den Himmel schauen—
Darum so klag' ich nicht.

. . . . .

Things change, whatever we look at,
Day sinks into sunset glow,
Desire has its own horror,
And everything dies.

Into life steals sorrow
As secretly as a thief,
We must all be separated
From everything that loves us.

What is there of value on earth,
Who could endure the misery,
Who would want to be reborn,
Dost Thou not promise a home above!

It is Thou, who, whatever we build,
Gently breakest down over us
That we may see Heaven—
And so I do not complain.

Why should this "suit" Gaye? Egorin sees Gaye's personal dilemma as hopeless and wants to offer him the consolation that things change: " 'Es wandelt.' Things do change sometimes, after all, don't they?" He wants to offer Gaye some way of enduring the suffering he cannot escape. The religious belief of Eichendorff, a Roman Catholic, is Egorin's solution to Gaye's personal problems as an artist.

Egorin can offer no consolation whatever to Gaye to help him out of his public dilemma. Because his conception of art forces him to separate it from politics, Egorin's attitude toward the possibility that art can change things in 1938, can make something happen, is completely defeatist:

> "Gaye," said Otto Egorin, "you know there's one other thing. This is not a good world for music, either. This world now, in 1938. You're not the only man who wonders, what's the good? who needs music, who wants it? Who indeed, when Europe is crawling with armies like a corpse with maggots, when Russia uses symphonies to glorify the latest boiler-factory in the Urals, when the function of music has been all summed up in Putzi playing the piano to soothe the Leader's nerves. By the time your Mass is finished, you know, all the churches may be blown into little pieces, and your men's chorus will be wearing uniforms and also being blown into little pieces. If not send it to me, I shall be interested. But I'm not hopeful. I am on the losing side, with you. . . . music is no good, no use, Gaye. Not any more. Write your songs, write your Mass, it does no harm. I shall go on arranging concerts, it does no harm. But it won't save us. . . . "

Perhaps because she has a hindsight Egorin does not have, Le Guin does not share his defeatism. And as we discover at the end of the tale, Gaye does not share Egorin's defeatism either. Music does save him, though not in the sense Egorin has in mind.

In the final scenes, Le Guin brings all the questions about the artist and art together, forces Gaye's tensions to the breaking point, and then resolves them not by answering any of the questions she has raised, but by creating an epiphany which transcends the questions. On the afternoon of the day that Chamberlain meets Hitler in Munich to give him the Sudetenland, Gaye is trying to finish his setting of *"Es wandelt"* and his wife is demanding that he do something about their son Vasli who has been caught with some other boys trying to set a cat on fire. Gaye's cry "let me have some peace" is both his and Europe's: private and public merge. A moment later, European politics, the coming war, his family problems, and his Mass all converge as he consoles Vasli, with the sound of his mother's radio coming from the next room:

> All cruelty, all misery, all darkness present and to come hung round them. . . . In the thick blaring of the trombones, thick as cough-sirup, Gaye heard for a moment the deep clear thunder of his Sanctus like the thunder between the stars, over the edge of the universe—one moment of it, as if the roof of the building had been taken off and he looked up into the complete, enduring darkness, one moment only.

In the evening, as he sits at the kitchen table with his wife, who is mending and listening to the radio (full of news of Munich, no doubt), Gaye tries to recapture the accompaniment to the last verse of *"Es wandelt"* so he can write it down and send it to Egorin in Krasnoy. At the moment when "the total impossibility of writing was a choking weight in him," at the moment when he thinks "nothing would ever change." he hears Lotte Lehmann on the radio singing Schubert's *"An die Musik."* The barrier between inner and outer worlds evaporates as he initially mistakes the music on the radio for the unwritten music in his mind:

> He thought it was his own song, then, raising his head, understood that he was actually hearing this tune. He did not have to write it. It had been written long ago, no one need suffer for it any more. Lehmann was singing it,
>
> Du holde Kunst, ich danke dir.
>
> He sat still a long time. Music will not save us, Otto Egorin had said. Not you, or me . . . ; not Lehmann who sang the song; not Schubert who had written it and was a hundred years dead. What good is music? None, Gaye thought, and that is the point. To the world and its states and armies and factories and Leaders, music says, 'You are irrelevant'; and, arrogant and gentle as a god, to the suffering man it says only, 'Listen.' For being saved is not the point. Music saves nothing. Merciful, uncaring, it denies and breaks down all the shelters, the houses men build for themselves, that they may see the sky.

Gaye's epiphany rises not only from the identification of

inner and outer music; it also depends on the conjunction of the words in the last stanza of Eichendorff's *"Es wandelt"* and the words in the lyric set by Schubert, Schober's *"An die Musik."* Here is Schober's poem:

Du holde Kunst, in wieviel grauen Stunden,
Wo mich des Lebens wilder Kreis umstrickt,
Hast du mein Harz zu warmer Lieb' entzunden,
Hast mich in eine bessre Welt entrückt!
   In eine bessre Welt entrückt.

Oft hat ein Seufzer, deiner Harf' entflossen
Ein süsser, heiliger Akkord von dir,
Den Himmel bessrer Zeiten mir erschlossen
Du holde Kunst, ich danke dir dafur!
   Du holde Kunst, ich danke dir.

O kindly Art, in how many a grey hour
when I am caught in life's unruly round
have you fired my heart with ardent love
and borne me to a better world!
   Borne me to a better world.

Often, has a sigh from your harp,
a chord, sweet and holy, from you
opened for me a heaven of better times;
O kindly Art, for that I thank you!
   O kindly Art, I thank you.

Gaye has been suffering, trying to write the music for the last stanza of Eichendorff's poem, which Le Guin renders as "It is Thou in thy mercy that breakest down over our heads all we build, that we may see the sky: and so I do not complain." In the afternoon, Gaye had heard the thunder of his Sanctus like thunder between the stars "as if the roof of the building had been taken off." Now, in the evening, as he hears his own unwritten tune in Schubert's, Gaye also hears Eichendorff's and Schober's lyrics simultaneously, the first inside his head and the second outside, sung by Lehmann on the radio. He experiences the synchronicity of a poem addressed to God and a poem addressed to Art: Eichendorff's God, who breaks down what men build that they may see heaven, becomes Schober's kindly Art, realized by Schubert and performed by Lehmann, opening for Gaye a heaven of better times. "Arrogant and gentle as a god," music, not God, "breaks down all the shelters, the houses men build for themselves, that they may see the sky." It fires his heart with love and carries him to a better world. Art renews the possibility of utopia. The paradox at the core of Gaye's epiphany is religious: what he suffers for releases him from suffering for it. Music does save him. Le Guin saves Gaye from the conflict of "public and private imperatives" as she merges inner and outer worlds in a palimpsest of art and religion, of immanence and transcendence.

Gaye's epiphany does not, however, unravel the Gordian knot of his ethical dilemmas. It cuts right through them. Otto Egorin, who believes that "music is no good, no use . . . not any more," has a defeatist attitude because he retains vestiges of a belief that music *is* of some good, that it is of some use. Gaye's flash of insight saves him from defeatism by wiping out entirely the question of the success or failure of an artist's attempts to do some good. The world's states, its armies, its factories, and its *Fuehrers* are all simply irrelevant; politics and economics are of no concern to the artist. The function of art is not to save anything or to make something happen or to change the world. Its function is to deny the world, to detach people from politics and history so they can receive visions of a better world, and perhaps redeem politics and history with that vision. Art mediates a negative dialectic; it removes the obstacles that block the way to a better world, but it does not bring that world into being. That is the task of the artist's audience.

So, as he sits in Foranoy, Orsinia, in September, 1938—as Hitler is meeting Chamberlain and as "Europe is crawling with armies like a corpse with maggots"—Gaye concludes that "music saves nothing." A few months later, after Chamberlain had returned to London proclaiming "peace with honour . . . peace for our time," W. B. Yeats died. Auden, who had wrestled throughout the thirties with the problem of the artist's duty, came to a position in his elegy on the death of Yeats that is nearly identical with Gaye's:

For poetry makes nothing happen: it survives
In the valley of its making where executives
Would never want to tamper, flows on south
From ranches of isolation and the busy griefs,
Raw towns that we believe and die in; it survives,
A way of happening, a mouth.

If poetry makes nothing happen, what then is the proper duty of the poet? What should he do in a world where

In the nightmare of the dark
All the dogs of Europe bark,
And the living nations wait,
Each sequestered in its hate;

Intellectual disgrace
Stares from every human face,
And the seas of pity lie
Locked and frozen in each eye.

Auden's answer is

Follow, poet, follow right
To the bottom of the night,
With your unconstraining voice
Still persuade us to rejoice;

With the farming of a verse
Make a vineyard of the curse,
Sing of human unsuccess
In a rapture of distress;

In the deserts of the heart
Let the healing fountain start,
In the prison of his days
Teach the free man how to praise.
      [from "In Memory of W. B. Yeats"]

This is, I would argue, what Le Guin does, not only in **"An die Musik,"** but throughout *Orsinian Tales* and the rest of her fiction as well. With "all cruelty, all misery, all darkness present and to come" hanging about him, Gaye hears his Sanctus and looks into "the complete, enduring darkness." In each volume of the Earthsea trilogy, Le Guin journeys into the "nightmare of the dark," to the "bottom of the night," and emerges to rejoice and to praise. Genly Ai and Estraven go into "The Place Inside the Blizzard" and Shevek's quest takes him into a cellar with a dying man. Each of the Orsinian tales describes a similar journey into darkness. And there is, moreover, a sense in which every story Le Guin tells is an Orsinian tale; they all bear her name. In that sense, the trip into darkness that most of her characters make is a trip she herself makes as an artist whenever she writes a story. Along with some other modern writers, Le Guin is a lineal descendant of Orpheus. Sometimes the map of her journey is historical, as in *Orsinian Tales*; sometimes it is psychological and ethical, as in the Earthsea trilogy; sometimes it is political, as in *The Word for World Is Forest* and *The Dispossessed.* It is always an aesthetic journey. In each case, the message Le Guin returns with is a version of the invocation Estraven murmurs every night as he goes to sleep: "Praise then darkness and Creation unfinished."

Le Guin has consistently occupied herself with her own inner life. She has always written fantasy, searching not in the outside world, but in her own creative unconscious, for the subjects of her fiction.

—*James W. Bittner*

If we could abstract from Le Guin's practice the ideas that define for her the proper duty of an artist, if we could formulate a statement of the ethics that guides her when she practices her art, it would probably come close to Rilke's definition of the artist's role:

> Art cannot be helpful through our trying to keep and specially concerning ourselves with the distresses of others, but in so far as we bear our own distresses more passionately, give now and then a perhaps clearer meaning to endurance, and develop for ourselves the means of expressing the suffering within us and its conquest more precisely and clearly than is possible to those who have to apply their powers to something else.

Le Guin has consistently occupied herself with her own inner life. She has always written fantasy, searching not in the outside world, but in her own creative unconscious, for the subjects of her fiction. The course of her development from the early sixties into the middle seventies has been a series of attempts to develop for herself the means of expressing her own suffering (which, of course, can be ethical and political as well as psychological) and its conquest more precisely and clearly. She would probably agree with Rilke's repeated assertion that we are "only just where we persist in praising." But she also feels the need to blame. The strength of her convictions and her ethical principles demands that. When her fiction blames, however, as *The Word for World Is Forest* does, it is less just.

Ultimately, the real subject of **"An die Musik"** and the rest of Le Guin's fiction that explores ethical problems is not a group of ethical questions. These are means, not ends. Her purpose is to ask them, not to answer them. The real subject of **"An die Musik"** is celebration; the tale is a celebration of Gaye's devotion to his art, and beyond that, a celebration of art itself. That is the meaning of its title. Like Estraven, Shevek, Kasimir Augeskar, and many other Le Guin characters, Gaye is an "enemy of the feasible." Le Guin places so many obstacles between him and his music not merely to wrestle with questions about the duty of the artist and the function of art, but to dramatize more vividly Gaye's capacity to endure and survive, and to pursue an ideal without compromising either himself or his goal. Like Auden's "In Memory of W. B. Yeats," which, in Samuel Hynes's words, "transforms calamity into celebration by an act of the imagination, and so affirms the survival of art in a bad time," **"An die Musik"** and *Orsinian Tales* are acts of imagination that transform the calamity of history that is Central Europe into a celebration of the individual's ability to survive bad times. (pp. 215-35)

James W. Bittner, "Persuading Us to Rejoice and Teaching Us How to Praise: Le Guin's 'Orsinian Tales'," in Science-Fiction Studies, *Vol. 5, No. 3, November, 1978, pp. 215-42.*

Le Guin on symbolism in her science fiction:

Writing **"The Stars Below,"** I thought I knew what I was doing. As in the early story **"The Masters,"** I was telling a story not about a gimmick or device or hypothesis, but about science itself—the idea of science. And about what happens to the idea of science when it meets utterly opposed and powerful ideas, embodied in government, as when seventeenth-century astronomy ran up against the Pope, or genetics in the 1930s ran up against Stalin. But all this was cast as a psychomyth, a story outside real time, past or future, in part to generalize it, and in part because I was also using science as a synonym for art. What happens to the creative mind when it is driven underground?

That was the question, and I thought I knew my answer. It all seemed straightforward, a mere allegory, really. But you don't go exploring the places underground all that easily. The symbols you thought were simple equivalences, signs, come alive, and take on meanings you did not intend and cannot explain. Long after I wrote [**"The Stars Below"**] I came on a passage in Jung's *On the Nature of the Psyche:*

"We would do well to think of ego-consciousness as being surrounded by a multitude of little luminosities. . . . Introspective intuitions . . . capture the state of the unconscious: The star-strewn heavens, stars reflected in dark water, nuggets of gold or golden sand scattered in black earth." And he quotes from an alchemist, *"Seminate aurum in terram albam foliatam"*—the precious metal strewn in the layers of white clay.

Perhaps [**"The Stars Below"**] is not about science, or about art, but about the mind, my mind, any mind, that turns inward to itself.

Ursula K. Le Guin, in her introduction to "The Stars Below" in The Wind's Twelve Quarters, *1975.*

James W. Bittner   (essay date 1979)

[*In the following excerpt, Bittner analyzes the short stories "Semley's Necklace" and "Schrödinger's Cat" as examples of the fusion of science and myth in Le Guin's fiction.*]

When Le Guin assembled *The Wind's Twelve Quarters,* she placed **"Semley's Necklace"** first because it is, she says in her headnote, "the most characteristic of [her] early science fiction and fantasy works, the most romantic of them all." **"Semley's Necklace"** is characteristic in that it combines fantasy and science fiction, myth and science. It is one of those early stories Le Guin elsewhere calls her "fairytales decked out in space suits." But **"Semley's Necklace"** is more than a characteristic and romantic early story; it was the germ of *Rocannon's World,* the first of six science fiction novels set in Le Guin's Hainish future history.

"Semley's Necklace," as it appears in *The Wind's Twelve Quarters,* was first published as "Prologue: The Necklace" in *Rocannon's World* (1966). "Prologue: The Necklace," in turn, is the revision of **"The Dowry of Angyar"** (1964). In her account of the genesis of *Rocannon's World* in her "Foreword" to *The Wind's Twelve Quarters,* Le Guin says,

> I had done with Semley when I had finished ["The Dowry of Angyar"], but there was a minor character, a mere bystander, who did not sink back obediently into obscurity when the story was done, but kept nagging me. "Write my story," he said. "I'm Rocannon. I want to explore my world" (pp. vii-viii).

Le Guin responded to Rocannon's nagging by writing parts I and II of what is now *Rocannon's World.* When her manuscript reached Ace books, it was not long enough to fill one-half of an Ace Double, so she revised thoroughly **"The Dowry of Angyar,"** added the opening paragraphs on fact and legend, and attached it to *Rocannon's World* as "Prologue: The Necklace."

By describing **"Semley's Necklace"** as the germ of *Rocannon's World,* Le Guin invites us to consider that novel and the subsequent stories and novels in the Hainish cycle as an organic growth from the story. **"Semley's Necklace,"** then, would be the formal and thematic source of the Hainish cycle, the root of the more complex and developed plots and statements in the later works. This does not mean that **"Semley's Necklace"** is the first of several serial-linear episodes set on Hainish worlds. Rather, it means that **"Semley's Necklace,"** although complete in itself, contains tensions and raises questions that its plot resolves only temporarily. **"Semley's Necklace"** is an aesthetic whole that synthesizes divergent elements, yet it is like the synthesis in any open-ended dialectical process; its internal tensions produce contradictory elements that require a new synthesis. Rocannon is one such element: he does not sink back into obscurity, but nags for further development.

"Semley's Necklace" opens with one of the most conventional situations in science fiction: the encounter with an alien. The original version of the story begins with Rocannon reading from his *Handy Pocket Guide to Intelligent Life-forms.* (At the same time Le Guin invites us to identify with Rocannon's point of view, seeing through his eyes as he reads, she also signals us not to trust too fully someone who uses a guidebook with so many telling adjectives in its title. *The Left Hand of Darkness* opens with a much more subtle use of the same technique). A stunningly beautiful woman (Semley) and four "dwarves" have come to the League museum in Kerguelen, capital of New South Georgia (a member world in the League of Worlds), and stand before Ketho and Rocannon. Rocannon has encountered the "dwarves" before, but because the League contacts with their home have been selective, he had no idea what or who the woman might be. So he consults his guide book and determines that she is an Angya escorted by four Gdemiar from Fomalhaut II, several light years away. Looking up from his book, Rocannon says, "Well, now at least we know what she is." Ketho, profoundly impressed by her beauty, replies, "I wish there were some way of knowing *who* she is. . . ." There is a way, but it is not available to Rocannon and Ketho. Le Guin offers it to us as she shifts from Rocannon's point of view to Semley's, and tells Semley's story, for she knows intuitively what Hannah Arendt explains in *The Human Condition:* "*who* somebody is or was we can only know by knowing the story of which he is himself the hero. . . . everything else we know of him. . . . tells us only *what* he is or was."

In the opening paragraphs of this germinal story, Le Guin uses a narrative technique and establishes a theme that she will return to again and again: the relationship between different kinds of knowledge or ways of knowing, and the use of multiple points of view to explore those relationships. On the one hand there is "what-knowledge," the product of an advanced technology based on rational, objective, scientific, and conscious thought. On the other hand, the "who-knowledge" we get from a story is grounded in intuitive, subjective, artistic, and unconscious modes. In **"Semley's Necklace"** these two modes are literally light years apart, even when they meet in the museum as Rocannon and Semley face each other; without a common language, they cannot communicate. But if the characters in the story cannot understand each other, the story itself gives us, its readers, ways of seeing the connections between them: the story itself is the mediation between the two modes of knowing, the metalanguage that can synthesize seemingly irreconcilable opposites into complementary aspects of a whole. Le Guin will use myth in *The Left Hand of Darkness* to the same effect. This is precisely one of the functions of storytelling: "the way of art," says Le Guin, "is . . . to keep open the tenuous, difficult, essential connections between the two extremes." Le Guin's principal tool for that integrative task is . . . the romance quest.

Although **"Semley's Necklace"** contains all the trappings of a quest, it is not a romance. It is a tragedy. Like the other heroes and heroines of the romance, though, Semley has experienced a loss of social status, and is acutely aware of her deteriorating identity as a pure descendant of the first kings of the Angyar. *Who* she is has become problematic for her; she does not feel at home. After her marriage to Durhal, her pride turns to envy and resentment as she discovers that she is not able to "outshine other women," especially those who defer to her because of her superior birth and rank, but who nevertheless display greater riches. The Angyar, described in Rocannon's guide book as a "feudal-heroic culture," have accumulated wealth as the Vikings did, in raids and wars on their neighbors, just as the Sealords of Pendor do in **"The Rule of Names,"** just as the Kargad Empire does in *A Wizard of Earthsea.* But since the League has been taxing the Angyar, they sit in their Revelhalls in "idle shame," their warlike spirits and their cultural identities broken. Semley remembers that her great-grandmother had worn a massive sapphire set in a solid gold necklace—lost now for three generations—and she hopes that by recovering it she will be able to restore the lost glory of her ancestral identity, just as Blackbeard had hoped to restore himself as a Sealord of Pendor by retrieving Inalkil the Greenstone. "Think, Durossa," Semley says to her sister-in-law, "if I could come into Hallan Revel and sit down by my husband with the wealth of a kingdom round my neck, and outshine the other women as he outshines all men!"

Impulsively brushing aside Durossa's suggestion that Durhal's pride is in his wife and not in what she wears, Semley leaves her three-year-old daughter with Durossa and sets out on a quest to recover the precious object she hopes will reestablish and reconfirm her identity. She flies to her father's home on a windsteed (a horse-sized flying cat) but finds him in a drunken stupor amid the ruins of his castle and of no assistance. . . . She visits the Fiia, an elfish people living an idyllic life in sunshine and happiness (Frye's "idyllic world"); they advise her against her quest. Single-mindedly intent on getting the necklace, she disregards their warnings and flies on to the caves of the Gdemiar, a race of dwarf-like people who made the necklace, sold it to Semley's ancestor, and are rumored to have stolen it back. Just as many questers cross a threshold into another world, enchanted or demotic, Semley enters a "cave-mouth, a toothless, yawning mouth from which a stinking warmth sighed out," the entrance to "the Realm of Night" (clearly, Frye's "demotic world," characterized by alienation). Semley is no less insistent than Blackbeard, though she is more polite, as she asks the Gdemiar for the Eye of the Sea (Seaheart in the original version). The Gdemiar, who had traded it to the League for an automatic-drive spaceship, agree to guide Semley to the necklace, knowing that the trip will take sixteen years, yet telling her that it will last "but one long night." They have recognized that Semley's single-minded commitment to recovering the necklace leaves her vulnerable to manipulation and they maliciously anticipate an opportunity to dupe and to take advantage of an arrogant and beautiful Angya. In due course, she receives the necklace from Rocannon (from Ketho in the original version), returns to her home planet, flies back to Hallan on her windsteed, only to discover Durhal has been dead for nine years, her sister-in-law Durossa is an old woman, and her daughter Haldre is as old as she is. These revelations overwhelm Semley; dropping the necklace on the stone floor, she runs into the forest, lost in madness. Like Blackbeard's quest, hers has not let to a recovery of identity, but to complete alienation and disaster.

When Ted White reprinted the story in *The Best from Amazing,* he introduced it with this headnote:

> the idea as such is now new. We've all played with the notion of time-dilation, with the Einsteinian principle of the contraction of time as one approaches the speed of light. But Ursula K. Le Guin—in a story which became the root of her first novel, and thus the entire series which has culminated in her superb *The Left Hand of Darkness*—has distilled this common concept into the purity of myth.

White's remarks, which embody a widely held belief that science fiction is the mythology of the modern world, and which imply that a science fiction writer makes myths from the materials of twentieth-century science, do not accurately describe what Le Guin is doing in **"Semley's Necklace."** On different occasions, when she was discussing the role of myth in science fiction, Le Guin has explained that in **"Semley's Necklace"** she was retelling a Norse myth, the story of Freya and the Brisingamen Necklace. So the purity of myth is clothed in science fiction, not distilled from it. Better than metaphors of extraction and purification or covering and disguising, however, the idea of chiasmus describes what Le Guin is doing in **"Semley's Necklace"**: myth and science are crossed with each other as the nerves from our eyes to our brains are, making left into right and right into left, or, they are crossed as homologous chromosomes are during meiosis, producing exchanges and recombinations of genres.

In the Norse story, Freya, the lascivious goddess of summer and love, leaves Asgard in a chariot drawn by cats, wanders into Midgard, and in a cave encounters four dwarves making the Brisingamen Necklace. The beauty of the necklace so impresses Freya that she has to have it at any price. The dwarves have all the gold and silver they want, and therefore reject her offer of hard currency. They are interested in Freya herself. So Freya exchanges her favors for the necklace, and returns to Asgard only to find that her husband Odur is gone. Broken by her loss, she runs from Asgard looking for him, dropping tears of gold (or flowers in some versions) wherever she goes. Like the Greek myth of Persephone's marriage to Pluto, Freya's story is connected with the end of summer; the tragic simplicity of her fate is rooted in the inevitability of seasonal change.

The Gdemiar, who have "grey-white skins, dampish looking like the skins of grubs," are Le Guin's version of the subterranean nocturnal dwarves who grew from maggots in the corpse of the giant Ymir, just as the Fiia are her version of the airy and benevolent elves of Norse myth and legend. The windsteeds have their source in the cats which pull Freya's chariot (crossed, perhaps, with something like Pegasus), and the necklace Semley quests for resembles not only the Brisingamen Necklace, but also the various rings in Norse myth and legend which exercise a baleful influence on their possessors and ultimately return to their makers, myths revived by Wagner in the nineteenth century and by Tolkien in the twentieth. Four dwarves receive Freya's favors; four Gdemiar escort Semley to Kerguelen, pawing and fondling her along the way. In addition to borrowing and transforming specific elements from Norse myth, Le Guin preserves the flavor of Norse poetic style with kennings: Semley's father is "gray and swollen as the web-spinner of ruined houses," and Semley herself is "Halla's bride, Kirien-lady, Windborne, and Semley the Fair." This orphic style contrasts sharply with the pedestrian speech of Ketho and Rocannon, and reinforces the divisions between the two worlds.

But it is less important to know Le Guin's sources than it is to understand the relationship between the myth and its science fiction setting. Le Guin said in an interview that her job as an artist "is not to use myths, but to be used by myths. . . . The real thing is to find the native symbology of your own creative unconscious . . . and try to integrate it in terms comprehensible to others, and aesthetically solid." Norse myths, she continued, "are part of my 'childhood lore,' they shaped my imagination." So Freya's story is part of the native symbology of Le Guin's creative unconscious, which she integrated with the idiom of science fiction, terms comprehensible to twentieth-century readers. In a sense, Norse myth is a heuristic device, a catalyst for freeing Le Guin's own creativity; she circled back to her "childhood lore," a circular return which was also an advance. What makes Semley's tragedy "aesthetically solid" is the tragic irony Le Guin creates from the intersection, the crossing and interaction of the myth and its science fiction setting, and from the mutually estranging interplay of the two points of view in the story. Frye says that the normal containing form of the romance is a possible future while archaism is the normal content; the science fiction and the myth in **"Semley's Necklace"** seem to fit this notion, and Le Guin consciously exploits the clash between the two. In a review of a Russian science fiction novel, she writes,

> The genre [of *Hard to be a God*] is one familiar to American SF readers: Terran observers of the future, bound to noninterference, among (extraterrestrial) human beings whose society and culture resemble that of medieval Europe. A double estrangement, and the best of both worlds—the romance of future technology, plus the romance of feudalism. Something similar has been done by several American authors . . . including myself.

But the science fiction in **"Semley's Necklace"** does not "contain" the myth, as Frye's formulation would suggest; rather, it is braided together with it, woven in and out of it. Because the two points of view estrange each other, and because we hold them both in our minds as we read the story, each event has at least two dimensions, mythic and scientific, unconscious and conscious. After we read (through Rocannon's eyes) the coldly "scientific" description of the races on Fomalhaut II, we then experience them mediated through Semley's eyes as we participate in her intense desire to recover the Eye of the Sea. And while we subjectively experience "one long night" with Semley, we objectively know that it is sixteen years long. With one "part" of our minds, we are actors in the story, and with another "part," we are spectators: acting with Rocannon, we watch Semley in the museum; acting with Semley, we arrive in the museum to watch Rocannon. The ironies are reciprocal. Fact and myth and scientific law and tragic

fate are intertwined so that (to shift the metaphor) the story becomes a Möbius strip: the two sides or "parts" may seem to be different, yet they are in fact the same. Through *coincidentia oppositorum,* the chiasmus becomes a figure-eight.

This is more a description of the potential of Le Guin's method; in practice, in this story, one side is decidedly weaker than the other. Rocannon the objective intellectual is a "mere bystander"; his main function is to embody the scientific point of view, to be a vehicle for introducing the notion of time-dilation so that Semley's mythic fate becomes rationally credible for readers who have come to expect scientific explanations. Crossed with relativity physics, a myth about seasonal change is readily accepted by readers who might otherwise dismiss it as a "mere story."

Just as Le Guin uses physics to translate Semley's fate for modern readers, she uses another science, anthropology, to translate mythic and fairy tale figures into the individuals, races, and cultures which give Semley's story a vividly imagined background. In the process of inventing the settings and cultures in which Semley enacts her quest, Le Guin placed her in a complex web of relationships on Fomalhaut II, and made the initial exploration of a theme which is developed more fully in the Hainish cycle: the relationship of part and whole.

Semley is a member of a culture which is part of a world of many separate cultures which in turn become part of the colonial empire of the League. When the League begins taxing the Angyar and developing the technological skills of the Gdemiar with only the most superficial knowledge and understanding of their cultural patterns and relationships, it upsets the balance of Fomalhaut II and thus dislocates the culture of which Semley is a part. Semley's quest is her response. It is reactionary in that she wants to recover a necklace which is a symbol of the old ways before the coming of the League when Angyar lords conquered fiefs, dressed their women in jewels, and bought husbands for their daughters with dowries of "heroic loot." Semley's quest is a denial of the new relationships with the League, a denial of something she is ignorant of. In a series of dialectical reversals, Semley's effort to deny the League carries her into the future. She does not understand, and because of her pride as an Angya does not want to understand, her culture's relationships with the Gdemiar and the League. The goal of her quest, like the goal of Blackbeard's quest, is self-aggrandizement, and the failure of her quest is a pointed ethical judgment of her motivation. Her sixteen-year-long journey is Le Guin's metaphor for the judgment that Semley's self-absorption and pride, her tragic flaws, cut her off from relationships with those around her, remove her from history, and form a breach between herself and her world that leads to madness. She ceases to be part of the whole.

The thematic statement that runs throughout the Hainish cycle, and the Earthsea trilogy as well, and is articulated first in **"Semley's Necklace"** is this: if people act without an understanding and appreciation of the web of relationships in which they are a strand, they will find their actions producing effects and consequences which are the opposite of those intended. But if one acts in harmony with the whole, he will be at home with himself and his world. And it seems that the only way one ever gets knowledge of the whole is to go on a quest, to go "there" in order to discover "here," to discover and confront the Other in order to find the Self.

But all the responsibility for Semley's failure to understand her part in the web of relationships on her world and between her world and the League cannot be assigned to her alone. She is also a victim of the manner in which the League cavalierly exploits Fomalhaut II without understanding the people there. In the Norse myth, Freya's tragedy is as natural as seasonal change. In **"Semley's Necklace,"** Le Guin has translated a myth of the end of summer into a story about the personal costs of cultural and militaristic imperialism. Ketho and Rocannon, mere bystanders, are in the story to represent the League's ignorance of its colonial subjects. Rocannon has to consult his guide book, a parody of ethnological knowledge, merely to identify *what* Semley is. *Who* she is is completely beyond his grasp because he does not know any of her culture's *stories*. . . . Not knowing who Semley is, Rocannon greets her with a silly gesture he calls his All-purpose Intercultural Curtsey. He corrects Ketho when he hears him using the label 'trogs" for the Gdemiar, and then nearly uses the same racial slur when he says, "I wish we could talk to her without these tr—Gdemiar as interpreters."

When Le Guin constructed the complex situation in which Semley's quest is played out, she created tensions and raised questions that the tragic resolution of the plot holds together only momentarily. The background of Semley's tragedy, the conflict between the feudal-heroic world of Angyar and the technological-militaristic world of the League, remains. If Le Guin were a writer with a tragic vision, she could rest there, for tragedy confirms the status quo as it bows to the inevitability of fate. But she is a Romantic, and therefore sensitive to the possibilities and potentialities that may be latent in the present situation. At the end of **"Semley's Necklace"** Rocannon is aware of a blind spot in the League's understanding of its colonial races and cultures. Twice Le Guin has Rocannon admit his lack of understanding: "I never feel I really understand these hieratic races," he says of the Gdemiar; and as Semley walks away from him, he feels as though he has "blundered through the corner of a legend, of a tragic myth, even, which I do not understand." Rocannon's new awareness of the League's limitations, combined with the erotic awe and curiosity Semley elicits from Rocannon, raise possibilities and expectations that are neither fulfilled nor dissipated at the end of the story.

What Le Guin needed after finishing **"Semley's Necklace"** was a structure capable of carrying the creative growth that resulted from her planting Freya's story in the conventions and traditions of science fiction. So after she finished with Semley, she responded to Rocannon's nagging by sending him to Fomalhaut II as the leader of an ethnographic survey team. Nowhere in the original version of **"Semley's Necklace"** does Le Guin identify Rocannon as an ethnologist. But when Rocannon nagged himself into existence as a fully fledged ethnologist, Le

Guin had a ready vehicle for exploring the details only hinted at in **"Semley's Necklace."** As an ethnologist, he can explore the cultures glimpsed only briefly in **"Semley's Necklace,"** he can in his own person as scientist and romance hero represent a combination of "what-knowledge" and "who-knowledge," and he can sublimate his desire to know more about Semley and her world in a romance quest that will bring together the two points of view that had been light years apart when they first met in the League museum. (pp. 63-71)

"Schrödinger's Cat" may seem, on a first reading, radically different from [**"Semley's Necklace"**] . . . , but it too weaves together myth and science in complementary patterns, even as it creates an entirely different world. Unlike the landscapes in Le Guin's outer space and in her inner lands, unlike Orsinian geography, the world we experience as we read **"Schrödinger's Cat"** resembles neither the conventional imaginary landscapes of fantasy and science fiction nor any familiar landscape we have experienced or might experience. There are, to be sure, allusions to Michelangelo, Bach, and Schumann; there are references to Democrats, Episcopalians, Methodists, and Baptists; there is an account of Erwin Schrödinger's famous *Gedanken-experiment,* "performed" originally in 1935, and a large fragment of the myth of Pandora's Box; and, finally, there are cans of sardines and pork and beans. But even if these people and things are familiar, the context in which we find them is entirely strange and anomalous: the whole world outside the house to which the narrator has retreated is heating up and speeding up. Recalling Jameson's distinction [in "Magical Narratives: Romance as Genre," *New Literary History,* 7 (1975)] between the technical and popular senses of the word *world,* we might say that while the *world* in the normal sense of nature, people, and things is familiar, the *world* in the phenomenological sense as a *Gestalt,* the "supreme category that permits all experience or perception in the first place," is strange. In **"Schrödinger's Cat,"** our normal categories of time and logic and causality do not apply. In most of her fiction, Le Guin positions invented cultures and beings and things in an environment which has been created according to familiar conventions or rules or paradigms, but in **"Schrödinger's Cat"** she seems to place familiar things in a world that exists wholly outside the horizons of our normal world. Instead of estranging a familiar conceptual framework by putting strange things in it, Le Guin seems to be estranging the familiar things in our world by putting them into a strange frame. Thus the relationship between the two senses of *world* is reciprocal; they are internally related and relative to each other.

If the two senses of *world* are relative to each other, so also are our notions of strangeness, our categories of reality and fantasy, objective and subjective, subject and object. The strange frame of **"Schrödinger's Cat,"** therefore, may not be the world outside the house, but rather may be in the house itself: the narrator's consciousness and its contents. We know from the relativity theory that our perception of time and velocity is relative to the time frame in which we are moving. To the extent that biological processes and heat (the velocity of molecules) are functions of time, they would be relative also. Thus if it appears to the narrator that the world inside the house is cooler and that things move more slowly there, then those impressions may be the result of the *narrator's* speeding up. Like Semley, who returns from "one long night" of near lightspeed travel to find her daughter sixteen years older than she was "yesterday," the narrator of **"Schrödinger's Cat"** may be in a time frame moving faster than the world around her (him?—we never know for certain). If that is the case, then the outside world with its increasing heat (kisses like a branding iron) and its accelerated biological process (children growing up before your eyes) would *appear* to be moving faster. Moreover, the suggestion at the end of **"Schrödinger's Cat"** that the narrator is mad—she recognized before the glue of her mandolin melted that the note she had been hearing on "the mandolin strings of the mind" was A, "the note that drove Robert Schumann mad" (implying that her mind has become unglued?)—parallels Semley's madness at the end of **"Semley's Necklace."** In one sense, then, **"Schrödinger's Cat"** may be a retelling of **"Semley's Necklace,"** this time wholly from the subjectivity of the time traveler's point of view. But all of this may be merely the metaphorical mechanics of science fiction, the literalization of metaphor and the concretizing of subjective perceptions in aesthetic imagery which we should not read literally. Even so, one gets the impression that the tenors of some metaphors come from one world while the tenors of others come from another world.

Indeed, one could just as easily account for the differences between the world outside the house and the narrator's world by reading the house as a metaphor for a dream world separated from the outside waking world. Dreamers may have the impression of living if not in a timeless world, then in a world that moves more slowly than their waking worlds. Even in our waking moments time passes more quickly at one "time," and more slowly at other "times." This reading would explain the dream-like qualities of the narrative, the sudden shifts and interruptions, the coincidences, and the overdramatizations, in sum, the absence of normal causality. The narrator's punning ambiguities about telling stories and sleeping and dreaming seem to support this:

> the impulse to narrate remains. Many things are not worth doing, but almost anything is worth telling. In any case, I have a severe congenital case of *Ethica laboris puritanica*, or Adam's Disease. It is incurable except by total decephalization. I even like to dream when asleep, and to try and recall my dreams: it assures me that I haven't wasted seven or eight hours just lying there. Now here I am, lying, here. Hard at it.

Is the narrator merely lying, there (making things up, telling a story), or is she lying here before us (asleep), while we see the world from her dream world?

The point of all this uncertainty is just that: Uncertainty. We could press an interpretation of the story in scientific terms, but that would displace the dream elements into the background. On the other hand, we could foreground the dreamy qualities of the narrative, sacrificing a full understanding of the purely scientific elements. We are in a position similar to the physicist's as he tries to observe the ve-

---

> Although **"Schrödinger's Cat"** is one of Le Guin's shortest stories, it has a density and a range of meaning that are as allusive and complex as what we encounter in difficult modern poetry.
>
> —*James W. Bittner*

---

locity and momentum of an electron at the same time: only one can be measured accurately. And what better position to be in while reading a story that deals with just these anomalies of quantum mechanics that arise from the relationships between the observing subject with his tools and the observed object? Only when we try to "measure" the story with our critical tools do we need an Uncertainty Principle. If *contraria sunt complementa* is a useful motto for physicists, it is equally useful for readers. In **"Schrödinger's Cat,"** literal and figurative, outside and inside, the language of science and the language of dreams—these are by no means mutually exclusive, but are rather complementary parts of an imaginative whole, the story itself, a metalanguage that incorporates apparently separate languages.

Although **"Schrödinger's Cat"** is one of Le Guin's shortest stories, it has a density and a range of meaning that are as allusive and complex as what we encounter in difficult modern poetry. It takes us to the heart of epistemological and ontological questions raised by the modern revolutions in physics at the same time that it engages pressing moral problems in its search for Hope in a world where marriages (Le Guin's "central, consistent theme") are "coming apart" and where people are reified into "hopelessly tangled" and chaotic fragments of themselves. Yet for all its complexity, **"Schrödinger's Cat"** has a classical simplicity: the implied equation of Pandora's Box and the box in Schrödinger's thought experiment has an elegance that matches the beauty Dirac and other physicists try to get in their equations. More than any other story Le Guin has written, it displays self-consciously the "thought-experimental manner proper to science fiction." Itself a thought experiment, the story contains a thought experiment that is one part of an aesthetic connection between an explorative, synthesizing scientific-mindedness and a fantasy-mindedness. Its yoking together of a Greek myth and quantum theory, a chiasmus of science and fantasy, is, Le Guin would say, "simply a way of thinking," a question, not an answer. "One of the essential functions of science fiction," said Le Guin as she compared it to the thought experiments of Einstein and Schrödinger, "is precisely this kind of question-asking: reversals of an habitual way of thinking, metaphors for what our language has no words for as yet, experiments in imagination." The question-asking Le Guin has in mind here is the same process George Steiner has recently described [in "After the Book?" in *On Difficulty and Other Essays* (1978)]:

> our asking is, in Hegel's incisive terminology, an *Aufhebung*. Asking is an action, a possible bring-

ing into view and into being of perspectives in which the question is seen to be trivial or falsely posed. Or, at its rare best, to ask is to provoke not the answer one actually fears or aims at, but the first contours of a new and better asking—which is then a first kind of answer.

This is precisely what happens in **"Schrödinger's Cat,"** whose plot, like the plots of Le Guin's romances, culminates in a moment of vision in which contradictions are *aufgehoben,* a moment that brings into view new perspectives. Like Le Guin's other science fiction, **"Schrödinger's Cat"** generates a "view in" as it reverses habitual ways of thinking.

The person who barges into the narrator's cool retreat accepts the orthodox Copenhagen interpretation of quantum theory, and wants to use the narrator's cat to prove that "if you desire certainty, any certainty, you must create it yourself!" Apparently unaware of the contradiction, he wants certain knowledge of uncertainty; he wants to prove Einstein wrong: he wants "to know for *sure* that God *does* play dice with the world." The narrator raises the same epistemological questions that [1963 Nobel Laureate in Physics] Eugene Wigner raised, but "Rover" brushes them aside. He does not want the issue complicated by involving the observer in his system. He wants to keep things restricted to the box and confined within the categorical boxes of his binary thinking. Either the cat will be dead or not dead. When the narrator flings back the lid of the box and the cat is not there, Rover's questions are *aufgehoben.* A new perspective has come into view, a perspective much larger than the one permitted by Rover's categorical boxes: Non-Being transcends both life and death and certainty and uncertainty. Because the answer he aimed at is not provoked by his questions, Le Guin is telling us, his questions have been falsely posed. There are always more than two alternatives. And then when the roof of the house is lifted off "just like the lid of a box," the *Aufhebung* of Rover's questions is itself *aufgehoben.* If the "unconscionable, inordinate light of the stars" that floods into the house carries our minds beyond the box of the house, beyond our Earth, our solar system, even beyond our galaxy, then we might also think of boxes larger than our universe. When Le Guin removed the cat from the box she was not only doing a conjuring trick, an inversion of pulling a rabbit out of a hat. Since this is a science fiction story, she may be suggesting that the cat is in an alternate universe. This hypothesis is not as fantastic as it might seem. The multiple universe interpretation of quantum theory—the "EWG metatheorem" proposed by Elliot, Wheeler, and Graham—would give that hypothesis scientific credibility. The EWG metatheorem posits not only the existence of "simultaneous, noninteracting, but equally real worlds"; it says there are [more than 10 raised to the hundredth power] of them!

If physicists can soberly conjure other worlds into existence and then support their theories with mathematical equations, the only language in which these ideas can be expressed, then their questioning of reality parallels the questionings of science fiction writers, who likewise hypothesize other worlds and then use stories, the only language in which their ideas can be expressed, to communi-

cate with an audience. It is at this point that the incomplete myth of Pandora takes on significance. If Hope is blocked from a world (in the popular sense of the word) by the categorical boxes that constitute that world as they make perception of it possible (world in the technical sense), then a new and larger perspective that includes other worlds (in both senses of the word) means that a world without hope is not the only answer, and certainly not the final answer. Science fiction can create those other, alternate worlds (again, in both senses of the word) and therefore can change the way we ask questions of this world. If the perspectives that constitute a world without Hope are *aufgehoben* by a new asking, by the estranging techniques of science fictional thought experiments, then we will see that grief and loss, fear and *Angst,* are not the final human condition, but on the contrary are only the answers to a specific and limited kind of questioning.

The narrator enters her cool retreat grieving over a loss; she seems "to have no other self, nothing further, nothing that lies outside the borders of grief." What she has lost and cannot remember, the Nothing that lies outside the borders of her grief—Hope itself—constitutes the horizons of her world by its absence as surely as it would by its presence. While the cat is in the box, the narrator muses:

> Nothing happened. Nothing would happen. Nothing would ever happen, until we lifted the lid of the box.
>
> "Like Pandora," I said in a weak whisper. I could not quite recall Pandora's legend. She had let all the plagues and evils out of the box, of course, but there has been something else, too. After all the devils were let loose, something quite different, quite unexpected, had been left. What had it been? Hope? A dead cat? I could not remember.

The world does not happen, or at least does not make sense, unless and until we look at it. *Esse est percipi,* as Berkeley said. Recalling Michelangelo's "Last Judgment," the narrator thinks of the fellow "who has clapped his hands over his face in horror as the devils drag him down to Hell." But she notes that he has covered only one eye: "the other eye is busy looking. It's all he can do, but he does it. He observes. Indeed, one wonders if Hell would exist if he did not look at it." Significantly, just as the narrator cannot remember what was left in Pandora's Box, she does not refer to the top half of the painting. It is as though she too is looking with just one eye. The mandolin strings of her mind have a limited range of notes.

In *The Dispossessed,* published the same year (1974) as **"Schrödinger's Cat,"** Shevek says that "the earth itself was uncertain, unreliable. The enduring, the reliable, is a promise made by the human mind." Similarly, in the world of total Uncertainty in **"Schrödinger's Cat,"** Hope is something that exists in the human mind, or it exists nowhere. Having forgotten a myth, the narrator has lost hope and is thus confined within the boundaries of her grief. The value free language of science cannot predict the future, at least on the quantum level. The multivalent languages of myth, however, determine the moral attitude toward the future that we adopt in the present, and if we forget parts of that language, we alienate ourselves from significant parts of reality. Recovery of that language is then a moral task, as seeing with both eyes is a moral imperative. Seeing with only one eye the devils, and evils in the world, we capitulate to despair and thereby help bring about the very conditions that we fear. But if we see with both eyes, along with an inner imaginative eye, if we use the complementary languages of myth and science when we interrogate the world, we make room for moral choice. "I shall miss the cat," says the narrator at the end of the story; "I wonder if he found what it was we lost?" If the cat is nowhere *(u-topia)*, in a world simultaneous with this one but equally real, then he may have found it. The message of **"Schrödinger's Cat"** is the message of Le Guin's "ambiguous utopia" *The Dispossessed:* for a full view of present reality, this world, we must see with hope as well as grief and fear, we must include utopia on our maps of this world. Because Hope is absent from the narrator's world, it is all the more present in our minds as we read the story, whose theme then appears as the theme of much of Le Guin's fiction: the necessity of Hope. Demogorgon's words at the end of Shelley's *Prometheus Unbound* may be the best gloss on this story as well as Le Guin's work as a whole:

> To suffer woes which Hope thinks infinite;
> To forgive wrongs darker than Death of Night;
> To defy Power which seems Omnipotent;
> To love, and bear; to hope, till Hope creates
> From its own wreck the thing it contemplates;
> Neither to change nor falter nor repent:
> This, like thy glory, Titan! is to be
> Good, great and joyous, beautiful and free;
> This is alone Life, Joy, Empire and Victory.

Myth and science are usually regarded as two mutually exclusive languages, each with its own vocabulary, grammar, and syntax, each with its own way of seeing the world, each constituting its own world. What Heisenberg says [in *Physics and Philosophy*] of scientific work in physics applies, *mutatis mutandis,* to one who uses myth or any other specialized language to understand nature:

> We have to remember that what we observe is not nature in itself but nature exposed to our method of questioning. Our scientific work in physics consists in asking questions about nature in the language that we possess and trying to get an answer from experiment by the means at our disposal. In this way quantum theory reminds us, as Bohr has put it, of the old wisdom that when searching for harmony in life one must never forget that in the drama of existence we are ourselves both players and spectators. It is understandable that in our scientific relation to nature our own activity becomes very important when we have to deal with parts of nature into which we can penetrate only by using the most elaborate tools.

Like physicists, Le Guin asks questions of nature—the primary question being "who are we?"—as she experiments with one of the most elaborate tools human beings have developed, the story, not so much to get an answer as to provoke an *Aufhebung* that brings into view the first

contours of a new and better asking. She knows that Mind and Nature are interdependent, perhaps even identical at some moments, and that the specialized tools made for exploring one will not yield results when they are used on the other. There are parts of nature—the imagination, the mind, the moral intelligence—which can be penetrated with the language of the night: the symbols and narrative logics of dreams and myths. Conversely, there are parts of nature that we know best with the language of the day: the concepts and logics of science and rationality. Recognizing that these several parts of nature are interdependent, that we are ourselves both players and spectators in the drama of existence, and that a view of the whole web of relationships in the drama requires complementary modes of thought and feeling, Le Guin has tried to fashion stories which, as they weave together the languages of myth and science, as they make connections between fantasy-mindedness and scientific-mindedness, become themselves a new language in which myth and science can communicate with each other. That language then becomes an elaborate tool in the search for harmony in life. (pp. 77-83)

> *James W. Bittner, in his* Approaches to the Fiction of Ursula K. Le Guin, *UMI Research Press, 1984, 161 p.*

Barbara J. Bucknall   (essay date 1981)

[*Bucknall is an English-born critic and educator specializing in the study of the French novelist Marcel Proust. In the following excerpt, Bucknall surveys short stories by Le Guin—particularly those collected in* The Wind's Twelve Quarters—*and discusses the relationship of individual short stories to each other and to Le Guin's novels.*]

"The Diary of the Rose" is only one of several short stories that Le Guin published between 1974 and 1978. Three stories that appeared before *The Dispossessed* are **"The Author of the Acacia Seeds and Other Extracts from the *Journal of the Association of Therolinguistics,*"** **"Intracom,"** and **"Schrödinger's Cat"** (all 1974). They are comic and highly entertaining. The first speculates about the possibility of studying the art forms of animals and plants. The second describes through the metaphor of the crew of a spaceship the thoughts of a young woman who has just realized she is pregnant. And the third is a takeoff on a famous "thought experiment" by the physicist Erwin Schrödinger. Suppose a cat is put in a box with a gun attached to the inside of the box. Depending on the behavior of a photon emitted inside the box, the gun may shoot the cat or it may not. Le Guin turns this demonstration of uncertainty into a lively narrative, full of unexpected twists.

The short stories she has written since *The Dispossessed* are on the whole much less exuberant. **"Mazes"** (1975), a horrifying little story, describes the last living moments of an alien whose culture attaches great importance to performing dances in mazes of increasing complexity. A human scientist is testing its intelligence by putting it through mazes, without in the least understanding what the alien is doing in them. He is also starving it to death by feeding it the wrong kind of food. **"SQ"** (1978), a grimly humorous story, tells how a psychologist with great political influence invents a test to measure levels of sanity and forces everyone in the world to take the test. More and more people are committed to mental hospitals as a result, including the psychologist himself. His secretary, who is imperturbably sane, is left to run the world, since the psychologist is no longer capable of doing it.

"SQ" is reminiscent of *The Lathe of Heaven,* while **"The Eye Altering"** (1976), which describes the adjustment of a colonist's vision to a new world, is reminiscent of the idea of genetic adaptation in *Planet of Exile.* **"No Use to Talk to Me"** (1976) depicts a conversation in a space ship that is about to crash, while **"Gwilan's Harp"** tells the story of a woman's life, from famous musician to wife and mother to widow. Both these stories depend much more on emotional tone than invention.

Two other stories represent a mingling of fantasy and realism. **"The First Report of the Shipwrecked Foreigner to the Kadanh of Derb"** (1978) is a deeply personal description of Venice in terms that make it seem at first like a fantasy. It is not unlike the descriptions of imaginary cities in Italo Calvino's *Le Città invisibili* (1972; translated as *Invisible Cities,* 1974). In contrast, a very sad short story, *The Water Is Wide* (1976), which was published as an entire book, starts realistically and then turns into complete fantasy. (pp. 129-30)

[A] new departure has been in the direction of complete realism, with the only fantasy element being the private fantasies of the characters. This is the case with *Very Far Away from Anywhere Else. The Eye of the Heron,* in contrast, continues the tradition of *The Dispossessed* in being a science-fiction story with a political subject, although it is much slighter and also less successful than *The Dispossessed.*

Le Guin has also responded to the public's interest in her work by having collections of earlier short stories published, in *The Wind's Twelve Quarters* and *Orsinian Tales;* poems, in *Wild Angels;* and essays and talks, in *The Language of the Night.* Besides this, she has gone back to her first subject for novels, Orsinia, and published *Malafrena.* And she has published a short piece for fairly young children, *Leese Webster.* (pp. 130-31)

Orsinian Tales and *Malafrena* concern Orsinia, which does not exist in the real world, but which is described as if it were real, with references to real places, such as Prague, and real historical personages, institutions, and events, such as Napoleon, Metternich, and Hitler, the Austro-Hungarian Empire, and the 1956 Hungarian uprising. Some reviewers have supposed that Orsinia is actually a real country, such as Hungary or Romania, in disguise, but in fact it cannot be identified as any particular Central European country.

For those who have acquired a taste for the marvelous and want all Le Guin's books to satisfy it, there is something a little thin about Orsinia, a little lacking in richness and density. However, this is more the case with *Orsinian Tales* than with *Malafrena,* which reads like an historical romance. *Orsinian Tales,* moving about in time, covers the history of Orsinia from 1150 to 1960. *Malafrena* is

about Europe between 1820 and 1830, when reactionary governments tried to impose order and young liberals dreamed of revolution. In both books, as in so many of Le Guin's works, love, friendship, integrity and fidelity play an important role.

Very Far Away from Anywhere Else is a very short book, but a moving one. It is written for young people, about young people, and concerns the attempt of a young man of seventeen and a young woman of eighteen to achieve excellence in their chosen fields, science and music, and integrity and respect in their relationship with each other. To do this, they have to resist pressure from society, which would like them to abandon excellence, for the sake of normality, and spoil their beautiful friendship for the sake of premature sex.

Because of their very intelligence and talent and the ways in which they plan to use that intelligence and talent, they are not yet ready for a full sexual relationship. But they share each other's thoughts and feelings. The young man, Owen Griffiths, tells his friend, Natalie Field, about an imaginary country he has invented, called Thorn, where he can be free and himself. She sympathizes with this fantasy and writes some music for Thorn. She also gets him interested in the Brontës, and he finds that they too had imaginary countries. So his private fantasy, which he had come to feel too old for, is accepted by his dearest friend instead of being dismissed as immature. This is the only fantasy element in *Very Far Away from Anywhere Else,* which is a wise, tender, and loving book, written with understanding and concern. It has been named an American Library Association Notable Book for Young Adults. (pp. 131-32)

The Wind's Twelve Quarters, which takes its title from a poem by A. E. Housman in *A Shropshire Lad* (1896), is a chronologically arranged retrospective of Le Guin's short stories, accompanied by an introduction and notes. The first story, **"Semley's Necklace,"** was published in 1964, and the last story, **"The Day before the Revolution,"** was published in 1974. . . . **"Semley's Necklace"** was the starting point for *Rocannon's World;* and two other stories, **"The Word of Unbinding"** and **"The Rule of Names,"** were starting points for the Earthsea trilogy, while **"Winter's King"** was the starting point for *The Left Hand of Darkness.* **"The Day before the Revolution,"** which is about Odo, the founder of Odonianism, was written after *The Dispossessed* (1974).

The stories in *The Wind's Twelve Quarters* may be divided into three groups: the earlier fantasies; rather surrealistic later fantasies that take place outside time, which Le Guin calls "psychomyths"; and science-fiction stories. Apart from the stories already mentioned, only one of the science-fiction stories is directly related to the Hainish cycle. It is **"Vaster than Empires and More Slow." "Nine Lives"** may be part of the same cycle, but it is hard to tell, because there is no mention of the Hainish. These two stories have attracted more critical attention than the others, but all the stories are accompanied by brief introductions by Le Guin herself, which makes up for any lack of attention from other critics. It also justifies discussing all the stories in this collection in some detail.

Because Le Guin has chosen to follow a roughly chronological order in her arrangement of these stories, it would seem as well to respect this in discussing them. The first story [is] **"Semley's Necklace"**. . . . The second, **"April in Paris,"** tells of lonely people who come together and are consoled in their loneliness. An American professor is transported to fifteenth-century Paris by a spell pronounced by a poor scholar. The American knows that no one is interested in his theories on François Villon, and the medieval Frenchman has turned to black magic in despair of success in science. Once together, they share information and become fast friends. Then they summon two women from the past and the future, and at the end of the story they are in love in Paris in the spring. This pleasant tale was Le Guin's first published fantasy story.

The next story, **"The Masters,"** her first published science-fiction story, is considerably less pleasant. It describes a world that denies science because of the harm it has caused and that severely limits the use of numbers. Only Roman numerals are used, and the Mechanics, who use measurements, are not allowed to compute. Arabic numerals are known as black numbers and are equated with black magic. Two Mechanics secretly study mathematics and are punished by a kind of inquisition. One of them is burned at the stake, and the other has his right hand crushed. The story is full of sorrow and loss and fear. But it is also full of the joy of using one's mind and sharing ideas with a kindred spirit, in spite of any danger involved. Of **"The Masters,"** Le Guin says, "The figure of the scientist is a quite common one in my stories, and most often a rather lonely one, isolated, an adventurer, out on the edge of things."

"Darkness Box" (1963) is a fantasy about a king who has stopped time by shutting up darkness in a box and throwing it into the sea, so that the battle between his two sons, one a rebel and the other loyal to his father, can never come to a conclusion. But the sea returns the box, the darkness escapes, and time, change, and mortality return again. This tale is full of standard fantasy elements, such as a witch, a gryphon, and a kind of never-never Middle Ages.

"The Word of Unbinding," which comes next, is Le Guin's first Earthsea story. . . . [It] describes a wizard's attempts to escape from a sinister enemy who has returned from the dead. The wizard has to die himself in order to defeat his enemy.

"The Rule of Names," which has also been mentioned in connection with the Earthsea trilogy, concerns a very inefficient wizard, Mr. Underhill, who is attacked by another wizard, Blackbeard. Blackbeard has come in search of his family's lost treasure, for he knows that Mr. Underhill has stolen it. He uses Mr. Underhill's true name, Yevaud, to gain power over him. On hearing that name, Mr. Underhill has to reveal his true nature. But unfortunately for Blackbeard, his true nature is that of a dragon. He was an inefficient wizard because he was not really a wizard at all, but he is a very efficient dragon. This is a light-hearted story, showing Le Guin in a humorous mood.

"Winter's King" [is] a science-fiction story. . . . In it, Le Guin makes use of the notion that people who go on space trips return looking quite young, while the people on their home planets have aged or died. It is an idea that seems to fascinate her, for she also uses it in **"Semley's Necklace"** and **"Vaster than Empires and More Slow."**

"The Good Trip" is not, strictly speaking, a fantasy, but a fantastic tale in a realistic setting. A young man whose wife has gone insane has joined with three friends to take LSD. He has a vision of climbing Mount Hood and meeting his wife up there. Finally they can communicate. He thinks his vision is due to the drug, but then he realizes that he has not taken it. His vision was due to his faithful love for his wife and not to any external cause.

"Nine Lives" is a science-fiction story that, as Le Guin remarks, uses an actual scientific discovery—cloning—but only as a point of departure. She is more interested in the psychological implications of cloning and its use as a metaphor than she is in the science involved. In this story, there is a strong contrast between Owen Pugh, a scrawny Welshman who had to be fitted out with a second lung and have his myopia corrected before he was sent out on planetary exploration, and the ten strong and beautiful young men and women who have been cloned from the genius John Chow. Pugh has a friend, Martin, who works with him in the exploratory mission base on the planet Libra, but the two of them cannot be closer than ordinary friends, while the tenclone is completely self-sufficient.

While the tenclone is mining for uranium on Libra, an earthquake traps and kills nine of them. The one survivor, Kaph, is totally at a loss for a while in dealing with Martin and Pugh, whom he thinks of as strangers, but at last he is able to break free from his utter dependence on the other members of his clone and accept Pugh's proffered friendship. The moral of this story is that it is hard to meet a stranger, but that real love and friendship come when the barrier between strangers is crossed.

The next story, **"Things,"** is a psychomyth. It takes place in some unknown land by the sea. In this land, people feel the end is near, and they are killing animals and destroying things in preparation for that end. The hero of the story, who is a brickmaker, has no wish to destroy his bricks and would like to leave for the islands across the sea, but he has no boat to take him there. With the help of a widow who has befriended him, he makes a causeway into the sea with his bricks. His neighbors leave him alone because they think he is just dumping the bricks into the sea. Then he and the widow, with her child, walk out along the causeway, and a boat comes to rescue them. But they have to take one last step off the causeway to reach the boat. In her note, Le Guin says that there is always that last step to be made, past the things we possess or are possessed by, past the things we build with, whether bricks or words.

"A Trip to the Head" is a psychomyth about a forest where there are no names. Two people are standing at its edge, and a fawn is walking into it, losing its name as it goes. For anyone who knows Lewis Carroll, this is a clear reference to *Through the Looking-Glass* (1872), in the third chapter of which Alice goes walking through a wood where there are no names, with her arm around a fawn. The fawn trusts her, as long as they are in the wood, because it does not know that it is a fawn and that Alice is a human child. But when they leave the wood, it bounds away. When one of the people in **"A Trip to the Head"** finally gives himself a name (which happens to be the wrong one), he calls himself Lewis D. Charles. This is an allusion to the pseudonym Lewis Carroll and to Lewis Carroll's real name, Charles Lutwidge Dodgson. But mixed up with the references to Lewis Carroll is a satire on Jean-Paul Sartre and his existentialist theory that you have to do in order to be. There is also an allusion to the first two lines of William Blake's poem, "The Tyger":

> Tyger! Tyger! burning bright
> In the forests of the night,

The whole story comes across as a commentary on the loss of the self in dreams, no matter how full of action they may be.

Literary allusions are also important in **"Vaster than Empires and More Slow."** This science-fiction story owes its title to Andrew Marvell's poem, "To His Coy Mistress." In her note, Le Guin quotes two lines from it:

> Our vegetable love would grow
> Vaster than empires and more slow.

This is the story of vegetable love—love for a vegetation that covers an entire planet, without animals or other living beings. The man who finds that love is called Osden, and he has been sent on a mission of exploration with the title of Sensor and the task of entering into empathetic contact with sentient beings on any planet his spaceship may come to. (He is an empath, not a telepath, for at this stage in the Hainish cycle news has only just come of the discovery of telepathy on Rocannon's World.)

Like Kaph in **"Nine Lives,"** Osden finds it very difficult to reach out, in love or friendship, to another human being. But, in Osden's case, it is not because he is already living in total contact with other selves. Osden is completely alone, because his gift of empathy with all living things makes him feel what other people feel when they meet him. Because what they feel is the instinctive revulsion and fear with which we meet a stranger and which, for most people, is covered over by good manners, Osden reacts to everyone he meets with aggressive rudeness. And it does not help very much that the other members of his crew are of unsound mind. Osden hates them all, and they hate him.

There is only one person Osden has ever loved, and that is Dr. Hammergeld, who cured him, as a child, of the autism into which he had retreated to protect himself from the consequences of his empathy. But by the time the spaceship has reached its first stopping point, a world far beyond the ken of the Hainish, Dr. Hammergeld has been left two hundred and fifty years behind, and there is no one for Osden to return to.

When Osden discovers that the vegetation on this world is sentient and that the forest-mind is afraid of the newcomers, he responds to its fear with fear. But then he realizes that the forest-mind can be loved, and that it forms

the only Other he can love. So he chooses to stay behind, because his love has made him whole.

> **As Le Guin says, physical action has to reflect psychic action [in her fiction] or she gets bored.**
>
> —*Barbara J. Bucknall*

Toward the end of this story, Osden says that on this planet he feels "one big green thought." This is an allusion to another poem by Andrew Marvell, "The Garden." In "The Garden," Marvell speaks of "a green thought in a green shade." He also tells of the love he feels for the garden:

> No white or red was ever seen
> So amorous as this lovely green.

Toward the end of the poem, Marvell speaks of his joy at being alone in the garden:

> Two paradises 'twere in one
> To live in Paradise alone.

Osden has opted to live in Paradise alone and is perfectly happy. This inner adventure is what gives interest and meaning to the outer adventure of the exploration of a planet. As Le Guin says, physical action has to reflect psychic action or she gets bored.

"The Stars Below" tells the story of Guennar, an astronomer whose observatory and instruments have been burned by order of the church. He escapes the burning and is taken by a friend to a silver mine, where he can hide. The mine is almost entirely worked out, and only a few old miners still work there. They befriend Guennar, who longs for the stars and looks for them underground with a kind of makeshift telescope. He actually finds what he calls a constellation under the rock, and leaves a mark there for the miners, while he disappears into the depths of the mine. The miners dig by his mark, and find a new lode of silver.

Here, as in **"The Masters,"** Le Guin is writing about science as an idea to be cherished, in spite of opposition from authorities. But she says in her note that she was also thinking of science as a synonym for art, and that she was attempting to show what happens to the creative mind when it is driven underground. Then she quotes a passage from Carl Gustav Jung's *On the Nature of the Psyche*, which compares the stars in the heavens and nuggets of gold in the earth to the introspective intuitions that surround ego-consciousness like little luminosities. From this she concludes that perhaps her story is about a mind turning inward to itself.

"The Field of Vision" expresses an atheist's impatience with religion. For an atheist, Le Guin has spent an inordinate amount of time inventing religions and religious modes of feeling and thinking, but here she shows how annoyed she gets when religion is forced on those who have no interest in it. She makes her point in terms of a science-fiction story. A spaceship returns from the planet Psyche with three astronauts aboard, one dead, one functionally deaf and one functionally blind. It turns out that the blind one, Hughes, is blind because he sees God all the time, and the deaf one, Temski, is deaf because he hears God all the time. On Psyche, they had entered a room constructed to teach religion and were converted in spite of themselves. Temski is perfectly happy listening to God, but Hughes resents having to see God, and would sooner see the world and people. He ends up committing suicide. The story is framed by two quotations from "The World," a poem by Henry Vaughan that expresses the belief that the vision of God is reserved for the elect.

For an atheist, Le Guin has spent an inordinate amount of time inventing religions and religious modes of feeling and thinking, but [in "Field of Vision"] she shows how annoyed she gets when religion is forced on those who have no interest in it.

—*Barbara J. Bucknall*

"**Direction of the Road**" is a fantasy about a tree beside a road, told from the point of view of the tree. Le Guin supposes that the tree is fully conscious of the way it appears to people moving along the road. In fact, the tree actually works at looming over an approaching person and dwindling behind a departing person. In a tone that is at once sad and comic, the tree describes how much more difficult life has become now that the road is full of cars and he has to loom and dwindle continually at high speeds. But what offends him most is that a motorist has died by crashing into his trunk, obliging him to take on the aspect of eternity. This story is a protest against human carelessness of life and an expression of affection for a tree—a particular tree that Ursula K. Le Guin identifies in her note.

"**The Ones Who Walk Away from Omelas**," which won a Hugo Award, has the subtitle, "Variations on a Theme by William James." In her note, Le Guin explains that the central theme of the psychomyth comes from a passage in William James's "The Moral Philosopher and the Moral Life." In this work, he says that one could not accept a happiness shared with millions if the condition of that happiness were the suffering of one lonely soul. "**The Ones Who Walk Away from Omelas**" describes a town whose inhabitants are all perfectly happy, but know that their happiness depends on the suffering of a feeble-minded child, locked up alone in a small, dark room. Most of them stay and enjoy their happiness, but some people walk away from Omelas—where to, it is not known.

"**The Day before the Revolution**" won a Nebula Award.

Le Guin says it is about one of the ones who walked away from Omelas. It describes the last day in the life of Odo, and is dedicated to the memory of Paul Goodman. It is the day before the General Strike, the start of the Odonian uprising on Urras. But Odo will not live to see the revolution for which she has worked all her life, because she will have her "private stroke" before the General Strike. The story is told with deep sympathy for the plight of an old woman, and may be taken as a blow against prejudice toward the aged, about which Le Guin had already had a few words to say in *The Word for World Is Forest,* as well as a tribute to those who refuse to rest while there is still suffering in the world.

So ends *The Wind's Twelve Quarters,* moving from tender, romantic stories to what Le Guin calls "something harder, stronger and more complex." It also shows a movement from private concerns to public ones, which parallels the development in her novels from *Rocannon's World* to *The Dispossessed.* And it maintains the Taoist theme by using the yin-yang symbol as a logo throughout. But now we have to turn to some of her most recent works. (pp. 133-41)

> *Barbara J. Bucknall, in her* Ursula K. Le Guin, *Frederick Ungar Publishing Co., 1981, 175 p.*

Le Guin on the origin of *Orsinian Tales*:

I was in college when I started the pieces that eventually became the *Orsinian Tales.* I was trying to write fiction rather than poetry, which is what I was mainly doing up to that point, and I was stuck in that old formula that everyone always tells you—to write about what you know, what you've experienced. This is a terrible thing to tell an 18-year-old. What does an 18-year-old know? I remember thinking finally, "To hell with it, I'll just make up a country." And since most of what I knew came out of books at that point—I'd read a lot more than I'd done—I made up a place that was like the places in books I liked to read. But as soon as I began work in Orsinia, I realized I didn't have to imitate Tolstoy. I had created a place I could write about in my own terms; I could make up just enough of the rules to free my imagination and my observations. This was a big breakthrough for me—to say, "All right, I don't give a shit whether I get published or not; I'm not going to write for anybody but myself; I'm going to make these stories good by standards I set for myself." It was a step out of the trap of feeling that I had to get published right away. It was a step inwards that finally led me out.

Ursula K. Le Guin, in an interview with Larry McCaffery and Sinda Gregory, The Missouri Review, *1984. The interview was conducted in 1982.*

Theodore Sturgeon (essay date 1982)

[*An American author of science fiction, Sturgeon is one of the first writers in the genre to imbue his works with emotional and psychological depth. His novel* More Than Human (*1953) is regarded a science fiction clas-*

sic, and the works Venus Plus X *(1960) and* Some of
Your Blood *(1961) are well known, but Sturgeon is primarily remembered as a writer of short fiction and received both the Nebula and Hugo Awards for the short
story "Slow Sculpture." In the following essay, he remarks that Le Guin successfully writes on various scales
about diverse subjects in her short story collection* The
Compass Rose.]

Ursula K. LeGuin's background—backgrounds—
includes anthropology, sociology, poetry, ethology, and
the techniques of writing. These are biographical facts, but
they all become evident in reading through her remarkable [collection **The Compass Rose**].

The author of the prestigious *The Left Hand of Darkness,*
and a National Book Award winner, here manifests this
wide spectrum of knowledge and understanding, and, in
addition, that truly rare ability to have achieved not only
a style, but styles. LeGuin composes, conducts and can
play all of the instruments in her literary orchestra.

One finds oneself thinking in metaphors here: The rose,
the compass rose of the title, has, according to the preface,
not four points but six. Add zenith and nadir; add everywhere, everything, add alternative worlds and universes
not only of place and scene, but of consciousness.

The rose as flower appears as an exquisite image in the
diary of a psychiatric technician; working with near-
future technology within a possible near-future dictatorship, discovering the value of one patient's strength and
freedom while loyally doing her job, ensuring his destruction. The rose appears as coda in a quote from Rilke in the
preface.

Read as entertainments, these 20 narratives, so very different, necessarily vary on a scale of excellence. **"Intracom,"**
for example, might be regarded as a forced whimsy; **"The
Wife's Story,"** one of those compositional exercises in
which the assignment is to rewrite an existing anecdote
making all the blacks white and the whites black. But to
avoid the presence of metaphor even here is to demonstrate a most improbable degree of determination. For example, a similar "exercise," **"Mazes,"** involves a captive
extraterrestrial and a scientist, each desperately anxious
to find a means of communication, each incapable of understanding that the sounds made by one and the movements made by the other are language. Herein is that
"shock of recognition" that, at base, is the quality that
makes good fiction good. How readily we understand the
inability of each of these to understand one another. As
for thee and me, friend. . . .

Many years ago, the late John W. Campbell devised a category that is not fiction, nor nonfiction, but the "non-fact
article." LeGuin provides two perfect specimens of these
carefully reasoned tongue-in-cheek exuberances. **"The
Author of the Acacia Seeds,"** written by a therolinguist,
goes from the translation of a "document" 'written' by an
ant by arranging acacia seeds to the "literature" of dol-
phins, penguins, zucchini, lichens and the Earth itself.

**"Some Approaches to the Problem of the Shortage of
Time"** posits that there exists a hole, possibly in the vicini-

ty of the Andromeda Nebula, through which, for millions
of years, time has been escaping.

All of the facets of LeGuin's background are brought together in the provocative **"The Pathways of Desire."** A
scientific expedition, two men and a woman, are doing a
cultural observation of happy "primitives" on an
Edenesque planet. This will seem at first an exceedingly
familiar situation, but as the LeGuin touch, the LeGuin
grip, is slowly brought to bear on it, the plot is formed into
sharply unexpected shapes and directions, leaving the
reader in an immeasurable meta-universe, braided of
space time, philosophy and consciousness.

Can one find a common denominator in the work and
thought of Ursula K. LeGuin? Probably not; but there are
some notes in her orchestrations that come out repeatedly
and with power. A cautionary fear of the development of
democracy into dictatorship. Celebrations of courage, endurance, risk. Language, not only loved and shaped, but
investigated in all its aspects; call that, perhaps, communication. But above all, in almost un-earthly terms Ursula
LeGuin examines, attacks, unbuttons, takes down and exposes our notions of reality.

> *Theodore Sturgeon, "On Earth, as It Is on
> More Peculiar Planets," in* Los Angeles Times
> Book Review, *September 5, 1982, p. 2.*

Howard Waldrop   (essay date 1983)

[*Waldrop is an American critic and author of science
fiction, primarily short stories. In the following excerpt,
he finds Le Guin's novella* The Eye of the Heron *trite.*]

[**The Eye of the Heron** is] not one of Le Guin's best. There
are some wonderful patches of description, a few good
characterizations, and Le Guin reminds you what it's like
to live in a society where everyone (but a select few) has
to walk everywhere.

The setting (especially the background, how the people
got there) doesn't make much sense. Essentially, her space
colony of Victoria was settled by two groups: a) prisoners,
who have turned into the Bosses and b) pacifists, who have
turned into peasants. The straw-man Boss society is set up
to fail, the peasant society to undergo a lot of grief in the
name of noncooperative, nonviolent protest. (It would
have been much more logical for the governments of Earth
that didn't want either the criminals or pacifists to set
them down in Antarctica, or the middle of a desert, or
anywhere in the solar system. This is a prison planet,
which is fine if you've got a galaxy-spanning civilization,
but all these people came from *Earth,* on *one-way* rockets.
This is real pulp thinking, something Le Guin has never
done before.) I hate to give it the oldest of genre criticism,
but here it is: except for a few alien bugs and some giant
rabbit-like beasts, there's no reason this couldn't have
taken place somewhere on Earth, just post-gunpowder,
perhaps during the Thirty Years' War.

The main character, Luz, is a Boss' daughter. **The Eye of
the Heron** is the old science fiction standby, the tale of
conversion-to-the-rebels, with an overlain consciousness-
raising, and some few hard truths about what it takes to

be a real pacifist and how far short people always fall of the ideal.

If you're a Le Guin collector, you'll get this anyway. If not, my advice is to wait for the next novel or story collection.

Howard Waldrop, "Lem, Le Guin and Spinrad: Other Worlds, Other Times," in Book World—The Washington Post, *February 27, 1983, p. 10.*

Gerald Jonas   (essay date 1983)

[*Jonas is an American author and a critic for the* New York Times Book Review. *In the following excerpt, Jonas asserts that* The Eye of the Heron "*has neither the rigor of a philosophical essay nor the immediacy of strong fiction.*"]

As a novelist of ideas, Ursula K. Le Guin has no peer in science fiction and few rivals outside the genre. In *The Left Hand of Darkness* (1969), she explored the question, what would human society be like if gender distinctions were erased? In *The Dispossessed* (1974)—which she classed as an "ambiguous utopia"—she contrasted a social system based on anarchistic communal principles with an acquisitive, competitive society. While Mrs. Le Guin's sympathies clearly lay with the anarchists, she scrupulously considered the weaker points in their system, especially the lack of privacy and a certain leveling of human passions. One problem she did not confront directly was how such an "undisciplined" society could resist a would-be conqueror. In *The Eye of the Hero*—first published in 1978 as part of a collection entitled "Millennial Women"—Mrs. Le Guin draws the lines even more clearly, by positing a conflict between two groups of human colonists, one pacifists and the other bullies, who have been dumped side by side on the same planet.

The scale is pleasingly human, and Mrs. Le Guin exercises considerable art in setting the stage. But the telling is marred by a didacticism that was masked in the earlier novels by richly detailed accounts of character and background. Precisely because the scale is so small and the style so economical in *The Eye of the Heron,* the bare bones of the argument keep poking through. In the end the drama is reduced to an either-or proposition: When bullies attack, can a dedicated, well-trained band of pacifists survive with their principles and lives intact? It's a good question, and Mrs. Le Guin's answer is far from simplistic. But because it has neither the rigor of a philosophical essay nor the immediacy of strong fiction, *The Eye of the Heron* ultimately fails to engage the reader on either level. (pp. 15, 37)

Gerald Jonas, "Inside Elsewhere," in The New York Times Book Review, *May 22, 1983, pp. 15, 37-8.*

Charlotte Spivack   (essay date 1984)

[*Spivack is an American educator and author whose works include several studies related to Renaissance*

drama, as well as Ursula K. Le Guin. *In the following excerpt from that work, she discusses several short stories by Le Guin as examples of the psychological orientation of her fiction.*]

Not all of Le Guin's short fiction has been collected in anthologies. Several of her stories are available only in the periodicals in which they were originally published. Many of these stories are in the category of the thought-experiment which the author referred to in her introduction to *The Left Hand of Darkness.*

An almost classic example is **"Schrödinger's Cat,"** a thought-experiment about a thought-experiment. Based on physicist Edwin Schrödinger's experiments with quantum theory, it involves putting a cat into a box containing a loaded gun. When the box lid closes, it activates an emitter designed to emit one photon which has a fifty-fifty chance of striking a mirror, thereby activating the trigger. If the photon strikes the mirror, the gun will shoot the cat; if the photon is deflected, the gun will not shoot the cat. The observer must open the box to find out what happened. Before the emission of the photon, the system of the universe on the quantum level seems quite clear, but after the emission of the unpredictable photon, the system depends on an unknowable combination of two waves. Thus no one can predict the outcome. As one character in the story puts it, "God plays dice with the world!" The only certainty possible in the universe is what the observer creates subjectively for himself.

With considerable humor and ingenuity, Le Guin combines the cat-in-the-box story with a number of other elements, including the theory of entropy. At the time of the story, the world is both heating up and speeding up. The narrator lists graphic details of the unbearable heat. Stove burners are turned on in a vain attempt to cool them off, and touch is virtually impossible: "a kiss was like a branding iron." Speed is evidenced in the movement of the worms like subway trains through "the writhing roots of roses." The narrator wants to report these events although nothing can possibly matter any more. He mocks his own "Ethica laboris puritanica, or Adam's disease," which is incurable except by "total decephalization."

Much of the humor derives from the style. Metaphorical language is literalized. While most things are burning to the touch, the cat's fur remains cool: "a real cool cat." The expostulation of the young mailman who suddenly appears in the narrative—"Yah!," "Wow"—leads the narrator to nickname him Rover and ever after refer to him in canine terms. A young woman characterized as "pretty well gone to pieces" supports her head in the crook of her right knee and hops on the toes of her right foot, leaving her left leg, arms, and trunk lying in a heap.

The theme of entropic process is deftly interwoven with the box experiment. At the end, the narrator and the mailman breathlessly open the box only to find that there is no cat in it at all. Just as they lift the lid of the box, the roof of the house lifts off. An end-of-the-world story with a difference, **"Schrödinger's Cat"** is a delightful tour-de-force.

A different kind of thought-experiment is recounted in the story with the unusual title, **"The Author of the Acacia**

Seeds and Other Extracts from the *Journal of the Association of Therolinguistics.*" The authors of the three journal extracts assume the existence of both art and language among the animal and plant species. The first extract introduces a tentative translation and interpretation of a manuscript found in an ant hill. The message is written in "touchgland exudation" on acacia seeds artfully laid in rows at the end of a tunnel leading off a deep level colony. The second extract announces an expedition to investigate the language of the Emperor Penguin. A research specialist, already an expert on Dolphin, has received a UNESCO grant for the purpose. The third and final extract, written by the president of the Therolinguistic Association, considers the nature of art and language. Challenging the theory that art, like language, must communicate, this writer postulates that plants, too, have art. He wishes to rally support for further study of "non-communicative, vegetative art" and in a visionary glimpse of the future foresees the geolinguist not only understanding the delicate lyrics of the lichen but even discovering the "atemporal, cold, volcanic poetry of the rocks."

The three journal extracts are written in precise language, with no hint of parody or exaggeration. The sympathetic descriptive adjectives applied to the language of insects and birds reveal real sensitivity, and the mystical speculation that plant poetry may use "the meter of eternity" suggests a oneness with nature that the empath Osden would admire.

"Selection" might be a more conventional "hardcore" SF story, were it not for its sly, wry ending. The narrative takes place in a future galactic bubble colony, where all marriages are arranged by a highly sophisticated sociometric computer. Operated by a trained specialist in sociometrics, the computer takes into account everything from DNA patterns to enzymes in order to assure both optimum-offspring and maximum contentment. The details are carefully supplied by the author, who concentrates on one recalcitrant couple opposed to the efficient system. Joan vehemently objects to marrying Harry, whom she loathes. In the given situation, however, she has no choice but compliance, and the marriage takes place in spite of her protestations. One day when the newlyweds are out skiing, Harry is seriously injured in an accident, and the emergency awakens a new sentiment in Joan. The marriage becomes a success after all, and a year later Joan proudly shows her infant son to the sociometrist who arranged the match. In the last paragraph of the story, the confident sociometrist returns to his computer cards, and the reader learns the final stage of his scientific spouse selection process. By-passing the complex computer, he drops the namecards of fifty young men into his hat and draws.

The tight narrative is well-sustained, and the final twist comes as a complete surprise. A balance between the ultraefficient, computerized system and the vagaries of human nature adds a dimension of meaning, making the story much more than a merely gimmicky SF yarn.

"The Diary of the Rose" has a biographical as well as literary interest for the Le Guin reader. After the story had been nominated for the annual Nebula award, Le Guin publicly withdrew it from further consideration in protest against an action taken by the Science Fiction Writers of America. That organization, of which she had been a member for several years, had revoked an honorary membership it had bestowed on the Polish writer Stanislas Lem because of some unfavorable remarks he had published about American science fiction. Le Guin resented this dishonoring of a fellow writer.

The story offers a compelling, somewhat chilling SF narrative with a psychological twist. It is a first person account in the form of a diary written by a woman doctor, Rosa Sobel, who deals with mental patients. She specializes in the psychoscope, a highly sophisticated machine that projects thoughts on to a screen in pictures. The psychoscopic projection of images helps her to understand what is going on in the disturbed minds of her patients. The educational and therapeutic purpose of the diary is to record all of her spontaneous thoughts while dealing with her patients, both for the benefit of her own development and for the future training of others. As a result the style is clinical, straight-forward, impersonal, with an attentive care to literal details and a meticulous avoidance of emotional response. The enterprise is by definition ironic, in that the writer is so highly trained professionally as to be almost incapable of the sort of spontaneity called for in a diary.

The immediate subjects of Dr. Sobel's diary are her two new patients, a depressed, middle-aged woman and a young engineer referred to the hospital after an outbreak of violent behavior. The woman proves easy to treat with conventional hormone therapy. Essentially a dull person, she even has dull dreams. The man, however, is quite different. It is not clear at first why he has been hospitalized because he denies having committed any violent acts. He claims instead that one night he was awakened, interrogated, beaten and drugged, after which he was arrested. He is cooperative with Dr. Sobel, whom he respects, but although he is willing to work with her and the psychoscope he confesses his horror of being subjected to the so-called ECT, an electric shock treatment. She assures him of her preference for psychoscopy as an "integrative rather than a destructive instrument." But he learns through her that a once renowned intellectual, Dr. Arca, has been subjected to the ECT and as a result has lost all memory and indeed all identity. It is not until she reports these confidential details to him that she herself becomes fully aware of the outrage that has actually occurred.

The relationship between doctor and patient is sensitively portrayed. As she ostensibly learns about him by watching his mental images on the screen of the psychoscope, she also learns about herself. Her training has made her too impersonal, even mechanical, in handling psychological problems, but the full humanity of this young engineer comes through to her as a profoundly new experience. At one point when she is watching the images he is producing, she sees on the screen a strikingly beautiful rose. "The shadows of one petal on another, the velvety damp texture of the petals, the pink color full of sunlight, the yellow central crown" are more like a living, growing flower than a "mentifact." She is moved by its vivid quality but does not yet connect it with her own name. Shortly after, when she sees some of the mental images of his childhood, she again feels deeply touched and realizes that she is not being as coldly analytical as she is supposed to be. "I can't say what it is, I feel honored to have shared in the childhood he remembered for me."

The developing relationship also signals a growing irony, for it is clear that her study of him through his mental images projected on the psychoscope produces more of an effect on her than on him. By opening up his inner thoughts and memories and sharing them with her, he is in effect contributing to her own personal growth. Whereas her diary was initiated as a clinical account to be used for professional training, it becomes more and more personal until she realizes that she will not be able to show it to her superior. At the point when she realizes that her patient has what she calls a "political psychosis," that is, he is a liberal in an authoritarian state that will not allow liberals, she realizes that she has no one to turn to for advice. She continues the diary but hides the loose pages which she feels are now potentially dangerous.

At this point she is, of course, a different person from the blindly obedient, well-trained psychoscope operator who started her new diary with a touch of pride in her new patients. She has worked inside a sane, integrated mind for several hours a day for six weeks, whereas in the past she had worked only with the mentally disturbed. She has discovered that the alienation of the political liberal is not the product of his mind but of the repressive society. With growing horror she knows that he will indeed be given the ECT treatment and follow the unfortunate Dr. Arca into oblivion. But there is nothing she can do.

At the end of the story, she greets the young man on the morning after the ECT. He does not recognize her. He has lost his memory and his identity, but he has conferred identity on her. "I am Rosa. I am the rose. The rose, I am the rose. The rose with no flower, the rose all thorns, the mind he made, the hand he touched, the winter rose."

"The Diary of the Rose" is typical of Le Guin's psychologically oriented science fiction. The futuristic prospect, the technological materials, and the laboratory setting are stock features of science fiction, but what makes the story a success is the characterization. Told from Rosa's point of view, the narrative leads the reader from her state of innocence to her growing awareness of the horrors taking place in her world. In her sessions with her patient, the reader becomes familiar with both the inner workings of his rich, well-integrated personality and of her as yet undeveloped potential for sympathy, understanding, and love. The ending is shocking, not only for the actual event but also for the reversal of human identity that has taken place. The mind that has been destroyed has created a new one in its place.

Although it is idle to speculate as to whether this story would have won the Nebula, it clearly has the power and originality that established it as a worthy candidate. Perhaps because it did not win, however, it has not been as frequently collected as some of Le Guin's other stories, but it is well worth the reading.

Le Guin's story **"The Eye Altering,"** published in the anthology *The Altered Eye,* is a product of a science-fiction writing workshop. The workshop itself was her own idea. With her experience as writer-in-residence at similar American events, she suggested this transglobal workshop to the 33rd annual World Science Fiction Convention held in Melbourne, Australia, in 1975. All of the twenty selected participants wrote their own stories and criticized the others, with the result that the initial draft in each case benefited—or suffered—from nineteen detailed critiques.

Le Guin's own contribution to this workshop, **"The Eye Altering,"** was written in two differing versions. The original story is printed along with the several separate commentaries of fellow workshoppers. Le Guin's response to their critiques is also included, and the somewhat revised story appears at the end of the volume. Le Guin acted on some of the suggested revisions but rejected others, and the second version is tighter in language and structure than the first.

"The Eye Altering" takes place on the planet New Zion, settled by Jewish refugees from Earth. Life is difficult for the settlers both psychologically because of the drab, gray sky and physically because of the allergic reactions that make adaptation dependent on continual dosages of metabolizing pills. Several settlers are sickly, including the central figure, Genya, who was born on the planet twenty-four years ago. The older settlers maintain one Living Room as a nostalgic retreat. In this room artificial lighting simulates Earth sunlight in piquant contrast to the depressing native atmosphere. On the walls are pictures of Earth, many of them enlarged photographs. The delicate youth Genya, who is talented artistically, paints a picture of Earth which is startling in its authenticity. Never having seen Earth, he has achieved the Earthlike scene while looking at the dismal prospect of New Zion. What the painting reveals is that Genya is actually better adapted to the new planet than are the older settlers. Taking "meta" pills all of his life has been, in fact, a serious mistake, for his eye is native to the natural beauty of the planet. For him it is not ugly and alien, and his supposedly intense allergic reactions are, in fact, produced by the pills. His is the "altered eye."

The two slightly dissimilar versions of the story offer a useful insight into the writing process. As Le Guin explains in her introductory comments, her published stories usually have undergone two thorough revisions. In this case the story has profited from the advice of several outside readers. Noting minor changes in wording is a valuable lesson in the art of literary revision. One reader objected to "warty" modifying "orange," but Le Guin retained the image as a valid simile. On the other hand, she removed the word "non-adaptive" used twice on the last page in favor of the less pseudo-technical phrase "fitting a pattern."

Either version of the story is entertaining reading, but would-be writers will want to read both. (pp. 143-49)

Charlotte Spivack, in her Ursula K. Le Guin, *Twayne Publishers, 1984, 182 p.*

Shoshana Knapp   (essay date 1985)

[*In the following essay, Knapp asserts that Le Guin's short story "The Ones Who Walk away from Omelas" compellingly and artistically presents the theme of absolute moral accountability.*]

Ursula K. Le Guin firmly asserts that, at the time she was writing **"The Ones Who Walk Away from Omelas,"** she had forgotten Dostoevsky and remembered only William James. "The fact is, I haven't been able to re-read Dostoevsky, much as I loved him, since I was twenty-five, and I'd simply forgotten he used the idea. But when I met it in James's 'The Moral Philosopher and the Moral Life,' it was with a shock of recognition." We are, however, entitled to be sceptical, and, as D. H. Lawrence suggests, to trust the tale instead of the teller. Lawrence's advice, in fact, has a special relevance to Le Guin's fable, a tale that involves and implicates the reader in the telling, and one in which the reader and narrator, just as surely as the characters in the story, are on trial as moral agents.

In presenting a country where universal joy—perfect, intelligent, and mature—depends on the confinement and deprivation of one innocent child, Le Guin is indicting her reader and her own narrator, who work together to construct the hideous moral universe of Omelas. Although this universe has parallels in the writings of both William James (whom Le Guin remembers) and Dostoevsky (whom she thinks she has forgotten), Le Guin goes beyond their formulations and beyond the moral-political lesson, usually assigned to her story, that "no society should rest on the misery of the unfortunate" [X. J. Kennedy, Instructor's Manual to Accompany *An Introduction to Fiction,* second edition, 1979]. Her actual subject is the proper morality of art itself. A genuinely moral artist, Le Guin implies, would articulate a coherent universe in which connections and loyalties are possible, the sort of place envisaged by Le Guin in *The Dispossessed* as "a landscape inhabitable by human beings." Omelas does not qualify, for reasons Dostoevsky, at least, would have understood.

William James's "certain lost soul," of course, was clearly useful to Le Guin as a starting point. There are several similarities. In "The Moral Philosopher and the Moral Life," James writes (and Le Guin quotes):

> Or if the hypothesis were offered us of a world in which Messrs. Fourier's and Bellamy's and Morris's utopias should all be outdone, and millions kept permanently happy on the one simple condition that a certain lost soul on the far-off edge of things should lead a life of lonely torture, what except a specific and independent sort of emotion can it be which would make us immediately feel, even though an impulse arose within us to clutch at the happiness so offered, how hideous a thing would be its enjoyment when deliberately accepted as the fruit of such a bargain?

The basic situation, for Le Guin and for James, is the promise of mass bliss in exchange for a unique torment.

In both cases, furthermore, people are held accountable for their response to the scapegoat only because they are able to formulate this response in full knowledge of the context. James says that our enjoyment of this happiness would be hideous because the bargain would be "deliberately accepted." Similarly, every child in Omelas is given the opportunity to see the scapegoat, at least once, and to understand why it has to suffer.

In both universes, finally, the decision to dissent seems to be based on something other than rational calculation. For James, the reason lies in "a specific and independent sort of emotion"; the narrator of Omelas can offer no rational explanation at all of the sudden, silent, solitary march of the ones who walk away.

The passage in James appealed to Le Guin immediately; she says she felt a "shock of recognition" when she first read it. Certainly she found his anti-utilitarian position congenial. Le Guin and James agree that the greatest happiness of the greatest number should not be used as a moral criterion. (We recall the exchange between Rocannon and Mogien in Le Guin's *Rocannon's World:* "One man's fate is not important." "If it is not, what is?") The philosophical background of the passage in James, however, seems at first to clash with the spirit of Le Guin's story.

James offers his hypothetical situation as an example of a moral instinct or intuition—as distinct from a maxim, a habit, or a calculation—"an innate preference of the more ideal attitude for its own pure sake. The nobler thing *tastes* better, and that is all that we can say." In Omelas, on the other hand, the nobler thing does not taste better; if it did, Omelas would be a ghost town. To reject the hideous bargain is, for James, the obvious and immediate thing to do; according to our narrator, however, to do so is "incredible." Le Guin's story, then, seems to refute the Jamesian assumption of an innate human decency; in Omelas, the mean and the vulgar are accepted as a necessary part of existence. The narrator would not understand William James, and vice versa.

By creating an unsympathetic, un-Jamesian narrator, who in turn creates an unsympathetic, un-Jamesian world, Le Guin makes the story much more than the political parable it at first appears to be. We are allowed, of course, to read the story according to the political interpretation; Le Guin herself encourages us to do so. Referring to James's essay in her introduction to her story, she writes: "The dilemma of the American conscience can hardly be better stated." The political interpretation is suggestive, but its value is limited, particularly when we attempt to make connections between the story and the contemporary world. Do Americans enjoy perfect happiness? Even if they did, how could their happiness depend absolutely on the suffering of a scapegoat? And how could their rescue of a scapegoat bring all joy to an end? These questions are rhetorical, of course; the essay by James is not reducible to the sort of dogma that could provide concrete political answers.

The story is similarly complex and irreducible, whatever the writer may say about it after the fact. As we look more closely at the craft of the story, at the details, the language, the point of view, and even the grammar, we shall see not only that Le Guin has, on some level, remembered Dostoevsky, but also that she has defined, by negative example, the nature of artistic responsibility.

As we read **"The Ones Who Walk Away from Omelas,"** we are lectured, seduced, and importuned by a narrator who wants to make us hear, feel, see, and, above all, believe. We are asked to experience the music, the colors, the movement of a festival, which is characterized by the mingling of the generations and the joint participation of the human, the animal (horses), and the vegetable (flowers, meadows). The descriptions are evocative rather than clinical because, in the long third paragraph, we are politely requested to complete them: "Perhaps it would be best if you imagined it as your own fancy bids, assuming it will rise to the occasion, for certainly I cannot suit you all." Reality itself, it seems, requires permanent quotation marks. The inhabitants of Omelas may have mechanical marvels, or they may have none. "As you like it." The narrator at first believes that there are no drugs, but later explains that this first idea was wrong and "puritanical." The reader is invited to share in giving shape to Omelas. "If an orgy would help, don't hesitate." Observe the imperative mood: "Let [the nudes] join the processions. Let tambourines be struck. . . ." We might be hearing an echo of the divine fiat, an echo full of the intoxicated intensity of unlimited creation.

Unlimited? Not entirely. Sometimes the narrator implies that this society has objective reality, that it is possible to have definite knowledge about it, even if this knowledge is not fully accessible to the narrator or to us. "I do not know the rules and laws of their society, but I suspect that they were singularly few." The description of the scapegoat contains both kinds of information, the factual and the optional. "It could be a boy or a girl" (optional). "It looks about six, but actually is nearly ten" (factual). "It is feeble-minded" (factual). "Perhaps it was born defective, or perhaps it has become imbecile through fear, malnutrition, and neglect" (optional). (Observe the pronoun "it," which makes the child seem less than human, and hence more available for objective inspection.) Sometimes knowledge about Omelas is based on general principles. "I think that there would be no cars or helicopters; this follows from the fact that the people of Omelas are happy people." As we read, though, we realize that even certain knowledge can be wrong; the people of Omelas "know that they, like the child, are not free." (The ones who freely walk away do not "know" that.) We are therefore entitled to treat as enigmatic a central statement of the narrator, called to our attention by unusual syntax: "One thing I know there is none of in Omelas is guilt." Maybe, maybe not. We do not, however, necessarily know everything that the narrator knows, although the narrator has tried most skillfully and persistently to implicate us in the creation of a have-it-your-way world.

Yet we ourselves are not entirely free. The narrator's invitation to us, of course, is fairly straightforward; we can take it or leave it. We can participate in the creation of Omelas, or we can walk away. The grammar of the story, however, traps us more subtly. The narrator begins with a description of the festival, in the past tense. As the description becomes more detailed and inventive, as the narrator adds detail and asks for our contributions, the mood becomes imperative and conditional. After the third paragraph, the story enters the present tense. We have become

stuck in the story, to be set free only when a few of the people of Omelas stride out of the land and the story, headed for a country that the narrator cannot describe and that, consequently, may not "exist"—a hint that description confers reality, and that Omelas exists only by our leave.

The evil in the story, then, begins with its creator, a figure who is absent from James's formulation. It is this emphasis that leads me to remember the Dostoevsky whom Le Guin has forgotten. There are other reminders, too. To begin with, Le Guin has replaced James's "certain lost soul," a being of indeterminate age, with the young child of Ivan Karamazov's conversation with his brother Alyosha [in *The Brothers Karamazov*] Le Guin also expands James's abstract "lonely torture" into a painfully concrete picture, similar to Ivan Karamazov's, of isolation, malnutrition, mental torment, and filth. Both artists, in fact, give us not only a philosophical formulation, but (raw) flesh and (clotted) blood. More importantly, both Le Guin and Dostoevsky provide a broader context for the situation James presents as a free-floating hypothesis. For Ivan, the central bargain, the payment for mass happiness with a child's tears amounts to an indictment of God, who has created a universe Ivan declines to inhabit:

> And if the sufferings of children go to swell the sum of sufferings which was necessary to pay for truth, then I protest that the truth is not worth such a price. . . . And so I hasten to give back my entrance ticket, and if I am an honest man I am bound to give it back as soon as possible. And that I am doing. It's not God that I don't accept, Alyosha, only I most respectfully return Him the ticket.

For James, the hideous bargain is a given, to be accepted or rejected. For Ivan, though, Someone is responsible for the existence of the bargain. There is Someone to Whom one can return one's ticket. When Ivan walks away from Omelas, he knows to Whom he should say goodbye.

At the end of the conversation, he refines the bargain and asks his brother, a deeply religious man, to render judgment on the Designer of the bargain and on the parties involved:

> " . . . Imagine that you are creating a fabric of human destiny with the object of making men happy . . . but that it was essential and inevitable to torture to death only one living creature . . . and to found that edifice on its unavenged tears, would you consent to be the architect on those conditions?" . . .
>
> "No, I wouldn't consent," said Alyosha softly.
>
> "And can you admit the idea that men for whom you are building it would agree to accept their happiness on the foundations of the unexpiated blood of a little victim? And accepting it would remain happy forever?"
>
> "No, I can't admit it. . . . "

The architect of Omelas, then, is supremely guilty, and so are the inhabitants—or so Ivan would say. Something he knows there is *much* of in Omelas is guilt, and the culprits are several: those who remain in the land of joy after their glimpse of the scapegoat, the narrator who is creating the world in the very process of describing it, and the readers who are drafted to be partners in creation.

How can creators be guilty? Because, in the world of Le Guin's fiction, creation, like all acts of freedom and wizardry, entails moral responsibility. In *The Tombs of Atuan,* a young woman learns an important lesson: "Freedom is a heavy load, a great and strange burden for the spirit to undertake. It is not easy. It is not a gift given, but a choice made, and the choice may be a hard one." To a large extent, Le Guin insists, the freedom of her own artistic creation lies in exploring her inner world: "[The character] exists, inside my head to be sure, but in his own right, with his own vitality. All I have to do is look at him. I don't plan him, compose him of bits and pieces, inventory him. I find him." (The reference to "bits and pieces" sounds like an echo of the unnatural creation of Frankenstein's monster.)

The use of the subconscious, however, does not absolve one from accountability. In **"Omelas,"** the world created is unfit for human habitation. The bargain on which it rests violates not only decency but logic. Why in hell or heaven should a child's suffering lead to anyone's happiness? The rationalization offered by the narrator—that the child makes the inhabitants aware of the "terrible justice of reality"—is a patent sophistry. To choose between torturing a child and destroying one's society (which includes other children) is a diabolical choice, not a human one.

Consider the crisis in *Sophie's Choice,* by William Styron: a member of the SS offers a prisoner the choice between two unacceptable (morally, psychologically) alternatives; a rejection of the choice offered, furthermore, amounts to the sum of the unacceptable alternatives. In a situation like this, evil is no longer banal. It becomes elegant. And in the creation of Omelas, an elegantly immoral, illogical universe, the mad artist replaces the Frankenstein, or the mad scientist, and becomes the new villain.

Let us hasten to distinguish between the narrator of the story and its author. Le Guin has written in persona on a number of occasions; in **"Schrödinger's Cat," "SQ," "The First Report of the Shipwrecked Foreigner to the Kadanh of Derb,"** *Very Far Away from Anywhere Else,* and large chunks of *The Left Hand of Darkness,* the first-person narrator is not speaking directly for the writer herself. If she identifies with anyone in our story, it is with the ones who walk away. (In her introduction to **"The Day before the Revolution,"** she tells us that Odo, her heroine, was one of the ones who walked away.) For that reason, the story comes to an end when they are introduced. Unable to tolerate the immoral universe created by the narrator, they walk straight out of the story.

Why don't they stay and fight? Why don't they play Samson and bring down their world in ruins around them? Because, after all, we need not stop the world when we have merely decided to get off. In *The Farthest Shores,* when the wizard Ged makes his escape, he frees his fellow slaves, but does not harm his enemies. He does not wish to be forced to act, he tells Arren. The apparently noble act may be a trap. His advice to a king (or any man), he says, would

be: "My lord, do nothing because it is righteous or praiseworthy or noble to do so . . . do only that which you must do and which you cannot do in any other way." To challenge Omelas might be righteous, but it would also require the challengers to acknowledge Omelas, thereby granting it a kind of sanction. In choosing exile instead, they pursue the limits of dissent.

The story itself can be seen as a similar act of dissent, a refusal to write stories that are rotten at the core. Le Guin says that she did not sit down to write a story about James's lost soul; to base a story on a diabolical premise would be wizardry at its most deadly. The wizard in question would be as guilty as the God condemned by Ivan Karamazov. Le Guin liberates her characters from the evil narrator by allowing them a different choice: either to function within the trap of an immoral fictional universe, or to vote (with their feet, not their fists) against it. And we, as readers, have the same choice, when we read this story and any other speculative fiction that allows us to build a brave new world.

When Margaret Fuller said "I accept the universe," Emerson tartly responded: "She'd better!" His retort is an oversimplification of an interesting problem. In **"The Ones Who Walk Away from Omelas,"** Le Guin makes the decision to embrace or decline the universe an intensely dramatic event. But beyond this fundamental choice, she also invokes the moral accountability of the creator of the fictional universe, a creator who also implicates us. (pp. 75-80)

Shoshana Knapp, "The Morality of Creation: Dostoevsky and William James in Le Guin's 'Omelas'," in The Journal of Narrative Technique, *Vol. 15, No. 1, Winter, 1985, pp. 75-81.*

Le Guin on the relationship between science and her fiction:

"The Masters" was my first published genuine authentic real virgin-wool science fiction story, by which I mean a story in which or to which the existence and the accomplishments of science are, in some way, essential. At least that is what I mean by science fiction on Mondays. On Tuesdays sometimes I mean something else.

Some science-fiction writers detest science, its spirit, method, and works; others like it. Some are anti-technology, others are technology-worshippers. I seem to be rather bored by complex technology, but fascinated by biology, psychology, and the speculative ends of astronomy and physics, insofar as I can follow them. The figure of the scientist is a quite common one in my stories, and most often a rather lonely one, isolated, an adventurer, out on the edge of things.

Ursula K. Le Guin, in her introduction to "The Masters" in The Wind's Twelve Quarters, *1975.*

Carol P. Hovanec   (essay date 1989)

[*In the following essay, Hovanec argues that the main characters in Le Guin's novella* The Word for World Is Forest *evince the prevailing American attitudes toward the environment.*]

In a chapter entitled "Nature: Dynamism and Change" in Lois and Stephen Rose's study *The Shattered Ring: Science Fiction and the Quest for Meaning,* the authors point out that "space travel in science fiction provides the most obvious avenue to an expanded perception of nature, both in terms of distance and of the visions of very different natural environments" because it "plays on the theme of transferability of energy and matter, the possibilities of other dimensions, other space-time complexes." However, these critics admit that they will not attempt to resolve what they call the "riddle of nature" whether the term means matter, energy, space—is subjective or objective, friend or enemy. Indeed, science fiction, which Ursula Le Guin calls [in her *Language of the Night*] "the mythology of the modern world," does not attempt to define nature as much as to warn of ecological catastrophe, often using other planets in other galaxies to offer theoretical case studies of what might happen in the future if humanity continues to exploit the environment. This is certainly one of Le Guin's purposes in a brief, yet stunning, work which she wrote in 1972, *The Word for World Is Forest;* for she says in the introduction:

> It was becoming clear that the ethic which approved of the defoliation of forests and grainlands and the murder of non-combatants in the name of "peace" was only a corollary of the ethic which permits the despoliation of natural resources for private profit or the GNP and the murder of the creatures of the earth in the name of "man." The victory of the ethic of exploitation, in all societies, seemed as inevitable as it was disastrous. It was from such pressures, internalized, that this story resulted.

She also states that this work was an outlet for her feelings about the American involvement in Vietnam and that it "must stand or fall on whatever elements it preserved of the yearning that underlies all specific outrage and protest, whatever tentative outreaching it made, amidst anger and despair, toward justice, or wit, or grace, or liberty." Not only is the novel political, but Le Guin admits elsewhere that it is also Taoist and implies it may be Jungian. Its particular distinction, however, lies in the complex vision of nature which appears; for with great succinctness and consistency, this author presents a future world in which the collective consciousness of the protagonists and antagonists contains the major American attitudes towards the environment, from the early explorers to the present. Le Guin's ability to integrate these philosophies into a swiftly-moving narrative with a shifting point of view, a completely detailed setting, and a pervasive theme of illusion versus reality is a major achievement.

Set sometime in the future, *The Word for World Is Forest* tells the story of New Tahiti, a planet which "might have been Idaho in 1950. . . . Or Kentucky in 1830. Or Gaul, in 50 B.C." It has been invaded by "Yumens" seeking lumber for Earth (Terran) which has been denuded of plants and animals (even hunters must now track "robodeer"). Most of the loggers and officials sent to this new world have no understanding of the local inhabitants, the Athsheans, small, green-furred, peace-loving forest dwellers who have perfected conscious dreaming to an art. Because the Yumens enslave and kill them, these natives are driven finally to rebel and destroy their captors. The principals in the action are the brutal, amoral Captain Davidson, the sensitive, concerned anthropologist Lyubov, and the intelligent, resourceful Athshean, Selver. Their composite reactions to New Tahiti mirror the American ecological experience which has ranged from rapture to fear to coexistence.

The first explorers to the Western Hemisphere described what they found in idyllic terms. Columbus called Hispaniola "marvelous. . . . most beautiful" with inhabitants who were "guileless and so generous," displaying "much love." Similarily, Verrazzano said the place was delightful with air "salubrious, pure, and temperate." One hundred years later, an Englishman, Arthur Barlowe, spoke of being in "the midst of some delicate garden" with "incredible abundance" and "handsome and goodly [natives] . . . as mannerly and civill as any of Europe. . . . such as live after the maner of the golden age." This image of the golden age was a popular one, for Michael Drayton in his "Ode to the Virginia Voyage" spoke of "Earth's only paradise . . . to whose the golden age/Still nature's laws doth give." These comments confirmed the European tradition that an earthly paradise lay somewhere to the west. But, "anticipations of a second Eden quickly shattered against the reality of North America" where the Puritans found "a hideous and desolate wilderness, full of wild beasts and wild men," a "howling desart" where the Indians acted "like wolves" [Roderick Nash, *Wilderness and the American Mind,* Third Edition, 1967; William Bradford, *Of Plymouth Plantation,* 1970; Perry Miller and Thomas H. Johnson, *The Puritans,* Vol. 1, revised edition, 1963; John Demos, ed., *Remarkable Providences: 1600-1760,* 1972].

The Puritans quickly moved to subdue this hostile environment, which was one of their strongest symbols of evil and displacement; for they felt "by the command of God man had been made master of the whole visible creation" (Morgan). As Roderick Nash notes in *Wilderness and the American Mind,* "if paradise was early man's greatest good, wilderness, as its antipode, was his greatest evil," a place which the Judeo-Christian tradition had for centuries regarded as the abode of demons and spirits, where "the limbs of trees became grotesque, leaping figures," a representation of "the Christian conception of the situation man faced on earth. . . . a compound of his natural inclination to sin." Later, Hawthorne's Young Goodman Brown encapsulates this concept when he speaks of the "lonely" and "gloomy" forest with "a devilish Indian behind every tree."

This enmity towards wilderness remained dominant in the centuries that followed, and accounted for the obsession to clear and cultivate the land; for Leo Marx says in *The Machine in the Garden* that the pastoral ideal was "used to define the meaning of America ever since the age of discovery." A few intellectuals did begin to associate nature with religion (in Deism and later transcendentalism), and when romanticism and the sublime became popular in the late eighteenth and early nineteenth centuries, many writers and explorers seemed to appreciate those qualities which had formerly been vilified. Bartram and Jefferson spoke in awe of mountains and vast landscapes. Bryant praised nature's solace in his "Forest Hymn"—"let me often to these solitudes/Retire, and in thy presence reassure/My feeble virtue," and Emerson speculated in *Nature* that "in the woods, we return to reason and faith. . . . an occult relation between man and the vegetable." However, Nash notes that these feelings were often ambivalent, for "while appreciation of wild country existed, it was seldom unqualified" and much fear remained locked in the subconscious of even the most avid lovers of natural scenery.

This fear was unleashed again as the industrial revolution swept over America, manifesting itself in severe environmental damage when plants and animals became valued only for what they could contribute to the wealth of nations. Melville's leviathans were reduced to oil for factories, the latter changing the forest into numerous consumable products (such as the envelopes in "The Tartarus of Maids"). Nature became an indifferent, deterministic antagonist, perhaps best represented in symbols such as the ocean in Stephen Crane's "The Open Boat" and the prairie in "The Blue Hotel." A few decades later in the 1920s and 1930s "landscapes of ruin" [as termed in *The American Landscape,* edited by John Conron, 1974] were expressed by images of devastation—the "dead trees" and "dry stones" in Eliot's *The Wasteland* and the "ashheaps" of Queens in Fitzgerald's *The Great Gatsby,* for example. However, the environmental movement of the 1960s and 1970s reversed this trend to some extent, and Conron says we have arrived at a period of coexistence, even celebration of nature which Leopold in *A Sand County Almanac* calls "the salvation of the world" and which has Annie Dillard in *Pilgrim at Tinker Creek* going "in and out of Shadow Creek, upstream and down, exultant, in a daze, dancing, to the twin silver trumpets of praise."

It is important to remember that these various impressions of the landscape always contrasted with the harmonious animism of the American Indians whom Stewart Udall has said were "bound together by the ties of kinship and nature. . . . with an emotional attachment for his woods, valleys, and prairies [which] was the very essence of life" ["The Land Wisdom of the Indians," *Environmental Decay in Its Historical Context* (1973)]. Tecumseh is often quoted as replying to the demands to sell land with these words: "Sell the country? . . . Why not sell the air, the clouds, the great sea?" and a line from a Navaho chant beautifully summarizes this philosophy by describing the horizon as a "house made of evening twilight."

In *The Word for World Is Forest,* the three main characters are symbolic representations of these major ideologies. When Davidson, the captain of the security forces, speaks of New Tahiti, the reader is reminded of the explorers and the Puritans; for he constantly broods about the former, "You mooched along thinking about conquista-

dors, and destiny and stuff." "It's Man that wins, every time. The old Conquistador." He and his men are frightened by the omnipresent forest which they call "dark," "meaningless," and "endless." Like the Plymouth colonists who felt themselves soldiers of God, Davidson says that when they had come here "there had been nothing . . . but men were here now to end the darkness"—to tame the planet: "For this world, New Tahiti, was literally made for men. Cleaned up and cleaned out, the dark forests cut down for open fields of grain, the primeval murk and savagery and ignorance wiped out, it would be a paradise, a real Eden. A better world than worn-out Earth." Ironically, the new world already has the qualities of a paradise, but Davidson cannot comprehend what he sees: "There was something about this damned planet, its gold sunlight and hazy sky, its mild winds smelling of leafmold and pollen, something that made you daydream." To him, destiny is conquest and destruction, and his words seem to be a crude restatement of the centuries-old Judeo-Christian policy of the domination of nature: "When I say Earth, Kees, I mean people. Men. You worry about deer and trees and fibreweed, fine, that's your thing. But I like to see things in perspective, from the top down, and the top, so far, is humans." Davidson regards the natives as animals, calling them "beetles," "fish," "rats," and using them not only as slaves but for hideous "recreational" raids during which he and his men incinerate their villages. His philosophy might be summed up in these lines: "Primitive races always have to give way to civilised ones. Or be assimilated. But we sure as hell can't assimilate a lot of green monkeys." In his desire to destroy the forest and convert it to products useful for Terran, he also resembles the deterministic industrialists who saw the environment as an expendable commodity. Davidson is the antagonist, the enemy of nature, like all those who have sought to subdue it in the name of God and mammon.

In stark contrast to Davidson, but with an equally extreme position, is the anthropologist Lyubov, who sees the natives as "noble savages" with no capacity for evil "a static, stable, uniform society, perfectly integrated, and wholly unprogressive. You might say that like the forest they live in, they've attained a climax state." His inability to view the Athsheans objectively renders him unable to accept actions which do not fit his initial characterization: "Nearly five E-years here, and he had believed the Athsheans to be incapable of killing men, his kind or their kind. He had written long papers to explain how and why they couldn't kill men. All wrong. Dead wrong." Also, his feelings about the new wilderness are ambivalent:

> At first on Athshe he had felt oppressed and uneasy in the forest, stifled by its endless crowd and incoherence of trunks, branches, leaves in the perpetual greenish or brownish twilight. The mass and jumble of various competitive lives all pushing and swelling outwards and upwards towards light, the silence made up of many little meaningless noises, the total vegetable indifference to the presence of mind, all this had troubled him, and like the others he had kept to clearings and to the beach. But little by little he had begun to like it.

Clearly, he has never completely understood what he has been observing on the planet, either its people or its surroundings. In addition, his friendship with Selver and the other Athsheans has been superficial, and he cannot bring himself to take a meaningful stand:

> It was not in Raj Lyubov's nature to think, "what can I do?" Character and training disposed him not to interfere in other men's business. His job was to find out what they did, and his inclination was to let them go on doing it. He preferred to be enlightened, rather than to enlighten; to seek facts rather than the Truth. But even the most unmissionary soul, unless he pretend he has no emotions, is sometimes faced with a choice between commission and omission. "What are they doing?" abruptly becomes "What are we doing?" and then, "What must I do?" That he had reached such a point of choice now, he knew, and yet did not know clearly why, nor what alternatives were offered him.

In a conference investigating an attack on a Yumen camp, he is humiliated when his theories are shown to have been erroneous—and he cannot defend himself or the natives. As a result, he is closed out of both societies and dies in a subsequent raid. His reactions to the new world have been idealized; and his actions, like those of the romantics, have had no lasting effect.

The natives to whom both men have such different responses live in perfect harmony with their environment, considering themselves simply an extension of nature—not a separate entity: "The substance of their world was not earth, but forest. Terran man was clay, red dust. Athshean man was branch and root. They did not carve figures of themselves in stone, only in wood." They live in houses built beneath the roots of trees, from which they take their family names: "Selver is my name. Of the Ash." So attuned are they to their surroundings that they consider it to have the same animate qualities they do; for when he sees trees cut down, Selver envisions that "a little blood ran out of the broken end." All of their images relate to this vast forest world, an old man saying, "I have had my whole life. Days like the leaves of the forest. I'm an old hollow tree, only the roots live." They practice conscious, controlled dreaming, which again Lyubov does not completely comprehend; for Selver says that he "understood me when I showed him how to dream, and yet even so he called the world-time 'real' and the dream-time 'unreal', as if that were the difference between them." At the end of the novel, Selver has managed to conquer the Yumens, and the officials who have read Lyubov's reports and conducted inquiries decide to ban further colonization, saying they're "not coming back. Your world has been placed under the League Ban." Although Selver has, in effect, won, the Athsheans have learned to kill, and his final words are a grim reminder that that lesson will have permanent repercussions on their society: "Maybe after I die people will be as they were before I was born, and before you came. But I do not think they will."

The limited omniscient point of view in the novel shifts back and forth between Davidson, Lyubov, and Selver with three chapters each for the Captain and the Ath-

shean, and two for the anthropologist, arranged in this pattern: Davidson/Selver/Lyubov/Davidson/Lyubov/Selver/Davidson/Selver. The action begins in Davidson's consciousness when he is in a position of power—and ends with a reversal when Selver has taken the dominant role, Lyubov having died and Davidson having been exiled to an island he has defoliated. Le Guin's device of changing her viewpoint in this manner not only enables her to retell the American Experience in the new world and to present a more comprehensive view of New Tahiti, but also it underscores her theme of illusion versus reality.

This underlying message is developed with particular clarity by her detailing of the Athshean dream control. They feel that they can change what they perceive by concentration, an ability Selver says that the Yumens do not have: "none of them are trained, or have skill in dreaming. . . ."

> A realist is a man who knows both the world and his own dreams. You're not sane: there's not one man in a thousand of you who knows how to dream. Not even Lyubov and he was the best among you. You sleep, you wake and forget your dreams, you sleep again and wake again, and so you spend your whole lives, and you think that is being, life, reality! You are not children, you are grown men, but insane.

After Lyubov is killed, Selver dreams him alive: "Lyubov came out of the shadows of Selver's mind and said, "I shall be here'."Thus, he has trained himself to alter experience to his own liking.

This merging of the conscious and unconscious, the concrete and the illusory, adds considerable psychological and mythic complexity to the novel. Symbolically, Selver is nature, both plant and animal, resembling the forest in his color and name, representing many evolutionary stages and all primitive tribesmen. Davidson is the warrior and merchant, city dweller and even farmer, who through the centuries has felt that his mission was to use the environment for his own self-interest. Lyubov is the intellectual, the poet and dreamer who idealizes nature but never has a realistic or in-depth understanding of its relationship to his world. Their conflict on New Tahiti condenses in a few years several centuries of struggle on the American continent, as natives with an instinctive harmony with nature encounter settlers with a conditioned fear or a romantic idealism. At the end of the story only Selver and Davidson remain: "We're both gods, you and I." Even though Selver seems to have won the war and banished Davidson to Dump Island, the Yumen is not dead. Throughout American history it has been the Davidsons who have had staying power and consistently returned to pose a significant threat to the environment. Perhaps Ursula Le Guin's meaning in this novel is that the current "coexistence" with nature may also be ephemeral and like Lyubov die off, leaving the enemies of nature again in the supremacy.

Thus, Le Guin's accomplishment in less than two hundred pages has been more than to present an interesting adventure story or a disguised Vietnam war novel or even a warning of ecological catastrophe. In addition to all these, she *has* been able to define nature as an essence which is both physical and mental, a vital element, not only in the American experience, but in the consciousness of all humankind. If we are going to discover new Edens, then we must come to realize that preservation is essential—to self-knowledge and to survival. As she says in *The Wind's Twelve Quarters,* "Obviously my intent is in what goes on inside. . . . We all have forests in our minds. Forests unexplored, unending." (pp. 84-90)

> Carol P. Hovanec, "Visions of Nature in 'The Word for World Is Forest': A Mirror of the American Consciousness," in Extrapolation, Vol. 30, No. 1, Spring, 1989, pp. 84-92.

Elizabeth Cummins   (essay date 1990)

[*In the following excerpt, Cummins claims that the thematic unity and narrative sequence of the stories in* Orsinian Tales *reflect the conception of time as both linear and cyclical.*]

The imaginary Central European country of Orsinia has stimulated Ursula K. Le Guin's creativity longer than any of her other invented worlds. She began her publishing career in Orsinia, and she has returned to it after Earthsea and the Hainish planets, which established her reputation, appear to be closed to her imagination. Of Earthsea she said that once the protagonist Ged disappeared, she no longer had a guide in that country and could write no more Earthsea stories. Of the Hainish planets she has recently stated that outer space journeys no longer interest her.

In the first of her rare autobiographical essays Le Guin notes that prior to the publication of her first science fiction in 1962 she had written four novels "set in an invented though nonfantastic Central European country, as were the best short stories I had done." Although apparently none of these novels has been published, Le Guin's first published poem ["Folksong from the Montayna Province"] (1959) and short story ["An die Musik"] (1961) were Orsinian pieces. Furthermore, it is in the Orsinian fiction that Le Guin mastered her craft. She once commented that when in her early twenties she finished the Orsinian story **"A Week in the Country,"** she felt she had finished her apprenticeship. After publishing individual Orsinian stories in the 1970s, she brought out a collection of short stories in 1976, **Orsinian Tales,** which was nominated for the National Book Award in 1977. She published an Orsinian novel, *Malafrena,* in 1979 and more short stories in the 1980s, primarily in *The New Yorker.*

The Orsinian pieces are essentially historical fiction in that they describe the matrix of a culture in a time prior to the years in which the stories were published. Le Guin has acknowledged their "literary origin" as being "the Russian novel . . . Tolstoy and Dostoyevsky" [Larry McCaffery and Sinda Gregory, "An Interview with Ursula Le Guin," *The Missouri Review* 7, No. 2 (1984)]. What is intriguing about Le Guin's continued interest in Orsinia is that her own Hainish works reveal her awareness of modern physics and mathematics where the theories of relativity and probability have shaped a world view radically different

---

> [In *Orsinian Tales*] Le Guin develops Orsinia with the specific detail that readers expect in her fiction. . . . Orsinia becomes a unique place with a unique history which is and is not continuous with consensus reality.
>
> *—Elizabeth Cummins*

---

from that of the eighteenth and early nineteenth centuries, when time and space were regarded as absolutes and when historical fiction was the dominant expression of this world view.

The great historical novelists of the nineteenth century tried to represent their empirical environment and reconstruct the details of the past, as Sir Walter Scott did with Norman England or Leo Tolstoy did with Russia in the Napoleonic era. Like other twentieth-century writers, well aware of the difficulty of defining "represent" in the absence of an objective reality, Le Guin uses the technique of distancing or estrangement to separate herself from the world of recorded history and to call attention to recorded history as a subjective construct.

Estrangement is a literary device by which the reader experiences [what Robert Scholes calls in his *Structural Fabulation: An Essay on Fiction of the Future*] a "radical discontinuity" between the world of consensus reality and the world in the fiction. Although all fictional worlds are in some way different from the reader's world, estranged fictional worlds are radically different in physical location, history, or world view. What distinguishes Orsinia from Le Guin's fantasy and science fiction worlds is that it can be located in Europe in the distant and near past of Western civilization. Since the Orsinian fiction predates her science fiction and fantasy, it was in its creation that Le Guin first recognized the need to distance herself from consensus reality. As she notes in [the interview with McCaffery and Gregory]:

> I was in college when I started the pieces that eventually became the **Orsinian Tales**. . . . I was stuck in that old formula . . . to write about what you know, what you've experienced. . . . I remember thinking finally, "To hell with it, I'll just make up a country." And since most of what I knew came out of books . . . I made up a place that was like the places in books I liked to read. But as soon as I began work in Orsinia, I realized I didn't have to imitate Tolstoy. I had created a place I could write about in my own terms; I could make up just enough of the rules to free my imagination and my observations.

Le Guin develops Orsinia with the specific detail that readers expect in her fiction. She provides history, geographical features, names of places and people from a nonexistent language, and details of the daily lives of varied characters. In contrast to this world that has no referent in the reader's consensus reality are references to familiar events from European history such as Neville Chamberlain's 1938 meeting with Hitler in Munich, the October 1956 revolution in Hungary, the practice of tatooing numbers on the arms of prisoners in German work camps. Orsinia becomes a unique place with a unique history which is and is not continuous with consensus reality.

Used in the Orsinian fiction, estrangement calls attention to the subjective nature of history. Although modern historians may agree that a certain event happened during a given year and in a given area, they recognize that an account of the event and an estimate of its historical significance is unavoidably an interpretation. By writing about an imaginary country but embedding it in the history of Central Europe, Le Guin has, in a sense, written an alternative history of Central Europe, particularly in *Orsinian Tales,* which will be the focus of this [essay].

Malafrena, even though published after *Orsinian Tales,* provides geographic and political background for the tales. Told from the viewpoint of the landed gentry, the novel depicts Orsinia in the early nineteenth century, caught up in the idealism and fervor that followed the French Revolution and in the desire for independence that followed the Congress of Vienna in 1815. The novel focuses on Itale Sorde as he develops into a political revolutionary, having left his father's lands and gone to Krasnoy, the capital city. From 1825 to 1831 Sorde and his friends become more outspoken in their challenge to the Austrian Empire's right to rule Orsinia and in their call for the restoration of Orsinia's constitutional monarchy. Sorde, in both his political and personal life, fights for self-determination and independence.

In pursuit of the ideal he adopts a motto from the French debates, "Live free or die." However, his own imprisonment, the suicides of friends, his lover's insincere liberalism, and a failed insurrection eventually bring him home to heal both body and spirit. His belief in Orsinia's independence remains, but he has experienced the gulf between idealism and achievement. Le Guin has stated that she worked on the ideas and the story for twenty years, trying to get it right. *Malafrena* does not reach the unity and complexity of *Orsinian Tales,* which both presents and questions history.

The narrative sequence that Le Guin uses in *Orsinian Tales* begins to define what the nature of Le Guin's alternative history is. Individual stories generally are told chronologically, but the arrangement of the eleven stories is nonchronological. Ranging from 1150 to 1965, the stories are arranged in the following order: 1960, 1150, 1920, 1920, 1956, 1910, 1962, 1938, 1965, 1640, 1935.

James Bittner has suggested [in his *Approaches to the Fiction of Ursula K. Le Guin*] that the arrangement, a moving backward and then forward in time, reflects the circular romance quest which he has argued is the aesthetic structure of Le Guin's fiction. The quest proceeds by "returns which are also advances." The circular quest takes on additional significance when one tries to understand Le Guin's concept of history. The nonchronological order of the collection coupled with the chronological order within individual stories reveal that Le Guin's historical fiction

is, like her science fiction, based on the perception of time as both succession and duration. *Orsinian Tales* is a more complex book than *Malafrena* because it offers the experience of this double vision of time.

Although a unified theory of time, such as Shevek discovered in *The Dispossessed,* does not yet exist, many writers—most recently Stephen Jay Gould in *Time's Arrow, Time's Cycle*—have argued for the necessity of viewing time both ways. Time as succession, often imaged as the arrow or river, is the perception of time as a series of moments, each separate and unrepeatable. This perception explains change and is experienced in people's conscious, daily activities. Time as sequence is the basis of narration, that powerful order used to make sense out of both fact and fiction. On the other hand, time as duration, often imaged as the cycle, is the perception of time as fundamental states which are always present or regularly repeated. This perception explains changelessness and connectedness; humans experience it in dreams and myths. Time as duration is the basis of immanence or a lawlike structure, that equally powerful structure used to account for a meaning beyond human existence.

Le Guin's temporal physicist Shevek recognizes the apparent contradiction of the two views of time but argues for the necessity of both: "There is the arrow, the running river, without which there is no change, no progress, or direction, or creation. And there is the circle or the cycle, without which there is chaos, meaningless succession of instants, a world without clocks or seasons or promises."

One of Le Guin's sources for her understanding of modern speculation about time is *The Voices of Time,* edited by J. T. Fraser. In his essay "Time as Succession and the Problem of Duration" in this collection Friedrich Kümmel argues that the acceptance of both perceptions is the only assurance for free and responsible actions. He writes:

> No act of man is possible with reference solely to the past or solely to the future, but is always dependent on their interaction. Thus, for example, the future may be considered as the horizon against which plans are made, the past provides the means for their realization, while the present mediates and actualizes both. . . . This interrelation of reciprocal conditions is a historical process in which the past never assumes a final shape nor the future ever shuts its doors. Their essential interdependence also means, however, that there can be no progress without a retreat into the past in search of a deeper foundation.

In *Orsinian Tales* the reader is challenged to "make sense" out of the obvious violation of the familiar chronological sequence. As the reader moves through the collection, the recurring question is, What does this story have to do with the preceding one? Thus, the reader's understanding of the text and of the Orsinian people becomes an accumulative experience; each story is reinterpreted as the next one is read. The reader not only experiences linear time (in each story and in the process of reading) but also cyclical time (for example, in relating a 1960 story to an 1150 story, and then both to a 1920 story).

The placement of the date at the end of each story suggests

that the date is less important than what precedes it. The story's relationship to the other stories rests less on what is datable and more on what is repeated, such as themes, images, characters, places. The skewed chronological order reveals that Orsinia is all of these things and all of these people. A chronological sequence would encourage the reader to apprehend Orsinia only in the reductive, causal mode; the events of the 1150 story would be read as the "causes" of what occurred in later Orsinian history. Coherence would be dependent on sequency; unity would develop from simplicity rather than from multiplicity.

The reader views Orsinia within the framework of Western civilization as well as within the chronological history of Central Europe. As if trying to express her sense of her own European heritage, which was closely tied to German and Polish culture and to specific locations, Le Guin named her country after herself. James Bittner explains, "The country's name . . . and its creator's name have the same root: *orsino,* Italian for 'bearish,' and *Ursula* come from the Latin *ursa.*" Furthermore, the Russian invasion of Czechoslovakia in 1947 was a traumatic political event for Le Guin. She wrote, "That's when I came of age, and realized I had a stake in this world. . . . Writing about Orsinia allowed me to talk about a situation that had touched my heart, yet I could distance it, which was very important at that time."

With such countries now known as Hungary, Czechoslovakia, Poland, Rumania, and Yugoslavia, Orsinia has shared medieval feudalism and the long struggle for independence. Central Europe has a long history of invasion, war, and oppression. Because it lacks major geographic borders, it has been overrun by its strong neighbors, Turkey in the South, Central Asia to the East, and Germanic tribes to the west. Orsinia shares with other European countries the dream of liberty that triggered the French Revolution. Not only did Napoleon march across it to invade Russia in 1812, opposing forces fought major battles of both world wars on its soil. The desire for political autonomy is evident in the uprisings, strikes, and revolutions of the last thirty years. The cost of imperialism is evident in the daily lives of the Orsinians.

The efficacy of Le Guin's technique of using both linear and cyclic sequence can be demonstrated by examining the first three stories in *Orsinian Tales.* "The Fountains," "The Barrow," and "Ile Forest," dated 1960, 1150, and 1920 respectively, introduce the reader to Le Guin's concept of history and the texture that is Orsinia. Each protagonist is different, but each faces choices which change his sense of who he is and what his commitments are to the human community, seen as Orsinia, one's immediate neighbors, or a particular geographic area.

"The Fountains" tells of the defection by a renowned Orsinian microbiologist attending an international conference in Paris. Although heavily shadowed by secret police, he suddenly finds, during a tour of Versailles, that he is alone. As he walks away from the fountains and into the estate forest, he gradually realizes that he must decide whether to become a permanent exile or return to his Parisian hotel, a symbolic return to Orsinia. To seek asylum in one of the foreign embassies in Paris will give him secur-

ity, but he will be forever locked out of Orsinia. To return to the hotel will be a free choice to return home, but he will be again under the scrutiny of a willful government. Standing on the Solferino Bridge in Paris, near midnight, he makes his choice: "But he had never cared much about being safe, and now thought that he did not care much about hiding either, having found something better: his family, his inheritance. . . . What turned him to his own land was mere fidelity. For what else should move a man, these days?"

There could hardly be a stronger contrast than to move from the humane love which Dr. Adam Kereth feels for his European ancestors and his Orsinian fellow citizens to the fear and guilt of Count Freyga in **"The Barrow"** which cause him to sacrifice a visiting priest and then establish and defend a Benedictine monastery in his province. Freyga's province is Montayna, a mountainous isolated region inhabited by Orsinian Christians and heathen barbarians. Freyga, twenty-three years old, count since barbarians killed his father three years ago, has his ears filled with his wife's cries from upstairs as she labors in childbirth. He fears for the life of his seventeen-year-old wife, and the winter darkness that fills the downstairs hall makes him suspicious of the foreign priest from the city. Overcome by his fears and suspicions, Freyga takes the priest to the heathen barrow, slits his throat, and disembowels him. Later that night when he sees his wife and son safe and well, he kneels by the bed and murmurs, "Lord Christ, be praised, be thanked." Torn by conflicting belief systems, the count has tried to appease both gods.

In the context of the first two stories, the trade of death for life is seen as a universal human response. In the background of **"The Fountains"** is the opulence of Versailles, one cause of the French Revolution, which was followed by republican and then imperialistic bloodbaths, deaths traded for life and power. In the background of **"The Barrow"** is Christianity, which begins with the sacrifice of Jesus so that his followers might have life everlasting. Horrible as Freyga's action is, it must be viewed as an act which may be the foundation for a religion or a government, as plausible a foundation as Kereth's act of fidelity.

"Ile Forest" is also a story about killing. The story of Galven Ileskar is told by a senior physician in response to his younger partner's unqualified assertion that "murder can't go unpunished." Although he has no memory of it, Ileskar, in a fit of jealous rage, killed his wife and her lover; he lives in "a half-ruined house at the end of nowhere." a self-imposed exile in punishment for what he cannot remember. The storyteller and his sister meet Ileskar when the physician comes to practice in the village; the only person who knows of Ileskar's deed is Martin, his hired man. When the sister falls in love with Ileskar, the physician, disturbed over Ileskar's passivity and isolated life style, forces the story out of Martin. The physician fears for his sister's well-being and tells her the story. Undaunted, experiencing "the sense of peril, which is the root of love," she marries Ileskar. Ileskar is capable of passionate rage and gentle love; he acted out the dark side of himself one time in his life, but it was so horrible to his more rational, ethical self that he can no longer remember the act. However, he is very aware of the absence of something in his memory, and it is that awareness of absence that makes him capable of love and gentleness.

As different as these three protagonists are, they represent the range of human emotion for fidelity, love, rage, fear. By violating the chronological order Le Guin helps the reader recognize the universal in the particular; if these stories had been arranged in chronological order ("**The Barrow,**" "**Ile Forest,**" "**The Fountains**"), the reader might think of Freyga as only the predecessor of Ileskar and be so overwhelmed with these accounts of murder that the love and fidelity of Kereth for his compatriots would seem incredible or inconsequential. Furthermore, having experienced the significant act of fidelity by Kereth at the beginning, the reader recognizes that Freyga and Ileskar also share this quality.

Both the protagonists and the readers discover that rethinking the past allows them to understand who they are and what their commitments and responsibilities will be to their geographic area and its human community. Without this reassessment, the individual would be imprisoned by the past, blindly committed to something not understood.

By insisting on a double vision of time—as both linear and cyclic—Le Guin refuses to privilege chronological order either in constructing history or in constructing fiction. Implicit in this collection of short stories is an examination of how historical fiction is made meaningful, and Le Guin both uses and calls into question the chronological beginning, middle, and end structure of a narrative.

By not following chronological order for the arrangement of the stories in the collection, Le Guin deemphasizes the beginning and end and emphasizes the middle. The first and the last stories are significant more for the ideas, themes, and images they share with the other stories than as an account of origin and resolution. They do function as a beginning and ending of the reading process for the audience by offering a way into and then out of Orsinia. The collection begins with "**The Fountains,**" the only story set outside of Orsinia. When Dr. Kereth decides not to defect, the reader's attention and curiosity turn to Orsinia. The collection ends with "**Imaginary Countries,**" the only story in which the omniscient narrator speaks to the reader. At the end of the story the narrator comments, "But all this happened a long time ago, nearly forty years ago; I do not know if it happens now, even in imaginary countries."

The selection of the first and last stories, then, is certainly not arbitrary; but at the same time the selection is not decisive. Rather, these two stories suggest a tentative beginning and ending; the reader could begin to reread the stories, following a circular pattern rather than a linear one, with the end blurring into the beginning. The reader could, using the dates, reread the stories in chronological order; "**The Fountains**" would become the ninth story, "**Imaginary Countries**" would become the middle story, "**The Barrow**" would be the first, and "**The House**" would be the last. A reexamination of the collection reveals other tentative qualities. The chronology of Orsinia is full of

gaps, as the dates emphasize: 1150, 1640, 1910, 1920, 1935, 1938, 1956, 1960, 1962, 1965. The title *Tales* suggests an oral original and the possibility that each is only one version of an oft-repeated story. The word *tale* is a more general term than *story* and may be applied to a narrative account of either fact or fiction. Furthermore, the omniscient narrator has stepped into the collection at the end of the last story as if for the sole purpose of qualification: "I don't know if it happens now."

Individual stories generally follow chronological order, but they also call attention to the importance of the middle. Although they too have functional beginnings and endings, because they are not preceded or followed by stories which are chronologically related to them their beginnings and endings are inconclusive. The ending is always open in that the story ends just as the protagonist begins to live with a new view of self, work, and human community. Usually the protagonist does not fully understand the implications of the new awareness; furthermore the story ends with unanswered or even unanswerable questions. Thus the middle is more significant than the beginning or the ending.

In the third story Le Guin suggests this emphasis on the middle. Nearing the end of his story, the senior physician says of his sister,

> "But my telling her forced her to take sides. And she did. She said she'd stay with Ileskar. They were married in October."
>
> The doctor cleared his throat, and gazed a long time at the fire, not noticing his junior partner's impatience.
>
> "Well?" the young man burst out at last like a firecracker—"What happened?"
>
> "What happened? Why, nothing much happened."

And then the physician tells his audience of the uneventful, happy years of Ileskar and his wife. The listener's question, "What happened?" implies that he is most interested in the outcome, perhaps expecting another murder. The storyteller, however, is absorbed in the events of the story, the process of living.

The suggestions of tentativeness and of things blurring into one another reinforce the idea that the structure of a historical narrative for Le Guin cannot be only the chronological beginning-middle-end but must also be a revolving spiral; all aspects of the narrative develop a central theme and examine it both in linear and in cyclic relationship to other things. In a 1980 essay on narration Le Guin used such a structure and quoted a description of it as "radial, circling about, repeating and elaborating the central theme. It is all middle." Apparent discontinuity, then, becomes continuity.

Le Guin's narrative structure in ***Orsinian Tales*** is consistent with a world view shaped by modern physics. Her account of Orsinia has neither beginning nor end nor completeness, for the present is ongoing, the past is always being reinterpreted, and the future is open. The individual life, the history of Orsinia, and the narrative gain meaning not merely by the nature of beginning or end but by the quality of the middle.

The collection of stories is further unified by a central theme that defines the quality of life. The history of Orsinia that is retold in these eleven tales reveals that in a world of change, catastrophe, and indeterminacy, Orsinians have survived and maintained some sense of integrity and self-worth by personal vows of fidelity. Le Guin's characters, settings, plots, resolutions, and images reflect the power of this moral principle. The principle may be called commitment, love, comradeship, or fidelity; regardless of its name, adherence to it provides constancy in a world of inconstancy. Le Guin makes very clear that constancy results from individual choices. Fidelity is the central theme around which the stories circle, "repeating and elaborating" its implications for individuals and for the country. One of her characters sings:

> Yet be just and constant still, Love may beget a
>   wonder,
> Not unlike a summer's frost or winter's fatal
>   thunder:
> He that holds his sweetheart dear until his day
>   of dying
> Lives of all that ever lived most worthy the envy-
>   ing.

The first three stories of the collection depict characters facing unexpected events and "fatal thunder" in Kereth's opportunity to defect, Count Freyga's need to save the lives of his wife and unborn child, the listener's discovery that a murderer can also be a brother. In each life meaningfulness resulted from how the characters reacted to these events. In keeping with Le Guin's emphasis on indeterminacy, however, each story ends with unanswered questions about the characters' future; there can be no "finished version" of a life.

The matrix of each story contains several elements that heighten the immediacy of change. As James Bittner has indicated, the karst area, which is the setting for **"Brothers and Sisters,"** is a reminder of the natural change occurring in the land itself. Karst is a limestone area where water action underground produces caverns, sinkholes, and underground streams. Further, almost all of the stories take place in the fall, October frequently being mentioned—"the month when things fall," Le Guin once called it. The equally constant and immanent change in the human world is emphasized by ruins and remnants of human things. The barrow is an abandoned altar of the barbarians, the top stone of which has become the altar in the nearby church. The count's tower is glimpsed in **"A Week in the Country"** by its 1962 protagonists as "the ruins of the Tower Keep." The family house in which the protagonist of **"The House"** was born and in which he lived with his wife for several years is empty, abandoned even by the government which once used it for offices. The people themselves are often maimed or scarred. These injuries, often a result of war or revolution, are a constant reminder of the cost of the struggles for autonomy in this landlocked Central European country.

Le Guin uses the image of the road to suggest the immediacy of change and the opportunity for either escape or ac-

tion that may improve the future of an individual or of Orsinia. Hope, she shows, is based on a belief in the openness of the future, which in turn is based on learning from the past. In **"The Road East,"** a story of events in October 1956, Le Guin recounts a few days in a young man's life when he is faced with the conflicting fidelities of commitment to his mother, who denies the existence of evil, and commitment to his friends and fellow Orsinians who are risking their lives to plan a revolution.

Maler Eray's technique for coping with the growing tension is to imagine walking eastward from Krasnoy to Sorg, a journey, he imagines, to a secure city, "early in the last century." Although in his imagination he can reject the idea that "home" must always be with his mother, he cannot act on this desire. In contrast to his mother, who lives literally and figuratively behind a closed door, tending her flowers and blithely announcing, "nothing is evil, nothing is wasted, if only we look at the world without fear," is a woman who is identified with the road. An enigmatic figure, almost at times seeming to be a figment of his imagination, she serves as a guide for Eray. For she has come from Sorg, walking west on the road which Eray had always thought of as "the road east." She makes Eray think about going in a different direction, about accepting the responsibility his friend Provin had held out to him: "There's nothing left to us, now, but one another." Realizing he cannot escape to the country, or to the past, Eray acts. He leaves his mother, "dazzled at first by the bright October sunlight, to join the army of the unarmed and with them to go down the long streets leading westward to, but not across, the river."

The closing words provide knowledge of Eray's newly pledged fidelity, but they give no certainty that he will even survive the revolution. Eray has created an open future because he has relinquished his concept of the past as a fixed condition and because he decides that his actions are meaningful for himself and for Orsinia.

Just as the road serves as a symbol of change, the house often serves as a symbol of duration. **"A Week in the Country"** uses both of these symbols in an account of coming-of-age experience for a university student from Krasnoy in 1962.

By taking the roads to the country, Stefan Kabbre encounters great change; he experiences familial love, vows fidelity that will lead to a marriage, sees his best friend shot by Orsinian soldiers, and endures torture and imprisonment. The Augeskar house in the country symbolizes the family unit and its regular summer gathering which reunites and nourishes them all. The autonomy symbolized by the house is a microcosm of that autonomy the country of Orsinia does not have. The unity and endurance of the family, however, is a microcosm of that unity and fidelity that Orsinians depend on for a sense of identity in spite of the domination of foreign powers.

Stefan is aware of being an outsider, not only because he is not one of the six Augeskar children, but also because his family is no longer intact. He relishes the memory of an April morning when he, his father, and his grandfather walked out on the karst plain so that the grandfather could vent his anger at being "yoked to the foreign plow" with no hope of aid from the West. While the grandfather talks, however, his hand rests on his grandson's shoulder, the tender touch conveying the values that remain, "obduracy" and "fidelity."

Stefan's memory takes him back to the past to recover that which is valuable, and the men's sharing with him their secret desires overshadows for Stefan the knowledge "that his grandfather had died in a deportation train and his father had been shot along with forty-two other men on the plain outside town in the reprisals of 1956."

The reader's memory also brings back something valuable, the previous story. **"Brothers and Sisters,"** which concerns events in 1910, is about Stefan's grandfather when the grandfather was twenty-three. The reader, from the privileged perspective of viewing the same struggle in two different generations of the same family, sees the stages of life repeated from one generation to another. In both narratives the coming-of-age experience involves, on the one hand, knowledge of one's own mortality and, on the other hand, knowledge of love, of the need to commit to other human beings. Both kinds of knowledge are essential to cross the threshold into adulthood, are essential to "sharing . . . the singular catastrophe of being alive." "What is it all for?" the young man wonders, and the reader sees at least a partial answer; it is not the nature of one's birth or death which holds the answer but rather the middle, how one deals with death, fear of failure, injustice, irrational acts by others, love, self-definition, self-determination.

Stefan's coming-of-age experience has been traumatic; ironically, he has had to experience the very unknowns of life that he had once welcomed when they were only imagined. What were words in an intellectual argument at the beginning of the vacation are words of personal commitment at the end of the vacation: "No good letting go." Like Maler Eray's experience in **"The Road East,"** Stefan's guide to action is a woman. Bruna is representative of many of the women in the Orsinian stories. Like Tenar in *The Tombs of Atuan* they often choose the more difficult road and guide their male companions on it.

In **"An die Musik,"** the next story, another way of coping with being borne down by oppressive human acts is offered. This story focuses on a music composer in 1938 who, hearing the radio news reports that suggest impending world war, wonders about the value of his life's task, which is to write a Mass. He is advised to write short songs that can be performed immediately. He is told, "This is not a good world for music . . . when Europe is crawling with armies like a corpse with maggots, when Russia uses symphonies to glorify the latest boiler-factory in the Urals. . . . Music is no good, no use. . . . Write your songs, write your Mass, it does no harm. . . . But it won't save us." He chooses to fulfill two vows of fidelity which will conflict in their demands on his time. He cannot give up his commitment to the Mass, nor can he give up his commitment to his wife and children. Like Stefan Fabbre, who senses that the linear view of time is not the only way to regard history, Gaye is finally able to recognize that everything that is significant cannot be incorporated into a human history which is viewed as progress.

> What good is music? None, Gaye thought, and that is the point. To the world and its states and armies and factories and Leaders, music says, "You are irrelevant"; and, arrogant and gentle as a god, to the suffering man it says only, "Listen." For being saved is not the point. Music saves nothing. Merciful, uncaring, it denies and breaks down all the shelters, the houses men build for themselves, that they may see the sky.

Music, or art in general, points to the presence of the world beyond human limits. As James Bittner explains, "The function of art . . . is to deny the world, to detach people from politics and history so they can receive visions of a better world, and perhaps redeem politics and history with that vision."

In *Orsinian Tales* Le Guin has indeed written historical fiction that is consistent with a world view shaped by modern physics. The technique of estrangement calls attention to the subjective nature of history. The narrative sequence reveals her acceptance of both linear and cyclic time. Her account of Orsinia has neither beginning nor end nor completeness, for the present is ongoing, the past is always being reinterpreted, and the future is open. Finally, by using the theme of fidelity to unify the collection, she reveals that individuals find meaning and constancy in the face of change and impermanence by personal vows of commitment. The individual life, like the history of Orsinia, gains meaning not by the nature of its beginning or end but by the quality of the middle.

The closing lines of the collection leave the reader also in the middle of the narrative. The narrator writes, "But all this happened a long time ago, nearly forty years ago; I do not know if it happens now, even in imaginary countries." Not only does "this" refer to the eleventh story, it also refers to all the Orsinian tales. The reader then wonders just what has occurred in these stories. So the ending is not a closure but instead is an unanswered question that initiates rereading.

The rereading occurs with the reader puzzling over other unanswered questions. The doubt in the statement "I don't know if it happens" may be referring to the whole act of creating art. What if the art of storytelling is lost? What is art for? More particularly, Le Guin's narrator may be questioning whether or not stories like these can still be imagined, written, and published. Over Orsinia, Central Europe, and therefore over all the human family hangs the threat of additional imperialism and oppression, as well as the threat of atomic warfare. The reader hears the question, Can the author create in a world like this, create stories where commitment to each other is of the greatest value and where people accept both change and duration, reason and imagination, history and fiction?

Orsinian Tales is as open-ended a book as *The Dispossessed*, valued for the questions it raises and for not providing simple answers. The reader is left in the middle of both narratives, an experience Le Guin offers again in the most recent novel [*Always Coming Home*] of her fourth world, the future American West Coast. (pp. 126-51)

Elizabeth Cummins, in her Understanding Ursula K. Le Guin, *University of South Carolina Press, 1990, 216 p.*

FURTHER READING

Alterman, Peter S. "Ursula K. Le Guin: Damsel with a Dulcimer." In *Ursula K. Le Guin,* edited by Joseph D. Olander and Martin Harry Greenberg, pp. 64-76. New York: Taplinger, 1979.

Contends that Le Guin's novella *The Word for World Is Forest* and short story "Vaster Than Empires and More Slow" are consonant with the Romantic tradition, "resolving a rational-irrational dialectical argument through recourse to the visionary."

Baggesen, Søren. "Utopian and Dystopian Pessimism: Le Guin's *The Word for World Is Forest* and Tiptree's 'We Who Stole the Dream'." *Science-Fiction Studies* 14, No. 1 (March 1987): 34-43.

Contrasts Le Guin's novella *The Word for World Is Forest* and James Tiptree's short story 'We Who Stole the Dream," works which Baggesen perceives as evincing different types of pessimism.

Cogell, Elizabeth Cummins. "Setting as Analogue to Characterization in Ursula Le Guin." *Extrapolation: A Journal of Science Fiction and Fantasy* 18, No. 2 (May 1977): 131-41.

Argues that setting is an integral part of characterization, plot, and theme in Le Guin's works set in the Hainish universe, including the novella *The Word for World Is Forest.*

Easton, Tom. "The Reference Library." *Analog: Science Fiction, Science Fact* CV, No. 2 (February 1985): 180-86.

Discusses Le Guin's novella *The Eye of the Heron,* which Easton recommends to "those who feel science fiction does not pay enough attention to peace."

Eder, Richard. "Once upon a Place: On Fictions of Fate, Meadows of Meaning." *Los Angeles Times: The Book Review* (16 January 1983): 1, 4.

Claims that *The Eye of the Heron* fails because Le Guin "has failed to make any of her characters very interesting or individual; they are personifications of ideas and arguments."

Garfield, Roger. "In Praise of Limestone." *The Times Literary Supplement,* No. 3926 (10 June 1977): 697.

Questions Le Guin's decision to set the stories of *Orsinian Tales* in an imaginary world but praises the work as evincing "descriptive skill, narrative power, and also moral power, a refreshed sense of human dignity."

Herbert, Rosemary. "Fantasy Reminiscent of Tolkien and Adams." *The Christian Science Monitor* (29 September 1982): 15.

Brief favorable review of *The Compass Rose,* which is described as "more varied in style, theme, and mood than any compilation of works by a single author is likely to be."

Johnston, Kelvin. Review of *The Eye of the Heron,* by Ursula K. Le Guin. *Observer* (19 December 1982): 31.

Dismisses *The Eye of the Heron* as "the old anthropological stuff, laced with primitive sociology, plus a faint whiff of fantasy epic for the more discerning palate."

Jonas, Gerald. Review of *Orsinian Tales,* by Ursula K. Le Guin. *The New York Times Book Review* (28 November 1976): 8, 44.

Asserts that the stories of *Orsinian Tales* authentically address the role of the imagination in human experience.

Korn, Eric. "So Many Notions to the Page." *The Times Literary Supplement,* No. 3930 (8 July 1977): 820.

Claims that the novella *The Word for World Is Forest* is "part of the Vietnam canon that survives its occasion" because of strong characterization.

LaFaille, Gene. "Science Fiction Universe." *Wilson Library Bulletin* 64, No. 5 (January 1990): 106-07.

Reviews an abridged audiocassette of Le Guin's novella *The Word for World Is Forest,* which LaFaille declares a "very important work" that "contains a great deal of social and political criticism."

Miller, Jane. "Doubtful Improvements." *The Times Literary Supplement,* No. 3881 (30 July 1976): 950.

Notes that Le Guin's collection *The Wind's Twelve Quarters,* while containing some "sterile exercises," largely comprises stories that "are not simply demonstrations of an idea, but explorations of the imagining mind, of the scope of memory and prediction and of the vagaries of human perception."

Raksin, Alex. Review of *Orsinian Tales,* by Ursula K. Le Guin. *Los Angeles Times: The Book Review* (27 September 1987): 14.

Praises the imagery of the short story collection *Orsinian Tales,* which is described as "ultimately religious."

Remington, Thomas J. "A Touch of Difference, a Touch of Love: Theme in Three Stories by Ursula K. Le Guin." *Extrapolation: A Journal of Science Fiction and Fantasy* 18 (December 1976): 28-41.

Identifies themes in Le Guin's short stories "Nine Lives" and "Vaster Than Empires and More Slow" and novella *The Word for World Is Forest* that, according to Remington, are common to her fiction as a whole.

Review of *The Eye of the Heron,* by Ursula K. Le Guin. *Science Fiction Review* 12, No. 46 (Spring 1983): 41.

Commenting on the didacticism of Le Guin's novella *The Eye of the Heron,* the critic concludes: "The problem might be that the story has so much of a Point To Make that the other aspects don't quite get going under their own steam."

Shippey, T. A. "Variations on Newspeak: The Open Question of *Nineteen Eighty-Four*." In *Storm Warnings: Science Fiction Confronts the Future,* edited by George E. Slusser, Colin Greenland, and Eric S. Rabkin, pp. 173-93. Carbondale: Southern Illinois University Press, 1987.

Claims that Le Guin is a "language-satirist" in the vein of George Orwell and demonstrates that her novella *The Word for World Is Forest* parallels Orwell's novel *Nineteen Eighty-Four* "by its demonstration of the ruinous effects of jargon."

Yoke, Carl. "Precious Metal in White Clay." *Extrapolation:*

A Journal of Science Fiction and Fantasy 21, No. 3 (Fall 1980): 197-208.

Presents Le Guin's novella *The Word for World Is Forest* and short story "The Day before the Revolution" as examples of "her ability to detail the worlds she creates, and more importantly, at least in some respects, her ability to perceive and subsequently project characters who are thoroughly human."

Additional coverage of Le Guin's life and career is contained in the following sources published by Gale Research: *Authors and Artists for Young Adults,* Vol. 9; *Concise Dictionary of American Literary Biography, 1968-1988*; *Contemporary Authors,* Vols. 21-24, rev. ed.; *Contemporary Authors New Revision Series,* Vols. 9, 32; *Contemporary Literary Criticism,* Vols. 8, 13, 22, 45, 71; *Children's Literature Review,* Vols. 3, 28; *Dictionary of Literary Biography,* Vols. 8, 52; *Major Authors and Illustrators for Children and Young Adults*; *Major 20th-Century Writers*; and *Something about the Author,* Vols. 4, 52.

Primo Levi

1919-1987

(Also wrote under the pseudonym Damiano Malabaila) Italian memoirist, short story writer, essayist, novelist, and poet.

INTRODUCTION

A survivor of the Nazi concentration camp at Auschwitz, Levi is best known for his first two books, the holocaust memoirs *Se questo è un uomo* (*If This Is a Man*) and *La tregua* (*The Reawakening*). *If This Is a Man* is generally regarded as the most powerful description of the Nazi camps ever written and, like all of his subsequent work, is noted for its extraordinary equanimity and lack of rancor. Despite the horrors he endured, Levi remained consistently hopeful about humanity, steadfastly refusing to "nourish hatred," and his work—particularly his short fiction and essays—displays an almost childlike curiosity about living and the processes of life. Maintaining simultaneous careers as an author and industrial chemist for much of his life, Levi addressed the major issues of the twentieth century in his short fiction with the objective scrutiny of a scientist, the linguistic grace of a poet, and the profound understanding of a philosopher.

Levi was born in Turin, Italy, in 1919. His family was part of a small, highly assimilated middle-class Jewish community, whose roots go back to the sixteenth century. Although all European Jews were affected by anti-Semitism, those in Italy generally did not experience the virulent racism that infected Germany and other European nations until Fascism spread through the country. Levi was twenty when dictator Benito Mussolini and his fascist junta established "racial laws" that called for the official persecution of Italian Jews. Those laws took effect when Levi was in college studying chemistry, the field he believed could unlock the secrets of the universe and bridge the worlds of art and science. When Levi graduated in 1943, it was extremely difficult for Jews to find work, so he joined a band of partisans affiliated with the Italian resistance movement called Justice and Liberty. His band was poorly trained and ill-equipped, and on 13 December 1943 it was ambushed by the fascist militia. While Levi was arrested as a partisan, he admitted he was Jewish during questioning and was sent to Fossoli, a camp near Modena in northern Italy. He wrote that Fossoli was "originally meant for English and American prisoners-of-war [but was used to collect] all the numerous categories of people not approved of by the new-born Fascist Republic." Jews greatly outnumbered the other internees, and their ranks swelled while Levi was there. The SS—the elite Nazi troops responsible for the concentration camps—inspected Fossoli in February 1944, and all the Jews were sent to Auschwitz. After a harrowing, bitterly cold journey on a freight train, five hundred of the prisoners—mostly women, children, the elderly, and the sick and disabled—were immediately forced into the gas chambers. Levi and the remaining prisoners, deemed "economically useful Jews," were spared immediate death only to endure slave labor and constant physical and emotional debasement. Levi explained that the daily routine in the *Lager,* a German word he used to imply both prison camp and the idea of slavery, was designed to bring about "the demolition of a man."

Levi maintained that his survival at Auschwitz was solely a matter of luck. Intimates of the author speculate that Levi's innate curiosity about his environment, his training as a dispassionate observer of phenomena, and his need to bear witness to the crime, enabled him to overcome the despair and sense of futility that broke so many of those who suffered the brutalities of the *Lager.* Auschwitz was liberated by the Soviet army in 1945, and, after a long, tortuous journey described in picaresque detail in *The Reawakening,* Levi returned home to Turin. He subsequently found work in a chemical factory and promptly began writing about his experiences, completing *If This Is a Man* within two years. In 1947 Levi got married and began working at SIVA, a large paint factory in Turin. Although he became the company's general manager in 1961 and established himself as an expert in the manufacture of synthetic resins, he continued to write in the 1950s and 1960s, contributing essays and stories to the newspaper *La Stampa* and publishing *The Reawakening*. Levi retired as a chemist in 1977 to devote himself to writing, and gained international prominence when *Il sistema periodico* (*The Periodic Table*) was published in English in 1984. The widespread praise the book received renewed interest in all of Levi's work and consequently he became internationally renowned as a lecturer and commentator. In 1987, at the height of his fame, Levi died after falling down the stairwell in his four-story apartment building. Italian authorities, as well as many people who knew him, ruled his death a suicide.

Because his first two books were nonfiction and dealt with what many historians consider the most important event of the twentieth century, Levi was ambivalent about the idea of writing fiction. His first short stories, which originally appeared in *La Stampa,* were collected in *Storie naturali* in 1966. The posthumously published English-language collections *The Mirror Maker* and *The Sixth Day, and Other Stories* are comprised of pieces from this edition. Sometimes labeled science fiction, these short stories are often metaphysical extrapolations that combine scientific fact with moral and ethical issues. For example, in "Westward" from *The Sixth Day,* a scientist discovers a substance that can restore people's will to live. The story's moral dilemma is presented when one character states that people should overcome their pain and problems by themselves; "But," another asks, "what about the weak?" In addition to tales that examine ambivalent views about technological progress, Levi also wrote short stories that deal directly with his experience in Auschwitz. The stories in *Lilit e altri racconti* (*Lilith, and Other Stories,* also published as *Moments of Reprieve*) are about Jews attempting to survive Nazi persecution. Essentially character studies, these tales examine humanity's capacity for virtue and evil by portraying both the innocent victims of the Nazis and those who responded to them in clearly despicable ways. In one of the stories, which critic Paul Bailey said "ends on a note of resonant irony," Levi describes a man named Rumkowski, a Jewish prisoner of the Lodz ghetto in Poland who, taking advantage of the Nazi's inattention, flaunts his relatively great wealth before the starving people around him. Bailey added that "[how] Rumkowski arrived at Auschwitz must be left to Primo Levi to relate. 'Virtue' is of the essence of that arrival."

The predominantly autobiographical stories in *The Periodic Table* are often considered Levi's greatest works. In composing these tales, Levi was not constrained by the limits of his history; he embellished certain facts and created composite characters, and took his titles from elements on the periodic table devised by the Russian scientist Dmitry Mendeleyev. Levi's seemingly personal relationships with the chemical elements inspired these reminiscences about the Jewish community in northern Italy, his family, his childhood, and his life before and after Auschwitz. For example, the story "Argon," which refers to one of the "inert" or "noble" gases, introduces the reader to Levi's love for his family and relatives and to the language and culture of this unique and vanishing Italian-Jewish community. Critics note that each story distinctively relates some aspect of an element—for example, the strength of "Iron," the lightness and volatility of "Hydrogen"—to an aspect of Levi's life and, by extension, to the human condition.

In his short stories, Levi never strayed far from the issues related to his experience of the Holocaust. He once said, expressing a certain ambivalence about writing fiction, that when one "is aware of a 'sin' . . . [one] should deepen its examination and the study of it, dedicating himself to it even through suffering . . . and not free himself from it by writing a story." Critics agree that even the stories that do not concern the Holocaust deepen our understanding of humanity in moral crises. Ultimately Levi realized that "from the *Lager* to these fictions, a continuity, a bridge exists."

PRINCIPAL WORKS

SHORT FICTION

Storie naturali [as Damiano Malabaila] 1966
Il sistema periodico 1975
 [*The Periodic Table,* 1984]
Lilit e altri racconti 1981
 [*Lilith, and Other Stories,* 1985; also published as *Moments of Reprieve,* 1986]
Racconti e saggi 1989
 [*The Mirror Maker,* 1989]
The Sixth Day, and Other Stories 1990

OTHER MAJOR WORKS

Se questo è un uomo (memoirs) 1947
 [*If This Is a Man,* 1959; also published as *Survival in Auschwitz: The Nazi Assault on Humanity,* 1961]
La tregua (memoirs) 1958
 [*The Reawakening,* 1965; also published as *The Truce: A Survivor's Journey Home from Auschwitz,* 1965]
Shema: Collected Poems of Primo Levi (poetry) 1976
La chiave a stella (novel) 1978
 [*The Monkey's Wrench,* 1986; also published as *The Wrench,* 1987]
Se non ora, quando? (novel) 1982
 [*If Not Now, When?,* 1985]
L'altrui mestiere (essays) 1986
 [*Other People's Trades,* 1989]
I sommersi e i salvati (essays) 1986
 [*The Drowned and the Saved,* 1988]
Dialogo [with Tullio Regge] (interview) 1989

CRITICISM

John Gross (essay date 1984)

[*In the following highly positive review of* The Periodic

Table, *Gross applauds Levi's imaginative use of the chemical elements as a point of departure for his semi-autobiographical sketches.*]

The Italian author Primo Levi is a chemist by profession, and in writing this remarkable memoir he has had recourse to one of the most basic tools of his trade—the periodic table, in which the chemical elements are arranged according to their atomic numbers. Instead of writing a conventional autobiography he casts his eye over the table, picking out now one element and now another—some 20 in all—and following up the memories or preoccupations they bring to mind. Chromium evokes a whole phase of his past, silver and tin recall particular incidents, zinc and potassium come to embody hard-earned lessons about life.

The Periodic Table is not the first autobiographical work that Mr. Levi has written. During the war he joined a resistance group in his native Piedmont, and when he was arrested in 1943 he was doubly doomed, both as a partisan and as a Jew, he was sent to Auschwitz, but survived to write two outstanding memoirs of his ordeal, which have been published in this country as *Survival in Auschwitz* (though I must say I prefer the title of the British edition, *If This Is a Man,* which sticks closer to the original Italian) and *The Re-awakening.*

These books were valuable acts of testimony, but they also made it clear that Mr. Levi is a true writer, with a fine gift for narrative and subtle insight into character. It is respect for a fellow artist rather than sympathy with a former victim that has won him high praise from such contemporaries as Umberto Eco and Italo Calvino.

In *The Periodic Table,* he writes no less incisively than in his earlier books, and with greater imaginative range. His approach matches the subject matter in its variety; each episode, like each element, has its own distinctive character.

Why does he entitle the opening section, **"Argon"** for instance? Because argon is one of the so-called inert or rare gases, and these gases remind him of his ancestors, who had to work hard enough to earn their bread, but who were "inert in their inner spirits, inclined to disinterested speculation, witty discourses, elegant, sophisticated, and gratuitous discussion."

They were also marginals among marginals, members of the Jewish community that arrived in Piedmont from Spain by way of Provence around 1500, bringing ancient traditions with them and developing new ones—including a patois (the local Piedmontese dialect inlaid with Hebrew) of which Mr Levi gives many fascinating examples. **"Argon"** illumines this drowsy but agreeable corner of the world as it was seen through the eyes of a child, presided over by legendary aunts and uncles, "tobacco-smelling patriarchs and domestic household queens."

All this is a far cry from the low comedy of the **"Nitrogen"** section. Mr. Levi, trying to get what work he can in the years just after the war (we are in the epoch of movies like *The Bicycle Thief*) is hired as a consultant by a shifty businessman who wants to find out why the cheap lipstick he manufactures won't stay stuck in place. It turns out that the missing ingredient can most readily be extracted either from chicken droppings or snake droppings, a discovery that gives Mr. Levi philosophical satisfaction—after all, "that is what nature does: it draws the fern's grace from the putrefaction of the forest floor." But further investigation in the countryside and at the zoo reveals that the waste products in question are much harder to procure than you might suppose, and far more expensive.

A more sinister atmosphere envelops the section in which the author is recruited under murky wartime conditions to take part in the search for a new cure for diabetes involving phosphorus—a crackpot affair inspired by a German professor called Kerrn whose textbook breathes the authentic spirit of the Third Reich. Yet Mr. Levi can readily understand how Kerrn, "half biochemist and half witch doctor," has fallen under the spell of the legends surrounding phosphorus, the bringer of light and will-o'-the-wisp.

"It is not an emotionally neutral element," he says—and neither are many others on the periodic table. He himself has a strong feeling for the traditional attributes and human associations of the elements, from nickel—"the entrails of the earth swarm with gnomes, koboids (cobalt!), nickel, German 'little demon' or 'sprite' "—to "the arsenic of Mithridates and Madame Bovary."

He also has a good deal to say about the chemist's vocation, and about the challenges, satisfactions and setbacks of his career. If matter has its magic, it still remains the adversary—"stupid matter, slothfully hostile as human stupidity is hostile." But both varieties of stupidity can be overcome, and *The Periodic Table* itself represents a clear case of intelligence carrying the day.

One chapter in particular stands out. In the 1960's Mr. Levi found himself in correspondence with his opposite number in a German company about a shipment of vanadium, used in making varnish; gradually he realized that by an eerie coincidence the Dr. Muller he was writing to was the same Muller who had been in charge of the laboratory where he was a slave laborer in Auschwitz. He revealed who he was, and in the letters that followed Muller finally emerged as not so much infamous as inadequate, "after filtering off the rhetoric and the lies in good or bad faith there remained a typically gray human specimen." The whole episode rings profoundly, miserably true.

The book concludes with the history of an atom of carbon—a fable about the infinitude of matter with which we somehow have to reconcile our sense of human uniqueness. And then at the very end of the last line of his last paragraph, Mr. Levi poses the problem of mind in relation to matter with a witty fancy which it would be unfair to give away in a review, but which rounds off a memorable book with a memorable flourish.

John Gross, in a review of "The Periodic Table," in The New York Times, *November 29, 1984, p. C21.*

Alvin H. Rosenfeld   (essay date 1984)

[*In the following review of* The Periodic Table, *Rosenfeld examines the combined literary and scientific approach Levi employs to elucidate personal and historical experiences.*]

To the beginning chemistry student, the periodic table is likely to seem little more than a checkerboard chart of the elements, whose atomic symbols, weights and numbers are so many ciphers to be memorized. To the initiated, however, as one learns from Primo Levi's *The Periodic Table,* the Mendeleevian system is poetry, a possible bridge between the world of words and the world of things, and hence an unexpected means of understanding the universe and ourselves.

As Mr. Levi, the Italian writer and chemist, distills these means, they are endlessly metaphorical, as they must be to afford the correspondences he seeks between the otherwise disparate worlds of physical and human nature. The 21 pieces in *The Periodic Table,* each named after an element, are, therefore, at one and the same time rigorous "confrontations with Mother-Matter" and vividly drawn portraits of human types—analytical "tales of militant chemistry" and imaginative probings of personal, social and political experience. It is rare to find such diverse aims in combination, and rarer still to find them so successfully integrated in a contemporary work of literature. Yet that is what we have in this beautifully crafted book, the most recent and in many ways the most original of Mr. Levi's three volumes of autobiographical reflection.

Primo Levi is known to American readers, if at all, as the author of *Survival in Auschwitz.* That book, an affirmation of lucid, humane intelligence in the face of Nazi barbarism, is one of the truly distinguished works of Holocaust literature and has become something of a classic. It was followed by *The Reawakening,* in which the author described his long and bizarre journey home after his liberation from Auschwitz. In his native Italy these volumes, along with several others, have won for Mr. Levi a considerable reputation, but because so little of his work has been available to English readers, he has remained all but unknown here. This situation has now happily changed with Raymond Rosenthal's admirable translation of *The Periodic Table.*

The book's first piece, **"Argon"** (named for a gas "so inert, so satisfied with [its] condition" that it does "not combine with any other element") is a homage to the author's Jewish ancestors, themselves a breed apart. Intent on retrieving his innumerable aunts and uncles from a legendary past, Mr. Levi at the same time rescues for posterity snatches of their lost language, a local version of Judeo-Italian that combined Hebrew roots with Piedmontese endings and inflections—"a skeptical, good-natured speech . . . rich with an affectionate and dignified intimacy with God." The revivification of this jargon (which Mr. Levi elsewhere refers to as a kind of "Mediterranean Yiddish") and of some of the people who once spoke it is a sizable accomplishment and, in its linguistic precision and playful wit, sets the tone and direction for the pieces that follow.

Like **"Argon,"** these are similarly patterned on analogies between the elements and a variety of human types and develop a mode of imagining reality that is striking in its fusion of physical, chemical and moral truths. To Mr. Levi there are no such things as emotionally neutral elements, just as there are no emotionally neutral men and women. Thus, whether a given story's focus is on friendship, mountain-climbing, early encounters with love or the troubled status of being a Jew in Mussolini's Italy, the author is able to strike a fitting correlation with one of the elements. Mercury, "always restless," is "a fixed and volatile spirit." Zinc, by contrast, is "a boring metal," "not an element which says much to the imagination" (it requires the presence of impurities to react, and in Fascist Italy, as Mr. Levi's imagination seizes upon the analogy, the Jew was to be the impurity—in his case, almost proudly so). There are elements, such as iron and copper, that are "easy and direct, incapable of concealment"; others, such as bismuth and cadmium, that are "deceptive and elusive." The point of these figurations is to revive "the millennial dialogue between the elements and man" and to show that in none of its aspects is nature impermeable to intelligence.

The intelligence made manifest throughout this book is a relentlessly inquisitive one, dedicated to understanding the most subtle dimensions of matter and of man. At once analytic and novelistic, it is the intelligence of a writer who has been able to forge an unusual synthesis of scientific learning and poetic sensibility, of rational procedures and moral perceptions. Its aim, therefore, is both to comprehend and to create, and thereby to keep from being victimized by all outward assaults, spiritual as well as material.

In following Mr. Levi in his pursuit of the elements, one comes to see how the insights of the analyst serve to illuminate a wide range of personal and historical experience, including the author's experiences as an anti-Fascist partisan and his subsequent arrest and incarceration in Auschwitz. To readers of the earlier work, **"Zinc," "Gold," "Cerium," "Chromium"** and **"Vanadium"** will be of particular interest, for they fill in or otherwise expand on episodes recounted in *Survival in Auschwitz.* **"Vanadium,"** the book's penultimate story and its most dramatic one, for instance, vividly describes an uncanny correspondence that Levi had after the war with a Dr. Müller, a German chemist who turns out to have been the chief of the laboratory in Auschwitz where, in 1944, the author slaved to stay alive. The confrontation in this story strikes to the heart of Mr. Levi's subject and shows him at his contemplative best—putting the questions, pondering their manifold implications and reaching a resolution that is both rigorous and humane.

Indeed, for all of its musings upon the enigmas of matter, *The Periodic Table* is best read as a historically situated book and will mean most to those readers who are alert to the mind's engagements with moral as well as physical truths. Thus **"Iron,"** dedicated to Sandro Delmastro, a fellow chemistry student (and the first Resistance fighter to be killed in the Piedmont), is primarily about the nobility of friendship, as **"Phosphorus"** is more a tale of sexual attraction than it is an anatomy of life in the laboratory.

Both pieces, set in the 1940's, have far more to do with the vagaries of human relationships under the Italian racial laws than with the laws of chemistry.

The real attraction of **The Periodic Table,** therefore, lies in the author's ability to probe human events with as much discriminating power as he probes nature and in his refusal to surrender the sovereignty of independent inquiry to either stolid matter or a stupid and savage politics. If one sees the book in this way, it is not difficult to understand how chemistry became for Mr. Levi as much a "political school" as a trade and how its terms might be grasped as an "antidote to Fascism . . . because they were clear and distinct and verifiable at every step, and not a tissue of lies and emptiness."

For all of its immersion in the most wrenching of historical circumstances, **The Periodic Table** is not an angry or a brooding book. On the contrary, it is a work of healing, of tranquil, even buoyant imagination. The meditative power of *Survival in Auschwitz* and *The Reawakening* is fully evident but is joined by a newly acquired power of joyful invention. No doubt every chemist is a bit of a wizard (as every writer wants to be) and looks to extract gold from gangue, though few manage to do so. By descending deep into the matrix of both physical and human nature, Primo Levi seems to have learned the secrets behind such transformations, and he has written what can only be described as a liberating book.

To see just how liberating, read **"Carbon,"** the concluding story, a wondrous tale of a single atom of carbon that traverses the universe, courses through the intricate processes of photosynthesis and comes to rest almost magically at the tip of the author's pen. What that pen has wrought with these stories as the result of that imperceptible but vital element is a new opening on to life, and one that validates the point of the Yiddish proverb used as an epigraph for the book: "Ibergekumene tsores iz gut tsu dertseylin" ("Troubles overcome are good to tell").

> *Alvin H. Rosenfeld, "Elements of a Life," in*
> The New York Times Book Review, *December 23, 1984, p. 9.*

Neal Ascherson   (essay date 1985)

[*In the following excerpt, Ascherson favorably reviews* The Periodic Table *and, while describing several of its stories, provides an overview of Levi's life.*]

Primo Levi was a chemist. Not an apothecary, not an academic or a supervisor of pharmaceutical production in some enormous multinational concern, but a struggling free-lance chemist who has moved from place to place, from isolated mines to dilapidated laboratories, staining his fingers and scorching his lungs in close-quarter work with that which is most universal of all: elements, salts, molecules. There can be few major writers who have supported themselves by this profession. But after reading **The Periodic Table,** one wonders why there are not more. As the sea imposed respect and its own severe morality on Conrad, imposed a nearly infallible test of character for people who tried to make a living from it, so Primo Levi

refers to an obstinate physical universe that reveals a truth about all who strive to make something useful out of it, to break it down, to challenge its identity, or—most absurd of all—to transcend it. The first thing about fascism that repelled Levi was its emphasis on the life of the spirit, distilled to an intoxicating purity. Levi liked the material world for its impurity, its obscene mixture of ashes and diamonds, its sullen reluctance to obey the abstract laws of chemistry and physics.

Each chapter of his enchanting, original book bears the name of an element. But the relationship of the element to the matter of the chapter is never constant, acting sometimes as a profound symbol, sometimes as a mere memory-tag used to develop a reminiscence. **"Argon,"** one of the "inert gases" that "do not combine," leads off the book with an account of Levi's Jewish ancestors in Piedmont, of their attitudes of "dignified abstention," their curious little dialect of Hebrew words with Piedmontese terminations, their taste for "elegant, sophisticated, and gratuitous discussion." They lived in an age and a community when there was room for inertness, when nobody insisted that they should "combine." The chapter **"Zinc"** introduces the young Levi in a Turin chemistry class, listening to the words of a detached, ironic professor whose skepticism about human perfectibility renders him a natural antifascist. They are studying zinc, that gray, boring material that can resist dissolving in acid only in its purest form. "Praise of purity, which protects from evil like a coat of mail; the praise of impurity, which gives rise to changes, in other words, to life."

By the time of **"Iron,"** Levi is twenty and the year is 1939. A second-year student, he is doing qualitative chemical analysis. He is impressed by the nature of iron, which is "easy and direct, incapable of concealment," and his friend Sandro, descendant of a line of peasant blacksmiths, takes him on strenuous walks in the mountains. Sandro was later to be killed after joining the antifascist partisans. But the notion of active resistance comes only gradually to Primo Levi, certainly no "man of iron." He and his other Jewish friends are, by 1941, already isolated. And yet the historic tolerance of the Italian society in which they grew up makes them incredulous about what is taking place. "Only a voluntarily deaf and blind man could have any doubts about the fate reserved for the Jews in a German Europe. . . . And yet, if we wanted to live, if we wished in some way to take advantage of the youth coursing through our veins, there was indeed no other resource than self-imposed blindness." This chapter is named **"Potassium."** Levi has found a safe little job preparing and purifying elements for analysis. He uses some potassium to take moisture out of benzene, overlooks a morsel of potassium left in the vessel, and—when he rinses it—produces a blast of flame which sets fire to the curtains.

As a Jewish scientist in wartime Italy, Levi led an existence not unlike that of a learned slave in the Roman world: courted for his indispensable talents, offered jobs which he cannot refuse, treated with a degree of nervous respect, and yet essentially unfree. He worked for a time at a nickel mine in a remote mountain valley, obsessed with his own formula for extracting the metal from mine spoil. He was hired at a large salary by a Milan factory producing hormone extracts and fell half in love with his impetuous, chaotic colleague Giulia, ferrying her about the city between air raids on the handlebars of his bicycle. At the hormone factory, he read Nazi works of science and decided that phosphorus, that sinister, will-o'-the-wisp stuff used by conjurers and illusionists, fitted into "the environment impregnated with black magic of the Nazi court."

For Levi and his little circle of Jewish friends from Turin, a long period of pupation was nearly over. The bombs fell nightly around them; they wrote their "sad, crepuscular poems" and savored their loneliness. Primo Levi says, cuttingly and memorably, that this mood was nothing especially Jewish but rather a variant of the effect of fascism on almost all Italians, "alienating us and making us superficial, passive, and cynical." But the chrysalis broke apart, once again in a fashion that reflects Italian experience rather than a specifically Jewish one: the Allies landed in North Africa, the battles for Stalingrad took place, and in September 1943 Italian fascism collapsed, to be replaced within a few days by full-scale German occupation. Levi and his friends went into active resistance.

The young chemist became a guerrilla, a member of "the most disarmed partisans in the Piedmont, and probably also the most unprepared." When the militia rushed their hideout, most of the partisans got away, but Levi, too sleepy to collect his wits in time, was taken. Torture and the firing squad appeared inevitable, as he sat in a freezing cell in Aosta: "I read a great deal, because I thought the time left me was short." (I believe that only an Italian writer from this century, from that "school" whose hallmark is thrift with the materials used to convey emotion, could have written that sentence.) But in the same cell there was a man arrested for illegal gold trading, whose family had lived for generations by panning specks of gold from the Dora river. Levi listened to his stories, listened in the cold night to the small sounds of the Dora running over its stones near the prison, and wanted with a new urgency to live and not to die. So this chapter is entitled **"Gold."**

Primo Levi was spared the firing squad and was sent to Auschwitz instead, where his qualifications saved his life. **"Cerium"** is about working in the gigantic IG-Farben chemicals plant a few miles from the camp, about hunger of an intensity difficult to convey. He tried eating fatty acids and glycerin stolen from the laboratory, or furtively toasting pads of sanitary cotton into "fritters," until he and his companion Alberto found some sticks of cerium—the material used for cigarette-lighter flints. Now they could enter with confidence the muttering whirlpool of the Auschwitz economy: somebody was making lighters and bartering them for food, and his minions would give a bread ration for a flint. The Russians were not far away by then. Through the queer properties of this "equivocal and heretical rare-earth group" mineral, added to a number of other strokes of luck, Levi was still alive when the camp was liberated.

Albert did not survive. Primo Levi himself took many years to assimilate what he had seen and suffered: "I felt closer to the dead than the living, and felt guilty at being a man," he writes about his own mood in the first year after the war. The **"Cerium"** theme, retreating underground for a stretch of this book, surfaces again in **"Vanadium."** Twenty years have passed. Levi is now working for a varnish factory which finds that a consignment of resins from West Germany is defective. The Germans recommend a vanadium compound as an additive, in a letter signed by Dr. Müller. Primo Levi wonders if it could possibly be . . . and indeed it does turn out to be that very Dr. Müller of IG-Farben who helped to run the Buna laboratory at Auschwitz and whom Levi so vividly remembers.

Not a brute, and not a hero either. He writes a long, muddled, sentimental letter to Levi about "overcoming the past" (that German cliché) and about mutual understanding. He neither excuses his own early attachment to National Socialism nor comprehends which injuries can reasonably be treated by apology and which cannot. Then, with a tactlessness that—one must say—belongs uniquely to his nation, Müller goes on to congratulate Levi for the way in which he has overcome his Judaism in order to fulfill the Christian precept of forgiving one's neighbor. Reading this, Levi repeats what he said to himself at Auschwitz when Dr. Müller, having ordered him some shoes, asked why he looked so anxious: *"Der Mann hat keine Ahnung"*—he doesn't begin to grasp what's going on.

A fable in this book, apparently written during or just after the war, tells of a barbarian metal-worker, originally from the Germanic tribes, who wanders the continent in search of lead deposits. When he discovers a new lode, he sells it to the nearest natives and moves on. This much resembles Levi's own life, especially in the decades after the liberation. He too kept on the move, a sort of packman-chemist, an alchemist on the road as Zampano was the nomadic showman of *La Strada*. He won a battle with a chromate monster that was turning cans of varnish into useless lumps with the consistency of liver. He lost an expedition to make alloxan, required by a mafioso lipstick manufacturer to dye mouths indelibly crimson; though Primo Levi and his new wife, in order to extract uric acid for the alloxan, collected bicycle-loads of chicken shit and went begging for the excreta of serpents, all that ever emerged from his efforts were "foul vapors, boredom, humiliation, and a black and murky liquid." Later, he and his friend Emilio became free-lance chemists and set up a laboratory for stannous chloride (a tin salt used by mirror makers) in the flat of Emilio's long-suffering parents. They brewed the stuff in chamber pots, soup tureens, bits of chandeliers. They contrived not to inhale too many fumes from hydrochloric acid ("you expel from your nose two short plumes of white smoke, like the horses in Eisenstein's movies"). They went broke, but without bitterness, and Levi moved on to become a traveling "customer service" representative, selling chemicals and listening to the complaints, the endless anecdotes and fantasies of bored Italian manufacturers.

Flamboyant chemicals, sullen human beings; women living adventurously and organic compounds that live timorously behind many locks, ready to bolt down the fire escape when the analyst rings the front doorbell. This cunning bringing-together of animal and mineral allows Levi entry into a wonderful store of irony, of humor and observation, of literary effect. And behind this is a certain perception that is indeed universal but, with a stylist as delicate as Primo Levi, it would be insulting to drag it out and subject it to tests. It's enough to point the reader's attention to the final chapter, **"Carbon"**: simply a history of how a carbon atom might journey through limestone, the lungs of a falcon, the upper air, a vine, a glucose molecule in a human liver, the compound eye of a moth on a Lebanese cedar . . . to the particular cell in the brain of the writer which at that instant decides to bring his book to its end. From the atom of carbon comes "a double snap, up and down, between two levels of energy [which] guides this hand of mine to impress on the paper this dot, here, this one." (pp. 8, 10)

> Neal Ascherson, "The Alchemist," in The New
> York Review of Books, *Vol. XXXI, Nos. 21 &
> 22, January 17, 1985, pp. 8, 10.*

Ann Snitow   (essay date 1985)

[*In the following excerpt, Snitow discusses* The Periodic Table *as a "representative narrative" about the horrors of the Auschwitz death camps.*]

The Periodic Table, an account by the Italian chemist Primo Levi of his lifelong passion for his trade, is a profoundly original contribution to the genre of "the life." Although the elements of the chemist's periodic chart are ostensibly his focus, he is a wonderful writer on whatever subject, and one soon comes to trust him to locate living matter in any compound of experience. However, the particular story history has forced on Levi is not his so much as it is the story of the very rationality he loves run amok, the incalculable violence of our whole century. Extreme circumstances have pushed and shoved this story into the form of a representative narrative, a study of what can be said, what inwardly known, about the ghastly experiences typical of our time.

In Piedmont in Levi's boyhood, being Jewish meant little more than having odd elderly relatives, inconspicuous but eccentric Jews who made do with the middling welcome of Turin but who could fall back on their own exotic jargon. Hebrew words entered the shops with the cloth delivered at the back door, where no one bothered to make the anti-Semitic gesture of resisting them, so that *na vesta a kinim* was a polka-dot dress, and the small fact that *kinim* are lice was comfortably forgotten.

World War II interrupted this bland and gradual pattern of assimilation. **The Periodic Table,** which should have been the life of a chemist madly in love with work, a happy hero enjoying a tussle with "stupid matter," with the "deception, fraud, bedazzlement" of a deliciously shifting world, became instead a story with a hole in it, and that hole is Auschwitz.

Wonderful in itself, **The Periodic Table** has as its necessary shadow book *Survival in Auschwitz.* Levi's life was

wrenched into these two parts, and he cannot get them together between one set of covers. Or, rather, he refuses the assimilation. Still, the books belong together, intractable countertales that they are, one about a man's yen to dismantle nature, the other about the dismantling of a man. And their very different power comes from essential similarities of style: both are organized in mysteriously potent clusters of association. (p. 86)

The Periodic Table, finished in 1975, many years after the Auschwitz memoir . . . , is a record of the man who has come through. Auschwitz was his nightmare, but he has awakened to find that instead of being doomed to waste himself, he is in full possession of his faculties, vital, intelligent, fascinated by the variety of experience waiting beyond the little death inside the prison walls. To be awake: this is in itself the greatest pleasure. Levi's autobiography vibrates with his delight at seeing, at understanding the hidden sources of what he sees, at finding the underground connections that link all matter. In *Survival in Auschwitz,* the material was organized around certain core experiences: "Initiation," "Our Nights," "The Work." Here, chapters are **"Argon," "Hydrogen," "Zinc," "Iron,"** and in their way, these words call up memories and long, looping trains of thought as rich and powerful as any evoked in the shadow book.

For example, under **"Zinc,"** Levi remembers first the ferocious Professor P., in whose laboratory he prepared zinc sulfate. Levi admired P., who was a savage, a hunter, a social Darwinist but who was also—out of sheer love of independence—an anti-Fascist. Levi remembers the delight in his own ability to stay the difficult course set by P., but he never shared his professor's taste for blood or his contempt for those weaker ones who failed in the attack on zinc.

> Zinc, Zinck, zinco: they make tubs out of it for laundry, it is not an element which says much to the imagination, it is gray and its salts are colorless, it is not toxic, nor does it produce striking chromatic reactions; in short, it is a boring metal.

But the savage hunter must not get so complacent. Zinc, which should have been easy to blend with acid, resisted the young Levi's assault: "The hour of the appointment with Matter, the Spirit's great antagonist, had struck." It turns out that the "so tender and delicate zinc," when very pure, obstinately resists yielding to the acid preparation.

> One could draw from this two conflicting philosophical conclusions: the praise of purity, which protects from evil like a coat of mail; the praise of impurity, which gives rise to changes, in other words, to life. I discarded the first, disgustingly moralistic, and I lingered to consider the second, which I found more congenial. In order for the wheel to turn, for life to be lived, impurities are needed . . . Fascism does not want them, forbids them, and that's why you're not a Fascist; it wants everybody to be the same, and you are not.

"Zinc" ends with Rita, who is also there, in the lab, working with zinc, so there can be a "small zinc bridge" to

Levi's other desire, "a woman's smile." Rita and Primo are almost uncombinable elements: he is "intoxicated," "disjointed," Jewish, "the impurity that makes the zinc react"; she is more inert, "thin, pale, sad, and sure of herself." The victory of the day is finally that over Rita's reluctance. When he takes her arm, two resistant elements join. Zinc is only the beginning in a lifetime tested by many surprising catalytic agents, enriched by unlikely moments of contact.

Auschwitz rarely comes closer to the center of Levi's memoir than this, yet *The Periodic Table* contains traces of all the traumas now digested. As a young man, Levi sought mastery, but his encounter with the *Übermenschen* refined his boyhood passions, leaving wisdom as the distillate in the clear glass flask. (pp. 86-7)

> *Ann Snitow, "Living Matter," in* The Nation, *New York, Vol. 241, No. 3, August 3-10, 1985, pp. 86-8.*

Ferdinando Camon on meeting Primo Levi:

Levi arrived, short, pale, courteous. He suggested we go immediately to a corner of the hotel lobby and begin the interview.

His hair and beard were white, the beard whiter than the hair. His look was almost ironic, his smile almost playful. A very orderly mind, with detailed, precise memories. At a certain point he picked up the sheet of paper with the questions and on the back drew the layout of Auschwitz: with the central concentration camp, the outlying ones, and the number of prisoners. He spoke in a low voice, without getting excited, with no outbursts—that is to say, without rancor.

I have often wondered about the reason for this mildness, this gentleness. The only answer that comes to mind, even today, is the following: Levi did not shout, did not assail, did not accuse, because he didn't *want* to shout. He wanted something much more: to *make* people shout. He renounced his own reaction in exchange for the reaction of the rest of us. He took a long-range view. His mildness, his gentleness, his smile—which had something shy, almost childlike about it—were actually his weapons.

> *Ferdinando Camon, in his* Conversations with Primo Levi, *The Marlboro Press, 1989.*

Fernanda Eberstadt (essay date 1985)

[*In the following excerpt from her controversial essay "Reading Primo Levi," Eberstadt discusses in broad terms the characteristics of Levi's finest writing and, using* Lilith, and Other Stories *as an example, examines what she sees as the serious limitations of Levi's insight into Jewish life in the Auschwitz death camps.*]

As a writer, Primo Levi represents a relatively unfamiliar combination in the literature of the Nazi concentration camps. He is a survivor without Jewish—or, more specifically, without East European—inflections, a memoirist endowed with all the fruits of a classical Mediterranean education, an aesthete, a skeptic, a mild, equable, and eminently civilized man who is more at home in Dante and Homer than in the Bible. Some of the qualities he brings to his work—secularism, cultivation, elitism (coupled with an attitude of amused affection toward the common man), and a lack of deep familiarity with Jewish history or religion—are typical of his generation of Italian Jewish writers. Virtues that are his alone include precision, economy, subtlety, a dry and rueful wit, an intimate understanding of the dramatic potential of understatement, and a certain frigidity of manner which combines effectively with the explosiveness of his subject matter. (p. 43)

[In] the volume of stories entitled *Lilith* [also published as *Moments of Reprieve*], Levi set out to portray the Jewish side of life in Auschwitz. *Lilith* is a collection of vignettes serving as footnotes or appendices to his tales of the camps. Some of these sketches are culled from Levi's later reading about the war and the Holocaust: the experiences of a Polish partisan who fought in Italy, or of a young Jew who survived the war disguised as a Hitler *Jugend*. Many are about religious Jews—cantors' and rabbis' sons who continued to practice their faith and to preserve their cultural and historical memories in the death camps.

These tales, told in a *faux-naif* manner reminiscent of Yiddish fabulists and utterly unlike Levi's characteristically polished and subtle style, are uneven, but although even at his worst Levi is deft and able to convey much in a few words, nevertheless he must be said to fail in his larger attempt to recreate something of the flavor of Jewish life in the camps. In part the problem is one of inauthenticity. Thus, in one tale a watchmaker from a remote Lithuanian village astounds his barracks chief—a German Communist—by refusing food on Yom Kippur since, as the narrator informs us, cooking on that day is labor considered "inadvisable" by "some commentators." (It is forbidden, and on no lesser authority than Leviticus; but perhaps more significantly, rabbinic authorities had actually laid a positive injunction upon Jewish inmates of the camps to eat on Yom Kippur, in order to preserve life.) But such missteps are no more than symptoms of a larger discomfort.

By his own admission, Primo Levi is the child of a peculiarly Italian credo that "nothing is of greater vanity than to force oneself to swallow whole a moral system elaborated by others, under another sky." In addition to this resistance to all "unproven revealed truths," Levi is simply cursed with a tin ear for religion, and is incapable of representing imaginatively the life of people who practice their faith "without any feeling of constraint, rebellion, or irony." The unfortunate literary consequence is that although he self-consciously sets out in these stories to reproduce the traditions of East European Jewry as they were preserved in the death camps of Poland, he unwittingly reduces that tradition's central component—the Jewish faith—to the status of an archaic cult, a magpie's nest of quaint fables and "maniacally subtle" prohibitions.

Lilith also bears witness to a new and puzzling variation on Levi's tendency to view the camps, in his own words, "as a distorted mirror of the present-day world." In the last story of the book (in its author's estimation, the most important) he describes the life and career of Mordechai Chaim Rumkowski, the Nazi-installed Eldest of the Jews who turned the Lodz ghetto into a miniature kingdom, printing his own currency and postage stamps, commissioning poems in his own praise, organizing an army of workers ten thousand strong, and, finally, negotiating with the Germans over the transportation of Jews to concentration camps.

Rumkowski's career is hardly unknown: it has been the subject of much scholarly attention, it has offered occasion for at least one novel (Leslie Epstein's *King of the Jews*), and most recently it has been brought to our attention once more in Lucjan Dobroszycki's masterful edition of *The Chronicles of the Lodz Ghetto*. Levi has nothing new to add to the lamentable story. Instead, his half-whimsical, half-solemn retelling of it deliberately deflects its historical particularity, urging an "allegorical" view of Rumkowski as an emblem of a universal human potentiality. In Levi's reading, this former orphanage director and bankrupt who was dismissed from the Zionist party for insubordination before he rose to power under the Nazis was no sport brought to prominence by the unnatural circumstances of ghetto life but rather a kind of everyman, whose bizarre and sorrowful career serves as "a metaphor for our civilization":

> We are all mirrored in Rumkowski, his ambiguity is ours, that of hybrids molded of clay and spirit; his fever is ours, that of our Western civilization which "descends to hell with trumpets and drums," and its miserable tinsel is the distorted image of our symbols of social prestige. . . . Like Rumkowski, we too are so dazzled by power and money as to forget our essential fragility, forget that all of us are in the ghetto, that the ghetto is enclosed, that beyond the enclosure wait the lords of death and that close by the train is waiting.

This statement, with its muddled sentimentality, its descent into educated cliché, and its note of hauteur disguised as an almost maudlin self-incrimination (somehow, one does not believe Levi means to include himself in the "we" under indictment here), sits startlingly at odds with the modesty, the rationality, the faith in human will, and above all the bent for exact discrimination which illuminate Levi's finest writing. (pp. 45-6)

Yet for all their grace, intelligence, and often poetical qualities of expression, the memoirs, novels, and short stories of Levi's middle age suffer from a certain inhibiting fastidiousness and insubstantiality, an inertia which stems perhaps from snobbery or timidity, perhaps from lack of conviction. Describing his ancestors in the opening story of *The Periodic Table*, Levi could be describing his own later books: "Though quite various, [they] have in common a touch of the static, an attitude of dignified abstention, of voluntary (or accepted) relegation to the margins of the great river of life."

Levi's finest work, a civilized man's record of the ultimate barbarity, recalls that of the poets of late Latin antiquity, the last fruits of a rich and eloquent culture, living on the edge of an "endless night." The classical scholar Helen Waddell writes of Ausonius, a 4th-century poet, consul, and memoirist, who after a full career settled on his estate in Bordeaux to grow Paestum roses, work on his memoirs of the provincial grand bourgeoisie, and compose poetry dallying in "anagram and compliment, enamelled fragments of philosophy, the fading of roses, the flavor of oysters." Levi is such an Ausonius, one who lived to see and tell of the Sack of Rome and who was, if alas only momentarily, endowed by the sight with a strange power of speech. (p. 47)

*Fernanda Eberstadt, "Reading Primo Levi,"
in* Commentary, *Vol. 80, No. 4, October, 1985,
pp. 41-7.*

Amanda Prantera   (essay date 1985)

[*In the following review of* The Periodic Table, *Prantera notes that the conflict among Levi's three personae—scientist, storyteller, and thinker—results in uneven writing.*]

Once in an unguarded moment when I was trying to illustrate the unbounded nature of human vanity, I shamefacedly admitted to my daughter that I, too, outwardly so cool-headed and realistic about my slender talents, cherished in the back of my mind a dream of being awarded the Nobel Prize. I could see myself, I confessed, walking up an aisle of red plush carpet, flanked by applauding onlookers and heralded by fanfares, dressed in my best, blushing becomingly as I prepared to receive this the highest accolade currently available in the profession. Strange to say, and pathetic though I must have sounded, my daughter did not scoff at me in the least. 'There's nothing wrong in that,' she said encouragingly, patting my arm. 'I know exactly what you mean. You're right. Why not? It would be *wonderful*'—here she stopped and became thoughtful—'only what do you suppose they could award it to you for?'

Much the same question, and with much the same genuine lack of irony, posed itself to me when I read on the back of the cover of this book that its author, Dr Primo Levi, was being spoken of as a possible candidate for the Nobel. Would it be for literature, I wondered? Or for chemistry? Or would it conceivably be the Peace Prize, seeing that in this book of his he strives so painstakingly to unite these two apparently divergent disciplines? For—and I had better be quick about saying this if my lack of irony is to be believed—Dr Levi is not merely a writer, nor even a writer plus thinker: he is writer plus thinker plus scientist all rolled into one, and judging from the wise and tolerant tone of his writing, he also appears to be an extremely clever and sympathetic human being. However, since the best books do not necessarily proceed from the best thinkers or the best scientists or the best human beings (or even, come to think of it, from the best writers), and if, as I suspect, it is the Nobel Prize for Literature that the blurb-writer has in mind, the claim made on Levi's behalf needs a little more investigating—at least in so far as this particular work of his is concerned.

The title of the book, *The Periodic Table*, is taken from

the name of a classificatory list of elements which form the basis of the chemist's stock-in-trade: a list which normally hangs—so I am told—neglected, dust-covered, taken for granted, in some corner of every practitioner's laboratory, as fundamental as a diagram of the human skeleton or venous network is to a doctor and as little consulted. Dr Levi seems to be one of the few who have consulted it, however, and after a long and successful scientific career, he has taken from the list a score or so of items—iron, lead, mercury, gold, uranium and so forth—and used them as aides-mémoire, not to mention chapter headings, drawing from each item a thread of reminiscence with which to weave an unusual autobiography. The result is not so much the story of a life—there is no full-scale coverage in the strict sense, although chronological order had been respected—as the contents of a photograph album: a series of independent and often barely related stills culled through the years; all of the same subject, of course, but in different poses and settings.

Starting with argon, an inert, gaseous element which serves as a metaphorical touchstone for their condition and behaviour, Dr Levi introduces us to his relatives and family, all respected members of Turin's Jewish community. We meet Uncles Gabriel, Aaron and Bonaparte, dignified and ineffectual, sheltering from reality behind inch-thick lenses or barriers of learned books, aunts with tormented pasts who never leave their rooms, gourmet grandmothers, great-aunts, uncles of grandmothers . . . The pick of an eccentric and cultivated community is sympathetically brought to life, its quirks and foibles carefully explained. The explanation, mind you, is a little over-careful in parts—there are explanations of single words and explanations of their derivations and explanations of the explanations themselves—but to my mind it is here, in these thumbnail sketches of the family oddballs, that Levi's photographic technique is at its liveliest and most effective. Accents, tricks of speech, jokes—Jewish jokes—are precisely recaptured.

The headings **'Hydrogen', 'Iron'** and **'Zinc',** with the memories that they evoke, take us through the years of school and university—years spent under the menace of a waxing but as yet not fully fledged Fascism; while the following chapters, with a few interruptions and exceptions, lead us into the war years, following the itinerary of a highly gifted and sensitive young man in search of work in an ever more hostile environment, and showing us how, slowly and painfully, from the rebuffs and humiliations he received, he awakens first to social and then to political awareness. From rock-climbing, one of the favourite pastimes of the young Turin bourgeoisie of the period, Levi graduates to a more earnest form of mountaineering, taking to the hills with the Partisans of the Italian resistance movement, though, unlike most Italian intellectuals who joined the Partisans, he is so modest about his exploits that the episode risks seeming insignificant. From the Resistance we are whisked on to a chapter concerning his captivity in Auschwitz; and then, with a disarmingly stoical shrug of the shoulders, to his post-war professional career. Dr Levi's account of the Thirties and Forties is that of an honest post-war intellectual. Unfortunately, his reserve, though unusual and in personal terms commend-

able, tends to trammel his narrative and to flatten it somewhat. The war episodes—which you would think were more or less guaranteed to give him his most stirring and interesting material—are among the least vivid and successful.

Each of the book's chapters has the inner structure of a self-contained story, or anecdote, and in those dealing with the post-war period the threads are pulled together in a more commanding way, moving to a climax in which, in the second-to-last episode, a figure from the past, a former inspector of the laboratory at Auschwitz where Levi worked as a prisoner, reappears in the author's present, occupying the position of manager of a firm of suppliers which has furnished Levi's own concern with faulty material. The confrontation between the two men, their roles now reversed by circumstance, never takes place except in the most roundabout way, but for all that, none of the potential drama is wasted or underplayed as it is in the preceding chapters. It is a bitter, pregnant, sad and fascinating piece of human experience, in the telling of which the author's remarkable powers of restraint are for once an unmixed asset. The book would still be worth reading if it contained this episode alone.

The last chapter, **'Carbon',** sets forth what we may call the author's philosophy or way of looking at the world, and acts as justification and framework for the somewhat uneven material which has preceded it. I should mention that, tucked in between the chronologically-ordered chapters of the life-history proper, there are fragments of purely imaginative writing—stories, flights of fancy—often of exquisite craftsmanship. My favourite, is the tale of a little girl captured by an impatient house-painter anxious to get on with his job but 'imprisoned' within a circle drawn on the floor. The theme is Brechtian, and so is the simplicity of its handling, but the whimsicality and the very Jewish delight in the magic of words and sounds, represents Levi's literary gift at its best.

Seeing that there are at least three of them, which of the Levis is it who is seated at the writing-desk: Levi the scientist, Levi the narrator or Levi the thinker? And is there friction between them? And if there is, who is it who ultimately gets the upper hand and resolves the friction? As regards matters of style, there can be little doubt that it is the man of science who predominates: the writing is purified, measured, distilled, controlled at every turn, almost as if the author had sat there with a sieve, throwing aside every phrase, expression or word that would not pass through the mesh of his exacting filter. How about subject-matter then? Well, here the narrator holds full sway. Chemistry comes into it a good deal, of course, but only as a pretext. It provides the author with a fount of inspiration, a novel way of getting purchase on things. Although, as I have already intimated, it is nearly always when he forgets about the label on his jar and escapes into the realm of pure storytelling that the inspiration he derives from his years of practice as a chemical researcher is most fecund.

So no friction here either: the artistic hierarchy is respected, and Levi's many-sidedness brings in its fruits. In fact friction—which there definitely is—only becomes noticeable when one considers the composition as a whole. Let me explain. As I said earlier, the structure all along is avowedly fragmentary, and it is for Levi the thinker to tie it up in his last chapter, to justify it and make it hold together. And it is here that things somehow go wrong. It could be that the thinker's thread, or glue or whatever it is, is not strong enough—that he should never have been entrusted with the work in the first place. Or it may be that the scientist with his microscope has taken over once again and contrived to rob the narrator of his macroscopic vision. In either case, the upshot is that when the finished work is held up to the light the rag-bag origin of Dr Levi's material—beautiful though some of the single pieces are—shows through, and on finishing the book one is left with the impression that all these episodes are in reality odds and ends that the author has found lying in a drawer somewhere after his other writings finished, and felt it was a pity to waste. If Levi the artist (and there undoubtedly is such a person) had been in charge when it came to the final assembly, I can't help feeling he could have made a better job of it.

> *Amanda Prantera, "Aaron, Gabriel and Bona-parte," in* London Review of Books, *Vol. 7, No. 22, December 19, 1985, p. 23.*

Meredith Tax   (essay date 1986)

[*In the following excerpt, Tax discusses* Moments of Reprieve *and* The Periodic Table *in the context of Levi's Holocaust literature.*]

How many ordinary people . . . have been ground in the mill of world history: survived the Holocaust or Cambodia; fled the war in Vietnam or Bangladesh; escaped from Argentina or the Soviet Union, Chile or South Korea, Haiti or El Salvador? For all these survivors, "the personal is political" in ways more terrible than feminists imagined when they coined the slogan. Yet few are able to write of world-historical tragedies so that we really feel the political dimensions of their personal experiences and take their politics personally.

One of them is Primo Levi.

More than anything else I've read or seen—more even than *Shoah*—Primo Levi's books helped me not only to grasp the reality of genocide, but to figure out what it means for people like me, who grew up sheltered from the storm. This is because he's a wonderful writer: deft, witty, and precise. The lightness of his touch enabled me to keep reading even when what he was saying was unbearable. That I could read him at all is a tribute to his power, for my terror of understanding was considerable; there were years when I could not open a book about the Holocaust without being overcome by such severe anxiety that I had to close it. I was grateful to people who said, "Why torture yourself? Is this really necessary?"

It is necessary. For what the Nazis did has shaped our world as much as any other event in modern history: they lifted up the cover of civilization and showed the horrors lurking under the bed. The horrors are still there. But if we can grasp what happened, we can begin to see how it might have been stopped or limited. We can also see the Nazi impulses that still exist and are a danger to all of us.

But for this to work, each of us must grasp what happened with her imagination, concretely on the level of individual experience. Reading Levi helps because he has done it himself. He has really experienced the things that happened to him, without blocking or distortion or self-dramatization. (p. 10)

The Periodic Table . . . is an effervescent gloss on Auschwitz in the form of meditations on various chemical elements; one might even call it a *Jew d'esprit*. One of Levi's most appealing traits is his playfulness, and surely this was another thing that enabled him to keep on and that makes him different from other Holocaust writers. He has a childlike wonder and delight in life, even in extremity; at one point, half dead with exhaustion, he passionately tried to teach another prisoner Ulysses' speech from Dante's *Inferno:* "Think of your breed; for brutish ignorance / Your mettle was not made; you were made men / to follow after knowledge and excellence."

It's great to read a Jew who's so Italian—what a combination. If Auschwitz was Levi's Inferno and the journey home described in *The Reawakening* his Purgatory, Italy itself is Paradise to him. He begins one of his stories in *Moments of Reprieve*: "It often happens these days that you hear people say they're ashamed of being Italian. In fact we have good reasons to be ashamed: first and foremost, of not having been able to produce a political class that represents us and, on the contrary, tolerating for thirty years one that does not. On the other hand, we have virtues of which we are unaware and we do not realize how rare they are in Europe and in the world."

One of those virtues is an absence of murderous prejudice: of all the countries in Europe, only Italy and Denmark protected their Jews. *If Not Now, When?,* Levi's novel, a tribute to what he calls "the moonstruck world of Ashkenazic Judaism" and an attempt to educate his countrymen about Jewish resistance, has a band of partisans, the Gedalists, fighting their way through an end-of-the-war no man's land toward Palestine. He ends the novel when they reach Turin and are told, "It's an oasis, this country." He knows they have to go to Palestine, but Italy is the promised land for him and he wants to take all the Eastern European Jews he loved, who died in the camps, home for a visit.

His new book, *Moments of Reprieve,* consists of character sketches, Levi's way of memorializing certain individuals from the camps, a way of fighting the dehumanization the Nazis visited even on the dead, leaving them only smoke and a number on a ledger. He says in his preface, "A great number of human beings especially stood out against that tragic background . . . begging me one after another to help them survive and enjoy the ambiguous perennial existence of literary characters." Like other survivors, Levi writes to remember, to exorcise, and to bear witness. And he keeps writing about the Holocaust because he cannot help it. (p. 11)

> *Meredith Tax, "Speak, Memory," in* VLS, *No. 43, March, 1986, pp. 10-14.*

George B. Kauffman   (essay date 1986)

[*In the following review of* The Periodic Table, *Kauffman praises Levi for rendering his experiences in a personal yet universal manner and for his poetic treatment of scientific topics.*]

As a chemist and as a Jew, I looked forward to reading this book, first published in Italy as *Il sistema periodica* [*The Periodic Table*] in 1975, with a mixture of anticipation and trepidation. Its author, a writer, chemist, and concentration camp survivor (Auschwitz No. 174517 [the number tattooed on Levi's wrist—prisoners were identified and addressed by number rather than name]), born in Turin in 1919, is the recipient of numerous literary prizes and is regarded in his native Italy as one of the most important and gifted men of letters of this century. The first book of Levi's to be translated into English in almost two decades, it had received rave reviews on both sides of the Atlantic. I am pleased to report that the volume fulfilled my most extravagant expectations.

This unique book virtually defies categorization. In a fascinating blend of autobiography, memoirs, history, scientific methodology and explication, character sketches, comedy, tragedy, romance, biblical quotations, psychology, poetry, philosophy, and fiction, the author uses Mendeleev's periodic table as a metaphor or framework on which he organizes, in roughly chronological order, the events of a life filled with triumphs and tragedies. Each of the book's twenty-one chapters or essays bears the name of a chemical element, which, like Proust's madeleine, serves to "trigger" Levi's recollections of a person, experience, or adventure from his past. Two of these vignettes, **"Lead"** and **"Mercury,"** are fiction—first-person short stories dealing with chemical or alchemical themes and set entirely in italics. In two essays, **"Sulfur"** and **"Titanium,"** Levi himself does not appear.

Though written in terse, simple prose, the book is nevertheless poetic and lyrical, strongly evoking vivid images and feelings, which anyone who has tried to write poetry on scientific topics (I did so with indifferent success during a sabbatical leave in 1979) cannot but admire, appreciate, and respect. Like a true poet, the author views life with awe and does not state the plan of his work, showing rather than explaining it. Thus it is only near the end of the book that he discloses its purpose:

> I told him that I was in search of events, mine and those of others, which I wanted to put on display in a book, to see if I could convey to the layman the strong and bitter flavor of our trade, which is only a particular instance, a more strenuous version of the business of living. I told him that it did not seem fair to me that the world should know everything about how the doctor, prostitute, sailor, assassin, countess, ancient Roman, conspirator, and Polynesian lives and nothing about how we transformers of matter live: but that in this book I would deliberately neglect the grand chemistry, the triumphant chemistry of colossal plants and dizzying output, because this is collective work and therefore anonymous. I was more interested in the stories of the solitary chemistry, unarmed and on foot,

at the measure of man, which with few exceptions has been mine: but it has also been the chemistry of the founders, who did not work in teams but alone, surrounded by the indifference of their time, generally without profit, and who confronted matter without aids, with their brains and hands, reason and imagination.

Levi tells what it is like to be both a scientist (in his case, a chemist) and a complete, multifaceted, and compassionate human being (in short, the *Mensch,* which all Jewish parents since Abraham and Sarah have encouraged their offspring to become). Thus his reminiscences are personal but at the same time universal; we can view the macrocosm in the microcosm. Though intended to bring science to life for the layman, the book will assume an added dimension for the reader who is a scientist or historian. Such readers can empathize and identify with the narrator as he imaginatively but articulately recounts emotions that they have felt but rarely expressed so vividly. For example, Levi describes his motivation for becoming a chemist as follows:

> That the nobility of Man, acquired in a hundred centuries of trial and error, lay in making himself the conqueror of matter, and that I had enrolled in chemistry because I wanted to remain faithful to this nobility. That conquering matter is to understand it, and understanding matter is necessary to understanding the universe and ourselves and that therefore Mendeleev's Periodic Table, which just during those weeks we were laboriously learning to unravel, was poetry, loftier and more solemn than all the poetry we had swallowed down in liceo; and come to think of it, it even rhymed! That if one looked for the bridge, the missing link, between the world of words and the world of things, one did not have to look far: it was there, in our Autenrieth, in our smoke-filled labs, and in our future trade.

In the essay **"Hydrogen,"** Levi's account of his youthful attempt to prepare nitrous oxide (laughing gas) and successful electrolysis of water in a makeshift laboratory recalled my own adolescent experiments under similar conditions, and each reader will encounter here and there scenes that will likewise awaken memories of his or her own experiences.

In his first chapter, **"Argon,"** Levi describes his "noble, inert, and rare" forebears beginning with the sixteenth century. Not contenting himself with subtle insights into personality, which he paints with deft strokes for all characters throughout the book, he describes the culture of Jewish Piedmont, including the "curious language"—a Hebrew-Piedmontese dialect (etymologists and devotees of Leo Rosten's *The Joys of Yiddish* may here find some unfamiliar expressions and piquant imprecations to add to their collections). Then in swift succession he describes the vicissitudes of his life—his education and instructors, his friends and acquaintances, his meeting with his future wife, conditions in pre- and post-World War II Italy, and, most of all, his diverse chemical occupations and his philosophical reflections upon their significance (not all his investigations are successful; his attempted synthesis of alloxane from "chicken shit," described with humor in **"Nitrogen,"** is a case in point).

Levi's portrayal of his professional activities ("fornicating with matter in order to support myself") is utterly free of pretentiousness, and with hylozoistic animism he brings to life—even for nonscientists—such common substances as ammonium chloride, hydrochloric acid, and even rocks ("the rock, which seems dead, instead is full of deception: sometimes it changes its nature even while you're digging, like certain snakes that change color so you won't see them"). During World War II Levi joined the partisans, and on 13 December 1943 he was captured and sent, along with 651 other Jews, only 31 of whom survived, to the Fossoli concentration camp and thence to Auschwitz. Inasmuch as he has already dealt with his Auschwitz experience in his two best-known books, *Se questo è un uomo* (1947; translated as *Survival in Auschwitz,* 1961) and *La tregua* (1963; translated as *The Reawakening* 1965), he deals with this time in only two of the essays, **"Cerium"** and **"Vanadium."** The last essay, **"Carbon,"** tells the story of an atom of carbon—its peregrinations and transformations from limestone through carbon dioxide, glucose, the wood of a cedar of Lebanon, the body of an insect, and so on. He concludes from this "life cycle" that "the death of atoms, unlike ours, is never irrevocable."

Except for a glaring mistake on page 3—unfortunately the first page of the book (Neil Bartlett was not awarded the Nobel Prize for his discovery of noble gas compounds)—I found only eight minor errors. The book is a perfect and pleasurable summer read, ideally suited for browsing and reflection (I read it during a half-dozen of my daily morning constitutionals with my dog Jezebel). I only hope that its title does not discourage laymen from reading this synthesis of Levi's life and work, which is a successful but all-too-rare attempt to bridge C. P. Snow's gap between the two cultures of science and the humanities. (pp. 330-32)

> *George B. Kauffman, in a review of "The Periodic Table," in Isis, Vol. 77, No. 287, June, 1986, pp. 330-32.*

Bruce Clarke   (essay date 1986)

[*In the following review of* The Periodic Table, *Clarke focuses on the story "Carbon" to show how Levi uses the form and subject matter of a research chemist's discourse to create a poetic, atomic-level tale of "quest romance."*]

Meredith Tax's recent characterization of Primo Levi's *The Periodic Table* as "an effervescent gloss on Auschwitz" misses the point of the book. It is true that every other book Levi has written centers on the Holocaust and phases of Jewish resistance to it, but what emerges from *The Periodic Table* is that Levi personally survived to tell of Auschwitz to a large extent because he was a chemist, and so had a skill he could trade for chances at survival. *The Periodic Table* is a payment on his personal and professional debts to the discipline of chemistry, and as such it is also a reprieve from Holocaust topics. As Levi makes very clear, the book is a celebration of the poetry of chemistry: "Mendeleev's Periodic Table . . . was poetry." So

here we need not read Levi strictly within the context and associations of Holocaust literature; we can also read him as a cannier, more literate, less moonbeamy Lewis Thomas. Levi is the bard of a scientific vision that transcends particular historical events, but speaks with a voice and message tempered by his personal immersion in historical tragedy.

The topic of chemistry is universal and universally daemonic: it releases Levi from the mode of prosaic memoir into the mode of poesis, and I believe it is this formula that has made *The Periodic Table* so appealing and such an immediate success. Even while adhering to the actual chemical qualities of elements, he can set his poetic muse quite free through personification of the shared qualities of matter and human character, and he does so in the fine old vein of Ovidian metamorphosis. As a chemist, Levi grants the indifference of given forms: "Matter is matter, neither noble nor vile, infinitely transformable"; and he places himself among the chemists, "we transformers of matter." Levi's daemonic overtones throughout the book are brought to a head in the last chapter, for here he tells "the saga of an atom of carbon, to make the people understand the solemn poetry, known only to chemists, of chlorophyll photosynthesis."

The story in **"Carbon"** is an elemental parallel to the cyclical narratives of quest-romance. The obvious question is: has Levi merely adapted the world to his text—"told a story"—or is the structural homology between the wanderings of carbon and the wanderings of the soul in quest-romance an actual insight into affairs? Levi's **"Carbon"** is in fact a metamorphic romance concerning a most metamorphic element: if water is the great metamorphic or transformational molecule, the medium for all biological processes, carbon is the great metamorphic atom. Allotropically it lends the same atomic structure to chemical forms as varied as pencil lead and diamonds—and combined with water, it issues into living tissue. Carbon "is the only element that can bind itself in long stable chains without a great expense of energy. . . . Therefore carbon is the key element of living substance: but its promotion, its entry into the living world, is not easy and must follow an obligatory, intricate path. . . ."

The coincidence of narrative romance with the description of the behavior of carbon begins with the ability of carbon to "promote" itself from inert to living matter, to insert itself into living processes. Thus the fate of the carbon atom literally parallels fictional or "figurative" promotions: just as the animated objects of romance—talking reeds, conscientious beasts, personified powers, superhuman agents—arise out of the promotion of terms from names to figures, life arises with the promotion of carbon from an inert compound to an organic participant. So Levi begins to describe the existence of this carbon atom during its primal sleep, "bound to three atoms of oxygen and one of calcium, in the form of limestone," with a personification: "Its existence . . . is a pitiless alternation of hots and colds . . . : an imprisonment, for this potentially living personage, worthy of the Catholic Hell."

By taking the carbon atom as a "potentially living personage," Levi endows that elemental identity with "soul," but as we have seen, carbon's allotropic possibilities, its metamorphic nature, already make it apt for such figurative endowment. And in terms of this personification, Levi elaborates a secular myth of incarnation: the fortunate fall of an elemental life principle. The first sublime crossing of Levi's tale is the leap taken by the carbon atom over the limen from physics to biochemistry, from matter to life: as carbon dioxide "it traveled with the wind . . . now high, now low, on the sea and among the clouds . . . ; then it stumbled into capture and the organic adventure." Now is the moment of transgression, of transcendental nomination: the carbon atom "had the good fortune to brush against a leaf, penetrate it, and be nailed there by a ray of the sun":

> Our atom of carbon enters the leaf, colliding with other innumerable (but here useless) molecules of nitrogen and oxygen. It adheres to a large and complicated molecule that activates it, and simultaneously receives the decisive message from the sky, in the flashing form of a packet of solar light. . . .

Levi has translated mythic intuition by way of scientific vision: Phoebus Apollo with his shafts of light, or Hermes, mercurial messenger from heaven carrying the celestial packets, photons of solar energy, into a daemonic world. "Now our atom is inserted: it is part of a structure . . . a beautiful ring-shaped structure, an almost regular hexagon," a molecule of glucose ($C_6H_{12}O_6$) in which carbon and water combine their individual daemonic potentials in the joint effort of organic life. But like the fate of the immortal soul in a Neoplatonic allegory, the carbon atom's organic residence is only a temporary, essentially magical accident.

Following out this saga, Levi traces a metamorphic series of forms worthy of the transformations of Proteus: the "organic adventure" of this carbon atom, from leaf to grape to wine, from mouth to stomach to liver to muscle fiber, there to be overtaken by oxidization.

> So a new molecule of carbon dioxide returned to the atmosphere, and a parcel of the energy that the sun had handed to the vine-shoot passed from the state of chemical energy to that of mechanical energy. . . . "Such is life," although rarely is it described in this manner: an inserting itself, a drawing off to its advantage, a parasitizing of the downward course of energy, from its noble solar form to the degraded one of low-temperature heat. In this downward course, which leads to equilibrium and thus death, life draws a bend and nests in it.

The vital romance of the carbon atom begins only when it enters "the narrow door of photosynthesis. . . . not only the sole path by which carbon becomes living matter, but also the sole path by which the sun's energy becomes chemically usable"; but this romance ends through any of the broad egresses of metabolic process, little deaths which only prepare for further cycles, endless adventures. So Levi concludes by narrating a cycle that ends where chemistry ends, picking up the story with the same atom having now found its way into a glass of milk:

> One, the one that concerns us, crosses the intes-

tinal threshold and enters the bloodstream: it migrates, knocks at the door of a nerve cell, enters, and supplants the carbon which was part of it. This cell belongs to a brain, and it is my brain, the brain of the *me* who is writing; and the cell in question, and within it the atom in question, is in charge of my writing, in a gigantic minuscule game which nobody has yet described. It is that which at this instant, issuing out of a labyrinthine tangle of yesses and nos, makes my hand run along a certain path on the paper, mark it with these volutes that are signs: a double snap, up and down, between two levels of energy, guides this hand of mine to impress on the paper this dot, here, this one.

We see Levi's contemporaneity in the way he brings his speculations down to the scene of writing, ingeniously turning the final period of his *Periodic Table* (written, one hopes, with a trace of graphite from a pencil) into an iconic sign standing for a carbon atom. "These volutes that are signs" trace a spiral path across the handwritten page that maps the recursive paths of carbon atoms in and out of the organic adventure. Moreover, in bringing this elemental romance to an end, Levi conducts us to the further limen at which point physics and biochemistry (at least so far) must pack their bags, and literature, linguistics, and psychology unpack theirs: that threshold between the brain and the mind, life and human consciousness. (pp. 576-79)

> *Bruce Clarke, in a review of "The Periodic Table," in* The Georgia Review, *Vol. XL, No. 2, Summer, 1986, pp. 576-79.*

Jefferson Hunter   (essay date 1986)

[*In the following excerpt, Hunter praises Levi for his simple, poetic interweaving of such complex topics as chemical reactions and wartime guilt in* The Periodic Table.]

The Yiddish saying *Ibergekumene tsores iz gut tsu dertseylin* appears in Levi's two most recent books, the memoir *The Periodic Table* (1984) and the novel *If Not Now, When?* (1985). Troubles overcome are good to tell because they please listeners and simultaneously teach them something practical about the art of overcoming despair. (p. 329)

In *The Periodic Table* Levi chiefly writes fact—episodes from the history of his career in chemistry—rather than fiction. But *The Periodic Table* is a more freely imagined book than *If Not Now, When?*, its language richer and more inventive, its scenes more satisfactorily contrived. Reality, Levi comments, "is always more complex than invention: less kempt, cruder, less rounded out," and the writer must approach its complexities with an art like that of the chemical analyst, who weighs and divides, measures and judges. Confronting reality, Levi feels the complex, intense pleasure of the student "penetrating the solemn order of differential calculus," and in fact *The Periodic Table* does justice to a world even fuller of multiple perspectives than mathematics or wartime experience, with its gunfire symbolic of menace and hope. In the chapter **"Vanadium,"** for example, Levi discovers that the imperturbable German chemist to whom he has been writing business letters is the same Dr. Müller whom he met in the laboratory at Monowitz-Auschwitz. When Levi points out their common history and asks for a comment on the morality of IG Farbenindustrie's wartime enterprises, Müller responds not with a "humble, warm, Christian letter" from a redeemed German, nor with a "ribald, proud, glacial letter" from an obdurate Nazi, but with a letter full of digressions and farfetched praises, clumsy exculpations and half-sincere apologies. A long-winded version of the mayor in *If Not Now, When?*, Müller finds that things between Christians and Jews (or between past and present) aren't that simple.

"Vanadium" is one of the book's many excursions into painful memories. Levi notes how Mussolini's racial laws kept professors from accepting him as an assistant; he movingly recalls Sandro Delmastro, the fellow-student who taught him mountain-climbing and later died at the hands of Fascist partisans. But none of these stories is strident, self-pitying, or oversimplified. Levi is protected from the vices of memory by his style, which is precise and speculative at the same time. He tells us that zinc is yielding to acid except when very pure, hence, generalizing, that impurity gives rise to changes, "in other words, to life." That is why Fascism cannot tolerate impurity or dissension, because it wants everybody to be the same. The Levi who cannot find a professor to sponsor him is the impurity that makes the zinc react. These chemical symbolisms are endlessly multiplied, in serious and comic applications. Iron stands for the strong-willed Sandro, whereas argon, a noble or inert gas, gives the clue to Levi's standoffish and spiritually inert Turinese ancestors, whose ingenious dialect he lovingly describes. Much of *The Periodic Table,* indeed, is comic. That in itself is an achievement: a book full of wit by an author who after World War II might well have thought nothing laughable. Polyethylene, Levi says, is "a bit too incorruptible," and not by chance God Almighty, although "a master of polymerization," has abstained from patenting it: He does not like incorruptible things. Views of the divine chemical plant alternate with ironic meditations on the human scene. The gangsterish owner of a lipstick factory thinks that a certain compound, alloxan, might turn lips *permanently* red; he sends Levi chasing after alloxan; and Levi discovers that it may be derived from uric acid, found abundantly in bird and reptile droppings. For a moment, in Levi's imagination, ladies' lips are touched with the excrement of chickens or pythons, and his heart is warmed by a return to the origins of his science, when alchemists extracted phosphorus from urine.

Levi's comic style is highly original. It entails persistent self-deprecation, bravura comparisons ("a curious, nar-

Levi, at the beginning of 1985 when The Periodic Table *started to bring him international fame.*

row, twisting alleyway which branched off Piazza della Crocetta and stood out in the obsessive Turinese geometry like a rudimentary organ trapped in the evolved structure of a mammalian"), and subtle allusiveness. Like all educated Italians Levi had Dante force-fed to him in the *liceo,* so there is perhaps nothing very distinctive about his parallel between an open-pit mine and the encircling tiers of Hell, nor even about his offhand comment that a ponderous rolling shutter stood at the bottom of the mine, "in Lucifer's place." What *is* distinctive is Levi's description of the locomotive in the mine, by which he carries us away from *The Divine Comedy* only to bring us wittily and delicately back: the locomotive "positioned the cars one by one under the shutter so that they could be filled, then dragged them out to look again at the stars." One could say a good deal about Levi and Dante. He uses the poet, as here, to expand a perspective, and elsewhere to define the meaning of humane culture. In the most moving episode of his concentration camp book, *If This Is a Man,* Levi quotes from rusty memory the twenty-sixth canto of the *Inferno* as he and a fellow inmate go to fetch their midday soup. Like the Ulysses of that canto, Levi is subject to the will of Another but not finally held in bondage, being free in his mind, free to assert his humanity. In *The Periodic Table* Levi remembers also that Dante was not without a certain prejudice, and pointed a Christian finger at the Jew, who "in your midst laughs at you."

The open-pit mine features in **"Nickel,"** one of the autobiographical vignettes of *The Periodic Table.* Other chapters are historical fables (**"Lead," "Mercury"**), more or less realistic short stories (**"Sulfur," "Titanium"**), or tales of chemical investigation (**"Chromium," "Silver," "Nitrogen"**) somewhat resembling Berton Roueché's annals of medical detection in *The New Yorker.* It is apparent that the book lacks one kind of unity, though it has the unities of a marked personal style and of a structural conceit—all those elemental titles set forthrightly down in emulation of Mendeleev's Periodic Table, the lofty and solemn poetry of which Levi admired as a young chemistry student. The Table and the book are poetic because they impose order on stupid matter and meaningless experience. They struggle against an adversary "slothfully hostile as human stupidity is hostile, and like it strong because of its obtuse passivity." In this war every accurate qualitative analysis marks a victory. So does every understanding of motive or speculation into a mystery. What is the fate of a single carbon atom? That mystery is investigated in Levi's last chapter [**"Carbon"**], which follows the smallest unit of organic matter from a limestone ledge and a lime kiln to the sky, and thence to a grapevine, a bottle of wine, and a breathing human being. Exhaled as part of a molecule of carbon dioxide, the atom is absorbed by a tree and allowed to form wood, then swallowed by a woodworm, then freed by decay and swept into the air again. Finally it settles in a glass of milk which Levi himself drinks. It enters a cell:

> This cell belongs to my brain, and it is my brain, the brain of the *me* who is writing; and the cell in question, and within it the atom in question, is in charge of my writing, in a gigantic minuscule game which nobody has yet described. It is that which at this instant, issuing out of a labyrinthine tangle of yeses and nos, makes my hand

run along a certain path on the paper, mark it with these volutes that are signs: a double snap, up and down, between two levels of energy, guides this hand of mine to impress on the paper this dot, here, this one.

It is an extraordinary passage at the end of an extraordinary book, a bringing together of imagination and science, of liking for human beings in their labyrinthine tangles and admiration for chemistry in its exactness, such as has marked every production of an outstanding career. (pp. 331-33)

> *Jefferson Hunter, "Troubles Overcome Are Good to Tell," in* The Hudson Review, *Vol. XXXIX, No. 2, Summer, 1986, pp. 329-33.*

Primo Levi [with Philip Roth]   (interview date 1986)

[*In the following interview, Levi discusses some of the major issues informing his work, including the meaning and value of work and professionalism, and the importance of "rootedness," or an intimate connection to one's country, home, and family.*]

On the September Friday that I arrived in Turin—to renew a conversation with Primo Levi that we had begun one afternoon in London the spring before—I asked to be shown around the paint factory where he'd been employed as a research chemist and, afterwards, until retirement, as factory manager. Altogether the company employs 50 people, mainly chemists who work in the laboratories and skilled laborers on the floor of the plant. The production machinery, the row of storage tanks, the laboratory building, the finished product in man-sized containers ready to be shipped, the reprocessing facility that purifies the wastes—all of it is encompassed in four or five acres a seven-mile drive from Turin. The machines that are drying resin and blending varnish and pumping off pollutants are never really distressingly loud, the yard's acrid odor— the smell, Levi told me, that clung to his clothing for two years after his retirement—is by no means disgusting, and the skip loaded with the black sludgy residue of the antipolluting process isn't particularly unsightly. It is hardly the world's ugliest industrial environment, but a very long way, nonetheless, from those sentences suffused with mind that are the hallmark of Levi's autobiographical narratives. On the other hand, however far from the prose, it is clearly a place close to his heart; taking in what I could of the noise, the stench, the mosaic of pipes and vats and tanks and dials, I remembered Faussone, the skilled rigger in *The Monkey's Wrench,* saying to Levi—who calls Faussone "my alter ego"—"I have to tell you, being around a work site is something I enjoy."

On our way to the section of the laboratory where raw materials are scrutinized before moving on to production, I asked Levi if he could identify the particular chemical aroma faintly permeating the corridor: I thought it smelled a little like a hospital corridor. Just fractionally he raised his head and exposed his nostrils to the air. With a smile he told me, "I understand and can analyze it like a dog."

He seemed to me inwardly animated more in the manner

of some little quicksilver woodland creature empowered by the forest's most astute intelligence. Levi is small and slight, though not quite so delicately built as his unassuming demeanor makes him at first appear, and still seemingly as nimble as he must have been at 10. In his body, as in his face, you see—as you don't in most men—the face and the body of the boy that he was. His alertness is nearly palpable, keenness trembling within him like his pilot light.

It is probably not as surprising as one might think to find that writers divide like the rest of mankind into two categories: those who listen to you and those who don't. Levi listens, and with his entire face, a precisely-modeled face tipped with a white chin beard that, at 67, is at once youthfully Pan-like but professorial as well, the face of irrepressible curiosity and of the esteemed *dottore*. I can believe Faussone when he says to Primo Levi early in *The Monkey's Wrench*, "You're quite a guy, making me tell these stories that, except for you, I've never told anybody." It's no wonder that people are always telling him things and that everything is recorded faithfully before it is even written down: when listening he is as focused and as still as a chipmunk spying something unknown from atop a stone wall.

In a large apartment house built a few years before he was born—and where he was born, for formerly this was the home of his parents—Levi lives with his wife, Lucia; except for his year in Auschwitz and the adventurous months immediately after his liberation, he has lived in this same apartment all his life.

The apartment is still shared, as it has been since the Levis met and married after the war, with Primo Levi's mother. She is 91. Levi's 95-year-old mother-in-law lives not far away, in the apartment immediately next door lives his 28-year-old son, a physicist, and a few streets off is his 38-year-old daughter, a botanist. I don't personally know of another contemporary writer who has voluntarily remained, over so many decades, intimately entangled and in such direct, unbroken contact with his immediate family, his birthplace, his region, the world of his forebears, and, particularly, with the local working environment which, in Turin, the home of Fiat, is largely industrial. Of all the intellectually gifted artists of this century—and Levi's uniqueness is that he is even more the artist-chemist than the chemist-writer—he may well be the most thoroughly adapted to the totality of the life around him. Perhaps in the case of Primo Levi, a life of communal interconnectedness, along with his masterpiece *Survival in Auschwitz*, constitutes his profoundly civilized and spirited response to those who did all they could to sever his every sustaining connection and tear him and his kind out of history.

In *The Periodic Table*, beginning with the simplest of sentences a paragraph describing one of chemistry's most satisfying processes, Levi writes, "Distilling is beautiful." What follows is a distillation too, a reduction to essential points of the lively, wide-ranging conversation we conducted, in English, over the course of a long weekend, mostly behind the door of the quiet study off the entrance foyer to the Levis' apartment. Levi's study is a large, simply furnished room. There is an old flowered sofa and a comfortable easy chair; on the desk is a shrouded word processor; perfectly shelved behind the desk are Levi's variously colored notebooks; on shelves all around the room are books in Italian, German and English. The most evocative object is one of the smallest, an unobtrusively hung sketch of a half-destroyed wire fence at Auschwitz. Displayed more prominently on the walls are playful constructions skillfully twisted into shape by Levi himself out of insulated copper wire that is coated with the varnish developed for that purpose in his own laboratory. There is a big wire butterfly, a wire owl, a tiny wire bug, and high on the wall behind the desk are two of the largest constructions—one the wire figure of a bird-warrior armed with a knitting needle, and the other, as Levi explained when I couldn't make out what the figure was meant to represent, "a man playing his nose." "A Jew," I suggested. "Yes, yes," he said, laughing, "a Jew, of course."

[*Roth:*] *In* **The Periodic Table,** *your book about "the strong and bitter flavor" of your experience as a chemist, you speak of a colleague, Giulia, who explains your "mania about work" by the fact that in your early 20's you are shy of women and don't have a girlfriend. But she was mistaken, I think. Your real mania about work derives from something deeper. Work would seem to be your obsessive subject, even in your book about your incarceration at Auschwitz.*

Arbeit Macht Frei—Work Makes Freedom—are the words inscribed by the Nazis over the Auschwitz gate. But work in Auschwitz is a horrifying parody of work, useless and senseless—labor as punishment leading to agonizing death. It's possible to view your entire literary labor as dedicated to restoring to work its humane meaning, reclaiming the word Arbeit *from the derisory cynicism with which your Auschwitz employers had disfigured it. Faussone says to you, "Every job I undertake is like a first love." He enjoys talking about his work almost as much as he enjoys working. Faussone is Man the Worker made truly* free *through his labors.*

[Levi:] I do not believe that Giulia was wrong in attributing my frenzy for work to my shyness at that time with girls. This shyness, or inhibition, was genuine, painful and heavy, much more important for me than devotion to work. Work in the Milan factory I described in *The Periodic Table* was mock-work which I did not trust. The catastrophe of the Italian armistice of Sept. 8, 1943, was already in the air, and it would have been foolish to ignore it by digging oneself into a scientifically meaningless activity.

I have never seriously tried to analyze this shyness of mine, but no doubt Mussolini's racial laws played an important role. Other Jewish friends suffered from it, some "Aryan" schoolmates jeered at us, saying that circumcision was nothing but castration, and we, at least at an unconscious level, tended to believe it, with the help of our puritanical families. I think that *at that time* work was actually for me a sexual compensation rather than a real passion.

However, I am fully aware that *after* the camp my work, or rather my two kinds of work (chemistry and writing) did play, and are still playing, an essential role in my life. I am persuaded that normal human beings are biologically built for an activity that is aimed toward a goal, and that idleness, or aimless work (like Auschwitz's *Arbeit*) gives rise to suffering and to atrophy. In my case, and in the case of my alter ego Faussone, work is identical with "problem-solving."

At Auschwitz I quite often observed a curious phenomenon. The need for *lavoro ben fatto*—"work properly done"—is so strong as to induce people to perform even slavish chores "properly." The Italian bricklayer who saved my life by bringing me food on the sly for six months hated Germans, their food, their language, their war; but when they set him to erect walls, he built them straight and solid, not out of obedience but out of professional dignity.

Survival in Auschwitz *concludes with a chapter entitled "The Story of Ten Days," in which you describe, in diary form, how you endured from January 18 to January 27, 1945, among a small remnant of sick and dying patients in the camp's makeshift infirmary after the Nazis had fled westward with some 20,000 "healthy" prisoners. What's recounted there reads to me like the story of Robinson Crusoe in hell, with you, Primo Levi, as Crusoe, wrenching what you needed to live from the chaotic residue of a ruthlessly evil island. What struck me there, as throughout the book, was how much* thinking *contributed to your survival, the thinking of a practical, humane, scientific mind. Yours doesn't seem to me a survival that was determined by either brute biological strength or incredible luck, but was rooted, rather, in your professional character: the man of precision, the controller of experiments who seeks the principle of order, confronted with the evil inversion of everything he valued. Granted you were a numbered part in an infernal machine, but a numbered part with a systematic mind that has* always *to understand. At Auschwitz you tell yourself, "I think too much" to resist, "I am too civilized." But to me the civilized man who thinks too much is inseparable from the survivor. The scientist and the survivor are one.*

Exactly—you hit the bull's-eye. In those memorable 10 days, I truly did feel like Robinson Crusoe, but with one important difference. Crusoe set to work for his individual survival, whereas I and my two French companions were consciously and happily willing to work at last for a just and human goal, to save the lives of our sick comrades.

As for survival, this is a question that I put to myself many times and that many have put to me. I insist there was no general rule, except entering the camp in good health and knowing German. Barring this, luck dominated. I have seen the survival of shrewd people and silly people, the brave and the cowardly, "thinkers" and madmen. In my case, luck played an essential role on at least two occasions: in leading me to meet the Italian bricklayer, and in getting sick only once, but at the right moment.

And yet what you say, that for me thinking and observing were survival factors, is true, although in my opinion sheer luck prevailed. I remember having lived my Auschwitz year in a condition of exceptional spiritedness. I don't know if this depended on my professional background, or

an unsuspected stamina, or on a sound instinct. I never stopped recording the world and people around me, so much that I still have an unbelievably detailed image of them. I had an intense wish to understand, I was constantly pervaded by a curiosity that somebody afterwards did, in fact, deem nothing less than cynical, the curiosity of the naturalist who finds himself transplanted into an environment that is monstrous, but new, monstrously new.

Survival in Auschwitz *was originally published in English as* If This Is a Man, *a faithful rendering of your Italian title,* Se Questo E un Uomo (*and the title that your first American publishers should have had the good sense to preserve*). *The description and analysis of your atrocious memories of the Germans' "gigantic biological and social experiment" is governed, very precisely, by a quantitative concern for the ways in which a man can be transformed or broken down and, like a substance decomposing in a chemical reaction, lose his characteristic properties.* If This Is a Man *reads like the memoirs of a theoretician of moral biochemistry who has himself been forcibly enlisted as the specimen organism to undergo laboratory experimentation of the most sinister kind. The creature caught in the laboratory of the mad scientist is himself the very epitome of the rational scientist.*

In The Monkey's Wrench—*which might accurately have been titled* This *Is a Man*—*you tell Faussone, your blue-collar Scheherazade, that "being a chemist in the world's eyes, and feeling . . . a writer's blood in my veins," you consequently have "two souls in my body, and that's too many." I'd say there's one soul, capacious and seamless; I'd say that not only are the survivor and the scientist inseparable but the writer and the scientist as well.*

Rather than a question, this is a diagnosis that I accept with thanks. I lived my camp life as rationally as I could, and I wrote *If This Is a Man* struggling to explain to others, and to myself, the events I had been involved in, but with no definite literary intention. My model (or, if you prefer, my style) was that of the "weekly report" commonly used in factories: it must be precise, concise, and written in a language comprehensible to everybody in the industrial hierarchy. And certainly not written in scientific jargon. By the way, I am not a scientist, nor have I ever been. I did want to become one, but war and the camp prevented me. I had to limit myself to being a technician.

I agree with you on there being only "one soul . . . and seamless," and once more I feel grateful to you. My statement that "two souls . . . is too many" is half a joke, but half hints at serious things. I worked in a factory for almost 30 years, and I must admit that there is no incompatibility between being a chemist and being a writer: in fact, there is a mutual reinforcement. But factory life, and particularly factory managing, involves many other matters, far from chemistry: hiring and firing workers; quarreling with the boss, customers and suppliers; coping with accidents; being called to the telephone, even at night or when at a party; dealing with bureaucracy; and many more soul-destroying tasks. This whole trade is brutally incompatible with writing. Consequently I felt hugely relieved when I reached retirement age and could resign, and so renounce my soul number one.

Your sequel to If This Is a Man (The Reawakening: *also unfortunately retitled by one of your early American publishers) was called in Italian* La Tregua, *the truce. It's about your journey from Auschwitz back to Italy. There is a real legendary dimension to that tortuous journey, especially to the story of your long gestation period in the Soviet Union, waiting to be repatriated. What's surprising about* La Tregua, *which might understandably have been marked by a mood of mourning and inconsolable despair, is its exuberance. Your reconciliation with life takes place in a world that sometimes seemed to you like the primeval Chaos. Yet you are so tremendously engaged by everyone, so highly entertained as well as instructed, that I wondered if, despite the hunger and the cold and the fears, even despite the memories, you've ever really had a better time than during those months that you call "a parenthesis of unlimited availability, a providential but unrepeatable gift of fate."*

You appear to be someone whose most vital needs require, above all, rootedness—in his profession, his ancestry, his region, his language—and yet when you found yourself as alone and uprooted as a man can be, you considered that condition a gift.

A friend of mine, an excellent doctor, told me many years ago, "Your remembrances of before and after are in black and white; those of Auschwitz and of your travel home are in Technicolor." He was right. Family, home, factory are good things in themselves, but they deprived me of something that I still miss: adventure. Destiny decided that I should find adventure in the awful mess of a Europe swept by war.

You are in the business, so you know how these things happen. *The Truce* was written 14 years after *If This Is a Man:* it is a more "self-conscious" book, more methodical, more literary, the language much more profoundly elaborated. It tells the truth, but a filtered truth. Beforehand, I had recounted each adventure many times, to people at widely different cultural levels (to friends mainly and to high school boys and girls), and I had retouched it en route so as to arouse their most favorable reactions. When *If This Is a Man* began to achieve some success, and I began to see a future for my writing, I set out to put these adventures on paper. I aimed at having fun in writing and at amusing my prospective readers. Consequently, I gave emphasis to strange, exotic, cheerful episodes—mainly to the Russians seen close up—and I relegated to the first and last pages the mood, as you put it, "of mourning and inconsolable despair."

As for "rootedness," it is true that I have deep roots, and that I had the luck of not losing them. My family was almost completely spared by the Nazi slaughter, and today I continue to live in the very flat where I was born. The desk here where I write occupies, according to family legend, exactly the spot where I first saw light. When I found myself "as uprooted as a man could be" certainly I suffered, but this was far more than compensated afterwards by the fascination of adventure, by human encounters, by the sweetness of "convalescence" from the plague of Auschwitz. In its historical reality, my Russian "truce" turned to a "gift" only many years later, when I purified it by rethinking it and by writing about it.

If Not Now, When? *is like nothing else of yours that I've read in English. Though pointedly drawn from actual historical events, the book is cast as a straightforward, picaresque adventure tale about a small band of Jewish partisans of Russian and Polish extraction harassing the Germans behind their eastern front lines. Your other books are perhaps less "imaginary" as to subject matter but strike me as more imaginative in technique. The motive behind* If Not Now, When? *seems more narrowly tendentious—and consequently less liberating to the writer—than the impulses that generate the autobiographical works.*

I wonder if you agree with this—if in writing about the bravery of the Jews who fought back, you felt yourself doing something you ought *to do, responsible to moral and political claims that don't necessarily intervene elsewhere, even when the subject is your own markedly Jewish fate.*

If Not Now, When? followed an unforeseen path. The motivations that drove me to write it are manifold. Here they are, in order of importance:

I had made a sort of bet with myself: after so much plain or disguised autobiography, are you, or are you not, a full-fledged writer, capable of constructing a novel, shaping characters, describing landscapes you have never seen? Try it!

I intended to amuse myself by writing a "Western" plot set in a landscape uncommon in Italy. I intended to amuse my readers by telling them a substantially optimistic story, a story of hope, even occasionally cheerful, although projected onto a background of massacre.

I wished to assault a commonplace still prevailing in Italy: a Jew is a mild person, a scholar (religious or profane), unwarlike, humiliated, who tolerated centuries of persecution without ever fighting back. It seemed to me a duty to pay homage to those Jews who, in desperate conditions, had found the courage and the skills to resist.

I cherished the ambition to be the first (perhaps only) Italian writer to describe the Yiddish world. I intended to "exploit" my popularity in my country in order to impose upon my readers a book centered on the Ashkenazi civilization, history, language, and frame of mind, all of which are virtually unknown in Italy, except by some sophisticated readers of Joseph Roth (the Austrian novelist who died in 1939), Bellow, Singer, Malamud, Potok and of course yourself.

Personally, I am satisfied with this book mainly because I had good fun planning and writing it. For the first and only time in my life as a writer, I had the impression (almost a hallucination) that my characters were alive, around me, behind my back, suggesting spontaneously their feats and their dialogues. The year I spent writing was a happy one, and so, whatever the result, for me this was a liberating book.

Let's talk finally about the paint factory. In our time many writers have worked as teachers, some as journalists, and most writers over 50 have been employed, for a while at least, as somebody or other's soldier. There is an impressive list of writers who have simultaneously practiced medicine and written books, and of others who have been clergymen.

An excerpt from "Afterword: The Author's Answers to His Readers' Questions"

How can the Nazis' fanatical hatred of the Jews be explained?. . . I must admit that [the] commonly accepted explanations do not satisfy me. They are reductive; not commensurate with, nor proportionate to, the facts that need explaining. In rereading the chronicles of Nazism, from its murky beginnings to its convulsed end, I cannot avoid the impression of a general atmosphere of uncontrolled madness that seems to me to be unique in history. This collective madness, this "running off the rails," is usually explained by postulating the combination of many diverse factors, insufficient if considered singly, and the greatest of these factors is Hitler's personality itself and its profound interaction with the German people. It is certain that his personal obsessions, his capacity for hatred, his preaching of violence, found unbridled echoes in the frustration of the German people, and for this reason came back to him multiplied, confirming his delirious conviction that he himself was the Hero prophesied by Nietzsche, the Superman redeemer of Germany. . . .

I do not find it permissible to explain a historical phenomenon by piling all the blame on a single individual (those who carry out horrendous orders are not innocent!). Besides, it is always difficult to interpret the deep-seated motivations of an individual. The hypotheses that have been proposed justify the facts only up to a point, explain the quality but not the quantity. I must admit that I prefer the humility with which some of the most serious historians (among them Bullock, Schramm, Bracher) confess to *not understanding* the furious anti-Semitism of Hitler and of Germany behind him.

Perhaps one cannot, what is more one must not, understand what happened, because to understand is almost to justify. Let me explain: "understanding" a proposal or human behavior means to "contain" it, contain its author, put oneself in his place, identify with him. Now, no normal human being will ever be able to identify with Hitler, Himmler, Goebbels, Eichmann, and endless others. This dismays us, and at the same time gives us a sense of relief, because perhaps it is desirable that their words (and also, unfortunately, their deeds) cannot be comprehensible to us. They are non-human words and deeds, really counter-human, without historic precedents, with difficulty comparable to the cruelest events of the biological struggle for existence. The war can be related to this struggle, but Auschwitz has nothing to do with war; it is neither an episode in it nor an extreme form of it. War is always a terrible fact, to be deprecated, but it is in us, it has its rationality, we "understand" it.

But there is no rationality in the Nazi hatred: it is a hate that is not in us; it is outside man, it is a poison fruit sprung from the deadly trunk of Fascism, but it is outside and beyond Fascism itself. We cannot understand it, but we can and must understand from where it springs, and we must be on our guard.

Primo Levi, in his The Reawakening, *Collier Books, 1987.*

T. S. Eliot was a publisher, and as everyone knows Wallace Stevens and Franz Kafka worked for large insurance organizations. To my knowledge only two writers of importance have ever been managers of a paint factory, you in Turin, Italy, and Sherwood Anderson in Elyria, Ohio. Anderson had to flee the paint factory (and his family) to become a writer; you seem to have become the writer you are by staying and pursuing your career there. I wonder if you think of yourself as actually more fortunate—even better equipped to write—than those of us who are without a paint factory and all that's implied by that kind of connection.

As I have already said, I entered the paint industry by chance, but I never had very much to do with the general run of paints, varnishes, and lacquers. Our company, immediately after it began, specialized in the production of wire enamels, insulating coatings for copper electrical conductors. At the peak of my career, I numbered among the 30 or 40 specialists in the world in this branch. The animals hanging here on the wall are made out of scrap enameled wire.

Honestly, I knew nothing of Sherwood Anderson till you spoke of him. No, it would never have occurred to me to quit family and factory for full-time writing, as he did. I'd have feared the jump into the dark, and I would have lost any right to a retirement allowance.

However, to your list of writer/paint manufacturers I must add a third name, Italo Svevo, a converted Jew of Trieste, the author of *The Confessions of Zeno,* who lived from 1861 to 1928. For a long time Svevo was the commercial manager of a paint company in Trieste that belonged to his father-in-law, and that dissolved a few years ago. Until 1918 Trieste belonged to Austria, and this company was famous because it supplied the Austrian Navy with an excellent antifouling paint, preventing shellfish incrustation, for the keels of warships. After 1918 Trieste became Italian, and the paint was delivered to the Italian and British Navies. To be able to deal with the Admiralty, Svevo took lessons in English from James Joyce, at the time a teacher in Trieste. They became friends and Joyce assisted Svevo in finding a publisher for his works.

The trade name of the antifouling paint was Moravia. That it is the same as the *nom de plume* of the noted Italian novelist is not fortuitous: both the Triestine businessman and the Roman writer derived it from the family name of a mutual relative on the mother's side. Forgive me for this hardly pertinent gossip. No, no, as I've hinted already, I have no regrets. I don't believe I wasted my time in the factory. My factory *militanza*—my compulsory and honorable service there—kept me in touch with the world of real things. (pp. 1, 40-1)

> *Philip Roth and Primo Levi, "A Man Saved by His Skills," in* The New York Times Book Review, *October 12, 1986, pp. 1, 40-1.*

Paul Bailey (essay date 1986)

[*In the following review of* Moments of Reprieve, *Bailey examines the issue of virtue by discussing those characters who affirm humanity and those who tolerate its degradation.*]

The stories in [**Moments of Reprieve**] were written over

a number of years. Each one was inspired by a particular enduring memory from the time Primo Levi was forced to spend in Auschwitz. The book is, in a sense, a companion volume to the two masterpieces (*If This Is a Man* and *The Truce*) that will guarantee Levi's literary survival, and is best appreciated if read in sequence.

[*Moments of Reprieve*] is a work which celebrates that peculiar virtue that is the will to live: a virtue, he explains in his preface, that is 'not always . . . approved of by common morality.' The people who appear in this book are all possessed of it, in their different ways.

There is a single exception, who happens to be the most heroic of these heroes. He is Lorenzo, the laconic mason from Fossano whose acts of kindness are described in *If This Is a Man.* During the war, Lorenzo was a voluntary civilian worker for the Nazis ('voluntary' was the official term), which meant that he enjoyed small privileges denied to the inmates of the Camps. His will to keep others alive persisted throughout the long nightmare. What happened to him on his return to Italy is recounted here with that intense sympathy for the complexities of human suffering that lends Levi's writing its unique distinction. Lorenzo had seen too much that was diabolical, and wanted only not to see.

Cesare, the joyous rogue Levi encountered on his trek home to Turin, is another old friend who reappears. In *The Truce,* Levi tells how Cesare made fish fatter with the aid of a syringe and sold them to gullible Russian peasants. Here the inventive man from the slums of Rome is up to even more ingenious—not to say, convoluted—tricks. Cesare's 'virtue' would never elicit the approval of those who function within the confines of a common morality, yet virtuous he surely is in his desire for the best that life can offer, after the worst it has afforded him.

In a story called **'The Quiet City,'** Levi chooses not to celebrate. It concerns a fellow chemist, Mertens: 'He was an almost-me, another myself, turned upside down. We were contemporaries, not dissimilar in education, not even in character.' Mertens was German and Catholic, and was employed in the Buna Works at Auschwitz: 'I was inside the barbed wire and he outside.' The greater part of the short narrative is set down in the present tense, with Mertens learning of the horrors that are being perpetrated inside the barbed wire. The decent Mertens and his decent wife elect to be silent. The story is a tiny reminder that tyrants grow on the backs of those who prefer not to see, who settle for the quotidian in the midst of the unspeakable. Lorenzo saw, and took to drink. Herr Martens and his Hausfrau collaborated, after their respectable fashion. It is Lorenzo who is virtuous.

The book ends on a note of resonant irony, with a brief account of the devious career of Chaim Rumkowski, who became president (or elder) of the ghetto in Lodz—rechristened Litzmannstadt by the Nazis. Rumkowski had 'a coach drawn by a skeletal nag, and it rode about his minuscule kingdom, through the streets swarming with beggars and petitioners. He wore a regal cloak, and surrounded himself with a court of flatterers, lackeys, and cut-throats; he had his post-courtiers compose hymns celebrating his "firm and powerful hand" . . . ' How Rum-

kowski arrived at Auschwitz must be left to Primo Levi to relate. 'Virtue' is of the essence of that arrival.

> Paul Bailey, *"After Auschwitz,"* in The Observer, *December 21, 1986, p. 21.*

Michiko Kakutani (essay date 1989)

[*In the following excerpt, Kakutani discerns "anger and a growing pessimism" in the later stories in* The Mirror Maker *and suggests that in light of his suicide the weight of Levi's death camp memories may have become unbearable.*]

On April 11, 1987, some 42 years after his liberation from Auschwitz, Primo Levi hurled himself down the central stairwell of the house where he was born in Turin, Italy. He was 67 years old.

Since his suicide, friends, colleagues and other writers have sought to reconcile his life and death, the luminous rationality of his writings with his violent, shocking end. What, people wondered, had brought a man whose own life and work seemed to speak of transcendence—of surviving the horrors of the Holocaust and testifying to his experience with such dignity and courage—to commit such a hopeless act?

There was talk about the stress of two minor operations, incorrect dosages of antidepressants, the stress of caring for aging, ailing relatives. William Styron wrote of the incalculable causes of depression. Levi's editor, Lorenzo Mondo, noted that the author had grown increasingly distressed during his last months about the spiritual state of the world. Another friend, the writer Alexander Stille, wrote about the terrible burdens of memory, of the emotional difficulties of surviving the Nazi death camps. In the last book published before Levi's death (*The Drowned and the Saved*), Cynthia Ozick discerned a sudden change of tone, the magisterial calm of his earlier Holocaust writings giving way to a long-suppressed eruption of rage—the sort of rage that, in Levi's own words, leaves one "incapable of finding joy in life, indeed of living."

Similar indications of anger and a growing pessimism surface in some of the later pieces included in **The Mirror Maker,** a new collection of Levi's newspaper stories and essays written during his last 20 years for *La Stampa* in Turin. Worried that the lessons of the Holocaust were being forgotten, Levi compared the refusal of today's society to acknowledge the atomic threat to the "I don't want to know about it" attitude initially taken toward Hitler. At the same time, he warned against the dangers of forgetting the uniqueness of the Holocaust, of seeing it as just another historical atrocity.

"That 'the gulag came before Auschwitz' is true," he wrote in January 1987,

> but one cannot forget that the aims of the two infernos were not the same. The first was a massacre among peers; it was not based on racial primacy and did not divide humanity into supermen and submen. The second was founded on an ideology saturated with a world split in two, "we" the masters on one side, all the rest on the

other: at their service or exterminated because racially inferior.

In his two masterpieces of autobiography, *Survival in Auschwitz* and *The Reawakening,* and in a series of other essays, Levi told and retold the story of his own imprisonment in the Nazi death camps. His reminiscences were always lucid, sober and precise, devoid of rhetoric and inflationary prose, and grounded in a welter of astonishing detail that attested both to his powers of observation (doubtless developed in his other career as a chemist) and to his inability to forget.

"At times," he writes in this volume, "but only for what concerns Auschwitz, I feel I am the brother of Ireneo Funes, 'el memorioso' described by [Jorge Luis] Borges, the man who remembered every leaf of every tree he had ever seen, and who 'by himself had more memories than all the men who ever existed since the world began.' "

Indeed, the ghosts of Auschwitz haunt many of the short stories and literary essays in this volume. **"Force Majeure,"** a tale published in July 1986, gives a graphic account of a sidewalk confrontation between a mild-mannered man and a thuglike sailor—a showdown in which the odds are anything but even. "The duel," the hero thinks, as he picks himself up from the street, "had not resembled its models: it had been unbalanced, unfair, dirty, and had dirtied him. The models, even the most violent, are chivalrous; life is not. He set out for his appointment, knowing that he would never be the same man as before."

As for the other pieces in *The Mirror Maker,* they cover a wide range of subjects that demonstrate Levi's interest as a scientist in the worlds of chemistry and nature, his curiosity as an artist in the power of words. There is a lyrical meditation on man's flight to the moon and the spider's web-weaving powers. There are essays on the importance of rhyme in poetry and on the insidious workings of gossip. There are also several sci-fi-like fictions about magical mirrors and fantastic medicines that enable people to make time go faster or slower.

Apparently made up of pieces left over from previous collections, this volume does not represent Levi at his finest. A series of imaginary interviews with animals representing different emotional types, for instance, feels like a pallid version of *The Periodic Table* (which found correlations between certain human types and assorted chemical elements)—a version that lacks the latter's rich autobiographical material and carefully observed detail.

In the end, though, Levi writes so eloquently and so powerfully about essential issues that even his minor work compels the reader's attention. Though this volume may not be the best introduction to his work, followers of his career will find that *The Mirror Maker* is necessary reading.

> Michiko Kakutani, "Primo Levi and the Ghosts of Auschwitz," in The New York Times, *December 12, 1989, p. C23.*

Wallis Wilde-Menozzi   (essay date 1990)

[*In the following excerpt from his analytical tribute to Levi, Wilde-Menozzi quotes the author at length on his ambivalence toward writing fiction and, focusing on Levi's first collection of short stories,* Storie naturali *(Natural Stories), addresses the essential elements that unite Levi's seemingly disparate autobiographical writing and his fiction.*]

In a telling passage that accompanies an introduction to a series of short stories published in 1966 [*Storie naturali*], at first under a pseudonym [Damiano Malabaila], Levi reveals a conflict inherent in the fact that he is becoming a writer.

> To talk about my stories creates a certain embarrassment for me; but perhaps the very description and analysis of this embarrassment will help answer your questions. Certainly in the act of writing them, I feel a vague sense of guilt, such as one who knowingly commits a transgression.
>
> What transgression? Let's see, maybe it's this: he who is aware of a "sin," of something that isn't right, should deepen its examination and the study of it, dedicating himself to it even through suffering, and making mistakes and not free himself from it by writing a story.
>
> I entered (rather unexpectedly) the world of writing with two books on concentration camps; it is not up to me to judge their value, though they were undoubtedly dedicated to a serious public. To propose to such a public a volume of light fiction, moral puzzles that are even amusing, but detached and cold, wouldn't that be a commercial fraud, not unlike those who sell bottles of wine for oil? These are questions I ask myself in facing the act of writing and publishing these **Natural Stories**. Well, I wouldn't be publishing them if I hadn't realized (not immediately, in fact) that from the Lager to these fictions, a continuity, a bridge exists. The Lager was the greatest sin, the most threatening of the monsters generated by the sleep of reason.

The bridge was Levi's life.

Writing as a witness was to be an absolute commitment. Like his tattoo, the Lager memories would deliberately not be erased. The tattoo wasn't hidden, nor was it always pointed out. It was just there on his skin. His sense of responsibility would always compel him to get the Lager's reading—its radioactive count—to place it inside other experiences, or alongside them, as well as to work slowly on seeing how endemic, how specific, how far-reaching it was. The sense of questioning, the scientist's integrity when facing facts, Levi's own resistance to simple reductionist arguments would guide his explorations. He would doubt analogy which comes easily in words, but can do so little in revealing truth. "Beware of analogies: for millennia they corrupted medicine and it may be their fault that today's pedagogical systems are so numerous, and after 3000 years of argument, we still don't know which is best."

With his publication of *The Truce* in 1963, an account of the long trip back from the Lager via Russia, Levi had begun to face the unstoppable flow of experiences that still remained after the first excruciating account. *The Truce,* with muted colors and unreal sense of time, is still a canvas weighed down by disorientation and chaos. But its experience, the feel of mud, cold and hunger, and also of the heartbreaking setbacks, are all of a different tenor. Survival itself begins to mean something else.

With *Natural Stories* (natural as opposed to Lager) the flow of life rushes forward, and Levi accepts the idea of crossing the bridge into the present, this other aspect of existence. He will find his way as witness. He will overcome his sense of uneasiness. The bridge is symbolic of the task Levi will attempt to take on, of its dangers and beauties. He will try to construct stories from the world he knows as a chemist and as a man. His commitment will be to explain certain things: work, for example, which if one loves it "represents the best, most concrete approximation of happiness on earth." (pp. 154-55)

Levi, in many of his books, assumes the character of a writer and exalts the writer's experience. But generally, in these fictional exchanges, he awards the greater certainty to other laborers and to the material world itself. "In the task of writing, the instruments, the alarm systems are rudimentary. There isn't even a trustworthy equivalent of the T Square, or the plumb line." He begins, though, to accept his feeling that he can write, and, moreover, in a light tone. He says of Rabelais: "in his enormous work it would be difficult to find a single sad page; even though the savant, Rabelais, knows human misery well he is quiet about it. Like the good doctor that he is, even when he writes, his wish is to heal." (pp. 155-56)

> *Wallis Wilde-Menozzi, "A Piece You've Touched Is a Piece Moved," in* The Tel Aviv Review, *Vol. 2, Fall, 1989 & Winter, 1990, pp. 149-65.*

Isa Kapp (essay date 1990)

[*In the following review of* The Mirror Maker, *Kapp relates the stories and essays to Levi's Holocaust literature and his suicide.*]

It is hard to believe, reading Primo Levi's remarkable *Survival in Auschwitz* (1947), that anyone subjected to the inhumanity of a Nazi death camp could write about it with such excruciating fairness and precision. As a chemist, Levi was trained to professional exactitude, but it required a special girding of mind to deal so circumspectly with the harrowing things human beings did to one another.

In *The Drowned and the Saved* (1986), written in Turin, Italy, 40 years after his imprisonment, he still meditates on the Holocaust and believes that more important than facts and judgments "were the motives and justifications: Why did you do this? Were you aware that you were committing a crime?" The book contains a forbidding portrait, "The Gray Zone," of that hierarchy of degradation the SS imposed on its victims in concentration camps, which in turn drove fellow sufferers to become rivals and abusers of their comrades. Levi makes the most painstaking moral distinctions among them, including those who rose in the

ranks as far as "Kapos" (section chiefs). Like a scale with many levers that must be delicately adjusted to show the right weight, he gives credit for a kind gesture, grants extenuation for a weakness. He wants us to know not that collaborators were corruptible, but how they became that way.

Nevertheless, after four decades, it is precisely the images of corruptibility that transfix this uncompromising observer. *The Mirror Maker,* a posthumous collection of Levi's very short stories, along with essays published in the Italian newspaper *La Stampa,* must have been to some extent an emotional reprieve for him. It leaves room for a few unconstrained outbursts against mankind's forgetfulness and inanition. The stories are pointed fables, the essays nutshell sermons, and in these casual compositions Levi can allow himself a more workaday prose. At times he is surprisingly comic, at others surprisingly righteous, though neither tone emerged in the by now classic recollections of his time in the camps. Here, his range is flawlessly represented by Raymond Rosenthal's translation.

But more heartening, we find Levi again pursuing his original interests, science and nature. They ground him and furnish a perspective from which he moves at ease, as in his charming and ingenious book *The Periodic Table,* where each reminiscence is associated with one of the basic elements in the universe. Unluckily, in the present collection, the natural world often echoes the ethos of Hitler's Germany—the once proud and daring herring gull of **"Five Intimate Interviews"** is a born rationalizer of his spiritual decline; the Queen in **"The Ant's Wedding"** admits that she eats her incipient young: "Yes, yes, you mustn't eat the eggs, it's not nice. But there are situations in which one must follow the sense of the State. . . . When food is scarce and eggs are too many, there is no room for moralisms."

On rare occasions the animal kingdom sounds a benign note. The journalist asks the giraffe how it deals with hypertension, discovers his subject's amazing expertise on valves and veins, the intricate detail of its singular physiology, but is moved to pay tribute instead to the giraffe's graceful gait and majestic rhythm. And science provides both poetry and suspense when the author describes, in his essay "The Spider's Secret," the exquisite process by which nature turns liquids into solids, water into web: "Now, this liquid is so fine and specific that a modest lengthening of its floss is sufficient to provoke its irreversible solidification. . . . No chemist has yet succeeded in reproducing so elegant, simple, and clean a process."

Levi's fascination with life guarantees touches of optimism in both the essays and the stories. In the [**"The Mirror Maker"**], the protagonist creates diverse, fantastic mirrors and finally invents one that displays his own image as seen by the person who stands before him. Presented to a cold-hearted mistress, the mirror returns an unflattering reflection. But held by the gentler girl who has often watched him work with enchantment, it makes him look like Apollo, his expression serene and merry.

More often, the writer is still listening to reverberations of Auschwitz. **"Force Majeure"** is a Kafkaesque nightmare of an unaccountable attack upon the slim, peaceable hero by a husky, aggressive, silent sailor. The essay "Translating Kafka" concludes that Joseph K. in *The Trial* "is ashamed of being a man." When Levi breaks away from his dark memories, he writes a beautifully formulated essay on our need for poetry—or an airy fantasy, **"The Great Mutation,"** about a girl who grows wings, with its tantalizing reminder that every person responds differently to the opportunities opened up by freedom and talent. It is almost impossible to accept that this gifted writer, with his empathy for his fellows and his curiosity about the human soul, decided to commit suicide three years ago at 67.

In fact, the sense of shame that he experienced in the Nazi camp never left him, and his book returns several times to the words of the philosopher Jean Améry, who wrote after his release from Auschwitz: "Faith in humanity, already cracked by the first slap in the face, then demolished by torture, is never acquired again." Améry killed himself in 1978. Levi had many reasons for faith in humanity, for feeling himself lucky. Yet perhaps he imagined that the impact of his warnings, of his moral force, was evaporating. The pieces in **The Mirror Maker** do not have the weight of his earlier work. But which of his readers would forgo a few more hours with this unusual man who willed us his conscience?

> *Isa Kapp, "Life Is Good, but Death Is Strong," in* The New York Times Book Review, *February 4, 1990, p. 15.*

Hugh Denman   (essay date 1990)

[*In the following review of* The Mirror Maker, *Denman discusses the differences between Levi's Holocaust writings and his short fiction.*]

Looking back across Primo Levi's *oeuvre* one is struck by the sharp contrast that seems to exist between his accounts of his experiences in Auschwitz and much of his fiction. At times one could be forgiven for thinking that the books had been written by two different authors. The discrepancy appeared problematic to Levi himself. His reputation had been established with *Se questo è un uomo* (*If This Is a Man,* 1947), and *La tregua* (*The Truce,* 1963) which dealt respectively with survival in the *Lager* and the chaotic odyssey that followed his liberation by the Red Army. When he came to write his third book, **Storie naturali** (1966), his début as a writer of wry fantasies inspired in some measure by his training as a professional scientist, he initially felt compelled to use a pseudonym [Domiano Malabaila] so as to avoid misleading his public. It took some time for Levi himself to identify the common denominator. He later described it as a preoccupation with "vizi di forma", formal defects whether in matter or human nature, but the link can equally well be found in the meticulous sensibility which Levi brought to his work both as an industrial chemist and as a writer.

If one wonders how it was that Levi managed to survive Auschwitz, the first answer must be by luck. He more than once described how at the end of the war he was abandoned in the camp by the fleeing SS because he had scarlet fever. His friend, Alberto, who had had the disease as a child, was immune to infection and was among the tens of thousands who, forced to march to Mauthausen, perished on the roadside. Levi's profession also played a vital role. As a chemist he knew some German and was eventually selected for special labour which entailed extra rations. In addition to this, however, it is clear that Levi's gift for precise, dispassionate observation—further honed by the training he had received at the Istituto Chimico of Turin University just before Jewish students were excluded—stood him in good stead as a survival technique in Auschwitz.

In a wide-ranging discussion with the Italian physicist, Tullio Regge, published under the title *Dialogo* in 1984, . . . Levi talks revealingly about the ways in which this training contributed to the techniques he employed as a writer and how it shaped his metaphors, his perspectives and above all his fundamental curiosity. Now **The Mirror Maker** provides a further opportunity to appreciate Levi's penetrating yet quizzical vision of the awesome universe we inhabit and of Auschwitz, its perverse microcosm. Broadly speaking, **The Mirror Maker** represents a translation of **Racconti e saggi** (1986), a collection of stories and essays which Levi contributed over a period of some twenty-five years to the Turin daily newspaper *La stampa.* Unfortunately some of the more charming stories in the Italian volume (such as **"Meccano d'amore"** and **"Ranocchi sulla luna"**) have been omitted from **The Mirror Maker,** while a number of essays which appeared in *La stampa* after the publication of **Racconti e saggi** are now included.

This is the most disparate of Levi's books, consisting to a large extent of occasional items and the paralipomena of other works. We find stories and episodes that could have fitted into *If This Is a Man, The Truce,* **The Periodic Table** (1985), **Moments of Reprieve** (1986) or even *The Drowned and the Saved* (1988). Some items are rather lightweight and one imagines that they might have remained uncollected but for the desire to bring out a volume of the pieces from *La stampa,* but even when Levi's parables are slightly simplistic, they are always redeemed by some fresh detail of observation. **"The Two Flags"**, for example, is a sub-Swiftian homily on the irrationality of racism (with sardonic linguistic comments reminiscent of the Struldbruggs passage that Levi included in his personal anthology, *La ricerca delle radici* in 1981). However, the physiological symptoms of advanced prejudice are very much his own and at the same time entirely convincing.

In stories like **"The Great Mutation"** one again encounters the disconcerting blend of whimsy and clinical precision that characterized **Storie naturali** and *Vizio di forma* (1971). It concerns a virus-induced mutation that causes humans to grow wings. Many of Levi's stories have something of the quality of computer-simulated experiments. What would be the consequences if one aspect of reality were to be drastically modified in the framework of an otherwise familiar environment? The *Verfremdung* generated by this technique renders the reader more aware of his own subliminal perceptions and has the curious effect of producing a kind of magical hyper-realism. In this context it is particularly interesting to read Levi's essay on his experience of translating Kafka. The juxtaposition of dream images and precisely observed realistic detail is common to both authors, but Levi's constant striving for lucidity is in complete contrast to Kafka's purposeful hermeticism.

Levi was not one for neat compartmentalization, indeed, he is quite specific about the epistemological benefit to be derived from transferring intuitions between apparently unrelated fields. It is not surprising, therefore, that the formal distinction between stories and essays is fairly tenuous. If narrative perspective occasionally suffers, we are more than compensated by his subtle percipience and eclectic brilliance on subjects as varied as entomology, literary form, disarmament and psychopathology. All this is only partially obscured here by a translation that is at best pedestrian, frequently insensitive to distinctions of register and at times grossly inaccurate ("sixteenth century" for *Settecento* etc). It is a pity that Methuen has not been able to find a translator capable of matching Levi's finely crafted prose.

> *Hugh Denman, "Versatile Invitations," in* The Times Literary Supplement, *No. 4536, March 9-15, 1990, p. 248.*

Gabriel Motola   (essay date 1990)

[*In the following excerpt, Motola discusses some of the stories in* The Mirror Maker, *and notes that the most engaging "address ethical and moral questions raised by political considerations and by [Levi's] literary readings and scientific studies."*]

Like those of its predecessor, *Other People's Trades,* the pieces in **The Mirror Maker,** written over a twenty-five-year period, were culled from the pages of *La Stampa.* While the earlier collection remains a richer and fuller one, more substantial and more informative about Levi's life and his philosophy, this collection yields further proof of Levi's extraordinary ability to probe the human condition in its myriad guises. The inclusion in **The Mirror Maker** (1989) of the initial publication dates of the stories and essays is a significant improvement over the editing of *Other People's Trades,* which lacks these details. Unfortunately the reader cannot determine who had ultimate control over the inclusion of the pieces and their arrangement.

Because of the introduction ("Premise") written by Primo Levi, you get the impression that the contents were arranged by the author himself or with his approval. Levi's introduction is dated October 1986, but some of the pieces collected from *La Stampa* were first published in early 1987. Let us hope that in future editions of **The Mirror Maker** the choices made by Levi and those made by the editor or publisher will be clearly shown as well as the dates of first publication.

Levi's most engaging stories and essays remain those that address ethical and moral questions raised by political considerations and by his literary readings and scientific studies. The tension in **"Through the Walls,"** one of the most complex stories in the book, is created by the conflicting demands of metaphysics and science. Memnone,

an alchemist, has been imprisoned for many years because he refuses to recant what he knows to be true: matter is *not* infinitely divisible and atoms do exist.

He devises a diet that ultimately enables him to pass his body through the stone walls of the prison. But because his body has lost its corporeity his feet now sink into the ground and the stone paths. With difficulty he reaches his old lover, Hecate. He and his theory have been vindicated. But instead of taking the proper nourishment his weakened body needs, he is carried away by desire and embraces Hecate, only to sink into her: "He again experienced the dizziness that had seized him while he was moving through the stone: no longer irritating now but delicious and mortal. He dragged the woman along with him into a perpetual night of impossibility."

The passion of the man is such that he unwittingly trades one prison for another: the stone walls of the dungeon for the soft flesh of the woman. This is not to say, however, that Levi placed the restraints of logic above the passion of love. What he feared was unbridled passion unmediated by loving kindness, as his satirical and humorous piece **"The Ant's Wedding"** illustrates. After saying she has laid a million and a half eggs despite being only fourteen years old and having made love only once, the queen ant says: "When food is scarce and eggs are too many, there is no room for moralism. We eat the eggs and I'm the first. . . . They are nutritious. . . . So what: Without logic there is no government."

Although it lacks the metaphysical complexity of **"Through the Walls"** and the allegorical satire of **"The Ant's Wedding,"** **"Force Majeure"** is nevertheless the most powerful and most disturbing story in the collection. Published in July 1986, the story recalls the experiences Levi suffered more than forty years earlier. The protagonist, identified simply as M., doubtless in tribute to Kafka, is a slight, bespectacled, bookish man who has an appointment with a library manager in an unfamiliar section of town. In order to reach his destination, M. must pass through an alley which is blocked by a powerful sailor who beats and humiliates M.—"who until then had lived a normal life strewn with joys, irritations and sorrows, successes and failures perceived a sensation he had never experienced before, that of persecution, *force majeure,* absolute impotence, without escape or remedy." Levi concludes the story with M. setting out "for his appointment, knowing that he would never be the same man as before."

In the newly issued volume that combines *Survival in Auschwitz* and *The Reawakening* Primo Levi wrote an afterword. There he says that his experiences in Auschwitz did not leave him with "any violent or dolorous emotions. On the contrary . . . the sum total is clearly positive: in its totality, this past has made me richer and surer."

Written at approximately the same time, these antithetical notions seem difficult, if not impossible, to reconcile. Having experienced "absolute impotence," M. "would never be the same man as before" seems to contradict categorically Levi's assertion that "this past has made me richer and surer." What must be borne in mind, however, is that Levi, on the one hand, was viewing the past as well as the future through a keen intellect influenced by scientific objectivity. Thus, even such a past, when filtered through the reasoning mind, may recollect in tranquility experiences which can make one "richer and surer." On the other hand, when the experiences are stirred up rather than recollected, when they are felt again and again, as they must be in defenseless dreams of the night or in the re-created stories and poems that roil the unconscious, then the "absolute impotence" constantly felt in his soul is a constant reminder "that he would never be the same man as before." Paradoxically this almost unresolvable stress between his emotion and his intellect largely provides the tension that informs and enriches his work. (pp. 509-11)

One of the last essays in **The Mirror Maker** is "The Spider's Secret." In it Levi wrote of his lifelong fascination with "producing varnishes." The essay is devoted to the process of solidification of liquids, similar to how varnish is made, by such creatures as caterpillars in building their cocoons or spiders in weaving their webs. "No chemist has yet succeeded in reproducing so elegant, simple and clean a process. We have surpassed and violated nature in many fields," he concludes, "but we still have much to learn from nature." As interesting as are his discussions of both the natural and physical sciences, the most intriguing sentence of the essay if not of the whole book is one he fails to develop. It comes in the first paragraph: "It seems to me . . . strange that varnishes are displacing Auschwitz in the 'ground floor' of my memory: I realize this from my dreams, from which the *Lager* has by now disappeared and in which, with increasing frequency, I am faced with a varnish maker's problem that I cannot solve."

A varnish is used to protect, to gloss over, to seal in whatever must not be exposed to the elements. If in fact varnish was displacing Auschwitz in his memory, if in fact the *Lager* had disappeared from his dreams and in its place was the "varnish maker's problem" that could not be solved, then one interpretation for what he terms as strange is that the varnish itself was covering but not displacing Auschwitz, concealing the *Lager* but not making it disappear. Whatever pain or frustration or depression Primo Levi was experiencing in the final months of his life, it seemed too strong finally for even the varnish to contain.

From his poetry and his prose, from the interview and the dialogue, a sharply focused picture of Primo Levi emerges: he is the twentieth-century victim who refuses to feel sorry for himself for having been in the camps or to see himself as a hero for having survived them, who depicts with relentless and unforgiving clarity those responsible by their actions or by their inactions for the destruction and humiliation of their fellow human beings. He is also the twentieth-century man who through his cultural and scientific awareness takes pride in man's achievement and progress, who knows that the fate of the earth is bound up in man's ultimate acceptance of his responsibility to all its creatures—who after all are made of the same materials as man himself. (pp. 513-14)

Gabriel Motola, "The Varnish-Maker's Dreams," in The Sewanee Review, *Vol. XCVIII, No. 3, Summer, 1990, pp. 506-14.*

Carole Angier   (essay date 1990)

[*In the following review of* The Sixth Day, and Other Stories, *Angier identifies Jewish courage as the major theme of Levi's work and observes that the stories in this collection exhibit a fine balance "between humanity and detachment, art and science, drama and meaning."*]

We have been getting Primo Levi's philosophical science fiction in reverse order. **The Sixth Day** translates stories from his first two collections, **Storie Naturali** (**Natural Stories**, 1967) and *Vizio di Forma* (*A Structural Defect*, 1971). They are among the first things he wrote after the long convalescence of home and work that followed his Auschwitz masterpiece, *If This Is a Man.*

And how extraordinary they are, testaments to recovery as triumphant as *If This Is a Man* was to survival. Anthony Rudolf, in his brief, intense tribute to Levi's work [*At an Uncertain Hour: Primo Levi's War against Oblivion*], says that he was never wittier or more inventive; it's true. And Rudolf is right, too, that these taut metaphysical fables are Levi's territory—indeed, I'd add, his invention. They are beautifully balanced between humanity and detachment, art and science, drama and meaning. In them, Levi balances between a scientist and (in the courtly sense) a fool: lightly, he runs reality through his literary laboratory, making a small change here, a small extrapolation there: and the delicate, dangerous balance of our real world is revealed.

Seven or eight of the stories are scientific *jeux d'esprit* on different themes—on memory, on a post-nuclear world, on water (one day it becomes viscous; and rain destroys the land, ice becomes "as elastic and tenacious as steel", people are torpid, can't weep, and die at 30 or 40 of fatigue). But the others, twice that number, are all in one way or another on the same theme. It is summed up, aptly, in **"The Servant"**, Levi's version of the Jewish legend of the *golem,* the clay figure brought to life by a man: when the *golem* stirs, his builder feels both joy and fear, because "the joy of the Jew contains a crumb of fear."

This theme is the theme of Prometheus. "You invent fire and make a gift of it to mankind," says one of Levi's scientists, "then a vulture gnaws at your liver for eternity." Partly because men are corrupt, and abuse their power over nature for money (**"Full Employment"**) or sex (**"The Sleeping Beauty in the Fridge"**) or simply to see what will happen (**"Some Effects of the Mimer"**); but mostly because this power is dangerous in itself, and exacts an equal and opposite cost. The most godlike ambition produces the most hellish consequence (**"Angelic Butterfly"**); even the best aim—for example, to increase communication between people—can produce the opposite of what was intended (**"For a Good Purpose"**).

The two most brilliant stories are also the key ones, attacking the question of pain head-on. In **"Westward"**, scientists synthesise a substance which creates the "will for life" in people who have lost it; in **"Versamina"**, a chemist discovers one that converts pain into pleasure. Levi does not deny the value of such (only slightly extrapolated) achievements: when Anna in **"Westward"** says that it is better to vanquish pain from one's own strength, and Walter asks, "But what about the weak?" Levi is, I think, in both of them. But, in the end, his Jewish fear outweighs his Jewish joy, and he is in both the narrators of **"Versamina"** too: in Dybowski, who says that everything must be paid for, and in Dessauer, who says that pain, though "a foolish guardian, because it is inflexible" is nonetheless "one with life, it is its custodian".

What Levi mainly stands for, therefore, here, as in all his work, is Jewish courage. He is most of all in the "unborn" S in **"The Hard-Sellers",** who refuses the guarantee of a good life, and chooses to take his chance with the rest of "defenceless and blind humanity"; and in the Arunde tribe of **"Westward",** who lack the illusions that lend the will to live, but who refuse Factor L because they "prefer freedom to drugs and death to illusion". This unillusioned, unsupported courage is, I think, the key to Primo Levi: to his art; to his life after Auschwitz; and to his death.

> Carole Angier, "Unillusioned Courage," in New Statesman & Society, *Vol. 3, No. 123, October 19, 1990, p. 32.*

Robert Gordon   (essay date 1990)

[*In the following excerpt, Gordon discusses major themes in* The Sixth Day, and Other Stories.]

The Sixth Day is a collection of Primo Levi's science-fantasy stories taken from *Storie naturali* (1966) and *Vizio di forma* ("Formal Defect"). They explore the sometimes awful, sometimes comic consequences of science's interference with the natural order, and their light inventiveness provides a fascinating counterpoint to the sombre tragedy of Levi's major autobiographical works. Nevertheless, many of the underlying concerns of the latter remain valid here. He continues to probe the limits of the human and the humane, by way of acute observation, deduction and hypothesis, so that he could fairly claim that "between the Lager and these inventions, a continuity, a bridge exists: the Lager was for me the greatest of all 'defects' . . . the most threatening of all monsters born of reason".

In **"The Servant"** the monster is a literal one, the Golem of Judaic mythology, but, more often, it is man who renders himself monstrous by transgressing implicit natural laws. **"Versamina",** for example, describes the catastrophic and ultimately fatal attempts by Kleber, a brilliant chemist, to transform pain into pleasure. Kleber is one of several Promethean inventors in the book who, absorbed by the power of manipulation and creation (or Creation), and unperturbed by problems of morality, innocently court disaster. Their archetype is Mr Simpson of the organization NATCA, tireless foil to the largely autobiographical narrator in several stories, who acknowledges with a sigh his mythological ancestry: "Same old story, right? You invent fire and make a gift of it to mankind, then a vulture gnaws at your liver for eternity."

Furthermore, as always in Levi, there is an implicit equivalence between scientific and poetic invention. The narrator of **"Psychophant"** says of the machine of that name,

"it didn't matter to me whether it told the truth or lied, but it created from nothing, invented: *found,* like a poet". Hence, careful control of language acts as a correlative to the central theme; language too is a tool of power. The parodies of bureaucratic jargon (**"The Sixth Day"**) or of research reports (**"Seen from Afar"**) and the stories which deal directly with communication (**"The Mnemogogues"**, **"Full Employment"**) reaffirm both the risks and pleasures of the creative impulse.

Although uneven, these vignettes show Levi thinking with lateral ingenuity, exploring many moral issues, experimenting through fiction. A ludic side to his style, already detectable in *The Truce* (1963), here comes to the fore, and may disappoint readers who look to him for searing moral authority. But for those open to what Primo Levi's friend and publisher Italo Calvino called "leggerezza" (lightness) in literature, there is much to enjoy in these cautionary tales.

> Robert Gordon, "Prometheus Unperturbed," in The Times Literary Supplement, *No. 4573, November 23-29, 1990, p. 1271.*

Anthony Rudolf   (essay date 1990)

[*In the following excerpt from his book* At an Uncertain Hour: Primo Levi's War against Oblivion, *Rudolf discusses the course of Levi's literary output and surveys the themes, plots, and style of his short stories.*]

Levi does not seem to have written much, if anything, in the fifties: certainly between the original publication of *If This is a Man* in 1947 and the publication of *The Truce* [the sequel to *If This Is a Man* which chronicles Levi's journey home from Auschwitz] in 1963, the only book to appear was the second edition of the former. What Levi was doing in the fifties was building a life with his loved and loving wife, raising a family, and working at a proper job as an industrial chemist in whose specialised techniques—concerning paint varnish—he would later become a world authority. In 1962 he wrote *The Truce* and was beginning to write his science fiction stories. When pushed in an interview to say what his Paradise (or promised land) might be—perhaps the professional and personal world of **The Periodic Table**—he said: "I don't think *The Periodic Table* describes a paradise unless you call normal life a paradise, which could be the case. If you are happy with daily life, living the life of a *mensch* freely, then yes you can describe it as my Paradiso".

The Truce is, as I have said, in many ways a happy book. Certainly it is an exuberant one, a book of hope and longing, of convalescence and adventure. I am convinced that Levi's long and unsought eight-month journey home was a kind of blessing. He grew back into normal life (normal relative to Auschwitz: occupied eastern Europe was no picnic, even for those outside the camps, as Levi well knew), and sharpened his wits and perceptions to accommodate his exceptionally broad yet focused and unsentimental sympathies for humankind. During those eight months *If This is a Man* was continuing to gestate. Home again, Levi was ready for love and ready for work. Had he gone straight home he might one day have written a book but not, perhaps, a masterpiece of world literature completed within two years of his time in Auschwitz.

In the early sixties, as I have said, Levi began writing his science fiction stories, virtual realities, unsolemn moralities which discuss and predict destructive uses of technology and echo his ongoing concern—after the hitherto worst monster of all—to prevent more and worse monsters begotten by or in the sleep of reason, or excess of reason. Collected in two volumes in Italy and published as **The Sixth Day** in English nearly quarter of a century later, Levi explores the fictional possibilities inherent in what are, fortunately, only metaphysical conceits, disturbing projections of present trends: these include *mnemogogues,* pharmacological 'arousers of memories' (one in the eye, or rather up the nose, for Proust); 'a hormone that inhibits the existential void'; a pill, *versamine,* which can reverse nature, turn dog into counterdog, convert pain into pleasure: 'if pain is life's guardian, pleasure is its purpose and reward'—the character Dessauer could be speaking for Levi himself.

There is a powerfully imagined and beautifully retold version—*midrash* if you like—of the Golem fable; and several stories about the *mimer,* a duplicator which is 'revolutionary . . . it does not imitate, it does not stimulate, but rather it reproduces the model, recreates it identically, so to speak from nothing . . . '. In the hands of the narrator's friend Gilberto it is extremely dangerous, for Gilberto is 'a noxious Prometheus . . . a child of the century. . . . I've always thought that, if the occasion arose, he would have been able to build an atom bomb and drop it on Milan "to see the effect it would have" '. Gilberto creates a second wife, and the narrator resolves to have nothing to do with 'the melancholy mess'. Gilberto, however, visits him two months later and says it's all been sorted out. About time, says the narrator. 'No, look, you didn't understand me. I'm not talking about myself; I'm talking about Gilberto the first'.

Then, in another story, the American company which patented the *mimer,* brings out a new product, a beauty meter or *kalometer* but the narrator's wife, a plainspoken everywoman, scandalised, says it should be called a *homeometer,* because it measures conformity. Elsewhere the sales rep of the company likens himself proudly to Prometheus. Undoubtedly the myth was crucial to Levi. It is deeply ironic that the etymology of the name Prometheus is—as all science fiction writers from Mary Shelley to Levi must know—"forethinker".

Other projections include: the *psychophant* which measures your inner image, and the *torec* which transmits total experiences not through the sensory organs but directly on the nervous system. Neither hallucination nor dream, it is 'indistinguishable from reality'. There are more than nine hundred titles, categorised under "Art and Nature", "War", "Wealth", etc. Levi explains how the tapes are prepared in the first place and has much fun describing the experiences of people playing them, including one man who puts the tape in backwards. This particular story looks forward to stories like **"Time Checkmated"** in **The Mirror Maker.**

Levi's imagination and wit are at their most inventive in these stories and in **The Mirror Maker.** As we know, he had already drafted **"Carbon"** (the last chapter of **The Periodic Table**) in Auschwitz, and several of these stories were written while Levi was drafting *The Truce* in 1962. This is a writer indeed, a fiction writer of the first rank, but a maker of miniatures like his friend [Italo] Calvino and [Jorge Luis] Borges, not a full-scale novelist. *The Wrench,* a quasi-novel, is a masterpiece but *If Not Now, When?,* Levi's only attempt at a proper novel, is surely his least successful book.

During the sixties and seventies he was writing regularly for *La Stampa,* which published stories and essays some of which have appeared in French in **Lilith** and in English in *Other People's Trades* and **The Mirror Maker.** In the early seventies, he must have started writing **The Periodic Table,** and perhaps **The Wrench.**

Real work, significant work, was of great importance to Levi, both in theory and in practice, and both theoretical and practical work—as we know from *The Wrench*—where work is the active ingredient—and **The Periodic Table** where it is never absent. These are two of the best books ever written on the subject. Through work he retrospectively and singlehandedly demolishes the gates of Auschwitz, though his spirit had been free even while his body was incarcerated, or he would have died: those gates, with their diabolically mendacious motto 'arbeit macht frei': work sets you free. As well as teaching us about the complex relationship between theory and practice—often in a very funny way—he sometimes seems to abolish the difference between art and science, between chemistry and alchemy, between art and work. These are two exhilarating books, mind blowing and mind sweeping. As Levi says, Dante was an astronomer, Galileo a great writer. There is no problem here about two cultures.

I have already mentioned the chapters in **The Periodic Table** on Vanadium and Carbon, the savage irony of the former, the moving and harmonious implications of the latter: to think that a meditation on photosynthesis could help keep you alive and sane, but it did. There is a kind of magical or, better, alchemical realism about Levi's use, in these autobiographical fictions, of universal metaphors derived from the seriously objective structure of the chemical elements—Levi returns to this subject in some essays in *Other People's Trades* and in the least substantial of all his books, *Dialogo,* to which he contributes only 20%. I wrote earlier about the chapter **"Cerium"** in **The Periodic Table** with its gloss on events in *If This is a Man.* **"Nickel"** describes the play of work with great love and fascination:

> For that rock without peace I felt a fragile and precarious affection: with it I had contracted a double bond, first in the exploits with Sandro, then here, trying as a chemist to wrest away its treasure. From this rocky love and these asbestos-filled solitudes, on some other of those long nights were born two stories of islands and freedom, the first I felt inclined to write after the torments of composition in high school: one story fantasized about a remote precursor of mine, a hunter of lead instead of nickel; the other, ambiguous, and mercurial, I had taken from a refer-

ence to the island of Tristan da Cunha that I happened to see during that period.

These two stories—**"Lead"** and **"Mercury"**—are real fables, and remind us of the territory of Calvino and other fabulists. Fable rather than realistic or documentary writing is his forte when it comes to fiction, and this is confirmed by some of the non-*Churban* subjects he writes about in his essays right through to the eighties, for example on bacteria and on gossip in *The Mirror Maker.* [*Churban* is the term Levi preferred. In a footnote, Rudolf explains: "In common with some other writers I shall use the term *Churban,* a Hebrew word for 'destruction' and one not laden with the wrong religious connotations of 'Holocaust' or even 'Shoah'. 'Ch' is pronounced as in 'loch' not 'church'."] The metaphysical possibilities, the sheer entertainment, inherent in extrapolations from science, in pseudo-scientific experimentation, in pushing scientific and technological models or physical structures beyond their natural limits: this is his territory. (pp. 24-9)

> *Anthony Rudolf, in his* At an Uncertain Hour: Primo Levi's War against Oblivion, *The Menard Press, 1990, 56 p.*

Peter Lewis   (essay date 1991)

[*In the following excerpt, Lewis examines the influences on and the general characteristics of Levi's short fiction.*]

Levi is now widely acknowledged to be one of the most searching and subtle analysts as well as chroniclers of what is usually called the *Holocaust,* although Levi himself disapproved of both this term and its synonym *Shoah* because they evoke the wrong religious connotations. He preferred the Hebrew word *Churban* ('destruction'), as some other Jewish writers have done, including Anthony Rudolf in his short monograph *At an Uncertain Hour: Primo Levi's War against Oblivion,* which is both a tribute to Levi and an excellent introduction to his achievement as a writer. Like [Elias] Canetti, Levi wrote non-autobiographical fiction, including the realistic novel *If Not Now, When?* and the metafictional stories contained in *The Sixth Day and Other Tales,* but his finest and most enduring work is either autobiographical (e.g. *If This Is a Man* and *The Truce*) or involves an important element of autobiography even though this is incorporated into a quasi-fictional form (e.g. *The Periodic Table*).

From the end of World War II until his suicide in 1987, which can be at least partly attributed to his experience as a victim of the Nazis in a death camp, Levi returned again and again to the problem of describing and understanding the *Churban*—if 'understanding' is possible. As one of the 'saved' as opposed to the 'drowned'—the words he uses in *The Drowned and the Saved*—Levi was driven to bear witness about the manmade *Inferno* he lived through: to speak for all the 'drowned' and against those who actively committed genocide and the many more who passively turned a blind eye to it. Levi compared himself to the Ancient Mariner—'And till my ghastly tale is told / This heart within me burns,'—and Rudolf appropriately takes as his title a phrase from Coleridge's poem. Rudolf 's study is not in the least academic and is far removed from

orthodox literary criticism. His three-part essay is a thoroughly engaged piece of work about a writer who has affected him deeply and altered his way of looking at the world. For Rudolph, Levi's books provide 'a renewed insight and outsight into what it means to be human'. An unexpected part of Rudolph's book is his comparison between Levi and the great poet Paul Celan, another Jewish survivor of the same age as Levi who also committed suicide (in 1970). In an essay in *Other People's Trades* Levi describes the difficulties he experienced in grappling with the complex poetry of Celan, a multilingual Jew born in Romania who chose to write in German, the language of those responsible for the Final Solution. In defending Celan against the charge of wilful obscurity, Rudolph shrewdly perceives the crucial difference between these two compelled and compelling writers:

> Primo Levi, trusting language, especially Italian, salvaged and reasserted truth through language, went *with* its grain. His life's work and work's life was to *say.* Celan, not trusting language or not trusting German, salvaged and reasserted truth *against* language, went *against* its grain. His life's work and work's life was to *unsay.* They are, both of them, breathtaking and breathgiving writers, *breath-turning/ atemwende,* to use the word Celan coined.

Most of Levi's writings are now available in English, thanks to the determined effort by translators, especially Raymond Rosenthal, during the past few years. Three recent additions are *The Sixth Day and Other Tales, The Mirror Maker: Stories and Essays* and *Other People's Trades.* The first of these is a compilation of two collections of stories written in the 1960s and published in Italy in 1966 and 1971. With their blend of fantasy, science fiction, fable and parable, these *tales,* a more accurate word than *stories,* reveal an indebtedness to [Jorge Luis] Borges and [Italo] Calvino, but their scientific and technological preoccupations are very much those of a professional scientist who was an international authority in his field of chemistry. A characteristic of metafiction is its ability to present the ordinary, everyday world in startlingly unexpected ways, opening up new perspectives as though seen in a radically distorting mirror. Levi makes the most of this potential to provoke his readers' imaginations and challenge their assumptions. In doing so, he often focuses on the divorce in our society between science and technology, on the one hand, and ethics and values, on the other. The *Churban* itself was a large-scale example of what can occur if a technology, with its accompanying bureaucracy, is completely severed from moral criteria. For its perpetrators, the Final Solution was a problem of organization and technology—the technology of annihilation. These provocative stories can be humorous and witty, but are also sinister and disturbing.

The Mirror Maker, too, contains a number of Levi's tales as well as a few poems, but about half the book is devoted to a selection of the essays he contributed to the newspaper *La Stampa* over a period of more than twenty years. *La Stampa* is also the source of almost all the articles collected in *Other People's Trades,* which contains no fiction. Most of the tales in *The Mirror Maker,* which date from the late 1970s and 1980s, employ fantasy even more freely than his earlier ones with a consequent reduction in the science-fiction element, although a few are realistic with a basis in personal experience. Like the tales, many of the essays in both books reflect the workings of a scientist's mind, sometimes in broadly speculative ways (especially in *Other People's Trades*), but sometimes focused sharply on the ethical implications of scientific research, as in 'Hatching the Cobra' (*The Mirror Maker*). Levi acknowledges the divide between human intelligence and wisdom, and the enormous dangers, including nuclear destruction, inherent in this separation, but he rejects the pleas of some prominent scientists, including the late Sir Martin Ryle, a Nobel Prize winner, for an end to some basic research for fear of the consequences. Risk, for Levi, is inevitable in the human condition, and if we were to deny ourselves the intellectual curiosity that manifests itself in scientific research 'we would betray our nature and our nobility as "thinking reeds," and the human species would no longer have any reason to exist'. Science and technology are by no means Levi's only concerns in his journalistic writings. He ranges far and wide, writing with great discernment on such literary topics as Rabelais, the writing of fiction, the translating of Kafka, and the importance of traditional poetic forms, techniques and devices.

Levi is particularly impressive, as is to be expected from his finest books, in treating aspects of the *Churban,* such as his tribute to the heroic but hopeless Jewish rising against the Germans in Warsaw in 1943, 'Defiance in the Ghetto'. Especially moving as well as forcefully argued is 'The Dispute among German Historians', written only a few months before his death. Here he takes issue with those recent 'revisionist' historians who deny the uniqueness of 'the Nazi slaughter' by placing it in a context of historical atrocities and by presenting it as Hitler's 'preventive defence' against a possible 'Asiatic' invasion. Levi also criticizes Western liberals for simplistically conflating German Nazism and Soviet Communism into a virtually indistinguishable totalitarianism. As an Italian who grew up during the Mussolini era, Levi knew very well that 'totalitarianism' is a clumsy word covering a considerable variety of possibilities. While deploring Stalin and Stalinism, Levi rightly insists on the crucial differences between what happened in the Soviet Union and in German-occupied Europe. After Solzhenitsyn, no justification of the gulag camps is possible, but, as Levi notes, they were certainly not death camps, black holes like Treblinka and Chelmno. To the very end of his life Levi, for whom, like the Ancient Mariner, the agony always returned, continued to bear witness on behalf of the twelve million civilians who perished in Nazi camps, not only the six million Jewish victims. Only by keeping their memory alive, could Levi win what Rudolf calls his 'war against oblivion', against the Nazi attempt to liquidate not only people but memory it-

self. 'The dead rely upon our fidelity', as Vladimir Jankélévitch wrote in 1986. (pp. 79-81)

> *Peter Lewis, "Speaking Out, Bearing Witness," in* Stand Magazine, *Vol. 32, No. 2, Summer, 1991, pp. 74-83.*

FURTHER READING

Biography

Atlas, James. "The Survivor's Suicide." *Vanity Fair* 51, No. 1 (January 1988): 78-84, 94.

Discusses Levi's life, work, and the circumstances of his death; although not completely certain, Atlas argues that Levi did in fact take his own life.

Criticism

Denby, David. "The Humanist and the Holocaust: The Poised Art of Primo Levi." *The New Republic* 195, No. 4 (28 July 1986): 27-33.

Surveys Levi's life and careers in chemistry and literature, focusing primarily on *Survival in Auschwitz, The Reawakening, The Periodic Table, If Not Now, When?,* and *Moments of Reprieve.*

Howe, Irving. "How to Write about the Holocaust." *The New York Review of Books* XXXII, No. 5 (28 March 1985): 14-17.

Extols Levi's life and literature and argues that he is unique among writing survivors of the Holocaust because his works display "an emotional restraint and a steadiness of creative purpose that [would] seem almost indecent to demand from survivors."

Levi, Primo. "Reflections on Writing." *Partisan Review* LVI, No. 1 (Winter 1989): 21-33.

Excerpts from *Other People's Trades* in which Levi discusses various aspects of writing, including fictional and critical topics as well as practical advice.

Morrison, Philip. Review of *The Periodic Table*. *Scientific American* 252, No. 2 (February 1985): 23, 27.

Positive review of *The Periodic Table* from a scientifically informed critic.

Wilde-Menozzi, Wallis. "A Piece You've Touched Is a Piece Moved." *The Tel Aviv Review* 2 (Fall 1989-Winter 1990): 149-65.

Commemorates and analyzes Levi's life and literature; cites examples from the major forms in which he wrote, including his memoirs and other autobiographical writings, essays, short stories, novels, and poetry. [See excerpt above]

Additional coverage of Levi's life and career is contained in the following sources published by Gale Research: *Contemporary Authors,* Vols. 13-16 rev. ed., 122 [obituary]; *Contemporary Authors New Revision Series,* Vols. 12, 33; *Contemporary Literary Criticism,* Vols. 37, 50; and *Major 20th-Century Writers.*

Saki

1870-1916

(Pseudonym of Hector Hugh Munro) English short story writer, novelist, journalist, and historian.

INTRODUCTION

The reputation of H. H. Munro (Saki) rests primarily on his short stories, which convey whimsical humor, fascination with the supernatural, and disillusionment with hypocrisy and banality. Saki's works memorialize the comfortable world of British upper-class town houses, tea parties, and weekends in the country that reached its peak between the end of Queen Victoria's reign in 1901 and the beginning of World War I. The clever remarks and cynical views of Saki's characters expose the arbitrariness and artificiality of the society in which they never completely lose faith. Saki's stories present individuals who, through capriciousness or eccentric behavior, get into odd situations from which they usually escape by means of their quick wits. His narratives often go beyond realism, however, when employing surprise endings or depicting strange anthropomorphic animals and children embattled with adults.

Munro began his writing career in 1894, but published little until 1900, when his first major work, *The Rise of the Russian Empire,* appeared. During the same year Munro collaborated with popular cartoonist Francis Carruthers Gould to produce a series of cartoons and comic sketches that use figures from Lewis Carroll's *Alice's Adventures in Wonderland* to satirize political events of their era. The cartoons by Gould and the comic sketches written under Munro's pseudonym, Saki—which was borrowed from Edward Fitzgerald's translation of Omar Khayyam's *Rubaiyat*—were an immediate success. In 1901 Munro began contributing short sketches to the *Westminster Gazette* in which he related the adventures of a witty, acerbic young man named Reginald. Collected in 1904 as the volume *Reginald,* these enormously popular stories established Munro's reputation as a cynical observer of upper-class manners and mores. From 1902 to 1909 Saki was a foreign correspondent for the *Morning Post* in the Balkans and Paris. He returned to London and published many short stories and novels prior to the outbreak of the First World War. Refusing a commission as an officer, Munro enlisted as a private and was killed in France in 1916.

The sketches collected in *Reginald,* which are often set in fashionable places where the wealthy congregate, are narrated by either Reginald himself or an older friend called "the Other," and reveal Reginald to be a humorous observer of upper-class manners as well as a dandified narcissist. Only the title story of Saki's second collection, *Reginald in Russia,* concerns Reginald. The rest of the tales continue Saki's satiric examination of upper-class country

life or venture into didactic fables. "Gabriel-Ernest" is about a man who finds a boy, referred to as Gabriel-Ernest, whom he suspects may be a werewolf. The man's aunt, knowing nothing of his suspicion, decides he should be taken to her Sunday school class. Gabriel-Ernest subsequently devours a child he has been entrusted to walk home. While the man suspects the truth, Gabriel-Ernest, like many Saki heroes, manages both to get his way and to preserve his spotless reputation in spite of his actions.

In *The Chronicles of Clovis* Saki introduced two new major characters, Clovis Sangrail and Bertie Van Tahn. Although both characters are similar to Reginald, Clovis is more likable than either Reginald or Bertie; while he delights in absurd situations and in deflating the pretensions of others, he often has sympathy for those in real trouble. By contrast, the perpetually adolescent Bertie fails to see how humor at the expense of others can turn into cruelty. Many of the stories in the collection feature animals and animal imagery. In "Tobermory," for example, a talking cat disrupts a weekend party by revealing the guests' secrets he has overheard.

Animal stories are again featured in the collection *Beasts and Super-Beasts.* Saki also introduced a new main character, Vera, whose name, suggesting truthfulness, contradicts her role in the stories as a practical joker. In "The Open Window," a frequently anthologized story, Vera tells a guest, Framton Nuttel, that her mother always leaves a French window open for her husband and brothers, who supposedly were lost in a bog while hunting three years ago to the day. When men are seen approaching, Nuttel runs madly from the house, leaving the reader to realize that he has been the victim of a fabricated ghost story.

Popular and respected as a virtuoso of the short story during his own lifetime, Saki has been ranked throughout the twentieth century with such acknowledged masters of the genre as Guy de Maupassant and O. Henry. Saki's work has influenced writers such as P. G. Wodehouse, whose farcical tales of affluent, scatterbrained young sophisticates are reminiscent of the Reginald stories. While commending his wit and adroit dialogue, critics often mention the apparent cruelty in Saki's stories. Elizabeth Drew justified this lack of compassion: "The cruelty is certainly there, but it has nothing perverted or pathological about it. . . . It is the genial heartlessness of the normal child, whose fantasies take no account of adult standards of human behavior. . . . The standards of these gruesome tales are those of the fairy tale; their grimness is the grimness of Grimm." Although terrible things happen in Saki's stories, he provides a satisfying sense of justice done and human decency restored. Modern commentators have argued that Saki usually goes beyond mere entertainment to explore such moral issues as the social responsibilities of the upper classes and the failure of humanity to live up to its potential.

PRINCIPAL WORKS

*SHORT FICTION

Reginald 1904
Reginald in Russia, and Other Sketches 1910
The Chronicles of Clovis 1912
Beasts and Super-Beasts 1914
The Toys of Peace, and Other Papers 1919
The Square Egg, and Other Sketches, with Three Plays
    (short stories and dramas) 1924

OTHER MAJOR WORKS

The Rise of the Russian Empire [as Hector H. Munro]
    (history) 1900
The Westminster Alice (satire) 1902
The Unbearable Bassington (novel) 1912
When William Came: A Story of London under the Hohen-
    zollerns (novel) 1914
The Works of Saki. 8 vols. (novels, short stories, satire,
    and dramas) 1926-27

*Six previously uncollected short stories are included in *Saki: A Life of Hector Hugh Munro* by A. J. Langguth, 1981.

CRITICISM

The New York Times Book Review (essay date 1919)

[*In the following review, the critic favorably appraises Saki's observations on human nature in the stories collected in* The Toys of Peace.]

Somewhere within the blood-sanctified soil of France lies the body of Hector Hugh Munro, who for a time adopted the pen name of "Saki." A successful author, a man over 40, and of slight physique, he nevertheless sought the fighting line, enlisted as a private soldier and was shot down while crossing No Man's Land on his way toward the enemy's trenches. Satirist and brilliant stylist, a writer whose gayety softened the sting of his wit, he was also one of those few who saw the danger to which most men were blind—extraordinarily, almost miraculously blind it seems to us now as we look back upon the years just preceding the great war—the danger of German aggression. So he wrote *When William Came,* a book whose very cleverness hid its seriousness from the majority of readers. That, indeed, was his way—a way to which [*The Toys of Peace*] bears witness—to cloak serious purpose with a glittering outer garment of wit and gayest irony.

Take, for instance, **"The Toys of Peace,"** well and wisely chosen as the opening tale in the book and the one which gives an appropriate name to the entire collection. In the nine or ten pages which so amusingly describe how the Bope children received their uncle's well intentioned gift of "peace toys" and what they did with it there lies beneath the fun a discerning comment on certain facts of child nature, which is but human nature in embryo. Most of the stories and sketches in the volume are short, and many of them are of the lightest and most amusing type— vers de société in prose. It is therefore with a certain shock that one comes across that grim story, **"Interlopers,"** or the pathetic, lovely little idyl called **"The Image of the Lost Soul."** Even in the trenches, when, as his friend, Rothay Reynolds, who prefaces the volume with an admirable and sympathetic memoir, tells us, the physical strain so taxed his strength, his gayety does not seem to have failed. The last tale in the book, written at the front and entitled **"For the Duration of the War,"** is the lively account of a literary hoax which this same war made possible. There are no less than thirty-three tales and sketches in the book, and to comment on all of them is obviously out of the question. They show an understanding of the foibles and weaknesses of human nature, but never a contempt for it, nor any degeneration into bitterness. The arrow of the satirist is winged with kindliness; always there is in his work that quality which enabled him to close the brilliantly ironical *When William Came* with a memorable picture of the boys of England flinging their indomitable defiance in the very face of the triumphant Kaiser. They are very gay, very amusing, these brief, witty little stories of the days before the war. Yet the very enjoyment with which one reads them but makes keener one's sense of the tragedy which occurred on that November day when their creator fell, shot through the head by a bullet from the Hun.

A review of "The Toys of Peace," in The New York Times Book Review, *July 6, 1919, p. 358.*

S. P. B. Mais   (essay date 1920)

[*Mais was an English author who wrote extensively on English life and literature. In the following excerpt, he describes the characteristic qualities of Saki's humor.*]

It was in the Christmas vacation of 1905 that I was presented with a copy of **Reginald** by a fellow-undergraduate. There are some debts that one can never repay in full; it is perhaps something that we never forget the friend who introduces us to an author who ultimately becomes a favourite: I shall feel that I have, in some degree, repaid him in this case if I can entice any reader . . . who may have missed Munro's work to love it as I do, for he who brings before our notice what exactly suits our temperament is a private benefactor of a very high order. "Saki's" humour—let it be admitted at once—is not for all tastes. There may be some who look upon such playing upon phrases as "There are occasions when Reginald is caviare to the Colonel," or "We live in a series of rushes—like the infant Moses"—as unworthy. These are they who refuse to laugh at the nimble-witted Nelson Keys, and prefer to reserve their merriment for an abstruse Shakespearean pun about "points" and "gaskins." Again, it may be urged that such a jest as the following may be found every week in the comic papers:

> There is my lady kitten at home, for instance: I've called it Derry . . . then if there are any unseemly noises in the night, they can be explained succinctly: Derry and Toms.

Whether or no that is a good joke I don't profess to judge. All I know is that I have remembered it for nearly fifteen years, and I have no memory whatever for stories of any kind. I am not ashamed to say that I laugh whenever I think of it. That is the type of humour that exactly appeals to me. How we laughed too over the deft, ironic touches that we afterwards came to regard as Munro's choicest gift, from the simple "Reginald considered that the Duchess had much to learn: in particular, not to hurry out of the Carlton as though afraid of losing one's last bus," or "she was one of those people who regard the Church of England with patronising affection, as if it were something that had grown up in their kitchen gardens," to the crisper, unforgettable "never be a pioneer: it's the Early Christian that gets the fattest lion," "the frock that's made at home and repented at leisure," "the stage can never be as artificial as life; even in an Ibsen drama one must reveal to the audience things that one would suppress before the children or servants"; "in a few, ill-chosen words she told the cook that she drank: the cook was a good cook, as cooks go; and as cooks go, she went": *c'est le premier pa qui compte,* as the cookoo said when it swallowed its foster-parent," "a young man whom one knew instinctively had a good mother and an indifferent tailor—the sort of young man who talks unflaggingly through the thickest soup, and smooths his hair, dubiously as though he thought it might hit back" . . . and so on. I am tempted to go on quoting, as we used to in those far-off days of

youth . . . but with me, at any rate, **Reginald** has stood the test of time. I read it to-day with just as many involuntary guffaws of mirth as I used to: it is no book for the railway carriage, if you are constituted as I am.

The sketch of Reginald, who is forced to spend Christmas at an intolerably dull house, planning some diversion (a favourite trick of Munro's), is almost a test example.

> I had been preceded [to bed] a few minutes earlier by Miss Langshan-Smith, a rather formidable lady, who always got up at some uncomfortable hour in the morning, and gave you the impression that she had been in communication with most of the European Governments before breakfast. There was a paper pinned on her door with a signed request that she might be called particularly early on the morrow. Such an opportunity does not come twice in a lifetime. I covered up everything except the signature with another notice, to the effect that before these words should meet the eye she would have ended a misspent life, was sorry for the trouble she was giving, and would like a military funeral. A few minutes later I violently exploded an air-filled paper-bag on the landing, and gave a stage moan that could have been heard in the cellars. Then I went to bed. The noise those people made in forcing open the good lady's door was positively indecorous; she resisted gallantly, but I believe they searched her for bullets for about a quarter of an hour, as if she had been an historic battlefield.

I find it impossible to copy that story down without laughing; to me, at any rate, it is irresistibly funny, and it is in Munro's peculiar vein: he is better at this practical-joke sort of fun than any man I know: you may legitimately urge that such a sense of humour connotes cruelty, and "Saki" seems to me to be, on occasion, one of the "hardest" writers I know.

After all, so far as I understand him, he sets out to scourge the foibles of Society: he is a sort of prose Pope: at times he is just as polished and his arrows are quite as well-barbed. "He died quite abruptly while watching a county cricket match: two and a half inches of rain had fallen for seven runs, and it was supposed that the excitement killed him." "Isn't there a bishop who believes that we shall meet all the animals we have known on earth in another world? How frightfully embarrassing to meet a whole shoal of whitebait you had last known at Prince's! I'm sure, in my nervousness, I should talk of nothing but lemons." "Whether the story about the go-cart can be turned loose in the drawing-room, or must be told privately to each member of the party, for fear of shocking public opinion." "She must have been very strictly brought up, she's so desperately anxious to do the wrong thing correctly. Not that it really matters nowadays, as I told her: I know some perfectly virtuous people who are received everywhere." "There's Marian Mulciber, who *would* think she could play bridge, now she's gone into a Sisterhood—lost all she had, you know, and gave the rest to Heaven." As you may, by this time, have gathered, Reginald is one of those flippant young men about town (not very common) who are as neat in their speech as they are in their clothes. I visualise Munro as very like his own Reginald in his youth, sardonic and rude at garden parties, never losing an opportunity of revenge on his enemies, conversationally brilliant in a way that unfortunately reminds one of Wilde at very rare intervals as in "That is the worst of tragedy, one can't hear oneself talk," and "Beauty is only sin deep," but he escapes from the sterile artificiality of the Wilde school very quickly, and Wilde never could have hit on the sort of humour one finds in such a sentence as: "Never be flippantly rude to any inoffensive, grey-bearded stranger that you may meet in pine forests or hotel smoking-rooms on the Continent. It always turns out to be the King of Sweden."

Reginald stage-managing a Sunday-school treat by depriving the choir-boys of their clothes and compelling them to form a Bacchanalian procession through the village with a he-goat and tin-whistles, but no covering beyond a few spotted handkerchiefs, provides us with an inexhaustible theme for mirth; Reginald telling tales about Miriam Klopstock, "who *would* take her Chow with her to the bath-room, and while she was bathing it was playing at she-bears with her garments. Miriam was always late for breakfast, and she wasn't really missed till the middle of lunch"; Reginald refusing to accept invitations from a sort of to-be-left-till-called-for cousin of his father on the ground that "the sins of the father should not be visited by the children"; Reginald "ragging" the Major who was for ever reminding his fellow-guests of things that he had shot in Lapland, "continually giving us details of what they measured from tip to tip as though he thought we were going to make them warm underthings for the winter"; whatever he is doing he is a sheer delight. What I cannot understand is why such a scintillating book should have so far failed to attract the public that a second edition was not called for until a year after publication, and a third edition was not printed until six years had passed. To me, this little book of 118 pages contains the cream of his work. True, it contains no example of his essays in the tragic muse, some of which are no whit inferior to his best in the comic vein, but in ***Reginald*** we see him at his most ingenuous, most naïve, and most youthful. (pp. 311-16)

Reginald in Russia, as so often happens in the case of sequels, was most disappointing and need not detain us.

The Chronicles of Clovis (1912) is, in the opinion of most of his admirers, his best book. It is certainly his most characteristic work. In it we see his understanding of and love for animals, his almost inhuman aloofness from suffering, his first-hand knowledge of house-parties and hunting, his astounding success in choice of names for his characters, his gift for epigram, his love of practical jokes, his power of creating an atmosphere of pure horror, his Dickensian appreciation of food and the importance of its place in life, his eerie belief in rustic superstitions, and his never-failing supply of bizarre and startling plots.

Clovis is, of course, only Reginald re-christened: he supplies the epigrams and is the prime instigator of most of the practical jokes.

For originality of theme it would be hard to beat **"Tobermory,"** the story of the cat who suddenly assumed human speech at a house-party and began to regale a drawing-room full of guests with precise extracts from the private opinions of each of those present about the others.

"What do you think of human intelligence?" asked Mavis Pellington lamely.

"Of whose intelligence in particular?" asked Tobermory coldly.

"Oh, well, mine, for instance," said Mavis, with a feeble laugh.

"You put me in an embarrassing position," said Tobermory. "When your inclusion in this house-party was suggested, Sir Wilfred protested that you were the most brainless woman of his acquaintance, and that there was a wide distinction between hospitality and the care of the feeble-minded. Lady Blemley replied that your lack of brain-power was the precise quality which had earned you your invitation, as you were the only person she could think of who might be idiotic enough to buy their old car. You know, the one they call 'The Envy of Sisyphus,' because it goes quite nicely up-hill, if you push it."

Once given the idea, which is brilliant, it is easy to see how, in the hands of an artist, there is no limit to the humour to be derived from it. It is like *Gulliver's Travels*.

There is a simplicity about his plots that makes one gasp at their effectiveness, as in the case of Lady Bastable, in whose house Clovis did not wish to stay longer, and so obtained permission to leave by the ruse of playing on Lady Bastable's weak spot. She was always in dread of a revolution: Clovis only had to rush into the servants' quarters and shout: "Poor Lady Bastable! In the morning-room! oh, quick!" and lead the butler, cook, page-boy, three maids, and a gardener still clutching a sickle, rapidly to the room where she was seated quietly reading the paper, to make her fly through the French windows in ignominious retreat.

"The Unrest Cure" is in much the same vein: Clovis, in this case, manages to disturb the even tenor of the existence of a "groovy" middle-aged bachelor and his sister by a "fake" massacre of the Jews in their neighbourhood. The plot, as usual, is ingenious and convincing.

But the story that stands out in this volume is the gruesome **"Sredni Vashtar,"** which tells of a delicate small boy (living under the strictest surveillance of a religious aunt), who managed to keep a Houdan hen and a great ferret in the recesses of a tool-shed unknown to his tyrannical overseer. The hen was found and destroyed. Other gods were suspected, and the woman made a personal investigation to discover the ferret while the boy prayed for vengeance, his face glued to the window which overlooked the garden and the tool-shed. After an interminable interval he saw a long, low, yellow-and-brown beast emerge with dark wet stains around the fur of jaws and throat . . . and, after a lull, during which he happily made himself some toast, he heard the scared sobbings and the shuffling tread of those who bore a heavy burden into the house. The atmosphere is as tense and awe-inspiring as it is in "Thrawn Janet" or "Markheim," or the mysterious tales of Richard Middleton. It is a relief to come down to the antics of Adrian of Bethnal Green, who amused himself by transferring the bath-room label in a German hotel to the adjoining bed-room-door belonging to Frau Hofrath Schilling, who, from seven o'clock in the morning onwards, had a stream of involuntary visitors. We rise to the purer regions of irony again in **"The Chaplet,"** where the chef of a famous restaurant plunged the head of the conductor of the orchestra into the almost boiling contents of a soup tureen because the guests had allowed his consummate dish of *Canetons à la mode d'Amblève* to grow cold on their plates while they listened to the strains of *The Chaplet.*

One begins to think that advertising agencies must have lost a gold mine by the death of "Saki," after one has read **"Filboid Studge,"** the story of the penurious young man who wanted to marry the daughter of a patent-food seller. Mark Spayley, the prospective bridegroom, steps in to save his future father-in-law from ruin. As "Pipenta" the food had failed to "catch on." Spayley re-christened it "Filboid Studge," and designed one huge, sombre poster depicting the damned in Hell suffering a new torment from their inability to get at the Filboid Studge, which elegant young fiends held out just beyond their reach. The scene was rendered more gruesome by a subtle suggestion of the features of the leading men and women of the day. The poster bore no fulsome allusions to the merits of the new breakfast food, but a single grim statement in bold letters along its base: "They cannot buy it now."

Spayley had grasped the fact that people will do things from a sense of duty which they would never attempt as a pleasure. Needless to say, he loses the wife he wants owing to the startling success of his poster. As Clovis said: "After all, you have this doubtful consolation, that 'tis not in mortals to countermand success."

From **"The Music on the Hill"** we learn that "Saki" held in very considerable awe the power of the great god Pan: his lonely life as a boy in North Devon must have led him to realise that the forces of Nature are relentless and terrible. This fact must have been seared into his heart, for he recurs to it again and again. The doing to death of the young city-bred wife by the hunted stag because of her disbelief in the power of the wood-gods is horribly effective in its irony. **"The Peace of Mowsle Barton"** is intended to prove that London may very well be more restful for the nerves than the depths of the country, where old women seem to have retained their witchcraft and possess some remnants of their legendary powers of magic and cursing.

"The Hounds of Fate" is exactly in the vein of Masefield's long narrative poems, and shows the slow, unchanging steps of doom tracking down the miscreant who thinks to escape vengeance. There is a quite sufficient sprinkling of the terrible in this book, which is, perhaps, all the more hair-raising by reason of its juxtaposition with the light and airy persiflage of Clovis. One word on his choice of names: a mere catalogue will suffice to show how perfectly they are invented. As an exercise in imagination, I would suggest that you try to visualise the appearance and characteristics of each, and then compare your results with the

reality. In every case you will, I think, very nearly approximate to his conception. I will begin by helping you.

> Constance Broddle (a strapping, florid girl of the kind that go so well with autumn scenery or Christmas decorations in church).
>
> The Brimley Bomefields (depressed-looking young women who have the air of people who have bowed to destiny and are not quite sure whether the salute will be returned).
>
> Septimus Brope (the Editor of *The Cathedral Monthly*).
>
> Groby Lington (a good-natured elderly man of recluse habits who kept a pet parrot).

Now try a few for yourself:

> Bertie Van Tahn, Odo Finsberry, Agnes Resker, Mrs Riversedge, Mrs Packletide, J. P. Huddle, Aristide Saucourt, Rose-Marie Gilpet, Duncan Dullamy, Betsy Croot, Mortimer Seltoun, Cocksley Coxon, Loona Birnberton, Martin Stonor.

Which is the witch, the unorthodox Dean, the chef, the old-fashioned hostess, the man who was reading for Holy Orders, the youth who was so depraved at seventeen that he had long given up trying to be any worse, the Christian Scientist, the Company Promoter, the solid, sedate man who discussed the prevalence of measles at the Rectory? . . . I maintain that their names fit them so exactly that you ought to be able to "spot" each of them at a glance.

I do not propose to dwell on *The Unbearable Bassington,* in which joy and pain are blended so inextricably that we find ourselves laughing through our tears at one moment, and weeping through our laughter the next. "Saki" was not a great novelist, even though we may claim that *When William Came* was a magnificent *tour de force.* If anything could have roused England to the menace of Prussian militarism in those days before the war this bitingly ironic fantasy should have succeeded; but we were too far sunken in our torpor, and the squib fizzled out. As propaganda this novel deserves lasting fame, but from the artistic point of view "Saki's" reputation will rest solely on his manipulation of the short story, in which branch of letters he was, as I am trying to show, a past master.

In *Beasts and Super-Beasts* he sometimes excels even the most witty chapters of *The Chronicles of Clovis:* as can be seen from the title, he specialises in animal stories, and by a queer trick now attributes his more effective practical jokes to the inventive genius of sixteen-year-old flappers instead of to young male "rips" of the Reginald-Clovis type.

His choice of beasts is as queer as his choice of names: they bear something of the same resemblance to ordinary animals and ordinary names as Heath Robinson's drawings do to the usual machine diagram. Just as Heath Robinson ridicules absurd inventions, so does "Saki" burn up with the white flame of his scorn all pretenders to occult powers: the man whose aunt averred that she had seen him actually turn a vegetable marrow into a wood-pigeon before her very eyes gets a very thin time at the hands of Clovis, "whom he would gladly have transformed into a cock-roach, and stepped on had he been given the chance." Munro was probably all the more bitter against the charla-tan because of his own belief in unaccountable phenome-na: he casts a wonderful air of verisimilitude over the story of Laura, who, at the point of death, declares that she is coming back as an otter to worry her friends, and does so: having been hunted and killed in that capacity, she next reappears in the guise of a naked brown Nubian boy, in-tent on mischief as ever.

Even the hoaxes in this book seem to depend on animals: there is the story of how the flapper kept the parliamenta-ry candidate from brooding over politics at night by com-mitting to his care a gamecock and a pig, on the plea that the outhouses had been flooded owing to the bursting of the reservoir: there is the delicious tale of the man in the train who always failed to capture the attention of any of his fellow-passengers until, at the instigation of a friend, he launched the following at their heads: "A snake got into my hen-run yesterday morning and killed six out of seven pullets, first mesmerising them with its eyes, and then biting them as they stood helpless. The seventh pullet was one of that French sort, with feathers all over its eyes, so it escaped the mesmeric snare and just flew at what it could see of the snake and pecked it to pieces." From that day his reputation as the Munchausen of the party was as-sured. The story of the tame otter that had a tank in the garden to swim in and whined restlessly whenever the water-rate was overdue, was scarcely an unfair parody of some of his wilder efforts. And then came Nemesis. His wife followed the example of her mother and great-grand-aunt by dying immediately after making a "Death's Head Patience" work out. At last something had really hap-pened in the romancer's life. He wrote out the full story only to find that he was disbelieved in every quarter. "Not the right thing to be Munchausening in a time of sorrow" was the general verdict, and he sank once more to conver-sation about canaries, beetroot, and potatoes, a chastened and lonely man.

There is irony enough and to spare in the story of how the family of Harrowcluff came to figure in the Honours' List. Basset, at the age of thirty-one, had returned to England after keeping open a trade route, quietening a province, enforcing respect . . . all with the least possible expense. He was likely to be thought much of in Whitehall: his elder half-brother, Lucas, was always feverishly engrossed in a medley of elaborate futilities, and bored him sadly with his constant discoveries of ideas that were "simply it." On this occasion the inspiration came to Lucas while he was dressing. "It will be *the* thing in the next music-hall revue. All London will go mad over it. Listen:

> Cousin Teresa takes out Caesar,
> Fido, Jock, and the big borzoi.

A lilting, catchy sort of refrain, you see, and big-drum business on the two syllables of bor-zoi. It is immense." It was: to the surprise of his family the song caught on, the name of Harrowcluff became more and more famous until at length, under the heading of "Merit in Litera-ture," Colonel Harrowcluff had the satisfaction of seeing his son's name in the List of Honours. But it wasn't Basset.

The story of Cyprian, who preferred to accompany his aunt on a shopping expedition without a hat and was seen by her at intervals to be deliberately pocketing the money for various articles from buyers who mistook him for a salesman, is in the best Reginald manner, as is the story of the young man who, having gambled all his own posses-sions, staked his mother's peerless cook and lost.

"The Story-Teller," in which Munro shows his complete understanding of children, ought to prove invaluable to those who want to know how to hold the attention of small boys and girls: the flick of the satiric whip at the end of the story when the aunt stigmatises the stranger's fable as "improper" is delightful.

> "Unhappy woman," [said the bachelor to him-self] "for the next six months or so those chil-dren will assail her in public with demands for an improper story."

There are tales of wolves (a favourite animal with "Saki"), elks, hunters, boar-pigs, whitebait, honey-buzzards, a most hilarious picture of a cow in a drawing-room, and of two Turkestan camels climbing a grand staircase: one be-gins to think that "Saki" must have felt some affinity with one of his own characters, an artist who always represent-ed some well-known place in London, fallen into decay, populated with wild fauna. "Giraffes drinking at the foun-tain pools, Trafalgar Square," "Vultures attacking dying camel in Upper Berkeley Street," "Hyænas asleep in Eus-ton Station," and "Sand-grouse roosting on the Albert Memorial" are some of his happiest titles, and it is not hard to think of "Saki" visualising some of his scenes in much the same way. His love for animals was great, his love of the incongruous even greater: a combination of these two passions would account for much of the merri-ment his animal stories cause us.

His last book, **The Toys of Peace,** published post-humously, is not so sustainedly successful as his earlier collections of short stories. He was so ardent a soldier that writing for *The Morning Post, The Westminster Gazette,* and *The Bystander* must have seemed but toying with life in comparison with the great vocation to which he was suddenly called to consecrate his time. His first story, ironic as ever, shows us parents of a pacific turn of mind endeavouring to divert their children's taste from blood-lust to the excitements of peace, from guns to ploughs, from toy soldiers to toy city councillors, by giving them figures supposed to represent Mrs Hemans, John Stuart Mill, and models of the Manchester branch of the Y.W.C.A. The result can easily be guessed.

> Peeping in through the doorway Harvey ob-served that the municipal dustbin had been pierced with holes to accommodate the muzzles of imaginary cannon . . . J. S. Mill had been dipped in red ink and apparently stood for Mar-shal Saxe.

> Louis orders his troops to surround the Y.W.C.A. and seize the lot of them. "Once back at the Louvre and the girls are mine," he ex-claims. "We must use Mrs Hemans again for one of the girls: she says 'Never!' and stabs Marshal Saxe to the heart."

As I said before, "Saki's" understanding of the psychology of childhood is profound. His old trick of happy simile returns with as good effect as ever, but on rarer occasions.

> Nowadays the Salvation Army are spruce and jaunty and flamboyantly decorative, like a geranium bed with religious convictions.

His brain never lost its cunning in coining perfectly fitting names: "Eleanor Bope" brings before us at once a realistic picture of the aunt with freak ideas about "peace" toys. "Crispina Umberleigh" could only be a woman of martinet habits, born to sit in judgment. "Octavian Ruttle" could not be other than amiable; you would expect Waldo Orpington to be frivolous and chirrup at drawing-room concerts; we know exactly the kind of novel to expect from Mark Mellowkent, while the home life of Mr and Mrs James Gurtleberry can be guessed without much explanation.

How far it is permissible to search for a serious design in the work of a humourist it is hard to say, but one story so far stands out from the rest of his work as epitomising his attitude to life, that one is tempted to base a theory on the ideas contained in it.

Why, we ask ourselves, does "Saki" so frequently have recourse to hoaxes for his plots? Why does he take an almost indecent delight in those of his characters who are fluent liars, who exercise their imagination at everybody else's expense? The reason, I think, will be found in **"The Mappined Life,"** which might almost have been written by Tchehov.

> "We are able to live our unreal, stupid little lives on our particular Mappin terrace, and persuade ourselves that we really are untrammelled men and women leading a reasonable existence in a reasonable sphere: we are trammelled by restrictions of income and opportunity and, above all, by lack of initiative. Lack of initiative is the thing that really cripples one, and that is where you and I and Uncle James are so hopelessly shut in. There are heaps of ways of leading a real existence without committing sensational deeds of violence. It's the dreadful little everyday acts of pretended importance that give the Mappin stamp to our life. Take my case: I'm not a good dancer, and no one could honestly call me good-looking, but when I go to one of our dull little local dances, I'm conventionally supposed to 'have a heavenly time,' to attract the ardent homage of the local cavaliers, and to go home with my head awhirl with pleasurable recollections. As a matter of fact, I've merely put in some hours of indifferent dancing, drank some badly-made claret-cup, and listened to an enormous amount of laborious light conversation. A moonlight hen-stealing raid with the merry-eyed curate would be infinitely more exciting."

That is "Saki's" secret. Behind the mask of the satirist and the elegant buffoon we can trace the features of one who so loved life that his affections always swayed his more sober reason, of one whose favourite companions were the Reginalds and Clovises of this world, because they, at least, could never grow up and worship at the shrine of routine.

"Saki" was not only a child-lover, he was a child himself, with all the imagination, the irresponsibility and the harsh cruelty of children fully developed in him: there is nothing sweet or mellow or restful in his genius: he surprises us just as "O. Henry" surprises us by turning a complete somersault in his last sentences after astonishing us with all manner of gymnastic capers in each paragraph before. It reminds one of music-hall acrobats who, after taking our breath away several times during their "turn," make their adieux by performing some incredible antic that leaves us too shattered even to applaud.

Such is the humour of "Saki," which never descends to caricature like so much of Dickens, is never aimless like that of W. W. Jacobs, is often bitter like his masters, Pope, Dryden, Swift, and (at times) Wilde, always verbally brilliant, polished, and cold: his exaggerations are all marked with a restraint which, of course, makes them all the more grotesque and mirth-provoking: his accents are as precise as those of the most prim governess or the most literal Scotsman:

> "There is a goat in my bedroom," observed the bishop.
>
> "Really," I said, "another survivor? I thought all the other goats are done for."
>
> "This particular goat is done for," he said, "it is being devoured by a leopard at the present moment. That is why I left the room: some animals resent being watched while they are eating."

It is here that he differs from Stephen Leacock, his transatlantic counterpart: both are prolific in verbal felicities, but Leacock is far less subtle: where "Saki" is giving full play to a wonderfully developed imagination, Leacock is confined by the bounds of his terrestial fancy; where "Saki" soars into the highest regions of the truly comic, Leacock is content with the slow, earth-borne car of Parody; the barbs of irony which "Saki" employed were aimed at foolish humanity straying pitiably from paths where they might be happy, while Leacock's sarcastic darts are levelled at a particular failing of foolish "cranks." Leacock has intermittent flashes of great brilliance, but his intellect is that of a highly talented professor; "Saki," like "O. Henry," rises quite frequently beyond cleverness into that inexplicable, rarefied atmosphere where only the genius can survive. Like "O. Henry," and only too many other geniuses, he escaped recognition in his lifetime: "Saki" had only an eclectic public: but the passion of the devoted few always keeps the reputation of great men burning until the time comes for posterity to acknowledge the master, and there is no doubt whatever that the time will come when "Saki" will be given his niche among the great humourists. (pp. 317-30)

S. P. B. Mais, "The Humour of 'Saki'," in his Books and Their Writers, *Grant Richards Ltd., 1920, pp. 311-30.*

Alexander Porterfield   (essay date 1925)

[In the following essay, Porterfield assesses Saki's literary career, viewing his short stories as his most enduring achievement.]

In his lively if not altogether satisfactory reply to Jeremy Collier's famous *Short View of the Profaneness and Immorality of the English Stage,* Sir John Vanbrugh has given us an admirably succinct, engaging definition of the function, the "business" of comedy. Sir John, it will be remembered, fared rather badly at the doctor's hands, and hit back with much commonsense and spirit. "The business of Comedy," he says in his *Vindication,* "is to shew people what they should do, by representing them upon the stage, doing what they should not." Now, this is excellent—considered solely in the light of sheer dexterity of definition. But the plain fact is, Sir John composed his comedies first and his explanations afterwards, and he no more wrote plays for the reformation of manners than Congreve did, or "Easy" Etherege. He was, in short, a comic writer pure and simple, like every other writer of his day and generation.

Jeremy Collier changed all that, however, substituting a moral footrule for the old, less positive, pragmatic standards—a substitution which Sir John and those who followed him accepted readily enough and which has worked the utmost mischief ever since. Indeed, one trouble with most comic writers is their failure to be chiefly and primarily comic; they have, apparently, too many other duties. They are anti-vivisectionists first, or Roman Catholics, and comic writers afterwards; story-tellers, dramatists, mainly by a kind of literary courtesy, an accident of label. That, nowadays, appears to be the rule. You must have quite pre-eminently some sort of moral *parti pris* before you can be humorous; but it is, luckily, a poor rule which has no exceptions, and *Saki*—the late H. H. Munro—is one of them. *Saki* is almost the Sir John Vanbrugh of this generation. In tone and feeling he is definitely Restoration; if, as he himself says somewhere, his tales point out an evil, they at least offer no solution; and, in an age given up almost entirely to such depressing earnestness in general, from its preoccupation with the problem of Hamlet to the latest crossword puzzle, they are doubly worth reading for that very reason. It is a great pity they are not better known. (p. 385)

Most of his stories which have been collected in book form were reprinted from the *Bystander,* the *Westminster* and the *Morning Post,* and most of them are rather more than good. In temper and intention, most of them are purely comic pieces, distinguished by a crisp insouciant elegance and easiness of manner, a fertility of invention and sparkling gaiety of dialogue and narrative—the temper and intention of the comedy of manners. They introduce us to an indolent, delightfully amusing world where nothing is ever solved, nothing altered, a world in short extremely like our own, only you are not asked to believe in it. It is the "fairy" world of Charles Lamb, a wholly comic world realistic merely in its imaginative resemblance to this present universe of ours—a world steeped in the classical, dry light of Restoration comedy.

Beasts and Superbeasts is easily the best collection of his stories. It is all foolery of the purest sort, unadorned by any dull tags of morality, from the tale about the lady who was turned into a wolf—instead of a fox, which is, I believe, the prevailing fashion—to the one about Sophie Chattel-Monkheim, who was a "Socialist by conviction and a Chattel-Monkheim by marriage"—from the very first story in the book, in fact, to the last. Sophie is particularly a joy. She

> had very advanced and decided views as to the distribution of money; it was a pleasing and fortunate circumstance that she also had money. When she inveighed eloquently against the evils of capitalism at drawing-room meetings and Fabian conferences she was conscious of a comfortable feeling that the system, with all its inequalities and iniquities, would probably last her time. It is one of the consolations of middle-aged reformers that the good they inculcate must live after them if it is to live at all.

Then there is the bachelor who entertains three small children in a train with a most "improper story," and Vasco Honiton, who was "blessed with a small income and a large circle of relatives, and lived impartially and precariously on both." The name Vasco, by the way, had

> been given him, possibly, in the hope that he would live up to its adventurous traditions, but he limited himself strictly to the home industry of adventurer, preferring to exploit the assured rather than explore the unknown.

It is just this sardonic, entertaining gift of irony and insight, this tightly-knit compactness of construction, that makes *Beasts and Superbeasts* so readable and gay a *tour de force* from beginning to end. And it is, too, something much more than that; it is the classical, dry comedy of ideas as opposed to the Dickensian comedy or farce of character.

"The Story-teller" illustrates this admirably. It is a first-rate example of the comedy of ideas as opposed to the comedy or farce of character, which is good not only as an idea but excellent as a story. Congreve himself might have written it, or Sir John Vanbrugh—the necessary changes as to theme and time, of course, having been made. The bachelor is *en route* to Templecombe and is being driven frantic by three restless, small children who completely occupy the carriage. They are nominally in charge of an aunt, most of whose remarks seem to the bachelor to begin with "Don't!"—the children's quite inevitably with "Why?"

> "Don't, Cyril, don't," exclaimed the aunt, as the small boy began smacking the cushions of the seat, producing a cloud of dust at each blow.
>
> "Come and look out of the window," she added.
>
> The child moved reluctantly to the window. "Why are those sheep being driven out of that field?" he asked.
>
> "I expect they are being driven into another field where there is more grass," said the aunt weakly.
>
> "But there's lots of grass in that field," protested

the boy; "there's nothing else but grass in that field. Aunt, there's lots of grass in that field."

"Perhaps the grass in the other field is better," suggested the aunt fatuously.

"Why is it better?" came the swift, inevitable question.

Having rather unsuccessfully encountered the difficulties of lucid explanation, the aunt starts telling the children a story, which is even more unsuccessful. It transpires to be an account of a small girl who was exceedingly good, and made immense numbers of friends by her goodness, and who was eventually rescued from a mad bull by a body of admirers who particularly esteemed her moral character.

"Wouldn't they have saved her if she hadn't been good?" demanded the bigger of the small girls. It was exactly the question the bachelor had wanted to ask.

"Well, yes," admitted the aunt lamely, "but I don't think they would have run quite so fast to help her if they hadn't liked her so much."

"It's the stupidest story I ever heard," said the bigger of the small girls, with immense conviction.

"I didn't listen after the first bit, it was so stupid," said Cyril.

And that is the keynote of the story, of all his stories—that blithe negation of the dull and laudable, that quiet derision of pretentiousness and cant. The bachelor observes that the aunt does not seem to be much of a success as a story-teller, and the aunt invites him to try his hand at it himself. He does:

"Once upon a time," began the bachelor, "there was a little girl called Bertha, who was extraordinarily good."

The children's momentarily aroused interest began at once to flicker; all stories seemed dreadfully alike, no matter who told them.

"She did all that she was told, she was always truthful, she kept her clothes clean, ate milk puddings as though they were jam tarts, learned her lessons perfectly, and was polite in her manners."

"Was she pretty?" asked the bigger of the small girls.

"Not as pretty as any of you," said the bachelor, "but she was horribly good."

There was a wave of reaction in favour of the story; the word horrible in connection with goodness was a novelty that commended itself. It seemed to introduce a ring of truth that was absent from the aunt's tales of infant life.

That is the true, the comic touch. Little Bertha's character is sketched in with consummate ease and irony, a delightful absence of detail, though the bachelor adds the intelligence that she was so good she was awarded three medals for goodness—one for obedience, another for punctuality, and a third for general good conduct. She was so good—so

"horribly good," says Cyril—that the prince of the country allowed her to walk in his garden, a privilege denied to ordinary children. But she promised beforehand, with tears in her eyes, that she would not pick any of the kind prince's flowers, consequently she felt a little silly when she discovered there were no flowers to pick.

"Why weren't there any flowers?"

"Because the pigs had eaten them," said the bachelor promptly. "The gardeners had told the prince that you couldn't have pigs and flowers, so he decided to have pigs and no flowers."

There was a murmur of approval at the excellence of the prince's decision; so many people would have decided the other way.

You feel instinctively that *Saki* himself was not one of them, that he was on the side of all children and animals in their struggle against the arbitrary, unscrupulous authority and domination of grown-ups and never on the side of the "angels."

Bertha's goodness is the cause of her undoing; she is overtaken in the prince's garden by a wolf in search of a succulent piggy for lunch, and hides unavailingly in the laurels, for the medal for good conduct clinked loudly against the medal for punctuality—she was trembling with terror—and gives her away. The wolf dashed into the laurels and devoured her entirely with the exception of her boots and her three medals for exemplary behaviour. Naturally the children—and a good many grown-ups as well—enjoy this unorthodox ending immensely.

"Were any of the little pigs killed?"

"No, they all escaped."

"The story began badly," said the smaller of the two girls, "but it had a beautiful ending."

"It is the most beautiful story I ever heard," said the bigger of the small girls with immense decision.

"It is the *only* beautiful story I ever heard," said Cyril.

It is all extraordinarily gay, sparkling and ingenious. The mood, the manner, have that co-relating sameness of originality and feeling as the Restoration comedies—a dry, impersonal comic spirit caught in the clear crystal of delightful witty prose. *Saki* was probably not conscious of this fundamental sameness; probably he was hardly so conscious or so complex an artist; but his Bertie van Tahns, his Clovis Sangrails, however, and the Sir Fopling Flutters and Mirabells, are—*mutatis mutantur*—definitely something rather "more than kin." They are each figures of the same imperturbable elegance and ease, animated by exactly the same qualities of temper and intention—a "characteristic irony displayed towards things of the spirit, a negligent pleasure in things of the flesh." His comedy, as I have said, is the comedy of ideas. He says in effect, as Comus says in *The Unbearable Bassington,* "it may sound unorthodox to say so, but this is going to hurt you much more than it will hurt me;" and this, possibly, is the secret of *Saki's* impish and sardonic humour. It is the classical re-action of all Restoration comedy. "Life," says Horace Walpole, "is a comedy to him who thinks, a tragedy to him who feels." That is probably one reason why *Saki* seems perhaps a little cruel to so many people, at least, upon a superficial examination, a first reading.

Stripped of all critical comparisons, however, *Saki's* humour is essentially the heedless, almost Nietzschean, non-moral humour of a child. It is with children especially, in fact, that he is at his best, not because they talk or act like children in his stories, since they do not particularly, but because they *think,* they re-act, like children. It is in their own imaginative world we move when we read **"The Story-teller,"** say, or **"The Lumber Room"**—a world of make-believe and escape. Paradoxes present themselves as reasonably as day and night; it is the grown-ups, in brief, who are fantastic and ridiculous, like the aunt in **"The Lumber Room,"** who organises a drive to Jagborough Sands by way of a punitive expedition:

> Nicholas was not to be of the party; he was in disgrace. Only that morning he had refused to eat his wholesome bread-and-milk on the seemingly frivolous ground that there was a frog in it. Older and wiser and better people had told him that there could not possibly be a frog in his bread-and-milk and that he was not to talk nonsense; nevertheless, he continued to talk what seemed the veriest nonsense, and described with much detail the colouration and markings of the alleged frog. The dramatic part of the incident was that there really was a frog in Nicholas's bread-and-milk; he had put it there himself so he felt entitled to know something about it. The sin of taking a frog from the garden and putting it into a bowl of wholesome bread-and-milk was enlarged upon at great length, but the fact that stood out clearest in the whole affair, as it presented itself to Nicholas, was that older, wiser and better people had been proved to be profoundly in error in matters about which they had expressed the utmost assurance.

Now, this is just the way a child would feel in such circumstances; and it is in all such similar passages that *Saki* is at his best, his surest of touch, his most sardonic—naturally enough, perhaps. His own experience was lamentable. It is, moreover, interesting to note that he has made the aunts, if not all the female relations, in his stories almost without exception represent "three-fifths of the world that are necessary and disagreeable and real," like the cousin in that extraordinarily gruesome tale **"Sredni Vashtar"** in *The Chronicles of Clovis.* She is exacting and pedantic, a bully and bigot and a coward withal—a figure corresponding to the jealous husband of the Restoration plays. The jealous husband of Congreve's comedies, say, represented something a little more than a merely ridiculous object; he represented everything the Restoration cordially detested because of what was then considered his intolerance in denying to his wife what he himself asserted, surreptitiously, perhaps, as his right; and, just as Wycherley and Vanbrugh made him their target of satire and ridicule, so *Saki* has fixed upon the aunt or cousin as representing in an eminent degree the object of tyrannical, intolerant authority. She is typical of everything that he dislikes.

"Sredni Vashtar" is *Saki* with a difference; even Mr. Jacobs has not written in "The Monkey's Paw" a more creepy, gruesome tale than this, and its effect is heightened by his usual restraint and admirable economy of words. Sredni Vashtar is a ferret that Conradin secretes in the tool-house at one end of the garden, where he is worshipped with

> mystic and elaborate ceremonial. . . . Red flowers in their season and scarlet berries in the winter time were offered at his shrine, for he was a god who laid some special stress on the fierce impatient side of things, as opposed to the Woman's religion, which, as far as Conradin could observe, went to great lengths in the contrary direction. And on great festivals powdered nutmeg was strewn in front of his hutch, an important feature of the offering being that the nutmeg had to be stolen. These festivals were of an irregular occurrence, and were chiefly appointed to celebrate some passing event. On one occasion when Mrs. de Ropp suffered from acute toothache for three days, Conradin kept up the festival during the entire three days, and almost succeeded in persuading himself that Sredni Vashtar was personally responsible for the toothache. If the malady had lasted for another day the supply of nutmeg would have given out.

But the "Woman" recovers and, what is more, discovers that Conradin has something in which he obtains some enjoyment hidden in the tool-house at the end of the garden. She orders him to remain behind and stalks down to investigate—and does not return. But Conradin

> knew that the Woman would come out presently with that pursed smile he loathed so well on her face, and that in an hour or two the gardener would carry away his wonderful god, a god no longer but a simple brown ferret in a hutch. And he knew that the Woman would triumph always as she triumphed now, and that he would grow ever more sickly under pestering and domineering and superior wisdom, till one day nothing would matter much more with him, and the doctor would be proved right. And in the sting and misery of his defeat, he began to chant loudly and defiantly the hymn of his threatened idol.—
>
> Sredni Vashtar went forth,
> His thoughts were red thoughts and his teeth
>   were white.
> His enemies called for peace but he brought
>   them death,
> Sredni Vashtar the beautiful.

Time slips by, however, and the "Woman" does not appear. He waits, presently hope begins to creep into his heart, presently he begins again that "paean of victory and devastation." Then, almost incredulously, his anxious gaze "is rewarded; out through that doorway came a long, low, yellow-and-brown beast with eyes ablink at the waning daylight, and dark wet stains around the fur of jaws and throat." The final effect of horror is obtained by that grimly sardonic touch at the story's end—the housemaid's loud foolish screaming, the

> answering chorus of wondering ejaculations from the kitchen regions, the scuttling footsteps and hurried embassies for outside help, and then after a lull, the scared sobbings and the scuffling tread of those who bore a heavy burden into the house. "Whoever will break it to the poor child? I couldn't for the life of me," exclaimed a shrill voice. And while they debated the matter among themselves Conradin made himself another piece of toast.

But, while in this instance and in *The Cobweb,* Saki achieves an authentic atmosphere of the macabre and horrible—and these and those stories of his dealing with the manifestations of mental relationship between man and animal seemed to suggest that he was finding a new source of inspiration—I do not think his essays in the supernatural were ever quite so good as his best comic pieces were. The introduction, for example, of the black dog which Comus sees in *The Unbearable Bassington* just before he sails for Africa, seems to me unnecessary if lamentably weak. It smacks a little of the mere theatrical, where **"Sredni Vashtar"** is completely sinister, effective and restrained.

For that matter, I do not think *The Unbearable Bassington* is particularly a success as a novel; it does not quite come off. Nevertheless, it is easily the most ambitious thing that *Saki* tried to do and important consequently for that reason. Strictly speaking, *Saki's* characters are not characters at all, but types, composite portraits drawn almost entirely from one specified class. What Bertie van Tahn says and does in **"A Touch of Realism"** is exactly what Clovis Sangrail might and probably would say in such conditions, or, say, Sir Lulworth Quayne. If there is a distinction at all, it is the somewhat myopic distinction between Sir Fopling Flutter and Mr. Sparkish. And there is something to be said for this kind of portraiture. In Comus Bassington, however, *Saki* has attempted character as character, and he has not quite succeeded in pulling it off; you feel that the fault, as a matter of fact, lies rather with Comus. Like the young lady in **Beasts and Superbeasts** who was "born during Goodwood Week, with an Ambassador staying in the house who hated babies" Comus is inconsiderate from the first—and especially to his creator. In spite of all this, though, the book manages to be at times infinitely touching, if not actually tragic, in that gaily flippant way of his which, with a rather complicated knowledge of geography, is so peculiarly his own. Structurally, *The Unbearable Bassington* is a little loosely written; it seems throughout half to suggest some difference between right and wrong in things which the author has forgotten but which is none the less vital, devastating; and in importance of achievement hardly measures up to the closely knit, compact artistry of **Beasts and Superbeasts,** but it is worth reading for all that—if not quite worth reading so much as **Beasts and Superbeasts.** (pp. 386-92)

Indeed, it is his stories rather than his novels which will be read and remembered, if he is to be read and remembered at all. His style, his wittiness becomes a little trying in a full length novel; it is like a dinner of thirteen courses

of caviare, or smoked salmon—excellent as a beginning, but somewhat monotonous after a while. True, most of his stories were merely occasional journalism, distinguished by a sparkling originality and animation, a freshness which was peculiarly his own, but it is these qualities exactly which make all the difference. (p. 393)

Saki was, possibly, not a great artist; he deserves, however, a good deal more critical recognition and reading than many other humorists whose slightest *obiter dicta* are treasured by everybody as so much revelation. As Mr. J. B. Priestley said of Mr. Jacobs, if his stories had been published in the *Pale Review* instead of the *Strand Magazine,* if they had been read by the few instead of giving pleasure to thousands, he would to-day have received that recognition to which he is surely entitled and **Beasts and Superbeasts** would be on every shelf.

It is difficult to see exactly to what extent he would have developed had he lived. His stories seemed to suggest, as I have already pointed out, a new source of interest and inspiration, and he himself seemed to think that after the war he would never be happy in his old surroundings—in fact, he planned or, rather, was talking about going to the steppes of Siberia to live. But the war, which seemed to have changed so much of the familiar world he knew and loved, really changed things very little, and people still play bridge in St. James's Street just as they used to. It is the tragedy of many young men to have died prematurely before their work was done or even started; it is the tragedy of many many more to have survived.

Saki had probably said everything he had to say; he had selected an artificial and brilliant and flippant philosophy for all his profound understanding of human nature, and, while he was interesting and important for his potentialities, I hardly think he would have gone on any further. After all, he made some delightful contributions to contemporary letters; he was never dull; and that is more than can be said for most modern comic writers. (p. 394)

Alexander Porterfield, "Saki," in The London Mercury, *Vol. XII, No. 70, August, 1925, pp. 385-94.*

Henry W. Nevinson   (essay date 1926)

[*In the following excerpt from the introduction to* Beasts and Super-Beasts, *Nevinson comments on Saki's cynical outlook in the stories collected in this volume.*]

The first time I met "Saki" was in St. Petersburg during the attempted revolution of 1905. We were staying in the same hotel, I as correspondent of the *Daily Chronicle,* he, I think, of the *Morning Post.* At all events he ought to have been for the *Morning Post,* since he was endowed with just the right touch of "educated scorn" which has always distinguished that superior paper. Like his paper, "Saki" was suspicious of all enthusiasm, especially of all Liberal enthusiasm, and stood ready to mock at the zeal and aspirations of all "faddists" and "cranks." His nature ranged him on the side of authority and tradition, while he despised the ideals of "progress" as amiable illusions. One saw the twist of cynicism clearly marked on his face. His aspect of the world was cynical. But the cynicism was humorous and charming, partly assumed as a protective covering to conceal and shelter feeling. That is our English way, and in the suppression of emotion, or of its outward signs, "Saki" was entirely English.

Even in [the stories collected in *Beasts and Super-Beasts*], so far removed from politics, one comes suddenly upon this shrewd distrust of theories and reforming ideals. Consider that sharp stroke in **"The Treasure Ship"**:

> "Somewhere on the west coast of Ireland the Dulverton property included a few acres of shingle, rock, and heather, too barren to support even an agrarian outrage."

Or consider the precautions of the lady who wished to give the candidate for election (obviously a Liberal) a respite from politics in **"The Lull"**:

> "I've had the picture of Cromwell dissolving the Long Parliament taken down from the staircase, and even the portrait of Lord Rosebery's 'Ladas' removed from the smoking-room."

Or take that phrase in **"The Unkindest Blow"**:

> "The Government of the day, which from its tendency to be a few hours behind the course of events had been nicknamed the Government of the afternoon, was obliged to intervene with promptitude and decision."

Or the description of the lady who was a Socialist by conviction:

> When she inveighed eloquently against the evils of capitalism at drawing-room meetings and Fabian Conferences she was conscious of a comfortable feeling that the system, with all its inequalities and iniquities, would probably last her time. It is one of the consolations of middle-aged reformers that the good they inculcate must live after them if it is to live at all."

There you get the pure satiric irony, and you will find more than a touch of it whenever Trade Unions and Strikes come into the story, as in that same **"Byzantine Omelette"** or **"The Unkindest Blow."** Something similar is the educated scorn of the vulgar herd in **"Cousin Teresa,"** with its wildly popular refrain of "The Big Borzoi."

In fact, the charm of cynical sanity enters into nearly all "Saki's" inventions. Rather than admit saints and heroes to sentimental adoration he tinges nearly all his characters with a delightful malice. In **"The Story-Teller"** he lets us into his own secret. There we are shown to perfection the nature of children and their persistent, unanswerable questions ("Why is the grass in the other field better?" and so on). But we also see the dislike that children and all human beings instinctively feel towards the uncommonly good, and the general joy when an evil fate overtakes them owing to their goodness. For if Bertha's three medals for goodness had not clinked together, the wolf would not have found and devoured her, and what a pity that would have been!

A delightful and ingenious wickedness gives a charm to

> There is only one tragic story in [*Beasts and Super-Beasts*] ("The Cobweb"), and a reader should be warned against swallowing the whole succession rapidly one after the other. That dulls the appetite for the wit and malice. It is worse than reading a whole volume of an old *Punch* on end, and there is little more depressing than that. "Saki" must be taken as an occasional spice, an exquisite *aperitif*. He is best as a defence against commonplace and sentimentality.
>
> —*Henry W. Nevinson*

nearly all the stories, and it is noticeable that the most wickedly malicious of the characters are dear, innocent little girls or even good, sweet women who ought to have been "ministering angel thous." On the whole, I think I like the girl in **"The Lull"** best. Her idea of distracting the politician's mind by bringing a little pig and a gamecock into his bedroom is most ingenious. And then her description of the imaginary flood that made the shelter necessary:

> "Good gracious! Have any lives been lost?"
>
> "Heaps, I should say. The second housemaid has already identified three bodies that have floated past the billiard-room window as being the young man she's engaged to. Either she's engaged to a large assortment of the population round here or else she's very careless at identification. Of course it may be the same body coming round again and again in a swirl; I hadn't thought of that."

And I love Matilda in **"The Boar-Pig"** story. Minx, liar, thief—Oh, yes! I know all that. But how ingenious! How lovable!

> "Shoo! Hish! Hish! Shoo!" cried the ladies in chorus.
>
> "If they think they're going to drive him away by reciting lists of the kings of Israel and Judah they're laying themselves out for disappointment," observed Matilda from her seat in the medlar tree.

Equally fine is the mendacious invention of Vera in **"The Quince Tree."** The malice of Eleanor in **"Fur"** almost surpasses her charm, but how pleasing is the final remark:

> "A cloud has arisen between the friendships of the two young women; as far as Eleanor is concerned the cloud has a silver-fox lining."

One naturally classes Max Beerbohm with "Saki." Their half-humorous, half-cynical attitude of mind is much the same. But even Max is not so consummate a liar as "Saki." I suppose "Saki" is the finest liar in literature. In *The Way of All Flesh* Samuel Butler showed himself a good liar, but his lies are not so rich in invention as "Saki's." Which is the most outrageous lie in this lot? It is hard to decide between **"The Lull,"** already mentioned, **"The Hen," "The Romancers,"** and **"A Defensive Diamond."** But on the whole I incline to **"The Schartz-Metterklume Method."** That has all the advantages of a splendid lie and a series of surprises. Surprise is one of "Saki's" favourite jests. In that story how startling is the answer of the pseudo-governess:

> "We got very satisfactory references about you from Canon Teep," she (Mrs. Quabarl, the employer) observed: "a very estimable man, I should think."

> "Drinks like a fish and beats his wife, otherwise a very lovable character," said the governess imperturbably.

And then I like the lie and the surprise in **"Dusk."** The story is so nearly a commonplace tract, but how charmingly it is saved by the malicious surprise of the last six words.

For mere wit of expression one might take the description of the Duke of Falvertoon in **"The Unkindest Blow"** (not in itself the best of the stories), as "One of those human *hors d'œuvres* that stimulate the public appetite for sensation without giving it much to feed on." Or of the soft and idle young man who was "one of those people who would be enormously improved by death" (**"The Feast of Nemesis"**). And what perfection of satire on the artistic taste of the British public is hidden in the account of Eshley (in **"The Stalled Ox"**) who won success by painting cattle drowsing picturesquely under walnut-trees, and was obliged by the public to go on painting the same subject for ever. How well I remember a Royal Academician who painted a cow by a willowy stream about the middle of last century and for fifty or sixty years continued to paint that cow beside a willowy stream without noticeable variation or sign of age.

There is only one tragic story in [*Beasts and Super-Beasts*] (**"The Cobweb"**), and a reader should be warned against swallowing the whole succession rapidly one after the other. That dulls the appetite for the wit and malice. It is worse than reading a whole volume of an old *Punch* on end, and there is little more depressing than that. "Saki" must be taken as an occasional spice, an exquisite *aperitif*. He is best as a defence against commonplace and sentimentality. To myself his works, like his conversation, have given so many happy moments that when I think with sorrow upon the friends that I lost in the war, his small and twisted face, in expression like a young and humorous bird's, stands among the first that rise before my mind. It stands beside Rupert Brooke's and Edward Thomas's. (pp. vii-xii)

> *Henry W. Nevinson, in an introduction to* Beasts and Super-Beasts *by "Saki" (H. H. Munro), 1914. Reprint by Core Collection Books, Inc., 1978, pp. vii-xii.*

Edith H. Walton (essay date 1930)

[*In the following review, Walton comments on the style, plots, and characterization of Saki's short stories, concluding that he is a "minor, if exquisitely entertaining, writer."*]

Around some authors a cult arises. This has been the case with Saki. A few years ago some one conceived the happy notion of republishing his works in this country, and at once they were enthusiastically endorsed by the initiate. So much did he become the fashion that even those who had not read him at least learned a convenient patter about him. By this time, for example, almost every one knows that Saki's real name was H. H. Munro, that he was killed in the war, and that his books are distinguished for their light, sophisticated wit.

Most cults are apt to be synthetic and to have their basis in a transitory snob appeal. There is, however, a legitimate foundation for the extravagant praise which Saki has evoked. Now that the first fervor has died down, and that his short stories have been collected in [*The Short Stories of Saki*], one has a better chance of judging his work as a whole and of judging it soberly. It stands the test well. His range was narrow and he lacked variety, but in his own field Saki is supreme and unique. Without him English literature would be the poorer by one enchanting by-path. To say this is to say a great deal. Few writers can boast that they are irreplaceable.

As Christopher Morley points out in his introduction, it is an unprofitable business to undertake a critical estimate of Saki. It is like puncturing a bright, floating bubble with a bludgeon. Again, the flavor of his wit cannot be tested vicariously. To convey any sense of its quality one would have to quote in detail the dazzling, malicious epigrams, the wry, surprising twists of phrase which he tosses off in such nonchalant abundance. It is not the plots of these stories that matter—though Saki is, when he chooses, a master of trick endings. (Witness **"Dusk"** or **"The Reticence of Lady Anne."**) It is the manner of telling, the irresistible, unmistakable stamp which Saki set upon everything that he wrote.

It would be instructive to hear from Mr. Upton Sinclair or Mr. Michael Gold on the subject of H. H. Munro. Surely they would find him deplorable. Except for an occasional peasant or shopkeeper with engaging oddities of character, the proletariat has no place in Saki's world. It is an idle and frivolous world, populated chiefly by baroque baronesses and eccentric dukes, by fluttered hostesses with unmanageable children, and by precocious young men about town with a fine taste for pranks and exotic food. These wastrels rejoice in such improbable names as Jocantha Bessbury, Wilfred Pigeoncote, Augustus Mellowkent, Sir Lulworth Quayne and Ada Spelvexit. It is enough to make any pious Communist shudder.

Certain types and situations repeat themselves again and again. One is always running cross gorgeous unscrupulous liars, who rid themselves of the attention of bores by the sheer flow and fertility of their inventions. Other prigs and bores fall victim to the malevolent designs of those shrewd, incorrigible children who were their inventor's particular joy. There was a strain of something approaching cruelty in Saki, a quality of mind akin to the casual heartlessness of a child. In his stories cleverness and insouciance invariably win out. He has no patience with stupid or stolid folk—whom he condemns to grotesque mishaps with a grin of delighted malice.

Only a moral zealot would seriously quarrel with Saki on such a score. It is his very malice which adds spice to the gayety of his tales. Nevertheless one suspects that it is this quality of mind which will contribute largely toward making Saki, in any permanent ranking, a minor if exquisitely entertaining, writer. His sister, in the memoir which is included in this volume, is inclined to minimize the touch of cruelty in Hector Munro's work and to stress his personal kindliness, generosity and charm. She quotes, however, a comment made by S. P. B. Mais on one of Saki's bitterest stories, **"The Mappined Life,"** a comment which is possibly more revealing than is immediately apparent:

> Here at last, behind the child, the buffoon, the satirist, the eclectic, the aristocrat, the elegant man of the world, we can trace the features of one who discovered that the only way to make life bearable was to laugh at it.

Very likely this is so. Very likely Saki's impish satire was a purge for disillusionment. It is equally probable, however, that the slightly inhuman hardness of his work, its lack of warmth and mellowness, will prevent him from achieving first rank. Although it is a platitude, and a smug-sounding one at that, it remains true that greatness usually belongs to those who laugh with the world and not at it.

> *Edith H. Walton, "The Impish Satire of H. H. Munro," in* The New York Times Book Review, *December 14, 1930, p. 9.*

Elizabeth Drew   (essay date 1940)

[*In the following essay, Drew asserts that Saki's wit in his short fiction is brilliant, polished, and artistically mature—though sometimes cruel.*]

Hector Hugh Munro, born in India in 1870, a delicate child who was not expected to live, was brought up from the age of two in a damp, dark country house in Devonshire, surrounded by high walls and hedges. Here he and his brother and sister, placed in the care of two dragonlike aunts, were virtually prisoners, mewed in behind closed windows at night and in all bad weather, and permitted to play only on the front lawn in summer—'the kitchen garden being considered too tempting a place, with its fruit trees.' Both the aunts, Miss Munro tells us in her memoir of her brother, 'were guilty of mental cruelty.' Their methods are described in those of the aunt in **'The Lumber Room.'**

> It was her habit, whenever one of the children fell from grace, to improvise something of a festival nature from which the offender would be rigorously debarred; if all the children sinned collectively they were suddenly informed of a circus in a neighbouring town, a circus of unrivalled merit and uncounted elephants, to which, but

for their depravity, they would have been taken that very day.

'We often longed for revenge with an intensity I suspect we inherited from our Highland ancestry,' says Miss Munro, and Hector 'sublimated' that longing in the finest of his sketches in the *macabre*—**'Sredni Vashtar.'** In that story we share all Conradin's feelings of exultant practical triumph over the aunt who made his life a misery, and the story itself remains as a symbol of Saki's own spiritual triumph over the Brontosauri rather than Montessori methods of his upbringing. For in his art, as in his life, there is no trace of the repressed or neurotic temperament which might have been expected.

He spent a cosmopolitan youth traveling on the continent with his father, a year in India with the Military Police, several years in Russia, the Balkans, and Paris as a newspaper correspondent, and then settled down as a free-lance journalist in London. At the outbreak of the Great War, when he was forty-four, he at once enlisted in the ranks, and he was killed in the attack on Beaumont-Hamel on November 13, 1916.

Admirers, in their natural wish to do justice to a man they loved, have pointed to passages in Saki's works in which he reveals his personality directly, and from which it is possible to construct the man of flesh and blood behind the mask of mockery he chose to wear. But such criticism does him no service. He deliberately chose a pseudonym for his writings—Sáki, the cupbearer whose 'joyous errand' was to serve the guests with wine in the *Rubáiyát* of Omar Khayyám. He never sought intimacy with his readers, or gave them his confidence. He asks nothing from them but lips that can laugh, flesh that can creep, and legs that can be pulled. Saki, in fact, agreed with the eighteenth-century essayist, Shaftesbury:—

> I hold it very indecent for anyone to publish his meditations, reflections and solitary thoughts. Those are the froth and scum of writing, which should be unburdened in private and consigned to oblivion, before the writer comes before the world as good company.

Saki is the most impersonal of artists. His private emotions and enthusiasms, meditations or thoughts, have no place in the world of his art. Saki is not Hector Munro, any more than Elia is Charles Lamb. But the methods of the two writers are completely opposed. Lamb dowered Elia with all his own most lovable characteristics: his warm heart, his genius for friendship, his love of life. Hector Munro, though he was richly endowed with all these qualities, denied them to Saki. That artist, in all his short sketches and stories, is allowed but three strains in his nature: the high spirits and malicious impudence of a precocious child; the cynical wit of the light social satirist; and the Gaelic fantasy of the Highlander. We meet these three in turns: the irresponsible imp who invents unlimited extravagant practical jokes to mystify and enrage and outwit the heavy-minded adult world; the ironic mocker who speaks in the quips of Clovis and Reginald and the Duchess; and the Celt who sees the kettle refuse to boil when it has been bewitched by the Evil Eye, or hears Pan's laughter as he tramples to death the doubter of his powers.

Hilaire Belloc once wrote a poem beginning,—

> Matilda told such awful lies
> It made you gasp and stretch your eyes.

Matilda came to a bad end, but Saki's child and adult liars never come to bad ends. Triumphantly they discomfit the forces of dullness and of feeble counter-deception opposed to them, and prove indisputably that fiction is stronger than fact. It must be owned that there are times when we tire of these *enfants terribles* of all ages, just as we can have too much of Mr. P. G. Wodehouse's dithering dukes and prize pigs; but at his best the fiendish capacity for unveracious invention with which Saki endows his children, and the amazing mendacities with which his young men and women confute the commonplace, are the fine art of lying at its finest. My own favorites are the story spun by the ingenious niece of the house to the nervous caller, with the innocent opening, 'You may wonder why we keep that window open on an October afternoon,' or the visit of the Bishop to organize a local massacre of the Jews, invented by Clovis to animate a family in need of an 'unrest cure.' This, since it involved action as well as equivocation, perhaps belongs more truly to the stories dealing with elaborate hoaxes and practical jokes—such as the tale of Leonard Bilsiter, who liked to hint of his acquaintance with the unseen forces of 'Siberian magic' but was somewhat horrified when it appeared that his powers had changed his hostess into a she-wolf; or that of the titled lady who was mistaken for the new governess and plays the part by teaching the children the history of the Sabine Women by the Schartz-Metterklume method of making them act it for themselves.

There is an element of cruelty in a practical joke, and many readers of Saki find themselves repelled by a certain heartlessness in many of his tales. The cruelty is certainly there, but it has nothing perverted or pathological about it. He is not one of those whose motto might be 'Our sweetest songs are those that tell of sadist thought.' It is the genial heartlessness of the normal child, whose fantasies take no account of adult standards of human behavior, and to whom the eating of a gypsy by a hyena is no more terrible that the eating of Red Ridinghood's grandmother by a wolf. The standards of these gruesome tales are those of the fairy tale; their grimness is the grimness of Grimm.

The other element in Saki's cruelty springs from a certain unsparing consistency of vision which will allow no sentiment to intrude. He speaks of one young man as 'one of those people who would be enormously improved by death,' and he never hesitates to supply that embellishment himself on suitable occasions. Stories such as **'The Easter Egg'** and **'The Hounds of Fate'** are tragedies entirely without pity, but their callousness is consistent with the hard cynical sanity which is behind even his lightest satire, and gives it its strength. His mockery is urbane but ruthless. His wit is in the tradition of Wilde and the lesser creations of E. F. Benson's *Dodo* and Anthony Hope's *Dolly Dialogues,* and in the modern world he has affinities with Noel Coward and the early Aldous Huxley. Like them, he creates an artificial world enclosed in an element outside of which it could no more exist than we could exist outside our envelope of ether. It is embalmed in the element of

Wit. To talk about Saki's 'characterization' is absurd. His characters are constructed to form a front against which his light satiric artillery can most effectively be deployed. The forces against him are the common social vices of Vanity Fair: humbug and hypocrisy, greed and grab, envy and uncharitableness, sheer dullness and fatuity. Comus Bassington, listening to scraps of conversation at an At Home, comments: 'I suppose it's the Prevention of Destitution they're hammering at. What on earth would become of all these dear good people if anyone should start a crusade for the prevention of mediocrity?' The crusade would be a disaster, for it would extinguish Lucas Bassett, the young poet who had the triumphant inspiration of the couplet

> Cousin Teresa takes out Caesar,
> Fido, Jock and the big borzoi,

and whom we see at the end of the story docketed for a knighthood under the letter L.

> 'The letter L,' said the secretary, who was new to his job. 'Does that stand for Liberalism or liberality?'

> 'Literature,' explained the minister.

And the crusade would probably eliminate all those ardent slum workers and society socialists 'whose naturally stagnant souls take infinite pleasure in what are called "movements" '; those Wodehouse-like moneyed aunts and impecunious and irresponsible nephews; those drones and butterflies 'to whom clear soup is a more important factor in life than a clear conscience'; and those odious children whose ghastly pranks turn us into keen supporters of the canonization of good King Herod.

But the situations and characters which, left to themselves, would develop into what Jane Austen called 'the elegant stupidity of a private party' develop instead into hilarious gayety and crackling brilliance, and it is Saki's wit and not his satirical material, or any of his other literary material, which will make him live. It is his sheer good fun and good spirits and capacity to be such persistent good company. His power to comment that 'so many people who are described as rough diamonds turn out to be only rough paste'; his power to describe the unsophisticated diner-out consulting the wine list 'with the blank embarrassment of a schoolboy suddenly called on to locate a Minor Prophet in the tangled hinterland of the Old Testament'; or his impudent morsels of dialogue.

> 'Such an exquisite rural retreat, and so restful and healing to the nerves. Real country scenery; apple blossom everywhere.'

> 'Surely only on the apple trees?'

'As a companion he was an unfailing antidote to boredom,' wrote one of his friends. It is an epitaph anyone might envy. (pp. 96-8)

Elizabeth Drew, "Saki," in The Atlantic Monthly, *Vol. 166, No. 1, July, 1940, pp. 96-8.*

Robert Drake   (essay date 1960)

[*In the following essay, Drake discusses how Saki used humor and satire in his short stories to express or imply social norms for behavior.*]

The short stories of Saki (H. H. Munro) have had their admirers ever since they began appearing in the *Bystander, Westminster Gazette,* and *Morning Post* in the late 1890's; and at least one of them is nearly always included in every short-story anthology. But he has hardly ever been made the subject of serious reappraisal. For many readers, he is still 'just a humorist'; and even Christopher Morley, in his introduction to the collected stories, implied that Saki is a sort of English O. Henry—an opinion which I believe does little justice to either writer.

By way of accounting for Saki's lack of critical attention we might note that the world he writes about is receding farther and farther into the romantic past. It was the world of Edwardian elegance and Wildean wit, in which trifles were tremendous and manners were almost morals. The tea-table, rather than the television 'panel', was the forum and the field of battle for the wits of the day; and the wits had not yet degenerated into vulgar jesters. This world knew nothing of nuclear fission and the graduated income tax; it still believed in a future and in house-parties.

To our more apocalyptic age this world may seem idyllic and even unreal. And its insistence on orders and degrees—and social forms in general—may appear to be archaic and undemocratic. Saki's particular brand of comedy, which I regard as essentially a comedy of manners, is practised by only a few writers today, the most notable instances being perhaps Evelyn Waugh and Noël Coward. Today we want our comedy 'straight'. Many of us are loth to believe that comedy can be the most serious business in the world; hence the unending spate of 'gags' and 'situation comedy' on our stages and television screens.

Comedy was a serious business for Saki—as serious as it was for the French philosopher Henri Bergson, who defined laughter as essentially a corrective measure aimed at bringing the deviant back into harmony with the norm. The fact that mid-twentieth-century society is often apt to mistake *averages* for *norms* is but one more reason why the comedy of manners is in eclipse today and why Saki's admirers, though always ardent, are nevertheless relatively few. But who or what are the norms in Saki's stories, and what is their significance? How can he be both serious and amusing? Such questions can be answered only by examining closely a variety of his stories.

At first there really seem to be no norms at all in Saki's humorous stories. It is at once apparent, though, that there are two violently opposed classes of people in most of them. On the one hand, there are Mrs Packletide, whose 'pleasure and intention [was] that she should shoot a tiger', and Teresa Thropplestance, whose manner 'in dealing with the world in general . . . suggested a blend between a Mistress of the Robes and a Master of the Foxhounds, with the vocabulary of both'. On the other hand, there are the Nut, as exemplified in such characters as Reginald and Clovis, and the Flapper, realized in girls like Vera Durmot, who provide violent contrast to the exceedingly proper, decorous, and stuffy world of upper-middle-class respectability.

Such 'impossible' young men as Reginald and Clovis seem (in the eyes of the 'proper' people) to be bound by no scruples, no repressions or inhibitions. For example, in '**The Feast of Nemesis**' Clovis suggests to his aunt—one of Saki's inevitable and impossibly proper aunts—that a Feast of Nemesis be instituted as a yearly occasion on which one may avenge himself on others for fancied offences during the previous year. He suggests to her that she might achieve such satisfactory vengeance on her neighbours ('who made such an absurd fuss when Ping Yang bit their youngest child') by getting up quite early on the morning of Nemesis Day and digging for truffles on their tennis court. 'You wouldn't find any truffles,' says Clovis, 'but you would find a great peace, such as no amount of present-giving would ever bestow.' He also suggests that vengeance might be taken on the odious Waldo Plubley, who is always coddling himself, by inciting a wasps' nest to riot over his head as he lies in a hammock. The aunt, it may be noted, has begun to see the possibilities of Nemesis Day; but she protests that the wasps might sting Waldo to death, to which objection Clovis replies: 'Waldo is one of those people who would be enormously improved by death.'

Vera Durmot in '**The Lull**' is adjured by her aunt to help divert a prospective M. P. who is staying with them overnight from worrying about the forthcoming election. She has a simple and amazingly forthright solution to this problem. She rushes into the young man's room in the middle of the night and tells him that a reservoir in the vicinity has burst, leaving the barnyard awash, and asks him to harbour a pet pig and cockerel in his room overnight.

But surely, we think, these characters—violently opposed though they be to the stuffy and primly proper ones—are not intended as norms to which the behaviour of the other people should be brought to conform. Perhaps, then, they are *beyond-norms,* to employ a prefix Saki uses on several occasions. But this term calls for a longer explanation.

The important thing about Reginald, Clovis, Bertie Van Tahn, Cyril Skatterly, the other Nuts and the Flappers is that they deprecate the importance of those things held up as important by the 'other' people and exalt what appears to the 'others' as trivial. In '**The Quest**' Clovis seems far more interested in what sort of sauce is to be served with the asparagus at dinner than in what has become of the Momebys' lost child. It is this unexpected, jolting exaggeration of the trivial and the deprecating of the seemingly weighty and important which amuses us. The Nut and the Flapper are constantly reversing the accepted scale of values, belittling the shibboleths of the 'proper' people, and glorifying the asparagus sauce. What is it that is amusing in this particular reversal? Perhaps it is the incongruity of the situation—that is, the implication that the asparagus sauce represents good sense as opposed to the unwarranted hysteria of the Momebys. What is also funny is that we know that Clovis does not *really* believe the asparagus sauce to be of supreme importance; rather, he is spoofing everything and everybody and in so doing seems to bring a degree of sanity to a confused and cluttered scene peopled by individuals who think they are acting rationally and in perfect decorum. It seems that Clovis is not only pulling our leg, but his own as well.

It is possible, then, that the characters of the Nut and Flapper serve as a sort of beyond-norms, who attempt to bring the pompous, self-deceived people to a reconciliation with the real norms of honesty and good sense. They thus serve in their ridicule of the others, whom we may call the uninitiated, as a sort of corrective influence, which Bergson says is the proper end of all laughter. It is not so much that this conduct is held up by Saki as a pattern to be followed; but there is a strong implication that there is far greater honesty and more good sense in the didoes the beyond-norms are up to than is found in the actions of the dowagers, ambitious society hostesses, and maiden aunts, who are all trying so desperately to be 'civilized'.

Through the whole of Saki's humorous stories—as through his stories of irony—there lies a profound distrust of the civilized, the artificial. Reginald and Clovis, in giving free rein to their impulses and free vent to their imaginations, seem to act more naturally—and therefore more sensibly—than the 'others'. They seem to realize quite clearly that they are only rather superior animals—with possibilities for rational behaviour —and the sensible thing to do is to behave in that fashion without all the sugar-coated rationalizing in which the 'others' indulge. To the extent that they act normally or naturally they may be considered Saki's norms, but in their taking to the extreme the idea of what they consider normal or natural they become beyond-norms rather than norms. In the last analysis the principal difference between the initiated and the uninitiated in the stories of Saki is that the initiated (in this case, Clovis, Reginald, and company) are aware of their predicament as imperfect beings and act accordingly. The 'others'—the uninitiated—remain blind to the truth and act in accordance with the conventional hypocrisies of society, though they may eventually be 'shocked' into this awareness by the beyond-norms.

From the standpoint of satirical humour Saki is at his best in describing the members of the cult of the uninitiated. His descriptive sentences are stripped bare of all non-essentials. They are as direct and to the point as a guided missile, and they are infused with an almost overpowering awareness of human folly and vanity. Even when Saki writes from the omniscient point of view we hear the mocking laugh of Clovis in the background. Of the irrepressible Mrs Packletide he says: 'In a world that is supposed to be swayed by hunger and by love Mrs Packletide was an exception; her movements and motives were largely governed by dislike of Loona Bimberton.' Of the Dowager Lady Beanford he notes that she 'was a vigorous old woman who had coquetted with imaginary ill-health for the greater part of a lifetime; Clovis Sangrail irreverently declared that she had caught a chill at the Coronation of Queen Victoria and had never let it go again'. In **'Filboid Studge, The Story of a Mouse that Helped'** when Duncan Dullamy, the breakfast-food king, cannot sell his new breakfast food, Pipenta, he asks Mark Spayley to design a poster that will help put the new preparation over:

Three weeks later the world was advised of the coming of a new breakfast food, heralded under the resounding name of 'Filboid Studge'. Spayley put forth no pictures of massive babies springing up with fungus-like rapidity under its forcing influence, or representatives of the leading nations of the world scrambling with fatuous eagerness for its possession. One huge sombre poster depicted the Damned in Hell suffering a new torment from their inability to get at the Filboid Studge which elegant young fiends held in transparent bowls just beyond their reach. The scene was rendered even more gruesome by a subtle suggestion of the features of leading men and women of the day in the portrayal of the Lost Souls; prominent individuals of both political parties, Society hostesses, well-known dramatic authors and novelists, and distinguished aeroplanists were dimly recognizable in that doomed throng; noted lights of the musical-comedy stage flickered wanly in the shades of the Inferno, smiling still from force of habit, but with the fearsome smiling rage of baffled effort. The poster bore no fulsome allusions to the merits of the new breakfast food, but a single grim statement ran in bold letters along its base: 'They cannot buy it now.'

Spayley had grasped the fact that people will do things from a sense of duty which they would never attempt as a pleasure. There are thousands of respectable middle-class men who, if you found them unexpectedly in a Turkish bath, would explain in all sincerity that a doctor had ordered them to take Turkish baths; if you told them in return that you went there because you liked it, they would stare in pained wonder at the frivolity of your motive.

It would seem, then, that what really binds the Nut and the Flapper and the other 'shockers' together in a common bond is this cognizance, this awareness. They know the inescapable facts of life—that man is an imperfect being with little in his favour except the potentiality of acting rationally. They are truly the initiated; they know the real facts of life and the way of the real world. The solution proposed by them to combat stuffiness and self-deception is to go to the other extreme; they represent not a norm but a beyond-norm.

The solutions advanced by the initiated characters in the humorous stories for bringing the uninitiated to their senses are varied. But we must be careful to note that the solutions are rarely looked on as solutions by their perpetrators. If they were, then Clovis, Reginald, and the rest would become sermonizers or even reformers and, by implication, Saki along with them. Under such an interpretation much of the humour of the stories would disintegrate. One solution—that of Nemesis Day—has already been mentioned. The solution of Lady Carlotta, whom the *nouveau riche* Mrs Quabarl has mistaken for a governess, is to teach history to the Quabarl children by what she calls the Schartz-Metterklume method, that is, by acting it out for themselves. And to our delight Lady Carlotta begins the lesson with the Romans and the Sabine women.

An ostensible solution is provided in **'The Unrest-Cure'**.

J. P. Huddle is complaining to a friend while riding on a train of the stuffiness of the dull complacent lives he and his sister are leading. They are so set in the life they lead in their country home that they are annoyed when the thrush which has been building its nest year after year in the catkin-tree changes its nesting-place to the ivy on the garden wall. 'We have said very little about it, but I think we both feel that the change is unnecessary.'

J. P. Huddle's travelling companion suggests that he and his sister get themselves out of this placidity by resorting to what he calls the 'Unrest-cure', as opposed to the rest cure for people who have been living under great tension and nervous strain. When Huddle asks how this cure may be undertaken, his friend replies:

> Well, you might stand as an Orange candidate for Kilkenny, or do a course of district visiting in one of the Apache quarters of Paris, or give lectures in Berlin to prove that most of Wagner's music was written by Gambetta; and there's always the interior of Morocco to travel in. But, to be really effective, the Unrest-cure ought to be tried in the home. How you would do it I haven't the faintest idea.

Clovis, who has been sitting opposite Huddle and his friend, decides to undertake the Unrest-cure for Mr Huddle and his sister. Accordingly, he arrives at their home in the guise of the Bishop's secretary, having sent a telegram to the Huddles invoking their hospitality on behalf of the Bishop. The Bishop is in the neighbourhood ostensibly examining a confirmation class, says Clovis; but really he is out for blood. The interchange of words between Clovis as the secretary and Huddle is somewhat illuminating:

> 'Tonight is going to be a great night in the history of Christendom,' said Clovis. 'We are going to massacre every Jew in the neighbourhood.'
>
> 'To massacre the Jews!' said Huddle indignantly. 'Do you mean to tell me there's a general rising against them?'
>
> 'No, it's the Bishop's own idea. He is in there arranging all the details now.'
>
> 'But—the Bishop is such a tolerant, humane man.'
>
> 'That is precisely what will heighten the effect of his action. The sensation will be enormous.'

Farther on, conversation is again in the familiar vein:

> '. . . after all, we've got men we can trust to do our job, so we shan't have to rely on local assistance. And we've got some Boy-scouts helping us as auxiliaries.'
>
> 'Boy-scouts!'
>
> 'Yes; when they understood there was real killing to be done they were even keener than the men.'

Later on, when Miss Huddle somewhat understandably develops a headache, though 'it was not her day for having a headache', Clovis reports to the terrified Huddles:

> 'The Bishop is sorry to hear that Miss Huddle

has a headache. He is issuing orders that as far as possible no firearms shall be used near the house; all killing that is necessary on the premises will be done with cold steel. The Bishop does not see why a man should not be a gentleman as well as a Christian.'

Blenkinthrope in 'The Seventh Pullet' is aware of the dull sameness of his life and, what is more, manages to find a solution for his problem so that a Nut or a Flapper is not really necessary in the story. His solution is to tell fantastic tales about his daily life to his fellow commuters—about his pullet, for instance, out of a flock of seven, who, unlike the other six, was not mesmerized and killed by a snake because its eyes were covered with feathers, and thus was able to peck the snake to death. There is a grim irony in the fact that, when his wife meets her death after having finally won a game of Death's Head patience, as her mother and great-grand-aunt had done before her, no one will believe his story. Perhaps, in a way, Blenkinthrope is one of Saki's few characters that are norms, not beyond-norms. (Possibly the same thing may be said about J. P. Huddle.) No beyond-norm is really needed here since Blenkinthrope is cognizant of the existing state of affairs and takes measures himself to combat them. His methods of improving his situation are indeed methods that a beyond-norm might use, though. And it is notable that his plan of attack is suggested to him by Gorworth, who is strongly suspect of being a beyond-norm—Gorworth who, 'since winning a prize for excellence in Scriptural knowledge at a preparatory school . . . had felt licensed to be a little more unscrupulous than the circle he moved in. Much might surely be excused to one who in early life could give a list of seventeen trees mentioned in the Old Testament.'

All Saki's beyond-norm characters have this cognizance, this knowledge of what is really going on in the world about them. What makes the pronouncements of the Nut and Flapper so jolting, though, is that they seem to be hitting so much nearer the truth—harsh though it may be—than the overstuffed dowagers and conservatively hidebound aunts. In other words, their solution to the same problem—that of bringing order and sanity to the disordered—is much more nearly rational than the 'civilized' solutions offered by the 'proper' people, if indeed these latter may be called solutions. And possibly this is where the real humour of Saki lies—in the paradox that the more rational solution is what seems the most irrational, and lies in what is farthest from 'conventional' thought and behaviour.

The use and treatment of children in Saki's stories is significant. It must be borne in mind that his own childhood was an unusual one. With his mother dead and his father overseas, he and the other children were cared for by a grandmother and a coterie of aunts who alternately tyrannized over them and devoured them with affection. In her biographical sketch of her brother the late Ethel Munro gave the impression that the aunts were actually cruel to the children and thus that Saki's childhood was a sad, lonely one. Though Miss Munro herself voiced violent objection to this inference, there is certainly an apparent antagonism between children and adults in many of Saki's stories.

The function of the children in the humorous stories seems to be similar to that of the Nuts and the Flappers; their role is that of the beyond-norm. The children in **'The Story-Teller'** appear as bloodthirsty little creatures and enjoy hearing about the death of a little girl who was 'horribly good'. There is a deadly sanity in them that is far more sophisticated than anything their proper aunt has to offer. Saki's continual thesis regarding children seems to be that their conduct is more nearly rational than that of decorous adults because they have not yet learned the deceptions and hypocrisies of civilization. Theirs is a sophistication that is truly artless, truly natural, and unsought for.

The children in **'The Penance'** successfully threaten Octavian Ruttle, a dignified gentleman of middle age, into standing for an hour in his shirt with a candle in his hand over the grave of their cat, which he has ordered to be killed. As he stands there, he must say: 'I'm a miserable beast.' The means they employ to coerce him into this act of contrition? They merely threaten to throw his little daughter Olivia into the pigsty to be devoured by the pigs or choked in the muck. Their 'inexorable child-logic' provides a perfect contrast to Octavian's superficial 'adult' dignity. Pigs figure prominently again in **'Hyacinth'**, where Hyacinth, the son of a parliamentary candidate, successfully blackmails the opposing candidate into conceding the election. His method is likewise direct, forthright, and untainted by the touch of civilization and adulthood. He threatens to throw the two sons of the other candidate into a pigsty.

Perhaps Saki's humorous stories can be thought of as falling into two subdivisions. The first subdivision would include those stories in which a beyond-norm is explicit and of great importance, such as the Reginald and Clovis stories. The second subdivision would include those stories in which a beyond-norm, if it exists in a story, is implied and of only secondary importance.

In the second subdivision may be placed **'Cousin Teresa'**. It is the story of Lucas Harrowcluff, who composes a very successful music-hall number after years of futile endeavour which has been subjected to ridicule on the part of his family. Lucas knows he will succeed in the end, and always has an unbridled optimism that is maddening to his hidebound middle-class family, and it is not necessary for any outside beyond-norm such as Clovis to come bring him to his senses. And his persistence does finally bring him a tremendous popular success.

There is some very effective implicit satire in Saki's portrayal of the reaction of the public to the turn. The number itself is really nonsensical, consisting of a song about Cousin Teresa, the chorus of which concludes with:

> Cousin Teresa takes our Caesar,
> Fido, Jock, and the big borzoi.

While this song is being sung, a group of mechanical dogs moves across the stage, then comes on again led by a Nut, and then once more led on by an actress impersonating

Cousin Teresa. On the word 'borzoi' there is a big double beat on the drums, and this double beat takes the public fancy to such a degree that people thump it out on the glasses in restaurants and in other public places. The popularity of the number is universal:

> . . . Nowhere and at no time could one get away from the double thump that brought up the rear of the refrain; revellers reeling home at night banged it on doors and hoardings, milkmen clashed their cans to its cadence, messenger boys hit smaller messenger boys resounding double smacks on the same principle. And the more thoughtful circles of the great city were not deaf to the claims and significance of the popular melody. An enterprising and emancipated preacher discoursed from his pulpit on the inner meaning of 'Cousin Teresa', and Lucas Harrowcluff was invited to lecture on the subject of his great achievement to members of the Young Men's Endeavour League, the Nine Arts Club, and other learned and willing-to-learn bodies. In Society it seemed to be the one thing people really cared to talk about; men and women of middle age and average education might be seen together in corners earnestly discussing, not the question whether Servia should have an outlet on the Adriatic, or the possibilities of a British success in international polo contests, but the more absorbing topic of the problematic Aztec or Nilotic origin of the Teresa motif.

> 'Politics and patriotism are so boring and so out of date,' said a revered lady who had some pretensions to oracular utterance; 'we are too cosmopolitan nowadays to be really moved by them. That is why one welcomes an intelligible production like "Cousin Teresa", that has a genuine message for one. One can't understand the message all at once, of course, but one felt from the first that it was there. I've been to see it eighteen times and I'm going again tomorrow and on Thursday. One can't see it often enough.'

Perhaps what Lucas *does* constitutes a beyond-norm method, but he is not a beyond-norm himself.

The beyond-norm is not always a person. In **'Tobermory'**, one of Saki's most popular stories, the beyond-norm is a cat. Cornelius Appin has perfected a method, after years of study, for teaching animals to talk. While he is a guest in Lady Blemley's house, he tries his art on her cat, Tobermory. He proudly proclaims his success to the assembled house guests, for in Tobermory he says he has found a true 'Beyond-cat' of a high degree of intelligence. Naturally, the other guests are sceptical; and so the cat is called in for proof.

Much to the surprise and chagrin of the house-party, Tobermory displays not only the power of speech but an extraordinarily good memory as well. This surprising virtuosity becomes embarrassing for all concerned:

> 'What do you think of human intelligence?' asked Mavis Pellington lamely.

> 'Of whose intelligence in particular?' asked Tobermory coldly.

'Oh, well, mine for instance,' said Mavis, with a feeble laugh.

'You put me in an embarrassing position,' said Tobermory, whose tone and attitude certainly did not suggest a shred of embarrassment. 'When your inclusion in this house-party was suggested Sir Wilfrid protested that you were the most brainless woman of his acquaintance, and that there was wide distinction between hospitality and care of the feeble-minded. Lady Blemley replied that your lack of brain-power was the precise quality which had earned you your invitation, as you were the only person she could think of who might be idiotic enough to buy their old car. You know, the one they call "The Envy of Sisyphus", because it goes quite nicely uphill if you push it.'

Lady Blemley's protestations would have had greater effect if she had not casually suggested to Mavis only that morning that the car in question would be just the thing for her down at her Devonshire home.

Again:

. . . Agnes Resker could not endure to remain too long in the background.

'Why did I ever come down here?' she asked dramatically.

Tobermory immediately accepted the opening.

'Judging by what you said to Mrs Cornett on the croquet-lawn yesterday, you were out for food. You described the Blemleys as the dullest people to stay with that you knew, but said they were clever enough to employ a first-rate cook; otherwise they'd find it difficult to get anyone to come down a second time.'

This display of Tobermory's vocal virtuosity is enough to convince both guests and hostess that Tobermory must be put out of the way. Consequently, a plate of fish scraps dosed with strychnine is put out for him. This group of unmasked pseudo-sophisticates shows little appreciation of Mr Appin's work in the field of animal elocution:

An archangel ecstatically proclaiming the Millennium, and then finding that it clashed unpardonably with Henley and would have to be indefinitely postponed, could hardly have felt more crestfallen than Cornelius Appin at the reception of his wonderful achievement. Public opinion, however, was against him—in fact, had the general voice been consulted on the subject it is probable that a strong minority vote would have been in favour of including him in the strychnine diet.

There is bitterness in the fact that the pseudo-sophisticated people deprive Appin of his greatest pupil; but the overall effect of the story is humorous, for it is implied that the pseudo-sophisticates have been jarred into a better insight into their situation.

This essay would be inadequate without some consideration of a story in which that super-Nut Reginald appears. Perhaps the best Reginald story is **'Reginald's Christmas**

Revel', in which that irrepressible young man spends Christmas with his relatives, the Babwolds. That the Babwold household was a respectable and solemn one Reginald leaves no doubt:

Mrs Babwold wears a rather solemn personality, and has never been known to smile, even when saying disagreeable things to her friends or making out the stores list. A state elephant at a Durbar gives one a similar impression. Her husband gardens in all weathers. When a man goes out in the pouring rain to brush caterpillars off rosetrees, I generally imagine his life indoors leaves something to be desired; anyway, it must be very unsettling for the caterpillars.

The guests are not stimulating nor is the entertainment which has been planned for them, according to Reginald. He can endure this ponderous festivity only a short while and finally, as do all the beyond-norms, takes matters into his own hands:

. . . As a crowning dissipation, they all sat down to play progressive halma, with milk-chocolate for prizes. I've been carefully brought up, and I don't like to play games of skill for milk-chocolate, so I invented a headache and retired from the scene. I had been preceded a few minutes earlier by Miss Langshan-Smith, a rather formidable lady, who always got up at some uncomfortable hour in the morning, and gave you the impression that she had been in communication with most of the European Governments before breakfast. There was a paper pinned on her door with a signed request that she might be called particularly early on the morrow. Such an opportunity does not come twice in a lifetime. I covered up everything except the signature with another notice, to the effect that before these words should meet the eye she would have ended a misspent life, was sorry for the trouble she was giving, and would like a military funeral. A few minutes later I violently exploded an airfilled paper bag on the landing, and gave a stage moan that could have been heard in the cellars. Then I pursued my original intention and went to bed. The noise those people made in forcing open the good lady's door was positively indecorous; she resisted gallantly, but I believe they searched her for bullets for about a quarter of an hour, as if she had been a historic battle-field.

It may easily be seen that Reginald is blood-brother to Clovis.

Perhaps the best illustration of this jarring of the self-deceived into sanity is **'Shock Tactics'**. Bertie Heasant's mother is a domineering woman, who insists on opening her son's mail. Bertie appeals to Clovis for help, and there is certainly no doubt that he has brought his problem to the right authority. Clovis immediately embarks on a plan designed literally to shock Mrs Heasant to her senses.

Clovis' solution is to send Bertie a series of counterfeited letters, for he knows that Mrs Heasant will be sure to read them. His letters progress from the provocative to the terrifying (to Mrs Heasant). First, there is:

Bertie, carissimo . . . I wonder if you will have the nerve to do it; it will take some nerve, too. Don't forget the jewels. They are a detail, but details interest me.

Yours as ever, Clotilde.

Your mother must not know of my existence. If questioned swear you never heard of me.

This is soon followed by a gory specimen:

So you have really done it! . . . Poor Dagmar. Now she is done for I almost pity her. You did it very well, you wicked boy, for the servants all think it was suicide, and there will be no fuss. Better not touch the jewels till after the inquest.
Clotilde.

By this time Mrs Heasant is on the verge of hysteria and commands Bertie to reveal his ghastly secret to her:

'Miserable boy, what have you done to Dagmar?'

'It's Dagmar now, is it?' he snapped; 'it will be Geraldine next.'

'That it should come to this, after all my efforts to keep you at home of an evening,' sobbed Mrs Heasant; 'it's no use you trying to hide things from me; Clotilde's letter betrays everything.'

Finally a letter from Clovis arrives, explaining the whole ruse. Bertie, who has locked himself in his bedroom during his mother's tirade, emerges and says he is going for the doctor. He says he thinks his mother is mentally ill because no sane person could have believed the letters from 'Clotilde'.

'But what was I to think of those letters?' whimpered Mrs Heasant.

'I should have known what to think of them,' said Bertie; 'if you choose to excite yourself over other people's correspondence it's your own fault. Anyhow, I'm going for a doctor.'

It was Bertie's great opportunity, and he knew it. His mother was conscious of the fact that she would look rather ridiculous if the story got about. She was willing to pay him hush-money.

'I'll never open your letters again,' she promised.

Perhaps in no other story of Saki's is the idea of the 'undeceiving' of the self-deceived by the beyond-norm more explicitly illustrated.

In **'Tobermory'** and **'Shock Tactics'**, as in the stories regarding children, is found the paradox which seems fundamental to Saki's humour—that the seemingly irrational and therefore objectionable is more nearly rational than that which purports to be so and is accepted as such by the world. Thus Saki uses the ostensible deviant—the beyond-norm—to prod the smugly decorous and complacent into closer conformity with the dictates of good sense.

The humour and satire of Saki are never condescending and therefore never offensive. The characters employed as instruments of satire realize their essential imperfection along with that of the persons against whom the satire is

directed. It is this cognizance, though, that sets them apart from the 'others' and makes them members of the cult of the initiated. It is their purpose to bring as many outsiders into the cult as possible, and to that end all their efforts are directed. Thus laughter is for Saki, as it was for Bergson, essentially a corrective measure. (pp. 61-73)

> Robert Drake, "The Sauce for the Asparagus: A Reappraisal for Saki," in The Saturday Book, *Vol. 20, 1960, pp. 60-73.*

Janet Overmyer (essay date 1964)

[*In the following essay, Overmyer maintains that Saki does not employ cruel humor in his short fiction gratuitously or sadistically, but to express disdain for the waste of human potential.*]

Hector Hugh Munro—who wrote under the apt pseudonym of Saki—has had a strange and interesting popularity. At no time during his life or after his death in battle in 1916 was he a best-selling author in the usual sense of the word. Several essays and book reviews, but no major critical studies of his work, have appeared. The only available information about his personal life is that contained in the comparatively brief biography written by his sister, Ethel M. Munro.

Yet he has attracted the attention of such literary figures as S. P. B. Mais, A. A. Milne, Christopher Morley, and Graham Greene. His popularity, if not outstanding, has been steady enough to cause two publishers to reprint his short stories while one also keeps in print his two novels and three plays. His public may be smaller than that of some authors, but it is faithful and growing. Saki would seem to be something of a specialized and acquired taste, like olives stuffed with anchovies.

That he is unique is at once obvious. Futile attempts to pin him down have at one time or another compared him to: the Restoration dramatists, John Dryden, Jonathan Swift, Alexander Pope, William Makepeace Thackeray, Robert Louis Stevenson, Rudyard Kipling, Max Beerbohm, Ronald Firbank, Charles Lamb, James Barrie, Eric Parker, Kenneth Grahame, Oscar Wilde, Aldous Huxley, Evelyn Waugh, and George Orwell. Other authors may also be added—Thomas Hardy and Roald Dahl, for instance. The very length of the list and diversity of authors indicate the difficulty of pigeon-holing Saki.

His trademark is his wit, and to this may, in part perhaps, be attributed the absence of effusive and widespread acclaim. Our Puritan heritage still insists that no one who is funny can at the same time be profound. Saki's subject matter also seems remote; he is the satirical chronicler of the leisurely Edwardian era, which was characterized by week-long house parties, proper afternoon teas, servant difficulties, and the suffragette movement—a way of life that died with the First World War. The upper classes with which Saki was familiar and of which he wrote almost exclusively are no longer, even in England, as much looked up to as pace setters as they once were. The stately homes of England that once echoed the clever conversations of titled guests now resound to the tramping of tourists.

Also, fiction today dwells on the common man, the Willy Lomans and the Walter Mittys. It concerns itself with the inactive, the trapped, the frustrated; it is not receptive to Saki's protagonists, uncommon to say the least, who strike out boldly and outrageously, if sometimes foolishly and blunderingly, attempt grandly to solve their problems, and frequently succeed.

Not only Saki's content but his style also seems to be at war with contemporary fiction. Saki is a succinct, precise story teller; no character sketches or slice-of-life incidents for him. He is not particularly concerned with characterization at all, except as it emphasizes his ideas and sharpens his satire. This slight dehumanization of his people serves his purpose well, but fiction today demands people first, story second. At first reading, Saki may seem to consist of little more than cleverness, an amusing but thin facade behind which no lasting ideas lurk. A look at Saki's short stories, which represent his best and most characteristic work, will show whether or not this is true.

The facade, if that is what it is, is well constructed; Saki is a delightfully easy author to read. His aptness of expression is perfect; his stories move rapidly and frequently end with a twist; and he is wondrously witty. His wit constantly sparks from the mouth of an outrageous protagonist named Reginald, Clovis Sangrail, or Bertie van Tahn—a frank, conceited, irreverent, and charming man about town. He comments openly on people and situations, gets himself and others into and out of embarrassing predicaments, and continually lands on his well-shod feet. He or his counterpart, who may be feminine, spouts such epigrams as "Waldo is one of those people who would be enormously improved by death"; "They have the air of people who have bowed to destiny and are not quite sure whether the salute will be returned"; and "The cook was a good cook, as cooks go; and as cooks go she went." This persona is fond of such practical jokes as disrupting a house party by placing a false suicide note on a respectable lady's door, supposedly turning a lady into a hyena for the benefit of a dinner party, and boarding a rooster and pig in a politician's bedroom to keep his mind off politics.

Saki is also fond of the macabre, and anticipates the current "theatre of the absurd" by blending it with wit. The result is such a story as **"Esmé,"** a tale of two ladies on horseback and their difficulties with a hyena which takes up with them, devours a gypsy child, is struck down and killed by an automobile, and buried by the driver under the impression that it was a pet dog. He makes restitution by presenting the supposed owner with a diamond brooch. Not only the situation but the dialogue maintains the delicate balance between the comic and the gruesome:

> " 'Do you think the poor little thing suffered much?' came another of her futile questions.

> " 'The indications were all that way,' I said; 'on the other hand, of course, it may have been crying from sheer temper. Children sometimes do.' "

But no matter how engaging, style is not, after all, its own

excuse for being. It should not be laid on, like frosting, to hide unbaked content. But Saki's stylistic blend of wit and cruelty is not used to cover, but to expose. This combination is daubed on the tips of pointed barbs which are carefully aimed to puncture the weaknesses and affections of those persons for whom Saki had an especial dislike, and who may all be included in the elastic category of fools. Saki did not suffer fools gladly; indeed, he did not suffer them at all. It might well have been his motto, emblazoned on his coat of arms, had he possessed a coat of arms.

Saki is impatient with the foibles of bores, cowards, the idle, useless rich, those lacking a sense of humor, "popular" poets, suffragettes, most women, especially aunts, politicians, and all the pompously self-righteous. He gives them such names as Ada Spelvexit, Hortensia Bavvel, Sir James Beanquest, Demosthenes Platterbaff, and Sir Wilfrid Pigeoncote. The ridiculous names and the absence of characterization in depth tend to so dehumanize them that the reader will not sympathize with them and the satire can then scathe more effectively.

Above all Saki recoils from "the mapped life," which is led by fools. The story of that name [**"The Mappined Life"**] defines it:

> "We are able to live our unreal, stupid little lives on our particular Mappin terrace, and persuade ourselves that we really are untrammelled men and women leading a reasonable existence in a reasonable sphere. . . . We are trammelled by restrictions of income and opportunity, and above all by lack of initiative. . . . We are just so many animals stuck down on a Mappin terrace, with this difference in our disfavour, that the animals are there to be looked at, while nobody wants to look at us. As a matter of fact there would be nothing to look at. . . . It's the dreadful little everyday acts of pretended importance that give the Mappin stamp to our life."

But as Saki is capable of biting satire he is also capable of its opposite, heartfelt compassion. His tender solicitude shows as he relates the bittersweet concern for the church mice in **"The Saint and the Goblin"**; the description of the "elderly gentleman" in **"Dusk"** who "belonged unmistakably to that forlorn orchestra to whose piping no one dances"; and the heartbreaking doomed friendship of the little bird and the effigy of the Lost Soul in **"The Image of the Lost Soul."**

His compassion and cruelty come into careful balance when he writes of children. Saki loved and understood children as only a few adult writers are privileged to do, but his view of childhood is dark. He does not sketch the carefree, merry existence that adults like to think children lead. Instead, the children inhabit their own private, often grim world, one which is perfectly understandable to another child, but rarely to an adult. Children revel in the grimness since it is one way of alleviating the very cruelty of their actual existence. Children are cruel to one another because they openly and reasonably express their feelings of dislike. They are cruel to adults because the entire adult world is against them, and they are helpless to resist. They must therefore snatch their revenge whenever the opportunity arises. Saki chronicles children's cruelty with compassion; and this is not a paradox. He pities them, for they need pity; they must retaliate in kind because it is all they know.

Interwoven with Saki's attitude toward fools and children are four main themes, all of which fall under the general heading of man in relation to his environment. The themes are: supernatural beings and events, religion, hypocrisy, and death. The first two have in common their suggestion of tentative answers to man's questions about the unknown; the latter two have in common their inevitability.

From evidence in the stories, and from an actual incident in his own life when he saw a black dog which appeared only to those to whom bad news was coming and which presaged the death of his father, it is apparent that Saki took the supernatural seriously. Saki's characters have dreams which predict horse race winners, see signs which foretell death, put spells on one another, turn into ghosts or animals, and are startled by animals which have supra-animal powers. At no time is a rational explanation for these occurrences offered, and no character doubts their other-worldly source.

Saki's opinion of religion connects with his opinion of hypocrisy. Men endlessly pretend to one another, for both trivial and serious reasons. They glibly utter the "polite" white lie of thanking the giver for a useless Christmas gift, as in **"Down Pens,"** and they just as readily dole out their friendship and pity openly to one of lower station only when it should be to their advantage, as in **"The Wolves of Cernogratz."**

Hypocrisy mars not only man's relation to man but man's relation to God. True Christians, actively practicing what they are supposed to believe, are almost impossible to find. Such stories as **"A Touch of Realism,"** in which two Jews are marooned on a moor in a snowstorm as part of a Christmas game, and **"The Story of St. Vespaluus,"** in which a supposed Christian near-martyr is actually a pagan, indicate that Saki distrusted genuine religious practices.

Polite tale-telling would thus seem to be necessary not only for a smooth-running society, but a smooth-running conscience. Man cannot face the truth about himself. Perhaps one reason why religion in Saki's stories is unworkable is that it will not permit man to lie to himself.

Saki loved and understood children as only a few adult writers are privileged to do, but his view of childhood is dark. He does not sketch the carefree, merry existence that adults like to think children lead. Instead, the children inhabit their own private, often grim world, one which is perfectly understandable to another child, but rarely to an adult.

—Janet Overmyer

References to death recur repeatedly. It may be referred to flippantly, as in **"The Lull,"** when a young girl describes the housemaid's identification of three bodies that have floated past the window during a supposed storm as her fiancé. At times it is unavoidable doom, as in **"The Hounds of Fate,"** when a young man is killed because of his resemblance to another; and at times it is a triumph of the human spirit as in **"The Easter Egg"** when a coward gives his life to save that of a prince. Saki's preoccupation with death would seem to say that an awareness of man's final end colors his every action. No matter how high he rises, death waits. But it need not be a total defeat; it may, in fact, be a victory. There is a correlation between this belief and the Christian philosophy, although the victory in Saki's stories refers to man's triumph over himself, not over death.

From a consideration of those persons Saki attacks and those themes that most interest him can be evolved an idea of his basic philosophy. All of his writing life Saki saw through a glass darkly. He attacks mercilessly because he sees life so clearly, both as it is and as he feels it should be. He cares so deeply about mankind that he cannot bear to see people dissipate their tastes and talents on the inconsequential. He so wants to incite them to productive action in order that they may achieve the great goals of which they are capable that he becomes cruel in pointing up their defects. And he finds it necessary to cover this bitter pill of cruelty with the jelly of wit. But the pill is still visible.

The jelly has two purposes. First, coating the bitterness makes the pill easier to swallow. For Saki attacks not *him*, but *me*, and no one enjoys having his own failings blatantly trumpeted. Saki's poker-faced satire exposes the faults of its reader as well as its victim, while it seems merely to be relating an amusing incident. While the reader is laughing, the rapier is slipping, almost unfelt, between his own shoulder blades. He must watch that he does not say, "How ridiculous he is," but "How ridiculous I am."

Wit is also a protection for Saki, as it is for Reginald-Clovis-Bertie—it wounds others before they can wound him. And it keeps the insensitive at a distance so they will not discover the sincere solicitude Saki felt for his fellows. For Saki, unlike Swift, can pity as hugely as he condemns because, as is evident from his many compassionate insights, he identifies himself with foolish, struggling, inept mankind.

But even while he is urging man on he says that, ironically, there is a barrier to complete success. Just as children can never win out against adults, so man can never win out against a force more powerful than he, which may be referred to as fate. Man may transcend himself for a moment and achieve a truly glorious triumph; but then he will be slapped back. And the final defeat is that of death. Nevertheless he must keep trying. The heroes are not those who win, for no one can win, but those who persist until they gain some small success before the greater power intervenes. It is the attempt that exalts.

It is not the purpose of this [essay] to reduce Saki's work to a serious philosophical treatise. For above all his stories are fun to read, they effervesce. But like all outstanding humorists, he is funny for a more trenchant purpose than to win the passing smile. The straw man of incontemporaneity set up originally has been demolished. Those characteristics of Saki's work that would seem to make it obsolete are mainly the surface ones of subject matter and style. The underlying philosophy is not trivial: Keep trying in the face of almost certain defeat. As a credo for modern man it is not outworn. (pp. 171-75)

Janet Overmyer, "Turn Down an Empty Glass," in The Texas Quarterly, Vol. VII, No. 3, Autumn, 1964, pp. 171-75.

Philip Stevick (essay date 1966)

[*In the following essay, Stevick provides a Freudian interpretation of the stories collected in* Beasts and Super-Beasts.]

Few writers, says Christopher Morley [in his introduction to **The Short Stories of Saki**], are "less profitable to write *about*" than H. H. Munro. "Saki exists only to be read. The exquisite lightness of his work offers no grasp for the solemnities of earnest criticism." In a sense, of course, Morley is right. Much of what matters most about Saki, his wit, his formal mastery, his stylistic acuteness, his bitter urbanity that never becomes mere cynicism—these are qualities immediately obvious and pointless to analyze. Yet it is unfortunate to leave Saki in the hands of the Christopher Morleys of this world, for whom it is the highest compliment for a host to place a volume of Saki on the guest's night table. For in another and equally legitimate sense, placing Saki on the night table is as dubious an act as supplying the house guest with Krafft-Ebing. There is, behind the facile gloss, an uncompromising honesty in much of Saki together with a remarkably prescient insight into the unconscious life of his characters.

Beasts and Super-Beasts (1914) collects many of those stories which display Saki at his most surreptitiously tough minded. It begins with a sentence, from the story **"The She-Wolf,"** which is worth taking as a statement of theme. "Leonard Bilsiter was one of those people who have failed to find this world attractive or interesting, and who have sought compensation in an 'unseen world' of their own experience or imagination—or invention." Leonard acquires a reputation for possessing "esoteric forces and unusual powers." Early in the story, the conversation goes like this:

"I wish you would turn me into a wolf, Mr. Bilsiter," said his hostess at luncheon the day after his arrival.

"My dear Mary," said Colonel Hampton, "I never knew you had a craving in that direction."

"A she-wolf, of course," continued Mrs. Hampton; "It would be too confusing to change one's sex as well as one's species at a moment's notice."

"I don't think one should jest on these subjects," said Leonard.

"I'm not jesting, I'm quite serious, I assure you."

Clovis, Saki's ubiquitous provocateur, contrives meanwhile to borrow a real wolf from a wild animal collection. And the afternoon of the collision between the spurious magic of Leonard and the mischief of Clovis approaches.

By the following day the house-party had swollen to larger proportions, and Bilsiter's instinct for self-advertisement expanded duly under the stimulant of an increased audience. At dinner that evening he held forth at length on the subject of unseen forces and untested powers, and his flow of impressive eloquence continued unabated while coffee was being served in the drawing-room preparatory to a general migration to the card-room. His aunt ensured a respectful hearing for his utterances, but her sensation-loving soul hankered after something more dramatic than mere vocal demonstration.

"Won't you do something to *convince* them of your powers, Leonard?" she pleaded. "Change something into another shape. He can, you know, if he only chooses to," she informed the company.

After this point, the story works toward the manifold nonsense of fainting women, defensive men, puzzled wolf, still more puzzled Leonard, and triumphant Clovis. But what is most significant about the story is not the cleverness of its plot and the wit of its presentation but its collection of images and symbols which give the story an instinctual dimension.

First there is the contrast between the beast and the garden party, a party in which the participants are over-civilized and ineffectual, with their comic names, their empty chatter, and their incapacity to act. (The comic incongruity of beast and gentry is a frequent one in **Beasts and Super-Beasts** with appearances by boar-pigs, an elk, an ox, a cat, a hen, and all manner of imagined animals from sheep to wild dogs.) Secondly, there is a heavily ironic emphasis on standards of decorum and propriety. Here Saki exploits the "sensation-loving" wish to become a beast; elsewhere he writes ironically of "sin" and "depravity." Finally, there is that amazing series of submerged metaphors in the paragraph quoted above and throughout the story, of potency and desire and inhibition, of seclusion and demonstration, of stimulation and swelling and flowing.

A few pages later in the collection, the same dimension recurs, in a story titled **"The Boar-Pig,"** which begins with a paragraph that sounds like an account of a dream in a psychoanalytic case-book.

"There is a back way on to the lawn," said Mrs. Philidore Stossen to her daughter, "through a small grass paddock and then through a walled fruit garden full of gooseberry bushes. I went all over the place last year when the family were away. There is a door that opens from the fruit garden into a shrubbery, and once we emerge from there we can mingle with the guests as if we had come in by the ordinary way. It's much safer than going in by the front entrance and running the risk of coming bang up against the hostess; that would be so awkward when she doesn't happen to have invited us."

Again, there is beast and garden party, secrets and prohibitions, entry and "the unyielding obstacle of the locked door," innocence and experience, and dialogue like this: " *'Une bete,'* corrected Matilda; 'a pig is masculine as long as you call it a pig, but if you lose your temper with it and call it a ferocious beast it becomes one of us at once. French is a dreadfully unsexing language.' "

Another story in ***Beasts and Super-Beasts,*** **"The Treasure-Ship,"** concerns Lulu, Duchess of Dulverton, "a believer in the existence of a sunken treasure of alluring proportions." Lulu finds a smalltime adventurer, named Vasco Honiton, who she hopes will recover the treasure.

> Lulu's intercourse with him had been restricted of recent years to the negative processes of being out of town when he called on her, and short of money when he wrote to her. Now, however, she bethought herself of his eminent suitability for the direction of a treasure-seeking experiment; if any one could extract gold from an unpromising situation it would certainly be Vasco—of course, under the necessary safeguards in the way of supervision.

Vasco operates the salvage apparatus and in due course discovers the sunken wreck of a fashionable motor boat, the *Sub-Rosa.* In the strong box of the wreck, he finds a list of prominent people, with Lulu at its head, who are all implicated in a compromising situation. And with this list, Vasco blackmails his way into comfort and opulence. Lulu is shocked at his guile, but she does not protest her innocence. The people on Vasco's list, roughly equivalent to the fatuous habituees of Saki's gardens elsewhere, are found implicitly guilty of some nameless depravity.

The most remarkable of these stories, remarkable as a complex and self-consistent chain of Freudian imagery, is one entitled **"The Lumber-Room."** Nicholas, a small boy, is to be denied a trip to the shore because he has put a frog into his bread and milk. The act is no more bizarre than a good many similar acts in other Saki stories. And it serves the fictional purpose of showing that the adults, who all along had insisted that there could *not* be a frog in the bowl, were wrong, and Nicholas was right. Saki describes Nicholas as being "in disgrace," as having "sinned," as suffering from "depravity"—all of this suggesting the absurd values and the hypocrisy of the adult world.

The other children now prepare to leave. The aunt, a forbidding representative of adulthood, expects that Nicholas will cry. However, "all the crying was done by his girl-cousin, who scraped her knee rather painfully against the step of the carriage as she was scrambling in." Bobby, another cousin, is not likely to enjoy himself either, says Nicholas, because "his boots are hurting him. They're too tight." The unlikelihood, that is, that the two cousins will enjoy themselves at the seashore, explicitly a symbol of pleasure and conceivably a Freudian landscape-symbol, is associated by Saki with tightness and pain in entry, two nearly gratuitous details that suggest sexual immaturity.

Nicholas, since he is being punished, must not enter the gooseberry garden, one of his favorite places to play, and his aunt stands guard, in effect, to keep him out. "Now the

Munro in uniform after transferring to the 22nd Battalion of the Royal Fusiliers in 1914.

gooseberry garden had two doors by which it might be entered, and once a small person like Nicholas could slip in there he could effectually disappear from view amid the masking growth of artichokes, raspberry canes, and fruit bushes." The gooseberry garden, that is, is the source of vague pleasures and occasional prohibitions; it is a "landscape" which is explicitly "entered"; it is a place which affords privacy and is conductive to fantasy; and its two doors suggest the anatomical confusion of the sexual imagination of children which Freud reports in *The Interpretation of Dreams.* Nicholas makes several diversionary attempts at the gooseberry garden, all of the time intending to outwit his aunt by exploring the forbidden lumber-room.

> By standing on a chair in the library one could reach a shelf on which reposed a fat, important-looking key. The key was as important as it looked; it was the instrument which kept the mysteries of the lumber-room secure from unauthorized instrusion, which opened a way only for aunts and such-like privileged persons. Nicholas had not had much experience of the art of fitting keys into keyholes and turning locks, but for some days past he had practiced with the key of the schoolroom door; he did not believe in trusting too much to luck and accident. The key turned stiffly in the lock, but it turned. The door

opened, and Nicholas was in an unknown land, compared with which the gooseberry garden was a stale delight, a mere material pleasure.

In the midst of such unremitting sexual symbolism, one is tempted to recall Christopher Morley and the reputation of Saki as a bland, innocuous charmer, the "English O. Henry."

The lumber-room is all Nicholas had ever expected. It is "large and dimly lit, one high window opening on to the forbidden garden being its only source of illumination." Besides the excitement of its darkness and mystery, the lumber-room contains abandoned treasures, the most conspicuous of which is a large tapestry. The central figure of the tapestry is a man, "dressed in the hunting costume of some remote period," who had just "transfixed a stag with an arrow." The hunter is not safe, however, for he fails to see four wolves who are coming upon him and his dogs from the wood. "Nicholas sat for many golden minutes revolving the possibilities of the scene; he was inclined to think that there were more than four wolves and that the man and his dogs were in a tight corner."

But Nicholas is excited by other discoveries. "There were quaint twisted candlesticks in the shape of snakes, and a teapot fashioned like a china duck, out of whose open beak the tea was supposed to come. How dull and shapeless the nursery teapot seemed in comparison! And there was a carved sandal-wood box packed tight with little brass figures, hump-necked bulls, and peacocks and goblins, delightful to see and to handle." Finally, his attention is taken by a book containing pictures of birds, generally birds with long legs and long beaks, herons and toucans and ibises, unlike birds he has seen.

Presently his aunt comes looking for him. Of course she looks in the gooseberry garden since it does not occur to her that Nicholas might have let himself into the lumber-room. But instead of finding him, she slips instead into the rainwater tank. Nicholas sees his opportunity for revenge and answers her calls for help by asking if she is really "the Evil One" tempting him to disobedience. After a brief exchange in which Nicholas pretends to be unconvinced that she is really his aunt, he leaves, and after thirty-five minutes she is rescued by a kitchen-maid.

The story ends with a summary of the three experiences—of the immature cousins, of the old, impotent, ineffectual aunt, and of the initiated Nicholas. The tide had been high, "so there had been no sands to play on." Bobby's tight boots had made him irritable. The aunt is mute, thoroughly humiliated by her experience in the rainwater tank. (If it is possible to take the aunt's encounter with a round container of liquid as being, in its way, sexually significant, then certainly the absurdly inordinate amount of time necessary for her to get out is significant too.) "As for Nicholas he, too, was silent, in the absorption of one who has much to think about; it was just possible, he considered, that the huntsman would escape with his hounds while the wolves feasted on the stricken stag."

That so heavy a concentration of forbidden pleasures and ineffectual punishments, of penetration and tightness, entry and delight, of keys and locks, candlesticks and spouts, of long slender objects and open containers—that all of this should be the chance result of Saki's imagining an incident involving a precocious child and a repressive adult is unbelievable. Surely the story is about the acquiring of sexual knowledge and the sexual fables of the adult world, whether such an intent were ever wholly conscious or not. Indeed, perhaps the question of conscious intentions is unanswerable. Saki's talent is not the sort to engage an intellectual biographer. Saki's sister, Ethel M. Munro, in her biographical sketch [in *The Short Stories of Saki*], recalls the circumstances of **"The Lumber-Room"**; the story is, in part, autobiographical and the lumber-room is drawn after a forbidden room in their childhood experience. But this account only confirms the depth of feeling which lies behind the rather facile exterior of the story, confirms the genuineness of Saki's resentment toward the repressive and hypocritical world of adults.

The question of a direct influence of Freud on Saki's work is an open one. The first English edition of *The Interpretation of Dreams* was in 1913, a year before the collection of **Beasts and Super-Beasts.** But it is, in any case, entirely believable that the penetrating, critical, passionately honest imagination of Saki should have, at one level or another of his consciousness, played its little joke on his genteel, newspaper-reading public by surreptitiously dealing with a level of experience which no one has ever suspected of him. (pp. 33-7)

> *Philip Stevick, "Saki's Beasts," in* English Literature in Transition: 1880-1920, *Vol. 9, No. 1, 1966, pp. 33-7.*

Peter Bilton   (essay date 1966)

[*In the following essay, Bilton argues that most critics have neglected the serious purpose underlying Saki's verbal wit in his fiction.*]

On November 14th, 1916, at Beaumont-Hamel—in no man's land—a sniper's bullet killed Lance-Sergeant Hector Hugh Munro of the 22nd Royal Fusiliers. His order that a light be put out had come a moment too late. Munro's enlistment at the age of forty-four as one of the first volunteers of the war, like his refusals to take a commission, must have surprised some of those who knew him as the clubman, political reporter and writer whose sketches, stories and two novels had appeared over the pseudonym Saki. Yet the soldiering was only principle put into practice.

For there *was* principle: one should not be misled by the apparent lack of it in Saki's protagonists. The way they speak or act for him, or provide our wish-fulfilment for us, shows an underlying attitude in their creator that comes across as strongly to-day as at any time in the last fifty years.

Certainly Saki has never disappeared from view—except in the literary histories. The list of fellow-writers who have been ready to praise him is quite a literary honour-roll, including Chesterton, Walpole, Baring, Waugh, Priestley and Greene. Saki appears as of right in the anthologies, and selections or collections of his stories are published at brief intervals. (He is fortunate in the fidelity of John Lane, his original publishers.) A few years ago, a Sunday paper included *The Unbearable Bassington* in its short-list of the best novels of the first half-century; and there was another press survey in which more than one notability chose Saki for the desert-island library. The final accolade has also been bestowed: TV adaptation in Great Britain and the United States.

Yet literary history and academic criticism largely ignore him (though he has found a foothold at Purdue). A divergence between popular and critical esteem is common, but seldom so wide as in Saki's case. Mere neglect might be partly explained by critics in terms of the famous *Punch* dictum about Wodehouse criticism, 'like taking a spade to a soufflé', but applied to Saki 'soufflé' would be a misnomer. It may be just such an identification of Saki with mere lightness—and hence with triviality—that has led such critics as do mention him to disapprove of the form or structure of many of the stories. Greater awareness of the serious attitude behind them might lead to greater respect for the economy with which Saki directed all his means to one end.

Verbal wit is the ingredient for which Saki's stories are most admired, and the level at which criticism often stops, with some comment on the bright surface beneath which little can be found. But when Clovis says 'Waldo is one of those people who would be enormously improved by death', the wit works—as wit does—through the trick it plays on our conditioned expectations and responses, which were what Saki constantly tried to break down. At the same time, the remark has a disquieting chill about it, appropriate to Saki's views. When the twists of plot or sudden endings of the stories take us unawares, they are functioning in the same way as the wit: conventional expectations are upset, and life is shown as Saki thought it ought to be seen, as a source of constant surprise, shock—and interest. While he thus defies the reader to feel complacent behind banalities or preconceptions, he is at the same time attacking catch-phrases and complacency within his ficitonal framework. While the reader is enjoying having his eyes opened to unconventional possibilities in language and life, the self-satisfied snob or prejudice-ridden prig in the story is being routed by repartee or humiliated by a practical joke. The medium of wit, the setting amid society conventions, the plot aimed at the discomfiture of dulness: at all levels Saki made logically coherent choices. (That, surely, is structure.)

Despite such single-mindedness, Saki avoided sameness by depicting a wide variety of platitudinous forms of life and creating a fantastic array of antagonists to unleash against it. No status-seeker, poseur, dilettante or mere dullard can sustain his illusions after the iconoclastic attentions of a Reginald or a Clovis; no cliché or hollow code is left without its weirdly illogical conclusion. When the fog of human folly grows too thick even for his outspoken children, wild animals are brought in to stab dramatically through it with tooth or claw, or simply to lurk in it, inconvenient presences not allowed for in well-regulated lives, like truth or death. The imaginative human being or upsettingly natural animal find other al-

lies in a casual werewolf or witch or an even more casual Fate.

Perhaps Saki came to feel that the Universal Darkness—in his particular upper-class version—was triumphing nevertheless, or simply that with his stories he could lead his bores to laughter but could not make them think. Whatever the reason, one finds in a chronological reading of the stories a gradual decrease in the verbal wit, a more and more earnest or even bitter tone of voice, and a gradual increase in physical assault on his victims to accompany the mental. (Here let me express my wonder at the use of the word 'sadistic' in descriptions of the stories. Saki never goes into gory detail; when one of his animals takes life it happens quickly, cleanly, and above all naturally. Besides, the charge of sadism must refer to the writer's intention rather than to his subject matter. The verbal lashings and practical jokes in Saki's stories leave the air cleaner afterwards; even the deaths, though sometimes macabre, are never morbid.)

> **Verbal wit is the ingredient for which Saki's stories are most admired, and the level at which criticism often stops, with some comment on the bright surface beneath which little can be found. But when Clovis says 'Waldo is one of those people who would be enormously improved by death', the wit works—as wit does—through the trick it plays in our conditioned expectations and responses, which were what Saki constantly tried to break down. At the same time, the remark has a disquieting chill about it, appropriate to Saki's views.**
>
> **—*Peter Bilton***

Finally, in a few late stories, a passionate declaration of true values is allowed to reinforce the concerted attack on the false. The explicit statements in **'The Cupboard of the Yesterdays'** or **'The Mappined Life'** bring out what has been implied all along. To Saki the prospect that fatuous and self-satisfied Sheep should dwell in the land and possess it was far from soothing. He saw that passions were 'fast becoming atrophied for want of exercise', felt the 'charm of uncertainty and landslide', and pitied the 'legion of men who were once young and unfettered and now eat out their souls in dustbins'. He knew that 'there are heaps of ways of leading a real existence without committing sensational deeds of violence. It's the dreadful little everyday acts of pretended importance that give the Mappin stamp to our life.' Succinct anticipations of modern drama, and previews of modern life. Saki's crystal ball showed all to-day's triviality and mass-thinking, from status to strikes, from politics to pop. Sheep-like people, their passions at third- or fourth-hand, ignorant of uncertainty or landslide, have been fruitful and multiplied. Perhaps

Saki was wrong about the eating out of souls, since to-day we know of nothing beyond the dustbins: our powers of self-deception are even greater than those Saki speaks of. To-day's Mappin terraces are the most comfortable yet, with all mod. cons. and no disturbing view.

Despite our confirmation of Saki's fears, the human qualities he admired have also survived, so far. There are people who live up to ideals 'not because they think they ought to, but because they want to', who share Saki's love of wild nature and things natural and his resentment at all laming and taming processes, who oppose themselves to what Saki must have regarded as the survival of the unfittest. But in life, and hence in fiction, what Saki stood for must have other outlets and applications than he envisaged fifty years ago. Slight deviations from sane norms lend themselves to satirical attack; our mid-century extremes do not, for they cannot be exaggerated: we have reached the illogical conclusions already. Ever more drastic measures are needed to get complacency to bat an eyelid. To-day's public would simply assimilate Clovis or Tobermory, Clovis as compère of a satirical TV show, and the talking cat as a Top Twenty hit—until the novelty wore off.

With the winged chariot of progress ever at our backs, we have also moved beyond the reach of Saki's positive approach. We have neither world enough nor time to follow the example of the rare Saki hero, to be alone or independent. (Saki did not see 1917; he had longed to settle in distant Russian wilds after the war.) The way Saki found of living up to his ideals because he wanted to could scarcely look less 'with it' to-day. Creating surprise by volunteering as a private, unconventionally refusing a commission, fighting the trench war with imagination, as an adventure, keeping always cheerful and kind, he was living an attractive part, so it seems, in one of his own stories. We may regret the shock ending, but with its ironic last words and its impersonal fatal bullet for the Wanderer in no man's land it, too, might have been written by Saki. His good stories and good sense survive him: long life to them. (pp. 439-42)

> *Peter Bilton, "Salute to an N.C.O.," in* English Studies, *Netherlands, Vol. XLVII, No. 6, December, 1966, pp. 439-42.*

Charles H. Gillen (essay date 1969)

[*In the following excerpt, Gillen provides an overview of the distinctive features of Saki's short stories.*]

A Most Original Imagination

One of Munro's writing distinctions is the manner in which he set out his truly unique fantasies. His straightfaced mendacity, for instance, was a frequent manifestation of this quality. Munro's readers knew, of course, that they were having their "legs pulled," but Munro did it with such appropriateness to his premises that the readers accepted it as slightly unfocused truth. Sir John Squire wrote of Munro's embroidery: " 'Saki' was a unique example of the man who tells lies with a grave face. . . . He related a fantastic fable with the most matter-of-fact air. . . . Mendacity and credulity were the spectacles in

which he chiefly delighted. . . . In the end the reader of 'Saki' is pleased in proportion to the magnitude of the lie." And Munro himself averred that "one-half of the world believes what the other half invents."

In his story **"The Background"** Munro told of Henri Deplis, a native of Luxemburg, who spends a legacy in Italy getting tattooed all over his torso with a masterly drawing of "The Fall of Icarus." It was acclaimed, wrote Munro, a masterpiece "by all those who had the privilege of seeing it." So beautiful, in fact, was the man's tattooed torso that Italy refused to let Deplis leave the country because he would be violating "the stringent law which forbids the exportation of Italian works of art." And Munro gravely added: "A diplomatic parley ensued between the Luxemburgian and Italian Governments, and at one time the European situation became overcast with the possibilities of trouble." Meanwhile, the tattooed man had joined the Italian anarchists; and at one of the anarchists' meetings "a fellow-worker, in the heat of debate, broke a phial of corrosive liquid over his back. . . . As soon as he was able to leave the hospital Henri Deplis was put across the frontier as an undesirable alien."

Munro's approbation of a character who lives out a lie is evident in the story of **"The Schartz-Metterklume Method."** A titled young lady who has missed her train at a remote country station is mistaken for the new governess awaited by a Mrs. Quabarl. This rather parvenu mother of four insists upon bundling the young lady off to the Quabarl mansion, where she is supposed to instruct the Quabarl children in languages and history. The young lady rather grimly accepts the mistaken identity; she informs Mrs. Quabarl that she teaches history by the Schartz-Metterklume method, under which the pupils act out events which actually happened in history, and Mrs. Quabarl agrees to the use of this spurious teaching method on her children. The next morning the young lady makes the four young Quabarls act out the Rape of the Sabine Women, which necessitates, among other curious enterprises, the kidnapping of the lodge keeper's two small daughters. This sample of the "Schartz-Metterklume Method" is enough for Mrs. Quabarl; she discharges the pseudo-governess at once, and the young lady, imperturbable as ever, resumes her interrupted train journey. Munro, who obviously approved her duplicity, makes her the one likable character in the story.

A typical handling of fantasy in a convincing manner is found in the story **"The Occasional Garden"** in which Munro invented a company called "The Occasional Oasis Supply Association." This company, he wrote, would come to the aid, whenever summoned, of those wealthy people who are embarrassed by their "backyards that are of no practical use for gardening purposes" whenever they give luncheons or dinner parties. The "O.O.S.A." will provide special though temporary gardens for luncheons: "a blaze of lilac . . . one or two cherry trees in blossom, and clumps of heavily flowered rhododendrons . . . in the foreground . . . a blaze of Shirley poppies." If a Bishop is coming to lunch, said Munro, then "you get an old-world pleasaunce, with clipped yew hedges and a sun-dial and hollyhocks . . . borders of sweet william and Canterbury bells, and an old-fashioned beehive or two. . . . ''

If, however, it is necessary to deflate a patronizing acquaintance, this company furnishes "E.O.N. service," meaning "envy of the neighborhood." A drab backyard "becomes voluptuous with pomegranate and almond trees, lemon groves, and hedges of flowering cactus, dazzling banks of azaleas, marble-basined fountains . . . where golden carp slithered and wriggled amid the roots of gorgeous-hued irises."

In **"The Occasional Garden"** Gloria Rapsley uses this exotic garden service to stun and silence the odious braggart Gwenda Pottington. And for a while Gwenda is quite subdued by this vision of horticultural splendor, but four days later, long after the garden has been taken back by the "O.O.S.A.," she bursts uninvited into Gloria's house and discovers that the fantastic garden is no longer there. Gloria calmly states that Suffragettes have broken into the garden and destroyed it while they were demonstrating.

In the story of **"Cousin Teresa"** Munro conveyed his vast amusement at the workings of London's Edwardian equivalent of Tin Pan Alley. A harebrained dabbler in get-rich-quick schemes strikes gold when he composes the couplet "Cousin Teresa takes out Caesar, / Fido, Jock, and the big borzoi." When the enterprising producers of a revue set this "doggerel" to music and introduce it into their show, the public accords it an hysterical success as Cousin Teresa walks across the stage " . . . followed by four wooden dogs on wheels; Caesar . . . an Irish terrier, Fido a black poodle, Jock a fox-terrier, and the borzoi, of course . . . a borzoi."

Munro added that "Packed houses on successive evenings confirmed the verdict of the first night audience . . . the magic of the famous refrain laid its spell all over the Metropolis. Restaurant proprietors were obliged to provide the members of their orchestras with painted wooden dogs on wheels . . . revellers reeling home at night banged it on doors and hoardings, milkmen clashed their cans to its cadence. . . . '' The intellectuals invested the jingle with much significance: preachers discoursed from their pulpits on its real meaning; and society dowagers debated "the problematic Aztec or Nilotic origin of the Teresa *motif*," opining that " 'Cousin Teresa' has a genuine message for one. One can't understand the message all at once, of course." So great was the success of **"Cousin Teresa"** that its author was rewarded by a grateful nation: he was knighted and named in the annual Honours list for his contribution to English literature.

Munro's name for the leading character in this story is typical of his fantastic invention: Bassett Harrowcluff. Munro's names for his characters—such as Waldo Plublely, Sir Lulworth Quayne, and Loona Bimberton—approached the Dickensian in their combination of aptness and improbability. In inventing these unlikely names Munro may have been motivated by the stringent British libel laws, and quite often his creations bear the names of British towns—Courtenay Youghal, Tony Luton, Murrey Yeovil.

Munro's ability first to ideate his fantasies, then to develop them with all sorts of logical additions and reasonable comments, is another of his literary hallmarks.

Jaundiced Observer of the Great World

Truly knowledgeable about the incidents and the backgrounds he was constantly observing in wealthy town houses and at weekend parties in the country, Munro wrote about these rarefied places and their habitués in a rather unflattering way. His was a sort of love-hate attitude; the milieu was Munro's own, the one into which he had been born, but he wrote about it in a dissociated and alienated way. The following passage in *When William Came* more than anything else he wrote expresses this distaste:

> People of our dominant world at the present moment, herd together as closely packed to the square yard as possible, doing nothing worth doing, and saying nothing worth saying, but doing it and saying it over and over again, listening to the same melodies, watching the same artistes, echoing the same catchwords, ordering the same dishes in the same restaurants, suffering each other's cigarette smoke and perfumes and conversation, feverishly, anxiously making arrangements to meet each other again tomorrow, next week, and the week after next, and repeat the same gregarious experience . . . herded together in a corner of western London.

Perhaps the most amusing treatment of this environment is found in **"Tobermory,"** the short story dealing with a cat which is taught to speak English. Tobermory reveals his astounding faculty at a house party, a background Munro knew intimately. Through the cat's observations Munro comments acidulously on the party's guests—the stupid, the calculating, the greedy, the philandering. The hilarious comments are heightened in wit because they are uttered by the cat. **"Tobermory,"** quite possibly the funniest story Munro ever wrote, combines unique fantasy with deep humor. A closer reading of the story, however, reveals the deprecation and the faint disgust Munro felt for all the characters in it, an example of how Munro could draw an attractive background with repulsive figures in the foreground.

In the story of **"The Treasure Ship"** Munro deals with an attempt to salvage reputed treasure aboard a galleon which has lain underwater off the Irish coast for three hundred years. The one-man salvager discovers not the galleon but the wreck of a modern motor boat, the *Sub-Rosa*, which had gone down a few years before. In a watertight strongbox in the locker of the motor boat the salvager found a list of prominent people who had committed "indiscretions" of an extortionary nature, together with the evidence of these sins. The salvager confronts the most prominent of the people compromised by the papers he has discovered and starts his blackmailing operations with her, implying that he intends to blackmail the other people on the list and to live in ease thereafter. **"The Treasure Ship"** is one of Munro's deeper probings of the decadence of Society, an implied revelation of the vicious life led by some of the Best People, although he describes none of these things in detail. "Man delights not me," he seems to be agreeing with Hamlet.

In **"The Stampeding of Lady Bastable"** Munro contrasts the chicanery of a youth who discovers he is about to be victimized with the stupidity of a self-centered dowager, against a background of Munro's specialty, a country house. Mrs. Sangrail wants to visit "up north, to the Mac-Gregors" and intrigues to have her son Clovis "boarded" at Lady Bastable's house for six days while visiting in Scotland. Lady Bastable, in spite of misgivings about Clovis' wildness, agrees to this boarding arrangement only after Mrs. Sangrail offers to cancel a bridge table debt. Clovis is informed at breakfast of this arrangement, which he feels is really a plot, because he also wants badly to visit the MacGregors "to teach the MacGregor boys, who could well afford the knowledge, how to play poker-patience." When Lady Bastable retires in lonely splendor to the morning room after breakfast, to scan the newspapers for any signs of upheaval which might destroy the existing social order, a theory she dearly subscribes to, Clovis rushes up to a knot of the household's servants, crying "Poor Lady Bastable! In the morning-room! Oh, quick."

The servants, including the gardener with his sickle, run after Clovis into the morning room. At the door, Clovis yells to Lady Bastable "The jacquerie! They're on us!" Lady Bastable, after one horrified glance at the onrushing servants, flees out through a French window to the lawn. After Lady Bastable realizes the enormity of this practical joke, she frigidly refuses to board Clovis and pointedly settles the bridge debt. Clovis accompanies his mother to the MacGregors after all.

In a good many of his other stories, in the majority perhaps, Munro took as models the people of this upper world; but he never wrote of them with kindness or approbation. He criticized their habits, their beliefs, their characters; but he never once criticized the social system that permitted such beings to rest on the top of it. Because Munro believed in the rightness and inevitability of the class system, he was incapable of making any fundamental criticism of it. As H. W. Nevinson has stated of Munro [in his introduction to **Beasts and Super-Beasts**], "His nature ranged him on the side of authority and tradition."

These "socialite" stories are the undistorted reflections of his feelings about the people in his own narrow little stratum of humanity. His disenchantment with his peculiarly personal milieu, the fashionable world, is expressed in a manner that transcends in its skepticism, cynicism, and bitter humor the writings of contemporaneous Society wits like Oscar Wilde, W. S. Gilbert, Max Beerbohm, and John Oliver Hobbes. It is not quite accurate, however, to group Munro with such modern writers; his mordancy, from an older tradition, is more akin to the outlook and humor of the Restoration playwrights, to Dryden, Wycherley, and Congreve. Munro felt much the same repelled fascination at the spectacles and excesses of his own Vanity Fair. He took much the same delight, too, in ripping aside the veil of hypocrisy in which the *beau monde* swathed itself. Munro observed the frivolities of the great world with incredulity often, with wry amusement always; his contempt for the pursuits, attitudes, and morals of this upper world invariably leaks through the glossy surface of his stories. Yet the anomaly is that Munro personally was

a devout practitioner of all that was conventional and "done."

This way of life was after all his own, and his obedience to its outward aspects went far back into his heritage. And for all Munro's comparative impecuniousness, no one could write more authoritatively than he of a world of stately homes, tailored clothes and handmade frocks, heavy-laden breakfast sideboards, glittering automobiles, elaborate balls and dinner parties, and hovering butlers, footmen, and maids. Munro's writing is archetypical of that halcyon prewar era of Edward VII and George V when, for the consumption of the wealthy and privileged, a caste of loving artisans labored in a small area of London's West End—the tailors, gunsmiths, bootmakers, vintners, hatters, tobacconists, jewelers, and haberdashers whose products play so large a part in Munro's fiction. No other writer has so fully bequeathed the feel and look of this vanished time of apparent solidity and order, when the happy few in Britain led their carefree lives in the country houses of "county" Society or in mansions in the sooty air of Town.

It certainly was not Munro's intention to be remembered solely as the recorder of these Golden Calf years, when the wealthy dissipated and lorded it over a world whose stability and imperviousness to social change seemed eternal. It is amusing that posterity has assigned Munro just this role of recorder of the revels, while it ignores his efforts to write seriously and even profoundly. There is an irony here that would fit well into one of his improbable plots.

Contempt for Routine Living

Another of the themes running through Munro's stories is his disdain of domesticity and a settled, ordered way of life. In **"The Mappined Life"** Munro deplored the caging of birds and beasts in the London Zoological Gardens, even though the creatures had just been given new and more natural quarters in the Garden's Mappin Terraces, and from this condition he drew a parallel with the self-imposed captivity of the middle-class Londoner. Into the mouth of a young lady who has just visited these new zoological quarters, Munro puts his estimate of her and her kind: "We are just so many animals stuck down on a Mappin terrace, with this difference in our disfavour, that the animals are there to be looked at, while nobody wants to look at us . . . there are heaps of ways of leading a real existence. . . . It's the dreadful little everyday acts of pretended importance that give the Mappin stamp to our life."

In the story **"Tea"** Munro wrote in more detail of this domestic disaffection: "Cushat-Prinkley detested the whole system of afternoon tea. . . . Thousands of women, at this solemn hour, were sitting behind dainty porcelain and silver fittings, with their voices tinkling pleasantly in a cascade of solicitous little questions. . . . 'Is it one lump? I forget. You do take milk don't you? Would you like some more hot water if it's too strong?' "

Munro made his character, James Cushat-Prinkley, fall in love with a girl because she makes a minimum of fuss when she serves tea: "Cushat-Prinkley found that he was enjoying an excellent tea without having to answer as many questions about it as a Minister for Agriculture might be called on to reply to during an outbreak of cattle plague." After Cushat-Prinkley marries this paragon, however, she reverts to type, serving her first tea as a married woman with a full panoply of porcelain and silver, and asking solicitously: "You like it weaker than that, don't you? Shall I put some more hot water to it? No?"

Munro's approval of a break with the ordered life, a reversal of stodgy living habits into a precarious but exhilarating existence, shines through in his story **"The Way to the Dairy."** A rather elderly single lady, who had spent a restricted life in very modest circumstances, is left a large inheritance from a distant relative who mentioned no one else in the family in his will. The elderly lady, upon receiving this fortune, is immediately cosseted by three of her nieces, the Brimley Bomefields, who had ignored her when she was poor: they expect now that she will leave her newfound money to them when she dies. Unfortunately, the Brimley Bomefields take her to France; there the nieces give the old lady a hortatory introduction to gaming tables and the life of casinos.

Instead of alarming the old lady, these gambling hells charm her, and she becomes a confirmed gambler. Moreover, she surrounds herself with other gamblers: "For the first time in her life the old thing was thoroughly enjoying herself; she was losing money, but she had plenty of fun and excitement in the process . . . her nieces . . . still remained in attendance on her, with the pathetic unwillingness of a crew to leave a foundering treasure ship which might yet be steered into port." At last, the aunt's continual gambling and her growing circle of raffish friends from the casinos drive the Brimley Bomefields back to England, leaving the old lady to enjoy her newfound way of life. This approbation of dangerous living was not, of course, the majority view; but it is firmly embedded in the "Saki" canon, and one must consider Munro's disgust of domesticity as essential to an understanding of his attitude and work.

A Passion for Wild Things

Another factor to be considered in assessing Munro is the frequency with which he introduced wild animals and birds with such knowledgeability into his short stories. E. V. Knox [in his introduction to *76 Short Stories*] has cogently described this aspect of Munro:

> "What an enormous number of animals!" might be the comment of a reader who looks casually through these pages. . . . There is in fact a Munro menagerie. It is not merely the god Pan nor his rout of sylvans who break into country houses and obstruct the purposes of men. The wild things run riot. They peep out in every plot. They peer from the corner of every conversation. . . . One creature or another, exotic or domesticated, is always playing a part in these tales, and sometimes a decisive part, terrible or whimsical, a *bestia ex machina.* Here is a world in which time after time in the author's eyes, human beings are a little lower than the animals.

And it is true that Munro contrasted the behavior of ani-

mals with the behavior of humans, always to the latter's discredit.

In his book ***Beasts and Super-Beasts,*** which mockingly echoes Shaw's title *Man and Super-Man,* he makes this passion for animals a recurring theme. In this book the short story **"On Approval"** makes animals the subjects of a series of paintings by a German immigrant artist in London:

> His pictures always represented some well-known street or public place in London, fallen into decay and denuded of its human population, in the place of which there roamed a wild fauna, which, from its wealth of exotic species, must have originally escaped from Zoological Gardens and travelling beast shows. "Giraffes drinking at the fountain pools, Trafalgar Square," was one of the most notable and characteristic of his studies, while even more sensational was the gruesome picture of "Vultures attacking dying camel in Upper Berkeley Street." . . . The large canvas on which he had been engaged for some months. . . . "Hyenas asleep in Euston Station" . . . the picture that he showed us last week, "Sand-grouse roosting on the Albert Memorial" . . . a more ambitious picture, "Wolves and wapiti fighting on the steps of the Athenaeum Club."

Perhaps the secret of Munro's love for animals is that, while he recognized their ruthless struggle for survival, he habitually contrasted their instinctive decency and bravery with the sorry spectacle of human behavior. A long expression of this sentiment is to be found in the story of **"The Achievement of the Cat"**:

> Confront a child, a puppy, and a kitten with a sudden danger; the child will turn instinctively for assistance, the puppy will grovel in abject submission to the impending visitation, the kitten will brace its tiny body for a frantic resistance. . . . The cat of the slums and alleys, starved, outcast, harried, still keeps amid the prowlings of its adversity the bold, free panther-tread with which it paced of yore the temple courts of Thebes, still displays the self-reliant watchfulness which man has never taught it to lay aside . . . it dies fighting to the last, quivering with the choking rage of mastered resistance.

One would think that, if Munro were ever offered a chance at reincarnation, he would return as some animal. He never lost his fascination with other orders of creatures, even amid the horrors of the battlefield; in his piece **"Birds on the Western Front,"** which appeared in the *Westminster Gazette* a few weeks before his death, he gratefully described the brave behavior of the birds in adversity; and he was ashamed that man's brutality had so gravely damaged their environment. Munro's feeling for birds and animals should not be dismissed as the usual Englishman's love of horses and dogs; it was a much deeper emotion than that. It may be explained as being a reaction to his misanthropy—he had a deep need to admire life, even if it was not that of his own species.

Mastery of the Surprise Ending

The editors of the early 1900's seem to have admired and often to have demanded short stories with surprise endings—a mechanism most notably used in that era by the American short story writer O. Henry (William Sydney Porter). Munro, however, used this device with even greater cleverness and aptness, which was to be expected from the more accomplished of the two writers. Munro and O. Henry both had seen the seamy side of life, the discreditable facets of human nature; but Munro, better educated, more widely traveled, and with a much more sophisticated mind, set his satiric sights higher and was more successful in annihilating his targets. Munro was the more polished stylist, the more original moralist, the more ambitious satirist; and he never stooped to the use of O. Henry's sometimes cloying sentimentality.

Munro may have deprecated this snapper-ending trick as being too facile, but it placated editors who demanded that Munro always write as that startling fellow "Saki." It is difficult to give examples of this aspect of Munro's writing without relating the entire plot of the story in point, so tightly knit was the preparation and skilled placing of false scents; the surprise ending of the story must be considered in relation to every little thing that has occurred before it. O. Henry, on the other hand, often sacrificed credibility in his characters or the careful development of his staging to achieve his trick endings.

In the story **"The Bag"** a wealthy Russian youth, Vladimir, is visiting an English "county" family that is very keen on fox hunting. Vladimir doesn't ride well enough to join the local hunt, but he does some shooting in nearby woods and fields. When he returns from one of his expeditions, he proudly announces that he has shot an animal that "lives in the woods and eats rabbits and chickens." The family is thunderstruck: "Merciful Heaven! he's shot a fox!" And to do so is just about the worst social blunder one can make in these parts. They order Vladimir to hide his unopened game bag since they are expecting the master of the local hunt to arrive at any minute. Munro skillfully developed the suspense of the inevitable discovery of Vladimir's heinous offense. The hunt master eventually deduces that a fox has been shot by the Russian, and he storms out of the house. Vladimir is then curtly ordered by the household to bury his kill. Munro ended the story: "And thus it came to pass that in the dusk of a November evening, the Russian boy, murmuring a few of the prayers of his church for luck, gave hasty but decent burial to a large polecat."

Another surprise ending capable of being summarized briefly is the ending of **"The Forbidden Buzzards."** A friend of Clovis Sangrail dearly wishes to propose marriage to Betty Coulterneb, but the girl is attracted to still another man, one Lanner. Clovis' friend appeals to him for help in this situation. When Lanner is invited to the girl's country home for a weekend, Clovis is also there; and he tells the hostess, Betty's mother, that Lanner is really visiting in order to steal the eggs from the nest of two "rough-legged buzzards . . . the only pair of rough-legged buzzards known to breed in this country." These birds have honored the Coulterneb home by nesting in the woods adjacent to it. The hostess is shocked and outraged

by Clovis' story, but he suggests that Mr. Lanner never be left alone long enough to perpetrate the egg theft. The hostess agrees to this suggestion, and Mr. Lanner is constantly, if involuntarily, in the company of the governess or the nine-year-old son, or he is being shown all the boring aspects of the house and grounds, or being dragged off to visit a nearby village or some allegedly historic farmhouse. Lanner never has the opportunity to propose to the girl, and Clovis' plot must be accounted successful. Munro ends his narrative thus: "The buzzards successfully reared two young ones, who were shot by a local hairdresser."

Munro's expertise with the surprise ending is testified to by the frequency with which some of his stories employing this device have been reprinted and anthologized: **"The Open Window," "Dusk,"** and **"The Reticence of Lady Anne."** This surprise ending was a literary trick, no doubt; but it took an able writer to make it credible. Present-day stories which eschew all hints of a plot and attempt to emerge as "mood pieces" or "slices of life" seem somehow skimped and underdone when they are compared with the tailor-made short story of 1910.

Use of the Uncanny

Munro was the only writer of his day who consistently used the unhackneyed subject of the uncanny and supernatural. Other writers were indifferent to this subject, perhaps because they lacked an inborn feeling for it and in any case could not fit it into their work. And by its nature the subject disqualified itself from use by the realists and social reformers, and probably could only be appreciated by a restricted and selective readership like Munro's. This subject might easily have degenerated into the merely silly, but Munro handled it with gravity and great writing skill, and he was helped in its development by something sympathetic in his nature.

In the story **"The Music on the Hill"** the sense of foreboding, of being watched by something supernatural, is credibly conveyed. A girl named Sylvia has inveigled wealthy Mortimer Seltoun into marriage; but, because she feels that he is too distracted by life in London, she wrenches him away to his country place, "a remote, wood-girt manor farm." Sylvia, a town-bred girl, does not appreciate this rural setting: " 'it is very wild,' she said to Mortimer, 'one could almost think that in such a place the worship of Pan had never quite died out.' "

Mortimer assures her that the worship of Pan has never disappeared thereabouts. Then, on an excursion into the woods, Sylvia stumbles upon

> a stone pedestal surmounted by a small bronze figure of a youthful Pan . . . a newly cut bunch of grapes had been placed as an offering at its feet. Grapes were none too plentiful at the manor house, and Sylvia snatched the bunch angrily from the pedestal. Contemptuous annoyance dominated her thoughts as she strolled slowly homeward . . . across a thick tangle of undergrowth a boy's face was scowling at her, brown and beautiful, with unutterably evil eyes. . . . "I saw a youth in the wood today . . . a gypsy lad, I suppose." . . . she went on to recount her finding of the votive offering. . . .

"Did you meddle with it in any way?" asked Mortimer . . . "I've heard it said that the Wood Gods are rather horrible to those that molest them. . . . I should avoid the woods and orchards if I were you, and give a wide berth to the beasts on the farm."

The next afternoon Sylvia rambles off, taking care to avoid the farmyard cattle and goats, and staying away from the woods. She climbed through open slopes of heather above the manor, "but across the wooded combes at her feet . . . Sylvia could presently see a dark body, breasting hill after hill . . . at last he broke through the outermost line of oak scrub and fern . . . a fat September stag carrying a well-furnished head." The stag was being pursued by a pack of hounds; but, instead of heading toward safety, he bounded up the hill where she stood:

> Pipe music suddenly shrilled around her . . . and at the same moment the great beast slewed round and bore directly down upon her. In an instant her pity for the hunted animal changed to wild terror at her own danger. . . . The huge antler spikes were within a few yards of her. . . . And then with a quick throb of joy she saw that she was not alone; a human figure stood a few paces aside. . . . "Drive it off!" she shrieked. But the figure made no answering movement. The antlers drove straight at her, but her eyes were filled with the horror of something else she saw other than her oncoming death. And in her ears rang the echo of a boy's laughter, golden and equivocal.

The central figure of the story **"Gabriel-Ernest"** is a creature who takes the form of a youthful human in daylight but changes into a wolf at night. This werewolf preys upon the wild and domesticated animals of the neighborhood and upon "children when I can get any; they're usually too well locked in at night." In **"The Soul of Laploshka,"** a miser dies suddenly; but, in a circumstantial and logical narrative, his ghost returns repeatedly to disturb his former tormentor.

The supernatural is used both as an actual occurrence and as an example of human credulity in **"The Hedgehog."** A country house, Exwood, is rented by the Norbury family from a Mrs. Hatch-Mallard. The Norburys are very fond of the house, so whenever necessary they try to please their landlady in the hope that she will renew the lease. The house is supposed to be haunted by a number of ghosts; when a highly clairvoyant woman, the seventh daughter of a seventh daughter, comes to it as a guest, some of the prominent people in the neighborhood wrangle about which ghost she will see. The landlady tells her tenant: "Mrs. Norbury, I shall take it as a deliberate affront if your clairvoyante friend sees any other ghost except that of my uncle."

The Norburys are apprehensive that their clairvoyant guest may see some other ghost; and sure enough, on the third night at Exwood she sees not the ghost of Mrs. Hatch-Mallard's uncle, but a white hedgehog with evil yellow eyes: it crawls across her bedroom, its loathsome claws clicking along the floor, its hideous eyes always staring at her. When it reaches a window, it climbs up on the

sill and vanishes. A local history book of the county identifies the hedgehog as the ghost of Nicholas Herison, who was hanged at Blatchford in 1763 for the murder of a farm lad. The tenants, the Norburys, are more than a little perturbed because they remember Mrs. Hatch-Mallard's promise of wrath if her uncle's ghost is not seen. Mr. Norbury thereupon tells a lie to the clairvoyant: the whole incident was only a practical joke; what she saw was really a stuffed albino hedgehog, which he had drawn on a string across the room and out the window, a prank often played on guests. Munro ended the story by noting that Mrs. Hatch-Mallard renewed the lease, but the clairvoyant never renewed her friendship with the Norburys.

Many other incidents and characters from the supernatural can be found in Munro; he dealt with the subject frequently and unexpectedly but in a way pertinent to his stories. The influences of his sojourn in the haunted Devon countryside and in half-pagan eastern Europe have already been marked. His heritage of Celtic blood from generations from the misty Highlands also explains to some extent his wild fancies and his liking for the eerie and macabre. In a true "original," this interest was perhaps the strangest of his writing peculiarities.

Some Other Themes

Some of Munro's short stories do not fit into any general classification; there is, for instance, the story of **"The Sheep."** Munro appears to have been a perceptive and quick-witted man, with a high degree of intolerance for people who were born with the opposite qualities of dullness and stupidity; and this story proves that he did not suffer fools gladly. In it Munro allowed his distaste for fools to turn into naked hatred.

The "sheep" of the story is a bungling, clumsy, stupid young man, whose unthinking folly is made all the more irritating by his ineffable self-satisfaction. He is described as ruining a partner's bridge hand, shooting a protected game bird, and losing a local election for a candidate by making a blundering remark at a political meeting. To compound his obnoxiousness, he has become engaged to a desirable and otherwise intelligent girl whose brother despises the "sheep." The terrible ending of the story—not the penultimate description of the fool's death beneath the ice of a skating pond—but the lovingly written details of how a dog which prevented the fool's rescue is thereafter cosseted and coddled by the girl's brother is absolutely counter to all Christian morality, although it is essential Munroism. The virulence of the writing in **"The Sheep"** which transcends this bitter quality found in so many other of his stories makes the reader doubt Munro's mental balance.

A story which shows that Munro never forgot his circumscribed childhood is **"Sredni Vashtar."** The central figure of this story, a ten-year-old orphaned boy Conradin is looked after in a house in the country by his middle-aged cousin and guardian Mrs. De Ropp. Mrs. De Ropp is an inept guardian who thwarts Conradin continually "for his own good." Conradin hates her bitterly, although he is able to dissemble his hatred. The only place on the property where he is his own master is an unused tool shed in a hidden corner of the garden; here he keeps a rather bedraggled hen, which he dotes on, and in a dark corner, securely caged, a large ferret "which a friendly butcher boy had once smuggled, cage and all, into its present quarters, in exchange for a long-secreted hoard of small silver."

Conradin, although terrified of the sharp-fanged ferret, adores it, and begins to worship it as a god. Conradin, who names it **"Sredni Vashtar,"** regularly brings it offerings of red flowers and scarlet berries. After a while Mrs. De Ropp notices Conradin's frequent trips to the tool shed. "It is not good for him to be pattering down there in all weathers" she says to herself; and, visiting the shed, she discovers the hen but not the ferret. When she sells the hen and it is taken away, Conradin's hatred becomes cold and murderous: "In the shed that evening . . . he asked a boon. 'Do one thing for me, Sredni Vashtar.' The thing was not specified. As Sredni Vashtar was a god he must be supposed to know."

Mrs. De Ropp notices that Conradin's visits to the tool shed have not ceased with the removal of the hen. "What are you keeping in that locked hutch?" she demands of Conradin; and, ransacking his bedroom, she finally finds the key to the cage. She marches into the tool shed but she does not come back out:

> Conradin stood and waited and watched. Hope had crept by inches into his heart, and now a look of triumph began to blaze in his eyes. . . . And presently, his eyes were rewarded: out through the doorway came a long, low, yellow-and-brown beast, with eyes a-blinking at the waning daylight, and dark wet stains around the fur of jaws and throat. Conradin dropped on his knees. The great polecat-ferret made its way down to a small brook at the foot of the garden, drank for a moment, then crossed a little plank bridge and was lost to sight in the bushes.

After a long wait Conradin hears the screaming of a maid and a great commotion among the other servants. And, while they argued about who should break the bad news to the poor child, Conradin made himself another piece of toast. **"Sredni Vashtar"** is one of the most frequently reprinted of Munro's stories; because of its balefulness and horror, it stays in a reader's memory ever afterward. Very clearly, it is Munro's sublimation of his own hatred for his aunt Augusta when he was her unruly ward at Broadgate.

Another of Munro's traits is the effortless display of his cosmopolitanism. In **"The Interlopers"** he used the background of a forest in the Carpathians for two *mitteleuropa* characters most credibly drawn in this sketch of the old Austro-Hungarian Empire. The story **"The Name-Day"** also deals with the old Habsburg dominions; and, like **"The Interlopers,"** it conveys the flavor of an exotic corner of the world. **"The Wolves of Cernogratz"** knowledgeably deals with the fulfillment of a legend in an east German castle, and in **"Wratislaw"** the badinage between a Gräfin and a Countess somehow imparts the gaiety of old Vienna. Munro casually injected Dieppe, Homburg, the Engadine, Novibazar, Paris, Pomerania, Burma, and other foreign places into his stories, always with the authenticity of having been to these places himself. Just as

casually he introduced characters from the Russian nobility, the revolutionaries of the Balkans, the smug merchant class of the Far East, or the bohemian world of Paris; like the exotic backgrounds, these characters were authentic. Munro had known such people.

Posterity's Verdict

Although Munro may have written his short stories to satisfy an exigent financial need, making them acceptable to editors rather than trying to make them into little gems of literary art, it is for these short stories that he is remembered today. Posterity, in its dogmatic way, has decided that Munro is to be considered solely as the creator of little, wryly humorous stories. This latter-day judgment can be seen in the extent to which Munro's short stories have been anthologized in collections of humorous stories. A few of Munro's stories, in surveys of modern English literature, have even been held up as worthy examples for the novice writer to imitate; Munro would surely have been amused at such canonization.

But the fact remains that through his short stories alone, and not his other literary achievements, the "Saki" name lives on today; this is borne out by an event of recent days when Munro's stories were given the ultimate accolade of this age—conversion to television material. Thirty-six of Munro's short stories, in eight one-hour programs, were "adapted" for British television audiences. They were later exported to the United States, where they were rather a success with viewers of "educational" stations. Yet, like wine that does not travel well, Munro's bouquet did not come through in this television transmogrification. Of necessity only Munro's dialogue could be used in these television adaptations. The dialogue which was used is amusing enough, but these playlets could not possibly introduce Munro's observations, asides, and comments; these are just the things that complement the dialogue in the short stories to give them the unique "Saki" cachet. At any rate, these television adaptations proved that Munro has some appeal for the latest generation, who would rather get their entertainment from television than from books.

There is a strong likelihood that Munro used some sort of system to help him turn out his short stories in a no-nonsense, workmanlike fashion. Despite his superficial languor—the affectation of the gentleman of that period—Munro was an organized, industrious writer who practiced his calling with seriousness. It is logical to assume that he kept a notebook of plots for possible use in the composition of his short stories, and that his friends and relatives told him anecdotes they thought would be helpful to him. An indication of this practice is in a passage written by the humorist Thomas Anstey Guthrie ("F. Anstey") in March, 1912: "I met Hector Munro (Saki) . . . and he had a soft and remarkably pleasant voice. I find a note of an anecdote he told me that afternoon of a man who when seized by a sudden and violent hunger found that he had nothing but a penny in his pocket. Fortunately, however, he came upon an automatic chocolate machine outside a shop, eagerly put in his penny and got a box of matches."

In Munro's time, editors wanted no part of stories which

experimented with plotless plots, stream-of-consciousness monologues, precious obscurity, or any other literary innovation. They were looking for the well-made story which did not flout any of the writing conventions, and Munro did not attempt to divert them from this insistence on the well-made story. Almost certainly Munro himself subscribed to this rationale, for Sir John Squire firmly believed in Munro's devotion to traditional writing: "He polished his sentences with a spinsterish passion for neatness and chose his words as the last of the dandies might choose his ties. Writing brief stories and sketches for evening newspapers he was as careful with the shaping of his paragraphs as the most anchorite of esthetes writing for an elect few with glass-fronted bookcases. He expended the pains of a poet upon modern fairy-tales."

On the other hand, A. A. Milne gave his opinion of Munro's craftsmanship in this pronouncement: "I do not think that he has that 'mastery of the *conte*' . . . which some have claimed for him. Such mastery infers a passion for neatness which was not in the boyish Saki's equipment. He leaves loose ends everywhere." But, as Munro himself observed, "Two of a trade never agree."

The "Saki" short stories seem certain to endure; the latter-day reader finds something familiar and pertinent in Munro's cynicism and unflattering view of humanity. Munro's people are alive and contemporaneous: one still sees today the stuffed shirt, the persistent sponger, the social climber, the ambitious young politician, the black sheep, the self-satisfied incompetent, the wealthy idler, the silly, exploited woman, and, even occasionally, the wit. Munro's attractiveness for the modern reader is his surprising modernity. (pp. 72-90)

> *Charles H. Gillen, in his* H. H. Munro (Saki), *Twayne Publishers, Inc., 1969, 178 p.*

John Daniel Stahl   (essay date 1977)

[*In the following essay, Stahl discusses images of rebellious children in Saki's short stories, particularly focusing on those in "The Open Window."*]

"The Open Window" is H. H. Munro's most frequently anthologized story, yet it has been almost entirely neglected by critics. It is a very brief story (only about 1200 words) and has the cameo quality and brisk wit so characteristic of Saki. A hasty reading of the story may confirm the opinion of those who, like A. A. Milne, believe that Saki is merely an entertainer. He is often considered a technically facile artisan whose plots, O. Henry-like, suffer from over-contrivance and whose elegance of expression is like a glaze on a thin and rather fragile pot.

Robert Drake, on the other hand, has argued for the deeper significance of Saki's work, distinguishing between the ironic and the humorous stories. In the ironic stories the unwillingness of a central character to face undesired aspects of reality (such as the supernatural, the bestial, Evil) is contradicted by events which humiliate or destroy the character concerned through a direct confrontation with the undesired reality. In the humorous stories (the distinction between the two kinds being one of degree, according

to Drake), a Bergsonian 'norm'—often represented by respectable, stuffy members of Society—is ridiculed by contrast with a seemingly cruel or amoral 'beyond-norm' which takes the shape of a character like Reginald or Clovis. Children, Drake says, also act as 'beyond-norm' in Saki's stories. The 'beyond-norm', as Drake indicates, is closer to a true norm than the 'norm'.

An imaginative child faced with an adult world of dull limitation such as Saki frequently satirized will escape into a world of phantasy, a pattern not rare in Edwardian literature—see E. M. Forster's "The Celestial Omnibus", for example. As Roger Fry once wrote, "The daydreams of a child are filled with extravagant romances in which he always is the invincible hero." "The Open Window" is a story with all the marks of a child's wish-fulfilling daydream; it is an expression of the fantasy of a child able to control the adult world—a world which is unattractive or even contemptible.

Vera, a girl of fifteen, entertains a guest, Framton Nuttel, a stranger who has just arrived for a nerve cure, for a few minutes before her aunt, Mrs. Sappleton, descends. In the brief time the niece is alone with the guest, she tells him about the aunt's tragedy: the deaths of the latter's husband and two brothers in a bog during a hunt, and her subsequent superstition that her husband and brothers will return through the open window as was once their habit. When the aunt appears and clearly expects someone to cross the fields and enter through the open window the guest is alarmed; when three figures that exactly fit the niece's description of the 'dead' trio actually appear, he panics and flees. When Mr. Sappleton inquires about the stranger who fled so precipitously, the niece invents a credible impromptu explanation.

Though on one level strictly realistic—the story could happen in every detail—the extreme purposeful opposition of child and adult gives the story an intensified, hallucinatory atmosphere. Vera, at fifteen, has the articulacy of an adult but the rôle of an adolescent child, as the story emphasizes by calling her both "young lady" and "child". Vera's romance is almost supernaturally clever. She, the child, is vastly superior in every way to Mr. Framton Nuttel (note the nutty name, so characteristic for Saki), the adult whom she has chosen as her adversary. Vera must make several crucial judgments on which the outcome of her romance rests. She must determine that Nuttel is the sort of man too fastidious to mention or even hint at the 'tragedy' to Mrs. Sappleton, and that he will be suggestible and superstitious enough to interpret the events that follow in the light in which Vera has represented them. She must discover how much Nuttel knows about the family and the vicinity in order to safeguard herself against discovery; his ignorance is of course a prerequisite for her scheme. Her judgements are all correct.

Vera's two fantasies for the benefit of the audience are brilliant and expertly told. She is adept at deception. She combines in her tale circumstances such as Ronnie's habit of singing, "Bertie, why do you bound?", and her aunt's accustomed expectation of her husband and brothers, which will seem to confirm the truth of what she has told Nuttel; she speaks with pity and a touch of susceptibility: " 'Poor aunt . . . poor dear aunt . . . Do you know, sometimes on still quiet evenings like this, I almost get a creepy feeling that they will all walk in through that window—' "

Not only her words but her actions as well convey what she desires to convey. At the fitting moment in her tale of the three lost hunters her voice "lost its self-possessed note and became falteringly human". When she has said just enough to suggest the uncanny, she breaks off "with a little shudder". When the hunters appear on the lawn, "The child was staring out through the open window with dazed horror in her eyes." She also knows when not to be dramatic; she presents her explanation of Nuttel's hasty departure with that calm finesse which convinces by its lack of insistence, and adds a note of sympathy, "enough to make anyone lose their nerve", which is a perfect camouflage for invention.

Vera is in fact in total control of the events of the story. By contrast, Framton Nuttel, the central adult figure, is being controlled. He is the victim of Vera's 'romance', but he does not arouse sympathy. The first few paragraphs of the story subtly reveal that he is dominated by his sister; he doubts the efficacy of his nerve cure and regrets having to visit strangers, yet is apparently too feeble-willed to object. He is a hypochondriac and a bore: he "laboured under the tolerable wide-spread delusion that total strangers and chance acquaintances are hungry for the least detail of one's ailments and infirmities, their cause and cure." As Janet Overmyer writes [in her essay "Turn Down an Empty Glass," *Texas Quarterly,* Autumn 1964], "Saki is impatient with the foibles of bores, cowards, the idle, the useless rich, those lacking a sense of humor . . . He gives them such names as Ada Spelvexit, Hortensia Bavvel, Sir James Beanquest, Demosthenes Platterbaff, and Sir Wilfred Pigeoncote—and one might add, Framton Nuttel— . . . the ridiculous names and the absence of characterization in depth tend so to dehumanize them that the reader will not sympathize with them and the satire can then scathe more effectively."

So we have in **"The Open Window"** a powerful, clever child in opposition to a weak, neurotic, suggestible adult. On first reading, the story may well appear to be a tale of the supernatural; at the latest by the last line that impression has been replaced by an amazed recognition of the truth of the statement, "Romance at short notice was her specialty." But the story has not become more realistic by an elimination of the supernatural; it has merely become more fantastic in another sense: it has taken on the quality of a daydream, a fantasy. The intensity of the story is also increased by the contrast between its content and its tone; the events of the plot, the deception and the intimation of supernatural horror are reminiscent of Poe (e.g., "The Cask of Amontillado") but the tone of the story does not emphasize the Gothic element for its own sake. Like Vera in presenting her inventions, the narrator presents unostentatiously and economically just what is necessary for his effect. At times, in fact, author and central character bear such similarities to each other that they merge; we as readers may be less likely to be frightened by the figures on the lawn, but if we are unacquainted with the ways of

Saki's imagination, Vera's story on first reading has the same capacity to fool us as it does for Nuttel.

Vera's romance is a clever practical joke of the highest caliber—without wires, strings, or mechanical contraptions. If, once we are initiated, the story appeals to us, if we laugh or feel any satisfaction at Framton Nuttel's hasty exodus, we are most likely participating in a fantasy that is peculiar to the mind of a child, and particularly a frustrated child, who is powerless to resist the encroachments or dictates of a cruel or boring adult world. According to Janet Overmyer, children in Saki's stories often are "cruel to adults because the entire adult world is against them, and they are helpless to resist. They must therefore snatch their revenge whenever the opportunity arises."

The impulse behind practical jokes often arises from urges against authority or the established order of things. The wishful fantasy of a child desiring to play havoc with adults is widespread. In one of Jack Harkaway's stories (a series of 'penny dreadfuls' for boys that began in 1871, the year after Munro's birth, and continued up to the end of the Victorian era) an episode occurs which bears some relation to intrigue of Vera's kind. Here, as quoted by E. S. Turner [in *Boys Will Be Boys*]:

> Fighting apart, there was little to do at Pomona House school except to rag as graceless a set of pedagogues as ever gathered under one roof. Jack, being a ventriloquist, had a head and shoulders start over the others. By causing Mr. Mole to say 'Frogs!' and 'Waterloo!' to M. Bolivant, the French master, he succeeded in making these excitable gentlemen fight in front of the class. Then the Head, Mr. Crawcour, entered and the fun really started:
>
> 'What is this?' exclaimed Mr. Crawcour. 'Mr. Mole with his fists clenched and Mr. Bolivant on his back. Disgraceful! How can you expect boys to be orderly when they have such a bad example? Gentlemen, I am ashamed of you!'
>
> 'Shut up', said Jack making his voice come from the senior master. . . .

Such practical joking is, like **"The Open Window"**, an entertaining fantasy but it is also symptomatic of a fascination with the domination of the adult world by a preternaturally powerful child.

That extraordinary children have a peculiar attraction and meaning for Saki is immediately evident on reading a cross-section of his stories. Munro's own early life has provided grounds for comparison with Thackeray, Kipling, and Dickens, writers "who never [shook] off the burden of their childhood." Munro was born in Burma, taken to England after his mother's death, when he was around two years old, and was raised by a household of women at Broadgate Villa in Pilton, North Devon. Drake writes of his childhood home: "This establishment was presided over during [Hector's father] Major Munro's nearly perpetual absence in the East by his mother and his two sisters, Charlotte ('Aunt Tom') and Augusta, fierce spinster ladies who ruled with an authoritarian hand and whom Saki depicted again and again in his stories with a mixture of hatred and affection." Greene emphasizes Munro's unhappy childhood in relation to his writings, and Drake, with some reservations, makes the point too: "It is tempting . . . to see in Saki the boy who never grew up, avenging himself on his aunts and possibly his sisters."

To connoisseurs of Saki, the idea of an avenging boy brings the story **"Sredni Vashtar"** immediately to mind. Conradin, a boy of ten, suffers under the dominion of his guardian, Mrs. De Ropp. To him "she represented those three-fifths of the world that are necessary and disagreeable and real; the other two-fifths, in perpetual antagonism to the foregoing, were summed up in himself and his imagination. One of those days Conradin supposed he would succumb to the mastering pressure of wearisome necessary things—such as illnesses and coddling restrictions and drawn-out dullness. Without his imagination, which was rampant under the spur of loneliness, he would have succumbed long ago." In a forgotten toolshed in the garden Conradin keeps two pets, a Houdan hen and a large polecat. The polecat, named Sredni Vashtar by the boy, becomes the center of his imaginative life and the object of his worship. When Mrs. De Ropp discovers the hen and abruptly sells it, Conradin scarcely reacts, but he prays to his god, " 'Do one thing for me, Sredni Vashtar.' " That one unspecified thing is done when Mrs. De Ropp, having found the key to the hutch, visits the shed to clear out what she supposes to be guinea pigs. Conradin scarcely dares to hope, but when, under his watchful eyes, the "Woman" does not emerge from the shed after a long interval but, instead, the beast, with "dark wet stains around the fur of jaws and throat", he luxuriously toasts and butters for himself a piece of bread, while the distraught servants below debate how to break the news to the "poor child". Mrs. De Ropp is so mean and philistine a woman that the story evokes no sympathy for her; on the contrary, the narrator's sympathies, as reserved and implicit as they are, side entirely with Conradin.

In **"The Boar-Pig"**, the child Matilda entraps two Society ladies who, lacking invitations, are trying to join "the garden party of the season" surreptitiously through the back yard, by loosing Tarquin, the boar-pig, in the paddock where he hinders retreat. Matilda is herself being detained away from the party as a punishment because she had force-fed her overly well-behaved cousin Claude in order to disprove the adults' assertion that "Claude never eats too much raspberry trifle". The intruders gain their freedom only after paying a cleverly extorted bribe to their young prison-keep.

Of the stories which pit child against adult, Philip Stevick has singled out **"The Lumber Room"** as being "remarkable as a complex and self-consistent chain of Freudian imagery". He writes [in his essay "Saki's Beasts" in *English Literature in Transition, 1880-1920,* 1966]:

> Nicholas, a small boy, is denied a trip to the shore because he has put a frog into his bread and milk. The act is no more bizarre than a good many similar acts in other Saki stories. And it serves the fictional purpose of showing that the adults, who all along had insisted that there could not be a frog in the bowl, were wrong and Nicholas was right. Saki describes Nicholas as being "in disgrace", as having "sinned", and suf-

fering from "depravity"—all of this suggesting the absurd values and the hypocrisy of the adult world.

Nicholas is forbidden to enter the gooseberry garden; by pretending to want to enter it he keeps the attention of his aunt focused on the 'forbidden paradise' while he explores the also off-limit lumber room, where he finds a wealth of treasures, especially a tapestry depicting a hunter who has just shot a stag. When the aunt, suspecting Nicholas' long absence, goes to search for him in the garden, she falls into a rain-water tank, and Nicholas, slyly tricking her into revealing that she has told a lie, pretends that she is the Devil and refuses to rescue her. Stevick in his reading of **"The Lumber Room"** dwells on the conflict between "a precocious child and a repressive adult".

In **"Sredni Vashtar"**, **"The Boar-Pig"**, and **"The Lumber Room"**, children of extraordinary sensitivity and imagination are oppressed and confined by narrow-minded, unimaginative adults, and assert themselves through some 'perverse' but effective countermeasure: in **"Sredni Vashtar"**, the imaginative elevation of an animal into a deity; in **"The Boar-Pig"**, a form of practical joke; in **"The Lumber Room"** the frustration of adult authority by outwitting it and by a selective literal obedience.

That the Victorian world of Munro's youth might provoke a child to more than ordinary rebellion is confirmed by a pattern too broad to ignore: [Graham Greene, in his introduction to *The Best of Saki*] points out the close parallel to **"Sredni Vashtar"** in the following passage:

> Kipling described the horror . . . in *Baa, Baa Black Sheep*—a story in spite of its sentimentality almost unbearable to read: Aunt Rosa's prayers, the beatings, the card with the word LIAR pinned upon his back, the growing and neglected blindness, until at last came the moment of rebellion.
>
> "If you make me do that", said Black Sheep very quietly, "I shall burn this house down and perhaps I will kill you. I don't know whether I can kill you—you are so bony, but I will try."
>
> No punishment followed this blasphemy, though Black Sheep held himself ready to work his way to Auntie Rosa's withered throat and grip there till he was beaten off.

One might add *Stalky & Co.* as an illustration of the battle between children and boorish adults. Samuel Butler's *The Way of All Flesh* depicts a cruelty and stupidity in the treatment of children which seems almost incredible today. Peter Coveney writes in *The Image of Childhood* that "the book contains a whole phase of English family development, and stands as an indictment of a whole epoch of English behavior towards children."

But it need not have been physical cruelty that incited Saki to create his rebellious children. Hector's sister Ethel Munro's assertion that "he and his brother and I managed to have a happy and often very amusing childhood", in reaction to Greene's conjectures, does not suffice to counteract the suspicion that Hector suffered an oppression which can be worse than the infliction of physical punishment:

the oppression of loveless prigs, of jejune and arbitrary petty tyrants. Katharine West, writing about Saki's portrayals of governesses [in her *Chapter of Governesses: A Study of the Governess in English Fiction, 1800-1949*], says: "Neglect stimulates resource; and a child brought up in a mental prison may (like Saki himself) fight its way to intellectual freedom." The adult world is overwhelmingly unattractive in Saki's work; the heroes of his stories—Reginald, Clovis, Comus—remain adolescents. Like Peter Pan, they dread the thought of growing up: Mr. Darling, the father figure in *Peter Pan* ("a good man as bread-winners go"), is part of the dreary adult world: "In the city where he sits on a stool all day, as fixed as a postage stamp, he is so like all the others on stools that you recognize him not by his face but by his stool, but at home the way to gratify him is to say that he has a distinct personality." It is no wonder Comus in *The Unbearable Bassington* does not marry and dies young, out in the colonies. When Comus, a handsome, irresponsible, cruelly compassionless boy, is still in boarding school, he and other boys like him are discussed by two of his masters: " 'They never do grow up,' said the housemaster; 'that is their tragedy. Bassington will certainly never grow out of his present stage.' 'Now you are talking in the language of Peter Pan', said the form-master. 'I am not thinking in the manner of Peter Pan', said the other." As Maurice Baring has pointed out [in his introduction to *The Unbearable Bassington*], neither does Saki think in the manner of Peter Pan. Saki never romanticizes childhood; the terrain of *Lord of the Flies* is closer to his fictional territory than Barrie's Never Land.

Perhaps one of the best clues to the source of the antagonism towards adult life in Saki can be found in the story **"The Mappined Life"**. It begins as a casual conversation between Mrs. Gurtleberry and her niece about the new terraces at the zoo which are intended to give the animals the illusion of being in their natural surroundings. The niece paints a view of what the world might look to a wild animal, in a manner similar to Virginia Woolf's *Flush*, then sets the caged life in contrast. Mrs. Gurtleberry finds her conclusion depressing; but her niece has an even more depressing commentary to make. " 'We are able to live our unreal, stupid little lives on our particular Mappin terrace, and persuade ourselves that we are really untrammeled men and women leading a reasonable existence in a reasonable sphere.' " To the aunt's protests, the niece replies, "We are trammeled by reasons of income and opportunity, and above all by lack of initiative . . . lack of initiative is the thing that really cripples one, and that is where you and I and Uncle James are so hopelessly shut in. We are just so many animals stuck down on a Mappin terrace, with this difference in our disfavour, that the animals are there to be looked at, while nobody wants to look at us." She very effectively details the lack of initiative and the drabness of their life, the exaggerated importance that trivialities such as the number of blossoms on the Gurtleberrys' magnolia bush and Mr. Gurtleberry's gossip at the tobacconist's assume. The niece does not spare herself: "Nearly everything about me is conventional make-believe. I'm not a good dancer, and no one could honestly call me good-looking, but when I go to one of our dull little local dances I'm conventionally supposed to 'have a

heavenly time', to attract the ardent homage of the local cavaliers, and to go home with my head awhirl with pleasurable recollections. As a matter of fact, I've merely put in some hours of indifferent dancing, drunk some badly-made claret cup, and listened to an enormous amount of laborious light conversation. A moonlight hen-stealing raid with the merry-eyed curate would be infinitely more exciting; imagine the pleasure of carrying off all those white minorcas the Chibfords are always bragging about." But she knows she will not go on any moonlight hen-stealing raids; she predicts a dull, decorous, and undistinguished future for herself. Even such a minor adventure is beyond the limits of her life; that is the curse of life, and when Mr. Gurtleberry enters with a typical inane remark about the political situation in Albania such as his niece has exposed for its empty self-importance, even Mrs. Gurtleberry acknowledges the truth of the matter by bursting into tears.

"The Open Window" certainly supports S. P. B. Mais' claim, made in 1920 [in *Books and Their Writers*], that "Munro's understanding of children can only be explained by the fact that he was in many ways a child himself; his sketches betray a harshness, a love of practical jokes . . . a lack of mellow geniality that hint very strongly at the child in the man." Framton Nuttel unquestionably belongs to the vapid adult world of the Gurtleberrys, but unlike Mrs. Gurtleberry's niece, Vera of **"The Open Window"** has not acquiesced to this world. Vera's practical joke is of a kind with the moonlight hen-stealing raid, which remains after all only the fantasy of Mrs. Gurtleberry's niece. Vera not only rejects but completely—and one might say, maliciously—dominates the feeble representative of adult life who crosses her path. (pp. 5-8)

> John Daniel Stahl, "Saki's Enfant Terrible in 'The Open Window'," in The USF Language Quarterly, *Vol. XV, Nos. 3-4, Spring-Summer, 1977, pp. 5-8.*

Miriam Quen Cheikin (essay date 1978)

[*In the following essay, Cheikin examines Saki's use of practical jokes as comic devices in his short stories.*]

" 'I love people who do unexpected things.' " This impertinent assertion by the hero of the **"Innocence of Reginald"** strikes the theme that is to be a constant in the short stories of Saki. From his first collection of short stories in 1904 to his last, published in 1924, the heroes and heroines of H. H. Munro (who assumed the name of "Saki") both "do" and "say" the unexpected. Presented either in the form of a startling word or an outrageous practical joke, the unexpected is a predictable delight for the devoted followers of Saki. Indeed, Saki's special mark, the device that cleverly captures the ingredients necessary to comedy is his use of the practical joke. Although this device has appeared before in literature, notably in Greek literature, in Chaucer and in Shakespeare, the complexity and the extent to which it is used makes it idiosyncratic to Saki. In addition, an examination of how the practical joke is used to create comedy in these short stories reflects some light on the nature of comic fiction and on the nature of comedy itself.

Although few critics have been concerned with the talents of H. H. Munro, those who have expressed interest, with few exceptions, have referred to the use of the practical joke as a manifestation of Saki's "lost childhood," of his never having grown up. Coupling this story device to his interest in children, animals and the supernatural, he is condemned to the role of a Peter Pan. Edith H. Walton mentions in a review of short stories that Saki had a "quality of mind akin to the casual heartlessness of a child." Even in an extremely appreciative essay like that of S. P. B. Mais [in his *Books and Their Writers*], the same note is sounded. Mais concludes that Munro was a child himself, "the irresponsibility and the harsh cruelty of children fully developed in him." In the same vein Alexander Porterfield, whose essay in 1925 tried to analyze Munro's art and place in literary history, called his humor the "non-moral humor of a child." V. S. Pritchett called him a "performing lynx," while Graham Greene reenforced these sentiments by claiming that Munro learned cruelty from his childhood, "a cruelty that is the source of his strength and his humor." There has been a failure to see that the practical joke, an apparently childish trick, is deliberately chosen by Saki because it can be put to such effective use in creating comedy.

Perhaps in an attempt to mitigate the conclusion that Munro's themes and devices are childish, more recent criticism deals with Munro's critical attitude toward the follies of mankind by focusing on his satirical bent. This serves to give an aura of seriousness to work that has been described as one of "exquisite lightness . . . that offers no grasp for the solemnities of earnest criticism." In 1959 Pritchett called Munro more than a "sub-Wildean drawing-room satirist," comparing him to Orwell as a social commentator while recognizing him as an "economical and accomplished comedian." Robert Drake, whose three articles on H. H. Munro are a major contribution, sees Munro is "dead earnest dramatizing his individual perception of man's plight." Drake compares Munro's humor to the standards set by Bergson as "corrective" and "normative." Charles H. Gillen's *H. H. Munro,* an extremely useful survey, alludes to these ideas, but his method is basically descriptive, rather than analytical. George Spears, as the name of his book *The Satire of Saki* indicates, attempts to relegate Saki to the solitary role of a satirist, overlooking the complexity of Munro's focus. Munro, despite all these assertions, is not a satirist—his interests are elsewhere.

The attempt to classify Munro as a satirist, however, merits a pause because it points us, through indirection, to that quality of his work that makes for his unique contribution to the comic art. Although Munro's stories are saturated with criticism of British high society and often have a satiric tone, they are not satires because his interest centers on the people, not on the exposure of follies. In satire the awareness of the vast separation between what is and what should be evokes feelings of anger or bitterness; the satirist displays his wares to arouse us to the need for reform rather than acceptance, contempt rather than plea-

sure. In contrast, comedy, although it arouses our intellectual awareness that human life often falls short of expectation, tends to surround man with an aura of acceptance. Comedy balances itself between humor's loving embrace of mankind and satire's bitter and hostile thrust, and it is the realm of comedy that is Saki's domain. For example, Saki's **"Reginald on Besetting Sins"** plays with the reversal of the commonplace that one should not lie, just as "A Modest Proposal" reverses the universally accepted idea that infants should be protected and cherished. Swift's essay is a satire because the interest is centered on the idea, first and foremost. In the Saki story, the focus is on the woman's behavior and how she unsuccessfully tries to resist telling the truth, to her utter undoing. Saki chooses to make it comic rather than satiric by focusing on the character while making the importance of the idea secondary.

Another useful example is Saki's **"Louise,"** in which Jane "misplaces" her niece while shopping and is trying to remember all the stops she made:

> "Fortunately, I didn't go to any place of devotion, although I did get mixed up with a Salvation army procession. It was quite interesting to be at close quarters with them, they're so absolutely different to what they used to be when I first remember them in the eighties. They used to go about then unkempt and dishevelled, in a sort of smiling rage with the world, and now they're spruce and jaunty and flamboyantly decorative, like a geranium bed with religious convictions."

Although philanthropic organizations are being satirized, the focus is on the scatterbrained Jane, whose thought processes are random and flyaway. The stories that are primarily satires in Saki's last collections, such as **"The Purple of the Balkan Kings"** in *Toys of Peace* and **"The Infernal Parliament"** in *The Square Egg,* are forced. Munro's interest is in people primarily, not ideas, political or social; consequently, his forays into pure satire are almost consistently unsuccessful.

In effect, Munro has been called a "satirist" as an indication that he has a critical attitude. He has been called a "humorist" to indicate that he makes us laugh. When his work is correctly described as "comedy," the word is often merely a casual catch-all to indicate anything that is "funny." There are many sources of comedy in the stories, including witty dialogue, clever plots with endings that often set our expectations on end, and amusing characters with improbable names. The freshness of Saki's wit, particularly in the early collections of **Reginald** and **Reginald in Russia,** parallels Wilde's best efforts; he could have based his success on witty dialogue and commentary. Graham Greene recognized this when he pointed out that "Reginald and Clovis are children of Wilde. The epigrams, the absurdities fly unremittingly back and forth, they dazzle and delight." The wit, by taking us unawares and upsetting our conventional expectations in the choice of words, functions as do the sudden turns in the plot, or the unexpected endings. Running through the stories are the other essentials of comedy, including the unexpected, the incongruous, and the action that breaks the rules of decorum. The characters are entertaining, but rarely sympathetic enough to engage our "gut" feelings; the reader mimics Munro's detached manner, a manner that reflects his lack of emotional involvement. The short story form lends itself to comedy because it minimizes the problem of sustaining the light tone, a concern of longer comic fiction. It allows the author to sketch out his situations and characters rapidly, point his comic gun, fire and leave the scene. No matter how threatening the twists of the plot in Saki's stories become, there are usually no serious consequences, another essential of comedy.

The most casual reading of Saki's words, therefore, shows that he had many means by which he could effectively produce comedy other than the practical joke. It must be concluded that Munro uses the strategem of the practical joke with great calculation; it does not issue from childishness nor from an inability to use other devices. In the two most successful collections, *The Chronicles of Clovis* and *Beasts and Super-Beasts,* H. H. Munro's inclination toward wit and his critical acumen are rendered through the medium of the practical joke, a device that almost becomes a personal comic convention. Noting the superficial smoothness of the life of the upper classes, the monotony of house parties and luncheons, the witty dialogue that is a game instead of communication, he uses the practical joke to explore the still surface of life—to reveal the incongruities that lie underneath. This artifice provides the diversion and excitement necessary to break through the texture of ennui that permeated Munro's social world. At the same time, the practical joke, as used by Saki had all the essentials of comedy. Saki states his intentions in using the practical joke very succinctly in **"The Mappined Life"**:

> "We are trammelled," said the niece, calmly and pitilessly, "by restriction of income and opportunity, and above all by lack of initiative."
>
> "It's the dreadful little everyday acts of pretended importance that give the Mappin stamp to our life . . . a moonlight hen-stealing raid with the merry-eyed curate would be infinitely more exciting."

For some, life is not sufficiently comic. While most comedy reveals incongruity, reveals reversals of expectation and violations of decorum, some comedy *creates rather than reveals:* this is true of the practical joke. Freud recognized this when he asserted that the need to create the comic is essential to mankind: "mankind has not been content to enjoy the comic where they have come upon it in their experience; they have sought to bring it about intentionally." This is exactly what Saki is doing. His practical jokes are a parody of life, an aggressive impersonation of life that deflates pretence. When Saki set up a practical joke he is demonstrating the incongruity of life, forcing it into the open where it must be seen and recognized. In **"The She-Wolf,"** when a guest claims that he can change a person into a wolf, Clovis brings in an actual wolf, pretending that the guest has been successful. It is a demonstration of absurdity. When Bertie's mother is fearful that her son is involved in romantic intrigues in **"Shock Tactics,"** Clovis turns the fear into reality by sending incriminating notes to Bertie that the mother intercepts. Again, by dramatizing the absurdity, by demonstrating it in action, Munro has flushed this absurdity into the open where

it is exposed and must be confronted. James Feibleman explains [in his *In Praise of Comedy*] that customs and institutions become accepted by virtue of their having existed over a period of time, but that "comedians soon correct this error in estimation, by actually demonstrating the forgotten limitations of all actuals." Saki, in effect, is using the practical joke in "demonstrating" or revealing something beneath the surface, or as Freud expressed it, "jokes must bring forward something that is concealed or hidden."

In addition, Saki's practical jokes are an act of creation that we witness unfolding, that we create with him almost simultaneously, or just a step behind. There is a burst of understanding when we realize what he is up to and that flash of perception, that small explosion of insight, gives us pleasure. The essence of these momentary perceptions is a bubble-like quality—a sparkle and a burst. The next insight comes, a pause and then the next explodes. Comedy seems to be make up of flashes of perception, small explosions of insight.

In *Jokes and Their Relation to the Unconscious* Freud explains that we derive pleasure from the activity of our minds, that joking "is an activity which aims at deriving pleasure from mental processes, whether intellectual or otherwise." It is interesting to note that this aspect of Freud's analysis of the mental pleasure derived from jokes has been largely ignored, while the aspects of relieved hostility and repression have become almost a commonplace. Freud pointed out very clearly that the sensation we derive from comedy is pleasure, and that the source is often the pleasure of using the mind. Koestler [in his *Act of Creation*] points out that "every good joke contains an element of the riddle . . . which the listener must solve." He goes on to say that in effect we are repeating "the process of inventing the joke, to recreate it in our imagination." While we are usually aware of better known aspects of comedy, such as Hobbes' moment of superiority, or "sudden glory," or Bergson's theory of comic man as mechanism, we forget the mental aspect of comedy. Recent studies in humor have shown that "getting the joke" is the real source of pleasure in humor. "The sudden discovery achieved by the reshuffling of the symbols and meanings into a surprisingly new relationship is the source of gratification."

Saki's unique practical jokes provide this high level of challenge to our intellect. The involvement of our mental processes would be impossible if Saki's practical jokes were on a level with the garden-variety practical joke. A bucket of water poised over a doorway to douse the unwary victim is hardly a joke that gives the sensible reader a jolt of understanding. Our intellectual processes must be engaged at the proper level for comedy to exist. Some people do find the joke of the bucket variety worthy of a good chuckle, but in a recent study of children's responses in humor, it was demonstrated that "the mirth response is greatest when the complexity of the child's cognitive structure is congruent." One study concludes that "as the development of the intelligence of these children matures, they demanded increasingly more difficult humorous stimuli for maximum appreciation." As the sophisticated reader is evidently responsive to Saki's practical jokes, his creations are ones that engage us intellectually.

There is no doubt that the urbane population has long considered the ordinary practical joke as the basest, least intellectual type of humor. Even George Eliot, never one to be associated with humor, takes a few lines in an essay to express disdain: "it is impossible to deny a high degree of humour to many practical jokes, but no sympathetic nature can enjoy them." Munro makes good comic use of this commonplace opinion, using it to build his effect, laying brick upon brick, into a massive comic structure. The foundation of this structure is the usual idea that this device is somewhat vulgar, and, therefore, indecorous. Upon this foundation Saki violates expectations by having the joke perpetrated by the super-sophisticated in the super-sophisticated setting that makes up his landscape (in effect, we watch the highjinks of practical jokes in high society). The effectiveness is further multiplied by having the person responsible for the deviltry the one least likely to be involved. By this means, the comic build-up becomes geometric in its effect rather than merely additive.

Often these jokes are devised by adolescents or children; Feibleman explains that "comedy is continual rebellion and a refusal, even when faced with the inability to change conditions, to accept the compromises meted out by actuality." Rebellion and a refusal to compromise are certainly characteristic of young people. These precocious youngsters understand the machinations of the adult world despite their age; they "see into the life of things" and set their bombs effectively. When the ruse is devised by an adult, as in **"The Schartz-Metterklume Method,"** the behavior is indecorous for an adult, upsetting expectations as to how the adult world functions. In addition, there is a disparity between what appears to be happening and what is actually happening. The joke is a "set-up," so that what appears on the surface results from reasons that are unsuspected and unexpected. Since incongruity, upended expectations and violations of decorum are essential to comedy, the device of the practical joke works.

As mentioned previously, essential to the comic mode is the understanding that no dire consequence will result despite the threatening nature of events, compared to tragedy in which the catastrophic is inevitable. As Cyrus Hoy expresses it [in his *The Hyacinth Room*], "through all the modes of comedy, life is proceeding, by fair means and by foul." In Saki's short stories this assurance of survival is achieved partially through our awareness that we are witnessing a comedy within a comedy. The Puck figure senses and seizes an irresistible opportunity and develops the idea before the eyes of the reader, literally controlling the actions of the characters through the manipulation of events. In **"The Unrest-Cure,"** despite the horrible idea of massacring all the Jews, we are really watching Clovis mastermind his elaborate scheme, therefore being assured that nothing dangerous will occur. The very elaborateness of the scheme, the details of working it out, help to keep that essential confidence. The preposterous extreme of the plan also serves to make us feel safe, assuring us that nothing dire can come of it. Clovis is in total control, satisfying that essential of comedy—the promise of survival. Not for

one moment do we doubt that Clovis can manipulate, trick and outsmart any adult in existence. We trust Clovis, if we have read the canon, and do not fear the ending. Survival is the outcome for both Clovis and his victim. The deceiver, it has been pointed out, "must be in a position not only to gratify his desires, but to escape the odium which gratification might ordinarily be expected to bring."

The role of observer of a creation, of a comedy within a comedy, helps satisfy another demand of comedy—that of sufficient distance from the subjects and the events so that the emotions are not really engaged. Elmer Blistein, in discussing comedy in the drama, explains [in his *Comedy in Action*] that the reason we can tolerate "the representation of a cruel act on the stage is that it is at least two, and probably three removes from reality." If the emotions are engaged by empathy, sympathy or fear of dire consequences, the intellectual perception is not objective enough; when emotions intrude, comedy vanishes. This intellectual distancing, however, does not mean indifference. We are amused, entertained and often amazed at the cleverness of the irreverent figures of Saki, but they do not touch our emotions deeply. The characters who are at the wrong end of the tricks are usually deserving of some sort of punishment, so we do not care, particularly as the perpetrator gives us no clue as to his deeper emotions. Our response is primarily an intellectual one—an appreciation of cleverness.

H. H. Munro's ingeniously wrought schemes fall into three categories that often overlap in part, if not totally. The first group is made up of conspiracies that drum up sheer fun. Included in this category are stories such as **"Reginald's Christmas Revels,"** a story in which a note is changed on a house guest's door to mislead others into thinking that she has suicidal plans; Reginald then retires to his room while all bedlam breaks loose. **"The Open Window,"** a favorite of anthologists, is certainly one of the best examples. A young girl convinces a visitor that her aunt is crazy and that her uncle and cousins will return as ghosts simply because "romance at short notice was her speciality." These stories appear to be a creation of exuberant animal spirits with no concrete motivation for the prank.

The second group is distinguished from the first in that the ingenious schemes in these stories have a definite end in mind. In some ways they are more tricks than practical jokes. Clovis, in **"The Stampeding of Lady Bastable,"** determined to make a visit with his mother, tricks Lady Bastable into believing that her worst fears have been realized—the masses have revolted and are attacking the aristocracy. Lady Bastable is so upset that she makes Clovis leave, which is exactly what he had in mind. In **"The Lull,"** the problem of keeping a politician's mind off the coming election is solved by convincing him that the house is surrounded by flood waters; he is given a rooster and a pig to keep in his room to safeguard them from the rising waters. The device works; the politician, with a pig and a rooster squabbling in his room, has no time to think of the oncoming election. Robert Drake suggests [in his essay "The Sauce for the Asparagus"] that "this is where the real humour of Saki lies—in the paradox that the rational solution is what seems the most irrational and lies in what is furthest from 'conventional' thought and behavior." In this group of stories, the problem is solved through manipulation of a situation in the most improbable manner. Although the reason for the practical jokes may differ from that of the first group, merrymaking, the methods are equally as outrageous.

In the third group of stories the role of the perpetrator of the practical joke changes to that of a punishing agent, or perhaps an agent of justice. The contrivance is as astonishing as in the other groups, but someone is punished in the process. When Reginald, in **"Reginald on House Parties,"** is the butt of ridicule because of his inability to bag any game, he shoots a treasured peacock to prove he can shoot. In **"The Boar-Pig,"** two women trying to crash a garden party are tricked by a young child into believing that they are trapped by a fierce boar-pig. They are both embarrassed and infuriated, but they are also clearly in the wrong. People who come to parties uninvited, hosts who mock their guests, are acting improperly and deserve to be punished.

In **"The Boar-Pig,"** another aspect of Saki's use of the practical joke as comic device comes more clearly into focus. The incongruity lies not only in the situation, but in the child's teaching and avenging herself through punishing the adult. The reversal of the child-adult role provokes a smile; it upsets our expectations, upsets the rules of proper decorum. Almost all the stories concerning Reginald and Clovis, boys in their adolescence, make use of this reversal to produce comedy. Additionally, our sympathies are not stirred because the victims are invariably pompous authority figures.

The three groups of stories often overlap combining sheer fun with trickery and punishment. In **"Shock Tactics,"** Clovis helps trick Bertie's mother so that she is cured of going through his mail. It is a trick in that a particular goal is specified; it is punishment in that Bertie's mother is made justly distraught and it is, of course, pure fun in the letters that Clovis directs, knowing that the prying mother will open them:

> "So you really have done it," the letter abruptly commenced; "Poor Dagmar. Now she is done for I almost pity her. You did very well, you wicked boy, the servants all think it was suicide, and there will be no fuss. Better not touch the jewels till after the inquest."

In **"The Occasional Garden,"** a woman driven to distraction by a neighbor's overbearing pride in her garden avenges herself by hiring a commercial outfit which makes instant exotic gardens. The neighbor is beside herself as she has been bettered by the formerly inept gardener. The neighbor, tricked by a garden shipped in for the occasion, is justly punished.

Punishment and trickery are not necessarily inimical to comedy, although they could have dire consequences. It is Saki's use of them that makes them comic. In all three groups, the pranks, the tricks and the enactments of punishment, there is a perpetrator and a victim. Blistein feels that both are essential to comedy, because we need some-

one to laugh with, such as Clovis or Reginald, and someone to laugh at, the hapless recipient of the perpetrator's ingenuity—the victim.

> The emotions that we seek to purge in comedy are those of scorn and mockery. We do not scorn, we cannot mock, the sympathetic comic character. We certainly are able to scorn and to mock the comic antagonist, the comic villain . . . For we can seldom, unless we are blind, feel superior to the sympathetic comic character; we can always feel superior to the comic antagonist.

We must feel that the antagonist has suffered no serious harm, Blistein is quick to add, so that the comic mode is not upset. Saki's use of the practical joke satisfies all these particulars by providing a "sympathetic" comic character and a "comic antagonist," and a safe landing for all.

The world that Munro inhabited was staid, self-satisfied and inflated with its own importance. The practical jokes served to deflate the importance of the people and rearrange the components of the world, although only temporarily. As Feibleman suggests, "the corrosive effect of humour eats away the solemnity of accepted evaluation, and thus calls for a revaluation of values." Munro places a colorful rocket in the middle of a stuffy, safe world and watches the fireworks that are sheer fun, sometimes punishing, sometimes corrective (*a la* Bergson's theory that comedy is corrective) but always startling and stimulating. And the reader cheers him on.

There are some important considerations that help explain Saki's success in turning us into accomplices rather than antagonists. Freud explains that in order to laugh at certain jokes we must be able to recognize what he calls the naive: "we must know that the internal inhibition is absent in the producing person. Only when this is certain do we laugh instead of being indignant." Saki's schemers are far from naive or innocent in the ordinary sense because even the children are extremely worldly and understanding of the "ways of the world," but in the sense that these characters consistently exhibit a lack of "internal inhibition" they function as if they were naive. Such "impossible young men as Reginald and Clovis seem (in the eyes of the 'proper people') to be bound by no scruples, no repressions or inhibitions." Not for one moment do they feel guilt or shame. The question of right or wrong simply does not occur to them; therefore, it does not occur to the reader. The reader allows himself to laugh at the intriguers because they supposedly function spontaneously and without inhibition, as children do. Comedy's only concern, according to [Joseph Meeker in his *The Comedy of Survival*], is a confirmation of man's ability to survive and a celebration of the continuity of life itself, despite all moralities.

Another vital reason that explains the humor in Saki's use of the practical joke is suggested by W. H. Auden: "a man asserts his freedom because the law he has disobeyed is an important one." It has been pointed out that "humor is the product of the imagination through creation of a 'humor illusion' wherein the rules of logic, time, place, reality and proper conduct are momentarily suspended." This statement is clearly derived from Freud's thesis that what is comic is usually tending towards the infantile. In other words, in thinking like a child we can escape the constraints of rationality and logic. Jokes are a comfortable way to relieve the pressures of being realistic and moral. Since our hostile impulses have been repressed by societal pressures, we can see that by utilizing "joke techniques we can re-establish old liberties and get rid of the burden of intellectual upbringing; they are psychical reliefs," as expressed by Freud.

Perhaps the critics who accuse Saki of behaving in a childish manner are right for the wrong reason; they use the expression as a pejorative. When Freud says that for *all* mankind the comic is in search to "re-establish" the old liberties of childhood, then for *all* men "the comic arises from the uncovering of a mode of thought that is exclusively proper to the unconscious." The critics who fail to include themselves and all of us in the childish aspects of comedy are perhaps denying their own desires to break the restriction of reason and critical judgments, denying their own desire to recapture the mood of their childhood.

When the reader allows himself to respond instinctively, delighting in the opportunity to vent hostility in a joke that cannot harm anyone, then the practical joke works effectively as a comic device in the stories of H. H. Munro. What could be safer than a joke on a printed page? We enjoy, vicariously, a lifting of inhibition and display of animosity with no sense of guilt.

As the comic is a mode of thought derived from the unconscious, another reason for the success of the practical joke in creating comedy becomes increasingly apparent. Munro's characters plan their elaborate designs with a spontaneity that suggests a direct communication with the unconscious. The unfolding of the device is most successful aesthetically when it appears to arise mysteriously without undue thought, like the impulse of a child. In one of Munro's best stories, **"The Unrest-Cure,"** Clovis' idea for injecting some variety into the lives of the Huddles seems to be almost instinctive. When Mrs. Huddle's friend suggests an "unrest-cure," he explains that this must be tried in the home, but offers no suggestion as to how this can be accomplished:

> It was at this point in the conversation that Clovis became galvanized into alert attention. After all, his two days' visit to an elderly relative at Slowborough did not promise much excitement. Before the train had stopped he had decorated his sinister shirt-cuff with the inscription, "J. P. Huddle, The Warren, Tilfield, near Slowborough."

The involved intricacies of the plot then unfold before our eyes as we observe Clovis' activities, but we do not know how the ideas developed; the joke, evidently, comes from the realm of the unconscious. The practical joker cares nothing for the horror that Mr. Huddle feels or the unbelievable lies that must be concocted. The reader, like Clovis, does not worry about right or wrong and becomes a child again doing exactly what he feels like doing for no reason other than a response to inner dictates. We laugh at Clovis' cleverness and respond with delight to the sense of freedom that we catch from the story. Poor Mr. Huddle

is not our concern because we know that nothing serious will happen to him.

The same technique of plunging into the scheme without warning is true of the other successful stories. In **"The Forbidden Buzzards,"** Clovis' friend asks him to keep a rival in love occupied so that he may propose marriage to a young lady. Clovis only promises, "I'll do my best for you, if the opportunity arises." Obviously there is no advance preparation, but an opportunity arises when his hostess suggests that his friend's rival, Mr. Lanner, has come down for particular reasons. Although she is referring to a marriage proposal, Clovis turns it around by suggesting that he is there to collect the eggs of the rough-legged buzzards, rare birds nesting on the manor. Clovis improvises:

> "Very few people know about them, but as a member of the league for protecting rare birds that information would be at his disposal. I came down in the train with him, and I noticed that a bulky volume of Dresser's *Birds of Europe* was one of the requisites that he had packed in his travelling kit. It was the volume dealing with short-winged hawks and buzzards."

> Clovis believed that a lie worth telling was worth telling well.

The hostess spends the day trailing Mr. Lanner to protect the birds, thereby effectively preventing the rival's success.

When the practical joke is set up with more overt planning, it is not as funny. Obviously, we respond the the spontaneity, to the freedom from inhibition. If the practical joke is contrived too self-consciously it becomes unsavory; when we have too much time to think our critical faculties come to the fore. Freud explains that "an awakening of the conscious intellectual interest usually makes the effect the joke impossible; a joke loses its effect of laughter as soon as [there is] an expenditure of intellectual work in connection with it." In **"For the Duration of War,"** the Rev. Gaskpilton has a wife whose intellectual reputation revolves around an English translation from the French that is always in process. He gets increasingly annoyed and it was "among the gooseberry bushes and beneath the medlar tree, that the temptation to the perpetration of a great literary fraud came to him." Munro has revealed a little too much. We know that there is a fraud planned, but we also know it is a literary fraud. The joy of discovery, the intellectual flash of recognition, is weakened as is the spontaneity of the action. This counteracts the comic in the practical joke. It evidently must be spontaneous, not premeditated, and it must be partially hidden so that we can enjoy the revelation.

For Saki the practical joke was far from a childish device; his unique contribution to the world of comedy was the method by which he manipulated these apparently simple tricks. The practical joke, for Saki, fulfilled the needs of comedy be revealing the incongruities that permeate our lives despite their silken surfaces. In its continual reversal of the expected or the probable and in its violation of decorum, the practical joke became for H. H. Munro the essence of comedy. Through the pleasure we derive from the activity of our minds, in our "getting the joke," from the delight in being free of the usual societal restrictions and repressions while vicariously enjoying the machinations of endlessly amusing characters, the practical jokes in Saki's stories give us the pleasurable sensations that we associate with comedy. The careful observer of the life-scene sees comedy all around him, sees the incongruities that provoke mirth and upset expectations. But for some, the comedy that life reveals is not enough, they need more:

> "But hang it all, my dear fellow," said Blenkinthrope impatiently, "haven't I just told you that nothing of a remarkable nature ever happens to me."
>
> "Invent something," said Gorworth.

And so Saki did. (pp. 121-31)

> *Miriam Quen Cheikin, "Saki: Practical Jokes as a Clue to Comedy," in* English Literature in Transition: 1880-1920, *Vol. 21, No. 2, 1978, pp. 121-31.*

Richard Harter Fogle   (essay date 1985)

[*Fogle is an American educator and critic whose work has focused on major figures of the Romantic movement in English and American literature. In the following excerpt, he examines major themes in Saki's short stories.*]

[Saki] is a romantic—in a simple version of romanticism, an escapist, a lover of the elemental, the strange, the exotic. He evidently doted on J. E. Flecker's *The Golden Journey to Samarkand* (see his story **"A Defensive Diamond"**): I do myself, but Flecker has undoubtedly been long overpassed. Saki's romanticism is a form of romantic irony: he craves the heart's desire, the lost Paradise. His intellect tells him that the Romantic Quest seeks impossibility, but he persists; World War I was his final quest, which he found, incredibly, romantic. His last word on reality is brief, too brief perhaps to bear great weight; it resembles the more persistent word of A. E. Housman in its unalterable rejection of all that is. The cat is Saki's favorite beast, and its glory is defiance: "it dies fighting to the last, quivering with the choking rage of mastered resistance, and voicing in its death-yell that agony of bitter remonstrance which human animals, too, have flung at the powers that may be; the last protest against a destiny that might have made them happy—and has not" (**"The Achievement of the Cat"**). (pp. 84-5)

[Saki's work] commences with the witty commentaries of "Reginald" on the London social scene, with an occasional look-in at country-house parties. He is Wildean, agreeably epicene, a dandy like the persona of Beerbohm's early prose, though a little more strident. Reginald is youth incarnate, and a comic figure; in Saki's pages he will not age. " 'To have reached thirty,' said Reginald, 'is to have failed in life,' " and he doesn't. He is wholly flippant, a characteristic brought out by interlocutors who are less so; he is, of course, the vehicle of Saki's wit, which develops into story through his interaction with them. He is charming, disarmingly selfish, and a rebel against the society to which he nevertheless firmly belongs; he knows the ropes too well to get in serious trouble. Some of his escapades,

always intentional and self-assertive, are outrageous, but he does not expose himself to real ostracism, only temporary coldness ("There was *rather* a breath of winter in the air when I left those Dorsetshire people.")

In this instance (**"Reginald on House-Parties"**) he has been invited for the shooting, at which he is inexpert: "And they tried to rag me in the smoking-room about not being able to hit a bird at five yards, a sort of bovine ragging that suggested cows buzzing around a gadfly and thinking they were teasing it." So he rises at dawn the next morning ("I know it was dawn, because there were larknoises in the sky, and the grass looked as if it had been left out all night"), and blazes away at the most conspicuous bird in sight, a peacock. "They said afterwards that it was a tame bird; that's simply *silly,* because it was awfully wild at the first few shots." He then has it dragged into the hall, where everybody must see it on the way to the breakfast room. "I breakfasted upstairs myself. I gathered afterwards that the meal was tinged with a very unchristian spirit. I suppose it's unlucky to bring peacock's feathers into a house; anyway, there was a blue-pencilly look in my hostess's eye when I took my departure."

The deed is horrific; it is clear that Reginald is guilty of deliberate "pavonicide," though he says not; and there is an added touch of demure perverseness in a particular touch: Reginald has remembered the jibe about hitting a bird at five yards, and has "measured the distance as nearly as it would let me." The *telling* of the deed is exquisite in its quiet precision, its undeviating pretense of innocence and gentleness. "What else," he seems to ask, "could I have done?"

Saki's "cruelty" is often mentioned; it is certainly responsible for some of his most striking effects. Reginald is his first comic protagonist, and most dominant in that the **Reginald** collection is wholly devoted to him. He is a shadowy figure compared to the later Clovis Sangrail, and the Reginald stories are slighter than those that came after, in which the "cruelty" theme is more noticeable. Yet we think first of Reginald when we think of Saki; he has a pristine freshness, a purer comic strain, self-delighting. One might find a parallel in another practitioner of cruelty, Evelyn Waugh, whose early *Decline and Fall* has a humor that exists for itself, unburdened by later responsibilities. To put the case differently, Saki had one hero, the brilliant and insouciant youth. Reginald is the prototype, and he is ever-young. Nothing can really touch him, he is as close to Paradise as a position in London society will permit. He is theoretically aware of the state of thirtyishness, but he will never reach it. His selfishness and insensitivity are attributes of youth, untouched by trouble, and his creator has endowed him with intelligence, taste, and enormous *savoir vivre*. This hero has no future; the later Clovis has some intimations of mortality. To see what Reginald would have become we go beyond the limits of the stories to a novel, *The Unbearable Bassington* (1912); Comus Bassington ends in dishonor, exile, and miserable death. He is not really Reginald, though; Reginald has never fallen.

The tales that celebrate him usually employ interlocutors. There are exceptions: the general theme is Reginald upon his world, and he sometimes monologizes on such topics as the Royal Academy, worries, house parties, besetting sins, and tariffs. Invariably, however, the presence of a listener is understood, even when silent, and there is always narrative, since he illustrates his mock-opinions with copious examples and anecdotes. At their simplest the Reginald stories are still tightly organized: apparent digressions are actually a device to display his inventiveness, and there are no loose ends. As structures they move from "turn" to "turn" without (since they are brief) relief or lapse, and conclude climactically with an O. Henry—like "snapper," a final twist at once relevant and surprising.

Thus in **"Reginald on Besetting Sins"** we have the sad example of "The Woman Who Told The Truth." "Not all at once, of course, but the habit grew upon her gradually, like lichen on an apparently healthy tree." Reginald kindly finds excuses: "her life was a rather empty one, and it is so easy to slip into the habit of telling the truth in little matters." The situation deteriorates, however, "until at last she took to telling the truth about her age; she said she was forty-two and five months—by that time, you see, she was veracious even to months. It may have been pleasing to the angels, but her elder sister was not gratified," and as a result gives her for her birthday a view of Jerusalem from the Mount of Olives, instead of the opera tickets she has hoped for. "The revenge of an elder sister may be long in coming, but, like a South-Eastern express, it arrives in its own good time."

Things go on worsening. "And after a while her friends began to thin out in patches. Her passion for the truth was not compatible with a large visiting list. For instance, she told Miriam Klopstock *exactly* how she looked at the Ilexes' ball. Certainly Miriam had asked for her candid opinion, but the Woman prayed in church every Sunday for peace in our time, and it was not consistent." She tries "to recall the artless mendacity of past days" with her prestigious and imperious dressmaker, but "habit had become too strong." As always, the result is disastrous. "Madame was not best pleased at being contradicted . . . , and when Madame lost her temper you usually found it afterwards in the bill."

The end arrives, capped by perhaps the most famous sentence in the Saki canon. "At last the dreadful thing came, as the Woman had foreseen all along that it must. . . . On a raw Wednesday morning, in a few ill-chosen words, she told the cook that she drank. . . . The cook was a good cook, as cooks go; and as cooks go she went." This would seem to be enough: turn after flashing, unexpected turn; but there is still the snapper, an added twist that tidies up one tiny piece of unfinished business. "Miriam Klopstock came to lunch the next day. Women and elephants never forget an injury."

The avenging Miriam appears in several stories, as a standard though presumably oversized member of Reginald's set. She "takes nines in voices," and "They had to stop her playing in the 'Macaw's' Hockey Club because you could hear what she thought when her shins got mixed up in a scrimmage for half a mile on a still day." As an interlocutor she is perhaps less significant than the also-recurrent Duchess because she calls forth fewer of Reginald's pow-

ers than that pretentious *grande dame* and is engaged chiefly in farce situations; in which, however, she is vigorous and entertaining. . . . [One] story pursues her, "poor Miriam Klopstock, who *would* take her Chow with her to the bathroom, and while she was bathing it was playing at she-bears with her garments. Miriam is always late for breakfast, and she wasn't really missed till the middle of lunch" (**"Reginald on Tariffs"**). This has its sequel: later on, Reginald plans a book of personal reminiscences, to the terror of most of his acquaintances, especially Miriam, who "began at once about the incident of the Chow dog in the bathroom, which she insisted must be struck out." He pretends to demur, at which she "snorted, 'You're not the boy I took you for,' as though she were an eagle arriving at Olympus with the wrong Ganymede" (**"The Innocence of Reginald"**). (pp. 85-8)

After **Reginald** the Munro collections vary in point of view. There is no strict progression, but in general the dominant figure is diffused into various storytellers in particular social situations, often glamorous. **Reginald in Russia** is appropriate only to the title story, since neither Reginald nor Russia appears again. Some others he could have told; some, such as **"The Blood-Feud of Toad-Water,"** do not fit him; a few are straight third person; and one, **"The Baker's Dozen,"** is arranged as a playlet. Taking the canon as a whole, there is *typically* a perceptible narrator, evident in confidential asides or engaged by an interlocutor. Saki does not use the framework of a general audience, as do Lord Dunsany in his Jorkins stories or Wodehouse at the Angler's Rest with Mr. Mulliner holding forth in the bar parlor. One might speculate that this device was so familiar that the fastidious Saki disdained it; and one cannot imagine a Saki audience that would sit still for a story; his atmosphere is too competitive. There would be Reginalds and Duchesses, or more exotically Baronesses and Gräfins, engrossed in outdoing each other. To return to **Reginald in Russia,** for various reasons it is the least homogeneous of the story collections of his lifetime; Munro's career as a political foreign correspondent distracted him, while at the same time he was developing as a writer. His increasing prestige made more space available to him in the journals and his stories grew longer, while his sense of the unifying narrator temporarily diminished.

To categorize Saki's tales is not particularly profitable. It might be possible to distinguish degrees of narrative development. Those who are interested in establishing his convictions could proceed by degrees of "seriousness," but very few of his stories are completely "straight," and these are least attractive. He was fond of allegorical sketches, usually political and topical; these appear occasionally from **Reginald in Russia** on. Their topicality dates them, along with their opinions—most of all the ones that derive from the Balkan wars of the early 1900s, of which Munro had firsthand experience as a correspondent on assignment. Concerning these he was most earnestly warlike, and his reminiscent **"The Cupboards of the Yesterdays"** (in **The Toys of Peace**) is one of his dullest productions.

To do them justice, these sketches are often witty and dramatic; they tend to be chiefly monologues, but with interlocutors who offer enough opposition to strike out sparks. It may be said, too, that as satirist it is Saki's function to attack the absurdities and illogicalities of all social and political life. He is not fond of activists of any kind, especially suffragettes, but their opposers do not escape unscathed either. His wit plays upon all society, even upon all civilization. In full narratives he is weakest when snobbish, as in **"The Wolves of Cernogratz"** (in *The Toys of Peace*), where it is evident that he has loved the *Almanach de Gotha* not wisely but too well, or in **"The Easter Egg"** (in *The Chronicles of Clovis*) too melodramatic, in which he commits the tactical error of being too respectful to a character both wise and courageous, Lady Barbara, whom he overexposes. The tale is perhaps prophetic as a serious treatment of propagandist terrorism, but it is well-known that people were planting bombs before World War I.

To venture a sweeping generalization, Saki's best and most characteristic short stories are founded on practical jokes. His youth had been full of them; in their embattled early years the Munro children had been severely repressed, and vented their explosiveness in their more privileged teens in elaborate and sometimes horrendous pranks, in which young Hector was an inventive leader. No doubt there are many psychological explanations, both simple and complex. The practical joke is an assertion; it may be revengeful and retributive, rebellious; an expression of superiority; a means of preserving threatened individuality; an act of aesthetic creation, pure and self-delighting; an embodiment of elemental and eternal disorder, like the medieval vice.

In the Saki tales there are many literal practical jokes: their general function is the preservation of flippancy against the threats of all conventional assumptions. They are particularly evident in the Reginald and Clovis collections: these young men are determined to take nothing seriously, to preserve their independence, and to master all conventional thinkers, whether sincere or, more frequently, hypocritical. (It is not always easy to distinguish.) On one memorable occasion (**"Reginald's Choir Treat"**), "the vicar's daughter undertook the reformation of Reginald" with considerable temporary success. At first repulsed by his pyrotechnic dialectics,

> Amabel began to realize that the battle is not always to the strong-minded. With the immemorial resource of her sex, she abandoned the frontal attack and laid stress on her unassisted labours in parish work, her mental loneliness, her discouragements—and at the right moment she produced strawberries and cream. Reginald was obviously affected by the latter, and when his preceptors suggested that he might begin the strenuous life by helping her to supervise the annual outing of the bucolic infants who composed the local choir, his eyes shone with the dangerous enthusiasm of a convert.

Unfortunately he is left to his own subversive devices: "The most virtuous women are not proof against damp grass, and Amabel kept her bed with a cold." After tricking them out of their clothes, he organizes the choristers into a Bacchanalian procession through the village, with the happy addition of "a he-goat from a neighbouring or-

chard. . . . " Properly, Reginald explained, "there should have been an outfit of panther skins; as it was, those who had spotted handkerchiefs were allowed to wear them, which they did with thankfulness." Of the tout ensemble he remarks mildly that "he had seen something like it in pictures; the villagers had seen nothing like it in their lives, and remarked as much freely." The effect on the unfortunate Amabel is left to the imagination, but "Reginald's family never forgave him. They had no sense of humour." (It is to be noted that he *has* a family, which is mentioned in several stories, but it seems to exist only to be helplessly scandalized by him.) Mythically Reginald is Bacchus, or Pan with his flair for Panics, or a Lord of Misrule; and his effect is enhanced by his imperturbable affectations of innocence, as in his account of his "pavonicide" in the similar tale of **"Reginald on Houseparties."** As a mortal he inflicts poetic justice on those who try to change his nature; in his defense it may be said that he protects his identity by leaving his attackers in confusion. To change would be to die—and from the point of view of his creator there would be an end to Reginald stories.

Saki's most famous practical joke is **"The Schartz-Metterklume Method"** (in *Beasts and Super-Beasts*), in which one Lady Carlotta is mistaken by an overbearing Mrs. Quabarl for the new governess she has come to meet at the railroad station.

> "You must be Miss Hope, the governess I've come to meet," said the apparition [Mrs. Quabarl], in a tone that admitted of very little argument.
>
> "Very well, if I must I must," said Lady Carlotta to herself with dangerous meekness.

The Quabarls are affluent social climbers with ill-based pretensions to position and culture; they are prepared to run roughshod over an expected docile and powerless governess for their young children. Lady Carlotta falls upon them like an avenging fury; she is the genuine social article, intrepid, intelligent, and endowed with a merciless sense of humor. In her brief stay with her employers she puts them utterly to rout. In her crowning exploit she resembles Reginald, a veritable deity of discord, or in Saki's words "a Goddess of Battles." She teaches history "on the Schartz-Metterklume method" of putting her charges to act out great events dramatically, and she chooses to start with the Rape of the Sabine Women, with explosive results. Interrupted ("Miss Hope, what on earth is the meaning of this scene?"), she explains: "Early Roman history; the Sabine women, don't you know? It's the Schartz-Metterklume method to make children understand history by acting it themselves; fixes it in their memory, you know. Of course, if, thanks to your interference, your boys go through life thinking that the Sabine women ultimately escaped, I really cannot be held responsible."

Dismissed, Lady Carlotta leaves further problems with the unhappy Quabarls: her (imaginary) luggage will need to be forwarded. "There are only a couple of trunks and some golf-clubs and a leopard cub," which is, according to her, actually "more than half-grown, you know. A fowl every day and a rabbit on Sundays is what it usually gets. Raw beef makes it too excitable." The arrival of the real governess causes "a turmoil which that good lady was quite unused to inspiring. Obviously the Quabarl family had been woefully befooled, but a certain amount of relief came with the knowledge."

As was earlier said, **"The Schartz-Metterklume Method"** is Saki's most famous joke, and there is a good deal more to say about the practical joke motif in his work—but first, a word about the story's special quality. Lady Carlotta herself is notable among Saki's women, more fully drawn than is usual in the tales; she is eccentric, powerful, and firmly moral, while she is also supremely witty, more so than a summary can reveal. She has more reverberations than most Saki characters; one is tempted to look for literary parallels, which he does not ordinarily evoke. In her case one might range from Dickens to Wilde, though as a *combination* she is unique. While relentless, she has no stain of cruelty; she does the Quabarls no actual harm, while she metes out comic retribution.

The Quabarls are of course fakes, and it is delightful to see them exposed. Yet the very completeness of their rout makes them objects of sympathy. One shares in their relief, participating with them in a kind of comic catharsis, when their nightmare ends. After all, they play their game like others in Saki's world of one-upmanship, and their failure endows them momentarily with innocence (we do not see how they treat the *genuine* governess). The tale reflects Munro's convictions and prejudices, no doubt. The aristocrat is not to be challenged; she knows the rules, her *savoir vivre* is absolute, and the justice of her world is not in question. The **"Schartz-Metterklume Method"** is a double-stab itself, at German pedantry, under the general assumption that Teutonism is comprehensively ridiculous, and at the sentimental fripperies of "progressive education," perhaps too democratic in its implications, and not the traditional and real thing. But in this story the wit carries all, and the cruel claws are sheathed.

The literal practical joke is very frequent in Saki, and more figuratively it could be magnified into a general principle; the tales are jokes upon the reader himself; the constant turns, the "snapper" conclusions, his startling metaphors, perpetually surprising, which jest even with language in their exploitation of clichés, the common, easy, thoughtless phrases we use to counterfeit meaning—all these are literally subversive of our expectations. If we seek for Munro's opinions behind them, we may come upon the cat's death yell, "that agony of bitter remonstrance which human animals, too, have flung at the powers that may be; the last protest against a destiny that might have made them happy—and has not." But this would be getting beyond a joke, and his own death was presumably not unhappy, though warlike.

Saki's practical jokes are undoubtedly sometimes cruel. Commentators have generally attributed them to a state of arrested development that made him an unsentimental Peter Pan. His recent biographer A. S. Langguth suggests that his writing has ceased to shock, and is prophetic of the absurdism and black humor of the later twentieth century. These are deep waters, as Sherlock Holmes was wont to remark; too deep for dogmatism. Saki achieves effects that are striking and unique; their source may be, as has been frequently suggested, in some inner lack, but his effects are calculated. Their context cannot be replaced; he wrote with a classical elegance that heightened their shock with its contrasting imperturbability, and his world itself is inimitable.

His style could be reproduced now only as parodic tour de force, though we can find similarities, British and Anglo-Irish. There were, of course, Wilde and Shaw, Beerbohm, Chesterton, Dunsany; later on Evelyn Waugh, who rivaled him in cruelty jokes. John Collier was more like him than any other twentieth-century writer, and a natural parallel because he specialized in short stories and had a similar audience to Saki's. Wodehouse . . . is similar in elegance and in wildly inventive figures, but he was pervasively a parodist, unlike Saki, and never by intent cruel, though his unvarying mockery and farcical plots can bring him to the verge. Lawrence Durrell belongs to the Saki tradition; in his case, however, there *is* absurdism, a wild humor beyond Saki's wit. The similarity is in elegance and virtuosity.

The practical joke, literal or figurative, is almost omnipresent in Saki, some degree of cruelty very frequent, and imperturbability invariable. **"Esmé"** (in *The Chronicles of Clovis*) is his most outrageous achievement in comic cruelty: a hapless gypsy child is devoured by a fortuitous hyena in the presence of the narrator and a companion, who represents the normal reaction.

> "How can you let that ravening beast trot by your side?" asked Constance.
>
> "In the first place, I can't prevent it," I said; "and in the second place, whatever else he may be, I doubt if he's ravening at the present moment."
>
> Constance shuddered. "Do you think the poor little thing suffered much?" came another of her futile questions.
>
> "The indications were all that way," I said; "on the other hand, of course, it may have been crying from sheer temper. Children sometimes do."

At the end of the story, after the hyena has been accidentally killed by a passing motorist, there are no repercussions. The hyena has strayed from a private menagerie, and for excellent reasons the owner never advertises his loss. The narrator (a Baroness), an imperturbable opportunist, herself poses as the owner of the dead beast, which she passes off as a valuable thoroughbred dog to the disturbed driver, disposing of the evidence by requiring him to bury it. "The gypsies were equally unobtrusive over their missing offspring; I don't suppose in large encampments they really know to a child or two how many they've got." In the sequel she profits to the extent of "a charming little diamond brooch" from the motorist, who is grateful for her forbearance. She does lose the friendship of her companion Constance, a setback she accepts with equanimity. "You see, when I sold the brooch I quite properly refused to give her any share of the proceeds."

The story is successful because, unlike its casualties, it is thoroughly alive. It moves lightly, and it has its decorum. It is drily told: the Baroness understates. To summarize where argument could be endless, **"Esmé"** holds comedy and horror in fruitful tension, each element supporting the other: it has many implications that are rigidly restrained, but linger in the mind. The Baroness herself, the narrator, has enough potentiality to furnish a Henry James novel— though perhaps it is the art of this highly compressed tale that it seems so, since Saki could not have written a Henry James novel, as he demonstrated in *The Unbearable Bassington*.

"Esmé" is at the outset a battle for dominance; the Baroness is evidently matching wits with the arrogant and formidable Clovis, who challenges her to interest him. She seems to have announced a "hunting story," which he immediately discourages: "All hunting stories are the same." "My hunting story isn't a bit like any you have ever heard," she replies, and proceeds to prove it: for some moments he tries to intervene, but is quickly forced into silence. She commences with a throw-away that is also a self-characterization. The Baroness dominates both Clovis and the story; she herself is horrifying and imperturbable. Yet she *might* be unhappy, and fascinating, if the reins were loosed.

> It happened quite a while ago, when I was about twenty-three. I wasn't living apart from my husband then: you see, neither of us could afford to make the other a separate allowance. In spite of everything that proverbs may say, poverty keeps together more homes than it breaks up. But we always hunted with different packs. All this has nothing to do with the story.

"The Story" is so compact that we do not learn her nationality, but it impels us to wonder. She may be foreign. She may be English but married to a foreign nobleman, probably French, at which she is proficient: "I stormed and scolded and coaxed in English and French and gamekeeper language" (she is certainly a huntress). The title **"Esmé"** is itself a French joke: not knowing the hyena's sex she gives it a name that may be either male or female. Her levity has the effect of cruelty, in contrast with the brainless normality of her English companion Constance Braddle. Whatever she is, she has a cosmopolitan flavor; it may be that Saki, writing for an English audience, plays for safety—the tale has its decorums, as has been suggested above. More deeply, it may be that she represents Munro's own ethos: this is a world of cruel accidents, which the wise accept undismayed; she is not unfeeling, but unshaken. Less favorably, it might be averred that she has the feelings of a huntress. Perhaps her sympathies are with the hyena. After the killing of the child, "When the beast joined us again, after an absence of a few minutes, there was an air of patient understanding about him, as though he knew that he had done something of which we disapproved, but which he felt to be thoroughly justifiable." Beasts will be beasts. In any event, **"Esmé"** is a most suggestive story.

As elsewhere, the joke motif is present in Saki's serious stories of cruelty and violence, but in these the joker is usually Nemesis, and the author's sympathies easier to discern than in his comedies. *Easier* rather than *easy*, perhaps; the distinction is relative between serious and comic, and the better "serious" tales are the more complex. The simpler verge on melodrama, although not devoid of wit and irony. As in the Reginald tales, violence and disorder intervene to save the protagonist from insensitive authority and tyrannical custom. In the celebrated **"Sredni Vashtar"** (in *The Chronicles of Clovis*) the struggle is mortal. Conradin, a ten year old, is being slowly stifled by his cousin and guardian, Mrs. De Ropp. "One of these days Conradin supposed he would succumb to the mastering pressure of wearisome necessary things—such as illnesses and coddling restrictions and drawn-out dulness. Without his imagination, which was rampant under the spur of loneliness, he would have succumbed long ago."

His only refuge from his guardian is a disused tool shed, which is peopled by phantoms of his imagination and two living creatures: a hen, "on which the boy lavished an affection that had scarcely another outlet," and, secreted away, "a large polecat-ferret," whom he makes his god under the name of Sredni Vashtar, and worships with strange ceremonies. Mrs. De Ropp, visited by hubris, uncovers his refuge, disposes of the hen, and finally and fatally discovers the ferret, which tears out her throat and escapes. The shock of the story lies in Conradin's unbounded exultation in this result. At the end, in the midst of the clamorous dismay of the household, he has leisurely toasted and buttered and eaten a piece of bread, which he had always been forbidden to do because Mrs. De Ropp had decided that toast was bad for him and troublesome to prepare. " 'Whoever will break it to the poor child? I couldn't for the life of me!' exclaimed a shrill voice. And while they debated the matter among themselves, Conradin made himself another piece of toast."

Like **"Esmé,"** **"Sredni Vashtar"** reverberates beyond its limits. Saki is never diffuse, but his account of the creation of the ferret-god in the boy's mind is sympathetic, acute, and objective. He originates in a dreadful necessity; we are convinced that without him Conradin cannot survive, and this strengthens the story, though hard on Mrs. De Ropp. The probability of a different conclusion is glanced at, with a blasphemous echoing of "Lord, I believe; help Thou my unbelief." "He knew as he prayed that he did not believe. He knew that the Woman would come out presently with that pursed smile he loathed so well on her face, and that in an hour or two the gardener would carry away his wonderful god, a god no longer, but a simple brown ferret in a hutch." Instead, his prayers are rewarded, his god confirmed. It is likely enough that **"Sredni Vashtar"** is a fantasy of the sickly boy Hector Munro, pursued by the worse of his two dreadful aunts; if so, Saki is able to find a context for it.

The other serious "cruelty" stories are slighter, though all of them are striking. Like **"Sredni Vashtar"** they are grim jokes played by Nemesis upon the insensitive and presumptuous, and like **"Sredni"** they are pagan, but they spring from a shallower fount; relatively, they are arbitrary and modish. We cannot accept the Wood Gods who wreak vengeance in **"The Music on the Hill"** (in *The Chronicles of Clovis*) as we accept Conradin, nor the good-looking werewolf in **"Gabriel-Ernest"** (in *Reginald in Russia*), the savage surrogate of Reginald and Clovis. Broadly, these tales can be accounted for by alluding to

Saki's simple and pervasive romanticism. He hated commonplace, he was primitivist; more profoundly, he was a depth-psychologist who found more in human nature than civilized creeds explain, though he did not *analyze*. This would describe his seriousness; what it leaves out is the all-important fact that his stories fundamentally are jokes. (pp. 88-96)

> *Richard Harter Fogle, "Saki and Wodehouse," in* The English Short Story, 1880-1945: A Critical History, *edited by Joseph M. Flora, Twayne Publishers, 1985, pp. 83-111.*

Joseph S. Salemi   (essay date 1989)

[*In the following essay, Salemi examines Saki's use of animals and animal imagery in* The Chronicles of Clovis.]

Of his six collections of short fiction, H. H. Munro's *The Chronicles of Clovis* is undoubtedly the most popular. Besides containing his most memorable and frequently anthologized stories, the book displays Munro's literary skills at their polished and mordant best: his flair for social caricature; his adept handling of the occult; his knack for making bizarre cruelties seem hilariously apt; and his ear for the euphemistic bitchery of the tea-table. Unlike the earlier *Reginald* stories, *The Chronicles of Clovis* is the work of a mature and brilliant satirist whose capacity for parody is both wide-ranging and precise. Saki—to use Munro's *nom de plume*—attains in this book a level of stylistic adroitness and acidulous, deadpan mockery that was to be unsurpassed in his later and posthumous collections.

Any careful reader of *The Chronicles of Clovis* is struck by the recurrence of animals and animal imagery in many of the stories. Saki's book teems with a remarkable number and variety of beasts. Hyenas, cats, tigers, goats, weasels, hens, stags, mice, ducklings, sparrows, swans, tortoises, and monkeys all make their appearance, sometimes just as decor but more often as integral parts of the action and meaning of the tales. Such fascination with wildlife is not as evident in the earlier *Reginald* collections, but even there, one notes Saki's inclination to dabble in beast fables and zoological metaphor—an inclination which in *The Chronicles of Clovis* (and later on, in *Beasts and Super-Beasts*) was to become a virtual signature of his work.

There are several plausible explanations for Saki's obsessive interest in animals. First, he spent his childhood in Devonshire, in close contact with all sorts of pets and livestock. Second, under his father's tutelage, he studied natural history and ornithology at home. Third, he was by temperament and breeding a member of the English rural gentry, a class with a proprietary fondness for horses, hounds, foxes, deer, and game birds of all types. Fourth, he moved in leisured patrician circles, where horse racing, dog shows, pampered cats, and exotic birds were part of life's furniture. Lastly, he was a denizen of an actively imperial Britain, for which elephants, camels, tigers, and all the fauna of Africa and the Orient were objects of both pride and enchantment. There is a more general point to be made as well: we today would be hard pressed to imagine the actual proximity to and familiarity with live animals

that obtained in the Western world a mere ninety years ago.

Any or all of these biographical facts could account for an abiding personal interest in the animal kingdom, but they are insufficient in themselves to explain why Saki makes such excessive literary use of beasts. I use the word *excessive* deliberately—reading through *The Chronicles of Clovis,* one becomes either amused or impatient with the growing menagerie of wild creatures. Saki was surely too good a writer to be dependent on a single literary device. But he seems, as a writer, to have been on the lookout for every possible turn of events—or of phrase—that could be an occasion for the entrance of some animal, or for a zoological reference. In many cases this practice has startling and effective results—as when Saki describes how a character dashes through an open window "like an escaping hawk," or when diners in a restaurant are said to be eating "in the nervous, detached manner of roebuck feeding in the open," or when an angry crowd is called "a great hive of bewildered and affronted bees." At other times, the intrusion seems willful or gratuitous: in one story, a child is disguised as a grunting and slobbering pig at an amateur theatrical; in another, a character suggests to the mother of a missing infant that her baby may have been carried off by an eagle or a wild beast. But whether the figure be appropriate or farfetched, it is sure to pop up, and the experienced reader of Saki comes to expect its presence. It is as if some strange, unconscious insistence were driving the author to these stylistic choices, demanding from his pen bestial and feral imagery at the expense of all other possibilities.

Critics who have noted this propensity in Saki have accounted for it in two ways. Some ascribe it to a misanthropic preference for animals over human beings, others to an old satiric tradition of contrasting human perversion with animal decency. In this vein, Charles H. Gillen writes [in his *H. H. Munro (Saki)*]: "Perhaps the secret of Munro's love for animals is that, while he recognized their ruthless struggle for survival, he habitually contrasted their instinctive decency and bravery with the sorry spectacle of human behavior." For my part, I do not see how either misanthropy or an idolization of animals can account for certain events in *The Chronicles of Clovis.* First of all, Saki's stories, through sometimes bitter, are not misanthropic. They certainly do not display the kind of thoroughgoing distaste for humanity and human society that one finds, say, in Swift or Kafka. Their comic elements save them from the totally despairing blackness that true misanthropy exudes. Secondly, in *The Chronicles of Clovis* animals are most definitely not presented as models of decent, upright behavior. In fact, what strikes one upon reading these stories is the disturbing frequency with which animals slaughter human beings. In no less than five of the the stories in *The Chronicles of Clovis* (that is, in nearly twenty percent of them), the action involves the death of persons who have run afoul of wild beasts. A perusal of these five tales reveals something different from either simple misanthropy or affectionate partiality for animals.

In the story **"Esmé,"** two upper-class Englishwomen on

horseback, who have lost their way during a fox hunt, come upon an escaped hyena. The beast follows them in a friendly enough manner, with no signs of ferocity or hostility, as they seek to find their way back to the other riders. But when a gypsy child appears on the road, the hyena seizes it and, despite some ineffectual shooings by the women, kills and devours it. The women continue on, still followed by the hyena, but they are complacently indifferent to the fate of the child, and much more concerned with returning to the comfort of their homes. The hyena is accidentally killed by a passing automobile, and this incident becomes the occasion for a brief flirtation between the repentant owner of the car and one of the women, who claims that the hyena was her prize dog Esmé. He later sends her an expensive diamond brooch by way of reparation, and when the brooch is sold, the two women fall out over the division of the proceeds.

"**Esmé**" is, of course, a grim satire on the callous indifference of the rich to anything other than their own comforts and interests. The rapaciousness of the hyena is simply a mirror image of the coldness and selfishness of the two women, whose petty squabbling over the diamond brooch reveals their predatory characters. In the story, Saki does not contrast noble beast and ignoble humans, but instead establishes a frightening identity between an animal's relentless hunt for food, and the human desire for comfort and money. This tale—the lead story in *The Chronicles of Clovis*—should have alerted critics to Saki's real views, which are confirmed again and again in subsequent stories: namely, that human beings and animals are not very different, and that the traits they share are more repulsive than endearing.

In the story "**Tobermory**," one of Saki's most famous, we encounter a cat who has been taught to speak correct English by an eccentric zoologist. The glow of this remarkable achievement is dimmed by the fact that the loquacious and utterly cynical cat proceeds to break every rule of tact and discretion at a house party. The scandalized guests agree that the cat must be put to death lest he instruct other animals in the art of human speech. But before this can be done, the cat is fortuitously slain in a back-alley confrontation with some other feline. The story ends with a brief mention of how the zoologist himself is later killed by an elephant, during a futile attempt to teach the beast to talk.

"**Tobermory**" is a highly improbable tale, but one that works by virtue of its amusing displacement of a sympathetic human perspective in favor of a dispassionate animal one. A cat who can speak is singularly suited to discuss human behavior and motives without the slightest scruple or polite evasion. And here we have a clue as to why animals play so large a role in Saki's fiction. They represent what human beings would be like without the veneer of etiquette and social grace—in fact, what human beings really are beneath the surface of upper-class manners, bourgeois respectability, and feigned solicitude for others. No wonder then, that the author kills off the errant zoologist at the end of "**Tobermory**"—in Saki's view, the playful conflict between man and beast represents the more serious and unremitting conflict between what we

are and what we strive to seem. Anyone who tries to heal this breach, by reconciling man's bestial inner self with his socialized exterior, dies at the hands (or perhaps the claws, tusks, and teeth) of one of the outraged antagonists.

This brings us to one of Saki's grimmest and most terrifying stories, "**Sredni Vashtar**." The tale is not just about animal violence, but a violence tinged with vindictive and unabashed paganism. A whiff of savagery hangs about "**Sredni Vashtar**," one that is wholly out of keeping with Saki's usual light tone. The story is frequently anthologized and was dramatized once for American television.

The tale hangs, in a characteristically Sakian manner, on the conflict between a child and an adult. A young and sickly boy named Conradin is the ward of his older female cousin, a domineering and smug bourgeoise who fills the boy's life with petty restrictions and schoolmarmish tyrannies. Conradin's only escape from this hated authority figure is in the garden toolshed, where he keeps two pets: a hen, and a caged polecat that he has secretly bought. This polecat becomes an object of religious worship for the boy, who calls it the god "Sredni Vashtar." Conradin carries out his ceremonial worship of Sredni Vashtar in secret, associating the sharp-fanged divinity with, as Saki says, "the fierce impatient side of things." The hidden polecat is clearly a symbol of the boy's muted but burning resentment and rejection of everything his cousin-guardian represents: regulation, submission, socialization, and continued sickness. One day the cousin—who is unaware of the polecat's existence—orders Conradin's beloved hen to be sold. The boy suppresses his rage, but continues the secret worship of Sredni Vashtar. Since Conradin persists in frequenting the toolshed, his cousin decides to go there herself, to see what holds her ward's interest. As he watches her descend to the garden, Conradin breathes a desperate prayer to Sredni Vashtar in an attempt to stave off the humiliation and defeat of seeing his animal-deity discovered and dethroned. His prayer is answered—when the cousin enters the toolshed and unwarily opens the cage within, the disturbed polecat-god tears her throat out. The story ends with Conradin making himself some buttered toast as he listens with profound satisfaction to the clamorous panic of the servants who have discovered his cousin's corpse.

There is nothing amusing about "**Sredni Vashtar**"; it is a thoroughly disturbing piece, a textbook case-history of the revenge of the repressed unconscious. I suggest that, of all the stories in *The Chronicles of Clovis*, this one best represents the author's settled judgment on the man-beast conflict. The "fierce impatient side of things" is the suppressed, instinctual animality that Saki sensed was trying to claw its way free behind the rigid social conventions of Victorian and Edwardian Britain. Like some caged beast, this drive lurked in a dark, forgotten corner, waiting to strike out viciously at those who would meddle with it. "**Tobermory**" tells, in a delightfully facetious way, how the frank honesty of bestial manners can never coexist with the hypocrisy that makes civilization possible. "**Sredni Vashtar**" tells essentially the same tale, but on a profounder and more troubling level; here Saki seems to say that the fury of our natural instincts is forever at war with the necessary repressions of the social order.

Sometimes animal violence in Saki is a reflection of his fondness for the occult or the preternatural. The story **"The Music on the Hill"** is a good example. A rather self-satisfied London woman, recently married, decides that she and her husband should live in his remote country house near the Devonshire-Somerset border. They settle there, but the husband warns his wife that the god Pan holds sway in those regions and that his divinity must be respected. The woman, a skeptical urban type, speaks disparagingly of such "superstition." Soon afterwards, however, she notices that the farm animals in the vicinity have become hostile to her in some undefined and subtle way. Later, during a walk in the woods, she unthinkingly despoils Pan's statue of an offering left there by her credulous husband, and as she walks home, she is frightened by the sight of a boy's face in the undergrowth, a boy "brown and beautiful, with unutterably evil eyes." Although her husband warns her to avoid the groves and orchards after this affront to Pan's dignity, she disregards his advice and continues her country strolls. On one such walk, she suddenly hears the whine of pipes, and watches in helpless horror as a hunted stag bounds out of the forest and impales her upon his antlers.

"The Music on the Hill" rings slightly different changes on the subject of man and beast. In this story we see Saki contrasting the pagan countryside and its dark wisdom with the superficial enlightenment of city dwellers. Several of his stories touch upon this polarity. For Saki, rural and wild areas (along with their beasts) were dangerous, haunting territory, presided over by uncanny chthonic powers that could be cruel when crossed. Like D. H. Lawrence, he believed in the "primal, dark veracity" of nature and animals, in all their inarticulate but potent vitality. Beside such primitive energies, reason and civilization must have seemed anemic indeed. **"The Music on the Hill"** confirms, to my satisfaction at least, that Saki's literary use of animals was more than a stylistic peculiarity or a quirk of personal taste. He was a strong believer in the irrational and its force in human affairs. But the upper-crust English milieu depicted in *The Chronicles of Clovis*—a milieu hedged in, as it was, with so many social conventions, fixed attitudes, and codified rituals—offered very little scope for spontaneity of any sort, let alone irrational impulse. Animals, however, could embody the pure force of nature's prompting in such a world; they were the "wild cards," so to speak, in the carefully stacked deck of correct and proper expectations that was Saki's Britain.

It is hard to ignore Saki's special perspective on his own society's limitations when we remember that he spent many years abroad as a correspondent for the *Morning Post.* As a journalist in eastern Europe, he was well placed to see a world rather different from his own. In the troubled Balkans of 1902, political violence, ethnic hatreds, and the constant threat of upheaval were facts of daily life. Some of his stories touch upon such issues. Later, on assignment in St. Petersburg, he witnessed the sanguinary but abortive 1905 Revolution. He was sent to Paris in 1906, close to the time when the long Dreyfus affair came to an end with the final exoneration of Dreyfus by the French court of cassation. He was certainly aware of the passionate partisanship that this controversy provoked, not just in France but in nearly all of Europe. The point is that Saki had enough experience with lands where volatility and hot blood had plenty of scope for expression to see that his staid and phlegmatic England restrained irrational impulse wisely, but perhaps too well.

There remains one final tale to discuss. The story **"Ministers of Grace"** is purely facetious, but it too has a bearing on my argument. A mischievous young nobleman with preternatural psychic powers replaces several English politicans and notables with perfectly duplicated angelic substitutes. These changelings then proceed to act in accordance with right reason and public spiritedness, as opposed to the usual temporizing and maneuvering of the men they have replaced. Meanwhile the real souls of the dispossessed politicians are placed in the bodies of various animals, where their energies are reduced to harmless chirping and barking. However, the utter sensation caused by the unaccountable change in behavior of so many public figures leads to sociopolitical turmoil, and ultimately to the threat of civil war. The story ends when a large swan, which harbors the soul of an aggressive Cabinet Minister, attacks the young nobleman and drags him to his death by drowning, thus breaking the magic spell and returning England to non-angelic rule.

One could hardly imagine a more absurd piece of trivia than **"Ministers of Grace,"** reminiscent, as it is, of the cheaper sort of science fiction. But the story confirms that Saki had no illusions about the supposed "decency" or "nobility" of animals *vis à vis* human beings. Animals in **"Ministers of Grace"** are not redemptive icons. They are simply receptacles wherein the imprisoned souls of venal and corrupt men can act out their vices. In order to imagine a rationally governed society, the author felt compelled to supply it with angelic rulers. But "the ruck of human beings," as Saki would have called us, remains unredeemed from its solipsism, visceral reactions, and reflexive egoism. The aggregate of men are "beasts," in the pejorative sense of that term. That is, we are creatures of cunning rather than intelligence, of ferocity rather than courage, of base appetites rather than noble yearnings. Our one saving grace—a fitful and tenuous sentimentality—only mitigates our inherent rapaciousness.

Profound pessimism of this sort has always been the occupational hazard of satirists, from Juvenal to Swift. And when a satirist despairs of humanity, his *saeva indignatio* can become an end in itself, rather than a means of promoting social reform or personal regeneration. But one of the hallmarks of Saki's style is a complete absence of any indignation, or even irritation. Human folly elicits not the slightest hint of his disapproval or distaste. We get instead that curiously cold-blooded detachment which has prompted so many of his readers to call him cruel or inhuman. I suggest that in Saki's writings, animals (and especially the violent acts of animals) are the principal manifestations of this detachment. They are symbols of a psychological nemesis that dishes out retribution, with mechanical impartiality, to a world hidebound in its repressions and strait jacketed in its social rituals. Combine this sort of vindictive zoology with epigrammatic point and *Galgenhumor,* and you have vintage Saki.

Those who read Saki for the first time are apt to describe his work as brittle, icy, or sharp-edged. What these terms share is a sense of the writer's aristocratic hauteur. Many of his best characters are cynically self-absorbed, verbally cutting, and glacially indifferent to the demands of compassion. But this patrician disdain is only one side of Saki. A more important fact about his fiction is the way in which it aspires to bring an utterly unsentimental perspective to human affairs, as if the author were a high-flying hawk, looking down with sharp but pitiless eye on man's pretentiousness and posturing. When Saki attains such perspective, it is easy to imagine him as one of his *enfants terribles,* or as the writer whom V. S. Pritchett [in his essay "The Performing Lynx," in *The New Statesman & Nation,* 1957] called "the teaser of hostesses, the shocker of dowagers, the mocker of female crises, the man in the incredible waistcoat who throws a spanner into the teacup." So he is—but he will often whimsically subcontract the work of devastation to bird or beast. It is a convenient way to make the punishment of folly swift, rigorous, and impersonal.

In ["**The Secret Sin of Septimus Brope**"] in *The Chronicles of Clovis,* a woman is described as having "the self-applauding air of one who has detected an asp lurking in an apple-charlotte." It would be hard to find another image more characteristic of Saki's pen, or more reflective of his peculiar frame of mind. In an apple-charlotte—that so very prim, proper, and English piece of pastry, sitting in its sublime complacency on a silver tea-tray—there lurks a fanged and venomous snake, ready to strike at whatever respectable matronly hand reaches for it. There could be no better description of what Saki accomplishes in his fiction. He lashes out, suddenly and unpleasantly, to subvert conventional expectations and to violate all propriety. He upsets the careful arrangements that human beings have made to cover up the facts of their ruthless self-interest. He exposes the core of concupiscence that lies behind the niceties of gentlemanly and ladylike behavior. Above all, he makes us aware that there is an animal within each of us, crouching and ready to spring—and that we are well advised to keep in mind its needs, its insistence, and its capacity for revenge. (pp. 423-30)

> Joseph S. Salemi, *"An Asp Lurking in an Apple-Charlotte: Animal Violence in Saki's*

'*The Chronicles of Clovis',*" in Studies of Short Fiction, *Vol. 26, No. 4, Fall, 1989, pp. 423-30.*

FURTHER READING

Biography

Langguth, A. J. *Saki: A Life of Hector Hugh Munro, with Six Stories Never Before Collected.* New York: Simon and Schuster, 1981, 366 p.

Biographical study.

Criticism

Abrams, Fred. "Onomastic Humor in Saki's 'Filboid Studge, The Story of the Mouse That Helped'." *Names* 19, No. 4 (December 1971): 287-88.

Interprets the meanings underlying the proper names in "Filboid Studge."

Davison, Edward. "An English Wit." *The Saturday Review of Literature* (New York) IV, No. 10 (1 October 1927): 147.

Reviews *The Chronicles of Clovis,* observing that the volume is "far from [Saki's] best book," while praising his dialogue and varied subjects.

Drake, Robert. "Saki: Some Problems and a Bibliography." *English Fiction in Transition* 5, No. 1 (1962): 6-26.

Biographical and critical sketch with an extensive annotated bibliography of secondary sources.

———. "Saki's Ironic Stories." *Texas Studies in Literature and Language* V, No. 3 (Autumn 1963): 374-88.

Attempts to demonstrate that "Saki's stories which are not humorous seem, if they have no other bond in common, to have a pervading irony." Drake adds: "This irony usually consists in the principal character's bringing about his own downfall by scorning as 'unreal' some aspect of total reality."

Thrane, James R. "Two New Stories by 'Saki' (H. H. Munro)." *Modern Fiction Studies* 19, No. 2 (Summer 1973): 139-51.

Reprints two previously uncollected short stories by Saki. Thrane also includes an introduction discussing Munro's work as a journalist.

Voltaire

1694-1778

(Born François-Marie Arouet) French novelist, short story writer, essayist, playwright, poet, historian, critic, and autobiographer.

INTRODUCTION

A principal figure of the French Enlightenment, Voltaire is best known for his philosophical tales, including *Candide; ou, l'optimisme* (*Candide; or, All for the Best*), his most famous work, as well as *Memnon: Histoire orientale*, also known as *Zadig, ou la destinée* (*Zadig, or the Book of Fate: An Oriental History*), *L'Ingénu: Histoire véritable, tirée des manuscrits de Père Quesnel* (*The Pupil of Nature*), and *Le Micromégas de Mr. de Voltaire, avec une histoire des croisades & un nouveau plan de l'histoire de l'esprit humain* (*Micromégas: A Comic Romance*). Throughout his life, Voltaire was both lauded and despised for his satirical writings directed at the philosophical and political trends of his day. At the same time, his work proceeds from his belief in humankind's ability to perfect itself, an ideal characteristic of the Enlightenment.

Voltaire began writing short fiction late in his career during a stay with the Duchesse du Maine at Sceaux, where he recited parts of his philosophical tales each evening. Most of his twenty-five tales are written in the oriental mode of exotic adventure stories made popular by Antoine Galland's translation of *The Arabian Nights,* published between 1704 and 1717, and Montesquieu's *Lettres persanes* of 1721. For Voltaire this narrative form was a useful vehicle for his criticism of political, religious, and social institutions, enabling him to safely discuss his ideas for reform by presenting them in a foreign context. Voltaire believed in effecting social progress through education, and the exotic settings in his fiction present his protagonists with the opportunity to confront the different philosophies associated with different cultures.

The best known of Voltaire's philosophical tales, such as *Candide, Zadig,* and *L'Ingénu,* feature naive protagonists whose innocence and inexperience allow them to convey to the reader a fresh perspective on the various societies in which they find themselves. Critics have observed that Voltaire's use of naive protagonists serves to illuminate one of the constant themes in his writings—the conflict between the quest for personal happiness and the desire to lead an ethical life. In *Candide* Voltaire presents a succession of moral, physical, and social evils in order to attack Gottfried Leibniz's philosophy of Optimism, as well as other viewpoints such as Manichaeanism. Throughout the story Candide discovers the flaws of each philosophy. Despite the consistent use of irony and satire to undercut different philosophies in *Candide,* many critics find the value of the work resides in its offering an alternative to the ni-

hilism that might seem to follow Voltaire's rejection of Optimism. The meliorism advocated in the conclusion of *Candide* has sparked much debate because Candide's admonition that one must cultivate one's garden is ambiguous: it may be read as both an argument for philosophical quietism as well as a call for political and social reform.

Zadig is a didactic tale that considers the role of Providence in human affairs. The protagonist, like others in Voltaire's fiction, is an ideal figure who, in his search for happiness, encounters a number of individuals who represent the potential for evil in human nature. At the same time, Zadig's experiences also teach him the divinely ordered nature of the universe; at the story's end, rather than despairing at his inability to change human nature, Zadig accepts his place in the cosmic order. In *Micromégas,* two extraterrestrial beings, one a giant, the other a dwarf, discover the earth in the course of their travels, and speculate on the disparity between humanity's abilities and achievements. A satire on anthropocentrism, *Micromégas* depicts the insignificance of human beings in an incomprehensibly large universe. Recalling *Candide* in the naive character of its protagonist, *L'Ingénu* focuses on the subject of religious persecution. Provoked by the execution of heretics that took place throughout France in the 1760s, *L'Ingénu* condemns religious intolerance through its portrayal of suffering and its appeal to common sense.

Voltaire's reliance upon reason defines the themes of his short fiction; he believed that injustice could be examined with detachment and thereby eliminated. Exploiting the didactic and philosophical potential of the short story, Voltaire argued for both religious and political tolerance and for social reform.

PRINCIPAL WORKS

SHORT FICTION

Memnon: Histoire orientale 1747; also published as *Zadig, ou la destinée,* 1749
[*Zadig, or the Book of Fate: An Oriental History,* 1749]
Le monde comme il va 1748; published in *Oeuvres de M. de Voltaire*
[*Babouc, or the World As It Goes,* 1754]
Le Micromégas de Mr. de Voltaire, avec une histoire des croisades & un nouveau plan de l'histoire de l'esprit humain 1752
[*Micromégas: A Comic Romance,* 1753]
Le deux consolés 1756; published in *Oeuvres de M. de Voltaire*
Candide; ou, l'optimisme, traduit de l'Allemand, de Mr. le Docteur Ralph 1759
[*Candide; or, All for the Best,* 1759]
Histoire d'un bon brahmin 1759; published in *Oeuvres de M. de Voltaire*
Le blanc et le noir 1764
Les aveugles juges des couleurs 1766
L'Ingénu: Histoire véritable, tirée des manuscrits de Père Quesnel 1767
[*The Pupil of Nature,* 1771; also published as *The Sincere Huron,* 1786]
L'homme aux quarante écus 1768
[*The Man of Forty Crowns,* 1768]
La princesse de Babylon 1768
[*The Princess of Babylon,* 1927]
Les lettres d'Amabed 1769
Le taureau blanc 1774
[*The White Bull: An Oriental History.* 2 vols., 1774]
Histoire de Jenni, ou l'athée et le sage 1775

OTHER MAJOR WORKS

Oedipe (drama) 1719
La ligue, ou Henry le Grand (poetry) 1723; also published as *La Henriade,* 1728
[*Henriade: An Epick Poem,* 1732]
Oeuvres de M. de Voltaire. 12 vols. (essays, dramas, philosophy, poetry, prose, history, and criticism) 1738-60
[*The Works of Voltaire.* 35 vols., 1761-69]
Poèmes sur le désastre de Lisbonne et sur la loi naturelle (poetry) 1756
Dictionnaire philosophique portatif (nonfiction) 1764;

revised editions 1765, 1767; also published as *La raison par alphabet* [revised edition], 1769
[*Philosophical Dictionary for the Pocket,* 1765]

CRITICISM

Dorothy Madeleine McGhee (essay date 1954)

[*In the following excerpt, McGhee examines the development of the protagonists of* Candide *and* L'Ingénu.]

Whether the character be hero or protagonist, "candide" or "ingénu", the problems of accounting for his name appear similar. (p. 11)

In the light of a considerable amount of scholarly research which has commented upon the difficulty of finding reference to the name Candide as chosen by Voltaire, it is interesting to note that scarcely more material nor corroborative evidence seems possible on a similar title of eight years later,—*L'Ingénu.* Similarity not only in name, but in type of hero might urge the reader to discover a probable origin and application of this second title.

The general formula of the "artfully guileless" protagonist had, as we know, become familiar in several genres, long before Voltaire's first use of the 'conte.' In an age which had taken for its motto the transmission of all knowledge to all men, it was natural that many heroes should approach their schools of experience with a naïvely ingenuous attitude, in order to have impressed upon them the various phases of human endeavor and conquest. One of their common ancestors had been the 'pícaro,' educated in a world of obstacles. This "artfully guileless" protagonist we might term a "naïf," as type determines him. In his most potent vehicle, the 'conte philosophique,' he is far from naïve, however, as we are well aware. Consultation of the *Dictionnaire Etymologique de la Langue Française* serves to elucidate the two title words "candide" and "ingénu," and also to save us from confusing what we shall term this typed "naïf" with the ordinary application of the adjective "naïve." Says the *Dictionnaire:*

> candide—XVe siècle, emprunté du latin *candidus,* proprement "d'un blanc éclatant";
> ingénu—fin XVIIe siècle (Bossuet) au sens juridique de "né libre";
> ingénuité—1541 (Calvin) dans un sens correspondant, encore chez Montesquieu. . . .

This one specific Voltairian version, then, of the hero becoming philosophized under surveillance of a mentor, had resulted in the ultra-successful Candide, the double-play hero who could doubt *while* refuting, or vice versa. Of the 'contes' between 1759 and 1767, not one had made use of this special application of the formula, to philosophize the apparently ingenuous 'naïf.' Hence it seems of interest to note that "ingénu," again an infrequent word, should be used to apply, after a period of eight years, to a similar type of protagonist, depicting the author's particular version of that 'naïf.'

If we first examine occurrences of the word "ingénu" in contemporary references or in Voltaire's own works, little seems available. Though cases be few, yet they may prove of value in attempting to limit our point. Regnard's *Sérénade,* scène 18, gives: "Voilà un garçon bien ingénu, . . . ,"; Chénier's *Elégies,* XXXII, yields:

Qu'un jeune homme, agité d'une flamme inconnue,
S'écrie aux doux tableaux de ma muse ingénue;
Ce poète amoureux, qui me connaît si bien,
Quand il a peint son coeur, avait lu dans le mien.

and Voltaire's own *Henriade,* IX, uses the word, though apparently with memories of J.-B. Rousseau: "Accordent à leurs voix leurs danses ingénues. . . ." It is certain that the references just cited will prove of but superficial value, and upon no single one could we logically base any claim to exactness of source.

What is more, we find that Voltaire himself had made absolutely no mention in his correspondence of either the word or the tale prior to its publication. Of course, we must bear in mind that the wary author, very probably anticipating some repercussions about such a grouping of "sensitive" subjects, might more than likely have refrained purposely from mentioning it even to friends.

Thus much for some negative phases. Our interest is aroused anew, however, upon reading the extensive analysis of the term "ingénuité" in the 1765 Neufchastel edition of the *Encyclopédie.* One begins to wonder whether "l'ingénu" might not have been constructed about this very definition, so near is the 'naïf' Huron to it: "L'Ingénuité est dans l'âme; la naïveté dans le ton. L'ingénuité est la qualité d'une âme innocente qui se montre telle qu'elle est, parce qu'il n'y a rien en elle qui l'oblige à se cacher. L'innocence produit l'ingénuité, et l'ingénuité la franchise. On est tenté de supposer toutes les vertus dans les personnes ingénues. Que leur commerce est agréable! Si elles ont parlé, on sent qu'elles devoient dire ce qu'elles ont dit. Leur âme vient se peindre sur leurs lèvres, dans leurs yeux, et dans leur expression. On leur découvre son coeur avec d'autant plus de liberté, qu'on voit le leur tout entier. Ont-elles fait une faute, elles l'avouent d'une manière qui feroit presque regretter qu'elles ne l'eussent pas commise. Elles paroissent innocentes jusque dans leurs erreurs; et les coeurs doubles paroissent coupables, lors même qu'ils sont innocens. . . ." Thus the 'ingénu' could be sincere, whareas the 'naïf,' generally speaking, might or might not be so. The Encyclopedists' preoccupation with an ideal is rather evident in the entire passage. The century was fully aware of the effectiveness of its typed 'naïf' or 'ingénu' or 'candide.' And for Voltaire the transformation of a 'naïf' into a 'philosophe' was a perfect 'conte' subject.

Voltaire actually did adapt characteristics of this formula to the latter tale *L'Ingénu,* subsequent to similar traits in *Candide. L'Ingénu* was evidently no casual return to the *Candide* idea. To compare adjectives and expressions used in evolving the two, chronologically:—In Candide, we have found a 'naïf' who is described as "doux," "simple"; he looks at life "avec modestie," at ideals "avec respect"; he accepts "conseils," though frequently enough "avec admiration" (wonderment). "Sage" though he be, or decide to be, he is overcome by events—"éperdu," "étourdi," "étonné," "bouleversé," "agité." If any suggestion does come to his mind, he makes it only with "discrétion," or "modestie," and limits his mental reaction thereupon to subsequent "réflexions." L'Ingénu, as a 'naïf' fulfilling a double thesis, presents qualities on both positive and negative sides,—an admirably ingenuous frankness of mind as contrasted with the lack of delicate sensibilities that accompany a civilized state. He casts himself ashore, literally—"simple et naturel," possessed also of Candide's "douceur." "Naïvement" he states the reason for his arrival; the auditors are charmed. Upon his arrest and incarceration in the Bastille, he *embarrasses* the Jansenist by his "naïveté." Because of his mental freedom from prejudice, he immediately begins his march toward progress. Here is a Candide reappearing,—minus, it is true, the constant adherence to a set doctrine, but nevertheless a really candid mind in the physical makeup of the "ingénu." In these two 'contes' are varying shades of the 'naïf'—the one, a direct protagonist of the thesis, the other a 'porte-parole' for it.

Thus do they assume very different rôles in the action of their 'contes.' Yet in one point they are basically bound together,—in their secret feelings of rebellion. To Candide, tradition is presented as a cult; to l'Ingénu, it may never have existed. Both submit in action, but rebel mentally. We note that both personages have tutors who endeavor to inculcate in their pupils either doctrine or reason. In accordance with his "douceur," and the qualities of a 'naïf,' Candide listens attentively, respectfully, or absently, as the case may be,—but he listens. For the time being, i.e., before the presentation of realistic Martin, he attempts no analysis whatsoever. L'Ingénu, from the very outset, travels differently on the path of progress. After listening, he questions, and furthermore, upon sensing the inability of his tutor to explain, or the futility of an explanation, he dares "ingenuously" to feel pity. Both are shades of the 'naïf' in progress toward "philosophism." A constantly wandering existence has been necessary to bring about disproof for Candide, whereas for l'Ingénu the exact opposite has been a necessity, if the 'philosophe' were to be developed by precept and growth of inner self.

The author's purpose in each tale has created its protagonist, essential 'naïf' though he always remains. There would seem to be a significance in Voltaire's reversion to a similar term to depict his particular version of this 'naïf.' Guilelessness had served to refute a doctrine through the complete impressionability of the first protagonist. In the second case it was to serve in a positive capacity, to reject those premises of Man's planned thought which mean tradition as such.

Proceeding then to link characteristics of the two 'naïfs' with the general exposition of their 'contes,' one may discover some further points of interesting similarity. Candide and l'Ingénu have been evolved either by direct dialogue or by means of adjectives or expressions describing resultant feelings in the personages themselves. For example, as reactions, witness Candide's being in turn "stupéfait," "bienfaisant," "épouvanté," "interdit," "éperdu," "palpitant," "étonné," again "éperdu," "stupéfait," "désespéré," "tremblant d'émotion," "étourdi," "choqué," "consolé," "entre la joie et la douleur," "charmé," "étonné," "plein de l'idée de retrouver Cunégonde," "le coeur agité," "l'esprit bouleversé." And after this gamut of emotions elicited by events, there is the usual synthesizing process so evident in Voltairian style,—the interweaving of these emotions with the thought sequences that either preceded or succeeded them.

Inasmuch as *L'Ingénu* is primarily a study of the savage versus civilized man on the one hand (for customs), and of the natural, versus cultivated feeling for religion on the other, the tale does not present this same reaction process of character exposition. Whereas Candide exercised little of either physical or mental force upon opinions presented to him, l'Ingénu is physically able and ready to execute the results which his ingenuous spirit has dictated as logical and right. The Huron therefore displays his characteristics through action,—an ever present spontaneity; hostility to tradition; a disputatious spirit conscious of its sincerity; an aversion to counsel; a sincere respect for mankind in return for a similar respect toward self; and lastly, intrepidity in logical reason. Candide we have seen *reacting;* his brother 'naïf' literally meets us in the midst of *action.* Events have evoked Candide's "naïveté," whereas l'Ingénu's guilelessness has served to motivate action.

Many are the moments in which we find both 'naïfs' departing from complete simplicity in their action sequences. Candide darts through his experiences with a justifiable "mais," in imminent danger of complicating matters for himself. It is more than frequently, even before the entry of Martin, that he departs momentarily from the path of completely ingenuous 'naïf' to interpose a balancing negative. He comments, at an early stage in the 'conte,' upon the excellence of free will; he shows a practical side of his nature in replying to Pangloss' lengthy preachments. He continues to assert, though it be with modification of some kind; he expresses curiosity; he even displays anger, though it is followed immediately by sadness.

We may point likewise to an inclusive "mais" in *L'Ingénu,* for neither is he by any means completely the guileless 'naïf.' Upon arrival, he accepts the newly discovered relationship to the Kerkabons, though he is convinced only as one member of the group pronoun "on"—"Enfin *on* était si persuadé, si convaincu de la naissance de l'Ingénu, qu'il consentit lui-même à être neveu . . . "; he censures inconsistencies on the part of his fellows; his 'naïveté' of observation embarrasses the Jansenist in search of words, and the Jansenist it is who becomes the object of pity; the Huron is himself instrumental in fortifying his already strong mind, and he ends by more than fulfilling philosophic expectations. Throughout the series of events befalling these two, there is one common point in which they do entertainingly announce their naïve quality, in mock Leibnitzian style. It is as though the author found himself unconsciously making them too clever for their circumstances, and hence caused them to utter at pronounced intervals the oft-quoted "if" exclamations.

As arguments for progress, the Voltairian 'candide' and 'ingénu' thus work constantly toward perfectibility. The fact of their being 'naïfs' has rendered them capable of being infused with "philosophism." "Ingénuité dans l'âme, . . . naïveté dans le ton"—as already remarked, the Encyclopedists in their analysis had quite evidently envisaged an ideal. In considering the 'contes' as a whole, we are often inclined to think of *L'Ingénu* as a pendant to *Candide,* and to agree with M. Bellessort, that, while the later tale is in no wise weak, yet the author refrains from approaching another Candide. But if we think of l'Ingénu as a 'naïf' on his way toward perfectibility, this 'conte' surely maintains a brilliant standard, in that it epitomizes an attitude of thought. It would seem to be a model for the protagonist of an entire century. Finding Candide and l'Ingénu interesting companions, then, in title meaning, one observes that the hero formula of the latter is in many ways a return to the earlier. Each becomes, according to his individual nuance of character, a 'philosophe',—Candide to modify and mature his thought processes by Realism—l'Ingénu supposedly to find his share of an elusive happiness in ordered thought.

The point concerning the author's love of the 'naïf' therefore seems again to revolve about the eternal quest for happiness. Is one happy reasoning or not reasoning? True, all of the 'contes' have contained shades of this query, but it will be recalled that not one between 1759 and 1767 had exhibited just this particular mode of philosophizing the "artfully guileless" 'naïf.' And "ingénu," as we have seen, like its predecessor "candide," was a decidedly infrequent word in contemporary reference.

Research and commentaries on the name Candide have all appeared to support the contention that the word was only a reading memory with Voltaire, and suggestions of *probable* sources have been the sole extent of possible conclusions. Could it have been, we now suggest for "l'Ingénu," that the 1765 Neufchastel tome of the *Encyclopédie,* with its painstakingly shaded definition of *Ingénuité,* had suggested to Voltaire a title? It would appear that the 'naïf,' whether the gullible one of 1759 or the 'homme naturel' of 1767, was his preference in title form for the same two reasons that had dictated this encyclopedia expression. On the one hand, while the protagonist is maintaining his seeming guilelessness of mien, he offers a perfect opportunity for assimilating the doctrines of an ideal 'philosophe' (Martin and the Jansenist). Also, when he begins his own progress toward the century goal of this "philosophism," after countless untoward events have befallen him, he profits by the perfect equipment of humility, to impress fellow beings undertaking the same journey. Candide exhibits a soul "trop pure pour trahir la vérité." With l'Ingénu, it is the absence of prejudice, as much as the quality of his being, that makes for progress. In a world admittedly lacking perfection, but nevertheless passable, Reality is to have its full sweep along with Idealism. Possessed of the latter, one must always be cognizant of the first. The 'naïf' is that being most capable of development,—hence it is upon him that Reality falls most profitably. He becomes l'Ingénu, rightful successor to his brother Candide. (pp. 11-17)

Dorothy Madeleine McGhee, "Voltaire's 'Conte' Title—'L'Ingénu'," in her Fortunes of a Tale: The Philosophic Tale in France, Bridging the Eighteenth and Nineteenth Centuries, *George Banta Publishing Company, 1954, pp. 11-17.*

André Maurois (essay date 1957)

[*Maurois was a distinguished French biographer and literary critic. He is best known for his biographies of Percy Bysshe Shelley, Benjamin Disraeli, George Gordon, Lord Byron, and Voltaire, among others. In the following essay, originally published in* Lecture mon doux plaisir *(1957), he explores the philosophical nature of Voltaire's fiction.*]

Philosophical fiction is a difficult, because a hybrid, literary form. Since the author uses it for the purpose of espousing or attacking certain accepted ideas, it belongs to the class of essays or pamphlets. But because it narrates a sequence of imaginary events, it can also claim the title of fiction. It cannot, however, have either the seriousness of the essay or the credibility of the novel. Not that it even pretends to be credible. On the contrary, it deliberately stresses the fact that it is an exercise in intellectual ingenuity. Not Voltaire when he created *Candide,* nor Anatole France when he wrote *L'Île des Pingouins,* nor Wells when he invented *The Island of Dr Moreau* believed for a moment that the reader would mistake these fictions for reality. On the contrary, it was their considered intention to present these stories with a philosophical content as fantastic tales.

But why, it may be asked, should an author have recourse to this whimsical and indirect method of philosophizing? In order to enjoy greater freedom in expressing ideas which, in an essay, might seem to be subversive, shocking and unacceptable to the reader. The more he can be made to feel that he has been transported into a world where nonsense reigns supreme, the more reassured will he feel, and the readier to digest many surprising truths. Swift was able to say a number of disturbing things about human nature and the England of his own day, merely by pretending to describe a nation of midgets, a kingdom of giants, or a country in which horses ruled over human beings. Montesquieu was able, through the mouth of an imaginary Persian, to mock at customs for which his birth and position compelled him to make a show of respect.

The philosophical tale, or novel, will, therefore, be peculiarly well suited to a period in which ideas are changing more quickly than institutions and manners. Writers, tormented by the need they feel to say what they think, but hampered by the severity of police regulations, censorship or an Inquisition, will be tempted to take refuge in the absurd, and to make themselves invulnerable by making their books incredible. Such was the position in the France of the eighteenth century. To all appearances the monarchy was still powerful. It was the protector of religious and philosophic orthodoxy. Its judges administered the Law

with a heavy hand. But, in fact, the writers and the members of the privileged classes had been won over to the new ideas, and were eager to air them. It was not altogether impossible for them to do so openly, as is proved by the publication of the *Dictionnaire Philosophique,* the *Essai sur les Moeurs* and the *Encyclopédie.* But there still remained a number of themes on which it was difficult to touch. There was, however, a good chance that, if treated as elements in a fictitious narrative, they could be brought to the notice of a more timorous and, therefore, a wider public, the more so since this type of reading matter was very much in the fashion. Ever since the publication of *The Arabian Nights* in Galland's translation (1704-1717) and of the *Lettres Persanes* (1721), the oriental mode had become the favoured and transparent mask of those who, in this way, could temper their audacities with prudence. Voltaire, more than anybody else, had recourse to it.

James Boswell compares *Candide* to Samuel Johnson's *Rasselas:*

Voltaire's *Candide,* written to refute the system of Optimism, which it has accomplished with brilliant success, is wonderfully similar in its plan and conduct to Johnson's *Rasselas;* insomuch, that I have heard Johnson say, that if they had not been published so closely one after the other that there was not time for imitation, it would have been in vain to deny that the scheme of that which came latest was taken from the other. Though the proposition illustrated by both these works was the same, namely, that in our present state there is more evil than good, the intention of the writers was very different. Voltaire I am afraid, meant only by wanton profaneness to obtain a sportive victory over religion, and to discredit the belief of a superintending Providence: Johnson meant, by shewing the unsatisfactory nature of things temporal, to direct the hopes of man to things eternal.

James Boswell, in his The Life of Samuel Johnson, *1791.*

It is a matter for no little surprise that he should have adopted this lively and, in both senses of the word, free form at a comparatively advanced age. Apart from the *Adventures du Baron de Gangan* which never found its way into print, though its existence is proved by a series of letters exchanged between the author and the Crown-Prince of Prussia, Voltaire's first philosophic tale was *Le Monde Comme il Va,* written in 1747. It was at this time that, as the result of an unfortunate episode, he, together with Mme du Châtelet, took refuge with the Duchesse du Maine at Sceaux. It was under her roof that *Babouc, Memnon, Scarmentado* and *Zadig* were composed. Voltaire wrote a chapter every day, which he showed to the Duchess in the evening. "Sometimes, after supper, he would read a tale or a short novel which he had written during the day for the express purpose of entertaining her. . . ."

These philosophic fictions, always contrived so as to illustrate some moral truth, were written in a gay and charming style, and the Duchesse du Maine took so great a delight in them that others soon expressed a wish to share her pleasure, with the result that Voltaire was compelled to read them aloud to a wider circle. This he did with the skill of a trained actor. The tales enjoyed a great success with his listeners, who begged that he would have them printed. For a long time he refused to do so, saying that such trivial works, designed for the amusement of a small and intimate circle, did not deserve to be perpetuated. Writers are bad judges of their own productions. At the age of eighteen Voltaire had believed that he would go down in literary history as a great tragic dramatist: at thirty, that he was destined to be a famous historian: at forty, an epic poet. He could not have foreseen, when he wrote **Zadig** in 1748, that it would still be regarded as entertaining reading, together with his other short tales, in 1958, whereas *La Henriade, Zaïre, Mérope* and *Tancrède* would be condemned to an eternal sleep on library shelves.

In this matter Voltaire's contemporaries were no less wrong than he was. They attached but little importance to frivolous stories in which what struck them most forcibly were numerous allusions to the author's personal enemies. "It is easy to recognize Voltaire under the disguise of the sagacious Zadig. The calumnies and spite of courtiers . . . the disgrace of the hero are so many allegories to be interpreted easily enough. It is thus that he takes revenge upon his enemies . . ." The abbé Boyer, who was the Dauphin's tutor and a powerful ecclesiastic, took in very bad part the attacks on one whose identity was but thinly concealed behind the anagram *Reyob.* "It would please me mightily if all this to-do about **Zadig** could be ended," wrote Mme du Châtelet, and it was not long before Voltaire disowned a book "which some there are who accuse of containing audacious attacks upon our holy religion". In point of fact the audacities of **Zadig** were pretty mild, and were limited to showing that men, at different times and in different places, have had different beliefs, though the solid basis of all religions is the same. Such a thesis was the most obvious common sense, but common sense was, at that time, most certainly not in general circulation.

Those who dared not attack Voltaire's theology accused him of plagiarism. That has always been an easy method of belittling a great writer. Everything has been said before—not excepting the statement that everything has been said before—and nothing is easier than to establish a connexion between passages in two different authors. Molière imitated Plautus who, in his turn, had imitated Menander who, no doubt, had imitated some earlier model unknown to us. Fréron (some twenty years later) charged Voltaire with having borrowed the best chapters of **Zadig** from sources "which that prize copyist took great pains to conceal". For instance, the brilliant *L'Ermite* chapter was borrowed from a poem by Parnell, and that entitled *Le Chien et le Cheval* (an anticipation of Sherlock Holmes) was lifted from *Le Voyage et les Adventures des Trois Princes de Serendip.* "Monsieur de Voltaire", wrote the treacherous Fréron, "reads often with intention, and much to his advantage, more especially in such books as he thinks have now been long forgotten. . . . From these obscure mines he brings a great many precious jewels to the surface."

Is that so terrible a crime? Must an author refuse to touch seams which have not been completely worked out? What honest critic has ever maintained that a writer can create *ex nihilo?* Neither Parnell's *The Hermit* nor *Le Voyage de Serendip* were original productions. "All these brief tales", says Gaston Paris, "were told long ago in many languages before being recast in that flexible and lively French which, today, gives them a seeming novelty . . . " The unique and brilliant character of Voltaire's *tales* lies not in originality of invention, but in that combination of diverse and seemingly contradictory qualities which are their author's own and unequalled contribution.

He had been educated by the Jesuits, and from them had learned intellectual discipline and elegance of style. During a temporary period of exile in England he had read Swift and studied his technique. "He is the English Rabelais," he had said of the author of Gulliver, "but without Rabelais' bombast." Under the influence of Swift he had developed a liking for strange fancies (whence **Micromégas** and **Babouc**), for travellers' tales which were no more than an excuse for satiric writing, and a literary variant of what we, today, should call a "poker face" which enabled him to give expression to the most monstrous propositions as though they were obvious and natural truths. Onto this living tree had been grafted the Galland of the *Arabian Nights.* "The combination of the classic French mind, with its love of proved statements, its lucid deduction of conclusions from strict logical premises, and the completely illogical view of life common in the fatalistic East, might have been expected to produce a new dimension: and this it did." The subject matter was provided by stories as old as the human race: the technique contained elements drawn from Swift, from Eastern story-telling and from Jesuit teaching: but it was the inimitable synthesis of all these influences that produced the tales which Voltaire continued to concoct over a long period of time.

It has already been pointed out that he began his experiments in this, for him, new literary form, in 1747, that is to say, when he was fifty-three. He wrote his masterpiece in that kind, **Candide,** when he was sixty-five; **L'Ingénu,** which is another of his most successful products, when he was seventy-four, in the same year that saw the publication of **La Princesse de Babylone;** and he was over eighty when he brought out such minor works as **L'Histoire de Fenni, Le Crocheteur Borgne** and **Les Oreilles du Comte de Chesterfield.** Hence, Paul Morand's generalization to the effect that French writers are never younger, never more free from constraint, than when they have passed their sixtieth birthday. By that time they have broken free from the romantic agonies of youth and turned their backs on that pursuit of honours which, in a country where literature plays a social rôle, absorbs too much of their energies during the years of maturity. Chateaubriand was never more "modern" than in his *Vie de Rancé,* and in the concluding sections of the *Mémoires d'Outre-Tombe.* Voltaire wrote his best book at sixty-five, and Anatole France his, *Les Dieux ont Soif,* at sixty-eight. The old writer, like the old actor, is a master of his craft. Youthfulness of style is no more than a matter of technique.

It has become customary to bring together under the blanket title of "Romans et Contes de Voltaire" a number of works greatly differing in kind and in value. Among them are such masterpieces as *Zadig, Candide* and *L'Ingénu*; there are the relatively unimportant *Princesse de Babylone* and *Le Taureau blanc;* there are *Cosi-Sancta* and *Le Crocheteur Borgne* which are no more than short stories of ten pages or so, and genuine novels of a hundred; there are rough sketches of the general type of *Les Voyages de Scarmentado,* which is really only a foretaste of *Candide; Les Lettres d'Amabel* which belongs to the tradition of *Lettres Persanes,* and dialogues like *L'Homme aux Quarante Ecus,* in which there is no fictional element at all, but only a discussion about political economy reminiscent of *Dialogues sur le Commerce des Blés,* by the abbé Galiani, or Voltaire's own *Oreilles du Comte de Chesterfield* in which theology is argued instead of economics.

What have all these odds and ends of writing in common? First and foremost, the *tone* which, in Voltaire, is always mocking, mercurial and, at least apparently, superficial. There is not, in all these fictions, a single character who is treated with genuine seriousness. All are either embodiments of an idea or a doctrine (Pangloss stands for optimism, Martin for pessimism), or fairy-tale heroes from a lacquer screen or a piece of Chinese embroidery. They can be tortured or burned to death without the author or the reader feeling any real concern for them. Even the beautiful Saint-Yves, when dying of despair because she has sacrificed what she calls her honour in order to save her lover, can weep without bringing the slightest hint of moisture to the eyes of anybody else. The stories, catastrophic though they may be, are always dominated by the author's wit, and so rapid is their *tempo* that the reader is given no time in which to be deeply distressed. A *prestissimo* has no place in a Funeral March or a Requiem Mass, and the *prestissimo* or the *allegretto* are Voltaire's favourite "movements".

Puppets, variously labelled, jig to this devil's tattoo. Voltaire delighted in bringing on to his stage priests, to whom he gave the name of *magi;* judges, whom he called *mufti;* financiers, inquisitors, Jews, innocents and philosophers. Certain routine enemies reappear in all the tales, variously disguised. Of women he has no very high opinion. To judge from his treatment of them, their minds are exclusively occupied by the prospect of making love to handsome young men with good figures, though, being both venal and timid, they are prepared to hire their bodies to old inquisitors or soldiers if, by so doing, they can save their own lives or amass riches. They are inconstant, and will gladly cut off the nose of a husband fondly mourned in order to cure a new lover. For such conduct he does not blame them. "I have", says Scarmentado, "seen all that the world can offer of the beautiful, the good and the admirable, and am determined for the future to confine my attention to my household gods. I took me a wife in my own country: I was cuckolded, and concluded that my state was the pleasantest that life can give."

It is from the author's philosophy that these writings truly derive a unity. It has been described as "a chaos of lucid ideas", in short, incoherent. Faguet accused Voltaire of having considered everything, examined everything, and

never gone deeply into anything. "Is he an optimist? Is he a pessimist? Does he believe in free-will or predestination? Does he believe in the immortality of the soul? Does he believe in God? Does he deny the validity of metaphysics? Is there something in him of the agnostic spirit, but only up to a certain point, in other words, is he really a metaphysician at heart? . . . I defy anybody to answer any of these questions with an unqualified yes or no."

All that is perfectly true. There is something of everything to be found in Voltaire, and also the opposite of everything. But the chaos is reduced to order as soon as one sees the apparent contradictions against the background of his times. In this case, as in that of most men, a personal philosophy was in a continuing state of evolution throughout his life. *La Vision de Babouc* and *Zadig* were written when Fortune was smiling on him. He was enjoying the favour and protection of Mme de Pompadour, and, consequently, of a considerable section of the Court. All the kings of Europe were inviting him to visit them. Mme du Châtelet was attending to his sensual needs, giving him affection and assuring his independence. He had every reason, therefore, for finding life tolerable. That is why the conclusions reached in *Babouc* are, relatively speaking, lenient.

"Would you have me chastise Persepolis or destroy it?" the djinn Ituriel asks him. Babouc has an observant and impartial eye. He is present at a bloody battle, in which, on neither side, do the soldiers know why they are killing and getting killed, but that same battle is the occasion for innumerable acts of bravery and humanity. He enters Persepolis and finds there a dirty and ill-favoured people, temples where the dead are buried to an accompaniment of harsh, discordant voices, and women of the town on whose activities the magistrates turn an indulgent eye. But, as he continues his tour, he comes upon finer temples, a wise and polished people who are deeply attached to their king, an honest merchant. It is not long before he comes to like the city which is, at once, frivolous, scandalmongering, pleasant, beautiful and intelligent. When he reports his findings to Ituriel, the latter decides not even to try to correct its shortcomings, but "to let the world go its way, since though everything is far from well, everything is not too bad".

Zadig sounds a somewhat deeper note. In it Voltaire shows, by a series of ingenious parables, that it would be a rash man indeed who would maintain that the world is bad because it contains a certain number of evils. The future is hidden from us, and we cannot be sure that from these seeming errors of the Creator salvation may not come. "There is no evil", says the Angel to Zadig, "of which some goodness is not born." "But", asks Zadig, "what if everything were good and nothing evil?" "Then", says the angel Jesrad, "this world would be a different place: the interconnexion of events would belong to a different order of wisdom, and this different order, which would be perfect, could exist only in the eternal dwelling-place of the Supreme Being . . . "—a form of reasoning which is far from being irrefutable, since, if God is good, why did He not confine the world within the bounds of that eternal dwelling-place? If He is all-powerful, why did He not, in creating the world, keep it free from suffering?

Voltaire was far too intelligent not to have asked himself these questions, and, in *Micromégas,* he gives them a disillusioned answer. Micromégas is an inhabitant of Sirius who travels from planet to planet in the company of a dweller in Saturn. One day, the giant discovers the Earth and the almost invisible animalculae who live upon it. He is amazed to find that these tiny creatures can talk, and is outraged by their presumption. One of these midgets, wearing a doctor's cap, tells him that he knows the whole secret of existence, which, he says, is to be found in the *Summa* of St Thomas. "He looked the two celestial beings up and down, and informed them that their persons, their worlds, their suns and their stars had been created for the sole purpose of serving Man." Hearing this, Micromégas gives vent to Homeric laughter.

This laughter is Voltaire's own. So, human beings complain that the world is ill-made, do they? But ill-made for whom? For Man, who, in the immense design of the Universe is no more than an unimportant mould! The probability is that everything in this world which we think is botched or erroneous has its reasons at a totally different level of existence. The mould endures, no doubt, a small amount of suffering, but somewhere there are giants who, huge in stature as in mind, live in a state of semi-divinity. This is Voltaire's answer to the problem of evil. It is not very satisfactory because the mould need never have been created, and, in the eyes of God, it may well be that mere size is of no importance.

But *Micromégas* is still comparatively optimistic. Ridiculous though these human insects may be when they presume to speak of philosophy, they astonish the celestial visitors when they apply the principles of their science, and measure with accuracy the exact size of Micromégas, and the distance of Sirius from the Earth. That these all but invisible mites should have penetrated so deeply into the mysteries of the Universe in which they are themselves, perhaps, no more than accidents, was already causing no little wonder in Voltaire's time, and would still more surprise a Micromégas who should make a similar voyage of discovery in our own day. Pascal had already said as much, and so had Bacon. Men may be no more than mites, but mites who dominate the Universe by obeying its laws. Their absurdities are counter-balanced by their intelligence.

In *Micromégas* we have the second Voltaire of the "tales". The third is a far sadder figure, for he has come to understand that Man is not only absurd but also extremely wicked. By that time he had had his own personal misfortunes. Mme du Châtelet had deceived him with his best friend, and, got with child by Saint-Lambert, had died in labour. The Kings, whether of France or Prussia, had treated him badly, and he found himself condemned to live in exile. True, it was a very comfortable exile. Neither Les Délices nor Ferney could be called unpleasing residences. But such happiness as he enjoyed there he owned to his own prudence, and not at all to his fellow men among whom he had met with such bitter persecution. But his worst sufferings resulted from public disasters. Too many wars, too much intolerance. Then, in 1755, to the cruelty of men was added the enmity of Nature. It was the year of the Lisbon earthquake which destroyed one of the finest cities in Europe. It had a profound effect upon him. No longer was it possible to maintain that everything is tolerable. The present, for him, was hideous.

> *One day, all will be well.* That is our hope.
> *All is well now,* that is an illusion.

One day all would be well, but only on condition that men set to work to transform society. In this poem we see the first sketch of a doctrine of progress and of the philosophy of *Candide.*

Candide was the outcome of Voltaire's own experiences and of the exasperation bred in him by the works of certain philosophers, such as Rousseau who had written: "If the Eternal Being has not done better, the reason is that he could not," or Leibnitz who laid it down that all was for the best in the best of all possible worlds. This generalization Voltaire put into the mouth of Pangloss, the teacher of optimism, and, to show how false it was, sent wandering about the world a simple-minded disciple of that same Pangloss, the young Candide, who saw at first hand armies, the Inquisition, murders, thievings and rapes, the Jesuits of Paraguay and conditions in France, England and Turkey. As a result of what he found in all these places, he came to the conclusion that everywhere and always Man is a very vicious animal. All the same, the last words of the book are: *Il faut cultiver notre jardin*—we must cultivate our garden—in other words, the world is mad and cruel: the earth trembles and the skies shoot lightning: kings engage in wars, and the churches tear one another to pieces. Let us limit our activities and try to do such humble work as many come our way, as best we can. That "scientific and bourgeois" conclusion was Voltaire's last world, as it was to be Goethe's. Everything is bad, but everything can be bettered. It sounds the prelude to our modern world, to the wisdom of the engineer, which may be far from complete, but is useful all the same. Voltaire, as Bainville said of him, "cleared the world of many illusions". On the ground thus swept and tidied it is possible to build anew.

Certain writers of our own day have discovered that the world is absurd. But in *Candide* Voltaire said all that can be said on that subject, and he said it with wit and intelligence, which is a good deal better than merely growing irritable, and leaves to us that legacy of courage which we need for action.

Candide was the high-point of Voltaire's art. Of the tales that followed it, *L'Ingénu* is the best. It still has the swiftness of the true Voltaire *tempo* and all his charm, but the themes round which it is constructed are of less importance than those of *Candide. L'Histoire de Fenni* is a defence of Deism, "the sole brake on men who are so shrewd in the committing of secret crimes. . . . Yes, my friends, atheism and fanaticism are the two poles in a Universe of confusion and horror." *Les Oreilles du Comte de Chesterfield* is a story which sets out to prove that fatality governs all things in this world. So, why reason and why worry? "Swallow hot drinks when you freeze, and cool drinks in the dog-days. Steer a middle course between the too much and the too little in all things. Digest, sleep and take your pleasure, all else is mockery." That is the conclusion of **Candide,** minus the poetry.

For the dominant quality of Voltaire's prose in his days of happiness is poetry. "There is", said Alain, "a prayer in every great work, even in Voltaire's tales." The poetry in all great writing is born, to a very large extent, of the fact that the madness of the universe is expressed by the disorder of ideas, but dominated by rhythm. In this, Shakespeare was a master with his witches' chants and his fairies' songs, so incoherent and so perfect. Voltaire's best work has the same two characteristics. Unforeseeable cascades of factual absurdities splash every page, yet the rapidity of the movement, the return at regular intervals of Martin's lamentations, of Candide's simplicities, of the misfortunes of Pangloss and of the Old Woman's stories, bring assurance to the mind of that tragic repose which only great poetry can give.

And so it is that Voltaire, who wanted to be a great poet in verse, and worked so hard at his tragedies and his epic, ended, though he did not know it, by finding pure poetry in his prose tales which he wrote for fun, and without, for a moment, thinking that they were important. Which proves, as he would have said, once again, that bad is good, good bad, and that fatality rules the world. (pp. 35-50)

> *André Maurois, "Voltaire: Novels and Tales,"*
> *in his* The Art of Writing, *translated by Gerard Hopkins, The Bodley Head, 1960, pp. 35-50.*

Roland Barthes   (essay date 1958)

[*A French critic, essayist, and autobiographer, Barthes was a leading exponent of the French "new criticism," "la nouvelle critique." His critical works helped usher structuralism to the forefront of French intellectual thought in the 1960s.* Le degré zéro de l'écriture *(1953;* Writing Degree Zero, *1967), considered to be Barthes's most influential and characteristic work, outraged many prominent French academics. In it Barthes presented his concept of* écriture, *the idea that a literary text has a meaning independent of, and possibly different from, the author's intentions. In the following essay, originally published in 1958, he appraises Voltaire's significance for the modern critic.*]

What have we in common, today, with Voltaire? From a modern point of view, his philosophy is outmoded. It is possible to believe in the fixity of essences and in the chaos of history, but no longer in the same way as Voltaire. In any case, atheists no longer throw themselves at the feet of deists, who moreover no longer exist. Dialectics has killed off Manicheanism, and we rarely discuss the ways of Providence. As for Voltaire's enemies, they have disappeared, or been transformed: there are no more Jansenists, no Socinians, no Leibnizians; the Jesuits are no longer named Nonotte or Patouillet.

I was about to say: there is no longer an Inquisition. This is wrong, of course. What has disappeared is the theater of persecution, not persecution itself: the *auto-da-fé* has been subtilized into a police operation, the stake has be-

come the concentration camp, discreetly ignored by its neighbors. In return for which, the figures have changed: in 1721 nine men and eleven women were burned at Grenada in the four ovens of the scaffold, and in 1723 nine men were burned at Madrid to celebrate the arrival of the French princess: they had doubtless married their cousins or eaten meat on Friday. A horrible repression, whose absurdity sustains Voltaire's entire *oeuvre*. But between 1939 and 1945, six million human beings were killed, among others, because they were Jews—they, or their fathers, or their grandfathers.

We have not had a single pamphlet against that. But perhaps it is precisely because the figures have changed. Simplistic as it may appear, there is a proportion between the lightness of the Voltairean artillery and the sporadic artillery of religious crime in the eighteenth century: quantitatively limited, the stake became a principle, i.e., a target: a tremendous advantage for its opponent: such is the stuff of which triumphant writers are made. For the very enormity of racist crimes, their organization by the State, the ideological justifications with which they are masked—all this involves today's writer in much more than a pamphlet, demands a philosophy rather than an irony, an explanation rather than an astonishment. Since Voltaire, history has been imprisoned in a difficulty which lacerates any committed literature and which Voltaire never knew: *no freedom for the enemies of freedom:* no one can any longer give lessons in tolerance to anyone.

In short, what separates us from Voltaire is that he was a happy writer. Better than anyone else, he gave reason's combat a festive style. Everything is spectacle in his battles: the adversary's name—always ridiculous; the disputed doctrine—reduced to a proposition (Voltairean irony is invariably the exposure of a disproportion); the points scored, exploding in every direction until they seem to be a game, dispensing the onlooker from all respect and all pity; the very mobility of the combatant, here disguised under a thousand transparent pseudonyms, there making his European journeys a kind of feinting farce, a perpetual Scapinade. For the skirmishes between Voltaire and the world are not only a spectacle but a superlative spectacle, proclaiming themselves such in the fashion of those Punchinello shows Voltaire loved so much—he had a puppet theater of his own at Cirey.

Voltaire's first happiness was doubtless that of his times. Let there be no mistake: the times were very harsh, and Voltaire has everywhere described their horrors. Yet no period has helped a writer more, given him more assurance that he was fighting for a just and natural cause. The bourgeoisie, the class from which Voltaire came, already held most of its economic positions; a power in commerce and industry, in the ministries, in culture and the sciences, it knew that its triumph coincided with the nation's prosperity and the happiness of each citizen. On its side, potential power, certainty of method, and the still-pure heritage of taste; against it, all a dying world could display of corruption, stupidity, and ferocity. It was indeed a great happiness, a great peace to combat an enemy so uniformly condemnable. The tragic spirit is severe because it acknowledges, by obligation of nature, its adversary's greatness: Voltaire had no tragic spirit: he had to measure himself against no living force, against no idea or individual that could induce him to reflect (except the past: Pascal, and the future: Rousseau; but he conjured them both away): Jesuits, Jansenists, or parliaments, these were great frozen bodies, drained of all intelligence and filled with no more than a ferocity intolerable to the heart and the mind. Authority, even in its bloodiest manifestations, was no more than a decor; merely subject such machinery to human eyes, and it would collapse. Voltaire had that sly and tender gaze (*Zaire's very heart,* Mme de Genlis tells us, *was in his eyes*), whose destructive power lay in simply bearing life among those great blind masks which still ruled society.

It was, then, a singular happiness to have to do battle in a world where force and stupidity were continually on the same tack: a privileged situation for the mind. The writer was on history's side, all the happier in that he perceived history as a consummation, not as a transcendence which risked sweeping him along with it.

Voltaire's second happiness was precisely to forget history, at the very moment it was supporting him. In order to be happy, Voltaire suspended time; if he has a philosophy, it is that of immobility. We know what he thought: God created the world as a geometer, not as a father. Which means that He does not bother to accompany His creation and that, once regulated, the world no longer sustains relations with God. An original intelligence established a certain type of causality once and for all: there are no objects without ends, no effects without causes, and the relation between one and the other is immutable. Voltairean metaphysics is therefore never anything but an introduction to physics, and Providence a mechanics. For once God has left the world He created (like the clockmaker his clock), neither God nor man ever moves again. Of course good and evil exist; but we are to translate them as happiness and misery, not sin or innocence; for they are merely the elements of a universal causality; they have a necessity, but this necessity is mechanical, not moral: evil does not punish, good does not reward: they do not signify that God is, that He surveys all, but that He has been, that He has created.

If man should take it upon himself to turn from evil to good by a moral impulse, it is the universal order of causes and effects which he injures; he can produce, by this movement, only a farcical chaos (as Memnon does, the day he decides to be wise). Then what can man do with regard to good and evil? Not much: in this machinery which is the Creation, there is room only for a *game,* that is, the very slight amplitude the constructor allows his pieces in which to move. This game is reason. It is capricious—i.e., it attests to no direction of history: reason appears, disappears, with no other law than the very personal effort of certain minds: among the benefits of history (useful inventions, great works) there is a relation of contiguity, never of function. Voltaire's opposition to any intelligence of time is very intense. For Voltaire, there is no history in the modern sense of the word, nothing but chronologies. Voltaire wrote historical works expressly to say that he did not believe in history: the age of Louis XIV is not an or-

ganism, it is a cluster of chance meetings, here the dragonnades, there Racine. Nature itself, of course, is never historical: being essentially art, i.e., God's artifice, it cannot move or have moved: the mountains were not wrought by the earth and the waters, God created them once and for all for the use of His creatures, and the fossil fishes—whose discovery so excited the age—are only the prosaic leavings of picnicking pilgrims: there is no evolution.

The philosophy of time will be the contribution of the nineteenth century (and singularly of Germany). We might assume that the relativist lesson of the past is at least replaced in Voltaire, as in his entire age, by that of space. At first glance, this is what occurs: the eighteenth century is not only a great age of travel, the age in which modern capitalism, then preponderantly British, definitively organizes its world market from China to South America; it is above all the age when travel accedes to literature and engages a philosophy. We know the role of the Jesuits, by their *Edifying and Curious Letters,* in the birth of exoticism. From early in the century, these materials were transformed and soon produced a veritable typology of exotic man: we have the Egyptian Sage, the Mohammedan Arab, the Turk, the Chinese, the Siamese, and most prestigious of all, the Persian. All these Orientals are philosophy teachers; but before saying which philosophy, we must note that just when Voltaire begins writing his Tales, which owe a great deal to Oriental folklore, the century has already elaborated a veritable rhetoric of exoticism, a kind of digest whose figures are so well formed and so well known that they can henceforth be utilized without troubling further over descriptions and astonishments; Voltaire will not fail to utilize them in this fashion, for he never troubled to be "original" (an entirely modern notion, moreover); for him, as indeed for any of his contemporaries, the Oriental is not the object, the term of a genuine consideration, but simply a cipher, a convenient sign of communication.

The result of this conceptualization is that the Voltairean journey has no density; the space Voltaire covers so obsessively (we do nothing but travel in his Tales) is not an explorer's space, it is a surveyor's space, and what Voltaire borrows from the allogeneous humanity of the Chinese and the Persian is a new limit, not a new substance; new habitations are attributed to the human essence, it flourishes from the Seine to the Ganges, and Voltaire's novels are less investigations than inspections of an owner whom we "orient" in no particular order because his estate never varies, and whom we interrupt by incessant stops during which we discuss not what we have seen but what we are. This explains why the Voltairean journey is neither realistic nor baroque (the picaresque vein of the century's first narratives has completely dried up); it is not even an operation of knowledge, but merely of affirmation; it is the element of a logic, the figure of an equation; these Oriental countries, which today have so heavy a weight, so pronounced an individuation in world politics, are for Voltaire so many forms, mobile signs without actual content, humanity at zero degrees (Centigrade), which one nimbly grasps in order to signify . . . oneself.

For such is the paradox of Voltairean travel: to manifest

an immobility. There are of course other manners, other laws, other moralities than ours, and this is what the journey teaches; but this diversity belongs to the human essence and consequently finds its point of equilibrium very rapidly; it is enough to acknowledge it in order to be done with it: let man (that is, Occidental man) multiply himself a little, let the European philosopher be doubled by the Chinese Sage, the ingenious Huron, and universal man will be created. To aggrandize oneself in order to confirm, not in order to transform oneself—such is the meaning of the Voltairean voyage.

It was doubtless Voltaire's second happiness to be able to depend upon the world's immobility. The bourgeoisie was so close to power that it could already begin not to believe in history. It could also begin to reject any system, to suspect any organized philosophy, that is, to posit its own thinking, its own good sense as a Nature which any doctrine, any intellectual system would offend. This is what Voltaire did so brilliantly, and it was his third happiness: he ceaselessly dissociated intelligence and intellectuality, asserting that the world is an order if we do not try too much to order it, that it is a system if only we renounce systematizing it: this conduct of mind has had a great career subsequently: today we call it anti-intellectualism.

Notable is the fact that all of Voltaire's enemies could be named, that is, their being derived from their certainty: Jesuits, Jansenists, Socinians, Protestants, atheists, all enemies among themselves, but united under Voltaire's attack by their capacity to be defined by a word. Conversely, on the level of denominative systems, Voltaire escapes. Doctrinally, was he a deist? a Leibnizian? a rationalist? Each time, yes and no. He has no system except the hatred of system (and we know that there is nothing grimmer than this very system); today his enemies would be the doctrinaires of history, of science (*vide* his mockery of pure science in *The Man with Forty Ecus*), or of existence; Marxists, existentialists, leftist intellectuals—Voltaire would have hated them, covered them with incessant *lazzi*, as he did the Jesuits in his own day. By continuously setting intelligence against intellectuality, by using one to undermine the other, by reducing the conflicts of ideas to a kind of Manichean struggle between stupidity and intelligence, by identifying all system with stupidity and all freedom of mind with intelligence, Voltaire grounded liberalism on a contradiction. As system of the nonsystem, anti-intellectualism eludes and gains on both counts, perpetually ricocheting between bad faith and good conscience, between a pessimism of substance and a jig of form, between a proclaimed skepticism and a terrorist doubt.

The Voltairean festivity is constituted by this incessant alibi. Voltaire cudgels and dodges at the same time. The world is simple for a man who ends all his letters with the cordial salutation *Ecrasons l'infâme* (i.e., dogmatism). We know that this simplicity and this happiness were bought at the price of an ablation of history and of an immobilization of the world. Further, it is a happiness which excluded many, despite its dazzling victory over obscurantism. Thus, in accord with the legend, the anti-Voltaire is indeed Rousseau. By forcefully positing the idea of man's corruption by society, Rousseau set history moving again, estab-

lished the principle of a permanent transcendence of history. But by doing so he bequeathed to literature a poisoned legacy. Henceforth, ceaselessly athirst and wounded by a responsibility he can never again completely honor nor completely elude, the intellectual will be defined by his bad conscience: Voltaire was a happy writer, but doubtless the last. (pp. 83-9)

> *Roland Barthes, "The Last Happy Writer," in his* Critical Essays, *translated by Richard Howard, Northwestern University Press, 1972, pp. 83-9.*

Giovanni Gullace   (essay date 1967)

[*In the following excerpt, Gullace discusses the conclusion of* Candide *as it illustrates the different aspects of Voltaire's belief in progress.*]

It is unquestionable that Voltaire believed in the material betterment of mankind through the advancement of knowledge; but it is most doubtful that he ever had any sincere faith in moral perfectibility, which is the very essence of human progress. And this is strongly suggested time and again by some of his writings which best express his mature views, despite the frequent inconsistencies of his thought. "We argue for ever," he wrote, "on the physical and the moral; but instinct will always govern the whole earth, for passions are the product of instinct, and passions will always reign." True human progress (if possible at all) should, therefore, be measured in terms of changes (for the better) in human instincts and passions, and not on the basis of the development of reason and the furtherance of knowledge. Reason and knowledge cannot be equated with human progress; at their best they are means and not an end. Thinking more rationally and knowing more do not automatically imply higher moral standards. The words of Medea in Ovid's *Metamorphoses*, "Video meliora proboque, deteriora sequor," confirm Voltaire's view on human instincts. Human nature has, for him, always been a mixture of good and evil, of wickedness and benevolence, and always will be: therefore, human progress is impossible. This is the conclusion implicit in his mature thought.

Before his stay in Prussia (1750-1753), Voltaire seemed more inclined to look at human events optimistically and to believe in a sort of meliorism, however ambiguous. In *Le Mondain* (1736) he had praised the march of progress with enthusiasm, contrasting life in his own times to primitive life when men walked barefooted, had long nails, slept on the bare ground, and ate acorns. Human progress had appeared to him then as an undeniable fact. His conception and treatment of history are permeated by the belief that mankind is marching toward enlightenment. The century of Louis XIV was presented (with the exception of the closing chapters) as the apotheosis of the human spirit: "The sound philosophy was known only during that time." The following stanza of his *Poème sur la loi naturelle* (1752) echoes a definite faith in progress (although the poem upholds the existence of a natural law whose universality and fixity conflict with the idea of progress):

> Enfin, grâce en nos jours à la philosophie,

> Qui de l'Europe au moins éclaire une partie,
> Les mortels, plus instruits, en sont moins inhu-
>   mains.

And his *Essai sur les mœurs* (1756) was conceived as a history of the progress of reason and of the gradual defeat of human folly and superstition, showing the transformations which had occurred through a long series of errors and prejudices. He wrote:

> It is to believe that reason and industry will always bring about new progress; that the useful arts will increase; that among the evils that have afflicted men, prejudices, which are not their least scourge, will gradually disappear in all those who are at the head of nations, and that philosophy, everywhere disseminated, will console a little human nature for the calamities it will undergo in all times.

However, despite his hopes in human betterment, Voltaire had to admit that human nature will undergo calamities "in all times," and that philosophy will only "console a little" for these calamities. His study of history and his personal experiences had gradually weakened his belief in progress. His sojourn at Potsdam was the last blow to his illusions. He realized that philosopher-kings like Frederick II were no better than other tyrants and that philosophy can never change their tyrannical instincts. His outlook on human nature and the world in general became thereafter increasingly gloomy. The *Poème sur le désastre de Lisbonne* (1756) and **Candide** (1759) clearly express the somber mood of his new attitude. His conception of history as the history of human progress was disproved by experience. While showing a process of material improvement in the conditions of mankind, history offers no proof that human nature has ever changed, that moral progress has ever been achieved. Man appears always to have been the same: "Before daring to say that we are better than our ancestors we should have to prove that under their conditions of life we would abstain with horror from the crimes of which they were guilty—and it is not demonstrated that in such a case we would be more humane than they." In his *Essai sur les mœurs* Voltaire expressed more or less the same views: "It is clear that everything which belongs intimately to human nature is the same from one end of the universe to the other." Man was born with certain feelings and instincts and he cannot rid himself of them; he is conditioned by these instincts, having no reserve of human resistance to hinder them. "Man, in general," Voltaire maintains, "has always been what he is: this does not mean that he has always had beautiful cities . . . But he has always had the same instinct. . . . This is what never changes from one end of the universe to the other." If man is governed by invariable instincts, he cannot possibly perfect himself: "Do we not see, indeed, that all animals, like other beings, invariably fulfill the law which nature gives to their kind? The bird makes his nest, as the stars round out their course, by a principle which never changes. How could man alone have changed?" Furthermore, Voltaire denies the natural goodness of man: "In general, men are senseless, ungrateful, jealous of another's good; they take advantage of their superiority when they are strong, and they become knavish when they are weak." The author,

however, concedes that men are neither good nor bad. But if they are not altogether good and they are not susceptible to improvement, moral progress is obviously impossible.

It seems that a theory of progress (intended as moral progress) has no foundation unless it is coupled with a theory of organic evolution, for only organic changes can effect modifications in man's moral behavior. In order to improve his moral habits, it is necessary to improve his physiological mechanism. Moral perfectibility would imply organic perfectibility. But, unfortunately, the physical nature of man cannot be modified; therefore, his moral character, being irresponsive to action from without, such as education or practice, remains completely inalterable. The present organic structure of man cannot afford any higher ethical principles than those displayed throughout history. Torn by conflicting instincts resulting from the basic laws of life, he is unable to be fairer or more benevolent than he is, without violating these laws. Any improvement would imply an alteration of the entire structure of nature. From the ethical point of view it is to be concluded that the so-called civilized man is no better than the primitive specimens of the human race. Man is and has always been a mixture of good and evil: it is his very nature to be so. On the other hand, human progress toward an ideal of happiness would break the barriers between man and God, between the human and the divine. If human nature could perfect itself indefinitely, it logically would reach the point of absolute perfection; it would thus become similar to God. Moral betterment conceived as a gradual increase of good and decrease of evil would alter the ratio on which the world rests. Evil, then, cannot end as long as the present reality exists. Wars, human cruelty, and all forms of man's intrinsic wickedness have in fact persisted throughout the ages. Human nature basically does not progress, since it is ruled by unchangeable laws. History is a succession of periods of greatness and periods of decadence: external conditions may favor the prevailing of the one or the other, but no moral gain is made in the flux of events.

> The world keeps on becoming a little more refined. But after having gotten out of one mess for a while, it falls back into another; centuries of barbarism follow upon centuries of politeness. Afterwards the barbarism is pushed out; then it reappears: it is the continual alternation of day and night.

Civilization changes the external appearance of things, not their essence. And if human folly has always been present in the world, it is evident that it is part of the structure of human nature. "But, said Zadig, if there was only good and no evil?" This, of course, would mean that the present world would no longer be the same. In its present structure it is inescapable that there will always be people destined to reason badly, others not to reason at all, and still others to persecute those who reason:

> We shall always have passions and prejudices since it is our destiny to be subject to prejudices and passions. We shall be certain that it no more depends on us to have great merit and talent than to have nice hair and a handsome hand. We shall be convinced that one must not take pride

in anything, and yet we shall always be vain. I am passionately fond of writing this; and you are passionately fond of condemning me: we are both equally foolish, equally the playthings of destiny. Your nature is to be evil, mine is to love truth and to publish it in spite of you.

This marked leaning toward determinism weakens further Voltaire's vague idea of progress. Human progress is not a natural process, but a planned effort whose success depends on the capacity of man's free will. If it were in the design of nature that things should move in a desired direction, human effort to achieve a perfectly happy existence would no longer be required. Voltaire believed that the world is so tied up, so rigorously organized that it admits no alterations, additions or omissions. If the laws of nature, to which man himself is subject, are prearranged, man cannot wilfully and consciously contribute to the march of events; he cannot improve the moral order. Voltaire's deterministic views leave no room for free will, which is the very instrument of human progress: "We are balloons pushed blindly and irresistibly by the hand of fate." Nature gave man the sense of pleasure and pain, and these are the only motives for his action: "We are but the blind instruments of nature."

Whether the world is ruled by organized laws or by blind forces, whether it follows a predetermined course or an unfathomable one, Voltaire's views sharply conflict with the idea of a universe molded by reason and free will. Human achievements are for him the result of fate or necessity. Since the plan of nature, if any, is completely unknown to man, a theory of progress would be on slippery ground, for no one can guarantee that such a plan would work for the best. Determinism in Voltaire has no teleological meaning, for it does not imply movement toward an ideal situation, but simply that events have mechanical causes intrinsic in the natural order of the universe.

The lack of a definite theory of progress accounts for his ambiguity and contradiction on the matter. In the introduction to the *Essai sur les mœurs* Voltaire takes issue with current ideas concerning man's pre-social state and the role of civilization. According to Rousseau, man lived alone in his natural state, having no family or social instincts. His family and social bonds are the result of a gradual degeneration from his primitive state—a degeneration characterized by the emergence of free will and the increasing resistance to physical impulses. "I do not believe," objects Voltaire, "that this solitary life attributed to our ancestors is intrinsic to human nature." Men were born with social instincts (Aristotle had already said so) like honeybees and ants. There is no primitive man living alone and "degenerating" toward social consciousness: "Has not every animal its irresistible urges which it obeys of necessity? What are these urges? The arrangement of the organs whose functions develop in the course of time." Therefore, man could not have changed: "If he had been destined, like the carnivorous animals, to a solitary life, could he have so contradicted the laws of nature as to live in society? And if he had been created to live in a herd . . . could he have so perverted his destiny as to live for centuries in solitude?" Man has not become a social animal

through a series of external accidents. He was destined to live in society and there has been no change in his state.

A theory of progress would conceive of morality as a degree of perfection acquired through education. But Voltaire, in his *Poème sur la loi naturelle,* stressed that the moral principle is innate in mankind, that is, inherent in man's nature and consequently instinctive. Voltaire, in fact, strongly objects to the assumption (coming from Locke) that man is the result of his upbringing and that only education is responsible for his intellectual and moral character. Man is not the imitator of his environment, learning justice through the example of others. He possesses the notion of good and evil before any experience: "We all have two sentiments which are the foundation of society—compassion and justice." In this case, one must conclude that the effort of enlightenment to inculcate them from without was completely useless. Voltaire disagrees with Montesquieu's deterministic theory according to which man's moral behavior is the result of climate and environment; likewise he rejects the view that remorse is to be attributed to education, maintaining that it is an instinctive and natural self-punishment for an evil action, since it springs from the intrinsic moral nature of man.

From all this it clearly emerges that Voltaire's thought is far from conducive to any faith in progress. He entertained a vague notion of human progress, while asserting the invariability of human nature. Human progress implies movement toward a definite goal, suggesting a dynamic world, whereas natural law implies fixity and universality, conveying the idea of a static world. If man is ruled by unchangeable instincts, he is not susceptible to perfection, and if his natural instincts made him cruel, foolish, unreasonable, egotistical, nothing can be done to improve his character. Improvements within the limits of nature are achieved through a spontaneous process; there is no need for education and enlightenment. Progress, on the contrary, begins where the natural process ends, and it operates beyond the sphere of natural laws, through the conscious effort of man. Voltaire's belief in human progress is no different from his belief in God—it is a profession of faith for public consumption. He concluded his *Essai sur les mœurs* with this pessimistic note:

> Since nature put self-interest, vanity and all passions in the heart of men, it is not astonishing that we have witnessed an almost continual series of crimes and disasters within a period of some ten centuries. If we go back to the times preceding, they are no better. Customs made it possible for evil to be perpetrated everywhere in different ways.

His words in *Les Lois de Minos* (1772), "The world slowly marches toward wisdom," should not mislead the reader concerning the author's real conviction. Voltaire's views on human progress are definitely pessimistic; and if he often took an ambivalent attitude in this respect, it was certainly prompted by this sad consideration: "The miserable human condition is such that truth is not always advantageous."

Some critics, none the less, interpreted the ending of *Candide* as the expression of a melioristic philosophy (if things are not good today, they will be better in the future). [In his *La Persée Francaise au XVIIIe siècle*] Daniel Mornet wrote that Candide "has still the courage to tend his garden, for, despite everything, he has faith in the future." [In his *Voltaire*] Gustave Lanson gave the ending of the novel a similar interpretation: "Life is not good, but it can be improved. How? Through work . . . from which everyone can profit." The same conclusion more or less was reached by others, who took for granted Voltaire's faith in human progress. But the author's inconsistency renders this melioristic interpretation completely unfounded. Meliorism is a "dynamic" optimism based on the hope in human betterment. It implies a theory of moral perfectibility, for only if man is capable of moral perfection can the world be improved. Meliorism, therefore, opposes itself to Leibniz's "static" optimism which considers the present world to be the best, despite the reality of evil. Voltaire does not seem to be far removed from Leibniz, whatever his bitter satire of Leibniz's philosophy. Leibniz's optimism is, in reality, an expression of deep pessimism. His assertion that this is the best world does not mean that it is absolute goodness, but simply that any other possible world would be worse. Therefore, if mankind is perverse and cruel, if nature is blind and merciless, if there is "a sufficient reason" for the existence of slavery, despotism, wars in the best structure of the universe, there is nothing one can do. Resignation is the only maxim of wisdom, since any change in the present order of things would result in more imperfections. The system of optimism is thus more frightening than pessimism, because it confronts us with a tragic and inescapable situation—the inevitability of evil in the inalterable structure of the universe. What led Leibniz to see his system as one of optimism were his teleological assumptions concerning the universal order. If one looks at the world from God's point of view, as Leibniz did, everything appears to be perfectly organized for the achievement of a universal goal; if one looks at the world from the point of view of the individual who suffers, as Voltaire did, things are not satisfactory at all. Voltaire's pessimism stems precisely from his narrow perspective. However, for both Leibniz and Voltaire moral improvement is impossible. Man, being what he is in the general order of nature, must resign himself to his lot. This is in fact what *Candide*'s conclusion seems to suggest. The call for action—"We must cultivate our garden"—is not the promise of a better world, but the expression of escape from the irremediable calamities of the present one. The fact that the garden is located at the margin of the world known by Candide may indicate a complete withdrawal. The concluding phrase of the work has, in the context, a negative sense. It expresses an aspiration to peace and oblivion. Voltaire seems to have abandoned the idea not only of explaining the world but also of correcting it. The garden is the antidote for the struggle and disappointment of life: the world is suffering, misery, injustice; the garden is peace and consolation.

[In his "Candide's Garden and the Lord's Vineyard," in *Studies on Voltaire* (1963)] Norman Torrey pointed out not long ago that the words "cultiver," "bâtir," "planter," which recur in Voltaire's writings after his return from Prussia, are always associated with the idea of living away from the folly of the world and of minding one's own busi-

ness, and that the references to the garden invariably show a desire for retreat. Voltaire's call for action sounds like a last resort, an act of resignation, the symbol of man's powerlessness in the face of evil. The atmosphere of the story is definitely pessimistic, despite the sprightly satire of men, institutions, and doctrines. The author's growing pessimism is already evident in his correspondence during the seven or eight years preceding the composition of *Candide.* In 1751, he wrote from Potsdam to Hénault: "The more I advance in life, the more I find work to be necessary. It becomes, in the long run, the greatest pleasure, replacing all of one's lost illusions." In 1754, he wrote to Roques that he regarded work as the "greatest consolation for the calamities inseparable from the human condition." Without mentioning the bitter pessimism of his *Poème sur le désastre de Lisbonne,* feelings of disappointment are invariably perceptible in his writings posterior to his sojourn in Prussia: "I know of nothing but work that can console the human race for existing" (letter to his niece); "I prefer my solitude to any court. Let us live in peace and let the heroes slaughter one another" (to Tronchin); "What, then, must be done? Nothing; keep silent, live in peace, and eat one's bread in the shade of one's fig tree; let the world go as it will" (to Bertrand).

After *Candide* Voltaire's feelings did not change. The pessimism of his *Poème sur le désastre de Lisbonne* became less bitter in *Candide,* the tragic mood turned into satire and irony, but his outlook remained unaltered. Though essentially a pessimist, he realized, nevertheless, the practical danger of an attitude that explicitly and completely closes the door to the hope for a better world. He recognized the social value of an illusion concerning the future, although evil appeared to him to be irremediable. What remedy against boredom, intrinsic to the human condition? Work is an anesthetic, and not a therapeutic treatment: "I imposed upon myself all this work so that I may not have any idle and sad moment" (to Madame du Deffand); "This world is a storm. Every man for himself !" (to Tronchin); "One must end up like Candide by cultivating one's garden" (to Damilaville). He strikes us not as an advocate of human progress, but as a disappointed Epicurean planning to withdraw from the world. His pessimism appears at times latent, at other times explicit, but it is persistent; and the devilish gaiety of *Candide* cannot dispel it. If social evils are the result of our natural limitations, there is no way of correcting them. This world was meant to be as it is: God "made this immense machine as perfect as he could; if he noticed any imperfection resulting from the nature of matter, he remedied it at the very beginning; thus he will never change anything in it." It is clear that the faith in human progress is absurd since it implies the violation of inflexible natural laws.

Some critics, however, contended that pessimism cannot be justified in a man like Voltaire who fought all his life for freedom and justice. How could he have suggested Epicurean indifference as the last word of wisdom? Here, of course, lies the great difficulty in the interpretation of *Candide*'s ending. But in Voltaire the theoretical and the practical orders do not seem to be logically connected. He is a skeptic by the very constitution of his mind. Skepticism is the ground for intellectual freedom; but it is also the ground for inconsistency, where it is possible to uphold the most conflicting principles without believing in any. He is a skeptic in theory, and as such he would lack a firm principle of action (how can one act rationally without knowing the ultimate end of action?), but in practice he takes a positivistic attitude. In fact, if he does not end his work on a note of despair, it is more from prudence than conviction. An explicitly pessimistic conclusion in **Candide** would not have attained any practical purpose from the social point of view. Pessimism paralyzes man's action and leads him into a sort of fatalism; Leibniz's optimism produces the very same results. And this is precisely what Voltaire strove to prevent. Man needs faith in certain values (even if these prove to be untrue) in order to act. Voltaire's call for action was prompted by social pragmatism rather than faith in the ultimate value of action. Did he not say, in reference to religion, that it "must be weighed on the political scale, after being weighed on the scale of truth"? It is hard to understand why, if not from his ingrained ambivalence, he employed all the resourcefulness of his mind in an attempt to destroy religious faith, which is the most powerful spring for moral action and the only source of consolation.

The meliorism which some critics claim to see in the conclusion of **Candide** becomes more and more questionable when related to Voltaire's view on the human condition. The retreat to the garden is in essence the expression of a gloomy outlook on life. Mankind suffers not only from physical evil, but also from metaphysical anguish, and even if physical evil could be obliterated from the face of the earth, there would always be the moral discomfort of a life without purpose. Civilization and wealth cannot alleviate boredom, which man bears within himself. The last chapter of **Candide** echoes the problem of boredom very eloquently. Man, in Martin's views, was born either to suffer or to be bored to death; in the garden, in fact, the first feeling was boredom:

> And when they were not arguing, the boredom was so excessive that one day the old woman dared to say to them:—I would like to know which is worse—to be raped a hundred times by Negro pirates, have a buttock cut off, run the gauntlet among the Bulgarians, be flogged and hanged in an auto-da-fé, be dissected, row in galleys, in short to undergo all the miseries we have all been through—or to stay here doing nothing?

All the justice that this world can afford would not eliminate boredom; nor would material prosperity. Work is an escape for those who are bored; it is a palliative, for it cannot improve the human condition or the nature of man: "Man," wrote Voltaire, "is more unfortunate than all the other animals together. He is continually prey to two scourges unknown to animals—anxiety and boredom, which are but repugnance for oneself. He loves life and he knows that he will die." What is, then, the advantage of enlightenment and the progress of knowledge, if they lead man to the consciousness and fear of his nothingness? Voltaire's meliorism must be interpreted as a march toward unhappiness:

> Beasts and men suffer almost ceaselessly, but men still more because not only is their gift of

thought quite often a torment, but because that faculty always makes them fear death, which beasts do not foresee. Man is a quite miserable being who has a few hours of respite, a few minutes of satisfaction and a lengthy succession of days of pain in his short life.

And here again the question could be asked: "Why cultivate reason if it is a source of inner misery?"

But Voltaire's pessimism is not nihilistic; it does not advise rest, or surrender to suffering. He advocates action which helps us forget our own absurd plight. The conclusion of **Candide** is that of an atheist who cannot count on God's help and who has to depend on his own resources:

> Let us end this miserable life as we are able, without recourse to a fantastic being whom no one has ever seen and to whom it would matter little, if he existed, whether we believed in him or not. What I think of him cannot affect him a whit more. . . . No relation between him and me, no link, no involvement. Either that being is not or he is an absolute stranger to me. Let us do as do nine hundred ninety-nine out of a thousand mortals: they sow, they plant, they work, they procreate, they eat, they drink, they sleep, suffer, and die without speaking of metaphysics, without knowing whether such a thing exists.

The question which Voltaire asks is not "Where are we going?" or "Where do we come from?" but simply "How must we live?" The answer to this question implies a definite answer to the two previous questions, for no maxim of practical wisdom can be established without knowing the goal. But Voltaire avoids the first two questions, and his answer to the third is that of a skeptic, not a skeptic like Montaigne, for whom agitation is senseless, but a skeptic like Voltaire himself who considers agitation to be the only way of making life bearable. Let us work without bothering about ultimate problems: absolute truth is beyond man's intellectual sphere. What purpose, then, does Voltaire assign to action? No ultimate purpose can be established and his call for action leads to blind pragmatism more distressing than pessimism. In rereading **Candide** Aldous Huxley remarked: "Il faut cultiver notre jardin. Yes, but suppose one begins to wonder why?" How can one be confident in human action, if the ultimate reason cannot be understood?

Gustave Lanson commented on **Candide**'s ending: "Reasoning on metaphysics does not serve any purpose: practical activity must replace empty speculation;" and he added that Voltaire's philosophy is only concerned with "the augmentation of welfare." But the welfare meant here is only material and far from solving the problem of the human condition. It renders man's lot more exasperating by showing that beyond material well-being there is nothing to hope for. It is true that in **Candide** everyone complains but no one kills himself; but is there anything more depressing than a mediocre life, which is hardly tolerable, in a world from which God has withdrawn? "Reasoning on metaphysics does not serve any purpose:" but is it not in the very nature of man to think, to philosophize, even if metaphysics should be inconclusive? In Arthur Schopenhauer's words, man is an *animal metaphysicum*

*Les Délices, where Voltaire lived from 1755 to 1758 on the outskirts
of Geneva. Today it houses the Institut et Musée Voltaire.*

committed to the search for knowledge beyond the world
of phenomenal appearances.

Voltaire dispelled traditional superstitions and illusions,
but he found no substitute for them. He tried to discredit
religion—the most consoling belief; he showed with lucidity the reality of evil; he bared the human condition; but
he offered no satisfactory remedy. His suggestion seems to
be: "Work and forget your plight!" Is man happier after
Voltaire's lesson? If we cultivate our garden, we want to
know why; if we must be just and beneficent, we want also
to know why. Pascal's teaching is, in this case, to be preferred to Voltaire's. Pascal's pessimism contains something consoling—hope; Voltaire's pessimism leads to
nothingness. Progress is a process of enrichment of life.
Voltaire impoverished life by stripping it of its religious dimension and by restricting man's aspirations to those of
a purely social animal.

Voltaire's alleged meliorism has also led critics to view the
conclusion of **Candide** as heralding the age of positivism
and the industrial revolution of the nineteenth century.
The last words of the novel seemed to foreshadow the civilization of machines and the scientific and technological
conquests of our times. Candide's departure from metaphysics and his turning entirely to practical activity was
interpreted as a sign of new cultural trends marked by a
more concrete attitude toward life. Lanson wrote of Voltaire:

> He is the philosopher who perhaps has done
> most to lay the foundation for the present form
> of civilization; he would have applauded the
> marvellous progress of our utilitarian and prac-
> tical century, the inventions of every sort which
> have made life easier, pleasanter, and at the same
> time more active and more intense. Civil law,

railroads, the electric telegraph, department
stores would have delighted him.

André Maurois echoed similar views [in his *Voltaire*]
when he wrote that in Voltaire there is an anticipation of
the "modern man and the wisdom of the engineer." The
phrase "we must cultivate our garden" appeared as the rehabilitation of manual labor. The theological conception
of work as punishment seemed to be reversed by a new
conception in which manual activity would no longer be
for enslaved classes but a religion for all, a means of progress and happiness capable of giving a meaning to life. The
famous garden, where the metaphysical and theological
ideals of the past came to an end, was interpreted to mark
the beginning of a new era—the era of technicians, engineers, and industry. Faust, like Candide, ends his fruitless
search for eternal truths by turning to practical work as
the only meaningful activity of life, to the work which con-
quers and transforms the earth.

But, even if Voltaire's enigmatic conclusion in **Candide**
could be read into a melioristic context, it should not be
taken without serious scrutiny. When the material progress realized in modern times is translated into terms of
human happiness one cannot repress a feeling of defeat.
The conquests of science and technology have intensified
the rhythm of life, but they have not changed man's lot.
No real progress has been achieved in the ethical domain.
A glimpse at the present world shows the level of bestiality
to which our "enlightened" civilization is descending. The
mythical reign of Saturn, promised by the prophets of
human progress, has not yet materialized; and their faith
in human betterment is more than ever confronted with
disappointing reality. And the optimists of our times are
more frightening than the pessimists of the past, their
promises being more diabolical and terrifying than any
past evils. The progress of automation, which they advocate, will perhaps atrophy human creative resources, and
we will gradually die as men in order to live as efficient
machines. If the material means at man's disposal are increased and improved without a corresponding improvement in his moral behavior, the so-called human progress
may become a march toward destruction.

If the ending of **Candide** foreshadows the age of the engineer and the opposition to abstract thinking, it must be
considered as a rather negative conclusion, since the narrow pragmatism implied in it is not in the least the final
word of human wisdom. Turning away from metaphysical
speculation and directing man's activity exclusively to
practicalities is not the answer to the deeper problem of
life. Such an attitude indicates a complete disregard for
man's inner desire to see beyond the physical world. The
trend to practicalities has led to the aberrations of modern
idolatry—the machine idolatry. We seem to have reached
the point where we need more priests and moralists than
engineers, more humanists than technicians, more sound
ethical principles than gadgets, more wisdom than power,
more distributive justice than production, more peace of
mind than material comfort. If Voltaire's garden is to be
taken as a positive program to combat evil, as the melio-
rists maintain, such a program is definitely short-sighted:
the remedy proposed is perhaps worse than the evil itself.

But it is doubtful that Candide, after all his sad experiences—with kings and commoners, with savages and civilized peoples, with the old and the new worlds—would believe in a better world. If moral progress had occurred, man's lot would have improved, and *Candide* would today be no more than a document of the past. Lanson's melioristic outlook prompted him to predict that the interest in Voltaire's novel would be, with the passing of time, purely stylistic. Instead, *Candide* still remains a living work appealing to us as it appealed to eighteenth century readers. Its call for action simply means that life is a perennial struggle and that man must fight in order to survive. It does not promise a better world, but it cautions us against the present one, eternally dominated by human folly. Life is a pendulum swinging between these two points—boredom and suffering. One must choose between the two. This is a pessimistic conclusion, but one of stoical resistance to evil, not one of future melioration. (pp. 168-85)

> Giovanni Gullace, "Voltaire's Idea of Progress and 'Candide's' Conclusion," in The Personalist, *Vol. XLVIII, No. 2, April, 1967, pp. 167-86.*

William F. Bottiglia   (essay date 1968)

[*Bottiglia is an American critic and educator who has written extensively on Voltaire and his times. In the following 1968 abridgment of a chapter in his* Voltaire's "Candide": Analysis of a Classic *(rev. ed., 1964), he delineates the qualities that make* Candide *a literary masterpiece.*]

A close analysis of the Conclusion of *Candide* will yield internal evidence which historians of ideas are prone to dismiss as beneath serious attention; but literary critics will accept it as objectively valid and will recognize in it the voice of Voltaire addressing his readers with authoritative immediacy. Once this analysis has been made, its results will be checked against, and correlated with, external considerations; and those results will be seen to shed light on the author's life and on his other writings. If the background of *Candide* helps illuminate its meaning, *Candide,* in turn, helps elucidate its historical context. This reciprocal relationship between art and history is a reality that needs to be constantly re-emphasized. *Candide* is not a mere passive product of "heredity, environment, and momentum." As a great literary statement, it has an agency of its own: it contributes to the making of history. More than this, as a work of art instinct with enduring values, it reflects and reveals the essential Voltaire in ways impossible to his humbler media of expression, such as his correspondence.

Since the Conclusion *is* a conclusion, and since the point at issue is one of meaning, it seems wise to begin by showing how the progression of ideas in the tale as a whole leads inevitably to the final climax. *Candide ou l'Optimisme* contains more—much more—than the promise of its subtitle. Voltaire is not on exhibition here as a systematic philosopher. He does not dialectically anatomize a doctrine and throw it piecemeal to the dogs as lacking in logical coherence or in correspondence to re-

ality. He displays himself as a theatrically self-aware artist, skillfully co-ordinating an atmosphere of clear ideas into a philosophic attitude charged with social dynamism. His central problem is that of human conduct in relation to the somber mystery of physical and social evil. His drive toward a solution of that problem develops as an assault on the vulnerable aspects of senescent classicism—its intellectual and its sentimental infirmities. But the assault alone, although it pervades the work from beginning to end, does not solve the problem. By routing the enemy and clearing the ground, it implies and prepares a positive solution. Meanwhile many hints are dropped along the way, prefiguring such a solution. Thus the great melioristic finale effectively concludes the tale by converging everything which has gone before into an epigrammatic statement of Voltaire's answer to the basic problem.

The intellectual presentation of physical evil in *Candide* includes natural disasters utterly beyond human control (e.g., tempest, earthquake), social calamities which outrun human responsibility (e.g., syphilis, plague), and misfortunes visited indiscriminately upon the good and the wicked (e.g., death of Jacques, naval battle)—all correlated with the view that the individual is helpless because completely predetermined by general laws. Throughout the tale there are repeated assertions that these workings of a "diabolical" principle mock the pursuit of happiness with miseries so numerous and so universal as to appear the normal lot of mankind, and so afflictive as to make one wonder at the tenacity of the will to live. Identical assertions are made with even greater frequency in the intellectual presentation of social evil, which occupies most of *Candide* with its grim catalogue of human ills rendered all the more execrable by their origin in human ignorance, weakness, and malice. A complete enumeration of these would rival the tale itself in length, and would show that Voltaire ranges with astonishing comprehensiveness through time and space as he satirizes man-made evils in their manifold appearances—metaphysical, theological, ecclesiastical, political, social, economic, and cultural.

Brilliantly interwoven with the intellectual presentation of physical and social evil is the complementary assault on the sentimental foibles of the age—an aspect of *Candide* either ignored or understressed by most critics. This takes the form of fictional parody, which saturates the work with ironic imitations of heroic, pastoral, picaresque, and utopian adventure-romances; also, by natural extension, of idealized travel-accounts. Numerous narrative devices, most of the character-types, many of the settings, and frequent turns of phrase are combined in this deliberate mimicry, which the author makes all the more amusing with occasional sly comments uttered through his personages. In mocking the sentimental ideals of his period, Voltaire powerfully rounds out his treatment of physical and social evil, for he is thereby enabled not only to enlarge the area of his illustrations but also to re-emphasize ironically the helplessness of the individual, driven as if fortuitously by the necessary specific effects of the general, immutable, unhuman laws of nature.

The bulk of *Candide* is an attack, in accordance with Voltaire's conception of "true *philosophes*" as "decent persons who have no fixed principles on the nature of things, who do not know what is, but who know very well what isn't. . . . " Yet the affirmation at the end is not thrust upon the reader suddenly, without preparation. To repeat, the attack itself is a preparation, in that it routs the enemy and clears the ground, thus implying a positive solution by elimination of its opposite. In addition, there are affirmative hints pointing in the same direction: two invincible biological drives, the will to live and the desire for food; the value of experience as a corrective for naïveté and as a means to practical wisdom; instinctive goodness, "conscience," and its normal civilized product, social goodness or "beneficence"; the benefits of culture, such as freedom of expression, good theater, good literature, good taste. And above and beyond all this, far-distant and half-lost in a luminous haze, the dream of Eldorado.

The final chapter of *Candide* funnels these many elements into an epigrammatic conclusion which summarizes and unifies the tale by answering the central problem. This answer, in keeping with the entire presentation, is not the scheme of a systematic philosopher, but the terse melioristic affirmation of a profound practical moralist doubled by a great literary artist.

Physical evil disturbs Voltaire for two reasons: (1) it calls into question the nature and purposes of a Creator whose general laws cause so much specific wretchedness for His predetermined creatures; (2) it gives rise to speculation which romances about the unknown as though it were the known, with disastrous effects on the moral motivation of mankind. The answer given by Voltaire through the dervish is no attempt to solve the insoluble. It is the resort of a pragmatist concerned with preserving the moral initiative. Physical evil is declared to be ultimately unknowable, and men are exhorted to resign themselves to that which they can never know, hence never control.

Social evil, on the other hand, is knowable and to some extent controllable. Much of what men have constructed in ignorance, weakness, and malice can be torn down and replaced by those who are willing to work for the betterment of the human family. To the entrenched ruthlessness of man-made evil the champions of social goodness must oppose disingenuous tactics which spring from the will to live combined with a sense of practical necessities. Thus, like the old Turk and Candide, they will turn their backs on public abominations in a gesture of philosophic disdain. They will assemble in small, like-minded groups safely removed from the centers of corruption. As members of model societies, they will work concretely, each at his appointed task, and with a minimum of windy theorizing, toward the diminution of social evil and the spread of social virtue. Already, in this way, men can enjoy the pleasures of good dinners seasoned with good conversation, as well as the precious benefits of culture. They can also legitimately envision an ideal State which, though beyond complete realization, may at least be more or less approached through co-operative work, through practical action—through the weeding and the cultivation of the garden and the sale of its produce in the market of the world.

The progression of ideas just outlined is significantly punc-

tuated by a series of symbolic gardens, or ways of life, culminating in the three which rapidly succeed one another at the very end:

1   the Westphalian "terrestrial Paradise,"
2   the kingdom of the Bulgares,
3   Protestant Holland,
4   Catholic Lisbon,
5   the Jesuit "vineyard" of Paraguay,
6   the primitive society of the Oreillons,
7   the model society of Eldorado,
8   Paris, the social and cultural hub of civilization,
9   Pococurante's ornamental garden,
10 Cacambo's accursed, backbreaking garden,
11 the modest garden of the old Turk,
12 Candide's garden, cultivated by a small model society.

Most of these are, of course, false Edens. Westphalia is the center of optimistic fatalism, sentimental quixotism, and petty aristocratic tyranny. The kingdom of the Bulgares is a naked military despotism, while Paraguay is a military despotism masquerading as a kingdom of God on earth. Holland is a mercantile utopia where "all are rich" and Christian charity is practised—with discrimination. Lisbon is the home of Inquisitorial fanaticism, with its attendant superstition and corruption. The country of the Oreillons is the habitat of state-of-nature savagery. The eighth garden symbolizes the tedium and the moral depravity of rootless and fruitless urban sophistication; the ninth, the sterile artificiality of blasé indolence; the tenth, the depression which accompanies work unillumined by a social purpose. Of the remaining three, Eldorado is negative in the sense that it is a myth, perfect and unreal; but it is also positive in the sense that it offers a philosophic ideal for human aspiration. Eldorado is the standard of perfection toward which the eleventh and twelfth gardens are dynamically directed. The old Turk's garden is a concrete example, however modest, of mankind advancing along the lines indicated above. Already less modest because involving a larger group than a family circle, and big with promise, is Candide's garden—a co-operative model society working ever so gradually, but with practical assurance, for the betterment of civilization.

The first and last gardens are specially related to each other by a common Biblical reference. The opening episode to some extent parodies the story of the Fall, with Candide, originally in a state of innocence, succumbing to temptation at the hands of a woman, and being expelled from the "terrestrial Paradise" by a very Teutonic Jehovah. In the final chapter the reader is reminded of the same story of Pangloss's quotation from the Vulgate. Before the Fall man was placed in the garden to dress it and to keep it. After the Fall he was condemned to work as a punishment. But the conclusion of *Candide* looks upon work as man's most wholesome activity . . . ; hence the ironical aptness of Pangloss's quotation, which seems to ignore the malediction of God following "man's first disobedience."

Before we look more closely at other key details of the finale, a few general observations are in order. In *Candide* the letter alone kills. Undeniably, the genre of the philosophic tale by its very nature invites interpretation that goes far beyond the naïve and unimaginative oversimplifications of Fundamentalist criticism. It is not quite true, however, to say that the literal invariably serves as nothing more than a pretext for the symbolical. If the symbolical rightly understood is always true in *Candide,* the literal may also contain a measure of truth; but due allowance must be made for overstatement, duplicity, inversion, etc. Another, and related, point involves the negative emphasis which pervades the tale, and concerning which [George R. Havens correctly says in the introduction to his 1934 edition of *Candide, ou l'Optimisme*]: "Of course *Candide* is intentionally one-sided. No carefully balanced account of good and evil could shock mankind into revolt." In other words, the tale is a deliberately exaggerated polemic, which sets an example by protesting vigorously against current evils, so that its negations imply corresponding affirmations. A third point, related to the second, is that there are a number of direct affirmations strewn through *Candide,* and that these are not swept away by the Conclusion, but gathered up into it. The tale does not recklessly destroy the good along with the bad. It is an exemplary exercise in creative, or constructive, criticism. A final point, connected with the third, is that *Candide* . . . is a *comic* work with a *happy* ending.

Now for those other key details of the finale. That the message conveyed by the dervish contains a certain degree of overstatement should be obvious. It is necessary to distinguish between what he literally says and what the author soberly means. Thus "be silent" appears to enjoin silence about ultimates, but actually would prohibit speculation on final problems only when it becomes a waste of time or is taken seriously enough to be exploited by power-hungry opportunists, to threaten moral initiative, to warp or obstruct social productivity. Earlier in the tale it was established that such discussion is permissible for purposes of intellectual stimulation and mutual consolation: "Candide continued his conversations with Martin. They argued unceasingly for two weeks, and at the end of two weeks they were as far advanced as on the first day. But after all they were expressing themselves, they were communicating ideas to one another, they were consoling one another" (Chapter XX). The dervish also prescribes resignation to physical evil on the ground that it can be neither known nor controlled. "His Highness" has instituted a certain general order and given men a certain basic equipment. The rest, it is implied, is strictly up to them. Let them carve out for themselves whatever destiny remains possible within these limits. Those critics who insist that there is an effect of contraction or shrinkage at the end of *Candide* are obviously right, since Voltaire makes it clear through the dervish that all ultimates, including physical evil, are fated to remain forever beyond human reach. The author is so utterly convinced of this that he presents his dervish accordingly, self-assured to a point of being impatient and even curt with those who think otherwise.

The role of Martin has often been misconstrued because of a critical failure to catch some of Voltaire's finer distinctions. The Manichaean's arrival on the scene is strategically timed to symbolize Candide's drift toward pessimism in Chapter XIX. He serves as a devil's advocate, arguing consistently that all is for the worst and that man is powerless to change the situation. Now, the fact that Voltaire is attacking optimism does not mean that he is embracing its opposite. If he rejects optimism, he does so not only on the ground of its metaphysical bluff but also on account of its "devitalizing agency," its discouraging fatalism. It is true that he treats Martin much more sympathetically than Pangloss, partly for polemical reasons, partly because the former's philosophy does less violence to the facts of life. But his handling of Martin in Chapter XXX shows plainly that pessimism does not triumph at the end. The author himself refers to Martin's principles as "detestable"—a valuation completely ignored by all critics who favor a pessimistic interpretation of the Conclusion. What is more, when Martin states that man was born to live "in the convulsions of anxiety, or in the lethargy of boredom," Candide *disagrees,* although he is not yet ready to voice a positive opinion of his own. Later, in the ripeness of time, it is Candide who makes the great affirmation, while Martin, like Pangloss, merely falls into line with an echoing judgment. Thus the pessimist and the optimist lose their respective identities to merge with their former disciple, now suddenly matured into the meliorist. In sum, Voltaire carefully shuns *both* extremes. Indeed, if, after his sustained assault on optimistic fatalism, he had concluded by adopting *pessimistic* fatalism, he would have perpetrated a glaring non sequitur, he would have killed the point of his tale, destroyed his case, lost the battle he had set out to win—the battle to preserve the moral initiative for his deistic humanism. In connection with Martin's echoing judgment, some scholars have understood the "let us work without arguing" to exclude from Candide's garden all forms of intellectual activity, philosophic or other. Actually, "without arguing" is the exact equivalent of the dervish's "be silent," which has already been explicated.

The first of the three gardens in Chapter XXX is Cacambo's. *Physically, it is the same garden as Candide's.* On this point [René Pomeau comments in *La Religion de Voltaire*]: "The survivors of the tale had been settled there for some time without knowing it. A profound lesson: all men are already in the only possible paradise. It is quite simply up to them to realize it." Voltaire's full meaning is richer than Pomeau suggests. Cacambo's garden and Candide's are physically identical, but the one precedes and the other follows the dawning of wisdom through consultation of the dervish and the old Turk. Before that dawning Cacambo works alone and curses his fate; after it the entire group finds happiness in co-operative labor. The example had been set for both him and Candide by the Eldoradans. Neither, however, was then mature enough to appreciate the contentment that comes from socially purposeful collaboration. [In *The Spirit of Voltaire,* Norman L. Torrey] says of Candide's garden that it reveals a Voltaire at "the bottom of his emotional curve." More accurately, it is Cacambo's garden which represents such a depression of spirits, along with the attitudes of Martin, of Pococurante, and of Candide at Surinam.

The second of the three gardens in Chapter XXX is the old Turk's. Here the author has blended *overstatement* with *duplicity,* hammering home the former—"I know nothing about it," "I have never known," "I know absolutely nothing," "I never make inquiries"—in order to prepare the reader for the latter—"I content myself with sending the fruits of the garden I cultivate to market there." The old Turk is no rude, untutored peasant. He is head of a well-bred, hard-working family, and he is a master of literary utterance, climaxing his series of incisive, elegantly turned observations with the magnificent aphorism: "work keeps away from us three great evils: boredom, vice, and want." If such a person insists that it is best to remain rigidly indifferent, even ignorant, respecting the world, Voltaire is soberly implying: 1) that men of good will should turn their backs on public abominations in a gesture of philosophic disdain; 2) that they should seek positions wherein they can maximize their personal safety and provide the fullest possible scope for their self-determination; 3) that they should work to banish the basic evils of boredom, vice, and want by producing for the market of the world. Once again there is an effect of shrinkage. The *philosophe* must dissociate himself from all corrupt governments, since they would embrace him only to stifle him; and he must withdraw to where he is secure from their abuses of power. But there is also countermovement, with potentially explosive overtones. After so much ironic emphasis on the helplessness of the individual, Voltaire now seriously suggests that men have a certain freedom of action. He further suggests that they can exert an influence for the better on the world at large, not by overt participation in its political affairs, but by supplying it with nutriment, as well as by setting a good example. Considering the heavy exaggeration of the old Turk's opening remarks, his traits of character, the many values directly or indirectly affirmed throughout the tale as worth salvaging, and its calculated symbolism, what critic would be so rash as to propose that the nutriment being supplied is restricted to food? The fruits of the old Turk's garden include more than legumes; they include intellectual pabulum.

A comparison of Candide's garden with those of Cacambo and the old Turk reveals *a deliberate progression from lone individual to family circle to small model group;* also, in all three (explicitly in the first two, implicitly in the third), the practical enterprise of selling their produce in the metropolitan market. The progression is objectively there, and it has profound implications. It proves that the effect of shrinkage is accompanied and balanced by an effect of expansion. The former, however, fulfills its function within the limits of the tale. The latter projects beyond those limits. The Conclusion of **Candide** is an ending with a vista. The vista is neither infinite nor insipidly roseate, but it does hold promise of solid humanistic advancement, of augmentative and ameliorative evolution in the direction of Eldoradan values. The pattern of the final chapter, no less eloquent than its language, informs the alert and sensitive reader that Candide's garden is not a terminus, but a commencement. Animated by an inherent dynamism, it will outgrow itself—*provided* its inhabitants continue to work together and are spared a natural catastrophe. This vista suffices by itself to destroy the Fundamentalist interpretation, for the future of the garden must entail something more than the growing of bigger and better vegetables.

As for interpretations which dwell on "selfish indifference" and "the doctrine of minding one's own business," they are refuted by Voltaire's own words. Candide's garden is co-operatively cultivated by "the entire little community." Pomeau contends that Pangloss constitutes an exception: "He alone escapes the final reformation of the little community. Still addicted to metaphysico-nigology, still 'arguing without working,' he remains imperturbably Pangloss, the man who is nothing but talk." The text of the tale, however, makes Pangloss a member of "the *entire* little community," and therefore one of its active workers. Moreover, it represents him as relapsing only "sometimes" into otiose speculation. Like his companions, then, he becomes socially useful in accordance with deistic doctrine. But social utility is not confined to the "little community." The garden is not "an Iland, intire of it selfe." The sale of produce establishes a connection with the big city—a connection wherein it is the small model group which influences the world, and not the other way around. But if the garden is to be understood symbolically as well as literally, then its yield must be such as to affect not only the bodies but also the minds of men.

In this regard it is a point of key importance that *Candide's garden involves more than gardening.* Each member of the group puts his particular talents to use. Cunégonde becomes a pastry cook, Paquette embroiders, the old woman takes care of the linen, Friar Giroflée does the carpentry. Cacambo presumably continues to grow vegetables and to market them in the metropolis. What of the remaining three members? Voltaire uses the others to illustrate very concretely the beginnings of specialized labor in a civilized society. Why does he say nothing specific about the work of Candide, Pangloss, and Martin? Several times in the course of the final chapter he focuses attention on them as *the intellectual subgroup* of the "little community." They undoubtedly help in the physical garden, but they, too, must have a specialty. Both Martin and Candide, applying the lesson taught by the dervish, discourage Pangloss from speculating about ultimates. That does not, however, preclude the composition and dissemination of socially useful literature. The activities of this civilization-in-minature not only go beyond literal gardening to the extent of including carpentry, laundering, embroidery, and baking; they also include the life of the mind concentrated on the spreading of utilitarian knowledge. To argue the opposite would, of course, be absurd. Does Candide achieve mature wisdom by repudiating the life of the mind and degenerating into a brute fellah? Voltaire's silence respecting the intellectual activity of Candide's model group is not a denial of its existence. Once again, his patterns powerfully convey his full meaning. I have just mentioned the pattern of the intellectual subgroup. There is, in addition, the pattern of *the disingenuous stance.* The duplicity of the old Turk's family circle prepares that of Candide's little band. Pomeau nonetheless flatly denies that there is any suggestion of "pamphletary activity" in the Conclusion of the tale. He does find in the garden an "engineering philosophy" whose goal is to "develop natural resources." This is in itself a large admission. A society devoted to applied science is a society that believes in socially useful knowledge and in the indispensability of book-learning, hence fosters the life of the mind. Pomeau is certainly right to find this in the garden. In my judgment, if he had closely examined the *form* of Chapter XXX, as well as *the language in relation to the form,* he would have found more. In fact, he would have found enough to prove that the wisdom of the Conclusion is not narrow and disappointing . . . , but excitingly dynamic, expansive, and challenging at every level of the civilized adventure.

There is still another pattern which contributes in an important way to the elucidation of Voltaire's closing message. *Voltaire has Candide state his conclusion, not once, but twice, the second time with dilated meaning.* In good music the restatement of a theme after an intervening development constitutes something more than a mechanical repetition. It enables the listener to hear the theme with a new understanding of its meaning, to appreciate it in a richer perspective. And so with Candide's conclusion. The first time he makes his affirmation, it is already charged with considerable significance. It chokes off Pangloss's pedantic prolixity, opposing the Deed to the Word. It dramatically underlines the antithesis between those who bloody the earth and those who cultivate it. It proclaims the immeasurable superiority of productivity to power politics. It invites to reflection on the values preached and practised by the old Turk and his family. And it casts a fitful light over the long, fantastic road traveled by Candide and his companions. But all this is not yet fully clear. The author has said too much and moved too swiftly for the reader to be able to absorb the final wisdom in one abrupt, climactic judgment. With great tactical skill he goes on to the elaboration of his theme. First he varies it. The variation sounded by Pangloss harks back to the beginning of the tale and, with consummate irony, to the beginning of the Scriptural Revelation. That voiced by Martin picks up the dervish's message and beautifully fuses the effect of shrinkage with that of expansion. The effect of expansion, however, still remains to be clarified. Having stated and varied his theme, Voltaire now proceeds to develop it. He shows us the little band purposefully hustling and bustling about its business, achieving co-operative contentment, serving as a miniature model for the world, and seeking to help make the world's business more like its own. The picture is much clearer now, provided the reader has been alert to the stylistic and structural devices which the master-storyteller is dynamically interweaving as he approaches the end of his story. The end takes the form of a summation in two contrasting speeches. That of Pangloss, a parody of periodic eloquence and a caricature of optimistic dialectic, nevertheless manages to provide a rapid review of several major motifs and episodes: namely, both the intellectual and the sentimental aspects of optimism, the inhumanity of man to man, religious fanaticism, the aimlessness of the South-American adventure, the visit by special dispensation to Eldorado, and the worthlessness of unearned wealth. This review rings a number of changes on social unproductiveness, while reminding us of its ideal opposite. Candide's response, quietly tolerant of his comrade's occasional aberrations, pointed, terse, lapidary, reaffirms the theme of productivity, which this time, because of the intervening development, renews, enriches, deepens, and broadens the meaning of the garden. The restatement flashes both back and forward. It is a wondrous epitome of the tale's wisdom, coined neither for mere show nor for mere contemplation, but for *use.*

Among other things, after mercilessly caricaturing love and woman throughout his narrative, Voltaire redresses the balance at the very end, but with subtlety, so as to preserve congruity of tone. If Candide reluctantly agrees to marry an ugly and shrewish Cunégonde whom he no longer loves, but who later develops into an excellent pastry cook, the author is soberly suggesting: 1) that sentimental quixotism warps or obstructs social productivity; 2) that the dignity and the moral value of the individual's life depend strictly on such productivity; 3) that a sound marriage demands mutual respect, and mutual respect becomes possible only through such productivity; 4) that a sound marriage further involves the procreation and proper upbringing of children who may eventually, *like the sons and daughters of the old Turk,* themselves become useful citizens.

Thus one of the Conclusion's many functions is to blunt the cutting edge of the satirical sword wielded up to the final moments of the battle with a bravura relish which might otherwise be mistaken for sadistic abandon. But in addition, from the very beginning Voltaire has taken care to sow his recital with salutary affirmatives, with examples of moral sanity and true civilized refinement; and this seed will bear fruit in Candide's garden. One reason why the message of Chapter XXX has been so often misread is that readers fail to appreciate the constructive character of Voltaire's criticism. He razes in order to rebuild more solidly, but he does not raze indiscriminately. While demolishing he picks out what is worth saving and makes ready to re-use it. The cultivation of the garden must therefore be understood to include immediately a humanitarian feeling for the wretched and the oppressed, and sooner or later the various cultural pursuits. This salvaging operation effectively illustrates Voltaire's belief in *the conservation and exploitation of all truly human resources.*

Pomeau raises the interesting and very important question of how the garden is socially and administratively organized. "Good humor," he states, "prevents the problem of social relationships from being posed. No leadership, no subordination in 'the little community.' Voltaire, easy-to-get-along-with fellow that he is, assumes that work organizes itself. . . . " Since it is Candide who makes the big decision while the others simply accept it, and since it is he who has the last word, I think it plain enough that he has now become the leader of the group. Moreover, Voltaire is under no obligation to do more than start the group on its way at the end. The rest is a matter of time, effort, intelligence, and good will. Nor must it be forgotten that the general direction of possible development may be inferred from the ideal society in the Eldorado episode. Voltaire definitely knows that it is men who organize work, and that in due course, if things go reasonably well, equality before the law will be preserved, but a social and economic hierarchy will take shape.

The nature of Candide's garden makes it dependent on those who work in it, to be sure, but also, as already noted, on the lucky avoidance of physical disasters, and, finally, on its security against destruction by hostile governments.

There is nothing automatic or certain about it, then. Its existence is precarious. It is a beautiful but fragile thing. Yet it represents man's best hope—indeed, his only hope *as* man; and it is therefore the only thing with which he has a human right to occupy himself.

One more point: Voltaire's conception of the garden is plural. Wherever a few persons gather in the name of social productivity, a garden comes into existence. Given enough of these developing, setting an example, and influencing the world, a global metagarden is conceivable. Conceivable, that is, as Eldorado is conceivable; but Voltaire is too much the realist to regard a global metagarden as fully realizable on this "globule." It is sufficient for him that men should move toward it, no matter how modestly, in attestation of their higher humanity.

The great mass of internal evidence proves that the meaning of the Conclusion is complex but not obscure, and that Voltaire does not end by abandoning the world to the wicked after flaying them with his verbal lash. He ends by affirming that social productivity of any kind at any level constitutes the good life, that there are limits within which man must be satisfied to lead the good life, but that within these he has a very real chance of achieving both private contentment and public progress.

Nothing outside *Candide* can be legitimately used to refute or to alter or to question what is actually expressed and communicated inside it by its author composing at a superconscious pitch of creative intensity. It is common sense to check the results of internal analysis against the available external evidence, to correlate the text of *Candide* with its historical context, to show how the work reflects the background and vice versa. But at no point should the work be treated as a mere result of mechanical forces functioning in time and space, hence susceptible of definitive measurement from without. The container theory of causation cannot be successfully applied to art, because the artist is a "sovereign Alchemist" who transmutes "Life's leaden metal into Gold," who creates new values. Investigations of origins and influences are therefore limited. Carefully conducted, they may prove highly suggestive. They should never be substituted for direct literary analysis of the work, and they should respect the great qualitative gap that separates the raw material from the finished product. This is why I have begun with a presentation of the internal evidence. What follows will serve to corroborate that evidence, both in general and in particular.

"Voltaire's tales," according to Torrey, "have a way . . . of summing up certain periods of his existence and certain problems with which he was then faced." In the case of *Candide* the period was the decade of the fifties; the central problem, as already stated, that of human conduct in relation to the somber mystery of physical and social evil. And viewed as a whole, *Candide* pursues a course of argument which parallels the evolution of its author's philosophic attitude during that decade—a decade wherein he irrevocably abandoned the relative complacency of his earlier years, inclined toward pessimism, and finally won through to a melioristic affirmation.

The pessimistic trend of the fifties is clearly perceptible in several important branches of Voltaire's production: in the correspondence; in the tales, from *Zadig* (1747-48) to *Scarmentado* (1753); in poetry, from the *Poème sur la loi naturelle* (1752) to the *Poème sur le désastre de Lisbonne* (1756). Surveyed in broad perspective, this gradual, cumulative movement assumes dominant proportions between 1752 and 1756. A mere enumeration of the major contributing factors will suffice to prove that this effect had its proper causes: the onset of old age coupled with poor health; the death of Mme. du Châtelet; the cynicism of Frederick's entourage; the rupture with His Majesty; the consequent sense of homelessness or exile; various literary and philosophic quarrels (Maupertuis, Rousseau, etc.); the Seven Years' War; the Lisbon disaster; the study of history, leading to disgust and skepticism; a painful awareness of the unresolvable conflict between the clocklike order of a rational, mechanical universe and the mad confusion of an illogical, capricious actuality. This last factor underlies the others. Metaphysics had become the unknowable. The purposes of God were inscrutable. Physical evil was a matter for stoical submission. Free will had been reluctantly abandoned in favor of determinism; yet optimistic fatalism was dispiriting and repugnant to one who could confront social evil only with programs of reform based on faith in man's progressive possibilities.

In the latter part of the decade, as the correspondence and the contributions to the *Encyclopédie* and *Candide* itself reveal, the pessimistic trend was checked and turned back upon itself by a melioristic countercurrent, which, gathering volume and momentum, swelled at last into an irresistible flood at Ferney. . . . Here again, sufficient reasons can be adduced to account for this fateful reversal of direction. The effect of Mme. du Châtelet's death wore off with time. Failing health and old age became conventional complaints, as Voltaire absorbed himself in active interests. He created for himself a secure haven, whence he was able to resume relations with Frederick at a safe distance. He attained genuine happiness through gardening and humanitarian projects. Confirmation of his genius all over the civilized world gave him renewed strength. Collaboration with the Encyclopaedists revived his confidence in at least a partial triumph of his ideas. And so his instinctive pugnacity spurred him on with increasing boldness against personal enemies, optimistic fatalism, "l'infâme," and social evil in general.

Thus the period of Voltaire's life which extends from the death of his mistress to the composition and publication of *Candide* can be summed up as a progression from relative complacency through pessimistic drift to meliorism. When due allowances have been made for literary license and accentuation, the movement of ideas in the tale is seen to follow pretty much the same line of development. Shortly after the beginning of the story Candide is ejected from his "terrestrial Paradise," the seat of optimism. The ensuing series of fantastically cumulated misadventures first disenchants, then disheartens him; until finally, in Chapter XIX, he renounces optimism as "the mania of maintaining that all is well when one is miserable," and is plunged into "a black melancholy," such that "the wickedness of men presented itself to his mind in all its ugliness, he harbored only gloomy thoughts." From this point on, symbolically accompanied by a devil's advocate in the person of Martin, he is drawn for a time toward pessimism; but concludes on a note which avoids both extremes by sounding the call to positive, practical action unobstructed by windy theorizing. This broad similarity between the evolution of Voltaire's philosophic attitude during the fifties and the movement of ideas in *Candide* lends no small degree of autobiographical distinctiveness and realism to its content.

There are certain principles of Voltaire's thought which, despite hesitations and vacillations, remain essentially consistent through the years. To see that this is so one need only look beneath the mercurial surface. As [Emmanuel Berl expresses it in the introduction to an edition of Voltaire's *Traité sur la tolérance*], "one needs but a minimum of intellectual discrimination to distinguish his caprices from his serious ideas and his petulant outbursts from his permanent views. So it is pointless to say: 'He is a chaos of clear ideas'; the chaos is made up of ideas solid enough to have endured intact through a meditation carried on for seventy years with undiminished energy." His attitude may evolve, as just shown, and it may even appear to shift from one pole to the other; yet invariably, in his serious moods, in his key works, it finds a way to avoid extremes. Thus he moves from free will to determinism, but interprets the latter as self-determination for purposes of human conduct, and so stays clear of fatalism. He attacks Jansenism from one direction and atheism from the opposite, again with the Golden Mean as his goal. What then, of *Candide?* Is it a spectacular exception? "His entire intellect was an engine of war," says Flaubert . . . of the satirist who never wrote but to act, who recognized that "he who takes pen in hand has a war on his hands," and who fought with a pen mightier than the sword for concrete social reforms. Did this same satirist, to indulge a fleeting mood of discouragement, compose his masterpiece on the problem of evil and pour into it all of his consummate artistry and ripened wisdom, only to arrive at a bucolic conclusion—the result of a paltry choice between cabbages and kings? Common sense tells us what the internal evidence and the evolution of Voltaire's attitude have already told us: that the Conclusion of *Candide* rejects pessimism no less than optimism, embracing instead a healthy, equilibrating meliorism.

Another permanent principle of Voltaire's thought is his social conception of morality. In his seventh *Discours envers sur l'homme* (1737) he had censured the piety of the hermit:

> Mais quel en est le fruit? quel bien fait-il au
>   monde?
> Malgré la sainteté de son auguste emploi,
> C'est n'être bon à rien de n'être bon qu'à soi

> [But what fruit does it yield? What good does he do the world? / Despite the holiness of his August occupation, / To be good only to oneself is to be good for nothing.]

In his *Traité de métaphysique* (1734) he had defined virtue as *"what is useful . . . to society."* On this point he remains perfectly consistent from start to finish of his long career.

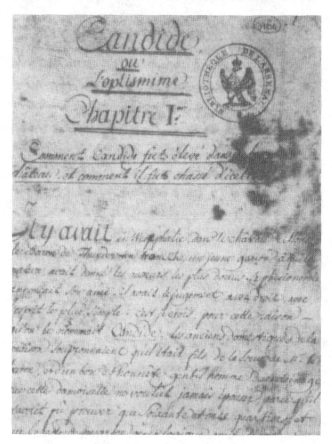

Opening page of the La Vallière manuscript of Candide.

Once more, what shall we say of *Candide*? Does his greatest work end in selfish withdrawal, indifference, escape, as some have maintained? The evidence inside the tale eloquently witnesses Voltaire's unbroken fidelity to his deistic ethic. Candide affirms that "we must cultivate *our* garden." Accordingly, the garden is co-operatively cultivated by the *entire* group. And what the group produces is fed to the *world*. Love of neighbor is thereby pursued in large as well as in small, and the meaning of "our garden" is expanded.

There are critics who defend a purely literal interpretation of that "garden" by reference to the author's gardening activities of 1758. Now, a Voltairean inclination toward allegorical and/or symbolical invention is clearly perceptible in as early a work as the *Henriade,* and has its roots deep in his psychology, his literary training, and his philosophic orientation. Long before 1758 this propensity had found apt raw materials for imaginative exploitation in the garden and the cultivation of the soil. In 1736 Voltaire has already utilized the Biblical garden of Eden in *Le Mondain,* contrasting its crudity with the "terrestrial paradise" of Cirey, and bantering Adam in these terms:

> Mon cher Adam, mon gourmand, mon bon père,
> Que faisais-tu dans les jardins d'Eden?
> Travaillais-tu pour ce sot genre humain?

> [My dear Adam, my glutton, my good father, / What were you doing in the garden of Eden? /

Were you working for our foolish human race?]

The Leningrad notebooks include the following entry: "The soil of Florence seemed made to produce Petrarchs, Galileos. We must cultivate ours, fertilize it, etc. Geniuses, like fruit, have come to France from Greece" (*Notebooks*, II, 277-78). Part IV of the *Poème sur la loi naturelle* (1752) contains a prolonged metaphor representing France as a garden, the king as the gardener, and his subjects as plants of various kinds and sizes, which he "cares for and prunes in the interests of a better garden." During the same year Voltaire writes to Argental, concerning his *Rome sauvée*: "It is by emendations that one must turn one's victory to account. This Roman soil was so unproductive that we must recultivate it after getting it, by dint of art, to bear fruit which was relished." A letter to Thieriot, dated 26 March 1757, affirms: "I have done everything I could throughout my life to help spread the spirit of philosophy and tolerance which seems today to characterize our century. That spirit, which inspires all decent Europeans, has successfully taken root in [this] country [Switzerland]. . . . " In a letter of 3 March 1758 to Cideville, he says of his theater at Lausanne: "The actors trained themselves in one year. They are fruits which the Alps and Mount Jura had not previously borne." In another, also to Cideville, dated 1 September 1758, he writes: "You are content to pick the flowers of Anacreon in your gardens."

The remarkable early pamphlet, *Ce qu'on ne fait pas et ce qu'on pourrait faire* (1742), reproduces a Roman citizen's imaginary memorandum containing a program of reform which definitely prefigures the conclusion of **Candide,** and closes with the words: "The obscure citizen's memorial turned out to be a seed which gradually germinated in the minds of great men." Also prefigurative is the following passage from the philosophic tale, **Lettre d'un Turc** (1750), with Omri saying to Bababec: "I value a man who sows vegetables or plants trees a hundred times more highly than all your comrades who stare at the tip of their nose or carry a pack out of excessive nobility of soul."

But the most astonishing anticipation of all is Voltaire's ode on *La Félicité des temps, ou l'Eloge de la France,* read before the French Academy on 25 August 1746. Stanzas VII, VIII, IX, and XI of this poem develop the following line of thought: in olden times a wilderness infested with intestine wars, France is today a peaceful commonwealth overlaid with splendid cities and ennobled by cultural pursuits; this immense progress was made possible by industrious tillage of the soil; work increased fertility, fertility produced wealth, wealth gave rise to all the benefits of higher civilization; such is the history and the promise of our nation, as indeed of all mankind.

> Loin ce discours lâche et vulgaire,
> Que toujours l'homme dégénère,
> Que tout s'épuise et tout finit:
> La nature est inépuisable,
> Et le Travail infatigable
> Est un dieu qui la rajeunit.

[Away with the craven and vulgar opinion / That man is constantly degenerating, / That everything is giving out and coming to an end: /

Nature is inexhaustible, / And tireless Work / Is a god who rejuvenates it.]

Here is one more fixed principle of Voltaire's thought, found from the *Lettres philosophiques* through the *Essai sur les mœurs* to the *Questions sur l'Encyclopédie.* Given time and good will, and unimpeded by earthquakes or invasions, human societies will advance by natural stages, beginning with agriculture and rising to culture in an ever more elaborate fusion of "pleasure" with "need." Agriculture is necessary for survival—which is why it has its indispensable place in the garden; but culture is necessary for higher civilization—which is why public works, the arts, and the general cultivation of the mind will sooner or later follow from the cultivation of the soil. In this connection I have already shown how the garden salvages the good seed from the experiences of the group in order to sow it for the future. Furthermore, in keeping with the values of the *Essai sur les mœurs,* the garden stands for every form of activity which helps produce civilization, as opposed to the criminally irresponsible and infertile practices of "the higher powers."

In addition to these inventions on the part of Voltaire, there is the striking passage from *Gulliver,* with which he had long been familiar, wherein the King of Brobdingnag expresses the opinion "that whoever could make two ears of corn or two blades of grass to grow upon a spot of ground where only one grew before, would deserve better of mankind, and do more essential service to his country than the whole race of politicians put together." There is the even more striking passage from a letter addressed to him by Bolingbroke as early as 27 June 1724. Writing from his "hermitage" at La Source, Bolingbroke develops at some length a comparison between the cultivation of the literal garden and that of "the mind," "the heart," and "the talents." Shortly before the composition of **Candide,** Voltaire, writing to Alembert from *his* "hermitage" at Les Délices, preaches a crusade of ideas against "l'infâme" and in favor of tolerance, speaks of the advances already made, and states that the vineyard of truth is being admirably cultivated by such *philosophes* as his correspondent, Diderot, Bolingbroke, Hume, etc. Bolingbroke had been dead for several years, yet Voltaire links him here with three other exemplary thinkers who are still alive and active. These associations, considered in the light of Voltaire's remarkable memory, fully justify, it seems to me, Besterman's suggestion that the Bolingbroke letter should be regarded as "one of the sources of Candide's final conclusion."

Since a majority of these inventions and readings—the above list is by no means exhaustive—antedate Les Délices by a number of years, and since they prove that the metaphorical use of the garden is a literary habit with Voltaire, there is no compelling biographical reason for arguing a one-to-one relationship between the author's literal garden and Candide's.

There is a much closer relationship between the author's philosophic activities of 1758 and the old Turk's garden. The latter's attitude toward news of public affairs is an absolute contradiction of Voltaire's irrepressible curiosity. In fact, as already pointed out, the Turk professes ignorance and indifference with an overemphasis which broadly hints at, and prepares the reader for, an effect of duplicity. It happens that "a certain form of duplicity was the necessary condition of Voltaire's life and works." . . . Now, the deceptions practised by Voltaire in his war against social evil, although they proved very effective in circumventing the established authorities, are never difficult to fathom. Like the author, the Turk and Candide do not withdraw completely from the world; they merely affect to do so. Actually, they turn their backs on public abominations in a gesture of philosophic disdain, and they retire to safe positions, where they will work concretely toward the spread of social virtue, and whence they will fight social evil with disingenuous tactics.

What was the justification for disingenuousness in 1758? Exile and homelessness were recent experiences and still-painful memories. The *Poème sur le désastre de Lisbonne,* issued in 1756, had had to be cautiously worded in order to avoid dangerous opposition. A royal decree of 1757 had restored the death penalty for writers and publishers convicted of attacking religion. In the very year 1758 the philosophic quarrel reached an acute stage, with the Encyclopaedic party deeply involved. Shortly before the publication of **Candide** a censorship of the mails was instituted. Voltaire was an eminently practical fighter. He believed that false heroics leading to martyrdom would only play into the hands of the enemy; hence his elaboration of the adroit stratagems usually associated with his Ferney period, but already being practised in connection with the composition and the publication of **Candide.**

As a disciple of Bayle, a contributor to the *Encyclopédie,* and a master-tactician in his own right, he established his "four paws." He wrote **Candide** in great secrecy. . . . He published it anonymously and denied his authorship. Shortly before its publication he feigned in his letters a loss of interest in the reading and writing of books. He included in the tale only a few anti-Biblical thrusts, and these mostly indirect. He scattered through his letters repeated affections of complete withdrawal from the world, and gave literary expression to this ruse in the final chapter of **Candide.** Finally, he may in part have chosen the metaphor of the garden because he could thereby screen an aggressive social intention behind a literal occupation. The old Turk's meaning, veiled yet strangely clear, shines through the following characteristic excerpts from the correspondence:

> (28 February [1757], to Diderot) "It is with pleasure that I forget in my retreat all those who are working to make men unhappy or to brutify them; and the more I forget those enemies of the human race, the more I remember you. I exhort you to diffuse as widely as possible through the *Encyclopédie* the noble freedom of your spirit";

> (26 March [1757], to Thieriot [the Damiens affair]) "We avert our eyes from those abominations in our little Romanic country. . . . We are doing here what one should be doing in Paris; we are living in tranquillity, we are cultivating literature without any cabals";

> (12 December [1757], to Alembert [the article *Genève*]) "there are some who accuse me of an

impious conspiracy with you. You know I am innocent";

> (24 December [1757], to Vernes [same subject]) "I haven't yet received the new volume of the *Encyclopédie* and I know absolutely nothing of what it's about. . . . Let's be neither Calvinists nor papists, but brothers, adorers of a merciful and just God";

> (15 May [1758], to Argental) "Do you have any news about the *Encyclopédie?* I prefer it to news of public affairs, which is almost always distressing";

> (3 September 1758, to Mme. Du Bocage [the Encyclopaedic party]) "The few sages, Madame, must not expose themselves to the wickedness of those who are mad. They must live together and shun the general public."

As most of these excerpts plainly show, Voltaire was vitally interested in the victory of the Encyclopaedic party. He declared himself the "admirer and . . . partisan to his dying day" of those who were compiling "the greatest work in the world," and contributed not a few articles of his own to the great enterprise. In 1757, and especially in 1758, when the opposition was making progress on the work increasingly difficult, Voltaire repeatedly exhorted his colleagues to strengthen themselves by forming a closely-knit philosophic group: "Gather the little flock. Courage.—Unite all the *philosophes* as best you can against the fanatics.—Form a group, gentlemen; a group always commands respect. . . . Get together, and you will be masters of the situation.—This is the moment when all the *philosophes* should join together.—All the *kakouaks* should form a pack, but they separate and the wolf devours them." Finally, recognizing the seriousness of their plight, he suggested that they flee from public life to where they could live together as free men, not in defeat, not in escapist retirement, but for the purpose of completing their task. To that end he even invited them to share his own retreat, just as in 1766 he was to recommend withdrawal to one of Frederick's southern provinces: (7 March [1758], to Alembert) "if we could reach an agreement, if we had courage, if we dared make a resolution, we could very well complete the *Encyclopédie* here. . . . If we were sufficiently detached from our age and our country to make this decision, I should contribute half of what I own to its execution. I should have the wherewithal to house you all, and very comfortably at that. I should like to see this project through and die happy."

The topical connection of the *Encyclopédie* with the conclusion of **Candide** is implicit in this epistolary evidence that Voltaire thought of the Encyclopaedists as a "little community," a model group of *philosophes,* who, like the old Turk and Candide—and Voltaire—should shelter themselves from exposure to public abominations, and work together toward the reduction of social evil and the spread of social virtue, by setting a concrete example and by enlightening the world. But the correspondence of the period immediately preceding **Candide** does more than imply such a connection; it explicitly links the Encyclopaedists with the metaphor of the garden:

(30 January [1755], to Gauffecourt) "Speaking of philosophy, do you still get to see my lords of the *Encyclopédie?* They are the proprietors of the greatest domain in the world. I hope they will always cultivate it with complete freedom; they are made to enlighten the world boldly, and to crush their enemies";

(6 December [1757], to Alembert) "I do as Cato did, I always end my harangue with the words: *Deleatur Carthago.* . . . It takes only five or six *philosophes* leagued together to overturn the colossus. It is not a question of preventing our lackeys from going to mass or attending Protestant services; it is a question of rescuing heads of families from the tyranny of impostors, and of inspiring a spirit of tolerance. This great mission is already enjoying success. The vineyard of truth is being well cultivated by Alemberts, Diderots, Bolingbrokes, Humes, etc.";

(7 March [1758], to Alembert) "If you again take up the ill-harnessed plow of the *Encyclopédie* and want some of those articles, I shall send them back proofread."

Torrey makes much of the fact that in his correspondence Voltaire differentiates the metaphor of the garden from that of the vineyard. Actually, before the publication of *Candide* there is no such pattern, for the figure of the vineyard appears but once in the letters that have survived. After the publication of *Candide* the "garden-vineyard" distinction does develop, and it is maintained with consistency, but it proves quite the opposite of what Torrey would have it prove. The "vineyard" metaphor becomes the ironic battle-cry of the philosophic party in its attack on "l'infâme": e.g., (13 February 1764, to Alembert) "so labor in the vineyard, crush 'l'infâme'." The "garden" figure, which tends to recur especially at times when "l'infâme" seems to be gaining the advantage over the philosophic party, becomes the symbol for an affectation of retreat accompanied by vigorous clandestine activity, so that, in the correspondence as in the Conclusion of *Candide, the garden includes the vineyard.* An excellent example of this fusion by absorption is found in Voltaire's letter of 2 April 1764 to Damilaville: "So we shall have to end like Candide by cultivating our garden. Good-bye, dear brother. Crush 'l'infâme' "; another, in his letter of 14 July 1773 to Alembert: "We must cultivate literature or our garden. . . . Please do not fail to remember me to Monsieur de Condorcet and your other friends who are very quietly supporting the good cause."

In fine, the correspondence posterior to *Candide* corroborates the message of its Conclusion as expressed and communicated in the text itself. The note of duplicity which is sounded in the letters echoes that of the old Turk's garden and Candide's, and so is necessarily present to Voltaire's mind. After the tale even more than before he is aware that the inherent dynamism of the garden inescapably compels its figurative extension. I have taken pains to describe the limitations which circumscribe and the dangers which attend that extension; but limitations and dangers notwithstanding, the basic, concrete example of gardening and/or farming has in it the stuff of expansion,

so that it cannot be confined within a purely literal conception.

It is difficult for historians of ideas to accept the principle that in a genuine work of art material and efficient causes are transcended by formal and final causes; but art critics know that to enter a work of art is to enter a sanctuary where the raw material of experience becomes aesthetically significant form-fused-with-content, and where quantitative measurement must accordingly be replaced by qualitative insight. I have been careful here to consider every kind of external evidence which has relevance either as raw material for *Candide* or as a subsequent reflection of *Candide,* and to consider it with a proper respect for its real importance—and a sensible appreciation of its limitations. My approach, in sum, has steered clear of both the Scylla of *in-vacuo* analysis and the Charybdis of unimaginative historicism in order to do full justice to a literary masterpiece risen out of time to timelessness. (pp. 87-111)

> William F. Bottiglia, *"Candide's Garden," in* Voltaire: A Collection of Critical Essays, *edited by William F. Bottiglia, Prentice-Hall, Inc., 1968, pp. 87-111.*

Priscilla P. Clark　(essay date 1973)

[*In the following essay, Clark contrasts the types of naïveté embodied by the protagonists of* Candide *and* L'Ingénu.]

One need not have read a great deal of Voltaire to notice his fondness for characters whose innocence with respect to one or another of the ways of the world is equalled only by their credulity. A perennial figure in various guises throughout Voltaire's *œuvre,* nowhere is the presence of the *naïf* so marked as in the *contes* where the combination of ignorance and candour makes him an unexcelled vehicle for social criticism.

What is a *naïf?* *Naïveté* and *naïf* derive from *nativus,* natural; [Maximilien-Paul-Émile] Littré equates the *naïf* with sincerity, candour and simplicity, an individual governed by feeling rather than reason: '[celui] qui retrace simplement la vérité, qui obéit à ses sentiments, qui dit sa pensée sans détour', while naïveté denotes that which is natural, lacking in artifice. Spontaneity of word and deed reflect the *naïf's* innate sincerity. On the other hand, depending on one's point of view, naïveté admits pejorative connotations too: simplicity may be seen as simple-mindedness; innocence and lack of guile may be equated with credulity and gullibility; candour may denote lack of foresight and restraint. All in all, the *naïf* is quite as susceptible to ridicule as to admiration. With great skill Voltaire plays on this ambiguity, emphasizing now the positive, now the negative side of naïveté and letting the nature of the satire determine the nature of the *naïf.*

As a literary device, however, the *naïf* has limitations. Most obviously, little more than a puppet, he cannot appeal directly to the reader, who discerns the author manipulating every string. The garden in *Candide,* we feel, will be cultivated as it was created, by Voltaire himself rather than by his eponymous hero. Clearly the *naïf* cannot serve as a positive model. Hence, when Voltaire wanted to make a positive statement with and through his protagonist and not just about his situation, he had to discard the *naïf.* Yet because it abstracts from reality, where the novel elaborates and develops, the *conte philosophique* requires the narrative simplicity to which the *naïf* is so admirably suited. And then too, Voltaire must have been reluctant to jettison a figure that he had used so often and to such effect. In *L'Ingénu* Voltaire resolved this dilemma by choosing a central character who is and at the same time is not a *naïf,* which resulted in a work that both is and is not a *conte philosophique.*

L'Ingénu is no ordinary *naïf,* and Littré tells us why. As one '[qui] laisse voir avec naïveté ses sentiments', *ingénu* overlaps with *naïf,* which l'Ingénu himself confirms: 'je suis assez accoutumé à dire ce que je pense, ou plutôt ce que je sens'. But the original meaning furnishes a significant nuance: under Roman law *ingénu* (*ingenuus*) referred to someone who had been born free and consequently had never known servitude. By extension the term refers to that which is worthy of a free man. L'Ingénu embodies just such a free man, free because uncontaminated by the prejudices of civilization. His ignorance of France and the French is as much a blessing as a disadvantage since, never having been 'enslaved' to this society's institutions, he sees them in a different, and perhaps, Voltaire is saying, a truer light. Despite his credulity, frankness and lack of sophistication, characteristics which unerringly mark him as a *naïf,* l'Ingénu is endowed with a dignity and a measure of autonomy that distinguish him from the more truly naïve Zadig and Candide.

In other respects as well, the naïveté of l'Ingénu differs from that of his predecessors. Unlike the Quaker in the *Lettres philosophiques,* whose simplicity is prompted by his philosophical principles, the innocence of l'Ingénu is a genuine manifestation of his ignorance. Like Zadig, he brings about his own quandaries, albeit unwittingly, but does not concern himself with the workings of Providence, the only domain in which Zadig, otherwise a very astute and definitely superior individual, can be considered naïve. Finally, in contrast to Candide, who more or less passively awaits the world's maledictions, l'Ingénu sallies forth to criticize whatever comes within his ken and undertakes to practise what he preaches.

Most important is that, for l'Ingénu as for none of the others, naïveté is relative and temporary. Whereas nature defines the *naïf* (*naïf* = natural), it is society that defines the *ingénu.* Thus **Candide,** with its hero as ignorant of the ways of man as he is innocent of those of God, represents above all an exploration of the *nature* of the universe and of the *nature* of man. Candide-Everyman exemplifies the human condition, which is to remain ignorant. In *L'Ingénu* Voltaire abjured metaphysics and restricted his scope to *social* criticism, choosing his protagonist accordingly. L'Ingénu speaks less from ignorance than from a different set of values, and since this ignorance is socially defined, it is not innate, not a permanent attribute. Like the Oriental visitors Montesquieu used as his foils in the *Lettres persanes,* l'Ingénu's naïveté, his innocence and ignorance represent no more than a passing phase in his de-

velopment, one which he, like Rica and Usbek, soon quits. Once a *naïf,* always a *naïf*—man cannot change what nature has decreed—but the *ingénu* may change, indeed by definition, he is destined to do so. (Thus *ingénue* in ordinary as well as theatrical parlance denotes a young girl: with age will come the experience that signals loss of naïveté.)

Whence l'Ingénu's transformation from untutored (though not uncivilized) half-savage to 'philosophe intrépide', a journey taken by none of the others. Besides the Quaker, whose brief appearance precludes development of any sort, Zadig and Candide too are more or less static, since despite achieving a certain understanding of life's workings and their own limitations, they personally change little. Zadig at the beginning of his saga is as wise and as intelligent and as honest as at the end, and he is really no more enlightened about the ways of Providence than Candide, whose solution to cultivate his garden tacitly acknowledges the impossibility of overcoming philosophical ignorance. Doomed never to know, Candide is necessarily condemned to eternal naïveté. L'Ingénu could not be more different. When his fiancée's good offices effect his release from the dungeons of Paris and he returns to Brittany, 'l'Ingénu [. . .] n'était plus l'ingénu', a transformation the young lady remarks upon in more detail: 'ce n'est plus le même homme; son maintien, son ton, ses idées, son esprit, tout est changé; il est devenu aussi respectable qu'il était naïf et étranger à tout'.

This evolution is not without its effects on the *conte philosophique,* since it alters one of its basic premises, namely the type of character used to illustrate the narrative. L'Ingénu's education, the more serious tone of the discussions with Gordon in prison, not to mention the lachrymose agony of Mlle de St. Yves, all attenuate the satire by diminishing the psychic distance characteristic of both the other *contes* and the beginning of *L'Ingénu.* Whereas in **Candide** we take Voltaire seriously, seeing the master's hand controlling every manœuvre, every absurdity, in *L'Ingénu* the focus perceptibly though not consistently shifts from Voltaire to his creature. Voltaire endowed l'Ingénu with an identity, and if this story begins as a philosophical tale, it comes perilously close to ending like a novel. This crossing of genres and the resulting ambiguity are no doubt responsible for some of the uneasy reactions of those who cannot decide how they should categorize this work or what standards they should apply.

That Voltaire chose to transform his *naïf* and the orientation of his *conte* tells us something about the uses and limitations of naïveté, and also the uses and the limitations of the *conte philosophique,* for l'Ingénu's changes alter the type and the source of criticism. In the first part of *L'Ingénu* Voltaire aims at the more blatant inconsistencies of 'civilized' society. Unlike **Candide,** where the satire is more comprehensive and more astringent, here Voltaire is almost benign in his comparisons between the 'natural' ethics promulgated by l'Ingénu and the entrenched customs of the French, or rather the Bretons. That it should be Brittany—the most backward or certainly the least sophisticated part of France (in the eyes of Voltaire's *mondain* readers at any rate)—which introduces l'Ingénu to civilization, only makes the contrast more ironical. The traits assigned by Voltaire to Breton society are basic characteristics which, with a few modifications, would be applicable to many different societies.

The glee with which he recounts l'Ingénu's unquenchable critical enthusiasm and his never-ending sallies might seem to place Voltaire in the rather paradoxical position of advocating 'nature' over civilization, were it not that l'Ingénu cannot be considered an avatar of even the most noble of savages. Quite the contrary, to counterbalance his lack of knowledge of things French, Voltaire takes care to base l'Ingénu's criticisms, like those of the Quaker, on a definite, though vague, set of values. Unpolished and unsophisticated, l'Ingénu nevertheless is far from inexperienced. No advocate of civilization was more ardent than Voltaire, and it is unlikely that he who would exclaim, 'Ô le bon temps que ce siècle de fer!' would choose as spokesman someone who contradicted that ideal.

Precisely because l'Ingénu's criticisms derive from his strong convictions—'la loi des Hurons valait pour le moins la loi des Bas-Bretons'—they are the more trenchant, reaching beyond the Quaker's indirect criticism to direct commentary and not infrequently to action as well. As he explains upon his arrival in Brittany, reticence is foreign to his nature: 'On m'a toujours appelé l'Ingénu [. . .] parce que je dis toujours naïvement ce que je pense, comme je fais tout ce que je veux'. The incompatibility of the two worlds grows particularly acute when it becomes necessary to reconcile l'Ingénu's amatory instincts with the conduct sanctioned by polite society. The thwarted swain may invoke the commandments and privileges of natural law to his heart's content, the shocked disapprobation of civilized society dooms his projects to failure.

It is in Brittany, however, that l'Ingénu takes the first step towards the civilized man he will eventually become when, albeit reluctantly, he recognizes the necessity of 'la loi positive' ('un frein que la vertu s'est donné elle-même'). Henceforth, instead of playing on the conflict between the natural laws of Huronie and those of civilized society, Voltaire directs his criticism against the society's failure to respect the very principles it endeavours to instil. In Versailles l'Ingénu faces, and with all the appalled zeal of a new convert criticizes, the abuses of those laws he has just accepted. From the amusing, relatively innocuous criticisms of the familiar absurdities of religious rites and social rituals, Voltaire moves to attack Church and State as powerful social institutions. The good-natured if ethnocentric Bretons are replaced by the 'coquins raffinés' who inhabit the capital.

As l'Ingénu learns more about society, his criticisms become more pointed and more appropriate, less frequently arising from an instinctive reaction to events and more often due to a measured judgment. Still, he retains enough of his naïveté to make remarks which were better not made, and he soon finds himself in prison. Here, under the tutelage of his Jansenist fellow-prisoner, Gordon, l'Ingénu 'faisait des progrès rapides dans les sciences, et surtout dans la science de l'homme'. He is more and more capable of voicing Voltaire's own views directly, hence less and less naïve. Gordon takes his pupil seriously, and the reader

is invited to do likewise: 'Il voyait les choses comme elles sont'.

At the same time l'Ingénu completes his education, in order to maintain the satiric tone, to keep the *conte* from turning into a philosophic discourse of sorts as well as to compensate for the lessening naïveté of his hitherto principal *naïf,* Voltaire shifts the focus slightly and, without abandoning his hero altogether, concentrates on the tribulations of Mlle de St. Yves, l'Ingénu's Breton fiancée, in her efforts to liberate l'Ingénu from prison. Since the problem that Jansenism poses in this tale is a purely ideological matter, Voltaire's attack on Jansenism is wholly directed toward its theological pretensions. Despite the absurdities of his doctrine, absurdities which l'Ingénu easily demonstrates as such by 'cette naïveté [qui] embarrassait fort le bonhomme', Gordon himself is very *sympathique*—'il avait été malheureux avec le jeune prisonnier et c'était un grand titre.' Jansenism is something else again, and not surprisingly the severe, distorted Jansenist ethics do not withstand comparison with the candid, honest judgments of the protagonist who has become Voltaire's spokesman. 'Pour dernier prodige un Huron convertissait un janséniste' who 'oublia pour jamais la grâce efficace et le concours concomitant'. The pupil learns, but the would-be converter is converted. 'Serait-il bien vrai, s'écria-t-il, que je me fusse rendu malheureux pour des chimères?'

The Jesuits constitute a far graver danger than one lone (and ultimately tractable) Jansenist, and to them accordingly Voltaire metes out proportionately harsher treatment. It is their efficient spy system that is responsible for l'Ingénu's prison sojourn. But l'Ingénu's prime opponent is Jansenism. Mlle de St. Yves is Voltaire's principal instrument for unmasking the immorality and corruption of the dastardly Jesuits into whose clutches she falls. Despite her firm command of the rules that governed the restricted world of her native Brittany, when she is transplanted to the more subtly malevolent world of Paris and Versailles, Mlle de St. Yves is utterly lost. The outrageous propositions of Monsieur de St Pouange, the adroit arguments of the aptly named Père Tout-à-tous, the perfidious counsel of her supposed friend—all contribute to her knowledge in precious little time.

The naïveté of Mlle de St. Yves in the labyrinths of Parisian *anti-chambres* mirrors the naïveté of l'Ingénu and his predicament on his arrival in Brittany, with the major difference that l'Ingénu's flexibility and native intelligence enable him to defeat his adversaries and surmount the problems posed by an unfamiliar environment, while his less fortunate and more naïve fiancée, incapable of adapting beliefs to a new situation, perishes. 'L'amour et le malheur l'avaient formée', true enough, even though she never is able to reconcile what she considers nothing less than treason with her love for l'Ingénu. 'Elle ne savait pas combien elle était vertueuse dans le crime qu'elle se reprochait': it is precisely this ignorance of true virtue as Voltaire defines it, this naïveté, that precipitates her untimely, not to say maudlin, death. Like Gordon, Mlle de St. Yves is a martyr to 'des chimères', technically losing her innocence, retaining her basic naïveté, and as with Gordon, Voltaire sympathizes with the plight of such a victim while yet judging him, and in this case her, adversely. (We may note that, elsewhere referred to as *Mademoiselle de St. Yves, la St. Yves* or perhaps *la belle* or *la tendre St. Yves,* during the seduction scenes with Monsieur de St Pouange, she becomes simply but dramatically *St. Yves,* and a reminder of her martyrdom).

Of the two *naïfs, L'Ingénu* pits against the world, the one, more credulous, more simple, more naïve, is vanquished by outside forces while the other, because he outgrows his naïveté, emerges victorious from his contest with these same forces. L'Ingénu's early instinctive observations when he first lands in Brittany ('[. . .] je n'étais alors qu'un sauvage'), differ greatly in tone and in content from the reasoned criticism of French institutions he offers after his return from Paris.

> Je soupçonne qu'il y a souvent de l'illusion, de la mode, du caprice, dans les jugements des hommes. J'ai parlé d'après la nature; il se peut que chez moi la nature soit très imparfaite; mais il se peut aussi qu'elle soit quelquefois peu consultée par la plupart des hommes.

The man who utters such sentiments is no *naïf.* Nor for that matter is he an *ingénu.* Even his manner has changed: 'il avait appris à joindre la discrétion à tous les dons heureux que la nature lui avait prodigués'. The nature of which he speaks is not 'la simple nature' which had already astonished Gordon in his first conversations with his fellow prisoner, but 'la nature, qui se perfectionnait en lui' during his incarceration. Because for Voltaire nature is capable of improvement, indeed that is the essence of civilization. If l'Ingénu is a positive figure as an *ingénu,* he is far more of one as a 'philosophe intrépide'. The Huron has become an enlightened man and a man of the Enlightenment, an ideal after Voltaire's own heart.

Because the forces which l'Ingénu combats are confined to the social and political spheres, because his problems concern the means of living rather than the ends, *L'Ingénu* is a more limited work than **Candide.** By the same token it is the more positive work, Candide's garden come to fruition. Instead of answering the questions posed in **Candide,** since no answer is possible, Voltaire responded with a programme of action and, most important, a programme of education. L'Ingénu wins his battles where the true *naïf* does little more than survive. The *naïf* may accumulate experience, the *ingénu* assimilates it.

In large measure the dynamic of *L'Ingénu* is the dynamic of development, and in a way this *conte* represents something of a **Philosophe's** Progress, a journey to which the *naïf* was clearly not equal. An *ingénu* was required. If, as many critics have observed, *L'Ingénu* veers from the *conte philosophique* to the novel, the reason is less the intrusion of sentimentality into a satiric genre than the more basic change wrought by the substitution of *ingénu* for *naïf.* The obvious affinity between the latter part of *L'Ingénu* and the sentimental novel is ultimately less significant than the connection of this *conte* as a whole to the *Bildungsroman.* For what is l'Ingénu but the archetypal young man from the provinces, however far off they may be, who enters society to learn about life? No Wilhelm Meister, l'Ingénu yet follows the same course. Both works, moreover, share a

meliorist orientation, a certain reconciliation with the world: 'Malheur est bon à quelque chose'.

Ought we perhaps to look to the title character himself and his education to resolve at least partially the disputes about the unity of *L'Ingénu*? In this perspective many of the incongruities that have troubled critics—the shift in tone, in characterization from the earlier *contes,* the shift from one part of *L'Ingénu* to the other, the historical setting—can be viewed as a function of Voltaire's goal to educate his *ingénu.* His sentimental education, which remains incomplete until the very end and Mlle de St. Yves's revelations, naturally brings into play different topics, requires a different tone from that of his formal education.

As l'Ingénu changes, so do his experiences. The political, social and religious satire, the more general criticism of the rigours and injustices necessarily perpetrated in an absolutist regime, the sentimentality, seem less heterogeneous when related to l'Ingénu's experience, which subsumes them all. If *L'Ingénu* has no revelatory subtitle, other than the fictional indication of 'Histoire véritable', might we not surmise that Voltaire thought that the title sufficed?

It would not do to exaggerate this point. If *L'Ingénu* is a *Bildungsroman,* it is a very schematic one. L'Ingénu never attains the plenitude associated with the protagonist of a novel, and his story remains close enough to the *conte philosophique* for that filiation to be the primary one. Notwithstanding such qualifications, l'Ingénu himself warrants more attention than critics have been inclined to accord him, for it is his variegated experiences that provide the *raison d'être* for everything that is satirized, it is his education that furnishes Voltaire with a rationale for his criticisms of French society, and it is his development that allows Voltaire to make a positive statement about the world and the possibilities open to man.

It was indeed advisedly that Voltaire baptised his Huron. Rejecting the *naïf* and its limitations, he opted for the potential inherent in the *ingénu.* The very title of this tale virtually implies the course it will take, and implies the transformations that will occur. Succinct as always, Voltaire once again shows himself master not only of words, but of the word, the significant detail, of an art which says so much by saying so little. (pp. 278-86)

> *Priscilla P. Clark, " 'L'Ingénu': The Uses and Limitations of Naïveté," in* French Studies, *Vol. XXVII, No. 3, July, 1973, pp. 278-86.*

David E. Highnam   (essay date 1975)

[In the following essay, Highnam analyzes the ways in which the satirical and sentimental strains complement each other in L'Ingénu.]

Because of Voltaire's attempt in *L'Ingénu* to evoke the reader's genuine sympathy for the tragic injustices suffered by its characters, this story is unique in his entire collection of philosophical tales. This very uniqueness is the source of a long-standing controversy among critics and scholars with regard to the work's aesthetic unity and its philosophical meaning. Voltaire himself perhaps initiated the debate with his remark that *L'Ingénu* is worth more than *Candide* because it is 'infiniment plus vraisemblable'. Nevertheless, in the large quantity of critical response which Voltaire's tale has elicited, few commentators have chosen to consider it in its entirety without emphasizing one of its two narrative tones—the sentimental or the satirical—to the detriment of the other or concluding that its 'two distinct and contrasting modes' are irreconcilable. The point of view of the present study is that the differing currents of inspiration in *L'Ingénu* are combined in an aesthetically and philosophically viable way and do not, in fact, constitute an undesirable dichotomy—nor is it necessary for one of the two narrative perspectives to be viewed as dominant in order to demonstrate the aesthetic unity of the work.

The evolution of narrative tone in *L'Ingénu* from *conte philosophique* to *roman sensible* can best be studied by examining the presentation and evolution of Voltaire's characters. Set in a precise geographical location at a specific date in recent French history, the minor characters of *L'Ingénu* are in general less schematic from the onset than their counterparts in other *contes*. Professor Hayden Mason has rightly asserted that the gap between their initial presentation and final state of development is therefore less radical than might appear at first glance.

Nevertheless, the dominant tone of the initial chapters is undeniably reminiscent of the familiar Voltairean irony and sarcasm at the expense of his fictional characters. Certain elements of the 'bas-Breton' setting where the Huron first sets foot, the geographic isolation and the narrow, provincial social hierarchy, remind us of the Wesphalia of *Candide.* One has the same general impression of a mockheroic world where the seriousness of the characters and the gravity of their emotions are undermined by the satirical distance so typical of Voltaire's narrative tone in the majority of the *contes*. The characters are essentially flat, stereotyped and mechanical, unaware of their obvious motivations and limitations, yet taking themselves seriously in the best Voltairean tradition.

Because of his calmness, his self-assurance and his natural nobility—the detachment he maintains, in effect—the Ingénu appears at first to be admirably three-dimensional in a society of excited marionettes. It soon becomes evident, however, that he is himself the illustration of a Voltairian thesis—an instrument for revealing the absurd and unjust aspects of French social organization, religious beliefs and political practices. Through the first six chapters, he is presented as a force of nature—his virility is prodigious, his reason untainted, his manners straightforward and uncivilized. From the time of his departure from Brittany in search of reward for his military exploits and the deliverance of mlle de St Yves until his imprisonment in the Bastille, he is only a slightly more credible version of Zadig or perhaps even of Candide. He is admirable in his innocence and candour, yet naïve and ignorant of the evils of the world. His quest is animated by the ideal of true love and the belief that, through truth and reason, he can put right the wrongs of society. Voltaire's satirical, distanced view of his character is evidenced by the Huron's mechanical repetition of stock ideas such as 'Vous n'avez donc

point de marraines que vous vouliez épouser' and 'Je verrai le Roi, je lui ferai connaître la vérité'.

The first significant change in narrative tone toward the Ingénu occurs during his prison education. The shift is brought about primarily by the critical distance which the Ingénu acquires toward his former self: 'La lecture agrandit l'âme, & un ami éclairé le console. Nôtre captif jouissait de ces deux avantages qu'il n'avait pas soupçonnés auparavant. Je serais tenté, dit-il, de croire aux métamorphoses, car j'ai été changé de brute en homme'.

In those chapters which relate the Ingénu's introduction to and criticism of numerous aspects of European civilization, the didactic role of the Ingénu as spokesman for Voltaire's own views eliminates the distance between author and character which is necessary for satire and irony.

Mlle de St Yves's evolution parallels for the most part that of the Ingénu. There is little significant evidence in the first twelve or thirteen chapters that she is individualized beyond the stereotyped figure of the young fiancée. The final paragraph of chapter 13 displays the curious mixture of *style satirique* and *style sensible* with which Voltaire still describes his heroine at this point in the story: 'La belle St. Yves partagée entre un peu de joye, et d'extrêmes douleurs, entre quelque espérance et de tristes craintes, poursuivie par son frère, adorant son amant, essuiant ses larmes et en versant encore, tremblante, affaiblie, et reprenant courage, courut vite chez Mr. de St. Pouage'. In the passage just quoted, the binary pairs which oppose each other and the triplets which juxtapose contrasting actions in a series create the jerky effect of marionettes. The rapid play of contrasting forces and emotions imposes on the reader a distanced, almost bemused perspective (as with the speeded-up and exaggerated melodrama of silent films).

Lacking the extreme character-modifying influence of a prison education, mlle de St Yves's evolution from puppet to tragic figure is not as well defined as that of the Ingénu. For example, in chapter 17, upon realizing that she is reduced to the terrible extremity of choosing death or dishonour, she cries out: 'Ah! quelle vertu, quel labyrinthe d'iniquités, quel païs, et que j'apprends à connaître les hommes! Un père de la Chaise, et un Bailly ridicule font mettre mon amant en prison; ma famille me persécute, on ne me tend la main dans mon désastre que pour me déshonorer. Un Jésuite a perdu un brave homme, un autre Jésuite veut me perdre; je ne suis entourée que de pièges, et je touche au moment de tomber dans la misère! Il faut que je me tue ou que je parle au Roi; je me jetterai à ses pieds sur son passage quand il ira à la Messe ou à la Comédie'. In spite of the humour which might be implied by the gesture which St Yves proposes, the reader's amusement results less from the melodramatic nature of the gesture than from the contrast which it forms with the hypocritical and insincere world in which it will be expressed. The king, riding meaninglessly in his coach on two contrasting missions, represents the absurdity enthroned at the summit of this society. In her ultimate distress, St Yves sees her appeal to the King as the only alternative to death. She retains this final hope, thus demonstrating her limited vision, while Voltaire's irony continues to engulf all.

It is not until the final three chapters of the book that the tone of serious, sentimental drama is free from interruption by Voltaire's characteristic tongue-in-cheek sarcasms such as those at the expense of mlle de St Yves just quoted. All of the characters are presented as sadder and wiser people as a result of the suffering which they have undergone. Voltaire, in fact, takes pains to distinguish his new, humanized characters from the schematic, comic figures of the previous chapters: 'L'Ingénu . . . n'était plus l'Ingénu', and mlle de St Yves 'n'était plus cette fille simple dont une éducation provinciale avait rétréci les idées. L'amour et le malheur l'avaient formée'. It has been previously noted that Voltaire narrates this portion of the story through a series of carefully constructed scenes of dramatic pathos: the reunion of the lovers, the liberation of Gordon, the illness and death of St Yves, the conversion of St Pouange and so forth. It would be an exaggeration to say, however, that Voltaire the ironic polemicist has completely disappeared in favour of Voltaire the edifying bourgeois dramatist. On the contrary, his irony has here elevated itself to an intensity of anger and indignation possible only in the 'serious' context of the story's conclusion. Thus when Gordon cries out in rage and horror, 'C'est donc ainsi qu' on traite les hommes comme des singes! On les bat et on les fait danser', the reader undergoes the full impact of the disproportion between the carefully developed humanity of the Ingénu and the inhumanity of the society which has unjustly persecuted him and which now seeks to reward him in such a petty and absurd manner. The particularly moving effect of this exclamation can only be explained by the successful convergence of the points of view of characters, author and reader at this stage in the story. The Ingénu has finally recognized that the world has treated him and continues to treat him like a puppet, without humanity, reason or justice. His point of view is now free of naivety and unjustified optimism. He sees the shortcomings of his contemporaries as Voltaire sees them: and his anguish, his rage and scorn for such a society (which he demonstrates by tearing the letter of invitation to shreds) are a powerful expression of Voltaire's own feelings—'la saillie d'une grande âme', in Voltaire's words. The Ingénu and his small circle, with their values of reason, justice and sensibility, now stand in dramatic contrast to the venality and vacuity of the courtly society in power.

At this point, we ask whether Voltaire's intention in *L'Ingénu* was indeed gradually to bring his characters convincingly to life enveloping them and his reader in a tragic finale which would fix the story's dominant mood. Following Voltaire's remark to Moultou in 1766 that he wished to compose a work which would move his readers to compassion, several commentators have maintained that *L'Ingénu* is, more than anything else, a *roman sensible*. Detailed parallels have been drawn between Voltaire's concept of tragedy and his techniques and apparent intentions in the final chapters of the work. In the same vein, professor Ridgway maintains [in his *Voltaire and Sensibility*] that *L'Ingénu* greatly suffers from the 'melodramatic exaggeration and an overemphasis on the externals of emotion' which mar the tragedies and comedies of the eighteenth century. These responses to the story are based on the assumption that Voltaire intended the ultimate lesson of *L'Ingénu* to be expressed by a *dénouement sensible*.

[In his *Voltaire*] Professor Mason, in fact, sees the evolution from philosophical tale to novel of sensibility as the organizing principle and 'raison d'être' of the work.

Such views would leave us with the conclusion that Voltaire intended from the start for his novel to culminate in a glorification of *sensibilité*. Even if this were true, no one—with the exception of Hayden Mason—has attempted to explain, using criteria relevant to the structure of the text, why Voltaire initiated his tale in a narrative tone so far removed from that appropriate to his eventual goal. And finally, even if we accept that Voltaire successfully transforms his tale from *conte philosophique* to *roman sensible*, we cannot dismiss lightly professor Ridgway's charge that as a novel of sensibility or a narrated *comédie larmoyante* Voltaire's tale displays all of the weaknesses of the genre—that it is a flawed masterpiece, in effect.

Given the great popular and critical success of *L'Ingénu*, we are forced to conclude, however, that the novel is not a flawed masterpiece and that its artistic secret must lie in a different direction. Those who see the work as a novel of sensibility have overlooked evidence which indicates that Voltaire did not intend for his story to be viewed in such a limited perspective. If we examine the character of mlle de St Yves, for example, we see that throughout the final pages of the book the author refers to her with a double epithet such as 'la tendre et infidèle' or 'l'heureuse et désolée' or 'la belle et infortunée St Yves'. Voltaire's treatment of St Yves's character is obviously still highly stylized, in spite of the change in narrative tone. The Ingénu, for his part, never acquires a more personalized designation than the comic and quickly forgotten Hercules of his unfortunate baptism or the sobriquet 'l'Ingénu', which by Voltaire's own admission is inappropriate following his prison education ('L'Ingénu . . . n'était plus l'Ingénu'). In the final chapters of the book, the succession of *tableaux*, as if drawn directly from the precepts of the *drame bourgeois*, is so obvious as to be distracting. It seems apparent, therefore, that Voltaire—an avowed literary opportunist—did no more than borrow the conventions of a currently popular genre, and exploited them for provisional advantage in the construction of his plot and the development of his characters. The melodramatic tone of this phase of the novel is not introduced for its absolute value as the determining character of the work, but rather as a means of deepening the impact and the intensity of the author's indignation at the abuses of power and the terrible examples of man's inhumanity which had personally touched him or come to his attention during this period.

In fact, if we examine our reactions to the story's ending, we distinguish in our feelings more the anger and scorn of satire than either the pity and fear of tragedy or the edifying sensibility of the Richardsonian novel. The serious tone of the final chapters has the effect of raising Voltaire's irony to a level which transcends not only the abuses suffered by the Ingénu but also those events in real life, such as the La Barre or Calas cases, which aided in provoking the story's composition. Voltaire's appeal in *L'Ingénu* is not primarily to our emotions, but to that cosmic sense of perspective within us which allows us to see the insignificance of an individual man in the totality of the universe.

This view of human history as an unbroken chain of short-comings is first put forward in the course of the Ingénu's prison education. The critical distance which the Ingénu acquires toward the past spectacle of human frailty ('Le monde lui parut trop méchant & trop misérable. En effet, l'histoire n'est que le tableau des crimes et des malheurs') anticipates Voltaire's own eventual ironic detachment from the misfortunes of the Ingénu. The sufferings of his exemplary characters are, after all, only the latest install-ment in the continuing saga of human vice and folly.

In this respect, it is significant that the intensity of the im-mediate tragedy of the Ingénu and his friends is not the last scene to occupy the reader's attention; and it is a mis-take to overlook, as many readers have done, the last two paragraphs of the novel in an assessment of its meaning, for here Voltaire again sweeps the reader into the perspec-tive of history. Louvois eventually makes a good officer of the Huron, St Yves is remembered, the *prieur* is rewarded, mlle de Kerkabon resigns herself to her nephew's military instead of ecclesiastical career, and *le père* Tout à Tous re-ceives sugar candy and devout books bound in morocco leather for his good services. The tone of this concluding paragraph clearly swings back toward the ironic detach-ment which preceded the sentimental phase of the novel. In the final analysis, then, the story goes beyond both the mode of satire and that of sensibility to reach a type of su-preme irony, deeper and yet more detached than that found in any of Voltaire's earlier *contes*. St Yves dies for having taken herself too seriously, Gordon recognizes that he has made himself miserable for no reason, and the In-génu is eventually made into a good officer—the opposite of a tragic hero and much removed from his former role as champion of natural law and the liberty of the individu-al.

The final paragraph thus puts the work into its proper per-spective which, it turns out, is not the puppet-like mecha-nization of the story's beginning, nor the providential world of the *comédie larmoyante,* which emerges near the end. For Voltaire, nothing is absolute. The miraculous conversions of errant members of society do not prove the existence of an overall pattern for good. They merely dis-play change in a particular perspective, while society in the eternal perspective (represented by *le père* Tout à Tous, the king who will nod to the Ingénu in his ante-chamber, and the court ladies who will admit him to their boudoir) has not changed at all. Even those characters in *L'Ingenu* whose unique humanity was built on their abili-ty to change, seem sadly arrested by the final paragraph which serves as the story's epilogue. The indications of ab-solute attitudes on the part of the main characters ('ne par-lait jamais'; 'jusqu'au dernier moment de sa vie'; 'jusqu'à sa mort'; 'oublia pour jamais'), which appear in the final paragraphs, are closer to the distanced narrative tone of the beginning of the story than the intense 'sensibilité' of the final chapter. This swing back toward the detachment of irony demonstrates that the structural pattern of oppos-ing ideas or movements in a series exists at all levels of the text. The concluding slogan adopted by Gordon, 'Malheur est bon à quelque chose', and its opposite number, 'Mal-heur n'est bon à rien', serve as the definitive expression of

Final page of the La Vallière manuscript of Candide.

unresolved paradoxes which have been brought out in every major episode of the Ingénu's story.

In the perspective of the present study, we can see that the 'dénouement brusqué' deplored by Wm R. Jones in the in-troduction to his critical edition is absolutely necessary for restoring the balance of the ironic perspective. The return to irony does not erase, however, the impact of the senti-mental phase of the novel. The two opposites combine to produce a third perspective which might be termed 'cos-mic' in its breadth and depth. The society which perse-cutes innocent people seems less a temporary and correct-ible incarnation of evil than the mindless agent of an over-riding absurd pattern. The prison episode is an appropri-ate symbol within the novel of the omnipotence of paradox and, ultimately, the omnipresence of the absurd as the basic element of the human condition: 'Nous sommes tous deux dans les fers, sans savoir qui nous y a mis, sans pou-voir même le demander'.

The question of the absurd and what one's response to it should be is strongly implied in the second half of the novel. One could say that all three of the major characters come to grips with the question and respond in different ways. Gordon's slogan shows that he chooses to believe the absurd does not exist, 'Malheur est bon à quelque chose'. Mlle de St Yves cannot live with the notion and in effect chooses to cease to exist, 'Son âme tuait son corps'. The choice of suicide is also entertained by the In-génu, and the very positive tone which Voltaire gives to the passage implies at least his respect, if not his approval, of such a decision calmly taken in the face of reality: 'Gordon se garda bien de lui étaler ces lieux communs fastidieux, par les quels on essaie de prouver qu'il n'est pas permis d'user de sa liberté pour cesser d'être quand on est horriblement mal, qu'il ne faut pas sortir de sa maison quand on ne peut plus y demeurer, que l'homme est sur la terre comme un soldat à son poste comme s'il importait à l'être des êtres que l'assemblage de quelques parties de matière fût dans un lieu ou dans un autre; raisons impuissantes qu'un desespoir ferme & réfléchi dédaigne d'écouter, & auxquelles Caton ne répondit que par un coup de poignard'.

If suicide as an expression of one's ultimate scorn for the absurdity of the human condition would not be out of place in the 'tragic' mood of the story's *dénouement,* it is obvious that Voltaire would not make this his personal choice, nor would he applaud it as an alternative. He refuses to be drawn into an absolute stance, either as regards the providential order of the universe or its systematic disorder. He chooses instead the perspective of the ironic consciousness which puts a saving distance between himself and the spectacle of human corruption and suffering. The maddeningly superficial and absurd society, which abuses power to persecute innocence and indiscriminately rewards evil-doing as well as virtue, will not push him to take his own life. His response is that of the Sisyphean man, who sees good as well as bad in the capricious unfolding of life, and who chooses to act with no illusions as to the ultimate goals to be achieved.

The key to understanding Voltaire's 'message' in *L'Ingénu* lies in an awareness of the total absence of any dominant, organizing pattern to life, either for good or bad. In the long history of human folly, vice, and superstition, change and evolution are an illusion. Every force has its opposite. The meaning of the work and its aesthetic unity are thus, as they should be, inextricably linked. On the philosophical plane, Voltaire says nothing new in *L'Ingénu:* the natural 'good' of the primitive must be tempered by culture and civilization, yet civilization, or life in highly organized social groups, produces the evils of intolerance, injustice and inhumanity.

The true originality of *L'Ingénu* lies in the way in which Voltaire subordinates his traditional message to an overriding awareness. Admittedly, all of his philosophical tales can be construed as caricatural representations of the human condition. Voltaire's ideas are wittily and humorously communicated in this code to his receptive reader. His marionnettes always imply, nevertheless, an authentic world which is that of the author and his audience. The true genius of *L'Ingénu* is that for once the distance between these two worlds is temporarily annihilated—the puppets have come to life, and they resemble us. The effect on the reader is neither the cleansing awe of tragedy nor the tearful sympathy of the bourgeois drama, but rather the profound realization of an enormous gulf between utopia and reality and the horror of those traits of human nature (vanity, avarice, cruelty, superstition, intolerance) which enlarge that gulf.

Voltaire's masterful innovation was to combine into one

aesthetic whole the intellectual 'philosophy' of the *conte* and the emotional empathy of the *drame. L'Ingénu* thus demonstrates the most profound and ultimately the most moving expression of Voltaire's wisdom. The smile of the patriarch has surpassed the sarcasm of the satirist and been mellowed by the sympathy of the humanist. Voltaire in this work has reached that rare and admirable summit of the ironic consciousness: commitment which does not blind and detachment which does not immobilize. (pp. 71-83)

> *David E. Highnam, "'L'Ingénu': Flawed Masterpiece or Masterful Innovation," in* Studies on Voltaire and the Eighteenth Century, *Vol. CXLIII, 1975, pp. 71-83.*

Frederick M. Keener   (essay date 1983)

[*In the following essay, Keener offers a detailed analysis of the motives and concerns of the characters in* Candide.]

> Enlightenment is man's leaving his self-caused immaturity. Immaturity is the incapacity to use one's intelligence without the guidance of another. . . . I do not have any need to think; if I can pay, others will take over the tedious job for me.
> —Kant, "What is Enlightenment?"

That Candide the character is a marionette has become a commonplace in criticism of the tale, despite infrequent though recurrent statements to the contrary by some commentators. Yet the primary meaning of the famous, iterated final words is "his" meaning, a matter of Candide's motives in speaking them. The nature of human motivation, the inner counterpart of the "chain of events" that increasingly occupied eighteenth-century thinkers, had, by the time of *Candide,* become a central subject for writers on ethics, politics, and the fledgling science of psychology. By mid-century, too, there was a new, developmental sense of change in embryology and physical cosmology. Was there a comparable new sense of the development of fictional characters?—of characters' not simply being changed but changing themselves, and of their doing so not *ex machina* but in relation to the tendencies, the inner processes, that characterize them? If there was—and I believe there was . . . —it was likely to be tentative and subtle, since representation of self-conscious development by characters would mark a distinct departure from the practices of romance writers and early novelists, and from what is typical of the romance and novel as genres.

"Motivation" is also a technical term in formalist analysis of narrative, indicating the propulsion of a plot toward its conclusion (not to be confused with the comparatively arbitrary "human" motivation of fictional characters, which serves to disguise, and ease a reader's acceptance of, a plot's necessities). A tale like *Candide,* however, presents problems to the formalist because the meaning of the ending is primarily a matter of what a character means to say, and the narrator does not tell us what that is; nor, definitively, does Candide. Those final words about the necessity of cultivating the garden are, according to Roman Jakobson's division, distinctly metonymical rather than metaphorical in their relation to the rest of Voltaire's tale, because Candide's statement differs considerably from, without directly contradicting, statements he has made earlier. Most notably, Candide insists that an action is necessary; he has not spoken so peremptorily before. Less obviously, he sets himself apart from not only Pangloss' way of thinking but also that of everyone else, including Martin, as I intend to show. Moreover, the clause "il faut cultiver notre jardin" may itself be metaphorical: the necessary cultivation of that garden may stand for more than agriculture. But that possibility, especially when elaborated, will seem more evident to the historian of Voltaire's ideas than to the critic mainly concerned with **Candide** as an example of eighteenth-century narrative fiction. What Voltaire may have meant by the clause is one question; what the character Candide, who is not given to poetry or eloquence, may mean in addition to what he says explicitly, is quite another.

A reading of the conclusion of the tale thus requires a reading of Candide's nature, to discover whether what he says there is linked to what he says earlier. But modern criticism, in its nearly relentlessly *a priori* emphasis on the difference between the philosophical tale (or apologue) and the nascent novel, has usually been unhistorically neat, too quickly ruling out possibilities of significant characterization in the tale, even though a tale like **Candide** is obviously less about philosophy itself than about the hero's peculiar use of it.

Candide's character is not so uninterestingly or insignificantly simple as it seems. Perhaps the comparison with a marionette has itself become too simple. There were other eighteenth-century models of near humanity that a critic might draw upon. Although Voltaire enjoyed marionettes, he was interested too in automata, such as the celebrated flutist, drummer, and duck manufactured by Jacques Vaucanson ("rival de Prométhée," Voltaire called him in the *Discours en vers sur l'homme*). Automata, it is true, only seem autonomous, though they manage to perform without visible strings, but there was still another, still more lifelike artificial Adam to converse about in the years just before **Candide,** the awakening statue which Condillac, in the *Traité des sensations* (1754), employed to demonstrate the conceivable derivation of thought from sense experience—an example put to similar use by Buffon and Charles Bonnet. The statue come to life presents additional evidence of the new, mid-eighteenth-century interest in self-conscious, although general, psychological development. But I mention this series of progressively more lifelike models mainly to suggest historical analogues for Candide other than the marionette, so as to promote reconsideration of him as a character, not to argue that Voltaire probably had one or more of these models in mind.

In reading a narrated philosophical tale one should be attentive to the character of the narrator, who himself may change in some important way, and whose comments are not necessarily more dependable than evidence drawn from what his characters say and do. Though Voltaire's narrator says in the first paragraph that Candide has the simplest of intellects, Candide's mind is certainly not so simple as it seems or as Candide himself regards it. When,

in the wilds of South America, he kills the apes pursuing two naked girls, and before he learns from his companion Cacambo that the victims were the girls' chosen lovers, his first response is of delivery from guilt: "Dieu soit Loué, . . . si j'ai commis un péché en tuant un inquisiteur et un jésuite, je l'ai bien réparé en sauvant la vie à deux filles" ("God be praised, . . . if I have sinned by killing an inquisitor and a Jesuit, I have made up for it well by saving the life of two girls"). Immediately, he has another thought: "Ce sont peut-être deux demoiselles de condition, et cette aventure nous peut procurer de très grands avantages dans le pays" ("These are perhaps two young ladies of quality, and this adventure can procure us very great advantages in the land"). The main chance does not escape him. At a later, prominent place in the book, the point of his decision to leave Eldorado, he seems swayed particularly by desire to rejoin Cunégonde, but the sentiment as he expresses it is again not single-minded:

> Si nous restons ici, nous n'y serons que comme les autres; au lieu que si nous retournons dans notre monde, seulement avec douze moutons chargés de cailloux d'Eldorado, nous serons plus riches que tous les rois ensemble, nous n'aurons plus d'inquisiteurs à craindre, et nous pourrons aisément reprendre mademoiselle Cunégonde.

> (If we remain here, we shall be only like the others; whereas if we go back to our world, with only twelve sheep bearing pebbles from Eldorado, we shall be wealthier than all kings put together, we shall not have any more inquisitors to fear, and we shall easily regain Mademoiselle Cunégonde.)

That Cunégonde figures as the bread and not the filling in this sandwich of motivation, the narrator insists in the one passage of the book that directly criticizes his hero: "on aime tant à courir, à se faire valoir chez les siens, à faire parade de ce qu'on a vu dans ses voyages, que les deux heureux résolurent de ne plus l'être, et de demander leur congé à Sa Majesté" ("people love so much to run around, to pride themselves among their friends, to make a show of what they have seen in their travels, that the two happy men decided to be happy no more and to ask his majesty for permission to go away").

The narrator generally speaks of Candide as an unfortunate innocent preyed upon by evildoers. Such is often the case, it seems, but Candide himself also seems eager to accept that explanation. In the ninth chapter, when surprised with Cunégonde by Don Issacar, who shares her with the Grand Inquisitor, Candide—"quoi-qu'il eût les mœurs fort douces" ("although he had the gentlest manners"), the narrator says—slays the interloper. Minutes later, with the Inquisitor's entrance, the narrator records Candide's thinking "to the moment":

> Si ce saint homme appelle du secours, il me fera infailliblement brûler, il pourra en faire autant de Cunégonde; il m'a fait fouetter impitoyablement; il est mon rival; je suis en train de tuer, il n'y a pas à balancer.

> (If this holy man cries for help, he will unquestionably have me burned, he will be able to do as much to Cunégonde; he has had me whipped

cruelly; he is my rival; I am already involved
with killing, there is nothing to hesitate about.)

The selflessness he would think typical of himself is again
mixed with less rarefied motives. He runs the Inquisitor
through. How could he do it? exclaims Cunégonde, "vous
qui êtes né si doux" ("you who were born so gentle"). Candide replies, "Ma belle demoiselle, . . . quand on est amoureux, jaloux, et fouetté par l'Inquisition, on ne se connaît plus" ("My sweet young lady, . . . when a person is
in love, jealous, and scourged by the Inquisition, he no
longer knows himself"). He does not readily acknowledge
ordinary, unedifying feelings, and his reluctance persists.
Five chapters later, he again looks down upon a man he
has stabbed, again astonished by himself: "Hélas mon
Dieu! dit-il, j'ai tué mon ancien maître, mon ami, mon
beau-frère; je suis le meilleur homme du monde, et voilà
déjà trois hommes que je tue . . . " ("Oh, my God! he
says; I have dispatched my former master, friend, brother-
in-law; I am the best of men, and already there are three
men I have killed . . . ").

"Le meilleur homme du monde"—an epithet amusingly
resonant in this tale about the best of worlds, chateaux,
philosophers, and so forth. It begins to appear that, if
there were no Pangloss, Candide would have to invent
him. Invent him in a root sense, Candide through much
of the book wishes he could do: to find or recover or resurrect him. It is a humorous obsession. Worlds burst; still
Candide yearns to know what Pangloss' explanation
would be. As late as the twenty-seventh chapter he is still
insisting that Pangloss was right and that all is well. Candide the child keeps fathering that man. And Candide's
having saddled himself with Pangloss is suggested also by
the hero's manner of replacing him: Candide does not fall
in with Martin, his alternate Mentor, accidentally.

After encountering the wretched slave of Surinam, after
being robbed of his last two Eldoradan sheep, after being
cheated by the judge to whom he complained, Candide
feels the deepest melancholy. "La méchanceté des hommes se présentait à son esprit dans toute sa laideur, il ne
se nourrissait que d'idées tristes" ("The wickedness of
men loomed in all its ugliness before his mind, he nurtured
only sad ideas"). But he cannot sustain such ideas by himself; he needs assistance of the sort he is used to, so he
sponsors an odd contest to select a traveling companion,
advertising for someone "le plus dégoûté de son état et le
plus malheureux de la province" ("the most revolted by
his own condition and the most wretched man in the province"); if it were practical, he would undoubtedly seek the
unhappiest person in the world. From the throng that replies, Candide chooses twenty and hears them out, with
gratifying misery, thinking of how embarrassed Pangloss
would be, until finally Martin is chosen, not because he
particularly deserves the prize but because, besides pro-
fessing to be miserable, he is a philosopher. The logic is
bluntly Hegelian: if this is not the best of all possible
worlds, it must be the worst. Candide still wishes to believe Pangloss, but if Martin can convince him of the truth
of the opposite position, Candide may assent. One way or
the other, he will arrive at the absolute truth of the matter.
Although constantly regarding himself as indivisible in his
sentiments, he is not.

The action of the next chapter, the twentieth, should be
seen as an oblique but telling commentary upon the procedures of "le meilleur homme du monde." Candide is protesting to Martin that the world has some good when the
noise of cannons interrupts them. They watch a naval engagement in which one ship suddenly sinks, all hands lost.
Candide tends to agree with Martin that the event is diabolical—but, something red is floating in the water where
a hundred men have just drowned, one of the Eldoradan
sheep. Candide, we are told, "eut plus de joie de retrouver
ce mouton, qu'il n'avait été affligé d'en perdre cent tous
chargés de gros diamants d'Eldorado" ("was more delighted in regaining this sheep than he had been afflicted
by the loss of a hundred sheep all carrying huge diamonds
from Eldorado"). The drowned men, the lost sheep, the
repetition of the number one hundred for them in so short
a space, Candide's sympathy for the dead so quickly followed by joy at recovery of his treasure: he is rather more
ordinary in his self-centeredness than he realizes. He fondles his sheep and supposes that, since he has regained it,
he may also regain Cunégonde.

The parallel is apt. Cunégonde, and indeed the women of
the tale in general, unblushingly reveal an animality that
Candide and Pangloss have also but rationalize away.
(Candide of course does not notice it in the women either).
Though beautiful at first, Cunégonde lacks other Petrar-
chan characteristics. It is she who takes the lead in Candide's first encounter with her, and later she eagerly receives him in the Grand Inquisitor's house, typically not
wondering about their safety together. She tells her tale:
a Bulgarian captain, having killed a soldier who was rap-
ing her, made her his slave; she adjusted herself to the situation, for "il me trouvait fort jolie, il faut l'avouer; et je
ne nierai pas qu'il ne fût très bien fait, et qu'il n'eût la peau
blanche et douce; d'ailleurs"—she is tellingthis to Candide—"peu d'esprit, peu de philosophie: on voyait bien
qu'il n'avait pas été élevé par le docteur Pangloss" ("he
thought me quite pretty, it must be said; and I shall not
deny that he was very well put together, and that his skin
was fair and smooth; otherwise, not much brain, not much
philosophy; a person could see very well that he had not
been taught by Doctor Pangloss"). Later, at the auto-da-
fé, she saw Pangloss hanged and she fainted.

> A peine reprenais-je mes sens que je vous vis dé-
> pouillé tout nu; ce fut là le comble de l'horreur,
> de la consternation, de la douleur, du désespoir.
> Je vous dirai, avec vérité, que votre peau est en-
> core plus blanche, et d'un incarnat plus parfait
> que celle de mon capitaine des Bulgares.

> (Hardly did I regain my senses when I saw you
> stripped entirely naked; that was the extremity
> of terror, vexation, sorrow, despair. I will say to
> you, truly, that your flesh is still whiter and of
> a finer rosiness, than my Bulgarian captain's.)

The flogging of Candide prompted her to recall all her
misfortunes, which she summarizes in one of those pell-
mell litanies of comically enchained events with which the
book abounds—massacres, degradation, "et surtout [le]
baiser que je vous avais donné derrière un paravent, le jour
que je vous avais vu pour la dernière fois" ("and especially
the kiss I had given you behind a screen, that day I saw

you the last time"). "Vous devez avoir une faim dévo-
rante," she concludes, no *non sequitur* for her; "j'ai grand
appétit; commençons par souper" ("You must have a ferocious appetite; I am awfully hungry; let us start by sup-
ping").

The old woman has a similar history and personality, this
once delectable daughter of a pope, beaten, robbed, mutilated, who wanted to kill herself a hundred times but still
loved life. More resilient than Candide, the women have
no need for a Pangloss or Martin. They have an amoral
authority all their own because they claim no authority
while simply doing as they like, as much as they can. They
even readily fall in with the ways of the world that exploits
them. Cunégonde resisted the first Bulgarian, she explains,
because she did not know that "tout ce qui arrivait dans
le château de mon père était une chose d'usage" ("everything that happened in my father's chateau was sanctioned
by custom"). The old woman, stripped and probed by cor-
sairs, was surprised, ignorant of the fact that everyone,
even the Knights of Malta, acts that way; "C'est une loi
du droit des gens à laquelle on n'a jamais dérogé" ("It is
an article of international law from which no one has ever
deviated"). Expostulating with cannibals, the somewhat
comparably flexible Cacambo declares, "En effet le droit
naturel nous enseigne à tuer notre prochain, et c'est ainsi
qu'on en agit dans toute la terre" ("As a matter of fact,
natural law instructs us to kill our neighbor, and it is thus
that everyone behaves throughout the world").

Candide, who never voices complacent classifications of
this kind, whose penchant is for acceptance of metaphysical cosmology rather than custom, seems to occupy a
place like that of Man in Pope's *Essay,* between the assert-
ive doctors, his light and dark angels, and the libidinal if
not brutal women. Even in respect to his feelings for Cunégonde, however, he is less simple than the narrator says,
not readily quixotic. He has not simply envisioned her as
a lady of romance, nor has he given disinterested attention
to philosophical Optimisim. He gave Pangloss his cre-
dence, the narrator says at the outset, "car il trouvait mademoiselle Cunégonde extrêmement belle." From the
first, his motives are consistently double and mixed, his
priorities transparent, to the narrator and the reader, not
to him. "Il concluait qu'après le bonheur d'être né baron
de Thunder-ten-tronckh, le second degré de bonheur était
d'être mademoiselle Cunégonde, le troisième, de la voir
tous les jours, et le quatrième, d'entendre maître
Pangloss . . . " ("He determined that next to the good
fortune of being born the Baron of Thunder-ten-tronckh,
the second greatest sort of happiness lay in being Mlle
Cunégonde, the third in gazing on her every day, and the
fourth in understanding Master Pangloss . . . ").

Though Candide would be the last to admit it, his love for
Cunégonde and his faith in Pangloss have, consistently,
much to do with his wish to be the best man in the best
possible world: to be discovered, for example, to be the
Baron's nephew, like that other obscure youth turned out
of paradise, the romantic, more single-minded Tom Jones.
That this is so seems still more probable when one considers Candide's final reason for marrying Cunégonde at the
end. To reverse his set of priorities, checked off by events:

fourth, Pangloss has become tedious to Candide; third and
second, Cunégonde is ugly, poor, and abrasive, now neither companionable nor enviable; but, first, her baronial
brother opposes the marriage as beneath her, so Candide,
with but not determined by Cunégonde's solicitations,
makes a point of going through with it.

Thus, repeatedly, though Candide thinks himself exceptional for his unselfishness, he acts upon self-regarding
motives which he resists acknowledging, and he avoids
such acknowledgment, systematically, either by displacing the object of his desires from one thing to another
somehow associated with it (despite the fact that, after
Locke, the main trend in psychology promoted critical
consciousness of mental associations) or by attaching himself to an authority, such as Martin, and thus displacing
the subject of his desires. Repeatedly it is shown that Candide's concern about whether the world is for the best or
for the worst is displaced concern about how the world
will deal with poor Candide. He is really more an automaton, brother to Vaucanson's duck—moved by a concealed
drive wheel, concealed from himself—than he is a marionette. Once in a while Voltaire ties a string to him and
jerks it, as when Candide, thinking he has killed the Jesuit,
worries about what the *Journal de Trévoux* will say. But
most of the time Candide goes by his own spring, an adequately motivated comic character whose traits, while too
thin for psychoanalysis, are not inhumanly mechanical.
He moves the comedy, is not simply moved by it, and he
does not simply carry about his favorite philosophical
proposition; he embodies and enacts it. Odd as the statement may seem at first, Candide is, energetically, ingeniously on Voltaire's part, a trope.

Considered as a trope in the conventional sense, as a device of communication, as the equivalent of a figure of
speech conceived by a rhetorician, Candide may seem a
metaphor. His name would give that impression. But as
I have tried to show, he is only partially *candide* (in one
sense of the word), for he is not so with himself. He may
be considered a figure of irony, and he is that much of the
time, but he does not seem so definitely that when he
speaks the concluding words. The other major tropes, besides metaphor and irony, are synecdoche and metonymy;
and, broadly speaking, synecdoche is everywhere in the
tale, but in saying that I use *synecdoche* not primarily in
the common rhetorical sense, to indicate devices mediating between writer and reader. I use the term, rather, to
indicate the way in which words are combined in sentences, ideas associated in the mind, by the characters and
narrator. As we have seen, Cunégonde and other characters constantly explain (one might say *naturalize*) strange
events by classifying them as species of general codes: custom, international law, natural law. The species-genus relation is especially synecdochic; the part-whole relation is
usually regarded as synecdochic too. And, at least in the
earlier sections of the tale, the narrator matches his characters in the production of broadly synecdochic associations, as in the particulars chosen to support faint praise
of the Baron's chateau, exceptional in Westphalia: "son
château avait une porte et des fenêtres."

The grand architects of synecdoche in the tale, however,

are the philosophical Optimists; "All are but parts of one stupendous whole," Pope had written. Part-whole classification becomes Candide's main occupation. His esteem for Pangloss derives, as that name suggests, precisely from the philosopher's ability to identify the whole of which Candide is a part, thus establishing rootless Candide *as* a part, deducing his estimable character and expectations from that best whole. The philosophy of Optimism, as Kenneth Burke points out [in his *A Grammar of Motives*], is essentially synecdochic:

> The "noblest synecdoche," the perfect paradigm or prototype for all lesser usages, is found in metaphysical doctrines proclaiming the identity of "microcosm" and "macrocosm." In such doctrines, where the individual is treated as a replica of the universe, and vice versa, we have the ideal synecdoche, since microcosm is related to macrocosm as part to whole, and either the whole can represent the part or the part can represent the whole. (For "represent" we could substitute "be identified with.") One could thus look through the remotest astronomical distances to the "truth within," or could look within to learn the "truth of all the universe without." Leibniz' monadology is a good instance of synecdoche on this grand scale.

It may be helpful to emphasize that the use of a trope by a metaphysician in this manner is not rhetorical but epistemological. Instead of employing the trope to illustrate a concept distinct from, antecedent to, the trope, he employs the trope to think. The metaphysics *is* a synecdoche. But statements about the philosophy are synecdochic in linguistic and rhetorical ways. In **Candide,** the various synecdochic associations constructed by the characters and the narrator have a splendid parodic symmetry. For the most part, the trope of irony persists rhetorically and dominates the epistemological and linguistic synecdoches, as in Cunégonde's unconsciously ironic recourse to custom, the narrator's deliberately ironic specification of door and windows, and mainly in comic transformations of Optimism.

A trope may have a mind of its own, like Alice's croquet mallet. Although in rhetoric *trope* means a turn or twist given to speech (one says "a sail" and means "a ship"), the figure may twist in one's hands, the resultant meaning not quite what one intended. The vitality of a trope may spring particularly from its instability as a compound, its tendency to be resolved in another trope—its tropism. A metaphor may reveal an implicit set of synecdoches. In Burke's example, initially the part is related to the whole; then it can be identified with it. But once the part has been so fully identified with the whole that it can stand for it, a curious turning occurs: the part tends to become the distinctive part of the whole, the really important part, even in a sense the *best* part. The trope of synecdoche, a kind of metaphor, tends to become pure metaphor by transforming the species that can stand for a genus, the part that can stand for a whole, into a new, more economical, higher genus or whole.

If, to return to **Candide,** the not so simple hero is categorized as a trope, his desires are seen to turn that way. Es-

tablishing himself as part of the best of all possible worlds, he would demonstrate that, far from being a nobody, he is not a microcosm but *the* microcosm: "le meilleur homme du monde." In the sense that Candide himself is synecdochic like Leibniz's noble synecdoche, the full title of the tale has its full significance: **Candide ou l'optimisme,** the philosophy and would-be philosopher are one.

But though synecdoche for the most part characterizes the hero and typifies much that the narrator says as well, the fundamental trope of the tale is metonymy, which, against some precedents, I should like to distinguish as much as possible from synecdoche as that term is usually understood. Synecdoche may verge on the metaphorical, as in Burke and in what I have said thus far. But it may verge instead on the metonymical. Whereas metaphor works with items that have an intrinsic similarity to or identify with each other, metonymy works with items extrinsic to each other: relations of before and after, above and below, cause and effect; relations often temporal rather than spatial. Metonymy is often a trope of movement and change, of calculus rather than algebra. It is also the trope of otherness, for each trope implies a point of view, the condition of the knower in regard to what is to be known; but whereas metaphor and the more metaphorical sort of synecdoche, by their predication of whole or partial resemblance or identity in the items related, tend to identify the knower with the known, metonymy tends to keep them separate. Synecdoche verging on the metonymical rather than the metaphorical will suggest that any resemblance between the part and the whole is slight, or that any predication of identity between them, even partial identity, is arbitrary. A person should be wary about the adequacy of any theory of genus and species. A person sees that this accompanies that but remains in doubt about relations of identity between them, beyond the notion that they "go together." Hume's epistemology is thus fundamentally metonymical and extremely cautious: *post quod* is no more than that, and causes, important as they are to us, represent no more than the effects of one principle governing our association of ideas.

> **Throughout the tale Candide is assaulted by discrete, unassimilable, pressing events. He strains to read them metaphorically, to give them a teleology assimilating them to the grand pattern of a world deserving the qualification "best." His reasoning is always really practical, not speculative, but in person or in spirit there is always at his shoulder, by his choice, one of his mentors to keep him in the dark.**
>
> **—Frederick M. Keener**

It is into something like Hume's world that Voltaire has dropped Candide, arranging the tale so that it is from the basic, alienated point of view of epistemological metonymy that characters attempt to read the universe, that is, to associate events by general formulae. Throughout the tale Candide is assaulted by discrete, unassimilable, pressing events. He strains to read them metaphorically, to give them a teleology assimilating them to the grand pattern of a world deserving the qualification "best." His reasoning is always really practical, not speculative, but in person or in spirit there is always at his shoulder, by his choice, one of his mentors to keep him in the dark. Pangloss radiates obscurity. "Remarquez bien," he argues in the first chapter, "que les nez ont été faits pour porter des lunettes, aussi avons-nous des lunettes" ("Note well that noses were made to hold eyeglasses, so we have eyeglasses"). This reasoning, comically trivial on the surface, becomes sillier when looked into. In the first place, Pangloss has omitted the necessary middle term if the proposition that all is for the best is to make sense as philosophical Optimism, that term being the proviso of a perfect Creator, "Wisdom infinite" (*An Essay on Man*); it is because of God's nature that all must be for the best. Second, the given example begins to make sense only if employed to justify the existence of noses, but Pangloss wrenches the argument to justify what we do with our noses, anything we do.

It is not simply the position in which man has been placed that Pangloss is busy accepting; it is what man wants to do there, still clearer in a succeeding example: "les cochons étant faits pour être mangés, nous mangeons du porc toute l'année" ("pigs being made to be eaten, we eat pork all through the year"). Pangloss neatly, gratifyingly, confuses the theological and teleological sense of "end" with the personal and moral sense and thus can adduce the nature of the universe, implicitly the nature of God, to explain the rightness of whatever Pangloss wants to do. He attracts Candide by glossing everything, seeing resemblance in all that happens, and locating his desires in the nature of things rather than in himself. Through the whole argument there is a telling balance in the omission of the First Mover and the neglect of the human agent's motivation. Pangloss could seem rather cunning in all this, but he is not: though given to abstractions, he resembles the women of the tale in completely lacking critical self-consciousness.

It is in the nature of things, not of Pangloss, that he eats pork or gives Paquette a lesson in experimental physics. And Martin resembles him by similarly displacing motives, only shifting them to the devil's shoulders much of the time. Neither philosopher makes room for specifically human desires. And Candide, employing first one and then the other to think for him, establishes for himself the best of possible fools' paradises by successfully shifting judgment from his own shoulders onto theirs. Event follows event, detail is added to detail; the empirical relations are extrinsic, mere relations of contiguity. Why does event B follow event A? Will C, success, follow B? Yes, says Pangloss. No, says Martin. Such is the world, they say in chorus. Each thinks he is associating events by cause and effect when he is only, tacitly, correlating them with his own desires, and, like Candide, correlating his reasoning with a high opinion of himself. Each, to resolve the metonymy of experience, rashly makes the wrong tropic turn.

Instead of inquiring into the relation between the whole of himself and the part constituted by his desires, he assumes he is a whole, all integrity, and concerns himself entirely with his relation to the whole universe.

However, metonymy forbids these flights and retaliates by promoting recognition of the most down-to-earth causes. In this respect the tale plays with the mechanistic explanation of human motives common in Swift. Cunégonde, spying Pangloss in the bushes with the chambermaid, "vit clairement la raison suffisante du docteur, les effets et les causes" ("clearly perceived the doctor's sufficient reason, the effects and the causes"). Descartes is being stood upon his head: men are machines, mechanically rationalizing animals. Given Cunégonde's regular animality, it follows that she would immediately find an opportunity for applying Pangloss' physics. Given Candide's innocence of natural rather than selfless human motives, he is particularly vulnerable to both manipulation and criticism in this mode.

Now it would seem that the tendency of metonymy is toward perception of chains of events as mechanical (the vogue of naturalistic fiction a century after *Candide* might seem the historical realization of that tendency, the empire of realism's metonymy). It would seem so, that is, if metonymy did not imply the point of view I have mentioned, that of extrinsicality. The would-be knower perceives one thing going with another; he may forge a causal link; but he does so, at his most self-conscious, with recognition that he has created the association, perhaps delusively.

There is definite movement in Voltaire's tale, in Samuel Johnson's *Rasselas* too, from the hero's expectation of full understanding of the world to fear that there can be no understanding of it, at least none warranting any contentment. At the beginning, Candide cheerfully accepts the notion that all is for the best with the implication that all shall be for his own personal good. Despite frustrations, he persists in seeking suitable evidence. "Isn't everyone happy?" he asks. Then, having discovered in the first third of the tale that everything European seems far from being for the best, and in the next third that the New World is little better, by chapter 19, Candide, near despair, hires Martin to prove that all is for the worst. Candide does not want to make that judgment, but his question has now become, "Isn't anyone happy?"—that wealthy, educated senator, or that seemingly jolly cleric with the girl on his arm? Martin's pessimism is repeatedly vindicated, and the metaphysical question falls to earth in the process. Martin seems an expert reader of this world's metonymies—until he ventures to ridicule Candide's faith in Cacambo: "Vous êtes bien simple, en vérité, de vous figurer qu'un valet métis, qui a cinq ou six millions dans ses poches, ira chercher votre maîtresse au bout du monde et vous l'amènera à Venise" ("You are really a simpleton to expect that a half-breed servant, with five or six million in his pockets, will go seeking your mistress to the end of the world and conduct her to you in Venice").

Candide could certainly profit from increased proficiency in reductive, mechanistic prediction of chains of human events, yet not in this instance, for of course his valet returns—without the money, it is true, but having acted in good faith and bringing news of Cunégonde's whereabouts. Martin's chain has broken. The tale moves inexorably toward an attitude of skepticism as explanation after explanation proves false, as metonymy outlasts noble synecdoches, yet there is no corresponding movement toward doctrinaire skepticism. The book moves toward skepticism conscious of and skeptical of itself. Explanations have failed but explanation itself has not been proven futile; what has, at most, been demonstrated is that explanation by unconscious wishful thinking is futile. Erich Auerbach's rather unsympathetic pages on **Candide** in *Mimesis,* summarized by the statement that "For Voltaire, it is a perfectly self-evident premise that no one in his senses can believe in . . . an inner justification for views," seem badly in need of qualification, the addition to the statement of "without first considering whether he is deluded about that inner justification." There the satirical stress falls; there Voltaire's ridicule comes to a point.

Candide may seem the helpless, passive object of a remarkable series of misfortunes. The misfortunes are remarkable, even an earthquake killing thousands, a natural disaster on a scale afflicting few fictional characters. The world seems Candide's nemesis. However, with the notable exception of that earthquake—which, for all its enormity, is an instance of natural evil virtually required in a work bearing on theodicy—the reader finds that Candide regularly, often actively, induces the world's nasty, morally evil reactions against him. As mimesis of probability in the objective world, the events loom unrealistically huge, frequent, and severe. Yet as mimesis of the probability of the world's responses to someone like Candide, the series of events comes to seem, at the least, less improbable; as mediated through a Candide the world takes on a different aspect. He invites misfortune at a rate very close to that of its occurrence, because, with Pangloss' spectacles on his nose, he insists upon secretly seeing "all things for my use," despite that warning about the wrong Optimistic turn in *An Essay on Man.*

It must be for the best when the Baron's daughter makes love to him, or when the Bulgarian press-gang attracts him by appealing eloquently to the same expectation. "Les hommes ne sont faits que pour se secourir les uns les autres" ("Men were made only so that each one could help out the others"), they say. Candide says that is just what Pangloss thinks. Even when Candide chooses to desert the army, he does so not out of a natural desire to be free and safe but out of the belief that "c'était un privilège de l'espèce humaine . . . de se servir de ses jambes à son plaisir" ("it was a right of human beings . . . for a man to have the benefit of using his own legs as he pleases"). Candide is a rigorist.

There is always, as Johnson said of Richardson's Clarissa, something which he prefers to truth, the truth of acknowledged desire. Given the choice of the gauntlet or the firing squad, he chooses by the divine gift of *"liberté,"* and asking to be killed he is neither desperate nor angry but polite, requesting of the Bulgarians "qu'on voulût bien avoir la bonté de lui casser la tête" ("that someone would kindly be gracious enough to crush his head"). This comment nicely illustrates the positivity of Candide as a character;

delivered in indirect discourse, it is obviously a sarcasm of the narrator's, yet the reader senses no sarcasm in what Candide seems to mean by it, and no improbability in *his* speaking this way. He has relative independence from his author. Having escaped, except mentally, Candide proceeds to deduce that the Dutch, being Christians, will take care of him, another Panglossian expectation to be frustrated, but he pays no attention to the anomaly presented by the kindness of the unbaptized Jacques; then, when Jacques is soon drowning, Candide allows himself to do nothing but look on, conveniently persuaded by Pangloss' assertion "que la rade de Lisbonne avait été formée exprès pour que cet anabaptiste s'y noyât" ("that the harbor of Lisbon had been shaped expressly for this Anabaptist to drown in"). And so forth; extremely unrealistic as Candide's credulity is, the chain of evil events, as significantly determined by his unrealistic longings, is not entirely without probability.

Although I have suggested in passing that Candide occupies a middle state between his doctors and the women, that vertical scale, that microcosmic Chain of Being, is illusory. Pangloss, Martin, Cunégonde, the old woman, all are in an important sense variations on the same theme. They think about different things, but the ways in which they think about them are fundamentally identical, for all these characters take the events they observe and mechanically reduce them to uniformity. To Pangloss they are all for the best; to Martin, for the worst; to Cunégonde, they are acceptable. (Belonging to a Bulgarian captain, or to Candide, or to a South American governor; it is all the same to her; at the end she does not recognize the change in her own appearance.) Each ancillary character processes experience as if by an assembly line. Each proceeds without introspection. Thus each, though enduring innumerable crises, inhabits a serenely uniform mental world, a world without change, all events linked by similarity. Toward such secure simplicity of world and mind, particularly as represented by the confident, authoritative philosophers, Candide is constantly propelled by his uneasy combination of self-esteem and self-regard. But at the end, whatever else he means by his closing remarks, he refuses to join his companions in continued mock-philosophizing.

In this late turn of events the hero is subtly but definitely seconded by the narrator (there is a parallel development in *Rasselas*). At the beginning of the tale the narrator had made himself prominent with continual, insistent irony, often sarcasm, but he plays a much subdued part as the tale progresses, particularly after the entrance of Martin in the nineteenth chapter. The narrator's earlier, extreme irony had made a witty, critical foil for the naive optimism of Pangloss and Candide, and for the complacency about cruelty and stupidity exhibited by most of the other characters. Martin, when he enters, is occasionally ironical (it is he who says, in chapter 23, that France and England "sont en guerre pour quelques arpents de neige vers le Canada"—"are at war for a plot of snow near Canada"), but in the main his is a direct critical voice, and he is in addition a pessimist. By contrast with this role, the narrator's, for much the most part toward the close of the tale, is that of an uneditorializing introducer of speakers and straightforward describer of actions. Directly or indirectly, the narrator of the latter part of the tale offers very few opinions, with the result that the irony lodged in his comments earlier now continues almost exclusively in the plot, and his earlier criticism is replaced by Martin's. Yet valid as Martin's criticism often is, he overreaches himself in his pessimism, which turns out to be similar in its affected omniscience about the chain of events, in kind if not in degree, to the optimism of Pangloss. When Cacambo defeats Martin's prediction by returning to Candide, the plot defeats Martin's philosophy too.

One rhetorical effect of the change whereby Martin takes on himself the judgmental responsibilities of the narrator is some attenuation of the tale's satire. The narrator's satirical reflections had worn the absoluteness and invulnerability of irony. Martin's criticism becomes vulnerable because based on a stated, then overstated doctrine; his point of view, unlike the narrator's, remains distinctly limited—formally, but also by consequences in the plot, by the limitations of his nature as fully revealed in the end, and perhaps even by one of the narrator's rare late judgments, the reference to Martin's "détestables principes." That is, part of the satire which continues in the tale after the narrator steps down from the bench qualifies Martin's utterances. And the narrator, who at the outset had taken the reader into his confidence, offering him the absolute assurance that only an omniscient narrator can provide, an assurance like that which Candide sought from Pangloss and metaphysics, toward the end ranges himself less closely with the reader and more closely with Candide, whom the narrator resembles increasingly when Candide finally refrains from explanation, from commentary.

In the final pages, the hero, the narrator, and the tale resist commentary as misreading, likely to be the product of covert egotism, like the philosophies of Pangloss and Martin. In the last page or so Candide says, twice, "il faut cultiver notre jardin." The narrator, who had earlier made such a point of uncovering the true motives of his blind, compulsive hero, does not explain these declarative, in effect imperative statements, but presents them to the reader as final, seemingly discrete items in the series constituted by Candide's words, thoughts, and actions throughout the tale, presents them to be motivated in meaning by the reader. To be interpreted, Candide's final statements must be associated with his history, and virtually the only way *that* can be accomplished is to construe them as negation. As part of the tale, not as a historic statement by the historical Voltaire, the clause in context resists all but the most elementary commentary. So often duped by unexamined, grandiose, metaphorical habits of thought, Candide here speaks as unmetaphorically, as literally, as possible.

In the history of interpretation, it is true, the resistance of the text has often been resisted itself. The image of cultivating one's garden is so historically poetical, so pregnant with iconic potentiality—one may even find it in a passage Leibniz wrote about the necessity of universal progress—that a scholar is hard put not to explode with learned associations. Surely, however, it ought to give an interpreter pause when he considers that the import of the remark in context, the final time Candide makes it, is precisely to re-

buff Pangloss' Optimistic assimilation of events up to this moment;

> Tous les événements sont enchaînés dans le meilleur des mondes possibles, [Pangloss exclaims] car enfin, si vous n'aviez pas été chassé d'un beau château, à grands coups de pied dans le derrière . . . —Cela est bien dit, répondit Candide, mais il faut cultiver notre jardin.
>
> (All events are enchained in this best of possible worlds, for if you had not been turned out of a fine chateau with strong kicks in the rear. . . . —Well said, answered Candide, but it is necessary to care for our garden).

That *bien dit,* implying the gap between words and things: has Candide come full circle, finally emulating the narrator's former sarcasm? Pangloss' last speeches compose a brief grammar of facile interpretation, a Panglossary: philosophical, as in the comment just quoted; historical a paragraph before, as he enumerated unfortunate rulers, prompting Candide's first "il faut cultiver," prefaced by the suspect "Je sais aussi"; mythological and typological in Pangloss' reply, "Vous avez raison, dit Pangloss; car quand l'homme fut mis dans le jardin d'Eden, il y fut mis, *ut operaretur eum,* pour qu'il travaillât . . . " ("Correct, says Pangloss; for when man was placed in the Garden of Eden, he was placed in it *ut operaretur eum,* in order to work. . . ."). At this point Martin cannot forbear affirming, as he thinks, what Candide has said: "Travaillons sans raisonner"—without arguing, also without reasoning or even without rationalizing in the manner of Pangloss. Yet Martin, being Martin, also cannot resist interpreting and revising Candide's statement and giving a reason for not reasoning, yin for Pangloss' yang: "c'est le seul moyen de rendre la vie supportable" ("it is the only way to make living bearable"). Candide says nothing.

There is now in Candide a resistance to potentially delusive naturalization of decisions. He is, one might say colloquially, more realistic about the world and himself. But there is a way, though a quite special way, in which he is a rare example of literary realism in this respect. The two philosophers persist to the end in providing absolute reasons for life as they would have it. Candide seems to have learned something from the old Turk with a modest farm and isolationist views, but Candide does not seek to attach himself to that philosopher and he does not parrot his reasoning" ("le travail éloigne de nous trois grands maux, l'ennui, le vice et le besoin"—"work keeps three great evils away from us: boredom, vice, and want"), just as Candide does not echo Martin's reasoning. Candide's final words are most unusual for him in omitting concern for reasoning, while the motive for his behavior that the narrative suggests is, he has come to regard the metonymical from the point of view of metonymy; that is, with recognition that he perceives external events from the outside and that they remain in large measure unknowable except insofar as he can give them modest, motivated, metaphorical meaning, of desire and attainable object, by attending to his own desires instead of resisting acknowledgment of them.

Every effect has a cause, Voltaire would say in the *Diction-*

naire philosophique ("Chaîne des événements"), but every effect does not necessarily cause further effects. In Candide's final words, he concentrates on causing rather than being caused. The implication of his words is that, by possibly recognizing the automaton in himself, he may have enabled himself to be different, though what he may become we are not told. He does not grandly rouse himself and shake invincible locks. His repeated "il faut" could be more personal. This is no messianic (or Minervan) moment. But he would not abandon the habits of thought of his philosophical companions if he had not begun to cultivate his mind. In the garden he pauses; everything that has gone before in the tale indicates that he pauses to rid himself of disabling preconceptions, as Condillac's newly conscious statue stops to realize that he is not himself the scent of a rose that was his first sensation.

Condillac's statue is meant to be taken as a fiction, a teaching model; but to understand it, the philosopher insists, we must share its point of view (as we must share Candide's). Condillac's prefatory "Avis important au lecteur" is urgent on the point: "J'avertis donc qu'il est très-important de se mettre exactement à la place de la statue que nous allons observer. Il faut commencer d'exister avec elle . . . : en un mot, il faut n'être que ce qu'elle est" ("I insist then that it is most important to place oneself exactly in the situation of the statue which we are going to observe. We must begin to exist with it . . . ; in a word, we must be only what it is"). Mental life being "une chaîne dont les anneaux sont tour à tour idées et desirs" ("a chain of which the links are by turns ideas and desires"), we have only to follow that chain "pour découvrir le progrès de toutes les connoissances de l'homme" ("to discover the progress of all the conceptions of man"). As in Locke, Gay, and others, a person must be very wary of, and curious about, the habits of thought he has formed, "Car, lorsqu'une fois nous avons contracté ces habitudes, nous agissons sans pouvoir observer les jugemens qui les accompagnent . . . " ("For once we have formed these habits, we act without being able to observe the judgments accompanying them . . . "). *Amour-propre* is the fundamental love felt by the statue; the mind has a certain natural bias, for example, whereby it tends to think that what pleases it intends to do so ("Elle pense donc que ce qui lui plaît, a en vue de lui plaire . . . "). The mind is also very apt to imitate what it sees: "Nous sommes si fort portés à l'imitation, qu'un Descartes à sa place [in the condition of a wild child] n'apprendroit pas à marcher sur ses pieds: tout ce qu'il verroit suffiroit pour l'en détourner" ("We are so forcefully drawn to imitate that a Descartes in his condition would not learn to walk on his feet; everything he would see would tend to turn him away from doing so"). These hazards are to be avoided so that the statue, conscious of the chain of his thinking, may declare: "Instruite par l'expérience, j'examine, je délibère avant d'agir. Je n'obéis plus aveuglément à mes passions, je leur résiste, je me conduis d'après mes lumières, je suis libre . . . " ("Instructed by experience, I examine, I deliberate before acting. I no longer obey my passions blindly, I resist them, I go by my own lights, I am free . . . ").

The finally enlightened, liberated Candide is a rare and distinguished person in eighteenth-century fiction. A work such as *Candide,* or *Rasselas,* supports the seemingly paradoxical observation that the blatantly unrealistic philosophical tale tends to be more realistic, in what I have called realism of psychological assessment, than the "novel of worldliness" in France or the then-new English novel, because the tale promotes attention to the hero as assessor of his own sense of reality. In *Candide,* unlike most novels of the time, the hero is quite imperfect; there is considerable emphasis, as also in contemporary associationist philosophy, upon his preconceptions as obstacles to knowledge of himself and the "real" world; self-knowledge, including non-rigorist recognition of the hero's own desires, is requisite for whatever happiness may be found (marvelous coincidences finally solve no crucial problems for the hero); and the narrator, prominently and satirically distant from the hero at the beginning of the tale, has become unobtrusive by the end while his judgmental function has been assumed by a less authoritative person, Martin. The mentor or mentors engage the hero in productive exchanges of opinion, dialectic usually only said to be present in novels, and the ending thwarts novelistic absorption of the reader, rhetorical stress there remaining on the dangers of mindless idealization, not the allure of the ideal. (pp. 194-216)

Frederick M. Keener, " 'Candide': Structure and Motivation," in his The Chain of Becoming, *Columbia University Press, 1983, pp. 194-216.*

Josephine Grieder (essay date 1984)

[*In the following essay, Grieder considers the function of paradox in* Candide.]

That critics should still continue to argue about *Candide* is scarcely surprising. To summarize it is wellnigh impossible; to isolate one idea is often to find that idea contradicted or betrayed further on. Underlying the apparent chaos, I would suggest, is in fact a venerable literary genre: that of paradox. In the epilogue to her distinguished study *Paradoxia Epidemica: The Renaissance Tradition of Paradox,* Rosalie Colie concludes that by the eighteenth century the "epidemic" had, in general, run its course. Nevertheless, her analysis of certain of its characteristics is equally germane to *Candide* and provides an orderly structure whose function is to accommodate what appears to be defiant disorderliness.

In the literary tradition of paradox, which embraces a host of techniques—encomia upon unworthy subjects, double-bind propositions like that of the Cretan who declares that all Cretans are liars—two seem especially appropriate to *Candide.* The first is that of *insolubilia,* that is, in Professor Colie's words, "the problems arising from the conventional existence of two realms, one of experience and one of discourse; what is real in the second may not be real in the first, with all the intellectual and moral problems thereupon pendant." She also identifies another looser sense of paradox, "a formulation of any sort running counter to received opinion." She continues, "the paradox is always somehow involved in dialectic: challenging some orthodoxy, the paradox is an oblique criticism of absolute judgment or absolute convention."

Candide is, in effect, a synthesis of these two aspects of this literary genre. The *insolubilia,* the conflict of discourse and experience, may be phrased in other ways: order and disorder, or stability and changeability; most general perhaps, the opposition of the ideal (here defined as what we wish to believe or are told by authorities that we should believe) and the real (what we in fact see and in which we participate). Fundamental to *Candide* is the intrusion, or more strongly, the irruption of the real world into the ideal. In the process the paradox (the experience, the real) challenges the orthodox (the discourse, the ideal) by dislocating its equilibrium and calling into question its capacity to deal with the world as it is. Paradox is all too apparent in the work; a more subtle question is the nature of the orthodox which it insists on upsetting. I would suggest that orthodoxy is attacked in at least four forms: rhetorical, logical, sentimental, and psychological.

What is orthodox rhetoric? In one sense it may be interpreted as verbal embellishment designed to elevate the ordinary to another, ideal plane. But in *Candide* the ordinary subtly but stubbornly refuses elevation, betraying, by a tiny detail, that the rhetoric is no more than a pompous euphemism for commonplace activity. Pangloss most eloquently describes his entry into a mosque: "il n'y avait qu'un vieux iman et une jeune dévote très jolie qui disait ses paternôtres; sa gorge était toute découverte: elle avait entre ses deux tétons un beau bouquet de tulipes, de roses, d'anémones, de renoncules, d'hyacinthes, et d'oreilles d'ours; elle laissa tomber son bouquet; je le ramassai, et je le lui remis avec un empressement respectueux." The scene is decorous, the description of the bouquet lavishly precise, the philosopher's courtesy apparently admirable. But Pangloss's own casual, perhaps even unwitting vulgarism, the "deux tétons," even though promptly overwhelmed by the catalogue of the flowers, defines plainly the "empressement" that animated him.

A scene in Chapter One, similar in construction, turns on the orthodox rhetoric of experimental science. Cunégonde, walking in the woods, sees Pangloss "qui donnait une leçon de physique expérimentale à la femme de chambre de sa mère, petite brune très jolie et très docile. Comme mademoiselle Cunégonde avait beaucoup de disposition pour les sciences, elle observa, sans souffler, les expériences réitérées dont elle fut témoin; elle vit clairement la raison suffisante du docteur, les effets, et les causes, et s'en retourna tout agitée, toute pensive, toute remplie du désir d'être savante." Omitted from the quotation is, of course, the crucial initial detail: Cunégonde sees them "entre des broussailles." What, limited to orthodox terminology, appears to be a laudable instructive endeavor is in fact the most elegantly discreet pornography.

Puncturing orthodox rhetoric with realistic detail produces a fine comic effect; more serious in intent is manipulation involving those elevated ideas with which rhetoric traditionally concerns itself. Stylistically, it operates in two ways. The rhetorical vocabulary of the ideal world may be substituted for vocabulary normally employed in describing the real world, or it may be made to explain an

inescapable, actual condition. The result in either case is a discreditation of the ideal world which orthodox rhetoric is assumed to express.

The discreditation arises, in the first instance, from the following: substitution of an ideal term for a real term necessitates its continual repetition, since the real occurs so frequently; and at last the repetition empties it of all its ideal sense. In Chapter Two, for example, the two Bulgar officers, identified in any case only as "Deux hommes habillés de bleu," see Candide and remark, "voilà un jeune homme très bien fait, et qui a la taille requise." After they persuade him to drink to the health of their king, "C'en est assez, lui dit-on, vous voilà l'appui, le soutien, le défenseur, le héros des Bulgares." In effect, Candide has become a soldier—but the word "soldat" is never used at all, being replaced, as necessary, with the term "héros." "Candide, tout stupéfait, ne démêlait pas encore trop bien comment il était un héros," and quite naturally goes for a walk. "Il n'eut pas fait deux lieues que voilà quatre autres héros de six pieds qui l'atteignent, qui le lient, qui le mènent dans un cachot." In Chapter Three, fleeing after a battle designated only as "cette boucherie héroïque," he passes through a village devastated by the troops and sees old men looking at their slaughtered wives and babies, and "des filles, éventrées après avoir assouvi les besoins naturels de quelques héros." What received opinion has been taught to accept as glorious is here, by compression and repetition, reduced to meaninglessness and, more serious, indicted as the cause of human suffering.

A variation on this is to explain a real effect by a rhetorically acceptable cause and simultaneously to surcharge the latter with such fulsome elaboration that its credibility is debased still further. Candide meets in Holland "un gueux tout couvert de pustules, les yeux morts, le bout du nez rongé, la bouche de travers, les dents noires, et parlant de la gorge, tourmenté d'une toux violente, et crachant une dent à chaque effort." It is Pangloss, in all his syphilitic misery. But how does he explain the cause of his condition? "c'est l'amour: l'amour, le consolateur du genre humain, le conservateur de l'univers, l'âme de tous les êtres sensibles, le tendre amour." The rhetoric of the ideal fails abysmally to ennoble the initial graphic reality.

Pangloss' rhetorical distortions are not unexpected because he is the established voice of the ideal world. His particular province, philosophy, introduces another form of orthodoxy: logic. As the spokesman for the laws of cause and effect, he is on perfectly sound, logical ground: there are no effects without causes. It might appear that his obviously faulty reasoning, which adds so much comic texture, can simply be dismissed as a display of the fallacy of false causes, e.g., *post hoc, ergo propter hoc.* I would suggest, however, that his errors are far more grave because they proceed from his essential conviction—rendered subtly by the passive voice—that each cause has been ordered, so as to produce a specific effect. We have spectacles not only because we first had noses but because "les nez ont été faits pour porter des lunettes," and we wear breeches because "les jambes sont visiblement instituées pour être chaussées." In short, as he says, "tout étant fait pour une fin, tout est nécessairement pour la meilleure fin." But made by whom or by what?

At issue here, by implication, is something far more profound than Pangloss' efforts to interpret the data of the world according to the logic of cause and effect. Consider his unshakable conclusion in the beginning that "Par conséquent, ceux qui ont avancé que tout est bien ont dit une sottise: il fallait dire que tout est au mieux." What is missing from this effect is its specific cause; and the cause, like the ordering principle which dictates that noses are made for glasses, would appear to be the deity. Pangloss' formulation would therefore seem to be that known in formal logic as *modus ponens*. His first premise may be phrased thus: "If God is all powerful and all good, then this is the best of all possible worlds." His position, so often reiterated, is that indeed, this is the best. It might thus seem to support what is actually his essential and unquestioned second premise: God is all powerful and all good.

Yet, precisely what *Candide* as a work demonstrates is the impossibility of accepting Pangloss' position: a world which is subject to or condones injustice, treachery, brutality, and suffering cannot possibly be described as "the best." Therefore, the formal logical equation passes to that known as *modus tollens* and the second premise is thereby invalidated: if God is all powerful and all good, then this is the best of all possible worlds; the work proves that it is not the best; therefore, God is either not all powerful or not all good. Paradox, paradoxically obeying orthodox logic, in effect challenges and refutes orthodox opinion about the nature of the deity; but such subversive calculation is discreetly left to the reader.

What is to be concluded about Pangloss and, by extension, about the ideal world whose spokesman he is? At the beginning, operating in the realm of pure logic, he succeeds only in justifying the unjustifiable: syphilis is essential to our enjoyment of chocolate and cochineal. At the end, he must explain the unexplainable: how he survived the auto-da-fé and has turned up aboard the Turkish ship. But when questioned by Candide on his views, he remains resolutely faithful to orthodoxy, "car enfin je suis philosophe: il ne me convient pas de me dédire." Yet, even he silently acquiesces in the bankruptcy of the ideal. "Pangloss avouait qu'il avait toujours horriblement souffert; mais ayant soutenu une fois que tout allait à merveille, il le soutenait toujours, et n'en croyait rien."

Both rhetorical and logical orthodoxy are situated in the text itself, either by characters or in commentary. Sentimental orthodoxy is broader in scope: it gives the work its shape and its hero his motivation. Consider, for example, the ideal *roman d'amour:* boy and girl meet, realize they are meant for each other, are separated by unavoidable castastrophes, are reunited, marry, and live happily ever after. Consider equally the character of its hero: devoted to Love and the Woman who embodies it; passionate but discreet, steadfast, courageous, triumphant. *Candide* the work corresponds exactly to the former definition and Candide the character to the latter. But it is reality—reality as sexuality in the form of Cunégonde and reality as the physicalness of the world—which, by intruding itself into this rather bloodless literary formula, gives the work its movement.

From the beginning Candide possesses "les mœurs les plus douces"; he combines "le jugement assez droit avec l'esprit le plus simple"; he listens attentively to Pangloss' lessons "car il trouvait mademoiselle Cunégonde extrêmement belle, quoiqu'il ne prît jamais la hardiesse de le lui dire." Cunégonde, however, "haute en couleur, fraîche, grasse, appétissante," is already more palpable than the orthodox sentimental heroine ought to be. Aroused by Pangloss' demonstration in the bushes, it is she who takes the initiative: she drops her handkerchief, he picks it up, she takes his hand. Behaving impeccably, he kisses hers "avec une vivacité, une sensibilité, une grâce toute particulière," but physical contact abruptly destroys any pretense of spirituality: "leurs bouches se rencontrèrent, leurs yeux s'enflammèrent, leurs genoux tremblèrent, leurs mains s'égarèrent"—until the baron puts a decisive halt to the scene, and, dislocating the equilibrium of the best of all possible worlds, "chassa Candide du château à grands coups de pied dans le derrière."

To say that Candide is forced out of the ideal world into the real is, as is paradoxically appropriate, simultaneously true and untrue. That this is the real world is verified in very orthodox fashion by places (Buenos Aires, Surinam, Venice), events (the earthquake, the execution of Admiral Byng), and people (the Jesuits, the six kings). That it cannot be the real world is due not only to the presence of mythical lands but also to the mythical talent of its characters to survive a disproportionate number of catastrophes.

What makes these contradictory statements mutually compatible, what gives them their equilibrium, is the function of the work's movement from known to unknown to known in terms of the education of its hero. The expulsion from Thunder-ten-tronckh signals the beginning of a quest—a quite unwitting one on Candide's part but evident to the reader—for the philosopher's best of all possible worlds. Exposure to the real world into which sexuality has thrust him teaches a harsh lesson to Pangloss' pupil; nonetheless, he refuses to disavow his master's instruction. The measure of his intellectual progress can be assessed during the voyage from Europe to South America: "Car il faut avouer qu'on pourrait gémir un peu de ce qui se passe dans le nôtre en physique et en morale," he tells Cunégonde; "C'est certainement le nouveau monde qui est le meilleur des mondes possibles." Reality being scarcely less rude in Argentina and Paraguay, however, Candide escapes into lands progressively more mythical: the country of the Oreillons (the state of pure nature), and Eldorado. Yet, when he at last discovers his quest's utopian goal—to which I shall return—he leaves it. The logic of the real world—exemplified by the one-handed, one-legged black slave who declares that "C'est à ce prix que vous mangez du sucre en Europe"—is now comprehensible. "O Pangloss! . . . c'en est fait, il faudra qu'à la fin je renonce à ton optimisme . . . [cette] rage de soutenir que tout est bien quand on est mal." Accompanied by Martin, whose pessimism he is at present equipped to understand even while he combats it, he re-enters the real, known world, made incongruous only by the reunion of so many acquaintances missing or presumed dead.

Thus, Candide's education, or at least one aspect of it, has consisted in his learning to accept and deal with the reality which so irrationally irrupts into the equilibrium of the ideal taught to him by Pangloss; yet, the end of the work demonstrates a return to orthodoxy, compromised though it has become. Reunited with his mistress, Candide is confronted by the effects of reality on the long-sought ideal: "sa belle Cunégonde rembrunie, les yeux éraillés, la gorge sèche, les joues ridées, les bras rouges et écaillés." Even he cannot fail to recognize what actually exists. "Le tendre amant . . . recula trois pas, saisi d'horreur"; but, stubbornly refusing to abandon the sentimental ideal to which he has so long dedicated himself, "[il] avança ensuite par bon procédé." He does indeed marry her, principally to spite her brother, but also because "Cunégonde le pressait si vivement qu'il ne pouvait s'en dédire." Like Pangloss, who is trapped by his commitment to logical orthodoxy, Candide is trapped by his own (and with the same verb) to the sentimental. Received opinion as to how the *roman d'amour* must conclude and its hero behave is obeyed; actual physical fact exposes the hollowness of the ideal construct.

However, in this confrontation between orthodoxy and paradoxy, there would appear to be one moment at which the ideal effectively triumphs over the real, maintaining its own integrity while the intruder shamefacedly skulks away. Eldorado, at the center of this work, is undeniably an Enlightenment utopia: an ancient civilization in which the arts are valued and the sciences esteemed, an undogmatic religion is respected, and government is benevolently organized to promote the general welfare of its citizens. Surrounded as it is by misfortune and disaster, the episode is a moment of tranquillity spent, as Candide recognizes, in "probablement le pays où tout va bien: car il faut absolument qu'il y en ait un de cette espèce." Yet he and Cacambo leave. Why?

In the context of orthodox and paradox, the answer lies in an opposition of mentalities. What animates Candide and Cacambo to depart is not necessarily admirable. Appropriately alleging his sentimental desire to recover Cunégonde, Candide continues more forthrightly, "Si nous restons ici, nous n'y serons que comme les autres." Cacambo is pleased with the suggestion, because "on aime tant à courir, à se faire valoir chez les siens, à faire parade de ce qu'on a vu dans ses voyages." But the outlook of the Eldoradans is not necessarily enviable, either. "Je suis fort ignorant, et je m'en trouve bien," says the innkeeper to Candide; "nous sommes tous du même avis," declares the old man; and the king chides them for wanting to leave because "quand on est passablement quelque part, il faut y rester."

Reality, represented by Candide and Cacambo, is thus resisting and rejecting a new sort of orthodoxy: the psychological orthodoxy that accepts with equanimity the stasis that perfection necessarily imposes so that it will not be disrupted. Reality can confront, fight, try to give the lie to the other orthodoxies—rhetorical, logical, sentimental—constructed by man. Reality cannot accept immuta-

bility based on mediocrity and ignorance, no matter how beneficial its consequences, and voluntarily withdraws.

If, at the end of the work, Pangloss and Candide continue to adhere verbally to the ideals in which they formerly believed, they do tacitly accept the real in which they must participate. "Il faut cultiver notre jardin" is also a sort of stasis, but human-imposed and of undeterminable duration: the midpoint of a see-saw on which paradox and orthodox are at opposing ends. A glance at the minor characters confirms this. Those who have been most buffeted by reality—Paquette, the old women, frère Giroflée—move usefully into this community to which Candide's formulation gives a certain stability; the last "même devint honnête homme." Relinquishing to a degree his orthodox pessimism, " 'Travaillons sans raisonner,' dit Martin; 'c'est le seul moyen de rendre la vie supportable.' " Only the baron refuses to abandon orthodoxy and he pays the price: the others spirit him away to the galley ship, to return to Rome, "et on eut le plaisir d'attraper un jésuite, et de punir l'orgueil d'un baron allemand."

This compromise between the real and the ideal has its rewards, even for the latter's two most doctrinaire spokesmen. "Cunégonde était, à la vérité, bien laide," as Candide must acknowledge, "mais elle devint une excellente pâtissière." As for Pangloss, it is only fitting that the work's final paradox should be that the philosopher is, for the first time, absolutely right: "car enfin si vous n'aviez pas été chassé d'un beau château à grands coups de pied dans le derrière pour l'amour de mademoiselle Cunégonde, si vous n'aviez pas été mis à l'Inquisition, si vous n'aviez pas couru l'Amérique à pied, si vous n'aviez pas donné un bon coup d'épée au baron, si vous n'aviez pas perdu tous vos moutons du bon pays d'Eldorado, vous ne mangeriez pas ici des cédrats confits et des pistaches." How is it possible that Pangloss can at last reason correctly? Because he is explaining the logic of a non-world: the work itself. (pp. 485-92)

Josephine Grieder, "Orthodox and Paradox: The Structure of 'Candide'," in The French Review, *Vol. LVII, No. 4, March, 1984, pp. 485-92.*

Carol Sherman   (essay date 1984)

[*In the following essay, Sherman treats* Zadig *as an allegory concerned with reading and interpretation.*]

By the time even the casual reader arrives at the end of **Zadig,** she has found little coherence in what has been offered as exemplary. The title, **Zadig, ou la destinée,** proposes a double reading, a fiction and a philosophy. The dedicatory epistle designates bad readers and good ones—among the latter are those willing to *parler raison*. Lesson-giving and lesson-seeking are performed and proposed by both the narrator and the protagonist who thus seem to be offering guidance in the quest for meaning. Rarely, however, is one allowed to feel confident of the instructions available; in many ways the text constantly undermines its own authority as guide, and frustrates rather than facilitates the search for meaning. It is against interpretation; it is also about interpretation, and I propose viewing it as an allegory of (mis)reading.

One of the deconstructive factors is the text's demolition and transformation of the idea or project of mimesis. Didactic literature offers the particular kind of reflection that consists in a lesson or a truth. Since the promise of instruction is continually renewed, the reader, believing a large part of the game to be the pleasurable discovery of the message, attempts to develop a strategy for its reception. At another moment of resistance, the subject, conscious of its own and the text's fragmentation, can be the locus where many kinds of "texts"—cultural, personal, etc.— unite. The reader, conscious of the processes of reception, brings to bear a multiplicity of factors in order to make sense of the tale; such an audience can thus try different strategies, juggle grids, respond selectively at each moment. In this activity, the undecidability or indeterminism of successful strategy is the primary deconstructing message of *Zadig;* and for the fragmented subject, it replaces any essentialist lesson that it is possible, even fragmentedly, to derive. Before the multiplicity of potential parodies of other texts and of specific practices, the critical reader has to perform more, i.e., to adjust grids more often; and she is frustrated in the performance because, ultimately, no certainty is offered. One might imagine that she willingly or conventionally puts aside the expectation of mimesis because she recognizes fairytale-form ("histoire orientale," "il y avait une fois," etc.). The didactic discourse-relation, however, constantly positions the fairytale-code in a referential code as well by inviting the assimilation of the oriental setting and the hero's predicament with the political system and philosophical dilemmas the reader herself knows. The folkloric aspects do not, therefore, prevent the expectation of some objective, reflected truth. That this prospect is always denied, however, means that the text is constantly "foregrounding" its own loss of innocence. In many ways it destroys itself as representation.

Deconstruction of this didactic and mimetic logic occurs, among other places, at that point where the story contrasts the hero's feeling of being helpless before the accidents of fate ("mais quel sera le serpent?") with the reader's observation that, besides being subject to destiny, the hero is also destiny for others. This perception is attributed twice to Zadig himself: once negatively and still in the perspective of his own bad fortune, he says, "Je vois . . . que les malheurs de ma destinée se répandent sur la tienne"; and once he sees himself as a positive instrument but complains of the lack of recompense: "O puissant Orosmade! . . . vous vous servez de moi pour consoler cet homme; de qui vous servirez-vous pour me consoler?" The numerous episodes in which Zadig acts as enabler for another character's desire gradually accumulate (the queen, the brigand, the fisherman). They magnify an insight that he does not completely share, but they nuance his perception of his own dilemma. One episode in particular represents this insight, for it contains signs that encourage it— those emitted by the fisherman (who calls him *ange sauveur*) and by the narrator. As didactic complexity increases, it becomes more accessible to the reader than to the hero, and indeed it is the narrator who summarizes the

imbalance in the exchange between the two characters. He does so in a way that encourages the realization of the hero's place in the scheme of accidents. He pronounces the emblematic sentence, "Ils se séparèrent: le pêcheur marcha en remerciant son destin, et Zadig courut en accusant toujours le sien."

Up to the very end, this double situation continues to be manifest; the hero is at the same time fate's victim and its agent for others. The hermit will finally tell them this, and he thereby takes for a special case what the reader could think about all of them: "Souviens-toi de ce pêcheur qui se croyait le plus malheureux de tous les hommes. Orosmade t'a envoyé pour changer sa destinée." The reader's omniscience comes from her complicity with the narrator, but it is limited to that domain and is thus only relative; she is not granted omniscience about her own destiny, and the text continually proves it. Viewed in this perspective, the title of the tale seems to suggest two truths. In *Zadig ou la destinée,* the conjunction *ou* can indicate not choice, but a double state: he is a factor in the destiny of others, but that is not the problem. In the sentence treating him and the fisherman, the hero is still an eiron, complaining of injustice; but the sign of his power is present, even though only in the reader's eventual, supratextual perception of the fact that, despite the rigorously contrasted elements, the syntactic proximity between *son destin* and *Zadig* suggests a semantic similarity as well. *A* is not to *a* as *B* is not to *b,* and so on:

$$A \quad B \quad C \quad D$$

Le pêcheur marcha en remerciant son destin et
Zadig courut en accusant le sien.

$$a \quad b \quad c \quad d$$

The syntactic parallelism of the two phrases produces contrast and emphasizes the linear, fragmented state of the two events while it insists upon the absence of understanding and of synthesis in the story and in the *récit.* In both, the two lines can continue without ever meeting. The second possibility that the title suggests is something like "Zadig or an experience/experiment in destiny," which makes an explicit contrast between the *exempla,* Zadig's adventures, and the general idea of providential fate. Positioned in the larger problem, the title reveals this duality by the ambiguity of *ou* and of *ou bien,* that is, the difference between *identity* and *exclusion.*

Two other codes come into play in the depiction of the protagonist, and they contribute to the destruction of the idea of hero. Logically, they exclude each other, yet they are both present: the code of tragedy and myth and that of comic eiron leading to parody. The plot-curve resembles that of myth, not that of literature or news—the hero's existence is a uniform given with an incident of loss and one of reparation demarcating the part recounted; and in the tent ("Les Combats"), he undergoes symbolic death and resurrection. Further insuring his membership in the class of the admirable, he shows both physical prowess and wisdom in many episodes. For those reasons and by his exalted governmental position, that of minister, he has the culturally-given right to dramatize himself in misfortune as a tragic victim of fate. A part of the episodic sequence also reinforces the mythical, even god-like, resonance of his adventures, for the minister is made a slave before becoming king. This incident, as well as the one in which he appears on the field of battle without his armor and is jeered, recall the precept according to which the humble are (sometimes) exalted; and they support in these further ways a possible view of Zadig as mythical hero.

At the same time, he is comical and his mythic potential mocks myth, for these very features can be reversed and degraded. The passage from minister to slave and from slave to king belongs also to the comic grotesque (he wears bonnet and nightcap on the field of battle), to carnival, and to traditions of the reversal of roles (Cador was a more valuable slave than Zadig, at first) that occur in certain privileged periods. Added to this way of deciphering the up-and-down movement of the hero's fate are the quasi-simultaneous lamentations and their minimizing *chutes* by which Zadig is made to deflate his own rhetoric and to appear foolish, even as he expresses the dilemma of mankind. The potential for the tragic and mythic reference co-exists with the comic and eironic, and both grids are offered by the same group of signs. Our interpretative strategies vacillate in this respect also. The mixed presentation of the hero as potentially both comic and tragic resonates with parody of the novel and of the epic. His destruction is both rhetorical and literary; by referring to those kinds of texts and to their heroes, the tale also disapproves of the hero as a literary personage and indirectly undermines both the comic and the tragic figure. The implicit opposition remains the one between literature and ethical or moral analysis, since questions of destiny are posed in natural not literary (religious) terms.

Another of the elements of intertextual construct is the hero's permanent wondering about generalized, global, agentless (in)justice. The status of these interrogations as serious reference to theodicy has its formal and deconstructive equivalent in the anecdotal schema itself, in the parabolic nature of the incidents. In the episodes ending in a *pointe,* the reader is subjected to a back-and-forth movement between the little paradoxes—revealed by attacks on specific individuals and by attacks on general traits of humanity—and the grand interrogation about fate and unhappiness in general, the cosmic paradox, and general irony. In this movement, two kinds of plot-logic conflict: 1) the innocence of the text—events seen as occurring and only accidentally pointing to a theme, and 2) the impurity of the text, in which the theme is seen as directing the selection of incidents. While it is true that many stories contain either suprise or paradox that gives them their point and that is primary in their being perceived as stories, this tale accumulates short stories that reiterate paradox and generate an insistent paradigm of life's quirkiness stressing unhappy (for the hero) fortune and accentuating the phenomenon of stories themselves. The critic detects the second, the impure logic named above. The reflection, the lesson, cannot be both *arranged* (having a beginning and an end) and *true,* especially given the existential demonstrations of Zadig's positive effect on others that go against the other demonstrations of fate's cruelty for him. An induction of truth from innocent evidence (the first logic named above), derives the lesson from real and chance happenings. The hero's displays

overtly opt for the lesson, and the tale's do too. Its unfolding resembles deductive process (the impurity named above), and the *conte philosophique* "foregrounds" it without naming the given from which all is derived. Events follow one logic, and meaning follows another—an illogic or a-logic that requires misreading. By radically separating the two logics, **Zadig** exposes particularly clearly this paradox of any attempt to discover meaning. It typifies and thematizes the difficulty. It combines two thematizations, one, *lack of meaning* (it is absurd that the good are punished), and two, *meaning assigned* (the angel says everything means something, and he simply assigns meaning as Meaning). His act gives to the *récit* primacy over the *histoire,* for his speech shows only that he *is saying* that there is meaning. This meta-assurance coincides with what any story-like signifier says to us also by the fact of its being divided into chapters and of its having words on the page. The conclusion (ch. 19), however, exhibits neither lack of meaning nor meaning assigned; the topic does not even come up, and it is not possible to choose. The good are rewarded, the evil are punished, happiness finally reigns because it is time to stop reading.

Most damaging to the claims the didactic-mimetic text makes for itself are the content and arrangement of the last three chapters. [In his *The Act of Reading: A Theory of Esthetic Response*] Wolfgang Iser has written on several occasions about the degrees of indeterminacy of different kinds of texts. He speaks of utopic and of ideological novels that finish with a *tour de force,* thereby compensating for their own indeterminacy, and he opposes this sort to the type that articulates the indeterminacy: "Which one, dear Reader . . . ?" The naive reading of **Zadig** may lead one to believe that it belongs to the first category, the scene of the angel and the last beatific vision constituting this *tour de force* that knots all the threads into a utopic ending. Since the hero's *mais* and the position of the chapter and the absence of deixis all aid in removing determinisms, the critic can, however, just as easily see that the text is a very determined one, in both senses of the word, and that the story ends in a *tour de force* of *in*determinacy, a sudden definitive hiding or disappearance of what was to be made evident and had always been hidden. The last chapter returns to the charge of determinacy by the nature of its discourse—deixis recaptured—by its content of heavy distribution of rewards and punishments, and by the announcement of eternal bliss; but its very certainty and solidity seem to sharpen the indetermined determination that it just abandoned.

The reader probably entertains the possibility that the hero's trials and perplexity may be the work of Providence. That word, associated with theodicy and the belief that all is for the good, appears four times in the tale; for example, just after the theft of Zadig's armor, it occurs twice:

> Il lui échapa enfin de murmurer contre la Providence, et il fut tenté de croire que tout était gouverné par une Destinée cruelle qui opprimait les bons et qui faisait prospérer les chevaliers verds [. . .]. Dans cet équipage, il cotoyait l'Euphrate, rempli de désespoir et accusant en secret la Providence, qui le persécutait toujours.

It appears again when the hero submits ("L'Ermite"), and when he and the queen live happily ever after: "La reine et lui adorèrent la Providence" ("Les Enigmes"). Before the three final chapters, Voltaire employs the words *fortune, sort, destin, destinée* without capital letters to refer to forces beyond the hero's control. This means of vindicating divine justice in the face of misfortune and suffering was being debated in Europe all through the eighteenth century, and it reflects the particular form taken at that time by the universal desire to make sense of what was perceived as undeserved misfortune. (The *Théodicée* of Leibniz appeared in 1710). This instinct or desire is as strong in certain readers as it appears to be in the exclamations of the hero. The text, however, does not long allow the reader the satisfaction of this position. If she has already tried to project meaning onto the previous incidents, the episode of the hermit probably puts it into question again. All the preceding episodes led her and the hero to doubt the good sense of Providence; now an agent appears, and a group of events rewarding the unjust and punishing the just is concentrated into the four supposedly exemplary and explanatory visits conducted by the hermit. Replaying the role he assumed in the tales of three other lives, Zadig is only an observer in the four visits. His reactions are rage and submission. The reader who, by imagining a providential agent, had already tried to create coherence in the same way as the hermit later proposes, will tend to be as scandalized as Zadig is by the acceleration of injustice and by its concentration. She will perhaps be obliged to reject her own accommodation with that degree of injustice distributed throughout the previous episodes. Another kind of reader, one who has resisted taking the step to theodicy, will probably feel confirmed in her suspended judgment when she follows the explanations given by Jesrad. Zadig's "Qui te l'a dit, barbare?" and his hope for the *correction* of the wicked find their echo in her.

The conversation with the hermit-angel juxtaposes those two possibilities without ever synthesizing them. It could have, for instance, presented a materialistic or deterministic view of causality, in which human will to change and to correct also figures as one of the forces affecting events. The passage offers no synthesis, only silence; and it thus frustrates, for an indefinite period, the search for meaning. The would-be interpreter's faculties are exercised in both directions without being permitted to resolve, to explain, or to erase the moral scandal that reason assigns to the kinds of injustice described. This constitutes the principal and perhaps the most memorable experience of this text; and it is a fact that renders particularly futile the search for its "right" reading. The critic can simply describe most of the forces and processes that are available and that occur in reading. Those who do not like living with uncertainty—this *and* that instead of this *or* that—will choose one way or the other, will *select* the sense that allows conclusion about meaning. It so happens that the reader who elects to retain the problem as unresolved thereby espouses the *contiguous* or discrete nature of the last three episodes. Cause and effect between them and between the moments they record are entirely suspended as is judgment. From the visit with the angel and the successful living out of the trials, Zadig passes to a reward, one predicted, already and in any case, by the inexorable movement

of fairytale sequence and delayed only by the supernatural apparition that teaches him only submission. Since his obedience to contingency was never in question—he was buffeted about by it through the first seventeen chapters—, nothing is changed except that he now graciously submits to more agreeable chance by becoming king and marrying the queen. The text might thus be said to invite a final solution anyway—that fate arranges things for the best—for agreeable chance might be thought just as fundamental to the story/life as the unpleasant sort; and there were earlier "lucky" moments recounted as well as this last triumph: the parrot finds the broken tablet, the letter from Astarté arrives in time to save Zadig from being poisoned, etc.

The sense of two quests is still present at the end, for while the reader may grasp the concrete happiness attained, she may also feel the absence of the wisdom sought by the hero and promised by the hermit. The folk and philosophical endings diverge, because it is expected that the former give a sense of completeness as well as closure; but the latter, the quest for wisdom, is simply abandoned. Narration gives it up; it is absent from the signifier but not necessarily from the signified. The lesson she constructs for herself is not necessarily the abandonment of the question. Completeness can come only *from* closure for those readers who wish it thus. The hero's last tasks are indeed the direct cause of his right to reward, but the trials imposed by the angel make him see only a concentrated version of what he has already lived through and heard about. The angel's explanation—"tout est épreuve, ou punition, ou récompense, ou prévoyance"—assigns meaning to everything, but it adds no new information. The reader has no reason to believe that the hero was changed or enlightened by it, for even as he lived through disastrous contingency, he was already presented as virtuous and wise. This too prevents her from believing that the angel's proofs have taught her anything she had not already observed.

The form of resolution without its content is one construct of the double questing paradigm of the philosophical story. The grammar is present; the rhetoric is not. Pursuing the analogy of the tale as sentence, one imagines it to resemble a long sentence the meaning of which one will see at the end when each word has been read and its syntactic function identified. We expect that all the parts will make sense once we have seen the whole and that the whole will be meaningful once we have seen all the parts.

The critical reader is, therefore, not satisfied that there is continuity, a relation from cause to effect and from part to whole as she passes from the combats to revelation to enigmas and to the hero's reward. Instead, their juxtaposition records the essential ambiguity of the angel's explanation. I use the term "ambiguity" not in the sense of openended, but as positively double; for the angel's discourse contains two discontinuous utterances: 1) everything is reward or punishment, that is, purposeful and meaningful, but 2) you cannot know which and when. It invites the leap of faith that can embrace totalitarian meaningfulness—once again a grammar without rhetoric, a form without fixable content.

This indetermination doubles itself: it reigns both in life for the hero and in the literary experience of the reader.

In anything larger than individual episodes, where cause, effect, and enablers are sometimes clear to the protagonist and where a manifest satiric message is clear to the reader, that is, in the larger view promised to Zadig by the angel and promised to the reader by the fact that she approaches the end of the story, both she and he are denied explanation and are frustrated in that part of their expectation. However, both are compensated, although not with understanding, but with the sense of an ending, that is with a form. Zadig wins everything, and the reader gets to read the expected "happily-ever-after." Life's signs fail the hero; trying to make sense of existence, he cannot know. The literary signs fail the reader: trying to make sense of this literature, she is not allowed to guess. She is constrained to accept ignorance. Like the book of destinies, this book is not blank either; it is simply unreadable and always already misread.

Satiric genres usually leave us with nothing. That might suffice to account for the various absences that one feels in *Zadig,* but the topic bears elaboration. The tale announced itself as philosophical, as teaching something, a solution that turns out not to be there. It is very funny, but teaches no positive moral; and so the *conte philosophique* is essentially a *divertissement* with a negative lesson— unreadability—similar in that respect to the book of destinies. The constant negative, negated moral intertexts are the Christian idea of rewards and punishments and history à la Bossuet. These are constantly replaced by a new view of history from which God is absent. Part of the narrator's commentary on chance occurrences (the parrot, the letter that saves Zadig, etc.) parodies another intertext, namely, the science of cause and effect. If both God and science are undependable, the only proper treatment of destiny may be ironic, that is, refusing to be drawn into the metaphysical question of forces and of agents (distance), while admitting that the concept is of no use (reversal).

However, even in the absence of a positive lesson, the question raised by the subtitle remains. The description of the hero's fate can be construed as an immanent theory of destiny; it can be seen as parody of one of the *conte*'s echoes: the tale that ends happily. As such, it is an immanent criticism of the concept of destiny as well. Even if one accepts the implied criticism, one can also seize upon the outcome and perceive in it a form of realistic optimism, that is, the idea that chance and gratuitous forces can make one lucky too. *Zadig* and *Candide* are true versions of *La Théodicée:* the optimism of both—unexpressed in *Zadig,* explicit in *Candide*—consists in making the best of circumstances. The character Candide will not be a caricature of optimism, he will *be* optimism, the only kind possible. The grammar of revelation, of solution, and of truth is present both in the *histoire* and in the *récit.* The *histoire* includes a hermit-angel, a book of destinies, promises, tests: both tradition and explicited content say that the long-awaited answer is due. The incident that announces itself as the key to everything does the most damage to that very pretention. The *récit* has its own grammar of resolution; one approaches the end of the signifier—and that is traditional form's promise of a chord resolving the tension and dissonance that have gone before—but revelation is absent. A further subversion of grammar is the interrup-

tion in the crescendo of both *récit* and *histoire:* the place and content of the chapter "L'Ermite" constitute syntactic deviance. Instead of preceding or following the two sets of tests, it separates them. It could either come before both and thus seem to equip the hero with the extra wisdom and prowess necessary to accomplish the tasks, or it could follow his successful performances and, by conferring understanding, consecrate his achievements. It does neither, and the critic receives the deviance as a refusal of teleology and of providential thinking. The overt messages—"tu étais celui . . . qui méritait le plus d'etre éclairé" and "tout est épreuve . . . "—are abolished by the twisted syntax. It lays to rest Nietzsche's fear that "we shall never get rid of God, for we still believe in grammar." The text that claims to offer representation and truth subverts Destiny's ethics and its grammar. (pp. 32-40)

Carol Sherman, "Voltaire's 'Zadig' and the Allegory of (Mis)reading," in The French Review, *Vol. LVIII, No. 1, October, 1984, pp. 32-40.*

Graeme Hunter (essay date 1985)

[*In the following essay, Hunter debates Voltaire's refutation in* Candide *of Leibniz's philosophy of optimism.*]

It is a commonplace among general readers to believe that the philosopher Leibniz is aptly and accurately portrayed as Pangloss in Voltaire's *Candide.* Such is the merit of that philosophical satire that it seems, as it were, to carry with it its own certificate of success. It is equally habitual and common, however, for historians of philosophy to repudiate Dr Pangloss as a weak caricature of the German master. Such a split between the partisans and non-partisans of Leibniz was indeed foretold as early as the critical notice of *Candide* which appeared in the *Journal Encyclopédique* in 1759:

> Les partisans de Leibniz, au lieu d'y voir une réfutation de l'optimisme, n'y verront d'une bout à l'autre qu'un plaisanterie qui fait beaucoup rire, et ne prouve rien; ses adversaires soutiendront que la réfutation est complete, parce que le système de Leibniz n'étant qu'un roman, on ne peut le combattre que par un autre roman.

Scholarly treatment of *Candide* has been extensive and has of course moved subtly between these poles. However, as is to be expected, it typically sets out to determine what the actual goal of this highly ambiguous work was. It has been maintained, for example, that really Voltaire wished to criticize the Wolffians rather than the Leibnizians, that it was really Shaftesbury or Pope, rather than either Wolff or Leibniz, who was at issue, or that it was optimistic *philosophy* rather than optimistic philosophers which was the butt of Voltaire's ridicule.

I shall approach things somewhat differently here. My question does not concern what Voltaire intended by *Candide,* but rather what he accomplished by it, in so far as it relates to the philosophy of Leibniz. Hypothesizing that Voltaire did set out to criticize Leibniz, I shall be concerned in the main with evaluating his success. That such an approach will yield no definite insight into Voltaire's intentions I admit from the start. But I will claim for it two very significant advantages. First, it will illustrate an important but undervalued aspect of Leibniz's views. Second, it will disclose, independently of its particular success or failure, the mechanisms by which a work of literature is able to criticize a philosophical doctrine at all.

My focus will be the sequence of events recounted in *Candide* and my question to what extent that sequence of events may be regarded as a criticism of the Leibnizian philosophy of optimism. This is a philosophical question and it asks, in other words, whether *Candide* constitutes an extended global counterexample to the philosophy of Leibniz, which, while meeting the general suppositions of Leibniz's theory, shows it to be false in its consequences.

The standard view of historians of philosophy is that *Candide* simply fails to meet even minimal standards of criticism. They think Pangloss to be not just a one-sided but a false representation of Leibniz, and of course if Pangloss is not Leibniz, then the critique attempted in *Candide* can never get started.

The claim that Leibniz is mis- (as opposed to under-) represented in *Candide* I hold to be false and shall illustrate my claim in what follows. More unfortunate than the falsity of this view, however, is that complacency in it forestalls an appreciation of how and why Voltaire's criticism *really* fails and makes appear trivial what is in reality rather interesting and worthy of investigation.

There is no doctrine attributed to Pangloss which is not in fact held by Leibniz, though naturally some of the consequences drawn from the doctrines (e.g. that noses were made to prop up spectacles) are not drawn by Leibniz. However, the following ten teachings propounded by Pangloss are all central points in Leibniz's *Theodicy*: (a) for every event there is a cause or reason why it occurred; (b) the ultimate reason for all things is that they are best; (c) the world is fully determinate, i.e. things in this world cannot occur other than the way they do; and hence (d) all things are interconnected. Pangloss also holds (e) that the evil of this world is an essential ingredient in it, in the sense that a world which lacked these particular evils would not be the best, and consequently (f) that the fall of man and original sin enter necessarily into the best possible world and (g) that individual evils make for the general good. Pangloss maintains (h) that evils are analogous to the shadows in a beautiful picture, an analogy similar to ones which Leibniz himself uses ('De rerum originatione radicali,' *Die philosophischen Schriften*) to illustrate his doctrine that evil is merely privative. Pangloss and Leibniz also agree (i) that free will is compatible with complete determinism, and lastly, and most famously, (j) that the actual world is the best possible world.

A single point of controversy is perhaps the claim made by the narrator of *Candide* that Pangloss was insincere in maintaining these doctrines. But even this has respectable antecedents stretching from Leibniz's own acquaintances in Hanover to the critical account of his philosophy given by Bertrand Russell in our own century. I shall disregard this point in what follows.

This bare list of Leibnizian doctrines will be of little signif-

icance to anyone unfamiliar with the baroque system of thought into which they fit. The basis of it is this: we recognize that we are members of a world in which things happen in a determinate way. If it were not so, ordinary life would be chaotic and science impossible. Yet, while we recognize determination in things to be necessary, the particular determinations which hold in our world seem to be merely contingent. For example, we can easily imagine that there could have been some different law for the acceleration of free-falling bodies, that light could have travelled at a different speed, that the Ptolemaic system of planetary motions could have been correct, etc. The truth about all these matters had to be discovered through experiment and experience, and is therefore not a matter of logic or of necessity. By considering this fact we may come to see that there are many possible alternative orders of the world, in fact an infinite number corresponding to the infinite variety of ways the world could have been structured.

We can imagine worlds with the same laws as ours but in which we and our ancestors do not occur. We can imagine worlds in which we occur but in which the natural laws are different, and we can imagine worlds which differ from ours both in the laws which govern and the individuals governed. Yet each such possible world is subject to some laws or others; hence all things within any given world are interconnected and determinate. One world is distinguished from another by the individuals which inhabit it and/or the laws which obtain in it.

Now if we believe that nothing is as it is without a reason (Leibniz's Principle of Sufficient Reason), then some reason is necessary to account for why this world, rather than another possible world, is actual. And since such a reason could not, ultimately, be found in any being which was itself contingent, or part of any given world, there must be a necessary being, or God, transcendent with respect to all the worlds, to account for the series of contingent beings which we know. Again, given the principle of sufficient reason, God cannot be supposed to prefer creating one world to another without there being a sufficient reason for his doing so, and such a reason could lie only in the degree of perfection of this world in comparison to rival worlds. Had no world been best, Leibniz says, God would not have created any. But there is an actual world, so it must be the best possible.

I hope that this sketch is sufficient to make clear that Leibniz has metaphysical reasons for thinking this world to be the best possible. He did not draw this conclusion because he thought his own circumstances particularly enviable, or base it on fanciful assumptions about the felicity of others. Thus it remained for him to explain, in the face of obviously countervailing experience, how God's choice can be said to reflect wisdom and justice. And this is the theme of the lengthy work which Voltaire knew and criticized, *La Theodicée,* published in 1710.

Given the degree to which the doctrines of Pangloss coincide with those of Leibniz, it is difficult to see how the former can fail, in the context of *Candide,* to produce a literary criticism of Leibnizian philosophy. What more can be required than that central doctrines of a philosophical system be stated, and then reduced, by the literary context in which they are set, to absurdity?

The reasons for the failure of Voltaire's 'philosophical story' to accomplish its critical objective lie rather deeper than is usually imagined. It is to these that I now turn. In the first chapter of **Candide,** Pangloss is introduced as a teacher of 'metaphysico-theologo-cosmolonigologie.' Let us disregard the clever slur involved in the inclusion of 'ni-gaud' in 'cosmologie.' That the term 'cosmology' was given currency by Leibniz's disciple, Christian Wolff, and was unknown in Leibniz's time, is also not important for understanding the spirit of this remark. What the grouping of these three headings suggested to the educated person of the eighteenth century was that Leibniz had failed to separate theological and metaphysical reflections from the hard-nosed, mathematical/physical inquiries of the natural sciences, thus repeating the stupidities and scientific crudities of the scholastic metaphysics upon which the major philosophers of the seventeenth century never tired of heaping scorn. The suggestion of chapter I is that Pangloss (Leibniz) is a retrograde philosopher in a German backwater looking backwards towards the Middle Ages. To the eighteenth-century reader lacking a first-hand acquaintance with Leibniz's writings, this would seem to be confirmed in the ten or so doctrines of Leibniz to which Voltaire appeals in the course of **Candide,** and by the examples of Pangloss's reasoning which we encounter from time to time. But is it true that Leibniz confused metaphysics and science? For Voltaire, and for his intended readers, such a confusion would entail an importation of reasoning from the apparent purposiveness of nature (called by philosophers 'final causes') into the realm of natural science itself, where all legitimate reasoning must be about mechanisms (and hence about 'efficient causes') alone. But is Leibniz guilty of this confusion?

Certainly in Leibniz's technical writings he makes it clear that final causes have no place in science proper, in the sense that everything in nature can be explained by mechanical or efficient causes alone. But for Leibniz everything must have an explanation, and he therefore rehabilitates final causes at the level of metaphysics, which, among other things, must account for why we have the particular physical laws we do. Still the question remains how much of this is apparent in the *Theodicy,* which was all that was widely known of Leibniz in the eighteenth century.

It is perhaps surprising to discover that Leibniz sets out his doctrine of causality quite clearly in the *Theodicy* itself, even though it is a popular exposition of his views. Sections 345-50 go into some detail on the relationship of final to efficient causes and there is the elegant summary at section 247 which speaks:

> du système de l'harmonie générale que je con-çois, et qui comporte que le règne des causes effi-cientes et celui des causes finales sont parallèles entre eux; . . . que la matière est disposée en sorte que les lois du mouvement servent au meil-leur gouvernement des esprits. . . .

Here the separation of the two types of causality into different spheres or 'realms' is quite in evidence.

But as the initial characterization of Pangloss's doctrine suggested, Voltaire portrays a Leibniz who confuses the physical with the metaphysical. This is done by the simple device of presenting his metaphysical views in isolation, while implying that his cosmological views are therewith accounted for as well, and is therefore foreshadowed in the barbarism 'metaphysico-theologo-cosmolonigologie.' That this really is Voltaire's assessment of Leibniz's weakness is suggested further by his most down-to-earth and serious criticism of Leibniz in the 'Metaphysics' section of 'Les éléments de la philosophie de Newton.' Here he writes:

> J'en appelle à votre conscience: ne sentez-vous pas combien un tel système est purement d'imagination? L'aveu de l'humaine ignorance sur les éléments de la matière n'est-il pas au-dessus d'une science si vaine? Quel emploi de la logique et de la géometrie, lorsqu' on fait servir ce fil à s'égarer dans un tel labyrinthe, et qu'on marche méthodiquement vers l'erreur avec le flambeau même destiné à nous éclairer!

The intent of this passage is clear enough; its situation in the context of an exposition and defence of Newtonian science makes it unmistakable. Voltaire sets himself unambiguously in the line of philosophers, including Galileo, the early Descartes, Locke, and Newton and culminating in Kant, who see the only genuine locus of knowledge to be in actual human experience, and who think that metaphysics is simply a false light tempting the pilgrim from the straight and narrow path of empirical virtue. (Classical statements of this view are to be found in the 'Epistle to the Reader' of Locke's *Essay* and in the A- and B-prefaces of Kant's first *Critique.*)

From this the strategy of **Candide** is also illuminated. What better way to unmask this 'science si vaine' than to reveal a world in which ignorance is preferable to it and in which only a methodical pursuit of temporary advantages is possible?

What would Leibniz have thought of that fictive world? I believe he would have confessed it to be like our own world in *appearance,* but denied that it is very like it in *reality.* Indeed Pangloss and his pupils are the only ones to suggest that there is a reality behind the appearances of their world, and the suggestion, in the context of the story, is ridiculous. The world of **Candide** is our world as it is taken to be by the empirical philosopher of the enlightenment—a world of objects in mechanical interaction, observable, in principle at least, down to the tiniest parts, and where the unique order is one of an indifferent mechanical necessity. Leibniz, however, while agreeing more or less with the empiricists as far as they go, believes that the empiricist world-picture includes only the mechanical aspect of a world which must finally be understood in metaphysical terms, that the kingdom of efficient causes in which the scientist is at home is ultimately grounded in the kingdom of final causes, which is the province of metaphysics. Plato's analogy of the cave is useful here. Those cave-dwellers who become adept at predicting the sequences of shadows are analogous to the empirical scientists. There is a genuine science there, but not the ultimate one. For that, one must leave the cave and understand the purposive activity which leads the people to move the objects back and forth before the mouth of the cave, creating the sequence of shadows observed within.

For Leibniz, then, the world of *Candide* would be a world of appearances only, and therefore a world fundamentally unlike our own. Nor could the failure of his metaphysical views to find application in such a world be regarded as a decisive refutation of them, since they do not purport to describe all possible worlds, but only the unique world which is best.

Yet it is equally clear why *Candide* is so persuasive to the general reader. Nothing is more fundamental to the modern outlook than the mistrust of metaphysics and the belief in the exclusive reality of the material things investigated by physical science. It is therefore natural for a reader, on the authority of *Candide,* to assume that Leibniz, like a superannuated scholastic, would have him continue to explain the movements of his watch by appeal to the purpose of timekeeping or the presence in it of a horodictic virtue, ignoring the simple and satisfactory explanation offered by its mechanism.

Of course the reality is quite different. Leibniz was most conscious of the advances which had been gained by the mechanical philosophy and even contributed to them. Yet he did not subscribe to the polemical extremism popular with the Cartesians, according to whom the doctrine of final causes was worse than an idle daydream, being positively obstructive to science. According to Leibniz, appearances could be investigated only by the new quantifiable methods, but the reality which lay behind them, and to which, at its best, metaphysics had always restricted itself, could only be understood in metaphysical terms. Thus when Leibniz claims that this is the best possible world, he does not intend to imply that it is a world devoid of suffering. The claim has a dual force: the world is metaphysically best and morally perfect. Its metaphysical bestness results from its allowing a maximal variety of being with a minimal complexity of law. The moral perfection of the universe is expressed in the degree to which the individual who is responsible for his own actions is perfected by his virtues and destroyed by his vices. That the world is so structured is itself, in a secondary way, confirmed in experience. For the hypothesis that it is so can lead, Leibniz argues, to discoveries which could never be made by empirical methods alone. And since neither the rich variety of our world, nor the simplicity of its laws, nor the moral law which seems discoverable in it can be shown to be logically necessary, it follows that if there is to be an explanation of why these things obtain, rather than some very different and less desirable order, it must arise from the metaphysical consideration that they were better than any alternative, thereby eliciting the creative impulse of a rational deity.

In his attempt to accord metaphysics a role in thought which was complementary to that played by the natural sciences, Leibniz projected a path very different from the one that history in fact took. The divorce of man from nature is not the ineluctable consequence that textbooks of science make it appear to be, but is rather the result of a choice to see the world as a world of appearances, without

the purposive or teleological unity which is essential to the metaphysical outlook. The Leibnizian alternative, to regard metaphysics not as a competitor but as a complement to natural science, is the aspect of his thought to which I alluded at the beginning and which I said was undervalued today.

Finally, I would like to return to the theoretical question which is at the centre of the philosophy of literature, that of how works of literature can be critical of philosophical systems. What can be learned from the example of *Candide*? A correct account of *Candide* would be one which explained how a story so successful from a literary point of view should have been so ineffective in persuading those who have a first-hand acquaintance with Leibniz.

It has already been shown that the first answer historians are inclined to give—namely that Pangloss is an inaccurate portrait of Leibniz—is simply false. And yet their instinctive diffidence towards *Candide* is, I wish to argue, well founded. It is not that the Leibniz of *Candide*'s world is misrepresented; rather, that world, unlike our own, is unambiguously lacking in metaphysical dimension. The events which no doubt occur there according to natural causes translate into no purposeful story, suggest no reality beyond themselves. It is the obvious inappropriateness of the doctrines of Leibniz to the world of *Candide* which provides the satirical vehicle for the story. We cannot but suppose that Pangloss is passing off edifying reflections as genuine science—wasting our time—when we should be cultivating our garden. Every attempt of Candide to discover a purpose in existence comes to nothing. For example, at the house of Madame de Parolignac the 'learned and tasteful' gentleman responds to Candide's question as to whether this world is physically and morally the best:

> Moi, monsieur, . . . je ne pense rien de tout cela; je trouve que tout va de travers chez nous, que personne ne sait ni quel est son rang, ni quelle est sa charge, ni ce qu'il fait, ni ce qu'il doit faire. . . .

Similarly the great philosophical dervish at the conclusion of the tale, in response to Candide's indignation at the amount of evil in the world, replies:

> Quand sa Hautesse envoie un vaisseau en Egypte, s'embarasse-t-elle si les souris qui sont dans le vaisseau sont à leur aise ou non? Que faut-il faire, dit Pangloss? Te taire, dit le derviche.

Of course Voltaire relies on our supposing the world of *Candide,* apart from its burlesque exaggerations, to be really our own world, and consequently that our own world, like its fictive counterpart, cannot be understood in metaphysical terms. Further, *Candide* insinuates that the pursuit of metaphysics in some way militates against one's coming to a satisfactory understanding of the human condition as it really is (i.e. as existence without transcendent purposes). The points are complementary. If the world lacks a design, then any inquiry which imposes design upon it will be a pseudo-inquiry, a distortion of the truth, from the very outset. Yet in our world, we might wish to say, the attempt to discover purpose is not just the occupation of madmen; the world is not so obstinately phenomenal that the search for an underlying reality is absurd, like looking for your *doppelgänger* behind the mirror. Yet it is this kind of absurdity, this kind of obstinate phenomenalism, which does the critical work in *Candide.* These are the unspoken premises which, in effect, carry the argument.

For literary purposes it is no doubt right that they be unspoken, for they are unquestionably part of the modern outlook, part of the Galilean-Cartesian-Newtonian tradition which Voltaire did much to further in the eighteenth century. But when they are made explicit, they are seen to be more postulates than theorems in the world of *Candide.* No justification is provided for assuming them to be true of the actual world. We are given no reason to believe that the pointless suffering in *Candide* is a possible sequence of our own world. Of course there may be independent reasons for thinking that it is, but they can be invoked only at the expense of the integrity of the story. If *Candide* is to criticize successfully, it must compel our assent on its own merits and not stand in need of prejudices or convictions independent of it. However, it is precisely such convictions or prejudices which are required to make *Candide* work, leaving the entire issue a begged question. The rejection of the metaphysical viewpoint by the tradition in which Voltaire stands was polemical in nature and was justified only in so far as that metaphysics was a barrier to natural science. Nothing resembling proof that metaphysical reflection has *no* application to reality was ever offered prior to Kant, and none is implicit in *Candide.* What happened in the seventeenth century was a shift in the burden of proof from the advocates of natural science to those of metaphysics. *Candide* therefore begs an open question, even though the question is begged on the side that history has taken. Leibniz would deny that the world of *Candide* is a genuine counterpart to our own; if he had lived in the world of *Candide,* he would not have been a Panglossian. (pp. 64-72)

> Graeme Hunter, *"Leibniz in Other Worlds,"* in University of Toronto Quarterly, *Vol. 55, No. 1, November, 1985, pp. 64-73.*

Jean Sareil   (essay date 1987)

[*In the following essay, Sareil notes the comic devices in* Candide.]

Candide is a masterpiece of comic literature, yet it has never been seriously analyzed from the comic point of view. Because it is a satire of eighteenth-century society, aimed at demolishing ideas and beliefs that Voltaire considered false and dangerous, it has been mostly studied for its meaning and philosophical content.

Unfortunately, comic propaganda stresses only the negative aspect of the author's thought: it ridicules and destroys and never pretends to build up on the ruins; otherwise it would have to turn serious. The negative aspect of *Candide* is nowhere more evident than in the last sentence, which seems to convey a message, but so cryptic that no two scholars have agreed on its meaning. In fact, it has no hidden meaning, for the very simple reason that the author, having destroyed a system, was not ready to offer a straight answer to unsolvable problems. We should note

that his silence did not affect the quality of the work or the efficiency of its propaganda.

Laughter is based on an incongruous double vision. Therefore, if the text is ambiguous, it will create countless comic situations and, in return, the comic will add to the ambiguity. As a result, it is difficult to know whether the author is serious, whether he is not poking fun at ideas that he respects and defended in some other writings.

The dichotomy is everywhere. For example, is it a novel or a short story? It could be an apologue; unfortunately, the story is made not to confirm a philosophical concept but to refute it. Is the tale a vehicle to introduce and ridicule a metaphysical system, or is the system one of the many evils that plague humankind? Accidents are the weapons with which Voltaire ridicules the philosophy of optimism, but they are also part of the plot; it is through them that the story progresses and maintains its swift pace.

For lack of space I will limit the scope of this article to studying how the comic vision modifies all the major components of the novel: plot, characters, ideas, settings, relation with the reader, duration, as well as stylistic elements such as rhythm and tone. (For a more complete discussion of problems raised by the comic, see Sareil, *L'écriture comique.*)

Candide is packed with action, but as the story is never taken seriously, it has often been considered a parody of the adventure novel. I do not share that opinion. Here we have another example of ambiguity: a book that scrupulously respects all the conventions of the genre and, at the same time, destroys all the components of an adventure novel.

Suspense vanishes as soon as it is created because it cannot coexist with laughter. The minute readers perceive an incongruity, their attention is taken away from the story to focus on the ludicrous elements purposely introduced. As a result, we do not read a comic text the way we read a serious one. If we are moved, it means that we have entered the protaganists' world, we want to know what will happen to them; our interest is geared toward the future (even when we know how the book will end). When we laugh, we are only concerned with what is coming next, what comic inventions will result from those incredible events; in short, our concern is about the present—or a very near future, not going beyond the current chapter.

The past in *Candide* is inconsequential because the characters seem to forget their terrible misfortunes immediately. When they allude to them, it is always in an unconvincing way, or they sum them up with amusing lapses and contractions. Finally, through clever manipulations, never mentioned, the reader's interest is limited to the present moment, whatever the verb tenses are.

When we think that duration is an essential part of a psychological or realistic novel, we immediately realize that the notion of time is absent from comic fiction. A reading of Rabelais or Queneau would confirm this point. Such a difference is sufficient to show how dangerous it would be to ask a work like *Candide* to conform to the standards of a three-dimensional novel for which rules have been firmly established.

The elimination of suspense does not affect our interest in the plot; simply, the objectives are different. Instead of creating emotions, the plot becomes a source of laughter. Therefore exaggerations of all kinds and unbelievable accumulation of catastrophes are welcomed. Tragedy implies a controlled violence: one death, two deaths are dramatic; twenty-five accidents in a row cannot be taken seriously.

The chapters are loosely connected. Many episodes interrupt the story and would constitute a digression in a serious novel. The link between them is found not in the plot but in the philosophical system under scrutiny. If readers do not object to those interferences, it is because they do not care much about the story and because such episodes are extremely funny. The only ones that might look digressive are those when the tempo slows down, like the Parisian chapter added in 1761. Voltaire needed a flexible plot with countless adventures that allowed him to maintain a fast rhythm and gave him the freedom of developing each scene according to its comic potentialities.

Just as *Candide* is an adventure novel, it is a love story, the quest of Cunégonde by Candide. But the book is chaste and cold in spite of passionate speeches and scabrous situations. Laughter annihilates sentimentality and eroticism the way it eliminates suspense. One could wonder why Voltaire put so much emphasis on love if he never intended to exploit it in either the sentimental or libertine traditions. The answer is simple: passion and lust are universal motivations; they are accepted without opposition. Love is irrational and sudden (*coup de foudre*); it does not require preparations or justifications. It is possible to reduce it to a statement, always repeated and, of course, contradicted by what is taking place.

Besides, sex, having to face many social and religious taboos, is the sacrilegious topic par excellence. An erotic scene cannot be described in plain language without becoming vulgar and pornographic. The required disguise will turn into a game, either because the author introduced a vocabulary that has nothing to do with the subject (the lesson of *physique expérimentale* in ch. 1) or because he is so vague that he leaves the reader to imagine what is happening. The constant use of euphemism, periphrasis, metaphor, and double entendre forces the public to read the passage on two levels, one explicit and innocent, the other implicit; of course the text is written in a way that the duality is perceived at once, because there is no laughter without an immediate understanding.

Any successful book implies a complicity between author and public. To obtain this result, the writer of a serious novel creates an atmosphere that will emotionally involve the reader in the characters' lives. In a book like *Candide,* where tragic events are turned into comedy, the participation is different and requires a detachment from the action in order to follow the story on two different levels. Voltaire manages to avoid the dramatic climate by never presenting his protagonists at the right distance, the one in which we would share their fears and anxieties. Situations are always shown from too close or too far. The distantiation—which is always found in an ironical context—gives us the impression of participating in a game; it is amusing to note that this impression of playfulness comes from the writer's refusal to follow the rules and questioning of their relevance.

Ideas are not treated with more respect than the plot. *Candide* is supposed to be a philosophical tale, but there is not a single solid philosophical argument. Metaphysics here consists of a jargon that, before being seriously tested, is used euphemistically in the description of an erotic scene. After Pangloss's ridiculous demonstration, the same jargon is used again to explain the battle between Abares and Bulgarians to prove that wars are part of the best possible world. Not once has the theory been given a chance to be seriously evaluated.

Pangloss the optimist and Martin the pessimist never have an opportunity to debate. The scene would lead nowhere; what could they say to each other? Both are equally wrong, and hence their predictions are never fulfilled. If Martin is a much less developed character than Pangloss, it is only because he lacks the comic virtues of his opposite. A pessimist who is sure that everything will turn badly is not funny when proved wrong, whereas an optimist is, because contradiction hits him full blast.

The question of free will, which is so difficult to conciliate with optimistic determinism, is brought forward twice and twice rejected. The suspension points indicate how futile and boring the discussion would be.

The theory of optimism is contradicted not by words but by upcoming catastrophes. The predictability of the events and our ignorance as to what they will be creates another force of duality: surprise versus expectation, which is an essential source of comic effects.

At this point, we realize that philosophy, far from burdening the plot with jargon and theories, becomes part of it by justifying the incredible accumulation of misfortunes that are the motor of the action.

A point constantly stressed in the novel is the relationship between effects and causes, with their disproportionate results. But, by an amusing paradox, the causal conjunctions (*c'est-à-dire, car,* etc.) introduce sentences that are never the normal development of what has just been said.

The characters are also ambiguous. At times, they look like three-dimensional heroes, and the minute after, they are puppets in the hand of the author. Their role is to testify to and show the universality of evil in the best possible world. Consequently they have all the qualities required from a good witness: they do not lie (although there are often comic deliberate inconsistencies in their stories), they are keen observers, their memories are flawless, and they are so objective that they behave as if their misfortunes had occurred to someone else. This resignation implies that their fate is part of the human fate; their submissiveness leads to a general condemnation of optimism. And of course, it prevents the reader from being emotionally involved in creatures who are so unconcerned with their own misery.

This detachment can become a source of comedy. For example, Candide listens without saying a word to Cunégonde's ordeal. When she mentions the scar on her left flank, his only reaction is to ask if he will see it, thus discreetly revealing the only subject that occupies his mind. Cunégonde understands, promises, and resumes her story exactly where she left it—that is, while she was being raped.

In the same vein, when later in the novel Cunégonde says that nobody suffered as much as she did, the old woman challenges her with her story. This strange rivalry sets the tone of her testimony; every calamity she reports is nothing compared to those that will happen to her later on.

If the characters are puppets, someone is pulling their strings, and that someone has to be the author. It has often been debated whether Voltaire was present in his *contes philosophiques*. The answer is yes and no. No, if we think that Voltaire uses his hero as a mouthpiece or that incidents of his life are transposed in the story: when there is an allusion, it is often well hidden and written for his own satisfaction. But Voltaire's voice (not necessarily Voltaire's opinions) can be heard in the short comments that accompany the action and cannot be disassociated from it. A rational justification—or a comparison—is always offered to give some sense to all that is irrational or unbelievable in the novel. The explanation generally looks acceptable and, in fact, means nothing. As a result, the book gives the impression of always being under the control of a rational, intelligent, sarcastic author.

All the destructive effects of laughter on the plot and characters, the different attitudes it requires from the reader, give the writer complete freedom to follow the inspiration of the moment, to develop a scene as long as it is rich in comic inventions, and to drop it as soon as the jokes are not coming with the same abundance.

Stylistic devices are also completely modified by the comic approach. Their role is not more important but only more conspicuous. In a serious work, in a tragedy, the style is always appropriate to the situation; it suggests an atmosphere in which everything becomes believable, where the reader shares the hopes and the anxieties of the characters. In a comic novel, in a comedy, however, the writing never corresponds to the situation. Things are always expressed the wrong way or at the wrong moment. This complex subject has attracted little attention. For lack of space, I will limit myself to studying briefly rhythm and tone, which are the most remarkable features of Voltaire's comic style.

His *contes philosophiques* are known for their swift pace, and none maintains its rhythm better than **Candide.** One reason for this rapidity is the linearity of the plot; all the complexities are eliminated. Each topic is treated separately. The relationship between causes and effects is direct, immediate, and of course out of proportion. You just have to read the first chapter, a model of exposition, to realize how the characters and events are presented in succession, without interferences of any kind.

Gravity requires slowness; swiftness implies a cheerful mood. To present a succession of catastrophes on a frantic tempo is a contradiction between the subject and its expression; its resolution has to be comical. Whenever the movement slows down—in Eldorado, in Paris, and in the last chapter—we do not laugh with the same abandon.

Not only has the story proceeded at a brisk pace, but it also gives an illusion of speed by the use of various literary devices. First of all, the plot does not unfold in a uniform tempo. A continuous rapidity would give an impression of monotony, not of movement. In each episode we can find many accelerations and retards, and I would say that retards are more effective than accelerations in creating a sense of quickness; they are also a greater source of comic effects.

Anything that disrupts the continuity of the narrative contributes to the impression of speed. It can be a detail so minute that it escapes even an attentive reading, like the constant shift of verb tenses in chapter 5.

Another technique to upset the rhythm is the frequent change of objective: in chapter 9, Candide has killed the Jew and wonders with Cunégonde and the old woman what to do. Then the door opens and the Inquisitor enters the room; suddenly the scene is seen through his eyes. Candide is the first to react, and Voltaire tells us what is going through his mind. He kills the Inquisitor. We have then a dialogue with Cunégonde before the story resumes. The whole episode takes no more than half a page.

Digressions are another excellent way of interrupting the flow of the narrative. Readers accept those manipulations because they enjoy the story. When you are amused, time flies. Consequently, comic devices foster a subjective feeling that the pace was fast.

Rabelais and Molière use a single device until they have fully exploited all its potential; this supposes a slow tempo. Voltaire proceeds through an accumulation of varied techniques that generally pass unnoticed. He discards some, introduces new ones, shuffles them so that they can be used again without attracting our attention. There is never a device that can be singled out and would force the reader to pause. **Candide** does not have one-liners, despite Voltaire's facility for making them (see his correspondence). Although the rhythm is constantly changing, the general movement of a chapter is never interrupted. Just like the comments, the jokes are incorporated in the narrative.

The tone, which so vividly complements the rhythm, is always discordant and in *total* opposition to the story. It agrees with the narration only when the timing is off and the circumstances impossible. Something always has to defuse the drama. What the protagonists say could be taken from one of Voltaire's tragedies, but in the context, the emotional speech sounds ludicrous.

The whole book is written under the sign of exaggeration. We are in the universe of the superlative, the best of all possible worlds. So the characters will shed streams of tears and fall to the feet of their tormentors. When Candide and Cunégonde are reunited, she faints, he faints. But this absurd double swooning is simply mentioned; it does not affect the story. Cunégonde tells her misfortunes and Candide listens carefully.

I mentioned the linearity of **Candide.** All that is lacking is compensated by the richness of the comic invention and the complexities of the writing. The work looks deceptively thin if one tries to judge it by the standards of the great philosophical and realist novels, but **Candide** is a comic masterpiece, and it is as such that it should be read and studied to be fully appreciated. (pp. 134-40)

> *Jean Sareil, "The Comic Writing in 'Candide'," in* Approaches to Teaching Voltaire's "Candide," *edited by Renée Waldinger, Modern Language Association of America, 1987, pp. 134-40.*

English Showalter, Jr. (essay date 1989)

[*In the following essay, Showalter explores the theme of language in Voltaire's tales.*]

> On ne plaisantait pas sur les chiffres dans l'entourage d'Emilie. Si **Micromégas** a été composé à Cirey, il n'est pas étonnant que Voltaire ait mis son point d'honneur à réaliser une fantaisie qui fût mathématiquement irréprochable.
> [Jacques Van den Heuvel, in his *Voltaire dans ses contes: de "Micromégas" à "L'Ingénu"*]

> It is a curious fact that there is not one single proportion in the whole story accurately given.
> [Ira O. Wade, in his *Voltaire's "Micromégas": A Study in the Fusion of Science, Myth, and Art.*]

Micromégas is a comic fantasy based on the idea of proportion and disproportion, as the title suggests by the juxtaposition of the Greek terms for small and large. Proportion is among other things a mathematical concept, and Voltaire begins by treating it as such, to the perplexity of many a reader. In the third sentence one reads: "Quelques algébristes, gens toujours utiles au public, prendront sur le champ la plume, et trouveront que, puisque monsieur Micromégas, habitant du pays de Sirius, a de la tête aux pieds vingt-quatre mille pas, qui font cent vingt mille pieds de roi, et que nous autres, citoyens de la terre, nous n'avons guère que cinq pieds, et que notre globe a neuf mille lieues de tour, ils trouveront, dis-je, qu'il faut absolument que le globe qui l'a produit ait au juste vingt-un millions six cent mille fois plus de circonférence que notre petite terre." And Voltaire does not spare similar figures and calculations throughout the tale.

Many critics have wondered about the function of such passages. One of the most learned and perceptive Voltaire scholars, the late Jean Sareil, observes that "le calcul est comique par sa précision et son manque d'intérêt." and he asks, "Quel est le lecteur qui a jamais vérifié l'exactitude des chiffres ainsi prodigués?" It is surely true that few readers have ever bothered to verify those figures, but with a simple electronic calculator anyone can easily confirm that they are not only precise and boring, but also inaccurate. Ira Wade, who had the impertinent curiosity to check, declared them all inaccurate, and I will rely on his authority to shirk the task of repeating all the computations here.

Wade showed that the source of the opening calculations,

quoted above, is a Latin passage by the German Leibnitzian Johann Christian Wolff, arguing that the inhabitants of Jupiter must be the same size as the Old Testament giant Og. The argument rests on a series of ratios, which can be summed up as follows: ratio of distances from the sun of different planets; ratio of distance to intensity of sunlight; ratio of light intensity to size of the eye; ratio of eye size to the size of the whole body. This is the same passage that Emilie Du Châtelet read in December 1738, sight translating into French, to an awed Françoise de Graffigny, who commented: "nous nous en sommes fort divertie en admirant la folie d'un homme qui employe tant de tems et de travail pour aprendre une chose si inutile." Graffigny thus confirms Sareil's explanation of the humor of these figures.

Although the figures are in one sense pointless, they bear an obvious relationship to one of the central themes of **Micromégas,** that of proportion. Mathematics, moreover, as Van den Heuvel correctly observes, was a subject that Voltaire and Emilie took very seriously. At the same time, they realized that there were Johann Christian Wolffs as well as Newtons and that mathematics was only a language, a possible vehicle for lies and misrepresentations, and therefore also for comedy. The precise, pointless, and wrong calculations constitute the first of several examples of specialized language in **Micromégas.** Voltaire uses mathematics like the macaronic Latin of Molière's doctors. The reader hears a familiar voice, that of the would-be expert or the self-styled authority, whose incomprehensible discourse implies, not a meaning so complex that it exceeds ordinary language, but rather an absence of meaning masked by jargon.

. . . . .

> Rien n'est si commun que de lire et de converser inutilement. Il faut répéter ici ce que Locke a recommandé: *Définissez les termes.*
> [Voltaire, "Abus des mots," in his *Dictionnaire philosophique*]

> Il n'est aucune langue complète, aucune qui puisse exprimer toutes nos idées et toutes nos sensations; leurs nuances sont trop imperceptibles et trop nombreuses.
> [Voltaire, "Langues," in his *Dictionnaire philosophique*]

Mathematics is not the only language of comparison. When Micromégas first arrives on Saturn, the Secretary of the Academy of Sciences speaks in similes: "La nature est comme un parterre dont les fleurs . . . . Elle est comme une assemblée de blondes et de brunes, dont les parures . . . Elle est donc comme une galerie de peintures dont les traits . . . ." The ellipses are in fact in the text, because Micromégas interrupts the Secretary in order to demand scientific precision: "commencez d'abord par me dire combien les hommes de votre globe ont de sens." Traditionally, the Secretary has been regarded as a caricature of Fontenelle, and Micromégas as Voltaire's spokesman in his criticism of the flowery style. This identification may require some qualification, but it is at least clear that the Saturnian speaks a second type of jargon.

When the two giants reach earth, languages proliferate.

Like many Voltairean heroes, Micromégas and the Secretary have linguistic gifts and they quickly master French. When they address the humans, however, French immediately disintegrates into three discourses: "L'aumônier du vaisseau récita les prières des exorcismes, les matelots jurèrent, et les philosophes du vaisseau firent un système." The giants are briefly dazzled by the humans' ability to measure them and conclude too hastily that creatures with so high a ratio of spirit to matter must be happy. Disabused on that score, but still impressed by the earthlings' knowledge, the two travelers ask about the soul, provoking a still further collapse in communication: "Le plus vieux citait Aristote, l'autre prononçait le nom de Descartes; celui-ci, de Malebranche; cet autre, de Leibnitz; cet autre, de Locke." One even quotes Aristotle in the original Greek—a joke similar to the algebra that nobody understands and therefore skips over, and some editions of the tale omit the Greek entirely. The Sirian, however, confesses his ignorance and asks why the scholar cites a language no one understands, to which he replies that "il faut bien citer ce qu'on ne comprend point du tout dans la langue qu'on entend le moins."

The still timely witticism might appear to be Voltaire's definitive comment, rejecting jargon in favor of the plain French of Micromégas and the narrator. But the presence of so many flawed and unintelligible languages ought to make us look closely at the narrator's own discourse. In many respects this is the authoritative master language that can contain all the others and expose their failures. It speaks to the reader on a plane of superiority to ordinary humans, and even to the two space travelers; yet the speaker seems to be one of us, and often uses the first person plural, as in the first sentence: "Dans une de ces planètes qui tournent autour de l'étoile nommée Sirius, il y avait un jeune homme de beaucoup d'esprit, que j'ai eu l'honneur de connaître dans le dernier voyage qu'il fît sur notre petite fourmilière." Many readers simply take the narrator's voice to be Voltaire's and readily identify "our little anthill" with the earth. As Jean Sareil has argued, however, the narrator's language grows increasingly strange; already in the first sentence the perspective from which earth resembles an anthill is not a human one. It is "ours" only if we are a group including both humans and superhumans.

In like manner, Sirian insects with hundred-foot diameters are called "petits" and are invisible to "microscopes ordinaires," the age of four hundred fifty years is termed "au sortir de l'enfance," and Saturnians nine hundred times the size of earthlings are referred to as "nains." The narrator's posture of moral and intellectual superiority to the entire universe of *Micromégas* is matched by a more or less proportional physical superiority, which adds to the tale's comic effect because the proportion is based on a false analogy of material to spiritual qualities. Moreover, the tale itself repeatedly disproves the analogy, when Micromégas acknowledges that Saturnians are not ridiculous for being only six thousand feet tall, when the two travelers realize that the mites or atoms they find on earth can think, and when they learn that a high level of mind relative to body does not correspond to a high level of self-knowledge and happiness. Despite its reassuring familiari-

ty, the narrator's voice is not one of ours, but a curious hybrid, the sport of a human and fallible imagination.

Furthermore, this voice indulges in the same lapses as the algebrists and the Saturnian. Most of the erroneous calculations in the tale are presented as the narrator's. The descriptions of Earth as an anthill, molehill, or little pile of mud and of its inhabitants as mites or atoms, are comparisons, as are many other images, such as: Micromégas went from globe to globe "comme un oiseau voltige de branche en branche"; the two giants pass by Mars "comme deux voyageurs qui dédaignent un mauvais cabaret de village"; the Saturnian chasing Micromégas resembles "un très petit chien de manchon qui suivrait un capitaine des gardes du roi de Prusse," etc. It would appear, then, that there is no stable language in *Micromégas.* Micromégas, the Saturnian, several of the mathematicians and philosophers, and the narrator are all capable of reason. They observe, and they learn. But they also make mistakes and none of them possesses the perfectly clear language that could reveal truth and record nature.

One might argue on that basis that *Micromégas* was inspired by an integral skepticism on Voltaire's part. Even to Micromégas, nature will always remain surprising and mysterious. Knowledge must always be tentative and partial. Even what is known cannot be reliably expressed because language is flawed. The founding relation of human knowledge, a proper proportion of language to the real phenomena it represents, proves to be elusive and perhaps even non-existent, just another faulty analogy. The final scene, moreover, has been interpreted in this way. Van den Heuvel argues that "le prétendu Livre de la Vérité, qui est remis solennellement aux hommes par Micromégas en guise de présent d'adieu, doit rester blanc à jamais, pour lui comme pour eux." [In her *Reading Voltaire's 'Contes': A Semiotics of Philosophical Narration*] Carol Sherman aptly recalls Locke's *tabula rasa,* suggesting that "book and mind are blank; on them experience will write, constructing its truths. The book of the world shall be read in nature and no longer in books."

Is it certain, however, that the book is blank? According to the text, Micromégas "leur promit de leur faire un beau livre de philosophie, écrit fort menu pour leur usage, et que, dans ce livre, ils verraient le bout des choses. Effectivement, il leur donna ce volume avant son départ: on le porta à Paris à l'Académie des sciences; mais, quand le secrétaire l'eut ouvert, il ne vit rien qu'un livre tout blanc: 'Ah! dit-il, je m'en étais bien douté.'" This is the second time in the tale that we have encountered a Secretary of the Academy of Sciences, and the man who actually held the position in 1737, when the expedition returned from the Arctic, was none other than Fontenelle, whose style was parodied in the Saturnian's speech. This is also the second time we have encountered this line of reasoning; the first was in chapter 4, which relates the two giants' first experiences on Earth: "Le nain, qui jugeait quelquefois un peu trop vite, décida d'abord qu'il n'y avait personne sur la terre. Sa première raison était qu'il n'avait vu personne. Micromégas lui fit sentir poliment que c'était raisonner assez mal. . . . " Experience soon proves that the earth is inhabited, but the Saturnian continues to leap to false conclusions, first that all the inhabitants are whales, then that the people on the ship are in the act of propagating, and finally, "il n'entendait point parler nos atomes, et il supposait qu'ils ne parlaient pas."

In short, the evidence for the Book of Truth actually being blank is very slight, and undermined in advance. The Secretary of the Paris Academy, a mere human and subject to human mistakes, reasons exactly as the Saturnian Secretary did when he drew a reproach from Micromégas. And the facts prove Micromégas right, the Saturnian wrong. At the end, however, the giants have departed; there is no one to verify or dispute the French Secretary's conclusion.

Approaching the question from another direction, it is hard to explain why Micromégas would have promised to give the philosophers such a book if he had nothing to say. Or, if he found that he could not keep his promise, it is equally hard to explain why he would resort to such a trick. And while one might very well doubt that Micromégas really knew "le bout des choses," it is odd to claim that he could not see what he had written himself, as Van den Heuvel seems to suggest. It is altogether more plausible to assume that Micromégas, whose knowledge and understanding, even though imperfect, were vastly greater than any human's, wrote something that the Secretary could not understand. Indeed, he could not recognize it as writing, just as Micromégas and the Saturnian could not originally recognize any living creatures on the earth.

To read the ending of *Micromégas* this way requires a fundamental change in the way one interprets the entire tale. As Sherman says, comparing *Micromégas* to *Zadig,* in which the Book of Destinies has indecipherable but visible characters: "The presence of a *blank* book would constitute a *referential* statement according to which there is no answer. This one, on the contrary, is simply unreadable and shows the hero's ignorance." Just so; and the question is then whether *Micromégas* suggests the absolute absence of answers, or merely the relative ignorance of those who seek them. Radical doubt was not in fact characteristic of Voltaire either in the 1730s, when *Micromégas* was probably first conceived, or in the early 1750s when it was published. Moreover, the mood of the tale seems ill suited to so bleak a conception; most readers sense that the narrator and the characters who use their reason well are making progress toward real knowledge and wisdom. As Van den Heuvel puts it, "Une certitude réconfortante se fait jour à travers tout le récit: c'est que l'univers est homogène. Il y a entre eux on ne sait quel mystérieux dénominateur commun; en d'autres termes, l'analogie est universelle." In individual cases, the proportions may be comically wrong and the comparisons grotesque; but efforts to understand are not foredoomed.

. . . . .

> On confond souvent le mot de *raison* avec celui
> de *proportion.*
>> [Voltaire, "Raison," in his *L'encyclopédie*]

Universal analogy is in fact at the root of all knowledge, in Voltaire's view. Mathematics demonstrated the validity of proportions for the material world, and at the same time showed the possibility of a pure language of reason where words were adequate to meanings. The equations by which the problems of metaphysics might be resolved were not yet known, but Voltaire had faith that they existed and might be discovered. Proportion would eventually explain apparent differences in the lot of human beings. In Voltaire's preliminary formulation, the burdens and pleasures of every station were balanced to achieve a constant ratio. The meaning of life would presumably turn out to be some sort of constant ratio on a universal scale.

Likewise, a particular speech may be inappropriate to its meaning; but Voltaire did not believe that language itself was fatally flawed. Rather, he held the view, promulgated by the grammarians of Port-Royal, that linguistic structures were based on reason, and that reason itself was a universal, the same everywhere, even if not always recognized or applied. Language was capable of expressing reality because the natural universe operated according to providential reason. If it was difficult to explain in human terms why there was such variety within the assumed order, one could simply postpone answering, maybe forever. Nonetheless, Voltaire believed that the answer existed. Furthermore, he believed that parts of the answer had been found, not through divine revelations like the angel's apparition to Zadig, but in the work of Newton and other scientists.

A similar principle was invoked to explain differences in style. As Voltaire put it, "Le grand art est dans l'à-propos." Nonetheless, just as his rhetoric on the equality of conditions never led him to change places with a beggar, he remained convinced of a hierarchy of genres. Language had its origin in a practical function—Voltaire thought that merchants had invented it to facilitate trade—and its highest manifestations continued to be those where it communicated its meaning most efficiently. Ultimately he reduced all styles to two, "le simple et le relevé." But any deviation from the simple was suspect; speaking of "esprit" he commented that "dans les grands ouvrages on doit l'employer avec sobriété, par cela même qu'il est un ornement." In all genres and in all languages the same qualities are necessary: "régularité, clarté, élégance."

Although Voltaire is often regarded as an advocate of linguistic reform, another logical consequence of his position is a stern conservatism. His reforms aimed only at reducing arbitrary and illogical practices. Otherwise, he worked to stabilize and preserve classical French, justifying the enterprise as follows: "Il me semble que, lorsqu'on a eu dans un siècle un nombre suffisant de bons écrivains, devenus classiques, il n'est plus guère permis d'employer d'autres expressions que les leurs, et qu'il faut leur donner le même sens, ou bien dans peu de temps le siècle présent n'entendrait plus le siècle passé."

In *Micromégas,* even though no character including the narrator realizes Voltaire's ideal of language use, a clear sense of right language permeates the text. The cacophonous chorus of voices demonstrates the need for a fixed and well-defined language, like the mathematics of Newton or the philosophy of Locke. To those who knew this language, the Book of Truths would no longer appear blank, even if it could not yet be fully deciphered. This implicit language constitutes the master discourse that is so powerfully felt in the tale. *Micromégas* is thus a tale where Voltaire comes close to espousing radical skepticism and cultural relativism, but in fact only plays at it.

In many other tales Voltaire draws on the theme of language for comic effects, although it is less central than in *Micromégas.* Some of the devices occur repeatedly. Many of the tales are presented as translations, for example. On one level, this merely imitates a common fictional practice of the eighteenth century; on another it enables Voltaire to talk about France from under a transparent mask. At the same time, it implies the universality of the discourse of reason that always lurks behind the narration.

Within the tales, the heroes are often polyglots, like Micromégas. Zadig is "instruit dans plusieurs langues," even though he cannot read the Book of Destinies. At the supper of Balzora he translates the diverse religious myths into a single principle that all adore; at the dénouement he solves the enigmas. The resourceful Cacambo and the admirable Ingénu also speak several languages. Téone impresses Babouc in part because "elle savait parler à chacun son langage." By contrast, one sign of Jeannot's folly is his family's trust in an author who affirms that "on parle beaucoup mieux sa langue quand on ne partage pas son application entre elle et les langues étrangères." Voltaire approves of polyglotism, not for the appreciation of exotic beauties, nor for the enjoyment of diversity, but as a way to erase difference. As at the supper of Balzora, there is a universal reason all can understand, if the superficial barriers to communication can be removed.

The moral of *Le Monde comme il va,* as expressed by Ituriel, is that "si tout n'est pas bien, tout est passable," and this attitude prevails in Voltaire's earlier tales. The "bien" constitutes a standard against which everything is measured, and the tales mock or attack those who fall short. Language differs little from other kinds of human behavior. There is a "style oriental" and a "style de la raison," which is Zadig's style. Zadig, however, is not admired for being reasonable, but rather for being vizir. Reason serves as a measure of human folly but folly seems tolerable, funny, or even lovable. Zadig's fortunes rise and fall, deviating from what reason would predict and justice would provide, but he pursues his course toward the predictable happy ending with steady cheerfulness, matched by the narrator's confidence that everything will come right in the end. Foolish utterances fill the pages, but Voltaire felt sure that truth could be filtered out of the imperfect expressions and that right usage would ultimately prevail.

. . . . .

> En parlant ainsi, il ne laissa pas de manger.
> [Voltaire, in his *Candide*]

> Que faut-il donc faire? dit Pangloss.—Te taire,
>   dit le derviche.
>
> [*Candide*]

Events in the 1750s shook Voltaire's naive optimism, as is well known. His frustration at Versailles and exile from France, his painful experience with the "philosopher king" Frederick the Great, the outbreak of the Seven Years' War, and the apparent failure of the *Encyclopédie,* all these contributed to a period of depression; but these were human crimes and errors. The Lisbon earthquake of November 1755 is generally regarded as the incident that shattered Voltaire's belief in a providential universe; here was a natural disaster on a scale that defied rationalization. Too many innocent victims had suffered and died to permit the claim that a greater good resulted. From this period issued the darkest and greatest of Voltaire's tales, *Candide.*

It is hardly an exaggeration to call *Candide* an extended comedy of euphemism. From beginning to end, appalling events occur, which the characters discuss in ludicrously inappropriate language. Pangloss is, to be sure, the worst offender. In the last paragraph, he still summarizes the story as an illustration of Optimism: "Tous les événements sont enchaînés dans le meilleur des mondes possibles: car enfin si vous n'aviez pas été chassé d'un beau château à grands coups de pied dans le derrière pour l'amour de mademoiselle Cunégonde, si vous n'aviez pas été mis à l'Inquisition, si vous n'aviez pas couru l'Amérique à pied, si vous n'aviez pas donné un bon coup d'épée au baron, si vous n'aviez pas perdu tous vos moutons du bon pays d'Eldorado, vous ne mangeriez pas ici des cédrats confits et des pistaches." Until the very end, of course, Candide himself repeats Pangloss's maxims and tries to persuade himself of their truth.

Cunégonde, although she does not share Pangloss's mania for generalizing and systematizing, tells her own lamentable story with equal lack of feeling and reaches an equally unpalatable moral. At their reunion in Lisbon, she tells Candide: ". . . j'avais la tête remplie du massacre de mon père, de ma mère, de mon frère, de l'insolence de mon vilain soldat bulgare, du coup de couteau qu'il me donna, de ma servitude, de mon métier de cuisinière, de mon capitaine bulgare, de mon vilain don Issachar, de mon abominable inquisiteur, de la pendaison du docteur Pangloss, de ce grand *miserere* en faux-bourdon pendant lequel on vous fessait, et surtout du baiser que je vous avais donné derrière un paravent, le jour que je vous avais vu pour la dernière fois. Je louai Dieu, qui vous ramenait à moi par tant d'épreuves."

There are, to be sure, voices on the other side, notably Martin and the old woman. The old woman tells her story only to prove that she is unhappier than Cunégonde; in conclusion she remarks, "je voulus cent fois me tuer, mais j'aimais encore la vie. Cette faiblesse ridicule est peut-être un de nos penchants les plus funestes . . . ." Martin becomes Candide's companion by winning a contest as the most unfortunate man in Surinam; like Pangloss, he was trained as a philosopher. He argues that the purpose of the world's creation was "pour nous faire enrager" and he has seen evil just as consistently as Pangloss saw good, so that he says "j'ai tant vu de choses extraordinaires qu'il n'y a plus rien d'extraordinaire." Just as Pangloss, Cunégonde, and Candide express a comically excessive version of the same optimism that prevails in *Zadig* and *Micromégas,* Martin and the old woman express a comically excessive negative version. *Candide* has no character like Micromégas or Zadig who speaks for a reasonable middle position.

Candide ends with a gesture of silencing. To Pangloss's summing up, Candide responds with the famous line, "Cela est bien dit, mais il faut cultiver notre jardin." He seems to echo Martin's "Travaillons sans raisonner," the Turk's profession of deliberate ignorance, and the dervish's injunction, "Te taire" a few lines earlier. Injustice and violence, always mitigated in the earlier tales by the brevity of their triumphs and the resilience of the victims, are brutally escalated and far more serious in *Candide*. The resilience of the victims has not diminished, but they only survive, they do not prevail. One might conclude that language has likewise proved a failure. If the little society tolerates Pangloss's prattle, they nonetheless ignore him. No one emerges to speak for the group at the end; everyone except Pangloss settles willingly for silence. Their language has failed utterly to give a satisfactory account of the world.

The ending of *Candide,* however, resembles that of *Micromégas.* The characters succumb to doubt and ignorance, but the narrator's voice is not necessarily implicated. One might be tempted to suppose that by naming Doctor Ralph, the ostensible author of *Candide,* and giving the date of his death, Voltaire makes him a less reliable narrator than the anonymous and disembodied narrator of *Micromégas.* Doctor Ralph has died at Minden, the site of a notorious battle; he thus shares the vulnerability of the characters and perhaps their fallibility. Despite his being given a sketchy biography, he nonetheless reveals much less about himself than does the narrator of *Micromégas,* who claims to have known the space travelers. One might infer from the opening lines of *Candide* that Doctor Ralph had known the baron of Thunder-ten-tronckh and been a guest at the château; but it is a tenuous inference. Virtually every line Doctor Ralph writes that seems to express a judgment can be explained as indirect free style, the ironic quotation of one of the characters. "Tout fut consterné dans le plus beau et le plus agréable des châteaux possibles" is fundamentally ambiguous, but to my ear seems more likely an ironic quotation of Pangloss than an opinion held by Doctor Ralph, for in several cases the distance is clearly marked: "un des plus puissants seigneurs de la Vestphalie, car son château avait une porte et des fenêtres. . . . Le vicaire du village était son grand aumônier"; "Madame la baronne, qui pesait environ trois cent cinquante livres, s'attirait par là une très grande considération . . . le petit bois qu'on appelait parc." Doctor Ralph clearly knows the right name and the wrong name for things.

Large parts of *Candide* are told in direct or indirect quotation. Most of the humor derives from the transparent unreliability of the characters as narrators, especially in evaluating events. Doctor Ralph himself, however, seems to maintain the posture of an uninvolved scholarly historian; at most he allows himself an occasional sarcasm. Thus at the end when he writes: "Toute la petite société entra dans ce louable dessein; chacun se mit à exercer ses talents. La petite terre rapporta beaucoup. Cunégonde était, à la vérité, bien laide; mais elle devint une excellente pâtissière; Paquette broda; la vieille eut soin du linge. Il n'y eut pas jusqu' à frère Giroflée qui ne rendît service; il fut un très bon menuisier, et même devint honnête homme," the

judgments should probably be taken at face value. That the plan is praiseworthy need not mean that cultivating the garden is Voltaire's final wisdom; but there is, from beginning to end in *Candide* as in *Micromégas,* a stable, reliable, authoritative narrative voice, that calls on a conception of reason shared with readers as a standard against which to measure the words and deeds of the characters.

In short, even in the despair represented by *Candide,* Voltaire did not abandon the vision of universal reason he had held all along. His despair resulted from a loss of hope that it could be realized in practical terms; Doctor Ralph died in midst of horrors, not on the dawn of a newly enlightened civilization. But Voltaire did not pursue the logic of the earthquake to the conclusion that the natural world possessed no order and no reason. Martin articulates such a view, but the narrator's stance implicitly contradicts it. In earlier works, Voltaire had found the human tendency to stray from reason's path mainly amusing; in *Candide* he condemns it more strongly, but he does not doubt that reason's path exists. In *Zadig, Micromégas, Le Monde comme il va,* and other tales, the story leads to a form of silencing, but this silence is the complacent acceptance of an existence that is passable. Anguished doubt and vehement protest are discouraged because they disrupt a pleasant existence. Patience will carry us through unhappy spells, reason will eventually lead us to full understanding. In *Candide,* futility and defeat silence most of the characters, but from beyond the grave Doctor Ralph's voice and vision of reason persist at the core of the pointless argumentation and vain quests. They may not be able to find or define truth and happiness, but Doctor Ralph and his readers know what they are anyway.

. . . . .

> On disputa un peu sur la multiplicité des langues, et on convint que, sans l'aventure de la tour de Babel, toute la terre aurait parlé français.
> [Voltaire, in his *L'Ingénu*]

> Dites-moi s'il y a des sectes en géométrie?— Non, mon cher enfant, lui dit en soupirant le bon Gordon; tous les hommes sont d'accord sur la vérité quand elle est démontrée.
>
> [*L'Ingénu*]

Focusing attention on languages in Voltaire's tales highlights a paradox of his art. He was a man of deep contradictions. In practice he was an exceptional polyglot, competent in several classical and modern languages; within French he wrote well in more genres than any other author ever has, except perhaps Victor Hugo: fiction, theater, poetry, history, criticism, science, essays, familiar letters. Yet he held to the conviction that in an ideal world the multiplicity of languages would be reduced to the single language of reason. His poetry has not stood the test of posterity in large part because he used it like prose, seeking clarity above all else. The use of figures and the exploitation of ambiguity that seem to us essential elements of poetry seemed to him flaws of expression; poetic devices like rhyme and versification, which serve to give precedence to language over message, seemed to Voltaire arbitrary obstacles to communication.

A similar tension existed in his attitude toward the past.

As a Modern, he had to believe in progress. Classical Antiquity was not an ideal from which civilization was doomed to a perpetual decline or inadequate repetition; the great writers of the Century of Louis XIV had surpassed the Ancients. Yet he allowed the seventeenth century to become his own Antiquity and admitted change only where it seemed to him that his models had failed to live up to their own ideal standards. As a philosophe, he presumably had faith in the perfectibility of humanity and human institutions; but he brought with him a preconceived idea of that perfection.

He admired the great scientists of his era and did much to popularize the discoveries of Newton in France and throughout Europe. He preached and practiced the experimental method and the need for observation. Repeatedly he denounced faith in revealed truth and mocked those whose judgment was tainted by bias. Nonetheless he could not profess integral skepticism, and so his own observation remained clouded by his belief in a providential universe. Even in the writing of **Candide,** when he had an intuition of chaos and horror, he could not give up his underlying faith in order and reason.

These inner tensions help account for the irony in Voltaire's reputation today, which rests on the tales that he himself disdained and did not claim as his own. The tales do not belong within Voltaire's discourse of reason. All the rules of good grammar are predicated on language as an instrument of truth; a fiction is by definition an abuse of language. When the Saturnian tries to justify his comparisons to Micromégas, the latter retorts, "Je ne veux point qu'on me plaise, je veux qu'on m'instruise." A tale can please, amuse, and even persuade; but it does not instruct. Voltaire might consent to write tales as a diversion or for political purposes, but he did not count them among his real works.

He could not really escape from his own ideal of language; the tales themselves are dominated by the master discourse of reason. Within the tale, however, Voltaire was free to imitate and parody the multiplicity of languages he heard around him. For one who harbored misgivings about linguistic figures, he used them supremely well, but never better than when he was mimicking someone else. Yet the freedom that he found seems to have remained unconscious; Voltaire did not become the other that he imitated, even fleetingly. He never seems to have appreciated the possibility that the other was not just a deviant, but rather a new self from which he might be led to new discoveries. Instead, as we have seen, Voltaire's tales move toward silencing the dissident voices.

Voltaire differs sharply from his near contemporaries Diderot and Rousseau in this regard. It is not that they had a greater variety of styles; Diderot had less gift for poetry than Voltaire and Rousseau wrote consistently in the same personal prose. Within **Candide** there are probably as many voices as in *Jacques le fataliste* or *Le Neveu de Rameau,* two of Diderot's most successful multivocal works. The difference lies in the quality that Bakhtin calls dialogism. In Diderot, the various points of view resist silencing, and the narrator's discourse calls itself into question. The debate overflows the work; not only the charac-ters but the narrator and the reader seem to be affected by the ongoing conversation; and they change. Likewise in Rousseau, the conflicting perspectives within *La Nouvelle Héloïse* never reach a resolution; the apparent victory of Wolmar's reason or Julie's virtue proves false.

In Voltaire's tales, the characters speak as puppets. They learn nothing except perhaps patience. There is little that they could learn because Voltaire did not believe in diversity of viewpoints. Had Babel not happened, the universal language might not have been French, as the Ingénu and his friends thought; but a universal language would be a good thing because it would reflect universal reason. Geometry might not provide the answer, either; but a small number of demonstrated truths on which all agree are far preferable to the disorder of competing sects. Everything tends toward the single lesson of reason. Fortunately, Voltaire did not write his stories so that the characters learn the lesson; had he done so, they would have seemed merely sentimental and predictable. Their success depends in large part on the fact that the narrative voice, which speaks reason, remains distinct from the characters and events. The characters come on stage and perform their parts, but there can be no resolution in the world of the tales. Instead, they move toward an eventual silence, in which they are subsumed within the narrator's master discourse of reason. (pp. 17-28)

English Showalter, Jr., "The Theme of Language in Voltaire's Tales," in French Forum, *Vol. 14, No. 1, January, 1989, pp. 17-29.*

Aram Vartanian   (essay date 1989)

[*In the following essay, Vartanian considers the philosophical dilemma generated by the conflicting themes advanced in* Zadig.]

The eighteenth century in France saw the rise not only of the *dilemme du roman,* but of the "roman à dilemme." The latter came into being when the philosophes applied their talents to the writing of narrative fiction. Since they did not cease to be philosophers on assuming the role of novelists, it is not surprising that their novels took the form of attempts to solve, in a different key, those problems of philosophy that most perplexed them. Thus, Montesquieu's *Lettres persanes,* by elaborating its parable of the seraglio regime, showed that despotism, however appropriate as a type of government best suited to vast empires, was nonetheless "corrompu par sa nature" and destined ultimately to fail. Rousseau's *La Nouvelle Héloïse* strove to overcome the conflict, fatal to morality, of "nature" and "culture" through an exemplary reconciliation of the two despite the prevailing decadence of European society. Diderot, in *Jacques le fataliste,* tried to escape from the vexing contradiction between his own theory of psychophysical determinism and his no less firm commitment to moral responsibility. Voltaire, as another philosophe turned novelist, was no exception. The best of his *contes philosophiques* were built on the stumbling-block he encountered whenever he set out to combine the notions of happiness, evil, and providence into a coherent and satisfying doctrine. Such is the standpoint from which we shall consider *Zadig.*

The philosophical theme central to the tale has been obvious, because the hero himself is given the task of stating it as a leitmotiv. At the end of chapter 8, after Zadig's luck takes a more catastrophic twist than usual, he soliloquizes:

> Qu'est-ce donc que la vie humaine? O vertu! à quoi m'avez-vous servi? . . . Tout ce que j'ai fait de bien a toujours été pour moi une source de malédiction, et je n'ai été élevé au comble de la grandeur que pour tomber dans le plus horrible précipice de l'infortune. Si j'eusse été méchant comme tant d'autres, je serais heureux comme eux.

The same quandary, evoked over and over by both protagonist and narrator, is summed up pointedly before the denouement in Zadig's bitter comment on his rival Itobad's successful cheating at the tournament: " 'Les sciences, les moeurs, le courage n'ont donc jamais servi qu'à mon infortune.' Il lui échappa enfin de murmurer contre la Providence, et il fut tenté de croire que tout était gouverné par une destinée cruelle qui opprimait les bons et qui faisaient prospérer les chevaliers verts." The plot of *Zadig* bears out, on the whole, this harsh indictment of fate. Voltaire's hero, whose name in Arabic means a "just" and "truthful" man, is a paragon of fairness and probity. Around this nucleus, we observe a cluster of positive qualities: Zadig is also generous, loyal, brave, helpful, enterprising, sincere, tolerant, compassionate—a person of active good will. The concept of virtue in his case is stretched to include, as well, intellectual gifts and an aptitude for romantic love. This composite of admirable traits makes Zadig a model human being who, in any morally well-run universe, ought, we feel, to enjoy the happiness he so richly deserves. Yet, as his disillusioned complaints attest, that is not at all what he gets—at least not until the very last chapter. The sort of no-win world in which Voltaire has placed him is epitomized by the ironic formula: "Le malheur de Zadig vint de son bonheur même, et surtout de son mérite."

Such a perverse state of affairs would, no doubt, be puzzling to most people. But for Voltaire it was far more serious, because it laid bare a dilemma at the heart of his philosophical vision. By the 1740s, he had come to see himself as a reformer of institutional evils, especially those of political misrule, aristocratic privilege, militarist policy, and religious oppression. The logic of his mission obliged him to single out, stress, and even to exaggerate—as all reformers must—what was fundamentally wrong with the social arrangements of eighteenth-century France. At the same time, Voltaire could not surrender the belief essential to his deism that the cosmos had been designed by a Supreme Intelligence, and therefore expressed a providential order. In the ethical sphere, this teleology translated itself into the idea of natural law, which was supposed, among the most vital of its functions, to guarantee the happiness of the righteous and the unhappiness of the wicked. The supposition seemed necessary because, if it was indifferent to individual happiness whether or not one behaved morally, and, much worse, if those who behaved badly were better off than those who behaved well, then Voltaire, who

accepted as axiomatic that everyone acts out of self-interest, would have had no means of persuading the public to side with virtue against vice, or with justice against injustice. In short, his calling to reform society would have been rendered futile. To his utilitarian mind, morality thus "made sense" only if it promoted happiness, individually and collectively. Virtue for its own sake, or suffering as a higher value, were preachments for which he had no patience. He required of an ethically intelligible world that the power—be it fate, nature, providence, or God—presiding over it should discriminate in favor of the good. Such an expectation may strike us at first as naive and unrealistic; but, on second glance, it can be viewed, in the context of religious faith, as hard-headed common sense. It was usually the latter for Voltaire, even if he had a lurking suspicion that it might really be the former—whence the characterization of his heroes (Zadig, Candide, the ingenuous Huron) as "innocents" whose mentality confirms the opinion that a system of "moral rewards" is an illusion peculiar to the immature. It was, notwithstanding this, Voltaire's own overriding need for an ethical order in which virtue and happiness would be linked as cause and effect that gave him, in *Zadig* and elsewhere, an ambivalent sympathy for such heroes and for the philosophical optimism they represented. Yet he remained receptive to that doctrine only if it was not carried to the absurd limit of denying altogether the reality of evil, in which case, as shown by *Candide,* he could turn savagely against it.

Voltaire was predisposed by his vocation of philosophe to regard institutions and customs that defeated personal and social well-being as something like a nasty, but neither chronic nor terminal, disease in an otherwise healthy body—a disease curable by the medicine of enlightened ideas and the aid of nature. But the more he searched out and denounced the evils rampant in his milieu, the more he constrained himself to recognize their omnipresence and recalcitrance, and to imagine that the moral malady of mankind was without remedy. In the end, Voltaire could no longer convince himself that, despite all the particular evils he had made it his business to discover and attack, there was a general providence in charge of human events. He was not, of course, the first to be scandalized by the conjunction of "le malheur des vertueux" and "le bonheur des méchants." A disturbing awareness of that situation had always been typical of Christianity, which, like all religions, liked to believe that those who obeyed God's commandments would prosper in life, while those who broke them would fare poorly. But if the Christian well knew, like Voltaire, that in practice such was far from actually being the case, he could avoid the contradiction by way of the eschatological loophole, taking it on trust that all moral accounts would be balanced for all eternity in an after-life. This recourse to double bookkeeping was not available to Voltaire, whose earnest attachment to both deism and empiricism did not allow him to countenance a supernatural closure. For him, a moral order, if it was not to be simply a fantasy or a lie, had to manifest itself to reason and experience in the *hic et nunc.* Given these strict conditions, the "problem of evil" resisted philosophical solution, and Voltaire consigned it after a time to the metaphysical limbo of insoluble riddles. Yet he did not entirely refuse its challenge. He transposed the basic dilemma to the domain of fictional thinking and literary discourse, in the hope of finding there an alternative solution. The purpose of *Zadig* (and, for the most part, of the *conte philosophique* as a genre) was to affirm that, despite overwhelming factual evidence to the contrary and the inability of reason to ignore it, human existence is subject to a moral law that joins happiness to goodness, and misery to vice. What remains to be seen is how Voltaire, by means of an esthetically plausible fiction, satisfied his desire thus to have things both ways.

Critical study of *Zadig* has long sought in the relationship between its hero and Voltaire a key with which to interpret the work. In the heyday of the biographical method, Zadig was routinely identified with the author; since then, the equivalence has been questioned and dismissed as false, misleading, or simplistic. From our own perspective, it is largely beside the point. Admittedly, many of Zadig's experiences are reminiscent of Voltaire's own, so that there is at least an allegorical kinship between the two. But it hardly follows from this that the tale is an *autofiction*—except in a very restricted sense. The principal manner in which Zadig may be said to resemble Voltaire is that he personifies and defines a dilemma which had acquired an obsessive importance in the latter's thought. *Zadig* is the fictionalization of a state of mind—that of Voltaire, beset by philosophical confusion and in search of a way out by means of telling a story, that is, by bringing fictive invention to the rescue of objective reason. This is not to suggest, however, that the character Zadig can be equated with the work *Zadig,* for the fictive hero, even when he speaks for his creator Voltaire, does so only within the restraints set by the *récit.* The meaning of the story extends beyond the vicissitudes of the hero's career, as well as beyond what he or others think or say about what happens to them. It is the narrator of *Zadig* who controls its full, or ulterior, meaning. He is described as an unnamed "oriental sage." But the characterization of this "technical" narrator does not add up to someone distinct from the author, for the narrative voice in the *conte* is unmistakably Voltaire's. Throughout, it is his style, his wit, his temperament and sensibility, his opinions, tastes, and *bêtes noires* that we are conscious of. It was for the sake of *vraisemblance* that Voltaire interposed in *Zadig* a neutral spokesman between himself and the narrative, because he could not claim to be privy to the annals of Babylon.

A Voltairean *conte* is ordinarily analyzed into its "thème philosophique" and "trame romanesque." The latter component of *Zadig,* made up of a more or less discrete series of episodes, serves to diversify, explore, complicate, but especially to reinforce and confirm its *thème philosophique,* which in turn serves to unify into a signifying pattern the scattered events and persons of the story. The harrowing catalogue of Zadig's mishaps, highlighted in the foreground of the narrative and of the reader's consciousness, fills the work almost from start to finish. It depicts a world in which the norms of conduct are selfishness, vanity, ambition, envy, greed, infidelity, superstition, treachery, charlatanism, hypocrisy, lust, cruelty, intolerance, and stupidity. Zadig, who is remarkably free of these defects, regularly falls victim to those who count on them to advance their interests at the cost of his. But this "philosoph-ical theme," which represents human affairs as abandoned to a chaotic and impersonal fate devoid of moral sense, does not have the field all to itself. In the background and on the periphery of the narrative, as also of the reader's consciousness, several other factors, amounting to a counter-theme, have the cumulative effect, as the tale unfolds, of opposing and modifying the *thème philosophique,* whose thrust is thereby deflected toward an "arrière-pensée" on the author's part. This contrapuntal movement of the narrative results from such aspects of the *conte* as its sub-plot, point of view, tonality, structuration of anecdote, style, characterization, and parafictional commentary. The consequent interplay of theme and counter-theme in *Zadig* leads one to suspect, well before its happy ending, that the story's intent cannot lie wholly, or even chiefly, in its disheartening message; and that, although the real world is all too often like Voltaire's grim exposure of it, he must have something up his sleeve, for the revelation of which the reader is being gradually prepared. The *conte* is told in such a way that its overall meaning emerges before long to semi-awareness from the network of tensions felt or glimpsed among its various elements placed at different depths and angles in the narrative.

One of the countervaling features of the tale is the hero's tragic—or, more exactly, tragicomic—flaw. We realize, on a closer look at Zadig's reverses, that sometimes these are largely of his own doing. Despite his monopoly of virtue and merit, he is no paradigm of *bon sens.* In fact, he can be quite foolhardy, not to say foolish, when blinded by his confidence that others will act as he himself would in similar circumstances. An imprudent naiveness which provokes fate is thus a family trait that Zadig shares (though to a much lesser extent) with Candide and "L'Ingénu." In the first episode of the work, the hero's courtship of the fickle Sémire proves a disaster through no fault of his own. But, although he should have learned from that sobering failure how fragile a woman's faithfulness can be, he decides soon after to put the same quality to a drastic test with his wife Azora. Concocting a scheme that can only be called asinine, he pretends to have died and pays his friend Cador handsomely to seduce his "widow." This hoax, as it deserves, boomerangs, and we are not astonished that, following the trick played on her sense of conjugal duty, Azora "était devenue difficile à vivre," and that the marriage has to be dissolved.

In the "detective story" of the missing dog and horse, Zadig cannot resist the urge to show off his talents as a Babylonian Sherlock Holmes. Not foreseeing the suspicion that his detailed knowledge of the "crime" was bound to arouse, he is himself accused of it; and, although his innocence is at length established, he nonetheless ends up paying 890 *onces d'or* in fines and legal expenses. Another instance of blundering is Zadig's omission to take the necessary steps to conceal his Platonic love-affair with the Queen from the curiosity of spectators and the jealousy of the King. The outcome of his negligence is that, while he has engaged in no act of adultery, he—and she—must suffer for it as if they had. On arriving next as a refugee in a foreign land (Egypt), the first thing Zadig does is to meddle in a violent quarrel between a man and a woman, and finds himself as a result obliged to kill, very much against the latter's wish, what turns out to be her lover. This high-minded bit of rashness causes our hero to be sold, as punishment, into slavery. A no less dangerous, though more humanitarian, lapse from common sense occurs when he attempts to abolish the custom of suttee in Arabia, where the victims do not object to it, and where a powerful clergy has a vested interest in its continuance. For his trouble, Zadig narrowly escapes being himself burned at the stake. On all these occasions, the hero is to some degree responsible for the scrapes he gets into. The general effect on the reader is that fate is relieved of some of its perversity and arbitrariness, and the dominant theme of "les infortunes de la vertu" (to borrow Sade's phrase, inspired by his reading of *Zadig*) seems attenuated, although not to the point of being discredited. For we notice that, even when Zadig behaves sensibly, things do not necessarily go better for him.

Since it is mainly in dealings with women that Zadig's reflexes are likely to trip him up, Voltaire takes advantage of this fact to treat his misfortunes as a lover with ironic pathos. In chapter 8, when his "romance" with Queen Astarté becomes known and he must hastily flee, the narrator remarks about his affective state: "Cet illustre fugitif, arrivé sur le bord d'une colline dont on voyait Babylone, tourna la vue sur le palais de la reine, et s'évanouit; il ne reprit ses sens que pour verser des larmes, et pour souhaiter la mort." While Voltaire's aim in this aside, as in others like it, was to deflate the growing vogue of preromantic sentimentality at the time, its function in terms of the story is to counteract the *thème philosophique* by weakening, through Zadig's excess of "sensibilité," the moral anomaly perceived in the unjust destiny of a meritorious lover.

More important as a counter-theme than Zadig's tragicomic flaws is a secondary motif that is introduced in direct contrast to the primary one. It first appears in chapter 5 ("Les Généreux"). Zadig, after having gained the favor of King Moabdor, competes successfully for the quinquennial "prize of generosity." The episode indicates that, not only is virtue not always persecuted, but there is even in Babylon an official program to reward and encourage it. The persistence of natural law is thus confirmed in spite of the prevalence of "les infortunes de la vertu": "Ce jour mémorable venu, le roi parut sur son trône, environné des grands, des mages, et des députés de toutes les nations, qui venaient à ces jeux où la gloire s'acquérait, non par la légèreté des chevaux, non par la force du corps, mais par la vertu." Contrary to what we have been led to infer from Zadig's previous misadventures, there exists also, we realize, a universal wish to honor the good qualities he possesses. The interlude of "Les Généreux" is an early anticipation of the denouement, whose idyllic mood and incidents it already conjures up.

Chapter 6 ("Le Ministre") augments the same counter-movement. Zadig, having become Prime Minister thanks to his superior qualifications, is shown carrying out his duties with exemplary wisdom and justice. These events, which may be taken as a sign that he is destined to be someday the ruler of Babylon, likewise prefigure the ending. It is worth noting, moreover, that chapter 7 ("Les

Disputes et les audiences") was an appendum published originally in 1756. Describing the Prime Minister, now at the height of his career, as the idol of a grateful public, it also has the function of strengthening the counter-theme: "Zadig montrait tous les jours la subtilité de son génie et la bonté de son âme; on l'admirait, et cependant on l'aimait. Il passait pour le plus fortuné de tous les hommes, tout l'empire était rempli de son nom . . . etc." The hero is here almost in the position of power he will occupy as a result of the denouement. In writing chapter 7, Voltaire must have felt that he had not yet made his narrative aim clear enough. This surmise is confirmed by chapters 14 ("La Danse") and 15 ("Les Yeux bleus"), both of them supplements first printed posthumously in the Kehl edition. They give an account of Zadig's activities in the "Ile de Sérendib," underscoring once again his political acumen and initiative. We learn that he was not long in Sérendib before being "regardé comme un homme extraordinaire. Il devint l'arbitre de tous les différends entre les négociants, l'ami des sages, le conseil du petit nombre de gens qui prennent conseil. Le roi voulut le voir et l'entendre. Il connut bientôt ce que valait Zadig." But the usual malice of fate threatens his well-earned success: "Ainsi Zadig, par ses conseils sages et heureux, et par les plus grands services, s'était attiré l'irréconciliable inimitié des hommes les plus puissants de l'Etat." Luckily, he leaves Sérendib just before his enemies have a chance to kill him. That Voltaire grafted these episodes onto his *conte philosophique* reveals his concern with a counter-theme of "le bonheur des justes," and with the need to bolster it so as to make the ending less unexpected.

But the counter-theme was already present as a subordinate teleology elsewhere in the original version. No sooner had Zadig been condemned to slavery, for instance, than he began to "work his way up" so effectively by dint of intelligence, knowledge, and a spirit of enterprise that, at the beginning of chapter 11, he was his master Sétoc's "ami intime." Sétoc himself turned out, happily, to have "un naturel porté au bien, beaucoup de droiture et de bon sens." This permits Zadig to win his master over to deism before he goes on to become the "bienfaiteur de l'Arabie" by reforming "en un jour une coûtume si cruelle, qui durait depuis tant de siècles," that is, "le bûcher du veuvage." In chapter 12 ("Le Souper"), the hero manages to reconcile all parties to a heated quarrel over the crucial question of what constitutes true religion. These incidents bear out the maxim that one cannot keep a good man down; and, while they do not suffice to cancel out the *thème philosophique* and its accompanying pessimism, they surely contest, even subvert, it. From this stage on, theme and counter-theme are in an overtly dialectical relation. Chapter 16 ("Le Brigand") shows Zadig being assaulted by the henchmen of the bandit Arbogad. He is not harmed because the latter, watching from his window "les prodiges de valeur que faisait Zadig, conçut de l'estime pour lui. Il descendit en hâte et vint lui-même écarter ses gens." Zadig's virtue (this time in the sense of prowess and courage) has positive effects, and, what is more significant, owing to a notorious criminal's respect for it. But if this occurrence evinces once more the idea of natural law, the chapter as a whole corroborates with special pertinence the *thème philosophique*, for Arbogad, who is said to be "le plus heureux des hommes," illustrates to perfection "la prospérité du vice." Zadig himself remarks bitterly on the situation: "L'empire est déchiré, et ce brigand est heureux: ô fortune! ô destinée! un voleur est heureux, et ce que la nature a fait de plus aimable a péri peutêtre d'une manière affreuse . . . O Astarté! qu'êtes-vous devenue?"

For the remainder of the tale, Zadig is no longer personally exposed to disaster. His protests are those of a worried lover separated from Astarté when he is depicted as "toujours déplorant sa destinée" and claiming to be "le modèle du malheur." It is at this moment that Voltaire introduces the "pêcheur," compared to whose abject misery Zadig is perceived to be doing rather well. He succors the wretched fisherman, who declares: "vous êtes un ange sauveur." Even so, Zadig continues to reproach providence in a reference to the unscrupulous but fortunate Orcan: "d'ordinaire ce sont ces gens-là qui sont les favoris de la destinée." But chapter 19 ("Les Combats") reaffirms the counter-theme of a return to rationality and justice, for it is decided there that the next king of Babylon will be chosen, not by the criterion of birth, but by determining who is "le plus vaillant et le plus sage"—a procedure that can only benefit Zadig. Voltaire has so arranged the narrative that, at this penultimate juncture, the force of destiny is seen to be working with, not against, his hero. The *thème philosophique* has now only the devious fool Itobad to support it. The happy ending of the *conte* is the eventual triumph of what has been all along its occulted but persistent counter-motif of "virtue rewarded."

The thematic reversal on which the tale concludes is legitimated by several other techniques proper to Voltairean fiction. One of these is its tonality. When the most sinister phase of Zadig's troubles begins with his sudden flight from Babylon, the events that will follow are set in a cosmic perspective. The passage where this takes place has caught the eye of many a critic:

> Zadig dirigeait sa route sur les étoiles. La constellation d'Orion et le brillant astre de Sirius le guidaient vers le pôle de Canope. Il admirait ces vastes globes de lumière qui ne paraissent que de faibles étincelles à nos yeux, tandis que la terre, qui n'est en effet qu'un point imperceptible dans la nature, paraît à notre cupidité quelque chose de si grand et de si noble. Il se figurait alors les hommes tels qu'ils sont en effet, des insectes se dévorant les uns les autres sur un petit atome de boue. Cette image vraie semblait anéantir ses malheurs, en lui retraçant le néant de son être et celui de Babylone. Son âmes s'élançait jusque dans l'infini, et contemplait, détachée de ses sens, l'ordre immuable de l'univers.

This oft-cited text, by both its strategic positioning in the *conte* and its exceptional length for a nonnarrative insertion, has a key function. In it the author's voice becomes particularly audible and eloquent. Voltaire's deistic interpretation of Newtonian science had made celestial physics the basis and proof of a providential plan which he then expected to find also in the moral world. The "ordre immuable de l'univers," which guides Zadig in his darkest hour, is a guarantee that human affairs are not at the mercy of haphazard causes. But more than that, contem-

plation of the heavens restores a correct sense of proportion regarding our puny planet. This makes possible, in turn, a euphoric distancing and detachment between the observer and the immediate object of his interest. Zadig, his "âme détachée de ses sens," is here the observer whose vision of the human race, *sub specie coeli,* as so many insects devouring one another "sur un atome de boue" lifts his spirits by giving him a paradoxical feeling of superiority, as if he were not himself one of them. But if the fictive hero experiences this as only a passing mood, for Voltaire it was a continuous one, pervading the *conte philosophique* generally and generically. In *Zadig,* it fixes the author's attitude toward what he recounts—an attitude colored by an Olympian aloofness and amusement. This tone is easily modulated, as the occasion demands, into that of satire. For what can be more natural, when one looks down like God on the frantic but futile struggles of an ant-heap, than to feel a reassuring contempt? Nor is the effect of this lost on the reader. Made to see things from the Voltairean vantage-point, he too realizes that the main philosophical theme of *Zadig* has been radically reduced in scale. And because, at the same time, the tale subjects an ethically anarchic world to a running satirical commentary, the anarchy itself is thereby diminished. For satire partly redeems the nihilism of the narrative by reordering disorder to the extent that it supposes, implicitly, a moral and rational norm in contrast to what it mocks as irrational and immoral.

Another technique that serves the same end of undercutting the central theme of *Zadig* is the two-dimensionality of its characters. These are always defined by a predominant trait: Arimaze, or *l'envieux;* Astarté, the "femme idéale"; Missouf, the "femme capricieuse"; Arbogad, the bandit; Sétoc, the "honnête commerçant"; "le pêcheur"; Moabdor, the King and "mari jaloux"; Itobad, the vainglorious aristocrat; Cador, the loyal friend; Ogul, the lazy, gluttonous *bon vivant;* bigoted and lascivious priests; medical charlatans; greedy judges. And, of course, Zadig himself, or "l'homme juste" and "l'homme de mérite" rolled into one. Such stereotyping was, in the first place, a requirement of the *conte philosophique*. A work like *Zadig* called for the allegorization of its protagonists as a means of stressing its conceptual intent; by contrast, flesh-and-blood imitation would have destroyed, by its concreteness and opacity, the abstract transparence of the ideas whose interplay the characters were meant to convey. But Voltaire's use of this method achieved a further result. The flatness of his fictional types, particularly of the hero himself, makes them appear like marionettes whose relationship to the author is essentially one of manipulation. The reader's awareness of this counteracts the *thème philosophique,* because the misfortunes of Zadig cannot be taken as the outcome of unthinking forces in a morally neutral universe. They are felt instead to depend on the will of an "omnipotent intelligence" engaged in the ordering of an imaginary world. Moreover, insofar as Voltaire's characters fail to give the illusion of suffering that only "real" persons are capable of doing, their mistreatment by fate is lessened. This aspect of the tale is connected to its tone of detachment, which it reinforces.

The ironic mode in *Zadig* brings its own support to the

counter-theme. Moral disorder is ironized from the very start, when Sémire not only penalizes Zadig for his beneficent virtue, but compensates the criminal boorishness of his rival Orcan. Thereafter, the same pattern recurs often, as, for example, in the episode of the ailing Ogul (chapter 18), whom the hero heals with the consequence that "après avoir été toujours puni pour avoir bien fait, il était près de périr pour avoir guéri un seigneur gourmand." Inasmuch as irony expresses an inverse symmetry, it is incompatible with a picture of anarchy in human affairs; for the symmetrical in any form is a manifestation of an underlying order. Because there can be no irony proper in a purblind, indifferent nature, the ironic effects in the *conte* "humanize" evil by bringing it under the sway of a structuring purpose. The same may be said of the cyclical rhythm typical of the narrative of *Zadig.* The hero's fortunes rise and fall with something like the alternation and regularity of the tides. Such a rhythm, referable to a hidden law, was a basic property that led Voltaire to see in Newton's cosmos the providential order which he extrapolated to moral phenomena. A rhythmic sequence of prosperity and its opposite betrays the presence of an overseer, however sardonic his humor, behind the vicissitudes of fate which Zadig undergoes. Finally, Voltaire's style, typified by its allegro and buoyancy, mitigates whatever inclination the reader might still have toward somber reflections on the sort of world being offered to his view. The stylistic effervescence of the *conte* is obviously in conflict with its primary, but in accord with its secondary, theme. These various methods of narration, which taken together determine how the story of *Zadig* is told, allow the narrator to insinuate himself into the account he pretends to be giving of an impersonal and implacable fate, thereby establishing himself in the role of destiny itself; that is, he achieves *de facto* control over what is presumably happening in defiance of both ethical values and a wise providence. Voltaire's grand strategy consists in this assumption of power despite appearances to the contrary—an authorial maneuver behind the scenes which, in the deepest sense, is what the tale is really about.

Let us now relate what has so far been said to the Jesrad episode, which many have found the most baffling of the *conte.* Its hermeneutic importance cannot be measured quantitatively, for although chapter 20 ("L'Ermite") comprises only a small portion of the work, its role is pivotal. Coming at a decisive turn just before the denouement, it purports to be a resolution of the philosophical dilemma that has been posed in cumulative fashion up to that point. Despite its crucial bearing on the story, however, Zadig's encounter with the angel Jesrad disguised as a hermit has itself no narrative function. It is a digression from the unfolding plot, without any causal tie to what will ensue afterward. Voltaire could just as well have had his hero, following the fiasco at the tournament, wander dejectedly along the banks of the Euphrates, meet no hermit at all, return to Babylon for the second part of the competition, and emerge victorious. The Jesrad section could thus have been omitted with no loss in narrative continuity or credibility. Had it been left out, the ending would in fact have been more, not less, credible. The chapter on "L'Ermite" makes what critics have blamed as a "fairytale" finale even more fantastic, because it brings to it a supernatural di-

mension which is otherwise absent, and leads the reader to associate the hero's crowning success with the kind of *merveilleux* peculiar to Jesrad's personality and actions. The Hermit episode has, if anything, the effect of avoiding a too folklorish, even a rather banal, unravelling of the narrative, by adding to it a new and complicating factor.

That factor has to do, of course, with Jesrad's lecture on Leibnizian optimism—a metaphysical *hors d'oeuvre* that almost all interpreters have had difficulty in digesting. The Hermit-Angel's theodicy appears, on the one hand, to agree neatly with the moral of the tale brought to light in the conclusion. On the other hand, there has been reluctance to believe that Voltaire meant seriously to endorse the notion that "tout est pour le mieux" and that every evil in life produces, infallibly, some greater good. If he had put stock in such a doctrine (not counting that he later demolished it in *Candide*), he could not in the first place have written a work like *Zadig,* which presupposes indignation, not complacency, on the author's part concerning the injustices and absurdities it catalogues. In that respect, the majority of scholars have no doubt been right to take the hero's repeated "mais" in reply to Jesrad's pronouncements as proof of Voltaire's own skepticism. The latter, moreover, far from being a disciple of Leibniz, rarely missed an opportunity to deride his philosophical opinions. What, then, is the German metaphysician, dressed up as an emissary of God, doing in the *conte?*

The lesson on Leibnizian theodicy given just before the denouement facilitates a shift from the narrative to a "meta-narrative" level of discourse. The angel explains, among other mysteries, that God

> a créé des millions de mondes dont aucun ne peut ressembler à l'autre. Cette immense variété est un attribut de sa puissance immense. Il n'y a ni deux feuilles d'arbre sur la terre, ni deux globes dans les champs infinis du ciel, qui soient semblables, et tout ce que tu vois sur le petit atome où tu es né devait être dans sa place et dans son temps fixe, selon les ordres immuables de celui qui embrasse tout.

Whether or not Voltaire himself subscribes, in this passage, to the principle of plenitude or that of indiscernables is not the question. The purpose of Jesrad's statement, seen in its fictional context, is to suggest a state of mind receptive to the creation of possible worlds. Such a possibility, whatever its validity as metaphysics, is plainly valid as poetics. The novelist, like Leibniz's deity, is in a position to "create" any one (or several) of innumerable worlds, for if he does not like "le monde comme il va," he is free to construct another more to his liking. Leibnizianism is introduced into chapter 20 because its affirmation of unlimited creative, i.e., imaginative, freedom coincides with the narrative situation in which Voltaire finds himself as he is about to set the stamp of destiny—that is, the choice of one among millions of possible worlds—to his own creation.

What the author of *Zadig* has most in common with Jesrad is the cosmic outlook to which he raises himself on the coattails of the heavenly envoy. The Hermit carries with him "le livre des destinées," which he offers to let Zadig read. The latter cannot decipher its text, because the exercise of such a prerogative belongs, not to him, but to his "creator." And so it is no coincidence that, while the angel of fate brandishes his book of destiny, Voltaire is composing another book whose subtitle is "la destinée." Here the roles of Hermit and author, both of whom act as manipulators and dispensers of fate, intersect and overlap. How, precisely, does Jesrad go about his business? He is patently not just an "executor" of preordained decrees that must be carried out, i.e., a figure of determinism. On the contrary, he rearranges the outcome of events in the world according to his own sense of poetic justice, as a novelist might be expected to do in a fictional world. The angel's first two interventions, concerning a miserly host and an ostentatious one, are intended to correct the fault of each. The third incident, involving a perfect host, rewards genuine hospitality. But it is from the fourth case, in which Jesrad causes an adolescent to drown, that we can infer more clearly what he is up to. His "livre des destinées" tells him the dire consequences that would have ensued if the young man had been permitted to live; and it is in order to avert these "necessary" fates that the Hermit chooses a lesser evil. "La destinée," in Jesrad's book as in Voltaire's, is an inchoate background reality against which the angel and the poet compose texts of their own, bringing into existence, by an act of will and imagination, a state of affairs closer to the moral order preferred by each. That is why Zadig, despite the objection of his reiterated *mais*, "adora la Providence, et se soumit." He bows, in effect, not so much to Jesrad's as, more appropriately, to Voltaire's wishes for his future. The function of the Hermit is not so much to instruct Zadig (or the reader) in Leibnizian philosophy, as it is to let Voltaire "play God." Jesrad enters upon the scene just when it is time for the author finally to step in and set everything right, with a happy ending made, if not quite in heaven, at least in his conscience—which suits the purpose almost as well. The Hermit furnishes the cue that is acted on by his "creator," who as a matter of fact is not God but the *conteur* Voltaire. The latter, like his celestial creature, manages events in such a way as to convert, providentially, a chaotic into an ordered moral universe. It is known that, for the contents of the chapter on "L'Ermite," Voltaire drew upon a literary tradition reaching back to the Middle Ages. But his special use of it directs attention to the nature of fiction-writing itself, and to the ontological status of that activity. The story becomes here the imposition of a human design on an "inhuman" world; and as such it supercedes, while paralleling, its theological model.

Because *Zadig* is an allegory of the creation of a possible moral order, the hero's fate concerns not just himself, but everyone in Babylon. His individual destiny is given a political, and ultimately a global, significance. With Zadig's ascension to the throne, "l'empire jouit de la paix, de la gloire, et de l'abondance; ce fut le plus beau siècle de la terre; elle était gouvernée par la justice et par l'amour." Voltaire's prescription, in this most cheerful of endings, was a popular and enlightened absolutism that combines the Lockean theory of a social compact with his own ideal of a philosopher-king. We are told that "dès que Zadig parut dans la ville, le peuple s'assembla autour de lui; les yeux ne se rassasient point de le voir, les bouches de le

bénir, les coeurs de lui souhaiter l'empire." Not only does he alone explain the enigmas put to each candidate, but he does better than all the others on a more relevant type of examination: "On proposa des questions sur la justice, sur le souverain bien, sur l'art de régner. Les réponses de Zadig furent jugées les plus solides." Thanks to his all-round merit, "il fut reconnu roi d'un consentement unanime." In 1748, Voltaire was convinced that the best means of building an ethical system into society was to entrust government to a wise and virtuous monarch with unrestricted powers (like those of Jesrad and the philosophical novelist) to reorganize the *enchaînement* of human events. He would later retreat from that oversimplified position, but without giving it up entirely.

The narrative structure and other modalities of *Zadig,* which, as we have seen, were behind the dialectical tension and final reversal between its theme and counter-theme, "solved" the moral dilemma that generated the *conte.* Voltaire was able to have things both ways: he could discover, describe, denounce, and ridicule evils and injustices as much as he pleased; yet, beyond it all, he could also preserve the belief that destiny obeys a just and rational will—God's, or (as is visual whenever God's designs are invoked) his own. He was inclined to see the history of *moeurs* as a recapitulation, on mankind's modest terms, of the original creation of a providential nature by divine fiat. But even if a Supreme Intelligence did not exist, Voltaire was ready to invent one, so that, by imagining himself in its place, he could reinvent the world. (pp. 149-64)

> *Aram Vartanian,* "*'Zadig': Theme and Counter-Theme," in* Dilemmes du Roman: Essays in Honor of Georges May, *edited by Catherine Lafarge, Anma Libri, 1989, pp. 149-64.*

FURTHER READING

Biography

Ayer, A. J. *Voltaire.* London: Weidenfeld and Nicolson, 1986. 182 p.
    Overview of Voltaire's career by a prominent modern philosopher.

Lanson, Gustave. *Voltaire.* Translated by Robert A. Wagoner. New York: John Wiley and Sons, 1960. 258 p.
    Standard biography of Voltaire.

Mason, Haydn. *Voltaire: A Biography.* Baltimore, Md.: Johns Hopkins University Press, 1981. 204 p.
    Focuses on Voltaire's intellectual development and character traits.

Criticism

Betts, C. J. "On the Beginning and Ending of *Candide.*" *The Modern Language Review* 80, No. 2 (April 1985): 283-92.
    Investigates the parallels between the beginning and ending of *Candide* and their thematic significance.

Bongie, Lawrence L. "Crisis and the Birth of the Voltairian *Conte.*" *Modern Language Quarterly* 23, No. 1 (March 1962): 53-64.

Considers the reasons Voltaire chose to write in the *conte* form.

Bottiglia, William F. "*Candide* and the Genre of the Philosophic Tale." In *Studies on Voltaire and the Eighteenth Century* Vol. 7, edited by Theodore Besterman, pp. 56-88. Geneva: Institut et Musée Voltaire, 1959.

Attempts to locate the origins of the philosophic tale and to distinguish it from other literary genres.

Carr, Thomas M. "Voltaire's Fables of Discretion: The *Conte Philosophique* in *Le taureau blanc.*" In *Studies in Eighteenth-Century Culture* Vol. 15, edited by O. M. Brack, Jr., pp. 47-65. Madison: University of Wisconsin Press, 1986.

Contrasts the different types of persuasive rhetoric used in *Le taureau blanc.*

Cherpack, Clifton. "Positivism, Piety, and the Study of Voltaire's Philosophical Tales." *The Eighteenth Century* 24, No. 1 (Winter 1983): 23-37.

Asserts that the inability of modern literary criticism to define Voltaire's philosophical tales reflects their parodic and ambiguous nature.

Dawson, Deidre. "In Search of the Real Pangloss: The Correspondence of Voltaire with the Duchess of Saxe-Gotha." *Yale French Studies,* No. 71 (1986): 93-112.

Examines the correspondence between Voltaire and the Duchess of Saxe-Gotha in an attempt to verify whether she was the inspiration for the character of Pangloss in *Candide.*

Henry, Patrick. "Raisonner in *Candide.*" *Romantic Review* 80, No. 3 (May 1989): 363-70.

Studies the significance of the different meanings attached to the word 'raisonner' in *Candide.*

Howells, Robin. "Processing Voltaire's *Amabed.*" *British Journal for Eighteenth-Century Studies* 10, No. 2 (Autumn 1987): 153-62.

Considers the aesthetic failure of *Les Lettres d'Amabed* as the result of different symbolic tendencies and associations throughout the text counteracting the action of the story.

James, JoAnn. "Childhood's End: Apocalyptic Resolution in *Candide.*" In *Apocalyptic Visions Past and Present: Selected Papers from the Eighth and Ninth Annual Florida State University Conferences on Literature and Film,* edited by JoAnn James and William J. Cloonan, pp. 67-76. Tallahassee: Florida State University Press, 1988.

Offers an allegorical reading of *Candide* based on the apocalyptic tendencies that develop from its Edenic beginnings and the movement of characters from innocence to experience.

Langdon, David. "On the Meanings of the Conclusion of *Candide.*" *Studies on Voltaire and the Eighteenth Century,* No. 238 (1985): 397-432.

Detailed analysis of the philosophical implications of the conclusion of *Candide* in relation to Voltaire's other philosophical tales.

Lynch, James J. "Romance Conventions in Voltaire's *Candide.*" *South Atlantic Review* 50, No. 1 (January 1985): 35-46.

Discusses the influence of the Heliodoran novel, which is a "synthesis of romance and epic" that "strives for a balance between unity and diversity, verisimilitude and the marvelous, instruction and delight."

Mason, Haydn T. "Voltaire's 'Contes': Etat Présént." *The Modern Language Review* 65, No. 1 (January 1970): 19-35.

Surveys the different critical approaches to Voltaire's contes.

———. "*Conteur.*" In his *Voltaire,* pp. 48-85. London: Hutchinson, 1975.

Detailed discussion of Voltaire's major fiction, with attention to the historical context in which they were written.

Nablow, Ralph Arthur. "Was Voltaire Influenced by Lucian in *Micromégas?*" *Romance Notes* 22, No. 2 (Winter 1981): 186-91.

Compares "striking points of resemblance" between *Micromégas* and Lucian's satiric dialogue *Icaromenippus.*

Scanlan, Timothy M. "Subliminal Obscenity in *Candide.*" *Maledicta* 3, No. 1 (Summer 1979): 29-36.

Discusses the consistent use of sexually suggestive language in *Candide.*

Topazio, Virgil W. "Voltaire's Philosophical Tales and Style." In *Voltaire: A Critical Study of His Major Works,* pp. 27-60. New York: Random House, 1967.

Describes the development of Voltaire's narrative style.

Trapnell, William H. "Destiny in Voltaire's *Zadig* and *The Arabian Nights.*" *Studies on Voltaire and the Eighteenth Century,* No. 278 (1990): 147-71.

Compares the notion of destiny in *Zadig* to that found in Antoine Galland's translation of *The Arabian Nights,* a work that influenced Voltaire in his writing of *Zadig.*

Wade, Ira O. *Voltaire's* Micromégas: *A Study in the Fusion of Science, Myth, and Art.* Princeton, N.J.: Princeton University Press, 1950. 190 p.

Well-informed discussion of the scientific background and context of *Micromégas,* including Voltaire's involvement with the scientific advances of his day.

Wellington, Marie. "Crossovers from Theatre to Narrative in a Voltairian conte." *Studies on Voltaire and the Eighteenth Century,* No. 278 (1990): 187-96.

Demonstrates the connection between Voltaire's fiction and his plays, concentrating on the lesser-known conte *Cosi-Sancta.*

Wolper, Roy S. "Voltaire's *Contes*: A Reconsideration." *Forum* 16, No. 1 (Winter 1978): 74-9.

Survey of Voltaire's fiction.

———. "The Final Foolishness of Babouc: The Dark Centre of *Le monde comme il va.*" *The Modern Language Review* 75, No. 4 (October 1980): 766-73.

Assesses the irony and satire in *Le monde comme il va.*

———. "The Toppling of Jeannot." *Studies on Voltaire and the Eighteenth Century,* No. 183 (1980): 69-82.

Refutes the commonly perceived didactic tendencies of *Jeannot et Colin.*

Additional coverage of Voltaire's life and career is contained in the following sources published by Gale Research: *Literature Criticism from 1400 to 1800,* Vol. 14; and *World Literature Criticism,* Vol. 6.

Appendix:

Select Bibliography of General Sources on Short Fiction

BOOKS OF CRITICISM

Allen, Walter. *The Short Story in English.* New York: Oxford University Press, 1981, 413 p.

Aycock, Wendell M., ed. *The Teller and the Tale: Aspects of the Short Story* (Proceedings of the Comparative Literature Symposium, Texas Tech University, Volume XIII). Lubbock: Texas Tech Press, 1982, 156 p.

Averill, Deborah. *The Irish Short Story from George Moore to Frank O'Connor.* Washington, D.C.: University Press of America, 1982, 329 p.

Bates, H. E. *The Modern Short Story: A Critical Survey.* Boston: Writer, 1941, 231 p.

Bayley, John. *The Short Story: Henry James to Elizabeth Bowen.* Great Britain: The Harvester Press Limited, 1988, 197 p.

Bennett, E. K. *A History of the German Novelle: From Goethe to Thomas Mann.* Cambridge: At the University Press, 1934, 296 p.

Bone, Robert. *Down Home: A History of Afro-American Short Fiction from Its Beginning to the End of the Harlem Renaissance.* Rev. ed. New York: Columbia University Press, 1988, 350 p.

Bruck, Peter. *The Black American Short Story in the Twentieth Century: A Collection of Critical Essays.* Amsterdam: B. R. Grüner Publishing Co., 1977, 209 p.

Burnett, Whit, and Burnett, Hallie. *The Modern Short Story in the Making.* New York: Hawthorn Books, 1964, 405 p.

Canby, Henry Seidel. *The Short Story in English.* New York: Henry Holt and Co., 1909, 386 p.

Current-García, Eugene. *The American Short Story before 1850: A Critical History.* Twayne's Critical History of the Short Story, edited by William Peden. Boston: Twayne Publishers, 1985, 168 p.

Flora, Joseph M., ed. *The English Short Story, 1880-1945: A Critical History.* Twayne's Critical History of the Short Story, edited by William Peden. Boston: Twayne Publishers, 1985, 215 p.

Foster, David William. *Studies in the Contemporary Spanish-American Short Story.* Columbia, Mo.: University of Missouri Press, 1979, 126 p.

George, Albert J. *Short Fiction in France, 1800-1850.* Syracuse, N.Y.: Syracuse University Press, 1964, 245 p.

Gerlach, John. *Toward an End: Closure and Structure in the American Short Story.* University, Ala.: The University of Alabama Press, 1985, 193 p.

Hankin, Cherry, ed. *Critical Essays on the New Zealand Short Story.* Auckland: Heinemann Publishers, 1982, 186 p.

Hanson, Clare, ed. *Re-Reading the Short Story.* London: MacMillan Press, 1989, 137 p.

Harris, Wendell V. *British Short Fiction in the Nineteenth Century.* Detroit: Wayne State University Press, 1979, 209 p.

Huntington, John. *Rationalizing Genius: Idealogical Strategies in the Classic American Science Fiction Short Story*. New Brunswick: Rutgers University Press, 1989, 216 p.

Kilroy, James F., ed. *The Irish Short Story: A Critical History*. Twayne's Critical History of the Short Story, edited by William Peden. Boston: Twayne Publishers, 1984, 251 p.

Lee, A. Robert. *The Nineteenth-Century American Short Story*. Totowa, N. J.: Vision / Barnes & Noble, 1986, 196 p.

Leibowitz, Judith. *Narrative Purpose in the Novella*. The Hague: Mouton, 1974, 137 p.

Lohafer, Susan. *Coming to Terms with the Short Story*. Baton Rouge: Louisiana State University Press, 1983, 171 p.

Lohafer, Susan, and Clarey, Jo Ellyn. *Short Story Theory at a Crossroads*. Baton Rouge: Louisiana State University Press, 1989, 352 p.

Mann, Susan Garland. *The Short Story Cycle: A Genre Companion and Reference Guide*. New York: Greenwood Press, 1989, 228 p.

Matthews, Brander. *The Philosophy of the Short Story*. New York: Longmans, Green and Co., 1901, 83 p.

May, Charles E., ed. *Short Story Theories*. Athens, Oh.: Ohio University Press, 1976, 251 p.

McClave, Heather, ed. *Women Writers of the Short Story: A Collection of Critical Essays*. Englewood Cliffs, N. J.: Prentice-Hall, 1980, 171 p.

Moser, Charles, ed. *The Russian Short Story: A Critical History*. Twayne's Critical History of the Short Story, edited by William Peden. Boston: Twayne Publishers, 1986, 232 p.

New, W. H. *Dreams of Speech and Violence: The Art of the Short Story in Canada and New Zealand*. Toronto: The University of Toronto Press, 1987, 302 p.

Newman, Frances. *The Short Story's Mutations: From Petronius to Paul Morand*. New York: B. W. Huebsch, 1925, 332 p.

O'Connor, Frank. *The Lonely Voice: A Study of the Short Story*. Cleveland: World Publishing Co., 1963, 220 p.

O'Faolain, Sean. *The Short Story*. New York: Devin-Adair Co., 1951, 370 p.

Orel, Harold. *The Victorian Short Story: Development and Triumph of a Literary Genre*. Cambridge: Cambridge University Press, 1986, 213 p.

O'Toole, L. Michael. *Structure, Style and Interpretation in the Russian Short Story*. New Haven: Yale University Press, 1982, 272 p.

Pattee, Fred Lewis. *The Development of the American Short Story: An Historical Survey*. New York: Harper and Brothers Publishers, 1923, 388 p.

Peden, Margaret Sayers, ed. *The Latin American Short Story: A Critical History*. Twayne's Critical History of the Short Story, edited by William Peden. Boston: Twayne Publishers, 1983, 160 p.

Peden, William. *The American Short Story: Continuity and Change, 1940-1975*. Rev. ed. Boston: Houghton Mifflin Co., 1975, 215 p.

Reid, Ian. *The Short Story*. The Critical Idiom, edited by John D. Jump. London: Methuen and Co., 1977, 76 p.

Rhode, Robert D. *Setting in the American Short Story of Local Color, 1865-1900*. The Hague: Mouton, 1975, 189 p.

Rohrberger, Mary. *Hawthorne and the Modern Short Story: A Study in Genre*. The Hague: Mouton and Co., 1966, 148 p.

Shaw, Valerie, *The Short Story: A Critical Introduction*. London: Longman, 1983, 294 p.

Stephens, Michael. *The Dramaturgy of Style: Voice in Short Fiction*. Carbondale, Ill.: Southern Illinois University Press, 1986, 281 p.

Stevick, Philip, ed. *The American Short Story, 1900-1945: A Critical History.* Twayne's Critical History of the Short Story, edited by William Peden, Boston: Twayne Publishers, 1984, 209 p.

Summers, Hollis, ed. *Discussion of the Short Story.* Boston: D. C. Heath and Co., 1963, 118 p.

Vannatta, Dennis, ed. *The English Short Story, 1945-1980: A Critical History.* Twayne's Critical History of the Short Story, edited by William Peden. Boston: Twayne Publishers, 1985, 206 p.

Voss, Arthur. *The American Short Story: A Critical Survey.* Norman, Okla.: University of Oklahoma Press, 1973, 399 p.

Ward, Alfred C. *Aspects of the Modern Short Story: English and American.* London: University of London Press, 1924, 307 p.

Weaver, Gordon, ed. *The American Short Story, 1945-1980: A Critical History.* Twayne's Critical History of the Short Story, edited by William Peden. Boston: Twayne Publishers, 1983, 150 p.

West, Ray B., Jr. *The Short Story in America, 1900-1950.* Chicago: Henry Regnery Co., 1952, 147 p.

Williams, Blanche Colton. *Our Short Story Writers.* New York: Moffat, Yard and Co., 1920, 357 p.

Wright, Austin McGiffert. *The American Short Story in the Twenties.* Chicago: University of Chicago Press, 1961, 425 p.

CRITICAL ANTHOLOGIES

Atkinson, W. Patterson, ed. *The Short-Story.* Boston: Allyn and Bacon, 1923, 317 p.

Baldwin, Charles Sears, ed. *American Short Stories.* New York: Longmans, Green and Co., 1904, 333 p.

Charters, Ann, ed. *The Story and Its Writer: An Introduction to Short Fiction.* New York: St. Martin's Press, 1983, 1239 p.

Current-García, Eugene, and Patrick, Walton R., eds. *American Short Stories: 1820 to the Present.* Key Editions, edited by John C. Gerber. Chicago: Scott, Foresman and Co., 1952, 633 p.

Fagin, N. Bryllion, ed. *America through the Short Story.* Boston: Little, Brown, and Co., 1936, 508 p.

Frakes, James R., and Traschen, Isadore, eds. *Short Fiction: A Critical Collection.* Prentice-Hall English Literature Series, edited by Maynard Mack. Englewood Cliffs, N.J.: Prentice-Hall, 1959, 459 p.

Gifford, Douglas, ed. *Scottish Short Stories, 1800-1900.* The Scottish Library, edited by Alexander Scott. London: Calder and Boyars, 1971, 350 p.

Gordon, Caroline, and Tate, Allen, eds. *The House of Fiction: An Anthology of the Short Story with Commentary.* Rev. ed. New York: Charles Scribner's Sons, 1960, 469 p.

Greet, T. Y., et. al. *The Worlds of Fiction: Stories in Context.* Boston: Houghton Mifflin Co., 1964, 429 p.

Gullason, Thomas A., and Caspar, Leonard, eds. *The World of Short Fiction: An International Collection.* New York: Harper and Row, 1962, 548 p.

Havighurst, Walter, ed. *Masters of the Modern Short Story.* New York: Harcourt, Brace and Co., 1945, 538 p.

Litz, A. Walton, ed. *Major American Short Stories.* New York: Oxford University Press, 1975, 823 p.

Matthews, Brander, ed. *The Short-Story: Specimens Illustrating Its Development.* New York: American Book Co., 1907, 399 p.

Menton, Seymour, ed. *The Spanish American Short Story: A Critical Anthology.* Berkeley and Los Angeles: University of California Press, 1980, 496 p.

Mzamane, Mbulelo Vizikhungo, ed. *Hungry Flames, and Other Black South African Short Stories.* Longman African Classics. Essex: Longman, 1986, 162 p.

Schorer, Mark, ed. *The Short Story: A Critical Anthology.* Rev. ed. Prentice-Hall English Literature Series, edited by Maynard Mack. Englewood Cliffs, N. J.: Prentice-Hall, 1967, 459 p.

Simpson, Claude M., ed. *The Local Colorists: American Short Stories, 1857-1900.* New York: Harper and Brothers Publishers, 1960, 340 p.

Stanton, Robert, ed. *The Short Story and the Reader.* New York: Henry Holt and Co., 1960, 557 p.

West, Ray B., Jr., ed. *American Short Stories.* New York: Thomas Y. Crowell Co., 1959, 267 p.

Short Story Criticism Indexes

Literary Criticism Series
Cumulative Author Index

SSC Cumulative Nationality Index
SSC Cumulative Title Index

How to Use This Index

The main references

Calvino, Italo
1923-1985.....CLC 5, 8, 11, 22, 33, 39,
73; SSC 3

list all author entries in the following Gale Literary Criticism series:

CLC = *Contemporary Literary Criticism*
CLR = *Children's Literature Review*
CMLC = *Classical and Medieval Literature Criticism*
DC = *Drama Criticism*
LC = *Literature Criticism from 1400 to 1800*
NCLC = *Nineteenth-Century Literature Criticism*
PC = *Poetry Criticism*
SSC = *Short Story Criticism*
TCLC = *Twentieth-Century Literary Criticism*

The cross-references

See also CANR 23; CA 85-88;
obituary CA 116

list all author entries in the following Gale biographical and literary sources:

AAYA = *Authors & Artists for Young Adults*
AITN = *Authors in the News*
BLC = *Black Literature Criticism*
BW = *Black Writers*
CA = *Contemporary Authors*
CAAS = *Contemporary Authors Autobiography Series*
CABS = *Contemporary Authors Bibliographical Series*
CANR = *Contemporary Authors New Revision Series*
CAP = *Contemporary Authors Permanent Series*
CDALB = *Concise Dictionary of American Literary Biography*
CDBLB = *Concise Dictionary of British Literary Biography*
DLB = *Dictionary of Literary Biography*
DLBD = *Dictionary of Literary Biography Documentary Series*
DLBY = *Dictionary of Literary Biography Yearbook*
HW = *Hispanic Writers*
MAICYA = *Major Authors and Illustrators for Children and Young Adults*
MTCW = *Major 20th-Century Writers*
SAAS = *Something about the Author Autobiography Series*
SATA = *Something about the Author*
WLC = *World Literature Criticism, 1500 to the Present*
YABC = *Yesterday's Authors of Books for Children*

Literary Criticism Series
Cumulative Author Index

A.
See Arnold, Matthew

A. E. .... **TCLC 3, 10**
See also Russell, George William
See also DLB 19

A. M.
See Megged, Aharon

Abasiyanik, Sait Faik 1906-1954
See Sait Faik
See also CA 123

Abbey, Edward 1927-1989 ...... **CLC 36, 59**
See also CA 45-48; 128; CANR 2, 41

Abbott, Lee K(ittredge) 1947- ...... **CLC 48**
See also CA 124; DLB 130

Abe, Kobo 1924-1993 .... **CLC 8, 22, 53**
See also CA 65-68; 140; CANR 24; MTCW

Abelard, Peter c. 1079-c. 1142 ... **CMLC 11**
See also DLB 115

Abell, Kjeld 1901-1961 .... **CLC 15**
See also CA 111

Abish, Walter 1931- .... **CLC 22**
See also CA 101; CANR 37; DLB 130

Abrahams, Peter (Henry) 1919- ..... **CLC 4**
See also BW; CA 57-60; CANR 26;
DLB 117; MTCW

Abrams, M(eyer) H(oward) 1912-... **CLC 24**
See also CA 57-60; CANR 13, 33; DLB 67

Abse, Dannie 1923-............. **CLC 7, 29**
See also CA 53-56; CAAS 1; CANR 4;
DLB 27

Achebe, (Albert) Chinua(lumogu)
1930- ..... **CLC 1, 3, 5, 7, 11, 26, 51, 75**
See also BLC 1; BW; CA 1-4R; CANR 6,
26; CLR 20; DA; DLB 117; MAICYA;
MTCW; SATA 38, 40; WLC

Acker, Kathy 1948- .... **CLC 45**
See also CA 117; 122

Ackroyd, Peter 1949-......... **CLC 34, 52**
See also CA 123; 127

Acorn, Milton 1923-.............. **CLC 15**
See also CA 103; DLB 53

Adamov, Arthur 1908-1970 ...... **CLC 4, 25**
See also CA 17-18; 25-28R; CAP 2; MTCW

Adams, Alice (Boyd) 1926- ... **CLC 6, 13, 46**
See also CA 81-84; CANR 26; DLBY 86;
MTCW

Adams, Douglas (Noel) 1952-... **CLC 27, 60**
See also AAYA 4; BEST 89:3; CA 106;
CANR 34; DLBY 83

Adams, Francis 1862-1893 ...... **NCLC 33**

Adams, Henry (Brooks)
1838-1918 .... **TCLC 4**
See also CA 104; 133; DA; DLB 12, 47

Adams, Richard (George)
1920- .... **CLC 4, 5, 18**
See also AITN 1, 2; CA 49-52; CANR 3,
35; CLR 20; MAICYA; MTCW;
SATA 7, 69

Adamson, Joy(-Friederike Victoria)
1910-1980 .... **CLC 17**
See also CA 69-72; 93-96; CANR 22;
MTCW; SATA 11, 22

Adcock, Fleur 1934-............. **CLC 41**
See also CA 25-28R; CANR 11, 34;
DLB 40

Addams, Charles (Samuel)
1912-1988 .... **CLC 30**
See also CA 61-64; 126; CANR 12

Addison, Joseph 1672-1719 .... **LC 18**
See also CDBLB 1660-1789; DLB 101

Adler, C(arole) S(chwerdtfeger)
1932-....................... **CLC 35**
See also AAYA 4; CA 89-92; CANR 19,
40; MAICYA; SAAS 15; SATA 26, 63

Adler, Renata 1938-............. **CLC 8, 31**
See also CA 49-52; CANR 5, 22; MTCW

Ady, Endre 1877-1919 .... **TCLC 11**
See also CA 107

Aeschylus 525B.C.-456B.C....... **CMLC 11**
See also DA

Afton, Effie
See Harper, Frances Ellen Watkins

Agapida, Fray Antonio
See Irving, Washington

Agee, James (Rufus)
1909-1955 .... **TCLC 1, 19**
See also AITN 1; CA 108;
CDALB 1941-1968; DLB 2, 26

A Gentlewoman in New England
See Bradstreet, Anne

A Gentlewoman in Those Parts
See Bradstreet, Anne

Aghill, Gordon
See Silverberg, Robert

Agnon, S(hmuel) Y(osef Halevi)
1888-1970 .... **CLC 4, 8, 14**
See also CA 17-18; 25-28R; CAP 2; MTCW

Aherne, Owen
See Cassill, R(onald) V(erlin)

Ai 1947-................... **CLC 4, 14, 69**
See also CA 85-88; CAAS 13; DLB 120

Aickman, Robert (Fordyce)
1914-1981 .... **CLC 57**
See also CA 5-8R; CANR 3

Aiken, Conrad (Potter)
1889-1973 ... **CLC 1, 3, 5, 10, 52; SSC 9**
See also CA 5-8R; 45-48; CANR 4;
CDALB 1929-1941; DLB 9, 45, 102;
MTCW; SATA 3, 30

Aiken, Joan (Delano) 1924-........ **CLC 35**
See also AAYA 1; CA 9-12R; CANR 4, 23,
34; CLR 1, 19; MAICYA; MTCW;
SAAS 1; SATA 2, 30, 73

Ainsworth, William Harrison
1805-1882 .... **NCLC 13**
See also DLB 21; SATA 24

Aitmatov, Chingiz (Torekulovich)
1928- .... **CLC 71**
See also CA 103; CANR 38; MTCW;
SATA 56

Akers, Floyd
See Baum, L(yman) Frank

Akhmadulina, Bella Akhatovna
1937-....................... **CLC 53**
See also CA 65-68

Akhmatova, Anna
1888-1966 .... **CLC 11, 25, 64; PC 2**
See also CA 19-20; 25-28R; CANR 35;
CAP 1; MTCW

Aksakov, Sergei Timofeyvich
1791-1859 .... **NCLC 2**

Aksenov, Vassily .... **CLC 22**
See also Aksyonov, Vassily (Pavlovich)

Aksyonov, Vassily (Pavlovich)
1932-....................... **CLC 37**
See also Aksenov, Vassily
See also CA 53-56; CANR 12

Akutagawa Ryunosuke
1892-1927 .... **TCLC 16**
See also CA 117

Alain 1868-1951 .... **TCLC 41**

Alain-Fournier................... **TCLC 6**
See also Fournier, Henri Alban
See also DLB 65

Alarcon, Pedro Antonio de
1833-1891 .... **NCLC 1**

Alas (y Urena), Leopoldo (Enrique Garcia)
1852-1901 .... **TCLC 29**
See also CA 113; 131; HW

Albee, Edward (Franklin III)
1928-... **CLC 1, 2, 3, 5, 9, 11, 13, 25, 53**
See also AITN 1; CA 5-8R; CABS 3;
CANR 8; CDALB 1941-1968; DA;
DLB 7; MTCW; WLC

Alberti, Rafael 1902-.............. **CLC 7**
See also CA 85-88; DLB 108

Alcala-Galiano, Juan Valera y
See Valera y Alcala-Galiano, Juan

Alcott, Amos Bronson 1799-1888 .. **NCLC 1**
See also DLB 1

Alcott, Louisa May 1832-1888 .... **NCLC 6**
See also CDALB 1865-1917; CLR 1; DA;
DLB 1, 42, 79; MAICYA; WLC;
YABC 1

Aldanov, M. A.
See Aldanov, Mark (Alexandrovich)

Aldanov, Mark (Alexandrovich)
1886(?)-1957 . . . . **TCLC 23**
See also CA 118

Aldington, Richard 1892-1962 . . . . . . **CLC 49**
See also CA 85-88; DLB 20, 36, 100

Aldiss, Brian W(ilson)
1925- . . . . **CLC 5, 14, 40**
See also CA 5-8R; CAAS 2; CANR 5, 28;
DLB 14; MTCW; SATA 34

Alegria, Claribel 1924- . . . . **CLC 75**
See also CA 131; CAAS 15; HW

Alegria, Fernando 1918- . . . . **CLC 57**
See also CA 9-12R; CANR 5, 32; HW

Aleichem, Sholom . . . . **TCLC 1, 35**
See also Rabinovitch, Sholem

Aleixandre, Vicente 1898-1984 . . . **CLC 9, 36**
See also CA 85-88; 114; CANR 26;
DLB 108; HW; MTCW

Alepoudelis, Odysseus
See Elytis, Odysseus

Aleshkovsky, Joseph 1929-
See Aleshkovsky, Yuz
See also CA 121; 128

Aleshkovsky, Yuz . . . . **CLC 44**
See also Aleshkovsky, Joseph

Alexander, Lloyd (Chudley) 1924- . . **CLC 35**
See also AAYA 1; CA 1-4R; CANR 1, 24,
38; CLR 1, 5; DLB 52; MAICYA;
MTCW; SATA 3, 49

Alfau, Felipe 1902- . . . . **CLC 66**
See also CA 137

Alger, Horatio, Jr. 1832-1899 . . . . . **NCLC 8**
See also DLB 42; SATA 16

Algren, Nelson 1909-1981 . . . . **CLC 4, 10, 33**
See also CA 13-16R; 103; CANR 20;
CDALB 1941-1968; DLB 9; DLBY 81,
82; MTCW

Ali, Ahmed 1910- . . . . **CLC 69**
See also CA 25-28R; CANR 15, 34

Alighieri, Dante 1265-1321 . . . . **CMLC 3**

Allan, John B.
See Westlake, Donald E(dwin)

Allen, Edward 1948- . . . . **CLC 59**

Allen, Roland
See Ayckbourn, Alan

Allen, Woody 1935- . . . . **CLC 16, 52**
See also AAYA 10; CA 33-36R; CANR 27,
38; DLB 44; MTCW

Allende, Isabel 1942- . . . . **CLC 39, 57**
See also CA 125; 130; HW; MTCW

Alleyn, Ellen
See Rossetti, Christina (Georgina)

Allingham, Margery (Louise)
1904-1966 . . . . **CLC 19**
See also CA 5-8R; 25-28R; CANR 4;
DLB 77; MTCW

Allingham, William 1824-1889 . . . **NCLC 25**
See also DLB 35

Allston, Washington 1779-1843 . . . . **NCLC 2**
See also DLB 1

Almedingen, E. M. . . . . **CLC 12**
See also Almedingen, Martha Edith von
See also SATA 3

Almedingen, Martha Edith von 1898-1971
See Almedingen, E. M.
See also CA 1-4R; CANR 1

Alonso, Damaso 1898-1990 . . . . **CLC 14**
See also CA 110; 131; 130; DLB 108; HW

Alov
See Gogol, Nikolai (Vasilyevich)

Alta 1942- . . . . **CLC 19**
See also CA 57-60

Alter, Robert B(ernard) 1935- . . . . . . **CLC 34**
See also CA 49-52; CANR 1

Alther, Lisa 1944- . . . . **CLC 7, 41**
See also CA 65-68; CANR 12, 30; MTCW

Altman, Robert 1925- . . . . **CLC 16**
See also CA 73-76

Alvarez, A(lfred) 1929- . . . . **CLC 5, 13**
See also CA 1-4R; CANR 3, 33; DLB 14,
40

Alvarez, Alejandro Rodriguez 1903-1965
See Casona, Alejandro
See also CA 131; 93-96; HW

Amado, Jorge 1912- . . . . **CLC 13, 40**
See also CA 77-80; CANR 35; DLB 113;
MTCW

Ambler, Eric 1909- . . . . **CLC 4, 6, 9**
See also CA 9-12R; CANR 7, 38; DLB 77;
MTCW

Amichai, Yehuda 1924- . . . . . . **CLC 9, 22, 57**
See also CA 85-88; MTCW

Amiel, Henri Frederic 1821-1881 . . **NCLC 4**

Amis, Kingsley (William)
1922- . . . . . . **CLC 1, 2, 3, 5, 8, 13, 40, 44**
See also AITN 2; CA 9-12R; CANR 8, 28;
CDBLB 1945-1960; DA; DLB 15, 27,
100; MTCW

Amis, Martin (Louis)
1949- . . . . **CLC 4, 9, 38, 62**
See also BEST 90:3; CA 65-68; CANR 8,
27; DLB 14

Ammons, A(rchie) R(andolph)
1926- . . . . **CLC 2, 3, 5, 8, 9, 25, 57**
See also AITN 1; CA 9-12R; CANR 6, 36;
DLB 5; MTCW

Amo, Tauraatua i
See Adams, Henry (Brooks)

Anand, Mulk Raj 1905- . . . . **CLC 23**
See also CA 65-68; CANR 32; MTCW

Anatol
See Schnitzler, Arthur

Anaya, Rudolfo A(lfonso) 1937- . . . . **CLC 23**
See also CA 45-48; CAAS 4; CANR 1, 32;
DLB 82; HW; MTCW

Andersen, Hans Christian
1805-1875 . . . . **NCLC 7; SSC 6**
See also CLR 6; DA; MAICYA; WLC;
YABC 1

Anderson, C. Farley
See Mencken, H(enry) L(ouis); Nathan,
George Jean

Anderson, Jessica (Margaret) Queale
. . . . **CLC 37**
See also CA 9-12R; CANR 4

Anderson, Jon (Victor) 1940- . . . . **CLC 9**
See also CA 25-28R; CANR 20

Anderson, Lindsay (Gordon)
1923- . . . . **CLC 20**
See also CA 125; 128

Anderson, Maxwell 1888-1959 . . . . . **TCLC 2**
See also CA 105; DLB 7

Anderson, Poul (William) 1926- . . . . **CLC 15**
See also AAYA 5; CA 1-4R; CAAS 2;
CANR 2, 15, 34; DLB 8; MTCW;
SATA 39

Anderson, Robert (Woodruff)
1917- . . . . **CLC 23**
See also AITN 1; CA 21-24R; CANR 32;
DLB 7

Anderson, Sherwood
1876-1941 . . . . . . **TCLC 1, 10, 24; SSC 1**
See also CA 104; 121; CDALB 1917-1929;
DA; DLB 4, 9, 86; DLBD 1; MTCW;
WLC

Andouard
See Giraudoux, (Hippolyte) Jean

Andrade, Carlos Drummond de . . . . . . **CLC 18**
See also Drummond de Andrade, Carlos

Andrade, Mario de 1893-1945 . . . . . **TCLC 43**

Andrewes, Lancelot 1555-1626 . . . . **LC 5**

Andrews, Cicily Fairfield
See West, Rebecca

Andrews, Elton V.
See Pohl, Frederik

Andreyev, Leonid (Nikolaevich)
1871-1919 . . . . **TCLC 3**
See also CA 104

Andric, Ivo 1892-1975 . . . . **CLC 8**
See also CA 81-84; 57-60; MTCW

Angelique, Pierre
See Bataille, Georges

Angell, Roger 1920- . . . . **CLC 26**
See also CA 57-60; CANR 13

Angelou, Maya 1928- . . . . **CLC 12, 35, 64, 77**
See also AAYA 7; BLC 1; BW; CA 65-68;
CANR 19; DA; DLB 38; MTCW;
SATA 49

Annensky, Innokenty Fyodorovich
1856-1909 . . . . **TCLC 14**
See also CA 110

Anon, Charles Robert
See Pessoa, Fernando (Antonio Nogueira)

Anouilh, Jean (Marie Lucien Pierre)
1910-1987 . . . . . . **CLC 1, 3, 8, 13, 40, 50**
See also CA 17-20R; 123; CANR 32;
MTCW

Anthony, Florence
See Ai

Anthony, John
See Ciardi, John (Anthony)

Anthony, Peter
See Shaffer, Anthony (Joshua); Shaffer,
Peter (Levin)

Anthony, Piers 1934- . . . . **CLC 35**
See also CA 21-24R; CANR 28; DLB 8;
MTCW

Antoine, Marc
See Proust,
(Valentin-Louis-George-Eugene-)Marcel

Antoninus, Brother
See Everson, William (Oliver)

Antonioni, Michelangelo 1912- ..... **CLC 20**
See also CA 73-76

Antschel, Paul 1920-1970...... **CLC 10, 19**
See also Celan, Paul
See also CA 85-88; CANR 33; MTCW

Anwar, Chairil 1922-1949 .... **TCLC 22**
See also CA 121

Apollinaire, Guillaume .... **TCLC 3, 8**
See also Kostrowitzki, Wilhelm Apollinaris
de

Appelfeld, Aharon 1932- ...... **CLC 23, 47**
See also CA 112; 133

Apple, Max (Isaac) 1941-....... **CLC 9, 33**
See also CA 81-84; CANR 19; DLB 130

Appleman, Philip (Dean) 1926-.... **CLC 51**
See also CA 13-16R; CANR 6, 29

Appleton, Lawrence
See Lovecraft, H(oward) P(hillips)

Apteryx
See Eliot, T(homas) S(tearns)

Apuleius, (Lucius Madaurensis)
125(?)-175(?) .... **CMLC 1**

Aquin, Hubert 1929-1977......... **CLC 15**
See also CA 105; DLB 53

Aragon, Louis 1897-1982....... **CLC 3, 22**
See also CA 69-72; 108; CANR 28;
DLB 72; MTCW

Arany, Janos 1817-1882........ **NCLC 34**

Arbuthnot, John 1667-1735......... **LC 1**
See also DLB 101

Archer, Herbert Winslow
See Mencken, H(enry) L(ouis)

Archer, Jeffrey (Howard) 1940- .... **CLC 28**
See also BEST 89:3; CA 77-80; CANR 22

Archer, Jules 1915- .... **CLC 12**
See also CA 9-12R; CANR 6; SAAS 5;
SATA 4

Archer, Lee
See Ellison, Harlan

Arden, John 1930- .... **CLC 6, 13, 15**
See also CA 13-16R; CAAS 4; CANR 31;
DLB 13; MTCW

Arenas, Reinaldo 1943-1990 .... **CLC 41**
See also CA 124; 128; 133; HW

Arendt, Hannah 1906-1975 .... **CLC 66**
See also CA 17-20R; 61-64; CANR 26;
MTCW

Aretino, Pietro 1492-1556 .... **LC 12**

Arguedas, Jose Maria
1911-1969 .... **CLC 10, 18**
See also CA 89-92; DLB 113; HW

Argueta, Manlio 1936-............ **CLC 31**
See also CA 131; HW

Ariosto, Ludovico 1474-1533........ **LC 6**

Aristides
See Epstein, Joseph

Aristophanes
450B.C.-385B.C........ **CMLC 4; DC 2**
See also DA

Arlt, Roberto (Godofredo Christophersen)
1900-1942 .... **TCLC 29**
See also CA 123; 131; HW

Armah, Ayi Kwei 1939-......... **CLC 5, 33**
See also BLC 1; BW; CA 61-64; CANR 21;
DLB 117; MTCW

Armatrading, Joan 1950-......... **CLC 17**
See also CA 114

Arnette, Robert
See Silverberg, Robert

Arnim, Achim von (Ludwig Joachim von
Arnim) 1781-1831 .... **NCLC 5**
See also DLB 90

Arnim, Bettina von 1785-1859.... **NCLC 38**
See also DLB 90

Arnold, Matthew
1822-1888 .... **NCLC 6, 29; PC 5**
See also CDBLB 1832-1890; DA; DLB 32,
57; WLC

Arnold, Thomas 1795-1842 ...... **NCLC 18**
See also DLB 55

Arnow, Harriette (Louisa) Simpson
1908-1986 .... **CLC 2, 7, 18**
See also CA 9-12R; 118; CANR 14; DLB 6;
MTCW; SATA 42, 47

Arp, Hans
See Arp, Jean

Arp, Jean 1887-1966.............. **CLC 5**
See also CA 81-84; 25-28R

Arrabal
See Arrabal, Fernando

Arrabal, Fernando 1932- ... **CLC 2, 9, 18, 58**
See also CA 9-12R; CANR 15

Arrick, Fran.................... CLC 30

Artaud, Antonin 1896-1948 ..... **TCLC 3, 36**
See also CA 104

Arthur, Ruth M(abel) 1905-1979.... **CLC 12**
See also CA 9-12R; 85-88; CANR 4;
SATA 7, 26

Artsybashev, Mikhail (Petrovich)
1878-1927 .... **TCLC 31**

Arundel, Honor (Morfydd)
1919-1973 .... **CLC 17**
See also CA 21-22; 41-44R; CAP 2;
SATA 4, 24

Asch, Sholem 1880-1957 .... **TCLC 3**
See also CA 105

Ash, Shalom
See Asch, Sholem

Ashbery, John (Lawrence)
1927- ..... **CLC 2, 3, 4, 6, 9, 13, 15, 25,**
41, 77
See also CA 5-8R; CANR 9, 37; DLB 5;
DLBY 81; MTCW

Ashdown, Clifford
See Freeman, R(ichard) Austin

Ashe, Gordon
See Creasey, John

Ashton-Warner, Sylvia (Constance)
1908-1984 .... **CLC 19**
See also CA 69-72; 112; CANR 29; MTCW

Asimov, Isaac
1920-1992 ...... **CLC 1, 3, 9, 19, 26, 76**
See also BEST 90:2; CA 1-4R; 137;
CANR 2, 19, 36; CLR 12; DLB 8;
DLBY 92; MAICYA; MTCW; SATA 1,
26, 74

Astley, Thea (Beatrice May)
1925-....................... **CLC 41**
See also CA 65-68; CANR 11

Aston, James
See White, T(erence) H(anbury)

Asturias, Miguel Angel
1899-1974 .... **CLC 3, 8, 13**
See also CA 25-28; 49-52; CANR 32;
CAP 2; DLB 113; HW; MTCW

Atares, Carlos Saura
See Saura (Atares), Carlos

Atheling, William
See Pound, Ezra (Weston Loomis)

Atheling, William, Jr.
See Blish, James (Benjamin)

Atherton, Gertrude (Franklin Horn)
1857-1948 .... **TCLC 2**
See also CA 104; DLB 9, 78

Atherton, Lucius
See Masters, Edgar Lee

Atkins, Jack
See Harris, Mark

Atticus
See Fleming, Ian (Lancaster)

Atwood, Margaret (Eleanor)
1939- .... **CLC 2, 3, 4, 8, 13, 15, 25, 44;**
SSC 2
See also BEST 89:2; CA 49-52; CANR 3,
24, 33; DA; DLB 53; MTCW; SATA 50;
WLC

Aubigny, Pierre d'
See Mencken, H(enry) L(ouis)

Aubin, Penelope 1685-1731(?)........ **LC 9**
See also DLB 39

Auchincloss, Louis (Stanton)
1917- .... **CLC 4, 6, 9, 18, 45**
See also CA 1-4R; CANR 6, 29; DLB 2;
DLBY 80; MTCW

Auden, W(ystan) H(ugh)
1907-1973 ..... **CLC 1, 2, 3, 4, 6, 9, 11,**
14, 43; PC 1
See also CA 9-12R; 45-48; CANR 5;
CDBLB 1914-1945; DA; DLB 10, 20;
MTCW; WLC

Audiberti, Jacques 1900-1965 ...... **CLC 38**
See also CA 25-28R

Auel, Jean M(arie) 1936-.......... **CLC 31**
See also AAYA 7; BEST 90:4; CA 103;
CANR 21

Auerbach, Erich 1892-1957 .... **TCLC 43**
See also CA 118

Augier, Emile 1820-1889 .... **NCLC 31**

August, John
See De Voto, Bernard (Augustine)

Augustine, St. 354-430........... **CMLC 6**

Aurelius
See Bourne, Randolph S(illiman)

Austen, Jane
1775-1817 . . . . **NCLC 1, 13, 19, 33**
See also CDBLB 1789-1832; DA; DLB 116;
WLC

Auster, Paul 1947- . . . . **CLC 47**
See also CA 69-72; CANR 23

Austin, Frank
See Faust, Frederick (Schiller)

Austin, Mary (Hunter)
1868-1934 . . . . **TCLC 25**
See also CA 109; DLB 9, 78

Autran Dourado, Waldomiro
See Dourado, (Waldomiro Freitas) Autran

Averroes 1126-1198 . . . . **CMLC 7**
See also DLB 115

Avison, Margaret 1918- . . . . **CLC 2, 4**
See also CA 17-20R; DLB 53; MTCW

Ayckbourn, Alan
1939- . . . . **CLC 5, 8, 18, 33, 74**
See also CA 21-24R; CANR 31; DLB 13;
MTCW

Aydy, Catherine
See Tennant, Emma (Christina)

Ayme, Marcel (Andre) 1902-1967 . . . **CLC 11**
See also CA 89-92; CLR 25; DLB 72

Ayrton, Michael 1921-1975 . . . . **CLC 7**
See also CA 5-8R; 61-64; CANR 9, 21

Azorin . . . . **CLC 11**
See also Martinez Ruiz, Jose

Azuela, Mariano 1873-1952 . . . . **TCLC 3**
See also CA 104; 131; HW; MTCW

Baastad, Babbis Friis
See Friis-Baastad, Babbis Ellinor

Bab
See Gilbert, W(illiam) S(chwenck)

Babbis, Eleanor
See Friis-Baastad, Babbis Ellinor

Babel, Isaak (Emmanuilovich)
1894-1941(?) . . . . **CLC 73**
See also CA 104; TCLC 2, 13

Babits, Mihaly 1883-1941 . . . . **TCLC 14**
See also CA 114

Babur 1483-1530 . . . . **LC 18**

Bacchelli, Riccardo 1891-1985 . . . . . **CLC 19**
See also CA 29-32R; 117

Bach, Richard (David) 1936- . . . . **CLC 14**
See also AITN 1; BEST 89:2; CA 9-12R;
CANR 18; MTCW; SATA 13

Bachman, Richard
See King, Stephen (Edwin)

Bachmann, Ingeborg 1926-1973 . . . . . **CLC 69**
See also CA 93-96; 45-48; DLB 85

Bacon, Francis 1561-1626 . . . . **LC 18**
See also CDBLB Before 1660

Bacovia, George . . . . **TCLC 24**
See also Vasiliu, Gheorghe

Badanes, Jerome 1937- . . . . **CLC 59**

Bagehot, Walter 1826-1877 . . . . . . **NCLC 10**
See also DLB 55

Bagnold, Enid 1889-1981 . . . . **CLC 25**
See also CA 5-8R; 103; CANR 5, 40;
DLB 13; MAICYA; SATA 1, 25

Bagrjana, Elisaveta
See Belcheva, Elisaveta

Bagryana, Elisaveta
See Belcheva, Elisaveta

Bailey, Paul 1937- . . . . **CLC 45**
See also CA 21-24R; CANR 16; DLB 14

Baillie, Joanna 1762-1851 . . . . **NCLC 2**
See also DLB 93

Bainbridge, Beryl (Margaret)
1933- . . . . **CLC 4, 5, 8, 10, 14, 18, 22, 62**
See also CA 21-24R; CANR 24; DLB 14;
MTCW

Baker, Elliott 1922- . . . . **CLC 8**
See also CA 45-48; CANR 2

Baker, Nicholson 1957- . . . . **CLC 61**
See also CA 135

Baker, Ray Stannard 1870-1946 . . . **TCLC 47**
See also CA 118

Baker, Russell (Wayne) 1925- . . . . . . **CLC 31**
See also BEST 89:4; CA 57-60; CANR 11,
41; MTCW

Bakshi, Ralph 1938(?)- . . . . **CLC 26**
See also CA 112; 138

Bakunin, Mikhail (Alexandrovich)
1814-1876 . . . . **NCLC 25**

Baldwin, James (Arthur)
1924-1987 . . . . . **CLC 1, 2, 3, 4, 5, 8, 13,**
15, 17, 42, 50, 67; DC 1; SSC 10
See also AAYA 4; BLC 1; BW; CA 1-4R;
124; CABS 1; CANR 3, 24;
CDALB 1941-1968; DA; DLB 2, 7, 33;
DLBY 87; MTCW; SATA 9, 54; WLC

Ballard, J(ames) G(raham)
1930- . . . . **CLC 3, 6, 14, 36; SSC 1**
See also AAYA 3; CA 5-8R; CANR 15, 39;
DLB 14; MTCW

Balmont, Konstantin (Dmitriyevich)
1867-1943 . . . . **TCLC 11**
See also CA 109

Balzac, Honore de
1799-1850 . . . . **NCLC 5, 35; SSC 5**
See also DA; DLB 119; WLC

Bambara, Toni Cade 1939- . . . . **CLC 19**
See also AAYA 5; BLC 1; BW; CA 29-32R;
CANR 24; DA; DLB 38; MTCW

Bamdad, A.
See Shamlu, Ahmad

Banat, D. R.
See Bradbury, Ray (Douglas)

Bancroft, Laura
See Baum, L(yman) Frank

Banim, John 1798-1842 . . . . **NCLC 13**
See also DLB 116

Banim, Michael 1796-1874 . . . . . . **NCLC 13**

Banks, Iain
See Banks, Iain M(enzies)

Banks, Iain M(enzies) 1954- . . . . **CLC 34**
See also CA 123; 128

Banks, Lynne Reid . . . . **CLC 23**
See also Reid Banks, Lynne
See also AAYA 6

Banks, Russell 1940- . . . . **CLC 37, 72**
See also CA 65-68; CAAS 15; CANR 19;
DLB 130

Banville, John 1945- . . . . **CLC 46**
See also CA 117; 128; DLB 14

Banville, Theodore (Faullain) de
1832-1891 . . . . **NCLC 9**

Baraka, Amiri
1934- . . . **CLC 1, 2, 3, 5, 10, 14, 33; PC 4**
See also Jones, LeRoi
See also BLC 1; BW; CA 21-24R; CABS 3;
CANR 27, 38; CDALB 1941-1968; DA;
DLB 5, 7, 16, 38; DLBD 8; MTCW

Barbellion, W. N. P. . . . . **TCLC 24**
See also Cummings, Bruce F(rederick)

Barbera, Jack 1945- . . . . **CLC 44**
See also CA 110

Barbey d'Aurevilly, Jules Amedee
1808-1889 . . . . **NCLC 1**
See also DLB 119

Barbusse, Henri 1873-1935 . . . . **TCLC 5**
See also CA 105; DLB 65

Barclay, Bill
See Moorcock, Michael (John)

Barclay, William Ewert
See Moorcock, Michael (John)

Barea, Arturo 1897-1957 . . . . **TCLC 14**
See also CA 111

Barfoot, Joan 1946- . . . . **CLC 18**
See also CA 105

Baring, Maurice 1874-1945 . . . . **TCLC 8**
See also CA 105; DLB 34

Barker, Clive 1952- . . . . **CLC 52**
See also AAYA 10; BEST 90:3; CA 121;
129; MTCW

Barker, George Granville
1913-1991 . . . . **CLC 8, 48**
See also CA 9-12R; 135; CANR 7, 38;
DLB 20; MTCW

Barker, Harley Granville
See Granville-Barker, Harley
See also DLB 10

Barker, Howard 1946- . . . . **CLC 37**
See also CA 102; DLB 13

Barker, Pat 1943- . . . . **CLC 32**
See also CA 117; 122

Barlow, Joel 1754-1812 . . . . **NCLC 23**
See also DLB 37

Barnard, Mary (Ethel) 1909- . . . . **CLC 48**
See also CA 21-22; CAP 2

Barnes, Djuna
1892-1982 . . . **CLC 3, 4, 8, 11, 29; SSC 3**
See also CA 9-12R; 107; CANR 16; DLB 4,
9, 45; MTCW

Barnes, Julian 1946- . . . . **CLC 42**
See also CA 102; CANR 19

Barnes, Peter 1931- . . . . **CLC 5, 56**
See also CA 65-68; CAAS 12; CANR 33,
34; DLB 13; MTCW

Baroja (y Nessi), Pio 1872-1956 . . . . **TCLC 8**
See also CA 104

Baron, David
See Pinter, Harold

Baron Corvo
See Rolfe, Frederick (William Serafino
Austin Lewis Mary)

Barondess, Sue K(aufman)
1926-1977 .... **CLC 8**
See also Kaufman, Sue
See also CA 1-4R; 69-72; CANR 1

Baron de Teive
See Pessoa, Fernando (Antonio Nogueira)

Barres, Maurice 1862-1923 .... **TCLC 47**
See also DLB 123

Barreto, Afonso Henrique de Lima
See Lima Barreto, Afonso Henrique de

Barrett, (Roger) Syd 1946- .... **CLC 35**
See also Pink Floyd

Barrett, William (Christopher)
1913-1992 .... **CLC 27**
See also CA 13-16R; 139; CANR 11

Barrie, J(ames) M(atthew)
1860-1937 .... **TCLC 2**
See also CA 104; 136; CDBLB 1890-1914;
CLR 16; DLB 10; MAICYA; YABC 1

Barrington, Michael
See Moorcock, Michael (John)

Barrol, Grady
See Bograd, Larry

Barry, Mike
See Malzberg, Barry N(athaniel)

Barry, Philip 1896-1949 .... **TCLC 11**
See also CA 109; DLB 7

Bart, Andre Schwarz
See Schwarz-Bart, Andre

Barth, John (Simmons)
1930- ...... **CLC 1, 2, 3, 5, 7, 9, 10, 14,
27, 51; SSC 10**
See also AITN 1, 2; CA 1-4R; CABS 1;
CANR 5, 23; DLB 2; MTCW

Barthelme, Donald
1931-1989 ..... **CLC 1, 2, 3, 5, 6, 8, 13,
23, 46, 59; SSC 2**
See also CA 21-24R; 129; CANR 20;
DLB 2; DLBY 80, 89; MTCW; SATA 7,
62

Barthelme, Frederick 1943-........ **CLC 36**
See also CA 114; 122; DLBY 85

Barthes, Roland (Gerard)
1915-1980 .... **CLC 24**
See also CA 130; 97-100; MTCW

Barzun, Jacques (Martin) 1907- .... **CLC 51**
See also CA 61-64; CANR 22

Bashevis, Isaac
See Singer, Isaac Bashevis

Bashkirtseff, Marie 1859-1884 ... **NCLC 27**

Basho
See Matsuo Basho

Bass, Kingsley B., Jr.
See Bullins, Ed

Bassani, Giorgio 1916-............. **CLC 9**
See also CA 65-68; CANR 33; DLB 128;
MTCW

Bastos, Augusto (Antonio) Roa
See Roa Bastos, Augusto (Antonio)

Bataille, Georges 1897-1962 .... **CLC 29**
See also CA 101; 89-92

Bates, H(erbert) E(rnest)
1905-1974 .... **CLC 46; SSC 10**
See also CA 93-96; 45-48; CANR 34;
MTCW

Bauchart
See Camus, Albert

Baudelaire, Charles
1821-1867 .... **NCLC 6, 29; PC 1**
See also DA; WLC

Baudrillard, Jean 1929-............ **CLC 60**

Baum, L(yman) Frank 1856-1919 ... **TCLC 7**
See also CA 108; 133; CLR 15; DLB 22;
MAICYA; MTCW; SATA 18

Baum, Louis F.
See Baum, L(yman) Frank

Baumbach, Jonathan 1933-...... **CLC 6, 23**
See also CA 13-16R; CAAS 5; CANR 12;
DLBY 80; MTCW

Bausch, Richard (Carl) 1945- ...... **CLC 51**
See also CA 101; CAAS 14; DLB 130

Baxter, Charles 1947-......... **CLC 45, 77**
See also CA 57-60; CANR 40; DLB 130

Baxter, George Owen
See Faust, Frederick (Schiller)

Baxter, James K(eir) 1926-1972 .... **CLC 14**
See also CA 77-80

Baxter, John
See Hunt, E(verette) Howard, Jr.

Bayer, Sylvia
See Glassco, John

Beagle, Peter S(oyer) 1939-........ **CLC 7**
See also CA 9-12R; CANR 4; DLBY 80;
SATA 60

Bean, Normal
See Burroughs, Edgar Rice

Beard, Charles A(ustin)
1874-1948 .... **TCLC 15**
See also CA 115; DLB 17; SATA 18

Beardsley, Aubrey 1872-1898 ..... **NCLC 6**

Beattie, Ann
1947- .... **CLC 8, 13, 18, 40, 63; SSC 11**
See also BEST 90:2; CA 81-84; DLBY 82;
MTCW

Beattie, James 1735-1803 .... **NCLC 25**
See also DLB 109

Beauchamp, Kathleen Mansfield 1888-1923
See Mansfield, Katherine
See also CA 104; 134; DA

**Beauvoir, Simone (Lucie Ernestine Marie
Bertrand) de**
1908-1986 ... **CLC 1, 2, 4, 8, 14, 31, 44,
50, 71**
See also CA 9-12R; 118; CANR 28; DA;
DLB 72; DLBY 86; MTCW; WLC

Becker, Jurek 1937-............. **CLC 7, 19**
See also CA 85-88; DLB 75

Becker, Walter 1950-............. **CLC 26**

Beckett, Samuel (Barclay)
1906-1989 ..... **CLC 1, 2, 3, 4, 6, 9, 10,
11, 14, 18, 29, 57, 59**
See also CA 5-8R; 130; CANR 33;
CDBLB 1945-1960; DA; DLB 13, 15;
DLBY 90; MTCW; WLC

Beckford, William 1760-1844 .... **NCLC 16**
See also DLB 39

Beckman, Gunnel 1910-.......... **CLC 26**
See also CA 33-36R; CANR 15; CLR 25;
MAICYA; SAAS 9; SATA 6

Becque, Henri 1837-1899........ **NCLC 3**

Beddoes, Thomas Lovell
1803-1849 .... **NCLC 3**
See also DLB 96

Bedford, Donald F.
See Fearing, Kenneth (Flexner)

Beecher, Catharine Esther
1800-1878 .... **NCLC 30**
See also DLB 1

Beecher, John 1904-1980.......... **CLC 6**
See also AITN 1; CA 5-8R; 105; CANR 8

Beer, Johann 1655-1700............ **LC 5**

Beer, Patricia 1924-.............. **CLC 58**
See also CA 61-64; CANR 13; DLB 40

Beerbohm, Henry Maximilian
1872-1956 .... **TCLC 1, 24**
See also CA 104; DLB 34, 100

Begiebing, Robert J(ohn) 1946-..... **CLC 70**
See also CA 122; CANR 40

Behan, Brendan
1923-1964 .... **CLC 1, 8, 11, 15**
See also CA 73-76; CANR 33;
CDBLB 1945-1960; DLB 13; MTCW

Behn, Aphra 1640(?)-1689 .... **LC 1**
See also DA; DLB 39, 80, 131; WLC

Behrman, S(amuel) N(athaniel)
1893-1973 .... **CLC 40**
See also CA 13-16; 45-48; CAP 1; DLB 7,
44

Belasco, David 1853-1931 .... **TCLC 3**
See also CA 104; DLB 7

Belcheva, Elisaveta 1893- .... **CLC 10**

Beldone, Phil "Cheech"
See Ellison, Harlan

Beleno
See Azuela, Mariano

Belinski, Vissarion Grigoryevich
1811-1848 .... **NCLC 5**

Belitt, Ben 1911-................. **CLC 22**
See also CA 13-16R; CAAS 4; CANR 7;
DLB 5

Bell, James Madison 1826-1902 ... **TCLC 43**
See also BLC 1; BW; CA 122; 124; DLB 50

Bell, Madison (Smartt) 1957- ...... **CLC 41**
See also CA 111; CANR 28

Bell, Marvin (Hartley) 1937-..... **CLC 8, 31**
See also CA 21-24R; CAAS 14; DLB 5;
MTCW

Bell, W. L. D.
See Mencken, H(enry) L(ouis)

Bellamy, Atwood C.
See Mencken, H(enry) L(ouis)

Bellamy, Edward 1850-1898 ...... **NCLC 4**
See also DLB 12

Bellin, Edward J.
See Kuttner, Henry

Bierce, Ambrose (Gwinett)
1842-1914(?) ..... **TCLC 1, 7, 44; SSC 9**
See also CA 104; 139; CDALB 1865-1917;
DA; DLB 11, 12, 23, 71, 74; WLC

Billings, Josh
See Shaw, Henry Wheeler

Billington, Rachel 1942-.......... **CLC 43**
See also AITN 2; CA 33-36R

Binyon, T(imothy) J(ohn) 1936- .... **CLC 34**
See also CA 111; CANR 28

Bioy Casares, Adolfo 1914-.... **CLC 4, 8, 13**
See also CA 29-32R; CANR 19; DLB 113;
HW; MTCW

Bird, C.
See Ellison, Harlan

Bird, Cordwainer
See Ellison, Harlan

Bird, Robert Montgomery
1806-1854 .... **NCLC 1**

Birney, (Alfred) Earle
1904- .... **CLC 1, 4, 6, 11**
See also CA 1-4R; CANR 5, 20; DLB 88;
MTCW

Bishop, Elizabeth
1911-1979 ..... **CLC 1, 4, 9, 13, 15, 32;
PC 3**
See also CA 5-8R; 89-92; CABS 2;
CANR 26; CDALB 1968-1988; DA;
DLB 5; MTCW; SATA 24

Bishop, John 1935-.............. **CLC 10**
See also CA 105

Bissett, Bill 1939-................. **CLC 18**
See also CA 69-72; CANR 15; DLB 53;
MTCW

Bitov, Andrei (Georgievich) 1937-... **CLC 57**

Biyidi, Alexandre 1932-
See Beti, Mongo
See also BW; CA 114; 124; MTCW

Bjarme, Brynjolf
See Ibsen, Henrik (Johan)

Bjornson, Bjornstjerne (Martinius)
1832-1910 .... **TCLC 7, 37**
See also CA 104

Black, Robert
See Holdstock, Robert P.

Blackburn, Paul 1926-1971 ...... **CLC 9, 43**
See also CA 81-84; 33-36R; CANR 34;
DLB 16; DLBY 81

Black Elk 1863-1950 .... **TCLC 33**

Black Hobart
See Sanders, (James) Ed(ward)

Blacklin, Malcolm
See Chambers, Aidan

Blackmore, R(ichard) D(oddridge)
1825-1900 .... **TCLC 27**
See also CA 120; DLB 18

Blackmur, R(ichard) P(almer)
1904-1965 .... **CLC 2, 24**
See also CA 11-12; 25-28R; CAP 1; DLB 63

Black Tarantula, The
See Acker, Kathy

Blackwood, Algernon (Henry)
1869-1951 .... **TCLC 5**
See also CA 105

Blackwood, Caroline 1931- .... **CLC 6, 9**
See also CA 85-88; CANR 32; DLB 14;
MTCW

Blade, Alexander
See Hamilton, Edmond; Silverberg, Robert

Blaga, Lucian 1895-1961 .... **CLC 75**

Blair, Eric (Arthur) 1903-1950
See Orwell, George
See also CA 104; 132; DA; MTCW;
SATA 29

Blais, Marie-Claire
1939- .... **CLC 2, 4, 6, 13, 22**
See also CA 21-24R; CAAS 4; CANR 38;
DLB 53; MTCW

Blaise, Clark 1940-.............. **CLC 29**
See also AITN 2; CA 53-56; CAAS 3;
CANR 5; DLB 53

Blake, Nicholas
See Day Lewis, C(ecil)
See also DLB 77

Blake, William 1757-1827 .... **NCLC 13**
See also CDBLB 1789-1832; DA; DLB 93;
MAICYA; SATA 30; WLC

Blasco Ibanez, Vicente
1867-1928 .... **TCLC 12**
See also CA 110; 131; HW; MTCW

Blatty, William Peter 1928-........ **CLC 2**
See also CA 5-8R; CANR 9

Bleeck, Oliver
See Thomas, Ross (Elmore)

Blessing, Lee 1949-.............. **CLC 54**

Blish, James (Benjamin)
1921-1975 .... **CLC 14**
See also CA 1-4R; 57-60; CANR 3; DLB 8;
MTCW; SATA 66

Bliss, Reginald
See Wells, H(erbert) G(eorge)

Blixen, Karen (Christentze Dinesen)
1885-1962
See Dinesen, Isak
See also CA 25-28; CANR 22; CAP 2;
MTCW; SATA 44

Bloch, Robert (Albert) 1917-....... **CLC 33**
See also CA 5-8R; CANR 5; DLB 44;
SATA 12

Blok, Alexander (Alexandrovich)
1880-1921 .... **TCLC 5**
See also CA 104

Blom, Jan
See Breytenbach, Breyten

Bloom, Harold 1930- .... **CLC 24**
See also CA 13-16R; CANR 39; DLB 67

Bloomfield, Aurelius
See Bourne, Randolph S(illiman)

Blount, Roy (Alton), Jr. 1941- ..... **CLC 38**
See also CA 53-56; CANR 10, 28; MTCW

Bloy, Leon 1846-1917............ **TCLC 22**
See also CA 121; DLB 123

Blume, Judy (Sussman) 1938-... **CLC 12, 30**
See also AAYA 3; CA 29-32R; CANR 13,
37; CLR 2, 15; DLB 52; MAICYA;
MTCW; SATA 2, 31

Blunden, Edmund (Charles)
1896-1974 .... **CLC 2, 56**
See also CA 17-18; 45-48; CAP 2; DLB 20,
100; MTCW

Bly, Robert (Elwood)
1926- .... **CLC 1, 2, 5, 10, 15, 38**
See also CA 5-8R; CANR 41; DLB 5;
MTCW

Bobette
See Simenon, Georges (Jacques Christian)

Boccaccio, Giovanni 1313-1375
See also SSC 10

Bochco, Steven 1943-............. **CLC 35**
See also CA 124; 138

Bodenheim, Maxwell 1892-1954 ... **TCLC 44**
See also CA 110; DLB 9, 45

Bodker, Cecil 1927- .... **CLC 21**
See also CA 73-76; CANR 13; CLR 23;
MAICYA; SATA 14

Boell, Heinrich (Theodor) 1917-1985
See Boll, Heinrich (Theodor)
See also CA 21-24R; 116; CANR 24; DA;
DLB 69; DLBY 85; MTCW

Bogan, Louise 1897-1970..... **CLC 4, 39, 46**
See also CA 73-76; 25-28R; CANR 33;
DLB 45; MTCW

Bogarde, Dirk .... **CLC 19**
See also Van Den Bogarde, Derek Jules
Gaspard Ulric Niven
See also DLB 14

Bogosian, Eric 1953- .... **CLC 45**
See also CA 138

Bograd, Larry 1953-.............. **CLC 35**
See also CA 93-96; SATA 33

Boiardo, Matteo Maria 1441-1494 .... **LC 6**

Boileau-Despreaux, Nicolas
1636-1711 .... **LC 3**

Boland, Eavan 1944-.......... **CLC 40, 67**
See also DLB 40

Boll, Heinrich (Theodor)
1917-1985 ... **CLC 2, 3, 6, 9, 11, 15, 27,
39, 72**
See also Boell, Heinrich (Theodor)
See also DLB 69; DLBY 85; WLC

Bolt, Lee
See Faust, Frederick (Schiller)

Bolt, Robert (Oxton) 1924-........ **CLC 14**
See also CA 17-20R; CANR 35; DLB 13;
MTCW

Bomkauf
See Kaufman, Bob (Garnell)

Bonaventura.................... **NCLC 35**
See also DLB 90

Bond, Edward 1934-.......**CLC 4, 6, 13, 23**
See also CA 25-28R; CANR 38; DLB 13;
MTCW

Bonham, Frank 1914-1989........ **CLC 12**
See also AAYA 1; CA 9-12R; CANR 4, 36;
MAICYA; SAAS 3; SATA 1, 49, 62

Bonnefoy, Yves 1923-........ **CLC 9, 15, 58**
See also CA 85-88; CANR 33; MTCW

Bontemps, Arna(ud Wendell)
1902-1973 . . . . **CLC 1, 18**
See also BLC 1; BW; CA 1-4R; 41-44R;
CANR 4, 35; CLR 6; DLB 48, 51;
MAICYA; MTCW; SATA 2, 24, 44

Booth, Martin 1944- . . . . **CLC 13**
See also CA 93-96; CAAS 2

Booth, Philip 1925- . . . . **CLC 23**
See also CA 5-8R; CANR 5; DLBY 82

Booth, Wayne C(layson) 1921- . . . . . **CLC 24**
See also CA 1-4R; CAAS 5; CANR 3;
DLB 67

Borchert, Wolfgang 1921-1947 . . . . . **TCLC 5**
See also CA 104; DLB 69, 124

Borges, Jorge Luis
1899-1986 . . . **CLC 1, 2, 3, 4, 6, 8, 9, 10,
13, 19, 44, 48; SSC 4**
See also CA 21-24R; CANR 19, 33; DA;
DLB 113; DLBY 86; HW; MTCW; WLC

Borowski, Tadeusz 1922-1951 . . . . . . **TCLC 9**
See also CA 106

Borrow, George (Henry)
1803-1881 . . . . **NCLC 9**
See also DLB 21, 55

Bosman, Herman Charles
1905-1951 . . . . **TCLC 49**

Bosschere, Jean de 1878(?)-1953 . . . **TCLC 19**
See also CA 115

Boswell, James 1740-1795 . . . . **LC 4**
See also CDBLB 1660-1789; DA; DLB 104;
WLC

Bottoms, David 1949- . . . . **CLC 53**
See also CA 105; CANR 22; DLB 120;
DLBY 83

Boucolon, Maryse 1937-
See Conde, Maryse
See also CA 110; CANR 30

Bourget, Paul (Charles Joseph)
1852-1935 . . . . **TCLC 12**
See also CA 107; DLB 123

Bourjaily, Vance (Nye) 1922- . . . . **CLC 8, 62**
See also CA 1-4R; CAAS 1; CANR 2;
DLB 2

Bourne, Randolph S(illiman)
1886-1918 . . . . **TCLC 16**
See also CA 117; DLB 63

Bova, Ben(jamin William) 1932- . . . . **CLC 45**
See also CA 5-8R; CANR 11; CLR 3;
DLBY 81; MAICYA; MTCW; SATA 6,
68

Bowen, Elizabeth (Dorothea Cole)
1899-1973 . . . . . **CLC 1, 3, 6, 11, 15, 22;
SSC 3**
See also CA 17-18; 41-44R; CANR 35;
CAP 2; CDBLB 1945-1960; DLB 15;
MTCW

Bowering, George 1935- . . . . **CLC 15, 47**
See also CA 21-24R; CAAS 16; CANR 10;
DLB 53

Bowering, Marilyn R(uthe) 1949- . . . **CLC 32**
See also CA 101

Bowers, Edgar 1924- . . . . **CLC 9**
See also CA 5-8R; CANR 24; DLB 5

Bowie, David . . . . **CLC 17**
See also Jones, David Robert

Bowles, Jane (Sydney)
1917-1973 . . . . **CLC 3, 68**
See also CA 19-20; 41-44R; CAP 2

Bowles, Paul (Frederick)
1910- . . . . **CLC 1, 2, 19, 53; SSC 3**
See also CA 1-4R; CAAS 1; CANR 1, 19;
DLB 5, 6; MTCW

Box, Edgar
See Vidal, Gore

Boyd, Nancy
See Millay, Edna St. Vincent

Boyd, William 1952- . . . . **CLC 28, 53, 70**
See also CA 114; 120

Boyle, Kay
1902-1992 . . . . . **CLC 1, 5, 19, 58; SSC 5**
See also CA 13-16R; 140; CAAS 1;
CANR 29; DLB 4, 9, 48, 86; MTCW

Boyle, Mark
See Kienzle, William X(avier)

Boyle, Patrick 1905-1982 . . . . **CLC 19**
See also CA 127

Boyle, T. Coraghessan 1948- . . . . **CLC 36, 55**
See also BEST 90:4; CA 120; DLBY 86

Boz
See Dickens, Charles (John Huffam)

Brackenridge, Hugh Henry
1748-1816 . . . . **NCLC 7**
See also DLB 11, 37

Bradbury, Edward P.
See Moorcock, Michael (John)

Bradbury, Malcolm (Stanley)
1932- . . . . **CLC 32, 61**
See also CA 1-4R; CANR 1, 33; DLB 14;
MTCW

Bradbury, Ray (Douglas)
1920- . . . . **CLC 1, 3, 10, 15, 42**
See also AITN 1, 2; CA 1-4R; CANR 2, 30;
CDALB 1968-1988; DA; DLB 2, 8;
MTCW; SATA 11, 64; WLC

Bradford, Gamaliel 1863-1932 . . . . . **TCLC 36**
See also DLB 17

Bradley, David (Henry, Jr.) 1950- . . **CLC 23**
See also BLC 1; BW; CA 104; CANR 26;
DLB 33

Bradley, John Ed 1959- . . . . **CLC 55**

Bradley, Marion Zimmer 1930- . . . . . **CLC 30**
See also AAYA 9; CA 57-60; CAAS 10;
CANR 7, 31; DLB 8; MTCW

Bradstreet, Anne 1612(?)-1672 . . . . **LC 4**
See also CDALB 1640-1865; DA; DLB 24

Bragg, Melvyn 1939- . . . . **CLC 10**
See also BEST 89:3; CA 57-60; CANR 10;
DLB 14

Braine, John (Gerard)
1922-1986 . . . . **CLC 1, 3, 41**
See also CA 1-4R; 120; CANR 1, 33;
CDBLB 1945-1960; DLB 15; DLBY 86;
MTCW

Brammer, William 1930(?)-1978 . . . . **CLC 31**
See also CA 77-80

Brancati, Vitaliano 1907-1954 . . . . . **TCLC 12**
See also CA 109

Brancato, Robin F(idler) 1936- . . . . . **CLC 35**
See also AAYA 9; CA 69-72; CANR 11;
SAAS 9; SATA 23

Brand, Max
See Faust, Frederick (Schiller)

Brand, Millen 1906-1980 . . . . **CLC 7**
See also CA 21-24R; 97-100

Branden, Barbara . . . . **CLC 44**

Brandes, Georg (Morris Cohen)
1842-1927 . . . . **TCLC 10**
See also CA 105

Brandys, Kazimierz 1916- . . . . **CLC 62**

Branley, Franklyn M(ansfield)
1915- . . . . **CLC 21**
See also CA 33-36R; CANR 14, 39;
CLR 13; MAICYA; SAAS 16; SATA 4,
68

Brathwaite, Edward (Kamau)
1930- . . . . **CLC 11**
See also BW; CA 25-28R; CANR 11, 26;
DLB 125

Brautigan, Richard (Gary)
1935-1984 . . . . **CLC 1, 3, 5, 9, 12, 34, 42**
See also CA 53-56; 113; CANR 34; DLB 2,
5; DLBY 80, 84; MTCW; SATA 56

Braverman, Kate 1950- . . . . **CLC 67**
See also CA 89-92

Brecht, Bertolt
1898-1956 . . . . . **TCLC 1, 6, 13, 35; DC 3**
See also CA 104; 133; DA; DLB 56, 124;
MTCW; WLC

Brecht, Eugen Berthold Friedrich
See Brecht, Bertolt

Bremer, Fredrika 1801-1865 . . . . . **NCLC 11**

Brennan, Christopher John
1870-1932 . . . . **TCLC 17**
See also CA 117

Brennan, Maeve 1917- . . . . **CLC 5**
See also CA 81-84

Brentano, Clemens (Maria)
1778-1842 . . . . **NCLC 1**

Brent of Bin Bin
See Franklin, (Stella Maraia Sarah) Miles

Brenton, Howard 1942- . . . . **CLC 31**
See also CA 69-72; CANR 33; DLB 13;
MTCW

Breslin, James 1930-
See Breslin, Jimmy
See also CA 73-76; CANR 31; MTCW

Breslin, Jimmy . . . . **CLC 4, 43**
See also Breslin, James
See also AITN 1

Bresson, Robert 1907- . . . . **CLC 16**
See also CA 110

Breton, Andre 1896-1966 . . . **CLC 2, 9, 15, 54**
See also CA 19-20; 25-28R; CANR 40;
CAP 2; DLB 65; MTCW

Breytenbach, Breyten 1939(?)- . . **CLC 23, 37**
See also CA 113; 129

Bridgers, Sue Ellen 1942- . . . . **CLC 26**
See also AAYA 8; CA 65-68; CANR 11,
36; CLR 18; DLB 52; MAICYA;
SAAS 1; SATA 22

Bridges, Robert (Seymour)
1844-1930 . . . . **TCLC 1**
See also CA 104; CDBLB 1890-1914;
DLB 19, 98

Buckler, Ernest 1908-1984........ **CLC 13**
See also CA 11-12; 114; CAP 1; DLB 68;
SATA 47

Buckley, Vincent (Thomas)
1925-1988 .... **CLC 57**
See also CA 101

Buckley, William F(rank), Jr.
1925- .... **CLC 7, 18, 37**
See also AITN 1; CA 1-4R; CANR 1, 24;
DLBY 80; MTCW

Buechner, (Carl) Frederick
1926- .... **CLC 2, 4, 6, 9**
See also CA 13-16R; CANR 11, 39;
DLBY 80; MTCW

Buell, John (Edward) 1927-........ **CLC 10**
See also CA 1-4R; DLB 53

Buero Vallejo, Antonio 1916- ... **CLC 15, 46**
See also CA 106; CANR 24; HW; MTCW

Bufalino, Gesualdo 1920(?)-........ **CLC 74**

Bugayev, Boris Nikolayevich 1880-1934
See Bely, Andrey
See also CA 104

Bukowski, Charles 1920-.... **CLC 2, 5, 9, 41**
See also CA 17-20R; CANR 40; DLB 5,
130; MTCW

Bulgakov, Mikhail (Afanas'evich)
1891-1940 .... **TCLC 2, 16**
See also CA 105

Bullins, Ed 1935- .... **CLC 1, 5, 7**
See also BLC 1; BW; CA 49-52; CAAS 16;
CANR 24; DLB 7, 38; MTCW

Bulwer-Lytton, Edward (George Earle Lytton)
1803-1873 .... **NCLC 1**
See also DLB 21

Bunin, Ivan Alexeyevich
1870-1953 .... **TCLC 6; SSC 5**
See also CA 104

Bunting, Basil 1900-1985.... **CLC 10, 39, 47**
See also CA 53-56; 115; CANR 7; DLB 20

Bunuel, Luis 1900-1983 .... **CLC 16**
See also CA 101; 110; CANR 32; HW

Bunyan, John 1628-1688 .... **LC 4**
See also CDBLB 1660-1789; DA; DLB 39;
WLC

Burford, Eleanor
See Hibbert, Eleanor Alice Burford

Burgess, Anthony
1917- ..... **CLC 1, 2, 4, 5, 8, 10, 13, 15,**
22, 40, 62
See also Wilson, John (Anthony) Burgess
See also AITN 1; CDBLB 1960 to Present;
DLB 14

Burke, Edmund 1729(?)-1797........ **LC 7**
See also DA; DLB 104; WLC

Burke, Kenneth (Duva) 1897- .... **CLC 2, 24**
See also CA 5-8R; CANR 39; DLB 45, 63;
MTCW

Burke, Leda
See Garnett, David

Burke, Ralph
See Silverberg, Robert

Burney, Fanny 1752-1840 .... **NCLC 12**
See also DLB 39

Burns, Robert 1759-1796....... **LC 3; PC 6**
See also CDBLB 1789-1832; DA; DLB 109;
WLC

Burns, Tex
See L'Amour, Louis (Dearborn)

Burnshaw, Stanley 1906- ..... **CLC 3, 13, 44**
See also CA 9-12R; DLB 48

Burr, Anne 1937-................ **CLC 6**
See also CA 25-28R

Burroughs, Edgar Rice
1875-1950 .... **TCLC 2, 32**
See also CA 104; 132; DLB 8; MTCW;
SATA 41

Burroughs, William S(eward)
1914- .... **CLC 1, 2, 5, 15, 22, 42, 75**
See also AITN 2; CA 9-12R; CANR 20;
DA; DLB 2, 8, 16; DLBY 81; MTCW;
WLC

Busch, Frederick 1941- ... **CLC 7, 10, 18, 47**
See also CA 33-36R; CAAS 1; DLB 6

Bush, Ronald 1946- .... **CLC 34**
See also CA 136

Bustos, F(rancisco)
See Borges, Jorge Luis

Bustos Domecq, H(onorio)
See Bioy Casares, Adolfo; Borges, Jorge
Luis

Butler, Octavia E(stelle) 1947- ..... **CLC 38**
See also BW; CA 73-76; CANR 12, 24, 38;
DLB 33; MTCW

Butler, Samuel 1612-1680 .... **LC 16**
See also DLB 101, 126

Butler, Samuel 1835-1902 ...... **TCLC 1, 33**
See also CA 104; CDBLB 1890-1914; DA;
DLB 18, 57; WLC

Butler, Walter C.
See Faust, Frederick (Schiller)

Butor, Michel (Marie Francois)
1926- .... **CLC 1, 3, 8, 11, 15**
See also CA 9-12R; CANR 33; DLB 83;
MTCW

Buzo, Alexander (John) 1944-...... **CLC 61**
See also CA 97-100; CANR 17, 39

Buzzati, Dino 1906-1972 .... **CLC 36**
See also CA 33-36R

Byars, Betsy (Cromer) 1928-....... **CLC 35**
See also CA 33-36R; CANR 18, 36; CLR 1,
16; DLB 52; MAICYA; MTCW; SAAS 1;
SATA 4, 46

Byatt, A(ntonia) S(usan Drabble)
1936- .... **CLC 19, 65**
See also CA 13-16R; CANR 13, 33;
DLB 14; MTCW

Byrne, David 1952-................ **CLC 26**
See also CA 127

Byrne, John Keyes 1926-.......... **CLC 19**
See also Leonard, Hugh
See also CA 102

Byron, George Gordon (Noel)
1788-1824 .... **NCLC 2, 12**
See also CDBLB 1789-1832; DA; DLB 96,
110; WLC

C.3.3.
See Wilde, Oscar (Fingal O'Flahertie Wills)

Caballero, Fernan 1796-1877..... **NCLC 10**

Cabell, James Branch 1879-1958 ... **TCLC 6**
See also CA 105; DLB 9, 78

Cable, George Washington
1844-1925 .... **TCLC 4; SSC 4**
See also CA 104; DLB 12, 74

Cabral de Melo Neto, Joao 1920-... **CLC 76**

Cabrera Infante, G(uillermo)
1929-.............. **CLC 5, 25, 45**
See also CA 85-88; CANR 29; DLB 113;
HW; MTCW

Cade, Toni
See Bambara, Toni Cade

Cadmus
See Buchan, John

Caedmon fl. 658-680............. **CMLC 7**

Caeiro, Alberto
See Pessoa, Fernando (Antonio Nogueira)

Cage, John (Milton, Jr.) 1912-..... **CLC 41**
See also CA 13-16R; CANR 9

Cain, G.
See Cabrera Infante, G(uillermo)

Cain, Guillermo
See Cabrera Infante, G(uillermo)

Cain, James M(allahan)
1892-1977 .... **CLC 3, 11, 28**
See also AITN 1; CA 17-20R; 73-76;
CANR 8, 34; MTCW

Caine, Mark
See Raphael, Frederic (Michael)

Calderon de la Barca, Pedro
1600-1681 .... **DC 3**

Caldwell, Erskine (Preston)
1903-1987 .... **CLC 1, 8, 14, 50, 60**
See also AITN 1; CA 1-4R; 121; CAAS 1;
CANR 2, 33; DLB 9, 86; MTCW

Caldwell, (Janet Miriam) Taylor (Holland)
1900-1985 .... **CLC 2, 28, 39**
See also CA 5-8R; 116; CANR 5

Calhoun, John Caldwell
1782-1850 .... **NCLC 15**
See also DLB 3

Calisher, Hortense 1911-.... **CLC 2, 4, 8, 38**
See also CA 1-4R; CANR 1, 22; DLB 2;
MTCW

Callaghan, Morley Edward
1903-1990 .... **CLC 3, 14, 41, 65**
See also CA 9-12R; 132; CANR 33;
DLB 68; MTCW

Calvino, Italo
1923-1985 .... **CLC 5, 8, 11, 22, 33, 39,**
73; SSC 3
See also CA 85-88; 116; CANR 23; MTCW

Cameron, Carey 1952-............ **CLC 59**
See also CA 135

Cameron, Peter 1959-............. **CLC 44**
See also CA 125

Campana, Dino 1885-1932........ **TCLC 20**
See also CA 117; DLB 114

Campbell, John W(ood, Jr.)
1910-1971 .... **CLC 32**
See also CA 21-22; 29-32R; CANR 34;
CAP 2; DLB 8; MTCW

Author Index

Campbell, Joseph 1904-1987 ...... **CLC 69**
See also AAYA 3; BEST 89:2; CA 1-4R;
124; CANR 3, 28; MTCW

Campbell, (John) Ramsey 1946- .... **CLC 42**
See also CA 57-60; CANR 7

Campbell, (Ignatius) Roy (Dunnachie)
1901-1957 .... **TCLC 5**
See also CA 104; DLB 20

Campbell, Thomas 1777-1844 .... **NCLC 19**
See also DLB 93

Campbell, Wilfred .... **TCLC 9**
See also Campbell, William

Campbell, William 1858(?)-1918
See Campbell, Wilfred
See also CA 106; DLB 92

Campos, Alvaro de
See Pessoa, Fernando (Antonio Nogueira)

Camus, Albert
1913-1960 ... **CLC 1, 2, 4, 9, 11, 14, 32,
63, 69; DC 2; SSC 9**
See also CA 89-92; DA; DLB 72; MTCW;
WLC

Canby, Vincent 1924- .... **CLC 13**
See also CA 81-84

Cancale
See Desnos, Robert

Canetti, Elias 1905- ...... **CLC 3, 14, 25, 75**
See also CA 21-24R; CANR 23; DLB 85,
124; MTCW

Canin, Ethan 1960-................ **CLC 55**
See also CA 131; 135

Cannon, Curt
See Hunter, Evan

Cape, Judith
See Page, P(atricia) K(athleen)

Capek, Karel
1890-1938 .... **TCLC 6, 37; DC 1**
See also CA 104; 140; DA; WLC

Capote, Truman
1924-1984 ..... **CLC 1, 3, 8, 13, 19, 34,
38, 58; SSC 2**
See also CA 5-8R; 113; CANR 18;
CDALB 1941-1968; DA; DLB 2;
DLBY 80, 84; MTCW; WLC

Capra, Frank 1897-1991.......... **CLC 16**
See also CA 61-64; 135

Caputo, Philip 1941-.............. **CLC 32**
See also CA 73-76; CANR 40

Card, Orson Scott 1951- .... **CLC 44, 47, 50**
See also CA 102; CANR 27; MTCW

Cardenal (Martinez), Ernesto
1925- .... **CLC 31**
See also CA 49-52; CANR 2, 32; HW;
MTCW

Carducci, Giosue 1835-1907....... **TCLC 32**

Carew, Thomas 1595(?)-1640........ **LC 13**
See also DLB 126

Carey, Ernestine Gilbreth 1908- .... **CLC 17**
See also CA 5-8R; SATA 2

Carey, Peter 1943- .... **CLC 40, 55**
See also CA 123; 127; MTCW

Carleton, William 1794-1869...... **NCLC 3**

Carlisle, Henry (Coffin) 1926- ..... **CLC 33**
See also CA 13-16R; CANR 15

Carlsen, Chris
See Holdstock, Robert P.

Carlson, Ron(ald F.) 1947-........ **CLC 54**
See also CA 105; CANR 27

Carlyle, Thomas 1795-1881 ..... **NCLC 22**
See also CDBLB 1789-1832; DA; DLB 55

Carman, (William) Bliss
1861-1929 .... **TCLC 7**
See also CA 104; DLB 92

Carossa, Hans 1878-1956........ **TCLC 48**
See also DLB 66

Carpenter, Don(ald Richard)
1931- .... **CLC 41**
See also CA 45-48; CANR 1

Carpentier (y Valmont), Alejo
1904-1980 .... **CLC 8, 11, 38**
See also CA 65-68; 97-100; CANR 11;
DLB 113; HW

Carr, Emily 1871-1945.......... **TCLC 32**
See also DLB 68

Carr, John Dickson 1906-1977 ...... **CLC 3**
See also CA 49-52; 69-72; CANR 3, 33;
MTCW

Carr, Philippa
See Hibbert, Eleanor Alice Burford

Carr, Virginia Spencer 1929-....... **CLC 34**
See also CA 61-64; DLB 111

Carrier, Roch 1937- .... **CLC 13**
See also CA 130; DLB 53

Carroll, James P. 1943(?)-........ **CLC 38**
See also CA 81-84

Carroll, Jim 1951- .... **CLC 35**
See also CA 45-48

Carroll, Lewis .... **NCLC 2**
See also Dodgson, Charles Lutwidge
See also CDBLB 1832-1890; CLR 2, 18;
DLB 18; WLC

Carroll, Paul Vincent 1900-1968.... **CLC 10**
See also CA 9-12R; 25-28R; DLB 10

Carruth, Hayden 1921- .... **CLC 4, 7, 10, 18**
See also CA 9-12R; CANR 4, 38; DLB 5;
MTCW; SATA 47

Carson, Rachel Louise 1907-1964... **CLC 71**
See also CA 77-80; CANR 35; MTCW;
SATA 23

Carter, Angela (Olive)
1940-1992 .... **CLC 5, 41, 76**
See also CA 53-56; 136; CANR 12, 36;
DLB 14; MTCW; SATA 66;
SATA-Obit 70

Carter, Nick
See Smith, Martin Cruz

Carver, Raymond
1938-1988 ... **CLC 22, 36, 53, 55; SSC 8**
See also CA 33-36R; 126; CANR 17, 34;
DLB 130; DLBY 84, 88; MTCW

Cary, (Arthur) Joyce (Lunel)
1888-1957 .... **TCLC 1, 29**
See also CA 104; CDBLB 1914-1945;
DLB 15, 100

Casanova de Seingalt, Giovanni Jacopo
1725-1798 .... **LC 13**

Casares, Adolfo Bioy
See Bioy Casares, Adolfo

Casely-Hayford, J(oseph) E(phraim)
1866-1930 .... **TCLC 24**
See also BLC 1; CA 123

Casey, John (Dudley) 1939-........ **CLC 59**
See also BEST 90:2; CA 69-72; CANR 23

Casey, Michael 1947-.............. **CLC 2**
See also CA 65-68; DLB 5

Casey, Patrick
See Thurman, Wallace (Henry)

Casey, Warren (Peter) 1935-1988 ... **CLC 12**
See also CA 101; 127

Casona, Alejandro................. **CLC 49**
See also Alvarez, Alejandro Rodriguez

Cassavetes, John 1929-1989....... **CLC 20**
See also CA 85-88; 127

Cassill, R(onald) V(erlin) 1919- ... **CLC 4, 23**
See also CA 9-12R; CAAS 1; CANR 7;
DLB 6

Cassity, (Allen) Turner 1929- .... **CLC 6, 42**
See also CA 17-20R; CAAS 8; CANR 11;
DLB 105

Castaneda, Carlos 1931(?)-........ **CLC 12**
See also CA 25-28R; CANR 32; HW;
MTCW

Castedo, Elena 1937- .... **CLC 65**
See also CA 132

Castedo-Ellerman, Elena
See Castedo, Elena

Castellanos, Rosario 1925-1974..... **CLC 66**
See also CA 131; 53-56; DLB 113; HW

Castelvetro, Lodovico 1505-1571..... **LC 12**

Castiglione, Baldassare 1478-1529 ... **LC 12**

Castle, Robert
See Hamilton, Edmond

Castro, Guillen de 1569-1631....... **LC 19**

Castro, Rosalia de 1837-1885 ..... **NCLC 3**

Cather, Willa
See Cather, Willa Sibert

Cather, Willa Sibert
1873-1947 ...... **TCLC 1, 11, 31; SSC 2**
See also CA 104; 128; CDALB 1865-1917;
DA; DLB 9, 54, 78; DLBD 1; MTCW;
SATA 30; WLC

Catton, (Charles) Bruce
1899-1978 .... **CLC 35**
See also AITN 1; CA 5-8R; 81-84;
CANR 7; DLB 17; SATA 2, 24

Cauldwell, Frank
See King, Francis (Henry)

Caunitz, William J. 1933- .... **CLC 34**
See also BEST 89:3; CA 125; 130

Causley, Charles (Stanley) 1917-..... **CLC 7**
See also CA 9-12R; CANR 5, 35; CLR 30;
DLB 27; MTCW; SATA 3, 66

Caute, David 1936-............... **CLC 29**
See also CA 1-4R; CAAS 4; CANR 1, 33;
DLB 14

Cavafy, C(onstantine) P(eter)...... **TCLC 2, 7**
See also Kavafis, Konstantinos Petrou

Cavallo, Evelyn
See Spark, Muriel (Sarah)

Christie
See Ichikawa, Kon

Christie, Agatha (Mary Clarissa)
1890-1976 . . . . . . **CLC 1, 6, 8, 12, 39, 48**
See also AAYA 9; AITN 1, 2; CA 17-20R;
61-64; CANR 10, 37; CDBLB 1914-1945;
DLB 13, 77; MTCW; SATA 36

Christie, (Ann) Philippa
See Pearce, Philippa
See also CA 5-8R; CANR 4

Christine de Pizan 1365(?)-1431(?) . . . . **LC 9**

Chubb, Elmer
See Masters, Edgar Lee

Chulkov, Mikhail Dmitrievich
1743-1792 . . . . **LC 2**

Churchill, Caryl 1938- . . . . **CLC 31, 55**
See also CA 102; CANR 22; DLB 13;
MTCW

Churchill, Charles 1731-1764 . . . . **LC 3**
See also DLB 109

Chute, Carolyn 1947- . . . . **CLC 39**
See also CA 123

Ciardi, John (Anthony)
1916-1986 . . . . **CLC 10, 40, 44**
See also CA 5-8R; 118; CAAS 2; CANR 5,
33; CLR 19; DLB 5; DLBY 86;
MAICYA; MTCW; SATA 1, 46, 65

Cicero, Marcus Tullius
106B.C.-43B.C. . . . . **CMLC 3**

Cimino, Michael 1943- . . . . **CLC 16**
See also CA 105

Cioran, E(mil) M. 1911- . . . . **CLC 64**
See also CA 25-28R

Cisneros, Sandra 1954- . . . . **CLC 69**
See also AAYA 9; CA 131; DLB 122; HW

Clair, Rene . . . . **CLC 20**
See also Chomette, Rene Lucien

Clampitt, Amy 1920- . . . . **CLC 32**
See also CA 110; CANR 29; DLB 105

Clancy, Thomas L., Jr. 1947-
See Clancy, Tom
See also CA 125; 131; MTCW

Clancy, Tom . . . . **CLC 45**
See also Clancy, Thomas L., Jr.
See also AAYA 9; BEST 89:1, 90:1

Clare, John 1793-1864 . . . . **NCLC 9**
See also DLB 55, 96

Clarin
See Alas (y Urena), Leopoldo (Enrique
Garcia)

Clark, (Robert) Brian 1932- . . . . **CLC 29**
See also CA 41-44R

Clark, Eleanor 1913- . . . . **CLC 5, 19**
See also CA 9-12R; CANR 41; DLB 6

Clark, J. P.
See Clark, John Pepper
See also DLB 117

Clark, John Pepper 1935- . . . . **CLC 38**
See also Clark, J. P.
See also BLC 1; BW; CA 65-68; CANR 16

Clark, M. R.
See Clark, Mavis Thorpe

Clark, Mavis Thorpe 1909- . . . . **CLC 12**
See also CA 57-60; CANR 8, 37; CLR 30;
MAICYA; SAAS 5; SATA 8, 74

Clark, Walter Van Tilburg
1909-1971 . . . . **CLC 28**
See also CA 9-12R; 33-36R; DLB 9;
SATA 8

Clarke, Arthur C(harles)
1917- . . . . . . **CLC 1, 4, 13, 18, 35; SSC 3**
See also AAYA 4; CA 1-4R; CANR 2, 28;
MAICYA; MTCW; SATA 13, 70

Clarke, Austin 1896-1974 . . . . **CLC 6, 9**
See also CA 29-32; 49-52; CAP 2; DLB 10,
20

Clarke, Austin C(hesterfield)
1934- . . . . **CLC 8, 53**
See also BLC 1; BW; CA 25-28R;
CAAS 16; CANR 14, 32; DLB 53, 125

Clarke, Gillian 1937- . . . . **CLC 61**
See also CA 106; DLB 40

Clarke, Marcus (Andrew Hislop)
1846-1881 . . . . **NCLC 19**

Clarke, Shirley 1925- . . . . **CLC 16**

Clash, The . . . . **CLC 30**
See also Headon, (Nicky) Topper; Jones,
Mick; Simonon, Paul; Strummer, Joe

Claudel, Paul (Louis Charles Marie)
1868-1955 . . . . **TCLC 2, 10**
See also CA 104

Clavell, James (duMaresq)
1925- . . . . **CLC 6, 25**
See also CA 25-28R; CANR 26; MTCW

Cleaver, (Leroy) Eldridge 1935- . . . . **CLC 30**
See also BLC 1; BW; CA 21-24R;
CANR 16

Cleese, John (Marwood) 1939- . . . . . **CLC 21**
See also Monty Python
See also CA 112; 116; CANR 35; MTCW

Cleishbotham, Jebediah
See Scott, Walter

Cleland, John 1710-1789 . . . . **LC 2**
See also DLB 39

Clemens, Samuel Langhorne 1835-1910
See Twain, Mark
See also CA 104; 135; CDALB 1865-1917;
DA; DLB 11, 12, 23, 64, 74; MAICYA;
YABC 2

Cleophil
See Congreve, William

Clerihew, E.
See Bentley, E(dmund) C(lerihew)

Clerk, N. W.
See Lewis, C(live) S(taples)

Cliff, Jimmy . . . . **CLC 21**
See also Chambers, James

Clifton, (Thelma) Lucille
1936- . . . . **CLC 19, 66**
See also BLC 1; BW; CA 49-52; CANR 2,
24; CLR 5; DLB 5, 41; MAICYA;
MTCW; SATA 20, 69

Clinton, Dirk
See Silverberg, Robert

Clough, Arthur Hugh 1819-1861 . . **NCLC 27**
See also DLB 32

Clutha, Janet Paterson Frame 1924-
See Frame, Janet
See also CA 1-4R; CANR 2, 36; MTCW

Clyne, Terence
See Blatty, William Peter

Cobalt, Martin
See Mayne, William (James Carter)

Coburn, D(onald) L(ee) 1938- . . . . . . **CLC 10**
See also CA 89-92

Cocteau, Jean (Maurice Eugene Clement)
1889-1963 . . . . **CLC 1, 8, 15, 16, 43**
See also CA 25-28; CANR 40; CAP 2; DA;
DLB 65; MTCW; WLC

Codrescu, Andrei 1946- . . . . **CLC 46**
See also CA 33-36R; CANR 13, 34

Coe, Max
See Bourne, Randolph S(illiman)

Coe, Tucker
See Westlake, Donald E(dwin)

Coetzee, J(ohn) M(ichael)
1940- . . . . **CLC 23, 33, 66**
See also CA 77-80; CANR 41; MTCW

Cohen, Arthur A(llen)
1928-1986 . . . . **CLC 7, 31**
See also CA 1-4R; 120; CANR 1, 17;
DLB 28

Cohen, Leonard (Norman)
1934- . . . . **CLC 3, 38**
See also CA 21-24R; CANR 14; DLB 53;
MTCW

Cohen, Matt 1942- . . . . **CLC 19**
See also CA 61-64; CANR 40; DLB 53

Cohen-Solal, Annie 19(?)- . . . . **CLC 50**

Colegate, Isabel 1931- . . . . **CLC 36**
See also CA 17-20R; CANR 8, 22; DLB 14;
MTCW

Coleman, Emmett
See Reed, Ishmael

Coleridge, Samuel Taylor
1772-1834 . . . . **NCLC 9**
See also CDBLB 1789-1832; DA; DLB 93,
107; WLC

Coleridge, Sara 1802-1852 . . . . **NCLC 31**

Coles, Don 1928- . . . . **CLC 46**
See also CA 115; CANR 38

Colette, (Sidonie-Gabrielle)
1873-1954 . . . . . . **TCLC 1, 5, 16; SSC 10**
See also CA 104; 131; DLB 65; MTCW

Collett, (Jacobine) Camilla (Wergeland)
1813-1895 . . . . **NCLC 22**

Collier, Christopher 1930- . . . . **CLC 30**
See also CA 33-36R; CANR 13, 33;
MAICYA; SATA 16, 70

Collier, James L(incoln) 1928- . . . . . **CLC 30**
See also CA 9-12R; CANR 4, 33;
MAICYA; SATA 8, 70

Collier, Jeremy 1650-1726 . . . . **LC 6**

Collins, Hunt
See Hunter, Evan

Collins, Linda 1931- . . . . **CLC 44**
See also CA 125

Collins, (William) Wilkie
1824-1889 . . . . **NCLC 1, 18**
See also CDBLB 1832-1890; DLB 18, 70

Collins, William   1721-1759 . . . . LC 4
See also DLB 109

Colman, George
See Glassco, John

Colt, Winchester Remington
See Hubbard, L(afayette) Ron(ald)

Colter, Cyrus   1910- . . . . CLC 58
See also BW; CA 65-68; CANR 10; DLB 33

Colton, James
See Hansen, Joseph

Colum, Padraic   1881-1972 . . . . CLC 28
See also CA 73-76; 33-36R; CANR 35;
MAICYA; MTCW; SATA 15

Colvin, James
See Moorcock, Michael (John)

Colwin, Laurie (E.)
1944-1992 . . . . CLC 5, 13, 23
See also CA 89-92; 139; CANR 20;
DLBY 80; MTCW

Comfort, Alex(ander)   1920- . . . . CLC 7
See also CA 1-4R; CANR 1

Comfort, Montgomery
See Campbell, (John) Ramsey

Compton-Burnett, I(vy)
1884(?)-1969 . . . . . . CLC 1, 3, 10, 15, 34
See also CA 1-4R; 25-28R; CANR 4;
DLB 36; MTCW

Comstock, Anthony   1844-1915 . . . . TCLC 13
See also CA 110

Conan Doyle, Arthur
See Doyle, Arthur Conan

Conde, Maryse . . . . CLC 52
See also Boucolon, Maryse

Condon, Richard (Thomas)
1915- . . . . CLC 4, 6, 8, 10, 45
See also BEST 90:3; CA 1-4R; CAAS 1;
CANR 2, 23; MTCW

Congreve, William
1670-1729 . . . . LC 5, 21; DC 2
See also CDBLB 1660-1789; DA; DLB 39,
84; WLC

Connell, Evan S(helby), Jr.
1924- . . . . CLC 4, 6, 45
See also AAYA 7; CA 1-4R; CAAS 2;
CANR 2, 39; DLB 2; DLBY 81; MTCW

Connelly, Marc(us Cook)
1890-1980 . . . . CLC 7
See also CA 85-88; 102; CANR 30; DLB 7;
DLBY 80; SATA 25

Connor, Ralph . . . . TCLC 31
See also Gordon, Charles William
See also DLB 92

Conrad, Joseph
1857-1924 . . . . . . TCLC 1, 6, 13, 25, 43;
SSC 9
See also CA 104; 131; CDBLB 1890-1914;
DA; DLB 10, 34, 98; MTCW; SATA 27;
WLC

Conrad, Robert Arnold
See Hart, Moss

Conroy, Pat   1945- . . . . CLC 30, 74
See also AAYA 8; AITN 1; CA 85-88;
CANR 24; DLB 6; MTCW

Constant (de Rebecque), (Henri) Benjamin
1767-1830 . . . . NCLC 6
See also DLB 119

Conybeare, Charles Augustus
See Eliot, T(homas) S(tearns)

Cook, Michael   1933- . . . . CLC 58
See also CA 93-96; DLB 53

Cook, Robin   1940- . . . . CLC 14
See also BEST 90:2; CA 108; 111;
CANR 41

Cook, Roy
See Silverberg, Robert

Cooke, Elizabeth   1948- . . . . CLC 55
See also CA 129

Cooke, John Esten   1830-1886 . . . . . NCLC 5
See also DLB 3

Cooke, John Estes
See Baum, L(yman) Frank

Cooke, M. E.
See Creasey, John

Cooke, Margaret
See Creasey, John

Cooney, Ray . . . . CLC 62

Cooper, Henry St. John
See Creasey, John

Cooper, J. California . . . . CLC 56
See also BW; CA 125

Cooper, James Fenimore
1789-1851 . . . . NCLC 1, 27
See also CDALB 1640-1865; DLB 3;
SATA 19

Coover, Robert (Lowell)
1932- . . . . CLC 3, 7, 15, 32, 46
See also CA 45-48; CANR 3, 37; DLB 2;
DLBY 81; MTCW

Copeland, Stewart (Armstrong)
1952- . . . . CLC 26
See also Police, The

Coppard, A(lfred) E(dgar)
1878-1957 . . . . TCLC 5
See also CA 114; YABC 1

Coppee, Francois   1842-1908 . . . . . . TCLC 25

Coppola, Francis Ford   1939- . . . . CLC 16
See also CA 77-80; CANR 40; DLB 44

Corcoran, Barbara   1911- . . . . CLC 17
See also CA 21-24R; CAAS 2; CANR 11,
28; DLB 52; SATA 3

Cordelier, Maurice
See Giraudoux, (Hippolyte) Jean

Corman, Cid . . . . CLC 9
See also Corman, Sidney
See also CAAS 2; DLB 5

Corman, Sidney   1924-
See Corman, Cid
See also CA 85-88

Cormier, Robert (Edmund)
1925- . . . . CLC 12, 30
See also AAYA 3; CA 1-4R; CANR 5, 23;
CDALB 1968-1988; CLR 12; DA;
DLB 52; MAICYA; MTCW; SATA 10,
45

Corn, Alfred   1943- . . . . CLC 33
See also CA 104; DLB 120; DLBY 80

Cornwell, David (John Moore)
1931- . . . . CLC 9, 15
See also le Carre, John
See also CA 5-8R; CANR 13, 33; MTCW

Corrigan, Kevin . . . . CLC 55

Corso, (Nunzio) Gregory   1930- . . . CLC 1, 11
See also CA 5-8R; CANR 41; DLB 5,16;
MTCW

Cortazar, Julio
1914-1984 . . . . . CLC 2, 3, 5, 10, 13, 15,
33, 34; SSC 7
See also CA 21-24R; CANR 12, 32;
DLB 113; HW; MTCW

Corwin, Cecil
See Kornbluth, C(yril) M.

Cosic, Dobrica   1921- . . . . CLC 14
See also CA 122; 138

Costain, Thomas B(ertram)
1885-1965 . . . . CLC 30
See also CA 5-8R; 25-28R; DLB 9

Costantini, Humberto
1924(?)-1987 . . . . CLC 49
See also CA 131; 122; HW

Costello, Elvis   1955- . . . . CLC 21

Cotter, Joseph S. Sr.
See Cotter, Joseph Seamon Sr.

Cotter, Joseph Seamon Sr.
1861-1949 . . . . TCLC 28
See also BLC 1; BW; CA 124; DLB 50

Coulton, James
See Hansen, Joseph

Couperus, Louis (Marie Anne)
1863-1923 . . . . TCLC 15
See also CA 115

Court, Wesli
See Turco, Lewis (Putnam)

Courtenay, Bryce   1933- . . . . CLC 59
See also CA 138

Courtney, Robert
See Ellison, Harlan

Cousteau, Jacques-Yves   1910- . . . . . . CLC 30
See also CA 65-68; CANR 15; MTCW;
SATA 38

Coward, Noel (Peirce)
1899-1973 . . . . CLC 1, 9, 29, 51
See also AITN 1; CA 17-18; 41-44R;
CANR 35; CAP 2; CDBLB 1914-1945;
DLB 10; MTCW

Cowley, Malcolm   1898-1989 . . . . CLC 39
See also CA 5-8R; 128; CANR 3; DLB 4,
48; DLBY 81, 89; MTCW

Cowper, William   1731-1800 . . . . NCLC 8
See also DLB 104, 109

Cox, William Trevor   1928- . . . CLC 9, 14, 71
See also Trevor, William
See also CA 9-12R; CANR 4, 37; DLB 14;
MTCW

Cozzens, James Gould
1903-1978 . . . . CLC 1, 4, 11
See also CA 9-12R; 81-84; CANR 19;
CDALB 1941-1968; DLB 9; DLBD 2;
DLBY 84; MTCW

Crabbe, George   1754-1832 . . . . NCLC 26
See also DLB 93

Dario, Ruben . . . . TCLC 4
See also Sarmiento, Felix Ruben Garcia

Darley, George 1795-1846 . . . . NCLC 2
See also DLB 96

Daryush, Elizabeth 1887-1977 . . . . CLC 6, 19
See also CA 49-52; CANR 3; DLB 20

Daudet, (Louis Marie) Alphonse
1840-1897 . . . . NCLC 1
See also DLB 123

Daumal, Rene 1908-1944 . . . . TCLC 14
See also CA 114

Davenport, Guy (Mattison, Jr.)
1927- . . . . CLC 6, 14, 38
See also CA 33-36R; CANR 23; DLB 130

Davidson, Avram 1923-
See Queen, Ellery
See also CA 101; CANR 26; DLB 8

Davidson, Donald (Grady)
1893-1968 . . . . CLC 2, 13, 19
See also CA 5-8R; 25-28R; CANR 4;
DLB 45

Davidson, Hugh
See Hamilton, Edmond

Davidson, John 1857-1909 . . . . TCLC 24
See also CA 118; DLB 19

Davidson, Sara 1943- . . . . CLC 9
See also CA 81-84

Davie, Donald (Alfred)
1922- . . . . CLC 5, 8, 10, 31
See also CA 1-4R; CAAS 3; CANR 1;
DLB 27; MTCW

Davies, Ray(mond Douglas) 1944- . . CLC 21
See also CA 116

Davies, Rhys 1903-1978 . . . . CLC 23
See also CA 9-12R; 81-84; CANR 4

Davies, (William) Robertson
1913- . . . . CLC 2, 7, 13, 25, 42, 75
See also BEST 89:2; CA 33-36R; CANR 17;
DA; DLB 68; MTCW; WLC

Davies, W(illiam) H(enry)
1871-1940 . . . . TCLC 5
See also CA 104; DLB 19

Davies, Walter C.
See Kornbluth, C(yril) M.

Davis, Angela (Yvonne) 1944- . . . . . . CLC 77
See also BW; CA 57-60; CANR 10

Davis, B. Lynch
See Bioy Casares, Adolfo; Borges, Jorge
Luis

Davis, Gordon
See Hunt, E(verette) Howard, Jr.

Davis, Harold Lenoir 1896-1960 . . . . CLC 49
See also CA 89-92; DLB 9

Davis, Rebecca (Blaine) Harding
1831-1910 . . . . TCLC 6
See also CA 104; DLB 74

Davis, Richard Harding
1864-1916 . . . . TCLC 24
See also CA 114; DLB 12, 23, 78, 79

Davison, Frank Dalby 1893-1970 . . . CLC 15
See also CA 116

Davison, Lawrence H.
See Lawrence, D(avid) H(erbert Richards)

Davison, Peter 1928- . . . . CLC 28
See also CA 9-12R; CAAS 4; CANR 3;
DLB 5

Davys, Mary 1674-1732 . . . . LC 1
See also DLB 39

Dawson, Fielding 1930- . . . . CLC 6
See also CA 85-88; DLB 130

Dawson, Peter
See Faust, Frederick (Schiller)

Day, Clarence (Shepard, Jr.)
1874-1935 . . . . TCLC 25
See also CA 108; DLB 11

Day, Thomas 1748-1789 . . . . LC 1
See also DLB 39; YABC 1

Day Lewis, C(ecil)
1904-1972 . . . . CLC 1, 6, 10
See also Blake, Nicholas
See also CA 13-16; 33-36R; CANR 34;
CAP 1; DLB 15, 20; MTCW

Dazai, Osamu . . . . TCLC 11
See also Tsushima, Shuji

de Andrade, Carlos Drummond
See Drummond de Andrade, Carlos

Deane, Norman
See Creasey, John

de Beauvoir, Simone (Lucie Ernestine Marie
Bertrand)
See Beauvoir, Simone (Lucie Ernestine
Marie Bertrand) de

de Brissac, Malcolm
See Dickinson, Peter (Malcolm)

de Chardin, Pierre Teilhard
See Teilhard de Chardin, (Marie Joseph)
Pierre

Dee, John 1527-1608 . . . . LC 20

Deer, Sandra 1940- . . . . CLC 45

De Ferrari, Gabriella . . . . CLC 65

Defoe, Daniel 1660(?)-1731 . . . . LC 1
See also CDBLB 1660-1789; DA; DLB 39,
95, 101; MAICYA; SATA 22; WLC

de Gourmont, Remy
See Gourmont, Remy de

de Hartog, Jan 1914- . . . . CLC 19
See also CA 1-4R; CANR 1

de Hostos, E. M.
See Hostos (y Bonilla), Eugenio Maria de

de Hostos, Eugenio M.
See Hostos (y Bonilla), Eugenio Maria de

Deighton, Len . . . . CLC 4, 7, 22, 46
See also Deighton, Leonard Cyril
See also AAYA 6; BEST 89:2;
CDBLB 1960 to Present; DLB 87

Deighton, Leonard Cyril 1929-
See Deighton, Len
See also CA 9-12R; CANR 19, 33; MTCW

Dekker, Thomas 1572(?)-1632 . . . . . . LC 22
See also CDBLB Before 1660; DLB 62

de la Mare, Walter (John)
1873-1956 . . . . TCLC 4
See also CA 110; 137; CDBLB 1914-1945;
CLR 23; DA; DLB 19; MAICYA;
SATA 16; WLC

Delaney, Franey
See O'Hara, John (Henry)

Delaney, Shelagh 1939- . . . . CLC 29
See also CA 17-20R; CANR 30;
CDBLB 1960 to Present; DLB 13;
MTCW

Delany, Mary (Granville Pendarves)
1700-1788 . . . . LC 12

Delany, Samuel R(ay, Jr.)
1942- . . . . CLC 8, 14, 38
See also BLC 1; BW; CA 81-84; CANR 27;
DLB 8, 33; MTCW

Delaporte, Theophile
See Green, Julian (Hartridge)

De La Ramee, (Marie) Louise 1839-1908
See Ouida
See also SATA 20

de la Roche, Mazo 1879-1961 . . . . . . CLC 14
See also CA 85-88; CANR 30; DLB 68;
SATA 64

Delbanco, Nicholas (Franklin)
1942- . . . . CLC 6, 13
See also CA 17-20R; CAAS 2; CANR 29;
DLB 6

del Castillo, Michel 1933- . . . . CLC 38
See also CA 109

Deledda, Grazia (Cosima)
1875(?)-1936 . . . . TCLC 23
See also CA 123

Delibes, Miguel . . . . CLC 8, 18
See also Delibes Setien, Miguel

Delibes Setien, Miguel 1920-
See Delibes, Miguel
See also CA 45-48; CANR 1, 32; HW;
MTCW

DeLillo, Don
1936- . . . . . CLC 8, 10, 13, 27, 39, 54, 76
See also BEST 89:1; CA 81-84; CANR 21;
DLB 6; MTCW

de Lisser, H. G.
See De Lisser, Herbert George
See also DLB 117

De Lisser, Herbert George
1878-1944 . . . . TCLC 12
See also de Lisser, H. G.
See also CA 109

Deloria, Vine (Victor), Jr. 1933- . . . . CLC 21
See also CA 53-56; CANR 5, 20; MTCW;
SATA 21

Del Vecchio, John M(ichael)
1947- . . . . CLC 29
See also CA 110; DLBD 9

de Man, Paul (Adolph Michel)
1919-1983 . . . . CLC 55
See also CA 128; 111; DLB 67; MTCW

De Marinis, Rick 1934- . . . . CLC 54
See also CA 57-60; CANR 9, 25

Demby, William 1922- . . . . CLC 53
See also BLC 1; BW; CA 81-84; DLB 33

Demijohn, Thom
See Disch, Thomas M(ichael)

de Montherlant, Henry (Milon)
See Montherlant, Henry (Milon) de

de Natale, Francine
See Malzberg, Barry N(athaniel)

Denby, Edwin (Orr) 1903-1983 . . . . . CLC 48
See also CA 138; 110

Denis, Julio
See Cortazar, Julio

Denmark, Harrison
See Zelazny, Roger (Joseph)

Dennis, John 1658-1734 . . . . **LC 11**
See also DLB 101

Dennis, Nigel (Forbes) 1912-1989 . . . . **CLC 8**
See also CA 25-28R; 129; DLB 13, 15;
MTCW

De Palma, Brian (Russell) 1940- . . . . **CLC 20**
See also CA 109

De Quincey, Thomas 1785-1859 . . . **NCLC 4**
See also CDBLB 1789-1832; DLB 110

Deren, Eleanora 1908(?)-1961
See Deren, Maya
See also CA 111

Deren, Maya . . . . **CLC 16**
See also Deren, Eleanora

Derleth, August (William)
1909-1971 . . . . **CLC 31**
See also CA 1-4R; 29-32R; CANR 4;
DLB 9; SATA 5

de Routisie, Albert
See Aragon, Louis

Derrida, Jacques 1930- . . . . **CLC 24**
See also CA 124; 127

Derry Down Derry
See Lear, Edward

Dersonnes, Jacques
See Simenon, Georges (Jacques Christian)

Desai, Anita 1937- . . . . **CLC 19, 37**
See also CA 81-84; CANR 33; MTCW;
SATA 63

de Saint-Luc, Jean
See Glassco, John

de Saint Roman, Arnaud
See Aragon, Louis

Descartes, Rene 1596-1650 . . . . **LC 20**

De Sica, Vittorio 1901(?)-1974 . . . . . **CLC 20**
See also CA 117

Desnos, Robert 1900-1945 . . . . **TCLC 22**
See also CA 121

Destouches, Louis-Ferdinand
1894-1961 . . . . **CLC 9, 15**
See also Celine, Louis-Ferdinand
See also CA 85-88; CANR 28; MTCW

Deutsch, Babette 1895-1982 . . . . **CLC 18**
See also CA 1-4R; 108; CANR 4; DLB 45;
SATA 1, 33

Devenant, William 1606-1649 . . . . **LC 13**

Devkota, Laxmiprasad
1909-1959 . . . . **TCLC 23**
See also CA 123

De Voto, Bernard (Augustine)
1897-1955 . . . . **TCLC 29**
See also CA 113; DLB 9

De Vries, Peter
1910- . . . . **CLC 1, 2, 3, 7, 10, 28, 46**
See also CA 17-20R; CANR 41; DLB 6;
DLBY 82; MTCW

Dexter, Martin
See Faust, Frederick (Schiller)

Dexter, Pete 1943- . . . . **CLC 34, 55**
See also BEST 89:2; CA 127; 131; MTCW

Diamano, Silmang
See Senghor, Leopold Sedar

Diamond, Neil 1941- . . . . **CLC 30**
See also CA 108

di Bassetto, Corno
See Shaw, George Bernard

Dick, Philip K(indred)
1928-1982 . . . . **CLC 10, 30, 72**
See also CA 49-52; 106; CANR 2, 16;
DLB 8; MTCW

Dickens, Charles (John Huffam)
1812-1870 . . . . **NCLC 3, 8, 18, 26**
See also CDBLB 1832-1890; DA; DLB 21,
55, 70; MAICYA; SATA 15

Dickey, James (Lafayette)
1923- . . . . **CLC 1, 2, 4, 7, 10, 15, 47**
See also AITN 1, 2; CA 9-12R; CABS 2;
CANR 10; CDALB 1968-1988; DLB 5;
DLBD 7; DLBY 82; MTCW

Dickey, William 1928- . . . . **CLC 3, 28**
See also CA 9-12R; CANR 24; DLB 5

Dickinson, Charles 1951- . . . . **CLC 49**
See also CA 128

Dickinson, Emily (Elizabeth)
1830-1886 . . . . **NCLC 21; PC 1**
See also CDALB 1865-1917; DA; DLB 1;
SATA 29; WLC

Dickinson, Peter (Malcolm)
1927- . . . . **CLC 12, 35**
See also AAYA 9; CA 41-44R; CANR 31;
CLR 29; DLB 87; MAICYA; SATA 5, 62

Dickson, Carr
See Carr, John Dickson

Dickson, Carter
See Carr, John Dickson

Didion, Joan 1934- . . . . . **CLC 1, 3, 8, 14, 32**
See also AITN 1; CA 5-8R; CANR 14;
CDALB 1968-1988; DLB 2; DLBY 81,
86; MTCW

Dietrich, Robert
See Hunt, E(verette) Howard, Jr.

Dillard, Annie 1945- . . . . **CLC 9, 60**
See also AAYA 6; CA 49-52; CANR 3;
DLBY 80; MTCW; SATA 10

Dillard, R(ichard) H(enry) W(ilde)
1937- . . . . **CLC 5**
See also CA 21-24R; CAAS 7; CANR 10;
DLB 5

Dillon, Eilis 1920- . . . . **CLC 17**
See also CA 9-12R; CAAS 3; CANR 4, 38;
CLR 26; MAICYA; SATA 2, 74

Dimont, Penelope
See Mortimer, Penelope (Ruth)

Dinesen, Isak . . . . **CLC 10, 29; SSC 7**
See also Blixen, Karen (Christentze
Dinesen)

Ding Ling . . . . **CLC 68**
See also Chiang Pin-chin

Disch, Thomas M(ichael) 1940- . . . **CLC 7, 36**
See also CA 21-24R; CAAS 4; CANR 17,
36; CLR 18; DLB 8; MAICYA; MTCW;
SAAS 15; SATA 54

Disch, Tom
See Disch, Thomas M(ichael)

d'Isly, Georges
See Simenon, Georges (Jacques Christian)

Disraeli, Benjamin 1804-1881 . . **NCLC 2, 39**
See also DLB 21, 55

Ditcum, Steve
See Crumb, R(obert)

Dixon, Paige
See Corcoran, Barbara

Dixon, Stephen 1936- . . . . **CLC 52**
See also CA 89-92; CANR 17, 40; DLB 130

Doblin, Alfred . . . . **TCLC 13**
See also Doeblin, Alfred

Dobrolyubov, Nikolai Alexandrovich
1836-1861 . . . . **NCLC 5**

Dobyns, Stephen 1941- . . . . **CLC 37**
See also CA 45-48; CANR 2, 18

Doctorow, E(dgar) L(aurence)
1931- . . . . . **CLC 6, 11, 15, 18, 37, 44, 65**
See also AITN 2; BEST 89:3; CA 45-48;
CANR 2, 33; CDALB 1968-1988; DLB 2,
28; DLBY 80; MTCW

Dodgson, Charles Lutwidge 1832-1898
See Carroll, Lewis
See also CLR 2; DA; MAICYA; YABC 2

Doeblin, Alfred 1878-1957 . . . . **TCLC 13**
See also Doblin, Alfred
See also CA 110; DLB 66

Doerr, Harriet 1910- . . . . **CLC 34**
See also CA 117; 122

Domecq, H(onorio) Bustos
See Bioy Casares, Adolfo; Borges, Jorge
Luis

Domini, Rey
See Lorde, Audre (Geraldine)

Dominique
See Proust,
(Valentin-Louis-George-Eugene-)Marcel

Don, A
See Stephen, Leslie

Donaldson, Stephen R. 1947- . . . . **CLC 46**
See also CA 89-92; CANR 13

Donleavy, J(ames) P(atrick)
1926- . . . . **CLC 1, 4, 6, 10, 45**
See also AITN 2; CA 9-12R; CANR 24;
DLB 6; MTCW

Donne, John 1572-1631 . . . . **LC 10; PC 1**
See also CDBLB Before 1660; DA;
DLB 121; WLC

Donnell, David 1939(?)- . . . . **CLC 34**

Donoso (Yanez), Jose
1924- . . . . **CLC 4, 8, 11, 32**
See also CA 81-84; CANR 32; DLB 113;
HW; MTCW

Donovan, John 1928-1992 . . . . **CLC 35**
See also CA 97-100; 137; CLR 3;
MAICYA; SATA 29

Don Roberto
See Cunninghame Graham, R(obert)
B(ontine)

Doolittle, Hilda
1886-1961 . . . . **CLC 3, 8, 14, 31, 34, 73;
PC 5**
See also H. D.
See also CA 97-100; CANR 35; DA;
DLB 4, 45; MTCW; WLC

Dorfman, Ariel 1942- . . . . **CLC 48, 77**
See also CA 124; 130; HW

Dorn, Edward (Merton) 1929- . . . **CLC 10, 18**
See also CA 93-96; DLB 5

Dorsan, Luc
See Simenon, Georges (Jacques Christian)

Dorsange, Jean
See Simenon, Georges (Jacques Christian)

Dos Passos, John (Roderigo)
1896-1970 . . . **CLC 1, 4, 8, 11, 15, 25, 34**
See also CA 1-4R; 29-32R; CANR 3;
CDALB 1929-1941; DA; DLB 4, 9;
DLBD 1; MTCW; WLC

Dossage, Jean
See Simenon, Georges (Jacques Christian)

Dostoevsky, Fedor Mikhailovich
1821-1881 . . . . **NCLC 2, 7, 21, 33; SSC 2**
See also DA; WLC

Doughty, Charles M(ontagu)
1843-1926 . . . . **TCLC 27**
See also CA 115; DLB 19, 57

Douglas, Ellen
See Haxton, Josephine Ayres

Douglas, Gavin 1475(?)-1522. . . . . . . **LC 20**

Douglas, Keith 1920-1944 . . . . **TCLC 40**
See also DLB 27

Douglas, Leonard
See Bradbury, Ray (Douglas)

Douglas, Michael
See Crichton, (John) Michael

Douglass, Frederick 1817(?)-1895. . **NCLC 7**
See also BLC 1; CDALB 1640-1865; DA;
DLB 1, 43, 50, 79; SATA 29; WLC

Dourado, (Waldomiro Freitas) Autran
1926- . . . . **CLC 23, 60**
See also CA 25-28R; CANR 34

Dourado, Waldomiro Autran
See Dourado, (Waldomiro Freitas) Autran

Dove, Rita (Frances) 1952- . . . **CLC 50; PC 6**
See also BW; CA 109; CANR 27; DLB 120

Dowell, Coleman 1925-1985. . . . . . . **CLC 60**
See also CA 25-28R; 117; CANR 10;
DLB 130

Dowson, Ernest Christopher
1867-1900 . . . . **TCLC 4**
See also CA 105; DLB 19

Doyle, A. Conan
See Doyle, Arthur Conan

Doyle, Arthur Conan
1859-1930 . . . . **TCLC 7; SSC 12**
See also CA 104; 122; CDBLB 1890-1914;
DA; DLB 18, 70; MTCW; SATA 24;
WLC

Doyle, Conan 1859-1930
See Doyle, Arthur Conan

Doyle, John
See Graves, Robert (von Ranke)

Doyle, Sir A. Conan
See Doyle, Arthur Conan

Doyle, Sir Arthur Conan
See Doyle, Arthur Conan

Dr. A
See Asimov, Isaac; Silverstein, Alvin

Drabble, Margaret
1939- . . . . **CLC 2, 3, 5, 8, 10, 22, 53**
See also CA 13-16R; CANR 18, 35;
CDBLB 1960 to Present; DLB 14;
MTCW; SATA 48

Drapier, M. B.
See Swift, Jonathan

Drayham, James
See Mencken, H(enry) L(ouis)

Drayton, Michael 1563-1631. . . . . **LC 8**

Dreadstone, Carl
See Campbell, (John) Ramsey

Dreiser, Theodore (Herman Albert)
1871-1945 . . . . **TCLC 10, 18, 35**
See also CA 106; 132; CDALB 1865-1917;
DA; DLB 9, 12, 102; DLBD 1; MTCW;
WLC

Drexler, Rosalyn 1926- . . . . **CLC 2, 6**
See also CA 81-84

Dreyer, Carl Theodor 1889-1968. . . . **CLC 16**
See also CA 116

Drieu la Rochelle, Pierre(-Eugene)
1893-1945 . . . . **TCLC 21**
See also CA 117; DLB 72

Drop Shot
See Cable, George Washington

Droste-Hulshoff, Annette Freiin von
1797-1848 . . . . **NCLC 3**

Drummond, Walter
See Silverberg, Robert

Drummond, William Henry
1854-1907 . . . . **TCLC 25**
See also DLB 92

Drummond de Andrade, Carlos
1902-1987 . . . . **CLC 18**
See also Andrade, Carlos Drummond de
See also CA 132; 123

Drury, Allen (Stuart) 1918- . . . . **CLC 37**
See also CA 57-60; CANR 18

Dryden, John 1631-1700 . . . . **LC 3, 21; DC 3**
See also CDBLB 1660-1789; DA; DLB 80,
101, 131; WLC

Duberman, Martin 1930- . . . . **CLC 8**
See also CA 1-4R; CANR 2

Dubie, Norman (Evans) 1945- . . . . . . **CLC 36**
See also CA 69-72; CANR 12; DLB 120

Du Bois, W(illiam) E(dward) B(urghardt)
1868-1963 . . . . **CLC 1, 2, 13, 64**
See also BLC 1; BW; CA 85-88; CANR 34;
CDALB 1865-1917; DA; DLB 47, 50, 91;
MTCW; SATA 42; WLC

Dubus, Andre 1936- . . . . **CLC 13, 36**
See also CA 21-24R; CANR 17; DLB 130

Duca Minimo
See D'Annunzio, Gabriele

Ducharme, Rejean 1941- . . . . **CLC 74**
See also DLB 60

Duclos, Charles Pinot 1704-1772 . . . . . **LC 1**

Dudek, Louis 1918- . . . . **CLC 11, 19**
See also CA 45-48; CAAS 14; CANR 1;
DLB 88

Duerrenmatt, Friedrich
1921-1990 . . . . . . **CLC 1, 4, 8, 11, 15, 43**
See also Durrenmatt, Friedrich
See also CA 17-20R; CANR 33; DLB 69,
124; MTCW

Duffy, Bruce (?)- . . . . **CLC 50**

Duffy, Maureen 1933- . . . . **CLC 37**
See also CA 25-28R; CANR 33; DLB 14;
MTCW

Dugan, Alan 1923- . . . . **CLC 2, 6**
See also CA 81-84; DLB 5

du Gard, Roger Martin
See Martin du Gard, Roger

Duhamel, Georges 1884-1966 . . . . **CLC 8**
See also CA 81-84; 25-28R; CANR 35;
DLB 65; MTCW

Dujardin, Edouard (Emile Louis)
1861-1949 . . . . **TCLC 13**
See also CA 109; DLB 123

Dumas, Alexandre (Davy de la Pailleterie)
1802-1870 . . . . **NCLC 11**
See also DA; DLB 119; SATA 18; WLC

Dumas, Alexandre
1824-1895 . . . . **NCLC 9; DC 1**

Dumas, Claudine
See Malzberg, Barry N(athaniel)

Dumas, Henry L. 1934-1968 . . . . . **CLC 6, 62**
See also BW; CA 85-88; DLB 41

du Maurier, Daphne
1907-1989 . . . . **CLC 6, 11, 59**
See also CA 5-8R; 128; CANR 6; MTCW;
SATA 27, 60

Dunbar, Paul Laurence
1872-1906 . . . . **TCLC 2, 12; PC 5; SSC 8**
See also BLC 1; BW; CA 104; 124;
CDALB 1865-1917; DA; DLB 50, 54, 78;
SATA 34; WLC

Dunbar, William 1460(?)-1530(?) . . . . **LC 20**

Duncan, Lois 1934- . . . . **CLC 26**
See also AAYA 4; CA 1-4R; CANR 2, 23,
36; CLR 29; MAICYA; SAAS 2;
SATA 1, 36

Duncan, Robert (Edward)
1919-1988 . . . **CLC 1, 2, 4, 7, 15, 41, 55;
PC 2**
See also CA 9-12R; 124; CANR 28; DLB 5,
16; MTCW

Dunlap, William 1766-1839 . . . . **NCLC 2**
See also DLB 30, 37, 59

Dunn, Douglas (Eaglesham)
1942- . . . . **CLC 6, 40**
See also CA 45-48; CANR 2, 33; DLB 40;
MTCW

Dunn, Katherine (Karen) 1945- . . . . . **CLC 71**
See also CA 33-36R

Dunn, Stephen 1939- . . . . **CLC 36**
See also CA 33-36R; CANR 12; DLB 105

Dunne, Finley Peter 1867-1936. . . . **TCLC 28**
See also CA 108; DLB 11, 23

Dunne, John Gregory 1932- . . . . **CLC 28**
See also CA 25-28R; CANR 14; DLBY 80

Dunsany, Edward John Moreton Drax
Plunkett 1878-1957
See Dunsany, Lord; Lord Dunsany
See also CA 104; DLB 10

Dunsany, Lord . . . . **TCLC 2**
See also Dunsany, Edward John Moreton
Drax Plunkett
See also DLB 77

du Perry, Jean
See Simenon, Georges (Jacques Christian)

Durang, Christopher (Ferdinand)
1949- . . . . **CLC 27, 38**
See also CA 105

Duras, Marguerite
1914- . . . . . . **CLC 3, 6, 11, 20, 34, 40, 68**
See also CA 25-28R; DLB 83; MTCW

Durban, (Rosa) Pam 1947- . . . . **CLC 39**
See also CA 123

Durcan, Paul 1944- . . . . **CLC 43, 70**
See also CA 134

Durrell, Lawrence (George)
1912-1990 . . . . **CLC 1, 4, 6, 8, 13, 27, 41**
See also CA 9-12R; 132; CANR 40;
CDBLB 1945-1960; DLB 15, 27;
DLBY 90; MTCW

Durrenmatt, Friedrich
. . . . **CLC 1, 4, 8, 11, 15, 43**
See also Duerrenmatt, Friedrich
See also DLB 69, 124

Dutt, Toru 1856-1877 . . . . **NCLC 29**

Dwight, Timothy 1752-1817 . . . . . . **NCLC 13**
See also DLB 37

Dworkin, Andrea 1946- . . . . **CLC 43**
See also CA 77-80; CANR 16, 39; MTCW

Dylan, Bob 1941- . . . . . . **CLC 3, 4, 6, 12, 77**
See also CA 41-44R; DLB 16

Eagleton, Terence (Francis) 1943-
See Eagleton, Terry
See also CA 57-60; CANR 7, 23; MTCW

Eagleton, Terry . . . . **CLC 63**
See also Eagleton, Terence (Francis)

Early, Jack
See Scoppettone, Sandra

East, Michael
See West, Morris L(anglo)

Eastaway, Edward
See Thomas, (Philip) Edward

Eastlake, William (Derry) 1917- . . . . . **CLC 8**
See also CA 5-8R; CAAS 1; CANR 5;
DLB 6

Eberhart, Richard (Ghormley)
1904- . . . . **CLC 3, 11, 19, 56**
See also CA 1-4R; CANR 2;
CDALB 1941-1968; DLB 48; MTCW

Eberstadt, Fernanda 1960- . . . . **CLC 39**
See also CA 136

Echegaray (y Eizaguirre), Jose (Maria Waldo)
1832-1916 . . . . **TCLC 4**
See also CA 104; CANR 32; HW; MTCW

Echeverria, (Jose) Esteban (Antonino)
1805-1851 . . . . **NCLC 18**

Echo
See Proust,
(Valentin-Louis-George-Eugene-)Marcel

Eckert, Allan W. 1931- . . . . **CLC 17**
See also CA 13-16R; CANR 14; SATA 27,
29

Eckhart, Meister 1260(?)-1328(?) . . **CMLC 9**
See also DLB 115

Eckmar, F. R.
See de Hartog, Jan

Eco, Umberto 1932- . . . . **CLC 28, 60**
See also BEST 90:1; CA 77-80; CANR 12,
33; MTCW

Eddison, E(ric) R(ucker)
1882-1945 . . . . **TCLC 15**
See also CA 109

Edel, (Joseph) Leon 1907- . . . . . . **CLC 29, 34**
See also CA 1-4R; CANR 1, 22; DLB 103

Eden, Emily 1797-1869 . . . . **NCLC 10**

Edgar, David 1948- . . . . **CLC 42**
See also CA 57-60; CANR 12; DLB 13;
MTCW

Edgerton, Clyde (Carlyle) 1944- . . . . **CLC 39**
See also CA 118; 134

Edgeworth, Maria 1767-1849 . . . . . . **NCLC 1**
See also DLB 116; SATA 21

Edmonds, Paul
See Kuttner, Henry

Edmonds, Walter D(umaux) 1903- . . **CLC 35**
See also CA 5-8R; CANR 2; DLB 9;
MAICYA; SAAS 4; SATA 1, 27

Edmondson, Wallace
See Ellison, Harlan

Edson, Russell . . . . **CLC 13**
See also CA 33-36R

Edwards, G(erald) B(asil)
1899-1976 . . . . **CLC 25**
See also CA 110

Edwards, Gus 1939- . . . . **CLC 43**
See also CA 108

Edwards, Jonathan 1703-1758 . . . . **LC 7**
See also DA; DLB 24

Efron, Marina Ivanovna Tsvetaeva
See Tsvetaeva (Efron), Marina (Ivanovna)

Ehle, John (Marsden, Jr.) 1925- . . . . **CLC 27**
See also CA 9-12R

Ehrenbourg, Ilya (Grigoryevich)
See Ehrenburg, Ilya (Grigoryevich)

Ehrenburg, Ilya (Grigoryevich)
1891-1967 . . . . **CLC 18, 34, 62**
See also CA 102; 25-28R

Ehrenburg, Ilyo (Grigoryevich)
See Ehrenburg, Ilya (Grigoryevich)

Eich, Guenter 1907-1972 . . . . **CLC 15**
See also CA 111; 93-96; DLB 69, 124

Eichendorff, Joseph Freiherr von
1788-1857 . . . . **NCLC 8**
See also DLB 90

Eigner, Larry . . . . **CLC 9**
See also Eigner, Laurence (Joel)
See also DLB 5

Eigner, Laurence (Joel) 1927-
See Eigner, Larry
See also CA 9-12R; CANR 6

Eiseley, Loren Corey 1907-1977 . . . . . **CLC 7**
See also AAYA 5; CA 1-4R; 73-76;
CANR 6

Eisenstadt, Jill 1963- . . . . **CLC 50**
See also CA 140

Eisner, Simon
See Kornbluth, C(yril) M.

Ekeloef, (Bengt) Gunnar
1907-1968 . . . . **CLC 27**
See also Ekelof, (Bengt) Gunnar
See also CA 123; 25-28R

Ekelof, (Bengt) Gunnar . . . . **CLC 27**
See also Ekeloef, (Bengt) Gunnar

Ekwensi, C. O. D.
See Ekwensi, Cyprian (Odiatu Duaka)

Ekwensi, Cyprian (Odiatu Duaka)
1921- . . . . **CLC 4**
See also BLC 1; BW; CA 29-32R;
CANR 18; DLB 117; MTCW; SATA 66

Elaine . . . . **TCLC 18**
See also Leverson, Ada

El Crummo
See Crumb, R(obert)

Elia
See Lamb, Charles

Eliade, Mircea 1907-1986 . . . . **CLC 19**
See also CA 65-68; 119; CANR 30; MTCW

Eliot, A. D.
See Jewett, (Theodora) Sarah Orne

Eliot, Alice
See Jewett, (Theodora) Sarah Orne

Eliot, Dan
See Silverberg, Robert

Eliot, George 1819-1880 . . . . **NCLC 4, 13, 23**
See also CDBLB 1832-1890; DA; DLB 21,
35, 55; WLC

Eliot, John 1604-1690 . . . . **LC 5**
See also DLB 24

Eliot, T(homas) S(tearns)
1888-1965 . . . . **CLC 1, 2, 3, 6, 9, 10, 13,**
15, 24, 34, 41, 55, 57; PC 5
See also CA 5-8R; 25-28R; CANR 41;
CDALB 1929-1941; DA; DLB 7, 10, 45,
63; DLBY 88; MTCW; WLC 2

Elizabeth 1866-1941 . . . . **TCLC 41**

Elkin, Stanley L(awrence)
1930- . . . **CLC 4, 6, 9, 14, 27, 51; SSC 12**
See also CA 9-12R; CANR 8; DLB 2, 28;
DLBY 80; MTCW

Elledge, Scott . . . . **CLC 34**

Elliott, Don
See Silverberg, Robert

Elliott, George P(aul) 1918-1980 . . . . . **CLC 2**
See also CA 1-4R; 97-100; CANR 2

Elliott, Janice 1931- . . . . **CLC 47**
See also CA 13-16R; CANR 8, 29; DLB 14

Elliott, Sumner Locke 1917-1991 . . . **CLC 38**
See also CA 5-8R; 134; CANR 2, 21

Elliott, William
See Bradbury, Ray (Douglas)

Ellis, A. E. . . . . **CLC 7**

Ellis, Alice Thomas . . . . **CLC 40**
See also Haycraft, Anna

Ellis, Bret Easton 1964- . . . . **CLC 39, 71**
See also AAYA 2; CA 118; 123

Ellis, (Henry) Havelock
1859-1939 . . . . **TCLC 14**
See also CA 109

Farley, Walter (Lorimer)
1915-1989 .... CLC 17
See also CA 17-20R; CANR 8, 29; DLB 22;
MAICYA; SATA 2, 43

Farmer, Philip Jose 1918- .... CLC 1, 19
See also CA 1-4R; CANR 4, 35; DLB 8;
MTCW

Farquhar, George 1677-1707 .... LC 21
See also DLB 84

Farrell, J(ames) G(ordon)
1935-1979 .... CLC 6
See also CA 73-76; 89-92; CANR 36;
DLB 14; MTCW

Farrell, James T(homas)
1904-1979 .... CLC 1, 4, 8, 11, 66
See also CA 5-8R; 89-92; CANR 9; DLB 4,
9, 86; DLBD 2; MTCW

Farren, Richard J.
See Betjeman, John

Farren, Richard M.
See Betjeman, John

Fassbinder, Rainer Werner
1946-1982 .... CLC 20
See also CA 93-96; 106; CANR 31

Fast, Howard (Melvin) 1914- ...... CLC 23
See also CA 1-4R; CANR 1, 33; DLB 9;
SATA 7

Faulcon, Robert
See Holdstock, Robert P.

Faulkner, William (Cuthbert)
1897-1962 .... CLC 1, 3, 6, 8, 9, 11, 14,
18, 28, 52, 68; SSC 1
See also AAYA 7; CA 81-84; CANR 33;
CDALB 1929-1941; DA; DLB 9, 11, 44,
102; DLBD 2; DLBY 86; MTCW; WLC

Fauset, Jessie Redmon
1884(?)-1961 .... CLC 19, 54
See also BLC 2; BW; CA 109; DLB 51

Faust, Frederick (Schiller)
1892-1944(?) .... TCLC 49
See also CA 108

Faust, Irvin 1924- .... CLC 8
See also CA 33-36R; CANR 28; DLB 2, 28;
DLBY 80

Fawkes, Guy
See Benchley, Robert (Charles)

Fearing, Kenneth (Flexner)
1902-1961 .... CLC 51
See also CA 93-96; DLB 9

Fecamps, Elise
See Creasey, John

Federman, Raymond 1928- ...... CLC 6, 47
See also CA 17-20R; CAAS 8; CANR 10;
DLBY 80

Federspiel, J(uerg) F. 1931- .... CLC 42

Feiffer, Jules (Ralph) 1929- .... CLC 2, 8, 64
See also AAYA 3; CA 17-20R; CANR 30;
DLB 7, 44; MTCW; SATA 8, 61

Feige, Hermann Albert Otto Maximilian
See Traven, B.

Fei-Kan, Li
See Li Fei-kan

Feinberg, David B. 1956- .... CLC 59
See also CA 135

Feinstein, Elaine 1930- .... CLC 36
See also CA 69-72; CAAS 1; CANR 31;
DLB 14, 40; MTCW

Feldman, Irving (Mordecai) 1928- .... CLC 7
See also CA 1-4R; CANR 1

Fellini, Federico 1920- .... CLC 16
See also CA 65-68; CANR 33

Felsen, Henry Gregor 1916- .... CLC 17
See also CA 1-4R; CANR 1; SAAS 2;
SATA 1

Fenton, James Martin 1949- .... CLC 32
See also CA 102; DLB 40

Ferber, Edna 1887-1968 .... CLC 18
See also AITN 1; CA 5-8R; 25-28R; DLB 9,
28, 86; MTCW; SATA 7

Ferguson, Helen
See Kavan, Anna

Ferguson, Samuel 1810-1886 ..... NCLC 33
See also DLB 32

Ferling, Lawrence
See Ferlinghetti, Lawrence (Monsanto)

Ferlinghetti, Lawrence (Monsanto)
1919(?)- .... CLC 2, 6, 10, 27; PC 1
See also CA 5-8R; CANR 3, 41;
CDALB 1941-1968; DLB 5, 16; MTCW

Fernandez, Vicente Garcia Huidobro
See Huidobro Fernandez, Vicente Garcia

Ferrer, Gabriel (Francisco Victor) Miro
See Miro (Ferrer), Gabriel (Francisco
Victor)

Ferrier, Susan (Edmonstone)
1782-1854 .... NCLC 8
See also DLB 116

Ferrigno, Robert 1948(?)- .... CLC 65
See also CA 140

Feuchtwanger, Lion 1884-1958 ..... TCLC 3
See also CA 104; DLB 66

Feydeau, Georges (Leon Jules Marie)
1862-1921 .... TCLC 22
See also CA 113

Ficino, Marsilio 1433-1499 .... LC 12

Fiedler, Leslie A(aron)
1917- .... CLC 4, 13, 24
See also CA 9-12R; CANR 7; DLB 28, 67;
MTCW

Field, Andrew 1938- .... CLC 44
See also CA 97-100; CANR 25

Field, Eugene 1850-1895 .... NCLC 3
See also DLB 23, 42; MAICYA; SATA 16

Field, Gans T.
See Wellman, Manly Wade

Field, Michael .... TCLC 43

Field, Peter
See Hobson, Laura Z(ametkin)

Fielding, Henry 1707-1754 .... LC 1
See also CDBLB 1660-1789; DA; DLB 39,
84, 101; WLC

Fielding, Sarah 1710-1768 .... LC 1
See also DLB 39

Fierstein, Harvey (Forbes) 1954- ... CLC 33
See also CA 123; 129

Figes, Eva 1932- .... CLC 31
See also CA 53-56; CANR 4; DLB 14

Finch, Robert (Duer Claydon)
1900- .... CLC 18
See also CA 57-60; CANR 9, 24; DLB 88

Findley, Timothy 1930- .... CLC 27
See also CA 25-28R; CANR 12; DLB 53

Fink, William
See Mencken, H(enry) L(ouis)

Firbank, Louis 1942-
See Reed, Lou
See also CA 117

Firbank, (Arthur Annesley) Ronald
1886-1926 .... TCLC 1
See also CA 104; DLB 36

Fisher, M(ary) F(rances) K(ennedy)
1908-1992 .... CLC 76
See also CA 77-80; 138

Fisher, Roy 1930- .... CLC 25
See also CA 81-84; CAAS 10; CANR 16;
DLB 40

Fisher, Rudolph 1897-1934 .... TCLC 11
See also BLC 2; BW; CA 107; 124; DLB 51,
102

Fisher, Vardis (Alvero) 1895-1968 .... CLC 7
See also CA 5-8R; 25-28R; DLB 9

Fiske, Tarleton
See Bloch, Robert (Albert)

Fitch, Clarke
See Sinclair, Upton (Beall)

Fitch, John IV
See Cormier, Robert (Edmund)

Fitgerald, Penelope 1916- .... CLC 61

Fitzgerald, Captain Hugh
See Baum, L(yman) Frank

FitzGerald, Edward 1809-1883 .... NCLC 9
See also DLB 32

Fitzgerald, F(rancis) Scott (Key)
1896-1940 .... TCLC 1, 6, 14, 28; SSC 6
See also AITN 1; CA 110; 123;
CDALB 1917-1929; DA; DLB 4, 9, 86;
DLBD 1; DLBY 81; MTCW; WLC

Fitzgerald, Penelope 1916- ...... CLC 19, 51
See also CA 85-88; CAAS 10; DLB 14

Fitzgerald, Robert (Stuart)
1910-1985 .... CLC 39
See also CA 1-4R; 114; CANR 1; DLBY 80

FitzGerald, Robert D(avid)
1902-1987 .... CLC 19
See also CA 17-20R

Flanagan, Thomas (James Bonner)
1923- .... CLC 25, 52
See also CA 108; DLBY 80; MTCW

Flaubert, Gustave
1821-1880 ..... NCLC 2, 10, 19; SSC 11
See also DA; DLB 119; WLC

Flecker, (Herman) James Elroy
1884-1915 .... TCLC 43
See also CA 109; DLB 10, 19

Fleming, Ian (Lancaster)
1908-1964 .... CLC 3, 30
See also CA 5-8R; CDBLB 1945-1960;
DLB 87; MTCW; SATA 9

Fleming, Thomas (James) 1927- .... CLC 37
See also CA 5-8R; CANR 10; SATA 8

Frost, Frederick
See Faust, Frederick (Schiller)

Frost, Robert (Lee)
1874-1963 . . . **CLC 1, 3, 4, 9, 10, 13, 15, 26, 34, 44; PC 1**
See also CA 89-92; CANR 33;
CDALB 1917-1929; DA; DLB 54;
DLBD 7; MTCW; SATA 14; WLC

Froy, Herald
See Waterhouse, Keith (Spencer)

Fry, Christopher 1907-. . . . . . **CLC 2, 10, 14**
See also CA 17-20R; CANR 9, 30; DLB 13;
MTCW; SATA 66

Frye, (Herman) Northrop
1912-1991 . . . . **CLC 24, 70**
See also CA 5-8R; 133; CANR 8, 37;
DLB 67, 68; MTCW

Fuchs, Daniel 1909-. . . . . **CLC 8, 22**
See also CA 81-84; CAAS 5; CANR 40;
DLB 9, 26, 28

Fuchs, Daniel 1934-. . . . . **CLC 34**
See also CA 37-40R; CANR 14

Fuentes, Carlos
1928-. . . . . . **CLC 3, 8, 10, 13, 22, 41, 60**
See also AAYA 4; AITN 2; CA 69-72;
CANR 10, 32; DA; DLB 113; HW;
MTCW; WLC

Fuentes, Gregorio Lopez y
See Lopez y Fuentes, Gregorio

Fugard, (Harold) Athol
1932-. . . . . . . **CLC 5, 9, 14, 25, 40; DC 3**
See also CA 85-88; CANR 32; MTCW

Fugard, Sheila 1932-. . . . . **CLC 48**
See also CA 125

Fuller, Charles (H., Jr.)
1939-. . . . . **CLC 25; DC 1**
See also BLC 2; BW; CA 108; 112; DLB 38;
MTCW

Fuller, John (Leopold) 1937-. . . . . . **CLC 62**
See also CA 21-24R; CANR 9; DLB 40

Fuller, Margaret . . . . **NCLC 5**
See also Ossoli, Sarah Margaret (Fuller
marchesa d')

Fuller, Roy (Broadbent)
1912-1991 . . . . **CLC 4, 28**
See also CA 5-8R; 135; CAAS 10; DLB 15,
20

Fulton, Alice 1952-. . . . . **CLC 52**
See also CA 116

Furphy, Joseph 1843-1912. . . . . . . **TCLC 25**

Fussell, Paul 1924-. . . . . **CLC 74**
See also BEST 90:1; CA 17-20R; CANR 8,
21, 35; MTCW

Futabatei, Shimei 1864-1909 . . . . . . **TCLC 44**

Futrelle, Jacques 1875-1912 . . . . . . **TCLC 19**
See also CA 113

G. B. S.
See Shaw, George Bernard

Gaboriau, Emile 1835-1873 . . . . . . **NCLC 14**

Gadda, Carlo Emilio 1893-1973 . . . . **CLC 11**
See also CA 89-92

Gaddis, William
1922-. . . . . **CLC 1, 3, 6, 8, 10, 19, 43**
See also CA 17-20R; CANR 21; DLB 2;
MTCW

Gaines, Ernest J(ames)
1933-. . . . . **CLC 3, 11, 18**
See also AITN 1; BLC 2; BW; CA 9-12R;
CANR 6, 24; CDALB 1968-1988; DLB 2,
33; DLBY 80; MTCW

Gaitskill, Mary 1954-. . . . . **CLC 69**
See also CA 128

Galdos, Benito Perez
See Perez Galdos, Benito

Gale, Zona 1874-1938 . . . . **TCLC 7**
See also CA 105; DLB 9, 78

Galeano, Eduardo (Hughes) 1940-. . . **CLC 72**
See also CA 29-32R; CANR 13, 32; HW

Galiano, Juan Valera y Alcala
See Valera y Alcala-Galiano, Juan

Gallagher, Tess 1943-. . . . . **CLC 18, 63**
See also CA 106; DLB 120

Gallant, Mavis
1922-. . . . . **CLC 7, 18, 38; SSC 5**
See also CA 69-72; CANR 29; DLB 53;
MTCW

Gallant, Roy A(rthur) 1924-. . . . . **CLC 17**
See also CA 5-8R; CANR 4, 29; CLR 30;
MAICYA; SATA 4, 68

Gallico, Paul (William) 1897-1976 . . . **CLC 2**
See also AITN 1; CA 5-8R; 69-72;
CANR 23; DLB 9; MAICYA; SATA 13

Gallup, Ralph
See Whitemore, Hugh (John)

Galsworthy, John 1867-1933. . . . **TCLC 1, 45**
See also CA 104; CDBLB 1890-1914; DA;
DLB 10, 34, 98; WLC 2

Galt, John 1779-1839. . . . . **NCLC 1**
See also DLB 99, 116

Galvin, James 1951-. . . . . **CLC 38**
See also CA 108; CANR 26

Gamboa, Federico 1864-1939. . . . . . **TCLC 36**

Gann, Ernest Kellogg 1910-1991. . . . **CLC 23**
See also AITN 1; CA 1-4R; 136; CANR 1

Garcia, Christina 1959-. . . . . **CLC 76**

Garcia Lorca, Federico
1898-1936 . . **TCLC 1, 7, 49; DC 2; PC 3**
See also CA 104; 131; DA; DLB 108; HW;
MTCW; WLC

Garcia Marquez, Gabriel (Jose)
1928-. . . **CLC 2, 3, 8, 10, 15, 27, 47, 55;
SSC 8**
See also Marquez, Gabriel (Jose) Garcia
See also AAYA 3; BEST 89:1, 90:4;
CA 33-36R; CANR 10, 28; DA;
DLB 113; HW; MTCW; WLC

Gard, Janice
See Latham, Jean Lee

Gard, Roger Martin du
See Martin du Gard, Roger

Gardam, Jane 1928-. . . . . **CLC 43**
See also CA 49-52; CANR 2, 18, 33;
CLR 12; DLB 14; MAICYA; MTCW;
SAAS 9; SATA 28, 39

Gardner, Herb. . . . . **CLC 44**

Gardner, John (Champlin), Jr.
1933-1982 . . . . **CLC 2, 3, 5, 7, 8, 10, 18,
28, 34; SSC 7**
See also AITN 1; CA 65-68; 107;
CANR 33; DLB 2; DLBY 82; MTCW;
SATA 31, 40

Gardner, John (Edmund) 1926-. . . . . **CLC 30**
See also CA 103; CANR 15; MTCW

Gardner, Noel
See Kuttner, Henry

Gardons, S. S.
See Snodgrass, William D(e Witt)

Garfield, Leon 1921-. . . . . **CLC 12**
See also AAYA 8; CA 17-20R; CANR 38,
41; CLR 21; MAICYA; SATA 1, 32

Garland, (Hannibal) Hamlin
1860-1940 . . . . **TCLC 3**
See also CA 104; DLB 12, 71, 78

Garneau, (Hector de) Saint-Denys
1912-1943 . . . . **TCLC 13**
See also CA 111; DLB 88

Garner, Alan 1934-. . . . . **CLC 17**
See also CA 73-76; CANR 15; CLR 20;
MAICYA; MTCW; SATA 18, 69

Garner, Hugh 1913-1979 . . . . **CLC 13**
See also CA 69-72; CANR 31; DLB 68

Garnett, David 1892-1981 . . . . **CLC 3**
See also CA 5-8R; 103; CANR 17; DLB 34

Garos, Stephanie
See Katz, Steve

Garrett, George (Palmer)
1929-. . . . . **CLC 3, 11, 51**
See also CA 1-4R; CAAS 5; CANR 1;
DLB 2, 5, 130; DLBY 83

Garrick, David 1717-1779 . . . . **LC 15**
See also DLB 84

Garrigue, Jean 1914-1972 . . . . **CLC 2, 8**
See also CA 5-8R; 37-40R; CANR 20

Garrison, Frederick
See Sinclair, Upton (Beall)

Garth, Will
See Hamilton, Edmond; Kuttner, Henry

Garvey, Marcus (Moziah, Jr.)
1887-1940 . . . . **TCLC 41**
See also BLC 2; BW; CA 120; 124

Gary, Romain . . . . **CLC 25**
See also Kacew, Romain
See also DLB 83

Gascar, Pierre . . . . **CLC 11**
See also Fournier, Pierre

Gascoyne, David (Emery) 1916-. . . . **CLC 45**
See also CA 65-68; CANR 10, 28; DLB 20;
MTCW

Gaskell, Elizabeth Cleghorn
1810-1865 . . . . **NCLC 5**
See also CDBLB 1832-1890; DLB 21

Gass, William H(oward)
1924-. . . **CLC 1, 2, 8, 11, 15, 39; SSC 12**
See also CA 17-20R; CANR 30; DLB 2;
MTCW

Gasset, Jose Ortega y
See Ortega y Gasset, Jose

Gautier, Theophile 1811-1872 . . . . . **NCLC 1**
See also DLB 119

Gawsworth, John
    See Bates, H(erbert) E(rnest)

Gaye, Marvin (Penze) 1939-1984 . . . **CLC 26**
    See also CA 112

Gebler, Carlo (Ernest) 1954- . . . . **CLC 39**
    See also CA 119; 133

Gee, Maggie (Mary) 1948- . . . . **CLC 57**
    See also CA 130

Gee, Maurice (Gough) 1931- . . . . **CLC 29**
    See also CA 97-100; SATA 46

Gelbart, Larry (Simon) 1923- . . . **CLC 21, 61**
    See also CA 73-76

Gelber, Jack 1932- . . . . **CLC 1, 6, 14**
    See also CA 1-4R; CANR 2; DLB 7

Gellhorn, Martha Ellis 1908- . . . **CLC 14, 60**
    See also CA 77-80; DLBY 82

Genet, Jean
    1910-1986 . . . **CLC 1, 2, 5, 10, 14, 44, 46**
    See also CA 13-16R; CANR 18; DLB 72;
    DLBY 86; MTCW

Gent, Peter 1942- . . . . **CLC 29**
    See also AITN 1; CA 89-92; DLBY 82

George, Jean Craighead 1919- . . . . . . **CLC 35**
    See also AAYA 8; CA 5-8R; CANR 25;
    CLR 1; DLB 52; MAICYA; SATA 2, 68

George, Stefan (Anton)
    1868-1933 . . . . **TCLC 2, 14**
    See also CA 104

Georges, Georges Martin
    See Simenon, Georges (Jacques Christian)

Gerhardi, William Alexander
    See Gerhardie, William Alexander

Gerhardie, William Alexander
    1895-1977 . . . . **CLC 5**
    See also CA 25-28R; 73-76; CANR 18;
    DLB 36

Gerstler, Amy 1956- . . . . **CLC 70**

Gertler, T. . . . . **CLC 34**
    See also CA 116; 121

Ghalib 1797-1869 . . . . **NCLC 39**

Ghelderode, Michel de
    1898-1962 . . . . **CLC 6, 11**
    See also CA 85-88; CANR 40

Ghiselin, Brewster 1903- . . . . **CLC 23**
    See also CA 13-16R; CAAS 10; CANR 13

Ghose, Zulfikar 1935- . . . . **CLC 42**
    See also CA 65-68

Ghosh, Amitav 1956- . . . . **CLC 44**

Giacosa, Giuseppe 1847-1906 . . . . . . **TCLC 7**
    See also CA 104

Gibb, Lee
    See Waterhouse, Keith (Spencer)

Gibbon, Lewis Grassic . . . . **TCLC 4**
    See also Mitchell, James Leslie

Gibbons, Kaye 1960- . . . . **CLC 50**

Gibran, Kahlil 1883-1931 . . . . **TCLC 1, 9**
    See also CA 104

Gibson, William 1914- . . . . **CLC 23**
    See also CA 9-12R; CANR 9; DA; DLB 7;
    SATA 66

Gibson, William (Ford) 1948- . . . **CLC 39, 63**
    See also CA 126; 133

Gide, Andre (Paul Guillaume)
    1869-1951 . . . . **TCLC 5, 12, 36**
    See also CA 104; 124; DA; DLB 65;
    MTCW; WLC

Gifford, Barry (Colby) 1946- . . . . **CLC 34**
    See also CA 65-68; CANR 9, 30, 40

Gilbert, W(illiam) S(chwenck)
    1836-1911 . . . . **TCLC 3**
    See also CA 104; SATA 36

Gilbreth, Frank B., Jr. 1911- . . . . **CLC 17**
    See also CA 9-12R; SATA 2

Gilchrist, Ellen 1935- . . . . **CLC 34, 48**
    See also CA 113; 116; CANR 41; DLB 130;
    MTCW

Giles, Molly 1942- . . . . **CLC 39**
    See also CA 126

Gill, Patrick
    See Creasey, John

Gilliam, Terry (Vance) 1940- . . . . **CLC 21**
    See also Monty Python
    See also CA 108; 113; CANR 35

Gillian, Jerry
    See Gilliam, Terry (Vance)

Gilliatt, Penelope (Ann Douglass)
    1932- . . . . **CLC 2, 10, 13, 53**
    See also AITN 2; CA 13-16R; DLB 14

Gilman, Charlotte (Anna) Perkins (Stetson)
    1860-1935 . . . . **TCLC 9, 37**
    See also CA 106

Gilmour, David 1944- . . . . **CLC 35**
    See also Pink Floyd
    See also CA 138

Gilpin, William 1724-1804 . . . . . . **NCLC 30**

Gilray, J. D.
    See Mencken, H(enry) L(ouis)

Gilroy, Frank D(aniel) 1925- . . . . **CLC 2**
    See also CA 81-84; CANR 32; DLB 7

Ginsberg, Allen
    1926- . . . . . **CLC 1, 2, 3, 4, 6, 13, 36, 69;**
                                                     PC 4
    See also AITN 1; CA 1-4R; CANR 2, 41;
    CDALB 1941-1968; DA; DLB 5, 16;
    MTCW; WLC 3

Ginzburg, Natalia
    1916-1991 . . . . **CLC 5, 11, 54, 70**
    See also CA 85-88; 135; CANR 33; MTCW

Giono, Jean 1895-1970 . . . . **CLC 4, 11**
    See also CA 45-48; 29-32R; CANR 2, 35;
    DLB 72; MTCW

Giovanni, Nikki 1943- . . . . . **CLC 2, 4, 19, 64**
    See also AITN 1; BLC 2; BW; CA 29-32R;
    CAAS 6; CANR 18, 41; CLR 6; DA;
    DLB 5, 41; MAICYA; MTCW; SATA 24

Giovene, Andrea 1904- . . . . **CLC 7**
    See also CA 85-88

Gippius, Zinaida (Nikolayevna) 1869-1945
    See Hippius, Zinaida
    See also CA 106

Giraudoux, (Hippolyte) Jean
    1882-1944 . . . . **TCLC 2, 7**
    See also CA 104; DLB 65

Gironella, Jose Maria 1917- . . . . **CLC 11**
    See also CA 101

Gissing, George (Robert)
    1857-1903 . . . . **TCLC 3, 24, 47**
    See also CA 105; DLB 18

Giurlani, Aldo
    See Palazzeschi, Aldo

Gladkov, Fyodor (Vasilyevich)
    1883-1958 . . . . **TCLC 27**

Glanville, Brian (Lester) 1931- . . . . . . **CLC 6**
    See also CA 5-8R; CAAS 9; CANR 3;
    DLB 15; SATA 42

Glasgow, Ellen (Anderson Gholson)
    1873(?)-1945 . . . . **TCLC 2, 7**
    See also CA 104; DLB 9, 12

Glassco, John 1909-1981 . . . . **CLC 9**
    See also CA 13-16R; 102; CANR 15;
    DLB 68

Glasscock, Amnesia
    See Steinbeck, John (Ernst)

Glasser, Ronald J. 1940(?)- . . . . **CLC 37**

Glassman, Joyce
    See Johnson, Joyce

Glendinning, Victoria 1937- . . . . **CLC 50**
    See also CA 120; 127

Glissant, Edouard 1928- . . . . **CLC 10, 68**

Gloag, Julian 1930- . . . . **CLC 40**
    See also AITN 1; CA 65-68; CANR 10

Gluck, Louise (Elisabeth)
    1943- . . . . **CLC 7, 22, 44**
    See also Glueck, Louise
    See also CA 33-36R; CANR 40; DLB 5

Glueck, Louise . . . . **CLC 7, 22**
    See also Gluck, Louise (Elisabeth)
    See also DLB 5

Gobineau, Joseph Arthur (Comte) de
    1816-1882 . . . . **NCLC 17**
    See also DLB 123

Godard, Jean-Luc 1930- . . . . **CLC 20**
    See also CA 93-96

Godden, (Margaret) Rumer 1907- . . . **CLC 53**
    See also AAYA 6; CA 5-8R; CANR 4, 27,
    36; CLR 20; MAICYA; SAAS 12;
    SATA 3, 36

Godoy Alcayaga, Lucila 1889-1957
    See Mistral, Gabriela
    See also CA 104; 131; HW; MTCW

Godwin, Gail (Kathleen)
    1937- . . . . **CLC 5, 8, 22, 31, 69**
    See also CA 29-32R; CANR 15; DLB 6;
    MTCW

Godwin, William 1756-1836 . . . . . . **NCLC 14**
    See also CDBLB 1789-1832; DLB 39, 104

Goethe, Johann Wolfgang von
    1749-1832 . . . . **NCLC 4, 22, 34; PC 5**
    See also DA; DLB 94; WLC 3

Gogarty, Oliver St. John
    1878-1957 . . . . **TCLC 15**
    See also CA 109; DLB 15, 19

Gogol, Nikolai (Vasilyevich)
    1809-1852 . . . . . **NCLC 5, 15, 31; DC 1;**
                                                     SSC 4
    See also DA; WLC

Gold, Herbert 1924- . . . . **CLC 4, 7, 14, 42**
    See also CA 9-12R; CANR 17; DLB 2;
    DLBY 81

Goldbarth, Albert 1948- .... **CLC 5, 38**
See also CA 53-56; CANR 6, 40; DLB 120

Goldberg, Anatol 1910-1982 .... **CLC 34**
See also CA 131; 117

Goldemberg, Isaac 1945- .... **CLC 52**
See also CA 69-72; CAAS 12; CANR 11,
32; HW

Golden Silver
See Storm, Hyemeyohsts

Golding, William (Gerald)
1911- ..... **CLC 1, 2, 3, 8, 10, 17, 27, 58**
See also AAYA 5; CA 5-8R; CANR 13, 33;
CDBLB 1945-1960; DA; DLB 15, 100;
MTCW; WLC

Goldman, Emma 1869-1940 ...... **TCLC 13**
See also CA 110

Goldman, Francisco 1955- .... **CLC 76**

Goldman, William (W.) 1931- .... **CLC 1, 48**
See also CA 9-12R; CANR 29; DLB 44

Goldmann, Lucien 1913-1970 ...... **CLC 24**
See also CA 25-28; CAP 2

Goldoni, Carlo 1707-1793 .... **LC 4**

Goldsberry, Steven 1949- .... **CLC 34**
See also CA 131

Goldsmith, Oliver 1728-1774 .... **LC 2**
See also CDBLB 1660-1789; DA; DLB 39,
89, 104, 109; SATA 26; WLC

Goldsmith, Peter
See Priestley, J(ohn) B(oynton)

Gombrowicz, Witold
1904-1969 .... **CLC 4, 7, 11, 49**
See also CA 19-20; 25-28R; CAP 2

Gomez de la Serna, Ramon
1888-1963 .... **CLC 9**
See also CA 116; HW

Goncharov, Ivan Alexandrovich
1812-1891 .... **NCLC 1**

Goncourt, Edmond (Louis Antoine Huot) de
1822-1896 .... **NCLC 7**
See also DLB 123

Goncourt, Jules (Alfred Huot) de
1830-1870 .... **NCLC 7**
See also DLB 123

Gontier, Fernande 19(?)- .... **CLC 50**

Goodman, Paul 1911-1972 .... **CLC 1, 2, 4, 7**
See also CA 19-20; 37-40R; CANR 34;
CAP 2; DLB 130; MTCW

Gordimer, Nadine
1923- .... **CLC 3, 5, 7, 10, 18, 33, 51, 70**
See also CA 5-8R; CANR 3, 28; DA;
MTCW

Gordon, Adam Lindsay
1833-1870 .... **NCLC 21**

Gordon, Caroline
1895-1981 .... **CLC 6, 13, 29**
See also CA 11-12; 103; CANR 36; CAP 1;
DLB 4, 9, 102; DLBY 81; MTCW

Gordon, Charles William 1860-1937
See Connor, Ralph
See also CA 109

Gordon, Mary (Catherine)
1949- .... **CLC 13, 22**
See also CA 102; DLB 6; DLBY 81;
MTCW

Gordon, Sol 1923- .... **CLC 26**
See also CA 53-56; CANR 4; SATA 11

Gordone, Charles 1925- .... **CLC 1, 4**
See also BW; CA 93-96; DLB 7; MTCW

Gorenko, Anna Andreevna
See Akhmatova, Anna

Gorky, Maxim .... **TCLC 8**
See also Peshkov, Alexei Maximovich
See also WLC

Goryan, Sirak
See Saroyan, William

Gosse, Edmund (William)
1849-1928 .... **TCLC 28**
See also CA 117; DLB 57

Gotlieb, Phyllis Fay (Bloom)
1926- .... **CLC 18**
See also CA 13-16R; CANR 7; DLB 88

Gottesman, S. D.
See Kornbluth, C(yril) M.; Pohl, Frederik

Gottfried von Strassburg
fl. c. 1210- .... **CMLC 10**

Gottschalk, Laura Riding
See Jackson, Laura (Riding)

Gould, Lois .... **CLC 4, 10**
See also CA 77-80; CANR 29; MTCW

Gourmont, Remy de 1858-1915 .... **TCLC 17**
See also CA 109

Govier, Katherine 1948- .... **CLC 51**
See also CA 101; CANR 18, 40

Goyen, (Charles) William
1915-1983 .... **CLC 5, 8, 14, 40**
See also AITN 2; CA 5-8R; 110; CANR 6;
DLB 2; DLBY 83

Goytisolo, Juan 1931- .... **CLC 5, 10, 23**
See also CA 85-88; CANR 32; HW; MTCW

Gozzi, (Conte) Carlo 1720-1806 .. **NCLC 23**

Grabbe, Christian Dietrich
1801-1836 .... **NCLC 2**

Grace, Patricia 1937- .... **CLC 56**

Gracian y Morales, Baltasar
1601-1658 .... **LC 15**

Gracq, Julien .... **CLC 11, 48**
See also Poirier, Louis
See also DLB 83

Grade, Chaim 1910-1982 .... **CLC 10**
See also CA 93-96; 107

Graduate of Oxford, A
See Ruskin, John

Graham, John
See Phillips, David Graham

Graham, Jorie 1951- .... **CLC 48**
See also CA 111; DLB 120

Graham, R(obert) B(ontine) Cunninghame
See Cunninghame Graham, R(obert)
B(ontine)
See also DLB 98

Graham, Robert
See Haldeman, Joe (William)

Graham, Tom
See Lewis, (Harry) Sinclair

Graham, W(illiam) S(ydney)
1918-1986 .... **CLC 29**
See also CA 73-76; 118; DLB 20

Graham, Winston (Mawdsley)
1910- .... **CLC 23**
See also CA 49-52; CANR 2, 22; DLB 77

Grant, Skeeter
See Spiegelman, Art

Granville-Barker, Harley
1877-1946 .... **TCLC 2**
See also Barker, Harley Granville
See also CA 104

Grass, Guenter (Wilhelm)
1927- .. **CLC 1, 2, 4, 6, 11, 15, 22, 32, 49**
See also CA 13-16R; CANR 20; DA;
DLB 75, 124; MTCW; WLC

Gratton, Thomas
See Hulme, T(homas) E(rnest)

Grau, Shirley Ann 1929- .... **CLC 4, 9**
See also CA 89-92; CANR 22; DLB 2;
MTCW

Gravel, Fern
See Hall, James Norman

Graver, Elizabeth 1964- .... **CLC 70**
See also CA 135

Graves, Richard Perceval 1945- .... **CLC 44**
See also CA 65-68; CANR 9, 26

Graves, Robert (von Ranke)
1895-1985 ..... **CLC 1, 2, 6, 11, 39, 44,
45; PC 6**
See also CA 5-8R; 117; CANR 5, 36;
CDBLB 1914-1945; DLB 20, 100;
DLBY 85; MTCW; SATA 45

Gray, Alasdair (James) 1934- ...... **CLC 41**
See also CA 126; MTCW

Gray, Amlin 1946- .... **CLC 29**
See also CA 138

Gray, Francine du Plessix 1930-.... **CLC 22**
See also BEST 90:3; CA 61-64; CAAS 2;
CANR 11, 33; MTCW

Gray, John (Henry) 1866-1934 .... **TCLC 19**
See also CA 119

Gray, Simon (James Holliday)
1936- .... **CLC 9, 14, 36**
See also AITN 1; CA 21-24R; CAAS 3;
CANR 32; DLB 13; MTCW

Gray, Spalding 1941- .... **CLC 49**
See also CA 128

Gray, Thomas 1716-1771 .... **LC 4; PC 2**
See also CDBLB 1660-1789; DA; DLB 109;
WLC

Grayson, David
See Baker, Ray Stannard

Grayson, Richard (A.) 1951- .... **CLC 38**
See also CA 85-88; CANR 14, 31

Greeley, Andrew M(oran) 1928- .... **CLC 28**
See also CA 5-8R; CAAS 7; CANR 7;
MTCW

Green, Brian
See Card, Orson Scott

Green, Hannah .... **CLC 3**
See also CA 73-76

Green, Hannah
See Greenberg, Joanne (Goldenberg)

Green, Henry .... **CLC 2, 13**
See also Yorke, Henry Vincent
See also DLB 15

Green, Julian (Hartridge)
1900- .... **CLC 3, 11, 77**
See also CA 21-24R; CANR 33; DLB 4, 72;
MTCW

Green, Julien 1900-
See Green, Julian (Hartridge)

Green, Paul (Eliot) 1894-1981...... **CLC 25**
See also AITN 1; CA 5-8R; 103; CANR 3;
DLB 7, 9; DLBY 81

Greenberg, Ivan 1908-1973
See Rahv, Philip
See also CA 85-88

Greenberg, Joanne (Goldenberg)
1932- .... **CLC 7, 30**
See also CA 5-8R; CANR 14, 32; SATA 25

Greenberg, Richard 1959(?)- .... **CLC 57**
See also CA 138

Greene, Bette 1934- .... **CLC 30**
See also AAYA 7; CA 53-56; CANR 4;
CLR 2; MAICYA; SAAS 16; SATA 8

Greene, Gael .... **CLC 8**
See also CA 13-16R; CANR 10

Greene, Graham (Henry)
1904-1991 ... **CLC 1, 3, 6, 9, 14, 18, 27,
37, 70, 72**
See also AITN 2; CA 13-16R; 133;
CANR 35; CDBLB 1945-1960; DA;
DLB 13, 15, 77, 100; DLBY 91; MTCW;
SATA 20; WLC

Greer, Richard
See Silverberg, Robert

Greer, Richard
See Silverberg, Robert

Gregor, Arthur 1923- .... **CLC 9**
See also CA 25-28R; CAAS 10; CANR 11;
SATA 36

Gregor, Lee
See Pohl, Frederik

Gregory, Isabella Augusta (Persse)
1852-1932 .... **TCLC 1**
See also CA 104; DLB 10

Gregory, J. Dennis
See Williams, John A(lfred)

Grendon, Stephen
See Derleth, August (William)

Grenville, Kate 1950- .... **CLC 61**
See also CA 118

Grenville, Pelham
See Wodehouse, P(elham) G(renville)

Greve, Felix Paul (Berthold Friedrich)
1879-1948
See Grove, Frederick Philip
See also CA 104

Grey, Zane 1872-1939 .... **TCLC 6**
See also CA 104; 132; DLB 9; MTCW

Grieg, (Johan) Nordahl (Brun)
1902-1943 .... **TCLC 10**
See also CA 107

Grieve, C(hristopher) M(urray)
1892-1978 .... **CLC 11, 19**
See also MacDiarmid, Hugh
See also CA 5-8R; 85-88; CANR 33;
MTCW

Griffin, Gerald 1803-1840 .... **NCLC 7**

Griffin, John Howard 1920-1980.... **CLC 68**
See also AITN 1; CA 1-4R; 101; CANR 2

Griffin, Peter .... **CLC 39**

Griffiths, Trevor 1935- .... **CLC 13, 52**
See also CA 97-100; DLB 13

Grigson, Geoffrey (Edward Harvey)
1905-1985 .... **CLC 7, 39**
See also CA 25-28R; 118; CANR 20, 33;
DLB 27; MTCW

Grillparzer, Franz 1791-1872...... **NCLC 1**

Grimble, Reverend Charles James
See Eliot, T(homas) S(tearns)

Grimke, Charlotte L(ottie) Forten
1837(?)-1914
See Forten, Charlotte L.
See also BW; CA 117; 124

Grimm, Jacob Ludwig Karl
1785-1863 .... **NCLC 3**
See also DLB 90; MAICYA; SATA 22

Grimm, Wilhelm Karl 1786-1859 .. **NCLC 3**
See also DLB 90; MAICYA; SATA 22

Grimmelshausen, Johann Jakob Christoffel
von 1621-1676 .... **LC 6**

Grindel, Eugene 1895-1952
See Eluard, Paul
See also CA 104

Grossman, David .... **CLC 67**
See also CA 138

Grossman, Vasily (Semenovich)
1905-1964 .... **CLC 41**
See also CA 124; 130; MTCW

Grove, Frederick Philip .... **TCLC 4**
See also Greve, Felix Paul (Berthold
Friedrich)
See also DLB 92

Grubb
See Crumb, R(obert)

Grumbach, Doris (Isaac)
1918- .... **CLC 13, 22, 64**
See also CA 5-8R; CAAS 2; CANR 9

Grundtvig, Nicolai Frederik Severin
1783-1872 .... **NCLC 1**

Grunge
See Crumb, R(obert)

Grunwald, Lisa 1959- .... **CLC 44**
See also CA 120

Guare, John 1938- .... **CLC 8, 14, 29, 67**
See also CA 73-76; CANR 21; DLB 7;
MTCW

Gudjonsson, Halldor Kiljan 1902-
See Laxness, Halldor
See also CA 103

Guenter, Erich
See Eich, Guenter

Guest, Barbara 1920- .... **CLC 34**
See also CA 25-28R; CANR 11; DLB 5

Guest, Judith (Ann) 1936- .... **CLC 8, 30**
See also AAYA 7; CA 77-80; CANR 15;
MTCW

Guild, Nicholas M. 1944-......... **CLC 33**
See also CA 93-96

Guillemin, Jacques
See Sartre, Jean-Paul

Guillen, Jorge 1893-1984......... **CLC 11**
See also CA 89-92; 112; DLB 108; HW

Guillen (y Batista), Nicolas (Cristobal)
1902-1989 .... **CLC 48**
See also BLC 2; BW; CA 116; 125; 129;
HW

Guillevic, (Eugene) 1907-......... **CLC 33**
See also CA 93-96

Guillois
See Desnos, Robert

Guiney, Louise Imogen
1861-1920 .... **TCLC 41**
See also DLB 54

Guiraldes, Ricardo (Guillermo)
1886-1927 .... **TCLC 39**
See also CA 131; HW; MTCW

Gunn, Bill .... **CLC 5**
See also Gunn, William Harrison
See also DLB 38

Gunn, Thom(son William)
1929- .... **CLC 3, 6, 18, 32**
See also CA 17-20R; CANR 9, 33;
CDBLB 1960 to Present; DLB 27;
MTCW

Gunn, William Harrison 1934(?)-1989
See Gunn, Bill
See also AITN 1; BW; CA 13-16R; 128;
CANR 12, 25

Gunnars, Kristjana 1948-......... **CLC 69**
See also CA 113; DLB 60

Gurganus, Allan 1947-............ **CLC 70**
See also BEST 90:1; CA 135

Gurney, A(lbert) R(amsdell), Jr.
1930- .... **CLC 32, 50, 54**
See also CA 77-80; CANR 32

Gurney, Ivor (Bertie) 1890-1937... **TCLC 33**

Gurney, Peter
See Gurney, A(lbert) R(amsdell), Jr.

Gustafson, Ralph (Barker) 1909-.... **CLC 36**
See also CA 21-24R; CANR 8; DLB 88

Gut, Gom
See Simenon, Georges (Jacques Christian)

Guthrie, A(lfred) B(ertram), Jr.
1901-1991 .... **CLC 23**
See also CA 57-60; 134; CANR 24; DLB 6;
SATA 62; SATA-Obit 67

Guthrie, Isobel
See Grieve, C(hristopher) M(urray)

Guthrie, Woodrow Wilson 1912-1967
See Guthrie, Woody
See also CA 113; 93-96

Guthrie, Woody.................... **CLC 35**
See also Guthrie, Woodrow Wilson

Guy, Rosa (Cuthbert) 1928-....... **CLC 26**
See also AAYA 4; BW; CA 17-20R;
CANR 14, 34; CLR 13; DLB 33;
MAICYA; SATA 14, 62

Gwendolyn
See Bennett, (Enoch) Arnold

H. D. .... **CLC 3, 8, 14, 31, 34, 73; PC 5**
See also Doolittle, Hilda

Haavikko, Paavo Juhani
1931- .... **CLC 18, 34**
See also CA 106

Habbema, Koos
See Heijermans, Herman

Hacker, Marilyn　1942-　.... **CLC 5, 9, 23, 72**
See also CA 77-80; DLB 120

Haggard, H(enry) Rider
1856-1925 .... **TCLC 11**
See also CA 108; DLB 70; SATA 16

Haig, Fenil
See Ford, Ford Madox

Haig-Brown, Roderick (Langmere)
1908-1976 .... **CLC 21**
See also CA 5-8R; 69-72; CANR 4, 38;
DLB 88; MAICYA; SATA 12

Hailey, Arthur　1920- .... **CLC 5**
See also AITN 2; BEST 90:3; CA 1-4R;
CANR 2, 36; DLB 88; DLBY 82; MTCW

Hailey, Elizabeth Forsythe　1938- ... **CLC 40**
See also CA 93-96; CAAS 1; CANR 15

Haines, John (Meade)　1924- .... **CLC 58**
See also CA 17-20R; CANR 13, 34; DLB 5

Haldeman, Joe (William)　1943- ..... **CLC 61**
See also CA 53-56; CANR 6; DLB 8

Haley, Alex(ander Murray Palmer)
1921-1992 .... **CLC 8, 12, 76**
See also BLC 2; BW; CA 77-80; 136; DA;
DLB 38; MTCW

Haliburton, Thomas Chandler
1796-1865 .... **NCLC 15**
See also DLB 11, 99

Hall, Donald (Andrew, Jr.)
1928- .... **CLC 1, 13, 37, 59**
See also CA 5-8R; CAAS 7; CANR 2;
DLB 5; SATA 23

Hall, Frederic Sauser
See Sauser-Hall, Frederic

Hall, James
See Kuttner, Henry

Hall, James Norman　1887-1951 ... **TCLC 23**
See also CA 123; SATA 21

Hall, (Marguerite) Radclyffe
1886(?)-1943 .... **TCLC 12**
See also CA 110

Hall, Rodney　1935- .... **CLC 51**
See also CA 109

Halliday, Michael
See Creasey, John

Halpern, Daniel　1945- .... **CLC 14**
See also CA 33-36R

Hamburger, Michael (Peter Leopold)
1924- .... **CLC 5, 14**
See also CA 5-8R; CAAS 4; CANR 2;
DLB 27

Hamill, Pete　1935- .... **CLC 10**
See also CA 25-28R; CANR 18

Hamilton, Clive
See Lewis, C(live) S(taples)

Hamilton, Edmond　1904-1977 ...... **CLC 1**
See also CA 1-4R; CANR 3; DLB 8

Hamilton, Eugene (Jacob) Lee
See Lee-Hamilton, Eugene (Jacob)

Hamilton, Franklin
See Silverberg, Robert

Hamilton, Gail
See Corcoran, Barbara

Hamilton, Mollie
See Kaye, M(ary) M(argaret)

Hamilton, (Anthony Walter) Patrick
1904-1962 .... **CLC 51**
See also CA 113; DLB 10

Hamilton, Virginia　1936- .... **CLC 26**
See also AAYA 2; BW; CA 25-28R;
CANR 20, 37; CLR 1, 11; DLB 33, 52;
MAICYA; MTCW; SATA 4, 56

Hammett, (Samuel) Dashiell
1894-1961 .... **CLC 3, 5, 10, 19, 47**
See also AITN 1; CA 81-84;
CDALB 1929-1941; DLBD 6; MTCW

Hammon, Jupiter　1711(?)-1800(?).. **NCLC 5**
See also BLC 2; DLB 31, 50

Hammond, Keith
See Kuttner, Henry

Hamner, Earl (Henry), Jr.　1923- ... **CLC 12**
See also AITN 2; CA 73-76; DLB 6

Hampton, Christopher (James)
1946- .... **CLC 4**
See also CA 25-28R; DLB 13; MTCW

Hamsun, Knut　1859-1952... **TCLC 2, 14, 49**
See also Pedersen, Knut

Handke, Peter　1942- .. **CLC 5, 8, 10, 15, 38**
See also CA 77-80; CANR 33; DLB 85,
124; MTCW

Hanley, James　1901-1985 ... **CLC 3, 5, 8, 13**
See also CA 73-76; 117; CANR 36; MTCW

Hannah, Barry　1942- .... **CLC 23, 38**
See also CA 108; 110; DLB 6; MTCW

Hannon, Ezra
See Hunter, Evan

Hansberry, Lorraine (Vivian)
1930-1965 .... **CLC 17, 62; DC 2**
See also BLC 2; BW; CA 109; 25-28R;
CABS 3; CDALB 1941-1968; DA;
DLB 7, 38; MTCW

Hansen, Joseph　1923- .... **CLC 38**
See also CA 29-32R; CAAS 17; CANR 16

Hansen, Martin A.　1909-1955 ..... **TCLC 32**

Hanson, Kenneth O(stlin)　1922- .... **CLC 13**
See also CA 53-56; CANR 7

Hardwick, Elizabeth　1916- .... **CLC 13**
See also CA 5-8R; CANR 3, 32; DLB 6;
MTCW

Hardy, Thomas
1840-1928 ..... **TCLC 4, 10, 18, 32, 48;
SSC 2**
See also CA 104; 123; CDBLB 1890-1914;
DA; DLB 18, 19; MTCW; WLC

Hare, David　1947- .... **CLC 29, 58**
See also CA 97-100; CANR 39; DLB 13;
MTCW

Harford, Henry
See Hudson, W(illiam) H(enry)

Hargrave, Leonie
See Disch, Thomas M(ichael)

Harlan, Louis R(udolph)　1922- ..... **CLC 34**
See also CA 21-24R; CANR 25

Harling, Robert　1951(?)- .... **CLC 53**

Harmon, William (Ruth)　1938- ..... **CLC 38**
See also CA 33-36R; CANR 14, 32, 35;
SATA 65

Harper, F. E. W.
See Harper, Frances Ellen Watkins

Harper, Frances E. W.
See Harper, Frances Ellen Watkins

Harper, Frances E. Watkins
See Harper, Frances Ellen Watkins

Harper, Frances Ellen
See Harper, Frances Ellen Watkins

Harper, Frances Ellen Watkins
1825-1911 .... **TCLC 14**
See also BLC 2; BW; CA 111; 125; DLB 50

Harper, Michael S(teven)　1938- .. **CLC 7, 22**
See also BW; CA 33-36R; CANR 24;
DLB 41

Harper, Mrs. F. E. W.
See Harper, Frances Ellen Watkins

Harris, Christie (Lucy) Irwin
1907- .... **CLC 12**
See also CA 5-8R; CANR 6; DLB 88;
MAICYA; SAAS 10; SATA 6, 74

Harris, Frank　1856(?)-1931 .... **TCLC 24**
See also CA 109

Harris, George Washington
1814-1869 .... **NCLC 23**
See also DLB 3, 11

Harris, Joel Chandler　1848-1908 ... **TCLC 2**
See also CA 104; 137; DLB 11, 23, 42, 78,
91; MAICYA; YABC 1

**Harris, John (Wyndham Parkes Lucas)
Beynon**　1903-1969 .... **CLC 19**
See also CA 102; 89-92

Harris, MacDonald
See Heiney, Donald (William)

Harris, Mark　1922- .... **CLC 19**
See also CA 5-8R; CAAS 3; CANR 2;
DLB 2; DLBY 80

Harris, (Theodore) Wilson　1921- .... **CLC 25**
See also BW; CA 65-68; CAAS 16;
CANR 11, 27; DLB 117; MTCW

Harrison, Elizabeth Cavanna　1909-
See Cavanna, Betty
See also CA 9-12R; CANR 6, 27

Harrison, Harry (Max)　1925- ...... **CLC 42**
See also CA 1-4R; CANR 5, 21; DLB 8;
SATA 4

Harrison, James (Thomas)　1937-
See Harrison, Jim
See also CA 13-16R; CANR 8

Harrison, Jim　........... **CLC 6, 14, 33, 66**
See also Harrison, James (Thomas)
See also DLBY 82

Harrison, Kathryn　1961- .... **CLC 70**

Harrison, Tony　1937- .... **CLC 43**
See also CA 65-68; DLB 40; MTCW

Harriss, Will(ard Irvin)　1922- ...... **CLC 34**
See also CA 111

Harson, Sley
See Ellison, Harlan

Hart, Ellis
See Ellison, Harlan

Hart, Josephine　1942(?)- .... **CLC 70**
See also CA 138

Hart, Moss　1904-1961 .... **CLC 66**
See also CA 109; 89-92; DLB 7

Harte, (Francis) Bret(t)
1836(?)-1902 . . . . . . TCLC 1, 25; SSC 8
See also CA 104; 140; CDALB 1865-1917;
DA; DLB 12, 64, 74, 79; SATA 26; WLC

Hartley, L(eslie) P(oles)
1895-1972 . . . . CLC 2, 22
See also CA 45-48; 37-40R; CANR 33;
DLB 15; MTCW

Hartman, Geoffrey H. 1929- . . . . CLC 27
See also CA 117; 125; DLB 67

Haruf, Kent 19(?)- . . . . CLC 34

Harwood, Ronald 1934- . . . . CLC 32
See also CA 1-4R; CANR 4; DLB 13

Hasek, Jaroslav (Matej Frantisek)
1883-1923 . . . . TCLC 4
See also CA 104; 129; MTCW

Hass, Robert 1941- . . . . CLC 18, 39
See also CA 111; CANR 30; DLB 105

Hastings, Hudson
See Kuttner, Henry

Hastings, Selina. . . . . CLC 44

Hatteras, Amelia
See Mencken, H(enry) L(ouis)

Hatteras, Owen . . . . TCLC 18
See also Mencken, H(enry) L(ouis); Nathan,
George Jean

Hauptmann, Gerhart (Johann Robert)
1862-1946 . . . . TCLC 4
See also CA 104; DLB 66, 118

Havel, Vaclav 1936- . . . . CLC 25, 58, 65
See also CA 104; CANR 36; MTCW

Haviaras, Stratis . . . . CLC 33
See also Chaviaras, Strates

Hawes, Stephen 1475(?)-1523(?) . . . . . LC 17

Hawkes, John (Clendennin Burne, Jr.)
1925- . . . . . . CLC 1, 2, 3, 4, 7, 9, 14, 15,
27, 49
See also CA 1-4R; CANR 2; DLB 2, 7;
DLBY 80; MTCW

Hawking, S. W.
See Hawking, Stephen W(illiam)

Hawking, Stephen W(illiam)
1942- . . . . CLC 63
See also BEST 89:1; CA 126; 129

Hawthorne, Julian 1846-1934 . . . . . TCLC 25

Hawthorne, Nathaniel
1804-1864 . . . . NCLC 39; SSC 3
See also CDALB 1640-1865; DA; DLB 1,
74; WLC; YABC 2

Haxton, Josephine Ayres 1921- . . . . CLC 73
See also CA 115; CANR 41

Hayaseca y Eizaguirre, Jorge
See Echegaray (y Eizaguirre), Jose (Maria
Waldo)

Hayashi Fumiko 1904-1951 . . . . . . TCLC 27

Haycraft, Anna
See Ellis, Alice Thomas
See also CA 122

Hayden, Robert E(arl)
1913-1980 . . . . . . CLC 5, 9, 14, 37; PC 6
See also BLC 2; BW; CA 69-72; 97-100;
CABS 2; CANR 24; CDALB 1941-1968;
DA; DLB 5, 76; MTCW; SATA 19, 26

Hayford, J(oseph) E(phraim) Casely
See Casely-Hayford, J(oseph) E(phraim)

Hayman, Ronald 1932- . . . . CLC 44
See also CA 25-28R; CANR 18

Haywood, Eliza (Fowler)
1693(?)-1756 . . . . LC 1

Hazlitt, William 1778-1830 . . . . . . NCLC 29
See also DLB 110

Hazzard, Shirley 1931- . . . . CLC 18
See also CA 9-12R; CANR 4; DLBY 82;
MTCW

Head, Bessie 1937-1986 . . . . CLC 25, 67
See also BLC 2; BW; CA 29-32R; 119;
CANR 25; DLB 117; MTCW

Headon, (Nicky) Topper 1956(?)- . . . CLC 30
See also Clash, The

Heaney, Seamus (Justin)
1939- . . . . CLC 5, 7, 14, 25, 37, 74
See also CA 85-88; CANR 25;
CDBLB 1960 to Present; DLB 40;
MTCW

Hearn, (Patricio) Lafcadio (Tessima Carlos)
1850-1904 . . . . TCLC 9
See also CA 105; DLB 12, 78

Hearne, Vicki 1946- . . . . CLC 56
See also CA 139

Hearon, Shelby 1931- . . . . CLC 63
See also AITN 2; CA 25-28R; CANR 18

Heat-Moon, William Least. . . . . CLC 29
See also Trogdon, William (Lewis)
See also AAYA 9

Hebert, Anne 1916- . . . . CLC 4, 13, 29
See also CA 85-88; DLB 68; MTCW

Hecht, Anthony (Evan)
1923- . . . . CLC 8, 13, 19
See also CA 9-12R; CANR 6; DLB 5

Hecht, Ben 1894-1964 . . . . CLC 8
See also CA 85-88; DLB 7, 9, 25, 26, 28, 86

Hedayat, Sadeq 1903-1951 . . . . TCLC 21
See also CA 120

Heidegger, Martin 1889-1976 . . . . . . CLC 24
See also CA 81-84; 65-68; CANR 34;
MTCW

Heidenstam, (Carl Gustaf) Verner von
1859-1940 . . . . TCLC 5
See also CA 104

Heifner, Jack 1946- . . . . CLC 11
See also CA 105

Heijermans, Herman 1864-1924 . . . TCLC 24
See also CA 123

Heilbrun, Carolyn G(old) 1926- . . . . . CLC 25
See also CA 45-48; CANR 1, 28

Heine, Heinrich 1797-1856 . . . . NCLC 4
See also DLB 90

Heinemann, Larry (Curtiss) 1944- . . CLC 50
See also CA 110; CANR 31; DLBD 9

Heiney, Donald (William) 1921- . . . . . CLC 9
See also CA 1-4R; CANR 3

Heinlein, Robert A(nson)
1907-1988 . . . . CLC 1, 3, 8, 14, 26, 55
See also CA 1-4R; 125; CANR 1, 20;
DLB 8; MAICYA; MTCW; SATA 9, 56,
69

Helforth, John
See Doolittle, Hilda

Hellenhofferu, Vojtech Kapristian z
See Hasek, Jaroslav (Matej Frantisek)

Heller, Joseph
1923- . . . . CLC 1, 3, 5, 8, 11, 36, 63
See also AITN 1; CA 5-8R; CABS 1;
CANR 8; DA; DLB 2, 28; DLBY 80;
MTCW; WLC

Hellman, Lillian (Florence)
1906-1984 . . . . . CLC 2, 4, 8, 14, 18, 34,
44, 52; DC 1
See also AITN 1, 2; CA 13-16R; 112;
CANR 33; DLB 7; DLBY 84; MTCW

Helprin, Mark 1947- . . . . . CLC 7, 10, 22, 32
See also CA 81-84; DLBY 85; MTCW

Helyar, Jane Penelope Josephine 1933-
See Poole, Josephine
See also CA 21-24R; CANR 10, 26

Hemans, Felicia 1793-1835 . . . . . . NCLC 29
See also DLB 96

Hemingway, Ernest (Miller)
1899-1961 . . . CLC 1, 3, 6, 8, 10, 13, 19,
30, 34, 39, 41, 44, 50, 61; SSC 1
See also CA 77-80; CANR 34;
CDALB 1917-1929; DA; DLB 4, 9, 102;
DLBD 1; DLBY 81, 87; MTCW; WLC

Hempel, Amy 1951- . . . . CLC 39
See also CA 118; 137

Henderson, F. C.
See Mencken, H(enry) L(ouis)

Henderson, Sylvia
See Ashton-Warner, Sylvia (Constance)

Henley, Beth . . . . CLC 23
See also Henley, Elizabeth Becker
See also CABS 3; DLBY 86

Henley, Elizabeth Becker 1952-
See Henley, Beth
See also CA 107; CANR 32; MTCW

Henley, William Ernest
1849-1903 . . . . TCLC 8
See also CA 105; DLB 19

Hennissart, Martha
See Lathen, Emma
See also CA 85-88

Henry, O. . . . . TCLC 1, 19; SSC 5
See also Porter, William Sydney
See also WLC

Henryson, Robert 1430(?)-1506(?). . . . LC 20

Henry VIII 1491-1547 . . . . LC 10

Henschke, Alfred
See Klabund

Hentoff, Nat(han Irving) 1925- . . . . . CLC 26
See also AAYA 4; CA 1-4R; CAAS 6;
CANR 5, 25; CLR 1; MAICYA;
SATA 27, 42, 69

Heppenstall, (John) Rayner
1911-1981 . . . . CLC 10
See also CA 1-4R; 103; CANR 29

Herbert, Frank (Patrick)
1920-1986 . . . . CLC 12, 23, 35, 44
See also CA 53-56; 118; CANR 5; DLB 8;
MTCW; SATA 9, 37, 47

Herbert, George 1593-1633 . . . . PC 4
See also CDBLB Before 1660; DLB 126

Holland, Isabelle 1920- .... **CLC 21**
See also CA 21-24R; CANR 10, 25;
MAICYA; SATA 8, 70

Holland, Marcus
See Caldwell, (Janet Miriam) Taylor
(Holland)

Hollander, John 1929- ...... **CLC 2, 5, 8, 14**
See also CA 1-4R; CANR 1; DLB 5;
SATA 13

Hollander, Paul
See Silverberg, Robert

Holleran, Andrew 1943(?)- .... **CLC 38**

Hollinghurst, Alan 1954- .... **CLC 55**
See also CA 114

Hollis, Jim
See Summers, Hollis (Spurgeon, Jr.)

Holmes, John
See Souster, (Holmes) Raymond

Holmes, John Clellon 1926-1988.... **CLC 56**
See also CA 9-12R; 125; CANR 4; DLB 16

Holmes, Oliver Wendell
1809-1894 .... **NCLC 14**
See also CDALB 1640-1865; DLB 1;
SATA 34

Holmes, Raymond
See Souster, (Holmes) Raymond

Holt, Victoria
See Hibbert, Eleanor Alice Burford

Holub, Miroslav 1923- .... **CLC 4**
See also CA 21-24R; CANR 10

Homer c. 8th cent. B.C.- .... **CMLC 1**
See also DA

Honig, Edwin 1919- .... **CLC 33**
See also CA 5-8R; CAAS 8; CANR 4;
DLB 5

Hood, Hugh (John Blagdon)
1928- .... **CLC 15, 28**
See also CA 49-52; CAAS 17; CANR 1, 33;
DLB 53

Hood, Thomas 1799-1845....... **NCLC 16**
See also DLB 96

Hooker, (Peter) Jeremy 1941-...... **CLC 43**
See also CA 77-80; CANR 22; DLB 40

Hope, A(lec) D(erwent) 1907- .... **CLC 3, 51**
See also CA 21-24R; CANR 33; MTCW

Hope, Brian
See Creasey, John

Hope, Christopher (David Tully)
1944- .... **CLC 52**
See also CA 106; SATA 62

Hopkins, Gerard Manley
1844-1889 .... **NCLC 17**
See also CDBLB 1890-1914; DA; DLB 35,
57; WLC

Hopkins, John (Richard) 1931-...... **CLC 4**
See also CA 85-88

Hopkins, Pauline Elizabeth
1859-1930 .... **TCLC 28**
See also BLC 2; DLB 50

Hopley-Woolrich, Cornell George 1903-1968
See Woolrich, Cornell
See also CA 13-14; CAP 1

Horatio
See Proust,
(Valentin-Louis-George-Eugene-)Marcel

Horgan, Paul 1903- .... **CLC 9, 53**
See also CA 13-16R; CANR 9, 35;
DLB 102; DLBY 85; MTCW; SATA 13

Horn, Peter
See Kuttner, Henry

Hornem, Horace Esq.
See Byron, George Gordon (Noel)

Horovitz, Israel 1939- .... **CLC 56**
See also CA 33-36R; DLB 7

Horvath, Odon von
See Horvath, Oedoen von
See also DLB 85, 124

Horvath, Oedoen von 1901-1938... **TCLC 45**
See also Horvath, Odon von
See also CA 118

Horwitz, Julius 1920-1986........ **CLC 14**
See also CA 9-12R; 119; CANR 12

Hospital, Janette Turner 1942-..... **CLC 42**
See also CA 108

Hostos, E. M. de
See Hostos (y Bonilla), Eugenio Maria de

Hostos, Eugenio M. de
See Hostos (y Bonilla), Eugenio Maria de

Hostos, Eugenio Maria
See Hostos (y Bonilla), Eugenio Maria de

Hostos (y Bonilla), Eugenio Maria de
1839-1903 .... **TCLC 24**
See also CA 123; 131; HW

Houdini
See Lovecraft, H(oward) P(hillips)

Hougan, Carolyn 19(?)- .... **CLC 34**
See also CA 139

Household, Geoffrey (Edward West)
1900-1988 .... **CLC 11**
See also CA 77-80; 126; DLB 87; SATA 14,
59

Housman, A(lfred) E(dward)
1859-1936 .... **TCLC 1, 10; PC 2**
See also CA 104; 125; DA; DLB 19;
MTCW

Housman, Laurence 1865-1959..... **TCLC 7**
See also CA 106; DLB 10; SATA 25

Howard, Elizabeth Jane 1923- ... **CLC 7, 29**
See also CA 5-8R; CANR 8

Howard, Maureen 1930- ..... **CLC 5, 14, 46**
See also CA 53-56; CANR 31; DLBY 83;
MTCW

Howard, Richard 1929- ...... **CLC 7, 10, 47**
See also AITN 1; CA 85-88; CANR 25;
DLB 5

Howard, Robert Ervin 1906-1936... **TCLC 8**
See also CA 105

Howard, Warren F.
See Pohl, Frederik

Howe, Fanny 1940- .... **CLC 47**
See also CA 117; SATA 52

Howe, Julia Ward 1819-1910 ..... **TCLC 21**
See also CA 117; DLB 1

Howe, Susan 1937-............... **CLC 72**
See also DLB 120

Howe, Tina 1937-................ **CLC 48**
See also CA 109

Howell, James 1594(?)-1666 .... **LC 13**

Howells, W. D.
See Howells, William Dean

Howells, William D.
See Howells, William Dean

Howells, William Dean
1837-1920 .... **TCLC 41, 7, 17**
See also CA 104; 134; CDALB 1865-1917;
DLB 12, 64, 74, 79

Howes, Barbara 1914- .... **CLC 15**
See also CA 9-12R; CAAS 3; SATA 5

Hrabal, Bohumil 1914-........ **CLC 13, 67**
See also CA 106; CAAS 12

Hsun, Lu .... **TCLC 3**
See also Shu-Jen, Chou

Hubbard, L(afayette) Ron(ald)
1911-1986 .... **CLC 43**
See also CA 77-80; 118; CANR 22

Huch, Ricarda (Octavia)
1864-1947 .... **TCLC 13**
See also CA 111; DLB 66

Huddle, David 1942- .... **CLC 49**
See also CA 57-60; DLB 130

Hudson, Jeffrey
See Crichton, (John) Michael

Hudson, W(illiam) H(enry)
1841-1922 .... **TCLC 29**
See also CA 115; DLB 98; SATA 35

Hueffer, Ford Madox
See Ford, Ford Madox

Hughart, Barry .... **CLC 39**
See also CA 137

Hughes, Colin
See Creasey, John

Hughes, David (John) 1930- .... **CLC 48**
See also CA 116; 129; DLB 14

Hughes, (James) Langston
1902-1967 .... **CLC 1, 5, 10, 15, 35, 44;**
DC 3; PC 1; SSC 6
See also BLC 2; BW; CA 1-4R; 25-28R;
CANR 1, 34; CDALB 1929-1941;
CLR 17; DA; DLB 4, 7, 48, 51, 86;
MAICYA; MTCW; SATA 4, 33; WLC

Hughes, Richard (Arthur Warren)
1900-1976 .... **CLC 1, 11**
See also CA 5-8R; 65-68; CANR 4;
DLB 15; MTCW; SATA 8, 25

Hughes, Ted 1930- ..... **CLC 2, 4, 9, 14, 37**
See also CA 1-4R; CANR 1, 33; CLR 3;
DLB 40; MAICYA; MTCW; SATA 27,
49

Hugo, Richard F(ranklin)
1923-1982 .... **CLC 6, 18, 32**
See also CA 49-52; 108; CANR 3; DLB 5

Hugo, Victor (Marie)
1802-1885 .... **NCLC 3, 10, 21**
See also DA; DLB 119; SATA 47; WLC

Huidobro, Vicente
See Huidobro Fernandez, Vicente Garcia

Huidobro Fernandez, Vicente Garcia
1893-1948 .... **TCLC 31**
See also CA 131; HW

Hulme, Keri 1947- . . . . CLC 39
  See also CA 125

Hulme, T(homas) E(rnest)
  1883-1917 . . . . TCLC 21
  See also CA 117; DLB 19

Hume, David 1711-1776. . . . . LC 7
  See also DLB 104

Humphrey, William 1924- . . . . CLC 45
  See also CA 77-80; DLB 6

Humphreys, Emyr Owen 1919- . . . . . CLC 47
  See also CA 5-8R; CANR 3, 24; DLB 15

Humphreys, Josephine 1945- . . . . CLC 34, 57
  See also CA 121; 127

Hungerford, Pixie
  See Brinsmead, H(esba) F(ay)

Hunt, E(verette) Howard, Jr.
  1918- . . . . CLC 3
  See also AITN 1; CA 45-48; CANR 2

Hunt, Kyle
  See Creasey, John

Hunt, (James Henry) Leigh
  1784-1859 . . . . NCLC 1

Hunt, Marsha 1946- . . . . CLC 70

Hunter, E. Waldo
  See Sturgeon, Theodore (Hamilton)

Hunter, Evan 1926- . . . . CLC 11, 31
  See also CA 5-8R; CANR 5, 38; DLBY 82;
  MTCW; SATA 25

Hunter, Kristin (Eggleston) 1931- . . . CLC 35
  See also AITN 1; BW; CA 13-16R;
  CANR 13; CLR 3; DLB 33; MAICYA;
  SAAS 10; SATA 12

Hunter, Mollie 1922- . . . . CLC 21
  See also McIlwraith, Maureen Mollie
  Hunter
  See also CANR 37; CLR 25; MAICYA;
  SAAS 7; SATA 54

Hunter, Robert (?)-1734. . . . . LC 7

Hurston, Zora Neale
  1903-1960 . . . . . . CLC 7, 30, 61; SSC 4
  See also BLC 2; BW; CA 85-88; DA;
  DLB 51, 86; MTCW

Huston, John (Marcellus)
  1906-1987 . . . . CLC 20
  See also CA 73-76; 123; CANR 34; DLB 26

Hustvedt, Siri 1955- . . . . CLC 76
  See also CA 137

Hutten, Ulrich von 1488-1523. . . . . . . LC 16

Huxley, Aldous (Leonard)
  1894-1963 . . CLC 1, 3, 4, 5, 8, 11, 18, 35
  See also CA 85-88; CDBLB 1914-1945; DA;
  DLB 36, 100; MTCW; SATA 63; WLC

Huysmans, Charles Marie Georges
  1848-1907
  See Huysmans, Joris-Karl
  See also CA 104

Huysmans, Joris-Karl. . . . . TCLC 7
  See also Huysmans, Charles Marie Georges
  See also DLB 123

Hwang, David Henry 1957- . . . . CLC 55
  See also CA 127; 132

Hyde, Anthony 1946- . . . . CLC 42
  See also CA 136

Hyde, Margaret O(ldroyd) 1917- . . . CLC 21
  See also CA 1-4R; CANR 1, 36; CLR 23;
  MAICYA; SAAS 8; SATA 1, 42

Hynes, James 1956(?)- . . . . CLC 65

Ian, Janis 1951- . . . . CLC 21
  See also CA 105

Ibanez, Vicente Blasco
  See Blasco Ibanez, Vicente

Ibarguengoitia, Jorge 1928-1983. . . . CLC 37
  See also CA 124; 113; HW

Ibsen, Henrik (Johan)
  1828-1906 . . . . . TCLC 2, 8, 16, 37; DC 2
  See also CA 104; DA; WLC

Ibuse Masuji 1898- . . . . CLC 22
  See also CA 127

Ichikawa, Kon 1915- . . . . CLC 20
  See also CA 121

Idle, Eric 1943- . . . . CLC 21
  See also Monty Python
  See also CA 116; CANR 35

Ignatow, David 1914- . . . . . . CLC 4, 7, 14, 40
  See also CA 9-12R; CAAS 3; CANR 31;
  DLB 5

Ihimaera, Witi 1944- . . . . CLC 46
  See also CA 77-80

Ilf, Ilya. . . . . TCLC 21
  See also Fainzilberg, Ilya Arnoldovich

Immermann, Karl (Lebrecht)
  1796-1840 . . . . NCLC 4

Inclan, Ramon (Maria) del Valle
  See Valle-Inclan, Ramon (Maria) del

Infante, G(uillermo) Cabrera
  See Cabrera Infante, G(uillermo)

Ingalls, Rachel (Holmes) 1940- . . . . . CLC 42
  See also CA 123; 127

Ingamells, Rex 1913-1955 . . . . TCLC 35

Inge, William Motter
  1913-1973 . . . . CLC 1, 8, 19
  See also CA 9-12R; CDALB 1941-1968;
  DLB 7; MTCW

Ingelow, Jean 1820-1897 . . . . NCLC 39
  See also DLB 35; SATA 33

Ingram, Willis J.
  See Harris, Mark

Innaurato, Albert (F.) 1948(?)- . . CLC 21, 60
  See also CA 115; 122

Innes, Michael
  See Stewart, J(ohn) I(nnes) M(ackintosh)

Ionesco, Eugene
  1912- . . . . CLC 1, 4, 6, 9, 11, 15, 41
  See also CA 9-12R; DA; MTCW; SATA 7;
  WLC

Iqbal, Muhammad 1873-1938 . . . . . TCLC 28

Ireland, Patrick
  See O'Doherty, Brian

Irland, David
  See Green, Julian (Hartridge)

Iron, Ralph
  See Schreiner, Olive (Emilie Albertina)

Irving, John (Winslow)
  1942- . . . . CLC 13, 23, 38
  See also AAYA 8; BEST 89:3; CA 25-28R;
  CANR 28; DLB 6; DLBY 82; MTCW

Irving, Washington
  1783-1859 . . . . NCLC 2, 19; SSC 2
  See also CDALB 1640-1865; DA; DLB 3,
  11, 30, 59, 73, 74; WLC; YABC 2

Irwin, P. K.
  See Page, P(atricia) K(athleen)

Isaacs, Susan 1943- . . . . CLC 32
  See also BEST 89:1; CA 89-92; CANR 20,
  41; MTCW

Isherwood, Christopher (William Bradshaw)
  1904-1986 . . . . CLC 1, 9, 11, 14, 44
  See also CA 13-16R; 117; CANR 35;
  DLB 15; DLBY 86; MTCW

Ishiguro, Kazuo 1954- . . . . . . CLC 27, 56, 59
  See also BEST 90:2; CA 120; MTCW

Ishikawa Takuboku
  1886(?)-1912 . . . . TCLC 15
  See also CA 113

Iskander, Fazil 1929- . . . . CLC 47
  See also CA 102

Ivan IV 1530-1584 . . . . LC 17

Ivanov, Vyacheslav Ivanovich
  1866-1949 . . . . TCLC 33
  See also CA 122

Ivask, Ivar Vidrik 1927-1992. . . . . . . CLC 14
  See also CA 37-40R; 139; CANR 24

Jackson, Daniel
  See Wingrove, David (John)

Jackson, Jesse 1908-1983 . . . . CLC 12
  See also BW; CA 25-28R; 109; CANR 27;
  CLR 28; MAICYA; SATA 2, 29, 48

Jackson, Laura (Riding) 1901-1991 . . CLC 7
  See also Riding, Laura
  See also CA 65-68; 135; CANR 28; DLB 48

Jackson, Sam
  See Trumbo, Dalton

Jackson, Sara
  See Wingrove, David (John)

Jackson, Shirley
  1919-1965 . . . . CLC 11, 60; SSC 9
  See also AAYA 9; CA 1-4R; 25-28R;
  CANR 4; CDALB 1941-1968; DA;
  DLB 6; SATA 2; WLC

Jacob, (Cyprien-)Max 1876-1944 . . . TCLC 6
  See also CA 104

Jacobs, Jim 1942- . . . . CLC 12
  See also CA 97-100

Jacobs, W(illiam) W(ymark)
  1863-1943 . . . . TCLC 22
  See also CA 121

Jacobsen, Jens Peter 1847-1885 . . NCLC 34

Jacobsen, Josephine 1908- . . . . CLC 48
  See also CA 33-36R; CANR 23

Jacobson, Dan 1929- . . . . CLC 4, 14
  See also CA 1-4R; CANR 2, 25; DLB 14;
  MTCW

Jacqueline
  See Carpentier (y Valmont), Alejo

Jagger, Mick 1944-. . . . . CLC 17

Jakes, John (William) 1932- . . . . CLC 29
  See also BEST 89:4; CA 57-60; CANR 10;
  DLBY 83; MTCW; SATA 62

James, Andrew
  See Kirkup, James

James, C(yril) L(ionel) R(obert)
    1901-1989 . . . . CLC 33
    See also BW; CA 117; 125; 128; DLB 125;
    MTCW

James, Daniel (Lewis)   1911-1988
    See Santiago, Danny
    See also CA 125

James, Dynely
    See Mayne, William (James Carter)

James, Henry
    1843-1916 . . . . . TCLC 2, 11, 24, 40, 47;
                                        SSC 8
    See also CA 104; 132; CDALB 1865-1917;
    DA; DLB 12, 71, 74; MTCW; WLC

James, Montague (Rhodes)
    1862-1936 . . . . TCLC 6
    See also CA 104

James, P. D. . . . . CLC 18, 46
    See also White, Phyllis Dorothy James
    See also BEST 90:2; CDBLB 1960 to
    Present; DLB 87

James, Philip
    See Moorcock, Michael (John)

James, William   1842-1910 . . . . . TCLC 15, 32
    See also CA 109

James I   1394-1437 . . . . LC 20

Jami, Nur al-Din 'Abd al-Rahman
    1414-1492 . . . . LC 9

Jandl, Ernst   1925- . . . . CLC 34

Janowitz, Tama   1957- . . . . CLC 43
    See also CA 106

Jarrell, Randall
    1914-1965 . . . . CLC 1, 2, 6, 9, 13, 49
    See also CA 5-8R; 25-28R; CABS 2;
    CANR 6, 34; CDALB 1941-1968; CLR 6;
    DLB 48, 52; MAICYA; MTCW; SATA 7

Jarry, Alfred   1873-1907 . . . . TCLC 2, 14
    See also CA 104

Jarvis, E. K.
    See Bloch, Robert (Albert); Ellison, Harlan;
    Silverberg, Robert

Jeake, Samuel, Jr.
    See Aiken, Conrad (Potter)

Jean Paul   1763-1825 . . . . NCLC 7

Jeffers, (John) Robinson
    1887-1962 . . . . CLC 2, 3, 11, 15, 54
    See also CA 85-88; CANR 35;
    CDALB 1917-1929; DA; DLB 45;
    MTCW; WLC

Jefferson, Janet
    See Mencken, H(enry) L(ouis)

Jefferson, Thomas   1743-1826 . . . . NCLC 11
    See also CDALB 1640-1865; DLB 31

Jeffrey, Francis   1773-1850 . . . . . . NCLC 33
    See also DLB 107

Jelakowitch, Ivan
    See Heijermans, Herman

Jellicoe, (Patricia) Ann   1927- . . . . . . CLC 27
    See also CA 85-88; DLB 13

Jen, Gish . . . . CLC 70
    See also Jen, Lillian

Jen, Lillian   1956(?)-
    See Jen, Gish
    See also CA 135

Jenkins, (John) Robin   1912- . . . . CLC 52
    See also CA 1-4R; CANR 1; DLB 14

Jennings, Elizabeth (Joan)
    1926- . . . . CLC 5, 14
    See also CA 61-64; CAAS 5; CANR 8, 39;
    DLB 27; MTCW; SATA 66

Jennings, Waylon   1937- . . . . CLC 21

Jensen, Johannes V.   1873-1950 . . . . TCLC 41

Jensen, Laura (Linnea)   1948- . . . . . . CLC 37
    See also CA 103

Jerome, Jerome K(lapka)
    1859-1927 . . . . TCLC 23
    See also CA 119; DLB 10, 34

Jerrold, Douglas William
    1803-1857 . . . . NCLC 2

Jewett, (Theodora) Sarah Orne
    1849-1909 . . . . TCLC 1, 22; SSC 6
    See also CA 108; 127; DLB 12, 74;
    SATA 15

Jewsbury, Geraldine (Endsor)
    1812-1880 . . . . NCLC 22
    See also DLB 21

Jhabvala, Ruth Prawer
    1927- . . . . CLC 4, 8, 29
    See also CA 1-4R; CANR 2, 29; MTCW

Jiles, Paulette   1943- . . . . CLC 13, 58
    See also CA 101

Jimenez (Mantecon), Juan Ramon
    1881-1958 . . . . TCLC 4
    See also CA 104; 131; HW; MTCW

Jimenez, Ramon
    See Jimenez (Mantecon), Juan Ramon

Jimenez Mantecon, Juan
    See Jimenez (Mantecon), Juan Ramon

Joel, Billy . . . . CLC 26
    See also Joel, William Martin

Joel, William Martin   1949-
    See Joel, Billy
    See also CA 108

John of the Cross, St.   1542-1591 . . . . LC 18

Johnson, B(ryan) S(tanley William)
    1933-1973 . . . . CLC 6, 9
    See also CA 9-12R; 53-56; CANR 9;
    DLB 14, 40

Johnson, Charles (Richard)
    1948- . . . . CLC 7, 51, 65
    See also BLC 2; BW; CA 116; DLB 33

Johnson, Denis   1949- . . . . CLC 52
    See also CA 117; 121; DLB 120

Johnson, Diane (Lain)
    1934- . . . . CLC 5, 13, 48
    See also CA 41-44R; CANR 17, 40;
    DLBY 80; MTCW

Johnson, Eyvind (Olof Verner)
    1900-1976 . . . . CLC 14
    See also CA 73-76; 69-72; CANR 34

Johnson, J. R.
    See James, C(yril) L(ionel) R(obert)

Johnson, James Weldon
    1871-1938 . . . . TCLC 3, 19
    See also BLC 2; BW; CA 104; 125;
    CDALB 1917-1929; DLB 51; MTCW;
    SATA 31

Johnson, Joyce   1935- . . . . CLC 58
    See also CA 125; 129

Johnson, Lionel (Pigot)
    1867-1902 . . . . TCLC 19
    See also CA 117; DLB 19

Johnson, Mel
    See Malzberg, Barry N(athaniel)

Johnson, Pamela Hansford
    1912-1981 . . . . CLC 1, 7, 27
    See also CA 1-4R; 104; CANR 2, 28;
    DLB 15; MTCW

Johnson, Samuel   1709-1784 . . . . LC 15
    See also CDBLB 1660-1789; DA; DLB 39,
    95, 104; WLC

Johnson, Uwe
    1934-1984 . . . . CLC 5, 10, 15, 40
    See also CA 1-4R; 112; CANR 1, 39;
    DLB 75; MTCW

Johnston, George (Benson)   1913- . . . CLC 51
    See also CA 1-4R; CANR 5, 20; DLB 88

Johnston, Jennifer   1930- . . . . CLC 7
    See also CA 85-88; DLB 14

Jolley, (Monica) Elizabeth   1923- . . . CLC 46
    See also CA 127; CAAS 13

Jones, Arthur Llewellyn   1863-1947
    See Machen, Arthur
    See also CA 104

Jones, D(ouglas) G(ordon)   1929- . . . . CLC 10
    See also CA 29-32R; CANR 13; DLB 53

Jones, David (Michael)
    1895-1974 . . . . CLC 2, 4, 7, 13, 42
    See also CA 9-12R; 53-56; CANR 28;
    CDBLB 1945-1960; DLB 20, 100; MTCW

Jones, David Robert   1947-
    See Bowie, David
    See also CA 103

Jones, Diana Wynne   1934- . . . . CLC 26
    See also CA 49-52; CANR 4, 26; CLR 23;
    MAICYA; SAAS 7; SATA 9, 70

Jones, Edward P.   1951- . . . . CLC 76

Jones, Gayl   1949- . . . . CLC 6, 9
    See also BLC 2; BW; CA 77-80; CANR 27;
    DLB 33; MTCW

Jones, James   1921-1977 . . . . CLC 1, 3, 10, 39
    See also AITN 1, 2; CA 1-4R; 69-72;
    CANR 6; DLB 2; MTCW

Jones, John J.
    See Lovecraft, H(oward) P(hillips)

Jones, LeRoi . . . . CLC 1, 2, 3, 5, 10, 14
    See also Baraka, Amiri

Jones, Louis B. . . . . CLC 65

Jones, Madison (Percy, Jr.)   1925- . . . CLC 4
    See also CA 13-16R; CAAS 11; CANR 7

Jones, Mervyn   1922- . . . . CLC 10, 52
    See also CA 45-48; CAAS 5; CANR 1;
    MTCW

Jones, Mick   1956(?)- . . . . CLC 30
    See also Clash, The

Jones, Nettie (Pearl)   1941- . . . . CLC 34
    See also CA 137

Jones, Preston   1936-1979 . . . . CLC 10
    See also CA 73-76; 89-92; DLB 7

Jones, Robert F(rancis)   1934- . . . . CLC 7
    See also CA 49-52; CANR 2

Jones, Rod 1953- .... **CLC 50**
    See also CA 128

Jones, Terence Graham Parry
    1942- .... **CLC 21**
    See also Jones, Terry; Monty Python
    See also CA 112; 116; CANR 35; SATA 51

Jones, Terry
    See Jones, Terence Graham Parry
    See also SATA 67

Jong, Erica 1942- .... **CLC 4, 6, 8, 18**
    See also AITN 1; BEST 90:2; CA 73-76;
    CANR 26; DLB 2, 5, 28; MTCW

Jonson, Ben(jamin) 1572(?)-1637...... **LC 6**
    See also CDBLB Before 1660; DA; DLB 62,
    121; WLC

Jordan, June 1936- .... **CLC 5, 11, 23**
    See also AAYA 2; BW; CA 33-36R;
    CANR 25; CLR 10; DLB 38; MAICYA;
    MTCW; SATA 4

Jordan, Pat(rick M.) 1941- .... **CLC 37**
    See also CA 33-36R

Jorgensen, Ivar
    See Ellison, Harlan

Jorgenson, Ivar
    See Silverberg, Robert

Josipovici, Gabriel 1940- .... **CLC 6, 43**
    See also CA 37-40R; CAAS 8; DLB 14

Joubert, Joseph 1754-1824 .... **NCLC 9**

Jouve, Pierre Jean 1887-1976...... **CLC 47**
    See also CA 65-68

Joyce, James (Augustine Aloysius)
    1882-1941 .... **TCLC 3, 8, 16, 35; SSC 3**
    See also CA 104; 126; CDBLB 1914-1945;
    DA; DLB 10, 19, 36; MTCW; WLC

Jozsef, Attila 1905-1937......... **TCLC 22**
    See also CA 116

Juana Ines de la Cruz 1651(?)-1695 ... **LC 5**

Judd, Cyril
    See Kornbluth, C(yril) M.; Pohl, Frederik

Julian of Norwich 1342(?)-1416(?) .... **LC 6**

Just, Ward (Swift) 1935- .... **CLC 4, 27**
    See also CA 25-28R; CANR 32

Justice, Donald (Rodney) 1925- .. **CLC 6, 19**
    See also CA 5-8R; CANR 26; DLBY 83

Juvenal c. 55-c. 127 .... **CMLC 8**

Juvenis
    See Bourne, Randolph S(illiman)

Kacew, Romain 1914-1980
    See Gary, Romain
    See also CA 108; 102

Kadare, Ismail 1936- .... **CLC 52**

Kadohata, Cynthia............... **CLC 59**
    See also CA 140

Kafka, Franz
    1883-1924 ...... **TCLC 2, 6, 13, 29, 47;
    SSC 5**
    See also CA 105; 126; DA; DLB 81;
    MTCW; WLC

Kahn, Roger 1927- .... **CLC 30**
    See also CA 25-28R; SATA 37

Kain, Saul
    See Sassoon, Siegfried (Lorraine)

Kaiser, Georg 1878-1945 .... **TCLC 9**
    See also CA 106; DLB 124

Kaletski, Alexander 1946- .... **CLC 39**
    See also CA 118

Kalidasa fl. c. 400- .... **CMLC 9**

Kallman, Chester (Simon)
    1921-1975 .... **CLC 2**
    See also CA 45-48; 53-56; CANR 3

Kaminsky, Melvin 1926-
    See Brooks, Mel
    See also CA 65-68; CANR 16

Kaminsky, Stuart M(elvin) 1934- ... **CLC 59**
    See also CA 73-76; CANR 29

Kane, Paul
    See Simon, Paul

Kane, Wilson
    See Bloch, Robert (Albert)

Kanin, Garson 1912-............ **CLC 22**
    See also AITN 1; CA 5-8R; CANR 7;
    DLB 7

Kaniuk, Yoram 1930-............ **CLC 19**
    See also CA 134

Kant, Immanuel 1724-1804 ...... **NCLC 27**
    See also DLB 94

Kantor, MacKinlay 1904-1977 ...... **CLC 7**
    See also CA 61-64; 73-76; DLB 9, 102

Kaplan, David Michael 1946- ...... **CLC 50**

Kaplan, James 1951- .... **CLC 59**
    See also CA 135

Karageorge, Michael
    See Anderson, Poul (William)

Karamzin, Nikolai Mikhailovich
    1766-1826 .... **NCLC 3**

Karapanou, Margarita 1946- .... **CLC 13**
    See also CA 101

Karinthy, Frigyes 1887-1938...... **TCLC 47**

Karl, Frederick R(obert) 1927- ..... **CLC 34**
    See also CA 5-8R; CANR 3

Kastel, Warren
    See Silverberg, Robert

Kataev, Evgeny Petrovich 1903-1942
    See Petrov, Evgeny
    See also CA 120

Kataphusin
    See Ruskin, John

Katz, Steve 1935-............... **CLC 47**
    See also CA 25-28R; CAAS 14; CANR 12;
    DLBY 83

Kauffman, Janet 1945-............ **CLC 42**
    See also CA 117; DLBY 86

Kaufman, Bob (Garnell)
    1925-1986 .... **CLC 49**
    See also BW; CA 41-44R; 118; CANR 22;
    DLB 16, 41

Kaufman, George S. 1889-1961..... **CLC 38**
    See also CA 108; 93-96; DLB 7

Kaufman, Sue .... **CLC 3, 8**
    See also Barondess, Sue K(aufman)

Kavafis, Konstantinos Petrou 1863-1933
    See Cavafy, C(onstantine) P(eter)
    See also CA 104

Kavan, Anna 1901-1968........ **CLC 5, 13**
    See also CA 5-8R; CANR 6; MTCW

Kavanagh, Dan
    See Barnes, Julian

Kavanagh, Patrick (Joseph)
    1904-1967 .... **CLC 22**
    See also CA 123; 25-28R; DLB 15, 20;
    MTCW

Kawabata, Yasunari
    1899-1972 .... **CLC 2, 5, 9, 18**
    See also CA 93-96; 33-36R

Kaye, M(ary) M(argaret) 1909-..... **CLC 28**
    See also CA 89-92; CANR 24; MTCW;
    SATA 62

Kaye, Mollie
    See Kaye, M(ary) M(argaret)

Kaye-Smith, Sheila 1887-1956..... **TCLC 20**
    See also CA 118; DLB 36

Kaymor, Patrice Maguilene
    See Senghor, Leopold Sedar

Kazan, Elia 1909-........... **CLC 6, 16, 63**
    See also CA 21-24R; CANR 32

Kazantzakis, Nikos
    1883(?)-1957 .... **TCLC 2, 5, 33**
    See also CA 105; 132; MTCW

Kazin, Alfred 1915- .... **CLC 34, 38**
    See also CA 1-4R; CAAS 7; CANR 1;
    DLB 67

Keane, Mary Nesta (Skrine) 1904-
    See Keane, Molly
    See also CA 108; 114

Keane, Molly.................... **CLC 31**
    See also Keane, Mary Nesta (Skrine)

Keates, Jonathan 19(?)-........... **CLC 34**

Keaton, Buster 1895-1966 .... **CLC 20**

Keats, John 1795-1821...... **NCLC 8; PC 1**
    See also CDBLB 1789-1832; DA; DLB 96,
    110; WLC

Keene, Donald 1922- .... **CLC 34**
    See also CA 1-4R; CANR 5

Keillor, Garrison .... **CLC 40**
    See also Keillor, Gary (Edward)
    See also AAYA 2; BEST 89:3; DLBY 87;
    SATA 58

Keillor, Gary (Edward) 1942-
    See Keillor, Garrison
    See also CA 111; 117; CANR 36; MTCW

Keith, Michael
    See Hubbard, L(afayette) Ron(ald)

Kell, Joseph
    See Wilson, John (Anthony) Burgess

Keller, Gottfried 1819-1890....... **NCLC 2**
    See also DLB 129

Kellerman, Jonathan 1949- .... **CLC 44**
    See also BEST 90:1; CA 106; CANR 29

Kelley, William Melvin 1937-...... **CLC 22**
    See also BW; CA 77-80; CANR 27; DLB 33

Kellogg, Marjorie 1922-............ **CLC 2**
    See also CA 81-84

Kellow, Kathleen
    See Hibbert, Eleanor Alice Burford

Kelly, M(ilton) T(erry) 1947-....... **CLC 55**
    See also CA 97-100; CANR 19

Kelman, James 1946-............. **CLC 58**

Kemal, Yashar 1923- . . . . **CLC 14, 29**
See also CA 89-92

Kemble, Fanny 1809-1893 . . . . **NCLC 18**
See also DLB 32

Kemelman, Harry 1908- . . . . **CLC 2**
See also AITN 1; CA 9-12R; CANR 6;
DLB 28

Kempe, Margery 1373(?)-1440(?) . . . . . **LC 6**

Kempis, Thomas a 1380-1471 . . . . **LC 11**

Kendall, Henry 1839-1882 . . . . **NCLC 12**

Keneally, Thomas (Michael)
1935- . . . . . . **CLC 5, 8, 10, 14, 19, 27, 43**
See also CA 85-88; CANR 10; MTCW

Kennedy, Adrienne (Lita) 1931- . . . . **CLC 66**
See also BLC 2; BW; CA 103; CABS 3;
CANR 26; DLB 38

Kennedy, John Pendleton
1795-1870 . . . . **NCLC 2**
See also DLB 3

Kennedy, Joseph Charles 1929- . . . . . . **CLC 8**
See also Kennedy, X. J.
See also CA 1-4R; CANR 4, 30, 40;
SATA 14

Kennedy, William 1928- . . . **CLC 6, 28, 34, 53**
See also AAYA 1; CA 85-88; CANR 14,
31; DLBY 85; MTCW; SATA 57

Kennedy, X. J. . . . . **CLC 42**
See also Kennedy, Joseph Charles
See also CAAS 9; CLR 27; DLB 5

Kent, Kelvin
See Kuttner, Henry

Kenton, Maxwell
See Southern, Terry

Kenyon, Robert O.
See Kuttner, Henry

Kerouac, Jack . . . . . **CLC 1, 2, 3, 5, 14, 29, 61**
See also Kerouac, Jean-Louis Lebris de
See also CDALB 1941-1968; DLB 2, 16;
DLBD 3

Kerouac, Jean-Louis Lebris de 1922-1969
See Kerouac, Jack
See also AITN 1; CA 5-8R; 25-28R;
CANR 26; DA; MTCW; WLC

Kerr, Jean 1923- . . . . **CLC 22**
See also CA 5-8R; CANR 7

Kerr, M. E. . . . . **CLC 12, 35**
See also Meaker, Marijane (Agnes)
See also AAYA 2; CLR 29; SAAS 1

Kerr, Robert . . . . **CLC 55**

Kerrigan, (Thomas) Anthony
1918- . . . . **CLC 4, 6**
See also CA 49-52; CAAS 11; CANR 4

Kerry, Lois
See Duncan, Lois

Kesey, Ken (Elton)
1935- . . . . **CLC 1, 3, 6, 11, 46, 64**
See also CA 1-4R; CANR 22, 38;
CDALB 1968-1988; DA; DLB 2, 16;
MTCW; SATA 66; WLC

Kesselring, Joseph (Otto)
1902-1967 . . . . **CLC 45**

Kessler, Jascha (Frederick) 1929- . . . . **CLC 4**
See also CA 17-20R; CANR 8

Kettelkamp, Larry (Dale) 1933- . . . . **CLC 12**
See also CA 29-32R; CANR 16; SAAS 3;
SATA 2

Keyber, Conny
See Fielding, Henry

Khayyam, Omar 1048-1131 . . . . . . **CMLC 11**

Kherdian, David 1931- . . . . **CLC 6, 9**
See also CA 21-24R; CAAS 2; CANR 39;
CLR 24; MAICYA; SATA 16, 74

Khlebnikov, Velimir . . . . **TCLC 20**
See also Khlebnikov, Viktor Vladimirovich

Khlebnikov, Viktor Vladimirovich 1885-1922
See Khlebnikov, Velimir
See also CA 117

Khodasevich, Vladislav (Felitsianovich)
1886-1939 . . . . **TCLC 15**
See also CA 115

Kielland, Alexander Lange
1849-1906 . . . . **TCLC 5**
See also CA 104

Kiely, Benedict 1919- . . . . **CLC 23, 43**
See also CA 1-4R; CANR 2; DLB 15

Kienzle, William X(avier) 1928- . . . . **CLC 25**
See also CA 93-96; CAAS 1; CANR 9, 31;
MTCW

Kierkegaard, Soeren 1813-1855 . . . **NCLC 34**

Kierkegaard, Soren 1813-1855 . . . . **NCLC 34**

Killens, John Oliver 1916-1987 . . . . . **CLC 10**
See also BW; CA 77-80; 123; CAAS 2;
CANR 26; DLB 33

Killigrew, Anne 1660-1685 . . . . **LC 4**
See also DLB 131

Kim
See Simenon, Georges (Jacques Christian)

Kincaid, Jamaica 1949- . . . . **CLC 43, 68**
See also BLC 2; BW; CA 125

King, Francis (Henry) 1923- . . . . . **CLC 8, 53**
See also CA 1-4R; CANR 1, 33; DLB 15;
MTCW

King, Stephen (Edwin)
1947- . . . . **CLC 12, 26, 37, 61**
See also AAYA 1; BEST 90:1; CA 61-64;
CANR 1, 30; DLBY 80; MTCW;
SATA 9, 55

King, Steve
See King, Stephen (Edwin)

Kingman, Lee . . . . **CLC 17**
See also Natti, (Mary) Lee
See also SAAS 3; SATA 1, 67

Kingsley, Charles 1819-1875 . . . . . **NCLC 35**
See also DLB 21, 32; YABC 2

Kingsley, Sidney 1906- . . . . **CLC 44**
See also CA 85-88; DLB 7

Kingsolver, Barbara 1955- . . . . **CLC 55**
See also CA 129; 134

Kingston, Maxine (Ting Ting) Hong
1940- . . . . **CLC 12, 19, 58**
See also AAYA 8; CA 69-72; CANR 13,
38; DLBY 80; MTCW; SATA 53

Kinnell, Galway
1927- . . . . **CLC 1, 2, 3, 5, 13, 29**
See also CA 9-12R; CANR 10, 34; DLB 5;
DLBY 87; MTCW

Kinsella, Thomas 1928- . . . . **CLC 4, 19**
See also CA 17-20R; CANR 15; DLB 27;
MTCW

Kinsella, W(illiam) P(atrick)
1935- . . . . **CLC 27, 43**
See also AAYA 7; CA 97-100; CAAS 7;
CANR 21, 35; MTCW

Kipling, (Joseph) Rudyard
1865-1936 . . . . **TCLC 8, 17; PC 3; SSC 5**
See also CA 105; 120; CANR 33;
CDBLB 1890-1914; DA; DLB 19, 34;
MAICYA; MTCW; WLC; YABC 2

Kirkup, James 1918- . . . . **CLC 1**
See also CA 1-4R; CAAS 4; CANR 2;
DLB 27; SATA 12

Kirkwood, James 1930(?)-1989 . . . . . . **CLC 9**
See also AITN 2; CA 1-4R; 128; CANR 6,
40

Kis, Danilo 1935-1989 . . . . **CLC 57**
See also CA 109; 118; 129; MTCW

Kivi, Aleksis 1834-1872 . . . . **NCLC 30**

Kizer, Carolyn (Ashley) 1925- . . . **CLC 15, 39**
See also CA 65-68; CAAS 5; CANR 24;
DLB 5

Klabund 1890-1928 . . . . **TCLC 44**
See also DLB 66

Klappert, Peter 1942- . . . . **CLC 57**
See also CA 33-36R; DLB 5

Klein, A(braham) M(oses)
1909-1972 . . . . **CLC 19**
See also CA 101; 37-40R; DLB 68

Klein, Norma 1938-1989 . . . . **CLC 30**
See also AAYA 2; CA 41-44R; 128;
CANR 15, 37; CLR 2, 19; MAICYA;
SAAS 1; SATA 7, 57

Klein, T(heodore) E(ibon) D(onald)
1947- . . . . **CLC 34**
See also CA 119

Kleist, Heinrich von 1777-1811 . . . . **NCLC 2**
See also DLB 90

Klima, Ivan 1931- . . . . **CLC 56**
See also CA 25-28R; CANR 17

Klimentov, Andrei Platonovich 1899-1951
See Platonov, Andrei
See also CA 108

Klinger, Friedrich Maximilian von
1752-1831 . . . . **NCLC 1**
See also DLB 94

Klopstock, Friedrich Gottlieb
1724-1803 . . . . **NCLC 11**
See also DLB 97

Knebel, Fletcher 1911-1993 . . . . **CLC 14**
See also AITN 1; CA 1-4R; 140; CAAS 3;
CANR 1, 36; SATA 36

Knickerbocker, Diedrich
See Irving, Washington

Knight, Etheridge 1931-1991 . . . . **CLC 40**
See also BLC 2; BW; CA 21-24R; 133;
CANR 23; DLB 41

Knight, Sarah Kemble 1666-1727 . . . . . **LC 7**
See also DLB 24

Knowles, John 1926- . . . . . . **CLC 1, 4, 10, 26**
See also AAYA 10; CA 17-20R; CANR 40;
CDALB 1968-1988; DA; DLB 6; MTCW;
SATA 8

La Guma, (Justin) Alex(ander)
1925-1985 .... CLC 19
See also BW; CA 49-52; 118; CANR 25;
DLB 117; MTCW

Laidlaw, A. K.
See Grieve, C(hristopher) M(urray)

Lainez, Manuel Mujica
See Mujica Lainez, Manuel
See also HW

Lamartine, Alphonse (Marie Louis Prat) de
1790-1869 .... NCLC 11

Lamb, Charles 1775-1834....... NCLC 10
See also CDBLB 1789-1832; DA; DLB 93,
107; SATA 17; WLC

Lamb, Lady Caroline 1785-1828.. NCLC 38
See also DLB 116

Lamming, George (William)
1927- .... CLC 2, 4, 66
See also BLC 2; BW; CA 85-88; CANR 26;
DLB 125; MTCW

L'Amour, Louis (Dearborn)
1908-1988 .... CLC 25, 55
See also AITN 2; BEST 89:2; CA 1-4R;
125; CANR 3, 25, 40; DLBY 80; MTCW

Lampedusa, Giuseppe (Tomasi) di ... TCLC 13
See also Tomasi di Lampedusa, Giuseppe

Lampman, Archibald 1861-1899 .. NCLC 25
See also DLB 92

Lancaster, Bruce 1896-1963....... CLC 36
See also CA 9-10; CAP 1; SATA 9

Landau, Mark Alexandrovich
See Aldanov, Mark (Alexandrovich)

Landau-Aldanov, Mark Alexandrovich
See Aldanov, Mark (Alexandrovich)

Landis, John 1950-............. CLC 26
See also CA 112; 122

Landolfi, Tommaso 1908-1979... CLC 11, 49
See also CA 127; 117

Landon, Letitia Elizabeth
1802-1838 .... NCLC 15
See also DLB 96

Landor, Walter Savage
1775-1864 .... NCLC 14
See also DLB 93, 107

Landwirth, Heinz 1927-
See Lind, Jakov
See also CA 9-12R; CANR 7

Lane, Patrick 1939-............. CLC 25
See also CA 97-100; DLB 53

Lang, Andrew 1844-1912........ TCLC 16
See also CA 114; 137; DLB 98; MAICYA;
SATA 16

Lang, Fritz 1890-1976 .... CLC 20
See also CA 77-80; 69-72; CANR 30

Lange, John
See Crichton, (John) Michael

Langer, Elinor 1939- .... CLC 34
See also CA 121

Langland, William 1330(?)-1400(?) ... LC 19
See also DA

Langstaff, Launcelot
See Irving, Washington

Lanier, Sidney 1842-1881 .... NCLC 6
See also DLB 64; MAICYA; SATA 18

Lanyer, Aemilia 1569-1645 .... LC 10

Lao Tzu .... CMLC 7

Lapine, James (Elliot) 1949-....... CLC 39
See also CA 123; 130

Larbaud, Valery (Nicolas)
1881-1957 .... TCLC 9
See also CA 106

Lardner, Ring
See Lardner, Ring(gold) W(ilmer)

Lardner, Ring W., Jr.
See Lardner, Ring(gold) W(ilmer)

Lardner, Ring(gold) W(ilmer)
1885-1933 .... TCLC 2, 14
See also CA 104; 131; CDALB 1917-1929;
DLB 11, 25, 86; MTCW

Laredo, Betty
See Codrescu, Andrei

Larkin, Maia
See Wojciechowska, Maia (Teresa)

Larkin, Philip (Arthur)
1922-1985 ... CLC 3, 5, 8, 9, 13, 18, 33,
39, 64
See also CA 5-8R; 117; CANR 24;
CDBLB 1960 to Present; DLB 27;
MTCW

Larra (y Sanchez de Castro), Mariano Jose de
1809-1837 .... NCLC 17

Larsen, Eric 1941- .... CLC 55
See also CA 132

Larsen, Nella 1891-1964 .... CLC 37
See also BLC 2; BW; CA 125; DLB 51

Larson, Charles R(aymond) 1938-... CLC 31
See also CA 53-56; CANR 4

Latham, Jean Lee 1902-.......... CLC 12
See also AITN 1; CA 5-8R; CANR 7;
MAICYA; SATA 2, 68

Latham, Mavis
See Clark, Mavis Thorpe

Lathen, Emma.................... CLC 2
See also Hennissart, Martha; Latsis, Mary
J(ane)

Lathrop, Francis
See Leiber, Fritz (Reuter, Jr.)

Latsis, Mary J(ane)
See Lathen, Emma
See also CA 85-88

Lattimore, Richmond (Alexander)
1906-1984 .... CLC 3
See also CA 1-4R; 112; CANR 1

Laughlin, James 1914-............ CLC 49
See also CA 21-24R; CANR 9; DLB 48

Laurence, (Jean) Margaret (Wemyss)
1926-1987 .. CLC 3, 6, 13, 50, 62; SSC 7
See also CA 5-8R; 121; CANR 33; DLB 53;
MTCW; SATA 50

Laurent, Antoine 1952- .... CLC 50

Lauscher, Hermann
See Hesse, Hermann

Lautreamont, Comte de
1846-1870 .... NCLC 12

Laverty, Donald
See Blish, James (Benjamin)

Lavin, Mary 1912-...... CLC 4, 18; SSC 4
See also CA 9-12R; CANR 33; DLB 15;
MTCW

Lavond, Paul Dennis
See Kornbluth, C(yril) M.; Pohl, Frederik

Lawler, Raymond Evenor 1922- .... CLC 58
See also CA 103

Lawrence, D(avid) H(erbert Richards)
1885-1930 ...... TCLC 2, 9, 16, 33, 48;
SSC 4
See also CA 104; 121; CDBLB 1914-1945;
DA; DLB 10, 19, 36, 98; MTCW; WLC

Lawrence, T(homas) E(dward)
1888-1935 .... TCLC 18
See also Dale, Colin
See also CA 115

Lawrence Of Arabia
See Lawrence, T(homas) E(dward)

Lawson, Henry (Archibald Hertzberg)
1867-1922 .... TCLC 27
See also CA 120

Lawton, Dennis
See Faust, Frederick (Schiller)

Laxness, Halldor.................. CLC 25
See also Gudjonsson, Halldor Kiljan

Layamon fl. c. 1200-............. CMLC 10

Laye, Camara 1928-1980........ CLC 4, 38
See also BLC 2; BW; CA 85-88; 97-100;
CANR 25; MTCW

Layton, Irving (Peter) 1912-..... CLC 2, 15
See also CA 1-4R; CANR 2, 33; DLB 88;
MTCW

Lazarus, Emma 1849-1887....... NCLC 8

Lazarus, Felix
See Cable, George Washington

Lazarus, Henry
See Slavitt, David R(ytman)

Lea, Joan
See Neufeld, John (Arthur)

Leacock, Stephen (Butler)
1869-1944 .... TCLC 2
See also CA 104; DLB 92

Lear, Edward 1812-1888 .... NCLC 3
See also CLR 1; DLB 32; MAICYA;
SATA 18

Lear, Norman (Milton) 1922- ...... CLC 12
See also CA 73-76

Leavis, F(rank) R(aymond)
1895-1978 .... CLC 24
See also CA 21-24R; 77-80; MTCW

Leavitt, David 1961-............. CLC 34
See also CA 116; 122; DLB 130

Leblanc, Maurice (Marie Emile)
1864-1941 .... TCLC 49
See also CA 110

Lebowitz, Fran(ces Ann)
1951(?)-................. CLC 11, 36
See also CA 81-84; CANR 14; MTCW

le Carre, John .... CLC 3, 5, 9, 15, 28
See also Cornwell, David (John Moore)
See also BEST 89:4; CDBLB 1960 to
Present; DLB 87

Lorenzo, Heberto Padilla
  See Padilla (Lorenzo), Heberto

Loris
  See Hofmannsthal, Hugo von

Loti, Pierre .... TCLC **11**
  See also Viaud, (Louis Marie) Julien
  See also DLB 123

Louie, David Wong 1954- .... CLC **70**
  See also CA 139

Louis, Father M.
  See Merton, Thomas

Lovecraft, H(oward) P(hillips)
  1890-1937 .... TCLC **4, 22**; SSC **3**
  See also CA 104; 133; MTCW

Lovelace, Earl 1935- .... CLC **51**
  See also CA 77-80; CANR 41; DLB 125;
  MTCW

Lowell, Amy 1874-1925 .... TCLC **1, 8**
  See also CA 104; DLB 54

Lowell, James Russell 1819-1891 .. NCLC **2**
  See also CDALB 1640-1865; DLB 1, 11, 64,
  79

Lowell, Robert (Traill Spence, Jr.)
  1917-1977 ... CLC **1, 2, 3, 4, 5, 8, 9, 11,
  15, 37**; PC **3**
  See also CA 9-12R; 73-76; CABS 2;
  CANR 26; DA; DLB 5; MTCW; WLC

Lowndes, Marie Adelaide (Belloc)
  1868-1947 .... TCLC **12**
  See also CA 107; DLB 70

Lowry, (Clarence) Malcolm
  1909-1957 .... TCLC **6, 40**
  See also CA 105; 131; CDBLB 1945-1960;
  DLB 15; MTCW

Lowry, Mina Gertrude 1882-1966
  See Loy, Mina
  See also CA 113

Loxsmith, John
  See Brunner, John (Kilian Houston)

Loy, Mina .... CLC **28**
  See also Lowry, Mina Gertrude
  See also DLB 4, 54

Loyson-Bridet
  See Schwob, (Mayer Andre) Marcel

Lucas, Craig 1951- .... CLC **64**
  See also CA 137

Lucas, George 1944- .... CLC **16**
  See also AAYA 1; CA 77-80; CANR 30;
  SATA 56

Lucas, Hans
  See Godard, Jean-Luc

Lucas, Victoria
  See Plath, Sylvia

Ludlam, Charles 1943-1987 ..... CLC **46, 50**
  See also CA 85-88; 122

Ludlum, Robert 1927- .... CLC **22, 43**
  See also AAYA 10; BEST 89:1, 90:3;
  CA 33-36R; CANR 25, 41; DLBY 82;
  MTCW

Ludwig, Ken .... CLC **60**

Ludwig, Otto 1813-1865 .... NCLC **4**
  See also DLB 129

Lugones, Leopoldo 1874-1938 ..... TCLC **15**
  See also CA 116; 131; HW

Lu Hsun 1881-1936 .... TCLC **3**

Lukacs, George .... CLC **24**
  See also Lukacs, Gyorgy (Szegeny von)

Lukacs, Gyorgy (Szegeny von) 1885-1971
  See Lukacs, George
  See also CA 101; 29-32R

Luke, Peter (Ambrose Cyprian)
  1919- .... CLC **38**
  See also CA 81-84; DLB 13

Lunar, Dennis
  See Mungo, Raymond

Lurie, Alison 1926- .... CLC **4, 5, 18, 39**
  See also CA 1-4R; CANR 2, 17; DLB 2;
  MTCW; SATA 46

Lustig, Arnost 1926- .... CLC **56**
  See also AAYA 3; CA 69-72; SATA 56

Luther, Martin 1483-1546 .... LC **9**

Luzi, Mario 1914- .... CLC **13**
  See also CA 61-64; CANR 9; DLB 128

Lynch, B. Suarez
  See Bioy Casares, Adolfo; Borges, Jorge
  Luis

Lynch, David (K.) 1946- .... CLC **66**
  See also CA 124; 129

Lynch, James
  See Andreyev, Leonid (Nikolaevich)

Lynch Davis, B.
  See Bioy Casares, Adolfo; Borges, Jorge
  Luis

Lyndsay, Sir David 1490-1555 .... LC **20**

Lynn, Kenneth S(chuyler) 1923- .... CLC **50**
  See also CA 1-4R; CANR 3, 27

Lynx
  See West, Rebecca

Lyons, Marcus
  See Blish, James (Benjamin)

Lyre, Pinchbeck
  See Sassoon, Siegfried (Lorraine)

Lytle, Andrew (Nelson) 1902- ...... CLC **22**
  See also CA 9-12R; DLB 6

Lyttelton, George 1709-1773 .... LC **10**

Maas, Peter 1929- .... CLC **29**
  See also CA 93-96

Macaulay, Rose 1881-1958 ..... TCLC **7, 44**
  See also CA 104; DLB 36

MacBeth, George (Mann)
  1932-1992 .... CLC **2, 5, 9**
  See also CA 25-28R; 136; DLB 40; MTCW;
  SATA 4; SATA-Obit 70

MacCaig, Norman (Alexander)
  1910- .... CLC **36**
  See also CA 9-12R; CANR 3, 34; DLB 27

MacCarthy, (Sir Charles Otto) Desmond
  1877-1952 .... TCLC **36**

MacDiarmid, Hugh ..... CLC **2, 4, 11, 19, 63**
  See also Grieve, C(hristopher) M(urray)
  See also CDBLB 1945-1960; DLB 20

MacDonald, Anson
  See Heinlein, Robert A(nson)

Macdonald, Cynthia 1928- ...... CLC **13, 19**
  See also CA 49-52; CANR 4; DLB 105

MacDonald, George 1824-1905 ..... TCLC **9**
  See also CA 106; 137; DLB 18; MAICYA;
  SATA 33

Macdonald, John
  See Millar, Kenneth

MacDonald, John D(ann)
  1916-1986 .... CLC **3, 27, 44**
  See also CA 1-4R; 121; CANR 1, 19;
  DLB 8; DLBY 86; MTCW

Macdonald, John Ross
  See Millar, Kenneth

Macdonald, Ross ..... CLC **1, 2, 3, 14, 34, 41**
  See also Millar, Kenneth
  See also DLBD 6

MacDougal, John
  See Blish, James (Benjamin)

MacEwen, Gwendolyn (Margaret)
  1941-1987 .... CLC **13, 55**
  See also CA 9-12R; 124; CANR 7, 22;
  DLB 53; SATA 50, 55

Machado (y Ruiz), Antonio
  1875-1939 .... TCLC **3**
  See also CA 104; DLB 108

Machado de Assis, Joaquim Maria
  1839-1908 .... TCLC **10**
  See also BLC 2; CA 107

Machen, Arthur .... TCLC **4**
  See also Jones, Arthur Llewellyn
  See also DLB 36

Machiavelli, Niccolo 1469-1527 ...... LC **8**
  See also DA

MacInnes, Colin 1914-1976 ...... CLC **4, 23**
  See also CA 69-72; 65-68; CANR 21;
  DLB 14; MTCW

MacInnes, Helen (Clark)
  1907-1985 .... CLC **27, 39**
  See also CA 1-4R; 117; CANR 1, 28;
  DLB 87; MTCW; SATA 22, 44

Mackenzie, Compton (Edward Montague)
  1883-1972 .... CLC **18**
  See also CA 21-22; 37-40R; CAP 2;
  DLB 34, 100

Mackintosh, Elizabeth 1896(?)-1952
  See Tey, Josephine
  See also CA 110

MacLaren, James
  See Grieve, C(hristopher) M(urray)

Mac Laverty, Bernard 1942- .... CLC **31**
  See also CA 116; 118

MacLean, Alistair (Stuart)
  1922-1987 .... CLC **3, 13, 50, 63**
  See also CA 57-60; 121; CANR 28; MTCW;
  SATA 23, 50

MacLeish, Archibald
  1892-1982 .... CLC **3, 8, 14, 68**
  See also CA 9-12R; 106; CANR 33; DLB 4,
  7, 45; DLBY 82; MTCW

MacLennan, (John) Hugh
  1907- .... CLC **2, 14**
  See also CA 5-8R; CANR 33; DLB 68;
  MTCW

MacLeod, Alistair 1936- .... CLC **56**
  See also CA 123; DLB 60

MacNeice, (Frederick) Louis
    1907-1963 . . . . **CLC 1, 4, 10, 53**
    See also CA 85-88; DLB 10, 20; MTCW

MacNeill, Dand
    See Fraser, George MacDonald

Macpherson, (Jean) Jay 1931- . . . . . . **CLC 14**
    See also CA 5-8R; DLB 53

MacShane, Frank 1927- . . . . **CLC 39**
    See also CA 9-12R; CANR 3, 33; DLB 111

Macumber, Mari
    See Sandoz, Mari(e Susette)

Madach, Imre 1823-1864 . . . . **NCLC 19**

Madden, (Jerry) David 1933- . . . . **CLC 5, 15**
    See also CA 1-4R; CAAS 3; CANR 4;
    DLB 6; MTCW

Maddern, Al(an)
    See Ellison, Harlan

Madhubuti, Haki R.
    1942- . . . . **CLC 6, 73; PC 5**
    See also Lee, Don L.
    See also BLC 2; BW; CA 73-76; CANR 24;
    DLB 5, 41; DLBD 8

Madow, Pauline (Reichberg) . . . . **CLC 1**
    See also CA 9-12R

Maepenn, Hugh
    See Kuttner, Henry

Maepenn, K. H.
    See Kuttner, Henry

Maeterlinck, Maurice 1862-1949 . . . **TCLC 3**
    See also CA 104; 136; SATA 66

Maginn, William 1794-1842 . . . . . . **NCLC 8**
    See also DLB 110

Mahapatra, Jayanta 1928- . . . . **CLC 33**
    See also CA 73-76; CAAS 9; CANR 15, 33

Mahfouz, Naguib (Abdel Aziz Al-Sabilgi)
    1911(?)-
    See Mahfuz, Najib
    See also BEST 89:2; CA 128; MTCW

Mahfuz, Najib . . . . **CLC 52, 55**
    See also Mahfouz, Naguib (Abdel Aziz
    Al-Sabilgi)
    See also DLBY 88

Mahon, Derek 1941- . . . . **CLC 27**
    See also CA 113; 128; DLB 40

Mailer, Norman
    1923- . . . . . . **CLC 1, 2, 3, 4, 5, 8, 11, 14,**
                     28, 39, 74
    See also AITN 2; CA 9-12R; CABS 1;
    CANR 28; CDALB 1968-1988; DA;
    DLB 2, 16, 28; DLBD 3; DLBY 80, 83;
    MTCW

Maillet, Antonine 1929- . . . . **CLC 54**
    See also CA 115; 120; DLB 60

Mais, Roger 1905-1955 . . . . **TCLC 8**
    See also BW; CA 105; 124; DLB 125;
    MTCW

Maitland, Sara (Louise) 1950- . . . . . . **CLC 49**
    See also CA 69-72; CANR 13

Major, Clarence 1936- . . . . **CLC 3, 19, 48**
    See also BLC 2; BW; CA 21-24R; CAAS 6;
    CANR 13, 25; DLB 33

Major, Kevin (Gerald) 1949- . . . . **CLC 26**
    See also CA 97-100; CANR 21, 38;
    CLR 11; DLB 60; MAICYA; SATA 32

Maki, James
    See Ozu, Yasujiro

Malabaila, Damiano
    See Levi, Primo

Malamud, Bernard
    1914-1986 . . . . . **CLC 1, 2, 3, 5, 8, 9, 11,**
                    18, 27, 44
    See also CA 5-8R; 118; CABS 1; CANR 28;
    CDALB 1941-1968; DA; DLB 2, 28;
    DLBY 80, 86; MTCW; WLC

Malcolm, Dan
    See Silverberg, Robert

Malherbe, Francois de 1555-1628 . . . . . **LC 5**

Mallarme, Stephane
    1842-1898 . . . . **NCLC 4; PC 4**

Mallet-Joris, Francoise 1930- . . . . . . **CLC 11**
    See also CA 65-68; CANR 17; DLB 83

Malley, Ern
    See McAuley, James Phillip

Mallowan, Agatha Christie
    See Christie, Agatha (Mary Clarissa)

Maloff, Saul 1922- . . . . **CLC 5**
    See also CA 33-36R

Malone, Louis
    See MacNeice, (Frederick) Louis

Malone, Michael (Christopher)
    1942- . . . . **CLC 43**
    See also CA 77-80; CANR 14, 32

Malory, (Sir) Thomas
    1410(?)-1471(?) . . . . **LC 11**
    See also CDBLB Before 1660; DA;
    SATA 33, 59

Malouf, (George Joseph) David
    1934- . . . . **CLC 28**
    See also CA 124

Malraux, (Georges-)Andre
    1901-1976 . . . . . . **CLC 1, 4, 9, 13, 15, 57**
    See also CA 21-22; 69-72; CANR 34;
    CAP 2; DLB 72; MTCW

Malzberg, Barry N(athaniel) 1939- . . . **CLC 7**
    See also CA 61-64; CAAS 4; CANR 16;
    DLB 8

Mamet, David (Alan)
    1947- . . . . **CLC 9, 15, 34, 46**
    See also AAYA 3; CA 81-84; CABS 3;
    CANR 15, 41; DLB 7; MTCW

Mamoulian, Rouben (Zachary)
    1897-1987 . . . . **CLC 16**
    See also CA 25-28R; 124

Mandelstam, Osip (Emilievich)
    1891(?)-1938(?) . . . . **TCLC 2, 6**
    See also CA 104

Mander, (Mary) Jane 1877-1949 . . . **TCLC 31**

Mandiargues, Andre Pieyre de . . . . . . **CLC 41**
    See also Pieyre de Mandiargues, Andre
    See also DLB 83

Mandrake, Ethel Belle
    See Thurman, Wallace (Henry)

Mangan, James Clarence
    1803-1849 . . . . **NCLC 27**

Maniere, J.-E.
    See Giraudoux, (Hippolyte) Jean

Manley, (Mary) Delariviere
    1672(?)-1724 . . . . **LC 1**
    See also DLB 39, 80

Mann, Abel
    See Creasey, John

Mann, (Luiz) Heinrich 1871-1950 . . . **TCLC 9**
    See also CA 106; DLB 66

Mann, (Paul) Thomas
    1875-1955 . . . **TCLC 2, 8, 14, 21, 35, 44;**
                           SSC 5
    See also CA 104; 128; DA; DLB 66;
    MTCW; WLC

Manning, David
    See Faust, Frederick (Schiller)

Manning, Frederic 1887(?)-1935 . . . **TCLC 25**
    See also CA 124

Manning, Olivia 1915-1980 . . . . . . **CLC 5, 19**
    See also CA 5-8R; 101; CANR 29; MTCW

Mano, D. Keith 1942- . . . . **CLC 2, 10**
    See also CA 25-28R; CAAS 6; CANR 26;
    DLB 6

Mansfield, Katherine . . . **TCLC 2, 8, 39; SSC 9**
    See also Beauchamp, Kathleen Mansfield
    See also WLC

Manso, Peter 1940- . . . . **CLC 39**
    See also CA 29-32R

Mantecon, Juan Jimenez
    See Jimenez (Mantecon), Juan Ramon

Manton, Peter
    See Creasey, John

Man Without a Spleen, A
    See Chekhov, Anton (Pavlovich)

Manzoni, Alessandro 1785-1873 . . **NCLC 29**

Mapu, Abraham (ben Jekutiel)
    1808-1867 . . . . **NCLC 18**

Mara, Sally
    See Queneau, Raymond

Marat, Jean Paul 1743-1793 . . . . **LC 10**

Marcel, Gabriel Honore
    1889-1973 . . . . **CLC 15**
    See also CA 102; 45-48; MTCW

Marchbanks, Samuel
    See Davies, (William) Robertson

Marchi, Giacomo
    See Bassani, Giorgio

Margulies, Donald . . . . **CLC 76**

Marie de France c. 12th cent. - . . . . **CMLC 8**

Marie de l'Incarnation 1599-1672 . . . . **LC 10**

Mariner, Scott
    See Pohl, Frederik

Marinetti, Filippo Tommaso
    1876-1944 . . . . **TCLC 10**
    See also CA 107; DLB 114

Marivaux, Pierre Carlet de Chamblain de
    1688-1763 . . . . **LC 4**

Markandaya, Kamala . . . . **CLC 8, 38**
    See also Taylor, Kamala (Purnaiya)

Markfield, Wallace 1926- . . . . **CLC 8**
    See also CA 69-72; CAAS 3; DLB 2, 28

Markham, Edwin 1852-1940 . . . . . . **TCLC 47**
    See also DLB 54

Markham, Robert
    See Amis, Kingsley (William)

Marks, J
See Highwater, Jamake (Mamake)

Marks-Highwater, J
See Highwater, Jamake (Mamake)

Markson, David M(errill) 1927- .... **CLC 67**
See also CA 49-52; CANR 1

Marley, Bob . . . . **CLC 17**
See also Marley, Robert Nesta

Marley, Robert Nesta 1945-1981
See Marley, Bob
See also CA 107; 103

Marlowe, Christopher
1564-1593 . . . . **LC 22; DC 1**
See also CDBLB Before 1660; DA; DLB 62;
WLC

Marmontel, Jean-Francois
1723-1799 . . . . **LC 2**

Marquand, John P(hillips)
1893-1960 . . . . **CLC 2, 10**
See also CA 85-88; DLB 9, 102

Marquez, Gabriel (Jose) Garcia . . . . . . **CLC 68**
See also Garcia Marquez, Gabriel (Jose)

Marquis, Don(ald Robert Perry)
1878-1937 . . . . **TCLC 7**
See also CA 104; DLB 11, 25

Marric, J. J.
See Creasey, John

Marrow, Bernard
See Moore, Brian

Marryat, Frederick 1792-1848 . . . . **NCLC 3**
See also DLB 21

Marsden, James
See Creasey, John

Marsh, (Edith) Ngaio
1899-1982 . . . . **CLC 7, 53**
See also CA 9-12R; CANR 6; DLB 77;
MTCW

Marshall, Garry 1934- . . . . **CLC 17**
See also AAYA 3; CA 111; SATA 60

Marshall, Paule 1929- . . **CLC 27, 72; SSC 3**
See also BLC 3; BW; CA 77-80; CANR 25;
DLB 33; MTCW

Marsten, Richard
See Hunter, Evan

Martha, Henry
See Harris, Mark

Martin, Ken
See Hubbard, L(afayette) Ron(ald)

Martin, Richard
See Creasey, John

Martin, Steve 1945- . . . . **CLC 30**
See also CA 97-100; CANR 30; MTCW

Martin, Webber
See Silverberg, Robert

Martin du Gard, Roger
1881-1958 . . . . **TCLC 24**
See also CA 118; DLB 65

Martineau, Harriet 1802-1876 . . . . **NCLC 26**
See also DLB 21, 55; YABC 2

Martines, Julia
See O'Faolain, Julia

Martinez, Jacinto Benavente y
See Benavente (y Martinez), Jacinto

Martinez Ruiz, Jose 1873-1967
See Azorin; Ruiz, Jose Martinez
See also CA 93-96; HW

Martinez Sierra, Gregorio
1881-1947 . . . . **TCLC 6**
See also CA 115

Martinez Sierra, Maria (de la O'LeJarraga)
1874-1974 . . . . **TCLC 6**
See also CA 115

Martinsen, Martin
See Follett, Ken(neth Martin)

Martinson, Harry (Edmund)
1904-1978 . . . . **CLC 14**
See also CA 77-80; CANR 34

Marut, Ret
See Traven, B.

Marut, Robert
See Traven, B.

Marvell, Andrew 1621-1678 . . . . **LC 4**
See also CDBLB 1660-1789; DA; DLB 131;
WLC

Marx, Karl (Heinrich)
1818-1883 . . . . **NCLC 17**
See also DLB 129

Masaoka Shiki . . . . **TCLC 18**
See also Masaoka Tsunenori

Masaoka Tsunenori 1867-1902
See Masaoka Shiki
See also CA 117

Masefield, John (Edward)
1878-1967 . . . . **CLC 11, 47**
See also CA 19-20; 25-28R; CANR 33;
CAP 2; CDBLB 1890-1914; DLB 10;
MTCW; SATA 19

Maso, Carole 19(?)- . . . . **CLC 44**

Mason, Bobbie Ann
1940- . . . . **CLC 28, 43; SSC 4**
See also AAYA 5; CA 53-56; CANR 11,
31; DLBY 87; MTCW

Mason, Ernst
See Pohl, Frederik

Mason, Lee W.
See Malzberg, Barry N(athaniel)

Mason, Nick 1945- . . . . **CLC 35**
See also Pink Floyd

Mason, Tally
See Derleth, August (William)

Mass, William
See Gibson, William

Masters, Edgar Lee
1868-1950 . . . . **TCLC 2, 25; PC 1**
See also CA 104; 133; CDALB 1865-1917;
DA; DLB 54; MTCW

Masters, Hilary 1928- . . . . **CLC 48**
See also CA 25-28R; CANR 13

Mastrosimone, William 19(?)- . . . . . . **CLC 36**

Mathe, Albert
See Camus, Albert

Matheson, Richard Burton 1926- . . . **CLC 37**
See also CA 97-100; DLB 8, 44

Mathews, Harry 1930- . . . . **CLC 6, 52**
See also CA 21-24R; CAAS 6; CANR 18,
40

Mathias, Roland (Glyn) 1915- . . . . . . **CLC 45**
See also CA 97-100; CANR 19, 41; DLB 27

Matsuo Basho 1644-1694 . . . . **PC 3**

Mattheson, Rodney
See Creasey, John

Matthews, Greg 1949- . . . . **CLC 45**
See also CA 135

Matthews, William 1942- . . . . **CLC 40**
See also CA 29-32R; CANR 12; DLB 5

Matthias, John (Edward) 1941- . . . . . . **CLC 9**
See also CA 33-36R

Matthiessen, Peter
1927- . . . . **CLC 5, 7, 11, 32, 64**
See also AAYA 6; BEST 90:4; CA 9-12R;
CANR 21; DLB 6; MTCW; SATA 27

Maturin, Charles Robert
1780(?)-1824 . . . . **NCLC 6**

Matute (Ausejo), Ana Maria
1925- . . . . **CLC 11**
See also CA 89-92; MTCW

Maugham, W. S.
See Maugham, W(illiam) Somerset

Maugham, W(illiam) Somerset
1874-1965 . . . . **CLC 1, 11, 15, 67; SSC 8**
See also CA 5-8R; 25-28R; CANR 40;
CDBLB 1914-1945; DA; DLB 10, 36, 77,
100; MTCW; SATA 54; WLC

Maugham, William Somerset
See Maugham, W(illiam) Somerset

Maupassant, (Henri Rene Albert) Guy de
1850-1893 . . . . **NCLC 1; SSC 1**
See also DA; DLB 123; WLC

Maurhut, Richard
See Traven, B.

Mauriac, Claude 1914- . . . . **CLC 9**
See also CA 89-92; DLB 83

Mauriac, Francois (Charles)
1885-1970 . . . . **CLC 4, 9, 56**
See also CA 25-28; CAP 2; DLB 65;
MTCW

Mavor, Osborne Henry 1888-1951
See Bridie, James
See also CA 104

Maxwell, William (Keepers, Jr.)
1908- . . . . **CLC 19**
See also CA 93-96; DLBY 80

May, Elaine 1932- . . . . **CLC 16**
See also CA 124; DLB 44

Mayakovski, Vladimir (Vladimirovich)
1893-1930 . . . . **TCLC 4, 18**
See also CA 104

Mayhew, Henry 1812-1887 . . . . . . **NCLC 31**
See also DLB 18, 55

Maynard, Joyce 1953- . . . . **CLC 23**
See also CA 111; 129

Mayne, William (James Carter)
1928- . . . . **CLC 12**
See also CA 9-12R; CANR 37; CLR 25;
MAICYA; SAAS 11; SATA 6, 68

Mayo, Jim
See L'Amour, Louis (Dearborn)

Maysles, Albert 1926- . . . . **CLC 16**
See also CA 29-32R

Maysles, David 1932- . . . . **CLC 16**

Montagu, Elizabeth 1917- .... **NCLC 7**
See also CA 9-12R

Montagu, Mary (Pierrepont) Wortley
1689-1762 .... **LC 9**
See also DLB 95, 101

Montagu, W. H.
See Coleridge, Samuel Taylor

Montague, John (Patrick)
1929- .... **CLC 13, 46**
See also CA 9-12R; CANR 9; DLB 40;
MTCW

Montaigne, Michel (Eyquem) de
1533-1592 .... **LC 8**
See also DA; WLC

Montale, Eugenio 1896-1981 ... **CLC 7, 9, 18**
See also CA 17-20R; 104; CANR 30;
DLB 114; MTCW

Montesquieu, Charles-Louis de Secondat
1689-1755 .... **LC 7**

Montgomery, (Robert) Bruce 1921-1978
See Crispin, Edmund
See also CA 104

Montgomery, Marion H., Jr. 1925- .. **CLC 7**
See also AITN 1; CA 1-4R; CANR 3;
DLB 6

Montgomery, Max
See Davenport, Guy (Mattison, Jr.)

Montherlant, Henry (Milon) de
1896-1972 .... **CLC 8, 19**
See also CA 85-88; 37-40R; DLB 72;
MTCW

Monty Python .... **CLC 21**
See also Chapman, Graham; Cleese, John
(Marwood); Gilliam, Terry (Vance); Idle,
Eric; Jones, Terence Graham Parry; Palin,
Michael (Edward)
See also AAYA 7

Moodie, Susanna (Strickland)
1803-1885 .... **NCLC 14**
See also DLB 99

Mooney, Edward 1951- .... **CLC 25**
See also CA 130

Mooney, Ted
See Mooney, Edward

Moorcock, Michael (John)
1939- .... **CLC 5, 27, 58**
See also CA 45-48; CAAS 5; CANR 2, 17,
38; DLB 14; MTCW

Moore, Brian
1921- .... **CLC 1, 3, 5, 7, 8, 19, 32**
See also CA 1-4R; CANR 1, 25; MTCW

Moore, Edward
See Muir, Edwin

Moore, George Augustus
1852-1933 .... **TCLC 7**
See also CA 104; DLB 10, 18, 57

Moore, Lorrie .... **CLC 39, 45, 68**
See also Moore, Marie Lorena

Moore, Marianne (Craig)
1887-1972 ... **CLC 1, 2, 4, 8, 10, 13, 19,
47; PC 4**
See also CA 1-4R; 33-36R; CANR 3;
CDALB 1929-1941; DA; DLB 45;
DLBD 7; MTCW; SATA 20

Moore, Marie Lorena 1957-
See Moore, Lorrie
See also CA 116; CANR 39

Moore, Thomas 1779-1852 .... **NCLC 6**
See also DLB 96

Morand, Paul 1888-1976 .... **CLC 41**
See also CA 69-72; DLB 65

Morante, Elsa 1918-1985 .... **CLC 8, 47**
See also CA 85-88; 117; CANR 35; MTCW

Moravia, Alberto ...... **CLC 2, 7, 11, 27, 46**
See also Pincherle, Alberto

More, Hannah 1745-1833 .... **NCLC 27**
See also DLB 107, 109, 116

More, Henry 1614-1687 .... **LC 9**
See also DLB 126

More, Sir Thomas 1478-1535 .... **LC 10**

Moreas, Jean .... **TCLC 18**
See also Papadiamantopoulos, Johannes

Morgan, Berry 1919- .... **CLC 6**
See also CA 49-52; DLB 6

Morgan, Claire
See Highsmith, (Mary) Patricia

Morgan, Edwin (George) 1920- ..... **CLC 31**
See also CA 5-8R; CANR 3; DLB 27

Morgan, (George) Frederick
1922- .... **CLC 23**
See also CA 17-20R; CANR 21

Morgan, Harriet
See Mencken, H(enry) L(ouis)

Morgan, Jane
See Cooper, James Fenimore

Morgan, Janet 1945- .... **CLC 39**
See also CA 65-68

Morgan, Lady 1776(?)-1859 ...... **NCLC 29**
See also DLB 116

Morgan, Robin 1941- .... **CLC 2**
See also CA 69-72; CANR 29; MTCW

Morgan, Scott
See Kuttner, Henry

Morgan, Seth 1949(?)-1990 .... **CLC 65**
See also CA 132

Morgenstern, Christian
1871-1914 .... **TCLC 8**
See also CA 105

Morgenstern, S.
See Goldman, William (W.)

Moricz, Zsigmond 1879-1942 ..... **TCLC 33**

Morike, Eduard (Friedrich)
1804-1875 .... **NCLC 10**

Mori Ogai .... **TCLC 14**
See also Mori Rintaro

Mori Rintaro 1862-1922
See Mori Ogai
See also CA 110

Moritz, Karl Philipp 1756-1793 ...... **LC 2**
See also DLB 94

Morland, Peter Henry
See Faust, Frederick (Schiller)

Morren, Theophil
See Hofmannsthal, Hugo von

Morris, Bill 1952- .... **CLC 76**

Morris, Julian
See West, Morris L(anglo)

Morris, Steveland Judkins 1950(?)-
See Wonder, Stevie
See also CA 111

Morris, William 1834-1896 ...... **NCLC 4**
See also CDBLB 1832-1890; DLB 18, 35, 57

Morris, Wright 1910-... **CLC 1, 3, 7, 18, 37**
See also CA 9-12R; CANR 21; DLB 2;
DLBY 81; MTCW

Morrison, Chloe Anthony Wofford
See Morrison, Toni

Morrison, James Douglas 1943-1971
See Morrison, Jim
See also CA 73-76; CANR 40

Morrison, Jim .... **CLC 17**
See also Morrison, James Douglas

Morrison, Toni 1931-..... **CLC 4, 10, 22, 55**
See also AAYA 1; BLC 3; BW; CA 29-32R;
CANR 27; CDALB 1968-1988; DA;
DLB 6, 33; DLBY 81; MTCW; SATA 57

Morrison, Van 1945- .... **CLC 21**
See also CA 116

Mortimer, John (Clifford)
1923- .... **CLC 28, 43**
See also CA 13-16R; CANR 21;
CDBLB 1960 to Present; DLB 13;
MTCW

Mortimer, Penelope (Ruth) 1918-.... **CLC 5**
See also CA 57-60

Morton, Anthony
See Creasey, John

Mosher, Howard Frank .... **CLC 62**
See also CA 139

Mosley, Nicholas 1923-........ **CLC 43, 70**
See also CA 69-72; CANR 41; DLB 14

Moss, Howard
1922-1987 .... **CLC 7, 14, 45, 50**
See also CA 1-4R; 123; CANR 1; DLB 5

Mossgiel, Rab
See Burns, Robert

Motion, Andrew 1952-............ **CLC 47**
See also DLB 40

Motley, Willard (Francis)
1912-1965 .... **CLC 18**
See also BW; CA 117; 106; DLB 76

Mott, Michael (Charles Alston)
1930- .... **CLC 15, 34**
See also CA 5-8R; CAAS 7; CANR 7, 29

Mowat, Farley (McGill) 1921- ..... **CLC 26**
See also AAYA 1; CA 1-4R; CANR 4, 24;
CLR 20; DLB 68; MAICYA; MTCW;
SATA 3, 55

Moyers, Bill 1934-............... **CLC 74**
See also AITN 2; CA 61-64; CANR 31

Mphahlele, Es'kia
See Mphahlele, Ezekiel
See also DLB 125

Mphahlele, Ezekiel 1919-........ **CLC 25**
See also Mphahlele, Es'kia
See also BLC 3; BW; CA 81-84; CANR 26

Mqhayi, S(amuel) E(dward) K(rune Loliwe)
1875-1945 .... **TCLC 25**
See also BLC 3

Mr. Martin
See Burroughs, William S(eward)

Mrozek, Slawomir 1930- .... **CLC 3, 13**
See also CA 13-16R; CAAS 10; CANR 29;
MTCW

Mrs. Belloc-Lowndes
See Lowndes, Marie Adelaide (Belloc)

Mtwa, Percy (?)-................ **CLC 47**

Mueller, Lisel 1924-.......... **CLC 13, 51**
See also CA 93-96; DLB 105

Muir, Edwin 1887-1959 .... **TCLC 2**
See also CA 104; DLB 20, 100

Muir, John 1838-1914 .... **TCLC 28**

Mujica Lainez, Manuel
1910-1984 .... **CLC 31**
See also Lainez, Manuel Mujica
See also CA 81-84; 112; CANR 32; HW

Mukherjee, Bharati 1940-........ **CLC 53**
See also BEST 89:2; CA 107; DLB 60;
MTCW

Muldoon, Paul 1951-......... **CLC 32, 72**
See also CA 113; 129; DLB 40

Mulisch, Harry 1927-............. **CLC 42**
See also CA 9-12R; CANR 6, 26

Mull, Martin 1943-.............. **CLC 17**
See also CA 105

Mulock, Dinah Maria
See Craik, Dinah Maria (Mulock)

Munford, Robert 1737(?)-1783 .... **LC 5**
See also DLB 31

Mungo, Raymond 1946-.......... **CLC 72**
See also CA 49-52; CANR 2

Munro, Alice
1931- .... **CLC 6, 10, 19, 50; SSC 3**
See also AITN 2; CA 33-36R; CANR 33;
DLB 53; MTCW; SATA 29

Munro, H(ector) H(ugh) 1870-1916
See Saki
See also CA 104; 130; CDBLB 1890-1914;
DA; DLB 34; MTCW; WLC

Murasaki, Lady................. **CMLC 1**

Murdoch, (Jean) Iris
1919- ...... **CLC 1, 2, 3, 4, 6, 8, 11, 15,**
22, 31, 51
See also CA 13-16R; CANR 8;
CDBLB 1960 to Present; DLB 14;
MTCW

Murphy, Richard 1927-........... **CLC 41**
See also CA 29-32R; DLB 40

Murphy, Sylvia 1937-............. **CLC 34**
See also CA 121

Murphy, Thomas (Bernard) 1935-... **CLC 51**
See also CA 101

Murray, Albert L. 1916- .... **CLC 73**
See also BW; CA 49-52; CANR 26; DLB 38

Murray, Les(lie) A(llan) 1938- ..... **CLC 40**
See also CA 21-24R; CANR 11, 27

Murry, J. Middleton
See Murry, John Middleton

Murry, John Middleton
1889-1957 .... **TCLC 16**
See also CA 118

Musgrave, Susan 1951- .... **CLC 13, 54**
See also CA 69-72

Musil, Robert (Edler von)
1880-1942 .... **TCLC 12**
See also CA 109; DLB 81, 124

Musset, (Louis Charles) Alfred de
1810-1857 .... **NCLC 7**

My Brother's Brother
See Chekhov, Anton (Pavlovich)

Myers, Walter Dean 1937- .... **CLC 35**
See also AAYA 4; BLC 3; BW; CA 33-36R;
CANR 20; CLR 4, 16; DLB 33;
MAICYA; SAAS 2; SATA 27, 41, 70, 71

Myers, Walter M.
See Myers, Walter Dean

Myles, Symon
See Follett, Ken(neth Martin)

Nabokov, Vladimir (Vladimirovich)
1899-1977 .... **CLC 1, 2, 3, 6, 8, 11, 15,**
23, 44, 46, 64; SSC 11
See also CA 5-8R; 69-72; CANR 20;
CDALB 1941-1968; DA; DLB 2;
DLBD 3; DLBY 80, 91; MTCW; WLC

Nagy, Laszlo 1925-1978............ **CLC 7**
See also CA 129; 112

Naipaul, Shiva(dhar Srinivasa)
1945-1985 .... **CLC 32, 39**
See also CA 110; 112; 116; CANR 33;
DLBY 85; MTCW

Naipaul, V(idiadhar) S(urajprasad)
1932- .... **CLC 4, 7, 9, 13, 18, 37**
See also CA 1-4R; CANR 1, 33;
CDBLB 1960 to Present; DLB 125;
DLBY 85; MTCW

Nakos, Lilika 1899(?)-............ **CLC 29**

Narayan, R(asipuram) K(rishnaswami)
1906- .... **CLC 7, 28, 47**
See also CA 81-84; CANR 33; MTCW;
SATA 62

Nash, (Frediric) Ogden 1902-1971 .. **CLC 23**
See also CA 13-14; 29-32R; CANR 34;
CAP 1; DLB 11; MAICYA; MTCW;
SATA 2, 46

Nathan, Daniel
See Dannay, Frederic

Nathan, George Jean 1882-1958 ... **TCLC 18**
See also Hatteras, Owen
See also CA 114

Natsume, Kinnosuke 1867-1916
See Natsume, Soseki
See also CA 104

Natsume, Soseki .... **TCLC 2, 10**
See also Natsume, Kinnosuke

Natti, (Mary) Lee 1919-
See Kingman, Lee
See also CA 5-8R; CANR 2

Naylor, Gloria 1950- .... **CLC 28, 52**
See also AAYA 6; BLC 3; BW; CA 107;
CANR 27; DA; MTCW

Neihardt, John Gneisenau
1881-1973 .... **CLC 32**
See also CA 13-14; CAP 1; DLB 9, 54

Nekrasov, Nikolai Alekseevich
1821-1878 .... **NCLC 11**

Nelligan, Emile 1879-1941........ **TCLC 14**
See also CA 114; DLB 92

Nelson, Willie 1933-.............. **CLC 17**
See also CA 107

Nemerov, Howard (Stanley)
1920-1991 .... **CLC 2, 6, 9, 36**
See also CA 1-4R; 134; CABS 2; CANR 1,
27; DLB 6; DLBY 83; MTCW

Neruda, Pablo
1904-1973 .... **CLC 1, 2, 5, 7, 9, 28, 62;**
PC 4
See also CA 19-20; 45-48; CAP 2; DA; HW;
MTCW; WLC

Nerval, Gerard de 1808-1855...... **NCLC 1**

Nervo, (Jose) Amado (Ruiz de)
1870-1919 .... **TCLC 11**
See also CA 109; 131; HW

Nessi, Pio Baroja y
See Baroja (y Nessi), Pio

Neufeld, John (Arthur) 1938- ...... **CLC 17**
See also CA 25-28R; CANR 11, 37;
MAICYA; SAAS 3; SATA 6

Neville, Emily Cheney 1919-...... **CLC 12**
See also CA 5-8R; CANR 3, 37; MAICYA;
SAAS 2; SATA 1

Newbound, Bernard Slade 1930-
See Slade, Bernard
See also CA 81-84

Newby, P(ercy) H(oward)
1918-..................... **CLC 2, 13**
See also CA 5-8R; CANR 32; DLB 15;
MTCW

Newlove, Donald 1928- .... **CLC 6**
See also CA 29-32R; CANR 25

Newlove, John (Herbert) 1938-..... **CLC 14**
See also CA 21-24R; CANR 9, 25

Newman, Charles 1938-.......... **CLC 2, 8**
See also CA 21-24R

Newman, Edwin (Harold) 1919- .... **CLC 14**
See also AITN 1; CA 69-72; CANR 5

Newman, John Henry
1801-1890 .... **NCLC 38**
See also DLB 18, 32, 55

Newton, Suzanne 1936-........... **CLC 35**
See also CA 41-44R; CANR 14; SATA 5

Nexo, Martin Andersen
1869-1954 .... **TCLC 43**

Nezval, Vitezslav 1900-1958 ...... **TCLC 44**
See also CA 123

Ngema, Mbongeni 1955- .... **CLC 57**

Ngugi, James T(hiong'o)........ **CLC 3, 7, 13**
See also Ngugi wa Thiong'o

Ngugi wa Thiong'o 1938-.......... **CLC 36**
See also Ngugi, James T(hiong'o)
See also BLC 3; BW; CA 81-84; CANR 27;
MTCW

Nichol, B(arrie) P(hillip)
1944-1988 .... **CLC 18**
See also CA 53-56; DLB 53; SATA 66

Nichols, John (Treadwell) 1940-.... **CLC 38**
See also CA 9-12R; CAAS 2; CANR 6;
DLBY 82

Nichols, Peter (Richard)
1927-................. **CLC 5, 36, 65**
See also CA 104; CANR 33; DLB 13;
MTCW

Nicolas, F. R. E.
See Freeling, Nicolas

Niedecker, Lorine 1903-1970.... **CLC 10, 42**
See also CA 25-28; CAP 2; DLB 48

Nietzsche, Friedrich (Wilhelm)
1844-1900 .... **TCLC 10, 18**
See also CA 107; 121; DLB 129

Nievo, Ippolito 1831-1861 ...... **NCLC 22**

Nightingale, Anne Redmon 1943-
See Redmon, Anne
See also CA 103

Nik.T.O.
See Annensky, Innokenty Fyodorovich

Nin, Anais
1903-1977 ..... **CLC 1, 4, 8, 11, 14, 60;
SSC 10**
See also AITN 2; CA 13-16R; 69-72;
CANR 22; DLB 2, 4; MTCW

Nissenson, Hugh 1933-.......... **CLC 4, 9**
See also CA 17-20R; CANR 27; DLB 28

Niven, Larry .... **CLC 8**
See also Niven, Laurence Van Cott
See also DLB 8

Niven, Laurence Van Cott 1938-
See Niven, Larry
See also CA 21-24R; CAAS 12; CANR 14;
MTCW

Nixon, Agnes Eckhardt 1927-...... **CLC 21**
See also CA 110

Nizan, Paul 1905-1940........... **TCLC 40**
See also DLB 72

Nkosi, Lewis 1936-............... **CLC 45**
See also BLC 3; BW; CA 65-68; CANR 27

Nodier, (Jean) Charles (Emmanuel)
1780-1844 .... **NCLC 19**
See also DLB 119

Nolan, Christopher 1965-......... **CLC 58**
See also CA 111

Norden, Charles
See Durrell, Lawrence (George)

Nordhoff, Charles (Bernard)
1887-1947 .... **TCLC 23**
See also CA 108; DLB 9; SATA 23

Norfolk, Lawrence 1963-.......... **CLC 76**

Norman, Marsha 1947- .... **CLC 28**
See also CA 105; CABS 3; CANR 41;
DLBY 84

Norris, Benjamin Franklin, Jr.
1870-1902 .... **TCLC 24**
See also Norris, Frank
See also CA 110

Norris, Frank
See Norris, Benjamin Franklin, Jr.
See also CDALB 1865-1917; DLB 12, 71

Norris, Leslie 1921- .... **CLC 14**
See also CA 11-12; CANR 14; CAP 1;
DLB 27

North, Andrew
See Norton, Andre

North, Captain George
See Stevenson, Robert Louis (Balfour)

North, Milou
See Erdrich, Louise

Northrup, B. A.
See Hubbard, L(afayette) Ron(ald)

North Staffs
See Hulme, T(homas) E(rnest)

Norton, Alice Mary
See Norton, Andre
See also MAICYA; SATA 1, 43

Norton, Andre 1912- .... **CLC 12**
See also Norton, Alice Mary
See also CA 1-4R; CANR 2, 31; DLB 8, 52;
MTCW

Norway, Nevil Shute 1899-1960
See Shute, Nevil
See also CA 102; 93-96

Norwid, Cyprian Kamil
1821-1883 .... **NCLC 17**

Nosille, Nabrah
See Ellison, Harlan

Nossack, Hans Erich 1901-1978..... **CLC 6**
See also CA 93-96; 85-88; DLB 69

Nosu, Chuji
See Ozu, Yasujiro

Nova, Craig 1945-.............. **CLC 7, 31**
See also CA 45-48; CANR 2

Novak, Joseph
See Kosinski, Jerzy (Nikodem)

Novalis 1772-1801 .... **NCLC 13**
See also DLB 90

Nowlan, Alden (Albert) 1933-1983 .. **CLC 15**
See also CA 9-12R; CANR 5; DLB 53

Noyes, Alfred 1880-1958 .... **TCLC 7**
See also CA 104; DLB 20

Nunn, Kem 19(?)-................ **CLC 34**

Nye, Robert 1939- .... **CLC 13, 42**
See also CA 33-36R; CANR 29; DLB 14;
MTCW; SATA 6

Nyro, Laura 1947- .... **CLC 17**

Oates, Joyce Carol
1938-..... **CLC 1, 2, 3, 6, 9, 11, 15, 19,
33, 52; SSC 6**
See also AITN 1; BEST 89:2; CA 5-8R;
CANR 25; CDALB 1968-1988; DA;
DLB 2, 5, 130; DLBY 81; MTCW; WLC

O'Brien, E. G.
See Clarke, Arthur C(harles)

O'Brien, Edna
1936-... **CLC 3, 5, 8, 13, 36, 65; SSC 10**
See also CA 1-4R; CANR 6, 41;
CDBLB 1960 to Present; DLB 14;
MTCW

O'Brien, Fitz-James 1828-1862... **NCLC 21**
See also DLB 74

O'Brien, Flann........ **CLC 1, 4, 5, 7, 10, 47**
See also O Nuallain, Brian

O'Brien, Richard 1942- .... **CLC 17**
See also CA 124

O'Brien, Tim 1946-......... **CLC 7, 19, 40**
See also CA 85-88; CANR 40; DLBD 9;
DLBY 80

Obstfelder, Sigbjoern 1866-1900... **TCLC 23**
See also CA 123

O'Casey, Sean
1880-1964 .... **CLC 1, 5, 9, 11, 15**
See also CA 89-92; CDBLB 1914-1945;
DLB 10; MTCW

O'Cathasaigh, Sean
See O'Casey, Sean

Ochs, Phil 1940-1976............. **CLC 17**
See also CA 65-68

O'Connor, Edwin (Greene)
1918-1968 .... **CLC 14**
See also CA 93-96; 25-28R

O'Connor, (Mary) Flannery
1925-1964 ... **CLC 1, 2, 3, 6, 10, 13, 15,
21, 66; SSC 1**
See also AAYA 7; CA 1-4R; CANR 3, 41;
CDALB 1941-1968; DA; DLB 2;
DLBY 80; MTCW; WLC

O'Connor, Frank.......... **CLC 23; SSC 5**
See also O'Donovan, Michael John

O'Dell, Scott 1898-1989.......... **CLC 30**
See also AAYA 3; CA 61-64; 129;
CANR 12, 30; CLR 1, 16; DLB 52;
MAICYA; SATA 12, 60

Odets, Clifford 1906-1963 .... **CLC 2, 28**
See also CA 85-88; DLB 7, 26; MTCW

O'Doherty, Brian 1934-.......... **CLC 76**
See also CA 105

O'Donnell, K. M.
See Malzberg, Barry N(athaniel)

O'Donnell, Lawrence
See Kuttner, Henry

O'Donovan, Michael John
1903-1966 .... **CLC 14**
See also O'Connor, Frank
See also CA 93-96

Oe, Kenzaburo 1935-.......... **CLC 10, 36**
See also CA 97-100; CANR 36; MTCW

O'Faolain, Julia 1932-....... **CLC 6, 19, 47**
See also CA 81-84; CAAS 2; CANR 12;
DLB 14; MTCW

O'Faolain, Sean
1900-1991 .... **CLC 1, 7, 14, 32, 70**
See also CA 61-64; 134; CANR 12;
DLB 15; MTCW

O'Flaherty, Liam
1896-1984 .... **CLC 5, 34; SSC 6**
See also CA 101; 113; CANR 35; DLB 36;
DLBY 84; MTCW

Ogilvy, Gavin
See Barrie, J(ames) M(atthew)

O'Grady, Standish James
1846-1928 .... **TCLC 5**
See also CA 104

O'Grady, Timothy 1951-.......... **CLC 59**
See also CA 138

O'Hara, Frank
1926-1966 .... **CLC 2, 5, 13, 77**
See also CA 9-12R; 25-28R; CANR 33;
DLB 5, 16; MTCW

O'Hara, John (Henry)
1905-1970 .... **CLC 1, 2, 3, 6, 11, 42**
See also CA 5-8R; 25-28R; CANR 31;
CDALB 1929-1941; DLB 9, 86; DLBD 2;
MTCW

Phillips, David Graham
1867-1911 . . . . **TCLC 44**
See also CA 108; DLB 9, 12

Phillips, Jack
See Sandburg, Carl (August)

Phillips, Jayne Anne 1952- . . . . . **CLC 15, 33**
See also CA 101; CANR 24; DLBY 80;
MTCW

Phillips, Richard
See Dick, Philip K(indred)

Phillips, Robert (Schaeffer) 1938- . . . **CLC 28**
See also CA 17-20R; CAAS 13; CANR 8;
DLB 105

Phillips, Ward
See Lovecraft, H(oward) P(hillips)

Piccolo, Lucio 1901-1969 . . . . **CLC 13**
See also CA 97-100; DLB 114

Pickthall, Marjorie L(owry) C(hristie)
1883-1922 . . . . **TCLC 21**
See also CA 107; DLB 92

Pico della Mirandola, Giovanni
1463-1494 . . . . **LC 15**

Piercy, Marge
1936- . . . . **CLC 3, 6, 14, 18, 27, 62**
See also CA 21-24R; CAAS 1; CANR 13;
DLB 120; MTCW

Piers, Robert
See Anthony, Piers

Pieyre de Mandiargues, Andre 1909-1991
See Mandiargues, Andre Pieyre de
See also CA 103; 136; CANR 22

Pilnyak, Boris . . . . **TCLC 23**
See also Vogau, Boris Andreyevich

Pincherle, Alberto 1907-1990 . . . **CLC 11, 18**
See also Moravia, Alberto
See also CA 25-28R; 132; CANR 33;
MTCW

Pinckney, Darryl 1953- . . . . **CLC 76**

Pineda, Cecile 1942- . . . . **CLC 39**
See also CA 118

Pinero, Arthur Wing 1855-1934 . . . **TCLC 32**
See also CA 110; DLB 10

Pinero, Miguel (Antonio Gomez)
1946-1988 . . . . **CLC 4, 55**
See also CA 61-64; 125; CANR 29; HW

Pinget, Robert 1919- . . . . **CLC 7, 13, 37**
See also CA 85-88; DLB 83

Pink Floyd . . . . **CLC 35**
See also Barrett, (Roger) Syd; Gilmour,
David; Mason, Nick; Waters, Roger;
Wright, Rick

Pinkney, Edward 1802-1828 . . . . . **NCLC 31**

Pinkwater, Daniel Manus 1941- . . . . **CLC 35**
See also Pinkwater, Manus
See also AAYA 1; CA 29-32R; CANR 12,
38; CLR 4; MAICYA; SAAS 3; SATA 46

Pinkwater, Manus
See Pinkwater, Daniel Manus
See also SATA 8

Pinsky, Robert 1940- . . . . **CLC 9, 19, 38**
See also CA 29-32R; CAAS 4; DLBY 82

Pinta, Harold
See Pinter, Harold

Pinter, Harold
1930- . . **CLC 1, 3, 6, 9, 11, 15, 27, 58, 73**
See also CA 5-8R; CANR 33; CDBLB 1960
to Present; DA; DLB 13; MTCW; WLC

Pirandello, Luigi 1867-1936 . . . . . **TCLC 4, 29**
See also CA 104; DA; WLC

Pirsig, Robert M(aynard)
1928- . . . . **CLC 4, 6, 73**
See also CA 53-56; MTCW; SATA 39

Pisarev, Dmitry Ivanovich
1840-1868 . . . . **NCLC 25**

Pix, Mary (Griffith) 1666-1709 . . . . **LC 8**
See also DLB 80

Pixerecourt, Guilbert de
1773-1844 . . . . **NCLC 39**

Plaidy, Jean
See Hibbert, Eleanor Alice Burford

Plant, Robert 1948- . . . . **CLC 12**

Plante, David (Robert)
1940- . . . . **CLC 7, 23, 38**
See also CA 37-40R; CANR 12, 36;
DLBY 83; MTCW

Plath, Sylvia
1932-1963 . . . . **CLC 1, 2, 3, 5, 9, 11, 14,
17, 50, 51, 62; PC 1**
See also CA 19-20; CANR 34; CAP 2;
CDALB 1941-1968; DA; DLB 5, 6;
MTCW; WLC

Plato 428(?)B.C.-348(?)B.C. . . . . **CMLC 8**
See also DA

Platonov, Andrei . . . . **TCLC 14**
See also Klimentov, Andrei Platonovich

Platt, Kin 1911- . . . . **CLC 26**
See also CA 17-20R; CANR 11; SATA 21

Plick et Plock
See Simenon, Georges (Jacques Christian)

Plimpton, George (Ames) 1927- . . . . . **CLC 36**
See also AITN 1; CA 21-24R; CANR 32;
MTCW; SATA 10

Plomer, William Charles Franklin
1903-1973 . . . . **CLC 4, 8**
See also CA 21-22; CANR 34; CAP 2;
DLB 20; MTCW; SATA 24

Plowman, Piers
See Kavanagh, Patrick (Joseph)

Plum, J.
See Wodehouse, P(elham) G(renville)

Plumly, Stanley (Ross) 1939- . . . . . . **CLC 33**
See also CA 108; 110; DLB 5

Poe, Edgar Allan
1809-1849 . . . **NCLC 1, 16; PC 1; SSC 1**
See also CDALB 1640-1865; DA; DLB 3,
59, 73, 74; SATA 23; WLC

Poet of Titchfield Street, The
See Pound, Ezra (Weston Loomis)

Pohl, Frederik 1919- . . . . **CLC 18**
See also CA 61-64; CAAS 1; CANR 11, 37;
DLB 8; MTCW; SATA 24

Poirier, Louis 1910-
See Gracq, Julien
See also CA 122; 126

Poitier, Sidney 1927- . . . . **CLC 26**
See also BW; CA 117

Polanski, Roman 1933- . . . . **CLC 16**
See also CA 77-80

Poliakoff, Stephen 1952- . . . . **CLC 38**
See also CA 106; DLB 13

Police, The . . . . **CLC 26**
See also Copeland, Stewart (Armstrong);
Summers, Andrew James; Sumner,
Gordon Matthew

Pollitt, Katha 1949- . . . . **CLC 28**
See also CA 120; 122; MTCW

Pollock, Sharon 1936- . . . . **CLC 50**
See also DLB 60

Pomerance, Bernard 1940- . . . . **CLC 13**
See also CA 101

Ponge, Francis (Jean Gaston Alfred)
1899-1988 . . . . **CLC 6, 18**
See also CA 85-88; 126; CANR 40

Pontoppidan, Henrik 1857-1943 . . . **TCLC 29**

Poole, Josephine . . . . **CLC 17**
See also Helyar, Jane Penelope Josephine
See also SAAS 2; SATA 5

Popa, Vasko 1922- . . . . **CLC 19**
See also CA 112

Pope, Alexander 1688-1744 . . . . **LC 3**
See also CDBLB 1660-1789; DA; DLB 95,
101; WLC

Porter, Connie 1960- . . . . **CLC 70**

Porter, Gene(va Grace) Stratton
1863(?)-1924 . . . . **TCLC 21**
See also CA 112

Porter, Katherine Anne
1890-1980 . . . . . **CLC 1, 3, 7, 10, 13, 15,
27; SSC 4**
See also AITN 2; CA 1-4R; 101; CANR 1;
DA; DLB 4, 9, 102; DLBY 80; MTCW;
SATA 23, 39

Porter, Peter (Neville Frederick)
1929- . . . . **CLC 5, 13, 33**
See also CA 85-88; DLB 40

Porter, William Sydney 1862-1910
See Henry, O.
See also CA 104; 131; CDALB 1865-1917;
DA; DLB 12, 78, 79; MTCW; YABC 2

Portillo (y Pacheco), Jose Lopez
See Lopez Portillo (y Pacheco), Jose

Post, Melville Davisson
1869-1930 . . . . **TCLC 39**
See also CA 110

Potok, Chaim 1929- . . . . **CLC 2, 7, 14, 26**
See also AITN 1, 2; CA 17-20R; CANR 19,
35; DLB 28; MTCW; SATA 33

Potter, Beatrice
See Webb, (Martha) Beatrice (Potter)
See also MAICYA

Potter, Dennis (Christopher George)
1935- . . . . **CLC 58**
See also CA 107; CANR 33; MTCW

Pound, Ezra (Weston Loomis)
1885-1972 . . . . . **CLC 1, 2, 3, 4, 5, 7, 10,
13, 18, 34, 48, 50; PC 4**
See also CA 5-8R; 37-40R; CANR 40;
CDALB 1917-1929; DA; DLB 4, 45, 63;
MTCW; WLC

Povod, Reinaldo 1959- . . . . **CLC 44**
See also CA 136

Powell, Anthony (Dymoke)
1905- . . . . **CLC 1, 3, 7, 9, 10, 31**
See also CA 1-4R; CANR 1, 32;
CDBLB 1945-1960; DLB 15; MTCW

Powell, Dawn 1897-1965 . . . . **CLC 66**
See also CA 5-8R

Powell, Padgett 1952-. . . . . **CLC 34**
See also CA 126

Powers, J(ames) F(arl)
1917- . . . . **CLC 1, 4, 8, 57; SSC 4**
See also CA 1-4R; CANR 2; DLB 130;
MTCW

Powers, John J(ames) 1945-
See Powers, John R.
See also CA 69-72

Powers, John R. . . . . **CLC 66**
See also Powers, John J(ames)

Pownall, David 1938- . . . . **CLC 10**
See also CA 89-92; DLB 14

Powys, John Cowper
1872-1963 . . . . **CLC 7, 9, 15, 46**
See also CA 85-88; DLB 15; MTCW

Powys, T(heodore) F(rancis)
1875-1953 . . . . **TCLC 9**
See also CA 106; DLB 36

Prager, Emily 1952- . . . . **CLC 56**

Pratt, Edwin John 1883-1964 . . . . . . **CLC 19**
See also CA 93-96; DLB 92

Premchand . . . . **TCLC 21**
See also Srivastava, Dhanpat Rai

Preussler, Otfried 1923-. . . . . **CLC 17**
See also CA 77-80; SATA 24

Prevert, Jacques (Henri Marie)
1900-1977 . . . . **CLC 15**
See also CA 77-80; 69-72; CANR 29;
MTCW; SATA 30

Prevost, Abbe (Antoine Francois)
1697-1763 . . . . **LC 1**

Price, (Edward) Reynolds
1933- . . . . **CLC 3, 6, 13, 43, 50, 63**
See also CA 1-4R; CANR 1, 37; DLB 2

Price, Richard 1949- . . . . **CLC 6, 12**
See also CA 49-52; CANR 3; DLBY 81

Prichard, Katharine Susannah
1883-1969 . . . . **CLC 46**
See also CA 11-12; CANR 33; CAP 1;
MTCW; SATA 66

Priestley, J(ohn) B(oynton)
1894-1984 . . . . **CLC 2, 5, 9, 34**
See also CA 9-12R; 113; CANR 33;
CDBLB 1914-1945; DLB 10, 34, 77, 100;
DLBY 84; MTCW

Prince 1958(?)- . . . . **CLC 35**

Prince, F(rank) T(empleton) 1912- . . **CLC 22**
See also CA 101; DLB 20

Prince Kropotkin
See Kropotkin, Peter (Aleksieevich)

Prior, Matthew 1664-1721. . . . . **LC 4**
See also DLB 95

Pritchard, William H(arrison)
1932- . . . . **CLC 34**
See also CA 65-68; CANR 23; DLB 111

Pritchett, V(ictor) S(awdon)
1900- . . . . **CLC 5, 13, 15, 41**
See also CA 61-64; CANR 31; DLB 15;
MTCW

Private 19022
See Manning, Frederic

Probst, Mark 1925- . . . . **CLC 59**
See also CA 130

Prokosch, Frederic 1908-1989. . . . **CLC 4, 48**
See also CA 73-76; 128; DLB 48

Prophet, The
See Dreiser, Theodore (Herman Albert)

Prose, Francine 1947-. . . . . **CLC 45**
See also CA 109; 112

Proudhon
See Cunha, Euclides (Rodrigues Pimenta) da

**Proust,
(Valentin-Louis-George-Eugene-)Marcel**
1871-1922 . . . . **TCLC 7, 13, 33**
See also CA 104; 120; DA; DLB 65;
MTCW; WLC

Prowler, Harley
See Masters, Edgar Lee

Prus, Boleslaw. . . . . **TCLC 48**
See also Glowacki, Aleksander

Pryor, Richard (Franklin Lenox Thomas)
1940- . . . . **CLC 26**
See also CA 122

Przybyszewski, Stanislaw
1868-1927 . . . . **TCLC 36**
See also DLB 66

Pteleon
See Grieve, C(hristopher) M(urray)

Puckett, Lute
See Masters, Edgar Lee

Puig, Manuel
1932-1990 . . . . **CLC 3, 5, 10, 28, 65**
See also CA 45-48; CANR 2, 32; DLB 113;
HW; MTCW

Purdy, A(lfred) W(ellington)
1918- . . . . **CLC 3, 6, 14, 50**
See also Purdy, Al
See also CA 81-84

Purdy, Al
See Purdy, A(lfred) W(ellington)
See also CAAS 17; DLB 88

Purdy, James (Amos)
1923- . . . . **CLC 2, 4, 10, 28, 52**
See also CA 33-36R; CAAS 1; CANR 19;
DLB 2; MTCW

Pure, Simon
See Swinnerton, Frank Arthur

Pushkin, Alexander (Sergeyevich)
1799-1837 . . . . **NCLC 3, 27**
See also DA; SATA 61; WLC

P'u Sung-ling 1640-1715 . . . . **LC 3**

Putnam, Arthur Lee
See Alger, Horatio, Jr.

Puzo, Mario 1920- . . . . **CLC 1, 2, 6, 36**
See also CA 65-68; CANR 4; DLB 6;
MTCW

Pym, Barbara (Mary Crampton)
1913-1980 . . . . **CLC 13, 19, 37**
See also CA 13-14; 97-100; CANR 13, 34;
CAP 1; DLB 14; DLBY 87; MTCW

Pynchon, Thomas (Ruggles, Jr.)
1937- . . **CLC 2, 3, 6, 9, 11, 18, 33, 62, 72**
See also BEST 90:2; CA 17-20R; CANR 22;
DA; DLB 2; MTCW; WLC

Qian Zhongshu
See Ch'ien Chung-shu

Qroll
See Dagerman, Stig (Halvard)

Quarrington, Paul (Lewis) 1953-. . . . **CLC 65**
See also CA 129

Quasimodo, Salvatore 1901-1968 . . . **CLC 10**
See also CA 13-16; 25-28R; CAP 1;
DLB 114; MTCW

Queen, Ellery. . . . . **CLC 3, 11**
See also Dannay, Frederic; Davidson,
Avram; Lee, Manfred B(ennington);
Sturgeon, Theodore (Hamilton); Vance,
John Holbrook

Queen, Ellery, Jr.
See Dannay, Frederic; Lee, Manfred
B(ennington)

Queneau, Raymond
1903-1976 . . . . **CLC 2, 5, 10, 42**
See also CA 77-80; 69-72; CANR 32;
DLB 72; MTCW

Quin, Ann (Marie) 1936-1973 . . . . **CLC 6**
See also CA 9-12R; 45-48; DLB 14

Quinn, Martin
See Smith, Martin Cruz

Quinn, Simon
See Smith, Martin Cruz

Quiroga, Horacio (Sylvestre)
1878-1937 . . . . **TCLC 20**
See also CA 117; 131; HW; MTCW

Quoirez, Francoise 1935-. . . . . **CLC 9**
See also Sagan, Francoise
See also CA 49-52; CANR 6, 39; MTCW

Raabe, Wilhelm 1831-1910 . . . . **TCLC 45**
See also DLB 129

Rabe, David (William) 1940-. . . **CLC 4, 8, 33**
See also CA 85-88; CABS 3; DLB 7

Rabelais, Francois 1483-1553 . . . . **LC 5**
See also DA; WLC

Rabinovitch, Sholem 1859-1916
See Aleichem, Sholom
See also CA 104

Radcliffe, Ann (Ward) 1764-1823 . . **NCLC 6**
See also DLB 39

Radiguet, Raymond 1903-1923 . . . . **TCLC 29**
See also DLB 65

Radnoti, Miklos 1909-1944 . . . . **TCLC 16**
See also CA 118

Rado, James 1939-. . . . . **CLC 17**
See also CA 105

Radvanyi, Netty 1900-1983
See Seghers, Anna
See also CA 85-88; 110

Raeburn, John (Hay) 1941-. . . . . **CLC 34**
See also CA 57-60

Ragni, Gerome 1942-1991 . . . . **CLC 17**
See also CA 105; 134

Rahv, Philip. . . . . **CLC 24**
See also Greenberg, Ivan

Raine, Craig 1944-............. CLC 32
  See also CA 108; CANR 29; DLB 40

Raine, Kathleen (Jessie) 1908- ... CLC 7, 45
  See also CA 85-88; DLB 20; MTCW

Rainis, Janis 1865-1929......... TCLC 29

Rakosi, Carl..................... CLC 47
  See also Rawley, Callman
  See also CAAS 5

Raleigh, Richard
  See Lovecraft, H(oward) P(hillips)

Rallentando, H. P.
  See Sayers, Dorothy L(eigh)

Ramal, Walter
  See de la Mare, Walter (John)

Ramon, Juan
  See Jimenez (Mantecon), Juan Ramon

Ramos, Graciliano 1892-1953 ..... TCLC 32

Rampersad, Arnold 1941-......... CLC 44
  See also CA 127; 133; DLB 111

Rampling, Anne
  See Rice, Anne

Ramuz, Charles-Ferdinand
  1878-1947 .... TCLC 33

Rand, Ayn 1905-1982....... CLC 3, 30, 44
  See also AAYA 10; CA 13-16R; 105;
  CANR 27; DA; MTCW; WLC

Randall, Dudley (Felker) 1914-...... CLC 1
  See also BLC 3; BW; CA 25-28R;
  CANR 23; DLB 41

Randall, Robert
  See Silverberg, Robert

Ranger, Ken
  See Creasey, John

Ransom, John Crowe
  1888-1974 .... CLC 2, 4, 5, 11, 24
  See also CA 5-8R; 49-52; CANR 6, 34;
  DLB 45, 63; MTCW

Rao, Raja 1909- .... CLC 25, 56
  See also CA 73-76; MTCW

Raphael, Frederic (Michael)
  1931- .... CLC 2, 14
  See also CA 1-4R; CANR 1; DLB 14

Ratcliffe, James P.
  See Mencken, H(enry) L(ouis)

Rathbone, Julian 1935- .... CLC 41
  See also CA 101; CANR 34

Rattigan, Terence (Mervyn)
  1911-1977 .... CLC 7
  See also CA 85-88; 73-76;
  CDBLB 1945-1960; DLB 13; MTCW

Ratushinskaya, Irina 1954-........ CLC 54
  See also CA 129

Raven, Simon (Arthur Noel)
  1927- .... CLC 14
  See also CA 81-84

Rawley, Callman 1903-
  See Rakosi, Carl
  See also CA 21-24R; CANR 12, 32

Rawlings, Marjorie Kinnan
  1896-1953 .... TCLC 4
  See also CA 104; 137; DLB 9, 22, 102;
  MAICYA; YABC 1

Ray, Satyajit 1921-1992........ CLC 16, 76
  See also CA 114; 137

Read, Herbert Edward 1893-1968.... CLC 4
  See also CA 85-88; 25-28R; DLB 20

Read, Piers Paul 1941- ...... CLC 4, 10, 25
  See also CA 21-24R; CANR 38; DLB 14;
  SATA 21

Reade, Charles 1814-1884 .... NCLC 2
  See also DLB 21

Reade, Hamish
  See Gray, Simon (James Holliday)

Reading, Peter 1946- .... CLC 47
  See also CA 103; DLB 40

Reaney, James 1926- .... CLC 13
  See also CA 41-44R; CAAS 15; DLB 68;
  SATA 43

Rebreanu, Liviu 1885-1944 ...... TCLC 28

Rechy, John (Francisco)
  1934-..............CLC 1, 7, 14, 18
  See also CA 5-8R; CAAS 4; CANR 6, 32;
  DLB 122; DLBY 82; HW

Redcam, Tom 1870-1933 .... TCLC 25

Reddin, Keith.................... CLC 67

Redgrove, Peter (William)
  1932-.................... CLC 6, 41
  See also CA 1-4R; CANR 3, 39; DLB 40

Redmon, Anne.................... CLC 22
  See also Nightingale, Anne Redmon
  See also DLBY 86

Reed, Eliot
  See Ambler, Eric

Reed, Ishmael
  1938- .... CLC 2, 3, 5, 6, 13, 32, 60
  See also BLC 3; BW; CA 21-24R;
  CANR 25; DLB 2, 5, 33; DLBD 8;
  MTCW

Reed, John (Silas) 1887-1920 ...... TCLC 9
  See also CA 106

Reed, Lou....................... CLC 21
  See also Firbank, Louis

Reeve, Clara 1729-1807 .... NCLC 19
  See also DLB 39

Reid, Christopher (John) 1949-..... CLC 33
  See also CA 140; DLB 40

Reid, Desmond
  See Moorcock, Michael (John)

Reid Banks, Lynne 1929-
  See Banks, Lynne Reid
  See also CA 1-4R; CANR 6, 22, 38;
  CLR 24; MAICYA; SATA 22

Reilly, William K.
  See Creasey, John

Reiner, Max
  See Caldwell, (Janet Miriam) Taylor
  (Holland)

Reis, Ricardo
  See Pessoa, Fernando (Antonio Nogueira)

Remarque, Erich Maria
  1898-1970 .... CLC 21
  See also CA 77-80; 29-32R; DA; DLB 56;
  MTCW

Remizov, A.
  See Remizov, Aleksei (Mikhailovich)

Remizov, A. M.
  See Remizov, Aleksei (Mikhailovich)

Remizov, Aleksei (Mikhailovich)
  1877-1957............... TCLC 27
  See also CA 125; 133

Renan, Joseph Ernest
  1823-1892 .... NCLC 26

Renard, Jules 1864-1910 .... TCLC 17
  See also CA 117

Renault, Mary.............. CLC 3, 11, 17
  See also Challans, Mary
  See also DLBY 83

Rendell, Ruth (Barbara) 1930- .. CLC 28, 48
  See also Vine, Barbara
  See also CA 109; CANR 32; DLB 87;
  MTCW

Renoir, Jean 1894-1979 .... CLC 20
  See also CA 129; 85-88

Resnais, Alain 1922-............. CLC 16

Reverdy, Pierre 1889-1960 .... CLC 53
  See also CA 97-100; 89-92

Rexroth, Kenneth
  1905-1982 ...... CLC 1, 2, 6, 11, 22, 49
  See also CA 5-8R; 107; CANR 14, 34;
  CDALB 1941-1968; DLB 16, 48;
  DLBY 82; MTCW

Reyes, Alfonso 1889-1959 .... TCLC 33
  See also CA 131; HW

Reyes y Basoalto, Ricardo Eliecer Neftali
  See Neruda, Pablo

Reymont, Wladyslaw (Stanislaw)
  1868(?)-1925 .... TCLC 5
  See also CA 104

Reynolds, Jonathan 1942- .... CLC 6, 38
  See also CA 65-68; CANR 28

Reynolds, Joshua 1723-1792........ LC 15
  See also DLB 104

Reynolds, Michael Shane 1937- .... CLC 44
  See also CA 65-68; CANR 9

Reznikoff, Charles 1894-1976 .... CLC 9
  See also CA 33-36; 61-64; CAP 2; DLB 28,
  45

Rezzori (d'Arezzo), Gregor von
  1914- .... CLC 25
  See also CA 122; 136

Rhine, Richard
  See Silverstein, Alvin

R'hoone
  See Balzac, Honore de

Rhys, Jean
  1890(?)-1979 .... CLC 2, 4, 6, 14, 19, 51
  See also CA 25-28R; 85-88; CANR 35;
  CDBLB 1945-1960; DLB 36, 117; MTCW

Ribeiro, Darcy 1922- .... CLC 34
  See also CA 33-36R

Ribeiro, Joao Ubaldo (Osorio Pimentel)
  1941- .... CLC 10, 67
  See also CA 81-84

Ribman, Ronald (Burt) 1932- .... CLC 7
  See also CA 21-24R

Ricci, Nino 1959-................. CLC 70
  See also CA 137

Rice, Anne 1941- .... CLC 41
  See also AAYA 9; BEST 89:2; CA 65-68;
  CANR 12, 36

Rice, Elmer (Leopold)
1892-1967 . . . . CLC 7, 49
See also CA 21-22; 25-28R; CAP 2; DLB 4,
7; MTCW

Rice, Tim 1944- . . . . CLC 21
See also CA 103

Rich, Adrienne (Cecile)
1929- . . . CLC 3, 6, 7, 11, 18, 36, 73, 76;
PC 5
See also CA 9-12R; CANR 20; DLB 5, 67;
MTCW

Rich, Barbara
See Graves, Robert (von Ranke)

Rich, Robert
See Trumbo, Dalton

Richards, David Adams 1950- . . . . . . CLC 59
See also CA 93-96; DLB 53

Richards, I(vor) A(rmstrong)
1893-1979 . . . . CLC 14, 24
See also CA 41-44R; 89-92; CANR 34;
DLB 27

Richardson, Anne
See Roiphe, Anne Richardson

Richardson, Dorothy Miller
1873-1957 . . . . TCLC 3
See also CA 104; DLB 36

Richardson, Ethel Florence (Lindesay)
1870-1946
See Richardson, Henry Handel
See also CA 105

Richardson, Henry Handel . . . . TCLC 4
See also Richardson, Ethel Florence
(Lindesay)

Richardson, Samuel 1689-1761 . . . . LC 1
See also CDBLB 1660-1789; DA; DLB 39;
WLC

Richler, Mordecai
1931- . . . . CLC 3, 5, 9, 13, 18, 46, 70
See also AITN 1; CA 65-68; CANR 31;
CLR 17; DLB 53; MAICYA; MTCW;
SATA 27, 44

Richter, Conrad (Michael)
1890-1968 . . . . CLC 30
See also CA 5-8R; 25-28R; CANR 23;
DLB 9; MTCW; SATA 3

Riddell, J. H. 1832-1906 . . . . TCLC 40

Riding, Laura . . . . CLC 3, 7
See also Jackson, Laura (Riding)

Riefenstahl, Berta Helene Amalia 1902-
See Riefenstahl, Leni
See also CA 108

Riefenstahl, Leni . . . . CLC 16
See also Riefenstahl, Berta Helene Amalia

Riffe, Ernest
See Bergman, (Ernst) Ingmar

Riley, Tex
See Creasey, John

Rilke, Rainer Maria
1875-1926 . . . . TCLC 1, 6, 19; PC 2
See also CA 104; 132; DLB 81; MTCW

Rimbaud, (Jean Nicolas) Arthur
1854-1891 . . . . NCLC 4, 35; PC 3
See also DA; WLC

Ringmaster, The
See Mencken, H(enry) L(ouis)

Ringwood, Gwen(dolyn Margaret) Pharis
1910-1984 . . . . CLC 48
See also CA 112; DLB 88

Rio, Michel 19(?)- . . . . CLC 43

Ritsos, Giannes
See Ritsos, Yannis

Ritsos, Yannis 1909-1990 . . . . . CLC 6, 13, 31
See also CA 77-80; 133; CANR 39; MTCW

Ritter, Erika 1948(?)- . . . . CLC 52

Rivera, Jose Eustasio 1889-1928 . . . TCLC 35
See also HW

Rivers, Conrad Kent 1933-1968 . . . . . . CLC 1
See also BW; CA 85-88; DLB 41

Rivers, Elfrida
See Bradley, Marion Zimmer

Riverside, John
See Heinlein, Robert A(nson)

Rizal, Jose 1861-1896 . . . . NCLC 27

Roa Bastos, Augusto (Antonio)
1917- . . . . CLC 45
See also CA 131; DLB 113; HW

Robbe-Grillet, Alain
1922- . . . . . . CLC 1, 2, 4, 6, 8, 10, 14, 43
See also CA 9-12R; CANR 33; DLB 83;
MTCW

Robbins, Harold 1916- . . . . CLC 5
See also CA 73-76; CANR 26; MTCW

Robbins, Thomas Eugene 1936-
See Robbins, Tom
See also CA 81-84; CANR 29; MTCW

Robbins, Tom . . . . CLC 9, 32, 64
See also Robbins, Thomas Eugene
See also BEST 90:3; DLBY 80

Robbins, Trina 1938- . . . . CLC 21
See also CA 128

Roberts, Charles G(eorge) D(ouglas)
1860-1943 . . . . TCLC 8
See also CA 105; DLB 92; SATA 29

Roberts, Kate 1891-1985 . . . . CLC 15
See also CA 107; 116

Roberts, Keith (John Kingston)
1935- . . . . CLC 14
See also CA 25-28R

Roberts, Kenneth (Lewis)
1885-1957 . . . . TCLC 23
See also CA 109; DLB 9

Roberts, Michele (B.) 1949- . . . . CLC 48
See also CA 115

Robertson, Ellis
See Ellison, Harlan; Silverberg, Robert

Robertson, Thomas William
1829-1871 . . . . NCLC 35

Robinson, Edwin Arlington
1869-1935 . . . . TCLC 5; PC 1
See also CA 104; 133; CDALB 1865-1917;
DA; DLB 54; MTCW

Robinson, Henry Crabb
1775-1867 . . . . NCLC 15
See also DLB 107

Robinson, Jill 1936- . . . . CLC 10
See also CA 102

Robinson, Kim Stanley 1952- . . . . . . CLC 34
See also CA 126

Robinson, Lloyd
See Silverberg, Robert

Robinson, Marilynne 1944- . . . . CLC 25
See also CA 116

Robinson, Smokey . . . . CLC 21
See also Robinson, William, Jr.

Robinson, William, Jr. 1940-
See Robinson, Smokey
See also CA 116

Robison, Mary 1949- . . . . CLC 42
See also CA 113; 116; DLB 130

Roddenberry, Eugene Wesley 1921-1991
See Roddenberry, Gene
See also CA 110; 135; CANR 37; SATA 45

Roddenberry, Gene . . . . CLC 17
See also Roddenberry, Eugene Wesley
See also AAYA 5; SATA-Obit 69

Rodgers, Mary 1931- . . . . CLC 12
See also CA 49-52; CANR 8; CLR 20;
MAICYA; SATA 8

Rodgers, W(illiam) R(obert)
1909-1969 . . . . CLC 7
See also CA 85-88; DLB 20

Rodman, Eric
See Silverberg, Robert

Rodman, Howard 1920(?)-1985 . . . . . CLC 65
See also CA 118

Rodman, Maia
See Wojciechowska, Maia (Teresa)

Rodriguez, Claudio 1934- . . . . CLC 10

Roelvaag, O(le) E(dvart)
1876-1931 . . . . TCLC 17
See also CA 117; DLB 9

Roethke, Theodore (Huebner)
1908-1963 . . . . . . CLC 1, 3, 8, 11, 19, 46
See also CA 81-84; CABS 2;
CDALB 1941-1968; DLB 5; MTCW

Rogers, Thomas Hunton 1927- . . . . . CLC 57
See also CA 89-92

Rogers, Will(iam Penn Adair)
1879-1935 . . . . TCLC 8
See also CA 105; DLB 11

Rogin, Gilbert 1929- . . . . CLC 18
See also CA 65-68; CANR 15

Rohan, Koda . . . . TCLC 22
See also Koda Shigeyuki

Rohmer, Eric . . . . CLC 16
See also Scherer, Jean-Marie Maurice

Rohmer, Sax . . . . TCLC 28
See also Ward, Arthur Henry Sarsfield
See also DLB 70

Roiphe, Anne Richardson 1935- . . . CLC 3, 9
See also CA 89-92; DLBY 80

Rolfe, Frederick (William Serafino Austin
Lewis Mary) 1860-1913 . . . . . . TCLC 12
See also CA 107; DLB 34

Rolland, Romain 1866-1944 . . . . . . TCLC 23
See also CA 118; DLB 65

Rolvaag, O(le) E(dvart)
See Roelvaag, O(le) E(dvart)

Romain Arnaud, Saint
See Aragon, Louis

Romains, Jules 1885-1972 . . . . **CLC 7**
  See also CA 85-88; CANR 34; DLB 65;
  MTCW

Romero, Jose Ruben 1890-1952 . . . **TCLC 14**
  See also CA 114; 131; HW

Ronsard, Pierre de 1524-1585 . . . . **LC 6**

Rooke, Leon 1934- . . . . **CLC 25, 34**
  See also CA 25-28R; CANR 23

Roper, William 1498-1578 . . . . **LC 10**

Roquelaure, A. N.
  See Rice, Anne

Rosa, Joao Guimaraes 1908-1967 . . . **CLC 23**
  See also CA 89-92; DLB 113

Rosen, Richard (Dean) 1949- . . . . **CLC 39**
  See also CA 77-80

Rosenberg, Isaac 1890-1918 . . . . **TCLC 12**
  See also CA 107; DLB 20

Rosenblatt, Joe . . . . **CLC 15**
  See also Rosenblatt, Joseph

Rosenblatt, Joseph 1933-
  See Rosenblatt, Joe
  See also CA 89-92

Rosenfeld, Samuel 1896-1963
  See Tzara, Tristan
  See also CA 89-92

Rosenthal, M(acha) L(ouis) 1917- . . . **CLC 28**
  See also CA 1-4R; CAAS 6; CANR 4;
  DLB 5; SATA 59

Ross, Barnaby
  See Dannay, Frederic

Ross, Bernard L.
  See Follett, Ken(neth Martin)

Ross, J. H.
  See Lawrence, T(homas) E(dward)

Ross, (James) Sinclair 1908- . . . . **CLC 13**
  See also CA 73-76; DLB 88

Rossetti, Christina (Georgina)
  1830-1894 . . . . **NCLC 2**
  See also DA; DLB 35; MAICYA;
  SATA 20; WLC

Rossetti, Dante Gabriel
  1828-1882 . . . . **NCLC 4**
  See also CDBLB 1832-1890; DA; DLB 35;
  WLC

Rossner, Judith (Perelman)
  1935- . . . . **CLC 6, 9, 29**
  See also AITN 2; BEST 90:3; CA 17-20R;
  CANR 18; DLB 6; MTCW

Rostand, Edmond (Eugene Alexis)
  1868-1918 . . . . **TCLC 6, 37**
  See also CA 104; 126; DA; MTCW

Roth, Henry 1906- . . . . **CLC 2, 6, 11**
  See also CA 11-12; CANR 38; CAP 1;
  DLB 28; MTCW

Roth, Joseph 1894-1939 . . . . **TCLC 33**
  See also DLB 85

Roth, Philip (Milton)
  1933- . . . . . . **CLC 1, 2, 3, 4, 6, 9, 15, 22,
                          31, 47, 66**
  See also BEST 90:3; CA 1-4R; CANR 1, 22,
  36; CDALB 1968-1988; DA; DLB 2, 28;
  DLBY 82; MTCW; WLC

Rothenberg, Jerome 1931- . . . . **CLC 6, 57**
  See also CA 45-48; CANR 1; DLB 5

Roumain, Jacques (Jean Baptiste)
  1907-1944 . . . . **TCLC 19**
  See also BLC 3; BW; CA 117; 125

Rourke, Constance (Mayfield)
  1885-1941 . . . . **TCLC 12**
  See also CA 107; YABC 1

Rousseau, Jean-Baptiste 1671-1741 . . . **LC 9**

Rousseau, Jean-Jacques 1712-1778 . . . **LC 14**
  See also DA; WLC

Roussel, Raymond 1877-1933 . . . . . **TCLC 20**
  See also CA 117

Rovit, Earl (Herbert) 1927- . . . . **CLC 7**
  See also CA 5-8R; CANR 12

Rowe, Nicholas 1674-1718 . . . . **LC 8**
  See also DLB 84

Rowley, Ames Dorrance
  See Lovecraft, H(oward) P(hillips)

Rowson, Susanna Haswell
  1762(?)-1824 . . . . **NCLC 5**
  See also DLB 37

Roy, Gabrielle 1909-1983 . . . . **CLC 10, 14**
  See also CA 53-56; 110; CANR 5; DLB 68;
  MTCW

Rozewicz, Tadeusz 1921- . . . . **CLC 9, 23**
  See also CA 108; CANR 36; MTCW

Ruark, Gibbons 1941- . . . . **CLC 3**
  See also CA 33-36R; CANR 14, 31;
  DLB 120

Rubens, Bernice (Ruth) 1923- . . . **CLC 19, 31**
  See also CA 25-28R; CANR 33; DLB 14;
  MTCW

Rudkin, (James) David 1936- . . . . . . **CLC 14**
  See also CA 89-92; DLB 13

Rudnik, Raphael 1933- . . . . **CLC 7**
  See also CA 29-32R

Ruffian, M.
  See Hasek, Jaroslav (Matej Frantisek)

Ruiz, Jose Martinez . . . . **CLC 11**
  See also Martinez Ruiz, Jose

Rukeyser, Muriel
  1913-1980 . . . . **CLC 6, 10, 15, 27**
  See also CA 5-8R; 93-96; CANR 26;
  DLB 48; MTCW; SATA 22

Rule, Jane (Vance) 1931- . . . . **CLC 27**
  See also CA 25-28R; CANR 12; DLB 60

Rulfo, Juan 1918-1986 . . . . **CLC 8**
  See also CA 85-88; 118; CANR 26;
  DLB 113; HW; MTCW

Runyon, (Alfred) Damon
  1884(?)-1946 . . . . **TCLC 10**
  See also CA 107; DLB 11, 86

Rush, Norman 1933- . . . . **CLC 44**
  See also CA 121; 126

Rushdie, (Ahmed) Salman
  1947- . . . . **CLC 23, 31, 55**
  See also BEST 89:3; CA 108; 111;
  CANR 33; MTCW

Rushforth, Peter (Scott) 1945- . . . . . **CLC 19**
  See also CA 101

Ruskin, John 1819-1900 . . . . **TCLC 20**
  See also CA 114; 129; CDBLB 1832-1890;
  DLB 55; SATA 24

Russ, Joanna 1937- . . . . **CLC 15**
  See also CA 25-28R; CANR 11, 31; DLB 8;
  MTCW

Russell, George William 1867-1935
  See A. E.
  See also CA 104; CDBLB 1890-1914

Russell, (Henry) Ken(neth Alfred)
  1927- . . . . **CLC 16**
  See also CA 105

Russell, Willy 1947- . . . . **CLC 60**

Rutherford, Mark . . . . **TCLC 25**
  See also White, William Hale
  See also DLB 18

Ruyslinck, Ward
  See Belser, Reimond Karel Maria de

Ryan, Cornelius (John) 1920-1974 . . . **CLC 7**
  See also CA 69-72; 53-56; CANR 38

Ryan, Michael 1946- . . . . **CLC 65**
  See also CA 49-52; DLBY 82

Rybakov, Anatoli (Naumovich)
  1911- . . . . **CLC 23, 53**
  See also CA 126; 135

Ryder, Jonathan
  See Ludlum, Robert

Ryga, George 1932-1987 . . . . **CLC 14**
  See also CA 101; 124; DLB 60

S. S.
  See Sassoon, Siegfried (Lorraine)

Saba, Umberto 1883-1957 . . . . **TCLC 33**
  See also DLB 114

Sabatini, Rafael 1875-1950 . . . . **TCLC 47**

Sabato, Ernesto (R.) 1911- . . . . . . **CLC 10, 23**
  See also CA 97-100; CANR 32; HW;
  MTCW

Sacastru, Martin
  See Bioy Casares, Adolfo

Sacher-Masoch, Leopold von
  1836(?)-1895 . . . . **NCLC 31**

Sachs, Marilyn (Stickle) 1927- . . . . . **CLC 35**
  See also AAYA 2; CA 17-20R; CANR 13;
  CLR 2; MAICYA; SAAS 2; SATA 3, 68

Sachs, Nelly 1891-1970 . . . . **CLC 14**
  See also CA 17-18; 25-28R; CAP 2

Sackler, Howard (Oliver)
  1929-1982 . . . . **CLC 14**
  See also CA 61-64; 108; CANR 30; DLB 7

Sacks, Oliver (Wolf) 1933- . . . . **CLC 67**
  See also CA 53-56; CANR 28; MTCW

Sade, Donatien Alphonse Francois Comte
  1740-1814 . . . . **NCLC 3**

Sadoff, Ira 1945- . . . . **CLC 9**
  See also CA 53-56; CANR 5, 21; DLB 120

Saetone
  See Camus, Albert

Safire, William 1929- . . . . **CLC 10**
  See also CA 17-20R; CANR 31

Sagan, Carl (Edward) 1934- . . . . **CLC 30**
  See also AAYA 2; CA 25-28R; CANR 11,
  36; MTCW; SATA 58

Sagan, Francoise . . . . **CLC 3, 6, 9, 17, 36**
  See also Quoirez, Francoise
  See also DLB 83

Sahgal, Nayantara (Pandit) 1927-... **CLC 41**
See also CA 9-12R; CANR 11

Saint, H(arry) F. 1941- .... **CLC 50**
See also CA 127

St. Aubin de Teran, Lisa 1953-
See Teran, Lisa St. Aubin de
See also CA 118; 126

Sainte-Beuve, Charles Augustin
1804-1869 .... **NCLC 5**

Saint-Exupery, Antoine (Jean Baptiste Marie
Roger) de 1900-1944 .... **TCLC 2**
See also CA 108; 132; CLR 10; DLB 72;
MAICYA; MTCW; SATA 20; WLC

St. John, David
See Hunt, E(verette) Howard, Jr.

Saint-John Perse
See Leger, (Marie-Rene) Alexis Saint-Leger

Saintsbury, George (Edward Bateman)
1845-1933 .... **TCLC 31**
See also DLB 57

Sait Faik .... **TCLC 23**
See also Abasiyanik, Sait Faik

Saki .... **TCLC 3; SSC 12**
See also Munro, H(ector) H(ugh)

Salama, Hannu 1936-............. **CLC 18**

Salamanca, J(ack) R(ichard)
1922- .... **CLC 4, 15**
See also CA 25-28R

Sale, J. Kirkpatrick
See Sale, Kirkpatrick

Sale, Kirkpatrick 1937- .... **CLC 68**
See also CA 13-16R; CANR 10

Salinas (y Serrano), Pedro
1891(?)-1951 .... **TCLC 17**
See also CA 117

Salinger, J(erome) D(avid)
1919- .... **CLC 1, 3, 8, 12, 55, 56; SSC 2**
See also AAYA 2; CA 5-8R; CANR 39;
CDALB 1941-1968; CLR 18; DA;
DLB 2, 102; MAICYA; MTCW;
SATA 67; WLC

Salisbury, John
See Caute, David

Salter, James 1925- .... **CLC 7, 52, 59**
See also CA 73-76; DLB 130

Saltus, Edgar (Everton)
1855-1921 .... **TCLC 8**
See also CA 105

Saltykov, Mikhail Evgrafovich
1826-1889 .... **NCLC 16**

Samarakis, Antonis 1919- .... **CLC 5**
See also CA 25-28R; CAAS 16; CANR 36

Sanchez, Florencio 1875-1910 ..... **TCLC 37**
See also HW

Sanchez, Luis Rafael 1936-........ **CLC 23**
See also CA 128; HW

Sanchez, Sonia 1934-.............. **CLC 5**
See also BLC 3; BW; CA 33-36R;
CANR 24; CLR 18; DLB 41; DLBD 8;
MAICYA; MTCW; SATA 22

Sand, George 1804-1876......... **NCLC 2**
See also DA; DLB 119; WLC

Sandburg, Carl (August)
1878-1967 ... **CLC 1, 4, 10, 15, 35; PC 2**
See also CA 5-8R; 25-28R; CANR 35;
CDALB 1865-1917; DA; DLB 17, 54;
MAICYA; MTCW; SATA 8; WLC

Sandburg, Charles
See Sandburg, Carl (August)

Sandburg, Charles A.
See Sandburg, Carl (August)

Sanders, (James) Ed(ward) 1939- ... **CLC 53**
See also CA 13-16R; CANR 13; DLB 16

Sanders, Lawrence 1920-.......... **CLC 41**
See also BEST 89:4; CA 81-84; CANR 33;
MTCW

Sanders, Noah
See Blount, Roy (Alton), Jr.

Sanders, Winston P.
See Anderson, Poul (William)

Sandoz, Mari(e Susette)
1896-1966 .... **CLC 28**
See also CA 1-4R; 25-28R; CANR 17;
DLB 9; MTCW; SATA 5

Saner, Reg(inald Anthony) 1931- .... **CLC 9**
See also CA 65-68

Sannazaro, Jacopo 1456(?)-1530...... **LC 8**

Sansom, William 1912-1976....... **CLC 2, 6**
See also CA 5-8R; 65-68; MTCW

Santayana, George 1863-1952 ..... **TCLC 40**
See also CA 115; DLB 54, 71

Santiago, Danny .... **CLC 33**
See also James, Daniel (Lewis); James,
Daniel (Lewis)
See also DLB 122

Santmyer, Helen Hooven
1895-1986 .... **CLC 33**
See also CA 1-4R; 118; CANR 15, 33;
DLBY 84; MTCW

Santos, Bienvenido N(uqui) 1911-... **CLC 22**
See also CA 101; CANR 19

Sapper .... **TCLC 44**
See also McNeile, Herman Cyril

Sappho fl. 6th cent. B.C.-.... **CMLC 3; PC 5**

Sarduy, Severo 1937-.............. **CLC 6**
See also CA 89-92; DLB 113; HW

Sargeson, Frank 1903-1982 .... **CLC 31**
See also CA 25-28R; 106; CANR 38

Sarmiento, Felix Ruben Garcia 1867-1916
See Dario, Ruben
See also CA 104

Saroyan, William
1908-1981 ..... **CLC 1, 8, 10, 29, 34, 56**
See also CA 5-8R; 103; CANR 30; DA;
DLB 7, 9, 86; DLBY 81; MTCW;
SATA 23, 24; WLC

Sarraute, Nathalie
1900- .... **CLC 1, 2, 4, 8, 10, 31**
See also CA 9-12R; CANR 23; DLB 83;
MTCW

Sarton, (Eleanor) May
1912- .... **CLC 4, 14, 49**
See also CA 1-4R; CANR 1, 34; DLB 48;
DLBY 81; MTCW; SATA 36

Sartre, Jean-Paul
1905-1980 ... **CLC 1, 4, 7, 9, 13, 18, 24,
44, 50, 52; DC 3**
See also CA 9-12R; 97-100; CANR 21; DA;
DLB 72; MTCW; WLC

Sassoon, Siegfried (Lorraine)
1886-1967 .... **CLC 36**
See also CA 104; 25-28R; CANR 36;
DLB 20; MTCW

Satterfield, Charles
See Pohl, Frederik

Saul, John (W. III) 1942- .... **CLC 46**
See also AAYA 10; BEST 90:4; CA 81-84;
CANR 16, 40

Saunders, Caleb
See Heinlein, Robert A(nson)

Saura (Atares), Carlos 1932-....... **CLC 20**
See also CA 114; 131; HW

Sauser-Hall, Frederic 1887-1961.... **CLC 18**
See also CA 102; 93-96; CANR 36; MTCW

Saussure, Ferdinand de
1857-1913 .... **TCLC 49**

Savage, Catharine
See Brosman, Catharine Savage

Savage, Thomas 1915- .... **CLC 40**
See also CA 126; 132; CAAS 15

Savan, Glenn .... **CLC 50**

Saven, Glenn 19(?)- .... **CLC 50**

Sayers, Dorothy L(eigh)
1893-1957 .... **TCLC 2, 15**
See also CA 104; 119; CDBLB 1914-1945;
DLB 10, 36, 77, 100; MTCW

Sayers, Valerie 1952-............. **CLC 50**
See also CA 134

Sayles, John (Thomas)
1950- .... **CLC 7, 10, 14**
See also CA 57-60; CANR 41; DLB 44

Scammell, Michael .... **CLC 34**

Scannell, Vernon 1922- .... **CLC 49**
See also CA 5-8R; CANR 8, 24; DLB 27;
SATA 59

Scarlett, Susan
See Streatfeild, (Mary) Noel

Schaeffer, Susan Fromberg
1941-.................. **CLC 6, 11, 22**
See also CA 49-52; CANR 18; DLB 28;
MTCW; SATA 22

Schary, Jill
See Robinson, Jill

Schell, Jonathan 1943-............ **CLC 35**
See also CA 73-76; CANR 12

Schelling, Friedrich Wilhelm Joseph von
1775-1854 .... **NCLC 30**
See also DLB 90

Scherer, Jean-Marie Maurice 1920-
See Rohmer, Eric
See also CA 110

Schevill, James (Erwin) 1920-....... **CLC 7**
See also CA 5-8R; CAAS 12

Schiller, Friedrich 1759-1805 .... **NCLC 39**
See also DLB 94

Schisgal, Murray (Joseph) 1926-..... **CLC 6**
See also CA 21-24R

Schlee, Ann 1934-................ CLC 35
See also CA 101; CANR 29; SATA 36, 44

Schlegel, August Wilhelm von
1767-1845 .... NCLC 15
See also DLB 94

Schlegel, Johann Elias (von)
1719(?)-1749 .... LC 5

Schmidt, Arno (Otto) 1914-1979.... CLC 56
See also CA 128; 109; DLB 69

Schmitz, Aron Hector 1861-1928
See Svevo, Italo
See also CA 104; 122; MTCW

Schnackenberg, Gjertrud 1953-..... CLC 40
See also CA 116; DLB 120

Schneider, Leonard Alfred 1925-1966
See Bruce, Lenny
See also CA 89-92

Schnitzler, Arthur 1862-1931 ...... TCLC 4
See also CA 104; DLB 81, 118

Schor, Sandra (M.) 1932(?)-1990 ... CLC 65
See also CA 132

Schorer, Mark 1908-1977 .... CLC 9
See also CA 5-8R; 73-76; CANR 7;
DLB 103

Schrader, Paul (Joseph) 1946-...... CLC 26
See also CA 37-40R; CANR 41; DLB 44

Schreiner, Olive (Emilie Albertina)
1855-1920 .... TCLC 9
See also CA 105; DLB 18

Schulberg, Budd (Wilson)
1914- .... CLC 7, 48
See also CA 25-28R; CANR 19; DLB 6, 26,
28; DLBY 81

Schulz, Bruno 1892-1942 .... TCLC 5
See also CA 115; 123

Schulz, Charles M(onroe) 1922- .... CLC 12
See also CA 9-12R; CANR 6; SATA 10

Schuyler, James Marcus
1923-1991 .... CLC 5, 23
See also CA 101; 134; DLB 5

Schwartz, Delmore (David)
1913-1966 .... CLC 2, 4, 10, 45
See also CA 17-18; 25-28R; CANR 35;
CAP 2; DLB 28, 48; MTCW

Schwartz, Ernst
See Ozu, Yasujiro

Schwartz, John Burnham 1965- .... CLC 59
See also CA 132

Schwartz, Lynne Sharon 1939-..... CLC 31
See also CA 103

Schwartz, Muriel A.
See Eliot, T(homas) S(tearns)

Schwarz-Bart, Andre 1928-....... CLC 2, 4
See also CA 89-92

Schwarz-Bart, Simone 1938-........ CLC 7
See also CA 97-100

Schwob, (Mayer Andre) Marcel
1867-1905 .... TCLC 20
See also CA 117; DLB 123

Sciascia, Leonardo
1921-1989 .... CLC 8, 9, 41
See also CA 85-88; 130; CANR 35; MTCW

Scoppettone, Sandra 1936-........ CLC 26
See also CA 5-8R; CANR 41; SATA 9

Scorsese, Martin 1942- .... CLC 20
See also CA 110; 114

Scotland, Jay
See Jakes, John (William)

Scott, Duncan Campbell
1862-1947 .... TCLC 6
See also CA 104; DLB 92

Scott, Evelyn 1893-1963.......... CLC 43
See also CA 104; 112; DLB 9, 48

Scott, F(rancis) R(eginald)
1899-1985 .... CLC 22
See also CA 101; 114; DLB 88

Scott, Frank
See Scott, F(rancis) R(eginald)

Scott, Joanna 1960-.............. CLC 50
See also CA 126

Scott, Paul (Mark) 1920-1978.... CLC 9, 60
See also CA 81-84; 77-80; CANR 33;
DLB 14; MTCW

Scott, Walter 1771-1832......... NCLC 15
See also CDBLB 1789-1832; DA; DLB 93,
107, 116; WLC; YABC 2

Scribe, (Augustin) Eugene
1791-1861 .... NCLC 16

Scrum, R.
See Crumb, R(obert)

Scudery, Madeleine de 1607-1701..... LC 2

Scum
See Crumb, R(obert)

Scumbag, Little Bobby
See Crumb, R(obert)

Seabrook, John
See Hubbard, L(afayette) Ron(ald)

Sealy, I. Allan 1951- .... CLC 55

Search, Alexander
See Pessoa, Fernando (Antonio Nogueira)

Sebastian, Lee
See Silverberg, Robert

Sebastian Owl
See Thompson, Hunter S(tockton)

Sebestyen, Ouida 1924-........... CLC 30
See also AAYA 8; CA 107; CANR 40;
CLR 17; MAICYA; SAAS 10; SATA 39

Secundus, H. Scriblerus
See Fielding, Henry

Sedges, John
See Buck, Pearl S(ydenstricker)

Sedgwick, Catharine Maria
1789-1867 .... NCLC 19
See also DLB 1, 74

Seelye, John 1931-............... CLC 7

Seferiades, Giorgos Stylianou 1900-1971
See Seferis, George
See also CA 5-8R; 33-36R; CANR 5, 36;
MTCW

Seferis, George .... CLC 5, 11
See also Seferiades, Giorgos Stylianou

Segal, Erich (Wolf) 1937- .... CLC 3, 10
See also BEST 89:1; CA 25-28R; CANR 20,
36; DLBY 86; MTCW

Seger, Bob 1945-................. CLC 35

Seghers, Anna .... CLC 7
See also Radvanyi, Netty
See also DLB 69

Seidel, Frederick (Lewis) 1936-..... CLC 18
See also CA 13-16R; CANR 8; DLBY 84

Seifert, Jaroslav 1901-1986..... CLC 34, 44
See also CA 127; MTCW

Sei Shonagon c. 966-1017(?) ...... CMLC 6

Selby, Hubert, Jr. 1928- ..... CLC 1, 2, 4, 8
See also CA 13-16R; CANR 33; DLB 2

Selzer, Richard 1928-............. CLC 74
See also CA 65-68; CANR 14

Sembene, Ousmane
See Ousmane, Sembene

Senancour, Etienne Pivert de
1770-1846 .... NCLC 16
See also DLB 119

Sender, Ramon (Jose) 1902-1982 .... CLC 8
See also CA 5-8R; 105; CANR 8; HW;
MTCW

Seneca, Lucius Annaeus
4B.C.-65. .... CMLC 6

Senghor, Leopold Sedar 1906-...... CLC 54
See also BLC 3; BW; CA 116; 125; MTCW

Serling, (Edward) Rod(man)
1924-1975 .... CLC 30
See also AITN 1; CA 65-68; 57-60; DLB 26

Serna, Ramon Gomez de la
See Gomez de la Serna, Ramon

Serpieres
See Guillevic, (Eugene)

Service, Robert
See Service, Robert W(illiam)
See also DLB 92

Service, Robert W(illiam)
1874(?)-1958 .... TCLC 15
See also Service, Robert
See also CA 115; 140; DA; SATA 20; WLC

Seth, Vikram 1952-.............. CLC 43
See also CA 121; 127; DLB 120

Seton, Cynthia Propper
1926-1982 .... CLC 27
See also CA 5-8R; 108; CANR 7

Seton, Ernest (Evan) Thompson
1860-1946 .... TCLC 31
See also CA 109; DLB 92; SATA 18

Seton-Thompson, Ernest
See Seton, Ernest (Evan) Thompson

Settle, Mary Lee 1918- .... CLC 19, 61
See also CA 89-92; CAAS 1; DLB 6

Seuphor, Michel
See Arp, Jean

Sevigne, Marie (de Rabutin-Chantal) Marquise
de 1626-1696 .... LC 11

Sexton, Anne (Harvey)
1928-1974 ... CLC 2, 4, 6, 8, 10, 15, 53;
PC 2
See also CA 1-4R; 53-56; CABS 2;
CANR 3, 36; CDALB 1941-1968; DA;
DLB 5; MTCW; SATA 10; WLC

Shaara, Michael (Joseph Jr.)
1929-1988 .... CLC 15
See also AITN 1; CA 102; DLBY 83

Shackleton, C. C.
See Aldiss, Brian W(ilson)

Shacochis, Bob . . . . **CLC 39**
See also Shacochis, Robert G.

Shacochis, Robert G. 1951-
See Shacochis, Bob
See also CA 119; 124

Shaffer, Anthony (Joshua) 1926- . . . . **CLC 19**
See also CA 110; 116; DLB 13

Shaffer, Peter (Levin)
1926- . . . . **CLC 5, 14, 18, 37, 60**
See also CA 25-28R; CANR 25;
CDBLB 1960 to Present; DLB 13;
MTCW

Shakey, Bernard
See Young, Neil

Shalamov, Varlam (Tikhonovich)
1907(?)-1982 . . . . **CLC 18**
See also CA 129; 105

Shamlu, Ahmad 1925- . . . . **CLC 10**

Shammas, Anton 1951- . . . . **CLC 55**

Shange, Ntozake
1948- . . . . **CLC 8, 25, 38, 74; DC 3**
See also AAYA 9; BLC 3; BW; CA 85-88;
CABS 3; CANR 27; DLB 38; MTCW

Shanley, John Patrick 1950- . . . . **CLC 75**
See also CA 128; 133

Shapcott, Thomas William 1935- . . . **CLC 38**
See also CA 69-72

Shapiro, Jane . . . . **CLC 76**

Shapiro, Karl (Jay) 1913- . . **CLC 4, 8, 15, 53**
See also CA 1-4R; CAAS 6; CANR 1, 36;
DLB 48; MTCW

Sharp, William 1855-1905 . . . . **TCLC 39**

Sharpe, Thomas Ridley 1928-
See Sharpe, Tom
See also CA 114; 122

Sharpe, Tom . . . . **CLC 36**
See also Sharpe, Thomas Ridley
See also DLB 14

Shaw, Bernard . . . . **TCLC 45**
See also Shaw, George Bernard

Shaw, G. Bernard
See Shaw, George Bernard

Shaw, George Bernard
1856-1950 . . . . **TCLC 3, 9, 21**
See also Shaw, Bernard
See also CA 104; 128; CDBLB 1914-1945;
DA; DLB 10, 57; MTCW; WLC

Shaw, Henry Wheeler
1818-1885 . . . . **NCLC 15**
See also DLB 11

Shaw, Irwin 1913-1984 . . . . . . **CLC 7, 23, 34**
See also AITN 1; CA 13-16R; 112;
CANR 21; CDALB 1941-1968; DLB 6,
102; DLBY 84; MTCW

Shaw, Robert 1927-1978 . . . . **CLC 5**
See also AITN 1; CA 1-4R; 81-84;
CANR 4; DLB 13, 14

Shaw, T. E.
See Lawrence, T(homas) E(dward)

Shawn, Wallace 1943- . . . . **CLC 41**
See also CA 112

Sheed, Wilfrid (John Joseph)
1930- . . . . **CLC 2, 4, 10, 53**
See also CA 65-68; CANR 30; DLB 6;
MTCW

Sheldon, Alice Hastings Bradley
1915(?)-1987
See Tiptree, James, Jr.
See also CA 108; 122; CANR 34; MTCW

Sheldon, John
See Bloch, Robert (Albert)

Shelley, Mary Wollstonecraft (Godwin)
1797-1851 . . . . **NCLC 14**
See also CDBLB 1789-1832; DA; DLB 110,
116; SATA 29; WLC

Shelley, Percy Bysshe
1792-1822 . . . . **NCLC 18**
See also CDBLB 1789-1832; DA; DLB 96,
110; WLC

Shepard, Jim 1956- . . . . **CLC 36**
See also CA 137

Shepard, Lucius 19(?)- . . . . **CLC 34**
See also CA 128

Shepard, Sam
1943- . . . . **CLC 4, 6, 17, 34, 41, 44**
See also AAYA 1; CA 69-72; CABS 3;
CANR 22; DLB 7; MTCW

Shepherd, Michael
See Ludlum, Robert

Sherburne, Zoa (Morin) 1912- . . . . . . **CLC 30**
See also CA 1-4R; CANR 3, 37; MAICYA;
SATA 3

Sheridan, Frances 1724-1766 . . . . **LC 7**
See also DLB 39, 84

Sheridan, Richard Brinsley
1751-1816 . . . . **NCLC 5; DC 1**
See also CDBLB 1660-1789; DA; DLB 89;
WLC

Sherman, Jonathan Marc . . . . **CLC 55**

Sherman, Martin 1941(?)- . . . . **CLC 19**
See also CA 116; 123

Sherwin, Judith Johnson 1936- . . . **CLC 7, 15**
See also CA 25-28R; CANR 34

Sherwood, Robert E(mmet)
1896-1955 . . . . **TCLC 3**
See also CA 104; DLB 7, 26

Shiel, M(atthew) P(hipps)
1865-1947 . . . . **TCLC 8**
See also CA 106

Shiga, Naoya 1883-1971 . . . . **CLC 33**
See also CA 101; 33-36R

Shimazaki Haruki 1872-1943
See Shimazaki Toson
See also CA 105; 134

Shimazaki Toson . . . . **TCLC 5**
See also Shimazaki Haruki

Sholokhov, Mikhail (Aleksandrovich)
1905-1984 . . . . **CLC 7, 15**
See also CA 101; 112; MTCW; SATA 36

Shone, Patric
See Hanley, James

Shreve, Susan Richards 1939- . . . . . . **CLC 23**
See also CA 49-52; CAAS 5; CANR 5, 38;
MAICYA; SATA 41, 46

Shue, Larry 1946-1985 . . . . **CLC 52**
See also CA 117

Shu-Jen, Chou 1881-1936
See Hsun, Lu
See also CA 104

Shulman, Alix Kates 1932- . . . . . . **CLC 2, 10**
See also CA 29-32R; SATA 7

Shuster, Joe 1914- . . . . **CLC 21**

Shute, Nevil . . . . **CLC 30**
See also Norway, Nevil Shute

Shuttle, Penelope (Diane) 1947- . . . . . **CLC 7**
See also CA 93-96; CANR 39; DLB 14, 40

Sidney, Mary 1561-1621 . . . . **LC 19**

Sidney, Sir Philip 1554-1586 . . . . **LC 19**
See also CDBLB Before 1660; DA

Siegel, Jerome 1914- . . . . **CLC 21**
See also CA 116

Siegel, Jerry
See Siegel, Jerome

Sienkiewicz, Henryk (Adam Alexander Pius)
1846-1916 . . . . **TCLC 3**
See also CA 104; 134

Sierra, Gregorio Martinez
See Martinez Sierra, Gregorio

Sierra, Maria (de la O'LeJarraga) Martinez
See Martinez Sierra, Maria (de la
O'LeJarraga)

Sigal, Clancy 1926- . . . . **CLC 7**
See also CA 1-4R

Sigourney, Lydia Howard (Huntley)
1791-1865 . . . . **NCLC 21**
See also DLB 1, 42, 73

Siguenza y Gongora, Carlos de
1645-1700 . . . . **LC 8**

Sigurjonsson, Johann 1880-1919 . . . **TCLC 27**

Sikelianos, Angelos 1884-1951 . . . . **TCLC 39**

Silkin, Jon 1930- . . . . **CLC 2, 6, 43**
See also CA 5-8R; CAAS 5; DLB 27

Silko, Leslie Marmon 1948- . . . . **CLC 23, 74**
See also CA 115; 122; DA

Sillanpaa, Frans Eemil 1888-1964 . . . **CLC 19**
See also CA 129; 93-96; MTCW

Sillitoe, Alan
1928- . . . . **CLC 1, 3, 6, 10, 19, 57**
See also AITN 1; CA 9-12R; CAAS 2;
CANR 8, 26; CDBLB 1960 to Present;
DLB 14; MTCW; SATA 61

Silone, Ignazio 1900-1978 . . . . **CLC 4**
See also CA 25-28; 81-84; CANR 34;
CAP 2; MTCW

Silver, Joan Micklin 1935- . . . . **CLC 20**
See also CA 114; 121

Silver, Nicholas
See Faust, Frederick (Schiller)

Silverberg, Robert 1935- . . . . **CLC 7**
See also CA 1-4R; CAAS 3; CANR 1, 20,
36; DLB 8; MAICYA; MTCW; SATA 13

Silverstein, Alvin 1933- . . . . **CLC 17**
See also CA 49-52; CANR 2; CLR 25;
MAICYA; SATA 8, 69

Silverstein, Virginia B(arbara Opshelor)
1937- . . . . **CLC 17**
See also CA 49-52; CANR 2; CLR 25;
MAICYA; SATA 8, 69

Snodgrass, William D(e Witt)
1926- . . . . **CLC 2, 6, 10, 18, 68**
See also CA 1-4R; CANR 6, 36; DLB 5;
MTCW

Snow, C(harles) P(ercy)
1905-1980 . . . . **CLC 1, 4, 6, 9, 13, 19**
See also CA 5-8R; 101; CANR 28;
CDBLB 1945-1960; DLB 15, 77; MTCW

Snow, Frances Compton
See Adams, Henry (Brooks)

Snyder, Gary (Sherman)
1930- . . . . **CLC 1, 2, 5, 9, 32**
See also CA 17-20R; CANR 30; DLB 5, 16

Snyder, Zilpha Keatley 1927- . . . . . . **CLC 17**
See also CA 9-12R; CANR 38; MAICYA;
SAAS 2; SATA 1, 28

Soares, Bernardo
See Pessoa, Fernando (Antonio Nogueira)

Sobh, A.
See Shamlu, Ahmad

Sobol, Joshua . . . . **CLC 60**

Soderberg, Hjalmar 1869-1941 . . . . **TCLC 39**

Sodergran, Edith (Irene)
See Soedergran, Edith (Irene)

Soedergran, Edith (Irene)
1892-1923 . . . . **TCLC 31**

Softly, Edgar
See Lovecraft, H(oward) P(hillips)

Softly, Edward
See Lovecraft, H(oward) P(hillips)

Sokolov, Raymond 1941- . . . . **CLC 7**
See also CA 85-88

Solo, Jay
See Ellison, Harlan

Sologub, Fyodor . . . . **TCLC 9**
See also Teternikov, Fyodor Kuzmich

Solomons, Ikey Esquir
See Thackeray, William Makepeace

Solomos, Dionysios 1798-1857 . . . **NCLC 15**

Solwoska, Mara
See French, Marilyn

Solzhenitsyn, Aleksandr I(sayevich)
1918- . . . **CLC 1, 2, 4, 7, 9, 10, 18, 26, 34**
See also AITN 1; CA 69-72; CANR 40;
DA; MTCW; WLC

Somers, Jane
See Lessing, Doris (May)

Sommer, Scott 1951- . . . . **CLC 25**
See also CA 106

Sondheim, Stephen (Joshua)
1930- . . . . **CLC 30, 39**
See also CA 103

Sontag, Susan 1933- . . . **CLC 1, 2, 10, 13, 31**
See also CA 17-20R; CANR 25; DLB 2, 67;
MTCW

Sophocles
496(?)B.C.-406(?)B.C. . . . **CMLC 2; DC 1**
See also DA

Sorel, Julia
See Drexler, Rosalyn

Sorrentino, Gilbert
1929- . . . . **CLC 3, 7, 14, 22, 40**
See also CA 77-80; CANR 14, 33; DLB 5;
DLBY 80

Soto, Gary 1952- . . . . **CLC 32**
See also AAYA 10; CA 119; 125; DLB 82;
HW

Soupault, Philippe 1897-1990 . . . . . **CLC 68**
See also CA 116; 131

Souster, (Holmes) Raymond
1921- . . . . **CLC 5, 14**
See also CA 13-16R; CAAS 14; CANR 13,
29; DLB 88; SATA 63

Southern, Terry 1926- . . . . **CLC 7**
See also CA 1-4R; CANR 1; DLB 2

Southey, Robert 1774-1843 . . . . **NCLC 8**
See also DLB 93, 107; SATA 54

Southworth, Emma Dorothy Eliza Nevitte
1819-1899 . . . . **NCLC 26**

Souza, Ernest
See Scott, Evelyn

Soyinka, Wole
1934- . . . . **CLC 3, 5, 14, 36, 44; DC 2**
See also BLC 3; BW; CA 13-16R;
CANR 27, 39; DA; DLB 125; MTCW;
WLC

Spackman, W(illiam) M(ode)
1905-1990 . . . . **CLC 46**
See also CA 81-84; 132

Spacks, Barry 1931- . . . . **CLC 14**
See also CA 29-32R; CANR 33; DLB 105

Spanidou, Irini 1946- . . . . **CLC 44**

Spark, Muriel (Sarah)
1918- . . . . **CLC 2, 3, 5, 8, 13, 18, 40;**
SSC 10
See also CA 5-8R; CANR 12, 36;
CDBLB 1945-1960; DLB 15; MTCW

Spaulding, Douglas
See Bradbury, Ray (Douglas)

Spaulding, Leonard
See Bradbury, Ray (Douglas)

Spence, J. A. D.
See Eliot, T(homas) S(tearns)

Spencer, Elizabeth 1921- . . . . **CLC 22**
See also CA 13-16R; CANR 32; DLB 6;
MTCW; SATA 14

Spencer, Leonard G.
See Silverberg, Robert

Spencer, Scott 1945- . . . . **CLC 30**
See also CA 113; DLBY 86

Spender, Stephen (Harold)
1909- . . . . **CLC 1, 2, 5, 10, 41**
See also CA 9-12R; CANR 31;
CDBLB 1945-1960; DLB 20; MTCW

Spengler, Oswald (Arnold Gottfried)
1880-1936 . . . . **TCLC 25**
See also CA 118

Spenser, Edmund 1552(?)-1599 . . . . **LC 5**
See also CDBLB Before 1660; DA; WLC

Spicer, Jack 1925-1965 . . . . . . **CLC 8, 18, 72**
See also CA 85-88; DLB 5, 16

Spiegelman, Art 1948- . . . . **CLC 76**
See also AAYA 10; CA 125; CANR 41

Spielberg, Peter 1929- . . . . **CLC 6**
See also CA 5-8R; CANR 4; DLBY 81

Spielberg, Steven 1947- . . . . **CLC 20**
See also AAYA 8; CA 77-80; CANR 32;
SATA 32

Spillane, Frank Morrison 1918-
See Spillane, Mickey
See also CA 25-28R; CANR 28; MTCW;
SATA 66

Spillane, Mickey . . . . **CLC 3, 13**
See also Spillane, Frank Morrison

Spinoza, Benedictus de 1632-1677 . . . . **LC 9**

Spinrad, Norman (Richard) 1940- . . . **CLC 46**
See also CA 37-40R; CANR 20; DLB 8

Spitteler, Carl (Friedrich Georg)
1845-1924 . . . . **TCLC 12**
See also CA 109; DLB 129

Spivack, Kathleen (Romola Drucker)
1938- . . . . **CLC 6**
See also CA 49-52

Spoto, Donald 1941- . . . . **CLC 39**
See also CA 65-68; CANR 11

Springsteen, Bruce (F.) 1949- . . . . . . **CLC 17**
See also CA 111

Spurling, Hilary 1940- . . . . **CLC 34**
See also CA 104; CANR 25

Squires, (James) Radcliffe
1917-1993 . . . . **CLC 51**
See also CA 1-4R; 140; CANR 6, 21

Srivastava, Dhanpat Rai 1880(?)-1936
See Premchand
See also CA 118

Stacy, Donald
See Pohl, Frederik

Stael, Germaine de
See Stael-Holstein, Anne Louise Germaine
Necker Baronn
See also DLB 119

Stael-Holstein, Anne Louise Germaine Necker
Baronn 1766-1817 . . . . **NCLC 3**
See also Stael, Germaine de

Stafford, Jean 1915-1979 . . . **CLC 4, 7, 19, 68**
See also CA 1-4R; 85-88; CANR 3; DLB 2;
MTCW; SATA 22

Stafford, William (Edgar)
1914- . . . . **CLC 4, 7, 29**
See also CA 5-8R; CAAS 3; CANR 5, 22;
DLB 5

Staines, Trevor
See Brunner, John (Kilian Houston)

Stairs, Gordon
See Austin, Mary (Hunter)

Stannard, Martin . . . . **CLC 44**

Stanton, Maura 1946- . . . . **CLC 9**
See also CA 89-92; CANR 15; DLB 120

Stanton, Schuyler
See Baum, L(yman) Frank

Stapledon, (William) Olaf
1886-1950 . . . . **TCLC 22**
See also CA 111; DLB 15

Starbuck, George (Edwin) 1931- . . . . **CLC 53**
See also CA 21-24R; CANR 23

Stark, Richard
See Westlake, Donald E(dwin)

Staunton, Schuyler
See Baum, L(yman) Frank

Stead, Christina (Ellen)
1902-1983 . . . . **CLC 2, 5, 8, 32**
See also CA 13-16R; 109; CANR 33, 40;
MTCW

Stead, William Thomas
1849-1912 . . . . **TCLC 48**

Steele, Richard 1672-1729 . . . . **LC 18**
See also CDBLB 1660-1789; DLB 84, 101

Steele, Timothy (Reid) 1948- . . . . . . **CLC 45**
See also CA 93-96; CANR 16; DLB 120

Steffens, (Joseph) Lincoln
1866-1936 . . . . **TCLC 20**
See also CA 117

Stegner, Wallace (Earle) 1909- . . . **CLC 9, 49**
See also AITN 1; BEST 90:3; CA 1-4R;
CAAS 9; CANR 1, 21; DLB 9; MTCW

Stein, Gertrude
1874-1946 . . . . **TCLC 1, 6, 28, 48**
See also CA 104; 132; CDALB 1917-1929;
DA; DLB 4, 54, 86; MTCW; WLC

Steinbeck, John (Ernst)
1902-1968 . . . . . **CLC 1, 5, 9, 13, 21, 34,
45, 75; SSC 11**
See also CA 1-4R; 25-28R; CANR 1, 35;
CDALB 1929-1941; DA; DLB 7, 9;
DLBD 2; MTCW; SATA 9; WLC

Steinem, Gloria 1934- . . . . **CLC 63**
See also CA 53-56; CANR 28; MTCW

Steiner, George 1929- . . . . **CLC 24**
See also CA 73-76; CANR 31; DLB 67;
MTCW; SATA 62

Steiner, Rudolf 1861-1925 . . . . **TCLC 13**
See also CA 107

Stendhal 1783-1842 . . . . **NCLC 23**
See also DA; DLB 119; WLC

Stephen, Leslie 1832-1904 . . . . **TCLC 23**
See also CA 123; DLB 57

Stephen, Sir Leslie
See Stephen, Leslie

Stephen, Virginia
See Woolf, (Adeline) Virginia

Stephens, James 1882(?)-1950 . . . . . . **TCLC 4**
See also CA 104; DLB 19

Stephens, Reed
See Donaldson, Stephen R.

Steptoe, Lydia
See Barnes, Djuna

Sterchi, Beat 1949- . . . . **CLC 65**

Sterling, Brett
See Bradbury, Ray (Douglas); Hamilton,
Edmond

Sterling, Bruce 1954- . . . . **CLC 72**
See also CA 119

Sterling, George 1869-1926 . . . . **TCLC 20**
See also CA 117; DLB 54

Stern, Gerald 1925- . . . . **CLC 40**
See also CA 81-84; CANR 28; DLB 105

Stern, Richard (Gustave) 1928- . . . **CLC 4, 39**
See also CA 1-4R; CANR 1, 25; DLBY 87

Sternberg, Josef von 1894-1969 . . . . . **CLC 20**
See also CA 81-84

Sterne, Laurence 1713-1768 . . . . **LC 2**
See also CDBLB 1660-1789; DA; DLB 39;
WLC

Sternheim, (William Adolf) Carl
1878-1942 . . . . **TCLC 8**
See also CA 105; DLB 56, 118

Stevens, Mark 1951- . . . . **CLC 34**
See also CA 122

Stevens, Wallace
1879-1955 . . . . **TCLC 3, 12, 45; PC 6**
See also CA 104; 124; CDALB 1929-1941;
DA; DLB 54; MTCW; WLC

Stevenson, Anne (Katharine)
1933- . . . . **CLC 7, 33**
See also CA 17-20R; CAAS 9; CANR 9, 33;
DLB 40; MTCW

Stevenson, Robert Louis (Balfour)
1850-1894 . . . . **NCLC 5, 14; SSC 11**
See also CDBLB 1890-1914; CLR 10, 11;
DA; DLB 18, 57; MAICYA; WLC;
YABC 2

Stewart, J(ohn) I(nnes) M(ackintosh)
1906- . . . . **CLC 7, 14, 32**
See also CA 85-88; CAAS 3; MTCW

Stewart, Mary (Florence Elinor)
1916- . . . . **CLC 7, 35**
See also CA 1-4R; CANR 1; SATA 12

Stewart, Mary Rainbow
See Stewart, Mary (Florence Elinor)

Still, James 1906- . . . . **CLC 49**
See also CA 65-68; CAAS 17; CANR 10,
26; DLB 9; SATA 29

Sting
See Sumner, Gordon Matthew

Stirling, Arthur
See Sinclair, Upton (Beall)

Stitt, Milan 1941- . . . . **CLC 29**
See also CA 69-72

Stockton, Francis Richard 1834-1902
See Stockton, Frank R.
See also CA 108; 137; MAICYA; SATA 44

Stockton, Frank R. . . . . **TCLC 47**
See also Stockton, Francis Richard
See also DLB 42, 74; SATA 32

Stoddard, Charles
See Kuttner, Henry

Stoker, Abraham 1847-1912
See Stoker, Bram
See also CA 105; DA; SATA 29

Stoker, Bram . . . . **TCLC 8**
See also Stoker, Abraham
See also CDBLB 1890-1914; DLB 36, 70;
WLC

Stolz, Mary (Slattery) 1920- . . . . **CLC 12**
See also AAYA 8; AITN 1; CA 5-8R;
CANR 13, 41; MAICYA; SAAS 3;
SATA 10, 70, 71

Stone, Irving 1903-1989 . . . . **CLC 7**
See also AITN 1; CA 1-4R; 129; CAAS 3;
CANR 1, 23; MTCW; SATA 3;
SATA-Obit 64

Stone, Oliver 1946- . . . . **CLC 73**
See also CA 110

Stone, Robert (Anthony)
1937- . . . . **CLC 5, 23, 42**
See also CA 85-88; CANR 23; MTCW

Stone, Zachary
See Follett, Ken(neth Martin)

Stoppard, Tom
1937- . . . **CLC 1, 3, 4, 5, 8, 15, 29, 34, 63**
See also CA 81-84; CANR 39;
CDBLB 1960 to Present; DA; DLB 13;
DLBY 85; MTCW; WLC

Storey, David (Malcolm)
1933- . . . . **CLC 2, 4, 5, 8**
See also CA 81-84; CANR 36; DLB 13, 14;
MTCW

Storm, Hyemeyohsts 1935- . . . . **CLC 3**
See also CA 81-84

Storm, (Hans) Theodor (Woldsen)
1817-1888 . . . . **NCLC 1**

Storni, Alfonsina 1892-1938 . . . . **TCLC 5**
See also CA 104; 131; HW

Stout, Rex (Todhunter) 1886-1975 . . . **CLC 3**
See also AITN 2; CA 61-64

Stow, (Julian) Randolph 1935- . . **CLC 23, 48**
See also CA 13-16R; CANR 33; MTCW

Stowe, Harriet (Elizabeth) Beecher
1811-1896 . . . . **NCLC 3**
See also CDALB 1865-1917; DA; DLB 1,
12, 42, 74; MAICYA; WLC; YABC 1

Strachey, (Giles) Lytton
1880-1932 . . . . **TCLC 12**
See also CA 110; DLBD 10

Strand, Mark 1934- . . . . . . **CLC 6, 18, 41, 71**
See also CA 21-24R; CANR 40; DLB 5;
SATA 41

Straub, Peter (Francis) 1943- . . . . . . **CLC 28**
See also BEST 89:1; CA 85-88; CANR 28;
DLBY 84; MTCW

Strauss, Botho 1944- . . . . **CLC 22**
See also DLB 124

Streatfeild, (Mary) Noel
1895(?)-1986 . . . . **CLC 21**
See also CA 81-84; 120; CANR 31;
CLR 17; MAICYA; SATA 20, 48

Stribling, T(homas) S(igismund)
1881-1965 . . . . **CLC 23**
See also CA 107; DLB 9

Strindberg, (Johan) August
1849-1912 . . . . **TCLC 1, 8, 21, 47**
See also CA 104; 135; DA; WLC

Stringer, Arthur 1874-1950 . . . . **TCLC 37**
See also DLB 92

Stringer, David
See Roberts, Keith (John Kingston)

Strugatskii, Arkadii (Natanovich)
1925-1991 . . . . **CLC 27**
See also CA 106; 135

Strugatskii, Boris (Natanovich)
1933- . . . . **CLC 27**
See also CA 106

Strummer, Joe 1953(?)- . . . . **CLC 30**
See also Clash, The

Stuart, Don A.
See Campbell, John W(ood, Jr.)

Stuart, Ian
See MacLean, Alistair (Stuart)

Stuart, Jesse (Hilton)
1906-1984 . . . . **CLC 1, 8, 11, 14, 34**
See also CA 5-8R; 112; CANR 31; DLB 9,
48, 102; DLBY 84; SATA 2, 36

Sturgeon, Theodore (Hamilton)
  1918-1985 . . . . **CLC 22, 39**
  See also Queen, Ellery
  See also CA 81-84; 116; CANR 32; DLB 8;
  DLBY 85; MTCW

Sturges, Preston 1898-1959 . . . . . . **TCLC 48**
  See also CA 114; DLB 26

Styron, William
  1925- . . . . **CLC 1, 3, 5, 11, 15, 60**
  See also BEST 90:4; CA 5-8R; CANR 6, 33;
  CDALB 1968-1988; DLB 2; DLBY 80;
  MTCW

Suarez Lynch, B.
  See Borges, Jorge Luis

Suarez Lynch, B.
  See Bioy Casares, Adolfo; Borges, Jorge
  Luis

Su Chien 1884-1918
  See Su Man-shu
  See also CA 123

Sudermann, Hermann 1857-1928 . . **TCLC 15**
  See also CA 107; DLB 118

Sue, Eugene 1804-1857 . . . . **NCLC 1**
  See also DLB 119

Sueskind, Patrick 1949- . . . . **CLC 44**

Sukenick, Ronald 1932- . . . . . **CLC 3, 4, 6, 48**
  See also CA 25-28R; CAAS 8; CANR 32;
  DLBY 81

Suknaski, Andrew 1942- . . . . **CLC 19**
  See also CA 101; DLB 53

Sullivan, Vernon
  See Vian, Boris

Sully Prudhomme 1839-1907 . . . . . . **TCLC 31**

Su Man-shu . . . . **TCLC 24**
  See also Su Chien

Summerforest, Ivy B.
  See Kirkup, James

Summers, Andrew James 1942- . . . . . **CLC 26**
  See also Police, The

Summers, Andy
  See Summers, Andrew James

Summers, Hollis (Spurgeon, Jr.)
  1916- . . . . **CLC 10**
  See also CA 5-8R; CANR 3; DLB 6

Summers, (Alphonsus Joseph-Mary Augustus)
  Montague 1880-1948 . . . . **TCLC 16**
  See also CA 118

Sumner, Gordon Matthew 1951- . . . . **CLC 26**
  See also Police, The

Surtees, Robert Smith
  1803-1864 . . . . **NCLC 14**
  See also DLB 21

Susann, Jacqueline 1921-1974 . . . . . . **CLC 3**
  See also AITN 1; CA 65-68; 53-56; MTCW

Suskind, Patrick
  See Sueskind, Patrick

Sutcliff, Rosemary 1920-1992 . . . . . . **CLC 26**
  See also AAYA 10; CA 5-8R; 139;
  CANR 37; CLR 1; MAICYA; SATA 6,
  44; SATA-Obit 73

Sutro, Alfred 1863-1933 . . . . **TCLC 6**
  See also CA 105; DLB 10

Sutton, Henry
  See Slavitt, David R(ytman)

Svevo, Italo . . . . **TCLC 2, 35**
  See also Schmitz, Aron Hector

Swados, Elizabeth 1951- . . . . **CLC 12**
  See also CA 97-100

Swados, Harvey 1920-1972 . . . . **CLC 5**
  See also CA 5-8R; 37-40R; CANR 6;
  DLB 2

Swan, Gladys 1934- . . . . **CLC 69**
  See also CA 101; CANR 17, 39

Swarthout, Glendon (Fred)
  1918-1992 . . . . **CLC 35**
  See also CA 1-4R; 139; CANR 1; SATA 26

Sweet, Sarah C.
  See Jewett, (Theodora) Sarah Orne

Swenson, May 1919-1989 . . . . **CLC 4, 14, 61**
  See also CA 5-8R; 130; CANR 36; DA;
  DLB 5; MTCW; SATA 15

Swift, Augustus
  See Lovecraft, H(oward) P(hillips)

Swift, Graham 1949- . . . . **CLC 41**
  See also CA 117; 122

Swift, Jonathan 1667-1745 . . . . **LC 1**
  See also CDBLB 1660-1789; DA; DLB 39,
  95, 101; SATA 19; WLC

Swinburne, Algernon Charles
  1837-1909 . . . . **TCLC 8, 36**
  See also CA 105; 140; CDBLB 1832-1890;
  DA; DLB 35, 57; WLC

Swinfen, Ann . . . . **CLC 34**

Swinnerton, Frank Arthur
  1884-1982 . . . . **CLC 31**
  See also CA 108; DLB 34

Swithen, John
  See King, Stephen (Edwin)

Sylvia
  See Ashton-Warner, Sylvia (Constance)

Symmes, Robert Edward
  See Duncan, Robert (Edward)

Symonds, John Addington
  1840-1893 . . . . **NCLC 34**
  See also DLB 57

Symons, Arthur 1865-1945 . . . . **TCLC 11**
  See also CA 107; DLB 19, 57

Symons, Julian (Gustave)
  1912- . . . . **CLC 2, 14, 32**
  See also CA 49-52; CAAS 3; CANR 3, 33;
  DLB 87; DLBY 92; MTCW

Synge, (Edmund) J(ohn) M(illington)
  1871-1909 . . . . **TCLC 6, 37; DC 2**
  See also CA 104; CDBLB 1890-1914;
  DLB 10, 19

Syruc, J.
  See Milosz, Czeslaw

Szirtes, George 1948- . . . . **CLC 46**
  See also CA 109; CANR 27

Tabori, George 1914- . . . . **CLC 19**
  See also CA 49-52; CANR 4

Tagore, Rabindranath 1861-1941 . . . . **TCLC 3**
  See also CA 104; 120; MTCW

Taine, Hippolyte Adolphe
  1828-1893 . . . . **NCLC 15**

Talese, Gay 1932- . . . . **CLC 37**
  See also AITN 1; CA 1-4R; CANR 9;
  MTCW

Tallent, Elizabeth (Ann) 1954- . . . . . **CLC 45**
  See also CA 117; DLB 130

Tally, Ted 1952- . . . . **CLC 42**
  See also CA 120; 124

Tamayo y Baus, Manuel
  1829-1898 . . . . **NCLC 1**

Tammsaare, A(nton) H(ansen)
  1878-1940 . . . . **TCLC 27**

Tan, Amy 1952- . . . . **CLC 59**
  See also AAYA 9; BEST 89:3; CA 136

Tandem, Felix
  See Spitteler, Carl (Friedrich Georg)

Tanizaki, Jun'ichiro
  1886-1965 . . . . **CLC 8, 14, 28**
  See also CA 93-96; 25-28R

Tanner, William
  See Amis, Kingsley (William)

Tao Lao
  See Storni, Alfonsina

Tarassoff, Lev
  See Troyat, Henri

Tarbell, Ida M(inerva)
  1857-1944 . . . . **TCLC 40**
  See also CA 122; DLB 47

Tarkington, (Newton) Booth
  1869-1946 . . . . **TCLC 9**
  See also CA 110; DLB 9, 102; SATA 17

Tarkovsky, Andrei (Arsenyevich)
  1932-1986 . . . . **CLC 75**
  See also CA 127

Tartt, Donna 1964(?)- . . . . **CLC 76**

Tasso, Torquato 1544-1595 . . . . **LC 5**

Tate, (John Orley) Allen
  1899-1979 . . . . **CLC 2, 4, 6, 9, 11, 14, 24**
  See also CA 5-8R; 85-88; CANR 32;
  DLB 4, 45, 63; MTCW

Tate, Ellalice
  See Hibbert, Eleanor Alice Burford

Tate, James (Vincent) 1943- . . . **CLC 2, 6, 25**
  See also CA 21-24R; CANR 29; DLB 5

Tavel, Ronald 1940- . . . . **CLC 6**
  See also CA 21-24R; CANR 33

Taylor, Cecil Philip 1929-1981 . . . . . **CLC 27**
  See also CA 25-28R; 105

Taylor, Edward 1642(?)-1729 . . . . **LC 11**
  See also DA; DLB 24

Taylor, Eleanor Ross 1920- . . . . **CLC 5**
  See also CA 81-84

Taylor, Elizabeth 1912-1975 . . . **CLC 2, 4, 29**
  See also CA 13-16R; CANR 9; MTCW;
  SATA 13

Taylor, Henry (Splawn) 1942- . . . . . . **CLC 44**
  See also CA 33-36R; CAAS 7; CANR 31;
  DLB 5

Taylor, Kamala (Purnaiya) 1924-
  See Markandaya, Kamala
  See also CA 77-80

Taylor, Mildred D. . . . . **CLC 21**
  See also AAYA 10; BW; CA 85-88;
  CANR 25; CLR 9; DLB 52; MAICYA;
  SAAS 5; SATA 15, 70

Unamuno (y Jugo), Miguel de
1864-1936 .... **TCLC 2, 9; SSC 11**
See also CA 104; 131; DLB 108; HW;
MTCW

Undercliffe, Errol
See Campbell, (John) Ramsey

Underwood, Miles
See Glassco, John

Undset, Sigrid 1882-1949......... **TCLC 3**
See also CA 104; 129; DA; MTCW; WLC

Ungaretti, Giuseppe
1888-1970 .... **CLC 7, 11, 15**
See also CA 19-20; 25-28R; CAP 2;
DLB 114

Unger, Douglas 1952-............ **CLC 34**
See also CA 130

Unsworth, Barry (Forster) 1930-.... **CLC 76**
See also CA 25-28R; CANR 30

Updike, John (Hoyer)
1932- ...... **CLC 1, 2, 3, 5, 7, 9, 13, 15,**
23, 34, 43, 70
See also CA 1-4R; CABS 1; CANR 4, 33;
CDALB 1968-1988; DA; DLB 2, 5;
DLBD 3; DLBY 80, 82; MTCW; WLC

Upshaw, Margaret Mitchell
See Mitchell, Margaret (Munnerlyn)

Upton, Mark
See Sanders, Lawrence

Urdang, Constance (Henriette)
1922- .... **CLC 47**
See also CA 21-24R; CANR 9, 24

Uriel, Henry
See Faust, Frederick (Schiller)

Uris, Leon (Marcus) 1924-...... **CLC 7, 32**
See also AITN 1, 2; BEST 89:2; CA 1-4R;
CANR 1, 40; MTCW; SATA 49

Urmuz
See Codrescu, Andrei

Ustinov, Peter (Alexander) 1921-.... **CLC 1**
See also AITN 1; CA 13-16R; CANR 25;
DLB 13

V
See Chekhov, Anton (Pavlovich)

Vaculik, Ludvik 1926-............. **CLC 7**
See also CA 53-56

Valenzuela, Luisa 1938-.......... **CLC 31**
See also CA 101; CANR 32; DLB 113; HW

Valera y Alcala-Galiano, Juan
1824-1905 .... **TCLC 10**
See also CA 106

Valery, (Ambroise) Paul (Toussaint Jules)
1871-1945 .... **TCLC 4, 15**
See also CA 104; 122; MTCW

Valle-Inclan, Ramon (Maria) del
1866-1936 .... **TCLC 5**
See also CA 106

Vallejo, Antonio Buero
See Buero Vallejo, Antonio

Vallejo, Cesar (Abraham)
1892-1938 .... **TCLC 3**
See also CA 105; HW

Valle Y Pena, Ramon del
See Valle-Inclan, Ramon (Maria) del

Van Ash, Cay 1918-............. **CLC 34**

Vanbrugh, Sir John 1664-1726 ...... **LC 21**
See also DLB 80

Van Campen, Karl
See Campbell, John W(ood, Jr.)

Vance, Gerald
See Silverberg, Robert

Vance, Jack .... **CLC 35**
See also Vance, John Holbrook
See also DLB 8

Vance, John Holbrook 1916-
See Queen, Ellery; Vance, Jack
See also CA 29-32R; CANR 17; MTCW

Van Den Bogarde, Derek Jules Gaspard Ulric
Niven 1921-
See Bogarde, Dirk
See also CA 77-80

Vandenburgh, Jane .... **CLC 59**

Vanderhaeghe, Guy 1951- .... **CLC 41**
See also CA 113

van der Post, Laurens (Jan) 1906- ... **CLC 5**
See also CA 5-8R; CANR 35

van de Wetering, Janwillem 1931- .. **CLC 47**
See also CA 49-52; CANR 4

Van Dine, S. S. .... **TCLC 23**
See also Wright, Willard Huntington

Van Doren, Carl (Clinton)
1885-1950 .... **TCLC 18**
See also CA 111

Van Doren, Mark 1894-1972..... **CLC 6, 10**
See also CA 1-4R; 37-40R; CANR 3;
DLB 45; MTCW

Van Druten, John (William)
1901-1957 .... **TCLC 2**
See also CA 104; DLB 10

Van Duyn, Mona (Jane)
1921- .... **CLC 3, 7, 63**
See also CA 9-12R; CANR 7, 38; DLB 5

Van Dyne, Edith
See Baum, L(yman) Frank

van Itallie, Jean-Claude 1936-....... **CLC 3**
See also CA 45-48; CAAS 2; CANR 1;
DLB 7

van Ostaijen, Paul 1896-1928 ..... **TCLC 33**

Van Peebles, Melvin 1932- ...... **CLC 2, 20**
See also BW; CA 85-88; CANR 27

Vansittart, Peter 1920-........... **CLC 42**
See also CA 1-4R; CANR 3

Van Vechten, Carl 1880-1964 ..... **CLC 33**
See also CA 89-92; DLB 4, 9, 51

Van Vogt, A(lfred) E(lton) 1912-..... **CLC 1**
See also CA 21-24R; CANR 28; DLB 8;
SATA 14

Vara, Madeleine
See Jackson, Laura (Riding)

Varda, Agnes 1928- .... **CLC 16**
See also CA 116; 122

Vargas Llosa, (Jorge) Mario (Pedro)
1936- .... **CLC 3, 6, 9, 10, 15, 31, 42**
See also CA 73-76; CANR 18, 32; DA;
HW; MTCW

Vasiliu, Gheorghe 1881-1957
See Bacovia, George
See also CA 123

Vassa, Gustavus
See Equiano, Olaudah

Vassilikos, Vassilis 1933-........ **CLC 4, 8**
See also CA 81-84

Vaughn, Stephanie................. **CLC 62**

Vazov, Ivan (Minchov)
1850-1921 .... **TCLC 25**
See also CA 121

Veblen, Thorstein (Bunde)
1857-1929 .... **TCLC 31**
See also CA 115

Venison, Alfred
See Pound, Ezra (Weston Loomis)

Verdi, Marie de
See Mencken, H(enry) L(ouis)

Verdu, Matilde
See Cela, Camilo Jose

Verga, Giovanni (Carmelo)
1840-1922 .... **TCLC 3**
See also CA 104; 123

Vergil 70B.C.-19B.C. .... **CMLC 9**
See also DA

Verhaeren, Emile (Adolphe Gustave)
1855-1916 .... **TCLC 12**
See also CA 109

Verlaine, Paul (Marie)
1844-1896 .... **NCLC 2; PC 2**

Verne, Jules (Gabriel) 1828-1905 ... **TCLC 6**
See also CA 110; 131; DLB 123; MAICYA;
SATA 21

Very, Jones 1813-1880........... **NCLC 9**
See also DLB 1

Vesaas, Tarjei 1897-1970......... **CLC 48**
See also CA 29-32R

Vialis, Gaston
See Simenon, Georges (Jacques Christian)

Vian, Boris 1920-1959 .... **TCLC 9**
See also CA 106; DLB 72

Viaud, (Louis Marie) Julien 1850-1923
See Loti, Pierre
See also CA 107

Vicar, Henry
See Felsen, Henry Gregor

Vicker, Angus
See Felsen, Henry Gregor

Vidal, Gore
1925- ..... **CLC 2, 4, 6, 8, 10, 22, 33, 72**
See also AITN 1; BEST 90:2; CA 5-8R;
CANR 13; DLB 6; MTCW

Viereck, Peter (Robert Edwin)
1916- .... **CLC 4**
See also CA 1-4R; CANR 1; DLB 5

Vigny, Alfred (Victor) de
1797-1863 .... **NCLC 7**
See also DLB 119

Vilakazi, Benedict Wallet
1906-1947 .... **TCLC 37**

Villiers de l'Isle Adam, Jean Marie Mathias
Philippe Auguste Comte
1838-1889 .... **NCLC 3**
See also DLB 123

Vincent, Gabrielle .... **CLC 13**
See also CA 126; CLR 13; MAICYA;
SATA 61

Warner, Sylvia Townsend
1893-1978 .... **CLC 7, 19**
See also CA 61-64; 77-80; CANR 16;
DLB 34; MTCW

Warren, Mercy Otis 1728-1814... **NCLC 13**
See also DLB 31

Warren, Robert Penn
1905-1989 ... **CLC 1, 4, 6, 8, 10, 13, 18,
39, 53, 59; SSC 4**
See also AITN 1; CA 13-16R; 129;
CANR 10; CDALB 1968-1988; DA;
DLB 2, 48; DLBY 80, 89; MTCW;
SATA 46, 63; WLC

Warshofsky, Isaac
See Singer, Isaac Bashevis

Warton, Thomas 1728-1790........ **LC 15**
See also DLB 104, 109

Waruk, Kona
See Harris, (Theodore) Wilson

Warung, Price 1855-1911........ **TCLC 45**

Warwick, Jarvis
See Garner, Hugh

Washington, Alex
See Harris, Mark

Washington, Booker T(aliaferro)
1856-1915 .... **TCLC 10**
See also BLC 3; BW; CA 114; 125;
SATA 28

Wassermann, (Karl) Jakob
1873-1934 .... **TCLC 6**
See also CA 104; DLB 66

Wasserstein, Wendy 1950-...... **CLC 32, 59**
See also CA 121; 129; CABS 3

Waterhouse, Keith (Spencer)
1929- .... **CLC 47**
See also CA 5-8R; CANR 38; DLB 13, 15;
MTCW

Waters, Roger 1944-............. **CLC 35**
See also Pink Floyd

Watkins, Frances Ellen
See Harper, Frances Ellen Watkins

Watkins, Gerrold
See Malzberg, Barry N(athaniel)

Watkins, Paul 1964-............. **CLC 55**
See also CA 132

Watkins, Vernon Phillips
1906-1967 .... **CLC 43**
See also CA 9-10; 25-28R; CAP 1; DLB 20

Watson, Irving S.
See Mencken, H(enry) L(ouis)

Watson, John H.
See Farmer, Philip Jose

Watson, Richard F.
See Silverberg, Robert

Waugh, Auberon (Alexander) 1939-.. **CLC 7**
See also CA 45-48; CANR 6, 22; DLB 14

Waugh, Evelyn (Arthur St. John)
1903-1966 ... **CLC 1, 3, 8, 13, 19, 27, 44**
See also CA 85-88; 25-28R; CANR 22;
CDBLB 1914-1945; DA; DLB 15;
MTCW; WLC

Waugh, Harriet 1944- .... **CLC 6**
See also CA 85-88; CANR 22

Ways, C. R.
See Blount, Roy (Alton), Jr.

Waystaff, Simon
See Swift, Jonathan

Webb, (Martha) Beatrice (Potter)
1858-1943 .... **TCLC 22**
See also Potter, Beatrice
See also CA 117

Webb, Charles (Richard) 1939-...... **CLC 7**
See also CA 25-28R

Webb, James H(enry), Jr. 1946-.... **CLC 22**
See also CA 81-84

Webb, Mary (Gladys Meredith)
1881-1927 .... **TCLC 24**
See also CA 123; DLB 34

Webb, Mrs. Sidney
See Webb, (Martha) Beatrice (Potter)

Webb, Phyllis 1927-............. **CLC 18**
See also CA 104; CANR 23; DLB 53

Webb, Sidney (James)
1859-1947 .... **TCLC 22**
See also CA 117

Webber, Andrew Lloyd............. **CLC 21**
See also Lloyd Webber, Andrew

Weber, Lenora Mattingly
1895-1971 .... **CLC 12**
See also CA 19-20; 29-32R; CAP 1;
SATA 2, 26

Webster, John 1579(?)-1634(?) .... **DC 2**
See also CDBLB Before 1660; DA; DLB 58;
WLC

Webster, Noah 1758-1843 .... **NCLC 30**

Wedekind, (Benjamin) Frank(lin)
1864-1918 .... **TCLC 7**
See also CA 104; DLB 118

Weidman, Jerome 1913-............ **CLC 7**
See also AITN 2; CA 1-4R; CANR 1;
DLB 28

Weil, Simone (Adolphine)
1909-1943 .... **TCLC 23**
See also CA 117

Weinstein, Nathan
See West, Nathanael

Weinstein, Nathan von Wallenstein
See West, Nathanael

Weir, Peter (Lindsay) 1944- .... **CLC 20**
See also CA 113; 123

Weiss, Peter (Ulrich)
1916-1982 .... **CLC 3, 15, 51**
See also CA 45-48; 106; CANR 3; DLB 69,
124

Weiss, Theodore (Russell)
1916- .... **CLC 3, 8, 14**
See also CA 9-12R; CAAS 2; DLB 5

Welch, (Maurice) Denton
1915-1948 .... **TCLC 22**
See also CA 121

Welch, James 1940-........ **CLC 6, 14, 52**
See also CA 85-88

Weldon, Fay
1933(?)- .... **CLC 6, 9, 11, 19, 36, 59**
See also CA 21-24R; CANR 16;
CDBLB 1960 to Present; DLB 14;
MTCW

Wellek, Rene 1903- .... **CLC 28**
See also CA 5-8R; CAAS 7; CANR 8;
DLB 63

Weller, Michael 1942-......... **CLC 10, 53**
See also CA 85-88

Weller, Paul 1958-............. **CLC 26**

Wellershoff, Dieter 1925-......... **CLC 46**
See also CA 89-92; CANR 16, 37

Welles, (George) Orson
1915-1985 .... **CLC 20**
See also CA 93-96; 117

Wellman, Mac 1945- .... **CLC 65**

Wellman, Manly Wade 1903-1986 .. **CLC 49**
See also CA 1-4R; 118; CANR 6, 16;
SATA 6, 47

Wells, Carolyn 1869(?)-1942 ...... **TCLC 35**
See also CA 113; DLB 11

Wells, H(erbert) G(eorge)
1866-1946 ...... **TCLC 6, 12, 19; SSC 6**
See also CA 110; 121; CDBLB 1914-1945;
DA; DLB 34, 70; MTCW; SATA 20;
WLC

Wells, Rosemary 1943-............ **CLC 12**
See also CA 85-88; CLR 16; MAICYA;
SAAS 1; SATA 18, 69

Welty, Eudora
1909- .... **CLC 1, 2, 5, 14, 22, 33; SSC 1**
See also CA 9-12R; CABS 1; CANR 32;
CDALB 1941-1968; DA; DLB 2, 102;
DLBY 87; MTCW; WLC

Wen I-to 1899-1946 .... **TCLC 28**

Wentworth, Robert
See Hamilton, Edmond

Werfel, Franz (V.) 1890-1945 ...... **TCLC 8**
See also CA 104; DLB 81, 124

Wergeland, Henrik Arnold
1808-1845 .... **NCLC 5**

Wersba, Barbara 1932-............ **CLC 30**
See also AAYA 2; CA 29-32R; CANR 16,
38; CLR 3; DLB 52; MAICYA; SAAS 2;
SATA 1, 58

Wertmueller, Lina 1928- .... **CLC 16**
See also CA 97-100; CANR 39

Wescott, Glenway 1901-1987....... **CLC 13**
See also CA 13-16R; 121; CANR 23;
DLB 4, 9, 102

Wesker, Arnold 1932- .... **CLC 3, 5, 42**
See also CA 1-4R; CAAS 7; CANR 1, 33;
CDBLB 1960 to Present; DLB 13;
MTCW

Wesley, Richard (Errol) 1945-....... **CLC 7**
See also BW; CA 57-60; CANR 27; DLB 38

Wessel, Johan Herman 1742-1785 .... **LC 7**

West, Anthony (Panther)
1914-1987 .... **CLC 50**
See also CA 45-48; 124; CANR 3, 19;
DLB 15

West, C. P.
See Wodehouse, P(elham) G(renville)

West, (Mary) Jessamyn
1902-1984 .... **CLC 7, 17**
See also CA 9-12R; 112; CANR 27; DLB 6;
DLBY 84; MTCW; SATA 37

West, Morris L(anglo) 1916-..... **CLC 6, 33**
See also CA 5-8R; CANR 24; MTCW

West, Nathanael
1903-1940 .... **TCLC 1, 14, 44**
See also CA 104; 125; CDALB 1929-1941;
DLB 4, 9, 28; MTCW

West, Paul 1930- .... **CLC 7, 14**
See also CA 13-16R; CAAS 7; CANR 22;
DLB 14

West, Rebecca 1892-1983 .. **CLC 7, 9, 31, 50**
See also CA 5-8R; 109; CANR 19; DLB 36;
DLBY 83; MTCW

Westall, Robert (Atkinson) 1929-... **CLC 17**
See also CA 69-72; CANR 18; CLR 13;
MAICYA; SAAS 2; SATA 23, 69

Westlake, Donald E(dwin)
1933- .... **CLC 7, 33**
See also CA 17-20R; CAAS 13; CANR 16

Westmacott, Mary
See Christie, Agatha (Mary Clarissa)

Weston, Allen
See Norton, Andre

Wetcheek, J. L.
See Feuchtwanger, Lion

Wetering, Janwillem van de
See van de Wetering, Janwillem

Wetherell, Elizabeth
See Warner, Susan (Bogert)

Whalen, Philip 1923- .... **CLC 6, 29**
See also CA 9-12R; CANR 5, 39; DLB 16

Wharton, Edith (Newbold Jones)
1862-1937 .... **TCLC 3, 9, 27; SSC 6**
See also CA 104; 132; CDALB 1865-1917;
DA; DLB 4, 9, 12, 78; MTCW; WLC

Wharton, James
See Mencken, H(enry) L(ouis)

Wharton, William (a pseudonym)
.... **CLC 18, 37**
See also CA 93-96; DLBY 80

Wheatley (Peters), Phillis
1754(?)-1784 .... **LC 3; PC 3**
See also BLC 3; CDALB 1640-1865; DA;
DLB 31, 50; WLC

Wheelock, John Hall 1886-1978 .... **CLC 14**
See also CA 13-16R; 77-80; CANR 14;
DLB 45

White, E(lwyn) B(rooks)
1899-1985 .... **CLC 10, 34, 39**
See also AITN 2; CA 13-16R; 116;
CANR 16, 37; CLR 1, 21; DLB 11, 22;
MAICYA; MTCW; SATA 2, 29, 44

White, Edmund (Valentine III)
1940- .... **CLC 27**
See also AAYA 7; CA 45-48; CANR 3, 19,
36; MTCW

White, Patrick (Victor Martindale)
1912-1990 .. **CLC 3, 4, 5, 7, 9, 18, 65, 69**
See also CA 81-84; 132; MTCW

White, Phyllis Dorothy James 1920-
See James, P. D.
See also CA 21-24R; CANR 17; MTCW

White, T(erence) H(anbury)
1906-1964 .... **CLC 30**
See also CA 73-76; CANR 37; MAICYA;
SATA 12

White, Terence de Vere 1912-...... **CLC 49**
See also CA 49-52; CANR 3

White, Walter F(rancis)
1893-1955 .... **TCLC 15**
See also White, Walter
See also CA 115; 124; DLB 51

White, William Hale 1831-1913
See Rutherford, Mark
See also CA 121

Whitehead, E(dward) A(nthony)
1933- .... **CLC 5**
See also CA 65-68

Whitemore, Hugh (John) 1936-..... **CLC 37**
See also CA 132

Whitman, Sarah Helen (Power)
1803-1878 .... **NCLC 19**
See also DLB 1

Whitman, Walt(er)
1819-1892 .... **NCLC 4, 31; PC 3**
See also CDALB 1640-1865; DA; DLB 3,
64; SATA 20; WLC

Whitney, Phyllis A(yame) 1903-.... **CLC 42**
See also AITN 2; BEST 90:3; CA 1-4R;
CANR 3, 25, 38; MAICYA; SATA 1, 30

Whittemore, (Edward) Reed (Jr.)
1919- .... **CLC 4**
See also CA 9-12R; CAAS 8; CANR 4;
DLB 5

Whittier, John Greenleaf
1807-1892 .... **NCLC 8**
See also CDALB 1640-1865; DLB 1

Whittlebot, Hernia
See Coward, Noel (Peirce)

Wicker, Thomas Grey 1926-
See Wicker, Tom
See also CA 65-68; CANR 21

Wicker, Tom .... **CLC 7**
See also Wicker, Thomas Grey

Wideman, John Edgar
1941- .... **CLC 5, 34, 36, 67**
See also BLC 3; BW; CA 85-88; CANR 14;
DLB 33

Wiebe, Rudy (H.) 1934-...... **CLC 6, 11, 14**
See also CA 37-40R; DLB 60

Wieland, Christoph Martin
1733-1813 .... **NCLC 17**
See also DLB 97

Wieners, John 1934-.............. **CLC 7**
See also CA 13-16R; DLB 16

Wiesel, Elie(zer) 1928-..... **CLC 3, 5, 11, 37**
See also AAYA 7; AITN 1; CA 5-8R;
CAAS 4; CANR 8, 40; DA; DLB 83;
DLBY 87; MTCW; SATA 56

Wiggins, Marianne 1947-......... **CLC 57**
See also BEST 89:3; CA 130

Wight, James Alfred 1916-
See Herriot, James
See also CA 77-80; SATA 44, 55

Wilbur, Richard (Purdy)
1921- .... **CLC 3, 6, 9, 14, 53**
See also CA 1-4R; CABS 2; CANR 2, 29;
DA; DLB 5; MTCW; SATA 9

Wild, Peter 1940-................ **CLC 14**
See also CA 37-40R; DLB 5

Wilde, Oscar (Fingal O'Flahertie Wills)
1854(?)-1900 .... **TCLC 1, 8, 23, 41;
SSC 11**
See also CA 104; 119; CDBLB 1890-1914;
DA; DLB 10, 19, 34, 57; SATA 24; WLC

Wilder, Billy .... **CLC 20**
See also Wilder, Samuel
See also DLB 26

Wilder, Samuel 1906-
See Wilder, Billy
See also CA 89-92

Wilder, Thornton (Niven)
1897-1975 ..... **CLC 1, 5, 6, 10, 15, 35;
DC 1**
See also AITN 2; CA 13-16R; 61-64;
CANR 40; DA; DLB 4, 7, 9; MTCW;
WLC

Wilding, Michael 1942-........... **CLC 73**
See also CA 104; CANR 24

Wiley, Richard 1944-............. **CLC 44**
See also CA 121; 129

Wilhelm, Kate .... **CLC 7**
See also Wilhelm, Katie Gertrude
See also CAAS 5; DLB 8

Wilhelm, Katie Gertrude 1928-
See Wilhelm, Kate
See also CA 37-40R; CANR 17, 36; MTCW

Wilkins, Mary
See Freeman, Mary Eleanor Wilkins

Willard, Nancy 1936-........... **CLC 7, 37**
See also CA 89-92; CANR 10, 39; CLR 5;
DLB 5, 52; MAICYA; MTCW;
SATA 30, 37, 71

Williams, C(harles) K(enneth)
1936- .... **CLC 33, 56**
See also CA 37-40R; DLB 5

Williams, Charles
See Collier, James L(incoln)

Williams, Charles (Walter Stansby)
1886-1945 .... **TCLC 1, 11**
See also CA 104; DLB 100

Williams, (George) Emlyn
1905-1987 .... **CLC 15**
See also CA 104; 123; CANR 36; DLB 10,
77; MTCW

Williams, Hugo 1942-............. **CLC 42**
See also CA 17-20R; DLB 40

Williams, J. Walker
See Wodehouse, P(elham) G(renville)

Williams, John A(lfred) 1925-.... **CLC 5, 13**
See also BLC 3; BW; CA 53-56; CAAS 3;
CANR 6, 26; DLB 2, 33

Williams, Jonathan (Chamberlain)
1929- .... **CLC 13**
See also CA 9-12R; CAAS 12; CANR 8;
DLB 5

Williams, Joy 1944-.............. **CLC 31**
See also CA 41-44R; CANR 22

Williams, Norman 1952- .... **CLC 39**
See also CA 118

Williams, Tennessee
1911-1983 .... **CLC 1, 2, 5, 7, 8, 11, 15, 19, 30, 39, 45, 71**
See also AITN 1, 2; CA 5-8R; 108;
CABS 3; CANR 31; CDALB 1941-1968;
DA; DLB 7; DLBD 4; DLBY 83;
MTCW; WLC

Williams, Thomas (Alonzo)
1926-1990 .... **CLC 14**
See also CA 1-4R; 132; CANR 2

Williams, William C.
See Williams, William Carlos

Williams, William Carlos
1883-1963 ... **CLC 1, 2, 5, 9, 13, 22, 42, 67**
See also CA 89-92; CANR 34;
CDALB 1917-1929; DA; DLB 4, 16, 54, 86; MTCW

Williamson, David (Keith) 1942-.... **CLC 56**
See also CA 103; CANR 41

Williamson, Jack .... **CLC 29**
See also Williamson, John Stewart
See also CAAS 8; DLB 8

Williamson, John Stewart 1908-
See Williamson, Jack
See also CA 17-20R; CANR 23

Willie, Frederick
See Lovecraft, H(oward) P(hillips)

Willingham, Calder (Baynard, Jr.)
1922- .... **CLC 5, 51**
See also CA 5-8R; CANR 3; DLB 2, 44;
MTCW

Willis, Charles
See Clarke, Arthur C(harles)

Willy
See Colette, (Sidonie-Gabrielle)

Willy, Colette
See Colette, (Sidonie-Gabrielle)

Wilson, A(ndrew) N(orman) 1950- .. **CLC 33**
See also CA 112; 122; DLB 14

Wilson, Angus (Frank Johnstone)
1913-1991 .... **CLC 2, 3, 5, 25, 34**
See also CA 5-8R; 134; CANR 21; DLB 15;
MTCW

Wilson, August
1945- .... **CLC 39, 50, 63; DC 2**
See also BLC 3; BW; CA 115; 122; DA;
MTCW

Wilson, Brian 1942- .... **CLC 12**

Wilson, Colin 1931- .... **CLC 3, 14**
See also CA 1-4R; CAAS 5; CANR 1, 22,
33; DLB 14; MTCW

Wilson, Dirk
See Pohl, Frederik

Wilson, Edmund
1895-1972 .... **CLC 1, 2, 3, 8, 24**
See also CA 1-4R; 37-40R; CANR 1;
DLB 63; MTCW

Wilson, Ethel Davis (Bryant)
1888(?)-1980 .... **CLC 13**
See also CA 102; DLB 68; MTCW

Wilson, John 1785-1854 .... **NCLC 5**

Wilson, John (Anthony) Burgess
1917- .... **CLC 8, 10, 13**
See also Burgess, Anthony
See also CA 1-4R; CANR 2; MTCW

Wilson, Lanford 1937-....... **CLC 7, 14, 36**
See also CA 17-20R; CABS 3; DLB 7

Wilson, Robert M. 1944-......... **CLC 7, 9**
See also CA 49-52; CANR 2, 41; MTCW

Wilson, Robert McLiam 1964- ..... **CLC 59**
See also CA 132

Wilson, Sloan 1920-.............. **CLC 32**
See also CA 1-4R; CANR 1

Wilson, Snoo 1948-.............. **CLC 33**
See also CA 69-72

Wilson, William S(mith) 1932- ..... **CLC 49**
See also CA 81-84

Winchilsea, Anne (Kingsmill) Finch Counte
1661-1720 .... **LC 3**

Windham, Basil
See Wodehouse, P(elham) G(renville)

Wingrove, David (John) 1954-...... **CLC 68**
See also CA 133

Winters, Janet Lewis .... **CLC 41**
See also Lewis, Janet
See also DLBY 87

Winters, (Arthur) Yvor
1900-1968 .... **CLC 4, 8, 32**
See also CA 11-12; 25-28R; CAP 1;
DLB 48; MTCW

Winterson, Jeanette 1959-........ **CLC 64**
See also CA 136

Wiseman, Frederick 1930-........ **CLC 20**

Wister, Owen 1860-1938 .... **TCLC 21**
See also CA 108; DLB 9, 78; SATA 62

Witkacy
See Witkiewicz, Stanislaw Ignacy

Witkiewicz, Stanislaw Ignacy
1885-1939 .... **TCLC 8**
See also CA 105

Wittig, Monique 1935(?)-.......... **CLC 22**
See also CA 116; 135; DLB 83

Wittlin, Jozef 1896-1976 .... **CLC 25**
See also CA 49-52; 65-68; CANR 3

Wodehouse, P(elham) G(renville)
1881-1975 ... **CLC 1, 2, 5, 10, 22; SSC 2**
See also AITN 2; CA 45-48; 57-60;
CANR 3, 33; CDBLB 1914-1945;
DLB 34; MTCW; SATA 22

Woiwode, L.
See Woiwode, Larry (Alfred)

Woiwode, Larry (Alfred) 1941-... **CLC 6, 10**
See also CA 73-76; CANR 16; DLB 6

Wojciechowska, Maia (Teresa)
1927- .... **CLC 26**
See also AAYA 8; CA 9-12R; CANR 4, 41;
CLR 1; MAICYA; SAAS 1; SATA 1, 28

Wolf, Christa 1929- .... **CLC 14, 29, 58**
See also CA 85-88; DLB 75; MTCW

Wolfe, Gene (Rodman) 1931-....... **CLC 25**
See also CA 57-60; CAAS 9; CANR 6, 32;
DLB 8

Wolfe, George C. 1954- .... **CLC 49**

Wolfe, Thomas (Clayton)
1900-1938 .... **TCLC 4, 13, 29**
See also CA 104; 132; CDALB 1929-1941;
DA; DLB 9, 102; DLBD 2; DLBY 85;
MTCW; WLC

Wolfe, Thomas Kennerly, Jr. 1930-
See Wolfe, Tom
See also CA 13-16R; CANR 9, 33; MTCW

Wolfe, Tom .... **CLC 1, 2, 9, 15, 35, 51**
See also Wolfe, Thomas Kennerly, Jr.
See also AAYA 8; AITN 2; BEST 89:1

Wolff, Geoffrey (Ansell) 1937- ..... **CLC 41**
See also CA 29-32R; CANR 29

Wolff, Sonia
See Levitin, Sonia (Wolff)

Wolff, Tobias (Jonathan Ansell)
1945- .... **CLC 39, 64**
See also BEST 90:2; CA 114; 117; DLB 130

Wolfram von Eschenbach
c. 1170-c. 1220 .... **CMLC 5**

Wolitzer, Hilma 1930-............. **CLC 17**
See also CA 65-68; CANR 18, 40; SATA 31

Wollstonecraft, Mary 1759-1797...... **LC 5**
See also CDBLB 1789-1832; DLB 39, 104

Wonder, Stevie .... **CLC 12**
See also Morris, Steveland Judkins

Wong, Jade Snow 1922-........... **CLC 17**
See also CA 109

Woodcott, Keith
See Brunner, John (Kilian Houston)

Woodruff, Robert W.
See Mencken, H(enry) L(ouis)

Woolf, (Adeline) Virginia
1882-1941 .... **TCLC 1, 5, 20, 43; SSC 7**
See also CA 104; 130; CDBLB 1914-1945;
DA; DLB 36, 100; DLBD 10; MTCW;
WLC

Woollcott, Alexander (Humphreys)
1887-1943 .... **TCLC 5**
See also CA 105; DLB 29

Woolrich, Cornell 1903-1968....... **CLC 77**
See also Hopley-Woolrich, Cornell George

Wordsworth, Dorothy
1771-1855 .... **NCLC 25**
See also DLB 107

Wordsworth, William
1770-1850 .... **NCLC 12, 38; PC 4**
See also CDBLB 1789-1832; DA; DLB 93,
107; WLC

Wouk, Herman 1915-........ **CLC 1, 9, 38**
See also CA 5-8R; CANR 6, 33; DLBY 82;
MTCW

Wright, Charles (Penzel, Jr.)
1935- .... **CLC 6, 13, 28**
See also CA 29-32R; CAAS 7; CANR 23,
36; DLBY 82; MTCW

Wright, Charles Stevenson 1932- ... **CLC 49**
See also BLC 3; BW; CA 9-12R; CANR 26;
DLB 33

Wright, Jack R.
See Harris, Mark

Wright, James (Arlington)
1927-1980 .... **CLC 3, 5, 10, 28**
See also AITN 2; CA 49-52; 97-100;
CANR 4, 34; DLB 5; MTCW

Wright, Judith (Arandell)
1915- . . . . CLC 11, 53
See also CA 13-16R; CANR 31; MTCW;
SATA 14

Wright, L(aurali) R. . . . . CLC 44
See also CA 138

Wright, Richard (Nathaniel)
1908-1960 . . . CLC 1, 3, 4, 9, 14, 21, 48,
74; SSC 2
See also AAYA 5; BLC 3; BW; CA 108;
CDALB 1929-1941; DA; DLB 76, 102;
DLBD 2; MTCW; WLC

Wright, Richard B(ruce) 1937- . . . . . . CLC 6
See also CA 85-88; DLB 53

Wright, Rick 1945- . . . . CLC 35
See also Pink Floyd

Wright, Rowland
See Wells, Carolyn

Wright, Stephen 1946- . . . . CLC 33

Wright, Willard Huntington 1888-1939
See Van Dine, S. S.
See also CA 115

Wright, William 1930- . . . . CLC 44
See also CA 53-56; CANR 7, 23

Wu Ch'eng-en 1500(?)-1582(?) . . . . LC 7

Wu Ching-tzu 1701-1754 . . . . LC 2

Wurlitzer, Rudolph 1938(?)- . . . CLC 2, 4, 15
See also CA 85-88

Wycherley, William 1641-1715 . . . . LC 8, 21
See also CDBLB 1660-1789; DLB 80

Wylie, Elinor (Morton Hoyt)
1885-1928 . . . . TCLC 8
See also CA 105; DLB 9, 45

Wylie, Philip (Gordon) 1902-1971 . . . CLC 43
See also CA 21-22; 33-36R; CAP 2; DLB 9

Wyndham, John
See Harris, John (Wyndham Parkes Lucas)
Beynon

Wyss, Johann David Von
1743-1818 . . . . NCLC 10
See also MAICYA; SATA 27, 29

Yakumo Koizumi
See Hearn, (Patricio) Lafcadio (Tessima
Carlos)

Yanez, Jose Donoso
See Donoso (Yanez), Jose

Yanovsky, Basile S.
See Yanovsky, V(assily) S(emenovich)

Yanovsky, V(assily) S(emenovich)
1906-1989 . . . . CLC 2, 18
See also CA 97-100; 129

Yates, Richard 1926-1992 . . . . . CLC 7, 8, 23
See also CA 5-8R; 139; CANR 10; DLB 2;
DLBY 81, 92

Yeats, W. B.
See Yeats, William Butler

Yeats, William Butler
1865-1939 . . . . TCLC 1, 11, 18, 31
See also CA 104; 127; CDBLB 1890-1914;
DA; DLB 10, 19, 98; MTCW; WLC

Yehoshua, Abraham B. 1936- . . . CLC 13, 31
See also CA 33-36R

Yep, Laurence Michael 1948- . . . . . . CLC 35
See also AAYA 5; CA 49-52; CANR 1;
CLR 3, 17; DLB 52; MAICYA; SATA 7,
69

Yerby, Frank G(arvin)
1916-1991 . . . . CLC 1, 7, 22
See also BLC 3; BW; CA 9-12R; 136;
CANR 16; DLB 76; MTCW

Yesenin, Sergei Alexandrovich
See Esenin, Sergei (Alexandrovich)

Yevtushenko, Yevgeny (Alexandrovich)
1933- . . . . CLC 1, 3, 13, 26, 51
See also CA 81-84; CANR 33; MTCW

Yezierska, Anzia 1885(?)-1970 . . . . . CLC 46
See also CA 126; 89-92; DLB 28; MTCW

Yglesias, Helen 1915- . . . . CLC 7, 22
See also CA 37-40R; CANR 15; MTCW

Yokomitsu Riichi 1898-1947 . . . . . . TCLC 47

Yonge, Charlotte (Mary)
1823-1901 . . . . TCLC 48
See also CA 109; DLB 18; SATA 17

York, Jeremy
See Creasey, John

York, Simon
See Heinlein, Robert A(nson)

Yorke, Henry Vincent 1905-1974 . . . CLC 13
See also Green, Henry
See also CA 85-88; 49-52

Young, Al(bert James) 1939- . . . . CLC 19
See also BLC 3; BW; CA 29-32R;
CANR 26; DLB 33

Young, Andrew (John) 1885-1971 . . . . CLC 5
See also CA 5-8R; CANR 7, 29

Young, Collier
See Bloch, Robert (Albert)

Young, Edward 1683-1765 . . . . LC 3
See also DLB 95

Young, Neil 1945- . . . . CLC 17
See also CA 110

Yourcenar, Marguerite
1903-1987 . . . . CLC 19, 38, 50
See also CA 69-72; CANR 23; DLB 72;
DLBY 88; MTCW

Yurick, Sol 1925- . . . . CLC 6
See also CA 13-16R; CANR 25

Zamiatin, Yevgenii
See Zamyatin, Evgeny Ivanovich

Zamyatin, Evgeny Ivanovich
1884-1937 . . . . TCLC 8, 37
See also CA 105

Zangwill, Israel 1864-1926 . . . . TCLC 16
See also CA 109; DLB 10

Zappa, Francis Vincent, Jr. 1940-
See Zappa, Frank
See also CA 108

Zappa, Frank . . . . CLC 17
See also Zappa, Francis Vincent, Jr.

Zaturenska, Marya 1902-1982 . . . . CLC 6, 11
See also CA 13-16R; 105; CANR 22

Zelazny, Roger (Joseph) 1937- . . . . . CLC 21
See also AAYA 7; CA 21-24R; CANR 26;
DLB 8; MTCW; SATA 39, 57

Zhdanov, Andrei A(lexandrovich)
1896-1948 . . . . TCLC 18
See also CA 117

Zhukovsky, Vasily 1783-1852 . . . . NCLC 35

Ziegenhagen, Eric . . . . CLC 55

Zimmer, Jill Schary
See Robinson, Jill

Zimmerman, Robert
See Dylan, Bob

Zindel, Paul 1936- . . . . CLC 6, 26
See also AAYA 2; CA 73-76; CANR 31;
CLR 3; DA; DLB 7, 52; MAICYA;
MTCW; SATA 16, 58

Zinov'Ev, A. A.
See Zinoviev, Alexander (Aleksandrovich)

Zinoviev, Alexander (Aleksandrovich)
1922- . . . . CLC 19
See also CA 116; 133; CAAS 10

Zoilus
See Lovecraft, H(oward) P(hillips)

Zola, Emile (Edouard Charles Antoine)
1840-1902 . . . . TCLC 1, 6, 21, 41
See also CA 104; 138; DA; DLB 123; WLC

Zoline, Pamela 1941- . . . . CLC 62

Zorrilla y Moral, Jose 1817-1893 . . NCLC 6

Zoshchenko, Mikhail (Mikhailovich)
1895-1958 . . . . TCLC 15
See also CA 115

Zuckmayer, Carl 1896-1977 . . . . CLC 18
See also CA 69-72; DLB 56, 124

Zuk, Georges
See Skelton, Robin

Zukofsky, Louis
1904-1978 . . . . CLC 1, 2, 4, 7, 11, 18
See also CA 9-12R; 77-80; CANR 39;
DLB 5; MTCW

Zweig, Paul 1935-1984 . . . . CLC 34, 42
See also CA 85-88; 113

Zweig, Stefan 1881-1942 . . . . TCLC 17
See also CA 112; DLB 81, 118

SSC Cumulative Nationality Index

SSC Cumulative Title Index

Title Index

Title Index

Title Index

Title Index

Title Index

Title Index

ISBN 0-8103-7955-4